Irish Laws of Evidence

AUSTRALIA
Law Book Co.
Sydney

CANADA and USA
Carswell
Toronto

HONG KONG
Sweet & Maxwell Asia

NEW ZEALAND
Brookers
Wellington

SINGAPORE and MALAYSIA
Sweet & Maxwell Asia
Singapore and Kuala Lumpur

Irish Laws of Evidence

by

John Healy
B.C.L., M.Litt., Barrister-at-Law

with a Foreword by

Mr Justice Adrian Hardiman
Judge of the Supreme Court

THOMSON ROUND HALL
2004

Published in 2004 by
Round Hall Ltd
43 Fitzwilliam Place
Dublin 2
Ireland

Typeset by
Gough Typesetting Services
Dublin

Printed by
MPG Books, Cornwall

ISBN 1-85800-381-4 (hb)
1-85800-380-6 (pb)

A catalogue record for this book
is available from the British Library

All rights reserved. No part of this publication may be reproduced or transmitted in any form or by any means, or stored in any retrieval system of any nature without prior written permission. Such written permission must also be obtained before any part of this publication is stored in a retrieval system of any nature.

© Thomson Round Hall and John Healy, 2004

*To Frederick and Rosaleen Healy,
my parents*

from Plato, *The Republic*
Book Four, Justice in the State

(trans. Lee)

'Then we must stand like hunters round a covert and make sure that justice does not escape us and disappear from view. It must be somewhere about. Try and see if you can catch sight of it before I can, and tell me where it is.'

'I wish I could,' he said. 'All you can reasonably expect of me is to follow your lead and see things when you point them out.'

'Then follow me and hope for the best.'

'I will,' he said; 'lead on.'

'It looks to me,' I said, 'as if we were in a pretty impassable and obscure spot; it's certainly dark and difficult to find a way through. But we must push on all the same.'

'Yes, we must,' he agreed.

I cast about a bit and then cried, 'Tally ho, Glaucon! I think we are on the track, and our quarry won't altogether escape us.'

'That's really good news.'

'We really are being a bit slow.'

'In what way?'

'Our quarry is lurking right under our feet all the time. And we haven't seen it but have been making perfect fools of ourselves. We are like people searching for something they have in their hands all the time; we're looking away into the distance instead of at the thing we want, which is probably why we haven't found it.'

TABLE OF CONTENTS

FOREWORD xiii
PREFACE xv
TABLE OF CASES xviii
TABLE OF LEGISLATION xlv

CHAPTER 1: EVIDENCE AND THE TRIAL 1
    I. INTRODUCTION 1
    II. EVOLUTION OF EVIDENCE LAWS AND THEORY 5
    III. EVIDENCE LAWS IN THE COMMON LAW TRIAL 6
    IV. KEY CONCEPTS AND TYPES OF EVIDENCE 8
    V. COURSE OF THE TRIAL 24
    VI. TESTIMONY 30
        Part III of the Criminal Evidence Act 1992 32
        Constitutionality of the Television Link Measures 33
        Taking Evidence in Advance of the Trial 36

CHAPTER 2: THE TESTIMONY OF WITNESSES 43
    I. COMPETENCE AND COMPELLABILITY 43
        General Principles 43
        Child Witnesses 47
        The Accused as a Witness 51
        The Spouse of the Accused as a Witness 54
        Witnesses with a Mental Disability 56
    II. HOSTILE WITNESSES 58
    III. REFRESHING A WITNESS' MEMORY 64
    IV. THE RULE AGAINST NARRATIVE 68
        General Principles 68
        The Complaint in Sexual Offence Cases 69

CHAPTER 3: CHALLENGES TO THE CREDIBILITY OF
           WITNESSES 76
    I. THE COLLATERAL ISSUE RULE 76
    II. A WITNESS' PREVIOUS INCONSISTENT STATEMENTS 79
    III. A WITNESS' BIAS 80
    IV. A WITNESS' PREVIOUS CONVICTIONS 81

V.	A Witness' Lack of Veracity	82
	A Witness' Reputation for Lies	82
	Lies Told by the Accused	83
VI.	A WITNESS' PHYSICAL OR MENTAL DISABILITY	85
VII.	SEXUAL HISTORY EVIDENCE	85
	Admissibility under the Common Law	85
	Current Provisions	86
	Reasons for Limiting Use of Sexual History Evidence	89
	The English Experience	91
VIII.	PRE-TRIAL DISCLOSURE BY THE PROSECUTION	94

CHAPTER 4: BURDENS AND STANDARDS OF PROOF 97
    I. GENERAL PRINCIPLES 97
    II. THE BURDENS OF PROOF 99
        The Legal Burden of Proof 99
        Evidential Burdens 101
        Presumptions of Law 103
        Distinguishing the Legal Burden from Evidential
            Burdens 104
    III. DEFENCES 106
        Defences in General 106
        Defence of Insanity 111
    IV. REVERSAL OF THE BURDENS OF PROOF 112
        Statutory Reversal of the Burdens 112
        Common Law Principle: Criminal Cases 121
        Common Law Principle and Res Ipsa Loquitur:
            Civil Cases 126
    V. STANDARDS OF PROOF 133
        Criminal Proceedings 133
        Civil Proceedings 136

CHAPTER 5: CORROBORATION 140
    I. GENERAL PRINCIPLES 140
    II. DEFINITION AND FORMS OF CORROBORATION 141
        The Strict Baskerville Definition 141
        Requirement of Independent Proof 142
    III. THE REQUIREMENT OF CORROBOATION 148
    IV. THE MANDATORY CORROBORATION WARNING 149
        Accomplice Witnesses 149
    V. THE DISCRETIONARY CORROBORATION WARNING 156
        Sexual Offence Proceedings 156
        Child Witnesses 165
        Mutual Corroboration 166

CHAPTER 6: IDENTIFICATION EVIDENCE 169
    I. GENERAL PRINCIPLES 169
    II. THE IDENTIFICATION EVIDENCE WARNING 171
        Reference to Supporting Evidence 172

Table of Contents

    Recognition Cases 173
    Sexual Offence Cases 175
    Mutual and Cumulative Identification 175
  III. MEANS OF IDENTIFICATION 176
    The Identification Parade 177
    Use of Photographs, Videos, and other Means of
      Identification 180
    Photofits and Identikits 183
    Voice Identification 184
  IV. PROSECUTOR'S DUTY TO DISCLOSE 185

CHAPTER 7: SIMILAR FACT EVIDENCE AND THE ACCUSED'S
    CRIMINAL PAST 188
  I. THE FORBIDDEN REASONING 188
  II. THE MAKIN AND BOARDMAN PRINCIPLES 189
  III. AMBIT OF SIMILAR FACT EVIDENCE RULES 196
  IV. THE ACCUSED'S CRIMINAL PROPENSITY 198
  V. SIMILAR FACT EVIDENCE IN JOINED TRIALS 201
  VI. EVIDENCE TO EXPLAIN THE BACKGROUND OF AN ACT 204
  VII. CIVIL CASES 205

CHAPTER 8: CROSS-EXAMINATION OF THE ACCUSED UPON BAD
    CHARACTER 208
  I. INTRODUCTION 208
  II. PARAMETERS OF SECTION 1(F) 210
  III. SECTION 1(F)(I): ADMISSIBLE SIMILAR FACT EVIDENCE 217
  IV. SECTION 1(F)(II): CHARACTER PUT IN ISSUE BY THE DEFENCE 219
    The Accused's Good Character 219
    Imputations against the Character of the Prosecutor 223
  V. SECTION 1(F)(III): EVIDENCE BY THE ACCUSED AGAINST A
    CO-ACCUSED 233

CHAPTER 9: THE RULE AGAINST HEARSAY 238
  I. PRINCIPLES AND DEFINITIONS 238
    Rationale of the Hearsay Rule 241
    Strictness of the Rule 243
    Right to Cross-Examine 245
  II. DISTINGUISHING HEARSAY FROM ORIGINAL EVIDENCE 247
  III. IMPLIED ASSERTIONS 252
  IV. DOCUMENTARY EVIDENCE 254
  V. HEARSAY IN CIVIL CASES 256
    Child Witnesses and Family Law 257
  VI. HEARSAY AT PRE-TRIAL AND INTERLOCUTORY STAGES 260
  VII. HEARSAY AND TRIBUNALS 262
  VIII. MISCELLANEOUS 263
    Expert Evidence 263
    Identification Evidence 263

IX. EXCEPTIONS TO THE HEARSAY RULE 265
    Statutory Exceptions 265
    Common Law Exceptions 266

CHAPTER 10: CONFESSION EVIDENCE 278
    I. GENERAL PRINCIPLES 278
        Confessions 278
        Form of Confession 280
        Persons in Authority 282
        Proof of Admissibility and the *Voire Dire* 283
        Tests of Admissibility 285
    II. THE JUDGES' RULES 286
    III. TREATMENT OF PERSONS IN CUSTODY REGULATIONS 291
    IV. REQUIREMENT OF VOLUNTARINESS 293
        Threats and Inducements 293
        Oppressive Questioning 295
        Threats, Inducements, and Oppression from
            Third Parties 296
        Causation 297
        The Subjective Test 297
    V. REQUIREMENTS OF FAIRNESS AND RELIABILITY 298
    VI. COMPLIANCE WITH THE CONSTITUTIONAL RIGHTS OF THE ACCUSED 301
        Rights of Access to Legal Advice 302
    VII. FRUIT OF THE POISONED TREE 307
    VIII. CONFESSION AS EVIDENCE AGAINST A CO-ACCUSED 308
    IX. "MIXED STATEMENTS" 310
    X. THE CORROBORATION WARNING 313

CHAPTER 11: EVIDENCE OBTAINED UNCONSTITUTIONALLY
    AND ILLEGALLY 317
    I. EVIDENCE OBTAINED IN BREACH OF THE ACCUSED'S
        CONSTITUTIONAL RIGHTS 317
        The Exclusionary Rule 317
        Constitutional Rights and the Obtaining of Evidence 321
        Proof of a Causative Link 324
        "Deliberate and Conscious Violation" 326
        "Extraordinary Excusing Circumstances" 328
    II. EVIDENCE OBTAINED ILLEGALLY OR IMPROPERLY 329
    III. GARDAÍ POWERS OF ARREST, DETENTION, SEARCH, AND SEIZURE 331
        Arrest and Detention 331
        Powers of Search and Seizure 343
    IV. APPLICATION OF THE EXCLUSIONARY RULE IN CIVIL CASES 350

CHAPTER 12: OPINION AND EXPERT EVIDENCE 353
    I. GENERAL PRINCIPLES 353
    II. THE EXPERT WITNESS 355
        Experts in the Criminal Trial 355
        Forensic Evidence and DNA 359

Expertise and its Limits 361
Expert Witnesses in Civil Proceedings 363
III. EXPERT EVIDENCE AND HEARSAY 366
IV. NON-EXPERT OPINION EVIDENCE 368

CHAPTER 13: PRIVILEGE 372
I. PRIVATE PRIVILEGE: GENERAL PRINCIPLES 372
Secondary Evidence 376
Waiver 377
Communications in Furtherance of Crime or Iniquity 378
Family Law Proceedings Affecting the Welfare of
Children 380
Proceedings under the Succession Act 1965 381
II. LEGAL PROFESSIONAL PRIVILEGE 382
Scope of Protected "Communications" 385
Disclosure of Expert Witness Reports 386
Distinction between Legal Advice and Legal Assistance 389
Communications in Furtherance of Settlement 390
Documents in Existence Prior to Legal Advice 391
Communications to Third Parties 392
Documents Created for Mixed Purposes 393
Advice to Remain Silent and Adverse Inferences 395
III. CONFIDENTIAL RELATIONSHIPS 396
Sacerdotal Privilege 396
Counsellors' Privilege 397
IV. PRIVILEGES AGAINST REVEALING INFORMANTS 398
Common Law Privileges 398
The Constitution: Executive and Parliamentary 402
V. MARITAL PRIVACY 404
VI. PUBLIC INTEREST PRIVILEGE 406
VII. PRIVILEGE AGAINST SELF-INCRIMINATION 411
The Right to Silence 413
Compulsorily Acquired Self-Incriminating Evidence 418
Adverse Inferences from Silence 421

APPENDICES 431

INDEX 643

FOREWORD

It is a pleasure to commend John Healy's work on evidence. This is the third Irish textbook on this subject to be published in the last few years, but that fact does not at all render it superfluous. It is a relatively long work but so clearly written and its exposition so detailed and so firmly based in principle as to recall the dictum of Professor Sir Rupert Cross that a long book on this subject might, in the end, prove more digestible than a shorter one.

The laws of evidence are what distinguish a trial at law from a mass meeting and still more from a lynch mob. The characteristic feature of a court is that it proceeds only on evidence and hears before it condemns. This of course is supremely important in criminal cases but almost equally so in civil trials: a trial of any sort must proceed according to formal, logically grounded and known rules of evidence if it is to be fair and if it is to be transparent. In our recent jurisprudence the importance of rigorous adherence to high evidential standards has been stressed—in the area of personal injuries law, in a series of cases commencing with *Vesey v Bus Éireann* [2001] 4 I.R. 192, in criminal law in a series of cases about new forms of evidence commencing with *Braddish v DPP* [2001] 3 I.R. 127, and in many other areas. The complexity of the process of ascertaining the truth about factual disputes, an ever present challenge for every legal system, has been thrown into prominence anew in the context of widespread attempts to prosecute very serious crimes decades after their commission. And individual cases continue to bring to sharp focus the exclusionary rule as applied for instance in *DPP v Kenny* [1990] 2 I.R. 110.

Despite the great importance of the law of evidence to the coherency and fairness of the legal system, it is something of a Cinderella amongst legal subjects. It is in fact (as the author's title indicates) not one subject but many. Some of its branches are of unique conceptual difficulty. I therefore welcome very heartily a work which is both practically oriented and very firmly grounded in an admirable knowledge of the theory and history of the subject. Mr Healy cast his net very wide. One often sees citations from Mr Justice Holmes of the Supreme Court of the United States but how often, on this side of the Atlantic, does one see a citation from his cases in the Supreme Court of Massachusetts?

Mr Healy spared no effort to make this a useful and important treatment of the law of evidence and I believe he has succeeded. I wish him every success.

Adrian Hardiman,
Supreme Court,
May 28, 2004.

PREFACE

Though indispensable to the law's application and practice, evidence law has long been regarded a subject difficult to digest upon first acquaintance yet tending to linger in the memory like the remnants of an unfinished puzzle. These were the qualities that drew me to it some years back when I set to writing a book that would frame its diffuse rules and precedents, its fine lines and distinctions, within their informing principles, logic, and origins. Writing it was not quite the canter I naively imagined at the outset. In its need for exactitude and deferment of dénouement, I was many times subdued by a line well remembered from Hopkins' *Windhover*—"shéer plód makes plough down sillion shine"—conveyed many years ago by an inimitable reader of literature, Marion Deane, but virtually shunned by me till immersed in the slow gradual work necessary for this book.

I am very grateful to Mr Justice Hardiman for kindly agreeing to write the foreword. His involvement is personally very gratifying to me, as I have had the highest regard for his judgments in the Supreme Court and Court of Criminal Appeal, and had hoped as far back as the book's inception that he would later assume this role. I am also very grateful to my colleagues in the law library for their advice and comments on draft chapters. I thank in particular Denis Vaughan Buckley S.C., Maire Whelan B.L., Martina Baxter B.L., and Shane Costello B.L. I thank also at work Alex Finn B.L., who suffered to hear the most of my angst-ridden monologues recounting the book's slow progress and sacrifice, and who was quickest to dispense *mots justes*, more often even than was required, though who vanished with alacrity when I was to be seen clutching lists of last citation checks. Without his arabesque wit, the journey would have felt much longer. To Tony McBride B.L. also heartfelt thanks; Tony who arrived as the second draft began and who actually helped with those lists whilst managing to gild his precision with dabs of classical flair and show-tune insouciance brightening fraught moments closing the manuscript. I thank my publishers and, in particular, at Thomson Round Hall, David McCartney and Martin McCann, who remained calm and adroit throughout the entire process despite my relentless bids to add and tweak text. I thank the staff at the issue desk of the law library who were very helpful and obliging and who do an exemplary job amid many competing demands on their services. I thank a number of my students at the King's Inns who combed drafts for typos and queries. I thank my brothers, Niall, Cormac, and Ciaran Healy, and friends Kyran Twomey and Rebecca O'Donnell, who were always on hand to give advice, and who are my grips in shifting sands. I thank Cherie and Ben and Marian, Denis and Breeda, and other blithe spirits in Dublin and Cork, too numerous, thankfully, to name individually, who I spared a fuller account of the book's labours, and who provide the *esprit* that prompts the motivation. Finally, I thank my mother and father for their support and trust over the years, and to whom this book is dedicated. My father, a quiet phenomenon to people who know him, worked many years as a garda sergeant, and by him I learned in formative years the necessity for suspension of judgment, neutral investigation of evidence, and the benefits of fair process. He nudged me in all the directions that led, at times surprisingly, to this book, upon which his mark is palpable.

I have striven to capture the law as it existed up to November 2003, beyond which point, and perhaps a short time before, the law surrendered to the exigencies of the edit. For the avoidance of doubt, no liability whatsoever is accepted towards any person arising from reliance upon the contents of this book, which is intended to serve as a guide for students and practitioners of the law but which remains in its detail and interpretation personal to the author.

Pragae, Die Sancti Isidori, AD MMIV.

TABLE OF CASES

A. (Minors: Disclosure of Material) *Re* [1991] 2 F.L.R. 473 .... 13–17n
Abbey National Mortgages Plc. v Key Surveyors Ltd., [1996]
   1 W.L.R. 1534 (CA) 12–22
Air Canada v Secretary of State for Trade (No.2) [1983] 2 A.C. 394
   (HL) 13–77
Alderson v Booth [1969] 2 Q.B. 216 .... 11–29n
Alfred Compton Amusement Machines Ltd. v Customs and Excise
   Commissioners (No.2) [1972] 2 Q.B. 102 (CA) 13–41n
Allhusen v Labouchere (1878) 3 Q.B.D. 654 (CA) 13–82n
Ambiorix v Minister for the Environment [1992] 1 I.R. 277 (SC) 13–71
Anderson v Bank of British Columbia (1876) 2 Ch. D. 644 (CA) 13–41n
Andrews v Northern Ireland Railways Co. Ltd. [1992] N.I. 1 13–44
Ares v Venner (1970) 14 D.L.R. (3d) 4 (SC) 9–62
Arnold and Arnold v Ireland and Attorney General [1988] I.L.R.M. 472
   (HC) 11–10n
Ashburton v Pape [1913] 2 Ch. 469 (CA) 13–08n
Attorney-General (Ruddy) v Kenny (1960) 94 I.L.T.R. 185 (SC) 12–03, 12–29
Attorney-General v Boylan [1937] I.R. 449 (CCA) 4–30
Attorney-General v Briant (1846) 15 M. & W. 169 13–54
Attorney-General v Byrne [1974] I.R. 1
   (CCA) 4–74, 4–75, 4–77, 4–78, 4–78n
Attorney-General v Campbell [1945] I.R. 237 (SC) 8–49
Attorney-General v Cleary (1938) 72 I.L.T.R. 84 (CCA) 10–33
Attorney-General v Duff [1941] I.R. 406 (HC) 4–47
Attorney-General v Ferguson (CCA, October 17, 1975) 4–40n, 12–28n
Attorney-General v Fleming [1934] I.R. 15 (CCA) 7–33
Attorney-General v Hamilton (No.1) [1993] 2 I.R. 250 (SC) 13–65
Attorney-General v Hamilton (No.2) [1993] 3 I.R. 227 (SC) 13–62n, 13–63
Attorney-General v Hitchcock (1847) 1 Excheq. 91 .... 1–13n, 3–04, 3–05, 3–10
Attorney-General v Ingram (1947) 82 I.L.T.R. 79
   (HC) 2–17, 2–17n, 2–20, 2–20n
Attorney-General v Joyce and Walsh [1929] I.R. 526 (CCA) 7–33
Attorney-General v Lannigan (1958) 24 Ir. Jur. Rep. 59 (CC) 1–26
Attorney-General v Linehan [1929] I.R. 19 (CCA) 5–21n, 5–26
Attorney-General v McCabe [1927] I.R. 129 (CCA) 7–28n, 10–10n
Attorney-General v O'Leary [1991] I.L.R.M. 454
   (HC) 4–08, 4–31n, 4–32n, 4–34, 4–36n, 4–40, 4–42,
                                4–44, 4–45, 4–49, 4–58, 12–28, 13–80n, 13–84n
Attorney-General v O'Shea [1931] I.R. 713 (CCA) 1–54n, 8–47
Attorney-General v O'Sullivan [1930] I.R. 553 (CCA) 2–14
Attorney-General v Paperlink [1984] I.L.R.M. 373 (HC) 13–90n
Attorney-General v Quinn (CCA, March 23, 1998) 13–84n, 13–100n

Attorney-General v Quinn [1965] I.R. 366
(SC) 4–19, 4–21, 4–23, 4–24, 4–25, 4–25n, 4–26, 4–27
Attorney-General v Shorten [1961] I.R. 304 (HC) 4–53, 4–54
Averill v UK (2001) 31 E.H.R.R. 839 13–106

B v DPP [1997] 3 I.R. 140
(HC) 1–44, 2–60n, 5–52, 6–37, 7–09n, 7–14, 7–28n, 7–30
Balabel v Air India [1988] 2 All E.R. 246 (CA) 13–25n
Belabel v Air India [1988] Ch. 317 (CA) 13–33n, 13–34n
Banco Ambrosiana S.P.A. v Ansbacher and Co. Ltd. [1987]
I.L.R.M. 669 (SC) 4–81, 4–81n
Barbera, Messegue and Jabardo v Spain (1988)
11 E.H.R.R. 360 .... 1–07n, 1–42n, 4–09
Barking and Dagenham LBC v O [1993] 4 All E.R. 59 .... 13–17n
Barkway v South Wales Transport Co. Ltd. [1950] 1 All E.R. 392 (HL) 4–62n
Barrett v Southern Health Board (HC, December 5, 1988) 4–71
Barry v Waldron (HC, May 23, 1996, ex tempore) 10–53n
Begley, Re [1939] I.R. 479 (SC) 4–80n
Berkeley Peerage Case (1811) 4 Camp. 401 .... 9–11n
BJ v DPP (HC, February 12, 2002) 12–08n
Blunt v Park Lane Hotel [1942] 2 K.B. 253 (CA) 13–80, 13–81n
Boardman v DPP [1974] 3 All E.R. 887
(HL) 7–07, 7–07n, 7–10, 7–13, 7–13n, 7–18, 7–22n, 7–23
Bolam v Friern Hospital [1957] 2 All E.R. 118 .... 12–19, 12–20,12–23n
Bolitho v City and Hackney H.A. [1998] A.C. 232 (HL) 12–19n
Bonis Doherty, Re [1961] I.R. 219 (HC) 4–14n
Bord na gCon v Murphy [1970] I.R. 301 (SC) 10–02n, 13–25
Borgers v Belgium [1993] 15 E.H.R.R. 92 .... 1–07n
Borges v Medical Council (March 5, 2003 (HC);
January 30, 2004 (SC)) 1–60n 9–18
Bostin v Carew (1824) Ry & M. 127 .... 1–53n
Bowes and McGrath v DPP [2003] 2 I.R. 25 (SC) 1–42n, 1–44, 1–44n, 1–45
Braddish v DPP [2001] 3 I.R. 127 (SC) 1–42, 1–43, 6–36, 6–37, 10–74
Brady v Group Lotus Car Co. [1987] 3 All E.R. 1050 (CA) 4–03n
Bratty v Attorney-General for N.I [1963] A.C. 386
(HL) 1–48n, 4–22, 4–29, 4–29n, 4–30, 4–33
Brazier v Ministry of Defence [1965] 1 Lloyd's Rep. 26 .... 4–65n
Breathnach v Ireland (No.3) [1993] 2 I.R. 458
(HC) 13–22, 13–22n, 13–73, 13–74, 13–79
Brennan v DPP [1996] 1 I.L.R.M. 267 (SC) 11–31
Brewer v Williams (1977) 430 U.S. 387 (SC) 11–08n
Bridlington Relay Ltd. v Yorkshire Electricity Board [1965] Ch. 436 .... 1–39n
British Columbia, Girard v Royal Columbian Hospital
(1976) 66 D.L.R. (3d) 676 .... 4–70n
Brogan v UK (1989) 11 E.H.R.R. 117 .... 11–41n
Brown v Eastern and Midlands Railway Co (1889) 22 Q.B.D. 391 .... 7–35n
Browne v Dunn (1893) 6 R. 67 .... 1–52n
Brozicek v Italy (1990) 12 E.H.R.R. 371 .... 1–07n
Buckley v Incorporated Law Society [1994] 2 I.R. 44 (HC) 13–57
Bula Ltd. (in receivership) v Crowley [1990] I.L.R.M. 756
(SC) 13–05, 13–22n
Bula Ltd. v Crowley (No.2) [1994] 2 I.R. 54 (SC) 13–15n, 13–34

Table of Cases xix

Bula Ltd. v Crowley (HC, December 19, 1989, Murphy J.,
    ex tempore) 13–26
Burke v Central Independent Television Plc [1994] 2 I.R. 61 (SC) 13–60
Burnwell v British Transport Commission [1956] 1 Q.B.D. 187 .... 13–11n
Bursill v Tanner (1883) 16 Q.B.D. 1 .... 13–20n
Butler v Board of Trade [1971] 1 Ch. 680 13–14
Buttes Gas & Oil Co. v Hammer (No.3) [1981] Q.B. 223
    (HL) 13–40, 13–40n
Byrne v Grey[1988] I.R. 31 (HC) 11–66
Byrne v Londonderry Tramway Co [1902] 2 I.R. 457 1–40

Calcraft v Guest [1898] 1 Q.B. 759 (CA) 13–02n, 13–08, 13–23, 13–40
Callaghan v Gleeson and Lavelle (HC, July 19, 2002) 12–21n
Camden v I.R.C. [1914] 1 K.B. 641 (CA) 1–39n
Canterbury v Spence (1972) 464 F 2d 772 12–21
Carey v Hussey (HC, December 21, 1999) 1–33n
Carroll v Law Society of Ireland (No.2) [2003] 1 I.R. 284 (HC) 13–83n
Cassidy v Ministry of Health [1951] 2 K.B. 343 (CA) 4–65n
Cathcart Ex p., *Re* (1870) 5 Ch. App. 703 (CA) 13–27n
Chadwick v Bowman (1886) 16 Q.B. 223 .... 13–40n
Chambers v Mississippi 410 U.S. 295 (1973) (SC) 10–05n
Chan Kau v R. [1955] A.C. 206 (PC) 4–20n
Chard v Chard [1955] 3 All E.R. 721 .... 4–14n
Christie v Leachinsky [1946] 1 K.B. 124 (CA);
    [1947] A.C. 573 (HL) 11–29, 11–30, 11–58
Clarke v Member in Charge [2001] 4 I.R. 173 (SC) 11–46n, 11–47, 11–47n
Coddington v DPP (CCA, May 31, 2001) 4–76
Commonwealth v Cleary (1898) 172 Mass. 175 .... 2–52n
Comptroller of Customs v Western Lectern Co Ltd [1966] A.C. 367
    (PC) 10–02n
Condron v UK [2001] E.H.R.R. 1 13–105
Convening Authority v Private Doyle [1996] 2 I.L.R.M. 213
    (CMAC) 4–30n, 4–37n, 4–44, 4–45
Conway v Rimmer [1968] A.C. 910 (HL) 13–70
Cook v Carroll [1945] I.R. 515 (HC) 13–49, 13–50, 13–51, 13–52, 13–61
Cooper Flynn v Radio Telefís Éireann [2000] 3 I.R. 344 (HC) 13–47n
Corbett v DPP [1999] 2 I.R. 179 (HC) 13–16, 13–24, 13–75
Cosgrove v E.S.B. [2003] 1 I.L.R.M. 544 (HC) 4–64
Coss v National Maternity Hospital (1949) 83 I.L.T. 103 (HC) 13–44n
Cracknell v Smith [1960] 3 All E.R. 569 (Q.B.D.) 5–12n
Crawford v Treacy (HC, November 4, 1998) 13–15, 13–19
Crescent Farm (Sidcup) Sports Ltd. v Sterling Offices Ltd.
    [1972] Ch. 553 .... 13–15n
Criminal Assets Bureau v Craft [2001] 1 I.R. 121 (HC) 11–49
Criminal Assets Bureau v Hunt (SC, March 19, 2003) 9–61
Cullen v Clarke [1963] I.R. 368 (SC) 1–32, 9–21n, 9–22, 9–33, 9–75
Cully v Governor of Portlaoise Prison [1998] 1 I.R. 443 (HC) 11–37n
Cummings v City of Vancouver (1911) 1 W.W.R. 31 .... 4–67n
Customglass Boats Ltd. v Salthouse Bros. Ltd. [1976] R.P.C. 589
    (SC, N.Z.) 9–73n
Cutts v Head [1984] 1 All E.R. 597 (CA) 13–38
Cutts v Head [1984] Ch. 290 .... 13–37n

D v DPP [1994] 2 I.R. 465 (SC) 1–76n
D v NSPCC [1978] A.C. 171 (HL) 13–54n, 13–57
D(V) v DPP (HC, November 23, 2001) 12–08n
Daniels v Heskin [1954] I.R. 73 (SC) 12–19n
Danville v Calwell [1907] 2 I.R. 617 (K.B.D.) 9–80n
Darwin v Connecticut (1968) 391 U.S. 346 10–59
Daubert v Merrell Dow Pharmaceuticals Inc. (1993) 113 S.C. 2786 12–16
Davie v Edinburgh Magistrates [1953] S.C. 34 12–01
Davies v DPP [1954] A.C. 378 (HL) 5–27, 5–30, 5–32
DB (a minor) v Minister for Justice [1999] 1 I.R. 29; [1999]
   1 I.L.R.M. 93 (HC) 1–53n
Delcourt v Belgium (1970) 1 E.H.R.R. 355 .... 1–07n
Dellow's Will Trusts, Re [1964] 1 All E.R. 771 .... 4–82n
Dental Board v O'Callaghan [1969] I.R. 181 (HC) 5–26
Deokinanan v R. [1969] 1 A.C. 20 (PC) 10–08n, 10–09
Dillon v O'Brien and Davis [1887] 20 L.R. I.R. 300 .... 1–42n
Dillon v Tobin (1879) 12 I.L.T.R. 32 (Prob) 9–80n
Director of Consumer Affairs v Sugar Distributors Ltd [1991]
   1 I.R. 225 (HC) 13–54, 13–54n
Domincan v R. (1992) 173 C.L.R. 555 (HC, Aust.) 6–11n
Donnelly v Ireland [1998] 1 I.R. 321
   (SC) 1–11n, 1–28n, 1–60, 1–60n, 1–61, 1–62, 1–71, 1–73
Doorson v Netherlands (1996) 22 E.H.R.R. 330 .... 1–28n
DPP (Hanley) v Holly [1984] I.L.R.M. 149 (HC) 13–56n, 13–74
DPP (Stratford) v Fagan [1994] 2 I.L.R.M. 349 (SC) 11–56
DPP v A & BC Chewing Gum Ltd [1968] 1 Q.B. 159 12–03
DPP v Barnwell (CCA, January 24, 1997) 4–11n
DPP v Barr (CCA, March 2, 1992) 3–02n
DPP v Best [2000] 2 I.R. 17 (SC) 1–48n, 4–31n, 4–33, 4–54n
DPP v Boardman [1975] A.C. 421 (HL) 3–36
DPP v Boylan [1991] 1 I.R. 477 (CCA) 11–46
DPP v Bradley (HC, December 9, 1999) 11–32n
DPP v Brophy [1992] I.L.R.M. 709 .... 2–55n
DPP v Byrne [1999] 1 I.L.R.M. 500 (SC) 10–21
DPP v Clifford (HC, July 22, 2002) 1–51n, 2–42n
DPP v Connell [1998] 3 I.R. 62 (HC) 11–29
DPP v Cremin (CCA, May 10, 1999) 4–25n, 4–77
DPP v Delaney [1996] 3 I.R. 556 (HC); [1997] 3 I.R. 453
   (SC) 11–05, 11–06, 11–21, 11–36
DPP v Doyle [1994] 2 I.R. 286 (SC) 1–46
DPP v Dunne [1994] 2 I.R. 337 (HC) 11–65n
DPP v Early [1998] 3 I.R. 158 (HC) 11–51n
DPP v Edgeworth (SC, March 29, 2001) 11–66n
DPP v Elliot [1997] 2 I.L.R.M. 156 (HC) 13–88
DPP v Finn [2003] 1 I.R. 372 (SC) 11–38
DPP v Forbes [1994] 2 I.R. 542 (SC) 11–35, 11–36, 11–36n
DPP v Gaffney [1987] I.R. 173 .... 11–35n
DPP v Healy [1990] 2 I.R. 73 (SC) 10–51, 10–52, 10–53, 11–21n
DPP v Hester [1973] A.C. 296 (HL) 5–33n, 5–49n
DPP v Keogh [1998] 4 I.R. 416; [1998] 1 I.L.R.M. 72 (HC) 7–19
DPP v Kilbourne [1973] A.C. 729
   (HL) 1–13, 5–06n, 5–33n, 5–51, 5–51n, 7–18n

Table of Cases

DPP v Kirwan (CCA, October 19, 1998) 2–56n
DPP v M (CCA, February 15, 2001) 1–50n, 4–11n
DPP v M [1998] 2 W.L.R. 604 2–14
DPP v McCreesh [1992] 2 I.R. 239 (SC) 11–29n, 11–35n
DPP v McGarrigle (SC, June 22, 1987) 11–31
DPP v McGuinness [1978] I.R. 189 at 191 (CCA) 3–23
DPP v McMahon [1987] I.L.R.M. 87 (SC) 11–26
DPP v McMahon, McMeel and Wright [1986] I.R. 393 (SC) 11–07n
DPP v McNamara (SC, June 21, 2002) 9–49
DPP v McNeice [2003] 2 I.R. 614 .... 11–38n
DPP v Molloy (SC, February 28, 2003) 11–36
DPP v Morgan [1975] 2 W.L.R. 913 (HL) 3–24n
DPP v Myers [1965] A.C. 1001 (HL) 9–38, 9–62
DPP v O'Connell [1995] 1 I.R. 244 (CCA) 11–20
DPP v O'Kelly (HC, February 10, 1998) 9–22, 9–23
DPP v O'Rourke (HC, February 17, 2003) 11–36n
DPP v P [1991] 2 A.C. 447 (HL) 7–09n, 7–13, 7–14, 7–15
DPP v Ping Lin [1976] A.C. 574 .... 10–40n, 10–41n
DPP v Rooney [1993] I.L.R.M. 61 (HC) 11–57n, 11–58n
DPP v Special Criminal Court [1999] 1 I.R. 60 (SC) 1–66, 3–38n
DPP v Spratt [1995] 1 I.R. 585 (HC) 10–50n
DPP v Spratt [1995] 2 I.L.R.M. 117 (HC) 10–27n
DPP v Sweeney (HC, March 26, 1996) 9–48
DPP v Yamanoha [1994] 1 I.R. 565 (CCA) 11–66
Dubai Aluminum Co. Ltd. v Al Alawi [1999] 1 All E.R. 703 .... 13–15n
Dubai Bank Ltd. v Galadari [1990] Ch. 98 (CA) 13–40n
Dully v North Eastern Health Board (HC, November 3, 1988) 4–71
Duncan v Governor of Portlaoise Prison [1998] 1 I.R. 433 (HC) 11–37n
Dunne v Clinton [1930] I.R. 366 (HC) 11–28n, 11–39, 11–39n, 11–40, 11–50n
Dunne v DPP [2002] 2 I.R. 305
    (SC) 1–11n, 1–42, 1–42n, 1–43, 1–44, 6–25n, 6–37
Dunne v National Maternity Hospital [1989] I.R. 91 (SC) 12–19, 12–20, 12–23
Dyer v Best (1866) 4 H. & C. 189 .... 2–45n

East Donegal Co-Operative v Attorney-General [1970] I.R. 317 (SC) 9–18n
Eastern Health Board v District Judge J.P. McDonnell
    [1999] 1 I.R. 174 (HC) 1–53n, 9–47n
Eastern Health Board v Mooney (HC, March 20, 1998) 1–53n
Edwards v UK (1992) 15 E.C.H.R. 417 .... 1–42n
Elias v Pasmore [1934] 2 K.B. 164 .... 11–63n
English and American Insurance Co. Ltd. v Herbert Smith & Co.
    [1988] F.S.R. 232 13–08
Enoch and Zaretsky, Bock & Co.'s Arbitration, *Re* [1910]
    1 K.B. 327 .... 1–53n
Entick v Carrington [1876] 2 Wils 275 .... 11–65n
ER v JR [1981] 1 I.L.R.M. 125 (HC) 13–48, 13–52
Estate of Fuld Deceased [1965] 2 All E.R. 657 .... 13–19, 13–40n
Ex. p. Fernandez (1861) 10 CBNS 3 .... 2–01n

F (a minor), *Re* [1993] Fam. 375 (CA) 1–39n
Falealilt [1996] 3 N.Z.L.R. 664 (CA) 8–33
FCB v Italy (1991) 14 E.H.R.R. 909 .... 1–07n

Federal Commissioners of Taxation v Coombes (1999) 164
   A.L.R. 131 .... 13–27n
Feldbrugge v Netherlands (1986) 8 E.H.R.R. 425 .... 1–07n
Fitzpatrick v Wymes [1976] I.R. 301 (SC) 2–01n
Flanagan v Fahy [1918] 2 I.R. 361 (CA) 2–51n
Flood v Russell (1891) 29 L.R. I.R. 91 .... 9–79n
Folens Co. v Minister for Education [1981] I.L.R.M. 21 (HC) 13–72
Foley v Quinnsworth (HC, April 10, 1992) 4–60, 4–61
Folkes v Chaad (1782) 3 Doug. K.B. 157 .... 12–01n
Forristal v Forristal (1966) 100 I.L.T.R. 182 (Cir. C.) 13–51
Fox v Gwent Chief Constable [1985] 1 W.L.R. 1126 (HL) 10–62n
Freeman v DPP [1996] 3 I.R. 565 (HC) 11–05, 11–21n, 11–35n
Freeman v R. [1994] 1 W.L.R. 1437 (PC) 6–11n
Funke v France (1993) 16 E.H.R.R. 257 13–99

G v DPP [1998] 2 W.L.R. 609 .... 2–11, 2–14n
G (A Minor) (Child Abuse: Standard of Proof), *Re* [1987]
   1 W.L.R. 1461 .... 7–35n
Gallagher v Revenue Commissioners [1995] 1 I.L.R.M. 241
   (SC) 9–54
Gallagher v Stanley & National Maternity Hospital [1998]
   2 I.R. 267 (SC) 13–34, 13–34n, 13–43
Galvin v Murray [2001] 2 I.L.R.M. 234 (SC) 13–29n, 13–31
Gamlen Chemical Co. (U.K.) Ltd. v Rochem Ltd. [1983] R.P.C. 1 .... 13–15n
Geoghegan v Harris [2000] 3 I.R. 536 (HC) 12–21n
Geraghty v Minister for Local Government [1975] I.R. 300
   (HC) 13–71n
Gertz v Fitchburg (1884) 137 Mass. 77 3–13
Getty (Sarah C.) Trust, *Re* [1985] Q.B. 956 .... 13–22n
Gilligan v Criminal Assets Bureau [1998] 3 I.R. 185 (HC);
   [2001] 4 I.R. 113 (SC) 4–49, 13–83, 13–83n
Glasbrook Brothers Ltd. v Glamorgan CC [1925] A.C. 270 .... 11–56n
Goddard v Nationwide Building Society [1987] Q.B. 670 (CA) 13–08n
Gold v Haringey H.A. [1988] 1 Q.B. 481 (CA) 12–20
Golder v UK (1979–80) 1 E.H.R.R. 524 .... 1–07n
Goodman International (No. 3) v Hamilton [1993] 3 I.R. 320
   (HC) 13–48, 13–55, 13–57
Goods of Ball (1890) 25 L.R. Ir. 556 9–82
Goods of Glynn Deceased v Glynn [1990] 2 I.R. 326 (SC) 4–80
Grant v Downs (1976) 135 C.L.R. 674 (HC, Aust.) 13–42n
Great Atlantic Insurance v Home Insurance Co. [1981]
   1 W.L.R. 529 (CA) 13–11
Greenough v Eccles (1859) 5 C.B.N.S. 786 .... 2–34, 2–35n
Greenough v Gaskell (1833) 1 My. & K. 98 .... 13–20n
Gresham Hotel v Manning (1867) I.R. 1 .... 9–74n

Hadjianastassiou v Greece (1993) 16 E.H.R.R. 219 .... 1–07n
Haines v Bellissimo (1977) 82 D.L.R. (3d) 215 .... 12–17n
Hanafin v Minister for the Environment [1996] 2 I.R. 321 (HC);
   [1996] 2 I.L.R.M. 161 (SC) 9–73n, 4–81n
Hanahoe v Hussey[1998] 3 I.R. 69 (HC) 11–65, 11–65n, 11–66n
Hannigan v District Judge Clifford [1990] I.L.R.M. 65 (SC) 11–39

Table of Cases

Hanrahan v Merck, Sharp & Dohme Ltd. [1988] I.L.R.M. 629
  (SC) 4–54n, 4–66, 4–67
Hardy v Ireland [1994] 2 I.R. 550 (SC) 1–48n, 4–30n, 4–32n, 4–33
Harmony Shipping Co. v Davis [1979] 3 All E.R. 177 (CA) 13–41n
Harris v DPP [1952] A.C. 694 (HL) 7–16n
Harris v Lambert H.C. [1932] I.R. 504 (HC) 9–80n
Harrison v Southcote and Moreland (1751) 2 Ves. Se. 389 (CA) 13–85n
Harvey v Ocean Accident and Guarantee Corporation [1905]
  2 K.B. 1 (CA) 4–14n
Haughey, Re [1971] I.R. 217 (SC) 1–76n, 9–21n, 13–80n
Heaney and McGuinness v Ireland [1996] I.R. 580;
  [1997] 1 I.L.R.M. 117 (SC) 13–80n, 13–84n, 13–87, 13–88,
                                                13–88n, 13–90, 13–92, 13–97
Hegarty v King (1880) 7 L.R. Ir. 18 .... 4–80n
Hehir v Commissioners of Police of the Metropolis [1982] 1 W.L.R. 715
  (CA) 13–11n, 13–77n
Herron v Haughton (SC, May 19, 2000) 1–16n
Hill v Baxter [1958] 1 Q.B. 277 .... 1–48n
Hill v Examiner [2001] 4 I.R. 219 (SC) 8–19n
Hockin v Cooke 4 T.R. 314 .... 1–39n
Holmes v Baddeley (1844) 1 Ph. 476 .... 13–20n
Holmes: Beamish v Smeltzer, Re [1934] I.R. 693 .... 9–81n
Horgan v Murray [1999] 1 I.L.R.M. 257 (HC) 13–22n, 13–36
Howlin v Morris Tribunal (HC, October 13, 2003) 13–55, 13–64
Huffman v Lindquist (1951) 234 P. 2d 34 .... 12–23n
Hughes v Garda Commissioner (HC, January 20, 1998) 13–74
Hughes v Staunton (HC, February 16, 1990) 9–39, 9–40
Hurch v Dublin Corporation [1992] I.L.R.M. 596 (SC) 4–54n
Huvig v France (1990) 12 E.H.R.R. 528 .... 11–11n

I.T.C. Film Distributors Ltd. v Video Exchange Ltd. [1982] 1 Ch. 431 13–08
IAC Deceased: C and F v WC and TC [1989] I.L.R.M. 815 (SC) 4–80n
Ibrahim v R. [1914] A.C. 599 (PC) 10–32
In the Matter of National Irish Bank [1999]
  1 I.L.R.M. 321 .... 10–39, 10–39n, 13–87, 13–92, 13–94, 13–96, 13–97
Incorporated Law Society of Ireland v Minister for Justice
  [1987] I.L.R.M. 42 (HC) 13–73
International Credit and Investment Co. (Overseas) Ltd. v Adham
  (Disclosure), The Times, February 10, 1997 .... 13–27n
Istel Ltd. v Tully [1993] A.C. 45 (HL) 13–83n

J O'C v DPP [2000] 3 I.R. 478 (SC) 2–60n
James v R (1970) 55 Cr. App. R. 299 (P.C.) 5–36n, 5–41
JB v Switzerland (European Court of Human Rights, May 3, 2001) 13–99
Jeffrey v Black [1978] 1 All E.R. 555 (QBD) 11–63
Jeffrey v Black [1978] Q.B. 490 (CA) 11–23n
Jennings v Quinn [1968] I.R. 305 (SC) 11–63n
JL v DPP [2000] 3 I.R. 122 .... 12–08n, 12–11n
John W [1998] 2 Cr. App. R. 289 (CA) 7–13
Johnston v Church of Scientology [2001] 1 I.R. 682 (HC, SC) 13–48, 13–52
Jones v DPP [1962] A.C. 635
  (HL) 8–04, 8–06, 8–12, 8–12n, 8–19, 8–46, 8–46n

Jones v Jones (1908) 24 T.L.R. 839 .... 13–19n

Kearney v Minister for Justice [1986] I.R. 116 (HC) 13–90n
Kennedy and Arnold v Ireland and Attorney-General [1988]
   I.L.R.M. 472 (HC) 11–10
Kennedy v Law Society of Ireland (No.3) [2002] 2 I.R. 458
   (SC) 11–07, 11–69n, 11–70n, 11–71
Kenning v Eve Construction [1989] 1 W.L.R. 1189 13–32
Kevin O'Kelly, Re (1974) 109 I.L.T.R. 97 (CCA) 13–60
Kiely v Minister for Social Welfare [1977] I.R. 267
   (SC) 9–17, 9–53, 9–54, 9–85n
Kincaid v Aer Lingus Teoranta [2003] 2 I.R. 314 (SC) 13–29, 13–31
King v Attorney-General [1981] I.R. 233 (SC) 7–19n
Klass v Germany (1978) 2 E.H.R.R. 214 .... 11–11n
Kostovski v The Netherlands (1990) 12 E.H.R.R. 434 .... 9–19n
Kraska v Switzerland (1994) 18 E.H.R.R. 188 .... 1–07n
Kremzow v Austria (1994) 17 E.H.R.R. 322 .... 1–07n
Krulevitch v US (1949) 336 U.S. 440 .... 7–27n
Kuruma v R. [1955] A.C. 197 (PC) 10–62n

L(T) v L(V) [1996] F.L.R. 126 (HC) 13–22n
L(T) v L(V) [1996] F.L.R. 126 (Cir. C.) 13–17
L(P) v DPP (HC, April 16, 2002) 12–01n
Lam Chi-Ming v R. [1991] 2 A.C. 212 (PC) 10–62n
Lavery v Member-in-Charge, Carrickmacross Garda Station
   [1992] 2 I.R. 390 (SC) 10–53n, 10–53n, 13–107
Lawrie v Muir (1950) S.C. 19 .... 11–23n
Leahy v Corboy [1969] I.R 148 (SC) 4–80, 4–80n
Leen v President of the Executive Council (No.1) [1926]
   I.R. 456 (HC) 13–69
Lindsay v Mid-Western Health Board [1993] I.L.R.M. 550
   (SC) 4–59n, 4–60, 4–62, 4–63, 4–64, 4–67, 4–70
Li-Shu-Ling v R. [1989] A.C. 270 (PC) 10–05n
Lloyd v Powell Duffryn Steam Coal Co. Ltd. [1914] A.C. 733 (HL) 9–75n
Lloyde v West Midlands Gas Board [1971] 2 All E.R. 1240 (CA) 4–62n
Lord Stafford's case (1680) 7 St. Tr. 1293 3–10
Lord Talbot de Malahide v Cussack (1864) 17 I.C.L.R. 213 .... 2–45n
Lowery v R. [1974] A.C. 85 (PC) 12–08, 12–10n
Lui Mei Lin v Queen [1989] 1 A.C. 288 (PC) 9–63n, 10–65

M (A Minor), Re [1994] 1 F.L.R. 59 .... 4–82n
M v D [1998] 3 I.R. 175 (HC) 9–50, 13–83, 13–83n
Madigan v Devally and DPP [1999] 2 I.L.R.M. 141 (SC) 11–31, 11–32n
Magee v UK (2001) 31 E.H.R.R. 822 13–106
Makin v Attorney-General for New South Wales [1894] A.C. 57
   (PC) 7–03, 7–04, 7–04n, 7–05, 7–06, 7–17,
                                                                          7–20, 7–23, 8–12, 8–24, 8–25
Malindi v R. [1967] 1 A.C. 439 (PC) 8–34n
Mallory v US (1957) 354 U.S. 449 .... 10–58n
Malone v Metropolitan Police Commissioners [1979] 2 All E.R. 620 .... 11–10n
Malone v UK (1984) 7 E.H.R.R. 14 .... 11–10n
Manchester Brewery v Combs (1900) 82 L.T. 347 9–76

Table of Cases

Mapp v Gilhooley (SC, April 23, 1991) 2–15, 9–43n
Marks v Beyfus (1890) 25 Q.B.D. 494 (CA) 13–58
Marsham, *Re* [1912] 2 K.B. 362 .... 2–05n
Maryland v Craig 497 U.S. 836 (1990) 1–61
Matter of a Ward of Court (HC, May 15, 1995) 4–81
Matter of M, S, & W Infants [1996] 1 I.L.R.M. 370 (HC) 9–44, 9–47, 9–62
Maxwell v DPP [1935] A.C. 309 (HL) 8–03n, 8–11, 8–19
McCarrick v Leavy [1964] I.R. 225 (SC) 10–17
McConnell v Commissioner of An Garda Síochána [2003] 2 I.R. 19
    (HC) 2–01n
McDonagh v West of Ireland Fisheries Ltd. (HC, December 19, 1986) 4–61
McDonald v RTÉ [2001] 2 I.L.R.M. 1 (SC) 13–77
McGhee v Attorney-General [1974] I.R. 284 (SC) 2–21, 13–66
McGinley and Egan v UK (1999) 27 E.H.R.R. 1 .... 1–07n
McGowan v Carville [1960] I.R. 330 (SC) 4–47n, 4–52
McGregor v Stokes [1952] V.L.R. 347 .... 9–30n
McHugh v Brennan & DPP (HC, April 14, 2000) 2–49n
McK (F) v F (A) (SC, January 30, 2002) 9–86n
McK v McK [1936] I.R. 177 (HC) 4–81n
McKenna v Deerey [1998] 1 I.R. 62 (SC) 11–26n
McKevitt v DPP (SC, March 18, 2003) 13–06n
McKevitt v Ireland and Attorney-General [1987] I.L.R.M. 541
    (SC) 4–11n
McLoughlin v DPP (CCA, February 22, 1999) 6–19n
McMahon v Judges of the Special Criminal Court (HC, July 30,
    1998) 10–05n
McMullen v Carty (SC, January 27, 1998) 13–11, 13–11n
McNabb v US (1942) 318 U.S. 332 .... 1–03n, 10–58n
McSorley v Governor Mountjoy Prison [1996] 2 I.L.R.M. 331 (HC) 10–54
Merriman v Greenhills Foods Ltd. [1997] 1 I.L.R.M. 46 (SC) 4–65, 4–67
Mexborough (Earl of) v Whitwood U.D.C. [1897] 2 Q.B. 111 (CA) 13–80n
Midland Bank Trust v Hett, Stubbs & Kemp [1978] 3 All E.R. 571 .... 12–23n
Miley v Flood [2001] 1 I.L.R.M. 489
    (HC) 13–21, 13–27, 13–27n, 13–34, 13–54n
Miller v Minister for Pensions [1947] 2 All E.R. 372 (CA) 4–72, 4–79n
Mills v R [1995] 3 All E.R. 865 (PC) 9–70, 9–78n
Minister for Industry & Commerce v Steele [1952] I.R. 304 (SC) 4–51
Minter v Priest [1929] 1 K.B. 655 .... 13–34n
Miranda v Arizona 384 U.S. 436 (1966) 10–53n
Mitchell v DPP [2000] 2 I.L.R.M. 396 (HC) 1–45, 6–38
Mitchell v Queen [1998] 2 W.L.R. 839 (PC) 10–13n
Moloney v Jury's Hotel Plc. (SC, November 12, 1999) 9–41, 9–51
Mood Music Publishing Company Ltd. v De Wolfe Ltd. [1976]
    Ch. 119 (CA) 7–35
Moore v Martin (HC, May 29, 2000) 10–21
Moore v Ransome's Dock (1898) 14 T.L.R. 539 .... 7–35n
Morris v Beardmore [1980] A.C. 446 (HL) 11–35n
Morris v Metriyakool (1981) 309 N.W. 2d 910 .... 12–23n
Mulhern v Clery [1930] I.R. 118 (SC) 4–13n
Mullen v Quinnsworth Ltd [1991] I.L.R.M. 439 (SC) 4–60
Murdoch v Taylor [1965] 1 All E.R. 406 (HL) 8–13n, 8–61n, 8–62, 8–65
Murphy v DPP [1989] I.L.R.M. 71 (HC) 1–42, 1–43, 6–36

Murphy v Dublin Corporation and Minister for Local Government
  [1972] I.R. 215 (SC) 13–71, 13–72, 13–74, 13–75
Murphy v GM PB PC Ltd. and GH (HC, June 4, 1999) 9–19n, 9–50
Murphy v Kirwan [1993] 3 I.R. 501 (SC) 13–15n, 13–16, 13–17
Murphy v Times Newspapers Ltd. [1996] 1 I.R. 169 (SC) 1–23n
Murray v UK (1995) 19 E.H.R.R. 193 13–109
Murray v UK (1996) 22 E.H.R.R.
  29 .... 1–07n, 5–13n, 10–57, 11–41,13–105, 13–105n, 13–106, 13–109n
Myers v DPP [1965] A.C. 1001 (HL) 9–12, 9–13
Myers v DPP [1997] 3 W.L.R. 552 (HL) 9–63

N (orse K) v K [1985] I.R. 733 (SC) 4–81n
N, Re (CA, March 14, 1996) 12–26
NC v DPP (SC, July 5, 2001) 12–11
Nea Kateria Maritime Co. Ltd. v Atlantic Corp. and Great Lakes Steamship
  (1981) COMM L.R. 138 .... 13–11n
Neill v Minister for Finance [1948] I.R. 88 (SC) 4–61
Neumeister v Austria (1979–80) 1 E.H.R.R. 91 .... 1–07n
Ng Chun Pui v Lee Cheun Tat [1988] R.T.R. 298 (PC) 4–63n
Nicholas v Penny [1950] 2 K.B. 466 .... 5–18n
Nichols v Digney [1921] V.L.R. 513 .... 5–37n
Nicolaou, Re [1966] I.R. 567 (SC) 2–21n, 13–66n
Nielson v Denmark (1988) 11 E.H.R.R. 175 .... 1–07n
Niemitz v Germany (1992) 16 E.H.R.R. 97 .... 13–21n
Northern Banking Co Ltd v Carpenter [1931] I.R. 268 (SC) 2–45n

O'Broin v District Judge Ruane and Attorney-General [1989]
  I.L.R.M. 732 (HC) 3–04n
O'C v TC (HC, December 8, 1981) 11–69
O'Callaghan v Ireland [1994] 1 I.R. 555 (SC) 11–57
O'Connor v Smith (HC, November 17, 1994) 2–60n
O'Flynn v District Judge Smithwick and DPP [1993] 3 I.R. 589 (HC) 2–36
O'Keeffe v Ferris [1997] 2 I.L.R.M. 161 (SC) 4–81n
O'Laighleis, Re [1960] I.R. 93 (SC) 11–29n
O'Leary v Attorney-General [1991] I.L.R.M. 454 (HC) 4–32n, 4–37n
O'R v B [1991] 1 I.R. 289 (SC) 4–81n
O'Reilly v Lavelle [1990] 2 I.R. 372 (HC) 4–60
O'Rourke v Darbshire [1920] A.C. 581 (HL) 13–16n
O'Shea v DPP [1988] I.R. 655 (SC) 1–48n, 4–10n
O'Shea v Tilman Anhold and Horse Holiday Farm Ltd (SC,
  October 23, 1996) 4–63n, 4–66n
O'Sullivan v Hamill (HC, February 25, 1998) 2–28
Ollett v Bristol Aerojet Ltd [1979] 1 W.L.R. 1197 .... 13–30, 13–32
Omychund v Barker (1745) 1 Atk. 21 .... 1–14n
Oregon v Elstad (1985) 470 U.S. 298 .... 10–59n
Oxfordshire CCC v M [1994] 2 All E.R. 269 (CA) 13–17

P, Re [1987] 2 F.L.R. 467 (CA) 7–36
P McG v AF (HC, January 28, 2000) 11–69
Pais v Pais [1970] W.L.R. 830 .... 13–52n
Parkes v R. [1976] 1 W.L.R. 1251 (PC) 5–12n
PB v AL [1996] 1 I.L.R.M. 154 (HC) 13–75n

Table of Cases xxvii

PC v CH (HC, January 11, 1996) 12–18n
PC v DPP [1999] 2 I.R. 25 (HC) 12–08n
Pearse v Pearse (1846) 1 De G. & Sm. 12 .... 13–20n
People (Attorney-General) v Casey (No. 2) [1963] I.R. 33 (SC) 10–75
People (Attorney-General) v McMahon [1946] I.R. 267 (HC) 1–36n
People (Attorney-General) v Ainscough [1960] I.R. 136 (CCA) 10–13
People (Attorney-General) v Bond [1966] I.R. 214 (CA) 8–13n, 8–14n
People (Attorney-General) v Carney [1955] I.R. 324 (SC) 5–31, 5–32
People (Attorney-General) v Casey (No.2) [1963] I.R. 33
    (SC) 5–48n, 6–01, 6–04, 6–04n, 6–10,
                                            6–18, 6–20, 6–20n, 6–23, 6–31, 6–33
People (Attorney-General) v Coleman
    [1945] I.R. 237 (CCA) 8–08n, 8–09n, 8–37, 8–47, 13–13
People (Attorney-General) v Cradden [1955] I.R. 130 (CCA) 2–56, 2–38n
People (Attorney-General) v Crosbie [1966] I.R. 490 (CCA) 9–67
People (Attorney-General) v Cummins [1972] I.R. 312
    (SC) 10–19, 10–30n, 11–25
People (Attorney-General) v Dempsey [1961] I.R. 288 (CCA) 7–05n
People (Attorney-General) v Dwyer [1972] I.R. 416 (SC) 4–28n
People (Attorney-General) v Fagan (CCA, May 13, 1974) 6–20n, 6–23n
People (Attorney-General) v Fennell (No.1) [1940] I.R. 445 (CCA) 4–30n
People (Attorney-General) v Ferguson (CCA, October 27, 1975) 12–28n
People (Attorney-General) v Flynn [1963] I.R. 255 (CCA) 10–33, 10–41
People (Attorney-General) v Hannigan [1941] I.R. 252 (CCA) 2–37n
People (Attorney-General) v Hughes (1958) 92 I.L.T.R. 179 (CCA) 6–04n
People (Attorney-General) v Kehoe [1951] I.R. 70 (HC) 2–02n, 2–27n
People (Attorney-General) v Kennedy [1946] I.R. 517 (CCA) 1–41n
People (Attorney-General) v Kirwan [1943] I.R. 279
    (CCA) 1–14n, 1–36n, 7–04, 7–04n, 8–12, 8–19
People (Attorney-General) v Martin [1956] I.R. 22 (SC) 6–09, 6–22
People (Attorney-General) v McCabe [1927] I.R. 129 (CCA) 10–31n, 10–32
People (Attorney-General) v Mills [1957] I.R. 106 (CCA) 6–26, 6–27
People (Attorney-General) v Murphy [1946] I.R. 236 (CCA) 10–10n
People (Attorney-General) v O'Brien (1969) 1 Frewen 343
    (CCA) 1–02, 1–06n, 1–26
People (Attorney-General) v O'Brien [1963] I.R. 65 (SC) 1–49n
People (Attorney-General) v O'Brien [1965] I.R. 142
    (SC) 10–43, 10–48, 10–51, 10–57, 11–01, 11–02, 11–03,
                            11–04, 11–05, 11–06, 11–07, 11–08, 11–09, 11–12,
                            11–14, 11–15, 11–16, 11–17, 11–18, 11–19, 11–20, 11–21,
                            11–22, 11–23, 11–26, 11–27, 11–28, 11–35n, 11–67, 11–69
People (Attorney-General) v O'Callaghan [1966] I.R. 501 (SC) 9–49
People (Attorney-General) v O'Shea [1931] I.R. 719 (CCA) 6–04n
People (Attorney-General) v Quinn [1965] I.R. 366 (SC) 4–74n
People (Attorney-General) v Sherlock (1975) 1 Frewen 383
    (CCA) 10–46n, 10–63
People (Attorney-General) v Shribman and Samuels [1946] I.R. 431
    (CCA) 2–17n, 4–47n
People (Attorney-General) v Taylor [1974] I.R. 97 (CCA) 2–32n, 2–39, 3–09
People (Attorney-General) v Trayers [1956] I.R. 110 (CCA) 2–18n
People (Attorney-General) v Williams [1940] I.R. 195 (SC) 5–04, 5–19n, 5–37
People (DPP) v Balfe [1998] 4 I.R. 50 (CCA) 11–20

People (DPP) v Bambrick [1999] 2 I.L.R.M. 71 (CCA) 4–26
People (DPP) v Behan (CCA, February 1, 1993, ex tempore) 6–20n
People (DPP) v BK [2000] 2 I.R. 199 (CCA) 7–05n, 7–13n, 7–15
People (DPP) v Braddish [2002] 1 I.L.R.M. 151 (SC) 6–03
People (DPP) v Breathnach (1981) 2 Frewen 43
  (CCA) 10–35, 10–41, 10–43n, 10–49
People (DPP) v Brophy [1992] I.L.R.M. 709 (CCA) 2–53, 2–57, 5–42n
People (DPP) v Buck [2002] 2 I.R. 268
  (SC) 10–55, 10–56, 10–57, 11–14, 13–107
People (DPP) v Buckley [1990] 1 I.R. 14 (CCA) 10–20, 10–59n
People (DPP) v Burke and O'Leary(1986) 3 Frewen 92 (CCA) 10–24
People (DPP) v Byrne (CCA, October 30, 2003) 11–68n
People (DPP) v Byrne [1987] I.R. 363 (SC) 11–66n
People (DPP) v Byrne [1989] I.L.R.M. 613 (SC) 11–28n
People (DPP) v Byrne [2001] 2 I.L.R.M. 134 (CCA) 9–37, 9–38
People (DPP) v Byrne [2002] 2 I.L.R.M. 68 (SC) 4–45
People (DPP) v C [2001] 3 I.R. 345 (CCA) 4–77, 5–40n, 5–46
People (DPP) v Cahill (CCA, July 30, 2001) 6–05n
People (DPP) v Cahill and Costello [2001] 3 I.R. 494 (CCA) 1–37
People (DPP) v Carroll (CCA, December 18, 2002, ex tempore) 6–20
People (DPP) v Clarke [1994] 3 I.R. 289
  (CCA) 4–25, 9–63, 10–68, 10–68n, 10–69, 10–71
People (DPP) v Cleary (HC, December 7,
  2001) 10–60, 10–60n, 11–09, 11–29n, 11–38n,
                                                            11–43, 11–46, 11–60, 11–61n
People (DPP) v Connaughton (CCA, April 5, 2001) 5–18
People (DPP) v Connolly [2003] 2 I.R. 1 (CCA) 2–18n, 10–05n, 10–07, 10–75
People (DPP) v Conroy [1986]
  I.R. 460 (SC) 1–10n, 1–25, 1–26, 2–02n 10–11,
                                                            10–12n, 10–13n, 10–43n, 10–51
People (DPP) v Cooney [1998] 1 I.L.R.M. 321 (SC) 6–15
People (DPP) v Cormack [1999] 1 I.L.R.M. 398 (SC) 10–46n
People (DPP) v Cornally (CCA, November 7, 1994) 5–48n
People (DPP) v Cotter (CCA, June 28, 1999) 4–28, 4–73
People (DPP) v Cullen (CCA, March 30, 1993) 11–13
People (DPP) v D (CCA, July 27, 1993, ex tempore) 5–41, 5–48n, 5–50
People (DPP) v Darcy (CCA, July 29, 1997) 10–17n, 10–18n, 10–55n
People (DPP) v Davis [2001] 1 I.R. 146 (CCA) 4–27
People (DPP) v Diemling (CCA, May 4, 1992) 5–32
People (DPP) v Dillon [2003] 4 I.R. 501 (CCA) 11–12
People (DPP) v Donnelly (CCA, February 22, 1999) 2–43, 5–41
People (DPP) v Doyle (CCA, March 22, 2002) 4–25n
People (DPP) v Duff [1995] 3 I.R. 296 (CCA) 6–12n, 6–20n
People (DPP) v Egan [1989] I.R. 681 (CCA) 10–37
People (DPP) v Egan [1990] I.L.R.M. 780 (SC) 1–22n, 5–19n
People (DPP) v Farrell [1978] I.R. 13
  (CCA) 10–18n, 11–46n, 11–09n, 11–16n, 11–47
People (DPP) v Farrell (CCA, July 13, 1998,
  ex tempore) 6–04, 6–04n, 6–10n, 6–20n
People (DPP) v Farrell (CCA, November 25, 2003) 5–40n
People (DPP) v Ferris (CCA, March 11, 1997, ex tempore) 10–63n
People (DPP) v Ferris (CCA, June 10, 2002) 5–38, 8–35

Table of Cases xxix

People (DPP) v Finnegan (CCA, July 15, 1997) 10–49, 10–53, 11–14
People (DPP) v Finnerty [1999] 4 I.R. 364 (SC) 13–84n, 13–100n, 13–101
People (DPP) v Flannery (Central Criminal Court, June 25, 1996) 3–38n
People (DPP) v Flynn and Keely [1996] 1 I.L.R.M. 317 (Cir. C) 13–06
People (DPP) v Foley [1995] 1 I.R. 267
    (CCA) 4–31n, 4–41, 4–42, 4–44, 5–13n, 13–87
People (DPP) v Gannon (CCA, April 2, 2003) 4–40n, 12–28
People (DPP) v Gavin [2000] 4 I.R. 557 (CCA) 2–54, 2–56n
People (DPP) v Geoghan and Bourke (Central Criminal Court,
    November 18, 2003) 1–23n, 10–05n, 10–34
People (DPP) v Gillane (CCA, December 14, 1998) 2–27, 5–02n
People (DPP) v Gilligan (Special Criminal Court, March 15, 2001) 5–23n
People (DPP) v Gilligan [1993] 1 I.R. 92 (CCA) 1–50n
People (DPP) v Halligan (CCA, July 13, 1998) 4–25n, 4–27
People (DPP) v Hand [1994] 1 I.R. 577 (SC) 11–31n
People (DPP) v Hardy [1994] 2 I.R. 550 (SC) 4–42, 4–44, 4–49
People (DPP) v Healy [1990] 2 I.R. 73 (SC) 10–43n, 10–50n
People (DPP) v Hoey [1987] I.R. 637 (SC) 10–31n, 10–42
People (DPP) v Hogan (CCA, January 12, 1994) 5–21, 5–27n, 6–04n
People (DPP) v Holland (CCA, June 15, 1998) 5–23n, 10–07n, 10–55n
People (DPP) v Horgan (Central Criminal Court, 2003) 12–14
People (DPP) v Howe (Central Criminal Court, October 14, 2003) 12–14
People (DPP) v Howley [1989] I.L.R.M. 629 (SC) 11–49
People (DPP) v JEM [2001] 4 I.R. 385 (SC) 5–35, 5–38, 5–40
People (DPP) v Jethi (CCA, February 7, 2000, ex tempore) 2–54n
People (DPP) v K (CCA, December 13, 1999) 4–76
People (DPP) v Kavanagh (CCA, February 26, 1996) 1–66n, 3–38n
People (DPP) v Kavanagh (CCA, July 7, 1997) 7–02n, 7–27n
People (DPP) v Keane (Central Criminal Court,
    October 30, 2003) 2–30n, 2–31n
People (DPP) v Kehoe [1992] I.L.R.M. 481 (CCA) 12–04, 12–06
People (DPP) v Kelly (No.2) [1983] I.R. 1 (SC) 11–46
People (DPP) v Kenny (CCA, November 19, 2002) 4–11n, 1–50n, 10–68n
People (DPP) v Kenny [1990] 2 I.R. 110;
    [1990] I.L.R.M. 569 (SC) 11–02, 11–06, 11–08, 11–15,
                                            11–16n, 11–18, 11–19, 11–67, 11–69n
People (DPP) v Kiernan (CCA, October 19, 1998) 5–39n
People (DPP) v Kiernan (CCA, March 11, 1994) 2–57
People (DPP) v Lawless (CCA, November 28, 1985) 11–07n, 11–21n
People (DPP) v Leacy (CCA, July 3, 2002) 1–50n
People (DPP) v Leahy (CCA, February 14, 2000) 1–49n
People (DPP) v LG [2003] 2 I.R. 517
    (CCA) 4–76n, 4–78n, 5–52n, 7–27n, 7–14n, 7–27n, 7–28
People (DPP) v Lynch [1982] I.R. 64 (SC) 10–32, 10–43n, 10–48
People (DPP) v MA [2002] 2 I.R. 601 (CCA) 2–56
People (DPP) v Madden [1977] I.R. 336
    (CCA) 10–48n, 10–49, 10–50, 11–09, 11–14, 11–16, 11–26n
People (DPP) v Maguire [1995] 2 I.R. 286 (CCA) 6–30
People (DPP) v Maleady and Grogan [1995] 2 I.R. 517 (CCA) 6–35
People (DPP) v Malocco (CCA, May 23, 1996) 12–02, 12–27
People (DPP) v Maples (CCA, February 26, 1996) 2–18n
People (DPP) v Maples [1999] I.L.R.M. 113 (SC) 6–18, 6–18n

People (DPP) v Marley [1985] I.L.R.M. 17 (CCA) 7–02n, 9–62n
People (DPP) v McCann (CCA, March 11, 1998) 1–27n
People (DPP) v McCann [1998] 4 I.R. 397
  (CCA) 10–08n, 10–37, 10–38, 11–21, 11–61, 11–62
People (DPP) v McD (CCA, July 27, 1994) 2–57n
People (DPP) v McDonagh (CCA, July 24, 1990) 3–28n
People (DPP) v McDonagh (CCA, May 29, 2003) 9–03
People (DPP) v McFadden [2003] 2 I.R. 105; [2003] 2 I.L.R.M. 201
  (CCA) 10–26, 11–53, 11–59
People (DPP) v McGinley [1987] I.R. 340 (CCA) 3–12
People (DPP) v McGinley [1998] 2 I.L.R.M. 233 (SC) 9–49
People (DPP) v McGrail [1990] 2 I.R. 38
  (CCA) 8–06n, 8–38n, 8–48, 8–49, 8–51, 8–53, 8–54, 8–55, 8–56, 10–14n
People (DPP) v McGrath (CCA, December 2, 2002) 11–47n
People (DPP) v McHugh [2002] 1 I.R. 352 (CCA) 4–31n
People (DPP) v McKeever [1994] 2 I.L.R.M. 186 (CCA) 10–25
People (DPP) v McNally and Breathnach (1981) 2 Frewen 43
  (CCA) 10–32, 10–33n
People (DPP) v McNamara (CCA, March 22, 1999) 6–04n, 6–10n, 6–20n
People (DPP) v Meehan (Special Criminal Court, July 29,
  1999) 5–23n, 6–15n
People (DPP) v Meleady (No.3) [2001] 4 I.R. 16 (CCA) 1–03n, 1–20n, 10–43n
People (DPP) v Molloy (CCA, July 28, 1995) 5–39n, 5–40, 5–48n
People (DPP) v Morgan (CCA, July 28, 1997) 10–22, 10–22n
People (DPP) v Morrissey (CCA, July 10, 1998) 1–50n, 5–06, 5–52, 7–31
People (DPP) v Murphy (CCA, November 3, 1997,
  ex tempore) 5–46, 6–12n
People (DPP) v Murphy (SC, July 12, 2001) 10–18n, 10–46n
People (DPP) v Murray [1977] I.R. 360 (SC) 4–28n
People (DPP) v Murtagh [1990] 1 I.R. 339 (CCA) 5–27n
People (DPP) v Myers [1965] A.C. 1001 (HL) 9–63n
People (DPP) v Nevin (CCA, March 14,
  2003) 1–37, 1–47n, 1–49n, 9–20n, 13–06n
People (DPP) v O'Brien (CCA, June 17, 2002) 1–23n
People (DPP) v O'Callaghan (CCA, December 18, 2000) 1–03n, 1–17n, 1–20n
People (DPP) v O'Connell [1995] 1 I.R. 244 (CCA) 10–18n, 10–54
People (DPP) v O'Connor (CCA, July 10, 1998) 5–40
People (DPP) v O'Connor (CCA, July 29, 2002) 4–73, 5–48n
People (DPP) v O'Donnell [1995] 3 I.R. 551 (CCA) 11–59
People (DPP) v O'Driscoll (CCA, July 19, 1999, ex tempore) 10–26n
People (DPP) v O'Hanlon (CCA, October 12, 1998) 6–19, 6–33n
People (DPP) v O'Loughlin [1979] I.R. 85 (CCA) 11–50
People (DPP) v O'Reilly [1990] 2 I.R. 415
  (CCA) 6–04n, 6–09n, 6–18, 6–19, 6–20n, 6–27
People (DPP) v O'Shea (1981) 2 Frewen 57 (CCA) 11–36n
People (DPP) v O'Toole and Tyndale (CCA, May 26, 2003) 6–09
People (DPP) v Owens [1999] 2 I.R. 17 (SC) 11–66n
People (DPP) v PC [2002] 2 I.R. 285 (CCA) 5–40, 5–41, 5–48n
People (DPP) v Palmer (CCA, March 22, 2002) 10–24, 10–63
People (DPP) v Pringle (1981) 2 Frewen 57 (CCA) 10–01n, 10–35n, 10–40,
  10–41, 10–53n, 12–01n, 12–07
People (DPP) v Prunty [1986] I.L.R.M. 716 .... 9–62n

Table of Cases

People (DPP) v Quillegan and O'Reilly (No.3) [1993] 2 I.R. 305
  (SC) 10–11, 10–70n, 11–41n
People (DPP) v Quillegan and O'Reilly [1987] I.L.R.M. 606 (SC) 11–48, 11–49
People (DPP) v Quinn (CCA, March 23, 1998,
  ex tempore) 1–27n, 10–10n, 10–47
People (DPP) v Quirke (HC, March 3, 2003) 12–29n
People (DPP) v Rapple [1999] 1 I.L.R.M. 113 (CCA) 6–22, 6–26
People (DPP) v Rawley [1997] 2 I.R. 265 (CCA) 4–78n
People (DPP) v Reddan [1995] 3 I.R. 560
  (CA) 10–25n, 10–29n, 10–50n, 10–55n
People (DPP) v Reid [1993] 2 I.R. 186 (CCA) 5–40, 5–43, 5–46
People (DPP) v Rose (CCA, February 21, 2002) 10–66n
People (DPP) v Roughan (CCA, June 23, 1997) 2–57, 2–58
People (DPP) v Scannell (CCA, June 18, 1996) 3–38n
People (DPP) v Shaw [1982] 1 I.R. 1
  (SC) 10–36, 10–43, 10–48, 11–03, 11–04, 11–05,
                                11–17, 11–18, 11–22, 11–32n, 11–39n, 11–40
People (DPP) v Shortt (CCA, July 23, 1996) 4–78n
People (DPP) v Shortt (No.1) [2002] 2 I.R. 686 (CCA) 1–17n, 7–35n
People (DPP) v Smith [1992] 2 I.L.R.M. 61 .... 6–20n
People (DPP) v Smith (CCA, November 16, 1998) 6–10
People (DPP) v Smith (CCA, November 22, 1999) 10–18n, 10–26n
People (DPP) v Stafford [1983] I.R. 165 (CCA) 6–04n, 6–10, 6–10n, 6–20n
People (DPP) v Synott (CCA, May 29, 1992) 2–57
People (DPP) v T (1988) 3 Frewen 141
  (CCA) 2–10n, 2–21, 2–21n, 2–22n, 2–23, 2–25,
                                           2–22, 2–27, 13–66n, 13–67, 13–67n
People (DPP) v Tuite (1983) 2 Frewen 175 .... 1–42n
People (DPP) v Wallace (SC, April 30, 2001) 5–38
People (DPP) v Walsh [1980] I.R. 294
  (SC) 11–16, 11–29n, 11–30, 11–32n, 11–38n, 11–39n, 11–46n
People (DPP) v Ward (Special Criminal Court, November 27, 1998; CCA,
  March 22, 2002) 2–17n, 5–23n, 5–24, 10–33, 10–38, 10–43, 10–45n
People v Abbott (1838) 19 Wend. 192 at 195 (N.Y.) 3–23n
People v Cummins [1972] I.R 312 (SC) 10–17
People v Farrell [1978] I.R. 13 (CCA) 10–51
People v Keane (1976) 110 I.L.T.R. 1 (CCA) 10–05n, 10–63n
People v Keating [1953] I.R. 200 (CCA) 2–02n
People v Kelly (No.2) [1983] I.R. 1 (CCA) 11–47
People v Lynch [1982] I.R. 64 (SC) 1–10n, 2–02n
People v McGuinness [1978] I.R. 189 (CCA) 1–53n
People v Murphy [1947] I.R. 236 (CCA) 10–08
People v O'Loughlin [1979] I.R. 85 (CCA) 11–21n
People v O'Mahoney [1985] I.R. 517 (SC) 4–30n
People v Radley (1945) 157 P. (2d) 426 .... 9–30n
People v Wallace (CCA, November 22, 1982) 7–27n
People v Ward (Special Criminal Court, October 23, 1998) 10–46
Perry v Gibson (1834) 1 A. & E. 48 .... 2–01n
PF v GO'M (orse GF) (SC, November 28, 2000) 4–81n
Pfenning v The Queen (1995) 182 C.L.R. 461 .... 7–22n
Phillion v R. [1978] 1 S.C.R. 18 .... 3–15n
Pickup v Thames Insurance Co. (1878) 3 Q.B.D. 594 4–17

PO'C v DPP [2000] 3 I.R. 87 (SC) 12–08n
Power City Ltd. v Monahan (HC, October 14, 1996) 13–44n
Power v United Dublin Tramways Co. [1926] I.R. 302 (SC) 9–80n
Pye v Butterfield 5 B. & s. 829 .... 13–80n

Queen v Edwards (1983) 77 Cr. App. R. 191 (CA) 2–47n
Quinlivan v Governor of Portlaoise Prison [1998] 1 I.R. 456
 (SC) 11–15n, 11–37
Quinn v South Eastern Health Board (HC, March 22, 2002) 4–65, 4–71, 4–74

R. (Ebrahim) v Feltham Magistrate's Court [2001] 1 All E.R. 831 .... 1–44n
R. (Sheahan) v Justices of Cork [1907] 2 I.R. 5 (KBD) 4–47
R. Griggs Group v Dunnes Stores (HC, October 4, 1996) 9–73
R. Hutchinson (1985) 82 Cr. App. R. 51 (CA) 1–49n
R. v A [1997] Crim. L.R. 883 (CA) 5–39n
R. v A [2001] 3 All E.R. 1 (HL) 3–36
R. v Abadom [1983] 1 W.L.R. 126 (CA) 9–45n, 9–55, 12–24
R. v Accused [1989] N.Z.L.R. 600 .... 1–60n
R. v Ananthanarayanan [1994] 2 All E.R. 847 (CA) 5–52, 7–31n
R. v Anderson [1988] Q.B. 678 (CA) 8–25
R. v Anderson and Neville [1971] 3 All E.R. 1152 (CA) 12–03
R. v Andrews [1987] A.C. 281 (HL) 9–25, 9–69, 9–70, 9–71, 9–78
R. v Andrews [1993] Crim. L.R. 590 (CA) 6–11n
R. v Argent [1997] 2 Cr. App. R. 27 (CA) 5–15n, 5–16n, 13–45n
R. v Armstrong [1922] 2 K.B. 555 (CA) 7–05n, 7–06
R. v Ataou [1988] Q.B. 709 (CA) 13–03, 13–03n
R. v Aziz [1995] 3 All E.R. 149 (HL) 8–30, 8–31, 10–70n
R. v B [1996] Crim LR 499 (CA) 1–69
R. v B [1997] Crim. L.R. 220 (CA) 7–33
R. v B (KG) [1993] 1 S.C.R. 740 (SC) 2–31n
R. v Bagshaw [1984] 1 W.L.R. 477 (CA) 5–34
R. v Ball [1911] A.C. 47. (HL) 7–33
R. v Barnes [1994] Crim. L.R. 691 (CA) 3–27
R. v Barnes [1995] 2 Cr. App. R. 491 (CA) 7–16n
R. v Barnes [1996] Crim. L. R. 39 (CA) 6–13
R. v Barrington [1981] 1 All E.R. 1132 (CA) 7–16n
R. v Baskerville [1916] 2 K.B. 658
 (CA) 5–04, 5–05, 5–06n, 5–07, 5–12, 5–22,
 5–41, 5–42, 5–46, 5–47, 6–12, 9–15
R. v Beck [1982] 1 W.L.R. 461 (CA) 5–34
R. v Beckles and Montague [1999] Crim. L.R. 148 (CA) 6–11n
R. v Bedingfield (1879) 14 Cox C.C. 341 9–66
R. v Beggs (1990) 90 Cr. App. R. 430 (CA) 7–09
R. v Bellamy (1985) 82 Cr. App. R. 222 .... 2–28n
R. v Bentley (1994) 99 Cr. App. R. 342 (CA) 6–11
R. v Bernadotti (1869) 11 Cox C.C. 316 .... 9–84n
R. v Berrada (1990) 91 Cr. App. R. 131 (CA) 8–28
R. v Berry [1985] 1 A.C. 246 (HL) 1–48n, 4–30, 4–30n
R. v Billings [1961] V.R. 127 (CA) 8–43
R. v Birks [2003] Crim. L.R. 401 (CA) 2–60
R. v Black (1922) 16 Cr. App. R. 118 (CA) 9–76
R. v Black [1995] Crim. L. R. 640 (CA) 7–28n

Table of Cases

R. v Blastland [1986] A.C. 41 (HL) 9–79n, 10–04, 10–65
R. v Blenkinsop [1995] 1 Cr. App. R. 7 (CA) 6–31n
R. v Boam [1998] Crim. L.R. 206 (CA) 9–86
R. v Bogie [1992] Crim. L.R. 301 (CA) 3–17n
R. v Bond [1906] 2 K.B. 389 7–32
R. v Bondy (1957) 121 C.C.C. 337 .... 5–12n
R. v Bowden [1999] 1 W.L.R. 823 (CA) 13–46
R. v Bowers [1998] Crim. L.R. 817 (CA) 5–14n
R. v Boyes (1871–3) All E.R. 172 .... 13–81n
R. v Brazier (1779) 1 Leach 199 .... 2–05n, 2–10
R. v Britzman & Hall [1983] 1 W.L.R. 350 (CA) 8–49, 8–52n, 8–56n
R. v Broadhurst [1964] A.C. 441 (PC) 3–18n
R. v Brophy [1982] A.C. 476 (CA) 10–12n
R. v Brown (1867) Cox C.C. 453 .... 3–15n
R. v Brown (1989) 89 Cr. App. R. 97 (CA) 3–31n, 5–39
R. v Brown [1998] A.C. 367 (HL) 3–39
R. v Browning [1995] Crim. L.R. 227 (CA) 12–11
R. v Browning [1994] Crim. L.R. 227 (CA) 2–42n
R. v Bruce [1975] 1 W.L.R. 1252 (CA) 8–63, 8–64
R. v Bryan (CA, November 8, 1984) 12–03n
R. v Bryant and Oxley (1978) 67 Cr. App. R. 157,
   [1978] 2 All E.R. 689 (CA) 8–28n
R. v Bryce (1992) 95 Cr. App. R. 320 (CA) 11–23n
R. v Buchan [1964] 1 All E.R. 502; 1 W.L.R. 365 (CA) 11–51n
R. v Burge [1996] 1 Cr. App. R. 163 (CA) 3–21n
R. v Burges (1956) 40 Cr. App. R. 144 (CA) 5–36n
R. v Burns [1996] Crim. L. R. 323 (CA) 7–18n
R. v Burrage [1997] Crim. L.R. 440 (CA) 7–25, 7–26
R. v Busby (1981) 75 Cr. App. R. 79 (CA) 3–11
R. v C [1996] Crim. L.R. 37 (CA) 3–34n
R. v Callan (1993) 98 Cr. App. R. 467 (CA) 10–04
R. v Callender [1998] Crim. L.R. 337 (CA) 9–71
R. v Camelleri [1922] 2 K.B. 122 2–53
R. v Campbell [1996] Crim. L.R. 500 (CA) 6–20n
R. v Cape [1996] 1 Cr. App. R. 191 (CA) 6–11
R. v Carr-Briant [1943] K.B. 607 (CA) 4–30n, 4–33, 4–38, 4–39, 4–44
R. v Carter [1956] Crim. L.R. 772 (CA) 7–07n
R. v Central Criminal Court Ex p. Francis [1989] A.C. 346
   (HL) 13–27
R. v Chance [1988] Q.B. 932 .... 5–39n, 6–12n
R. v Chard (1971) 56 Cr. App. R. 268 (CA) 12–08
R. v Chatwood (1980) 70 Cr. App. R. 39 (CA) 10–01
R. v Chauhan (1962) 46 Cr. App. R. 319 (CA) 5–43n, 5–44
R. v Chaulk [1990] 3 S.C.R. 1303 (SC, Can.) 4–40
R. v Cheema [1994] 1 W.L.R. 147 (HL) 5–29
R. v Chief Constable West Midlands Police Ex p. Wiley [1994]
   2 W.L.R. 433 13–77
R. v Ching (1976) 63 Cr. App. R. 7 (CA) 4–72n
R. v Christie [1914] A.C. 545 (HL) 7–01n, 8–46n
R. v Christie [1980] A.C. 402 (HL) 1–03n, 1–20n, 10–62n
R. v Clark [1955] 2 Q.B. 469 .... 8–43, 8–48
R. v Clarke (1977) 67 Cr. App. R. 398 (CA) 7–12n

R. v Clarke [1995] 2 Cr. App. R. 425 .... 6–28n
R. v Clay (1851) 5 Cox C.C. 147 .... 3–23n
R. v Cleary (1963) 48 Cr. App. R. 116 (CA) 10–37n
R. v Cockcroft (1870) Cox C.C. 410 .... 3–23n
R. v Cohen (1990) 91 Cr. App. R. 124 (CA) 8–28n
R. v Cokar [1960] 2 Q.B. 207 (CA) 8–11n
R. v Condron [1997] 1 W.L.R. 827 (CA) 13–45n
R. v Condron and Condron [1997] 1 Cr. App. R. 185 (CA) 13–104n
R. v Constantinou (1990) 91 Cr. App. R. 74 (CA) 6–32
R. v Cook [1959] 2 Q.B. 340 (CA) 8–43, 8–58n
R. v Cook [1987] Q.B. 147; [1987] 1 All E.R. 1049 (CA) 6–32
R. v Coulman (1927) 20 Cr. App. R. 106 .... 8–34n
R. v Cowan [1995] 3 W.L.R. 818 (CA) 5–15
R. v Cowan [1995] 4 All E.R. 939 (HL) 13–103n
R. v Cox (1884) 14 Q.B.D. 153 13–14
R. v Cox (1987) 84 Cr. App. R. 132 (CA) 3–36n
R. v Crampton (1991) 92 C.A.R. 369 (CA) 10–46
R. v Curbishley [1963] Crim. L.R. 778 (CA) 8–57n
R. v D [1995] T.L.R. 592 (CA) 2–11
R. v D [1996] Q.B. 283 (CA) 1–74n
R. v Da Silva [1990] 1 W.L.R. 31 (CA) 2–44
R. v Daniel [1998] 2 Cr. App. R. 373 (CA) 5–15n, 13–104n
R. v Darby [1989] Crim. L.R. 817 (CA) 2–38n
R. v Davies [1962] 3 All E.R. 97 (CMAC) 12–03
R. v Davinson-Jenkins [1997] Crim. L.R. 816 (CA) 8–17
R. v Day [1940] 1 All E.R. 402 (CA) 1–49n
R. v Deakin [1994] 4 All E.R. 769 (CA) 1–26n
R. v Derby Magistrates Ex p. B [1996] A.C. 487 (HL) 13–03, 13–21
R. v Desmond [1999] Crim. L.R. 313 (CA) 8–45n
R. v Despard (1803) 28 State Tr. 346 .... 5–23n
R. v Dickman (1910) 5 Cr. App. R. 135 (CA) 6–19n
R. v Director of Serious Fraud Ex p. Smith [1993] A.C. 1 (HL) 13–87n
R. v Dodd (1981) 74 Cr. App. R. 50 (CA) 8–07n
R. v Dodson and Williams (1984) 79 Cr. App. R. 220 (CA) 6–28n
R. v Dolan [2003] Crim. L.R. 41 (CA) 7–33
R. v Donaldson (1976) 64 Cr. App. R. 59 (CA) 10–70
R. v Dossett 2 C. & K. 306 .... 7–04n
R. v Dowley [1983] Crim. L.R. 168 (CA) 5–43n, 5–44n
R. v Downey [1995] 1 Cr. App. R. 547 (CA) 7–16n, 7–28n
R. v Duffield (1851) 5 Cox C.C. 404 .... 10–66n
R. v Duncan (1981) 73 Cr. App. R. 359 (CA) 9–63
R. v Duncan [1994] 3 I.R. 289 (CCA) 10–69
R. v Edwards (1848) 3 Cox C.C. 82 .... 1–53n
R. v Edwards (1872) 12 Cox C.C. 230 9–74
R. v Edwards [1975] Q.B. 27 (CA) 4–54, 4–55, 4–57, 4–58
R. v Edwards [1991] 1 W.L.R. 207 (CA) 3–03n, 3–05
R. v Edwards (2001) 9 Archbold News 1 (CA) 12–03n
R. v Effick (1992) 95 Cr. App. R. 427 (CA) 10–46n
R. v Ellis [1961] 1 W.L.R. 1064; [1961] 2 All E.R. 928 (CA) 8–65n
R. v Emery (1993) 14 Cr. App. R. 394 (CA) 12–08n
R. v Evans [1965] 2 Q.B. 295 (CA) 5–28n
R. v Everett [1988] Crim. L.R. 826 (CA) 10–47

Table of Cases

R. v Ewing [1983] 2 All E.R. 645 (HL) 8–58n
R. v Exall (1866) 4 F. & F. 922 1–37
R. v Fegan [1972] N.I. 80 (CA) 1–48n, 4–30n, 4–43n
R. v Ferguson (1909) 2 Cr. App. R. 250 .... 8–34n
R. v Ferguson [1925] 2 K.B. 799 .... 6–26n
R. v Fitzpatrick (1912) 46 I.L.T.R. 173 .... 9–84n
R. v Fitzpatrick [1998] Crim. L.R. 63 (CA) 8–62n
R. v Fletcher (1913) 9 Cr. App. R. 53 (CA) 8–46n
R. v Flynn [1963] 1 Q.B. 729 (CA) 8–03n, 8–42, 8–53
R. v Fotheringham (1976) 119 S.J. 613 (CA) 2–42
R. v France [1979] Crim L.R. 48 (CA) 8–20
R. v Friend [1997] Crim L.R. 817 (CA) 13–103
R. v Frost (1839) 4 St. Tr. N.S. 85 .... 1–49n
R. v Funderburk [1990] 1 W.L.R. 587 (CA) 3–03n, 3–06n, 3–29
R. v Galbraith [1981] 2 All E.R. 1060 (CA) 1–50n, 4–11n
R. v Garbett (1847) 1 Den. 236 .... 13–81n, 13–92n
R. v Garland (1941) 29 Cr. App. R. 46 (CA) 2–20n
R. v Genus & Britton [1996] Crim. L.R. 502 (CA) 3–20
R. v George [2003] Crim. L.R. 282 (CA) 6–24
R. v Gilfoyle (CA, December 20, 2000) 12–16n
R. v Gill [1963] 2 All E.R. 688 (CA) 4–20n
R. v Gillespie (1967) 51 Cr. App. R. 172 (CA) 3–08n
R. v Goldenberg (1988) 88 Cr. App. R. 285 (CA) 10–46n
R. v Golder, Jones, & Porritt [1960] 1 W.L.R. 1169 (CA) 2–38
R. v Goodway [1993] 4 All E.R. 894 (CA) 2–37n, 3–21n, 6–09n
R. v Grafton [1993] Q.B. 101 (CA) 1–53n
R. v Graham [1973] Crim. L.R. 628 (CA) 2–42
R. v Gray [1995] 2 Cr. App. R. 100 (CA) 10–66
R. v Gregg (1934) 24 Cr. App. R. 13 (CA) 5–45
R. v Griffin [1998] Crim. L.R. 418 (CA) 13–104n
R. v Gunewardene [1951] 2 K.B. 600 (CA) 12–09
R. v Gunning (1980) Cr. App. R. 303 at 306 (CA) 1–53n
R. v H [1995] 2 A.C. 596; [1995] 2 W.L.R. 737 (HL) 1–26n, 5–52, 7–29, 7–30
R. v Hampshire [1995] 2 Cr. App. R. 319 .... 1–74n
R. v Hampshire [1996] Q.B. 1 (CA) 2–14n
R. v Hardy (1794) 24 St. Tr. 199 .... 10–01n
R. v Harris (1927) 20 Cr. App. R. 144 (CA) 2–37n
R. v Harron [1996] Crim. L.R. 581 (CA) 3–20n
R. v Hatton (1977) 64 Cr. App. R. 88 (CA) 8–64
R. v Hawkins (CA, February 20, 1995) 1–74n
R. v Hayden & Slattery [1959] V.R. 102 .... 2–30n
R. v Hayes [1977] 1 W.L.R. 234 (CA) 2–07
R. v Hersey [1998] Crim. L.R. 281 (CA) 6–33
R. v Hester [1973] A.C. 296 (HL) 5–47
R. v Hill (1851) 2 Den. 254 .... 2–27, 2–27n
R. v Hill [1996] Crim. L.R. 419 (CA) 3–19
R. v Hills [1980] A.C. 27 (CA) 8–69, 8–70
R. v Hilton [1972] 1 Q.B. 421 (CA) 2–19
R. v Hodges and Walker [2003] Crim. L.R. 472 (CA) 12–03n
R. v Holmes (1871) L.R. 1 C.C.R. 334 .... 3–23n
R. v Honeyghon and Sayles [1999] Crim. L.R. 221 (CA) 2–33
R. v Hookway [1999] Crim. L.R. 750 .... 6–28n

R. v Horne [1990] Crim. L.R. 188 (CA) 5–12n
R. v Horwood [1970] 1 Q.B. 133 (CA) 7–22n
R. v Howell [2003] Crim. L.R. 405 (CA) 13–45n
R. v Hudson [1912] 2 K.B. 464 (CA) 8–41, 8–43, 8–45
R. v Hunt [1987] A.C. 352; [1987] 1 All E.R. 1 (HL) 4–55, 4–57, 4–58
R. v Hunting and Ward (1908) 1 Cr. App. R. 177 (CA) 2–20n
R. v Imran and Hussain [1997] Crim. L.R. 754 (CA) 5–16
R. v Islam [1999] 1 Cr. App. R. 22 (CA) 2–57n
R. v Jackson [1953] 1 W.L.R. 591 (CA) 5–12n
R. v Jeffries [1997] Crim. L.R. 819 (CA) 12–03n
R. v Jenkins (1869) 11 Cox C.C. 250 (CA) 9–84
R. v Johannsen (1977) 65 Cr. App. R. 101 (CA) 7–11
R. v John W [1998] 2 Cr. App. R. 289 (CA) 6–11n, 6–13
R. v John Wright (1990) 90 Cr. App. R. 325 (CA) 7–27n
R. v Jones (1827) Car. & P. 629 .... 10–70n
R. v Josephine Smith [1995] Crim. L.R. 305 (CA) 3–20n
R. v JP [1999] Crim. L.R. 401 (CA) 12–10
R. v Keane [1994] 1 W.L.R. 746 (CA) 1–42n
R. v Kearly [1992] 2 W.L.R. 656
    (HL) 9–11n, 9–12n, 9–14, 9–16, 9–28, 9–30, 9–30n, 9–33, 9–35, 9–63n
R. v Kelsey (1982) 74 Cr. App. R. 213 (CA) 2–48, 9–58
R. v Kemble [1990] 1 W.L.R. 1111 2–06
R. v Khan (1981) 73 Cr. App. R. 190 (CA) 2–13n
R. v Khan [1991] Crim. L.R. 51 (CA) 8–22n
R. v Khan [1996] 2 Cr. App. R. 440 (CA) 10–62n
R. v Kilbourne [1973] A.C. 729 (HL) 5–47
R. v King [1967] 2 Q.B. 338 (CA) 5–07n, 7–22n
R. v King [1983] 1 All E.R. 929 (CA) 13–39
R. v Kirkpatrick [1998] Crim. L.R. 63 (CA) 8–63n
R. v Krausz (1973) 57 Cr. App. R. 466 (CA) 8–41n
R. v Lake (1976) 64 Cr. App. R. 172 (CA) 10–63n
R. v Lamb (1980) 71 Cr. App. R. 198 (CA) 6–27n
R. v Land [1998] Crim. L.R. 70 (CA) 12–03n
R. v Lauchlan (CCA, June 15, 1976) 8–68
R. v Lawrence [1995] Crim. L.R. 815 (CA) 8–15n
R. v Lawrence [1977] Crim. L.R. 492 (CA) 3–34n
R. v Layton (1949) 4 Cox C.C. 149 .... 4–29n
R. v Lewes Justices Ex p. R [1973] A.C. 388 (HL) 13–54n
R. v Lewis (1983) 76 Cr. App. R. 33 (CA) 7–23
R. v Lillyman [1896] 2 Q.B. 167 .... 2–53, 2–56, 2–57
R. v Lin, Hung and Tsui [1995] Crim. L.R. 817 (CA) 11–23n
R. v Ling [1987] Crim. L.R. 495 (CA) 8–07n
R. v Liverpool Juvenile Court Ex p. R [1988] Q.B. 1 .... 10–10n
R. v Lucas [1981] 3 W.L.R. 121 (CA) 3–18, 3–21, 5–07, 5–08
R. v Lupien [1982] W.A.R. 171 (SC, Can.) 12–08
R. v Lushington Ex p. Otto [1894] 1 Q.B. 420 .... 1–42n
R. v M [2001] Crim. L.R. 911 (CA) 3–35
R. v M and R. v Sonia B [1996] Crim L.R. 499 (CA) 1–69n
R. v M'Naghten (1843) 4 St. Tr. 847 .... 4–29, 4–29n, 12–08, 12–08n
R. v Mackenney (1981) 76 Cr. App. R. 271 (CA) 12–10n, 12–14n
R. v Makanjuola [1995] 1 W.L.R. 1348
    (CA) 2–50n, 5–05n, 5–35, 5–38, 5–40, 5–42n, 5–50n

Table of Cases xxxvii

R. v Manchester Crown Court Ex p. Rogers [1999]
1 W.L.R. 832 .... 13–34n, 13–35
R. v Manley (1962) 126 J.P. 316 (CA) 8–59n
R. v Mansfield [1978] 1 All E.R. 134 (CA) 7–08
R. v Maqsud Alf [1966] 1 Q.B. 688 .... 1–11n
R. v May (1952) 36 Cr. App. R. 91 (CA) 10–17n
R. v McCay [1990] 1 W.L.R. 645 (CA) 9–57
R. v McGovern (1990) 92 Cr. App. R. 229 (CA) 10–59
R. v McIlkenny (1991) 93 Cr. App. R. 287; [1992]
2 All E.R. 417 (CA) 1–09n, 12–14
R. v McKay [1967] N.Z.L.R. 139 .... 3–15n
R. v McLean (1968) 52 Cr. App. R. 80 (CA) 9–58n
R. v McLeod [1994] 3 All E.R. 257 (CA) 8–16n
R. v McLintock [1962] Crim. L.R. 549 (CA) 10–08n, 10–10n
R. v McQuiston [1998] 1 Cr. App. R. 139 (CA) 1–70
R. v Melaney (1923) 18 Cr. App. R. 2 (CA) 6–26
R. v Mendy (1976) 64 Cr. App. R. 4 (CA) 3–11
R. v Merry (1990) 19 Cox C.C. 442 .... 2–58n
R. v Miller [1952] 2 All E.R. 667 (CA) 8–04n
R. v Miller [1997] Crim. L.R. 217 (CA) 8–60
R. v Miller [1998] Crim. L.R. 209 (CA) 10–18n, 10–22n
R. v Millikin (1969) 53 Cr. App. R. 330 (CA) 1–49n
R. v Mills and Lemon [1947] 1 K.B. 297 (CA) 10–23n
R. v Mills and Rose (1962) 1 W.L.R. 1152 .... 9–58n
R. v Minihane (1921) 16 Cr. App. R. 38 (CA) 13–68n
R. v Moore (1852) 2 Den. 522 .... 10–09n
R. v Morhall [1996] 1 A.C. 90 (HL) 12–08n
R. v Morris [1998] Crim. L.R. 416 (CA) 1–72
R. v Moseley (1825) 1 Mood C.C. 97 .... 9–83n
R. v Moshaid [1998] Crim. L.R. 420 (CA) 5–14n
R. v Myers [1997] 3 W.L.R. 552 (HL) 10–01n, 10–65
R. v Nagrecha [1997] 2 Cr. App. R. 401 (CA) 3–23n
R. v Noakes (1832) 5 C. & P. 326 .... 5–06n
R. v Norcott [1917] 1 K.B. 347 .... 2–58n
R. v Northam (1967) 52 Cr. App. R. 97 (CA) 10–34, 10–34n
R. v Novac (1976) 65 Cr. App. R. 107 (CA) 7–11
R. v O'Brien (CA, January 25, 2000) 12–09
R. v O'Doherty [2002] Crim. L.R. 761 (CA) 6–34
R. v O'Hadhmaill [1996] Crim. L.R. 509 (CA) 1–49n
R. v Okoye [1964] Crim. L.R. 416 (CA) 5–44n
R. v Osborne [1905] 1 K.B. 551 .... 2–53n, 2–58n
R. v Osbourne and Virtue [1973] 1 Q.B. 678 (CA) 9–56
R. v Osman (1881) 15 Cox C.C. 1 (CCR) 9–83n
R. v Owen (1986) 83 Cr. App. R. 100 (CA) 8–37n
R. v Paine (1696) 5 Mod. 163 .... 10–70n
R. v Palmer [1994] Crim. L.R. 122 (CA) 2–17n
R. v Paraskeva (1983) 76 Cr. App. R. 162 (CA) 3–14n, 3–39n
R. v Parker [1995] Crim. L.R. 511 (CA) 1–74n
R. v Peterborough Justices [1978] 1 All E.R. 225 13–39
R. v Pike (1829) 3 C. & P. 598 .... 9–78n
R. v Pitt [1982] 3 All E.R. 63 (CA) 2–03n, 2–04, 13–68
R. v Pointer [1997] Crim. L.R. 676 (CA) 5–16

R. v Powell (1985) 82 Cr. App. R. 167 (CA) 8–16, 8–17
R. v Prager (1972) 56 Cr. App. R. 151 (CA) 10–35
R. v Prater [1960] 2 Q.B. 464 (CA) 5–33n, 5–34n
R. v Preston [1909] 1 K.B. 568 (CA) 8–40, 8–43n
R. v Priestly (1966) 51 Cr. App. R. 1 (CA) 10–35, 10–41
R. v Prince [1990] Crim. L.R. 49 (CA) 8–57n
R. v Quinn and Bloom [1962] 2 Q.B. 245 (CA) 1–14n
R. v R. [1995] 1 Cr. App. R. 183 (CA) 13–27n
R. v Raghip [1991] T.L.R. 562 (CA) 12–09n
R. v Rappolt (1911) 6 Cr. App. R. 156 (CA) 8–39
R. v Rasheed (CCA, May 20, 1994) 3–39n
R. v Ratten [1972] A.C. 378 (PC) 9–78n
R. v Rawlings [1995] 1 W.L.R. 178 (CA) 1–68n, 1–70n
R. v Redd [1923] 1 K.B. 104 (CA) 8–34n
R. v Redgrave (1982) 74 Cr. App. R. 10 (CA) 7–17, 8–27
R. v Redpath (1962) 46 Cr. App. R. 319 (CA) 5–43
R. v Rennie [1982] 1 W.L.R. 64 (HL) 10–38n
R. v Reynolds [1950] 1 K.B. 606 (CA) 1–26, 1–26n
R. v Rice [1963] 1 Q.B. 857 (CCA) 9–26
R. v Richards [1967] 1 All E.R. 829;
   [1967] 1 W.L.R. 653 (CA) 10–33n, 10–34n
R. v Richardson and Longman [1969] 1 Q.B. 299 (CA) 3–15, 3–16
R. v Richens [1993] 4 All E.R. 877 (CA) 5–09, 5–15
R. v Rider (1986) 83 Cr. App. R. 207 (CA) 5–18n
R. v Riley (1990) 91 Cr. App. R. 14 (CA) 3–29n
R. v Riley 18 Cox C.C. 285 (CCR) 10–03n
R. v Roberts [1936] 1 All E.R. 23 (CA) 8–68
R. v Roberts (John Marcus) (1984) 80 Cr. App. R. 89 (CA) 1–53n
R. v Roberts [1942] 1 All E.R. 187 (CA) 2–51n
R. v Robinson (1953) 37 Cr. App. R. 95 (CA) 7–07n
R. v Robinson [2001] Crim. L.R. 478 (CA) 8–34n
R. v Roble [1997] Crim. L.R. 448 (CA) 13–45
R. v Rockman (CCA, November 22, 1977) 8–68
R. v Rouse [1904] 1 K.B. 184 (C.C.R.) 8–39
R. v Row (1809) Russ. & Ry. 153 .... 10–09n
R. v Rowton (1865) Le. & Ca. 520 .... 7–17, 8–27
R. v Royce-Bentley [1974] 1 W.L.R. 535 (CA) 5–22n
R. v Rudd (1948) 32 Cr. App. R. 138 .... 2–20n
R. v Samuel (1956) 40 Cr. App. R. 8 (CA) 8–16n, 8–29n
R. v Sanders (1961) 46 Cr. App. R. 60 (C.M.A.C.) 5–39n
R. v Sang [1980] A.C. 402 (HL) 10–62n, 11–23n
R. v Sartori [1961] Crim. L.R. 397 (CA) 10–10n
R. v Sat-Bhambra (1988) 88 Cr. App. R. 55 (CA) 10–13n
R. v Scarrott [1978] 1 All E.R. 672 at 676 (CA) 7–12
R. v Secretary of State Transport and Factortame Ltd
   (Divisional Court, May 6, 1997) 13–12
R. v Selvey [1970] A.C. 305 (HL) 8–41n
R. v Setz-Dempsey [1994] Crim. L.R. 123 (CA) 2–29
R. v Sharp [1988] 1 W.L.R. 7 (HL) 9–63n, 10–69n
R. v Simons 6 C. & P. 540 .... 13–68n
R. v Sims [1946] 1 K.B. 534 (CA) 5–33n, 7–27n
R. v Slater [1995] 1 Cr. App. R. 584 (CA) 6–11

Table of Cases

R. v Smith (1908) 1 Cr. App. R. 203 (CA) 6–19n
R. v Smith [1915] W.N. 309 7–06
R. v Smith (1966) 51 Cr. App. R. 22 (CA) 10–01n
R. v Smith [1976] Crim. L.R. 511 (CA) 9–56n
R. v Smith [1995] Crim. L.R. 304 (CA) 3–21, 3–21n
R. v Smith (Morgan) [2000] 4 All E.R. 289 (HL) 12–08n
R. v Smithies 5 C. & P. 321 .... 13–68n
R. v Smurthwaite [1994] 1 All E.R. 898 (CA) 11–23n
R. v South Ribble Magistrates' Court Ex p. Cochrane [1996]
    2 Cr. App. R. 544 .... 2–44n
R. v Spencer [1987] A.C. 128 (HL) 5–34
R. v Springer [1996] Crim. L.R. 903 (CA) 1–71
R. v Stannard [1965] 2 Q.B. 1 .... 5–34n
R. v Stockwell (1993) 97 Cr. App. R. 260 (CA) 6–28n, 6–33n
R. v Stokes (1848) 3 Car. & Kir. 185 .... 4–29n
R. v Straffen [1952] 2 Q.B. 911 (CA) 7–06
R. v Stronach [1988] Crim. L.R. 48 (CA) 8–34n
R. v Sumners (1952) 36 Cr. App. R. 14 (CA) 4–75
R. v Sutton (1969) 53 Cr. App. R. 504 (CA) 8–07n
R. v Sweeting and Thomas [1999] Crim. L.R. 75 (CA) 1–74n
R. v T and H [2002] 1 W.L.R. 632; [2002] 1 All E.R. 683 (CA) 3–27
R. v Taylor (1928) 21 Cr. App. R. 20 (CA) 1–37n
R. v Taylor [1998] Crim. L.R. 77 (CA) 13–100n
R. v Taylor [1999] Crim. L.R. 407 (CA) 3–14n
R. v Taylor [1999] Crim. L.R. 77 (CA) 5–13n
R. v Taylor and Taylor (1994) 98 Cr. App. R. 361 (CA) 3–38n
R. v Teper [1952] A.C. 480 (PC) 1–36, 9–11, 9–32
R. v Thomas [1985] Crim. L.R. 445 (CA) 2–38n
R. v Thompson (1976) 64 Cr. App. R. 96 (CA) 2–35
R. v Threlfall (1914) 10 Cr. App. R. 112 (CA) 5–18n
R. v Tompkins (1977) 67 Cr. App. R. 181 (CA) 13–08
R. v Toner (1991) 93 Cr. App. R. 382 (CA) 12–08
R. v Toohey [1965] A.C. 595 (HL) 12–08n, 12–09
R. v Tregear [1967] 2 Q.B. 574 (CA) 1–53n
R. v Tricoglus (1977) 65 Cr. App. R. 16 (CA) 7–16n
R. v Trigg (1963) 47 Cr. App. R. 94 (CA) 6–12n
R. v Trigg [1963] 1 W.L.R. 305 (CA) 5–39n
R. v Turnbull [1977] 1 Q.B. 224
    (CA) 3–21n, 5–12n, 5–48n, 6–01, 6–05n, 6–08, 6–11, 6–32, 6–33
R. v Turner (1816) 5 M. & S. 206 4–50
R. v Turner [1944] K.B. 463 (CA) 8–41, 8–41n
R. v Turner [1975] 1 Q.B. 834
    (CA) 6–33n, 12–04, 12–05, 12–06, 12–10n, 12–12
R. v Turner [1980] Crim. L.R. 305 (CA) 5–33n
R. v Tyndale [1999] Crim. L.R. 320 (CA) 2–59
R. v Tyrer (The Times, October 13, 1988) 8–07n
R. v Underwood [1999] Crim. L.R. 227 (CA) 7–33
R. v Valentine [1996] 2 Cr. App. R. 213 (CA) 2–57n
R. v Varley [1982] 2 All E.R. 519 (CA) 8–62n, 8–64n
R. v Vincent and Taylor [1983] Crim. L.R. 173 (CA) 5–21n
R. v Viola [1982] 1 W.L.R. 1138 (CA) 3–34n
R. v Virgo (1978) 67 Cr. App. R. 323 (CA) 2–46, 2–47, 5–05n

R. v Voisin [1918] 1 K.B. 531 .... 10–17, 10–18
R. v Vye [1993] 3 All E.R. 241 (CA) 8–30, 8–32
R. v Wait [1998] Crim. L.R. 68 (CA) 6–19n
R. v Walker [1996] Crim. L.R. 742 (CA) 1–74n, 5–39
R. v Walker [1998] Crim. L.R. 211 (CA) 10–44n, 10–46n
R. v Ward (1993) 96 Cr. App. R. 1 (CA) 12–09n
R. v Ward [1915] 3 K.B. 696 4–39
R. v Warickshall [1783] 1 Leach 263 .... 10–62n
R. v Warkentin [1977] 2 SCR. 355 .... 5–47n
R. v Watson (1817) 2 Stark 116 .... 3–15n
R. v Watson [1980] 2 All E.R. 293 (CA) 10–13n
R. v Watson [1997] Crim. L.R. 680 (CA) 9–07
R. v Wattam (1941) 28 Cr. App. R. 80 (CA) 8–07n
R. v Watts [1983] 3 All E.R. 101 (CA) 8–14n, 8–15, 8–16, 8–57n
R. v Weaver [1968] 1 Q.B. 353 (CA) 8–07n
R. v Weeder (1980) 71 Cr. App. R. 228 (CA) 6–05n, 6–07n, 6–13n
R. v Weekes (1980) 74 Cr. App. R. 161 (CA) 2–17n
R. v Weightman (1991) 92 Cr. App. R. 291 (CA) 12–09
R. v Welstead [1996] 1 Cr. App. R. 59 (CA) 1–68
R. v West (1996) 2 Cr. App. R. 374 (CA) 7–13n
R. v Westwell [1976] 2 All E.R. 812 (CA) 2–41n, 2–43
R. v Whitaker (1976) 63 Cr. App. R. 193 (CA) 5–34n
R. v Whitehead [1929] 1 K.B. 99 .... 2–56n, 5–42
R. v Whitehouse [1996] Crim. L.R. 50 (CA) 5–51n, 5–52n
R. v William Boughton (1910) 6 Cr. App. R. 8 (CA) 10–08n
R. v Williamson [1964] Crim. L.R. 126 (CA) 10–24
R. v Wood [1920] 2 K.B. 179 (CA) 8–09n
R. v Woodcock (1789) 1 Leach 500 9–83
R. v Worrall Ex p. (1820) 1 Buck 531 (CA) 13–85n
R. v Wright (1990) 90 Cr. App. R. 325 (CA) 7–24, 7–25, 7–26, 8–14n
Ramstead v R. [1999] 2 W.L.R. 698 (PC) 1–22n
Ratten v R. [1972] A.C. 378 (PC) 9–04, 9–24, 9–25, 9–27,
                                                                                                9–64, 9–68, 9–71, 9–78
Rawlinson v Westbrook, The Times, January 25, 1995 .... 12–23n
Rex v Jarvis (1754) 1 East 643 .... 4–50n
Reynolds v Llanelly Associated Tinplate Co. Ltd. [1948]
    1 All E.R. 140 .... 1–39n
Reynolds v Times Newspapers Ltd. [1999] 1 All E.R. 609 (HL) 13–61n
Rice v Connolly [1966] 2 Q.B. 414 .... 11–56n
Rio Tinto Zinc Corp. v Westinghouse Electric [1978] A.C. 547 (HL) 13–81n
Rock v Ireland [1997] 3 I.R. 484; [1998] 2 I.L.R.M. 35 (SC) 5–13, 13–91
Rothwell v M.I.B.I. [2003] 1 I.R. 268 (SC) 4–54n, 4–66, 4–68
Ruiz-Mateos v Spain (1993) 16 E.H.R.R. 505 .... 1–07n
Rumping v DPP [1964] A.C. 814 (CA) 10–02n
Rush & Tomkins Ltd. v Greater London Council [1989] A.C. 1280
    (HL) 13–38n
Russell v Jackson (1851) 9 Hare 387 .... 13–23n
Russell v Walsh (HC, April 3, 1995) 4–70n, 4–71
Ryan v Connolly [2001] 2 I.L.R.M. 174 (SC) 13–37

S v E [1967] 1 Q.B. 371 .... 13–81n
S v Switzerland (1991) E.H.R.R. 670 .... 10–53n

Table of Cases

S, M & W (Infants) (Wardship) (Eastern Health Board Intervening), *Re*
[1996] I.F.L.R. 87 .... 1–53n
Saunders v UK (1996) 23 E.H.R.R. 313 .... 1–07n, 13–85, 13–92,
13–93, 13–95, 13–96, 13–98
Savage v Chief Constable of Hampshire [1997] W.L.R. 1061 (CA) 13–78
Schneider v Leigh [1955] 2 Q.B. 195 (CA) 13–23n
Scott Paper Co. v Drayton Paper Works Ltd. (1927) 44 R.P.C. 151 13–38
Scott v London and St Katherine Docks Co. (1865)
3 H. & C. 596 .... 4–59, 4–59n, 4–62, 4–67
Scott v Sampson (1882) 8 Q.B.D. 491 .... 3–17n
Selvey v DPP [1970] A.C. 304
(HL) 8–36n, 8–39, 8–44, 8–46, 8–51, 8–53, 8–55, 8–56
Shand v R. [1996] 1 W.L.R. 67 (PC) 6–11n
Shelley-Morris v Bus Atha Cliath [2003] 1 I.R. 232 (SC) 9–40n
Silver Hill Duckling Ltd. and Steele v Minister for Agriculture, Ireland,
and the Attorney General [1987] I.R. 289 (HC) 13–24
Skeffington v Rooney [1997] 2 I.L.R.M. 56 (SC) 13–75
Skinner v Shew [1894] 2 Ch. D. 581 9–74
Smith v Police [1969] N.Z.L.R. 856 .... 9–62n
Smithkline Beecham Plc. v Antigen Pharmaceuticals Ltd [1999]
2 I.L.R.M. 190 (HC) 9–52, 9–73
Smurfit Paribas Bank v A.A.B. Export Finance [1990] 1 I.R.
469 (SC) 13–02n, 13–04, 13–27, 13–33, 13–34, 13–57
Smyth and Genport v Twomey (SC, April 8, 1997) 7–35n
Snell v Farrell (1990) 72 D.L.R. (4th) 289 (SC) 4–70n
Sodeman v R. [1936] 2 All E.R. 1138 (PC) 4–30, 4–30n
Solosky v R. (1979) D.L.R. (3d) 745 (SC, Can.) 13–02
Southern Health Board v CH [1996] I.L.R.M. 142,
[1996] 1 I.R. 219 (SC) 1–53n, 9–45, 9–47, 12–25
Spano v New York (1959) 360 U.S. 315 (CA, NY) 11–02
Sparks v R. [1964] A.C. 964 (A.C.) 2–54n
State (Comerford) v Governor of Mountjoy Prison [1981]
I.L.R.M. 86 (HC) 13–56n
State (D and D) v Groarke [1990] 1 I.R. 305 (SC) 9–45n, 12–25n
State (Healy) v Donoghue [1976] I.R. 325 (SC) 10–51n
State (McGee) v O'Rourke [1971] I.R. 205 (SC) 13–81n
State (Taylor) v Circuit Court Judge for Wicklow [1951] I.R. 311
(HC) 1–41
State (Trimbole) v Governor of Mountjoy Prison [1985] I.R. 550
(SC) 11–15, 11–27n
State (Walsh) v Maguire [1979] I.R. 372 (SC) 11–47n
State v Treanor [1924] 2 I.R. 193 (CCA) 10–32
Statue of Liberty [1968] 2 All E.R. 195 (CA) 6–31n
Steel v Goacher [1983] R.T.R. 98 .... 11–56n
Stirland v DPP [1944] 2 All E.R. 13 (HL) 8–08n, 8–10, 8–46n
Sturla v Freccia (1880) 5 App. Cas. 623 (HL) 9–78n, 9–85
Subramaniam v Public Prosecutor [1956] 1 W.L.R. 965
(PC) 9–21, 9–22, 9–25, 9–27, 9–72
Sullivan v Robinson [1954] I.R. 161 (SC) 10–08n
Sumners v Mosely (1834) 2 Cr. & M. 477 .... 2–01n
Supreme Court of Canada in Descoteaux v Mierzwinksi (1982)
141 D.L.R. (3d) 590 .... 13–21n

Surujpaul v R. [1958] 1 W.L.R. 1050 (PC) 10–01
Swaine v DPP (SC, April 26, 2002) 1–46
Sweeney v Director of Rape Crisis Centre [2001] 4 I.R. 101 (SC) 13–06
Swindler and Berlin v US (1998) 118 S. Ct. 2081 (US, SC) 13–23

Teper v R. [1952] A.C. 480 (PC) 9–67
Thake v Maurice [1984] 2 All E.R. 513; [1986] 1 All E.R. 497 (CA) 12–23n
The Queen v Justices of Antrim [1895] 2 I.R. 603 .... 1–39n
Thomas v Commissioner of Police of the Metropolis [1997]
 2 W.L.R. 593 (CA) 3–13n
Thomas, *Re* (Disclosure order) [1992] 4 All E.R. 814 (CA) 13–83n
Thompson v R. [1918] A.C. 221 (HL) 7–04, 7–21, 7–22, 7–22n
Thorpe v Chief Constable of Greater Manchester Police [1989]
 2 All E.R. 827 (CA) 1–09n
Tomlin v Standard Telephones and Cables Ltd. [1969] 3 All E.R. 201
 (CA) 13–38n
Toohey v Metropolitan Police Commissioner [1965] A.C. 595 (HL) 3–15n, 3–22
Travers v Ryan [1985] I.R. 586 (HC) 10–28n
Tromso Sparebank v Beirne [1989] I.L.R.M. 257 (HC) 13–40
Tucker v Oldbury Urban Council [1912] 2 K.B. 317 (CA) 9–79

Unilever plc. v Proctor & Gamble Co. [2001] 1 All E.R. 783 (CA) 13–38
United States of America v Mammoth Oil Company [1925] 2 D.L.R. 966 .... 13–27n
Universal City Studios Inc v Mulligan (No.2) [1999] 3 I.R. 392
 (HC) 11–69n, 11–71
US v Antonelli Fireworks Co. (1946) 155 F. 2d 631 .... 8–14n
US v Callandra (1974) 414 U.S. 338 (SC) 11–08n
US v Leon (1983) 468 U.S. 897 (SC) 11–08n
US v Long (1990) 905 F. 2d 1572 .... 9–35n
US v Zenni (1980) 492 F. Supp. 464 .... 9–30n

Vetrovec v Queen [1982] 1 S.C.R. 811 .... 5–47n
Vesey v Bus Éireann [2001] 4 I.R. 192 (SC) xiii

W. (A.) v DPP (HC, November 23, 2001) 12–08n
Walker v Ireland [1997] 1 I.L.R.M. 363 (HC) 13–72
Walsh v District Judge O'Buachalla & DPP [1991] 1 I.R. 56 (HC) 11–13
Walsh v Harrison [2003] 2 I.L.R.M. 161 (HC) 9–50n
Walshe and Bedford (HC, May, 2003) 11–43
Walton v R. (1989) 166 C.L.R. 283 (HC, Aust.) 9–35n
Ward v Special Criminal Court [1998] 2 I.R. 493 (SC) 13–59
Ward v Special Criminal Court and DPP [1999] 1 I.R. 77 (SC) 2–17n
Warren v Warren [1996] 4 All E.R. 664 (CA) 2–02n
Waugh v British Railways Board [1980] A.C. 521 (HL) 13–04n, 13–42
Wentworth v Lloyd (1864) 10 HL Cas. 589 .... 13–07n
West Midlands Passenger Executive v Singh [1988] 2 All E.R. 873
 (CA) 7–35n
Wheeler v Le Marchant (1881) 17 C. D. 675 .... 13–22n, 13–34, 13–49n
White v Ireland [1995] 2 I.R. 268 (HC) 1–11n, 1–28n, 1–60, 1–60n, 1–61,
 1–62, 1–62n, 1–63n, 1–71, 1–73
White v Queen [1998] 3 W.L.R. 992 (PC) 2–53n, 2–54n, 2–55
Wilkinson v Vesey (1972) 295 A. 2d 676 .... 4–70n

Table of Cases

Willey v Synan (1937) 57 C.L.R. 200 .... 9–77n
Williams v Powell [1894] W.N. 141 .... 10–03n
Williams v Quebrada Railway, Land and Copper Ltd. [1895]
    2 Ch. 751 .... 13–15n
Wong Kam Ming v R. [1980] A.C. 427 (PC) 10–12
Wong Sun v US (1963) 371 U.S. 471 .... 10–58n
Woodhouse v Hall (1981) 72 Cr. App. R. 39 (CA) 9–27
Woolmington v DPP [1935] A.C. 462 (HL) 4–07, 4–09, 4–17, 4–20,
                                          4–30n, 4–32, 4–34, 4–49, 4–50, 4–57
Wright v Doe d. Tatham (1838) 7 Ad. & E. 313 .... 9–31, 9–33, 9–34

Ybarra v Spangard (1944) 25 Cal. 2d 486, 154 P. 2d 687 .... 4–70n

Z v DPP [1994] 2 I.R. 476; [1994] 2 I.L.R.M. 481 (SC) 1–44, 12–15

TABLE OF LEGISLATION

TABLE OF CONSTITUTIONAL PROVISIONS

1937 Bunreacht na hÉireann	1–53n, 1–62n
Art.15	13–55, 13–64
(10)	13–64
(12)	13–55, 13–62, 13–63, 13–64
(13)	13–62, 13–63, 13–64
Art.28	13–65
Art.38	13–96
(1)	1–06n, 1–20, 1–25, 1–60, 1–73, 1–76, 4–08, 4–35, 5–02, 7–02, 10–39, 10–43, 11–27, 13–90, 13–91, 13–94
Art.40	2–21, 11–16, 13–66, 13–66n
(1)	11–10
(3)	1–06n, 10–39, 13–66
(1)	2–21
(4)(1)	4–10, 10–49, 11–09, 11–27, 11–40
(5)	10–49, 11–06, 11–07, 11–35n, 11–65, 11–69
(6)	13–90
Arts 41–44	2–21
Art.41	2–21, 2–25, 13–66, 13–66n
(3)(1)	2–25

TABLE OF STATUTES

Adoption Acts 1952–1991	1–57n
Age of Majority Act 1985	
s.2	1–55n
Bankers Books Evidence Act 1879	9–86n
s.5	2–01n
Bankers' Books Evidence (Amendment) Act 1959	2–01n, 9–61, 9–86n
Child Care Act 1991	1–53n, 1–57n
s.20	9–44n, 9–47n
s.24	1–53n
Child Trafficking and Pornography Act 1998	
s.2(3)	4–31n, 12–03n
ss.3–6	4–31n, 12–03n
s.7	11–64
Children Act 1908	
s.30	2–12n
Children Act 1997	1–64, 2–29, 2–50n, 9–43, 9–59, 12–25, 12–26
s.8	9–37

Children Act 1997—*contd.*
    ss.20–22 .... 1–55n
    s.20(b) 1–57n
    s.21 .... 1–55n, 1–57n
        (5) 1–57n
    s.22 .... 1–55n, 1–58n
    ss.23–25 2–09
    ss.23, 24 .... 9–46, 9–47
    s.25 9–46
    s.28 2–15
    Pt III 1–55, 1–58
Children Act 2001 .... 1–64, 1–67n, 2–31
    ss.56–63 10–28
    s.57 10–28
    s.66 .... 10–28n
        (4) 10–28n
    s.253 .... 9–59n
    s.254 11–32
    s.255 .... 1–56n, 1–57, 2–09
Common Law Procedure Act 1854
    s.22 .... 2–35n
Companies Acts 1963–1990 13–88
Companies Act 1990
    s.8 .... 10–39n
    s.10 .... 13–94, 13–95
    s.18 13–94
Competition (Amendment) Act 1996
    s.2 12–28
    s.4 12–28
Contempt of Court Act 1981
    s.10 .... 13–61n
Control of Horses Act 1996
    s.4 11–32
Copyright and Related Rights Act 2000
    s.127 .... 9–06n
County Officers and Courts (Ireland) Act 1877
    s.78 .... 4–46, 4–47, 4–47n
Courts Act 1988 .... 1–11n
Courts and Court Officers Act 1995
    s.45 .... 13–28n
        (3) 13–28
Criminal Assets Bureau Act 1996
    s.8 9–61
        (5) 9–61
        (7) 9–61
    s.14 11–68
    s.16 11–32
Criminal Evidence Act 1992 .... 1–11n, 1–55n, 1–64, 2–23, 2–25, 9–43
    s.2 .... 1–55n, 9–36n
    s.5(1), (2) 9–36n
    ss.7, 9, 10 .... 9–37n
    s.12 .... 1–55n, 1–59, 1–60, 1–62, 1–66

Table of Legislation

Criminal Evidence Act 1992—*contd*.
- s.13 .... 1–57, 1–60, 1–61, 1–62, 1–62n
  - (1) 1–55n
  - (2), (3) 1–57n
- s.14(1) 1–58n
- s.15(1) 1–66n
- s.16 .... 1–56, 1–65n, 1–75, 12–26
- s.16(1) 1–65, 1–65n
  - (a) 1–67
  - (b) 1–57, 1–65, 1–66, 1–67, 1–74, 9–59n
  - (2)–(3) 1–65n
  - (2) 1–65n, 1–67n
- s.18 .... 1–57n, 1–60, 6–17
- s.19 .... 1–55n, 1–57n, 1–58, 1–62n
- s.22 .... 2–23, 2–24, 2–25
  - (2) 2–24
- s.23 .... 2–23n, 13–67
- s.26 13–67
- s.27 .... 2–10, 2–12, 2–13, 2–29, 5–49n
- s.28 .... 1–65, 2–07, 5–49, 5–50
  - (3) 5–49
- s.29(1) 1–55
- s.30 1–33
- s.39 .... 1–55n
- Pt II 9–36, 9–37, 9–38, 9–60
- Pt III 1–28, 1–55, 1–55n, 1–57,
  1–59, 2–09, 2–29, 2–31
- Pt IV 2–23, 13–67

Criminal Justice Act 1964
- s.4(2) 4–28n

Criminal Justice Act 1984
- s.4 .... 6–36, 10–29, 10–60, 11–09, 11–41,
  11–42, 11–43, 11–44, 11–46, 13–101
  - s.7 10–26
    - (3) 10–50n, 11–24, 11–53
- s.10 .... 11–51, 13–88
- ss.18–19 .... 1–48n, 5–11n, 5–13, 5–14,
  13–89, 13–91, 13–100, 13–101
  - s.20(1) 1–47n
  - s.21 9–60
  - s.22 .... 1–14n, 10–03n
  - s.24(1) 1–48n
    - (1)(a) 1–48n
  - s.27 10–06

Criminal Justice Act 1990
- s.2 .... 5–18n

Criminal Justice Act 1994
- s.31 .... 4–31n
- s.64 11–65

Criminal Justice Act 1999 .... 1–48n, 1–56n, 1–64, 1–67n, 2–31
- s.9 .... 1–11n, 1–28, 1–48n, 1–50n, 1–56,
  1–57, 1–66n, 2–01, 2–09, 9–59n

Criminal Justice Act 1999—contd.
    s.14 .... 1–56n
        (2) 1–58
    s.15 .... 1–56n, 3–26n
    s.16(1) 1–48n
    s.17(1) 1–48n
    s.19 .... 1–66n
        (2), (3) 1–65n
    s.39 1–55
        (5) 6–17
    s.41 .... 3–27n
        (4) 3–27n
    Pt III 1–48n
Criminal Justice (Administration) Act 1914
    s.28(2) 2–12n
Criminal Justice (Drug Trafficking) Act 1996 .... 10–57, 13–101, 13–102
    s.2 11–41
    s.4 .... 11–51, 11–51n
    s.7 .... 5–11n, 5–14, 13–89, 13–100
    s.8 11–64
        (2) 11–68
Criminal Justice (Evidence) Act 1924 .... 2–16, 8–25, 8–70, 13–66
    s.1 .... 1–02, 2–16, 2–21, 8–06, 13–66
        (a)–(b) 8–01n
        (b) 2–18, 2–21, 13–84n, 13–100n
        (c) 2–22
        (e) 8–01, 8–04, 13–10n, 13–84n
        (f) 2–19, 7–24, 8–01, 8–02, 8–03, 8–04,
                                8–05, 8–06, 8–08, 8–09, 8–11, 8–15n, 8–19,
                                8–20, 8–29, 8–34, 8–34n, 8–59, 8–60, 10–64
            (i) 6–08, 8–06, 8–13, 8–15, 8–22, 8–23, 8–24
            (ii)–(iii) 1–52, 8–08, 8–23
            (ii) 1–25, 3–14, 8–13, 8–16, 8–26, 8–34,
                                8–35, 8–36, 8–38, 8–40, 8–41, 8–43, 8–45,
                                8–46, 8–46n, 8–47, 8–50, 8–51, 8–52n, 8–53,
                                8–54, 8–55, 8–55n, 8–56, 8–60, 8–61, 8–68, 10–14
            (iii) 8–13, 8–16, 8–61, 8–62, 8–65,
                                8–66, 8–67, 8–68, 8–69
    s.4 2–22
Criminal Justice (Forensic Evidence) Act 1990
    s.3 .... 5–11n, 13–89
        (1)(a)(i) 1–48n
Criminal Justice (Miscellaneous Provisions) Act 1997 4–10
    s.2 11–45
    s.5(4) 4–10
    s.6(1), (2) 9–60
        (4) 9–60n
    s.9 4–10
    s.10 11–64
    s.11(2) 9–60
Criminal Justice and Public Order Act 1994
    s.8 11–32

Table of Legislation xlix

Criminal Justice and Public Order Act 1994—*contd.*
    s.32 .... 5–21n
        (1) 5–35n
    s.34–35 .... 5–12n, 5–47n
    s.35(2) 5–13n
    Sch.9, para.33 .... 2–13n
Criminal Law Act 1976
    s.7 13–88
        (1) 11–13
    s.8 11–55
Criminal Law Act 1997 .... 11–32, 11–35
    s.4(1)–(2) 11–32, 11–32n
        (4)–(5) 11–32n
        (3) 11–32n
    s.6(1), (2) 11–33
Criminal Law (Amendment) Act 1935 1–26
Criminal Law (Jurisdiction) Act 1976
    s.18 .... 1–56n
Criminal Law (Jurisdiction) Act 1984
    s.14(4) 4–41n
Criminal Law (Rape) Act 1981
    s.3 .... 3–25, 3–26, 3–28, 3–29, 3–37
        (2) 3–26, 3–28
    s.4 3–25
        (1) 1–56n
    s.4A 3–25, 3–28
    s.13 3–25
Criminal Law (Rape) (Amendment) Act 1990
    s.7 .... 5–36, 5–37, 5–38, 5–39, 5–40
Criminal Law (Sexual Offences) Act 1993
    s.8(1) 7–19
Criminal Procedure Act 1865 (Denman's Act)
    s.1 .... 2–35n
    s.3 .... 2–35, 2–35n, 2–36
    s.4 3–07
    s.5 3–08
    s.6 .... 3–13, 3–13n, 8–03, 8–03n
    s.8 12–27
Criminal Procedure Act 1967 .... 1–48n, 2–49, 13–06
    s.4 .... 2–31, 4–31n, 4–36n
        (a)–(b) 1–56n
    s.4E 1–48n, 1–50n, 1–56, 4–10
    s.4F 1–57n, 2–29
    s.4F–G 1–11n, 1–56, 1–56n, 1–57,
                                        1–67, 2–09, 2–29, 9–59n
    s.4G 2–29
    s.4K–L 2–01
    s.4K 2–01n
        (1)(b) 2–01n
    s.4L 2–01n
        (1)(b) 2–01n
    s.5 9–37

Criminal Procedure Act 1967—contd.
    s.6 .... 1–66n, 9–37
        (1) 9–37
        Pt IA 3–26n
Criminal Procedure Act 1993
    s.10 .... 5–20, 5–10n, 10–07,
                                                                        10–72, 10–73, 10–75
Customs Consolidation Act 1876 13–88
Defences Act 1954
    s.135 4–44
Diplomatic Relations Immunities Act 1967
    s.5 .... 2–01n
Domestic Violence Act 1996 .... 1–53n, 1–57n
    s.3(4)(b) 12–28
    s.18 11–32
Dublin Police Act 1842
    s.29 11–55
Emergency Powers Act 1939 .... 1–41n
Evidence Amendment Act 1853
    s.3 13–66
Evidence Further Amendment Act 1869
    s.4 .... 2–06n
European Convention on Human Rights Act 2003 1–06
    s.2 1–06
    s.4 1–41
    s.5(1) 1–06
Explosive Substances Act 1883
    s.4 11–59
    s.4(1) 4–42, 4–43
Family Home Protection Act 1976 .... 1–57n
Family Law Act 1995 .... 1–53n, 1–57n
    s.47 .... 9–44n
Family Law (Divorce) Act 1996 .... 1–53n, 1–57n, 2–24
Family Law (Maintenance of Spouses) Act 1976 .... 1–57n
Firearms Act 1964
    s.27A 4–41, 13–87n
Garda Síochána (Complaints) Board Act 1986
    s.12 .... 13–75n
Greyhound Industry Act 1958 13–25
Guardianship of Infants Act 1964 .... 1–53n, 1–57n, 9–47, 13–17
    s.3 .... 1–53n, 9–47, 13–17
Illegitimate Children (Affiliation Orders) Act 1930
    s.3 .... 5–18n
Interception of Postal Packets and Telecommunications Messages (Regulation)
    Act 1993 11–12
    s.2(1) 11–11
        (5), (7) 11–11n
    s.8 .... 11–11n
Interpretation Act 1937
    s.6(1) 1–41
Intoxicating Liquor Act 1960
    s.22(3) 11–54n

Table of Legislation

Judicial Separation and Family Law Reform Act 1989 .... 1–53n, 2–24
    s.20 2–29
    ss.21–23 2–29
    ss.23–25 2–29
    s.28 2–29
    s.33 .... 1–57n
    s.45 .... 1–57n
Larceny Act 1861
    s.58 .... 4–39n
Larceny Act 1916
    s.28 .... 4–39n
    s.41(1) 11–35n
Litter Pollution Act 1997
    s.23(6) 11–32
Marriages (Ireland) Act 1844 .... 9–86n
Married Women's Status Act 1957 2–22
Medical Practitioners Act 1978 9–18
Misuse of Drugs Act 1977 .... 11–41, 11–66n
    s.4 .... 4–31n
    s.15 .... 4–31n
    s.15A(2) 4–36n
    s.23 11–57
        (1), (1)(b) 11–55
    s.25 11–32
    s.26(1) 11–66
        (2) 11–64
    s.29 .... 4–31n
Non-Fatal Offences Against the Person Act 1997
    s.2 12–03
Oaths Act 1888 2–06
    s.1 .... 2–01n, 2–05n
    s.3 2–06
Oaths Act 1909
    s.2(1) 2–05n
        (2) 2–05n, 2–06n
Offences Against the State Act 1939 .... 11–55n
    s.3 4–40
    s.12 4–34
    s.21 .... 4–34, 4–40, 11–59, 12–28
    s.24 .... 4–34, 4–36, 4–40, 4–45
    s.30 .... 10–41, 10–42, 11–09, 11–16, 11–41,
                                 11–41n, 11–43, 11–46n, 11–48,
                                 11–49, 11–59, 13–88, 13–107
        (1) 11–32, 11–55
        (2) 11–55
    s.30A 11–51
    s.52 .... 13–88, 13–92, 13–97
        (2) 13–88, 13–97
Offences Against the State (Amendment) Act 1972
    s.3 .... 4–40n
        (2) 4–34n, 12–28
    s.21 .... 4–34n

Offences Against the State (Amendment)
    Act 1998 .... 10–53, 10–57, 13–06n, 13–101, 13–102
        s.3 .... 1–47n
        s.5 .... 5–11n, 5–14, 13–89, 13–100
        s.10 11–41
        s.11 .... 11–51n
Partition Acts 1868–1876 .... 1–57n
Perjury Act 1911 .... 5–18n
Postal and Telecommunications Services Act 1983
        s.98 11–12
Proceeds of Crime Act 1996 13–93
        ss.2–3 4–49
        s.2(3) 4–49
        s.3 9–50
            (3) 4–49
        s.8(1)(b) 9–06n, 9–86
            (5) 9–06n
        s.9 13–83
Referendum Act 1994
        s.42 4–81
Registration of Births and Deaths (Ireland)
    Act 1883 .... 9–86n
Road Traffic Act 1933
        s.22 4–52
        Pt III 1–41
Road Traffic Act 1961
        s.49(8) 11–29, 11–31, 11–31, 11–34
        s.50(8) 4–31, 4–45
            (10) 11–34
        s.105 .... 5–18, 12–29n
        s.106(3A) 11–34
        s.107 13–88
        s.109 11–56
Road Traffic Act 1978 11–31
Road Traffic Act 1994 11–35
        s.10 .... 11–29, 11–31
        s.11 .... 4–31, 4–45
        s.13 .... 11–31, 11–36, 13–88
            (1)(b) 11–31
        s.15 13–88
        s.34 .... 11–36n
        s.39(1) 11–34
            (2) 11–34
        s.49(8) 11–29
School Attendance Act 1926
        s.4(2)(b) 4–31n
        s.18(2) 4–31n, 4–54n
Sex Offenders Act 2001
        s.34 .... 3–25, 3–25n, 3–28
Sexual Offences (Amendment) Act 1976
        s.2 3–26
Social Welfare (Consolidation) Act 1993 13–88

Table of Legislation

Status of Children Act 1985
    s.25 .... 5–18n
Succession Act 1965 .... 13–09, 13–15, 13–19
    s.117 .... 4–80, 4–80n
Treason Act 1939
    s.1(4) 5–18n
    s.2(2) 5–18n
Treason Act 1795
    s.1 .... 5–18n
Wildlife Act 1976
    s.45 .... 11–54n
    s.47 .... 11–54n
    s.51 .... 11–54n
    s.53 .... 11–54n
    Pt II 11–54n
Workmen's Compensation Act 1934 9–75

TABLE OF STATUTORY INSTRUMENTS

Criminal Evidence Act 1992 (Commencement) Order 1993
    (S.I. No. 288 of 1993) 1–57n
Criminal Evidence Act 1992 (Commencement) Order 1993
    (S.I. No. 38 of 1993) 1–57n
Criminal Justice Act 1984 (Electronic Recording of Interviews)
    Regulation 1997 .... 10–06n
        art.3(1) 10–07n
        art.4(3)(b) 10–07n
Criminal Justice Act 1999 (Part III) (Commencement) Order 2001 .... 1–48n
Criminal Justice Act 1984 (Treatment of Persons in Custody in
    Garda Síochána Stations Regulations)
    1987 .... 10–16, 10–17, 10–26, 10–27, 10–36, 10–45, 10–50, 10–55, 11–24
        reg.6 10–26
        reg.7 10–26
        reg.12(6) 10–55
        reg.17(1) 11–53
        art.2(4) 10–28n
        art.4(3) 10–50n
        art.8 9–23
        art.8(1)(b) 10–50
        art.9(2) 10–50n
        art.11(1) 10–50
        art.11(3) 10–50n
        art.12 10–29
        art.12(6) 10–50n
        art.13(1) 10–28n
Emergency Powers (Control of Export) Order 1940 4–47
Rules of the Superior Courts (No. 6) (Disclosure of Reports
    and Statements) 13–28n
Social Welfare Regulations of 1952
    Art.11(5) 9–53

RULES

District Court (Criminal Justice) Rules 2001
    r.8 .... 1–56n, 1–66n
        Schs 11–13 .... 1–66n
        Sch.11 .... 1–56n
District Court Rules 1997
    Ord.24
        r.7 .... 1–66n
        rr.15–17 .... 1–56n
        Sch.B, forms 24.3–24.7 .... 1–66n
Judges' Rules 10–16, 10.17, 10–18, 10–19, 10–20,
                                                        10–26, 11–09, 11–23n, 11–53
    r.1 10–21
    r.2 10–21
    r.3 .... 10–19, 10–22
    r.8 .... 10–20, 10–23
    r.9 .... 10–05, 10–06, 10–25
Rules of the Superior Courts 1986 13–28
    Ord.20, rr.20–24 .... 2–50n
    Ord.25, r.8(1)(b) 13–32n
    Ord.38, r.38 .... 13–30n
    Ord.39 .... 2–01n
        rr.45–51 .... 13–28n
        r.45(1)(e) 13–30n
        r.46(1) 13–28n
        r.48 .... 13–28n
    Ord.40, r.4 9–50
Rules of the Supreme Court (Ireland) 1905 13–06

EUROPEAN LEGISLATION

Convention on Human Rights and Fundamental Freedoms 1–06, 1–41, 2–31
    Art.6 .... 1–07, 1–28, 1–76, 3–36,
                                            10–57 13–21, 13–91, 13–106
        (1) 13–65
        (2) 4–09
        (3) 9–15, 9–19
            (c) 10–53
    Art.8 .... 1–28, 11–10n

OTHER LEGISLATION

International Conventions
Vienna Convention on Diplomatic Relations of April 18, 1961 .... 2–01n

Australia
Crimes Act 1900–74
    ss.413A–B 8–55n
Crimes Act 1958
    s.400 .... 2–26n
Evidence Act 1995 .... 8–55n
Uniform Evidence Acts 1995
    s.59(1) 9–35n

India
Indian Evidence Act 1872 1–05

UK
Children Act 1989 13–17
Civil Evidence Act 1968 .... 9–12n
    s.16(1)(a) 13–80n
Civil Evidence Act 1972 .... 9–12n
Civil Evidence Act 1995 .... 2–50n, 9–12n, 9–42
    s.1(1) 9–14n, 9–40n
    s.13 .... 9–36n
Companies Act 1985
    s.434 13–92
Crime and Disorder Act 1998
    s.120(2) 5–18n
Criminal Evidence Act 1965 .... 9–12n
Criminal Evidence Act 1979
    s.1 .... 8–70n
Criminal Evidence (Northern Ireland) Order 1988 .... 5–13, 13–102n, 13–105n
Criminal Justice Act 1988 .... 9–12n, 9–36n
    ss.23–25 .... 2–29n
    s.33A(2A) 2–13n
    s.34(2) 5–35n
Criminal Evidence Act 1898 .... 8–01, 8–53, 13–66
    s.1 .... 2–16n
        (f) 7–24
        (f)(iii) 8–70
    s.7(1) 2–16n
Criminal Justice (Public Order) Act 1994
    ss.34–35 13–103
    s.34 13–102
Family Law Reform Act 1987
    s.17 .... 5–18n
Human Rights Act 1998
    s.3 3–27
Misuse of Drugs Act 1971
    s.5(2) 4–55, 4–56

Police and Criminal Evidence Act 1984 1–05
        s.10(1) 13–27n
        s.72 .... 10–38n
        s.76 .... 10–62n
                (2) 10–09
        s.78 .... 10–10n
                (2) 10–44
        s.80(9) 13–67
Prevention of Corruption Act 1916
        s.2 .... 4–38, 4–39
        s.21 .... 4–40n
Youth Justice and Criminal Evidence Act 1999 .... 3–27, 3–28, 3–30, 3–34, 3–36
        s.3 3–27
        s.13 3–27
        ss.16–33 .... 1–59n
        s.41 .... 3–27, 3–35
        s.41(3)(c) 3–36
        s.41(4) 3–35
        s.53 .... 2–13n
        s.53(3) 2–10n
        s.54(1) 2–02n

US
Federal Rules of Evidence
        US Rule 801 .... 9–35n
US Constitution
        Fourth Amendment 11–08
        Fifth Amendment 10–53, 13–85
        Sixth Amendment 1–61n

CHAPTER 1

EVIDENCE AND THE TRIAL

I. Introduction	1–01
II. Evolution of Evidence Laws and Theory	1–08
III. Evidence Laws in the Common Law Trial	1–09
IV. Key Concepts and Types of Evidence	1–13
V. Course of the Trial	1–48
VI. Testimony	1–55
Part III of the Criminal Evidence Act 1992	1–57
Constitutionality of the Television Link Measures	1–59
Taking Evidence in Advance of the Trial	1–64

I. INTRODUCTION

1–01 The laws, principles, and rules of evidence determine the admissibility and function of evidence in judicial proceedings. Although now numerous and sourced more disparately, they derive from fundamental tenets and assumptions protective of the rights of the citizenry and of persons who stand accused of crime. The laws of evidence formally constitute a panoply of exceptions and counter-exceptions to the general principle that all relevant evidence is admissible; upon this basis, they have been categorised as the exclusionary rules of evidence. They do not necessarily share the same concerns, however, and their various premises and assumptions are increasingly supplemented or superceded by statute in response to the shifting exigencies of modern society. The laws and rules remain dynamic, and this has never been more apparent in Ireland than in the last decade when traditional forms of receiving evidence have been complemented by new alternatives such as the giving of evidence by television link from outside the courtroom, and by provision for the taking of evidence in advance of the trial—each breaking fundamentally with the temporal sequence of the trial steadfastly required by the common law for centuries.[1]

1–02 Although each rule of evidence assumes a particular concern with respect to evidence, proof, or investigation, the dominant concern of the common law has been the intrinsic unreliability of certain types of evidence. The fear of unreliable evidence was once reflected in a principle, long

---

[1] *cf.* para.**1–55** *et seq.*

abandoned, that the parties to a dispute were not competent to tender evidence in their own cause, since their evidence would inevitably be self-serving, therefore of low probative value and liable to encourage perjury. Indeed, until s.1 of the Criminal Justice (Evidence) Act 1924, the accused was not entitled to give sworn evidence in his own cause, and was restricted to making unsworn statements from the dock where permitted by judicial discretion to do so.[2] Whilst each of the classic rules of evidence explored in this book evoke reliability concerns, the rules have been developed in recent years to achieve other goals; notably the public interest in promoting due process at the investigative stage, reflected in a rule that accounts for the bulk of Irish appeals upon evidence issues, the strict *O'Brien* exclusionary rule proscribing evidence obtained by law-enforcers in breach of the accused's constitutional rights.[3]

1–03 Historically, the dominant concern of evidence law has been the criminal trial. Due to the severe consequences that may flow from a criminal charge and prosecution—potentially imprisonment, "the punishment par excellence" in a culture that exalts the principle of liberty[4]—the law is predominantly concerned to ensure that the accused benefits from the presumption of innocence enforced by the common law and, in more recent times, the Irish Constitution. One of the means by which it achieves this is to require proof by the prosecution to a higher standard, beyond reasonable doubt. This is further achieved by the rule in criminal proceedings that the accused is incompetent as a witness for the prosecution and non-compellable as a witness for the co-accused;[5] by the requirement that certain evidence, if uncorroborated, be viewed with caution;[6] and by the principle that the trial judge has an inherent discretion to exclude relevant and otherwise admissible evidence where its prejudicial effect is likely to outweigh its probative force.[7] Thus, in criminal proceedings, vital evidence may be excluded from the trial for reasons that have nothing to do with its cogency but instead respond to concern for the fairness of the trial or for future investigative and trial practices. In this light, it is often asserted that "the history of liberty has largely been the history of its procedural safeguards".[8] This emphasis is further justified on the basis that the litigator or prosecutor in criminal cases is also the fact-finder and investigator, with greater access to resources than the accused, and with an inbuilt impetus to prosecute successfully.

---

[2] *cf.* para.**8–01**.
[3] *cf.* para.**11–01** *et seq.*
[4] Foucault, *Discipline and Punish: The Birth of the Prison* (Penguin Books, London) at p.232.
[5] *cf.* para.**2–16** *et seq.*
[6] *cf.* para.**5–01** *et seq.*
[7] *People (DPP) v Meleady (No. 3)* [2001] 4 I.R. 16 at 31, *per* Geoghegan J. (CCA); *People (DPP) v O'Callaghan* (CCA, December 18, 2000); *R v Christie* [1980] A.C. 402 (HL).
[8] *McNabb v US* 318 U.S. 332 (1943), *per* Frankfurter J., where the US Supreme Court set the so-called "civilian standard" for interrogators as a prerequisite to admissibility of confession statements repudiated in a trial by the accused.

1-04 The rules of evidence apply strictly to civil proceedings involving private litigants, although there is sometimes more flexibility in this context insofar as parties are often permitted to waive a strict rule of evidence by mutual consent.[9] The failure to adhere to a strict rule of evidence in civil proceedings—most of which are now decided by judge alone—is less likely to have the critical impact often evident in serious criminal cases, although much depends upon the context and, in particular, how prejudicial or decisive the disputed evidence was for the outcome of the hearing. Whilst the rules of evidence are often, in practice, more relaxed for tribunals and arbitrations, statutory tribunals of enquiry that may consequentially give rise to prosecution are expected to adopt strict compliance with the rules of evidence adopted for ordinary criminal prosecutions, and further by the constitutional requirements of fair procedures and natural justice.[10]

1-05 Evidence law has been categorised as *adjectival* law, since it defines the procedures, pleadings, and proof by which the substantive law is to be applied.[11] Despite its sprawl and, some would say, its miscellaneousness—although to the extent this exists, it is due to the undeveloped status of a number of the older rules and exceptions—the laws of evidence have not been codified in Ireland or England to date. Numerous recent statutes in England, such as the Police and Criminal Evidence Act 1984, have effected comprehensive enactment of the rules of evidence and procedure for criminal proceedings. Elsewhere in the common law, codification of the laws of evidence and procedure has flourished. The Indian Evidence Act of 1872 was followed as a template in many colonies and former colonies of Britain. In America, the Federal Rules of Evidence were adopted by a majority of North American states. In Australia, codification of evidence rules was successfully achieved by the Evidence Act 1995.

1-06 In Ireland, the laws, principles, and rules of evidence have been drawn from the common law, the Constitution, and statutes. The Constitution has been responsible for strengthening and developing the Irish judiciary's commitment to core values of the common law, such as the presumption of innocence and the strict application of the rules of evidence in criminal proceedings.[12] This is particularly evident in the law governing the admissibility of confession statements and the effect upon evidence of infringements of the accused's constitutional rights.[13] The constitutionalisation of Irish evidence

---

[9] *cf.* para.**9-40** *et seq.*
[10] *cf.* para.**9-54** *et seq.*
[11] *Phipson on Evidence* (Howard ed., 15th ed., Sweet & Maxwell, London, 2000) at p.1.
[12] This has been achieved chiefly by developing the constitutional right to a fair trial and the constitutional right more generally to due process and fair procedures, rights which have been deemed implicit in Arts 38(1) and 40(3) respectively: *cf.* paras **9-19** and **11-27**. Additionally, the violation of the accused's constitutional right to personal liberty, bodily integrity, or inviolability of his dwelling have strict effect upon the admissibility of evidence obtained by gardai under the strict *O'Brien* exclusionary rule developed by the Irish courts: *cf.* para.**11-01** *et seq.*
[13] *cf.* paras **10-48** *et seq.* and **11-09** *et seq.*

law distinguishes it in many instances from English law precedent, which lacks the principled framework of a written constitution and has increasingly proceeded by reference to statute and piecemeal judicial qualification to fundamental tenets of an earlier age. The Convention on Human Rights and Fundamental Freedoms, and the case law of the European Court of Human Rights, now constitute an important additional source of evidence law. This will inevitably redouble in the coming years following enactment of the European Convention on Human Rights Act 2003. By virtue of s.2, the Irish courts are obliged to interpret statutory provisions and the common law in a manner compatible with the European Convention "in so far as is possible"; by virtue of s.5(1), the High Court, or the Supreme Court when exercising its appellate jurisdiction, may make a declaration that a statutory provision or rule of law is incompatible with the State's obligations under the Convention, in circumstances "where no other legal remedy is adequate and available".

1–07 Article 6 of the Convention sets out a number of non-exhaustive guarantees for procedural fairness, including: the right to adversarial proceedings;[14] the right to equality of arms;[15] the right to be present at court hearings;[16] the right to know the grounds upon which a court decision is based;[17] the right of a person accused of a crime to remain silent and not to incriminate himself;[18] and access to information necessary to bring or defend a case.[19] The right to a fair trial has been construed to be the *fons origo* of these specific safeguards;[20] and in more recent years, the European Court of Human Rights has tended to appraise allegations of specific breaches of Art.6 in terms of the net effect for unfairness in the trial.[21] Until the 1980s, the Court of Human Rights acted in the manner of a "sleeping beauty, frequently referred to but without much impact".[22] In the 1970s, the court delivered a mere 26 judgments compared to 169 in the 1980s, 809 in the 1990s, and 2,428 from 2000–2002.[23] The court is observed in recent years to have become

---

[14] Considered in *Feldbrugge v Netherlands* (1986) 8 E.H.R.R. 425; *Kraska v Switzerland* (1994) 18 E.H.R.R. 188; and *Ruiz-Mateos v Spain* (1993) 16 E.H.R.R. 505.
[15] Considered in *Delcourt v Belgium* (1970) 1 E.H.R.R. 355; *Neumeister v Austria* (1979-80) 1 E.H.R.R. 91; and *Borgers v Belgium* [1993] 15 E.H.R.R. 92.
[16] Considered in *Brozicek v Italy* (1990) 12 E.H.R.R. 371; *FCB v Italy* (1991) 14 E.H.R.R. 909; and *Kremzow v Austria* (1994) 17 E.H.R.R. 322.
[17] Considered in *Hadjianastassiou v Greece* (1993) 16 E.H.R.R. 219.
[18] Considered in *Murray v United Kingdom* (1996) 22 E.H.R.R. 29 and *Saunders v United Kingdom* (1996) 23 E.H.R.R. 313: cf. paras **13-92** *et seq.*, **13-105** *et seq.*
[19] Considered in *McGinley and Egan v United Kingdom* (1999) 27 E.H.R.R. 1.
[20] *Golder v United Kingdom* (1979-80) 1 E.H.R.R. 524 at para.36.
[21] Grosz *et al*, *Human Rights: The 1998 Act and the European Convention* (Sweet & Maxwell, London, 2000), at p.244. See: *Nielson v Denmark* (1988) 11 E.H.R.R. 175 at para.52; *Barbera, Messegue and Jabardo v Spain* (1988) 11 E.H.R.R. 360; *Murray v United Kingdom* (1996) 22 E.H.R.R. 29.
[22] Frowein, "European Integration through Fundamental Rights" (1994) 18 *Journal of Law Reform* 8.
[23] Council of Europe, *Survey of Activities of the European Court of Human Rights 2002* at p.31.

Evidence and the Trial

"fiercely expansionist" and "unquestionably interventionist",[24] now not merely engaged in judicial creativity but flaunting it, suddenly ready and willing to admonish signatory states for infringements of rights that are not formally stated in the Convention such as the privilege against self-incrimination and the right to silence.[25]

II. Evolution of Evidence Laws and Theory

1–08 The Anglo-American system of evidence, which is the earliest foundation of evidence laws in Ireland, derives from the post-Enlightenment philosophic tradition of Rationalism formatively applied between 1770 and 1830. Constructed upon concepts of reason and rationality acceptable at the time, the system consciously broke from old traditions reliant upon faith, creed, and practice. As remarked by Thayer: "What was formerly 'tried' by the method of force or the mechanical following of form [was] now tried by the method of reason".[26] Individual principles and rules of evidence have always tended to emerge spasmodically in response to prevailing concerns, and this process clearly continues apace in a common law world now governed to a greater extent by legislation. As a system of trial by proof, it was never fully subjected to an empirical analysis, although from the mid-eighteenth century on, a number of celebrated jurists sought to devise unitary treatises upon which the rules could be rationalised,[27] and many of whose thoughts and expressions are now assimilated into mainstream discourse. Most influential amongst the early publications were the writings of Wigmore and Thayer, the latter signalling current thoughts upon the matter, namely that the laws of evidence amount to a panoply of disparate exceptions to the general rule of free proof by relevant evidence.[28] By the twentieth century, treatises on evidence law had fallen out of favour—in part because ongoing changes to the laws of evidence stripped many of the published treatises of their relevance, but also because an increase in recourse to trials and litigation created a preference and an appetite for exploration and dissemination of the pith of the law, a shift most apparent in the format adopted by Cross in his influential work on *Evidence* published in 1958, and in which theory and treatise was referred to minimally.

---

[24] Munday, "Inferences from Silence and European Human Rights Law" [1996] Crim. L. Rev. 370 at 383.
[25] *cf.* paras **13–93, 13–105** *et seq.*
[26] Thayer, *A Preliminary Treatise on Evidence at the Common Law*, 1898 at p.199.
[27] The first published work, *The Law of Evidence* (1754), was by Lord Chief Baron Gilbert. This was followed by: Bathurst, *The Theory of Evidence* (1761); Buller, *An Introduction to the Law Relative to Trials at Nisi Prius* (1772); Peake, *A Compendium of the Law of Evidence* (1801); Bentham, *Rationale of Judicial Evidence* (1827); Greenleaf, *A Treatise on the Law of Evidence* (1843); Taylor, *Treatise on the Law of Evidence* (1848); *Stephen's Digest of the Law of Evidence* (1879); Phipson, *The Law of Evidence* (1892); Thayer, *A Preliminary Treatise on Evidence at the Common Law* (1898); and Wigmore, *A Treatise on the Anglo-American System of Evidence in Trials at Common Law* (1904–8).
[28] *cf.* para.**1–17**.

III. EVIDENCE LAWS IN THE COMMON LAW TRIAL

1–09 The elaborate nature of the laws of evidence that were incrementally applied to the modern trial from its evolution at the close of the seventeenth century, is often said to derive from the common law's mistrust of juries,[29] notwithstanding that trial by jury is regarded as the foundation of the criminal justice system operated by the common law.[30] In this light, Damaska has observed that many of the rules appear to reflect the perceived "need to compensate for the alleged intellectual and emotional frailties of amateurs cast in the role of occasional judges".[31] This perspective is acknowledged occasionally by the judiciary. Dillon L.J. once observed: "Where there is a jury the court must be more careful about admitting evidence which is in truth merely prejudicial than is necessary where there is a trial by a judge alone who is trained to distinguish between what is probative and what is not".[32] It is a frequent complaint of modern evidence law, however, that the rules have become so technical they are more likely to confuse than assist juries. This danger is especially evident with respect to the slew of judicial directions and guidelines emanating in recent years as a result of the demise of fixed corroboration requirements[33] and the increased use of pre-trial statements permitted to underscore a witness' inconsistency or unreliability.[34] On the other hand, the technicality of evidence laws derives necessarily in part from the temporally concentrated nature of the common law trial; further from the absence of a pre-trial stage dedicated to examination and testing of contemplated evidence; and yet further from the "inscrutability of the jury verdict, and the minimal possibility of reconsidering factual issues on appeal".[35]

1–10 Many of the rules of evidence and their underpinning concerns may be understood by distinguishing the common law trial from other systems of adjudication. The accusatorial form and adversarial dynamic of the trial constructed by the common law tend to be illustrated by the following characteristics (though many of them tempered in recent decades). The format of the trial is often likened to a gladiatorial combat whose ultimate aim is to persuade the triers of fact that the party's assertions and propositions have been proved. Structurally, the court contemplated by the common law rules of evidence is bifurcated, with a strict, though overlapping, division of labour between judge and jury.[36] The trial judge acts akin to an umpire required to

---

[29] In *A Preliminary Treatise on Evidence at the Common Law* (1898), Thayer associated the origins and continuance of evidence laws with the survival of the jury trial. For a contrary view, however, see Morgan, *Some Problems of Proof under the Anglo-American System of Litigation* (Columbia University Press, New York, 1956).
[30] *R. v McIlkenny* [1992] 2 All E.R. 417 at 425, *per* Lloyd L.J. (CA).
[31] Damaska, *Evidence Law Adrift* (Yale University Press, 1997) at p.28.
[32] *Thorpe v Chief Constable of Greater Manchester Police* [1989] 2 All E.R. 827 at 831 (CA).
[33] *cf.* para.**5–19** *et seq.*
[34] *cf.* paras **2–30** *et seq.*, **3–07** *et seq.*
[35] Damaska, *op. cit.* n.31 at p.65.
[36] *cf.* para.**1–22** *et seq.* Judges have on occasion expressed a preference for a unitary model

Evidence and the Trial

ensure that the rules of the game are adhered to.[37] Each party to the dispute has autonomy over the running of his case. Evidence and witnesses are viewed in a proprietary manner from the perspective of the side tendering the evidence, with the result that a witness whose testimony transpires to be "adverse" to the interests of the calling side is often deemed "hostile" as though a turncoat.[38] The rules of evidence have been developed not to *assist* a party in bringing evidence before the court helpful to his case, but rather to prohibit him from tendering certain types of evidence deemed strictly inadmissible by a particular rule because it is inherently or potentially unreliable or carries a clear risk of prejudice. The common law favours the reception of oral evidence in open court, and mistrusts documentary evidence by declarants not available on the day to be cross-examined. In particular, the rules against hearsay[39] and against narrative[40] "shore up the *oral tradition* of criminal trials—a tradition based on a deep-seated belief in the common law world that oral evidence is best. Common lawyers, like vegans, are firmly convinced that 'first hand is first rate'".[41] The common law favours live concentrated proceedings—evidence must be given *en bloc* by each party, and the trial or hearing is followed swiftly by judgment, from which a full appeal on the factual questions is often not possible. The resulting process presumes that "the 'dialectical immediacy' of oral presentation and confrontation is the best means of arriving at rectitude of decision on questions of fact and law".[42]

1–11 Many of these features have been eroded in specific contexts in recent years. The proposition that the trial judge acts akin to a passive umpire does not apply to family law proceedings, and not always in criminal or other civil proceedings.[43] New modes of scientific proof have been approved.[44] Alternative means of giving testimony during the trial have been implemented, prompted largely by concerns to secure the testimony of vulnerable witnesses and to prosecute child abusers and organised criminals more effectively. The rarely exercised option of using screens in court to shield complainants has been transformed into a complex closed-circuit televisual link between the

---

in particular contexts such as the *voire dire* determination of the admissibility of evidence: e.g. *People v Lynch* [1982] I.R. 64 (SC) and *People (DPP) v Conroy* [1986] I.R. 460, per Walsh J., dissenting (SC) (*cf.* appendix 29).

[37] *cf.* paras **1–22** *et seq.*, **1–53** *et seq.*
[38] Damaska, *op. cit.* n.31 at 77; *cf.* para.**2–30**.
[39] *cf.* para.**9–01** *et seq.*
[40] *cf.* para.**2–50** *et seq.*
[41] Spencer, "Orality and the Evidence of Absent Witness" (1994) Crim. L.R. 628.
[42] Twining, *Rethinking Evidence: Exploratory Essays* (Basil Blackwell Ltd., Oxford, 1990) at p.183.
[43] *cf.* paras **1–23**, **1–53**.
[44] The judges have not been reluctant to embrace the greater range of options provided by technological advances. In *Dunne v DPP* [2002] 2 I.R. 305 at 310 (SC), Hardiman J. commented: "The balance has long been struck in favour of the use of technology in the search for the perpetrators of crime, even when the processes involved are minimally invasive or transiently painful or undignified for innocent people. The greater good prevails". See also *R. v Maqsud Alf* [1966] 1 Q.B. 688 for the view that it is "wrong to deny to the law of evidence advantages to be gained by new techniques and new devices".

courtroom and the witness.[45] Notwithstanding the entrenched common law rule that statements made prior to the trial are inadmissible unless falling within an exception, the legislative trend in recent years in the UK and Ireland has been to enable evidence in certain circumstances to be taken in advance of the criminal trial by videotape or deposition.[46] A mixed system has resulted, although it is one that continues to require oral evidence save where a statutory exception applies. The right to a hearing by jury has all but vanished from civil hearings, and is retained chiefly for cases seeking damages solely for false imprisonment, intentional trespass to the person, and defamation;[47] the right to a jury trial in criminal proceedings on indictment is at the accused's election.

1–12 The common law trial, possessed in a rough-hewn way of the *indicia* identified above, may usefully be contrasted with the inquisitorial system of law operating in civil law jurisdictions across continental Europe. A judge is typically involved at the pre-trial stage, and references are made to this judge at all relevant stages for directions and decisions on whether certain evidence may be tendered at the trial, so that by the time of the trial the judge is very familiar with the evidence and has foreknowledge of what is likely to be the best evidence in the case. The judge often examines witnesses in advance, and may even attend the scene of a crime or be involved in formal identification of the suspect. A proprietary view is not taken of witnesses, particularly expert witnesses who are appointed and instructed by the court and who may even direct their own questions at ordinary witnesses in the proceedings. Where judges are given a pro-active role, and the proceedings are less formal and more amenable to adjournment, there are correspondingly fewer exclusionary rules of evidence and less mistrust of documentary evidence.[48]

IV. KEY CONCEPTS AND TYPES OF EVIDENCE

Evidence and Proof

1–13 Although the evidence that may be tendered in judicial proceedings—also called judicial evidence—by practice takes the form of witness testimony, objects (real evidence), and documents, there have been few attempts to define evidence. One of the respected definitions is that evidence is "any matter of fact, the effect, tendency or design of which is to produce in the mind a persuasion, affirmative or disaffirmative, of the existence of some other matter

---

[45] *cf.* para.**1–59** *et seq.*, *White v Ireland* [1995] 2 I.R. 268 (HC), and *Donnelly v Ireland* [1998] 1 I.R. 321 (SC), where the High Court and Supreme Court upheld the constitutionality of provisions of the Criminal Evidence Act 1992 enabling child witnesses to give their testimony by television link.
[46] *e.g.* the Criminal Procedure Act 1967, s.4F-G, inserted by the Criminal Justice Act 1999, s.9: *cf.* paras **1–56, 1–64** *et seq.*
[47] Courts Act 1988, brought into force on August 1, 1988.
[48] Beardsley, "Proof of Fact in French Civil Procedure" (1986) 34 Am. J. Comp. L. 459.

of fact".[49] This expresses proof in propositional form, and has been justified pragmatically. According to Rolphe B: "if we lived for a thousand years instead of about sixty or seventy, and every case was of sufficient importance, it might be possible, and perhaps proper ... to raise every possible enquiry as to the truth of statements made ... In fact mankind finds it to be impossible".[50] There has thus been little support by the common law judges for the ideal of certainty of proof, since subjective factors affect the bulk of evidence, being the live personal reconstruction of events by a witness. When determining the facts proven by a witness' testimony, the court is necessarily influenced by the credibility and demeanour of the witness, by how persuasive or truthful he appeared. As a result, the standards of proof are phrased according to probability and reasonable possibility. Evidence is that which *tends to prove* a fact in dispute. According to Lord Simon of Glaisdale in *DPP v Kilbourne*, relevant evidence is that "which makes the matter which requires proof more or less probable".[51]

1–14 Proof, aside from argument and inferences drawn by the triers, may be effected by evidence, or in certain circumstances by the operation of presumptions of law,[52] by formal admission,[53] or by judicial notice.[54] At one stage, but to limited effect, the common law courts recognised a "best evidence" principle, which operated to render inferior evidence inadmissible in the trial. Rooted in a statement by Lord Hardwicke in 1745,[55] and applied rarely in modern times,[56] the "best evidence" principle has had no significant effect on the laws of evidence. There has been no attempt to establish a hierarchy of evidence that would favour, for instance, direct evidence over circumstantial evidence, real evidence over testimonial evidence, and so forth,[57] although such a principle may be taken to be implicit in distinct rules such as the rule against hearsay. Concerns over the relative strength and merits of relevant admissible evidence are instead voiced in the context of persuasive submissions

---

[49] Best, *A Treatise on the Principles of the Law of Evidence* (1849) (8th ed., J.M. Lely, London, 1893) at s.11.
[50] *Attorney-General v Hitchcock* (1947) 1 Excheq. 91 at 105.
[51] [1973] A.C. 729 at 756 (HL).
[52] *cf.* para.**4–13** *et seq.*
[53] This facility was introduced to criminal proceedings by s.22 of the Criminal Justice Act 1984, which provides that the admission of a fact by either the prosecution or the accused before or during the trial may be accepted as "conclusive" evidence of that fact, save that, where made by the accused prior to the trial, the admission must be in writing and signed by the accused and with the approval of his solicitor or counsel.
[54] *cf.* para.**1–39** *et seq.*
[55] *Omychund v Barker* (1745) 1 Atk. 21 at 49, to wit that "the judges and sages of the law have laid it down that there is but one general rule of evidence, the best that the nature of the case will allow".
[56] A very rare application occurred in *R. v Quinn and Bloom* [1962] 2 Q.B. 245 (CA), with the effect that a private reconstruction attempted prior to the trial for the purpose of generating evidence was deemed inadmissible. The best evidence principle was also adverted to by Murnaghan J. in *People (Attorney-General) v Kirwan* [1943] I.R. 279 at 295–6 (CCA).
[57] Twining, *op. cit.* n.42 at p.196.

upon the weight properly to be attached to the various pieces of evidence in the case.

The Facts at Issue

1–15 Also called the principal facts or the *facta probantia*, these are the facts in dispute between the parties which must be proved in order to enable the prosecution/plaintiff or the defence to succeed in their respective claims. In criminal prosecutions, these are first propounded in statements, summonses or indictments, and in the book of evidence prepared by the prosecution for charges upon indictment. In civil proceedings, they are first formally set out in the pleadings (being the summons or civil bill, and/or statement of claim and affidavits). The facts at issue are determined by the substantive law upon which the charge or claim is based. In a prosecution for rape, the facts at issue, where the accused denies everything, are the fact of sexual intercourse, the identity of the offender, and the absence or presence of consent. In civil proceedings alleging negligence, the facts at issue are whether the defendant owed the plaintiff a duty of care, whether he breached the duty of care in the given circumstances, whether the plaintiff suffered a form of recoverable injury, whether the injury was caused by the defendant's breach of duty, and, if raised as a defence, whether the plaintiff was contributorily negligent.

Relevant Fact

1–16 A relevant fact, also called *evidential fact*, is any fact tending to prove the facts at issue. Such proof may be direct or indirect, and where indirect it is proven by *circumstantial* evidence—such as that, prior to his death, the deceased had been locked in a dispute with the accused over land. For some time, it was presumed by jurists that what was relevant was determined by ordinary common sense logic. It is now viewed as a matter of *legal* relevance, since it is the trial judge who must determine whether or not evidence or facts are relevant. In so doing, the judge will be guided by the need to conduct the trial efficiently[58] and sometimes by public policy.[59]

1–17 All evidence relevant to a fact at issue is receivable unless rendered inadmissible by an exclusionary rule of evidence such as the rule against hearsay and opinion assertions or against evidence disclosing the accused's criminal record or bad character. By contrast, irrelevant evidence is never admissible.[60]

---

[58] *cf.* the collateral issue rule at para.**3–02**. In *Herron v Haughton* (May 19, 2000), the Supreme Court approved a trial judge's refusal to permit the defence to call as witness the chief state solicitor working for the prosecution (in furtherance of the defence's allegation of garda harassment with respect to various road traffic charges). Barron J. reasoned that the decision had properly been within the trial judge's "powers to control the proceedings" in court.

[59] e.g. with respect to sexual history evidence: *cf.* para.**3–23** *et seq.*

[60] *People (DPP) v O' Callaghan* (CCA, Decmber 18, 2000); *People (DPP) v Shortt (No.1)* [2002] 2 I.R. 686 at 693, *per* Hardiman J. (CCA).

Facts Relevant to the Credibility of a Witness

1–18 These are facts introduced on the basis that they are relevant to a witness' credit, credibility, or consistency, and that they enable the court properly to determine if the witness should be believed under oath. The credibility of witnesses is of fundamental concern in the common law trial, given the concentrated nature of these proceedings. The capacity for recall and reasoning will differ for each witness. In this sense, a witness' evidence is largely an interpretation or reconstruction of reality through the witness' senses and mind, and the court is concerned to know how far it should trust that reconstruction. In many cases, the credibility challenge entails cross-examining the witness upon discrepancies between his testimonial account in court and an account provided by him in a statement prior to the trial. In such scenarios, where the jury hears the content of pre-trial statements, or is offered the statement as evidence, the statement becomes evidence in a limited capacity only. Unless admissible under a recognised exception to the hearsay rule, the statement may only be considered by the jury as evidence bearing upon the witness' lack of credibility (or consistency), but not as evidence probative of any of the facts at issue in the trial. The failure of the trial judge to explain that the witness' pre-trial account may not be considered when determining proof of the accused's guilt has led to the overturning of conviction on numerous occasions.[61] Credibility challenges are notoriously frequent in proceedings that admit little direct proof, such as sexual offences cases wherein the verdict will substantially depend upon the balance of credibility between the parties and who the court finally believes.[62] In an effort to restrict the extent to which counsel can drag the court into proliferating credibility-based sub-issues, a special rule exists restricting cross-examination of witnesses upon collateral questions.[63]

Collateral Fact

1–19 A collateral fact is that which is neither directly nor indirectly relevant to the facts at issue; or, if indirectly relevant, is so incidental to proof of the facts at issue as to be deemed collateral. Collateral facts are often raised and permitted in the context of challenges to the credibility of a particular witness—as a means of discrediting or undermining his testimony, by establishing that the witness suffers a bias, a propensity to lie or cheat, poor eyesight, and so forth.[64] Collateral facts may also affect the admissibility of evidence determined by the trial judge in the *voire dire*[65] (*e.g.* where the facts suggest that the confession statement, upon which the prosecution relies, was obtained after intimidation or physical force).

---

[61] *cf.* paras **2–38** *et seq.*, **3–08**.
[62] *cf.* paras **3–23** and **5–42** *et seq.*
[63] *cf.* para.**3–02**.
[64] *cf.* para.**3–06**.
[65] *cf.* para.**1–24** *et seq.*

Admissibility v Weight of Evidence

1–20 However relevant or probative evidence may be, the court must decline to accept it where strictly inadmissible under a rule of evidence. By contrast, the trial judge has an inherent discretion to exclude admissible evidence, however probative, from the criminal trial, where its admission may compromise the accused's constitutional right to a fair trial under Art.38(1).[66] The likely effect of the disputed evidence upon the ultimate verdict will influence, though not necessarily determine, whether the conviction or decision ought to be overturned upon appeal. The rules of evidence are adhered to for the greater good, not necessarily to achieve justice or accuracy in the instant case; this is often phrased as the conflict between criminal *procedure* or *process* and criminal *justice*. The question whether or not evidence is admissible is often decided by the trial judge by weighing the *probative* nature of the evidence against its likely *prejudicial* effect or its possible unreliability—'probative' referring to the weight or evidential force of the evidence, 'prejudicial' referring to "the capacity [of the evidence] to unfairly predispose the triers of fact toward a particular outcome".[67] This analysis is implicit in some of the rules of evidence, such as govern similar fact evidence.[68]

1–21 The weight of evidence, by contrast, refers to the factual cogency or probative force of the evidence in light of the facts at issue in the trial. This is ultimately a question of degree to be assessed having regard to all the evidence, inferences, and submissions in the case. The weight is not scientifically assessed, and much depends upon the credibility of witnesses, and the accumulation and combination of evidence finally generated in the trial.

1–22 Whereas the weight of evidence is a question of fact to be determined by the jury, where they sit, admissibility is a question of law reserved to the trial judge. The division of function between judge and jury flows from the maxim *ad quaestionem facti non respondent judices, ad quaestionem juris non respondent juratores*.[69] It is reflected in the principle that a trial judge may not collaborate with the jury prior to their verdict,[70] and further in the principle that an appellate court has no jurisdiction to substitute its own subjective view of the evidence for that of the trial court or to overturn its verdict where there is credible evidence to support it and where the verdict cannot be said to be "perverse".[71]

---

[66] *People (DPP) v Meleady (No.3)* [2001] 4 I.R. 16 at 31, *per* Geoghegan J. (CCA); *People (DPP) v O'Callaghan* (CCA, December 18, 2000); *R v Christie* [1980] A.C. 402 (HL).
[67] Damaska, *op. cit.* n.31 at p.15.
[68] *cf.* para.**7–01** *et seq.*
[69] *British Launderers' Research Association v Hendon Rating Authority* [1949] 1 K.B. 462 at 471–2 (CA).
[70] In *Ramstead v R.* [1999] 2 W.L.R. 698 (PC), the trial judge's private discussions with the foreman on the significance of the jury's deliberations to date constituted a material irregularity in the trial, due to which conviction was quashed.
[71] *People (DPP) v Egan* [1990] I.L.R.M. 780 (SC).

Evidence and the Trial

1–23 Despite the division of function between the judge and jury, the trial judge is permitted when summing-up to comment upon the relative strength and weakness of the evidence,[72] and is obliged to caution the jury as to the proper scope of the evidence in question (for example, that evidence by an accomplice, however convincing it appears, must be treated with special caution).[73] Ultimately, however, the jury is instructed that they are finally responsible to decide the weight to be given to the evidence and to determine whether the prosecution has proved its case to the requisite standard.[74] If the evidence is probative and stands unrebutted, the trial judge may give a *directed verdict*, requesting that the jury acquit the accused,[75] or may find him guilty as charged. The trial judge may also withdraw an issue from the jury, usually at the expense of the prosecution, but sometimes against the defence if it bears an evidential burden upon the issue—although, in principle, this is effected as a question of law on the basis that there are insufficient facts (whether primary, inferential, or evaluative)[76] in support of the issue.

The *Voire Dire*

1–24 When fundamental admissibility issues arise in the trial, they are determined in the *voire dire*. The words derive from the old Norman French words *voire* (the antecedent to *vrai*, meaning truth) and *dire* (meaning to speak),[77] and together referred to the oath a witness traditionally swore in the "trial within a trial" constructed to test the admissibility of primary evidence by the adduction of relevant secondary evidence.

1–25 The *voire dire* has been developed in Ireland chiefly as a device to forestall prejudice to the accused by the jury's exposure to evidence whose admissibility is in question; since its contemporary focus is upon potential prejudice to the accused, it has assumed an additional constitutional aspect for the purpose of achieving a fair trial under Art.38(1).[78] In *People (DPP) v Conroy*[79]—speaking generally on the *voire dire* enquiry of admissibility, and specifically on confession statements—the Supreme Court confirmed that constitutional justice requires that the *voire dire* enquiry be conducted in the absence of the jury, in order to prevent the jury's exposure to prejudicial information that may later be declared inadmissible. This further enables the accused to challenge and make imputations against a witness for the prosecution without losing his protection from cross-examination upon bad character

---

[72] Although he may not take a slanted view in favour of either party: *Murphy v Times Newspapers Ltd.* [1996] 1 I.R. 169 (SC).
[73] *cf.* para.5–21 *et seq*.
[74] *People (DPP) v O'Brien* (CCA, June 17, 2002).
[75] e.g. *People (DPP) v Geoghan and Bourke* (Central Criminal Court, November 18, 2003).
[76] Williams, "Law and Fact" (1976) Crim. L.R. 472 at p.482.
[77] Although *voire* has long since disappeared from modern French, its retention in the laws of evidence helps to distinguish it, etymologically, from the modern French word *voir* (meaning "to see").
[78] [1986] I.R. 460 , *per* Finlay C.J. (SC): *cf.* appendix 29.
[79] *ibid.*

bestowed upon him by virtue of s.1(f)(ii) of the Criminal Justice (Evidence) Act 1924.[80] The decision in *Conroy* was also justified in terms of the division of labour between judge and jury in the bifurcated common law court, whereby the judge alone is entrusted to decide questions of law.[81]

1–26 By contrast, English law has accepted that as a general rule the jury should be present during the *voire dire* enquiry so long as there is no risk that they will hear the disputed evidence.[82] Lord Goddard asserted in *R. v Reynolds*: "it should be regarded as most exceptional that any evidence should be given in a criminal trial otherwise than in the presence of the jury".[83] The view that the competence of a potential witness ought to be conducted in the presence of the jury is premised upon the assumption that in this context there is no risk of exposure to inadmissible primary evidence, and further in the belief that secondary evidence relevant to a witness' competence may also be relevant later to enable the jury to evaluate the weight to attach to that witness' evidence. The first premise clearly does not hold where the witness whose competence is being tested is a complainant in the proceedings. The risks of prejudice were stark in *Attorney-General v Lannigan*[84] where the accused had been charged with rape and unlawful carnal knowledge of a "feeble minded" woman, contrary to the Criminal Law (Amendment) Act 1935. Fawsitt J. of the Circuit Court accepted that a *voire dire* enquiry, in the presence of the jury, of the complainant's mental competence to testify would prejudice the jury when they came subsequently to considering whether or not she was "feeble minded" (which clearly was a fact at issue). Although Fawsitt J. also spoke of the accused "voluntarily electing to forego his right" to have the jury absent,[85] the view that a decision on this might depend upon the accused's election must be discounted in light of more recent assertions by the courts in *Conroy*[86] and *People (Attorney-General) v O'Brien*[87] where Kenny J. wisely observed that if the accused could unilaterally request trials-within-trials in the presence of the jury, the jury would likely be exposed to prejudicial information later declared inadmissible, culminating either in their discharge or the quashing of conviction, scenarios clearly beneficial to the accused.

1–27 Admissibility challenges are frequently made to the voluntariness of confession statements signed by the accused prior to his trial, to the admissibility

---

[80] *ibid. per* Henchy J. *cf.* para.**8–01** *et seq.*
[81] [1986] I.R. 460 at 492–3, *per* Griffin J. (SC).
[82] On this point, however, as elsewhere throughout its modern laws of evidence, the principle has splintered into many qualifications. Numerous ad hoc exceptions have been recognised since *R. v Reynolds* [1950] 1 K.B. 606 (CA), such as that the jury should be absent if and when it is necessary to hear expert psychiatric evidence on the issue of a witness' competence (*R. v Deakin* [1994] 4 All E.R. 769 (CA)) and in cases where a risk of collusion between witnesses has been established (*R. v H* [1995] A.C. 596 (HL)).
[83] [1950] 1 K.B. 606 at 611 (CA)
[84] (1958) 24 Ir. Jur. Rep. 59 (CC).
[85] *ibid.* at 61.
[86] [1986] I.R. 460 (SC).
[87] (1969) 1 Frewen 343 (CCA).

of evidence obtained in alleged violation of the accused's constitutional rights, and to the competence of intended witnesses. If too numerous and protracted, *voire dire* admissibility challenges may inhibit the efficacy of trials, given that juries are sometimes absent from court for long stretches, with consequent loss to the immediacy of the trial and the freshness of evidence heard prior to the *voire dire*.[88] This dilemma was addressed recently in the Fennelly Report,[89] which prudently recommends that as many admissibility challenges as possible should be addressed at a dedicated pre-trial stage, before the jury sits to hear the evidence. The proposal acknowledges, however, that the need to make admissibility challenges often arises in an ad hoc way throughout the trial, and it does not seek to restrict those challenges.

Vive Voce Evidence or Testimony

1–28 This is evidence given in open court, under oath or solemn affirmation, and offered by the witness as a true account of the relevant events. The common law has traditionally required the witness to testify in open court in the presence of the accused and parties to the proceedings. This had long been assumed essential to enable the judge and jury to assess the demeanour and credibility of witnesses as they are telling their story, and in the criminal context to facilitate physical confrontation between the accused and his accusers. Direct physical confrontation has been interpreted in recent cases never to have constituted a distinct right of the accused, and modifications to the requirement of open-court testimony have been undertaken, and upheld, to alleviate the trauma suffered by children appearing as complainants or other vulnerable witnesses.[90] These "protected witnesses" are now permitted, by Pt III of the Criminal Evidence Act 1992 and s.9 of the Criminal Justice Act 1999, to give their testimony from a separate room, displayed live in the court through a television link to monitors, and observed from a variety of angles by the court and the parties.[91] Such alternatives to traditional open-court testimony have been upheld domestically and internationally. The European Court of Human Rights has acknowledged that the right to examine witnesses (protected by Art.6) falls to be balanced against the interests of the particular witnesses (protected by Art.8), particularly where "their life, liberty and security ... may be at stake"; further that "contracting States should organise their criminal procedure in such a way that those interests are not unjustifiably imperilled".[92]

Direct Evidence

1–29 Also called *percipient evidence*, this is evidence of facts perceived

---

[88] This dilemma was highlighted by the Court of Criminal Appeal in *People (DPP) v McCann* (March 11, 1998) and *People (DPP) v Quinn* (*ex tempore*, March 23, 1998).
[89] Report of the Working Group on the Jurisdiction of the Courts July 15, 2003, at para.774, p.204.
[90] *White v Ireland* [1995] 2 I.R. 268 (HC); *Donnelly v Ireland* [1998] 1 I.R. 321 (SC) *cf.* paras **1–59**, *et seq.*
[91] *cf.* paras **1–55, 1–57** *et seq.*
[92] *Doorson v Netherlands* (1996) 22 E.H.R.R. 330, at para.70.

first-hand by the witness through one of his senses, and of which the witness has personal knowledge. It includes not only the witness' observation of events, but also the actual production in court of a thing or fact requiring proof. Direct evidence may be contrasted with hearsay evidence, which is second-hand evidence of what another person claimed to have perceived. Where A observes an assault, and tells B that he saw the accused assault the complainant, and the prosecution is unable to contact A to require him to give direct evidence of his observation, the court may not hear evidence from B as to what A had apparently told him.[93]

Hearsay v Original Evidence

1–30 The common law leans against admissibility of statements, whether written or oral, made prior to the trial or hearing, and has by tradition required all evidence to be given afresh from the witness box, save where the evidence "speaks for itself" in the form of objects or real evidence. The dominant rule in this respect is the rule against hearsay—which precludes not only third-party statements, but also all pre-trial statements made by any witness present in the trial where offered as evidence probative of any assertion expressed or implied in the statement.[94] In recent decades, the courts have recognised that a statement may alternatively be admissible as original evidence where the statement is tendered not to establish the truth of any assertion in the statement, but to establish a specific fact relevant to the proceedings that does not require the court to consider or accept the truth of any of the statement's assertions.[95] This distinction is supported by the definition and chief concern of the hearsay rule, which derives from a fear that a hearsay statement is more likely to be false or inaccurate and not necessarily the fear that the statement had never been made.

1–31 For instance, if A is charged with fraudulently obtaining charity monies by misrepresenting himself as mute, and was overheard by B conversing with a punter about the weather, B may legitimately testify to having heard A converse with the absent punter. The purpose of the attempted reference to A's statements to the punter clearly is not to prove that anything said by him was *true* or *accurate*, but instead to establish a relevant fact, namely that A spoke words. In this capacity, details of the conversation may be admitted as original evidence. Where the statement is excessively prejudicial to the case against the accused, however, the evidence should not be admitted, or, in appropriate cases where admitted, the trial judge may be required to explain to the jury that the statement is probative only of the relevant fact that justified its admission, and that it is not more broadly relevant or admissible to establish other facts at issue in the trial.

---

[93] *cf.* para.**9–02**.
[94] *cf.* para.**9–03**.
[95] *cf.* para.**9–20** *et seq.*

Evidence and the Trial 17

1–32 Some judges, such as Kingsmill Moore J. in *Cullen v Clarke*,[96] have asserted that the general rule is that all statements are admissible save where they infringe the rule against hearsay. To the extent that the exclusionary rules of evidence constitute exceptions to the general principle that all relevant evidence is admissible, this perspective is formally correct. To the extent, however, that statements are more commonly tendered in judicial proceedings on the basis that they are relevant and accurate, and less on the basis that their utterance is relevant irrespective of their truth, the proposition appears dissonant.

Documentary Evidence

1–33 This refers to the content of relevant documents, although it does not include affidavits or depositions, since these are sworn statements and therefore more akin to testimony. Documentary evidence encompasses all permanent legible information, including computer records, films, videotaped statements etc., where deemed admissible in trials and hearings (typically by virtue of legislation).[97] As a general rule, the party relying on the documents must, if possible, produce original copies (*primary* documentary evidence) in favour of copies (*secondary* documentary evidence). Section 30 of the Criminal Evidence Act 1992 ensures that trial judges have a broad discretion to accept copies of original documents, however. It provides that where information contained in a document is admissible in evidence in criminal proceedings, the information may be given in evidence whether or not the document is still in existence, by producing a copy of the document or a material part of the document, where authenticated to the satisfaction of the court.[98]

Circumstantial Evidence

1–34 Bentham wrote that "[c]ircumstances ... are facts placed round some other fact; each fact may be considered as a centre, and all others as ranged round it".[99] Circumstantial evidence tends to prove relevant facts that indirectly prove or infer the existence of a fact at issue. It may serve to eliminate possibilities or to indicate motives, and is often of the following type: (1) to establish motive (*e.g.* words of enmity, or a will recently changed); (2) to show planning and preparation (*e.g.* tickets for a flight abroad, or the recent purchase of arsenic); (3) to show state of mind (*e.g.* depression, hallucinations, or drug abuse); (4) to establish alibi or an opportunity to commit the crime; (5) to establish identity (*e.g.* fingerprints on the door-knob); or (6) to show a likely continuance of events (*e.g.* that it was the accused's habit to have a drink in his local every Wednesday evening).

---

[96] [1963] I.R. 368 at 378, *per* Kingsmill Moore J. (SC): *cf.* appendix 8.
[97] *cf.* para.**9–36** *et seq.*
[98] See *Carey v Hussey* (HC, December 21, 1999), affirming a decision of the District Court to accept, in its discretion, a photocopy of an original order instead of adjourning proceedings to procure a certified copy.
[99] *A Treatise on Judicial Evidence* (1825) at p.143.

1–35 Circumstantial evidence is often contrasted with *direct evidence*. For instance, a witness who saw the accused in flight from the bank may give *direct* evidence of that observation, which may then constitute *circumstantial* evidence showing his proximity to the bank at the time of the robbery and his guilty behaviour, indirectly to establish, cumulatively with other evidence in the case, that the accused robbed the bank. Direct evidence requires no inferential reasoning of the triers of fact, who are asked whether to accept the account or not; circumstantial evidence, by contrast, asks the court not only to accept it, but further to draw some inference arising from it.[100]

1–36 Although a person may in principle be convicted upon circumstantial evidence,[101] the evidence must be highly probative due to the natural fear that indirect proof may be manufactured or misconstrued.[102] Lord Normand expressed the dangers well in *R. v Teper*:[103]

> "Circumstantial evidence may sometimes be conclusive, but it must always be narrowly examined, if only because evidence of this kind may be fabricated to cast suspicion on another. ... It is also necessary before drawing the inference of the accused's guilt from circumstantial evidence to be sure that there are no other co-existing circumstances which would weaken or destroy the inference ..."

1–37 In *People (DPP) v Cahill and Costello*,[104] conviction was quashed (*inter alia*) because the trial judge had directed the jury that circumstantial evidence "is evidence of surrounding circumstances which by undesigned coincidence is capable of proving a proposition with the accuracy of mathematics".[105] This gave the jury an "erroneous impression as to the weight of circumstantial ... evidence", in the view of Keane C.J., who favoured instead dicta by Pollock C.B. in *R. v Exall*,[106] to wit: "There may be a combination of circumstances, no one of which would raise a reasonable conviction or more than a mere suspicion; but ... taken together, may create a conclusion of guilt, ... with as much certainty as human affairs can require or admit of". In *People (DPP) v Nevin*[107]—where the evidence relied upon by the prosecution was predominantly of a circumstantial nature (chiefly to show motive, planning, and opportunity)—one of the grounds of appeal was that the trial judge had

---

[100] Bentham, *Rationale of Judicial Evidence* (Book III, 1827) at pp.7–8.
[101] Affirmed in *People (Attorney-General) v Kirwan* [1943] I.R. 279 (CCA).
[102] See *People (AG) v McMahon* [1946] I.R. 267 at 272 (CCA), where Maguire P. warned that where the prosecution relies upon circumstantial evidence to establish guilt, the court must take care to ensure that the evidence is "inconsistent with any rational hypothesis consistent with innocence".
[103] [1952] A.C. 480 at 489 (PC).
[104] [2001] 3 I.R. 494 (CCA).
[105] This perspective had been taken from *ex tempore* observations of the Court of Appeal in *R. v Taylor* (1928) 21 Cr. App. R. 20, subsequently cited in Sandes, *Criminal Law and Procedure in the Republic of Ireland* (3rd ed.) at p.177, and Charleton, McDermott and Bolger, *Criminal Law* (Butterworths, Dublin, 1999) at p.118.
[106] (1866) 4 F. & F. 922 at 929.
[107] CCA, March 14, 2003.

failed when summing-up to advise the jury as to alternative explanations for the evidence. The Court of Criminal Appeal rejected the application, and approved Carroll J.'s directions, which had advised the jury as follows:—that they were required to consider individually whether or not to accept each piece of circumstantial evidence, and to resolve any doubts arising therefrom in favour of the accused, given the presumption of innocence; thereafter, that they were entitled to consider the "cumulative weight" of the circumstantial evidence and any inferences it engendered in the case, although they were required to exclude the possibility of coincidence or fabrication before deciding to convict the accused of murder upon the evidence.

Real Evidence

1–38 This refers to items of evidence that may be presented to the court and are objectively capable of being seen and examined by it. Real evidence therefore covers material objects such as weapons and drugs. It is not limited to physical evidence, however, and includes all evidence deriving from the court's own observations and inferences, and thus includes the court's inferences arising from its assessment of the credibility and demeanour of witnesses, intonations of voice on a tape recording, how the accused appears in court by contrast with previous descriptions of the offender, etc.

Judicial Notice

1–39 In some circumstances, judicial notice may, in the absence of formal proof, constitute sufficient proof of a fact that is well known or a matter of public knowledge or record. The trial judge's notice may be of a relevant fact or the contents of a document, although it is more usual for judicial notice to be taken of matters not seriously in dispute, to spare the court the unnecessary delay and expense of requiring strict proof. The notice—depending on whether the fact is being contended—may take the form of a prima facie assumption of fact or of conclusive evidence. The principles permitting judicial notice form an exception to the general rule that a court or tribunal is not entitled to decide disputed facts by reference to information within its own knowledge that was not first presented to the court by the respective parties.[108] A trial judge may direct questions at a witness that spring from his own special knowledge of facts; however, the judge is not entitled to act upon his own private knowledge, unless that knowledge was received as evidence in the case under oath amenable to cross-examination.[109] If the trial judge takes judicial notice of any fact in contradiction of evidence adduced by the parties to the action, fair procedures and natural justice require that he notify the parties of his intention to do so.

1–40 The exception, founded upon a difficult point of distinction, permits a judge to apply his own general or local knowledge of relevant matters. Lord

---

[108] *Phipson on Evidence* (15th ed.) *op. cit.* n.11 at p.5.
[109] So held in *The Queen v Justices of Antrim* [1895] 2 I.R. 603.

Greene M.R. phrased the principle to permit notice of a "type of knowledge ... of quite a general character [which] is not liable to be varied by specific individual characteristics of the individual case".[110] Judicial notice may be, and is routinely, taken of facts clearly and notoriously known—such as weights and measures,[111] the meaning and usage of common words used in statutes,[112] the function of television,[113] and in one case the fact that a person's genetic make-up may affect his susceptibility to a particular illness.[114] Judicial notice was approved in *Byrne v Londonderry Tramway Co.*[115] where Holmes L.J. found that "[b]oth judges and jurors must bring to the consideration of the questions they are called on to decide their knowledge of the common affairs of life, and it is not necessary on the trial of an action to give formal evidence of matters with which men of ordinary intelligence are acquainted".

1–41 Aside from facts required to be established by evidence, judicial notice may be taken of the relevant provisions of the substantive law, although naturally it is expected that counsel for the parties present complete and accurate accounts of the law to the court. Section 6(1) of the Interpretation Act 1937 provides that every Act of the Oireactas *shall* be judicially noticed. Section 4 of the European Convention on Human Rights Act 2003 obliges the courts to take judicial notice of the provisions of the European Convention on Human Rights, and further, where made within jurisdiction, of any declaration, decision, advisory opinion or judgment of the European Court of Human Rights, any decision or opinion of the European Commission of Human Rights, and any decision of the Committee of Ministers established under the Statute of the Council of Europe. Other examples have been created on a piecemeal basis. The principle of judicial notice of the substantive law appears for the most part to be founded upon an appreciation of the trial judge's familiarity with the law. Upon the basis that a judge would not necessarily be familiar with statutory orders and instruments, convictions have been overturned in cases where the prosecution omitted formally to prove that relevant statutory orders were in force at the time of the alleged offence.[116] In *State (Taylor) v Circuit Court Judge for Wicklow*,[117] however, Davitt J. approved a District judge's judicial notice of the statutory order bringing Pt III of the Road Traffic Act 1933 into force, since the judge has been entitled to apply his general knowledge and experience "gained by administering the provisions of the Road Traffic Act over a period of years".

---

[110] *Reynolds v Llanelly Associated Tinplate Co. Ltd.* [1948] 1 All E.R. 140 at 143 (CA).
[111] *Hockin v Cooke* 4 T.R. 314.
[112] *Camden v I.R.C.* [1914] 1 K.B. 641 (CA), finding that the court was competent to assess what "nominal rent" meant in a statute and that expert evidence on the meaning of these words was inadmissible *cf.* para.**12–01** *et seq.*
[113] *Bridlington Relay Ltd. v Yorkshire Electricity Board* [1965] Ch. 436.
[114] *Re F. (a minor)* [1993] Fam. 375 (CA).
[115] [1902] 2 I.R. 457 at 480 (CA).
[116] e.g. in *People (Attorney-General) v Kennedy* [1946] I.R. 517 (CCA), with respect to Emergency Orders adopted under the Emergency Powers Act 1939.
[117] [1951] I.R. 311 at 322 (HC).

Prosecutor's Pre-Trial Duty to Seek Out, Preserve, and Disclose Material Evidence

1–42 Pre-trial disclosure by the prosecution of material evidence and information has been recognised as fundamental to the constitutional requirement of fair procedures and a fair trial,[118] and to the accused's human rights.[119] In *Braddish v DPP*,[120] the Supreme Court authoritatively declared that it "is the duty of the gardaí, arising from their unique investigative role, to *seek out* and *preserve* all evidence having a bearing or potential bearing on the issue of guilt or innocence". In so finding, the court approved an earlier ruling by Lynch J. in *Murphy v DPP*,[121] finding that the prosecutor must disclose and make available to the accused all relevant evidence in its possession whether or not it intends to tender that evidence in the trial, and though it may advance the interests of the accused.[122] In *Dunne v DPP*,[123] a majority of the Supreme Court granted the applicant orders restraining further prosecution of a case in which the investigators had failed to seek out potentially probative evidence. Framed by an impressive exploration of the issues by Hardiman J., the decision differs from *Braddish* to the extent that it concerned the failure to *obtain*, rather than *retain*, a videotape of surveillance footage habitually taken from cameras installed at the filling station the accused was alleged to have robbed. The extension—though Hardiman J. preemptively disagreed with the notion that this was an innovation in the law[124]—was logically necessary since, if the duty were construed to be limited to the *retention* of evidence, there would be a "positive incentive to investigators not to seize or request permission to take

---

[118] *People (DPP) v Tuite* (1983) 2 Frewen 175 at 180–1; *Dunne v DPP* [2002] 2 I.R. 305 (SC); *Bowes and McGrath v DPP* [2003] 2 I.R. 25 (SC).
[119] In *Barbera, Messegue and Jabardo v Spain* (1988) 11 E.H.R.R. 360 at para.77, the European Court of Human Rights reasoned that the presumption of innocence entails adequate pre-trial disclosure by the prosecution: "It ... follows that it is for the prosecution to inform the accused of the case that will be made against him, so that he may prepare and present his defence accordingly, and to adduce evidence sufficient to convict him." This view was repeated in *Edwards v United Kingdom* (1993) 15 E.H.R.R. 417 at para.36, where the court found that "it is a prerequisite of fairness ... that the prosecution authorities disclose to the defence all material evidence for and against the accused". For a fuller account of the extent of the obligations on the prosecution to disclose evidence and information in advance of the trial, see Walsh, *Criminal Procedure* (Thomson Round Hall, Dublin, 2003) at pp.715–33, and Mullan, "The Duty to Disclose in Criminal Prosecutions" (2000) 5(4) *Bar Review* 174.
[120] [2001] 3 I.R. 127 (SC) at 133, *per* Hardiman J. (SC) (emphasis added): *cf.* appendix 63.
[121] [1989] I.L.R.M. 71 (HC). The court quashed conviction due to the prosecution's failure to notify the accused of its intention to destroy the stolen car he had allegedly been driving. It is of note that in this case, by contrast with *Bowes and McGrath v DPP* [2003] 2 I.R. 25 (SC), the car had been destroyed before adequate forensic analysis had been made of the vehicle.
[122] The English Court of Appeal identified a similar duty in *R. v Keane* [1994] 1 W.L.R. 746, where it held that the prosecution must disclose unused evidence if relevant, or possibly relevant, to a fact at issue in the case, or if it possibly raises a new issue not apparent from the prosecution's case to date.
[123] [2002] 2 I.R. 305 (SC).
[124] Citing in favour of the proposition: *Dillon v O'Brien and Davis* [1887] 20 L.R. I.R. 300 and *R. v Lushington Ex p. Otto* [1894] 1 Q.B. 420.

evidence which might contradict their suspicions or undermine the reliability of other evidence".[125] With respect to the view that an accused may seek to restrain his trial because the gardaí failed adequately to seek out evidence that might exonerate him, Fennelly J. disagreed.

1–43 The courts have considered the prosecutor's duty to seek out, preserve, and disclose material evidence and information in the specific contexts of witness statements, identifications of the accused, and confession statements, considered elsewhere in this book.[126] Although convictions have been quashed in recent decisions on the duty to disclose, each of the judges in *Murphy*, *Braddish*, and *Dunne* cautioned against sketching the pre-trial duty too widely. The need for pragmatism, and due regard for public resources, was highlighted by Hardiman J., who acknowledged in *Braddish* that the duty "cannot be interpreted as requiring the gardaí to engage in disproportionate commitment of manpower or resources in an exhaustive search for every conceivable kind of evidence" and therefore that the "duty must be interpreted realistically on the facts of each case".[127] In *Dunne*, the learned judge expressed the view that the investigators' duty does not oblige them to pursue every "remote, theoretical or fanciful possibility".[128]

1–44 The respective rights and duties do not exist *in vacuo*, however, and the Irish courts have rejected a test based upon the prosecutor's fault.[129] Formally, the demarcation line is drawn in cases by a consideration of the effect of the prosecutor's breach of duty for fairness in the specific trial. In *Dunne*, both Hardiman J. and Fennelly J. (who dissented) approved Denham J.'s assertion in *B v DPP*,[130] to wit: "The community's right to have offences prosecuted is not absolute but is to be exercised constitutionally, with due process. If there is a real risk that the applicant would not receive a fair trial then, on the balance of these constitutional rights the applicant's right would prevail". In *Bowes and McGrath v DPP*,[131] Hardiman J. approved the following test for assessing prospective unfairness, expressed by Finlay C.J. in *Z v DPP*, and which an applicant must establish to the satisfaction of the court: whether there is a "real risk of an unfair trial ... which cannot be avoided by appropriate rulings and directions on the part of the trial judge. The ... unfairness of trial must be an unavoidable unfairness of trial."[132]

1–45 In *Mitchell v DPP*,[133] Geoghegan J. rejected the applicant's contention

---

[125] *ibid.* at 313.
[126] *cf.* paras **1–66, 3–38, 6–35** *et seq.*, **10–73**.
[127] [2001] 3 I.R. 127 at 135 (SC).
[128] [2002] 2 I.R. 305 at 323 (SC).
[129] In *Bowes and McGrath v DPP* [2003] 2 I.R. 25 (SC), Hardiman J. repeated this view, rejecting the approach favoured in *R. (Ebrahim) v Feltham Magistrate's Court* [2001] 1 All E.R. 831.
[130] [1997] 3 I.R. 140 at 196 (SC).
[131] [2003] 2 I.R. 25 at 34–35 (SC).
[132] [1994] 2 I.R. 476 at 507 (SC).
[133] [2000] 2 I.L.R.M. 396 (HC).

that his right to a fair trial would be infringed in circumstances where the prosecution had not afforded the accused an opportunity to inspect garda surveillance videotapes of public activity in the Temple Bar area of Dublin on the night of the alleged offence. Geoghegan J. considered that the specific right to notification of videotaped evidence prior to its destruction extended no further than to cases "where it was genuinely considered that such tapes might be relevant to the criminal proceedings".[134] In *Bowes and McGrath v DPP*,[135] the first applicant failed in his attempt to restrain prosecution against him, on the basis that destruction of the car in which he had been discovered with drugs was unlikely to deprive him of fairness at his trial since all appropriate forensic tests had been conducted on the car prior to its destruction and had been furnished to the defence. By contrast, the court granted the second applicant orders restraining her trial for dangerous driving causing death. Whereas the car in Bowes' case had been destroyed one year after his arrest, the motorbike in McGrath's case had been destroyed, at the request of the deceased's family, two and a half months before proceedings were instituted against her. The court accepted McGrath's submission that destruction of the motorbike had deprived the defence of any opportunity to inspect the mechanical state of the bike for the purpose of attempting rebuttal of the prosecution's allegation that the cause of the accident had been dangerous driving and not mechanical fault.

1–46 The pre-trial duty of disclosure is notably more attenuated for summary proceedings, although it is subject to a strict requirement of fairness and due process, and, according to the Supreme Court in *Swaine v DPP*,[136] equally in summary proceedings "there is always a duty on the prosecution not to hold back material evidence that would be helpful to a defendant". Owing to the fact that there "are hundreds [of summary prosecutions] every day of the week and in which there is a right of appeal by way of re-hearing on the one hand and a serious prosecution upon indictment on the other hand",[137] the accused is not entitled to the production of statements on demand, and may have to apply to the court of trial for directions to receive certain statements. When determining the scope of the duty in individual cases, Denham J. favoured the following applicable factors in *DPP v Doyle*:[138] (1) the seriousness of the charge; (2) the importance of the statement or document to the accused; (3) whether the accused had already adequately been informed of the nature and substance of the accusation against him; and (4) the likelihood of any risk of injustice by the failure to furnish the document.

1–47 The accused bears no general duty to disclose aspects of his defence in advance of the criminal trial,[139] save: to notify the prosecution of his intention

---

[134] *ibid.* at 399.
[135] [2003] 2 I.R. 25 (SC).
[136] SC, April 26, 2002, *per* Geoghegan J.
[137] *ibid.*
[138] [1994] 2 I.R. 286 (SC).
[139] Recognised recently in *People (DPP) v Nevin* (CCA, March 14, 2003).

to raise the defence of alibi and to disclose particulars of the alibi;[140] and, where prosecuted for membership of an unlawful organisation, to identify witnesses intended to be called in his defence.[141]

V. COURSE OF THE TRIAL

1–48 In its basic form, the trial[142] or hearing begins with preliminary submissions by counsel for the prosecution or plaintiff, who bears an evidential burden to open a prima facie case before the court.[143] This is followed by the propounding party's evidence, for the most part given by witnesses who are examined by counsel and then cross-examined by opposing counsel. If the

---

[140] Criminal Justice Act 1984, s.20(1), providing that where notice of alibi particulars is not duly made, "the accused shall not without the leave of the court adduce evidence in support of an alibi".

[141] Offences Against the State (Amendment) Act 1998, s.3, providing that where notice of the intended witness' name and address is not duly made, "the accused shall not without the leave of the court call any other person to give evidence on his or her behalf".

[142] Prior to the Criminal Justice Act 1999, brought into force by the Criminal Justice Act 1999 (Part III) (Commencement) Order 2001, the accused was entitled to request a preliminary examination in the District Court for the purpose of deciding whether to send him forward to the court of trial. Thought to be beneficial as an additional filter, it was abandoned largely in the belief that it had become procedurally unnecessary and wasteful. Although it entitled the accused to call upon the prosecution to "raise its case" and produce testimonial evidence at an early stage in the proceedings, it had been interpreted *not* to reflect a constitutional right to same: *O'Shea v DPP* [1988] I.R. 655 (SC). Part III of the Criminal Justice Act, amending the Criminal Procedure Act 1967, creates an alternative stage with significantly different consequences for the early adduction of evidence. Section 4E of the 1967 Act, inserted by s.9 of the 1999 Act, provides that at "any time after the accused is sent forward for trial, the accused may apply to the trial court to dismiss one or more of the charges against the accused". For a comprehensive account of the relevant practice and procedure, see Walsh, *Criminal Procedure* (Thomson Round Hall, Dublin, 2003) at pp.685–92. Textually, s.9 may presuppose application of the normal rule that the party who brings an application bears the burden of proof. Walsh takes the view (p.690) that s.9 casts a burden upon the accused, and that this falls to be discharged according to the criminal standard, beyond reasonable doubt. This is unlikely to be the case, however, as the common law has traditionally mitigated any imposition of a burden of proof upon the accused by providing that proof must meet the lower civil standard of the balance of probabilities: *DPP v Best* [2000] 2 I.R. 17 at 43, *per* Denham J. (SC); *Hardy v Ireland* [1994] 2 I.R. 551 (SC), approving *R. v Fegan* [1972] N.I. 80 and *R. v Berry* [1985] A.C. 246; *Hill v Baxter* [1958] 1 Q.B. 277 at 282; *Bratty v Attorney-General for Northern Ireland* [1963] A.C. 386 at 407, *per* Kilmuir L.C. (HL): *cf.* para.**4–33**. During the application to dismiss, oral evidence may be taken only with the leave of the trial judge having regard to "the interests of justice". Restrictions on questions relating to the sexual history of the complainant apply: *cf.* para.**3–25** *et seq*. Where the trial court may draw adverse inferences from the accused's silence or non-cooperation under ss.18–19 of the Criminal Justice Act 1984 or s.3(1)(a)(i) of the Criminal Justice (Forensic Evidence) Act 1990, it may do so during the application to dismiss: Criminal Justice Act 1999, ss.16(1), 17(1).

[143] This is the initial *evidential burden* to "raise a case". The prosecution and the plaintiff typically bear, from the initial to the final stages, a burden to persuade the court to find in its favour, otherwise known as the *legal burden of proof*: *cf.* para.**4–07**.

accused intends to tender evidence, his case is presented next,[144] followed by the defence's closing address,[145] followed, at the discretion of counsel for the prosecution or plaintiff, by a replying address. If the defence elects not to call any witnesses, the procedure traditionally is to follow evidence for the prosecution or plaintiff by this party's closing address,[146] followed by the defence's closing address and, at the discretion of counsel, by an address in reply, and finally by the trial judge's summing-up, being a review of the evidence, and directions upon the relevant substantive law, rules of evidence, and burden and standard of proof for the jury's guidance. The course of the trial or hearing is interrupted episodically by submissions bearing upon the relevance or admissibility of evidence and upon any risks of prejudice to the accused's right to a fair hearing. Challenges to the admissibility of prejudicial evidence are determined by the trial judge in the absence of the jury in the *voire dire*.[147]

1–49 In Ireland, the trial judge retains a residual discretion to hear further evidence up to the time when the jury return their verdict.[148] In practice, this is likely not to be exercised in cases where the jury have already retired to consider a verdict. Despite this discretion, it may be stated as a general rule that each side must present its evidence *en bloc*, and is not entitled to revisit or complete it in stages.[149] To this, however, there are a number of exceptions. The most frequently applied of these permits a party to tender evidence to rebut unanticipated issues raised by an opponent during his evidence: these

---

[144] If the defence does not intend to call witnesses aside from the accused or a character referee, the practice has been to commence the defence's case by proceeding to examination in-chief and cross-examination of the accused and/or referee, to be followed by the prosecution's closing address and then the defence's closing address: Ryan and Magee, *The Irish Criminal Process* (Mercier Press, Dublin, 1983) at p.344.

[145] The defence has a right to make a closing speech after the prosecution's case in all instances: Criminal Justice Act 1984, s.24(1)(a).

[146] The prosecution may make a closing speech prior to the defence's closing speech, unless the accused has not been legally represented in the proceedings and has not called witnesses (save to testify to his character): Criminal Justice Act 1984, s.24(1).

[147] *cf.* para.**1–24** *et seq.*

[148] *People (Attorney-General) v O'Brien* [1963] I.R. 65 (SC). The Irish courts adopt a more flexible view of the discretion than exists in England, and the focus—consistent with many recent statutory formulations—is on "the interests of justice". A classic example of the need to permit evidence after the formal close of the prosecution's case arose in *People (DPP) v Leahy* (CCA, February 14, 2000). The accused had been charged with forging bank drafts, and the prosecution had tendered evidence establishing that his fingerprints had been identified on one of the forged drafts. During the trial, the accused testified that he had been shown the very same bank drafts when interviewed by gardai investigating that and other related offences (information the prosecution had avoided revealing till then, since it would prejudicially disclose that the accused had been a garda suspect with respect to other offences). The Court of Criminal Appeal upheld the trial judge's decision to permit the prosecution, "in the interests of justice", to tender this further evidence in rebuttal.

[149] *e.g. R. v Day* [1940] 1 All E.R. 402 (CA), where conviction was overturned due to the trial judge's decision to permit the prosecution to call a handwriting expert as witness after the evidence for the prosecution and defence had been presented to the court.

may concern contentious or unresolved propositions of fact;[150] or they may bear upon the credibility of the witness giving evidence for the opponent.[151] Other exceptions are recognised for: formal matters that require to be proved throughout the trial or hearing; proof of matters whose relevance was not foreseeable when the case was earlier presented to the court (although traditionally the common law viewed this basis restrictively, particularly in criminal trials);[152] and evidence that was not in existence or obtained when the case was earlier presented to the court.

1–50 At the close of the case for the prosecution or plaintiff, or later, the defence may seek a direction from the trial judge that the prosecution has failed to establish a prima facie case, or that the defence has no case to answer.[153] If through lack or insufficiency of evidence, and taking the prosecution's case at its height, the trial judge decides that a jury, properly directed, would not reasonably be justified in finding the accused guilty as charged, the trial judge may direct an acquittal or, in a trial without jury, may dismiss one or more of the charges.[154] In determining this question, the trial

---

[150] As in *People (DPP) v Nevin*, approved by the Court of Criminal Appeal, March 14, 2003.
[151] *cf.* para.**3–06**.
[152] In exceptional cases where a fresh or unresolved issue is raised in a closing speech to the jury, the opposing party may be entitled to tender evidence or call witnesses in rebuttal: *e.g. R. v O'Hadhmaill* [1996] Crim. L.R. 509 (CA), where the accused's closing address implied that over the relevant period there had been no bombings in England, from which one could infer that the I.R.A.'s policy had changed. The test traditionally applied in England required satisfaction that the matters proposed to be put in evidence were ones whose relevance "no human ingenuity" could have foreseen when the case was originally presented to the court: *R. v Frost* (1839) 4 St. Tr. N.S. 85 at 86, *per* Tindall C.J. In more recent times, it has been acknowledged that this formulation, if strictly applied, would have the effect of depriving the court of cogent, useful evidence; in this sense, modern case law tends to require satisfaction that the issues were not reasonably foreseeable when the evidence was originally presented by the party: *R. v Millikin* (1969) 53 Cr. App. R. 330 at 333 (CA); *R. Hutchinson* (1985) 82 Cr. App. R.51 at 59 (CA).
[153] With respect to the right of the accused to apply for a dismissal of the charges against him under s.4E of the Criminal Procedure Act 1967 (inserted by the Criminal Justice Act 1999, s.9), s.4E does not impose any time limit for the bringing of such an application, or indeed applications, nor for an appeal from the trial judge's decision. Walsh (*op. cit.* n.142 at 691) proposes that this leaves intact the right of the accused under common law rules of procedure to make subsequent applications to dismiss—although the trial judge will have considerable discretion in this regard—and the defence may do so during the trial, typically at the close of the prosecution's case.
[154] *R. v Galbraith* [1981] 2 All E.R. 1060 (CA), *per* Lord Lane C.J. The criteria identified in *Galbraith* were applied by the Court of Criminal Appeal in *People (DPP) v Gilligan* [1993] 1 I.R. 92, where the court rejected the submission that the trial judge should have granted the application for a directed verdict due to inconsistencies in the prosecution's case. When deciding the application, the trial judge is required to ascertain whether the prosecution has established "a *prima facie* case—looking at the case from the high point of the prosecution case", but this does not require the judge to accept or reject evidence, which is the task reserved ultimately for the jury (*per* O'Flaherty J., at 97). See also *DPP v M* (CCA, February 15, 2001) and *People (DPP) v Kenny* (CCA, November 19, 2002). In *Kenny*, the court rejected submissions upon appeal that the

Evidence and the Trial

judge is concerned to find no more than "the necessary minimum evidence" in support of the charges, and is required to entrust to the jury the task of evaluating the weight of evidence and proof. If the trial judge rejects the defence's submission of "no case to answer", the proceedings continue. The trial judge may, however, suspend his decision on this application until all the evidence has been heard and the jury has delivered their verdict (in which case the judge overrules the jury), so that in the event of subsequent applications and appeals, retrial may be avoided.

1–51 When one party calls a witness, the witness ordinarily is sworn in and evidence elicited from him by calling counsel under *examination-in-chief*.[155] Counsel is precluded from asking *leading questions*, being questions that imply or suggest a certain answer. Although the difference between a leading and a non-leading question often seems semantic, it is at root logical and principled. The difference between saying to the witness "when you saw the accused by the lake, was he with the girl?" and saying to him "did you see the accused by the lake?" followed by "was he with anyone?" is more than phraseology. The rule pragmatically seeks to ensure that the witness establishes his own recollection of events logically from first principles, with few assumptions or givens tolerated, so that an opponent can observe and later test the method and scope of the witness' recollection. The principle further ensures that a witness has not been coached or unduly influenced prior to the trial. Exception is routinely made for: questions relating to issues not in dispute between the parties, questions relating to the identity of persons or objects presented to the court, and questions directed to a witness who has been deemed hostile.[156] When being examined in-chief, witnesses must not repeat or be asked about statements or utterances they made prior to the trial and consistent with their version in court; they must give their testimony naturally from memory and may not consult notes or statements, save where leave has been given by the trial judge.[157]

1–52 When examination-in-chief is complete, any opposing party is entitled,

---

trial judge, when deciding the application, had been obliged to reconcile any inconsistencies in the evidence tendered by that stage in the trial (since this was a matter for resolution by the triers of fact at the end of the case after all the evidence had been considered). It is clear from other decisions on this issue, however, that where the inconsistencies are very significant, the trial judge is entitled to reject the evidence on the basis that it does not provide a prima facie case against the accused and would place the court in danger of a "perverse" decision: *e.g. People (DPP) v Morrissey* (CCA, July 10, 1998). By contrast, in *People (DPP) v Leacy* (CCA, July 3, 2002), the inconsistencies in the complainant's evidence related to peripheral matters of relevance to the credibility of the witness more properly to be decided by the jury.

[155] In some cases, a witness may be called and made available for cross-examination without being examined in-chief—typically to avoid replication of evidence already given by a witness in the case (where the two witnesses were privy to the same observations or events, *e.g.* two or more arresting gardaí).

[156] *cf.* para.**2–30**.

[157] To the extent that *DPP v Clifford* (HC, July 22, 2002) appears not to require advance leave from the trial judge, that decision may be questioned: *cf.* para.**2–41** *et seq*.

as of right, to *cross-examine* the witness. Under cross-examination, questioning is permissibly more aggressive since its accepted aim is to undermine or discredit the evidence given by the witness in-chief. When cross-examining a witness, leading questions may be asked; although these may suggest or insinuate a desired answer, they may be disallowed where they presume the existence of as yet unproven facts. Where the accused is cross-examined—having first elected to give evidence in the case—as a general rule, only matters upon which the prosecution has tendered evidence may be put to him, except where cross-examination upon bad character or criminal record has been permitted by the trial judge pursuant to s.1(f)(ii)–(iii) of the Criminal Justice (Evidence) Act 1924.[158] During cross-examination, counsel must put to the witness any matter raised in-chief upon which evidence will later be tendered to contradict him. As a general rule, a party who fails, at least formally, to cross-examine a witness upon a particular issue may not later be entitled to invite the court to reject the witness' evidence in-chief upon that issue.[159] When cross-examination is complete, the calling side may seek leave to re-examine the witness as to matters raised under cross-examination, and when this is complete the other party may be permitted to cross-examine a second time. By this stage and hereafter, the trial judge possesses considerable discretion in deciding whether to permit the questioning to continue, although leave is routinely granted for the purpose of addressing fresh or insubstantially tested issues raised by the other side in its most recent examination.

1–53 The trial judge enjoys a rarely invoked discretion to call a witness in a criminal trial where neither party has already done so.[160] It is a power, however, that is at odds with the supervisory role the trial judge characteristically assumes in the adversarial system of law, and may only be invoked exceptionally as a last resort for the purposes of achieving justice or fairness in the case but not to supplement or to take over the prosecution's case.[161] In civil cases, save for family law proceedings,[162] it would appear that the trial judge has a common law power to call a witness only by consent of the parties.[163] The trial judge enjoys a more frequently (but sparingly) exercised discretion to direct a question

---

[158] *cf.* para.**8–13** *et seq.*
[159] *Browne v Dunn* (1893) 6 R. 67.
[160] *R. v Edwards* (1848) 3 Cox C.C. 82; *R. v Roberts (John Marcus)* (1984) 80 Cr. App. Rep. 89 (CA).
[161] In *R. v Tregear* [1967] 2 Q.B. 574 (CA), the trial judge was criticised upon appeal for "taking over the prosecution" by intervening to call the final witness. In *R. v Grafton* [1993] Q.B. 101 (CA), the prosecution had established a prima facie case to answer, but had rested at a point when vital issues such as identity remained to be proved. In this situation, the trial judge invoked his power to call a witness, whose effect for the prosecution's case was more than formal but provided a vital link for proof of the accused's guilt. Upon appeal, the Court of Appeal considered (at 107, *per* Taylor L.J.) that "by proceeding as he did, the judge was no longer holding the ring. He took over the prosecution. There was no other prosecutor. The reaction of any neutral bystander could only be that the judge had become the adversary of the defence."
[162] *Eastern Health Board v Mooney* (HC, March 20, 1998).
[163] *Re Enoch and Zaretsky, Bock & Co.'s Arbitration* [1910] 1 K.B. 327.

Evidence and the Trial

to a witness,[164] a facility exercised notably more in family law proceedings affecting the welfare of children, which the courts rightly regard to be less adversarial and more inquisitorial.[165]

1–54 The trial judge's "summing-up" for the jury at the close of the trial is more akin to a series of directions and guidelines for the proper determination of the issues being tried and the evidence tendered in the case. A pragmatic approach to appellate review of the trial judge's closing directions was once advocated by the Court of Criminal Appeal: "In general, [the court] should not approach the consideration of a trial judge's charge to a jury at the end of a trial as a written document to be read and examined as it appears before us on paper, but ... should consider and value it for what it was—the living, spoken word of the judge, addressed to the minds of the jurors through their ears, uttered once only, to produce certain immediate effects and impressions, and delivered in the atmosphere of the trial created by the evidence, the speeches

---

[164] *Bostin v Carew* (1824) Ry & M. 127. Many decisions caution against overusing this discretion to the point that the judge behaves less like an umpire than the bowler or batsman: *R. v Gunning* (1980) Cr. App. R. 303 at 306 (CA), *per* Cumming-Bruce L.J. In *People v McGuinness* [1978] I.R. 189 at 190 (CCA), conviction was quashed on appeal due to excessive intervention by the trial judge, despite an acknowledgment that the prosecution had advanced sufficient evidence to lead reasonably to conviction. 123 out of 423 questions put to the complainant under cross-examination had been directed by the trial judge, and this had conveyed an inappropriate impression that the judge took a particular view of the complainant's evidence in-chief. According to Kenny J., the "judge must be patient and confine his intervention to the minimum necessary for a fair trial".

[165] The Irish courts have creatively developed an extensive, and on occasions, controversial, jurisdiction as guardian of the child's constitutional rights (a role which is not specifically articulated in the Constitution). As recent examples, see *Eastern Health Board v District Judge J.P. McDonnell* [1999] I.R. 174 (HC), *per* McCracken J. and *DB (a minor) v Minister for Justice* [1999] 1 I.R. 29, [1999] 1 I.L.R.M. 93 (HC), *per* Kelly J. The Irish judges have lately regarded their role, in cases affecting the welfare of a child, to be more hands-on and extensive, particularly in family law proceedings, whether public or private. This has been justified on the basis that many of these proceedings are not, or should not be, fully adversarial. In *Re S, M & W (Infants) (Wardship) (Eastern Health Board Intervening)* [1996] I.F.L.R. 87, the High Court emphasised that wardship proceedings involving the "welfare" of a child are inquisitorial. More extensively, in *Southern Health Board v CH* [1996] I.L.R.M. 142, [1996] 1 I.R. 219, the Supreme Court reasoned that any proceedings which affect s.3 of the Guardianship of Infants Act 1964—providing that in proceedings affecting the custody, guardianship, upbringing, or administration of the property of a child, the welfare of the child shall be the court's first and paramount consideration—are not to be regarded as *lis inter partes* (with all the concomitant restrictions on the course and conduct of the dispute) but instead as an enquiry into the welfare of the child, within which generally the judge may assume more responsibility for the course and conduct of the proceedings. This is strengthened by s.24 of the Child Care Act 1991 (interpreted by McCracken J. in *Eastern Health Board v District Judge J.P. McDonnell* [1999] I.R. 174 (HC) to impose a non-delegable duty on the courts to act as protectors of the child's welfare), and the cross-applicability of the Child Care Act 1991 in family law proceedings (facilitating orders under the 1991 Act at any time in proceedings under a wide range of statutes, including the Family Law (Divorce) Act 1996, the Family Law Act 1995, the Judicial Separation and Family Law Reform Act 1989, the Guardianship of Infants Act 1964, and the Domestic Violence Act 1996).

of counsel, and the whole conduct of the proceedings".[166] Notwithstanding these remarks, past decades have illustrated the critical effect which the summing-up and closing directions may have upon the jury's verdict, and the crucial need for accuracy; the following chapters each illustrate the countless times when trial judges' closing directions have successfully grounded appeals against conviction.

VI. TESTIMONY

1–55 The common law traditionally required *viva voce* testimony to be given live in the courtroom. The law in Ireland and England now provides that in certain circumstances testimony may be given from a different room or place and displayed simultaneously to the court via live television link.[167] The legislative machinery for this facility was first introduced in Ireland by Pt III of the Criminal Evidence Act 1992, designed to ameliorate the stressful experience for children of testifying, and thereby to encourage the reception of testimonial evidence by child complainants in cases of sexual and violent abuse.[168] The facility first applied only to child witnesses under 17 years— including witnesses of any age suffering a mental disability[169] and any witness "with the leave of the court"[170] —in criminal proceedings for sexual offences and acts of violence or the threat of violence to a person, including attempts or conspiracies to commit, aid, abet, counsel, procure, or incite the commission of said offences.[171] Section 29(1) created a general power to accept in any criminal proceedings the evidence of a witness (other than the accused) who is outside the State, via live television link, with the leave of the court. Part III of the Children Act 1997[172] extended the television link facility (and the use of an intermediary) to child witnesses (from within or outside the State) in any civil proceedings concerning the welfare of a child. More recently, s.39 of the Criminal Justice Act 1999[173] enables the court, in any criminal proceedings

---

[166] *Attorney-General v O'Shea* [1931] I.R. 713 at 726–27, *per* Kennedy C.J (CCA).
[167] The Fennelly Report has recommended that this facility be extended to facilitate experts living in different jurisdictions, and further to permit gardai to give their evidence establishing preservation of the crime scene televisually from their stations, to reduce unnecessary commutes and wastage of public resources: *op. cit.* n.89 at para.739, p.192.
[168] See 416 *Dáil Debates*, March 5, 1992, at 1695.
[169] Section 19.
[170] Section 13(1).
[171] Sections 12, 2.
[172] Sections 20–22 of the Children Act 1997 similarly enable children "not of full age" (*i.e.* under 18 years, *per* Age of Majority Act 1985, s.2) to give testimony by live television link, and similarly provide for the use of an intermediary, the mandatory videotaping of the evidence, and the removal of the need to re-identify the accused in court: *cf.* para.1– 57 *et seq*. These differ from the provisions in the Criminal Evidence Act 1992, to the extent that under s.21 testifying by television link is contingent upon the trial judge's grant of leave, and under s.22, the trial judge may assume the initiative to direct that questions be put to the child by an intermediary.
[173] Section 39 replicates provisions first enacted under Pt III of the Criminal Evidence Act 1992 for the mandatory videotaping of television link evidence, and for the dispensing of re-identification where the accused was known to the complainant prior to the offence

Evidence and the Trial 31

for indictable offences, to direct that a witness give testimony by live television link where he is "likely to be in fear or subject to intimidation in giving evidence otherwise".

1–56 Section 4F–G of the Criminal Procedure Act 1967—inserted by s.9 of the Criminal Justice Act 1999—provides that at any time after the accused has been sent forward for trial, an application may be made by either party to the trial court requesting that a witness give his evidence in advance of the trial before a District Court judge[174] and in the presence of the accused.[175] The justification for such measures was explained well by Spencer: "The law is bound to recognise at least some exceptional cases where the courts can hear the evidence of absent witnesses, because if it did not, criminal justice would be paralysed in the face of some of the most dangerous criminals, and also some of the most obnoxious ones. If the court is unable to receive as evidence anything except oral testimony at trial, threatening or killing witnesses will produce acquittals: which means that where organised crime is involved, witnesses are more likely to be killed, and guilty defendants correspondingly more likely to go free".[176] The District Court that the witness is ordered to attend has the power to secure attendance and compliance by any named witness including the accused,[177] except where the person whose attendance is required is outside the State or where it is not reasonably practicable to secure his attendance before the court.[178] The evidence may be given by live television link or by means of a sworn deposition—provided the witness may be cross-examined and (if necessary) re-examined in the presence of the accused, and provided the full extent of the witness' examination is recorded and signed by the witness. The provisions that elsewhere restrict cross-examination upon the complainant's sexual history apply.[179] The deposition may be tendered as evidence for the purpose of a pre-trial application under s.4E to dismiss charges, or as the witness' evidence in the trial where it is established that the witness is dead, or is unable to attend the trial, or is prevented from attending the trial by fear, intimidation, or otherwise, subject at all times to "the interests of

---

or where the complainant has already identified the accused at an identification parade or otherwise (for which purpose evidence by another person recalling the positive identification shall be admissible).

[174] The Fennelly Report has recommended that this evidence should be taken in the court of trial, owing to the heavy workload already faced by District courts: *op. cit.* n.89 at para.727, p.189.

[175] The 1999 Act was amended by the Children Act 2001, s.255, enabling the District Court to order that a child complainant give his evidence in advance of the trial, subject to the requirements in s.4F–G of the Criminal Procedure Act 1967.

[176] Spencer, *op. cit.* n.41 at p.636. When the Italian legislature enacted new "anglo-saxon" provisions in the Code of Criminal Procedure 1988, they did so out of concerns that witnesses were being killed by members of organised crime: *Nuovo Codice di Procedura Penale*, at art.512.

[177] Criminal Procedure Act 1967, s.4(a)–(b); District Court Rules 1997, Ord.24, rr.15–17, as amended by the District Court (Criminal Justice) Rules 2001, rr. 8 and Sch.11.

[178] Criminal Law (Jurisdiction) Act 1976, s.18, as amended by the Criminal Justice Act 1999, s.14.

[179] Criminal Law (Rape) Act 1981, s.4(1), as amended by Criminal Justice Act 1999, s.15; *cf.* para.**3–25** *et seq.*

justice". The videotaped evidence is likewise admissible as evidence at the trial—but not for the purposes of a section 4E pre-trial application to dismiss—upon proof that this is in "the interests of justice". The provisions are subject to s.16 of the Criminal Evidence Act 1992 (where the witness is a child) and the witness' attendance at the trial for cross-examination (which may be conducted via live television link).

Part III of the Criminal Evidence Act 1992

1–57 Part III of the Criminal Evidence Act 1992 laid the foundations for the television link facility in the State,[180] and from which subsequent Acts drew selectively. Under Part III, whenever the testimony of a witness is taken by television link, it must be videotaped by the court.[181] The various references to the age of the child in Part III apply to persons of any age suffering a mental disability.[182] Where a witness gives evidence by live television link under s.13, neither judge nor lawyer may wear a wig or gown when examining the witness.[183] The complainant is not required to re-identify the accused in court—unless against the "interests of justice"—where the prosecution gives evidence that the complainant knew the accused before the alleged offence, or where the complainant previously identified the accused at an identification parade or otherwise (for which purpose evidence by another person recalling the positive identification shall be admissible).[184] Section 16(1)(b) provided the first (limited) means for receiving a child's evidence in advance of the trial, by permitting interviews with complainants under 14 years to be admissible later in-chief. By virtue of s.4F-G of the Criminal Procedure Act 1967—inserted by s.9 of the Criminal Justice Act 1999 and amended by s.255 of the Children Act 2001—an application may now be made to the District Court for a direction that a child complainant formally give his evidence in advance of the trial, by deposition or videotaped television link evidence, where satisfied upon the evidence of a registered doctor that his attendance "would involve serious danger to the safety, health or well-being of the child". The facility is otherwise

---

[180] Brought into force (for the Dublin Metropolitan District of the District Court) on September 30, 1993 by the Criminal Evidence Act 1992 (Commencement) Order 1993 (S.I. No.288 of 1993), and for the Central Criminal Court and the Dublin Circuit Court on February 15, 1993 by the Criminal Evidence Act 1992 (Commencement) Order 1993 (S.I. No.38 of 1993).
[181] Section 13(2). The same is required by the Children Act 1997, s.21, and the Criminal Justice Act 1999, s.4F.
[182] Section 19. Similar provision exists under the Children Act 1997, s.20(b).
[183] Section 13(3). This had already been required—by virtue of the Judicial Separation and Family Law Reform Act 1989, ss.33, 45—in civil proceedings affecting the welfare of the child under a range of statutes including the Child Care Act 1991, the Domestic Violence Act 1996, the Family Law Act 1995, the Family Law (Divorce) Act 1996, the Guardianship of Infants Act 1964, the Adoption Acts 1952–1991, the Family Home Protection Act 1976, the Family Law (Maintenance of Spouses) Act 1976, and the Partition Acts 1868–1876.
[184] Section 18. Section 21(5) of the Children Act 1997 dispenses with the need of the child witness to re-identify a person in court, upon proof that the person was already known to, or identified by, the witness.

subject to the requirements in s.4F-G of the Criminal Procedure Act 1967, chiefly that the evidence must be in the presence of the accused, the witness must be available for cross-examination and re-examination, and the evidence must be recorded and signed.

1-58 Where the witness is under 17 years, and giving his evidence by television link pursuant to Pt III of the 1992 Act, the court may, "having regard to the age or mental condition of the witness" and "the interests of justice", accede to a request to re-put questions to the witness through an intermediary appointed by the court.[185] Section 14(2) has the effect that questions asked by examining counsel may either be *restated* by the intermediary or, presumably in exceptional cases, *rephrased* in words more appropriate to "the age or mental condition" of the witness. The potentially intrusive effect of rephrasing and restating by an intermediary will naturally be a cause for concern in the trial. Given that pace and pressure are intrinsic to effective cross-examination, the trial judge may come under a particular duty to ensure that the defence is not unduly hampered in the course of its challenges to the veracity and credibility of its accusers. It is submitted, given the significant effect an intermediary is likely to have upon the course and efficacy of cross-examination, that it should be availed of in few cases where it is clear that the witness lacks the mental or emotional ability to withstand direct and unmediated questioning.

Constitutionality of the Television Link Measures

1-59 The television link provisions introduced by the Criminal Evidence Act 1992 for s.12 offences were based upon a similar model adopted in England[186] which had emerged as a compromise to a scheme proposed in an 1989 report of a Home Office Committee chaired by Judge Pigot.[187] The initial report recommended that the child's testimony (examination-in-chief, cross-examination by defence lawyer, etc.) be taken entirely in advance of the trial by videotape, and later played at the trial. The compromise model requires the child to give testimony at the trial, though via television link and with the involvement of an intermediary.[188] In broadly following this approach, the Irish legislators were clearly influenced by the Law Reform Commission's

---

[185] Section 14(1). Similar provision exists under the Children Act 1997, s.22.
[186] Current provision in England for television link facilities are set down in the Youth Justice and Criminal Evidence Act 1999, ss.16–33. These provisions differ from current Irish law to the extent that witnesses suffering from a physical disability or disorder are formally eligible, and the trial judge has a discretionary power to give a non-eligible witness the benefit of the television link facility.
[187] Home Office, *Report of the Advisory Group on Video Evidence* (Home Office, London, 1989).
[188] The compromise was effective to the extent that the pre-recorded evidence model has not since proved popular. A Working Group established by the Home Office in England recently criticised the over-use of videotaped pre-trial interviews as evidence, and recommended that this facility not be extended to adult witnesses who suffer intimidation: Home Office, *Speaking Up for Justice: Report of the Interdepartmental Working Group on the Treatment of Vulnerable Witnesses in the Criminal Justice System* (Home Office, London, 1998).

cautions that some options (such as the appointment of a *guardian ad litem* for the child complainant in sexual abuse cases) ran the risk of favouring the prosecution at the expense of the accused, thereby jeopardising his constitutional right to a fair trial.[189] Although Pt III of the 1992 Act emerged as a compromise, and in a climate never more concerned to prosecute cases of child sexual abuse, some of its provisions ought to engender ongoing concern to members of the legal community.

1–60 The assumed right of physical confrontation[190] between accused and accuser in court had been decried by many writers as imposing unnecessary trauma and humiliation on the complainant, particularly in sexual offence proceedings.[191] The two constitutional challenges to Pt III—*White v Ireland*[192] and *Donnelly v Ireland*[193]—centred on the consequences of the removal of confrontation from the trial in circumstances where ss.12, 13, and 18 are applied with the effect that the complainant gives his testimony via television link from beyond the courtroom and is not obliged to identify, face, or observe the accused at any point throughout the trial. In both cases it was submitted for the applicants that direct physical confrontation constituted a right of the accused protected under the common law and the Constitution, and that confrontation is necessary to enable the defence to test the courtroom demeanour and credibility of the complainant, as an essential incident of the right to a fair trial under Art.38(1).

1–61 In both cases, the High Court—approved on appeal in *Donnelly* by the Supreme Court—considered, after a review of the authorities, that no such stand-alone right to direct or "eyeball to eyeball" confrontation existed under the common law or the Constitution. In *White*, Kinlen J. was influenced by Wigmore's assertion that "the right of confrontation is provided 'not for the idle purpose of gazing upon the witness, or of being gazed upon by him', but,

---

[189] Law Reform Commission, *Consultation Paper on Child Sexual Abuse*, 1987, at paras 7.32–34.

[190] To some extent this right (or facility) has been assumed in the context of criminal proceedings, although any claim to such a right in civil proceedings would suffer significantly from the findings of the courts in *White* and *Donnelly*: *cf.* para.**1–59** *et seq*. Of more concern is the right and opportunity to cross-examine one's accusers, whether in criminal, civil, or disciplinary proceedings, as illustrated recently in *Borges v Medical Council* (HC, March 5, 2003): *cf.* para.**9–17**.

[191] The New Zealand Court of Appeal memorably asserted: "Confrontation in the sense of being in the presence of one's accuser is one thing; but confrontation merely to provide the opportunity to glower and thereby intimidate the witness is another": *R. v Accused* [1989] N.Z.L.R. 600 at 672, *per* McMullin J. In "The Protection of Vulnerable Witnesses in Court: An Anglo-Dutch Comparison" (1999) 3 Int. J. Evid. & Proof 29, Ellison criticises the traditional preference of the common law for live trials and the concomitant premium this places on physical observation and demeanour as indicators of veracity or reliability. She argues that this is not rooted in fact, citing one psychological study—Wellborn, "Demeanour" (1991) 76 *Cornell Law Review* 1104—to propose that guilty behaviour is an indicator of stress and not untruthfulness. See also Lee, "Judicial Rape" (1993) 16 *Women's Studies International Forum* 26.

[192] [1995] 2 I.R. 268 (HC).

[193] [1998] 1 I.R. 321 (SC): *cf.* appendix 56.

rather, to allow for cross-examination".[194] In *Donnelly*, the submissions were dominated by an investigation of the vagaries of the right to eyeball confrontation in the US, where the right had been given protected status under the Constitution, precipitating difficulties when State legislatures sought to facilitate television link testimony. Case law had shifted in the US, from the view that the right to confrontation inhered in the right of the accused to be faced with oral and not written evidence, to the view that it inhered in his right to ensure that his accusers faced the jury to enable them to assess the credibility and demeanour of the accusers; and latterly, after numerous successful challenges to statutory attempts to balance the competing rights, the US Supreme Court had decided in *Maryland v Craig*[195] that the right to confrontation inheres in the right only to have reliable evidence tendered against the accused, but that any statutory attempt to interfere with direct physical confrontation was required to be specifically justified in each case. Mr Donnelly's strongest argument was that s.13 does not require an enquiry upon a case-by-case basis as to whether the witness or accuser would be traumatised by the experience of confrontation, but instead places an onus upon the accused to show why the television link should *not* be used by the court. The parallels with US case law were in this instance fruitless, however. The requirement of case-by-case enquiry had been necessarily required in the US because its Constitution expressly recognises the right to confrontation in trials.[196]

1–62 The High Court and Supreme Court acknowledged that s.13 of the 1992 Act is based upon an *assumption* that the witness under 17 years, especially where he is the complainant, is likely to suffer additional trauma from direct confrontation with the accused in the courtroom whilst giving his testimony. It does not require that the trial judge ascertain in each case if trauma is likely; in fact, it provides that testimony should normally be given via television link where a witness under 17 years is testifying in s.12 offence proceedings "unless the court sees good reason to the contrary". In *White*, Kinlen J. accepted that the trial judge may exercise his discretion in appropriate cases to direct that only the voice of the accused, without his image, be transmitted to the complainant via television link when the accused testifies. This in fact occurred in *Donnelly*, where the 14 year-old complainant viewed his questioners when examined and cross-examined, but was not required to view the accused at any time. Neither court considered that the ability to challenge a witness' credibility depends upon the physical presence of the accuser in the court.[197] Fair procedures were ensured by requiring the witness to take the oath, and to be cross-examined live via television link so that the

---

[194] [1995] 2 I.R. 268 at 279 (HC)..
[195] 497 U.S. 836 (1990).
[196] The Sixth Amendment to the US Constitution guarantees the right of an accused "to be confronted with the witnesses against him".
[197] In *White* [1995] 2 I.R. 268 (HC) Kinlen J. expressed the opinion that even if the right to direct confrontation was safeguarded by the Irish Constitution, that right had validly yielded to the rights of the young child under Pt III of the 1992 Act.

parties and the jury could observe the witness' demeanour and his response to questioning.[198]

1–63 In concluding that the accused's rights to cross-examination and assessment of the witness' credibility and demeanour were not infringed by the television link provisions, the courts were influenced by the technical flexibility of the system in place,[199] the practice of giving defence lawyers an opportunity to inspect the facilities a day before the trial, the opportunities for defence lawyers to request adaptation of the monitors and views, and the overarching requirement that the trial judge conduct the examination "in accordance with constitutional and natural justice".[200]

Taking Evidence in Advance of the Trial

1–64 Some of the new provisions under the Criminal Evidence Act 1992, Criminal Justice Act 1999, Children Act 2001, and, in the context of civil proceedings, the Children Act 1997,[201] permit the prosecution/applicant to tender pre-recorded statements and evidence *in lieu* of the child complainant's testimony in-chief. On occasion, these provisions may benefit the accused, insofar as they provide him with material in advance of the trial to enable him better to anticipate the prosecution's case and to prepare a defence. On the other hand, they raise numerous exigent concerns of undue prejudice, which it is the trial judge's responsibility to mitigate having regard to the constitutional right of the accused to a fair trial.

1–65 Section 16(1)(b) of the 1992 Act provides that a videotaped interview between a complainant under 14 years[202] and a member of the gardaí (or other

---

[198] For a contrary view of s.13, see Duffy (1994) at pp.184, 186, describing it as "at best an example of bad draftsmanship and at worst a constitutionally impermissible transfer of an onus of proof to the accused by requiring him to show why the proposed child witness should not testify under the subsection ... leaving it to the accused to "pluck at straws", as it were, by either raising generalities such as the characteristics of children in general or by seeking to call his own psychiatric evidence in rebuttal".

[199] In *White* [1995] 2 I.R. 268 (HC), Kinlen J. heard expert evidence given by the principal officer for the Department of Justice and by an engineer asserting that the system in place in Ireland was superior to most comparable systems operating around the world. The judge can control what is seen of the witness by the court, the lawyers, and the jury, through switching on any of the three monitors showing the witness above the shoulders. Judge and lawyers have the same view (unlike in England and Northern Ireland), and have the alternative of viewing the witness aerially from the ceiling of the room. The accused can share these views, since the monitors are on swivels. Through picture-in-picture facilities, the witness can see counsel and/or the accused at the same time through one monitor, or the judge can exclude the accused from the picture if considered appropriate.

[200] *ibid.* at 281.

[201] *cf.* para.**9–43** *et seq.*

[202] Section 16 does not identify when the child must have been under the age of 14 years, whether by the time of the interview or by the time of the trial. A purposive interpretation might favour the view that the child must be 14 years at the time of the application or the trial. A textual reading would reasonably favour this as being the date of the interview. Where a significant time lapse exists between the date of the interview and the trial,

Evidence and the Trial

competent person), taken before the trial, shall be admissible evidence at the trial (or for the purposes of the application to dismiss charges),[203] subject otherwise to the ordinary rules of relevance and admissibility, and provided that the complainant is available for cross-examination at the trial. Since the videotaped interview, where admitted, is generally admissible in the trial and probative of the facts at issue, it is capable of constituting corroboration of another witness' account, or of constituting evidence which, if accepted by the jury, may alone prove guilt (given that s.28 of the same Act abolished the old rules requiring corroboration for evidence by children).[204] As such, the provisions constitute another statutory exception to the rule against hearsay; although beyond the hearsay issue, the evidence must abide by the rules of evidence that ordinarily apply to testimony. Section 16(1) applies only to indictable offences where guilt is denied, and it is a prerequisite that the child complainant is available to be cross-examined at the trial following the playing of the tape (although cross-examination may be via television link and using an intermediary). An edited version of the videotape may instead be played, with the consent of the accused and leave of the court.[205] The trial judge may decide not to admit the videotape of either type "in the interests of justice" having regard to "any risk that its admission will result in unfairness to the accused".[206]

1–66 The prosecution must serve notice of its intention to admit a videotaped interview in evidence under s.16(1)(b),[207] and must give the accused a reasonable opportunity to view the videotape.[208] The requirement of pre-trial disclosure of the videotaped interview is phrased to apply to a videotape "proposed to be given at the trial" and not to other taped interviews with the child. Prior inconsistent interview statements given by the child, however, will clearly be critical to the defence for the purpose of launching a challenge to the admissibility, or subsequently to the weight, of the videotape actually tendered by the prosecution, and for the purposes of general challenges to the credibility of that witness. Recent judicial interpretations of this duty—

---

however, the trial judge may be expected to consider it inappropriate to admit the tape under s.16(2)–(3) having regard to the child's age and maturity by the time of the trial.
[203] Criminal Justice Act 1999, s.19(2).
[204] *cf.* paras **2–09, 5–49**.
[205] This may be in the context of an application to dismiss the charges by virtue of the Criminal Justice Act 1999, s.19(3), or during the trial by virtue of the Criminal Justice Act 1992, s.16(1).
[206] Section 16(2).
[207] This is in addition to all the documents and notices required to be served upon the defence after the accused has been sent forward for trial, pursuant to s.6 of the Criminal Procedure Act 1967, as amended by s.9 of the Criminal Justice Act 1999. Collectively called the book of evidence, these include: a statement of the charges against him; a copy of any sworn information in writing upon which the proceedings were initiated; a list of the witnesses proposed to be called at the trial; a statement of the evidence to be given by each of the proposed witnesses; a list of exhibits (if any); and a further statement of the evidence to be given by any witness who has already supplied a statement. See District Court Rules 1997, Ord.24, r.7 and Sch.B, forms 24.3–24.7, as amended by the District Court (Criminal Justice) Rules 2001, r.8, Schs 11–12.
[208] Section 15(1), as amended by the Criminal Justice Act 1999, s.19.

specifically the duty to disclose a copy of any information in writing upon which the proceedings were initiated (although s.6 refers only to "sworn information")—assert that the prosecution is under an important duty, as a matter of constitutional justice, to disclose the transcripts and videotapes for all interviews with the child.[209] The prosecutor's common law duty to disclose requires disclosure to the defence of any previous statements made by an intended witness, and any report materially bearing upon the witness's credibility or reliability.[210] In *DPP v Special Criminal Court*,[211] the Supreme Court recognised that this duty extends to disclosing to the defence a statement of a witness it no longer intends to call, and to give the accused an opportunity to call that person as a witness. If the statement is subject to informer privilege, a ruling upon this issue should first be obtained from the trial judge.[212]

1–67 In deciding whether to admit a videotape of evidence received in advance of the trial by television link under s.16(1)(a) of the Criminal Evidence Act 1992 or s.4F-G of the Criminal Procedure Act 1967,[213] or to admit a videotape of an interview with a child younger than 14 years under s.16(1)(b) of the 1992 Act, the trial judge must evaluate whether it is in "the interests of justice" to do so.[214] There have been numerous challenges in England to the trial judge's application of this discretion. Each case cautions against the danger that juries may attach disproportionate weight to the videos, particularly where they have been permitted to read the accompanying transcripts or to view the video a second time. Permanent evidence taken in advance of the trial potentially disrupts the temporal sequence of the trial operated by the common law for centuries. If the videotape is replayed or its accompanying transcript reread, *after* cross-examination of the witness has concluded, there is a real risk of disproportionate emphasis upon the complainant's evidence with extreme prejudicial effect for the defence.

1–68 The Court of Appeal has decided that the transcripts that accompany videotaped evidence should not be left with the jury—except temporarily where requested to enable them to clarify what specific words were spoken—and that if the trial judge decides in exceptional circumstances to permit the jury to retain the transcripts, this should be by consent of the accused, and the jury should be cautioned about the limited evidentiary value of the transcripts and be reminded of the other evidence in the case.[215] The court in *R. v Welstead*[216] upheld the trial judge's decision to give the jury the transcript whilst hearing

---

[209] *cf.* paras **1–42** *et seq.*, **3–38**.
[210] *People (DPP). v Kavanagh* (CCA, February 26, 1996), where conviction was quashed because a social welfare report—wherein the complainant was reported to give a version of events inconsistent with the account she gave later in the trial—had not been disclosed to the defence until after the accused had been convicted.
[211] [1999] 1 I.R. 60 (SC).
[212] *cf.* para.**13–53** *et seq.*
[213] As amended by the Criminal Justice Act 1999 and the Children Act 2001.
[214] Section 16(2).
[215] *R. v Rawlings* [1995] 1 W.L.R. 178 (CA).
[216] [1996] 1 Cr. App. R. 59 (CA).

the videotape to decipher the witness' mumblings, but stressed that transcripts of this sort should be used only for limited purposes, principally to enable the jury to comprehend the witness; they should not be left with the jury when they deliberate over a verdict, and in all cases the trial judge must caution the jury not to attach disproportionate weight to the transcript.

1–69 In *R. v B*,[217] evidence given in-chief by the children via television link conflicted with medical evidence presented to the court. Upon this basis, videotapes of their original interviews were played in court, following which the children were cross-examined via television link. The appeal centred on the trial judge's decision to permit the prosecution to play the videotapes a second time. The appeal succeeded upon the basis that the replaying had given an irregular slant to one party's evidence: crucially, the trial judge gave no reasons why he thought this necessary; nor had he cautioned the jury against attaching disproportionate weight to the recording; nor had he reminded them to recall the points established under cross-examination.

1–70 In *R. v McQuiston*,[218] the appeal centred on the fact that the trial judge had repeated *verbatim* most of the transcript accompanying the complainant's videotaped evidence in-chief, which had occupied about 70 per cent of the time and words spent when summing-up at the close of the trial. In deciding that there had been a mistrial, Otton L.J. recognised the following guidelines for the future handling of videotaped evidence in trials.[219] The guidelines are likely to be of persuasive assistance in Ireland:

> If at a later stage in the trial the jury requests to be reminded of the witness' evidence, it is sufficient that the trial judge remind them from his own note of the evidence.
> If the jury is concerned to be reminded of *how* the words were spoken, the trial judge may exercise his discretion to allow part or all of the videotape to be replayed.
> If the trial judge decides to replay the videotape, it should be replayed in court with judge, counsel, and the accused present.
> The trial judge should warn the jury not to give the complainant's evidence in-chief disproportionate weight simply because it was repeated and is most recent to memory, and should warn the jury to take care to consider the other evidence in the case.
> The trial judge should specifically remind the jury from his own notes of any challenges or points established under cross-examination or re-examination of the complainant.

1–71 It is clear, from a reading of *White* and *Donnelly*[220] and an appreciation

---

[217] Heard with *R. v M* and *R. v Sonia B* [1996] Crim L.R. 499 (CA).
[218] [1998] 1 Cr. App. R. 139 (CA): *cf.* appendix 54.
[219] Drawn from the court's earlier decisions in cases such as *R. v Rawlings* [1995] 1 W.L.R. 178 (CA).
[220] *cf.* para.**1–59** *et seq.*

of the courts' experience to date in England, that the trial judge's duties when giving closing directions to the jury is more rigorous and specific where televised or videotaped evidence has been employed in the trial. In *R. v Springer*,[221] conviction was overturned due to the trial judge's failure to warn the jury not to attach disproportionate weight to the transcript accompanying the videotaped evidence, and further due to his failure to remind them that the accused had objected to admission of the videotaped interviews upon the basis that the child had been told what to say by his mother (a challenge that had been rejected earlier by the trial judge on the question of admissibility, but that had remained relevant in the trial as a challenge to the weight of the interviews).

1–72 In light of the problems experienced in these and other cases, it has become a fixed rule in England that where, for one reason or another, transcripts of the videotaped or televised evidence are left with the jury, the trial judge must specifically warn the jury on the limited evidential use and relevance of the transcripts. The failure to do so has led routinely to the overturning of conviction in England, as in *R. v Morris*[222] where defence counsel had requested that the jury read copies of the transcript of the complainant's original interview whilst the complainant was giving her live testimony. If the jury were to be left with the transcript while they attempted to reach a verdict (a situation the Court of Appeal regarded as unusual and exceptional), it was incumbent upon the trial judge to warn them not to attach disproportionate weight to the transcript, particularly in a case where the complainant's account was uncorroborated, and to regard the complainant's live evidence throughout the hearing as that witness' evidence in the case.

1–73 As the courts confirmed in *White* and *Donnelly*, responsibility for the fair and just application of these provisions rests with the trial judge throughout the trial, and though this burden will be considerable in many cases, as the English cases indicate, the trial judge has a broad discretion to ensure that the trial has been fairly conducted and that pre-recorded evidence is admitted only where consistent with the "interests of justice" and constitutional requirements of fairness and due process.

1–74 The trial judge may be expected to exercise his discretion not to admit pre-trial videotapes of the complainant's interview or evidence, and instead to require the witness to give his evidence in-chief afresh, via television link or not, where the witness has subsequently retracted or revised the version of events given in his pre-trial statement or evidence. There is a particular need to proceed with caution to ensure that the inconsistent child witness is not treated significantly more favourably than a "non-protected witness" who might, in similar circumstances, be declared a hostile witness.[223] Generally, in this event, the hostile witness' *viva voce* version of events must alone, if at all, constitute his evidence, where admissible and relevant to proof of the facts at

---

[221] [1996] Crim. L.R. 903 (CA).
[222] [1998] Crim. L.R. 416 (CA).
[223] *cf.* para.**2–30**.

issue. His pre-trial versions, whether set out in statements, depositions, or videotaped evidence, are relevant at the behest of the non-calling party, but only as evidence relevant to the credit (or discredit) of the inconsistent witness. The statement or interview admitted under s.16(1)(b) of the 1992 Act is generally admissible, however. Amongst the English decisions on the matter, some have asserted that, as a general rule, videotaped evidence which was subsequently retracted or revised should not be admitted;[224] although in some instances already the appellate courts have defended the trial judge's right to admit the statement upon the basis that it was material that the jury were entitled to consider,[225] or upon the basis that it sought to spare the young witness the trauma of narrating the facts again prior to cross-examination.[226] In such circumstances, however, the trial judge may be required to give a stronger than usual warning to the jury of the dangers of accepting such a version of events at face value.[227]

1–75 The trial judge may also exercise his discretion not to admit the interview or complaint of the child under 14 years pursuant to s.16 of the 1992 Act where the child's accusations were made in response to leading questions or where they appear not to be his voluntary and unprompted assertions. There is clearly a need to address, by statutory instrument or practice guidelines, the procedural delicacies of taking and videotaping the child's complaints in this way—the need to avoid solicitous or leading questions, the use of anatomical dolls and photographs, etc.—if they are properly and fairly to function as admissible evidence later.

1–76 The trial judge must ensure that the protected witness is not treated with undue favouritism or that his evidence is not given disproportionate emphasis during the trial. He should not replay any video evidence—whether of the original interview or televised testimony—without carefully restoring the balance by pointing out the issues and premises established by the defence under cross-examination, or indeed facilitating further cross-examination. Except where foreclosed by the statutory provisions, the defence should have the benefit of all the ordinary procedural safeguards open to it. The range of facilities now available to the prosecution arguably heightens the burden of discretion imposed upon the trial judge to ensure a fair trial for the purposes of Art.38(1) of the Constitution and Art.6 of the European Convention on Human Rights, bearing in mind, in particular, the customarily weighty emphasis given to this right in Ireland, expressed by Denham J. as the certainty that the "right to fair procedures is superior to the community's right to prosecute".[228]

---

[224] *R. v Hampshire* [1995] 2 Cr. App. Rep. 319; *R. v Parker* [1995] Crim. L.R. 511 (CA); *R. v Sweeting and Thomas* [1999] Crim. L.R. 75 (CA).
[225] *R. v D.* [1996] Q.B. 283 (CA).
[226] *R. v Hawkins* (CA, February 20, 1995).
[227] *R. v Walker* [1996] Crim. L.R. 742 (CA).
[228] *D v DPP* [1994] 2 I.R. 465 at 474 (SC), applying *Re Haughey* [1971] I.R. 217 (SC).

Further Reading

Birch, "A Better Deal for Vulnerable Witnesses" [2000] Crim. L.R. 223.

Birks (ed.), *Pressing Problems in the Law: Criminal Justice and Human Rights* (Oxford University Press, Oxford, 1995).

Cashmore, "The Use of Video Technology for Child Witnesses" (1990) 40 Oklahoma L.R. 69.

Dennis, "Codification and Reform of Evidence Law in Australia" [1996] Crim. L.R. 477.

Dent and Flin, *Children as Witnesses* (Chicester, Wiley, 1992).

Duffy, "Televised Testimony and Constitutional Justice" (1994) I.C.L.J. 178.

Ellison, "Cross-examination and the Intermediary: Bridging the Language Divide" [2002] Crim. L.R. 114.

Fennell, *Crime and Crisis in Ireland: Justice by Illusion* (Cork University Press 1993).

Friedman, "Thoughts from across the Water on Hearsay and Confrontation" [1998] Crim. L.R. 697.

Glasser and Spencer, "Sentencing Children's Evidence and Children's Trauma" [1990] Crim. L.R. 371.

Goodman and Bottoms, *Child Victims' Child Witnesses* (Guilford Publications, London, 1993).

Home Office, *Speaking Up for Justice: Report of the Interdepartmental Working Group on the Treatment of Vulnerable Witnesses in the Criminal Justice System* (Home Office, London, 1998).

Hoyano, "Striking a Balance between the Rights of Defendants and Vulnerable Witnesses" [2001] C.L.R. 984.

Jones, "The Evidence of a Three Year Old Child" [1987] Crim. L.R. 677.

Kuhn, Weinstock, and Flaton, "How Well do Jurors Reason?" (1994) 5 *Psychological Science* 289.

Law Reform Commission, Consultation Papers on Child Sexual Abuse 1987, 1989.

McEwan, "On The Box?" [1990] Crim. L.R. 363.

O'Floinn, "Banquo's Ghost at the Commercial Banquet: Some Old and New Alternatives to the Live Witness" (1998) 4(1) *Bar Review* 39.

Sharpe, "Article 6 and the Disclosure of Evidence in Criminal Trials" [1999] Crim. L.R. 272.

Spencer and Flin, *Evidence of Children: The Law and the Psychology* (Blackstone Press, London, 1993).

Spencer, "Orality and the Evidence of Absent Witnesses" [1994] Crim. L.R. 628.

Williams, "Law and Fact" [1976] Crim. L.R. 472.

Zuckerman, "Miscarriage of Justice and Judicial Responsibility" [1991] Crim. L.R. 492.

CHAPTER 2

THE TESTIMONY OF WITNESSES

    I. Competence and Compellability 2–01
        General Principles 2–01
        Child Witnesses 2–08
        The Accused as a Witness 2–16
        The Spouse of the Accused as a Witness 2–21
        Witnesses with a Mental Disability 2–27
   II. Hostile Witnesses 2–30
 III. Refreshing a Witness' Memory 2–41
 IV. The Rule Against Narrative 2–50
        General Principles 2–50
        The Complaint in Sexual Offence Cases 2–52

I. COMPETENCE AND COMPELLABILITY

General Principles

2–01 Although the testimonial evidence of a witness is ordinarily admissible in judicial proceedings, its admissibility is in principle contingent upon the witness' *competence* to testify. Challenges to competence are comparatively rare where the witness is not a child or suffering a mental disability. In the event of challenge, common law principle once required witnesses to understand the nature and consequences of the oath, although latterly, and prior to the emergence of statutory rules, it had centred on the witness' ability to provide an intelligible account.[1] The requirement that the witness recognise and swear an oath was first developed as a safeguard against falsity; the oath has long since ceased to be the critical focus, however, and the prospect of prosecution for perjury exists equally for evidence given falsely under solemn affirmation as for evidence given falsely under oath.[2] A witness is *compellable* if he may be required by law to testify at the behest of one party to a trial or hearing. Under the common law, and still in civil proceedings,[3] this was achieved by means of the subpoena *duces tecum*, for the purpose of bringing a

---

[1] *cf.* para.**2–06** *et seq.*
[2] Oaths Act 1888, s.1.
[3] Rules of the Superior Courts, Ord.39. Given that the subpoena *duces tecum* requires a party to attend court to produce documentation upon pain of contempt of court, it should

document to court, or the subpoena *ad testificandum*, for the purpose of obtaining oral evidence. Section 4K–L of the Criminal Procedure Act 1967, inserted by s.9 of the Criminal Justice Act 1999, now governs the means by which witnesses may be compelled to testify at a criminal trial. A witness summons may be sought from the trial court by either the prosecution or the accused to secure the attendance at the trial of a named person, upon pain of contempt of court.[4] The court may make a witness order requiring the attendance at the trial of a person whose statement was served upon the accused or whose deposition was taken at an earlier date.[5] The person may be ordered to appear for the purpose of giving oral testimony, or for the purpose of producing a document.[6] Whilst by practice witnesses are assumed to be competent, and by principle competent witnesses are also compellable,[7] specific competence and compellability rules have been developed for certain classes of witness of more regular concern, for example: the accused; the spouse of the accused; children; the mentally ill; and with less contentiousness: diplomats;[8] bankers;[9] and judges.[10]

2–02 The onus of proof of a witness' competence to testify, where challenged,

---

not be granted unless it is established to the satisfaction of the court that the party's evidence is material: *Fitzpatrick v Wymes* [1976] I.R. 301 (SC). In *McConnell v Commissioner of An Garda Síochána* [2003] 2 I.R. 19 (HC), a subpoena *duces tecum* was set aside upon the basis that it had been granted in overly wide terms, and it had been sought in the context of an application to court unsupported by affidavit and before attempting to obtain the documents by way of discovery.

[4] Section 4L.
[5] Section 4K.
[6] Sections 4K(1)(b) and 4L(1)(b). By way of common law exception, a person who is compelled to attend court to produce a document is not required to give sworn testimony to authenticate or identify it, if there is another party who can do so: *Perry v Gibson* (1834) 1 A & E 48. In such a case, the producing person may not be required to undergo cross-examination, at the discretion of the trial judge: *Sumners v Mosely* (1834) 2 Cr. & M. 477.
[7] *Ex parte Fernandez* (1861) 10 CBNS 3.
[8] Under s.5 of the Diplomatic Relations Immunities Act 1967, incorporating the Vienna Convention on Diplomatic Relations of April 18, 1961, diplomats are competent but non-compellable. Non-compellability extends to the administrative and technical staff of a diplomatic mission, and to household members who have lived with the diplomat and are not nationals of the host country. The immunity belongs in practice to the State or Government employing the diplomat. For the first time in Ireland, in *People (DPP) v McKevitt*, an English diplomat—former British ambassador, Sir Ivor Roberts—agreed to testify as expert witness in an Irish court, on the role of MI5 in monitoring IRA terrorists, the British Government having dropped its claim to immunity: *Irish Times*, October 6, 2002.
[9] Under the Bankers' Books Evidence Act 1879, s.5, as amended by the Bankers' Books Evidence (Amendment) Act 1959, bankers are non-compellable, except by order of the court, to produce the banker's book "the contents of which can be proved", and all entries in a banker's book shall constitute prima facie proof of such entries where so entered in the ordinary course of the business of the bank.
[10] By common law rule, judges are competent but non-compellable to give evidence of any matters which have come to their knowledge as a result of the performance of their judicial function: applied recently in *Warren v Warren* [1996] 4 All E.R. 664 (CA).

rests upon the party who called the person as a witness.[11] It has elsewhere been reasoned that despite the imposition of a persuasive burden on the calling side, the party who challenges the witness' competence may bear an initial evidential burden of proof to substantiate its challenge,[12] a view that appears harmonious with the presumption of competence the law otherwise enforces. In criminal proceedings, where the witness is called by the prosecution, competence must be proven beyond reasonable doubt; where called by the defence, the requisite standard of proof would appear to be the balance of probabilities.[13] The enquiry takes place in the absence of the jury in the *voire dire*,[14] which often entails examination of new witnesses, typically doctors, psychiatrists, and psychologists. The trial judge is responsible to direct the enquiry, and finally to decide as a question of law whether the witness is competent to testify.

2–03 The competence and compellability of a witness is distinct from privilege, which operates in the ordinary way to modify the questions a witness must answer or the documents he may be required to produce.[15] The past non-compellable status of the accused's spouse derived in part from a common law (and later in Ireland, a constitutional) form of marital privacy; although to the extent that a spouse agreed to waive his non-compellable status, he also waived this form of marital privacy.[16]

2–04 The general rule holds that when a witness elects to waive his non-compellability, he must thereafter be treated as an ordinary witness. Upon this basis, Peter Pain J. emphasised in *R. v Pitt*[17] that if such a witness—here the wife of the accused—refuses to answer questions properly put to her, she may be deemed hostile. Given this possibility, trial judges should caution any non-compellable witness of the implications of his decision to waive non-compellability, prior to taking the oath or affirmation.

2–05 Prior to testifying, the witness ordinarily swears an oath upon the New Testament[18] or takes the solemn affirmation.[19] Evidence given by affirmation

---

[11] *People (Attorney-General) v Kehoe* [1951] I.R. 70 (HC).
[12] Tapper, *Cross & Tapper on Evidence* (9th ed., Butterworths, London, 1999) at p.207.
[13] This view of the common law was proposed in *Cross & Tapper on Evidence* (*ibid.* at p.207) prior to the enactment in England of the Youth Justice and Criminal Evidence Act 1999, s.54(1), which clarifies that proof of testimonial competence, where borne by the defence, should be discharged according to the civil standard.
[14] *cf.* para.**1–24** *et seq*. The Supreme Court authoritatively decided in *People (DPP) v Conroy* [1986] I.R. 460 (*cf.* appendix 29) that the *voire dire* must take place in the absence of the jury, overruling numerous earlier decisions requiring the presence of the jury: *People v Keating* [1953] I.R. 200 (CCA); *People v Lynch* [1982] I.R. 64 (SC).
[15] *cf.* para.**13–01**.
[16] *R. v Pitt* [1982] 3 All E.R. 63 (CA).
[17] *ibid*.
[18] If the witness is Jewish, he swears an oath upon the Old Testament: Oaths Act 1909, s.2(1). If the witness is neither Christian nor Jew, "the Oath shall be administered in any manner which is now lawful"; Oaths Act 1909, s.2(2).
[19] Oaths Act 1888, s.1. See, *e.g. R. v Brazier* (1779) 1 Leach 199.

has the same effect as evidence given by oath, in terms of carrying the same weight and attracting the same liability for perjurious falsehood.[20] The failure to take the oath or solemn affirmation, even if inadvertent, has the effect of nullifying the witness' evidence unless special provision exists under the common law or statute for the admissibility of the unsworn evidence.[21]

2–06 Traditionally under the common law, only witnesses who understood the moral imperative of the oath were competent to give sworn evidence, and at one time atheists were not entitled to testify.[22] These impediments were replaced by Parliament's endorsement of the solemn affirmation, the secular alternative to the oath introduced by the Oaths Act of 1888. Section 3 of the 1888 Act ensured that the fact that a witness swearing upon the oath lacks a genuine religious belief has no effect upon the validity of the oath (and therefore none upon the admissibility of the evidence taken from the witness). When swearing upon a religious oath prior to testifying, the witness is not confined to the Christian oath.[23] In *R. v Kemble*[24]—where a muslim witness was permitted to swear upon the Koran in Arabic—the test favoured by Lord Lane C.J. employed broad principles subjective to the witness:

> "[I]s the oath an oath which appears to the court to be binding upon the conscience of the witness? ... [I]f so, secondly, and most importantly, is it an oath which the witness himself considers to be binding upon his conscience?"

2–07 The common law courts have not by rule or practice gainsaid the adult witness' actual belief in the moral imperative of the oath since the nineteenth century. Until recently, this was otherwise for the child witness, against whom challenges were quite common, encouraged by the fact that the common law discriminated against unsworn evidence in terms of its probative and evidential effect. This was formally achieved by means of strict corroboration rules, which were eventually dismantled in Ireland by s.28 of the Criminal Evidence Act 1992,[25] thereby ensuring that any future front-line challenges to the admissibility of the child witness' evidence would take the form of challenges to his *competence to testify* (whether or not under oath). In some of the earlier decisions on child competence, the judges had identified a shift in legal and social sensibility with respect to the oath in general. In *R. v Hayes*,[26] the trial judge asked the 11-year-old child if he had been taught about religion, the Bible, God, or Jesus, to which the child answered in the negative. Notwithstanding, the Court of Appeal was satisfied that the child had been properly permitted to take the oath since he had answered that he thought

---

[20] Oaths Act 1888, s.1.
[21] *Re Marsham* [1912] 2 K.B. 362.
[22] This existed until the Evidence Further Amendment Act 1869, s.4.
[23] Oaths Act 1909, s.2(2).
[24] [1990] 1 W.L.R. 1111 at 1114 (CA).
[25] *cf.* para.**5–49**.
[26] [1977] 1 W.L.R. 234 (CA).

there was a God and knew it was very bad to tell lies. Lord Justice Bridge's observations on the oath provide a useful expression of its contemporary function, as well as suggesting apt principles to guide a trial judge when deciding whether to require a witness to take the oath or instead to receive his evidence unsworn:

> "It is unrealistic not to recognise that, in the present state of society, amongst the adult population the divine sanction of an oath is probably not generally recognised. ... [It was enough that the child appreciated the] solemnity of the occasion, and the added responsibility to tell the truth, which is involved in taking an oath, over and above the duty to tell the truth which is an ordinary duty of normal social conduct".[27]

Child Witnesses

2–08 Before considering recent reform to the rules governing the child's competence to testify, it is worthwhile bearing in mind that for most of its history the common law treated the evidence of children with considerable and, it is now felt, unjustified suspicion.[28] Many of the grounds for concern have been discredited in recent years, although some are likely to continue to present themselves in individual cases, for the most part now as challenges to the weight of the child's evidence, and in far fewer cases affecting competence and admissibility. Prior to this reform, it had been reasoned by the common law judges and jurists of the day that children were inherently unreliable, having bad memories and undeveloped logic, and tending to be egocentric, suggestible, and prone to falsehood or fantasy with respect to the accusation of sexual offence.[29] The law's former suspicion of children's evidence was deeply rooted in cultural stereotype, and was certainly influenced by a collective memory of the Salem Witch Trials conducted in America towards the end of the seventeenth century—the first recorded legal proceedings there to receive the evidence of children.[30]

---

[27] [1977] 1 W.L.R. 234 at 237.
[28] Discussed comprehensively in Spencer and Flin (1993).
[29] Heydon, *Evidence: Cases and Materials* (2nd ed., Butterworths, London, 1984) at p.84. See also Goodman, Golding, and Haith, "Jurors' Reaction to Children" (1984) 40 J. Social Issues 104.
[30] The magistrates convicted and executed 19 local women for witchcraft and devil worship, upon foot of the testimony of local girls aged between five and 16 years who claimed to have witnessed the accused levitate, transmorph, speak with animals, fly on broomsticks, and cast spells. The trials were conducted against a backdrop of social fretfulness and heightened superstition; witness statements were prompted by leadings questions; and confessions were extracted from many of the accused anxious to avoid hanging. The episode has since become a potent allegory of the forms that false accusation can take, and the ruinous consequences of the abandonment of fair procedures for evidence and proof. One of the better accounts of the trials and the period is given in: Hill, *A Delusion of Satan: The Full Story of the Salem Witch Trials* (Penguin, London, 1996).

2–09 The climate has changed dramatically in recent years.[31] It is now asserted that children are capable of accurately recollecting and conveying observed events,[32] and that their capacity emerges at a young age.[33] In this light, children are not inherently less reliable than adult witnesses, and it is wrong that they do not benefit from a presumption of competence as do adult witnesses whose potential unreliability or inconsistency is a matter throughout, but not before, the trial. The recent provisions liberalising the rules of child competence and corroboration broadly reflect this view, causing most of the concerns formerly associated with the child's evidence to engender questions of weight rather than admissibility. This transformation in Ireland was prompted chiefly by a concern that if the child was divested of his right to testify, by reason of age or instability, his version of events could not, due to the hearsay rule, be repeated in court by another party such as a child counsellor. The hearsay rule has since been suspended in civil proceedings affecting the "welfare" of a child with respect to statements made by a child prior to the hearing where the child has been judged unfit to testify, pursuant to ss.23–25 of the Children Act 1997.[34] Part III of the Criminal Evidence Act 1992 enables a child witness in sexual offence proceedings to give his evidence via television link from an off-court room, thereby avoiding the stress of having to confront the accused.[35] Under s.4F-G of the Criminal Procedure Act 1967, as inserted by s.9 of the Criminal Justice Act 1999 and supplemented by s.255 of the Children Act 2001,[36] the child may in advance of the trial give his evidence in the District Court by deposition or by videotaped television link, and should he later prove unable to attend the trial for one of the specified reasons (where: dead; unable to attend to give evidence at the trial; prevented from so attending; or refusing to give evidence at the trial due to fear or intimidation), the deposition or videotape is generally admissible in the trial, provided that the accused was in attendance when the original evidence was taken and was in a position to cross-examine the witness.

2–10 The common law rules on child competency retain their currency, notwithstanding provision under s.27 of the Criminal Evidence Act 1992 for the taking of unsworn evidence of children under 14 years. As a general common law rule, persons under 18 years of age are potentially competent

---

[31] Recent analysis argues that society has tended inappropriately to view the child as a miniature or undeveloped adult rather than as an entity qualitatively different from the adult and with a claim to distinct (rather than attenuated) rights: Martin, *The Politics of Children's Rights* (Cork University Press, Cork, 2000).
[32] Accepted by the Law Reform Commission in its report *Child Sexual Abuse* (32–1990): "children's ability to answer questions about witnesses or experienced events is better than both the law and common belief has up to now recognised."
[33] Foley and Johnson, "Differentiating Fact from Fantasy: The Reliability of Children's Memories" (1984) 40 J. Social Issues 33; Jones, "The Evidence of a Three Year Child" [1987] Crim. L.R. 677; Flynn, "Child Witnesses: The Psychological Evidence" [1998] N.L.J. 608.
[34] *cf.* para.**9–43** *et seq.*
[35] *cf.* para.**1–57** *et seq.*
[36] *cf.* paras **1–56, 1–64**.

The Testimony of Witnesses 49

and compellable to testify. Enquiry into the child's competence in the past tended to determine both competence to testify and ability to take the oath: where the child was shown to lack the maturity to give sworn testimony, he was permitted to give unsworn testimony, then of lesser worth. In determining eligibility to give evidence under oath, the common law until relatively recently had required the child to understand the nature and consequences of the oath and to be able to provide a reliable and intelligible account. This required the child to display a full understanding of the religious or divine implications of falsehood under oath. When this level of theological apprehension was finally perceived to be unrealistic and inappropriate, the courts shifted to the lesser test of comprehension of the "impiety of falsehood". The development was marked by the decision in *R. v Brazier*[37] which asserted that in the case of children, "their admissibility depends upon the sense and reason they entertain of the danger and impiety of falsehood, which is to be collected from their answers to questions propounded by the court". The trial judge was expected to ascertain what the child thought would or might happen if he lied. Although judges varied in their formulation of the requirements, it is fair to conclude that until recently the judges required proof that the child could give both an intelligible and reliable account.[38] The additional requirement of reliability may now be considered at odds with the legislative preference for assessment only of the child's ability to give an intelligible account, with respect to giving unsworn evidence in Ireland under s.27 of the 1992 Act and with respect to competence in England.[39]

2–11 The shift from requiring demonstration of reliability to demonstration of intelligibility as a prerequisite to admissibility, and the transfer of reliability concerns to the weight of evidence, is evident in a number of decisions. In *G v DPP*,[40] the English High Court observed that competence is assessed by reference to whether or not "the evidence can be *understood*". The court rejected the submission that the trial judge was wrong to refuse to entertain expert evidence by psychiatrists on this point: whether or not a child is competent is an issue that can properly be understood by the trial judge.[41] Despite this shift, however, trials judges are sometimes apt to consider the question of the child's potential reliability when assessing intelligibility. In *R. v D*,[42] for instance, the Court of Appeal phrased the appropriate test as whether the child

---

[37] (1779) 1 Leach 199 at 238.
[38] In upholding the trial judge's decision to accept the sworn evidence of the complainant in *People (DPP) v T* (1988) 3 Frewen 141 (CCA), Walsh J. commented that "even though, as appears in the evidence, she was to some extent afflicted by Down's Syndrome, there is nothing in the case to suggest that she was unable to understand the nature of the evidence she gave or indeed that her recollection could not be relied upon".
[39] Under the Youth Justice and Criminal Evidence Act 1999, s.53(3), a person is not competent to give evidence in criminal proceedings if it appears to the court that "he is not a person who is able to (a) understand questions put to him as a witness, and (b) give answers to them which can be understood".
[40] [1998] 2 W.L.R. 609 at 614, *per* Philips L.J. (CA) (emphasis added).
[41] *cf.* para.**12–05** *et seq.*
[42] [1995] T.L.R. 592.

was able to understand the questions put to him and to give a coherent, comprehensible account in response, although it acknowledged that the trial judge will also be concerned to establish that the child has the ability to distinguish fact from fiction. When the judge is satisfied on this point, the question of reliability and truth is thereafter relevant to the weight of the evidence as determined by the jury.

2–12 Section 27 of the Criminal Evidence Act 1992[43] provides that "in any criminal proceedings the evidence of a person under 14 years of age may be received otherwise than on oath or affirmation if the court is satisfied that he is capable of giving an intelligible account of events which are relevant to those proceedings". The provisions apply equally to persons of any age suffering a mental disability where capable of giving an *intelligible* account. Intentional falsehood exposes the child to penalties for perjury. The section does not refer to the duty to tell the truth—although this had been identified as a requirement in the earlier common law decisions. By identifying intelligibility as the sole criterion when considering whether to receive the unsworn evidence of a child under 14 years, the legislature signalled a vital shift in policy, which is to encourage and receive the evidence of children, where relevant, with any concerns in individual cases instead affecting the evidence's weight or value by the close of the trial.

2–13 Whether and to what extent 14 years is intended either as a cut-off point or as a guide is less clear. Section 27 must be taken intentionally to have chosen different wording to the otherwise equivalent provision in England (since repealed), by which a witness under 14 years "shall" give unsworn evidence.[44] The provision is clearly enabling, and it does not appear to intend to oust the trial judge's discretion to accept the sworn evidence of a child under 14 years or the unsworn evidence of a child over 14 years, although it may be expected that a stronger case would need to be made for either. The common law tends against operating a fixed chronological scale for competence or capacity with respect to testifying and most other actions.[45]

2–14 There would not appear to be any fixed or absolute rule that the trial judge must always conduct a *voire dire* of the child's competence as a

---

[43] This repeals s.30 of the Children Act 1908, as amended by s.28(2) of the Criminal Justice (Administration) Act 1914, which had provided that if a child of *tender years* did not understand the nature and consequences of the oath, the court could receive his unsworn evidence if it considered that the child had enough intelligence to justify it and understood the duty to speak the truth.

[44] Criminal Justice Act 1988, s.33A (2A), inserted by the Criminal Justice and Public Order Act 1994, Sch.9, para.33; since replaced by the Youth Justice and Criminal Evidence Act 1999, s.53.

[45] The choice of 14 years appears prompted by antecedent English provisions, which in turn responded to a Court of Appeal decision in *R. v Khan* (1981) 73 Cr. App. R. 190; to wit that as a working rule a *voire dire* enquiry of competence should be conducted where the potential witness is younger than 14 years.

preliminary issue.[46] In *Attorney-General v O'Sullivan*,[47] the sworn evidence of a 10-year-old boy formed the basis of a conviction of sodomy. It was held upon appeal that a preliminary test of the boy's competence to testify had not been necessary if the trial judge had already been satisfied of his competence.[48] Where the child is very young, however, the trial judge may be obliged by reason of the circumstances to conduct a specific enquiry into competence under *voire dire*. This is evident in a few recent English decisions. In *DPP v M*,[49] the High Court allowed appeal against conviction for the sexual assault of a four-year-old girl, on the basis that the trial judge should not automatically have refused to ascertain whether or not the complainant was competent, but should have ascertained whether she could give an intelligible, coherent, or comprehensible account.

2–15 Until recently, the Irish courts were not permitted to accept the unsworn testimony of children in civil cases. This was the reluctant conclusion of the Supreme Court in *Mapp v Gilhooley*.[50] Section 28 of the Children Act 1997 eventually addressed this lacuna, and provides that the trial judge may accept the unsworn testimony of children under 14 years in any civil proceedings, if satisfied that the child can give an intelligible account.

The Accused as a Witness

2–16 At common law and in Ireland until the enactment of the Criminal Justice (Evidence) Act 1924,[51] the accused was an incompetent witness for the defence and the prosecution. That such a fundamental transformation in status occurred relatively recently continues to surprise many; further that the old rule assumed that a man speaking in his own defence upon pain of criminal liability would inevitably lie (an assumption that extended to his spouse). Section 1 of the 1924 Act rendered the accused for the first time a competent but non-compellable witness in his own cause.

2–17 The accused remains an incompetent witness for the prosecution, whether charged solely or jointly. He is a competent but non-compellable witness for any co-accused. If tried separately for his part in a jointly committed offence, he retains his non-compellable status—described by Gavan Duffy P. in *Attorney-General v Ingham* as a privilege[52]—with respect to proceedings against the other participants; however, he may be compelled to testify at the behest of the prosecution or defence where he himself no longer stands accused. This is at the discretion of the trial judge, where proceedings are still pending

---

[46] *R. v Hampshire* [1996] Q.B. 1 (CA).
[47] [1930] I.R. 553 (CCA).
[48] The decision was also influenced by counsel's omission at the time to object to the failure to conduct a *voire dire* assessment of competence.
[49] [1998] 2 W.L.R. 604. See also *G v DPP* [1998] 2 W.L.R. 609.
[50] SC, April 23, 1991.
[51] *cf.* paras **1–2, 8–01**. This was modelled on s.1 of the Criminal Evidence Act 1898 enacted in England but not of application in Ireland, *per* s.7(1).
[52] (1947) 82 I.L.T.R. 79 (HC).

against the potential witness for his part in the offences. His compellability may arise in the following circumstances, where: (1) he has pleaded guilty; (2) he has been acquitted (through lack of evidence or by direction of the trial judge); (3) the indictment has been severed (although the trial judge may, and usually will, refuse where proceedings are still pending against him); or (4) a *nolle prosqui* has been entered (which, though not an absolute bar to re-entry of proceedings, is sufficient to render an accomplice compellable). Where the prospective witness has already pleaded guilty, and has agreed to testify against a former accomplice in a separate trial, the preference in England, and to some extent in Ireland,[53] has been to take the evidence of the witness accomplice prior to his sentencing, as a matter of fairness upon the basis that the trial judge in the witness' proceedings will lack a rounded view of the situation in which the two were implicated until all the associated evidence has been received.[54] This, however, exposes the accused in his trial to a prosecution witness motivated to testify by the hope of leniency at the sentencing stage in his own proceedings. The incentive to deceive the court in the expectation of a softer sentence—which is one of the chief concerns of the corroboration rules that govern accomplice witnesses[55]—is exigent, and the recent experiences of accomplice witnesses in the prosecutions that followed the assassination of Veronica Guerin must surely heighten those concerns.[56]

2–18 The non-compellable status of the accused has since proved harmonious with the constitutional right to silence.[57] Under s.1(b), the prosecution may not comment upon the failure of the accused or his spouse to testify, and conviction is likely to be overturned if the prosecution is permitted to do so.[58] It is now well-established that the trial judge must remind the jury of the accused's right to silence, and that his decision not to testify must not be taken to indicate that he is guilty or has anything to hide.[59] It has been accepted, however, that the trial judge is entitled to refer to the failure of the accused to testify, although this must be exercised "discretely"; and conviction may be quashed where it is possible that the jury mistook the reference to mean that the accused had borne an onus to exonerate himself from the charges.[60] Counsel

---

[53] *People (Attorney-General) v Shribman* [1946] I.R. 431 (CCA); approving the taking of an accomplice's evidence in the trial of a former accomplice, prior to the witness' sentencing, although expressing the view that it would be better that sentencing take place first; *cf.* para.**5–21** *et seq.*

[54] As in the case of Charles Bowden, who had been sentenced for drug related activities prior to testifying in *People (DPP) v Ward* Special Criminal Court, November 27, 1998. The accused's conviction was later quashed by the Supreme Court in *Ward v Special Criminal Court and DPP* [1999] 1 I.R. 77 (SC): *cf.* para.**5–24** *et seq.* See also *R. v Weekes* (1980) 74 Cr. App. Rep. 161 (CA): applied in *R. v Palmer* [1994] Crim. L.R. 122 (CA).

[55] *cf.* para.**5–23**.

[56] *cf.* para.**5–24** *et seq.*

[57] *cf.* paras **4–15** and **13–84** *et seq.*

[58] As in *People (DPP) v Maples* (CCA, February 26, 1996).

[59] *cf.* para.**13–84**.

[60] *People (Attorney-General) v Trayers* [1956] I.R. 110 (CCA). A similar view was expressed by Hardiman J. in *People (DPP) v Connolly* [2003] 2 I.R. 1 at 5 (CCA). The trial judge's

for a co-accused is generally free to invite adverse inference, although it is customary for the trial judge to redirect the jury to the core principles that the accused has the benefit of a constitutionally protected right to silence and a presumption of innocence, and that the prosecution bears the burden of proving his guilt beyond reasonable doubt.

2–19 If the accused elects to give evidence in his defence, he is required to take the oath or affirmation and, following his evidence in-chief, to submit to cross-examination. Evidence given by the accused as a witness in his own defence may also constitute evidence against or for any co-accused. Once the accused elects to give testimony, the prosecution and any co-accused may, as of right, cross-examine him with respect to the evidence he has given. The only significant limitation on the right to cross-examine him is contained in s.1(f) of the Criminal Justice (Evidence) Act 1924, which gives the accused his so-called shield of protection from questions tending to reveal his bad character or criminal record.[61] The shield may be lost in certain circumstances, which include giving evidence that implicates a co-accused.[62] The ability of counsel for a co-accused to cross-examine an accused is not dependent upon the loss of his shield, however, a point emphasised in *R. v Hilton*.[63]

2–20 English authority holds that where an accused gives evidence for his defence "what he says becomes evidence for all the purposes of the case including the purpose of being evidence against his co-defendant".[64] The Irish courts have likewise adopted the view that evidence given by one co-accused is cross-admissible for the purposes of the prosecution's case against another co-accused. Reported observations on this issue have been scarce, although such a view is implicit in Gavan Duffy P.'s comments in *Attorney-General v Ingham*: "Whilst a man was free to run the risk of *helping to convict himself on cross-examination by testifying voluntarily for an alleged confederate* who is a co-defendant ... the governing principle was that an accused man charged with other accused, was the only person recognised by law as having the right to decide for or against presenting himself as a witness".[65] Cross-admissibility of evidence in this way sits uneasily with the principle that an accused may not be compelled to testify. On this, Cross and Tapper write that "if it is sound policy to prohibit the prosecution from calling accused persons to testify against each other, it is pertinent to remember that the policy is likely to be circumvented whenever the prosecution is allowed to rely on the statements of an accused elicited in cross-examination as evidence against his co-accused".[66]

---

directions were upheld, since he had emphasised to the jury that they were not to draw adverse inferences from the accused's decision not to testify and that there were "many varied and multiple reasons why an accused person might not elect to give evidence".
[61] *cf.* para.**8–01** *et seq.*
[62] *cf.* para.**8–61**.
[63] [1972] 1 Q.B. 421 (CA).
[64] *R v Rudd* (1948) 32 Cr. App. R. 138 at 140, *per* Humphreys J. See also *R v Hunting and Ward* (1908) 1 Cr. App. R. 177 (CA); *R v Garland* (1941) 29 Cr. App. R. 46 (CA).
[65] (1947) 82 I.L.T.R. 79 at 84 (emphasis added).
[66] *Cross and Tapper on Evidence* (8th ed., Sweet & Maxwell, London, 1995) at p.246.

The Spouse of the Accused as a Witness

2–21 The spouse of the accused was traditionally under the common law incompetent to testify for or against him in criminal proceedings, subject to special exceptions. Although s.1 of the Criminal Justice (Evidence) Act 1924 rendered the spouse of the accused competent to testify at the behest of the accused, and although s.1(b) provided that the prosecution may not invite adverse inferences from the failure of the spouse to testify, the spouse remained non-compellable at the behest of the accused for policy reasons, chiefly to promote marital harmony and to minimise the prospect of intimidation between spouses.[67] This form of marital privacy did not extend under the common law to unmarried partners or to persons in polygamous relationships. It received additional strength in Ireland by reason of the weighty protection bestowed upon the married family by the Constitution, specifically by Arts 41–42. Marital privacy was first identified in its constitutional form by the Supreme Court in *McGhee v Attorney-General*.[68] Although a majority reasoned that the right derived from Art.40(3)(1) as an unenumerated personal right, Walsh J. considered that marital privacy was protected by Art.41 as an incident of the status afforded to the married family. In *People (DPP) v T*[69] Walsh J. expressed the further view that with respect to children born out of wedlock and the compellability of their parents, the child's family "is within the provisions of Art. 40",[70] and may be subject to the court's orders having regard to personal constitutional rights and duties developed under that article. The current rationale for the application of marital privacy to testifying is based upon upholding the institution of marriage, although this basis has come under considerable attack in recent years.[71]

2–22 Section 4 of the Criminal Justice (Evidence) Act 1924 had qualified the rule in s.1(c) by providing that the spouse was competent to testify for the prosecution or co-accused if the offence was a scheduled one (including cruelty to children and various sexual offences). Later, under the Married Women's Status Act 1957, the spouse was rendered competent to testify against the accused where the case concerned the protection and security of family property. Within this framework of piece-meal statutory exception, the spouse could be competent—and, by implication, compellable[72]—to testify with respect to specified offences such as rape or indecent assault but not including buggery or incest, the scenario faced in *People (DPP) v T*.[73]

---

[67] For a thoughtful analysis of the vagaries of these rules under the common law and the Irish constitution, see the judgment of Walsh J. in *People (DPP) v T* (1988) 3 Frewen 141 (CCA).
[68] [1974] I.R. 284 (SC).
[69] (1988) 3 Frewen 141 (CCA).
[70] Following *Re Nicolaou* [1966] I.R. 567 (SC).
[71] Criticised by: the Law Reform Commission (1985; 1989, at p.57); Jackson (1993); O'Connor, "Competence and Compellability of Spouses as Witnesses for the Prosecution" (1985) I.L.T. 204; and Creighton (1990).
[72] According to Walsh J. in *People (DPP) v T* (1988) 3 Frewen 141 at 162 (CCA).
[73] *ibid*.

2–23 The rules were streamlined recently by the Criminal Evidence Act 1992, which repealed the latter provisions. Under Pt IV, the spouse of the accused is in all cases competent for the prosecution (unless jointly charged—subject to that spouse pleading guilty or being acquitted, etc.), for the defence, and for a co-accused. Overturning the common law, the spouse is also generally compellable at the behest of the accused in any criminal proceedings, unless jointly charged.[74] Section 22 controversially provides that the spouse of an accused can be compelled to testify as a witness for the prosecution or co-accused in proceedings for specific offences. In explaining this direction—which ran counter to the Law Reform Commission's proposal that in no circumstances should the spouse of an accused be compellable to testify for the prosecution[75]—the Minister for Justice explained to the Dáil that the Court of Criminal Appeal had indicated in *People (DPP) v T* that common law or statutory rules limiting compellability of the spouse may, at least in cases of suspected child abuse, be unconstitutional.[76] The spouse, where not jointly charged, is now compellable at the behest of the prosecution or the co-accused where the accused is charged with a s.22 offence (of a type often committed in domestic settings):

(1) cases of violence (actual or threatened) to the spouse or to a child of the spouse or the accused or to any child under the age of 17 years at the material time;
(2) cases of sexual offence (as defined in s.2) against a child of either the spouse or the accused or any child under the age of 17 years at the material time; and
(3) attempts or conspiracies to commit, or the aiding, abetting, counselling, procuring, or inciting of the commission of the above two types of offence.

2–24 Under s.22(2), former spouses, unless jointly tried, are compellable at the behest of the accused, the prosecution, or a co-accused in proceedings for all criminal offences, unless the offence was allegedly committed while the former marriage was subsisting *and* it is not a s.22 offence. Thus, the former spouse is now compellable for all s.22 offences whether they allegedly occurred before or after the separation; and for non-s.22 offences only where they allegedly occurred after the separation (to preserve the vestiges of the marital privacy rule). Former spouses include: parties to a decree of divorce under the Family Law (Divorce) Act 1996; a foreign divorce recognised in the State; a nullified marriage; but also parties who have concluded a legally enforceable separation agreement or who have obtained a decree of separation under the Judicial Separation and Family Law Reform Act 1989.

2–25 In decisively breaking with the common law tradition against compellability of spouses, the legislators of the 1992 Act were clearly motivated to protect the constitutional rights of children. Yet by providing compellability

---

[74] Section 23.
[75] LRC, 13–1985, at p.49.
[76] 416 *Dáil Debates* Cols 1287–1288, March 3, 1992. For further discussion of this, see Jackson (1993).

for s.22 offences and withholding it for other offences, and by not instead creating a general discretion in the trial judge to declare compellability on a case-by-case basis, the legislators feared the constitutional implications of a general erosion of the marital privilege. Whilst this concern is inevitable given the wording of Art.41.3.1—which requires the State, including the judiciary, to afford special protection to the institution of marriage[77]—it has the effect of introducing artificiality and, potentially, inequality in the application of the rules of evidence. It also encourages conflict between the sources of law, particularly when one considers the effect of Walsh J.'s decision in *People (DPP) v T*,[78] which must be interpreted to assert that the courts are not restricted to the exceptions set out in the statutes, but can enforce the rights and interests of the respective parties in light of the Constitution:

> "In the form of a common law rule the law has recognised a rule to the effect that one spouse may not give evidence against the other in a criminal prosecution. Insofar as that may be based upon the view that it would tend to rupture family relationships it must be set against that the public interest in the vindication of the innocent who may have been subjected to injustice. As both may be said to fall within the provisions of Art. 41 of the Constitution it is the view of the court that the interests of the child must prevail".

2–26 Of note in this regard is an approach adopted in the Australian State of Victoria, which eschews the categorical approach to compellability in favour of determination upon a case-by-case basis having regard to the range of competing interests in the case.[79] Capable of application to most offences and with respect to spouses, former spouses, *de facto* spouses and domestic partners, the trial judge may decide the issue of the witness' compellability in individual cases having regard to: the type of offence; likely significance of the evidence sought; state of relationship; and the likely impact of testifying upon the spouse.

Witnesses with a Mental Disability

2–27 Formerly under the common law and in the crude parlance of the day, "lunatics" and persons suffering a form of insanity were automatically incompetent and ineligible to testify. In *R. v Hill*,[80] the rules changed to enable the issue of mental incompetence to be investigated by the trial judge in the *voire dire*, having regard to the person's appreciation of the divine implications of the oath and his ability to give an intelligible account.[81] Since then, the

---

[77] 416 *Dáil Debates* Cols 1287–1288, March 3, 1992, at 797, *per* Mr O'Dea.
[78] (1988) 3 Frewen 141 (CCA).
[79] Crimes Act 1958, s.400: for a discussion of this, see Creighton (1990).
[80] (1851) 2 Den. 254. Approved in *People (Attorney-General) v Kehoe* [1951] I.R. 70 (HC).
[81] In *Hill, ibid.*, the witness was an inmate of an asylum who suffered specific delusions that spirits spoke to him, a malady which did not affect his ability to give intelligible sworn evidence.

common law has favoured a test based upon the witness' *specific* competence to provide intelligible evidence, as opposed to a test of his general competence in medical or psychiatric terms. Thus witnesses who have been diagnosed with a mental or psychiatric disability are not automatically incompetent to testify. If the witness' disability does not appear to affect his ability to understand and communicate intelligibly the events in question, the witness may be deemed competent to testify. In *People (DPP) v Gillane*,[82] the irrational belief of a "down and out" that he had had a microchip inserted in his head by doctors, enabling others to read his mind, was not serious enough to require a finding of testimonial incompetence; the admissibility of his evidence was upheld upon appeal. In *People (DPP) v T*[83] a challenge was made to the trial judge's decision to accept the sworn evidence of the complainant, the defendant's 20-year-old daughter, in light of evidence that she appeared to suffer a mild form of Down's Syndrome retardation. In assessing her competence, the trial judge had asked her questions about the oath and the duty to tell the truth. Throughout her testimony, she had displayed sufficient knowledge of the genitalia and sexual organs, and had been assisted later in her evidence by anatomical dolls. The trial judge's decision was upheld by the Court of Criminal Appeal—the girl had clearly understood what she was saying and what she had been asked, and for the most part had suffered from embarrassment when giving her testimony.

2–28 The test of the competence of a person suffering a form of mental impairment has been equated with the test of a child's competence to testify,[84] and recent legislation appears to assume this correlation, although the qualitative differences between the two categories suggest this association is not sustainable. It is of note, however, that in *O'Sullivan v Hamill*,[85] the High Court observed (*obiter*) that in the case of a person suffering a mental disability, the trial judge is obliged to conduct a *voire dire* assessment prior to permitting the witness to give unsworn evidence. This requirement is sensible, although a similarly strict requirement no longer exists with respect to children.

2–29 The provisions under s.27 of the Criminal Evidence Act 1992[86] and s.28 of the Children Act 1997[87] apply equally to enable the reception of unsworn evidence by persons of any age suffering a mental disability. This is also the case for the option of giving evidence by television link under Pt III of the 1992 Act, but not under the Children Act 1997 with respect to civil proceedings affecting the welfare of a child. Whilst the proceedings to which the Children Act 1997 apply are defined by s.20 to include persons suffering a mental disability of any age, "child" is not so defined in ss.21–22 for the purpose of witnesses who are eligible to give evidence by television link under the Act. This appears anomalous, and it has been suggested that it was a draftsman's

---

[82] CCA, December 14, 1998.
[83] (1988) 3 Frewen 141 (CCA).
[84] *R. v Bellamy* (1985) 82 Cr. App. Rep. 222 at 226, *per* Simon Brown J. (CA).
[85] HC, February 25, 1998.
[86] *cf.* para.**2–12**.
[87] *cf.* para.**2–15**.

slip;[88] if this was the case, it was likely precipitated by concern to avoid extending to persons suffering a mental disability the exception to the hearsay rule facilitated for statements by children under ss.23–25. Section 4F-G of the Criminal Justice Act 1999[89] may in some cases apply to render a pre-trial deposition or videotaped television link evidence admissible later in the trial upon the basis that in the interim the witness became incompetent or "unable" to testify due to a mental illness. Clearly the s.4G declaration of general admissibility depends for its effect upon the prosecution acting to secure the witness' evidence in a timely fashion while he is still competent. There does not appear to be any requirement to persuade the District Court to receive the evidence by deposition or by videotaped television link under s.4F, which merely requires that the accused be present and have an opportunity to cross-examine the witness. Section 4G provides that the deposition or videotape is admissible in the trial unless "not in the interests of justice". The effect of this might be thought to cast a burden upon the accused to show cause why the canned evidence should not be admitted in the trial, although in practice both parties will tend to make submissions upon the issue. Recent English case law rightly suggests that this type of provision imposes a duty upon the trial judge to ascertain—as a preliminary issue—whether the evidence is admissible having regard to its quality and to the likely prejudice to the accused.[90] The trial judge's failure to satisfy himself independently of this in *R. v Setz-Dempsey*[91] — specifically that the mental illness might have begun to take root when the witness made the relevant statement—and the likely prejudice to the accused by the unavailability of the witness for cross-examination, were deemed to constitute material errors in the trial.

II. HOSTILE WITNESSES

2–30 In principle, a hostile witness is a witness who at some point after he is sworn in appears "unwilling, if called by a party who cannot ask him leading questions, to tell the truth and the whole truth".[92] An application to the trial judge to deem the witness hostile is often made at a point when it becomes clear to calling counsel that the witness has made a *volte face* with critical implications for the case. This tends to arise where the witness' testimony under oath begins to diverge materially from an account he provided earlier in

---

[88] This view is adopted in Canon and Nelligan, *Evidence* (Round Hall Sweet & Maxwell, Dublin, 2002) at p.74.
[89] *cf.* paras **1–56, 1–64**.
[90] Governed in England by the Criminal Justice Act 1988, s.25, providing that if the court, "having regard to all the circumstances ... is of the opinion that in the interests of justice a statement which is admissible by virtue of section 23 or 24 above nevertheless ought not to be admitted, it may direct that the statement shall not be admitted".
[91] [1994] Crim. L.R. 123 (CA).
[92] *R. v Hayden & Slattery* [1959] V.R. 102 at 103, *per* Sholl J. Stephen, often cited in court on this issue, wrote that the hostile witness was one "not desirous of telling the truth to the court at the instance of the party calling him" (*Digest of the Law of Evidence* (12th ed.) at Art.147).

a pre-trial statement or deposition. Alternatively, the witness becomes "mute" and refuses to answer relevant questions. Tactically, it is often in the best interests of the calling side to have the witness deemed hostile—since in this event, counsel is given a relatively free hand to cross-examine the witness, as an exception to the general common law rule that counsel cannot impeach his own witness. When cross-examining the witness, counsel may attempt to undo the damage done to his case by highlighting the witness' inconsistency and lack of credit; alternatively, where possible, an attempt may be made to bring the witness "back to proof" by reconciling and explaining any points of divergence. Where the witness refuses to assist counsel or the court in the attempt to resolve the impasse, the witness may be ordered into custody for contempt of court pending expurgation of his contempt.[93]

2–31 The hostile witness' pre-trial version of events—whether set out in signed statements, videotaped testimony, or sworn depositions—may not be entered into evidence, except where deemed to be relevant to credibility, or unless admissible by statutory exception such as under Pt III of the Criminal Evidence Act 1992, the Children Act 2001, or the Criminal Justice Act 1999.[94] The witness' sworn testimony in the trial—under examination in-chief and cross-examination—alone constitutes his evidence in the proceedings. Amid public interest in the dramatic collapse of a trial in 2003,[95] the Minister for Justice announced plans to consider making provision to enable juries to consider a witness' pre-trial statement where later repudiated by the witness under oath.[96] In this debate, reference was made to decisions by the Canadian Supreme Court to admit unsworn pre-trial witness statements where the trial judge was satisfied that the statements were reliable in light of surrounding circumstances in the case.[97] This possibility had been addressed by the Law Reform Commission in its working paper on *The Rule Against Hearsay*[98] two decades prior to enactment of the Criminal Justice Act 1999 creating criminal liability and penalties for the intimidation of witnesses and enabling the taking of testimonial evidence in advance of trials. The Commission for good reason rejected the alternative option of receiving unsworn pre-trial statements, which would "[open] the door to the manufacture of evidence or to the perpetuation of previously told lies or inaccuracies".[99] It took the view that a provision of this nature would depart perilously from the best evidence principle, and would likely act counter-productively in deterring witnesses against giving testimony less from their fear of reprisal than their fear of exposing a false or inaccurate account of events. The Commission concluded that such a direction was fraught with risks of prejudice and unfairness for the trial, given that statements are unsworn and made in the absence of the accused, and would certainly precipitate

---

[93] This option was exercised for three witnesses who repudiated their pre-trial statements in *People (DPP) v Keane* (Central Criminal Court, October 30, 2003).
[94] *cf.* paras **1–56, 1–64** *et seq.*
[95] *People (DPP) v Keane* (Central Criminal Court, October 30, 2003).
[96] *Irish Times*, November 5, 2003.
[97] See *R v B (KG)* [1993] 1 S.C.R. 740 (SC).
[98] *The Rule Against Hearsay*, Working Paper 9–1980.
[99] Words used by the Criminal Bar Association: *ibid.* at p.34.

questions of constitutionality and, further, of compliance with the European Convention on Human Rights. Moreover, it implicitly assumes the ability of judicial warnings on the limited probative use of statements to surmount the prejudice caused by their admissibility. Provision already exists to enable intimidated witnesses to give their evidence before the trial, by deposition or via television link, in the presence of the accused under s.4 of the Criminal Procedure Act 1967, as amended by the Criminal Justice Act 1999. Although this is certainly not capable of removing the prospect of intimidation, it is likely to reduce that prospect by enabling evidence to be taken shortly after charges are brought, and by the threat of separate prosecution for the crime of intimidating a witness.

2–32 Upon application by calling counsel, the trial judge decides whether or not the witness is hostile by *voire dire* in the absence of the jury.[100] The *voire dire* avoids occurrence of a dilemma experienced in England, namely where the hostile witness, upon challenge, modifies his testimonial account to bring it in line with his pre-trial account. Where the hostile witness has been "brought back to proof" in this way, should he remain a "hostile" witness for the purposes of his examination and the subsequent weight of his evidence? To a considerable extent, this scenario is foreclosed in Ireland by the requirement of assessment by *voire dire* in the jury's absence. Where the witness' divergence is not material, and is adequately explained and justified, the trial judge may decide that the witness is not hostile; where the divergence is material and the witness is deemed hostile, the limits the trial judge chooses to impose upon examination of this witness are likely to be influenced by the extent of his hostility as appraised during the *voire dire*.

2–33 The trial judge's decision on the hostility of the witness is based to a greater extent upon a live impression of the witness' demeanour and credibility; as such, appellate courts are reluctant, in the absence of clear error, to substitute a new opinion for that of the trial judge. The trial judge's failure to conduct a *voire dire* enquiry on this issue is a stronger basis for appeal, particularly if as a result of the failure the jury were unnecessarily exposed to prejudicial information against the accused. This occurred in *R. v Honeyghon and Sayles*,[101] where the partly successful argument was that if the trial judge had conducted a *voire dire* in the absence of the jury, he would have established that the witness would persist in his refusal to testify, and the jury would not have heard the prejudicial details set out in his pre-trial statement.

2–34 A hostile witness must be contrasted with an *unfavourable witness*, being a witness who has merely disappointed the interests of the calling party. Typically, this witness unintentionally damages or weakens the case by his answers under cross-examination. At common law, counsel could choose to tender further evidence contradicting evidence given by the unfavourable witness. In *Greenough v Eccles*,[102] Williams J. spoke of an inherent right to

---
[100] *People (Attorney-General) v Taylor* [1974] I.R. 97 at 99 (CCA): *cf.* appendix 21.
[101] [1999] Crim. L.R. 221 (CA).
[102] (1859) 5 C.B.N.S. 786.

tender evidence to rebut or contradict one's own witness, which right is founded upon "plain common sense". The calling side cannot, however, proceed to cross-examine a merely *unfavourable* witness. In practice, this is an important distinction, since the hostile witness can be cross-examined—by means of leading questions and reference to pre-trial statements—and by this route discredited or brought "back to proof".[103]

2–35 Although this process is considered for the most part in the context of common law rules and case law, s.3 of the Criminal Procedure Act 1865— which applies equally to civil proceedings[104]—has recognised the right to impeach one's own witness where he "proves adverse", by directing the witness to previous statements inconsistent with the testimonial version he advances in court.[105] Section 3 employed terminology which failed to correspond, then or since, with criminal practice,[106] specifically in its use of the word "adverse".[107] A number of cases, old and recent, have attempted the argument that the trial judge's management of the hostile witness is limited to the circumstances identified in s.3; the response of the courts in Ireland and England, however, has been consistently to affirm the discretion of the trial judge to manage the conduct of the trial and specifically the examination of witnesses. In *R. v Thompson*,[108] the accused argued that his daughter should not have been deemed a hostile witness, since she had refused to answer questions and s.3 was worded to apply only to cases where the witness contradicted a pre-trial statement; it was further argued that if she had not been treated as a hostile witness, she would not have been prompted to accept her pre-trial statement alleging incest by her father. Rejecting the argument, Widgery L.C.J. reasoned that common law principles govern *recalcitrant* witnesses generally, and that it is right and necessary that the trial judge should have discretion in the mode of examination of hostile witnesses so that fairness and justice is best served.

---

[103] See further Newark (1986).
[104] Criminal Procedure Act 1865, s.1.
[105] Section 3 provides: "A Party producing a Witness shall not be allowed to impeach his Credit by general Evidence of bad Character, but he may, in case the Witness shall, in the Opinion of the Judge, prove adverse, contradict him by other Evidence, or, by Leave of the Judge, prove that he has made at other Times a Statement inconsistent with his present Testimony; but before such last-mentioned Proof can be given the Circumstances of the supposed Statement, sufficient to designate the particular Occasion, must be mentioned to the Witness, and he must be asked whether or not he has made such Statement".
[106] Reference in s.3 to the ability to "contradict by other evidence" one's witness who proves "adverse" was decided not to detract from the general common law rule that counsel is free to contradict or rebut his own witness in any case whether the witness is hostile or merely unfavourable: *Greenough v Eccles* (1859) 5 C.B.N.S. 786 at 806, where Cockburn C.J., considering similar provision under s.22 of the Common Law Procedure Act 1854, proposed there had been "a great blunder in the drawing" of the provision.
[107] The term "adverse" failed to enter into common currency, and at any rate was declared synonymous with the word "hostile": *Greenough v Eccles* (1859) 5 C.B.N.S. 786, considering similar provision under s.22 of the Common Law Procedure Act 1854.
[108] (1976) 64 Cr. App. Rep. 96 (CA).

2–36 In *O'Flynn v District Judge Smithwick and DPP*,[109] the appeal was fought upon the basis that the District Judge at the preliminary examination had failed to confine cross-examination of the hostile witness to divergences between his interview with the police and his sworn depositions. It was asserted that s.3 gave the calling side a right to cross-examine the hostile witness with respect to prior inconsistent statements only, but not more broadly upon his bad character. Costello J. in the High Court affirmed the broad common law discretion in the trial judge to supervise cross-examination of the hostile witness, and disagreed that it had been restricted in this way by s.3:

> "[T]he issue of the hostility of a witness is a procedural one and different to that in the substantive proceedings against an accused. The court of trial has a wide discretion as to what matters are relevant on the procedural issue and it is not confined to considering hostility in relation to matters contained in a previous oral statement which a witness may have made".[110]

2–37 When supervising cross-examination of the hostile witness, the trial judge has considerable discretion over the extent of references that may be made to the witness' pre-trial statements.[111] Inconsistent pre-trial accounts may, by common law principle, be received by the court for the limited purpose of bearing upon the witness' lack of credibility,[112] but, owing to the rule against hearsay (which applies in the absence of statutory exception), not to establish the truth of any facts asserted therein.[113] The prosecution may not properly invite the jury to consider a witness' pre-trial account as evidence supplementing or replacing his oral evidence in the trial. Where the hostile witness has repudiated aspects of his prior statement, and is adamant about the truth of his revised account given from the witness box, the revised account constitutes that witness' testimony and in principle the jury is free to act upon it—although invariably it will be argued that the witness is now unworthy of belief, and the trial judge may be obliged to indicate to the jury at the close of the case that the witness' evidence has been shown to be inconsistent and therefore may be unreliable.[114] Thus in most events, the witness' account given testimonially in the trial constitutes that witness' evidence, whether or not probative of the accused's guilt.

2–38 It is consistently recognised that where a pre-trial statement is admitted in evidence to assist the jury with respect to a specific issue, the trial judge is obliged to warn the jury that the statement is not evidence tending to prove

---

[109] [1993] 3 I.R. 589 (HC).
[110] *ibid.* at 596.
[111] Affirmed in *People (Attorney-General) v Hannigan* [1941] I.R. 252 (CCA).
[112] *cf.* para.**3–07** *et seq.*
[113] In *R. v Harris* (1927) 20 Cr. App. Rep. 144 at 147 (CA), Hewart L.C.J. put it that: "it was permissible to cross-examine this girl upon the assertions she had previously made, not for the purpose of substituting those unsworn assertions for her sworn testimony, but for the purpose of showing that her sworn testimony, in the light of those unsworn assertions, could not be regarded as being of importance".
[114] See *R. v Goodway* [1993] 4 All E.R. 894 (CA).

any of the facts at issue in the trial, and that when considering the accused's guilt as charged they must disregard the statement. The failure adequately to direct the jury on this point has led to the quashing of conviction on numerous occasions. For instance, in *R. v Golder, Jones, & Porritt*,[115] a key witness repudiated an earlier deposition in which she incriminated the accused of burglary, and was deemed a hostile witness. She persisted in her denial of the truth of the deposition. The trial judge in his summing-up directed that the jury could, if they chose, act upon the evidence contained in the earlier deposition. Upon appeal, Parker L.C.J. disagreed, citing authority for the common law principle that a witness may be directed to earlier statements to establish that his sworn evidence in court is of little value, but no more. This restriction extended to all earlier sworn statements.[116]

2–39 The potential for manipulation of the hostile witness facility is significant, given that the jury may be presented with information masked as a credibility challenge which in reality attempts to sidestep the hearsay rule by planting a favourable version of events in their minds; therefore, as a general rule, statements are not admitted after the fact of the witness' *volte face* is established. In *People (Attorney-General) v Taylor*,[117] Walsh J. carefully set out the steps a trial judge should follow when a witness is accused of materially contracting his pre-trial statement. In the case, an important witness for the prosecution changed her mind and testified that the accused had stabbed her husband with a pair of scissors and not, as claimed in her statement, with a knife. The trial judge approved the request to deem her a hostile witness. In this scenario, as is sometimes the case, the witness' change of mind on one aspect of her account was a blessing in disguise for the prosecution, enabling it to discredit her testimony, part of which would have laid the basis for the defence of provocation (since scissors suggested unpremeditated action). The critical error in the trial, identified by the Court of Criminal Appeal, was to admit the witness' pre-trial statement in evidence without explaining to the jury that it was not evidence probative of any of the facts at issue in the case. In these circumstances, the appellate court could not be certain that the defence of provocation would have been rejected had the statement not been admitted in evidence. According to Walsh J., the procedure that should be adopted is as follows.

2–40 (1) The trial judge should consider whether the witness is hostile in the absence of the jury. (2) In the presence of the jury, it should then be put to the witness that he made an earlier statement materially contradicting his present testimony. (3) If the witness persists to deny the earlier account, or to recognise the contradiction, he should be asked to step down, and the garda who took the statement should be called to testify to its authenticity, without referring to the contents of the statement. (4) The witness should then be recalled, the

---

[115] [1960] 1 W.L.R. 1169 (CA).
[116] See also *People (Attorney-General) v Cradden* [1955] I.R. 130 at 138 (CCA); *R. v Darby* [1989] Crim. L.R. 817 (CA); *R. v Thomas* [1985] Crim. L.R. 445 (CA).
[117] [1974] I.R. 97 (CCA): *cf.* appendix 21.

statement produced for his identification, and his attention drawn to the relevant passage. (5) If the witness accepts the contradiction, this is as far as counsel may go in terms of impugning his credibility since the witness has admitted his inconsistency and change of mind. At the trial judge's discretion, and mindful of potential prejudice to the defence, the statement may be put in evidence, as relevant to whether the witness' testimony ought to be believed, although this is not strictly necessary where the witness has admitted the inconsistencies. (6) If the witness persists in denying a contradiction between his earlier statement and present testimony, then the statement may be put in evidence to enable the jury to establish whether the witness made a contradictory statement before the trial and whether therefore he is to be believed under oath. (7) In any case where the statement is put in evidence, the jury should be reminded that the statement is not proof of anything it asserts, nor is it evidence probative of guilt, but is relevant in the trial only to enable the jury to determine if the witness' testimonial account under oath is to be credited with any weight.

III. REFRESHING A WITNESS' MEMORY

2–41 A dedicated rule permits some witnesses to refresh their memory in the witness box by drawing upon contemporaneous notes. The rule emerged as an exception to the general principle that courtroom testimony must be given by a witness *de novo*, unsupported by pre-trial statements and documents. It is founded on a recognition that certain witnesses, such as gardaí and doctors, may be expected to forget the finer details of a single case, particularly where there has been a lengthy interval between the incident and the trial, and that in these circumstances it is inappropriate to test their memory of events in court without recourse to notes compiled closer to the time of the events under trial. The rationale for the rule was well put by Bridge L.J: "We have all, from time to time, seen the plight of an apparently honest witness, subjected to captious questioning about minor differences between his evidence in the witness box and the statement he made long ago and has never seen since, although his tormentor has it in his hand and has studied it in detail".[118]

2–42 Although the rule is designed to serve parties who have ongoing experience with different suspects and clients, and whose true recollection of events is restricted to notes and records made at the relevant time, any witness (except the accused) is permitted to refresh his memory in the witness box by consulting notes, provided that the notes were made more or less contemporaneously with the material facts.[119] Permission should first be obtained from

---

[118] *R. v Westwell* [1976] 2 All E.R. 812 at 814 (CA).
[119] Controversially, in the US throughout the 1960s and 1970s it was common practice to accept hypnotically induced recollections of complainants—in many cases purporting to recall buried experiences of sexual abuse—by an analogy with notes used as an aid to memory. The practice was briefly endorsed in England following the influential findings of Dr Howard and Professor Ashworth in "Same Problems of Evidence Obtained by Hypnosis" [1980] Crim. L.R. 469; but, at least with respect to complainants, it has since been discredited as unreliable and ungovernable. Conviction was quashed in *R. v*

The Testimony of Witnesses 65

the trial judge.[120] It is customary to ascertain from the witness that the events were fresh in his mind when he wrote the notes, that the information therein is the only true source of his recollection, and that the notes were made by, or under the supervision of, the witness. In considering whether the statement is sufficiently contemporaneous, the court will be concerned to ascertain that it was made at the first practicable opportunity or shortly thereafter, and that, when written down, the events were fresh in his mind. Although the nature of the information will be relevant to these issues—irregular, vivid occurrences may be expected to fade slower from memory—the actual time lag in the case is likely to be of most concern to the court. In England, this aspect has formed the basis of numerous appeals, though not in Ireland. In *R. v Graham*,[121] the Court of Appeal considered 27 days too long to constitute contemporaneity; however, in *R. v Fotheringham*, it accepted that a statement written 22 days after the events in question was contemporaneous.[122]

2–43 The rule is best considered to apply to the witness as he is giving testimony, and would be ungovernable at present if it sought to proscribe the witness' recourse to *aides-memoires* prior to being called as a witness. With respect to the rereading of statements or notes prior to the trial, it was acknowledged in *R. v Westwell*[123] that there is no general rule that witnesses may not inspect statements before giving their testimony, although the prosecution should inform the defence if any of its witnesses have been given access to their statements prior to the trial. *Westwell* was approved in *People (DPP) v Donnelly*,[124] where the Court of Criminal Appeal regarded this issue as unproblematic, save for the case of a witness who learns his statement by heart and then recites it in evidence. *Westwell* had further cautioned, however, that although a witness may ask, or accept an offer, to reread his statement shortly before the trial, in some cases—if there be "some sinister or improper purpose" behind the request—he ought not to be allowed to do so.

2–44 In *R. v Da Silva*,[125] the Court of Appeal addressed the rereading issue

---

Browning [1994] Crim. L.R. 227 (CA) in a case where a chief witness had been hypnotised so that she could recollect the registration number of the car she observed at the scene of the murder. The appeal succeeded on the grounds that the prosecution had failed to disclose the use of hypnosis or to follow Home Office guidelines of the day; *cf.* paras **12–10** *et seq.*

[120] The failure to do so prompted the District judge in *DPP v Clifford* (July 22, 2002) to declare the witness' evidence inadmissible and to strike out proceedings against the accused. The High Court considered that a dismissal of the charges had been inappropriate since the garda witness had been entitled to draw from his notebook. The court did not expressly address the necessity to obtain advance permission from the trial judge for reference to notes, although such a request appears implicit in the rule by virtue of its constant threat to the rule against hearsay.

[121] [1973] Crim. L.R. 628 (CA).
[122] (1976) 119 S.J. 613 (CA). This was considered to be "the utmost limit" by Newark and Samuels (1978) at p.40, n.2.
[123] [1976] 2 All E.R. 812 (CA).
[124] CCA, February 22, 1999.
[125] [1990] 1 W.L.R. 31 (CA).

by adding a new rule permitting witnesses to consult non-contemporaneous notes in court prior to giving their testimony. If the witness establishes to the court's satisfaction that the non-contemporaneous note is necessary to refresh his memory of a past event, that the note represents his true recollection of the event, and that he did not consult the note before entering the witness box (this last requirement since abandoned for practical reasons),[126] the witness may be given an opportunity (either before or during the trial) to reread it, but where the note is not a contemporaneous one, he is not permitted to consult it whilst giving testimony from the witness box.

2–45 The phrase "refreshing a witness' memory" has become common currency in evidence law, suggesting that notes are used by a witness in a mnemonic capacity; the practice, however, is to apply it much less discriminately, sidestepping the hearsay rule, by enabling a witness to consult notes less as a spur to memory than an original supply of information that was never fully committed to the witness' memory.[127] This was judicially acknowledged as far back as 1864, when Hayes J. observed that "it is a very inaccurate expression; because in nine times out of ten the witness' memory is not at all refreshed; he looks at the document again and again; and he recollects nothing of the transaction; but, seeing that it is in his own handwriting, he gives credit to the truth and accuracy of his habits, and though his memory is a perfect blank, he nevertheless undertakes to swear to the accuracy of his notes".[128] As such, the use of notes ought to be strictly minimised and carefully vetted in judicial proceedings. In principle, notes do not constitute or supplement the witness' evidence, since a dedicated exception to the hearsay rule has not been provided for contemporaneous notes, though often proposed. Although practice sometimes belies the theory in this regard, the notes are permitted only to refresh the witness' memory and to enable him to give more accurate evidence orally from the witness box. The judge, and sometimes the jury, are permitted to inspect copies of the notes while the witness is giving his testimony, but in such cases the notes are withdrawn from the jury since they are not probative evidence in the case and their admission may engender unnecessary prejudice.

2–46 Because the notes are inadmissible as probative evidence, they are incapable of supplying corroborating evidence. The possiblity that the jury were confused on this issue was critical to the appeal in *R. v Virgo*.[129] The accused was the head of the Obscene Publications Squad, charged with

---

[126] *R. v South Ribble Magistrates' Court Ex p. Cochrane* [1996] 2 Cr. App. R. 544.
[127] e.g. *Dyer v Best* (1866) 4 H. & C. 189, where a witness was permitted to refer to a newspaper account which he recorded the day when another set of proceedings had been taken and which he had read at the material time.
[128] *Lord Talbot de Malahide v Cussack* (1864) 17 I.C.L.R. 213 at 220. In general, the Irish courts do not consider this problematic. In *Northern Banking Co Ltd v Carpenter* [1931] I.R. 268 at 276 (SC), Kennedy C.J. reasoned that "if the witness can say that, from seeing his own writing, he is sure of the fact stated therein, such statement by him is admissible in evidence of the fact".
[129] (1978) 67 Cr. App. R. 323 (CA).

conspiracy and corruption by accepting bribes. The chief prosecution witness was a self-confessed dealer in pornography; since he constituted an accomplice at law, his evidence attracted corroboration rules.[130] The witness was permitted to refresh his memory by drawing from diaries he had kept around the time of his dealings with the accused. The trial judge directed the jury that the diary entries constituted powerful evidence against the accused, and that although they could not corroborate the accomplice's evidence, since they did not technically constitute evidence in the case, they were nonetheless very important. Because of the prejudicial and damaging effect of this direction for the accused, conviction was overturned by the Court of Appeal. The court stressed that the notes should never have been referred to by the trial judge when discussing proof of the charges and corroboration concerns.

2–47 Opposing parties are free to cross-examine the witness upon his testimonial reliance on notes;[131] but since the notes are not intended to go into evidence, cross-examination should be confined to specific passages in the notes adverted to by the witness. If cross-examination with respect to the notes, and the witness' inconsistency, becomes detailed, the trial judge may order that the notes be received by the jury as evidence relevant to the witness' credibility, but not as probative evidence, owing to the rule against hearsay. In this sense, rigorous examination or cross-examination upon the notes may prove counter-productive. A salutary warning was given in *Virgo* by Geoffrey Lane L.J: "There is always a danger in circumstances such as these when attention has been focused on a particular document for a long period of time, and when the document has been subjected to a minute and line by line analysis, as these diaries were, that the document will achieve an importance which it does not warrant".[132]

2–48 Related issues have emerged in cases where witnesses informally gave information to the police—such as the registration number of a car—but later at the trial could not remember the number and were forced to rely on what the policeman recorded. In such cases, the record had not been given, confirmed, and signed in the presence of police officers under controlled conditions such as exist for the taking of witness statements. A number of English decisions ruled that the evidence was defeated by the hearsay rule; a détente was eventually signalled by the decision in *R. v Kelsey*,[133] where the Court of Appeal decided that the rule is excluded where the observer had an opportunity at the time to verify his account by either rereading the record taken by the policeman or hearing it read back to him. In that event, the witness may be allowed to refresh his memory from the policeman's record without infringing

---

[130] *cf.* para.5–21 *et seq.*
[131] According to *Queen v Edwards* (1983) 77 Cr. App. R. 191 (CA), the right to cross-examine a witness with respect to his dependence upon notes extends to notes a witness was seen consulting outside the doors of the court before he gave his testimony. The court did not state how long the gap before the testimony must be to render the rule inoperative.
[132] (1978) 67 Cr. App. R. 323 at 328 (CA).
[133] (1982) 74 Cr. App. R. 213 (CA).

the hearsay rule. Where the policeman did not himself see the vehicle, the note of the witness' observations is inadmissible with respect to his own evidence upon an application of the rule against hearsay.

2–49 The right to pre-trial disclosure and a reasonable opportunity in advance to inspect the notes a witness hopes to consult in the trial—stricter than the general practice of revealing notes such as garda notebook entries on the morning of trials—has not so far been required under the Criminal Procedure Act 1967.[134] The failure to provide adequate advance notice, however, particularly in cases where the notes contain extraneous prejudicial information, may cause the trial judge to decide against recourse to the notes in the trial.[135]

IV. THE RULE AGAINST NARRATIVE

General Principles

2–50 According to the rule against narrative, a witness may not repeat, or be asked about, a statement he made prior to the trial or hearing for the purpose of showing *consistency* with his testimonial version of events; nor may a second witness give evidence of any statement made prior to the trial by the first witness which is consistent with the testimony given by the first witness in the trial. The rule is wedded to the logic that witnesses ought to be prevented from manufacturing consistent evidence by effecting or repeating self-serving statements to a number of people before the trial, in a bid to lend a false consistency and credibility to the version they later advance in court. The rule endures today, but will continue to do so only to the extent that statute does not provide for the general or limited admissibility of pre-trial statements.[136] As such, the rule against narrative co-exists with the rule against hearsay. Each rule is directed at statements made prior to the trial, and reflects the age-old

---

[134] *McHugh v Brennan & DPP* (HC, April 14, 2000).
[135] Newark and Samuels, "Refreshing Memory" [1978] Crim. L.R. 408 at 415.
[136] The Civil Evidence Act 1995 in England provided for the general admissibility of pre-hearing statements in civil proceedings, subject to due notice to the opposing party and to the requirement of competence; in all criminal cases, a witness can opt to submit a witness statement, furnished to the other side in advance of the trial, *in lieu* of examination in-chief, although the statement only becomes evidence when the witness verifies it on oath at the trial and has made himself available for cross-examination (R.S.C., Ord.20, rr.20–24). Irish law has not so far provided for the general admissibility of pre-trial or pre-hearing statements, and has opted instead to focus on alternative means of securing the traditional forms of testimonial evidence from certain classes of vulnerable witnesses, such as children and intimidated witnesses—during the trial by television link, or prior to the trial by means of deposition or videotaped television link evidence, in the presence of the accused and subject to a right to cross-examine: *cf.* paras **1–56, 1–64**. In civil proceedings affecting the welfare of a child, the Children Act 1997 provides that statements made by a child prior to the hearing are admissible in the hearing *in lieu* of testimony where the child is too young or otherwise unable to testify; the 1997 Act also enables a child witness to give his evidence via television link with the involvement of an intermediary: *cf.* para.**1–55**.

common law fear of manufactured evidence. The narrative rule, however, directs itself to the attempt to refer to a pre-trial statement to establish the witness' *credit*, through consistency; whereas the hearsay rule directs itself to the attempt to refer to a pre-trial statement as evidence *probative* of its content and the facts at issue—a distinction of consequence chiefly for the use to which the statement may properly be put where admitted, for one reason or another, in the trial or hearing. There is, clearly, a thin line between the two rules, especially given that the hearsay rule is in part founded on the principle against self-corroboration,[137] although this aspect of the hearsay rule is directed at the attempt to introduce consistent pre-trial statements as *further* probative evidence.[138]

2–51 The courts have recognised two general exceptions to the rule against narrative.[139] First, where the statement was made at the time of, or contemporaneous to, the material events, it may be admitted as a *res gestae* exception—an exception shared by the rule against hearsay[140]—upon the basis that such a statement is likely to have been a spontaneous uncritical response to the event in circumstances where the risk of contrivance is low. Second, where it is put to the accused under cross-examination that he concocted his version of events, the statement may be admissible to rebut the challenge to his credibility.[141] Under the first exception, the statement is entered into evidence without restriction. As such, it is capable of constituting evidence probative of any fact expressed or implied in the statement. Under the second exception, the statement constitutes evidence bearing only upon the witness' credibility, and may not be treated as probative of anything asserted in the statement; it is incumbent upon the trial judge to explain the distinction to the jury in this event.

The Complaint in Sexual Offence Cases

2–52 As a special exception to the rule against narrative, reference was permitted to the complainant's first complaint of sexual offence in cases of rape, for the purpose of rebutting the adverse inference a court could, and was likely to, draw when trying a case in which an immediate "hue and cry" was absent. Although memorably castigated by Oliver Wendell Holmes as "a

---

[137] *cf.* paras **9–03, 9–05**.
[138] The distinction is occasionally misconstrued: *e.g. R. v Makanjoula* [1995] 1 W.L.R. 1348 at 1355 (CA), where Lord Taylor wrongly identified the complaint in sexual offence cases as an exception to the rule against hearsay and not instead narrative.
[139] *R. v Roberts* [1942] 1 All E.R. 187 (CA). The court applied the rule to a conversation the accused had with his father two days after the deceased was shot, and in which he mentioned that his defence would be based on accident. The rule against narrative precluded either the accused or his father referring to this conversation.
[140] *cf.* para.**9–59** *et seq.*
[141] *cf.* paras **2–58, 3–01** *et seq.* In *Flanagan v Fahy* [1918] 2 I.R. 361 (CA), the trial judge had properly allowed the witness' employer to testify to an earlier conversation in which the witness had given an account consistent with his testimony, since this was admissible to rebut an allegation by the plaintiff that the witness had fabricated his allegations of fraud and bribery in the execution of the contended will.

perverted survival of the ancient requirement that a woman should make hue and cry"[142]—in practice, a prerequisite to prosecution under the common law until the eighteenth century—it has nonetheless survived as a special exception, now a rule in its own right, rendering the fact and details of a complaint admissible in sexual offence proceedings upon proof that the complaint was made voluntarily and at the first reasonable opportunity.

2–53 First articulated in its modern form in *R. v Lillyman*[143]—the decision most identified with the early complaint rule in England—it has since been extended to sexual offences not involving the issue of consent,[144] such as unlawful carnal knowledge of a minor, and all sexual offences so defined by statute and the common law. Application of the rule to male complainants was confirmed in *R. v Camelleri*.[145] The rule has not been extended beyond the remit of sexual offences, although its rationale may be considered equally to apply to cases of violence. It is perhaps best explained beyond reference to its historical lineage, but by the nature of sexual offence proceedings, which tend to hinge critically upon credibility and consistency of the witnesses. The rule has been very strictly applied by the courts in Ireland and England, however, where admissibility depends upon evidence that the complaint was made promptly. In this sense, the rule assumes that where issues of credibility are critically important to the trial, greater is the necessity to guard against the threat of affected consistency. The preventative approach to evidence of the complaint and its surrounding circumstances was evident in *People (DPP) v Brophy*,[146] where O'Flaherty J. emphasised that in sexual offence proceedings, where the evidence is often contentious and uncorroborated, the jury must be absent when the trial judges considers whether evidence of the complaint is admissible.

2–54 The formal purpose of the early complaint rule is to facilitate proof of *consistency* between the complainant's present version of events and the first complaint, as a matter of credit. On this basis, it has traditionally been reasoned that the rule applies only where the complainant testifies.[147] In *People (DPP) v Gavin*,[148] the Court of Criminal Appeal affirmed the credit-function of the rule by finding that details of the complaint should not have been admitted where they were not fully consistent with the complainant's evidence. Although divergent pre-trial statements are usually sought to be admitted by the defence, in *Gavin* details of the complaint and the description of the assault had been given by a garda appearing as a witness for the prosecution. In this instance, the evidence had wrongly been allowed to supplement the complainant's sworn testimony.

---

[142] *Commonwealth v Cleary* (1898) 172 Mass. 175 at 176.
[143] [1896] 2 Q.B. 167. See discussion in *White v The Queen* [1998] 3 W.L.R. 992 (PC).
[144] *R. v Osborne* [1905] 1 K.B. 551.
[145] [1922] 2 K.B. 122.
[146] [1992] I.L.R.M. 709 at 716 (CCA): *cf.* appendix 41.
[147] *Sparks v R.* [1964] A.C. 964 (A.C.); *White v Queen* [1998] 3 W.L.R. 992 at 995 (P.C.).
[148] [2000] 4 I.R. 557 (CCA). See also *People (DPP) v Jethi* (CCA, *ex tempore*, February 7, 2000).

2–55 Once the fact of the complaint has been deemed admissible, so too are the details of the complaint as communicated to the third party, "subject to the discretion of the trial judge to prevent unnecessary prejudicial repetition".[149] Where the prosecution wishes to emphasise that the complainant made an early complaint, the person to whom the complaint was made must give evidence of this fact under examination in-chief. It is not appropriate for the complainant to make reference to having discussed the incident with any persons not in court to testify to this fact. If such reference is made, the trial judge should direct the jury to ignore it. This very scenario led to the quashing of conviction in *White v Queen*.[150]

2–56 In cases where the allegations in the initial complaint are repeated in court, the trial judge must direct the jury at the close of the trial that they may consider the details to be relevant only to establish consistency in the complainant's story, but that they are not to be considered as evidence tending to prove the truth of the complainant's account[151] nor to corroborate the complainant's sworn testimony[152]—so emphasised in *People (Attorney-General) v Cradden*[153] and *People (DPP) v MA*[154] where *Lillyman* was applied and convictions overturned.

2–57 Given that the complaint is admitted as an exception to the rule against narrative, which aims to prevent witnesses manufacturing *consistent* evidence, the law generally requires proof that the complaint was voluntarily made at the earliest or first reasonable opportunity. The *Lillyman* principles were endorsed by the Court of Criminal Appeal in *People (DPP) v Brophy*.[155] The prosecution had conceded at an early stage in the trial that the complaint had not been made at the first reasonable opportunity, insofar as the complainant had met her mother shortly after the alleged indecent assault, and had reported nothing nor looked distressed, and had made no complaint until later in the evening when she discussed the matter with school friends and her father. *Brophy* was applied in *People (DPP) v Synott*,[156] where it was "quite clear" to Finlay C.J. that a complaint delayed by one year was inadmissible. This strict

---

[149] *DPP v Brophy* [1992] I.L.R.M. 709 at 715, *per* O'Flaherty J. (CCA): *cf.* appendix 41.
[150] [1998] 3 W.L.R. 992 (CA).
[151] See *R. v Whitehead* [1929] 1 K.B. 99.
[152] In *DPP v Kirwan* (CCA, October 19, 1998)—the second trial of the accused arising from the proceedings—the trial judge inadvertently referred to the date when the complainant first made her complaint, despite the fact that an appellate court had earlier ruled that this complaint was inadmissible by reason of delay and that a new jury would have to be empanelled. The trial judge's instructions to the second jury that they were to disregard what he had just said about the complaint was considered by the Court of Criminal Appeal to be effective in the circumstances to undo the error.
[153] [1955] I.R. 130 (CCA). Conviction was also quashed upon this basis in *People (DPP) v Gavin* [2000] 4 I.R. 557 (CCA), with respect to the trial judge's omission to direct the jury not to regard the complaint as corroborative evidence of the complainant's testimony.
[154] [2002] 2 I.R. 601 (CCA). The failure of defence counsel to requisition the trial judge upon this omission was not a bar to appeal on such a fundamental issue.
[155] [1992] I.L.R.M. 709 (CCA): *cf.* appendix 41.
[156] CCA, May 29, 1992.

approach to timing was adopted also in *People (DPP) v Kiernan*,[157] where the complaint was deemed inadmissible because the complainant had not told her boyfriend about the rape until two days later despite having met him the previous day. When considering whether the complaint was made at the first *reasonable* opportunity, the courts have sometimes, but rarely, excused short periods of delay where adequately justified. In *People (DPP) v Roughan*,[158] a delay of one day by an adult complainant was excused in the light of the extreme pressure she was under following the incident, since, according to her account, she had been raped by her sister's partner, a man described as having a violent temper, one night when she and her husband had visited.

2–58 The complaint may also be deemed inadmissible for lack of spontaneity due to prompting, where the allegation was first conveyed in response to another person's demands[159] or in response to leading questions.[160] The principle only precludes questions of a suggestive or leading nature (such as "did that man do this to you?" or "have you been raped?"). According to Ridley J.,[161] in considering this question, the trial judge may consider: "the character of the question put, as well as other circumstances, such as the relationship of the questioner to the complainant ... If the circumstances indicate that but for the questioning there probably would have been no voluntary complaint, the answer is inadmissible". A "but for" approach appears unnecessarily limiting, however, and the fact alone that the person to whom the complaint was made actively or passively precipitated the complaint ought not automatically foreclose admissibility. The Court of Criminal Appeal so ruled in *Roughan*[162] in a case where the complainant had initiated a conversation with her husband by the words "Denis is no gentleman", about which her husband enquired, in response to which questions the complainant made her first complaint.

2–59 It has been recognised in some cases that the complainant's pre-trial complaint or statement may alternatively be admissible for the limited purpose of rebutting an allegation or claim made by the accused. It is unclear to what extent this is permissible in Ireland. It is surely open to reason that a general allegation by the defence that the complainant has fabricated or falsified his account—a common adversarial assertion where consent is claimed in defence—ought not to cause such a dramatic shift in the rules of procedure and evidence applicable in the case. (This perspective appears harmonious with the approach of the Irish courts in declining to interpret the accused's repudiation of a confession as an imputation sufficient to lose him his shield

---

[157] CCA, March 11, 1994. See also *People (DPP) v McD* (CCA, July 27, 1994); *R. v Islam* [1999] 1 Cr. App. R. 22, *per* Buxton L.J. (CA); and *R. v Valentine* [1996] 2 Cr. App. R. 213, *per* Roch L.J. (CA).
[158] CCA, June 23, 1997.
[159] *R. v Norcott* [1917] 1 K.B. 347.
[160] *R. v Merry* (1990) 19 Cox C.C. 442.
[161] *R. v Osborne* [1905] 1 K.B. 551 at 556. In the case, the young girl made the complaint to her friend after she was asked why she was going home; the information in response was deemed voluntary and admissible.
[162] CCA, June 23, 1997.

of protection from questions on bad character.)[163] On the other hand, the trial judge may consider that the complaint has become an integral aspect of the trial by reason of how the case has been run; by this route, a complaint not made "early" enough permissibly to be narrated in evidence may yet be admitted to rebut a claim by the accused that the allegations have been fabricated. This occurred unwittingly as a consequence of the defence's trial strategies in *R. v Tyndale*.[164] The complainant, aged 11 years old, had delayed informing her mother that her mother's former boyfriend had sexually interfered with her until the mother's relationship with the man was at an end. Although there was evidence that the girl had confided in her sister and brother closer to the time, the trial judge ruled from the outset that the complaints were inadmissible upon the basis that they were not shown to have been made at the first reasonable opportunity. When during the trial the accused asserted that the girl's complaint was prompted by a family vendetta against him, the trial judge decided that the complaint could be admitted as evidence relevant to rebut the specific defence allegation.

2–60 The complaint rule/exception is apt to work mischief and injustice in many cases by virtue of its continued requirement of immediate or early hue and cry. Although the courts have excused delays in the *prosecution* of sexual offences—where justified (*inter alia*) by the tender age of the complainant or the complainant's unawareness that the sexual acts were improper;[165] or by the relationship of dominion exercised over the complainant by an elder[166]—they have resisted attempts to broaden the common law rule to permit admissibility in the trial of the fact and details of the consistent complaint. In *R. v Birks*,[167] the Court of Appeal reluctantly enforced the rule in its strict form, resisting submissions that it should be broadened to accommodate what we now know about the many ways in which traumatic experiences of abuse are buried by complainants. Although the court felt bound by earlier authorities, in which very short delays had rendered complaints inadmissible, the court nodded in the direction of the legislature, and expressed sympathy for the view that the law should change to enable juries to hear evidence explaining the circumstances of the complaint and the reasons for delaying it, so that the jury may construct a more complete narrative and chronology of events. In its current form, the rule may appear to reflect a sense that proof of an early

---

[163] *cf.* para.**8–55** *et seq.*
[164] [1999] Crim. L.R. 320 (CA).
[165] e.g. *O'Connor v Smith* (HC, November 17, 1994) where the 13-year-old complainant made her first complaint against her uncle one year after the offence. See also *J. O'C. v DPP* [2000] 3 I.R. 478 (SC).
[166] e.g. *B v DPP* [1997] 3 I.R. 140 (SC), where prosecution was brought some 20–30 years after the last alleged incident of abuse, and was justified upon the basis that the accused's daughters had delayed in airing their complaints until their mother died, so to spare her the inevitable shame.
[167] [2003] Crim. L.R. 401 (CA). Conviction was overturned in a case where the complaint had wrongly been admitted. The complaint had been made a number of months after the last alleged abuse, triggered when the complainant watched a television programme addressing child sexual abuse.

complaint continues to be considered important to proof of sexual offences, despite broad acceptance of the view that victims of rape often do not articulate their experience in the immediate aftermath.[168] In its application, the rule has been accused of wrongly assuming that proof of a complaint made some time after the alleged offence is not relevant to showing consistency; further, in proceedings where the complaint may not be referred to, of risking adverse inferences against the complainant (the latter to be avoided by prohibiting reference in front of the jury to the necessity to conduct a *voire dire* on the issue or to the result of that enquiry). This is neither the assumption nor logic of the rule of early complaint, which in its current, rather straitened form is best understood in terms of its formal lineage as an exception to the rule against narrative: a rule that justifies exceptions by requiring preliminary evidence to establish that the risks the statement was contrived or manufactured are low. It is anomalous in practice, however, and utterly ill-suited to the realities of sexual abuse and the trying of those offences. Omission of reference to the circumstances surrounding the first making of the complaint, and explanations for its delay, critically disrupts the narrated chronology of relevant events, and as such is likely to confound rather than protect juries when embarking upon an objective appraisal of the issues of fact and credit in cases of alleged sexual offence. Such trials would be better served by the creation of an inclusionary discretionary rule permitting limited credit-relevant admissibility of the complaint subject to the trial judge's discretion to exclude it in the "interests of justice".

---

[168] Adler, *Rape on Trial* (London, Routledge & Kegan Paul, 1987).

Further Reading

Adler, *Rape on Trial* (Routledge & Kegan Paul, London, 1987).
Birch, "Children's Evidence [1992] Crim. L.R. 263.
Creighton, "Spouse Competence and Compellability" [1990] Crim. L.R. 34.
Foley, "The Doctrine of Recent Complaint Revisited" (2001) 11 I.C.L.J. 20.
Foley, "Hearsay and Recent Complaint" (2001) 15 I.L.T. 234.
Jackson, "Part IV of the Criminal Evidence Act 1992" (1993) 15 D.U.L.J. 202.
Law Reform Commission, *Report on Competence and Compellability of Spouses as Witnesses* (13–1985).
Law Reform Commission, *Report on Child Sexual Abuse* (32–1990).
Lewis and Mullis, "Delayed Criminal Prosecutions for Childhood Sexual Abuse: Ensuring a Fair Trial" (1999) 115 L.Q.R. 265.
McEwan, "Children's Testimony: More Proposals for Reform" [1988] Crim. L.R. 813.
Mundy, "Calling a Hostile Witness" [1989] Crim. L.R. 866.
Murphy, "Previous Consistent and Inconsistent Statements: A Proposal to Make Life Easier for Juries" [1985] Crim. L.R. 270.
Newark, "The Hostile Witness and the Adversary System" [1986] Crim. L.R. 441.
Newark and Samuels, "Refreshing Memory" [1978] Crim. L.R. 408.
Spencer, "The Evidence of Children—the English Experience" (1997) *Bar Review* 382.
Spencer and Flin, *Evidence of Children: The Law and the Psychology* (Blackstone Press, London, 1993).

CHAPTER 3

CHALLENGES TO THE CREDIBILITY OF WITNESSES

I. The Collateral Issue Rule	3–01
II. A Witness' Previous Inconsistent Statements	3–07
III. A Witness' Bias	3–10
IV. A Witness' Previous Convictions	3–13
V. A Witness' Lack of Veracity	3–15
A Witness' Reputation for Lies	3–15
Lies Told by the Accused	3–18
VI. A Witness' Physical or Mental Disability	3–22
VII. Sexual History Evidence	3–23
Admissibility under the Common Law	3–23
Current Provisions	3–25
Reasons for Limiting Use of Sexual History Evidence	3–30
The English Experience	3–34
VIII. Pre-trial Disclosure by the Prosecution	3–38

I. THE COLLATERAL ISSUE RULE

3–01 Given the centrality of live oral testimony, or *viva voce* evidence, in the common law trial, it is critically important as a matter of procedural fairness that opposing parties are permitted to test the accuracy and reliability of the witness' evidence by effective cross-examination. Fundamental to this process is the facility to make particular challenges to a witness' credibility. Given the high likelihood that an unrestricted right to discredit or impeach witnesses testifying for an opponent would expose the trial to a labyrinth of splitting issues and delay, a rule exists which chiefly operates at the cross-examination stage to restrict the extent and sometimes the nature of credibility challenges against witnesses. Also more cumbersomely known as the rule governing the finality of answers to collateral questions, the collateral issue rule provides that where an answer is given by the witness to a "collateral" question, his answer is final and may not be contradicted by evidence in rebuttal. The rule applies notwithstanding that his answer may be false, although the witness risks penalty for contempt of court and prosecution for perjury.

3–02 The collateral issue rule reflects a concern that the longer the trial is allowed to deviate from the facts at issue, the more likely the jury will become side-tracked and the less likely the court will reach an effective decision. The rule is inherently pragmatic, and encourages the court to avoid a "multiplicity of issues" arising in the trial.[1] Lord Lane explained that the rule "is necessary to confine the ambit of a trial within proper limits and to prevent the true issue from becoming submerged in a welter of detail".[2] The range of evidence before the court, and the scope of challenges that may be made to the evidence, must be determined within convenient limits, which are imposed from time to time by the trial judge as part of his function to manage and direct the course and conduct of the evidence.

3–03 "Collateral" is best understood contextually by reference to the facts at issue and the cumulative evidence and contentious issues in the case. Henry J. put it that the "utility of the test may lie in the fact that the answer is an instinctive one based on the prosecutor's and the court's sense of fair play rather than any philosophical or analytic process".[3] To a greater extent, then, the question is one best governed upon a case-by-case basis, subject to the few rules which seek to lay down basic markers, derived from the broad discretion vesting in the trial judge "to control cross-examination and keep it within reasonable bounds".[4]

3–04 One of the few early English authorities to assay a test of "collateral" was *Attorney-General v Hitchcock*.[5] The Crown witness denied having previously told a third party he had been offered a bribe to testify against the accused. The defence wished to contradict the witness on his denial by calling another witness. The trial judge's refusal to allow the defence to rebut was upheld on appeal, on the grounds that calling other witnesses to establish that an *offer* of bribery had been made would not ultimately have "qualified or contradicted [the witness'] statement" that the offence had been committed. Pollock C.B. phrased the appropriate test as follows:

> "[I]f you ask a witness whether he has not said so and so, and the matter he is supposed to have said would, if he had said it, contradict any other part of his testimony, then you may call another witness to prove that he had said so, in order that the jury may believe the account of the transaction which he gave to that other witness to be the truth, and that the statement he makes on oath in the witness box is not true ... [I]f the answer of a witness is a matter which you would be allowed on your part to prove in evidence—if it have such a connection with the issue that

---

[1] *DPP v Barr* (CCA, March 2, 1992), *per* O'Flaherty J. In a case of indecent assault, the court decided that the complainant's denial of having been at the scene of the assault on a previous occasion had rightly been deemed final, and the prosecution had not been entitled to rebut it, since the matter was collateral and insufficiently relevant to the trial.
[2] *R. v Edwards* [1991] 1 W.L.R. 207 (CA).
[3] *R. v Funderburk* [1990] 1 W.L.R. 587 (CA).
[4] Affirmed in *O'Broin v District Judge Ruane and Attorney-General* [1989] I.L.R.M. 732 at 734, *per* Lynch J. (HC).
[5] (1847) 1 Excheq. 91.

you would be allowed to give it in evidence—then it is matter on which you may contradict him".[6]

3–05 Despite its surface circularity, the test has since been interpreted to mean that the cross-examiner must justify the challenge by reference to the specific facts at issue in the trial, and an insufficient link with those issues will entitle the trial judge to call a halt to the line of questioning upon the basis that it is collateral and insufficiently relevant to the trial. This view of the *Hitchcock* test was confirmed in *R. v Edwards*,[7] where Lord Lane suggested that the rule ultimately hinges on the distinction between issue-relevance and credibility: whether or not the jury are likely to be reaching their verdict upon the basis of the contended issue, or whether instead that issue bears only, and no further, upon the credibility of the particular witness. It has rightly been pointed out, however, that relevance in this context is not technically limited to the facts at issue identified by the substantive law—but that it is a moveable notion best understood in terms of being *relative to*, "about or around the facts in issue",[8] and in terms of making "a sufficient contribution to the determination of the issue".[9]

3–06 There are a number of special exceptions to the collateral issue rule, facilitating specific challenges to a witness' credibility subject to the trial judge's discretion to restrict their extent and duration. They relate to: (1) previous inconsistent statements made by a witness; (2) bias on the part of the witness; (3) previous convictions of the witness; (4) veracity of the witness; and (5) physical or mental disability of the witness. Cross-examination of complainants upon their sexual history or experience had once routinely been permitted in sexual offence cases, although it is now limited to exceptional cases owing to the construction of statutory "rape shields" across the common law world. Although judges on occasion have remarked that the list of exceptions is not closed,[10] English jurists appear to recognise this to be the case. Cross had made the case for an open list of exceptions,[11] whilst others such as Newark[12] and Zuckerman[13] have argued that the rule and the exceptions should be abandoned and replaced by a general principle for all cases acknowledging the trial judge's discretion, and indeed often duty, to restrict the nature and scope of credibility challenges, having regard to the broad principles upon which the collateral issues rule was first formulated. There is much to be said for this view—or indeed, more simply, for denying that the list of exceptions thus far recognised is closed—particularly when one considers that the

---

[6] (1847) 1 Excheq. 91 at 99.
[7] [1991] 1 W.L.R. 207 (CA).
[8] Seabrooke, "The Vanishing Trick—blurring the line between credit and issue" [1999] Crim. L.R. 387 at 390.
[9] Zuckerman, *The Principles of Criminal Evidence* (1989) at p.101.
[10] *R. v Funderburk* [1990] 1 W.L.R. 587 at 599, *per* Henry J. (CA).
[11] Cross, *Evidence* (7th ed., Butterworths, London, 1990) at p.310.
[12] Newark, "Opening Up the Collateral Issue Rule" (1992) 43 N.I.L.Q. 166 at 177.
[13] Zuckerman [1990] All E.R. Annual Review at p.122.

exception once identified for sexual history evidence is now much more controversial and much less tolerated evidence than it was when its place was first confirmed on the list so-called.

II. A WITNESS' PREVIOUS INCONSISTENT STATEMENTS

3–07 A witness may generally be cross-examined with respect to any statement he made prior to the trial that contradicts his testimony given in court under oath. The pre-trial statement may be sworn or unsworn, signed or unsigned. Section 4 of the Criminal Procedure Act 1865 laid the basis for this facility:

> "If a witness, upon cross-examination as to a former statement made by him relative to the subject-matter of the indictment or proceeding, and inconsistent with his present testimony, does not distinctly admit that he has made such statement, proof may be given that he did in fact make it; but before such proof can be given the circumstances of the supposed statement, sufficient to designate the particular occasion, must be mentioned to the witness, and he must be asked whether or not he has made such statement".

3–08 Section 5 provides that where reference is made to a witness' pre-trial statement to show that it contradicts aspects of his testimony, the witness must first be directed to the contradictory passages. The trial judge may receive the statement in evidence and make "such use of it for the purposes of the trial as he may think fit". According to well-entrenched common law rule, however, a pre-trial statement may be entered into evidence only if the witness refuses to admit to the inconsistency or to the fact that he has provided a confusing account.[14] It may only constitute evidence relevant to establish the witness' lack of credibility, and is not probative of any facts asserted therein owing to the rule against hearsay.[15] The trial judge must explain the distinction adequately to the jury when summing-up, and the failure to do so, particularly if the witness assumed importance in the case, may constitute a serious and fundamental misdirection.[16]

3–09 Where the witness has been deemed hostile, the court is particularly vigilant to ensure that minimal revelation of the substance of his statement is made in the presence of the jury, since in this context the cross-examiner often has an incentive to release the witness' pre-trial version of events into evidence or into the minds of the jury.[17] The procedure to be followed is as identified by Walsh J. in *People (Attorney-General) v Taylor*.[18]

---

[14] *cf.* para.**2–30** *et seq.*
[15] *cf.* para.**9–03**.
[16] *R. v Gillespie* (1967) 51 Cr. App. R. 172 (CA).
[17] *cf.* para.**2–39** *et seq.*
[18] [1974] I.R. 97 (CCA): *cf.* appendix 21.

III. A WITNESS' BIAS

3–10 Evidence can be tendered to rebut a witness' denial of bias, incentive, or partiality. The founding authority for the principle is *Lord Stafford's case* of 1680,[19] where evidence was allowed to rebut the particular witness' denial that he had suborned other witnesses by bribing them to provide a certain version of events. This outcome may be contrasted with *Attorney-General v Hitchcock*,[20] where counsel was not permitted to rebut a witness' denial that he had been *offered* a bribe, since proof of the claim that he had been offered a bribe would not have contradicted the rest of the witness' testimony.

3–11 The reported cases on bias tend to involve witnesses whose behaviour suggests that they are concerned to save the accused from conviction (by bribing others), or to secure the conviction of the accused (by manufacturing evidence or bribing others). In *R. v Mendy*,[21] the Court of Appeal upheld the trial judge's decision to facilitate a challenge to a witness, the husband of the accused, who had been observed receiving somebody else's notes of a preceding witness' evidence prior to being called into court to testify. In *R. v Busby*,[22] the appeal against the trial judge's decision not to allow rebuttal evidence also succeeded upon the basis that the jury should have been permitted to consider whether the prosecution witnesses (members of the police) had been prepared to go to improper lengths to secure a conviction, as alleged by the accused.

3–12 If the witness is himself a criminal and former accomplice of the accused, cross-examination upon the witness' motives and incentive to testify against the accused constitutes a permissible challenge on grounds of bias. In *People (DPP) v McGinley*,[23] a retrial was ordered upon the basis that the trial judge had wrongly deprived the accused of his right to cross-examine and rebut the chief prosecution witness, an accomplice. The defence wished to question him with respect to the suspended sentence he had already received for his part in the same crimes, and to ascertain if he had received the suspended sentence because of his undertaking to cooperate in the prosecution of the accused. Finlay C.J. recognised that this line of questioning had taken place "within the general category of questioning seeking to lead to the establishing of partiality, bias or improper motive on the part of the witness, as distinct from a general assertion of lack of credit".[24] Counsel for the accused had been entitled to cross-examine this witness "in considerable detail as to his motives and as to what was said at his trial which would tend to establish what those motives were".[25]

---

[19] (1680) 7 St. Tr. 1293.
[20] (1847) 1 Excheq. 91.
[21] (1976) 64 Cr. App. R. 4 (CA).
[22] (1981) 75 Cr. App. R. 79 (CA).
[23] [1987] I.R. 340 (CCA).
[24] *ibid*. at 345.
[25] *ibid*.

IV. A Witness' Previous Convictions

3–13 Under s.6 of the Criminal Procedure Act 1865,[26] the previous convictions of a witness may be proved in court. The conviction need not have any relevance to the facts at issue, nor need the crime be directly relevant to the question of the witness' honesty. The principle behind this type of provision was encapsulated by Holmes J. in *Gertz v Fitchburg*,[27] where he said that such evidence may be introduced to show that the witness has a general readiness to do wrong and thus that he is capable of lying under oath—namely, that he is of bad character and unworthy of credit or belief. The extent to which the witness may be cross-examined upon his convictions is a matter for the trial judge, balancing fairness to the accused against the need to avoid collateral issues proliferating in the trial. In civil proceedings, which lack punitive consequences, the judge's discretion has more primacy, with one difference. When deciding the nature and extent of cross-examination upon the witness' convictions, the trial judge must have equal regard to the interests of both parties to the dispute;[28] in the criminal context, by contrast, the trial judge is concerned to a greater extent to ensure that the accused has an effective opportunity to cross-examine a witness with a criminal past called by the prosecution to give evidence tending to establish his own criminal guilt.

3–14 The prosecution in indictable proceedings owes a pre-trial duty to disclose to the defence information material to any witnesses it intends to call.[29] If a witness has been convicted of any offences, the prosecution must disclose the witness' criminal record.[30] In light of the prosecution's burden of proof in criminal proceedings,[31] it is customary for the prosecution to inform the court, in advance of the witness' testimony, of any offences for which he has been convicted. Defence cross-examination of a prosecution witness upon his criminal record does not ordinarily expose the accused to cross-examination upon his bad character for the purposes of s.1(f)(ii) of the Criminal Justice (Evidence) Act 1924.[32] This would be inappropriate in principle: if the

---

[26] Section 6 provides: "A Witness may be questioned as to whether he has been convicted of any Felony or Misdemeanor, and upon being so questioned, if he either denies or does not admit the Fact, or refuses to answer, it shall be lawful for the cross-examining Party to prove such Conviction; and a Certificate containing the Substance and Effect only (omitting the formal Part) of the Indictment and Conviction for such Offence, purporting to be signed by the Clerk of the Court or other Officer having the Custody of the Records of the Court where the Offender was convicted, or by the Deputy of such Clerk or Officer, (for which Certificate a Fee of Five Shillings and no more shall be demanded or taken) shall, upon Proof of the Identity of the Person, be sufficient Evidence of the said Conviction, without Proof of the Signature or official Character of the Person appearing to have signed the same".
[27] (1884) 137 Mass. 77.
[28] *Thomas v Commissioner of Police of the Metropolis* [1997] 2 W.L.R. 593 at 608, per Evan L.J. (CA).
[29] *cf.* para.**1–42** *et seq.*
[30] *R. v Paraskeva* (1983) 76 Cr. App. R. 162 (CA).
[31] *cf.* para.**4–07**.
[32] This point was clarified in *R. v Taylor* [1999] Crim. L.R. 407 (CA).

prosecution calls witnesses of dubious reliability and morality, it is appropriate that the accused be entitled to challenge those witnesses with impunity. If the challenge is to be construed to amount to an "imputation" against the character of a prosecution witness for the purposes of s.1(f)(ii)—although logically this is not necessarily so, given that a witness' conviction is a fact and matter of public record—then alternatively the situation is one where the trial judge should usually exercise discretion to disallow the questioning.

V. A Witness' Lack of Veracity

A Witness' Reputation for Lies

3–15 Given that untruthfulness is not *per se* a criminal offence—save, after the event, for corroborated perjury in judicial proceedings—the court lacks any structured means of knowing if a witness is prone to lying.[33] The approach favoured in England to the difficult issue of ascertaining a witness' propensity to lie was summarised by Edmund Davies L.J. in *R. v Richardson and Longman*[34] and is common law in origin.[35]

3–16 The *Richardson* rules refer to the type of questions that can properly be put to a second witness regarding the untruthfulness of a first witness. The second witness may be asked to explain his knowledge of the first witness' general lack of repute, and may further express his personal opinion as to the first witness' untruthfulness under oath. He is not permitted to detail the events or circumstances grounding these opinions, however. The details may only be elicited under cross-examination by counsel for the discredited witness. This last rule places counsel for the opposing party in a delicate situation, and reflects a policy that where a witness is called who may be suspected of dishonesty, the risk of any prejudice should be borne by the calling side. If an attempt to rehabilitate the witness is not made by the calling side, the jury may suspect that the witness has something to hide. If counsel decides to cross-examine the second witness, the allegation of untrustworthiness may be shown to lack foundation, and thus no damage is done; on the other hand, cross-examination risks the release of unanticipated prejudicial information regarding the first witness, which, for reasons of ambush or an application by the trial judge of the collateral issue rule, may not be amenable to rebuttal.

3–17 There is no reported analysis of the rules and procedures that should

---

[33] Lie detector test results are assumed inadmissible in Ireland and England, potentially offending the rules against hearsay and opinion evidence, although they have been deemed admissible in Canada (*Phillion v R.* [1978] 1 S.C.R. 18) and New Zealand (*R. v McKay* [1967] N.Z.L.R. 139): *cf.* Hirst, *Andrews and Hirst on Criminal Evidence* (4th ed., Jordans, Bristol, 2001) at p.643.

[34] [1969] 1 Q.B. 299 (CA), approved by the House of Lords in *Toohey v Metropolitan Police Commissioner* [1965] A.C. 595.

[35] *R. v Watson* (1817) 2 Stark 116; *R. v Brown* (1867) Cox C.C. 453.

Challenges to the Credibility of Witnesses 83

be followed in Ireland, and it is by no means certain that each of the *Richardson* rules would or should be affirmed in Ireland, though they continue to be applied in England, albeit rarely.[36] The rules may be criticised for encouraging the prejudicial dissemination of bare opinion and multiple hearsay. As Cave J. put it: "Rumour is a lying jade, begotten by gossip out of hearsay, and is not fit to be admitted to audience in a court of law".[37] Wigmore too cautioned against turning the witness box into a "place of dread and loathing".[38] The *Richardson* rules, although extant in England, may indeed be viewed as "a rather desperate tactic by a cross-examiner short of other ammunition".[39]

Lies Told by the Accused

3–18 The accused is often shown to have lied at some point during the investigation or trial, proof of which may emerge when the accused is cross-examined upon discrepancies between his original statements and his evidence in-chief (or where the accused has elected not to testify, by evidence from an independent source). Whether or not the mistruth relates to a material issue, the prosecution is likely to fix upon it as further evidence of the accused's present guilt. The English courts have developed special rules governing the use to which lies may legitimately be put in the criminal trial, largely due to a fear that juries may be prompted to attach disproportionate weight to proof of the lie, when in reality lies are often told for innocent reasons (out of panic, to bolster a weak but true defence, or to shield others, etc.).[40] The rules are anchored in the Court of Appeal's decision in *R. v Lucas*,[41] which establishes various criteria to be satisfied before a proven lie may be treated as evidence corroborative of the prosecution's case against the accused.[42] In terms of lies relevant to the accused's credibility as a witness, the court accepted that where the lie relates only to a peripheral matter, it may be accepted, with proper direction, as evidence relevant to the accused's discredit, revealing his general lack of veracity as a witness. The decision further establishes that in all cases where the accused's lie relates to a *peripheral* or *collateral* issue, the trial judge is under a specific duty to caution the jury that the lie may have been told for any one of a number of innocent reasons, and that the jury should not attach disproportionate weight to the lie when deciding the accused's guilt as charged.

---

[36] In *R. v Bogie* [1992] Crim. L.R. 301 (CA), five witnesses were called by the accused to testify to the complainant's reputation for untruthfulness.
[37] *Scott v Sampson* (1882) 8 Q.B.D. 491 at 503.
[38] *A Treatise on the Anglo-American System of Evidence in Trials at Common Law* (3rd ed., Boston, 1940). Wigmore proposed that if witnesses are to be challenged and discredited in this fashion, they ought to be allowed to rehabilitate themselves, to counter the "publicity of one's discredit on the stand".
[39] Dennis, *The Law of Evidence* (Sweet & Maxwell, London, 1999) at p.460.
[40] *R. v Broadhurst* [1964] A.C. 441 (PC).
[41] [1981] 3 W.L.R. 121 (CA).
[42] *cf.* para.**5–08**.

3–19 Numerous recent appeals in England have been fought on the adequacy of the trial judge's warning as to the effect of peripheral lies. The necessity for a special warning was justified by the Court of Appeal in *R. v Hill*[43] upon the basis that an alleged lie relevant to a central fact at issue will inevitably be discussed by the trial judge when summing-up, rendering a special warning otiose, whereas in the case of a lie relating to a peripheral or collateral issue, a danger arises that the jury will attach disproportionate weight to the lie when considering the accused's guilt. Thus, where an accused trims his early version of events in a bid to render it consistent with the prosecution's evidence (in *Hill*, forensic evidence of blood on the walls, contradicting the accused's early statement that the deceased fell from a back-handed blow), there is no need for a special lies direction so long as the trial judge's general directions and summing-up properly directs the jury to the central conflicts of evidence.

3–20 It would appear that a special direction is not an invariable requirement in every case but is required only where there is a clear danger that the jury will attach disproportionate weight to the lie.[44] The warning is not strictly necessary where it is already clear that the lie is proven only to undermine the accused's credibility.[45] In *R. v Genus & Britton*,[46] the Court of Appeal overturned the conviction upon the basis that the trial judge had failed to give a lies-warning in a case that "cried out" for one. The lies in question had emerged from material differences between what was said in interview and what was said from the witness box, but these related to collateral issues only, such as what the accused was wearing upon arrest. Because the misrepresented facts were not directly relevant to the facts at issue (intent to supply and the defence of duress), it was imperative to caution the jury against embarking upon a false line of logic rooted merely in peripheral issues.

3–21 The *Lucas* rules have been extended to lies relied upon to disprove the accused's alibi. A special direction is now required in England to caution the jury that an alibi is sometimes fabricated to bolster a genuine defence, and that ultimately they must determine not whether the accused's alibi amounts to a lie, but whether the prosecution has proved its case against the accused beyond a reasonable doubt.[47] Only when the jury has concluded that the accused's false alibi was calculated to deceive the court, may it then consider the lie as potential corroboration.[48] It has also been decided that the *Lucas* direction is required when a lie told by the accused is relied upon as supporting evidence to bolster identification evidence: the jury is not entitled to accept the lie as evidence supporting the identification unless first satisfied that the accused did not tell the lie for innocent reasons.[49] A warning need not be given, however,

---

[43] [1996] Crim. L.R. 419 (CA).
[44] *R. v Harron* [1996] Crim. L.R. 581 (CA).
[45] *R. v Josephine Smith* [1995] Crim. L.R. 305 (CA).
[46] [1996] Crim. L.R. 502 (CA).
[47] *R. v Burge* [1996] 1 Cr. App. R. 163 (CA).
[48] *R. v Turnbull* [1977] Q.B. 224 at 230 (CA).
[49] *R. v Goodway* [1993] 4 All E.R. 895 (CA): *cf.* para.**6–09**.

where the lie is presented not as proof of the accused's guilt, but as evidence establishing some other relevant fact, such as in *R. v Smith*[50] where the accused's fiscal dishonesty was explored for the purpose of his claim that he suffered from psychiatric illness and diminished responsibility.

VI. A WITNESS' PHYSICAL OR MENTAL DISABILITY

3–22 Evidence may be tendered to show that the witness' testimony is unreliable due to a physical or mental disability suffered by the witness. This was reviewed by the House of Lords in *Toohey v Metropolitan Police Commissioner*.[51] Lord Pearce found that "when a witness through ... disease or abnormality is not capable of giving a true or reliable account to the jury, it must surely be allowable for medical science to reveal the vital hidden facts to them".[52]

VII. SEXUAL HISTORY EVIDENCE

Admissibility under the Common Law

3–23 The old common law rule was that counsel could not contradict a witness' denial of having had sexual intercourse outside of marriage.[53] Sexual promiscuity was considered a matter of grave ill repute, and public policy sought to avoid the airing of scandalous accusation in court. Where, however, there was evidence that the complainant in a sexual offence case had led a promiscuous lifestyle or was "notorious for want of chastity",[54] the floodgates opened to a full-scale attack upon the complainant's truthfulness and credibility. From the close of the nineteenth century, increased use came to be made of sexual evidence history, based upon an equation the common law then drew between promiscuity and untruthfulness. As was stated in 1838: "Will you not more readily infer consent in the practiced Messalina, in loose attire, than in the reserved and virtuous Lucretia?"[55] It was also then, and now, of concern to the courts that accusations of rape are difficult to defend. Hale once famously wrote that rape "is an accusation easily to be made and hard to be proved, and harder to be defended by the party accused, tho never so innocent".[56] Until recently, there was a broad acceptance of the defence's right to enquire into the complainant's sexual past in any case of rape or sexual offence where consent was denied. In *DPP v McGuinness*,[57] Kenny J. remarked: "When the

---

[50] *R. v Smith* [1995] Crim. L.R. 304 (CA).
[51] [1965] A.C. 595 (HL).
[52] *ibid.* at 608.
[53] *R. v Cockcroft* (1870) Cox C.C. 410.
[54] *R. v Clay* (1851) 5 Cox C.C. 147; *R. v Holmes* (1871) L.R. 1 C.C.R. 334.
[55] *People v Abbott* (1838) 19 Wend. 192 at 195 (N.Y.).
[56] Hale, *Historia Placitorum Coronae* (1734) at p.635.
[57] [1978] I.R. 189 at 191 (CCA).

defence is consent the judge must allow unpleasant charges to be made against the complainant in connection with her past; he should not indicate to the jury that he disapproves of this being done". One of the more popular explanations for the potential relevance of sexual history evidence in England was provided by Cross in the following terms:

> "It has also been remarked that sexual intercourse, whether or not consensual, most often takes place in private, and leaves few visible traces of having occurred. Evidence is often effectively limited to that of the parties, and much is likely to depend on the balance of credibility between them. This has important effects for the law of evidence since it is capable of reducing the difference between questions going to credit and questions going to the issue to vanishing point."[58]

3–24 Recourse to questioning on sexual history or experience has rightly become subject to strict restrictions in recent years. Although the view expressed above by Cross retains limited support, the more recent justification for the limited admissibility of sexual history evidence is that the complainant's sexual history may be specifically relevant in the circumstances of a case to the issue of consent or some other fact at issue such as whether the accused's assumption of consent was genuinely mistaken.[59]

Current Provisions

3–25 Section 3 of the Criminal Law Rape Act 1981, as amended by s.13 of the Criminal Law Rape (Amendment) Act 1990, provides that where the defence seeks to introduce evidence of the complainant's "sexual experience" in a trial for rape, aggravated sexual assault, or sexual assault,[60] whether by adducing evidence or cross-examining the complainant, an application must

---

[58] *Cross and Tapper on Evidence* (8th ed., Butterworths, London, 1995) at p.341. This passage was applied by the Court of Appeal in *R. v Nagrecha* [1997] 2 Cr. App. R. 401, where it ruled that evidence of previous complaints by the complainant against other men was relevant and admissible. The decision, it is submitted, rests upon false relevance logic. Evidence of prior complaint against other parties is not relevant to the issue of consent, nor to any of the facts at issue. It is potentially relevant to the person's credibility as a witness, and for this purpose alone sexual history evidence is currently inadmissible under English law: *cf.* para.**3–34**. It is of note that Adler (1982) at 668 reported, from her survey of 50 rape trials in England from 1978–79, that in all cases where cross-examination upon prior complaints was sought, the application "was invariably based on the assumption that prior complaints were false allegations". Both the decision in *Nagrecha*, and the passage by Cross, have been criticised by Seabrooke (1999) at p.388 on the basis that "the difference between credit and issue never reaches vanishing point; what may properly be said to vanish is the significance of that difference".

[59] This was construed in *DPP v Morgan* [1975] 2 W.L.R. 913 (HL) to constitute an element of the *mens rea* of the offence, which must be established by the prosecution.

[60] This was extended by s.34 of the Sex Offenders Act 2001 to cases of attempted aggravated sexual assault, aiding, abetting, counselling and procuring aggravated sexual assault or attempted aggravated sexual assault, incitement to aggravated sexual assault, and conspiracy to commit any of the foregoing offences.

first be made to the trial judge in the absence of the jury. The prosecution must give the accused notice of its intention to make an application under s.3 or s.4 "before, or as soon as practicable after, the commencement of the trial". By virtue of s.4A—inserted by s.34 of the Sex Offenders Act 2001—the complainant is now entitled to be heard and to be legally represented during the hearing of this application.

3–26 Evidence of the complainant's sexual history or experience is inadmissible in the trial,[61] save in cases where the trial judge decides that not to admit the evidence would be "unfair" to the accused. Section 3 was closely modelled upon s.2 of the Sexual Offences (Amendment) Act 1976, then in force in England, although it differed in one significant respect. The Irish provision, by defining "unfair", opted for a strict statutory test of admissibility. The failure of the English legislature to make similar provision in 1976 was a direct cause of the uncertainty and controversy that bedevilled sexual history evidence issues there over the following two decades. Under s.3(2) "unfair" contemplates a situation where, on the one hand, "if the evidence or question was not allowed the jury might reasonably be satisfied beyond reasonable doubt that the accused is guilty", and, on the other hand, "the effect of allowing the evidence or question might reasonably be that they would not be so satisfied". This test of admissibility implies that the trial judge must be satisfied that the sexual history evidence will be critical to the jury's verdict—that it appears to him that the accused may well be convicted and it is reasonably possible that the sexual history evidence will tip the balance from conviction to acquittal. Thus, a central concern of the trial judge will be the probative force of the line of questioning, having regard to the facts at issue, the circumstances of the case, and the nature of the defence. If the trial judge forms the view that to deny the evidence would be "unfair", it would appear from the wording of s.3 that a decision must be taken to permit the evidence.

3–27 "Sexual experience" has not been defined by the legislation. Under English case-law prior to the Youth Justice and Criminal Evidence Act 1999, it had been limited to previous acts of penetrative sexual intercourse. Cross-examination of the complainant upon sexual or erotic activities falling short of intercourse had been permitted, so long as sufficiently relevant, although it was refused in *R. v Barnes*[62] with respect to the complainant's use of a vibrator. Section 13 deleted the words "about any sexual experience of a complainant with a person other than the accused" from s.3, indirectly to broaden the category of non-examinable sexual experience to include prior sexual relations with the accused. English law courted controversy recently for doing the same by s.41 of the Youth Justice and Criminal Evidence Act 1999, although s.41 ostensibly subjects questioning on "sexual behaviour" (an apparently broader category) to a more restrictive admissibility test based upon similarity and a

---

[61] The prohibition applies also at the hearing of a pre-trial application by the accused to have the charges dismissed under Pt IA of the Criminal Procedure Act 1967, inserted by s.15 of the Criminal Justice Act 1999.
[62] [1994] Crim. L.R. 691 (CA).

showing of high probative force.[63] In an obvious effort to uphold the fairness of these new provisions from the perspective of the accused—made necessary by the requirement of conformity with the European Convention on Human Rights under s.3 of the Human Rights Act 1998—the Court of Appeal in *R. v T and H*[64] interpreted the prohibition not to include questioning on prior complaints or inconsistent statements made by the complainant with respect to the alleged or other instances of sexual abuse.[65]

3–28 There have been no reserved judgments of note on the relevant Irish provisions,[66] and no authoritative review of the parameters between issue and credit or of the evidentiary function of evidence elicited of the complainant's sexual history or experience. Clearly, this owes much to the wording of s.3, which implicitly conveys that recourse to such evidence is exceptional. It has also been suggested that this may be because defence counsel in Ireland has tended to side-step the formal mechanism and instead to engage in innuendo and hint.[67] If so, it may well be that the more formalised process introduced by s.4A, inserted by s.34 of the Sex Offenders Act 2001,[68] will precipitate the issues increasingly in Irish trials, although it is hoped that this will not work counter-productively to increase recourse to sexual history evidence in trials for rape and sexual assault. It is, of course, also the case that reference to the complainant's sexual history in the trial is prejudicial to the prosecution and not the defence—if it leads to the accused's acquittal, the prosecution is not in a position to bring an appeal upon the sexual history issue. Whatever the cause, the dearth of analysis in Ireland brings with it uncertainty. Whilst s.3(2) identifies a test for admissibility, it does not indicate to any extent the range of issues or circumstances that may make sexual history evidence probative to establish consent, identity, mistaken belief, or other facts at issue. Given that Irish law formally operated a much stricter test for the admissibility of sexual history evidence than applied in England prior to the severe retrenchment marked by the Youth Justice and Criminal Evidence Act 1999, the English decisions are of much looser relevance, although the comparative abundance of reported decision and published analysis on this issue there make it nonetheless a necessary and rewarding study.

3–29 Section 3 operates only to restrict evidence tendered by the accused of

---

[63] *cf.* para.**3–35** *et seq.*
[64] [2002] 1 W.L.R. 632, 1 All E.R. 683 (CA).
[65] Since these did not constitute "sexual behaviour" for the purposes of s.41, they were not subject to the prohibition under s.41(4) against questioning on sexual experience for the purposes of establishing the complainant's lack of credibility. Thus, the questions raised an ordinary challenge to the complainant, permissible as an exception to the collateral issues rule: *cf.* para.**3–6**.
[66] Brief comments were made in *People (DPP) v McDonagh* (CCA, July 24, 1990) *per* Finlay C.J.
[67] Law Reform Commission (1987); Adler, "Rape—the Intention of Parliament and the Practice of the Courts" (1982) 45 M.L.R. 664 at 674.
[68] This implemented an early proposal by the Law Reform Commission (*ibid.* at paras 94–96).

the complainant's sexual experience (either by way of cross-examination or evidence in-chief by other witnesses), but it does not restrict the prosecution from raising it expressly or impliedly in the trial. The complainant may unwittingly be exposed to questioning about sexual experience if the prosecution is run in such a way as to express or imply that he had no or little sexual experience. In other words, in this situation the evidence may be admissible to rebut any contrary proposition or suggestion raised by the prosecution. In *R. v Funderburk*,[69] the evidence was admissible to rebut a suggestion carefully created by the prosecution that the complainant had been a virgin at the time of the alleged intercourse. The accused alleged that the 13 year-old complainant had had a crush on him for the duration she and her mother shared lodgings with him, and that she had ultimately made the complaint out of spite after her mother quit the place under a cloud. The defence wished to question the complainant on her sexual experience with a view to showing that she had already had sexual relations with a local boy. In this context, Henry J. of the Court of Appeal concluded that the prosecution had created an impression in the trial that the complainant had been a virgin before the alleged intercourse with the accused, and this had implicitly become a critical question of credit in the trial. If the defence were to be denied the chance to rebut it, "there would be a danger that the jury would make their decision as to credit on an account of the original incident in which the most emotive, memorable and potentially persuasive fact was, to the knowledge of all in the case save the jury, false".[70]

Reasons for Limiting Use of Sexual History Evidence

3–30 Rape shield provisions implicitly take the view that, irrespective of the potential relevance of sexual history evidence (whether to issue or credit), public policy is against the admissibility of this type of evidence, as the social cost incurred by routine reception of the evidence (in terms at least of deterring complaint and prosecution of sexual offences) would outweigh any evidential gains in particular cases. The dangers arising from recourse to this type of evidence in sexual offence trials are many and obvious. The complainant may be required to endure a second ordeal in court if the prosecution is permitted to engage in a fishing expedition into his sexual history. The statistics have always suggested significant under-reporting of sexual offences. A sense that the law permits an open investigation into the complainant's sexual history is likely further to inhibit the cooperation of rape victims with the prosecution services. A laissez-faire approach to the reception of sexual history evidence would undoubtedly secure the acquittal of many rapists. For these reasons, in 1975 the Heibron Committee Report in England advocated prohibiting cross-

---

[69] [1990] 1 W.L.R. 587 (CA). See also *R. v Riley* (1990) 91 Cr. App. R. 14 (CA), where evidence was admitted to show that the complainant had had sex with her previous partner while her child was asleep in the next room, to rebut her specific assertion that she would never have had sex with someone while her child was in the other room.
[70] *ibid*. at 598.

examination upon the complainant's sexual history, save upon proof of "similarity" between the event under trial and the complainant's sexual past.[71] The proposal was not implemented in this form in England until the Youth Justice and Criminal Evidence Act 1999.

3–31 Although it has been judicially remarked that a jury is unlikely to be influenced any more by the fact alone of the complainant's sexual promiscuity[72] (a view, at any rate, very much to be doubted), it is difficult to resist concluding that one of the purposes of this kind of questioning is to appeal to the double standard that tends to cloud people's attitudes and responses to sexuality. Temkin described this dynamic well: "Within the enclosed and cut-off realm of the court-room, a jury may accept an account of the world as set out by the defence which in no way corresponds to the actual sexual mores of today's society but exemplifies the double standard of sexual morality in its most virulent form".[73] Also of this view, Zuckerman argues that sexual history evidence has been used in rape trials more often than not to show the complainant's lack of *moral* credibility as opposed to his *probative* credibility. It is being used to "show the complainant to be so morally inferior as either not to deserve the court's sympathy or not to provide a suitable foundation for punishing the accused".[74] It is also very possible that knowledge of the complainant's sexual past will greatly prejudice the jury against his account. According to McColgan: "Knowledge of a woman's sexual activities can also contribute to a process of shifting the blame away from the aggressor to the object of aggression."[75] The complainant may be imagined to have "led the accused on", or the accused to have been duped. The focus of the jury may be caused to shift from that of rape to that of the sexual act: "Once the complainant is established as a sexual woman, the door is opened to express or implied suggestions that the sexual contact at issue fell into the category of 'sex' ".[76]

3–32 One of the most persuasive arguments against admissibility of sexual history evidence is that, generally, it is not relevant evidence. Originally admissible by way of exception to the collateral issue rule, it was permissible to prove the complainant's "promiscuous" past only because the law then equated evidence of sexual promiscuity with untruthfulness in the witness. This association has not been evident for some time. McColgan persuasively argued that the law in England prior to the reform in 1999 was inconsistent with ordinary common law notions of relevance. The fact that a complainant is prepared to have sex consensually with numerous persons is no basis for an inference that he consented to sex with the accused: "Is it more likely that a man with a reputation for generosity consented to the appropriation of his

---

[71] *Report of the Advisory Group on the Law of Rape* (H.M.S.O., London, 1975) at para.137.
[72] *R. v Brown* (1989) 89 Cr. App. R. 97, *per* May L.J. (CA).
[73] Temkin,"Sexual History Evidence—the Ravishment of Section 2" [1993] Crim. L.R. 3 at 4–5.
[74] *The Principles of Criminal Evidence* (1989) at pp.248–9.
[75] McColgan, "Common Law and the Relevance of Sexual History Evidence" (1996) 16 *Oxford Journal of Legal Studies* 275 at 305.
[76] *ibid.*

possessions, in a case where he alleges theft by the appropriator, than a man who has a reputation for meanness?"[77]

3–33 The rules of evidence have strictly protected the accused from exposure to similar fact evidence and cross-examination upon bad character and criminal record in his own trial, based upon an appreciation of the danger that the jury might infer guilt of the instant crime from evidence of his past behaviour or general propensity.[78] Since sexual history evidence also encourages a forbidden reasoning—that because the complainant consented to the sexual act before, he did so on the occasion in question—the possibility of a *quid pro quo* approach has been mooted, which would expose the accused to cross-examination upon bad character if he chooses to cross-examine the complainant upon his sexual past.[79]

The English Experience

3–34 In opting for a statutory prohibition on sexual history evidence save where critically probative in the case, Irish law appears to have avoided undue recourse to this type of questioning. The failure to define "unfair" in England engendered too many variations of the appropriate test, and ultimately a permissive approach to sexual history evidence by the English courts.[80] The Advisory Group on the Law of Rape, or Heibron Committee, established in England in 1975, had concluded: "A woman's sexual experience with partners of her own choice are neither indicative of untruthfulness nor of a general willingness to consent".[81] Its proposal for a framework of stricter limitations based upon an appeal to "similarity" was implemented belatedly in the form of the Youth Justice and Criminal Evidence Act 1999, although this has courted similar controversy, now for being unduly restrictive for the defence.

3–35 Section 41 prohibits the defence from asking any question in cross-examination, or adducing any evidence, about "any sexual behaviour of the complainant", other than sexual behaviour which forms part of the event being

---

[77] *ibid.* at 285.
[78] *cf.* paras **7–01** *et seq.* and **8–01** *et seq.*
[79] This was considered but not recommended by the Law Reform Commission (1987) at para.26.
[80] One of the most popular tests was stated by May J. in *R. v Lawrence*—[1977] Crim. L.R. 492 at 493 (CA): approved in *R. v Viola* [1982] 1 W.L.R. 1138 (CA)—to wit that cross-examination on sexual history should be permitted where "it is more likely than not that the particular question or line of cross-examination, if allowed, *might reasonably lead the jury*, properly directed in the summing-up, *to take a different view of the complainant's evidence* from that which they might take if the question or series of questions were not allowed". In *R. v C* [1996] Crim. L.R. 37, the Court of Appeal decided that the test to be applied was "are the questions relevant to the facts in issue?" The decision was rightly criticised, for seeming, however unintentionally, to suggest that the basic prerequisite for the receivability of any evidence (relevance) is the only constraint upon sexual history evidence (whereas in fact public policy is decidedly against its general admissibility).
[81] *op. cit.*, n.71 at para.131.

tried, without the leave of court. When leave is sought on grounds of consent, it may be given only where the sexual behaviour took place "at or about the same time" as the event being tried, or where the previous sexual behaviour was "so similar" to the complainant's sexual behaviour at or about the same time as the event being tried that it "cannot reasonably be explained as a coincidence". The trial judge must also conclude that a refusal "might have the effect of rendering unsafe a conclusion of the jury". In the context of a different issue—such as identity, or the accused's belief in consent, or the fact of intercourse—the court may grant leave only if satisfied that a refusal to do so might result in the jury making an unsafe decision on any relevant issue in the trial. Section 41(4) declares the general thrust of the provision (depending upon one's view of where credit ends and issue begins), namely that questions may not be asked about the complainant's previous sexual behaviour if the sole or main purpose is to impugn the complainant's credibility as a witness. The provisions were applied strictly in *R v M*,[82] where the accused was not permitted to cross-examine the complainant with respect to prior sexual activity between her and the accused's brother. The Court of Appeal reasoned that the information was not relevant to consent to intercourse with the accused, and that it would not have improved the accused's defence.

3–36 In opting for a statutory test of consent-relevant admissibility centred on similarity, the English legislature clearly had in mind the number of cases in which sexual history evidence had appropriately been admitted to establish an unusual pattern or *modus operandi* on the part of the complainant in denying consent.[83] Reference was initially made by the Heibron Committee in 1975, and the sponsors of the Bill preceding the 1999 Act, to "striking similarity"— a concept incorporated into similar fact evidence rules by *DPP v Boardman*.[84] The word "striking" was dropped after fears that it would prove too erratic a barometer. The new provisions have been criticised for being too rigid, however.[85] Although the similarity-based test suggests that the prior sexual experience must disclose unusual characteristics or a peculiar *modus operandi* in denying consent and claiming rape, the House of Lords in *R. v A*[86] has interpreted the test more broadly to require proof that the questioning would disclose a very high degree of probative force sufficient to justify the resulting prejudice to the complainant. The accused argued that s.41(3)(c) infringed his right to a free trial protected under Art.6 of the European Convention on Human Rights, since the prohibition applied equally to the complainant's prior sexual relationship with the accused. The House upheld s.41(3)(c), but only after adopting a highly strained interpretation of the provision. It expressed the view

---

[82] [2001] Crim. L.R. 911 (CA).
[83] *e.g. R. v Cox* (1987) 84 Cr. App. R. 132 (CA), where evidence was admitted to establish that the complainant had also, on a prior occasion, had sex with a friend of her partner's and had afterwards claimed rape in similar circumstances to the event under trial.
[84] [1975] A.C. 421 (HL): *cf.* para.7–**05** *et seq.*
[85] Andrews and Hirst *op. cit.*, n.33 at p.210; Eliot, "Rape Complainants' Sexual Experience with Third Parties" [1984] Crim. L.R. 4 at 8.
[86] [2001] 3 All E.R. 1 (HL).

that reference to similarity should be taken to mean that the evidence must possess sufficient probative force to justify the likely prejudicial effect for the complainant. The judgments in *R. v A* demonstrate the changed nature of public and legal policy with respect to sexual history evidence in England. Lord Hutton said as follows:

> "[W]here the crime charged is that of rape, the law must have [another] objective which is also of great importance: it is to ensure that the woman who complains that she has been raped is treated with dignity in court and is given protection against cross-examination and evidence which invades her privacy unnecessarily and which subjects her to humiliating questioning and accusations which are irrelevant to the charge against the defendant. The need to protect a witness against unfair questioning applies, of course, to all trials but it is of special importance in a trial for rape".[87]

3–37 Amongst the formidable critical literature devoted to this issue in England, few writers have braved a less absolutist perspective. The new provisions in England, considered to tilt the scales unduly at the expense of the defence, are more likely to generate analysis of the potential relevance of sexual history evidence to the facts at issue from the perspective of the defence. Geddes, a Circuit Court judge in England, has written that figures and assertions have been exaggerated in England over the past years, and the "argument that the [pre-1999 Act] law [was] not working is so weak that one is tempted to the conclusion that political pressure rather than rational thought was the driving force for change".[88] Of the new provisions, he believes "the resulting rigidity, which cannot take into account the myriad factual situations which daily face the courts, will result in miscarriages of justice".[89] Geddes criticises in particular the decision to extend the prohibition to all sexual behaviour of the complainant predating the incident under trial, whether with the accused or other persons. Although the Irish provisions opted for a similar definition of sexual experience (by deleting appropriate words from s.3 in 1990), s.3 of the 1981 Act provides for admissibility only in cases where the evidence is so probative as to raise a critical reasonable doubt. The new English provisions would subject the sexual history of the complainant's relationship with the accused (who could be a spouse, partner, cohabitee, former partner, etc.) to an apparently more straitened similarity-based test. Giving as an example the case of a former partner whose relationship with the complainant was stormy, but who had resumed sexual relations with the complainant prior to the night of the alleged rape, Geddes writes: "If the jury were unaware that there had been a long history of the complainant consenting to sexual intercourse with the accused after they had separated, before the sexual intercourse in question ... there must be a real

---

[87] *ibid.* at 46.
[88] Geddes, "The exclusion of evidence relating to a complainant's sexual behaviour in sexual offence trials" (1999) New L.J. 1084 at 1086.
[89] *ibid.* at p.1084.

danger that they would convict where otherwise they would acquit".[90] Elliot asserts that rape cases are objectively likely to suffer a higher rate of false evidence; given that the evidence is often limited to the complainant and the accused, there is "an opportunity to lie with impunity".[91] He draws attention to a number of *sui generis* motivations to lie in the context of regretted sexual intercourse, including the extrication from blame or guilt, anger after contracting a venereal disease, revenge, blackmail, or selective recall.[92]

VIII. PRE-TRIAL DISCLOSURE BY THE PROSECUTION

3–38 In terms of its content, the prosecutor's duty to the defence to disclose material information in advance of the trial is under construction both in Ireland and England.[93] Thus far the duty has been recognised to require disclosure of all information material to the evidence proposed to be given by the prosecution, and to other relevant evidence that the prosecutor does not intend to tender. The prosecutor's pre-trial duty also certainly includes information revealing any previous convictions of prosecution witnesses, and, importantly, previous statements or interviews (consistent or inconsistent) given by any proposed witness,[94] but also statements given by persons the prosecution no longer intends to call as witnesses but who may be of use to the defence.[95] The duty to disclose relevant witness statements and material evidence is a continuing one. All further statements made by a witness after service of the Book of Evidence must be disclosed to the defence in advance of the trial.[96]

3–39 In England, some decisions have construed the duty further to include information bearing upon the bad character of the proposed witness[97] or disclosing any potential bias or incentive on his part (such as that he requested a reward).[98] The House of Lords in *R. v Brown*[99] considered whether the duty

---

[90] *ibid.* at p.1084.
[91] Elliot, "Rape Complainants' Sexual Experience with Third Parties" [1984] Crim. L.R. 4 at 13.
[92] *ibid.*
[93] *cf.* para.**1–43** *et seq.*
[94] *People (DPP) v Kavanagh* (CCA, February 26, 1996); *R. v Taylor and Taylor* (1994) 98 Cr. App. R. 361 (CA): *cf.* para.**1–66**.
[95] *DPP v Special Criminal Court* [1999] 1 I.R. 60 (SC): *cf.* para.**1–66**. Conviction was quashed in *People (DPP) v Kavanagh* (CCA, February 26, 1996) due to the failure of the prosecution to disclose to the accused a report by a social welfare worker based upon an interview with the complainant in which a materially different account of events had been conveyed. In *People (DPP) v Flannery* (Central Criminal Court, June 25, 1996), the case was withdrawn from the jury due to the failure of the gardai to secure and disclose necessary statements from other relevant witnesses, which would have been likely to clarify concerns about the consumption of drugs and alcohol by the accused and other witnesses on the night of the alleged murder. In one of the undisclosed statements the witness claimed to have seen the deceased after the alleged date of his death.
[96] *People (DPP) v Scannell* (CCA, June 18, 1996).
[97] *R. v Paraskeva* (1983) 76 Cr. App. R. 162 (CA).
[98] *R. v Rasheed* (CCA, May 20, 1994).
[99] [1998] A.C. 367 (HL).

extends further to require the prosecution to disclose information relevant to the credibility of witnesses proposed to be called on behalf of the defence—in other words, whether the prosecution is required to give advance notice of the nature of the credibility challenge it intends to make against a defence witness, including the accused. The case specifically concerned disclosure of information that one of the prosecution's intended witnesses had told the police he withdrew his first statement after receiving threats from the accused, and that another had told the police that he was drunk at the material time and no longer able to comment on the accused's alibi. The House refused to approve an extension of the prosecutor's duty to disclose upon the basis that neither principle nor fairness justified it.

Further Reading

Adler, "Rape—the Intention of Parliament and the Practice of the Courts" (1982) 45 M.L.R. 664.
Adler, *Rape on Trial* (Routledge & Kegan Paul, London, 1987).
Connolly, *Gender and the Law* (Oak Tree Press, Dublin, 1993).
Elliot, "Rape Complainants' Sexual Experience with Third Parties" [1984] Crim. L.R. 4.
Elliot, "Consent and Belief in Trials for Sexual Offences" (2000) 150 New L.J. 1150.
Ellison, "Vulnerable Witnesses in Court" (1999) *International Journal of Evidence & Proof* 35.
Ellison, "Cross-examination in Rape Cases" [1998] Crim. L.R. 605.
Geddes, "The exclusion of evidence relating to a complainant's sexual behaviour in sexual offence trials" (1999) New L.J. 1084.
Kibble, "The Sexual History Provisions: Charting a Course between Inflexible Legislative Rules and Wholly Untrammelled Judicial Discretion" [2000] Crim. L.R. 274.
Law Reform Commission, *Rape: Consultation Paper* CP 1–1987.
Lees, *Carnal Knowledge Rape on Trial* (Hamish Hamilton, London, 1996).
McColgan, *The Case for Taking Date out of Rape* (Pandora, London, 1996).
McColgan, "Common Law and the Relevance of Sexual History Evidence" (1996) 16 *Oxford Journal of Legal Studies* 275.
McEwan, "The Rape Shield Askew? *R. v A*" (2001) 5(4) *International Journal of Evidence & Proof* 257.
Newark, "Opening Up the Collateral Issue Rule" (1992) 43 N.I.L.Q. 166.
O'Malley, *Sexual Offences Law, Policy and Punishment* (Round Hall Sweet & Maxwell, Dublin, 1996).
Rumney, "Male Rape in the Courtroom" [2001] Crim. L.R. 205.
Seabrooke, "The Vanishing Trick—blurring the line between credit and issue" [1999] Crim. L.R. 387.
Smith and Holdenson, "Comparative Evidence: Admissibility of Evidence of Relationship in Sexual Offence Prosecutions" (1999) 73 Aust. L.J. 432 & 494.
Tempkin, *Rape and the Legal Process* (Sweet & Maxwell, London, 1987).
Temkin, "Sexual History Evidence—the Ravishment of Section 2" [1993] Crim. L.R. 3.

CHAPTER 4

BURDENS AND STANDARDS OF PROOF

I. General Principles	4–01
II. The Burdens of Proof	4–05
The Legal Burden of Proof	4–05
Evidential Burdens	4–10
Presumptions of Law	4–13
Distinguishing the Legal Burden from Evidential Burdens	4–15
III. Defences	4–19
Defences in General	4–19
Defence of Insanity	4–29
IV. Reversal of the Burdens of Proof	4–31
Statutory Reversal of the Burdens	4–31
Common Law Principle: Criminal Cases	4–50
Common Law Principle and *Res Ipsa Loquitur*: Civil Cases	4–59
V. Standards of Proof	4–72
Criminal Proceedings	4–72
Civil Proceedings	4–79

I. GENERAL PRINCIPLES

4–01 Analysis of the burdens and standards of proof is chiefly concerned with questions of preliminary and final proof during the trial or hearing, the standard of proof that must be met, and the consequences of statutory provisions and presumptions of law for the parties. There is a very close nexus between judicial directions on the burdens of proof and the jury's decision to convict or acquit in criminal proceedings, and many reported cases demonstrate that if the closing directions suffer even minor deviation or ambiguity on so critical an issue, the conviction is unsafe and likely to be overturned upon appeal.

4–02 It is a fundamental principle common to most legal systems that he who wants the court to take action or to alter the status quo on his behalf must prove his case to the court's satisfaction: the *onus propandi* is said to be upon him. The *standard of proof* determines the degree to which the prosecution or plaintiff must satisfy the court that its case is proved. For reasons of public and legal policy,[1] the law insists that proof of criminal guilt must be beyond reasonable doubt, whereas generally in non-criminal proceedings the requisite standard is the balance of probabilities or a preponderance of the evidence.

4–03 Critical exploration of the burdens of proof has been beset in past years by a lack of consensus amongst commentators and an abundance of theory questing for a definitive analysis of the mechanics of proof, inference, and rebuttal in the trial. Although this has certainly enriched scholarship devoted to the subject, it seems to have had less impact on courtroom practice or its representation in the reported case law, certainly in Ireland. In England, by the first half of the twentieth century, the courts had recognised the application of presumptions of fact and presumptions of law, the former generated by specific facts proved in the case, the latter of general and automatic application such as the presumption of death after an absence of seven years.[2] In 1945, Denning published an article of particular influence in England,[3] in which he advocated a new classification of burdens and presumptions of proof inspired by Thayer's landmark analysis at the turn of the century.[4] Denning identified a provisional burden of proof, a legal burden of proof, and an ultimate burden of proof; he divided presumptions into provisional, compelling, and conclusive presumptions. Each of these concepts has been subjected to critical scrutiny, and few have survived it; the notions of provisional burdens,[5] conclusive presumptions,[6] and the ultimate burden[7] have not.

---

[1] *cf.* para.**1–03**.
[2] *cf.* para.**4–14**.
[3] Denning, "Presumptions and Burdens" [1945] 61 L.Q.R. 379.
[4] Thayer, *A Preliminary Treatise on Evidence at the Common Law* (1898), at chaps 8–9. See also Thayer and Stone, "Burden of Proof and the Judicial Process" (1944).
[5] In an article criticising Denning's model, Nigel Bridge, "Presumptions and Burdens" [1949] 12 M.L.R. 273—subsequently Lord Bridge—argued that the "provisional" burden was too vague to constitute a legal concept. Cross, *Evidence* (7th ed., Butterworths, London, 1990) at p.117 agreed, arguing that "it is devoid of legal significance because there is no means of telling when it has been brought into existence or when it has been discharged".
[6] Cross (*ibid.*) rejected the existence of a *conclusive* unrebuttable presumption—*i.e.* one which must be accepted by the court even if rebutted, such as the presumption against criminal responsibility of a young person; in his view, this was not evidence, but instead the application of a rule fixed by the substantive law.
[7] Denning defined the "ultimate" burden as "the burden on the ultimate issue"—by which he meant the issue upon which the court's decision ultimately swings: *e.g.* in a murder trial, whether the accused intentionally killed the deceased. Whereas each *legal burden of proof* remains fixed in the trial, and different legal burdens of proof may arise between the parties, the *ultimate burden of proof* shifts back and forth according to whether the parties have discharged their other burdens of proof. It seems likely that Denning considered it necessary to identify one further burden as a means of clarifying the nature of the legal burden of proof, although in doing so, the dynamics became unduly abstracted from courtroom realities. For a criticism of its use, see *Brady v Group Lotus Car Co.* [1987] 3 All E.R. 1050 at 1059, *per* Mustill J. (CA). Commentators and judges have often described the "legal" burden of proof as the "ultimate" burden, so it is safe to assume the demise of this as a further burden.

4–04 Since the publication of Denning's article, and despite the subsequent proliferation of classification and scholarship, the courts in recent decades have preferred contrastingly to identify the legal burden of proof and the evidential burden of proof. The legal burden of proof corresponds to the burden placed on the propounding party to prove the facts at issue[8] to the satisfaction of the court and to gain his relief or verdict. The evidential burdens of proof correspond to preliminary burdens of proof of the issues and thereafter to the number of transitional burdens upon propositions of fact that arise intermittently throughout the trial or hearing according to the vicissitudes of proof and the application of presumptions of law in the case.[9] These have become convenient—if often opaque—tools to comprehend the potential workings of inference and proof throughout the trial of the action.

II. THE BURDENS OF PROOF

The Legal Burden of Proof

4–05 The *legal burden of proof* has also variously been called the risk of non-persuasion, the obligation to persuade, the probative burden, the ultimate burden, the fixed burden, and the burden of proof upon the pleadings. It characteristically refers to the burden upon the prosecutor or plaintiff to prove all the essential elements of his case, and at the final hurdle to persuade the triers of fact of the accused's criminal guilt as charged or of the plaintiff's entitlement to the relief as sought in the writ. As a matter of law, logic, and policy, the legal burden of proof is imposed upon, and remains with, the proponent of the issue, namely the prosecutor in criminal trials and the plaintiff in civil hearings. Much is gleaned of the legal burden by considering its *nom de guerre*, "the risk of non-persuasion". The party bearing the legal burden must, by the close of the proceedings, persuade the court to the requisite standard that he has proved his case. If he declines to rebut evidence tendered by the opposing party, he risks failing to persuade the court that his case has adequately been proved. The prosecution or plaintiff assumes the risk of non-persuasion once the evidence for its case is concluded, and, following final submissions, when the judges or jury retire to consider their decision in light of the evidence adduced and the substantive law.

4–06 The *extent* of the legal burden in particular cases is determined by reference to the rules of substantive law applicable to the dispute. For instance, generally in cases of rape, the prosecution must establish the facts of penetrative sexual intercourse of the complainant by the accused forcibly or without the complainant's consent. Where the plaintiff sues the accused for damages due

---

[8] *cf.* paras **1–15, 4–06**.
[9] Bridge, "Presumptions and Burdens" [1949] 12 M.L.R. 273 at 275 favoured reference to "evidential burdens" instead of "provisional burdens". Less successful was his proposition that the "legal burden" should instead be referred to as the "fixed burden" since the "legal burden" misleadingly suggests that this is the only type of burden determined by substantive law.

to negligence, the plaintiff will be required to prove the following facts at issue, unless conceded: that the defendant owed the plaintiff a duty of care; that the defendant breached his duty of care; that the plaintiff suffered loss or injury of a type actionable at law; and that the plaintiff's loss or injury was caused by the defendant's breach of duty.

4–07 Given the immense practical and symbolic importance of the presumption of innocence for the common law criminal justice system, and given the nature and consequences of criminal charges and convictions, there is far more concern in criminal proceedings to ensure that the legal burden is imposed and remains upon the prosecution. This was famously articulated by Viscount Sankey L.C. in *Woolmington v DPP*:[10]

> "Throughout the web of the English criminal law one golden thread is always to be seen, that it is the duty of the prosecution to prove the prisoner's guilt subject to ... the defence of insanity and subject also to any statutory exception. ... No matter what the charge or where the trial, the principle that the prosecution must prove the guilt of the prisoner is part of the common law of England and no attempt to whittle it down can be entertained".

4–08 In *Attorney-General v O'Leary*,[11] the presumption of innocence was acknowledged by Costello J. to have protected constitutional status under Art.38(1), despite the absence of express reference to it in the Constitution: "It seems to me that it has been for so long a fundamental postulate of every criminal trial in this country that the accused was presumed to be innocent of the offence with which he was charged that a criminal trial held otherwise than in accordance with this presumption would, prima facie, be one which was not held in due course of law under Article 38." The presumption of innocence has likewise been construed to constitute a fundamental human right, embedded in Art. 6(2) of the European Convention of Human Rights. In *Barbera, Messegue and Jabardo v Spain*,[12] the European Court of Human Rights reasoned that the presumption of innocence entails the non-admission of prejudicial evidence (such as evidence of past crimes), adherence to the principle that the prosecution bears the burden of proving guilt beyond reasonable doubt, and adequate pre-trial disclosure by the prosecution:

> "It requires, *inter alia*, that when carrying out their duties, the members of a court should not start with the preconceived idea that the accused has committed the offence charged; the burden of proof is on the prosecution, and any doubt should benefit the accused. It also follows that it is for the prosecution to inform the accused of the case that will be made against him, so that he may prepare and present his defence accordingly, and to adduce evidence sufficient to convict him."

---

[10] [1935] A.C. 462 at 481 (HL): *cf.* appendix 5.
[11] [1991] I.L.R.M. 454 at 459 (HC).
[12] (1988) 11 E.H.R.R. 360 at para.77.

4–09 The substantive law recognises in exceptional cases, however, that sometimes the accused may be caused to bear a legal burden of proof upon a specific issue. For instance, by way of well-entrenched common law rule—known in England as the first exception to the *Woolmington* principle—where the accused raises the defence of insanity in trials for murder, he bears a legal burden of proof upon that issue, and if he fails to persuade the jury to the appropriate degree, he must be convicted of murder.[13]

Evidential Burdens

4–10 The evidential burden has broadened as a concept to embrace two general dynamics of proof in the hearing or trial. The first alone constitutes a *burden* of proof in the obligatory sense of the word. This is the obligation to tender evidence in support of an issue the party is propounding. As a general principle, applicable to a much greater extent in civil proceedings, an evidential burden lies upon the party who states an affirmative (not a negative or denial) in substance (not form), and who would benefit if no evidence were tendered upon that issue.[14] Since the legal burden of proof of the facts in issue is generally upon the party who initiated the proceedings—whether prosecutor, plaintiff, or applicant—this party is required at the preliminary stage of the trial or hearing to make a sufficient case (also roughly described as a prima facie case) in support of the particular issues advanced before the court. Until recently in the context of criminal proceedings upon indictment, the initial proof of prima facie case took place at the election of the accused by way of preliminary examination in the District Court. This was recently abolished by s.5(4) of the Criminal Justice (Miscellaneous Provisions) Act 1997. Section 9 of the 1997 Act inserted s.4E into the Criminal Procedure Act 1967 as an alternative device enabling him to apply to the court of trial, prior to the trial date, to have one or more charges against him dismissed.[15] The section does not expressly state that the accused bears a burden to show cause, though it is ordinarily amenable to that interpretation, and may imply it; since not specified, however, it is open to the judiciary to develop it *in tandem* with previous common law and statutory rules enabling the accused to request an early showing of prima facie case in support of the criminal charges. The statutory right of an accused prior to the 1997 Act to require a preliminary examination of the charges in the District Court had been interpreted by the Supreme Court not to constitute a constitutional right.[16] Upon this basis, it may be deduced that constitutional concerns are not exigent on this issue, although such an assumption is questionable having regard to the Constitution's express commitment to personal liberty under Art.40.4.1°.

---

[13] *cf.* para.**4–29** *et seq.*
[14] *Phipson on Evidence* (15th ed., Sweet & Maxwell, London, 2000) at p.60; Heydon, *Evidence Cases & Materials* (3rd ed., Butterworths, London, 1991) at p.16.
[15] *cf.* para.**1–50**.
[16] *O'Shea v DPP* [1988] I.R. 655 (SC).

4–11 In terms of proof of evidential facts *during* the trial or hearing, the defence can request, as a matter of common law right at least, an early ruling on whether the prosecution or plaintiff has raised a prima facie case by tendering sufficient evidence upon which a jury, properly directed, could reasonably find in its favour.[17] This application, where made during a trial, is usually made at the close of the prosecution's or plaintiff's case, although a determination of this nature may be made by the trial judge at any stage in the trial or hearing prior to the deliberation. If the trial judge considers by the close of the hearing or trial that insufficient evidence has been tendered in support of a fact at issue—whether a charge, claim, or defence—the trial judge may decide to withdraw that issue from the jury or strike out a charge against the accused, upon the basis that a decision on the issue in the absence of adequate evidence would be unreasonable and perverse.

4–12 Aside from the logical obligation to raise an arguable case in support of a proposition or issue introduced in the proceedings, a second type of evidential burden has been identified by judges and jurists, although this corresponds to burdens distinguished previously as "provisional", "tactical", and "transitional" burdens. It is necessary to identify this additional dynamic chiefly to enable the court to distinguish between the legal burden of proof and other types of burden. It has helpfully been likened to a "tactical burden" that may fall upon one party after his opponent has successfully advanced evidence raising an evidential inference adverse to the other. In some cases, as a matter of tactics, the party may decide not to rebut the adverse inference, where, for instance, the attempt to rebut might precipitate more damage to his case than silence. This "burden" is tactical or evidential in the criminal context only where the defence may decide not to rebut the inference without necessarily incurring an adverse decision on the ultimate issues; in other words, where the accused's failure to rebut the inference does not affect the placement of the legal burden resting upon the prosecution. Because the tactical "burdens" are said to shift back and forth creating temporary inferences until and unless rebutted, they are often also called *provisional burdens*.[18] As part of proving its case or of supporting its version of events, either party will seek to establish various favourable relevant facts. In a negligence action, the plaintiff may seek to establish that he had made it known to the defendant he was relying

---

[17] A direction of this kind is not appropriate where the weakness of the prosecution's case depends upon an assessment of a witness's reliability, or where it is possible to take a reasonable view of the prosecution's evidence and find in its favour. The appropriate criteria were set out in *R. v Galbraith* [1981] 2 All E.R. 1060, *per* Lord Lane C.J. (CA) (*cf.* appendix 28), and were applied by the Court of Criminal Appeal in *DPP v Barnwell* (CCA, January 24, 1997), *DPP v M* (CCA, February 15, 2001), and *People (DPP) v Kenny* (CCA, November 19, 2002). The principles were applied in civil proceedings in *McKevitt v Ireland and Attorney General* [1987] I.L.R.M. 541, where they divided the Supreme Court: *cf.* paras **1–23, 1–50**.

[18] A reference favoured by Denning, "Presumptions and Burdens" [1945] 61 L.Q.R. 379 at 380: "As the case proceeds the evidence may first weigh in favour of the inference and then against it, thus producing a burden, sometimes apparent, sometimes real, which may shift from one party to the other as the case proceeds or may remain suspended between them".

exclusively upon his financial advice, whereas the defendant will seek to establish he undertook no responsibility with respect to the plaintiff's finances. In a rape case, the prosecution will establish the context of the offence and the circumstances in which the complainant encountered the accused. These facts are part of the building blocks of each case, and may be referred to as *evidential facts*. If we visualise the trial in the abstract, we can see that the aim of each side is to adduce prima facie evidence so that an *inference* of a fact arises in its favour on as many relevant facts as possible—thereby causing the tactical or provisional burden on the proposition to pass, temporarily or permanently, to his opponent. If the opponent succeeds in rebutting the inference, the provisional burden upon the proposition returns to the other side, and so on. The reality of course is that we hardly know during a trial or hearing precisely when a provisional evidential burden has been discharged by one side and when it has been caused to pass to the other, except where the issue between the parties is a net one and, owing to evidential gaps in the case, there is little evidence in support of, or against, the issue. The attempt to describe this aspect of the evidential "burden", though it poorly reflects the actual ebb and flow of issues in the trial, is chiefly necessary in cases where statute has redistributed the burdens of proof, and in cases where presumptions of law are invoked causing one side unexpectedly to bear a burden of disproof of a prima facie inference permitted or required to arise by operation of the law.

Presumptions of Law

4–13 Presumptions of law require or enable certain inferences to be drawn by the court, usually upon proof of prescribed grounding facts. The resulting inference constitutes evidence in the case, and prevails in the hearing or trial unless and until rebutted by the other party.[19] Most of the presumptions of law not already discussed in this chapter apply to civil proceedings. Where the inference is a fact at issue in the hearing and the presumption requires the court to accept the inference if unrebutted, a *persuasive* presumption is said to have been raised which has the effect of re-allocating an aspect of the plaintiff's legal burden of proof. Where the court may or may not accept the unrebutted inference, a *provisional* presumption is said to have arisen casting an evidential burden upon the opponent. The failure of the trial judge to recognise and apply the appropriate principles is likely to constitute a fundamental error in the hearing where bearing upon the ultimate decision.

4–14 Some presumptions apply automatically without proof of any grounding fact, *e.g.* the presumptions of innocence and sanity in criminal proceedings,[20] and the presumption of competence in succession cases.[21] Most presumptions, however, require proof initially of one or more grounding facts. For instance,

---

[19] An interestingly diverse range of perspectives emerged in *Mulhern v Clery* [1930] I.R. 118 (SC) with respect to the evidence necessary to initiate and to rebut the old presumption of "common law marriage" raised by evidence of "co-habitation and repute or tradition".
[20] *cf.* paras **4–07** *et seq.*, paras **4–29** *et seq.*
[21] *cf.* para.**4–80**.

to invoke the presumption of death after a seven years' absence, there must first be evidence before the court establishing an absence of communication for seven years or more, with people in court to testify to this fact, and further that every reasonable attempt to contact the person was made.[22] To invoke the presumption of accidental death, the proponent of the issue is required to establish that the causes of death are unknown, whereupon the opponent bears a burden to rebut the inference by establishing suicide.[23] To invoke the *res ipsa loquitur* maxim, considered above, the plaintiff must usually establish that the event that gave rise to the injury was under the management of the defendant, and that it was of a type that ordinarily does not occur if those exercising control of the event exercised due care.[24]

Distinguishing the Legal Burden from Evidential Burdens

4–15 The necessity to distinguish between legal and evidential burdens arises chiefly in cases where, by virtue of common law rule or statute, a burden is imposed upon the accused in his own trial, which if not discharged exposes him to adverse inferences or in exceptional cases to conviction. The failure to discharge an evidential burden upon a particular proposition is only as significant in the trial as the proposition. In principle, the legal burden upon the prosecution in criminal proceedings is unaffected by the failure of the accused to attempt to rebut various evidential facts and inferences established by the prosecution. The accused can put the prosecution fully to proof by exercising his right to silence and electing not to testify,[25] and he may yet be acquitted if the prosecution fails to prove its case beyond reasonable doubt.

4–16 The imposition of the legal burden of proof upon the accused or defendant is an altogether more serious matter. We recognise that the legal burden has been affected where: (1) a burden of disproof of the facts at issue (*e.g.* that the accused intentionally killed the deceased as charged, or that the defendant was negligent as pleaded) has been transferred to the defence; *and* (2) the consequence of the defence's failure to rebut the inference (or to discharge the burden upon the issue) is that the court is obliged to rule in the prosecution's or the plaintiff's favour. As a general rule, one knows that the legal burden has been redistributed where the ordinary effect is that the accused should be convicted in the absence of exculpatory evidence to rebut the inference. In this case, the burden is clearly not a provisional or tactical burden but corresponds to the risk of non-persuasion.

---

[22] *Chard v Chard* [1955] 3 All E.R. 721. The presumption was successfully applied in *Re Bonis Doherty* [1961] I.R. 219 (HC) in the context of an application by the Minister for Finance for a declaration that the relevant person was dead and that the Minister was entitled in *bona vacantia* to various shares registered in the person's name.

[23] Applied against an assurance company in *Harvey v Ocean Accident and Guarantee Corporation* [1905] 2 K.B. 1 (CA), where the court reasoned, in circumstances where the deceased's body had been discovered drowned in the river Lee, that the evidence was evenly balanced, and so therefore the presumption of death by accident prevailed.

[24] *cf.* para.**4–59**.

[25] *cf.* paras **2–16** *et seq.*, **13–84** *et seq.*

4–17 In such matters, the niceties of theory must swiftly be put to the service of practical necessity. In the few cases where the dominant issue at the close of the trial or appeal is the burden of proof, the consequences of misapplying the relevant principles are stark, as a quick trawl through the reported case law demonstrates. In *Pickup v Thames Insurance Co.*,[26] an action upon a policy of insurance on freight, the defence was that the vessel had been unseaworthy. The judge directed the jury that the fact that the ship had been unable to continue shortly after sailing gave rise to a presumption of unseaworthiness, shifting a burden of disproof to the accused. This was rightly rejected on appeal, upon the basis that any presumption of unseaworthiness that may have arisen from the facts established in evidence was provisional only, in the sense that it did not oblige the court to make that finding if the presumption remained uncontradicted. The legal burden of proof had remained on the plaintiffs. Most memorably, in *DPP v Woolmington*[27]—where in a trial for his wife's murder the accused based his defence upon accidental shooting—the trial judge wrongly caused the jury to believe that once it was proved that the accused had killed the deceased, the jury was obliged to presume murder unless and until the accused proved he was not guilty. The words used by the trial judge were as follows: "If the Crown satisfies you that the woman died at the prisoner's hands, [the accused] has to show you that there are circumstances to be found in evidence given from the witness box which show that it was manslaughter or that there was no homicide". The trial judge's logic was approved by the Court of Criminal Appeal—a stark indication of the disarray into which these issues had slipped. The appeal to the House of Lords succeeded upon the basis that proof of the killing gave rise to a provisional inference of the accused's guilt, but that this inference was provisional only and it did not require or oblige the jury to accept it: the legal burden of proof had remained upon the prosecution to prove the accused's guilt beyond reasonable doubt.

4–18 It is necessary next to consider when and with what effect an evidential or a legal burden may be imposed upon the accused or a defendant by reason of: (i) the defences that he runs; or (ii) the application of statutory provision and common law principle. There is now a great need in Ireland, given recent legislative trends, to understand the effect of statutory provision attaching adverse consequences to the accused's failure to rebut inferences or to tender exonerating evidence. Not alone are such provisions structurally inconsistent with the common law accusatorial model of criminal justice and process—and most obviously with the presumption of innocence and the right to silence—they have the potential to expose the accused upon minimal evidence to conviction due to his failure or, worse, his inability to rebut the charges.

---

[26] (1878) 3 Q.B.D. 594.
[27] [1935] A.C. 462 (HL): *cf.* para.**4–07**, appendix 5.

III. DEFENCES

Defences in General

4–19 As a general principle, though applicable more clearly in civil proceedings, the defendant bears an evidential burden to adduce evidence in support of issues raised in defence that are not in substance mere denials of the proponent's claims.[28] When considering the question of defences raised by the accused in criminal proceedings, we are most concerned about the possible imposition upon him of an evidential burden in the obligatory sense of the word, as a burden that may need to be discharged in order to raise the issue evidentially—often called making a prima facie case—before the court. In the criminal context, this is often described as a burden upon the accused to establish a reasonable doubt in the minds of the jury with respect to the defence issue when raised. The Irish courts have conspicuously avoided this rationalisation, however, upon the basis that it is apt to mislead juries and cause them to overlook the fundamental necessity for proof by the prosecution of criminal guilt beyond reasonable doubt. This is most evident in Walsh J.'s weighty ruling in *Attorney-General v Quinn*.[29]

4–20 For some time, there was little direct authority on the nature of the obligations or burdens, if any, upon the accused in his trial. It has been pointed out, however, that for some time after *Woolmington* the courts continued to impose an evidential burden of proof of defence issues upon the accused.[30] There has been some support for the view that the accused bears an evidential burden to establish affirmative or fresh-issue defences (such as duress, provocation, self-defence, alibi) upon the basis that these are not mere denials of the charges[31] and sufficient evidence may not necessarily be before the court on such issues. On the other hand, it has been pointed out that few fresh-issue defences (such as accident, alibi, self-defence) are not essentially mere denials of an element of the charges, and it is logically impossible that each party bears a burden on the same issue.[32] The consequences for an accused of bearing a burden or obligation to tender evidence upon the issue are two-fold. First, he must adduce a minimum of evidence to justify submitting the issue to the jury for their decision and to avoid a decision by the trial judge withdrawing the issue. Second, given that any such burden on the accused has been interpreted to be evidential—save for the defence of insanity, which imposes a legal burden of proof upon the accused—the mere raising of the defence is not

---

[28] Glanville Williams, *Criminal Law* (2nd ed., Stevens & Sons, London) at pp. 909–10; *Phipson on Evidence* (15th ed., Sweet & Maxwell, London, 2000) at p.60; Heydon, *Evidence Cases & Materials* (3rd ed., Butterworths, London, 1991) at p.16.

[29] [1965] I.R. 366 (SC): *cf.* para.**4–23** *et seq.* and appendix 13.

[30] Smith, "The Presumption of Innocence" (1987) 38 N.I.L.Q. 223 at 225. Post-*Woolmington* decisions continued to impose an onus upon the accused to prove self-defence and duress, and were not overruled until, respectively, *Chan Kau v R.* [1955] A.C. 206 (PC) and *R. v Gill* [1963] 2 All E.R. 688 (CA).

[31] Cross, *Evidence* (7th ed., Butterworths, London, 1990) at p.122.

[32] Glanville Williams, *Criminal Onus & Exculpations.*

enough by itself to warrant an acquittal in the absence of rebuttal evidence by the prosecution. The jury is reminded instead that the prosecution must prove its case beyond a reasonable doubt, which inevitably will require removing any reasonable doubts raised by the defence.

4–21 Although this is the inexorable logic of the burdens of proof, the practice of the Irish courts, since Walsh J.'s defining judgment in *Attorney-General v Quinn*,[33] has been to steer clear of reference to burdens of proof upon the accused in criminal proceedings, and instead to recharacterise the question as whether the court has sufficient evidence upon which it may reasonably decide the issue raised by the accused, whether that evidence comes from the accused or the prosecution. This approach broadly takes the view that on any issue placed before the court for its decision, sufficient evidence must in any event be adduced to raise an arguable case upon which the court can reasonably decide the question, one way or the other. Although admirable for requiring the trial judge's closing directions to focus on the legal burden and standard of proof upon the prosecution, and for seeking to avoid confusion in the minds of the jury on so critical a dynamic, the validity of this approach rests upon an acceptance that the accused may tender evidence in support of the defence as a matter of discretion and not obligation, a theoretic nicety that denies the underlying aim of a rule forcing him to proof on any issue.

4–22 The groundwork for this approach had been lain earlier in *Bratty v Attorney-General for N.I.*[34] The House of Lords decided that where the accused bases his defence on accident or provocation or "non-insane automatism" (in other words where he raises an affirmative or fresh-issue defence), he is obliged to lay a "proper foundation" for the defence or he risks not having the issue put to the jury. This was described by Viscount Kilmuir L.C. as requiring "positive evidence which would justify a finding by the jury" in his favour or "evidence ... on which a reasonable jury could act".[35] The Court of Appeal had explained its decision in terms of onus or burden upon the accused; the House of Lords wisely made little reference to onus in this context, although the court did not rule it out. It is clear that the speeches in *Bratty* are similarly motivated by a concern that the jury be presented with adequate evidence on each fact at issue, whether from the defence or the prosecution, to justify the court embarking upon a decision with respect to the issue: "the defence must be able to point to some evidence, whether it emanates from their own or the Crown's witnesses, from which the jury could reasonably infer that the accused acted in a state of automatism".[36]

4–23 In *Attorney-General v Quinn*,[37] the accused appealed against conviction for the manslaughter of a neighbour with whom he had been drinking in a

---

[33] [1965] I.R. 366 (SC): *cf.* appendix 13.
[34] [1963] A.C. 386 (HL): *cf.* appendix 10.
[35] *ibid.* at 405.
[36] *ibid.* at 406, *per* Kilmuir L.C.
[37] [1965] I.R. 366 (SC): *cf.* appendix 13.

local pub on the night in question. Although they had been seen leaving the pub on a friendly footing, they were witnessed shortly after arguing over a fork that one had borrowed from the other. According to the medical evidence, the deceased man died as a result of a single blow from the fist causing him to fall to the ground and fracture his skull. The accused claimed he had acted in self-defence, striking a blow to the deceased only after he had avoided a hit. When giving closing directions upon the burdens and standards of proof, the trial judge had used words suggesting the case hinged upon proof by the accused that he had acted in self-defence: "The case for the prosecution is that there is no question of self-defence. They must satisfy you it was manslaughter. The defence need not satisfy you it was self-defence, if you have a real doubt about it. The State says that you should have no doubt".[38] The Supreme Court quashed the accused's conviction solely upon the basis that the direction "might reasonably have left [the jury] under the impression that while there was no onus upon the defence to establish self-defence beyond reasonable doubt or as a matter of certainty yet there was some obligation to make a sufficient impression in the jury's mind to create at least a doubt about the State's case".[39] According to Walsh J:

> "When the evidence in a case, whether it be the evidence offered by the prosecution or by the defence, discloses a possible defence of self-defence the onus remains throughout upon the prosecution to establish that the accused is guilty of the offence charged. The onus is never upon the accused to establish a doubt in the minds of the jury. In such case the burdens rests on the prosecution to negative the possible defence of self-defence which has arisen and if, having considered the whole of the evidence, the jury is either convinced of the innocence of the prisoner or left in doubt whether or not he was acting in necessary self-defence they must acquit".[40]

4–24 Walsh J. proceeded to explain that where the accused introduces an issue in his defence, it is necessary, but also sufficient, that he adduce "some evidence" on that issue "from which the jury would be entitled to find that issue in [his] favour".[41] Although theoretically this places some kind of obligation upon him to establish an inference in favour of his proposition,[42] at most it could be said to be tactical or evidential. On the other hand, the attractiveness of the rule in *Quinn* against characterising this as "onus" or "burden", and its appropriateness to Irish criminal justice, lies in its decision to address defences from the perspective of evidence finally before the triers of fact and not the *burden* of proof, which is apt in the minds of juries and

---

[38] [1965] I.R. 366 at 380.
[39] *ibid.* at 381, *per* Walsh J.
[40] *ibid.* at 382.
[41] *ibid.* at 383.
[42] For instance, McAuley and McCutcheon, *Criminal Liability* (Round Hall Sweet and Maxwell, Dublin, 2000) at p.851 write that the accused bears a "burden ... [to] show that provocation is a live issue" and he must establish "a credible narrative of events suggesting the presence of the various elements of the defence".

occasionally judges to be confused with the overarching principles underpinning proof by the prosecution of criminal guilt and the presumption of innocence:

> "Before the possible defence can be left to the jury as an issue there must be some evidence from which the jury would be entitled to find that issue in favour of the appellant. If the evidence for the prosecution does not disclose this possible defence then the necessary evidence will fall to be given by the defence. In such a case, however, where it falls to the defence to give the necessary evidence it must be made clear to the jury that there is a distinction, fine though it may appear, between adducing the evidence and the burden of proof and that there is no onus upon the accused to establish any degree of doubt in their minds. In directing the jury on the question of the onus of proof it can only be misleading to a jury to refer to 'establishing' the defence 'in such a way as to raise a doubt.' No defence has to be 'established' in any case apart from insanity. In a case where there is evidence, whether it be disclosed in the prosecution case or in the defence case, which is sufficient to leave the issue of self-defence to the jury the only question the jury has to consider is whether they are satisfied beyond reasonable doubt that the accused killed the deceased (if it be a case of homicide) and whether the jury is satisfied beyond reasonable doubt that the prosecution has negatived the issue of self-defence".[43]

4–25 Numerous recent appeals have been taken against directions by the trial judge on defence issues. In some of these cases, the matter was disposed of by reference to the absence of evidence essential to establish the elements of the defence under the substantive law.[44] The framework provided by the *Quinn* decision has strengthened over the years. By the case of *People (DPP) v Clarke*,[45] the Court of Criminal Appeal was requesting trial courts to adhere strictly to the observations in *Quinn*, whenever a fresh-issue defence, such as self-defence, was raised by the accused. In *Clarke*, the only evidence in support of self-defence—the accused having elected not to testify—emanated from parts of statements made by him upon his arrest, which had been deemed admissible in the trial due to inculpatory content capable of rendering the statements confessions.[46] The trial judge accepted that self-defence had thereby been raised by the accused, but directed the jury that "a statement made to the guards is not at all in the same category as a statement made on oath subject to cross-examination," and whilst the jury could in theory acquit the accused on

---

[43] [1965] I.R. 366 at 382–83 (SC).
[44] e.g. *People (DPP) v Doyle* (CCA, March 22, 2002) and *People (DPP) v Halligan* (CCA, July 13, 1998), where there was no evidence before the courts tending to establish a "sudden and temporary loss of self control" for the purposes of the defence of provocation.
[45] [1994] 3 I.R. 289 (CCA). See also *DPP v Cremin* (CCA, May 10, 1999), applying the *Quinn* principle and finding that the accused never bears an onus to prove the defence to the satisfaction of the court.
[46] *cf.* para.**10–67** *et seq.*

grounds of self-defence, the facts hardly admitted of that possibility. The Court of Criminal Appeal quashed the conviction. O'Flaherty J. recognised that "once a [confession] statement is put in evidence, as in this case by the prosecution, it then and thereby becomes evidence in the real sense of the word, not only against the person who made it but for him as to facts contained in it favourable to his defence, or case".[47] Once the defence had been raised, a charge along the lines of *Quinn* had been required.

4–26 In *People (DPP) v Bambrick*,[48] conviction was overturned because of a reference by the trial judge when summing-up to the need to ascertain whether the defence of provocation had been established as "likely" or "probable". Lynch J. of the Court of Criminal Appeal accepted that these words may have suggested a burden upon the accused. Reference instead should have been made to the need to ascertain the reasonable possibility of the existence of the facts upon which the defence was based, and which might in turn raise a reasonable doubt in the minds of the jury. Although the decision accepts the need to avoid reference to any formal burden upon the accused, it appears finally, but without consequence in the case, to conflate two stages, and to deviate from the view clearly expressed in *Quinn* that the "onus is never on the accused to establish a doubt in the minds of the jury".[49] The question whether sufficient evidence has been tendered in support of an issue (phrased variously as "raising an arguable case", "tendering sufficient evidence upon which a jury could reasonably decide", etc.) is an initial evidential concern preceding the trial judge's decision to submit or to withdraw the particular issue to or from the jury. When the issue is evidentially raised and alive in the case, it properly falls to be considered by the jury and, in light of all the evidence in the case, accorded weight as appropriate; but it should feature in the trial judge's closing directions only in the context of the question whether the prosecution has proven the crimes beyond all reasonable doubt.

4–27 In *People (DPP) v Davis*,[50] the Court of Criminal Appeal—whilst apparently approving the views of McAuley and McCutcheon[51] that the accused bears a burden evidentially to raise the defence of provocation—expressed the need to ensure that there is evidence before the jury tending to establish the presence of all the elements of the defence of provocation, whether arising from evidence adduced by the accused or from inferences in the case as a whole. The view favoured by *Quinn*—that the grounding evidence may derive from any inferences or evidence adduced in the case, whether from the defence or prosecution—was repeated in *People (DPP) v Halligan*.[52]

---

[47] [1994] 3 I.R. 289 at 303 (CCA).
[48] [1999] 2 I.L.R.M. 71 (CCA).
[49] [1965] I.R. 366 at 382 (SC): *cf.* appendix 13.
[50] [2001] 1 I.R. 146 (CCA).
[51] *op. cit.* n.42.
[52] CCA, July 13, 1998.

4–28 Conviction was overturned in *People (DPP) v Cotter*[53] due to the possibility that the trial judge's directions might have been construed by the jury to indicate that the accused bore a burden to disprove the presumption that he intended the natural and probable consequences of his acts.[54] Lynch J. considered it would be better that trial judges advised as follows: "If you are satisfied beyond a reasonable doubt that the presumption of intending the natural and probable consequences of conduct has not been rebutted then that presumption applies and you may convict of murder. If, however, you are not so satisfied, then you must have a reasonable doubt as to whether or not the presumption applies and you should acquit of murder. There is no onus on the accused to establish anything".

Defence of Insanity

4–29 Under the entrenched common law exception, derived from Rule 2 of the *M'Naghten rules*,[55] the accused bears a legal burden of proof of his insanity where raised as a defence to the charge of murder. The burden imposed upon the accused is a legal burden of proof, and if he fails to discharge it, he is presumed to have intended the natural consequences of his act and is therefore guilty of the murder. In *Bratty v Attorney-General for N.I.*,[56] where the accused's defence to the charge of murdering an 18-year-old woman by strangulation was based on insanity and automatism arising from a defect of reason caused by mental disease, the House of Lords decided that the imposition of the legal burden applied equally to the defence of insane automatism where the insanity was alleged to arise from "a defect of reason from disease of the mind".[57]

4–30 The imposition of the legal burden upon the accused exposes him to conviction if he fails to persuade the triers of fact in his favour. Since this is regarded as an exceptional and severe occurrence, the courts have tended to require proof by the accused according to the civil standard, upon the balance of probabilities.[58] The House of Lords confirmed this view in *Bratty*[59] and *R*.

---

[53] CCA, June 28, 1999.

[54] The rebuttable common law presumption that the accused intended the natural and probable consequences of his acts is enshrined in s.4(2) of the Criminal Justice Act 1964. Section 4(2) was interpreted in *People (Attorney-General) v Dwyer* [1972] I.R. 416 (SC) and *People (DPP) v Murray* [1977] I.R. 360 (SC), and found to impose an *evidential* burden upon the accused; therefore, the prosecution bears the burden of establishing that the presumption has not been rebutted.

[55] *R. v M'Naghten* (1843) 4 St. Tr. 847. Rule 2 reads: "Every man is to be presumed to be sane and to possess a sufficient degree of reason to be responsible for his crimes until the contrary is proved." This was subsequently interpreted to cast the legal burden upon the accused in trials for murder: *R. v Stokes* (1848) 3 Car. & Kir. 185; *R. v Layton* (1949) 4 Cox C.C. 149; *Bratty v Attorney-General for Northern Ireland* [1963] A.C. 386 (HL).

[56] [1963] A.C. 386 (HL).

[57] *ibid.* at 404–05.

[58] *Woolmington v DPP* [1935] A.C. 462 at 475 (HL); *Sodeman v R.* [1936] 2 All E.R. 1138 (PC); *R. v Carr-Briant* [1943] K.B. 607 (CA).

[59] [1963] A.C. 386 (HL).

v Berry,[60] and it has since functioned as a general principle for all cases in which the legal burden of proof of an issue is cast upon the accused. According to Lord Kilmuir where the accused seeks to found his defence upon insanity, he "must prove on the preponderance of probabilities, first a defect of reason from a disease of the mind, and, secondly, as a consequence of such a defect, ignorance of the nature and quality (or the wrongfulness) of the acts".[61] The Court of Criminal Appeal incorporated this approach in *Attorney-General v Boylan*,[62] endorsing *Sodeman v R.*,[63] and finding that the burden on the accused is "not higher than that which rested upon a plaintiff or defendant in civil proceedings". Although the court once erroneously considered the criminal standard of proof applicable,[64] the civil standard principle has prevailed for some time with respect to the defence of insanity[65] and to any instance when a legal burden is imposed upon the accused in criminal proceedings.[66]

IV. Reversal of the Burdens of Proof

Statutory Reversal of the Burdens

4–31 A statute may determine which party bears the burden of proving or disproving a specified fact, and frequently does so expressly[67] or implicitly by means of reverse-onus clauses enabling an early inference in support of a proposition "unless the contrary is proved". In effect, reverse-onus clauses and other like devices work to relieve the prosecution of proof of a particular issue by recasting that issue as a statutory defence, often for reasons of public policy and expediency, and sometimes to put the accused on proof of matters more peculiarly within his knowledge (a criterion that formerly functioned in criminal proceedings as a separate common law principle).[68] This dynamic is evident in the structuring of s.50(8) of the Road Traffic Act 1961, as inserted by s.11 of the Road Traffic Act 1994, which relieves the prosecution of proving that a person found to be "in charge" of his vehicle whilst under the influence

---

[60] [1985] 1 A.C. 246 (HL).
[61] [1963] A.C. 386 at 403 (HL).
[62] [1937] I.R. 449 at 458 (CCA).
[63] *Sodeman v R.* [1936] 2 All E.R. 1138 (PC).
[64] *People (Attorney-General) v Fennell (No.1)* [1940] I.R. 445 (CCA). O'Sullivan C.J.'s decision was subsequently criticised by the Court of Appeal in *R. v Carr-Briant* [1943] K.B. 607 at 611 for having mistaken submissions by counsel as judicial findings in *Sodeman v R.* [1936] 2 All E.R. 1138 (PC).
[65] *People v O'Mahoney* [1985] I.R. 517 (SC).
[66] *Convening Authority v Doyle* [1996] 2 I.L.R.M. 213 (C.M.A.C.), approving *R. v Carr-Briant* [1943] K.B. 607 (CA); *Hardy v Ireland* [1994] 2 I.R. 550 (SC), Egan and Murphy J.J. approving *R. v Fegan* [1972] N.I. 80 (CA) and *R. v Berry* [1985] A.C. 246 (HL).
[67] *e.g.* School Attendance Act 1926, s.18(2), which expressly imposes a burden upon an accused parent to show "reasonable excuse" for his child's non-attendance at school, and which may be discharged upon proof that the child was receiving "suitable elementary education" for the purposes of s.4(2)(b); considered in *DPP v Best* [2000] 2 I.R. 17 (SC).
[68] *cf.* para.**4–50** *et seq.*

of alcohol had an intention to drive the car: "In a prosecution for an offence under this section, it shall be presumed that the Defendant intended to drive or attempt to drive the vehicle concerned until he shows the contrary".[69]

4–32 It is sometimes stated that if the inference enabled by the statute is "provisional", an *evidential* burden of disproof has arisen, whereas if the inference or presumption is "compelling", a legal burden of disproof has been cast upon the accused. Where the effect of a statutory inference is to impose an evidential or provisional burden upon the accused or defendant, his failure to rebut the inference does not oblige the court to convict or give judgment against him, nor does it relieve the prosecution or plaintiff of full proof of the facts at issue. It is an altogether different matter when the effect of a statutory provision, or indeed common law principle, is to impose a legal burden of proof of a fact at issue upon the accused in criminal proceedings, since this exposes him to criminal conviction if he does not exonerate himself, and as such is apposite, systemically and symbolically, to the presumption of innocence developed by the common law, beatified in *Woolmington*, and acknowledged to have constitutional standing in Ireland.[70]

4–33 By way of mitigation, whenever a legal or persuasive burden is imposed upon the accused in criminal proceedings, the courts have required him to discharge it not to the higher criminal standard but upon a preponderance of the evidence or the balance of probabilities. This was clarified by the House of Lords in *Bratty*,[71] the Court of Appeal in *R. v Carr-Briant*,[72] and by the Supreme Court in *Hardy v Ireland*[73] and *DPP v Best*.[74]

---

[69] See also, as a recent example of statutory evidential inferences, s.2(3) of the Child Trafficking and Pornography Act 1998, which on a reading of *O'Leary* (*cf.* para.**4–34** *et seq.*) would be interpreted not to affect the legal burden of proof. In proceedings for an offence under ss.3, 4, 5 or 6 of the Act: "a person shall be deemed, unless the contrary is proved, to be or have been a child, or to be or have been depicted or represented as a child, at any time if the person appears to the court to be or have been a child, or to be or have been so depicted or represented, at that time". Section 4 of the Criminal Justice Act 1999 inserts new provisions into s.15 and s.29 of the Misuse of Drugs Act 1977, enabling the court to accept an evidential inference of possession of drugs with intent to supply "having regard to the quantity" of the drugs found in the accused's possession, and where the court is "satisfied that it is reasonable to assume that the controlled drug was not intended for his immediate personal use". The accused may, under s.29 of the 1977 Act, seek to rebut the inference by showing that he was in lawful possession of the drugs by virtue of the regulations made under s.4 of the 1977 Act. Reference in s.4 to "reasonable" assumption and "until the court is satisfied to the contrary" would be interpreted to cast an evidential, rather than legal, burden upon the accused, having regard to the reasoning adopted in *O'Leary* (*cf.* para.**4–34** *et seq.*) and *Foley* (*cf.* para.**4–41**) See also Criminal Justice Act 1994, s.31, with respect to the offence of handling property constituting the proceeds of crime; considered, without reference to the burdens of proof, in *People (DPP) v McHugh* [2002] 1 I.R. 352 (CCA).
[70] *O'Leary v Attorney-General* [1991] I.L.R.M. 454 at 461, *per* Costello J; *Hardy v Ireland* [1994] 2 I.R. 550 (SC).
[71] [1963] A.C. 386 (HL): *cf.* appendix 10.
[72] [1943] K.B. 607 (CA).
[73] [1994] 2 I.R. 550, *per* Egan and Murphy J.J. (SC): *cf.* appendix 44 and *cf.* para.**4–43**.
[74] [2000] 2 I.R. 17 at 43, *per* Denham J. (SC).

4–34 The courts have been required to address the effect of a number of reverse-onus clauses in recent years. In the first of these, *Attorney-General v O'Leary*,[75] Costello J. of the High Court addressed the distinction between legal and evidential burdens in the context of a constitutional challenge to s.24 of the Offences Against the State Act 1939.[76] Section 24 provides that proof of possession of an "incriminating document" (in this case, IRA posters) "shall, without more, be evidence until the contrary is proved that such person was a member of the said organisation at the time alleged in the said charge". In his trial for membership of the IRA contrary to s.21 of the Act, as amended, and for having in his possession "incriminating documents" contrary to s.12, the prosecution invoked s.24 to establish his guilt. Before the High Court, the accused argued that s.24 amounted to an unconstitutional interference with the presumption of innocence and the *Woolmington* principle.

4–35 Considering the constitutionality of statutory reversals of the burdens of proof in general, Costello J. expressed the view that where an evidential burden has been cast upon the accused—in the sense that he may choose not to rebut any resulting inference and still "be entitled to an acquittal if the evidence adduced does not establish his or her guilt beyond a reasonable doubt"–no question of constitutional invalidity arises.[77] His view of statutory reversals of the legal burden of proof was: (1) that we recognise this has occurred when "the effect of the statute is that the court *must* convict an accused should he or she fail to adduce exculpatory evidence" to rebut the inference; and (2) that this *may* give rise to a question of constitutional invalidity, but that in many cases the statute will merely be giving "legal effect to an inference which it is reasonable to draw from facts which the prosecution establish. The presumption of the accused's innocence is therefore rebutted not by the statute but by the inference".[78] Costello J. found that the presumption of innocence, protected by the constitutional requirement of due process under Art.38(1), was not absolute but could be qualified "in accordance with law", and he rejected the argument that statutory interference with the legal burden of proof was necessarily impermissible.

4–36 Costello J.'s exploration of the burdens of proof was impressive, although his application of the principles to the provisions under scrutiny was logically less compelling. Section 24 of the 1939 Act *enabled* but did not

---

[75] [1991] I.L.R.M. 454 (HC): *cf.* appendix 39.
[76] The accused also challenged the constitutionality of s.3(2) of the Offences Against the State (Amendment) Act 1972, providing that where a garda officer not below the rank of chief superintendent gives evidence in s.21 proceedings that he believes the accused was a member of an unlawful organisation at the material time, his statement of belief shall be evidence of that fact. Costello J. rightly found that this merely rendered "admissible in evidence in certain trials statements of belief which would otherwise be inadmissible" (owing to the rule against opinion evidence: *cf.* para.12–01 *et seq.*), and that, despite the use of mandatory words in s.3(2), it renders the garda's opinion admissible as evidence relevant to the accused's guilt but not conclusive thereof.
[77] [1991] I.L.R.M. 454 at 460 (HC).
[78] *ibid*. at 460–61.

compel the court to draw an inference of membership from proof of possession of an incriminating document such as a poster;[79] in other words, the court was not required to convict the accused of the crime of membership in the absence of exculpatory evidence. Costello J.'s view of the words "until the contrary is proved" was that the court is not obliged to accept the inference of membership if any evidence coming from *either party* proves otherwise.[80] Costello J.'s analysis was upheld upon appeal by O'Flaherty J.[81] who construed the s.24 inference to constitute ordinary evidence in the case, which could be accepted or rejected by the court having regard to other evidence and inferences arising in the case: s.24 engendered a provisional rather than compelling or mandatory inference, and the trial judge would direct the jury accordingly at the close of the trial that the burden rested upon the prosecution to prove the accused's guilt as charged.

4–37 Although Costello J.'s reasoning has attracted criticism,[82] it has the support of one line of authority. Bridge, subsequently Lord Bridge, asserted in 1949: "whenever an accused person is required by statute to prove some matter in his defence, in terms which stop short of expressly requiring that he shall satisfy the jury, the effect is merely to relieve the prosecutor of the initial necessity of giving evidence on that issue, but by no means to relieve him of the fixed [or legal] burden of proof, when the prisoner, by evidence upon the issue, has removed the effect of the presumption".[83] Bridge was of the view that much of the complication surrounding reverse-onus clauses stems from the failure to appreciate that "proof" or "proven" as iterated in statutes may be construed to refer to any one of a number of standards or degrees of proof.[84] Proof may be interpreted to be indicative (such as "establishing a reasonable possibility of the fact") or prima facie, in which case, generally, evidential burdens have been affected. Proof may be upon the balance of probabilities or

---

[79] As a basis upon which to distinguish an evidential from a legal burden, this does not dispose of the matter, as the accused may in principle bear a legal burden with respect to one element of a criminal offence, and though he may not attempt to discharge it, he may still be entitled to an acquittal if the prosecution fails to prove the other elements of the offence beyond reasonable doubt: Hirst, *Andrews and Hirst on Criminal Evidence* (4th ed., Jordans, Bristol, 2001), at p. 68.
[80] This logic would be applied to provisions such as s.15A(2) of the Misuse of Drugs Act 1977, inserted by s.4 of the Criminal Justice Act 1999. Although s.15A(2) creates a compelling presumption of intent to supply drugs upon proof that the accused was found in possession of controlled drugs with a street value of at least £10,000, the words "until the court is satisfied to the contrary" avoid characterising this as something the accused must prove, and according to the *O'Leary* logic, it therefore imposes an evidential but not a legal burden upon the accused. For the preferable view that such measures in reality cast a legal burden of proof upon the accused, see Ní Raifeartaigh (1998) at pp.18–19.
[81] [1993] 2 I.L.R.M. 259 (SC).
[82] Ní Raifeartaigh, "The Criminal Justice System and Drug Related Offending: Some Thoughts on Procedural Reforms" (1998) 4 *Bar Review* 15 at 18–19; Cannon and Nelligan, *Evidence* (Round Hall, Sweet & Maxwell, Dublin, 2002) at p.22.
[83] Bridge, "Presumptions and Burdens" [1949] 12 M.L.R. 273 at 286.
[84] *ibid.* at p.285.

beyond reasonable doubt, where they refer to legal burdens of proof. According to this view, unless the statutory provision expressly imposes the legal burden of proof upon the accused—which is not constitutionally prohibited,[85] although will naturally engender suspicions of unconstitutionality—the statute should not be interpreted to do so by implication.

4–38 English law has been beset by a similar level of disagreement on the classification of burden affected by various statutes. In *R. v Carr-Briant*,[86] the Court of Appeal reasoned that the words "unless the contrary is proved" in s.2 of the Prevention of Corruption Act 1916[87] created a "compelling" statutory presumption, passing the legal burden of proof on the issue to the accused, who became obliged upon the balance of probabilities to persuade the jury in his favour on the issue:

> "In our judgment, in any case where, either by statute or at common law, some matter is presumed 'unless the contrary is proved', the jury should be directed that it is for them to decide whether the contrary is proved, that the burden of proof required is less than that required at the hands of the prosecution in proving the case beyond a reasonable doubt, and that the burden may be discharged by evidence satisfying the jury of the probability of that which the accused is called upon to establish."[88]

4–39 Although s.2 of the Prevention of Corruption Act 1916 is assumed without controversy by English lawyers and jurists[89] to impose a legal burden upon the accused to rebut the statutory presumption, Bridge[90] criticised *Carr-Briant* for wrongly assuming that the statute did not instead affect the evidential burden of proof: to the extent that the judges commented upon more than the standard of proof required of the accused (to which counsels' submissions were restricted), Bridge argued that the findings of the court were *obiter* and in conflict with a preferable approach adopted in *R. v Ward*.[91]

---

[85] *Attorney-General v O'Leary* [1991] I.L.R.M. 454 at 461, *per* Costello J. (HC).
[86] [1948] K.B. 607 (CA).
[87] Providing that where money, gifts, or other consideration are given to officials to whom the Act applies, it "shall be deemed to have been paid or given and received corruptly ... unless the contrary is proved".
[88] [1948] K.B. 607 at 612, *per* Humphreys J. These *dicta* were approved in *Convening Authority v Private Doyle* [1996] 2 I.L.R.M. 213 (C.M.A.C.): *cf.* para.**4–44**.
[89] Andrews and Hirst, *op. cit.* n.79 at p.111; Murphy, *Murphy on Evidence* (6th ed., Blackstone, London, 997) at p.102.
[90] Bridge, "Presumptions and Burdens" [1949] 12 M.L.R. 273 at 286.
[91] [1915] 3 K.B. 696. The accused had been charged with possession of an implement of housebreaking by night "without lawful excuse (the proof of which shall lie upon such person)" pursuant to s.58 of the Larceny Act 1861, as amended by s.28 of the Larceny Act 1916. The accused gave evidence that he had had the implements in his possession because he was a bricklayer and had been carrying the tools of his trade with him on his way to work when apprehended. The court rejected the submission that the accused had to satisfy the jury that he was lawfully in possession of the implements at the time (that he bore a legal burden to persuade the jury on the issue), and instead favoured the view that evidence showing that he was a bricklayer was sufficient to rebut the statutory inference, and that he did not further have to prove an absence of guilty intent.

4–40 The view that the words "unless the contrary is proved" require the accused to go no further than raise a reasonable doubt (or discharge an evidential burden) is not favoured in England, however, and nor was it adopted by the Canadian Supreme Court in *R. v Chaulk*,[92] which construed the words to impose a legal or persuasive burden upon the accused.[93] Whilst Costello J.'s view of the s.24 inference as provisional may textually be sustained (upon a narrow literal reading), it is contingent upon assumptions of prosecutorial practice, such as that the prosecution will only proceed under s.21 if it has hard evidence of membership that is not dependent solely upon s.24 or s.3,[94] and that an accused will never be "set up" by the planting of "incriminating documents". If one does not assume this, it is naturally of concern that these provisions enable the prosecution to proceed against a target with minimal evidence, and that it is a device effectively to put the accused upon disproof of his guilt. Whilst this may be tolerable for the trials of exceptional subversive offences, the true effect of the provisions should be acknowledged—in the sense that they are more inquisitorial than accusatorial—as a means of clarifying that they apply only to very exceptional cases. Despite these concerns, and notwithstanding Costello J.'s assertion in *O'Leary* that statutory reversal of the legal burden is not necessarily unconstitutional, subsequent Irish decisions have resisted the temptation to interpret statutory inferences to affect the legal burden, even where textually it appears otherwise.

4–41 In *People (DPP) v Foley*,[95] the Court of Criminal Appeal construed s.27A of the Firearms Act 1964[96] to cast an evidential but not a legal burden upon the accused. Section 27A provides that a person is guilty of an offence if a firearm or ammunition is found in his possession or under his control such as to "give rise to a reasonable inference that he has not got it in his possession or under his control for a lawful purpose". The applicant had been discovered in a bed-sit by the gardaí with two other men, surrounded by rifles, guns, and surveillance equipment. Only one of the three men testified—to the effect that his visit to the bed-sit had been innocent—and he was acquitted. The applicant and the other man were convicted of offences under s.27A by the Special Criminal Court, and sentenced to eight years imprisonment each. Upon leave for appeal to the Court of Criminal Appeal, the applicant argued that the trial court had paid insufficient regard to his right to silence under the Constitution and the common law, and that by exercising this right and not testifying, in

---

[92] [1990] 3 S.C.R. 1303 (SC, Can.).
[93] According to Lamer C.J. (*ibid.*), "the words 'until the contrary is proved' cannot be interpreted to require an accused merely to discharge an evidentiary burden (i.e., raise a reasonable doubt as to insanity); the words ... clearly impose a persuasive burden on the accused".
[94] *cf.* para.**4–34**, n.76. It is of note in this regard that the courts have acknowledged that an accused may be convicted of the s.21 crime of membership of an unlawful organisation upon foot solely of the testimonial opinion of a chief superintendent admissible by virtue of s.3 of the Offences Against the State (Amendment) Act 1972: *Attorney-General v Ferguson* (CCA, October 17, 1975); *People (DPP) v Gannon* (CCA, April 2, 2003).
[95] [1995] 1 I.R. 267 (CCA).
[96] As amended by Criminal Law (Jurisdiction) Act 1984, s.14(4).

effect the appellant had been penalised. On the facts of the case, the Court of Criminal Appeal decided that the court had been entitled ordinarily to infer possession and knowledge from the "ample evidence of the applicant's proximity to and presence in the room with the firearms and ammunition which were openly visible".[97] In this respect, the conviction was secure without reference to the inference enabled by s.27A. In considering whether the effect of the provision was to compel an accused person to abandon his "right to silence" and to testify in order to exonerate himself, Budd J. adopted a practical, non-doctrinal view of the consequences of the statutory inference for the right to silence:

> "What the 'right to silence' amounts to is that an accused is entitled in the first instance to call on the prosecution to prove its case. *Prima facie*, his situation is that he does not have to give an explanation or give evidence. But if proof of guilt is forthcoming—if circumstances are laid before the court of trial that point to the guilt of the accused—then an accused must attempt to rebut the prosecution case by evidence or else suffer the consequences".[98]

4–42 In *People (DPP) v Hardy*,[99] the Supreme Court considered s.4(1) of the Explosive Substances Act 1883. Textually, under s.4(1), a mandatory or compelling inference of unlawful intent is generated upon proof that the accused had control or possession of an explosive substance, and a burden is specifically cast upon the accused by virtue of the words "unless he can show". Since the provision refers to the necessity first to establish "such circumstances as ... give rise to a reasonable suspicion that he is not making it or does not have it in his possession or under his control for a lawful object", it becomes amenable to the provisional inference logic adopted by Budd J. in *Foley*.[100] In *Hardy*, the Supreme Court unanimously dismissed the appeal and rejected submissions that s.4(1) was unconstitutional. In their findings of law, the judges differed, however. A majority led by Hederman J. (with whom O'Flaherty J. and Blayney J. agreed) adopted reasoning similar to *O'Leary* and *Foley*, and considered that the onus upon the prosecution to prove circumstances of reasonable suspicion required the prosecution further to prove, beyond reasonable doubt, that "the accused could not show that he had it in his possession for a lawful object". Hederman J. did not see any conflict between the presumption of innocence and a statutory provision enabling inferences to be drawn upon proof of reasonable circumstances. The learned judge considered that s.4(1) created a prima facie inference of guilt, despite use of the word "shall" (which textually suggests a mandatory or compelling inference symptomatic of the legal burden).

4–43 Egan J. and Murphy J. adopted reasoning more faithful to the text of

---

[97] [1995] 1 I.R. 267 at 289, *per* Budd J. (CCA).
[98] *ibid.* at 292.
[99] [1994] 2 I.R. 550 (SC): *cf.* appendix 44.
[100] *cf.* para.**4–41**.

s.4(1) and the logic of the burdens of proof. According to Egan J: "*Prima facie* these words place an onus on the accused but they are in a saving or excusatory context and this is of relevance".[101] Murphy J. drew at length from observations by Lord McDermott C.J.[102] to wit, that this type of statutory provision (similar to misuse of drugs legislation) seeks to remove the mental element from the definition of the offence (thereby avoiding the creation of an offence of possession for an unlawful purpose), and to transfer proof of the mental element to the accused, upon the basis that proof of guilty intent is likely to be a matter of inherent difficulty for the prosecution. The judges tersely disposed of the constitutional challenge by reasoning that there was nothing in the Constitution absolutely prohibiting the shifting of the legal onus in criminal trials, nor with a statute that provides the accused with a particular defence where he proves the material facts upon the balance of probabilities.

4–44 By contrast with *O'Leary*, *Foley*, and a majority in *Hardy*, the Courts Martial Appeal Court in *Convening Authority v Private Doyle*[103] considered s.135 of the Defences Act 1954 to cast a legal burden upon the accused. Section 135 provides, for the purpose of the crime of desertion, that "a person who has been absent without authority for a continuous period of six months or more shall, unless the contrary is proved, be presumed to have had the intention of not returning to his unit or formation or the place where his duty requires him to be". Approving the decision of the English Court of Appeal in *R. v Carr-Briant*,[104] O'Flaherty J. implicitly accepted that the effect of the words "unless the contrary is proved" in s.135 was to cast a legal onus upon the accused to prove that he had not absented himself from his unit with intent not to return. By way of mitigation, however, it was noted in *Carr-Briant* that the accused is not required to discharge that burden beyond reasonable doubt, but may discharge it "by evidence satisfying the jury of the probability of that which the accused is called upon to establish".[105]

4–45 In *People (DPP) v Byrne*,[106] the Supreme Court considered s.50(8) of the Road Traffic Act 1961, as inserted by s.11 of the Road Traffic Act 1994. Section 50(8) appeared to provide a clearer illustration of reversal of the legal burden than was the case in *Doyle*, since it specifically refers to rebuttal proof by the accused: "In a prosecution for an offence under this section, it shall be presumed that the Defendant intended to drive or attempt to drive the vehicle concerned until he shows the contrary". Upon proof that the accused was found "in charge" of his vehicle whilst under the influence of alcohol, the section creates a compelling presumption of criminal guilt that "shall" prevail "unless rebutted" specifically by the accused (by contrast with s.24 of the Offences Against the State Act 1939 considered in *O'Leary*, which did not refer to

---

[101] [1994] 2 I.R. 550 at 566 (SC): *cf.* appendix 44.
[102] *R. v Fegan* [1972] N.I. 80 at 82 (CA).
[103] [1996] 2 I.L.R.M. 213 (C.M.A.C.).
[104] [1943] 1 K.B. 607 (CA).
[105] *ibid.* at 612.
[106] [2002] 2 I.L.R.M. 68 (SC).

proof by the accused). Despite the appearance of reversal, Murray J. interpreted the provision not to affect the legal burden of proof, but instead to generate an evidential inference of the driver's intention to drive upon proof that he was found "in charge" of the vehicle whilst under the influence of alcohol. The effect of s.50(8) was to require the accused "to raise a reasonable doubt in the mind of the trial judge" (in other words, to raise an evidential burden).

4–46 Reverse-onus clauses and like forms of drafting, which seek to re-channel the legal burden of proof of a particular issue from the prosecution to the defence, may be viewed from another perspective—less an attempt to force the accused to proof on the issue, and more an attempt to avoid a closing direction that if the prosecution fails to prove the particular fact at issue beyond reasonable doubt, despite an absence of explanation by the accused, the accused must be acquitted. This was self-evident in the drafting of s.78 of the County Officers and Courts (Ireland) Act 1877, which applies to proof of non-indictable offences:

> "In all cases of summary jurisdiction any exception, exemption, proviso, qualification or excuse, whether it does or does not accompany the description of the offence complained of, may be proved by the defendant, but need not be specified or negatived in the information or complaint, and if so specified or negatived no proof in relation thereto shall be required from the complainant unless evidence shall be given by the defendant concerning the same".

4–47 The effect of this is to relieve the prosecution, in summary proceedings, of the burden of pleading and establishing that the accused does not come within the terms of the exception, exemption, etc. The provision was considered in *R. (Sheahan) v Justices of Cork*,[107] where Gibson J. favoured a test distinguishing between exceptions that render a prima facie offence innocent, and exceptions that convert a prima facie lawful act into an offence. In the latter case, but not the former, the exception forms part of the definition or gist of the offence, with respect to which the prosecution bears at least an initial evidential burden of proof. In the former case, the accused bears the legal burden of proof of the exception. Section 78 was applied in *Attorney-General v Duff*,[108] in the context of the Emergency Powers (Control of Export) Order 1940 which prohibited various acts in relation to the export of specified goods "unless ... (a) exported under and in accordance with a licence issued by a Minister under this Order, and (b) such licence is prior to exportation delivered to the appropriate officer".[109]

---

[107] [1907] 2 I.R. 5 (KBD).
[108] [1941] I.R. 406 (HC).
[109] Maguire P. further considered (*ibid.* at 413) that apart from s.78, the "existence of a licence properly used [was] a matter peculiarly within the knowledge of the defendant" and upon this basis also justified a finding that "the onus of proving its non-existence [did] not rest upon the complainant". Maguire P. repeated this view in *People (Attorney-General) v Shribman and Samuels* [1946] I.R. 431 (CCA) in the context of proceedings upon indictment. His remark to this effect in *Duff* was marginalised by the Supreme

4–48 In recent years, the legislature has withdrawn aspects of the accused's right to silence in proceedings for specified serious offences—such as, drugs trafficking and offences against the State—enabling the court to draw unspecified inferences from the accused's failure to convey information withheld when arrested that he later relied upon in his defence. These inferences are stated to be capable of amounting to corroboration in the trial, and are considered in the following chapter.[110] Each such provision states that the accused cannot be convicted solely upon the basis of the inference. Therefore, in terms of their effect upon the burdens of proof, they give rise to provisional inferences affecting the evidential but not the legal burden of proof. Their significance is more pronounced in terms of their effect upon the right to silence.[111]

4–49 The High Court has confirmed that the imposition of a legal burden of proof or disproof upon the defendant in civil proceedings does not necessarily engender constitutional anxieties. In *Gilligan v Criminal Assets Bureau*,[112] the court considered the effect of the Proceeds of Crime Act 1996, which, by ss.2–3, enables the court in civil proceedings to confiscate and freeze property upon proof on the balance of probabilities that the property constitutes the proceeds of crime. Under s.2(3) and s.3(3), it falls to the respondent to rebut the inference that he committed the crimes as alleged. Despite the cross-over into determination of criminal culpability, the High Court rationalised that the imposition of the burden of disproof of this central fact at issue was justifiable upon the basis that the proceedings were not criminal and therefore the *Woolmington* principle did not strictly arise; alternatively, the court observed that the Supreme Court had ruled in *Hardy* and *O'Leary* that statutory imposition of the legal burden of proof upon the accused in criminal proceedings was constitutionally permissible where necessary and proportionate.

Common Law Principle: Criminal Cases

4–50 Throughout the seventeenth century in England, common law principle determined that the prosecution bore the legal burden of proof of the non-application of any "exception" created to a statutory offence, as an element of the offence to be pleaded by way of negative averment; by contrast, where the accused sought to bring himself within a "proviso" created to the statutory offence, he bore the legal burden of proof of that issue.[113] Therefore, the prosecution's failure to disprove the application of the exception would attract a directed acquittal, whereas the raising of a proviso by the accused did not require rebuttal by the prosecution and obliged the accused to persuade the triers of fact on that issue to the requisite standard, generally accepted to be

---

Court later in *McGowan v Carville* [1960] I.R. 330 (*cf.* appendix 9), where the court restricted the decision to a consideration of statutory and not common law rule.
[110] *cf.* para.**5–11** *et seq.*
[111] *cf.* para.**13–100** *et seq.*
[112] [1998] 3 I.R. 185 (HC).
[113] *Rex v Jarvis* (1754) 1 East 643.

the civil standard. The distinction gradually fell out of favour by the early nineteenth century, when the courts appear to have reoriented from rule to rationale; and in this climate the controversial principle of *peculiar knowledge* or *means of knowledge* drifted into judicial reasoning, following views expressed in *R. v Turner*.[114] The peculiar knowledge principle, when successfully invoked, had the effect of shifting the legal burden on a particular issue to the accused, with the effect that the prosecution was not obliged (as part of its burden of proof) to tender evidence rebutting the particular defence and the accused bore the burden to persuade the jury on that issue. With the endorsement of a smattering of decisions, and acknowledgment by Cross, Phipson, and others, it was dubbed in England "the third exception to the *Woolmington* rule", after the defence of insanity and express statutory reversal. It appears finally, and rightly, to have collapsed in the 1970s under the weight of consistent judicial unease with the implications of such an open-ended principle in criminal proceedings.

4–51 The peculiar knowledge principle had been employed on occasion by the Irish courts to relieve the prosecution of proving an element of the offence, where proof was believed to lie peculiarly or exclusively in the accused's knowledge or means of knowledge. In *Minister for Industry & Commerce v Steele*,[115] a post-war prosecution of a butcher for breaches of an Emergency Powers (Pork Sausages and Sausage Meat) Order, the prosecution had failed to prove one element critical to proof of the offence, namely the composition of pork in the meat used in the sausages. The Supreme Court accepted that the peculiar knowledge principle applied in the case, requiring the accused to prove that not less than 65 per cent of the meat in the sausages was pork, with the effect that his failure to adduce evidence upon the issue entitled the court to draw an inference against him and in the circumstances of the case to find his guilt proved. O'Byrne J. acknowledged the view expressed in *Stephen's Digest of the Law of Evidence* (9th ed.), that the "burden of proof as to any particular fact ... may in the course of a case be shifted from one side to the other, and in considering the amount of evidence necessary to shift the burden of proof the Court has regard to the opportunities of knowledge with respect to the fact to be proved which may be possessed by the parties respectively".

4–52 The principle was considered again by the Supreme Court in *McGowan v Carville*.[116] The accused was charged with driving without a licence contrary to s.22 of the Road Traffic Act 1933. The prosecution tendered no evidence

---

[114] (1816) 5 M. & S. 206 at 210. Rejecting the proposition that the prosecution was required to prove the non-application of an exception merely because it was required to be negatively averred in the pleadings (in the case, to show that the accused had had no authority or qualification to possess hares and pheasants of the realm), Bayley J. asserted: "if a negative averment be made by a party, which is peculiarly in the knowledge of the other, the party within whose knowledge it lies, and who asserts the affirmative, is to prove it, and not he who asserts the negative".
[115] [1952] I.R. 304 (SC).
[116] [1960] I.R. 330 (SC): *cf.* appendix 9.

with respect to whether the accused had or had not produced his licence to the gardaí, when required to do so, prior to the bringing of the charges. Although the High Court approved the peculiar knowledge principle, it did so only upon the basis that its application, especially in criminal proceedings, was exceptional and limited. A majority of the Supreme Court gave qualified support to its application in cases where the prosecution had already established a prima facie case against the accused on the issue. Its effect in the case was that the prosecutor was not required to "prove" that the accused was not in possession of the requisite licence, once it tendered sufficient "evidence as will, if not displaced by further evidence offered by the defendant, justify a finding that he had not a licence".[117] Dissenting, Maguire C.J. took the view that in all cases, whether by construction of the legislation or application of the peculiar knowledge principle, the accused bears the burden of proving he had the requisite licence.

4–53 The dangers of ad hoc recourse to the peculiar knowledge principle in criminal proceedings were sounded again in *Attorney-General v Shorten*.[118] The accused was charged with knowingly having made a false statement when applying for a driving licence. The statement in question was that his car had not been used by him or by anyone else with his consent over the past four months. The prosecution based its case upon one sighting of the car in an untaxed state by a garda. The defence was that the accused had been away from his home on the day and night of the sighting, and that on his return the car was still in the garage. The District Justice rejected a defence submission that no prima facie case had been established; he considered that once a use of the car had been established, an onus shifted to the accused to prove that neither he nor anyone else had used the car with his consent at the material time. In the High Court, to which the case was stated, counsel for the prosecution argued that actual knowledge could be "inferred circumstantially, from the fact that a party had reasonable *means of knowledge*".[119] Davitt P. disapproved of the application of the peculiar knowledge principle in this way: "I am unable to agree, as a general proposition, that the best way of proving that a person who has made a false statement knew it to be false is to show that he had the means of such knowledge".[120] In the context of the facts of the case, he commented that the owner of an untaxed car does not normally take special precautions to ensure that nobody uses it.

4–54 By 1975, in *R. v Edwards*,[121] the Court of Appeal had rejected the peculiar knowledge principle upon similar grounds to the High Court in *Shorten*. Lawton L.J. wisely asserted: "If there was any such rule, anyone charged with doing an unlawful act with a specified intent would find himself having to prove his innocence because if there ever was a matter which could

---

[117] *ibid.* at 356, *per* Lavery J.
[118] [1961] I.R. 304 (HC).
[119] Quoting *Phipson on Evidence* (9th ed., Sweet & Maxwell, London, 1952) at p.146.
[120] [1961] I.R. 304 at 308 (HC).
[121] [1975] Q.B. 27 (CA).

be said to be peculiarly within a person's knowledge it is the state of his own mind".[122] The peculiar knowledge principle has not for some time been pursued or indulged by the courts in Ireland and England in the context of criminal proceedings; it is preferable to presume its demise as a self-supporting common law principle in that context, at least.[123] This is to a significant extent due to the fact that legislatures have tended to address issues of proof and disproof more directly in recent years, and many statutory presumptions and reverse-onus clauses implicitly rest upon assumptions that the accused is in the best position to prove or disprove some relevant matters.[124]

4–55 A new wave of common law principle emerged in England with the Court of Appeal's decision in *Edwards*, and broke, to much publicity and debate, with the House of Lord's exploration of the issues in *R. v Hunt*.[125] The effect finally of these two decisions was to broaden the focus of the courts' discretion from the parties' respective means of knowledge and proof to a range of considerations including, in particular: what is expressed and what may be implied in the text of the statute; policy; principle; and practical exigencies. In *Hunt*, the accused was prosecuted for possession of a controlled drug contrary to s.5(2) of the Misuse of Drugs Act (U.K.) 1971. The provision was not stated to be subject to a proviso or exception, although the Act was stated to be subject to regulations adopted thereunder. Under one of those regulations, an "exemption" or "exception" was recognised for possession of a preparation comprising no more than 2 per cent of morphine. In the case, the prosecution tendered evidence to prove that the accused had been in possession of a compound containing morphine mixed with non-controlled substances, but no evidence as to the proportion.

4–56 The House of Lords decided in the case that the exemption in question, though appearing in a separate statutory instrument, bore upon the definition of the offence, and its non-application therefore was a fact at issue the prosecution was required to prove. The House was influenced to a significant extent by the fact that the Act had expressly cast a legal or persuasive burden upon the accused to establish any of the defences recognised by s.5(2); the non-inclusion of the exemption in s.5(2) therefore could reasonably be interpreted to imply that neither the Act nor the regulation intended to cast the legal burden of proof upon the accused. The House recommended that when construing statutory offences, the court should have regard to the mischief the statute addresses, and to the ease or difficulty a party would have in discharging the burden of proof (thereby assimilating an aspect of the peculiar knowledge

---

[122] [1975] Q.B. 27 at 35 (CA).
[123] Reference to the peculiar knowledge principle has emerged in some civil proceedings: e.g. in *Hurch v Dublin Corporation* [1992] I.L.R.M. 596 at 599 (SC), and (in the context of *res ipsa loquitur*) in *Hanrahan v Merck, Sharp & Dohme Ltd.* [1988] I.L.R.M. 629 (SC) and *Rothwell v M.I.B.I.* [2003] 1 I.R. 268 (SC): *cf.* paras **4–66** *et seq.*
[124] Accepted by Denham J. in *DPP v Best* [2000] 2 I.R. 17 (SC), when considering the effect of the imposition of a burden upon the accused by s.18(2) of the School Attendance Act 1926.
[125] [1987] A.C. 352, [1987] 1 All E.R. 1 (HL).

principle). The House emphasised, however, that trial courts should bear in mind that there is a presumption that parliament did not intend to impose an overly onerous burden upon the accused, and there is also a presumption against onus-shifting in criminal cases.

4–57 The *Edwards/Hunt* development has been criticised by many jurists[126] for encouraging a random dismantling of the golden thread identified in *Woolmington*, although some have given it their qualified support.[127] Stone had written, prior to this development, that there can be no material difference between "a quality of a class as contained in the definition of the class, and a quality of a class as contained in an exception to the class ... Every qualification of a class can equally be stated without any change of meaning as an exception to the class so qualified".[128] Zuckerman's response to *Edwards* was that it is wrong to assume that the legislature wishes to impose a burden of proof upon the accused when it drafts an offence creating a distinction between the offence and the exceptions or exemptions to the offence.[129] If there is no such distinction in form or in meaning, the distinction, if it exists at all, must be founded upon judicial policy.

4–58 The *Edwards/Hunt* approach has not yet been authoritatively examined by the Irish courts. In *O'Leary*,[130] one of the few judicial explorations of these issues in Ireland, Costello J. signalled that it is not constitutionally impermissible for a statute to cause the legal burden of proof on an issue to fall upon the accused. Costello J. did not express a view on whether this dynamic could be *implied* from the structuring or phrasing of a statute and/or regulations upon an application of common law principle, although the tone of the judgment and various asides suggest that this would be inappropriate—in other words, that if a statute purports to characterise an offence by redirecting proof of a fundamental element of the offence to the accused, it must do so expressly, and, unless proportionate and justified in the particular context, it may give rise to a "breach of the accused's constitutional rights".[131] Instead of pursuing a direction similar to *Hunt*, the Irish courts appear to favour the view that unless statute expressly provides otherwise, the court should interpret the

---

[126] Roberts, "Taking the Burden of Proof Seriously" [1995] Crim. L.R. 783 at 787–88 insists: "A policy of reversing the burden of proof in criminal proceedings might commend itself to a totalitarian regime which, for reasons of domestic order or foreign diplomacy, wished to retain the bare window-dressing of legality, but it is not the badge of an administration which values and respects its citizens' freedom." Mirfield(1988) at p.29 bemoans the loss of such "an important buffer between the practical power of the State and the comparative weakness of the individual". Healy, "Proof and Policy: No Golden Threads" [1987] Crim. L.R. 355 criticises the loss of principle and coherence.
[127] Birch, "The Hunting of the Snark" (1988) at p.226 queries the "court's extreme devotion to *Woolmington*". See also Bennion, "Statutory Exceptions: A Third Knot in the Golden Thread" (1988).
[128] Stone J., "Burden of Proof and the Judicial Process: A Comment on *Joseph Constantine Steamship Ltd. v Imperial Smelting Corp. Ltd.* (1944) 60 L.Q.R. 262 at 280.
[129] Zuckerman, "The Third Exception to the Woolmington Rule" (1976).
[130] [1991] I.L.R.M. 454 (HC): *cf.* para.**4–34** *et seq.* and appendix 39.
[131] [1991] I.L.R.M. 454 at 460 (HC).

relevant statutory provision to affect an evidential, but not a legal, burden of proof of the issue.

Common Law Principle and *Res Ipsa Loquitur*: Civil Cases

4–59 The *res ipsa loquitur* maxim or doctrine permits the court in exceptional cases to draw an inference of a fact at issue—in the bulk of cases, an inference of negligence—at an early stage in the hearing, upon proof of circumstantial evidence of a highly suggestive nature.[132] Literally, *res ipsa loquitur* means "the acts speak for themselves". Fleming put it that the "maxim contains nothing new; it is based on common sense, since it is a matter of ordinary observation and experience in life [that] sometimes a thing tells its own story".[133] The effect of an early inference may be severe and unjust for the defendant, particularly where the evidential gaps in the case are unbridgeable and it is not within the defendant's means to explain the cause of the plaintiff's injuries. Accordingly, the courts have consistently restricted *res ipsa loquitur* to exceptional cases, deferring to the criteria implicit in the *dicta* of Erle C.J. in *Scott v London & St. Katherine Docks Co.*,[134] to wit, that where the event that gave rise to the plaintiff's injury is:

> "shown to be under the management of the defendant or his servants, and the accident is such as in the ordinary course of things does not happen if those who have the management use proper care, it affords reasonable evidence, in the absence of explanation by the defendants, that the accident arose from want of care".[135]

4–60 The courts usually require evidence of an extraordinary event that would not be expected to occur if due care had been exercised by the defendant. A clear example arose in *Lindsay v Mid-Western Health Board*,[136] where a young girl had undergone a conventional operation to remove an appendix during the course of which she fell into a deep coma. The courts have applied the maxim to less extreme events, however. In *O'Reilly v Lavelle*,[137] it was applied to the case of a collision between the plaintiff's car and the defendant's farm animals that had strayed onto a public road. In *Mullen v Quinnsworth Ltd.*[138]— a case where a 74-year-old pensioner slipped on vegetable oil on the defendant's supermarket floor—the Supreme Court overturned the High Court's decision to dismiss her claim; evidence establishing the circumstances of the plaintiff's fall had been sufficient to raise an inference of negligence in the plaintiff's

---

[132] For a rigorous exploration of the maxim, see McMahon and Binchy, *Law of Torts* (3rd ed., Butterworths, Dublin, 2000) at pp.187–201.
[133] Fleming, *The Law of Torts* (7th ed., Sydney, Law Book Co., 1987) at p.291: cited by the Irish Supreme Court in *Lindsay v Mid-Western Health Board* [1993] I.L.R.M. 550 at 555: *cf.* appendix 43.
[134] *Scott v London and St Katherine Docks Co.* (1865) 3 H. & C. 596.
[135] *ibid.* at 601.
[136] [1993] I.L.R.M. 550 (SC): *cf.* appendix 43.
[137] [1990] 2 I.R. 372 (HC).
[138] [1991] I.L.R.M. 439 (SC).

favour, and it had not been necessary at that stage for the plaintiff to establish the defendant's breach of duty by tendering evidence of how other supermarkets operated their cleaning system. By contrast, in *Foley v Quinnsworth*,[139] the High Court refused to draw the early inference in a case where the plaintiff had slipped on a floor on which no spillages were discovered in the aftermath.

4–61 As suggested by the outcome in *Foley*, the maxim is incompatible with cases in which there may be other plausible explanations for the accident aside from the defendant's conduct. As a basis for rejection of the inference, this was expressed by Black J. in *Neill v Minister for Finance*,[140] a case where the plaintiff, a toddler, had injured his hand after a postman shut a van door on it: "I cannot see how the principle can be applied in the present case. The gap which exists between the evidence as to the movements of the driver and the injury of the child could reasonably be filled in a number of ways". This is reflected in numerous other decisions. In *McDonagh v West of Ireland Fisheries Ltd.*,[141] the plaintiff had established that his fishing boat had been removed from its berth and later re-berthed by the defendant, where it had been found damaged: in the circumstances of the case thus far established, the "thing" did not speak for itself.

4–62 Where *res ipsa loquitur* is deemed to arise, the plaintiff has effectively discharged his early burden of raising a prima facie case against the defendant, causing a burden of proof to pass to the defence to rebut the inference of negligence. According to prevailing authority, if the defendant fails to discharge his burden, the court is not obliged to rule in the plaintiff's favour—thus an evidential but not a legal burden of proof is affected by the maxim. In support of this approach, it is reasoned that *res ipsa loquitur* constitutes an inference arising from circumstantial evidence, and as such it should not cause elements of the legal burden of proof to pass to the defendant.[142] Indeed, the view is suggested in Erle C.J.'s reference in *Scott* to the inference supplying "*reasonable* evidence, in the absence of explanation by the defendant that an accident arose from want of care". Thus the maxim permits but does not compel the court to find in the plaintiff's favour where the defendant has failed adequately to rebut the inference of his negligence. In this light, *res ipsa loquitur* is less a rule of the substantive law than a lever to encourage the provision of evidence and explanation in the case. This view of the maxim appears rooted in an understandable judicial unwillingness to pin liability on a defendant for injuries he has not been proved to have caused. This view was reflected by the Supreme Court in *Lindsay v Mid Western Health Board*,[143] where O'Flaherty J. asserted that it would be wrong of the court to conclude that the defendant had caused the accident, in the absence of any explanation as to how the injury actually occurred.

---

[139] HC, April 10, 1992.
[140] [1948] I.R. 88 at 92 (SC).
[141] HC, December 19, 1986.
[142] *Lloyde v West Midlands Gas Board* [1971] 2 All E.R. 1240 (CA); *Barkway v South Wales Transport Co. Ltd.* [1950] 1 All E.R. 392 (HL).
[143] [1993] I.L.R.M. 550 (SC): *cf.* appendix 43.

4–63 The courts have consistently emphasised that at the end of the day, the court retains a discretion to evaluate whether or not the inference has been successfully rebutted.[144] How it does so is important. If the court decides that the inference has been rebutted by the defendant, the plaintiff is once more on proof, which may be critical to the case if the plaintiff was forced to rely upon the maxim in the first place. In principle, the defence is not required by way of rebuttal to prove *how* the plaintiff's injuries occurred, only that the injuries were not caused by a lack of due care on the defendant's part.[145] To impose a more onerous burden upon the defendant would be unjust, according to *Lindsay*,[146] as there may be many cases where no satisfactory explanation for the accidental injury exists. The defendant was therefore not required to take the further step of proving upon the balance of probabilities what had brought about the patient's comatose state. Since the defendants had displaced the early inference of their negligence by tendering expert evidence to show that the anaesthetic procedure had been performed competently, the burden of proof had returned to the plaintiff to prove the defendant's negligence, which she had failed to do.

4–64 In *Cosgrove v E.S.B.*,[147] the High Court again highlighted the fundamental distinction between *res ipsa loquitur* and proof of causation. The plaintiff, an agricultural contractor, sued for injuries suffered when his silage harvester came into contact with one of the defendant's electricity lines. Murphy J. reiterated the principle that the *res ipsa* maxim, as interpreted in *Lindsay*, does not require the defendant to prove what caused the injuries—in other words, it does not pass the burden of proof on causation from plaintiff to defendant. It passes the burden of proof only on the issue of whether or not the defendant exercised reasonable care and skill. An inference arises that the defendant acted unreasonably, which he is asked to rebut; the defendant is not required further to establish what or who caused the injury.

4–65 It may well be the case, however, depending on the circumstances, that the defendant's failure to establish an alternative explanation for the injuries will bear upon the efficacy of his attempt to rebut the inference of his own negligence. There have been numerous indications of judicial unease with restricting the scope of rebuttal merely to disproof of the specific allegation of negligence.[148] A majority of the Supreme Court recently found in *Merriman v*

---

[144] *Ng Chun Pui v Lee Cheun Tat* [1988] R.T.R. 298 at 301 (PC). Lord Griffiths added that resort to the burden of proof "is a poor way to decide a case", and at the end of the day the court remains free to evaluate all the evidence and to decide whether negligence is established.
[145] Upon which distinction, see Healy, "Issues of Causation in Recent Medical Negligence Litigation" (2003) 8 *Bar Review* 188.
[146] [1993] I.L.R.M. 550 at 556 (SC): *cf.* appendix 43. See also *O'Shea v Tilman Anhold* (SC, October 23, 1996).
[147] [2003] 1 I.L.R.M. 544 (HC).
[148] In *Brazier v Ministry of Defence* [1965] 1 Lloyd's Rep. 26, McNair J.'s view of the law was that a defendant did not have to rebut the inference by affirmatively establishing the absence of negligence, but that he would have to present an explanation of how the

Greenhills Foods Ltd.,[149] that the effect of the maxim in the case was properly to require the defendant not only to disprove the allegation of negligence on his part but also to shed light upon the possible cause of the truck's malfunction. Blayney J. found: "The explanation offered [by the defendants] did not go far enough. It did not explain why the leaf of the spring broke". The court justified its view by emphasising that *res ipsa loquitur* creates an evidential, but not a compelling, presumption, and so the effect of casting the burden upon the defendant is not to compel him to explain the accident upon pain of an adverse judgment. On the other hand, in his dissent, Murphy J. took the view that "neither the general principles of law nor the maxim of *res ipsa loquitur* compel a defendant to give evidence simply for the purpose of satisfying the curiosity or concern of the plaintiff. It is sufficient for the defendant's purpose to meet the case made against it".[150] The High Court in *Quinn v South Eastern Health Board*[151] appears to have adopted a similar approach to the findings of the majority in *Merriman*. Despite accepting evidence that in a majority of cases of meralgia parasthetica it is not possible to establish the cause, O'Caoimh J. ruled that since the defendants had failed to explain "how what should have been a benign procedure ended up causing the condition of meralgia parasthetica," the inference of negligence enabled by the maxim prevailed, and negligence was proven with respect to the operation.

4–66 The answer to the apparent inconsistencies in recent decisions may perhaps be reconciled in future cases by recourse to Henchy J.'s *dicta* in *Hanrahan v Merck, Sharpe and Dohme Ltd.*[152]—which at the time were very much doubted,[153] but endured as an accurate and elegant restatement of the implicit rationale of the *res ipsa loquitur* maxim. In *Rothwell v M.I.B.I.*,[154] a recent decision potentially of significant consequence for civil proceedings, the dicta were approved by the Supreme Court. Henchy J. had reasoned as follows in *Hanrahan*:

> "The ordinary rule is that a person who alleges a particular tort must, in order to succeed, prove (save where there are admissions) all the necessary ingredients of that tort and it is not for the defendant to disprove anything.

---

injury could have occurred without negligence. As it happened, this was discharged in the case by showing that proper surgical procedure had been followed, and that the surgical needle probably broke due to a latent defect in the shaft of the needle. In *Cassidy v Ministry of Health* [1951] 2 K.B. 343 at 366 (CA), Denning L.J. attached importance to the fact that the defence had "nowhere explained how [the injury] could happen without negligence. They have busied themselves in saying that this or that member of their staff was not negligent. But they have called not a single person to say that the injuries were consistent with due care on the part of all the members of their staff".
[149] [1997] 1 I.L.R.M. 46 at 50 (SC).
[150] *ibid*. at 56.
[151] HC, March 22, 2002.
[152] [1988] I.L.R.M. 629 (SC).
[153] McMahon and Binchy, *Law of Torts* (2nd ed., Butterworths, Dublin, 1990) at pp.142–44 and (3rd ed., 2000) at pp.199–201; *O'Shea v Tilman Anhold and Horse Holiday Farm Ltd.* (SC, October 23, 1996) *per* Keane J.
[154] [2003] 1 I.R. 268 at 275 *per* Hardiman J. (SC).

Such exceptions as have been allowed to that general rule seem to be confined to cases where a particular element of the tort lies, or is deemed to lie, pre-eminently within the defendant's knowledge, in which case the onus of proof as to that matter passes to the defendant. Thus, in the tort of negligence, where damage has been caused to the plaintiff in circumstances in which such damage would not usually be caused without negligence on the part of the defendant, the rule of *res ipsa loquitur* will allow the act relied on to be evidence of negligence in the absence of proof by the defendant that it occurred without want of due care on his part. The rationale behind the shifting of the onus of proof to the defendant in such cases would appear to lie in the fact that it would be palpably unfair to require a plaintiff to prove something which is beyond his reach and which is peculiarly within the range of the defendant's capacity of proof".[155]

4–67 Although this passage was called into question for its transference of focus from the grounding facts identified in *Scott* to apparently broader criteria that have regard to fairness and the parties' respective means of proof, the criteria appear broadly consistent with decisions since *Hanrahan*, and to an appreciable extent were already implied by the requirement in *Scott* that the plaintiff first establish that the event giving rise to injury was under the "management" or control of the defendant. The parties' respective access to relevant information critical to proof has often influenced the courts when deciding placement of the onus in tort cases.[156] In *Lindsay*, the Supreme Court acknowledged: "Disparity between the situation of the respective parties is crucial" to *res ipsa loquitur*.[157] This perspective was confirmed by the Supreme Court in *Merriman v Greenhills Foods Ltd.*,[158] a case where an employee's truck had malfunctioned and veered into a bog, and the maxim was applied upon the basis that the facts relevant to proof of causation and due care were unknown to the appellant and were, or ought to have been known, to the respondent.

4–68 In *Rothwell v M.I.B.I.*,[159] Hardiman J. of the Supreme Court specifically approved Henchy J.'s view that the maxim requires "not merely that a matter in respect of which the onus is to shift is within the exclusive knowledge of the defendant, but also that it is 'peculiarly within the range of the defendant's capacity of proof'". This was a case taken against the M.I.B.I. seeking compensation for injuries in an accident on the road when the plaintiff's car skidded on an oil spill. The M.I.B.I. is bound by agreement with the Minister to compensate road traffic casualties where the driver who negligently caused

---

[155] [1988] I.L.R.M. 629 at 634–35 (SC).
[156] According to Stephens (*Digest, Evidence Act 1896*, as cited in *Cummings v City of Vancouver* (1911) 1 W.W.R. 31 at 34): "In considering the amount of evidence necessary to shift the burden of proof, the Court has regard to the opportunities of knowledge with respect to the fact to be proved, which may be possessed by the parties respectively."
[157] [1993] I.L.R.M. 550 at 554, *per* O'Flaherty J. (SC): *cf.* appendix 43.
[158] [1997] 1 I.L.R.M. 46 (SC).
[159] [2003] 1 I.R. 268 at 275–6.

an accident is untraced or unidentified. The plaintiff was unable to prove that the oil spill had been left by a negligent driver with no defence—thus his case depended upon an application of *res ipsa loquitur* to invoke the inference that the spill had been left by a negligent driver with no defence. The court found the maxim not to apply in a case of this nature where it could not be said that knowledge of the source of the oil spill was a matter peculiarly within the knowledge of the defendant.

4–69 Inequality of means of proof is clearly inadequate as a formal criterion for the application or non-application of the maxim, however. The fact that the defendant is *merely* in a better position than the plaintiff to explain how the injuries occurred should not in itself be sufficient to raise an early inference of his negligence. The better view of *res ipsa loquitur* is that it gives rise to an inference of negligence in circumstances where the facts of the accident, without more, point strongly to the defendant's negligence, but that in considering whether or not the maxim applies in the case, the court *may* have regard to the means of knowledge on either side, and to whether or not the defendant exercised control of the event that gave rise to injury.

4–70 It is difficult to assess whether Hardiman J.'s ringing endorsement of Henchy J.'s *dicta* will effect significant change in the operation of *res ipsa loquitur* in Ireland, since disparity of knowledge had been implicit in the case law on the maxim to date. Of particular concern is the potential ascent of the maxim in cases of alleged medical negligence, since it is raised routinely in this context as a means of bridging difficult evidential gaps. The *res ipsa loquitur* plea had proved popular in the US for a time as a lever in medical negligence cases to "loosen the defendant's tongue" and to pierce a "conspiracy of silence".[160] It has sometimes been applied in response to the fact that the defendant doctor was in the best position to establish what occurred.[161] Yet the fact that medical injuries can stem from a number of factors not derivative from the defendant's negligence may make cases of iatrogenic injury intrinsically ill-suited to the application of *res ipsa loquitur*. On this basis, it has been asserted that "medicine is recognised as an inexact science from the practice of which serious complications can arise that cannot, without proof of some negligent act, be charged to the physician".[162] This view had been articulated by the Irish courts in a number of medical negligence decisions. In *Lindsay*, O'Flaherty J. drew support from the following *dicta* by Andrews J.[163]

> "The human body is not a container filled with material whose

---

[160] *Ybarra v Spangard* (1944) 25 Cal. 2d 486, 154 P. 2d 687.
[161] *Snell v Farrell* (1990) 72 D.L.R. (4th) 289 at 300 (SC). See further: Healy, *Medical Negligence: Common Law Perspectives* (Sweet & Maxwell, London, 1999).
[162] *Wilkinson v Vesey* 295 A. 2d 676 at 691, *per* Kelleher J. (1972).
[163] British Columbia, *Girard v Royal Columbian Hospital* (1976) 66 D.L.R. (3d) 676 at 691. The passage was endorsed further by Johnson J. in *Russell v Walsh* (HC, April 3, 1995).

performance can be predictably charted and analysed. It cannot be equated with a box of chewing tobacco or a soft drink ... Thus, while permissible inferences may be drawn as to the normal behaviour of these types of commodities, the same kind of reasoning does not necessarily apply to a human being. Because of this, medical science has not yet reached the stage where the law ought to presume that a patient must come out of an operation as well or better than he went into it".

4–71 In *Dully v North Eastern Health Board*,[164] the plaintiff had undergone a successful operation on his left knee, but suffered post-operative numbness in his left hand caused by pressure exerted to the left ulnar nerve. In deciding that the plaintiff had failed to establish the injury was of a type that does not in the ordinary course of events occur if due care is exercised, Hamilton P. was influenced by the fact that the medical evidence indicated that the injury could have been sustained at any time during his hospital stay, and by the failure of the plaintiff to tender evidence establishing negligence on the part of the defendants. In *Russell v Walsh*,[165] the plaintiff suffered a uretero-vaginal fistula and other complications following a simple abdominal hysterectomy. Expert medical evidence was divided on the merits of palpitating the ureter during the operation, but it was agreed that in approximately 0.5 per cent of cases damage can occur in that area without fault on the part of the surgeon. In these circumstances, Johnson J. decided that the maxim did not arise. A similar view was adopted by Blayney J. in *Barrett v Southern Health Board*: "This doctrine has no application in the context of an operation which necessarily involved risk and where the evidence is that in more than 7 per cent of the cases some nerve damage is sustained. Where such damage could occur without any negligence on the part of the surgeon, the mere fact that there was damage is not evidence of negligence".[166] In a recent break from this trend, the High Court applied the maxim in *Quinn v South Eastern Health Board*.[167] The patient had been advised at the age of 14 years to undergo an appendicectomy, and she emerged from the operation suffering meralgia parasthetica. The court accepted that in the majority of cases of meralgia parasthetica it is not possible to establish the cause, although when a cause is found it is usually compression of a nerve through or under the inguinal ligament during an operation. O'Caoimh J. found that since meralgia parasthetica is "not something that results in the ordinary course of things if those who have the management exercise reasonable care" the maxim applied to the case.

---

[164] HC, November 3, 1988.
[165] HC, April 3, 1995.
[166] HC, December 5, 1988.
[167] HC, March 22, 2002.

V. STANDARDS OF PROOF

Criminal Proceedings

4–72 The standard or degree to which the prosecution must prove the guilt of the accused in the criminal trial is beyond all reasonable doubt. Despite its fame and currency, judicial exploration of the phrase has suffered mixed results over the years, and there is now a decisive preference against tampering with a traditional formula already deeply embedded in the collective consciousness.[168] One of the few attempts at elaboration to endure was given by Denning J. in *Miller v Minister for Pensions*:[169]

> "Proof beyond reasonable doubt does not mean proof beyond the shadow of doubt. The law would fail to protect the community if it admitted fanciful possibilities to deflect the course of justice. If the evidence is so strong against a man as to leave only a remote possibility in his favour which can be dismissed with the sentence 'of course it is possible but not in the least probable' the case is proved beyond reasonable doubt, but nothing short of that will suffice".

4–73 Similar formulations were expressed by the trial judges in *People (DPP) v Cotter*[170] and *People (DPP) v O'Connor*,[171] which were approved upon appeal. In *Cotter*, the defence submitted that the prosecution was required to establish a moral certainty; the trial judge responded to this when summing-up by instructing the jury that the prosecution was required to establish "something short of a moral certainty: something which is in the phrase beyond a reasonable doubt—that is to say you must not have a doubt of a real nature". In *O'Connor*, the trial judge instructed the jury that they were to be "concerned with reasonable doubts ... you don't require mathematical certainty and you are not to be concerned with whimsical or fanciful doubts". Although in *Cotter* the Court of Criminal Appeal approved the direction because it had also made frequent reference to "beyond reasonable doubt", in *O'Connor* it stated the view that the trial judge is not required to repeat the phrase in the manner of a mantra.

4–74 Minor deviations or ambiguities in the trial judge's closing directions to the jury upon so critical an issue as the burdens and standards of proof tend to jeopardise the resulting conviction. This is especially so where the directions may have caused the jury to consider that the accused bore a burden to persuade or to establish any of the facts at issue—a situation which the rule in *Quinn* seeks to curtail, to the point of eschewing reference to "obligation" or "onus" even where an affirmative or fresh-issue defence has been raised by the

---

[168] In *R. v Ching* (1976) 63 Cr. App. R. 7 at 11, the Court of Appeal asserted: "If judges stopped trying to define that which is almost impossible to define, there would be fewer appeals".
[169] [1947] 2 All E.R. 372 at 373.
[170] CCA, June 28, 1999.
[171] CCA, July 29, 2002.

accused.[172] In *Attorney-General v Byrne*,[173] the trial judge had repeatedly directed the jury that the State bore the burden to *satisfy* them of the accused's guilt—an expression he preferred to the conventional "beyond reasonable doubt"—adding that "if you have a reasonable doubt you cannot be satisfied". In the Court of Criminal Appeal, Kenny J. lamented the interference with the time-honoured formula, which was likely to result only in confusion. A retrial was ordered upon the basis that the trial judge had failed to stress to the jury that the accused must be given the benefit of any doubt, and because, further, "one may be satisfied of something and still have a reasonable doubt."[174]

4–75 The trial judge's restatement of the standard of proof in *Byrne* had credible support from earlier authority, however, and had expressly been approved by Lord Goddard C.J. in *R. v Sumners*: "If a jury is told that it is their duty to regard the evidence and see that it satisfies them so that they can feel sure when they return a verdict of guilty, that is much better than using the expression 'reasonable doubt' and I hope in the future that that will be done."[175] Although the word "satisfied" continues to be used in Irish decisions as "shorthand" for proof beyond reasonable doubt, the trial judge must be more elaborate and explanatory in his closing directions to the jury on the burden and standard of proof imposed upon the prosecution.

4–76 In *People (DPP) v K*,[176] one of the problems identified upon appeal appears to have been the brevity of the trial judge's directions when summing-up. The trial judge had directed the jury that the onus of proof remained on the prosecution throughout the case, and that the jury had to be satisfied of the guilt of the accused beyond reasonable doubt. Barron J. considered that this failed to put the real issue before the jury—that the prosecution was required to prove the case to the criminal standard, notwithstanding the evidence given by the accused—and it may have suggested to the jury that they should find the accused guilty if they accepted, without regard to evidence given by the accused, that the prosecution had proved guilt beyond reasonable doubt. The court also criticised the direction that the jury were entitled to convict the accused if they did not believe him: the trial judge should instead have explained that they were required to be satisfied of the accused's guilt beyond all reasonable doubt in light of the evidence tendered by both the prosecution and the defence. Conviction was also overturned in *Coddington v DPP*,[177] upon the basis that reference by the trial judge in his closing directions to the accused's failure to explain his possession of a large sum of money (bearing traces of

---

[172] *People (Attorney-General) v Quinn* [1965] I.R. 366 (SC): *cf.* para.**4–23** *et seq.*
[173] [1974] I.R. 1 (CCA): *cf.* appendix 22.
[174] *ibid.* at 9.
[175] (1952) 36 Cr. App. R. 14 at 15 (CA).
[176] CCA, December 13, 1999. The trial judge's directions were similarly criticised by Keane C.J. in *People (DPP) v LG* [2003] 2 I.R. 517 (CCA). The directions did not explain what a "reasonable doubt" was for the purposes of the criminal standard and by contrast with the standard in civil cases, and they was "not as clear and detailed as they should have been".
[177] CCA, May 31, 2001.

cannabis on it) may have suggested to the jury that an adverse inference had arisen against the accused. The jury should instead have been directed to the burden upon the prosecution to prove beyond reasonable doubt, having regard to all the evidence and inferences in the case, possession by the accused of drugs with intent to supply.

4–77 In *Attorney-Geneal v Byrne*, Kenny J. expressed the need to explain to the jury what "reasonable doubt" meant, and specifically, where one or more possible views of the evidence are reasonably open, that the jury should resolve any conflict in favour of the accused.[178] As explained in *People (DPP) v C*,[179] however, this does not necessarily require the trial judge always to direct the jury to resolve any conflicts in the evidence in favour of the accused. In sexual offence cases, the verdict often ultimately depends upon the balance of credibility between the accused and the complainant—who the jury believes—and in such cases, a direction advising the jury to interpret any conflicts of evidence in favour of the accused would be tantamount to usurping the power of the jury to accept one aspect of the evidence over another. The court recommended instead that the jury be directed that they should accept the evidence most favourable to the accused unless satisfied beyond a reasonable doubt that the other evidence or inferences against him should be accepted. Ambiguities in the trial judge's references to "reasonable" doubt led to the overturning of conviction in *DPP v Cremin*.[180] The trial judge had correctly stated that the onus lay upon the prosecution, and that it never shifts to the accused, but had proceeded to say that this did not mean that doubt on any one matter entitled the accused to an acquittal. The trial judge's error lay in failing to explain that doubts on a "peripheral" issue did not entitle an acquittal, whereas any reasonable doubt on an "essential" issue did. In a case where there had been a serious conflict of evidence and much depended upon the credibility of the parties, this had amounted to a serious misdirection.

4–78 In *Attorney-General v Byrne*, Kenny J. also considered it beneficial to explain to jurors the rigours of the criminal standard of proof by contrasting it with the degree of proof required in civil cases.[181] Despite the number of convictions quashed in recent years over ambiguities and omissions in the trial judge's charge to the jury upon the criminal standard of proof, the Court of Criminal Appeal has avoided interpreting the observations and findings in *Byrne* to require formulaic adherence.[182] Thus, although it is preferable that he does so,[183] the trial judge is not required in every case to contrast the criminal

---

[178] [1974] I.R. 1 at 9 (CCA): *cf.* appendix 22.
[179] [2001] 3 I.R. 345 (CCA).
[180] CCA, May 10, 1999.
[181] [1974] I.R. 1 at 8 (CCA).
[182] *People (DPP) v Shortt*, CCA, July 23, 1996; *People (DPP) v Rawley* [1997] 2 I.R. 265 (CCA). In *Rawley*, the trial judge's charge, upheld upon appeal, had emphasised the prosecutor's burden to prove guilt beyond reasonable doubt but had omitted to state that any doubt was required to be resolved in favour of the accused (a statement the court in *Byrne* considered "essential").
[183] *People (DPP) v LG* [2003] 2 I.R. 517 (CCA).

standard with the lower civil preponderance standard to accentuate the difference.

Civil Proceedings

4–79 As a general rule, in non-criminal proceedings the standard of proof on the plaintiff, applicant, or petitioner is a preponderance of the evidence or the balance of probabilities. This requires the plaintiff to establish the facts at issue as being "more probable" or "more likely" than not.[184] The phrasing of the standard in this way appears to be quite recent in origin, and it belies the greater need in civil proceedings for a more sophisticated approach to probability.[185] Numerous more rigorous qualifications to the basic standard have been recognised on a piecemeal basis by statute and case law for specific causes of action, often in response to strong presumptions or inferences the law requires the court to draw.

4–80 Various higher standards have been recognised in the context of wills, stemming from the strong presumptions of the validity of a will, of testamentary capacity, and against intestacy. In *Leahy v Corboy*,[186] the Supreme Court identified a higher standard of proof that must be met by the propounder of a will who was involved in its drafting or execution *and* who stands to benefit by it, particularly in circumstances where the will purports to revoke an earlier will. It has also been recognised that a higher standard of proof applies to applications under s.117 of the Succession Act 1965—since this, brought by a child of the deceased, essentially seeks to redraft a duly executed will upon the basis that the testator failed in his lifetime to discharge his moral duty towards the child.[187] The array of presumptions applicable to succession law engendered striking disagreement amongst the Supreme Court in *Goods of Glynn Deceased v Glynn*, in terms of their requirements, effect, and ranking.[188] The deceased had given specific instructions on the drafting of his will to a lawyer and one other independent person, but prior to its execution he had suffered a massive stroke. Two weeks after the stroke, when still disorientated and unable to communicate, the draft will was read over to him, in response to which he nodded his head and signed the will with an "x". The applicant, standing to inherit the entire estate under intestacy rules, issued proceedings to have the will declared invalid by reason of the testator's incapacity. The High Court, and a majority of the Supreme Court, upheld the will. The majority accepted that owing to the strong presumption of testamentary capacity and

---

[184] Where the probabilities are equal, the standard has not been met: *Miller v Minister of Pensions* [1947] 2 All E.R. 372 at 374, *per* Denning L.J. (CA).
[185] Redmayne, "Standards of Proof in Civil Litigation" (1999) 62 M.L.R. 167 at 168.
[186] [1969] I.R 148 (SC). The principle applies equally to relatives as it does to strangers propounding the will: *Hegarty v King* (1880) 7 L.R. Ir. 18.
[187] In *IAC Deceased: C and F v WC and TC* [1989] I.L.R.M. 815 at 819 (SC), Finlay C.J. found as follows: "I am satisfied that the phrase contained in s.117(1) 'failed in his moral duty to make proper provision for the child in accordance with his means' places a relatively high onus of proof on an applicant for relief under the section".
[188] [1990] 2 I.R. 326 (SC).

Burdens and Standards of Proof 137

the validity of a will, the party challenging its validity bore the burden of proof, which required nothing short of the clearest and most satisfactory evidence in rebuttal.[189] Where evidence established that the deceased had suffered a massive stroke prior to signing the will, the presumption was displaced, and the onus had passed to the propounder of the will to establish testamentary capacity. Walsh J. based his dissent upon the view that in circumstances where the deceased suffered a stroke prior to executing a will,[190] the presumption of testamentary capacity does not arise unless there is evidence before the court that the content of the will had been read over to him and that he indicated his agreement.[191] Categorically, the point of difference between the majority and minority was with respect to whether testamentary capacity is an automatic presumption or, in cases where the testator suffered a stroke prior to drafting or executing the will, contingent upon proof that he understood and accepted the contents of the will.

4–81 Owing to the strong common law presumption of the validity of a marriage, the petitioner in nullity proceedings was once understood to bear a standard akin to the criminal standard.[192] Although the Supreme Court eventually clarified the application of the ordinary civil standard in nullity proceedings,[193] reference to proof suggestive of a higher standard is still routine.[194] Owing to the strong constitutional (and common law) presumption of the sanctity or *status quo* of life, in *Matter of a Ward of Court*, the High Court and Supreme Court required more stringent proof of the patient's best interests where a request was made on her behalf to discontinue artificial medical life-support. In the High Court, Lynch J. acknowledged "the gravity of the matter for decision" and the need to establish "clear and convincing" proof that such a decision would accord with the best interests of the ward, a woman who had remained in a coma for 26 years[195] In the Supreme Court, the issue was addressed by Denham J. who affirmed the civil standard but cautioned that "the court should not draw its conclusions lightly or without due regard to all the circumstances".[196] Owing to the great respect that must constitutionally

---

[189] *ibid.* at 330, *per* Hamilton P.
[190] Drawing an analogy with *Leahy v Corboy* [1969] I.R. 148 at 167 (SC).
[191] Approving *Re Begley* [1939] I.R. 479 (SC).
[192] In *McK v McK* [1936] I.R. 177 (HC), the petitioner was required to establish his case "clearly, unequivocally and beyond reasonable doubt."
[193] *N (orse K) v K* [1985] I.R. 733 (SC).
[194] In *O'R v B* [1991] 1 I.R. 289 at 303 (SC), Hederman J. emphasised that before declaring a marriage legally null and void, the court must be "cautious and examine all the evidence before it with great vigilance". See also *PF v GO'M (orse G.F.)* (SC, November 28, 2000).
[195] HC, May 15, 1995.
[196] [1995] 2 I.L.R.M. 401 at 453 (SC). Denham J. adopted these words from a decision affirming a higher civil standard for proof of fraud: *Banco Ambrosiano S.P.A. v Ansbacher & Co. Ltd.* [1987] I.L.R.M. 669 at 691 (SC). Blayney J. disagreed with reference in the *Ward of Court* case to the burden and standard of proof—this was a wardship application under the *parens patria* jurisdiction of the courts: as such it was not adversarial but instead a *lis inter partes*, and therefore the court had a freer hand to request evidence, information, and reports.

be given to the outcome of a referendum decided by the People of Ireland, any application under s.42 of the Referendum Act 1994 to declare the result null and void is an "awesome undertaking".[197] Although formally no higher standard applies than for other civil proceedings, the "court will be particularly vigilant in examining serious allegations".[198] In arriving at this view, the Supreme Court acknowledged its earlier decision in *Banco Ambrosiana S.P.A. v Ansbacher and Co. Ltd.*,[199] where it had refused to follow earlier authority asserting the need for a higher standard of proof in cases giving rise to allegations of fraud.

4–82 Thus, it appears settled in Ireland that the ordinary civil standard applies to all civil proceedings, even to cases of serious and weighty concern, but that, for one reason or another, the courts may require particularly cogent evidence before it finds for the proponent. In other words, rather than formally raising the standard in specific cases, the court will instead insist upon stronger, more compelling evidence—a distinction elsewhere criticised as "academic"[200] and "one of expression only".[201]

---

[197] *Hanafin v Minister for the Environment* [1996] 2 I.L.R.M. 161 at 195, *per* O'Flaherty J. (SC).
[198] *ibid., per* Barrington J., at 211.
[199] [1987] I.L.R.M. 669 (SC): applied in *O'Keeffe v Ferris* [1997] 2 I.L.R.M. 161 (SC).
[200] *Re Dellow's Will Trusts*[1964] 1 All E.R. 771 at 773, *per* Ungoed Thomas J.
[201] *Re M. (A Minor)* [1994] 1 F.L.R. 59 at 67, *per* Waite L.J.

Further Reading

Ashworth & Blake, "The Presumption of Innocence in English Criminal Law" [1996] Crim. L.R. 306.
Bennion, "Statutory Exceptions: A Third Knot in the Golden Thread" [1988] Crim. L.R. 31.
Birch, "The Hunting of the Snark" [1988] Crim. L.R. 19 & 221.
Bridge, "Presumptions and Burdens" [1949] 12 M.L.R. 273.
Denning, "Presumptions and Burdens" [1945] 61 L.Q.R. 379.
Doran, "Alternative Defences: The Invisible Burden on the Trial Judge" [1991] Crim. L.R. 878.
Healy, "Proof and Policy: No Golden Threads" [1987] Crim. L.R. 355.
Healy, "Issues of Causation in Recent Medical Negligence Litigation" (2003) 8 *Bar Review* 188.
Jones, ""Insanity, Automatism, and the Burden of Proof on the Accused" (1995) 111 L.Q.R. 475.
Kaye, "Clarifying the burden of persuasion: what Bayesian decision rules do and do not" (1999) 3(1) Int. J. Evid. & P. 1.
Mirfield, "The Legacy of Hunt" [1988] Crim. L.R. 355.
Ní Raifeartaigh, "Reversing the Burden of Proof in a Criminal Trial: Canadian and Irish Perspectives on the Presumption of Innocence" [1995] Ir. Crim. L.J. 135.
Ní Raifeartaigh, "The Criminal Justice System and Drug Related Offending: Some Thoughts on Procedural Reforms" (1998) 4 *Bar Review* 15.
Redmayne, "Standards of Proof in Civil Litigation" (1999) 62 M.L.R. 167.
O'Higgins & O'Braonain, "Section 4 of the Criminal Justice Act 1964: a constitutional presumption?" (1992) I.C.L.J. 179.
Roberts, "Taking the Burden of Proof Seriously" [1995] Crim. L.R. 783.
Smith, "The Presumption of Innocence" (1987) 38 N.I.L.Q. 223.
Stein, "After Hunt: the Burden of Proof, Risk of Non-Persuasion and Judicial Pragmatism" (1991) 54 M.L.R. 570.
Thayer and Stone, "Burden of Proof and the Judicial Process" (1944) 60 L.Q.R. 262.
Williams, "The Mathematics of Proof" [1979] Crim. L.R. 296.
Zuckerman, "The Third Exception to the Woolmington Rule" (1976) 92 L.Q.R. 402.

CHAPTER 5

CORROBORATION

I. General Principles	5–01
II. Definition and Forms of Corroboration	5–04
The Strict *Baskerville* Definition	5–04
Requirement of Independent Proof	5–05
III. The Requirement of Corroboration	5–17
IV. The Mandatory Corroboration Warning	5–19
Accomplice Witnesses	5–21
V. The Discretionary Corroboration Warning	5–35
Sexual Offence Proceedings	5–36
Child Witnesses	5–49
Mutual Corroboration	5–51

I. GENERAL PRINCIPLES

5–01 The English common law eschewed a general requirement of corroborated proof of criminal offence;[1] however, strict corroboration rules were developed upon an exceptional basis for prosecutors by operation of the law and latterly by judicial practice with respect to certain offences and witnesses, chiefly due to reliability concerns. Although many of the categories formerly targeted by the law—such as complainants in sexual offence cases and child witnesses—are no longer subject to mandatory corroboration rules, corroboration issues remain of concern, where the witness is potentially misleading (as in the case of accomplices) or evidence probative of the issue is unsupported (as if often the case in sexual offence trials). Some new categories have been brought into the fold in recent years, such as confession statements,[2] and others have been consolidated, such as accomplice witnesses.[3]

5–02 The principle that potentially suspect evidence should be corroborated is a sound one, and inheres in the *genus* principle, shared by the common law

---

[1] By contrast with Scots law, which continues to require corroboration for proof of criminal guilt (though adopting a looser definition of corroboration than has operated in England and Ireland): see Wilkinson, *The Scottish Law of Evidence* (Edinburgh, 1996) at pp.203–10.
[2] *cf.* paras **5–20** and **10–73** *et seq.*
[3] *cf.* para.**5–21** *et seq.*

and the Irish Constitution *per* Art.38(1), that the trial of an accused must be fair. It cannot safely be said that the accused has a right, discernible under the common law, to have only *actually* reliable evidence tendered against him.[4] Suspect witnesses are permitted to testify so long as the jury is adequately directed to the witness' potential unreliability and are urged to exercise caution when evaluating his evidence. Notwithstanding this rationale, strict corroboration rules appeared to flounder recently in England, freighted by excessive technicality and a sense that the rules were not always directed at the right targets; by the close of the last century, a shift had become evident in many cases from rule to discretion, a process also reflecting the correlative increase in credibility rules by this time.[5] As a broad concern, however, corroboration rules perform vital checks on the prosecution, encouraging it to substantiate the charges by better evidence, and latterly encouraging the jury to exercise caution when deciding the accused's guilt by reference to uncorroborated evidence.

5–03 Although some few offences, such as perjury, continue to attract an outright corroboration requirement, corroboration rules are now for the most part concerned with the trial judge's discretion, and in some cases, duty to caution the jury against convicting the accused upon the uncorroborated evidence in question. Before considering the implications of these rules, and the evidence to which they apply, an exploration of the definition and nature of corroboration evidence is essential, in light particularly of the fact that a great many appeals are successfully grounded in the trial judge's failure correctly to identify, when summing-up, evidence in the case that is capable of constituting corroboration.

II. Definition and Forms of Corroboration

The Strict *Baskerville* Definition

5–04 In cases where a corroboration rule technically applies, and in other cases where corroboration has been canvassed as an issue by the defence or the prosecution, the trial judge is required when summing-up to direct the jury's attention to the evidence in the case capable of amounting to corroboration if accepted by the jury. The task of defining corroborative evidence is not always straightforward, and terminological confusion and hesitancy persists with respect to notions of "corroboration" and "supporting evidence". The root of present difficulties is the strict definition of corroboration originally proposed by Lord Reading C.J. in *R. v Baskerville*,[6] to wit that corroboration is independent evidence which confirms "a material circumstance of the crime and of the identify of the accused in relation to the crime". The *Baskerville* definition was first accepted in Ireland by Sullivan C.J. in *People (Attorney-*

---

[4] *People (DPP) v Gillane* (CCA, December 14, 1998).
[5] *cf.* para.**3–01**.
[6] [1916] 2 K.B. 658 at 665 (CA).

General) v Williams,[7] and found to connote "independent evidence of material circumstances tending to implicate the accused in the commission of the crime with which he was charged". Despite numerous judicial qualifications and inconsistency in its application, the *Baskerville* decision is still ubiquitously cited in modern cases. Whilst in some contexts, a looser formulation is implicitly preferred, particularly in sexual offences cases—where proof tends by its nature to be more circumstantial, cumulative, and non-corroborative in the *Baskerville* sense—in other cases where policy still requires it, such as the testimony of accomplice witnesses, the courts rightly adhere to the stricter notion of independent proof envisaged by *Baskerville*.[8] Although Lord Reading C.J. explained towards the end of his judgment in *Baskerville*[9] that corroboration does not have to be supplied by direct evidence but may derive from circumstantial evidence establishing the accused's connection with the crime, in practice the requirement that corroboration be supplied from an independent source that *materially implicates* the accused has created most of the difficulties in administering the rules and will be considered further in the context of sexual offence proceedings.

Requirement of Independent Proof

5–05 The requirement of *independent* proof lies at the heart of the *Baskerville* formulation of corroboration, requiring that a first piece of evidence (or one witness' testimonial version) be confirmed in a material respect by evidence from some other source. As such, it reflects the principle that a party cannot self-corroborate, which is rooted in evidential concerns that a party may concoct falsely plausible evidence to bolster his own cause. The rule is routinely applied to documents and notes which a witness has been allowed to consult whilst giving testimony: such notes are inadmissible in the trial as evidence probative of any fact asserted therein, and, as a corollary, they are incapable of supplying corroboration of the witness' account to any extent.[10] Similarly, where a complainant in a sexual offence case has been permitted to testify to having made an early complaint shortly after the alleged offence, the jury is customarily instructed in watertight terms that the complaint may not be taken to constitute corroboration of the complainant's testimonial assertions.[11] The requirement of independent evidence creates peculiar difficulties for proof of sexual offences, considered later in the context of the discretionary corroboration warning now applicable to these cases. In such proceedings, the court rarely has the advantage of independent third-party proof, and is typically forced to evaluate the varying weight of circumstantial, indicative facts. In this context, it may now be more appropriate to refer to the law's preference for evidence that supports, rather than corroborates, the complainant's allegations of sexual

---

[7] [1940] I.R. 195 at 200 (SC).
[8] *cf.* para.**5–33**.
[9] [1916] 2 K.B. 658 at 667 (CA), *cf.* appendix 2.
[10] *R. v Virgo* (1978) 67 Cr. App. R. 323 (CA), *cf.* para.**2–45**.
[11] *cf.* para.**2–53** *et seq*. This was confirmed by the Court of Appeal in *R. v Makanjuola* [1995] 1 W.L.R. 1348 at 1355.

offence, which is the direction currently favoured in England.[12]

5–06 The requirement of independent proof has the logical effect that witnesses who each attract corroboration concerns due to their potential unreliability, such as accomplice witnesses, may not corroborate each other.[13] Whilst the courts have signalled a disinclination to apply this rule to witnesses no longer subject to the full rigours of corroboration law (namely, complainants in sexual offence cases and children),[14] they have been prepared to justify its continued application to accomplices, who attract a mandatory corroboration warning, and recent experience of accomplice testimony in Ireland can only serve to strengthen this stance.[15] A judicial direction that certain witnesses may not be taken to corroborate each other in a particular case may be required as a necessary exercise of judicial discretion having regard to the trial judge's constitutional duty to ensure that the accused receives a fair trial. This may arise, in particular, in cases where the evidence suggests that complainants or witnesses may have an axe to grind, or may have colluded prior to giving their testimony. This perspective was evident in the Court of Criminal Appeal's decision in *People (DPP) v Morrissey*,[16] where the accused had been convicted on foot of evidence by the complainant and her mother (with whom the accused had once lived). In light of the fact that there was an allegation that the two witnesses had conspired against the accused, and in light of inconsistencies between their accounts, the evidence should not have been treated as mutually corroborative. According to Barron J: "Corroboration must come from independent evidence. The mere fact that two parties in conspiracy with each other give the same evidence does not make the evidence of one corroboration of the evidence of the other".

5–07 A mere allegation by an accomplice witness that the accused has lied may not be treated as corroboration of his own testimonial version of events. Independent proof, as envisaged by *Baskerville*, is evidence from some source other than the witness who asserts the lie.[17] This issue was in dispute in an appeal against convictions for drugs importation in *R. v Lucas*.[18] An accomplice to the offences testified that the accused had lied in court about her non-involvement. The trial judge gave a customary corroboration warning of the dangers of convicting on foot of an accomplice's uncorroborated testimony, but obscurely suggested to the jury that they were entitled to treat the accused's lies, if found to be proven, as corroboration of the accomplice witness' account. This, then, was a case of assertion against assertion, in circumstances where the accomplice's assertion attracted concern to ensure that it was proven by evidence from an independent source. Alternatively, it was a case where an

---

[12] *cf.* para.**5–48** *et seq.*
[13] *R. v Noakes* (1832) 5 C. & P. 326; *R. v Baskerville* [1916] 2 K.B. 658 (CA), *cf.* appendix 2; *DPP v Kilbourne* [1973] A.C. 729, *per* Hailsham L.C. (HL), *cf.* appendix 20.
[14] *cf.* paras **5–43, 5–46**.
[15] *cf.* para.**5–24** *et seq.*
[16] CCA, July 10, 1998.
[17] *R. v King* [1967] 2 Q.B. 338 (CA).
[18] [1981] 3 W.L.R. 121 (CA).

accomplice, by the mere allegation of a lie, attempted in effect to self-corroborate. In overturning conviction, Lord Lane rightly recognised the circular nonsense of the occurrence: "If the belief that the accomplice is truthful means that the accused was untruthful and if that untruthfulness can be used as corroboration, the practical effect would be to dispense with the need of corroboration altogether".[19]

5–08 According to English law, as yet unexplored in Ireland, where the prosecution wishes to treat the lie as corroboration of aspects of its case against the accused, it is essential that specific criteria be satisfied before the false statement is properly presented to the jury in a corroborative capacity. In *Lucas*, the Court of Appeal established four: (1) the lie must be, or appear to be, deliberate (lessening the chance that it was innocently or mistakenly made); (2) the lie must relate to a material issue (beyond merely showing the accused to be generally untruthful); (3) the motive for the lie must appear to be a realisation of guilt and a fear of the truth (the behaviour of a guilty man); and (4) the lie must be proven by independent evidence.

5–09 The case of *R. v Richens*[20] well illustrates the need for special caution before the jury is invited to treat the accused's lies as corroborative evidence. The accused, a 17-year-old student, was charged with the murder of a fellow student who had allegedly raped the accused's girlfriend. When questioned, the accused initially denied any involvement in the death, but weeks later admitted to the killing. At his trial for murder and manslaughter, the accused explained that he had lied at first to protect his girlfriend, who had nothing to do with the incident and had since left the country. He further testified that he had postponed his confession so that his family would be shielded from disgrace until the Christmas season was over. In his summing-up, the trial judge gave no particular warning, and instead invited the jury to consider the lie as corroboration of the prosecution's case, probative of murder and an indication that the accused was a calculating liar. The Court of Appeal quashed conviction for murder and replaced it with a conviction for manslaughter, finding that the issue of the accused's lies has domineered in his trial and the trial judge's misdirection had critically affected the court's verdict.

5–10 Other forms of corroboration may emanate from the accused. Inculpatory admissions made by the accused during his trial—in most cases under cross-examination—may where relevant corroborate elements of the prosecution's case against him. Similarly, a voluntary confession made by an accused prior to the trial, and deemed admissible as an exception to the rule against hearsay,[21] may, if accepted by the jury to be true, corroborate all or part of the prosecution's case.[22] Evidence of the accused's previous misconduct

---

[19] *ibid.* at 123.
[20] [1993] 4 All E.R. 877 (CA).
[21] *cf.* para. **10–01** *et seq*.
[22] Confession evidence attracts a mandatory corroboration warning, pursuant to the Criminal Procedure Act 1993, s.10, *cf.* paras **5–20** and **10–72** *et seq*.

Corroboration

or convictions, where admitted in exceptional cases as "similar fact evidence",[23] may be relied upon by the prosecution as potential corroboration of its case. This type of evidence, once admitted, constitutes evidence probative of the facts at issue, controversially tending to prove the accused's guilt in the present instance by reference to past offences and bad character.

5–11 Notwithstanding that the accused attracts a right to silence and privilege against self-incrimination, numerous statutes now provide in specific circumstances that adverse inferences may be drawn at the trial arising from his refusal to cooperate (*e.g.* to consent to the taking of bodily samples),[24] or his refusal to explain his possession of objects or presence at a place,[25] or his failure to mention facts later relied upon in his defence.[26] Under each provision, the inference may amount to corroboration against him, although he may not be convicted solely upon the inference. This type of evidence has for good reason courted attention and controversy in recent years, chiefly because it is evidence that has unwittingly been produced by the accused and not independently by the prosecution; further because the provisions consciously exert pressure upon suspects to co-operate in criminal investigations; and further because they encourage inferential evidence in the trial of an unknown, ungovernable nature. The measures are clearly designed to extract proof from the accused in his own trial, and as such share more in common culturally with the inquisitorial model of law operating in mainland Europe. Since they dramatically affect the accused's right to silence and privilege against self-incrimination, they are considered in more detail in Chapter 13.[27]

5–12 Thus far in Ireland these qualifications to the right to silence have been maintained within limits, whereas a general facility to draw inferences from silence has been created by statute in England.[28] The English courts have faced numerous difficulties with respect to the effect and implication of these inferences.[29] Although there are many important differences between the Irish and English provisions, they each proceed on the basis that, as for proof that the accused told lies, the accused's silence ought to become circumstantial evidence of his guilty behaviour, and in appropriate cases to engender inferences against him. It is worth noting that the Irish provisions expressly acknowledge that the inferences may "corroborate" some aspect of the prosecution's evidence against the accused, whereas the English provisions wisely avoided reference to this problematic term, favouring instead a more generalised approach to the drawing of "such inferences as appear proper". It is questionable whether silence or non-cooperation is intrinsically capable of

---

[23] *cf.* para.**7–02**.
[24] Criminal Justice (Forensic Evidence) Act 1990, s.3.
[25] Criminal Justice Act 1984, ss.18–19.
[26] Criminal Justice (Drug Trafficking) Act 1996, s.7; Offences Against the State (Amendment) Act 1998, s.5.
[27] *cf.* para.**13–100** *et seq.*
[28] Criminal Justice and Public Order Act 1994, ss.34–35.
[29] *cf.* para.**13–103** *et seq.*

amounting to corroboration in the *Baskerville* sense of the word,[30] since neither supplies independent evidence tending to implicate the accused or to establish his guilt to a *material* degree. Silence and non-cooperation is equivocal.[31] The approach traditionally favoured in England was "to take [the accused's silence] into consideration ... in considering the weight to be attached" to other items of evidence.[32] In a similar vein, it has been decided in England that the accused's decision not to testify may not be accepted as "supporting evidence" (a broader base than corroboration) capable of bolstering an identification, although the trial judge may direct the jury that when considering the adequacy of the identification they may take into account the fact that the accused has not contradicted it.[33]

5–13 In *Rock v Ireland*,[34] where the accused had been discovered by gardaí in a toilet cubicle next to a bag stuffed full of forged bank notes, the Supreme Court confirmed that the power to draw inferences under ss.18–19 of the Criminal Justice Act 1984 is a permissive one.[35] It entitles but does not compel the trial judge to direct the jury that they may or may not draw such inferences as appear "proper". Thus the judge retains a general discretion to direct the jury that they may or may not draw inferences, as the case may be, in light of the particular circumstances. Conviction based solely upon inferences from pre-trial silence is expressly foreclosed by the relevant provisions in Ireland and England, a fact the European Court of Human Rights considered important when it rejected a challenge to the power to draw inferences from silence under the Criminal Evidence (Northern Ireland) Order 1988.[36] It is distinctly possible, however, that the provisions, whether intentionally or not, may cause some convictions to be secured *mainly* on foot of adverse inferences—where for example the accused persists in maintaining his silence and then chooses not to testify at his trial.[37]

---

[30] On rare occasions, the courts had treated silence coupled with evidence of the accused's flight as corroborative evidence: *R. v Bondy* (1957) 121 C.C.C. 337.

[31] Heydon, *Evidence: Cases & Materials* (Butterworths, London, 1991) at p.149.

[32] *Cracknell v Smith* [1960] 3 All E.R. 569 at 571, *per* Lord Parker C.J. (QBD); *R. v Jackson* [1953] 1 W.L.R. 591 (CA); *Parkes v R.* [1976] 1 W.L.R. 1251 (PC); and *R. v Horne* [1990] Crim. L.R. 188 (CA).

[33] *R. v Turnbull* [1977] Q.B. 224 at 230 (CA): *cf.* appendix 24.

[34] [1997] 3 I.R. 484, [1998] 2 I.L.R.M. 35 (SC): *cf.* appendix 55.

[35] The English provisions have been interpreted to trigger mandatory directions by the trial judge, largely because s.35(2) of the Criminal Justice and Public Order Act 1994 requires the trial judge to inform the accused during the trial that if he adheres to his decision not to testify, inferences may be drawn against him: *R. v Taylor* [1999] Crim. L.R. 77 (CA).

[36] *Murray v UK* (1996) 22 E.H.H.R. 29 *cf.* appendix 49. Although the court decided the case on another ground—that the accused's right of access to a lawyer had been violated—a majority of the judges reasoned that the right to silence is not an absolute, that it may be subject to public policy requirements and the common good, and that the practice of drawing inferences from silence is justifiable if the inferences are "reasonably" made: *cf.* para.**13–105** *et seq.*

[37] See the submissions made in the context of a statutory reverse-onus clause in *People (DPP) v Foley* [1995] 1 I.R. 267 (CCA): *cf.* para.**13–87**.

5–14 In this regard, it may be queried whether the Irish provisions are limited to trials in which the accused elects to testify. Sections 18–19 of the Criminal Justice 1984 Act cast a wide net, and entitle the court generally to draw inferences from the accused's silence in response to specific questions posed at the time the accused was summarily arrested. The sections are not limited to the question of discrepancies between the accused's version at trial and his silence or evasiveness at the pre-trial stage. By contrast, s.7 of the Criminal Justice (Drug Trafficking) Act 1996 and s.5 of the Offences Against the State (Amendment) Act 1998 create a specific power to draw inferences from the accused's failure to provide information later "relied on in his or defence" which he would "reasonably have been expected to mention when ... questioned, charged or informed". With respect to the words "any fact relied on in his defence" at the trial, the English courts have adopted a literal approach. If the defence adduces no evidence, the accused's pre-trial silence may not engender inferences.[38] This is not the case, however, where the defence calls witnesses or cross-examines witnesses for the prosecution even though the accused does not himself testify.[39]

5–15 According to emerging English case-law, the inevitable purpose of drawing adverse inferences from pre-trial silence is to suggest that the accused has fabricated his trial defence.[40] The trial judge, however, should caution the jury that the accused may have remained silent for a host of reasons other than guilt or fear of the truth. The accused might not have had time to consider the events that took place, or may not have been able at the time to provide an innocent explanation for behaviour that appeared highly incriminating. The accused might have refused to answer certain questions to shield others from blame or involvement in the investigation, as in *R. v Richens*.[41] The facts he "would reasonably be expected" to disclose when questioned by the police fall to be considered in light of the specific circumstances of the case. The court should assess the likely subjective effect of those circumstances on the accused, including his age, mental capacity, experience, health, tiredness, sobriety, knowledge, personality, and the legal advice he received.[42] According to the specimen direction endorsed in *R. v Cowan*,[43] the jury should be asked to consider whether the accused's silence "can only sensibly be attributed" to his having no defensible answer. Where the accused invites the court *not* to draw adverse inferences from his pre-trial silence, he will ordinarily be expected to show cause. It was made clear in *Cowan*, however, that merely establishing a good reason for his silence does not entitle the accused to a direction that no adverse inferences must be drawn; the jury is free to evaluate the respective weight of his silence, the potential inferences, and his explanation, having regard to other evidence in the case.

---

[38] *R. v Moshaid* [1998] Crim. L.R. 420 (CA).
[39] *R. v Bowers* [1998] Crim. L.R. 817 (CA).
[40] *R. v Daniel* [1998] 2 Cr. App. R. 373 (CA).
[41] *cf.* para.**5–09**.
[42] *R. v Argent* [1997] 2 Cr. App. R. 27 (CA).
[43] [1995] 3 W.L.R. 818 at 824 (CA).

5–16 According to the Court of Appeal in *R. v Pointer*,[44] it is technically improper to put questions to the accused for the purpose of raising adverse inferences from his silence where the prosecution already possesses a strong case against him. It would appear to be the case, however, that where the police are shown to have withheld all or some information before the accused was invited to comment in interview, his silence may yet be relied upon to ground an inference, although its weight may be regarded as less.[45] In *R. v Imran and Hussain*,[46] the court reasoned that it is "totally wrong to submit that an accused should be prevented from lying by being presented with the whole of the evidence against him prior to the interview".

III. THE REQUIREMENT OF CORROBOATION

5–17 Where a rule requires certain charges or evidence to be corroborated, the court is not permitted to convict the accused unless the evidence tendered against him is corroborated. Where no evidence has been produced capable of amounting to corroboration, the defence is entitled to a direction that the prosecution has failed to prove its case. Where evidence has been tendered by the prosecution that is reasonably capable of constituting corroboration, the trial judge is entitled to give the jury a conditional corroboration direction: to wit, that the jury may convict the accused if they first accept as reliable and true the second piece of evidence offered as corroboration of the first.

5–18 In recent years, the legislative trend has been to repeal full corroboration requirements,[47] although the common law requirement of corroborative proof of perjury[48] and the statutory requirement of corroborative proof of treason,[49] has been retained. Under s.105 of the Road Traffic Act 1961, proof of speeding on the road must be corroborated: "Where the proof of the commission of an offence under this Act involves the proof of the speed at which a person (whether the accused or another person) was driving ... the uncorroborated evidence of one witness stating his opinion as to that speed shall not be accepted as proof of that speed". Corroboration may be provided by additional witnesses to the car's speed or by a contemporaneous reading of the car's speedometer

---

[44] [1997] Crim. L.R. 676 (CA).
[45] *R. v Argent* [1997] Crim. L.R. 346 (CA).
[46] [1997] Crim. L.R. 754 (CA).
[47] For instance, s.25 of the Status of Children Act 1985 repeals the Illegitimate Children (Affiliation Orders) Act 1930, which, by s.3, had provided that declarations of paternity could not be made unless the mother's evidence was corroborated in "some material particulars". In England, this repeal was accomplished by s.17 of the Family Law Reform Act 1987.
[48] *R. v Threlfall* (1914) 10 Cr. App. R. 112 (CA); *R. v Rider* (1986) 83 Cr. App. R. 207 (CA). In England, this is governed by the Perjury Act 1911.
[49] The crime of treason attracts a mandatory sentence of life imprisonment, pursuant to the Criminal Justice Act 1990, s.2. Sections 1(4) and 2(2) of the Treason Act 1939 provide that an accused may not be convicted of the crime of treason or related offence upon uncorroborated evidence. In England, this requirement, formerly under the Treason Act 1795, s.1, was repealed by the Crime and Disorder Act 1998, s.120(2).

Corroboration

or like device.[50] In *People (DPP) v Connaughton*,[51] the Court of Criminal Appeal decided that the requirement in s.105 does not apply to prosecutions for dangerous driving causing serious bodily harm, and that the accused had been properly convicted upon the evidence of witnesses testifying to the *general* speed at which the car was going.

IV. THE MANDATORY CORROBORATION WARNING

5–19 The corroboration warning was developed as a judicial rule of practice that latterly became a fixed requirement in some cases. Where such a warning is mandatory, the trial judge is obliged to caution the jury that the witness or evidence is of a type considered potentially unreliable or suspect by the law, and that the jury should be slow to convict the accused upon this evidence unless corroborated by a second witness or piece of evidence. Once the dangers of acting upon the uncorroborated evidence are adequately expressed, and accurate guidance given as to what may constitute corroboration in the case, the jury is free to convict or not upon the uncorroborated evidence.[52]

5–20 The law now prefers not to restrict judges to a set-piece formula of words, and the modern tendency of legislators is to provide for mandatory warnings that do not have to be given in any fixed form of words. This is illustrated by s.10 of the Criminal Procedure Act 1993, which introduced a mandatory corroboration warning requirement in any case on indictment where evidence of a confession is tendered by the prosecution. The jury must be warned in appropriate cases to have "due regard to the absence of corroboration" in the case, although the trial judge need not express this in "any particular form of words".[53]

Accomplice Witnesses

5–21 By strict common law rule, the evidence of accomplice witnesses attracts a mandatory corroboration warning.[54] Because of the highly prejudicial nature of accomplice evidence, the failure to give an adequate warning to the jury is always likely to constitute a strong base for an appeal.[55] Once a warning has

---

[50] *Nicholas v Penny* [1950] 2 K.B. 466.
[51] CCA, April 5, 2001. The witnesses had observed the car to be driving "at speed" and "quite fast".
[52] *People (DPP) v Egan* [1990] I.L.R.M. 780 (SC), endorsing and applying *People (Attorney-General) v Williams* [1940] I.R. 195 (SC).
[53] *cf.* para.**10–72** *et seq.*
[54] By contrast, in England the mandatory warning was repealed under the Criminal Justice and Public Order Act 1994, s.32.
[55] The rule was strictly applied in *Attorney-General v Linehan* [1929] I.R. 19 (CCA). In *R. v Vincent and Taylor* [1983] Crim. L.R. 173 (CA), the trial judge's instruction that "a great deal of care was needed" with respect to the witness' evidence (expressed as part of his general directions) was not strong or forthright enough. Conviction was reversed since founded upon the uncorroborated evidence of an accomplice in respect of whom an adequate warning had not been given.

properly been given, however, the jury is free to evaluate the probity and weight of the accomplice's evidence and, if they so choose, to act upon it when deciding to convict the accused. In *People (DPP) v Hogan*,[56] the appeal against the trial judge's corroboration warning was based to a large extent on the fact that the accomplice's sentence had been reduced upon appeal due to his co-operation with the police, and that, being an accomplice to the robbery, he had been in a good position to know that the other party had incriminating evidence at his house. O'Flaherty J. refused to deem the trial judge's direction defective, because it had properly drawn the jury's attention to the reasons why corroboration was preferred. The fact that the accomplice had had insider knowledge of the incriminating evidence, and that he had cooperated with the police, were matters adequately emphasised in court under cross-examination.

5–22 As for all corroboration requirements, the accomplice witness rule applies only to witnesses called by the prosecution. According to *Baskerville*, given that the burden of proof is upon the prosecution, if it calls a witness of dubious reliability, the jury should be adequately warned of the dangers of acting upon that witness' uncorroborated evidence. The corollary of this is that the accused may choose to waive his entitlement to a warning if, for example, the accomplice's evidence proves favourable to the defence.[57]

5–23 There are many reasons why the law should generally treat accomplice evidence with suspicion, although it is more usually argued that: (1) accomplices may attempt to evade or to minimise their own liability by falsely diverting the blame to another; (2) accomplices are already morally culpable, so they are more likely to lie and deceive the court; and (3) accomplice testimony may appear artificially convincing because of the accomplice's familiarity with the accused and the events in question. Despite its potential unreliability, accomplice evidence is increasingly regarded as critical to the prosecution of large-scale organised crime and conspiracies, "the discovery whereof can properly only come from the conspirators themselves".[58] In the aftermath of the assassination of the celebrated investigative journalist Veronica Guerin in 1997, the State established the Witness Protection Programme, and much reliance was placed on accomplice witnesses in the prosecutions of Ward,[59] Holland,[60] Meehan,[61] and Gilligan.[62]

---

[56] CCA, January 12, 1994.
[57] As in *R. v Royce-Bentley* [1974] 1 W.L.R. 535 (CA).
[58] *Per* Lord Holt C.J., quoted in *R. v Despard* (1803) 28 State Tr. 346 at 489. See also Elliot (1999) at p.362 who argues that "as much as possible should be used of "insiders" who are in a position to help ... Many a convict owes his incarceration to betrayal by his former partners; the law must be astute to maintain or increase the frequency of such betrayals".
[59] *People (DPP) v Ward* (Special Criminal Court, November 27, 1998; CCA, March 22, 2002).
[60] *People (DPP) v Holland* (CCA, June 15, 1998).
[61] *People (DPP) v Meehan* (Special Criminal Court, July 29, 1999). The court rejected the evidence of a number of accomplices, due to their unreliability, but convicted the accused upon the evidence of an accomplice who had been corroborated independently by a credible witness unrelated to him.
[62] *People (DPP) v Gilligan* (Special Criminal Court, March 15, 2001).

Corroboration

5–24 The experience in the case of *People (DPP) v Ward*[63] is starkly illustrative of the perils occasioned by reliance upon discredited witnesses, and will surely serve to heighten corroboration concerns in future proceedings of this nature. When reviewing the evidence of the accomplice Bowden, Barr J. of the Special Criminal Court accepted that he was "a self-serving, deeply avaricious and potentially vicious criminal" with a self-confessed propensity to lie. The court further accepted that the witness lied when he told the court that part of the reason he came forward was remorse over the killing of Veronica Guerin. The court concluded that his motivation was, instead, self-interest. When evaluating concerns that his evidence might be misleading or unreliable, the court focused principally on the witness' motive and incentive to deceive, whether and to what extent it was in his interests to lie. The learned judge felt that the witness' obvious self-interest—in making "probably the best bargain he could hope to achieve from the State in all the circumstances"—lent greater credibility to his account of events, given that he must have known and feared that the State could have withdrawn his protection if his story was shown to be false, and given the low likelihood that Bowden would wrongly have cast the accused as the gun disposer since he had nothing to gain (having already implicated himself as an accessory to murder) and everything to lose (his life) by implicating the accused, and faced at all times the prospect of retaliation from former criminal associates.

5–25 The Court of Criminal Appeal quashed the appellant's conviction for accessory to murder after the fact.[64] In light of the inadmissibility of the confession statement—as found earlier by Barr J. for the Special Criminal Court[65]—the evidence against the appellant was entirely that of Bowden, the accomplice witness. Although the potential dangers of his testimony had been identified by the Special Criminal Court (sitting, *per force*, without a jury), it had erred by progressing to convict the appellant upon that evidence. The court noted in particular that: Bowden had been imprecise about important dates, had lied in earlier statements and in his sworn testimony, and had admitted in his own evidence that he was an "inveterate liar". The trial court should not have concluded that the gun had been received at the accused's house after the murder, since this claim was unsubstantiated and unproven; there was no evidence to show the accused's planning of the assassination; and the trial court must have been "misled by the confusing evidence and voluminous documentation preceding it".

5–26 Irish law favours a broad definition of accomplice for the purposes of deciding the status of the witness' evidence. This approach accords with the dominant justification for applying corroboration rules to accomplice witnesses: the witness' incentive to lie and deflect blame. When deciding, for instance, in *Dental Board v O'Callaghan*[66] that a police entrapper or *agent provocateur*

---

[63] Special Criminal Court, November 27, 1998.
[64] CCA, March 22, 2002.
[65] Special Criminal Court, October 23, 1998.
[66] [1969] I.R. 181 (HC).

was not an accomplice, the High Court observed that such witnesses do not lie for reasons of self-interest. In *Attorney-General v Linehan*,[67] Kennedy C.J. considered that it would not be wise to lay down a fixed definition of accomplice. Since "the degree and gravity of such complicity may vary, and inasmuch as the extent of the effect of such complicity upon the credit of the witness or the weight of his uncorroborated testimony will vary accordingly, so should the degree and gravity of the warning be measured".[68]

5–27 A much narrower concept is preferred in England, whose leading authority is *Davies v DPP*.[69] Lord Simonds of the House of Lords identified three broad types of accomplice. The first accords with the natural and primary meaning of "accomplice"—that is, persons who are *participes criminis*, whether as principals or accessories before or after the fact, and those who have procured, aided, or abetted with respect to the offence being tried. The second two relate to the "anomalous" scenarios of: receivers of stolen goods, since the two crimes of theft and receipt are in a relationship of "one-sided dependence";[70] and participants in *previous* crimes, where evidence of the previous crimes has been admitted in the trial under similar fact evidence rules. *Davies* is also authority for the view that the accomplice question is to be assessed in relation to the witness' involvement in the specific offence being tried. The accused and seven youths had set upon another gang, and in the midst of the fight the accused had unexpectedly brandished a knife stabbing a gang member to death. The court reasoned that when a member of the accused's own gang testified against him, he did not do so as accomplice to the crime of murder, since the evidence showed no intention amongst the gang to commit a murder; if the accused had been charged with common assault, then and only then would the witness have been an accomplice of the accused.

5–28 A person who has already been convicted for his involvement in the relevant events remains an accomplice for the purpose of giving testimony against an associate.[71] The rule reflects the likelihood that the accomplice's version at his own trial was given to avoid conviction, and that even if he perjured himself he is likely to stick to that story later at the trial of a fellow accomplice.[72] An accomplice's spouse may corroborate the accomplice, but in most cases the jury is likely to attach less weight to it.[73]

---

[67] *Attorney-General v Linehan* [1929] I.R. 19 (CCA).
[68] *ibid*. at 23.
[69] [1954] A.C. 378 (HL).
[70] A like approach was adopted in *People (DPP) v Murtagh* [1990] 1 I.R. 339 (CCA) with respect to the co-dependent offences of perjury and subornation (or inducement) of perjury, so that the perjurer is an accomplice of the suborner and *vice versa*; similarly, for the offences of perjury and perverting the course of justice by inciting another to make a false statement to the police, the person who has allowed himself to be incited is an accomplice to the crime, and *vice versa*.
[71] *People (DPP) v Hogan* (CCA, January 12, 1994).
[72] Heydon, *op. cit.* n.31 at p.95.
[73] *R. v Evans* [1965] 2 Q.B. 295 (CA).

5–29 Evidence given by a co-accused against a fellow co-accused (even if both are former accomplices) does not necessarily attract a corroboration warning, according to the Court of Appeal in *R. v Cheema*.[74] The prosecution's case was that the appellant and her son had arranged with two of his hit-men acquaintances to have her husband killed, and that two unsuccessful attempts had been made before the fatal attempt. In the trial of mother and son for murder and attempted murder, the prosecution claimed that the son's evidence in his own defence was capable of corroborating evidence against the appellant given by the two hit-men accomplices in an earlier trial. The trial judge directed that care needed to be taken with the son's evidence since he might have an axe to grind, but that his evidence was capable of corroborating the evidence of the two separately tried co-accused. In upholding the warning, the court based most of its reasoning on the prejudice that pejorative corroboration warnings are likely to cause for a co-accused's defence (here, with respect to the son). Instructing the jury that they should not act upon a co-accused's evidence, unless it is corroborated, devalues the co-accused's evidence and thus his defence. It would also tend to confuse juries, especially where there are numerous parties who are accused or implicated in the offence.

5–30 The Irish courts have occasionally considered whether the trial judge is entitled or obliged to decide the witness's status, or whether the jury may be invited to do so. The answer carries implications for the type of accomplice warning the judge is obliged to give—whether an absolute corroboration warning (that the witness is an accomplice and the jury should be slow to convict upon his uncorroborated evidence), or a conditional corroboration warning (that if the jury accepts the witness is an accomplice, they should be slow to convict upon his uncorroborated evidence). As the House of Lords conceded in *Davies*, the fact that the witness is an accomplice is often self-evident and non-contentious, where for example the witness himself has confessed to involvement in crimes with the accused. In other cases: (1) the trial judge may decide that there is not enough evidence upon which the jury could reasonably decide that the witness is an accomplice; and (2) where there is evidence that may reasonably be interpreted to lead to the conclusion that the witness is an accomplice, the trial judge *may* submit the question to the jury for their decision (whereupon he will give a conditional corroboration warning). The House of Lords did not directly consider whether the judge is entitled to decide unilaterally that the witness is an accomplice, although this may be taken to be the logical corollary of his power to decide unilaterally that the witness is not an accomplice.

5–31 The accomplice witness issue, it is submitted, raises a question of law strictly for the trial judge to decide, and, given its critical significance for the trial, this decision should be effected clearly. Nonetheless, this issue proved divisive in *People (Attorney-General) v Carney*.[75] The two accused had been

---

[74] [1994] 1 W.L.R. 147 (HL).
[75] [1955] I.R. 324 (SC).

convicted of receiving stolen goods, chiefly upon the evidence of an accomplice witness. Upon appeal, the defence argued that the trial judge should not have permitted the jury to decide whether the witness was an accomplice, but should have decided that point himself and given an absolute corroboration warning. The Court of Criminal Appeal decided that even where the evidence points strongly to the witness being an accomplice, it falls to the jury to resolve that question. On further appeal, O'Byrne J. for the Supreme Court decided that the accomplice issue should not have been left to the jury. On any reasonable view of the evidence, the witness was an accomplice—to the extent that he was involved in the crimes under investigation—and an absolute corroboration warning should have been given. Dixon J., dissenting, concluded that this was an issue properly to be addressed by the jury.

5–32 *Carney* may be contrasted with a decision by the Court of Criminal Appeal in *People (DPP) v Diemling*,[76] where the court decided that the trial judge had erred by *not* permitting the jury to consider whether the witness was an accomplice. The accused was charged with false imprisonment and murder. His daughter testified for the prosecution. The trial judge rejected an application to treat her as an accomplice witness despite evidence strongly implicating her in the offences: she had been aware that her father had kidnapped the deceased; she had purchased medical supplies to tend to his injuries; and she had helped to hide evidence of the crime, repainting the blood splattered walls of his confinement. Upon appeal, the court rejected the narrow view that an accessory-after-the-fact must give direct assistance and possess actual knowledge of the crime. The court was entitled to fix her constructively with knowledge, since even a slight degree of complicity was sufficient to render an accessory-after-the-fact an accomplice. Although *Diemling* may appear on the surface to accord with Dixon J.'s dissent in *Carney*, preferring to leave the issue to the jury, it is important to consider the decision in its true context. *Diemling* was an appeal from an obvious error not to treat the witness as an accomplice. It is possible to extract the following propositions from *Davies*, *Carney*, and *Diemling*:

> where the witness is clearly an accomplice, the trial judge should give an absolute corroboration warning that cautions the jury against convicting upon the uncorroborated testimony of that witness;
>
> where the witness is clearly not an accomplice, the accomplice issue does not arise and the trial judge is not required to give a special accomplice warning; and
>
> where there is evidence which could *reasonably* be interpreted to establish that the witness is an accomplice, but the evidence does not unequivocally establish it, and the trial judge prefers not to decide the question unilaterally, the trial judge should submit the issue to the jury for their determination, and should give a conditional corroboration warning.

---

[76] CCA, May 4, 1992.

5-33 The traditional view is that fellow accomplices (who are *particeps criminis*) cannot corroborate each other, since there is a greater risk that the conspirators colluded to shift the blame to the accused,[77] but that other types of accomplice may.[78] There are many reasons why this rule should be preserved, some practical and others legalistic. First, it is right to treat the evidence of co-conspirators with suspicion, particularly where two or more present a united front against the accused. Depending upon the circumstances, it may be particularly difficult to disprove the co-conspirators' spin on events. The courts should continue to encourage verification of the gist of their story by some independent source of evidence. Second, the requirement of independent confirmation is the cornerstone of corroboration principles, and reflects the view that where a corroboration concern arises, the court is effectively asked to seek confirmation from some extraneous source to lessen the chance that the witnesses' version of events was concocted or misleading.

5-34 It is often proposed in England, perhaps as a response to the narrowness of its definition of accomplice witness, that the law should instead encourage corroboration warnings to be given in any case where a witness is shown to have a vested interest in blaming the accused, whether or not the witness amounts, by definition at law, to an accomplice.[79] Thus, if an agent provocateur or entrapper is shown to have some particular self-interest in prosecuting the accused, such as retaliation or attainment of promotion, a warning as to motive and potential unreliability should be given.[80] This approach was adopted in *R. v Bagshaw*,[81] where the Court of Appeal overturned conviction upon the basis that though the witnesses did not fall squarely within a category of witness to which corroboration rules traditionally applied, the witnesses in question (mentally ill criminals) fulfilled the general criteria that attract the corroboration warning. This non-categorical approach was rejected by the Court of Appeal in *R. v Beck*,[82] however, where the witnesses were fellow officers of a finance company who, though clearly not accomplices, were shown to have an interest in covering up various false representations. In support of the need for a special warning, the appellant invoked Archbold for the view that where any witness for the prosecution is shown to have "some purpose of his own to serve which may lead him to give false evidence against an accused, the judge should warn the jury of the danger of convicting that accused on that witness' evidence unless it is corroborated".[83] The court resisted the temptation to articulate further special rules, and preferred to view this case as raising issues that a trial judge may and sometimes should incorporate into his general directions

---

[77] *R. v Sims* [1946] K.B. 531 (CA).
[78] *R. v Prater* [1960] 2 Q.B. 464 (CA); *DPP v Hester* [1973] A.C. 296 at 326 & 330 (HL); *DPP v Kilbourne* [1973] A.C. 729 at 748 (HL); and *R. v Turner* [1980] Crim. L.R. 305 (CA).
[79] English Criminal Law Revision Committee, cited in Heydon, *op. cit.* n.31 at p.94.
[80] Heydon, *ibid.* at p.95.
[81] [1984] 1 W.L.R. 477 (CA). See also *R. v Prater* [1960] 2 Q.B. 464; *R. v Stannard* [1965] 2 Q.B. 1; and *R. v Whitaker* (1976) 63 Cr. App. R. 193 (CA).
[82] [1982] 1 W.L.R. 461 (CA).
[83] Archbold, *Criminal Pleading Evidence & Practice* (40th ed., 1979) at para.1425a.

when summing-up: "Whilst we in no way wish to detract from the obligation upon a judge to advise a jury to proceed with caution where there is material to suggest that a witness' evidence may be tainted by an improper motive, and the strength of that advice must vary according to the facts of the case, we cannot accept that there is an obligation to give an accomplice warning with all that that entails, when it is common ground that there is no basis for suggesting that the witness is a participant or in any way involved in the crime the subject matter of the trial".[84] *Beck* was affirmed by the House of Lords in *R. v Spencer*.[85]

V. THE DISCRETIONARY CORROBORATION WARNING

5–35 In Ireland and England, the mandatory corroboration warning that formerly applied to the evidence of complainants in sexual offence cases and child witnesses has been transformed by statute into an optional warning to be given at the discretion of the trial judge.[86] This reflects a shift in critical view, to wit, that such witnesses should no longer systematically be singled out as unreliable, nor their testimony unnecessarily undermined by formal corroboration warnings. Speaking of equivalent provisions in England in *R. v Makanjuola*,[87] a decision affirmed by the Supreme Court in *People (DPP) v JEM*,[88] Lord Taylor C.J. confirmed that a non-categorical approach would henceforth be taken with respect to the evidence of these witness, and he proposed that before a trial judge should give such a warning, there ought "to be an evidential basis for suggesting that the evidence of the witness may be unreliable". Recent case-law in this and other areas suggests, however, that expressing a rule or preference of the law in discretionary terms is no guarantee that fewer appeals will be fought upon corroboration issues in cases suffering evidential gaps. Corroboration issues are still frequently contested upon appeal, whether in terms of the adequacy of warning or the definition of corroborative evidence given in the case. It is clear in particular that the conversion from rule to discretion has not diminished anxieties over the frailty of evidence in sexual offence cases.

Sexual Offence Proceedings

5–36 Traditionally, the evidence of complainants in trials for sexual offences attracted a specific corroboration rule. The trial judge was obliged to administer a strong warning cautioning the jury against convicting the accused upon the

---

[84] [1982] 1 W.L.R. 461 at 469, *per* Ackner L.J. (CA)
[85] [1987] A.C. 128 (HL).
[86] In England, s.34(2) of the Criminal Justice Act 1988 and s.32(1) of the Criminal Justice and Public Order Act 1994 abolished the obligation to give a full corroboration warning "merely because" the witness is an accomplice, or a child, or a complainant in a sexual offence case. Irish law differs to the extent that it has not abolished the mandatory corroboration warning requirement for accomplice evidence: *cf.* para.**5–21**.
[87] [1995] 1 W.L.R. 1348 at 1352 (CA).
[88] [2001] 4 I.R. 385 (SC): *cf.* appendix 60.

uncorroborated testimony of the complainant.[89] The trial judge was further required to identify any evidence the jury might properly consider to be corroborative of the complainant's case.[90] Section 7 of the Criminal Law (Rape) (Amendment) Act 1990 now provides that such a warning is no longer mandatory, but that the trial judge may choose to give it "in his discretion" although not necessarily in any "particular form of words". Notwithstanding this welcome re-alignment in the rules, the state of corroboration law with respect to sexual offence cases is not yet clear-cut, and it may still be useful to identify the rationale for the former rules, in light particularly of the fact that evidential concerns in specific cases may require the trial judge to exercise his discretion to give a warning tailored to the special circumstances and evidence of the case.

5–37 Section 7 responded to widespread dissatisfaction with the manner in which this and other rules of evidence have worked in the past to discredit and undermine complainants of sex crimes. Many of the reasons advanced in support of the corroboration requirement had focused on the possibility that female complainants might plausibly deceive the court: this is evident in Sullivan C.J.'s judgment in *People (Attorney-General) v Williams*,[91] despite his acceptance that a complainant is not by type a discredited witness, as is an accomplice. The rule was sometimes justified by the fear that complaints of sexual offence may sometimes be the product of spite, jealousy, psychological denial of having consented, or a reaction to be having been jilted;[92] that women with nothing to lose might seek to subject a man of high social standing to blackmail;[93] and that the accusation of rape is easily made but difficult to defend.[94] These sentiments are rarely expressed today, save in the context of particular cases where the facts reveal an evidential basis for suspicion. They were not then, however, the only reasons in support of corroboration rules in sexual offence cases.

5–38 Corroboration law has been equally concerned with the difficulty of disproving allegations of sexual offence and the obvious potential for miscarriage of justice. It is in the nature of sexual offence cases that the verdict depends substantially upon the balance of credibility between the parties. Sex crimes often occur in covert unwitnessed settings, leaving little independent or direct evidence of their occurrence. The victim may have been unable or

---

[89] Until recently, reference was made only to female complainants, although the English Court of Appeal made it clear in *R. v Burges* (1956) 40 Cr. App. R. 144 that the rules applied with equal effect to males.
[90] *James v R* (1970) 55 Cr. App. R. 299 (P.C.).
[91] [1940] I.R. 195 at 200–1 (SC).
[92] Heydon, *op. cit.* n.31 at p.99.
[93] In affiliation proceedings (where a woman sought to deem a man the father of her illegitimate child for the purposes of financial contribution), corroboration was required as a safeguard against women who sought "to shield their paramours or to impose burdens on some persons who are better able to bear them": *Nichols v Digney* [1921] V.L.R. 513 at 515, *per* Irvine C.J.
[94] Hale, *Pleas of the Crown 1*, at pp.635–6.

too terrified physically to struggle against the assailant; the victim may have showered immediately after the rape. When evidence in support of the sexual assault is weak, the jury should specifically be directed to look for evidence that tends independently to support the complainant's assertions. The Supreme Court endorsed the *Makanjoula* interpretation of the optional statutory corroboration warning in *People (DPP) v JEM*[95] and *People (DPP) v Wallace*.[96] In the context of s.7 of the 1990 Act, the court reasoned that such provisions mark a shift from rule to discretion. In *People (DPP) v Ferris*,[97] Fennelly J. elaborated further, stating that "the court should not interfere unless it appears either than the decision was made upon an incorrect legal basis or was clearly wrong in fact". He rejected the view that a corroboration warning had been necessary in light of the defence's allegation that the complainant had been angry with the accused after he turned up at his father's funeral. He added that it would be better that the trial judge not inform the jury of his decision to omit a corroboration warning.

5–39 Where the trial judge decides to give a corroboration warning in a sexual offence case, he should, given the wording of s.7, refrain from cautioning the jury that they must treat the complainant's evidence with particular caution due to the fact that many false allegations of a sexual nature have been made by complainants in the past. The statutory shift from mandatory to optional corroboration warning reflects the view that complainant witnesses must no longer be singled out as potentially unreliable by type.[98] It is no longer appropriate to discredit the complainant's evidence by recourse to a warning that refers to the potential duplicity of the complainant and not instead to the specific items of evidence produced in the case.[99] The defence should be required to adduce an evidential basis for the necessity to warn the jury that the evidence of the complainant must be treated with particular caution.[100] For instance, the complainant may be shown to have made false claims against sexual partners in the past, as was the case in *R. v Brown*.[101] Material

---

[95] [2001] 4 I.R. 385 (SC): *cf.* appendix 60.
[96] SC, April 30, 2001.
[97] SC, June 10, 2002.
[98] This view was recently confirmed by the English Court of Appeal in *R. v Chance* [1988] Q.B. 932. The court reasoned that where the allegation of rape is not contested or cross-examined, it would be "gratuitously offensive to the complainant" to insist that a full corroboration warning be given. Where the sole issue at the trial is proof of identity, the court should at most administer the special warning for identification evidence, namely that the jury should look for *supporting evidence* (a wider category than corroboration) to bolster any identifications made: *cf.* para.**6–06** *et seq.*
[99] In this respect, Andrews and Hirst, *Criminal Evidence*, (3rd ed., Sweet & Maxwell, London, 1995) at p.254 have written that "the warning requirement applies only in respect of the complainant's own evidence". Their view is expressed in the context of *R. v Sanders* (1961) 46 Cr. App. R. 60 (C.M.A.C.), where it was decided that corroboration rules did not apply to the evidence of another witness who claimed to have been similarly assaulted by the accused.
[100] This approach is implicit in the Court of Appeal's decision in *R. v A* [1997] Crim. L.R. 883.
[101] (1989) 89 Cr. App. R. 97 (CA).

discrepancies in the complainant's version of events,[102] or evidence disclosing a particular motive to lie about the offence, may and sometimes *must* cause the judge to direct the jury to exercise special caution with respect to the evidence where unsupported.[103] In *R. v Walker*,[104] for instance, the trial judge should have drawn the jury's attention to the possibility that the complainant falsely accused the defendant in a bid to secure the return of the complaina.nt's natural father to the family home, and to the fact that she had earlier retracted and then reinstated her complaint.

5–40 This view of the necessity for corroboration warnings in particular cases has been confirmed by recent case-law in Ireland.[105] In *People (DPP) v Reid*,[106] Keane J. expressly acknowledged that notwithstanding s.7, trial judges may consider it necessary in some cases to give the corroboration warning. More recently, in *People (DPP) v Molloy*,[107] Flood J.'s view of the necessity of a corroboration warning in the case stemmed from the inconsistent nature of the testimonial evidence tendered against the accused. Despite the statutory shift from mandatory to optional warning, the learned judge felt that "where the charge is essentially supported by the evidence of the complainant alone without collateral forensic evidence or any other form of corroboration, it is a prudent practice for the trial judge to warn the jury that unless they are very satisfied with the testimony of the complainant ... they should be careful not to convict in the absence of corroborative evidence". Specifically in the case, the trial judge should have directed the jury's attention to the complainant's mental status, inconsistencies between the versions of events provided by the girl and her mother, and their unusual domestic context. In light of the perversity of the jury's decision—finding the accused not guilty of the first count and guilty of the second, despite the almost identical nature of the allegations—conviction was quashed with no retrial. In *People (DPP) v PC*,[108] the Court of Criminal Appeal likewise found that a corroboration warning is necessary in any proceedings for sexual offence where independent evidence is absent and the verdict depends substantially upon the credibility of the parties.[109] This approach had been adopted by the trial judge in *People (DPP) v O'Connor*,[110] where "the sum total of the evidence was allegation and denial" of sexual abuse. The Court of Criminal Appeal upheld the trial judge's warning of the

---

[102] *People (DPP) v Molloy* (CCA, July 28, 1995), *cf.* para.**5–40**.
[103] *R. v Trigg* [1963] 1 W.L.R. 305 (CA). This approach to the warning was implicitly adopted in *People (DPP) v Kiernan* (CCA, October 19, 1998, O'Flaherty J.)
[104] [1996] Crim. L.R. 742 (CA).
[105] With the exception of *People (DPP) v C* [2001] 3 I.R. 345 (CCA), where the court observed that a central conflict of evidence between accused and complainant did not of itself necessitate a warning. It is of note that the court was also influenced by the failure of defence counsel to requisition the trial judge upon the necessity for a corroboration warning during summing-up.
[106] [1993] 2 I.R. 186 (CCA).
[107] CCA, July 28, 1995.
[108] [2002] 2 I.R. 285 (CCA).
[109] A view repeated in *People (DPP) v Farrell* (CCA, November 25, 2003).
[110] CCA, July 10, 1998.

dangers of convicting upon the uncorroborated evidence of the complainant unless "very, very satisfied" of the accused's guilt. This, Fennelly J. accepted, had been "sufficiently clear and strong". Thus, despite the discretionary approach advocated in *Makanjuola* and approved by the Supreme Court in *JEM*, the case-law confirms the view that although trial judges now have a discretion whether or not to warn juries in sexual offence cases of the dangers of convicting upon the uncorroborated testimony of the complainant, in many such cases they may be obliged to administer some such warning by reason of the evidence in the case.

5–41 In all cases where a corroboration warning is given, it must be accurate and appropriately worded. In the context of sexual offences, numerous appeals have been brought against the trial judge's failure correctly to identify evidence in the case capable of supplying corroboration of particulars of the complainant's account. The strict *Baskerville* view of corroboration is that it is a second source of evidence independently confirming elements of the first evidence whilst also materially implicating the accused in the offence with which he is charged. The trial judge erred in *People (DPP) v D*,[111] when he directed the jury that gynaecological evidence that the girl had been sexually interfered with could be accepted as corroboration against the accused: the evidence disclosed that an offence had been committed, but not that it had been committed by the accused; further, the medical examination revealing rupturing of the complainant's hymen had been performed a year after the offences as alleged. The trial judge similarly erred in the English case of *James v R.* when he directed the jury that gynaecological evidence showing the complainant had had sexual intercourse at the relevant time could be taken to corroborate her evidence against the accused. It proved no more than that she had had sexual intercourse at the material time, but did not further prove the identity of the other party or that she had been penetrated without consent. In *People (DPP) v PC*,[112] the state of the complainant's bedroom had become an issue of credibility in the trial, owing to ambiguities in the complainant's description. The trial judge's reference to the positioning of the curtains as potentially corroborative of "what the complainant says happened" constituted a material misdirection justifying retrial: the physical arrangement of the room was "so commonplace and anodyne a feature that ... [it was] not of sufficient particularity nor ... of a sufficiently material nature, independent of the complainant's version of events so as to make it corroboration that the offence had been committed and also that the defendant committed it".[113] Upon a similar basis in *People (DPP) v Donnelly*,[114] the trial judge erred by referring to the bloodstained state of the complainant's bedclothes as potential corroboration in the case: this was a fact that could be circumstantially inferential of a number of different propositions, and it "created more prejudice than probative value".

---

[111] CCA, *ex tempore*, July 27, 1993.
[112] [2002] 2 I.R. 285 (CCA).
[113] *ibid*. at 303.
[114] CCA, February 22, 1999.

5–42 The requirement in *Baskerville* that corroboration evidence be a second source of evidence, independent of the complainant's claim, creates peculiar difficulties for sexual offence cases where evidence and proof tend by nature to be indirect and circumstantial. Strict adherence to the requirement of independent proof stems from the principle against self-corroboration, and logically entails that evidence that to any extent emanates from the complainant is incapable of amounting to corroboration. It is, for instance, trite law that evidence of the complainant's original complaint and its surrounding circumstances cannot be considered by the court as potential corroboration of the allegations.[115] As explained in *R. v Whitehead*: "In order that evidence may amount to corroboration it must be extraneous to the witness who is to be corroborated. A [witness] cannot corroborate herself, otherwise it is only necessary to repeat her story some twenty-five times in order to get twenty-five corroborations of it".[116]

5–43 A number of decisions have consciously adopted a more relaxed, case-oriented approach, however, particularly with respect to the corroborative capacity of the complainant's distress as observed by another, and evidence of bruising or marking on the complainant's body. Technically, evidence of distress raises a hearsay question—since the principle against self-corroboration (itself one of the formative concerns of the hearsay rule)[117] potentially proscribes the tendering of the observed behaviour as a non-verbal implied assertion that the complainant was assaulted or in fear of the accused. In a number of English decisions permitting evidence of distress to function as corroboration of aspects of the complainant's case, the courts articulated the concerns underpinning the principle against self-corroboration, namely the fear of concocted, self-manufactured evidence. In *R. v Redpath*,[118] for instance, the court stressed that where bruises and marks are presented as corroborative evidence, the jury should be encouraged to satisfy themselves that the bruising was not self-inflicted or that the sexual intercourse in question was not intentionally rough. The court was also prepared to acknowledge that in exceptional cases, evidence of the distress of a complainant may be capable of corroborating the allegations. In a brief judgment, the court accepted the danger that complainants may "well put on an act and simulate distress", but it felt that this was not one such case.[119] The complainant was only seven years old; she had emerged from the moor shortly after the accused had left it; she was not about to make a complaint at that moment; and she was unaware of being observed by an independent bystander. The court seemed to regard these last criteria as important, although they were abandoned in subsequent decisions upon a case-by-case basis having

---

[115] Applied in *People (DPP) v Brophy* [1992] I.L.R.M. 709 at 716 (CCA) (*cf.* appendix 41); and *R. v Makanjuola* [1995] 1 W.L.R. 1348 at 1355 (CA).

[116] [1929] 1 K.B. 99 at 102, *per* Hewart L.C.J. (CA). Evidence of the making of a prompt voluntary complaint, and its detail, may however be admitted as evidence to show the complainant's credibility (although not as evidence probative of a fact at issue): *cf.* para.2–52 *et seq.*

[117] *cf.* paras **9–03, 9–08**.

[118] (1962) 46 Cr. App. R. 319 (CA)..

[119] *ibid*. at 322.

regard to the court's sense of whether the distress was reliable in the context of the surrounding circumstances.[120] Such concerns were not adverted to by the Court of Criminal Appeal in *People (DPP) v Reid*,[121] where reference was made to the complainant's observed distress, along with numerous other circumstantial facts, potentially as cumulative corroboration.

5–44 The concerns upon which the principle against self-corroboration are based clearly stem from a sense that evidence of consistent pre-trial statements or conduct is more likely to have been manufactured. If the distress was observed at or around the time the complainant first made complaint of sexual offence to another, there is a greater danger that the anguish was feigned or exaggerated to enlist the other's outrage and support. Where, on the other hand, there is reliable evidence suggesting that the complainant was unaware of being observed, or was still bound up in the immediate aftermath of the assault, the risk of concoction diminishes.[122] As indicated, however, in *R. v Chauhan*,[123] where the trial judge accepts that evidence of the complainant's distress may be considered by the jury potentially as partial corroboration of the allegations, he must direct the jury that they may only consider the distress in this capacity when they have first ruled out the possibility that the distress was affected or feigned.

5–45 In *R. v Gregg*,[124] evidence that both accused and complainant now suffered the same sexually transmitted disease was accepted as evidence independent of the complainant. This type of development is not without its dangers. If a sexually transmitted disease is comparatively common, the chance increases that the assumed link between the complainant's condition and the accused's is falsely based. Moreover, if the defence's request to enquire into the complainant's sexual history is denied,[125] the association may not sufficiently be tested. In a case where evidence of this nature is admitted, there is a heightened duty on the trial judge to ensure that the jury is properly directed upon the limits of such evidence, that it is circumstantial evidence merely suggesting the possibility that the disease was passed from one to the other but not that sexual intercourse was non-consensual. The decision in *Gregg* may best be understood by reference to its facts. Since the complainant was merely seven years old, evidence that she had contracted gonorrhoea, and that the accused himself tested positive for the disease, was highly probative in the circumstances.

---

[120] *e.g., R. v Chauhan* (1962) 46 Cr. App. R. 319 (CA) where it did not matter that the complaint was made to the person who observed the complainant's condition, since the complainant had not known she was observed by this person. Further, in *R. v Dowley* [1983] Crim. L.R. 168 (CA), evidence of observed distress was accepted even though bound up at the time with the complaint and taking place some time after the alleged event. The evidence was admitted because it was apparent to the court that the distress was real and not feigned.
[121] [1993] 2 I.R. 186 at 197 (CCA).
[122] *R. v Dowley* [1983] Crim. L.R. 168 (CA); *R. v Okoye* [1964] Crim. L.R. 416 (CA).
[123] (1962) 46 Cr. App. R. 319 (CA).
[124] (1934) 24 Cr. App. R. 13 (CA).
[125] *cf.* para.**3–23** *et seq.*

5–46 In more recent years, the courts have shown themselves willing in sexual offence cases to evaluate various evidential facts cumulatively as partial or complete corroboration of the complainant's account, even where the corroborative value of each established fact is low. This approach was implicitly adopted by Keane J. in *People (DPP) v Reid*,[126] where the court identified, as potential corroboration of the complainant's testimony, the state of her genitalia, the high volume of the accused's television set at the time of the alleged offence, and the distressed state of the complainant observed by her parents in the aftermath. Although Keane J. cited *Baskerville* with apparent approval, the learned judge adopted a much looser approach than was there intended, particularly with respect to the notions of independent proof and evidence specifically implicating the accused. The learned judge wisely focused instead on Hales' reference to evidence of "concurring circumstances which give greater probability to the evidence of the prosecutrix".[127] A similar approach was evident in *People (DPP) v Murphy*,[128] where the court considered evidence that the accused's jeans had been dirtied to be potentially corroborative of the complainant's allegation that a "fracas" had taken place on the way home from a disco. In *People (DPP) v C*,[129] the complainant testified that she had been facing the wall at the time the accused entered the room; the court considered this to be corroborative of her assertion that she thought the man was her boyfriend. Murphy J. observed: "Corroborative evidence does not mean that the evidence of the complainant must be corroborated in *every* material respect".[130] In upholding the trial judges' directions to the juries upon potential corroboration of the charges in *Murphy* and *C*, the Court of Criminal Appeal was influenced by the specific role each item of evidence was ascribed within the range of issues in contention before the court. In other cases, convictions have been overturned because the trial judge misled the jury into assuming that evidentially limited evidence was capable of supplying corroboration more generally of the central facts at issue.[131]

5–47 In the broad sense, a departure from reference to the strict sense of "corroboration" in sexual offence cases would be consistent with developments in other jurisdictions. From the 1970s on, the English courts consciously distanced themselves from the definitional approach to corroboration by then synonymous with the *Baskerville* decision. In *R. v Hester*,[132] Lord Pearson insisted that "the word 'corroboration' in itself has no special legal meaning: it is connected with the Latin word 'robur' and the English word 'robust' and it means 'strengthen': perhaps the best synonym is 'support' ". Lord Diplock observed that in six of the seven cases approved in *R. v Baskerville*, the words "corroboration" and "confirmation" were used interchangeably. What the

---

[126] [1993] 2 I.R. 186 (CCA).
[127] *ibid*. at 196.
[128] CCA, *ex tempore*, November 3, 1997.
[129] [2001] 3 I.R. 345 (CCA).
[130] *ibid*. at 362 (emphasis added).
[131] *cf*. para.**5-41**.
[132] [1973] A.C. 296 at 321 (HL): *cf*. appendix 19.

common law ultimately requires "is confirmation from some other source that the suspect witness is telling the truth in some part of his story which goes to show that the accused committed the offence with which he is charged".[133] The House of Lords repeated this view in *R. v Kilbourne*, going one step further: "The word 'corroboration' is not a technical term of art, but a dictionary word bearing its ordinary meaning; since it is slightly unusual in common speech the actual word need not be used, and in fact it may be better not to use it. Where it is used it needs to be explained".[134] The avoidance of reference to the word "corroboration" is now conspicuous in England. For example, recent provisions enabling the court to draw inferences from the accused's silence make no reference to the probative scope of such inferences.[135] The Canadian Supreme Court abandoned the *Baskerville* test some time ago, and favours the view that corroboration can be provided by an accumulation of individual pieces of evidence, notwithstanding the fact that none of the pieces separately satisfy the requirements in *Baskerville*.[136]

5–48 A number of Irish decisions have recently reasserted the *Baskerville* approach to corroboration: some of them in response to the trial judge's misleading suggestion that an evidential fact was corroborative of the complainant's allegation of sexual offence;[137] others, in response to the omission to caution the jury of the court's preference for corroboration.[138] On the other hand, there has occasionally been welcome reference to "supporting evidence" in preference to corroboration, in this context.[139] As a category of evidence, "supporting evidence" was first identified by the courts in the context of the special identification warning that trial judges must administer to the jury in cases where the prosecution relies upon identification evidence disputed by the defence.[140] In choosing to refer to the court's preference for evidence that "supports" rather than "corroborates" the identification, the courts cautiously sought to disassociate identification issues from the rigidity of the *Baskerville* test, perceived in the end to have spawned an excess of appeals against technically inaccurate judicial references to evidence capable of constituting corroboration. There is good reason why the law should do likewise in the context of sexual offence proceedings, given the centrality in this context of circumstantial facts critical to the jury's assessment of the respective credibility of the parties and in turn to the facts at issue. In Ireland, reference continues to be made to corroboration in the statutory provisions, sometimes needlessly so, in the case of sexual offences and child witnesses. The law in

---

[133] *ibid.* at 325.
[134] [1973] A.C. 729 at 741, *per* Lord Hailsham L.C. (HL): *cf.* appendix 20.
[135] Sections 34–35, Criminal Justice and Public Order Act 1994: *cf.* para.**13–103** *et seq.*
[136] *R. v Warkentin* [1977] 2 SCR. 355; *Vetrovec v Queen* [1982] 1 SCR. 811.
[137] *People (DPP) v P.C.* [2002] 2 I.R. 285 (CCA); *People (DPP) v D* (CCA, *ex tempore*, July 27, 1993); *People (DPP) v Cornally* (CCA, November 7, 1994); *cf.* para.**5–41**.
[138] *People (DPP) v Molloy* (CCA, July 28, 1995); *People (DPP) v P.C.* [2002] 2 I.R. 285 (CCA).
[139] *People (DPP) v O'Connor* (CCA, July 29, 2003), *per* Fennelly J.
[140] *People (Attorney-General) v Casey (No. 2)* [1963] I.R. 33 (SC); *R. v Turnbull* [1977] 1 Q.B. 224 (CA): *cf.* para.**6–06** *et seq.*

consequence appears wedded to the terminology, although it would seem, as often as not, that lip-service is paid to the *Baskerville* notion of corroboration, and that the courts are prepared to accept lesser forms of supporting proof as cumulative corroboration of the complainant's account in sexual offence trials. It is fully arguable that the definition of corroboration advanced in *Baskerville*, a case concerned with accomplice evidence, was not intended to apply equally, or ought not to apply equally, in sexual offence cases. A shift to supporting evidence in cases that now attract an *optional* "corroboration" warning would have the advantage of preserving the strict *Baskerville* test of corroboration only for cases where it is still strictly necessary to enforce it, such as for accomplice testimony.

Child Witnesses

5–49 As a class of witness, children had characteristically been singled out by the common law as being potentially unreliable.[141] In recent years, many of the assumptions of unreliability have been discredited, and the law has undergone a rapid liberalisation of rules, which in the past operated to hinder the child witness from telling his story in court. Far more flexible, discretionary rules currently operate with respect to the child's competence as a witness and the provision of sworn and unsworn testimony.[142] The child may now testify from an off-court room transmitted live to the court by closed-circuit television.[143] The mandatory corroboration rules that formerly existed have been replaced by an optional corroboration warning which the trial judge may choose to give in appropriate circumstances. Formerly, a child's unsworn evidence could only be accepted where the jury found it to be corroborated, and a child's sworn evidence attracted a mandatory corroboration warning. The unsworn evidence of a child was not capable of corroborating the unsworn evidence of another child (but could corroborate the sworn evidence of an adult or a child).[144] Section 28 of the Criminal Evidence Act 1992 abolished the corroboration requirement for unsworn testimony and the mandatory corroboration warning for sworn testimony. It further provided that the trial judge retains a discretion to give a corroboration warning, although in doing so he is not obliged to adhere to any "particular form of words". Section 28(3) provides for mutual corroboration as between unsworn children, sworn and unsworn children, and, by implication between sworn children.[145]

5–50 In the light of recent and continuing exposure of widespread child abuse in Ireland, these developments have rightly been welcomed. It is, however, important not to lose sight of problems that might emerge in particular cases,

---

[141] *cf.* para.**2–08**.
[142] *cf.* para.**2–10** *et seq.*
[143] *cf.* para.**1–57**.
[144] *DPP v Hester* [1973] A.C. 296 (HL); *cf.* appendix 19.
[145] Under s.27 of the 1992 Act, the unsworn evidence of a child under 14 years may be received where he is capable of giving an intelligible account of matters relevant to the proceedings.

where the facts disclose real doubts about the reliability of the child witness, whether because of emotional immaturity or motive against the accused. Although the trial judge must no longer administer a corroboration warning in every case, the special facts of a case may impose an appealable duty upon him to exercise that discretion to direct the jury accordingly at the close of the trial. Corroboration concerns remain relevant. According to s.28, the corroboration warning is no longer obligatory "by reason only that the evidence is the evidence of a child". Of this it may be said that children no longer automatically attract the corroboration warning by reason of their status as a child, and that the defence may need evidentially to establish particular reasons to doubt their testimony before the trial judge is obliged to administer the cautionary warning.[146] In all cases where corroboration is put in issue—whether by prosecution, defence, or the trial judge by way of warning—the trial judge must carefully identify evidence that is capable of corroborating other evidence in the case, and his failure to do so correctly may endanger the conviction, discretion notwithstanding, as cases such as *People (DPP) v D*[147] illustrate.

Mutual Corroboration

5-51 The prosecution is sometimes responsible for canvassing the corroboration issue, where it is reluctant to let the evidence of one child complainant stand or fall by itself.[148] Instead it may seek to strengthen its case by reference to mutual corroboration as between multiple complainants in the same trial, or by reference to similar fact evidence of previous offences deemed admissible and corroborative of the present complainant's testimony.[149] Mutual corroboration by its nature raises specific concerns. The basic scenario envisaged by the corroboration concept is that the jury is asked to decide whether or not to accept a witness' version, and, if they accept it, to ascertain if the version can be independently confirmed. As explained by Lord Hailsham C.J. in *DPP v Kilhourne:* "Corroboration is only required or afforded if the witness requiring corroboration or giving it is otherwise credible ... If a witness's testimony falls of its own inanition the question of his needing, or being capable of giving, corroboration does not arise".[150] This is otherwise where the jury is invited to decide that the accounts provided by two or more witnesses—each attracting corroboration rules—are mutually corroborative. As was explained by the House of Lords in *Kilbourne*, in this situation the jury may not properly be able to evaluate the reliability of one witness' account without observing it for points of consistency or inconsistency with the other witness' account. Mutually corroborative evidence of sexual offences conducted in private is necessarily co-dependent evidence.[151] It is also highly prejudicial and difficult to rebut, particularly in cases of sexual offence, proof

---

[146] *R. v Makanjuola* [1995] 1 W.L.R. 1348 (CA).
[147] CCA, *ex tempore*, July 27, 1993, *cf.* para.**5-41**.
[148] *DPP v Kilbourne* [1973] A.C. 729 at 736 (HL): *cf.* appendix 20.
[149] *cf.* para.**7-27** *et seq.*
[150] [1973] A.C. 729 at 746 (HL): *cf.* appendix 20.
[151] *R. v Whitehouse* [1996] Crim. L.R. 50 at 51 (CA).

of which tends, by its nature, to be sparse and indirect. In some cases, the similarity in accounts that first justified the joinder of indictments against the accused may later prove to be the very element giving rise to suspicion of collusion or complicity between the complainants.

5–52 In cases of co-dependent evidence attracting corroboration concerns, it is necessary that the court caution the jury that they should seek separately to assess the cogency of each complainant's account before proceeding to establish consistency or corroboration between the numerous accounts provided at the trial. The necessity to consider the possibility of collusion when evaluating the weight of co-dependent evidence was confirmed by Budd J. in *B v DPP*.[152] In *People (DPP) v Morrissey*,[153] the Court of Criminal Appeal ruled that in a case where the accused claimed the complainant had falsely accused him in collusion with another witness (in the case, the complainant's mother), the trial judge may not direct the jury that the evidence of the witnesses is capable of supplying mutual corroboration, since neither source of evidence is independent from the other. The English Court of Appeal likewise ruled in *R. v Ananthanarayanan*[154] that where an allegation of complicity has been made by the defence in a trial with multiple complainants, and the trial judge concludes that the risk of contamination or collusion is "real", he must decide that the evidence is incapable of supplying mutual corroboration because it is not "truly independent" from the other evidence or because it has been contaminated by collusion from a third party or between the complainants to make false or exaggerated allegations. The trial judge may further, in his discretion and having regard to other evidence and the circumstances of the case, find the evidence inadmissible due to its unreliability. The House of Lords emphasised in *R. v H*,[155] however, that only in exceptional cases should the risk of collusion between multiple complainants affect the admissibility of their evidence and that, in general, the risk is adequately addressed by raising the possibility of collusive accusation with the jury at the close of the trial.

---

[152] [1997] 3 I.R. 140 at 157 (HC), *cf.* para.**7–14**.
[153] CCA, July 10, 1998. See also *People (DPP) v LG* [2003] 2 I.R. 517 *per* Keane C.J. (CCA).
[154] [1994] 2 All E.R. 847 (CA), in the context of multiple complaints against the accused, which had been solicited by a local social services department. See also *R. v Whitehouse* [1996] Crim. L.R. 50 (CA).
[155] [1995] 2 A.C. 596 (HL).

Further Reading

Birch, "Corroboration: Goodbye to All That?" [1995] Crim. L.R. 524.
Dennis, "Corroboration Requirements Reconsidered" [1984] Crim. L.R. 316.
Doherty, "Recent Cases on Hearsay Evidence in Child Sexual Abuse Proceedings" [1992] I.L.T. 91.
Elliot, "Securing the Evidence of Criminal Associates" [1999] Crim. L.R. 349.
Hanley, "Corroborating Rape Charges" (2001) 11(1) I.C.L.J. 2.
Heydon, "The Corroboration of Accomplices" [1973] Crim. L.R. 264.
Heydon, "Can Lies Corroborate?" (1973) 89 L.Q.R. 552.
Ingoldsby, "Supergrass Testimony and Reasonable Doubt: An Examination of *D.P.P. v Ward*" 2 Trinity College L.R. 29 (1999).
Jackson, "Credibility, Morality and the Corroboration Warning" [1988] C.L.J. 428.
McGrath, "Two Steps Forward, One Step Back: the Corroboration Warning in Sexual Cases" (1999) I.C.L.J. 22.
McGrath, "The Accomplice Corroboration Warning" (1999) 34 Ir. Jur. 170.
Mirfield, "An Alternative Future for Corroboration Warnings" (1991) 107 L.Q.R. 450.
Mirfield, "Corroboration' after the 1994 Act" [1995] Crim. L.R. 448.
Palmer, "Guilt and the Consciousness of Guilt: The Use of Lies, Flight and Other 'Guilty Behaviour'" (1997) 21 Melbourne L.R. 95.
Spencer and Flin, *The Evidence of Children: The Law and the Psychology* (2nd ed., Blackstone, London, 1990).
Stephenson, "Should Collaborative Evidence be Permitted in Courts of Law?" [1990] Crim. L.R. 302.

CHAPTER 6

IDENTIFICATION EVIDENCE

I. General Principles 6–01
II. The Identification Evidence Warning 6–04
    Reference to Supporting Evidence 6–06
    Recognition Cases 6–10
    Sexual Offence Cases 6–12
    Mutual and Cumulative Identification 6–13
III. Means of Identification 6–15
    The Identification Parade 6–18
    Use of Photographs, Videos, and other Means of
        Identification 6–25
    Photofits and Identikits 6–32
    Voice Identification 6–33
IV. Prosecutor's Duty to Disclose 6–35

I. GENERAL PRINCIPLES

6–01 Identification evidence now demands the application of special rules of evidence to address the distinct issues and concerns arising from the means by which identification was obtained and the use to which the evidence is later put at the trial. The centre-piece of the rules is the identification evidence warning, the need for which was first established by the Supreme Court in *People (Attorney-General) v Casey (No.2)*,[1] some years prior to a comparable ruling by the English Court of Appeal in *R. v Turnbull*.[2] The warning requires the trial judge to advise the jury to exercise caution with respect to identification evidence disputed by the defence, owing to the fact that innocently mistaken identifications have in the past led wrongly to conviction, and to have regard not only to the general concerns arising from identification evidence but also to any specific weaknesses and strengths in the manner in which the accused was identified by a witness in the case.

6–02 The prospect of false-positive identification had been under-appreciated by the common law judges for centuries, and in England development of particular judicial principles did not begin in earnest until the findings of the

---
[1] [1963] I.R. 33 (SC): *cf.* appendix 11.
[2] [1977] 1 Q.B. 224 (CA): *cf.* appendix 24.

Devlin Committee were published in 1973,[3] revealing that in the preceding year for England and Wales, mistaken identifications had accounted for almost one-tenth of identifications made at formally conducted identification parades. The Committee in particular identified the tendency of jurors to accept the correctness of a positive identification at face value when the witness was considered to be honest and trustworthy. The impenetrability of positive identification, even under exacting cross-examination, in cases where the accused lacked a corroborated alibi, was a particular dilemma highlighted by the Committee:

> "A witness says that he recognises the man, and that is that or almost that. There is no story to be dissected, just a simple assertion to be accepted or rejected. If a witness thinks that he has a good memory for faces when in fact he has a poor one, there is no way of detecting the failing. ... Demeanour in general is quite useless. The capacity to memorise a face differs enormously from one man to another, but there is no way of finding out in the witness box how much of it the witness has got; no one keeps a record of his successes and failures to submit to scrutiny".[4]

6–03   Heydon, who has written well on the subject, adds that "identification is a matter about which witnesses are most confident and dogmatic, even where their grounds are slight, and in which personal pride, leading to stubbornness, becomes easily involved".[5] Despite the assertiveness of the witness' own faith in the identification, his recollection of the observation is susceptible to distortion according to the circumstances in which he first observed the offender, such as the state of light, distance from the object, length of time to observe, and the witness' eyesight, state of mind, and powers of recall. On a more subtle level, it is often observed that a recollection may be distorted by prejudice and preconception; that is, by associations the witness may subconsciously have drawn between the type of person likely to commit the crime and the appearance or behaviour of the accused when subsequently identified. There is the further concern that distortions of this nature may coalesce later with the witness' suggestibility when encouraged by investigators and shown photographs and identikits of suspects. Although often vital to the investigative process, suspect-narrowing procedures carry the additional ever-present danger that mistaken details may self-propagate inaccurately into fact and assume the fixed status of truth. It is due to this last concern that the Supreme Court recently decided in *People (DPP) v Braddish*[6] that inadmissible suspect-narrowing material may not be destroyed by the prosecution, but must be preserved and disclosed to the defence, to whom it may be highly relevant. In light of all the foregoing concerns, the Irish and English judges have acknowledged the

---

[3] Report to the Secretary of State for the Home Department of the Departmental Committee on Evidence of Identification in Criminal Cases (chairman: Lord Devlin) (1976) HC 338.
[4] *ibid*. at paras 1.24 and 4.25.
[5] Heydon, *Evidence: Cases and Materials* (3rd ed., Butterworths, London, 1991) at p.74.
[6] [2002] 1 I.L.R.M. 151 (SC): *cf*. para.6–36 and appendix 63.

necessity for a special warning reminding the jury of the hidden dangers posed by identification evidence.

II. THE IDENTIFICATION EVIDENCE WARNING

6–04 The Irish Supreme Court pre-empted later developments in England when it recognised in *People (Attorney-General) v Casey (No.2)* that owing to the special nature of identification evidence, juries ought to be warned at the close of the trial that positive identifications have in the past proved erroneous, even where made by more than one witness, and that for reasons general to identification evidence and specific to the circumstances of each case, special caution must be exercised when deciding whether or not to accept a witness' identification.[7] Kingsmill Moore J. referred throughout to the need for a strong direction in any case where the identification is challenged and the prosecution's case against the accused depends "wholly or substantially on the correctness of such identification".[8] To this he added that in "any case which depends on visual identification", a "minimum warning" should be given, although this is not intended to function as a "stereotyped formula" and its weight and content should vary according to the facts of each case.[9] The Irish courts have applied the *Casey* ruling strictly, and they readily regard omitted or inadequate warnings as serious misdirections justifying the quashing of conviction.[10] Flexibility instead exists with respect to the terms and extent of the warning, which the case law consistently states must vary according to the facts of each case.[11] According to O'Flaherty J. in *People (DPP) v Farrell*,[12] "the nuts and bolts of the evidence in a trial is clearly a matter for the trial judge. ... The very thing that Mr. Justice Kingsmill Moore warned against was that his judgment was not to be used as a ritualistic formula".

6–05 Where the identification evidence is weak and unsupported, the trial judge is entitled, and may be obliged, to withdraw the issues from the jury or

---

[7] [1963] I.R. 33 (SC): *cf.* appendix 11. In so finding, the learned judge drew support from two earlier decisions by the Irish courts adverting to the need to caution juries before convicting the accused upon the identification evidence of one witness: *People (Attorney-General) v Hughes* (1958) 92 I.L.T.R. 179 (CCA) and *People v Keffard* (unreported, CCA).
[8] [1963] I.R. 33 at 39 (SC).
[9] *ibid.* at 40.
[10] As in *People (Attorney-General) v Casey (No.2)* [1963] I.R. 33 (SC); *People (DPP) v Stafford* [1983] I.R. 165 (CCA); and *People (DPP) v McNamara* (CCA, March 22, 1999). Note, however, that the appellate courts have frequently signalled that the failure of defence counsel to requisition the trial judge upon the terms of the warning may militate against the argument that the warning was inadequate: *People (Attorney-General) v O'Shea* [1931] I.R. 719 at 726 (CCA); *People (DPP) v Stafford* [1983] I.R. 165 at 169, *per* Hederman J. (CCA); *People (DPP) v O'Reilly* [1990] 2 I.R. 415 at 423, *per* O'Flaherty J. (CCA); and (in the context of the accomplice corroboration warning) *People (DPP) v Hogan* (CCA, January 12, 1994, *per* O'Flaherty J.)
[11] *People (Attorney-General) v Casey (No.2) ibid.* at 40; *People (DPP) v Farrell* (CCA, July 13, 1998).
[12] *ibid.*

direct an acquittal upon the basis that the prosecution has failed to make a prima facie case by tendering adequate admissible evidence.[13] Where the case is appropriately before the jury, they are given an identification warning and advised of the law's preference for evidence that might lend support to the witness' identification, but thereafter they are free to convict the accused, even in the absence of supporting evidence.

Reference to Supporting Evidence

6–06 Whilst Kingsmill Moore J. drew an appropriate analogy between identification evidence and other types of evidence that traditionally attracted corroboration rules,[14] he clearly dissociated the identification evidence warning from corroboration rules, evidently in a wise bid to avoid burdening it with the rgidity of which those rules had long been accused: "An item of evidence falling within this formula may, according to its nature have very little or very great probative value".[15] Accordingly, the trial judge should advise the jury to seek confirmation of the identification "in the light of all the circumstances, and with due regard to all the other evidence in the case".[16]

6–07 The need to avoid reference to corroboration in the direction is abundantly clear in the judgment, and rests upon more than the avoidance of undue technicality but further upon sound logic. As the learned judge observed, a warning should be given even in cases where more than one identification has been made of the accused. This is because a second witness' identification of the accused would in principle amount to corroboration of the first witness' identification, and mutually corroborative identification between witnesses does not of itself address the concerns with respect to identification evidence, and may even compound the dangers with which this special warning is concerned. As has since been recognised in England, the fact alone that three mutually supportive witnesses claim to have observed the accused in flight from a passing bus does not dispense with the need to caution the jury that the identification may have been mistaken for a range of general and specific reasons.[17]

6–08 The avoidance of corroboration and reference instead to supporting evidence was specifically approved by the Court of Appeal in its own groundbreaking decision in *R. v Turnbull*, where Lord Widgery C.J. usefully elaborated on the distinction. Whereas corroboration strictly denotes evidence from some source independent of the witness that confirms the material particulars of the witness' account and implicates the accused in the offence as charged, supporting evidence is not subject to definitional limitations beyond

---

[13] *R. v Turnbull* [1977] 1 Q.B. 224 at 230 (CA): affirmed in *R. v Weeder* (1980) 71 Cr. App. R. 228 (CA). This view was taken in *People (DPP) v Cahill* (CCA, July 30, 2001) with respect to inconclusive identifications of the applicants.
[14] *cf.* para.**5–01** *et seq.*
[15] [1963] I.R. 33 at 40 (SC).
[16] *ibid.*
[17] *R. v Weeder* (1980) 71 Cr. App. R. 228 (CA).

that the evidence must be relevant and must to some degree reduce the likelihood that the identification was mistaken. In one of the numerous examples given by Lord Widgery, the witness caught only a fleeting glance of the robber running from the scene of the crime, but he also saw the robber enter a building that was later discovered by the police to be the house occupied by the father of the man selected by the witness at an identification parade.[18] This latter fact, though classically circumstantial, supplies a useful link between the robber fleetingly observed at the scene of the crime and the person who was identified at the formal parade, rendering it less likely that the witness was mistaken in his identification.

6–09 Accordingly, when examining the reliability of an identification, the court is first concerned to understand all its weaknesses, actual[19] and potential, and its strengths, having regard to whether it is bolstered or *supported* by other evidence in the case that reduces the likelihood the identification was mistaken. In *People (Attorney-General) v Martin*,[20] for instance, the witness' identification of the accused was supported by evidence that he had a scar on his leg and a rent in his trousers, features the witness had observed earlier at the time of the robbery. The accused's failure to testify is not capable of supporting an identification, given his right to silence and presumption of innocence. According to English authority, proof that the accused supplied a false alibi or otherwise lied, is capable of constituting evidence in support of an identification, with careful direction indicating the possibility that the accused may have lied for reasons other than the concealment of his guilt.[21] In *People (DPP) v O'Toole and Tyndale*,[22] the witnesses' identification of the first accused as the robber of their house was supported by evidence of an injury to the accused's hands, a baseball bat found at his house, and a conversation he had had with the victims' neighbours prior to the robbery.[23]

Recognition Cases

6–10 That the *Casey* direction applies equally to cases of identification by recognition was confirmed in *People (DPP) v Stafford*.[24] Upholding the appeal, Hederman J. rejected the argument that where, as here, a policeman recognised the accused, the question had become one of veracity and not identification. In *People (DPP) v Smith*,[25] the Court of Criminal Appeal again asserted that

---

[18] [1977] 1 Q.B. 224 at 230 (CA): *cf.* appendix 24.
[19] Failure to discuss the specific deficiencies of the prosecution's identification evidence (in the context of the general dangers associated with same) was deemed a misdirection in *People (DPP) v O'Reilly* [1990] 2 I.R. 415 at 423 (CCA).
[20] [1956] I.R. 22 (SC).
[21] *R. v Goodway* [1993] 4 All E.R. 894 (CA): *cf.* para.5–08.
[22] CCA, May 26, 2003.
[23] A retrial was ordered, however, on the basis that the trial judge had failed to emphasise the inconsistencies in the evidence, and had focused unduly on the supporting evidence in the case.
[24] [1983] I.R. 165 (SC).
[25] CCA, November 16, 1998. *Stafford* was followed in *People (DPP) v McNamara* (CCA,

identification based upon recognition equally attracts a *Casey* direction to warn the jury "unequivocally" as to the dangers in relying upon identification at face-value without additional supporting evidence. Whilst recognition evidence is generally more reliable, the distinction did not, in the court's view, justify "abandoning or neglecting the rules in *Casey's* case". In light of these findings, it is thus more likely that the extent to which an identification may reasonably be questioned, and the extent to which the defence's challenge to the identification is more a challenge to the truthfulness or credibility of the identifying witness, will naturally affect the detail and pitch of the warning required to be given.

6–11 This attempted distinction between questions of veracity or credibility on the one hand and questions of identification on the other has unwisely seduced the English courts, which generally have tended to toy unnecessarily with concern over when an identification warning must be given and when it may or may not be given. In *R. v Slater*,[26] the Court of Appeal explained that the possibility of *mistaken* identification is a prerequisite for the *Turnbull* warning, and that the need for a special direction must depend upon the circumstances of each case. *R. v Bentley*[27] drew a distinction between "fleeting-glance identification", with which *Turnbull* was primarily concerned and where a warning is especially necessary, and the recognition of a familiar face in good conditions where a full warning need not be given. *R. v Cape*[28] decided that where on the facts of the case it appears that the issue is less about identification than of credibility (typically where the witness recognised the accused engaging in criminal activity, but later at the trial the accused claims that the witness is either mistaken or lying due to a grudge), a *Turnbull* warning is not strictly necessary. These decisions have already been construed as categorical qualifications of *Turnbull* in England, yet they are probably demonstrative at most of a belatedly defensive stance by the English courts against overturning convictions upon grounds alone that the trial judge failed to administer an adequate warning.[29] This ambivalent conception of the use and function of the identification evidence warning is plainly at odds with the tenor of the *Turnbull* judgment which continues nonetheless to be held in high esteem. It is at odds with the response in other jurisdictions,[30] and contrasts greatly with the approach taken in this jurisdiction, which, in the spirit of evidence law generally, tends towards the preventative.

March 22, 1999), where conviction was quashed, and *People (DPP) v Farrell* (CCA, July 13, 1998).

[26] [1995] 1 Cr. App. R. 584 (CA).

[27] (1994) 99 Cr. App. R. 342 (CA).

[28] [1996] 1 Cr. App. R. 191 (CA). See also *R. v Beckles and Montague* [1999] Crim. L.R. 148 (CA).

[29] *Freeman v R.* [1994] 1 W.L.R. 1437 (PC); *Shand v R.* [1996] 1 W.L.R. 67 (PC); and *R. v John W* [1998] 2 Cr. App. R. 295 (CA). By contrast, a notably stricter approach was taken by the Court of Appeal in *R. v Andrews* [1993] Crim.L.R. 590.

[30] The Australian High Court, for instance, tends to allow the appeal unless it appears from other evidence in the case that the jury would inevitably have convicted the accused: *Domincan v R.* (1992) 173 C.L.R. 555 (HC, Aust.).

Sexual Offence Cases

6–12 In a case that raises both corroboration and identification issues—commonly, in a sexual offence case where the defence challenges the identification and additionally argues that the complainant's testimony ought to be corroborated—the jury is required at least to receive an identification warning, since this is mandatory. Some early authority opted for the full corroboration warning, upon the basis that many erroneous identifications of sexual assailants have been made in the past.[31] Recent authority, arguably for the better, favours the view that a sensitively worded identification warning, stating the preference for evidence in *support* of the identification, is the appropriate course.[32] This approach has been adopted generally in England by statute and precedent, in light of the immense difficulties experienced there in trials and appeals wrought by the strict definition of corroboration famously espoused in *R. v Baskerville*.[33] A realignment of terminology—from corroboration to supporting evidence—would be highly beneficial in Ireland for those categories of evidence no longer subject to a mandatory application of corroboration rules (namely, complainants in sexual offence cases and child witnesses).[34] Whilst in Ireland, reference persists to be made to corroboration, though fortunately not in the context of identification evidence,[35] this is to a large degree due to the draftsman's unconsidered use of the word in recent enactments that otherwise strive to import flexibility into this aspect of evidence law.[36]

Mutual and Cumulative Identification

6–13 It has been accepted that one witness' identification may be mutually supportive of another witness' identification, although a warning cautioning the jury against the possibility of mistake must still be given,[37] and indeed may require even more elaboration, given the greater danger that the evidence is accepted by the jury conclusively and at face-value. The Court of Appeal has recognised in England that multiple identifications are capable of cumulative effect—that is to say that each witness' account, though separately incomplete, may be viewed together to establish identity. In *R. v Barnes*,[38] the court rejected the contention that in trials of joined indictments with multiple complainants, the jury must always be directed that they are required first to consider whether there is sufficient evidence on each count to establish the accused's guilt, before they may properly proceed to consider if the various identifications are mutually

---

[31] *R. v Trigg* (1963) 47 Cr. App. R. 94 (CA).
[32] *People (DPP) v Murphy* (CCA, *ex tempore*, November 3, 1997); *R. v Chance* [1988] Q.B. 932.
[33] [1916] 2 K.B. 658 (CA): *cf.* para.**5–42** *et seq.* and appendix 2.
[34] *cf.* para.**5–35** *et seq.*
[35] Note, however, that in *People (DPP) v Duff* [1995] 3 I.R. 296 at 301 (CCA), counsel erroneously referred to the need for corroboration, not supporting evidence (which was not commented upon on by Finlay C.J. in his brief judgment).
[36] *cf.* para.**5–47** *et seq.*
[37] *R. v Weeder* (1980) 71 Cr. App. R. 228 (CA).
[38] [1996] Crim. L. R. 39 (CA).

supportive. The court considered that identifications may be mutually and cumulatively supportive where there are striking similarities between them. This reference to striking similarity—a concept developed in the context of similar fact evidence[39]—was more recently abandoned by the English Court of Appeal as a prerequisite for cumulative proof of identity in *R. v John W*.[40]

6–14 Cumulative identification by its nature is fraught with fresh difficulty, but these are best viewed as general difficulties of proof that will not necessarily be rectified by rigid rules and categorically different warnings on how the jury must assess the evidence. Such questions of proof will be critical at all stages— from the point at which it is decided to prosecute and try multiple indictments in a joined trial, to the close of the trial—and, depending upon the specific details of the evidence, may be expected to be reflected in a trial judge's decision to withdraw a case from the jury or to sever the indictments, or in his closing directions giving careful advice on the strengths and weaknesses of the evidence.

III. MEANS OF IDENTIFICATION

6–15 As a general rule, save for cases where the accused is known to the witness,[41] identification of the accused must be made by a witness before the trial. The common law disfavours formal identification for the first time in court (or dock identification), since by this stage in the proceedings the witness may feel under pressure to make a positive identification. In *People (DPP) v Cooney*,[42] the Supreme Court accepted that dock identification is highly prejudicial and irregular. The trial judge had been entitled to accept it in this case, however (though required to issue a more strongly worded warning), since the witness had already identified the accused positively at two formal identification parades (which had been rendered technically inadmissible due to the illegality of the accused's arrest and re-arrest), and since there was no suggestion in the case that the gardai had acted *male fides*.

6–16 The longer that the pre-trial identification is deferred, the more likely it becomes that the witness will forget and confuse important details, and, for a multiplicity of reasons, that the identification becomes potentially and actually unreliable. Delays or defects at any stage from the witness' first observation of the wrongdoer to his formal identification will affect the weight subsequently to be given to the identification, and if serious enough may affect its admissibility.

6–17 A second identification is usually made in open court to confirm the pre-trial identification. Exceptions to this exist for certain vulnerable witnesses

---

[39] *cf*. para.7–27 *et seq*.
[40] [1998] 2 Cr. App. R. 289 (CA).
[41] *People (DPP) v Meehan* (Special Criminal Court, July 29, 1999).
[42] [1998] 1 I.L.R.M. 321 (SC).

Identification Evidence 177

giving their testimony by television link[43]: under s.18 of the Criminal Evidence 1992, for child witnesses in cases of sexual offence or violence against children; and under s.39(5) of the Criminal Justice Act 1999, for witnesses intimidated by the accused. In these cases, where the accused was known to the witness before the alleged offence, the witness is not required to identify him during the trial; and where he has already identified him at a parade, another person may give evidence to that effect, unless in "the interests of justice" the court directs otherwise.

The Identification Parade

6–18 The chief advantage of conducting a formal parade is that identification may be made under controlled circumstances in the presence of the accused and his lawyer who may later inform the court of any inadequacies in the parade or the procedures employed. As O'Flaherty J. acknowledged in *People (DPP) v O'Reilly*,[44] the suspect who is identified informally is by contrast "seriously inhibited in challenging its unfairness at the trial". Although the courts have resisted characterising the need to identify the accused formally in a properly constituted parade as a distinct constitutional right of the accused, the right to be so identified is an important element of the fundamental (but general) constitutional right to fair procedures, whose content varies contextually according to the circumstances of each case.[45] Most pre-trial identifications are made at a formal identification parade, such that there is now something of a presumption that one should be organised in each case to avoid difficulties arising later at the trial. Furthermore, as explained by O'Flaherty J. in *People (DPP) v Maples*,[46] the failure to conduct a parade may require a stronger *Casey* warning in the trial judge's closing directions to the jury.

6–19 Prior to identification, the witness should not see the accused being arrested, where this can reasonably be avoided, or taken from custody to the parade room.[47] The Court of Criminal Appeal accepted in *O'Reilly*[48] that if several witnesses are requested to attempt identification, they should be kept apart before and after the parade to minimise consultation between them.[49] The court further accepted that at the parade, the witness should be asked to identify the culprit from a line of eight to 12 people chosen because they look

---

[43] *cf.* paras **1–28, 1–55**.
[44] [1990] 2 I.R. 415 at 421 (CCA): *cf.* appendix 42.
[45] *People (DPP) v Maples* [1999] I.L.R.M. 113, *per* O'Flaherty J. (SC).
[46] *ibid.*
[47] For which convictions were quashed in *R. v Smith* (1908) 1 Cr. App. R. 203 (CA); *R. v Dickman* (1910) 5 Cr. App. R. 135 (CA); and *R. v Wait* [1998] Crim. L.R. 68 (CA).
[48] [1990] 2 I.R. 415 (CCA).
[49] In *McLoughlin v DPP* (CCA, February 22, 1999), further prosecution of the accused was prohibited after it emerged that the identifying witness had consulted with a garda prior to testifying and had ascertained that the accused had a tattoo: the witness' identification in court, which was to be the prosecution's key evidence against the accused, was tainted "irremediably".

physically and sartorially similar to the suspect,[50] so far as is reasonably possible. It is sufficient that the foils look "roughly similar" to the suspect, according to the Court of Criminal Appeal in *People (DPP) v O'Hanlon*,[51] in which case a parade was not defective merely because some of its participants were a few inches shorter or taller than the suspect. If the witness fails to identity the accused, this fact should be disclosed by the prosecution to the defence.

6–20 Sometimes, practicalities may militate against the holding of a parade: for instance, the suspect may be of singular appearance, and it may be impossible to gather together a sufficient number of similar people.[52] The witness may already know the accused,[53] in which case a formal parade is not required,[54] though a *Casey* warning must still be given.[55] Where the only evidence implicating the accused in the offence is identification by one witness, there is a greater need to ensure that the procedures adopted for the identification were fair. The courts have criticised recourse by the gardai to informal procedures in cases where an identification parade could have been conducted, and have condemned the garda practice of asking witnesses to identify the accused as he enters or leaves a courthouse building,[56] surroundings that earmark the accused in advance of identification as a criminal type. In *People (DPP) v Carroll*,[57] the Court of Criminal Appeal was unimpressed by the garda's explanation that it would have been difficult to arrange a parade of scruffy males in their 40s or 50s in Cork city, and it quashed convictions in a case where informal identification was the only evidence against the accused. The garda had not explained why it would have been difficult to arrange a parade, such as that the accused was of singular appearance, and appeared not

---

[50] Ryan and Magee write that where there are two accused, a decision may be taken to include both of them in a parade of 12 volunteers, unless there are marked differences in their appearance necessitating separate parades with eight volunteers for each: *The Irish Criminal Process*, (Mercier Press, Dublin, 1983) at pp.139–40.
[51] CCA, October 12, 1998.
[52] So recognised by O'Flaherty J. in *People (DPP) v O'Reilly* [1990] 2 I.R. 415 at 420 (CCA): *cf.* appendix 42.
[53] As in *People (DPP) v Behan* (CCA, *ex tempore*, February 1, 1993), where the witness had recognised the accused amongst a group of people in the precincts of a District court. Conviction was upheld in light of the fact that the witness had known the accused previously and the trial judge had adequately discussed identification concerns when administering the *Casey* warning. In *R. v Campbell* [1996] Crim. L.R. 500 (CA), the witness accidentally bumped into the accused before a parade was arranged, and he recognised his face from school; whether or not the chance confrontation was an administrative slip-up, the Court of Appeal was prepared to uphold the identification.
[54] *People (DPP) v O'Reilly* [1990] 2 I.R. 415 at 420 (CCA); *People (DPP) v Farrell* (CCA, *ex tempore*, July 13, 1998).
[55] *People (DPP) v Stafford* [1983] I.R. 165 (SC); *People (DPP) v Smith* [1992] 2 I.L.R.M. 61. See also *People (DPP) v McNamara* (CCA, March 22, 1999), where a retrial was ordered due to the trial judge's failure to administer a *Casey* warning in a case where the identifying witness had claimed to recognise the accused.
[56] *People (Attorney-General) v Fagan* (CCA, May 13, 1974); *People (DPP) v O'Reilly* [1990] 2 I.R. 415 at 420 (CCA); *People (DPP) v Duff* [1995] 3 I.R. 296 at 301 (CCA).
[57] CCA, *ex tempore*, December 18, 2002.

Identification Evidence

to have made any attempt to arrange a parade before recourse to informal means (in this case, identifying the accused from a crowd gathered in Grand Parade, Cork, by night).

6–21 Identification parades have not been brought within the compass of statute or regulation in Ireland; indeed, to a significant extent in Ireland, procedures for obtaining identification evidence have been distilled in response to precedents and decisions of the courts. Ryan and Magee write that the identification parade should be conducted by a garda officer who is unconnected with the crime under investigation but who has been made familiar with the circumstances of the case and information relevant to the witnesses.[58] Only the garda member in charge of the investigation should be present at the parade. When the volunteers have been arranged in a line, the suspect should be asked if he has any objections to the composition or appearance of the parade. When the parade has been completed, the accused and his solicitor should be asked whether he has any comment to make with respect to the parade. Details of the parade, and any objections made by the accused or his solicitor, must "meticulously" be recorded by the officer responsible for conducting the parade.[59]

6–22 Since the identification parade is chiefly a matter of procedural fairness to the accused, it is naturally dependent upon his cooperation. Where the accused refuses to participate in a parade, the gardai are entitled to obtain identification by less formal means: for instance, in *People (Attorney-General) v Martin*[60] (where a make-shift parade was sprung on the accused in prison), and *People (DPP) v Rapple*[61] (where the accused was identified from the passenger seat of a car as he walked down a road). Thus, the failure to hold a full parade is not automatically a basis for quashing conviction. According to *People (Attorney-General) v Martin*,[62] the question is whether the conviction can properly stand in the light of all the evidence. In *Martin*, the witnesses had had ample time to observe the two accused men at the scene of the crime, the reliability of their testimony had been scrupulously tested under cross-examination, and the identification was supported by other evidence—that when first apprehended, the garda observed a rent in one of the men's trousers and a scar on his leg, later discovered to tally with his condition upon formal identification of the criminal.

6–23 In cases where the quality of the identification evidence withstands any defects in the procedures used to obtain it, the identification is likely to be admissible, although a stronger *Casey* warning is warranted to address the need to seek other evidence to support the problematic identification.[63] If the

---

[58] *op. cit.* n.50 at pp.139–40.
[59] In England, the Code of Practice (Code D 2.15 and Annex A to Code D, para.19) requires identification parades to be photographed or video-recorded.
[60] [1956] I.R. 22 (SC).
[61] [1999] 1 I.L.R.M. 113 (CCA).
[62] [1956] I.R. 22 (SC).
[63] As in *People (Attorney-General) v Fagan* (CCA, May 13, 1974).

defects in identification coincide with other procedural and evidential complications in the case, the case may be one that ought to be withdrawn from the jury or risk censure upon appeal.

6–24 A witness' failure positively to identify the accused at an identification parade is not a bar against the witness subsequently giving evidence in the trial of the accused to describe what he observed of the offender—although in the absence of other identifying witnesses or cogent supporting evidence, a case of this nature clearly risks dismissal of charges or a directed verdict. In *R. v George*,[64] the Court of Appeal upheld conviction upon the basis that the witness' qualified identification of the accused in evidence was consistent with accounts given by other witnesses of how the offender had behaved and was supported by circumstantial evidence in the case. The court rejected the challenge to the admissibility of the witness' evidence, but cautioned that where a witness has failed to make a positive identification of the accused prior to the trial, his testimonial evidence should be received on that footing, and questioning in-chief should not be permitted to excuse his failure to identify the accused nor to remove the court's reservations about his pre-trial identification.

Use of Photographs, Videos, and other Means of Identification

6–25 It is common case that identification may additionally or alternatively be proved by evidence of fingerprints or body samples,[65] and in more recent years by DNA profiling.[66] The courts have displayed moderate enthusiasm for new means of proof of identity, and in doing so have been prepared to develop *in tandem* the duty on the prosecutor "to seek out and preserve" evidence potentially relevant to the guilt or innocence of the accused in criminal trials.[67] In a recent decision of clear consequence, Hardiman J. observed:

> "If science or technology can provide certainty in matters of great importance which would otherwise be determined on human testimony which may be fallible or worse, who but a guilty man would not willingly invoke its aid? ... The balance has long been struck in favour of the use of technology in the search for the perpetrators of crime, even when the processes involved are minimally invasive or transiently painful or undignified for innocent people. The greater good prevails. This development is due in large measure to the development of techniques of previously unimagined sophistication, from the telephoto lens and the video camera to the extraordinary precision of DNA analysis."[68]

---

[64] [2003] Crim. L.R. 282 (CA).
[65] The failure to provide which, in contravention of a statutory requirement, may ground corroborative inferences against the accused: *cf.* para.**5–11**.
[66] *cf.* para.**12–12** *et seq.*
[67] *cf.* para.**6–35** *et seq.*
[68] *Dunne v DPP* [2002] 2 I.R. 305 (SC).

Identification Evidence

6–26 Although the showing of suspect photographs to witnesses makes the process greatly more vulnerable to false-positive identification, their use during the initial stages of investigation is inevitable and often critically important to police work. The obvious danger posed by recourse to such photographs is that the witness is being presented with a greatly reduced pool of faces known to have courted police suspicion, and a witness may be unwilling after the fact to concede the extent to which he was reliant on the photographs to enable him recollect the offender. A detailed description should first be obtained from the witness as a means of recording the parameters of the witness' memory of the offender prior to inspection of the photographs. In *People (Attorney-General) v Mills*,[69] the Court of Criminal Appeal sanctioned the practice of showing a witness photographs to prompt his memory, so long as the witness is shown photographs of numerous possible suspects. More recently in *People (DPP) v Rapple*,[70] Barron J. accepted the usefulness of photographs in the search for a suspect, but condemned the "clearly prejudicial and unfair" practice of showing a witness photographs as a means of ascertaining whether or not he is likely to make a positive identification of the suspect later at a duly conducted identification parade.[71] The court affirmed Lord Hewart's condemnation in *R. v Melaney*[72] of the use of photographs when "the person has not been arrested and the police are in the greatest doubt who is the culprit".

6–27 *Mills* acknowledges that the fact that a witness was shown a photograph of the accused taken from garda files prior to identification is a matter that may only be raised by the defence, due to the prejudicial suggestion of criminal record that this fact entails.[73] On the other hand, Maguire C.J. also accepted that where it has been prompted by photographs, identification should be taken subject to a reservation, and therefore "the jury's attention should be called to the fact that the witness' evidence may be coloured by having seen the photographs".[74] A seemingly irreconcilable conflict exists between these two premises; and as later acknowledged in *O'Reilly*, defence counsel is placed in an awkward dilemma. O'Flaherty J. suggested that counsel should raise the issue of the photographs privately with the judge, who may decide whether in the light of that fact and other frailties the resulting identification is admissible. Beyond this, defence counsel must inevitably choose the route less likely to damage the accused's case.

---

[69] [1957] I.R. 106 (CCA); applying *R. v Ferguson* [1925] 2 K.B. 799.
[70] [1999] 1 I.L.R.M. 113 at 118 (CCA).
[71] Reflected in England in Code of Practice D, para.2.18, Annex D, para.5, whereunder it is stated that police photographs may be shown where no suspect is yet known, but that where a suspect is known or where one witness has already made a positive identification, the police should not show the photographs to other witnesses (who should be asked instead to identify the suspect at an identification parade).
[72] (1923) 18 Cr. App. R. 2 at 3 (CA).
[73] If reliance has been placed upon photographs of the accused at any stage in the identification process, the prosecution must disclose this fact to the defence: *R. v Lamb* (1980) 71 Cr. App. R. 198 (CA).
[74] [1957] I.R. 106 at 109 (CCA).

6–28 Video footage and stills raise numerous specific concerns. Where randomly or continually recorded, they do not *per se* suggest that the person taped has been under suspicion or implicated in charges before. Video surveillance footage recording the accused *in flagrante delicto* may constitute admissible real evidence of identification in its own right. Where sufficiently clear, the jury may be permitted to compare the recorded image of the offender to the accused in the trial.[75] The concerns posed by this type of evidence relate chiefly to its quality, the possibility that the person shown on the video bears merely a compelling likeness to the accused, the possibility that the footage has been digitally manipulated (a matter yet to be raised before the Irish courts, and upon which expert evidence would likely be exigent),[76] and concern to gauge the extent to which an identifying witness was shown videotaped footage prior to or after making his formal identification. Although the video and the witness' own experience of the events can together constitute the prosecution's identification evidence against the accused, the court must know what details were provided independently by the witness, and what the video has specifically added to the witness' recollections. Thus it is vital that the court know the full extent of the witness' exposure to videotaped footage of the criminal in action prior to, and after, alternative identification.

6–29 On occasion, though with caution, video footage has been used to assist a witness in his identification and to supplement his observations. In *People (DPP) v O'Callaghan*,[77] surveillance footage was allowed to complete a security man's version of the incident (after the moment he was forced to the floor), and to enable him to confirm his first vague recognition of the thief. O'Hanlon J. clearly regarded the use of video footage in this way as exceptional, but upheld it in the case specifically in light of the fact that the witness was an experienced security man whose confidence had withstood rigorous cross-examination, and further because the jury had been able to view the two tapes and decide for themselves whether the man's disguise was or was not "impenetrable".

6–30 In *People (DPP) v Maguire*,[78] the Court of Criminal Appeal recognised that video footage may be tendered in evidence to show whether or not a witness had a reasonable opportunity to observe the criminal, or to show why the witness could not have made an independent identification of the criminal in the circumstances. Barron J. considered that where a video is permitted to supplement a witness' evidence in this way, it constitutes evidence bearing upon the witness' credit, for the purpose of establishing whether the witness' evidence is credible and his identification consistent. The court recognised, however, that in exceptional cases such as the present, where no identifying

---

[75] *R. v Dodson and Williams* (1984) 79 Cr. App. R. 220 (CA).
[76] The English courts have approved the use of experts in facial-mapping: *R. v Stockwell* (1993) 97 Cr. App. R. 260; *R. v Clarke* [1995] 2 Cr. App. R. 425; *R. v Hookway* [1999] Crim. L.R. 750.
[77] CCA, July 30, 1990.
[78] [1995] 2 I.R. 286 (CCA).

Identification Evidence 183

witnesses had come forward, the prosecution may rely on the videotaped footage in its own right (even though unsupported) as evidence probative of a fact at issue, namely identity of the culprit.

6–31 Barron J. also addressed the prejudicial aspects of surveillance footage and its associated dangers. The security man is in a similar position to the police officer; as persons in authority, both may recognise the accused from previous incidents, which if conveyed to the court might tend to reveal that the accused has a criminal record or is of a criminal type. The learned judge made it clear that if, having regard to all the circumstances of the case, the trial judge forms the view that the prejudicial effect of the identification exceeds its probative value, the evidence should not be admitted.[79] In all cases, the accused must be "protected from obvious prejudice" arising from such evidence. Further, in any case where videos are relied upon to establish or supplement identification, "the usual and proper warnings required in relation to identification evidence must be given to the jury".[80] In the light of *Casey* and decisions discussed above, this requires in each case a full discussion of any specific flaws and uncertainties with respect to the video representations and the testimony of witnesses. In any case where the jury is asked to identify the accused from the video, the warning must emphasise the dangers in relying upon unsupported video footage and the possibility that the videotaped person merely bears a strong resemblance to the accused.[81]

Photofits and Identikits

6–32 Whilst photographs and videos are potentially admissible as ordinary items of real evidence, upon due authentication, uncertainty persists with respect to the status of sketches and computerised photofits or identikits. In *R. v Cook*,[82] the Court of Appeal controversially placed the identikit on a similar footing to photographs, despite the obvious hearsay concerns arising from the translated expression into graphic form of a description orally provided by a witness. According to Watkins L.J., the production of sketches and photofits is "a graphic representation of a witness' memory" and "another form of the camera at work, albeit imperfectly and not produced contemporaneously with the material incident".[83] Although the court considered the photofit to be *sui generis*, it clearly regarded the item as more akin to real evidence that "speaks for itself". The reasoning instantly appears unsound, and has been roundly condemned by commentators who considered the point.[84] The Court of Appeal surprisingly

---

[79] [1995] 2 I.R. 286 at 289.
[80] *ibid.* at 290.
[81] Also decided in: *Statue of Liberty* [1968] 2 All E.R. 195 (CA) and *R. v Blenkinsop* [1995] 1 Cr. App. R. 7 (CA).
[82] [1987] Q.B. 147, [1987] 1 All E.R. 1049 (CA).
[83] *ibid.* at 1054.
[84] Andrews and Hirst, *Criminal Evidence* (4th ed., Jordans, Bristol, 2001) at p.294; *Cross and Tapper on Evidence,* (Tapper ed., 9th ed., Butterworths, London, 1999) at p.676; Dennis, *The Law of Evidence* (Sweet & Maxwell, London, 1999) at p.219; and Uglow, *Evidence: Text and Materials* (Sweet & Maxwell, London, 1997) at pp.308–09. By

followed *Cook* in *R. v Constantinou*,[85] deciding not alone that photofit identifications are admissible, but that the trial judge is not required to give a *Turnbull* direction in cases where they are admitted. Unlike photographs and videos, neither the sketch nor the photofit or identikit is automatically created. It is the composite production of the witness' description at a later date and an interpretation by the sketch artist or computer. As such, it is an assertion by a person, an impression that does not systematically come into being or "speak for itself". Thus, if offered as evidence of a witness' identification, a sketch or photofit offends the rule against hearsay; if offered to show the witness' consistency, it offends the rule against narrative, as well as begging questions of relevance; lacking the critical element of contemporaneity, it is intrinsically unlikely to benefit from a *res gestae* exception.[86]

Voice Identification

6–33 The identification evidence rules developed by the Irish and English courts have thus far addressed eye-witness identification, upon the basis that this in particular is fraught with hidden dangers of distortion. The *Casey* rules have not yet tackled voice identification,[87] of which there is little reported authority, although the need for carefully regulated procedures and practice guidelines is clear, as was demonstrated recently by the confusion caused in England over *R. v Hersey*.[88] During the robbery, the offender's face had been concealed by a balaclava helmet, and he had spoken at length. One of three witnesses, the shopkeeper, believed he recognised the voice as that of the accused, a long-standing customer, and he selected his voice from a range of 12 voices. An expert for the defence claimed that 12 voices were too many; that the 11 volunteers had read their passages at an artificially high pitch; and that only the accused had read the passage in a way that made sense. The Court of Appeal upheld the trial judge's decision not to admit this expert opinion upon the basis that the specific issues in this case were matters within the experience and competence of the jury,[89] although the court was prepared to accept that expert opinion on voice identification may be appropriate in other cases. In terms of the identification evidence warning necessary since *Turnbull*, the Court of Appeal concluded that the trial judge must adapt it to the particular dangers presented by voice identification.

---

contrast, *Murphy on Evidence* (6th ed., Blackstone Press, London, 1997) at p.456 takes the view that the photofit should be admissible where compiled contemporaneously with the witness' observation, whence it may function as a note to refresh the witness' memory: *cf.* para.**2–41** *et seq.*
[85] (1990) 91 Cr. App. R. 74 (CA).
[86] *cf.* paras **2–51** and **9–65** *et seq.*
[87] Voice identification is sometimes permitted in the context of parades when participants are requested to utter particular phrases, as in *People (DPP) v O'Hanlon* (CCA, October 12, 1998).
[88] [1998] Crim. L.R. 281 (CA).
[89] Applying *R. v Turner* [1975] Q.B. 834 (CA) and *R. v Stockwell* (1993) 97 Cr. App. R. 260 (CA); *cf.* para.**12–04**.

6-34 These dangers have not yet been sufficiently investigated, and it would seem that English law currently awaits further clarification on issues such as: how best to safeguard against the disguising or manipulation of voice; how to determine the appropriate numerical composition of the voice parade (based upon the extent to which similar voices can be obtained and on the number of voices a witness is typically able to digest and contrast); how to determine what text is played and whether and how often a certain voice may be replayed afterwards.[90] In *R. v O'Doherty*,[91] where a fundamental divergence in view between auditory experts had underscored the potential for false positive auditory associations, the Court of Appeal adopted a rigorous stance to voice identification. Two expert witnesses for the prosecution expressed the view that the voice recorded on the 999 emergency call was probably that of the accused. An expert witness for the defence criticised the prosecution's decision to restrict itself to an auditory phonetic analysis (chiefly of dialect and accent) and not to supplement it by a quantitative acoustic analysis (assessing acoustics by the likely effect of the speaker's vocal tract, mouth, and throat). Allowing the appeal, the Court of Appeal ruled that prosecutions should not be brought in reliance upon voice identification supported by auditory but not acoustic analysis. The court further found, owing to the uncertain nature of scientific technology on voice recognition, that juries should specifically be cautioned against the dangers in assuming an association between a voice recording and the accused, and of relying upon their own untrained ears.

IV. Prosecutor's Duty to Disclose

6-35 A key element of the duty on the prosecutor to disclose material evidence and information prior to trials upon indictment[92] is the disclosure of videotapes or photographs a witness consulted prior to, or as a means of, identifying the accused. In *People (DPP) v Maleady and Grogan*,[93] conviction was quashed on foot of the prosecution's failure to disclose the fact that the identifying witness had seen a book of photographs of suspects prior to identifying the accused at a parade. In recent cases, the courts have further considered the ambit of this duty in the context of evidence (such as surveillance footage) not preserved by the prosecutor.

6-36 In *Braddish v DPP*,[94] the Supreme Court found that the prosecution had breached its duty by failing to preserve a videotape the witness consulted prior to formal identification. The court further considered, in these circumstances, that the identification (by means of oral testimony and stills taken from the destroyed tape) had been inadmissible evidence, since the primary material upon which it was based was no longer in existence, and

---

[90] Commentary [1998] Crim. L.R. at 283.
[91] [2002] Crim. L.R. 761 (CA).
[92] *cf.* para.**1–42** *et seq.*
[93] [1995] 2 I.R. 517 (CCA).
[94] [2001] 3 I.R. 127 (SC): *cf.* appendix 63.

therefore the identification could not adequately be tested. The court approved an earlier decision of Lynch J. in *Murphy v DPP*,[95] finding that the prosecutor's duty extends to preservation and disclosure of "articles which may give rise to the reasonable possibility of securing relevant evidence". The fact that the accused in *Braddish* had signed a confession in custody was of no consequence to the prosecution in this case, since he had subsequently repudiated it, and in the absence of admissible identification the confession was uncorroborated.[96] Hardiman J. further found that because the videotape had been destroyed, the accused was inhibited in making any challenge to his detention, which in the circumstances of the case could only have been upon the basis that the gardai lacked a reasonable suspicion for his arrest and detention under s.4 of the Criminal Justice Act 1984.

6–37 In *Dunne v DPP*,[97] a majority of the Supreme Court granted the applicant orders restraining further prosecution of a case in which the investigators had failed to seek out potentially probative evidence. The case differed from *Braddish* to the extent that it concerned the failure to obtain, rather than retain, a videotape of surveillance footage habitually taken from cameras installed at the filling station the accused was alleged to have robbed. Hardiman J. considered the scope of this duty to be "to take reasonable steps to seek out material evidence". The effect for the prosecution or trial of a failure on the part of the public investigators to discharge this duty was best evaluated by applying the test proposed by Denham J. in *B v DPP*,[98] to wit, where "there is a real risk that the applicant would not receive a fair trial then, on the balance of these constitutional rights the applicant's right would prevail".

6–38 In *Mitchell v DPP*,[99] however, Geoghegan J. rejected the applicant's contention that his right to a fair trial would be infringed in circumstances where the prosecution had not afforded the accused an opportunity to inspect garda surveillance videotapes of public activity in the Temple Bar area of Dublin on the night of the alleged offence. The court was influenced by the fact that the prosecution had not deemed the tapes relevant to the investigation, and that the accused had not requested their production until 14 months after the charges, by which time the tapes has been destroyed. In terms of duties and rights, the learned judge preferred to assess the matter in terms of its direct effect upon fairness in the trial—this being the right of the accused and an issue which the trial judge was competent to decide in light of all the circumstances of the case. Geoghegan J. considered that the specific right to notification of videotaped evidence prior to its destruction extended no further than to cases "where it was genuinely considered that such tapes might be relevant to the criminal proceedings".[100]

---

[95] [1989] I.L.R.M. 71 at 76 (HC).
[96] *cf.* para.**10–72** *et seq.*
[97] [2002] 2 I.R. 305 (SC): *cf.* appendix 65.
[98] [1997] 3 I.R. 140 at 196 (HC).
[99] [2000] 2 I.L.R.M. 396 (HC).
[100] *ibid.* at 399.

Further Reading

Carey, "Recognition and Visual Identification Warnings, Provisos and Exceptional Circumstances—Irish Law and the Privy Council" [1999] 17 I.L.T. 69.

Clifford, "The Relevance of Psychological Investigation to Legal Issues in Testimony and Identification" [1979] Crim. L.R. 153.

Cutler and Penrod, *Mistaken Identification: The Eyewitness, Psychology, and the Law* (Cambridge University Press, 1995).

Elliot, "Video Tape Evidence: The Risk of Over-Persuasion" [1998] Crim. L.R. 159.

Jackson, "The Insufficiency of Identification Evidence Based on Personal Impression" [1986] Crim. L.R. 203.

Lambert, "Swearing Blind with Pointed Fingers: The Psychology of Identification Parades and Eyewitness Identification" (2000) 10 I.C.L.J. 11.

McKenzie, "Psychology and Legal Practice: Fairness in Identification Parades" [1995] Crim. L.R. 200.

Ormerod, "Sounding Out Expert Voice Identification" [2002] Crim. L.R. 771.

CHAPTER 7

SIMILAR FACT EVIDENCE AND THE ACCUSED'S CRIMINAL PAST

I. The Forbidden Reasoning 7–01
II. The *Makin* and *Boardman* Principles 7–03
III. Ambit of Similar Fact Evidence Rules 7–16
IV. The Accused's Criminal Propensity 7–20
V. Similar Fact Evidence in Joined Trials 7–27
VI. Evidence to Explain the Background of an Act 7–32
VII. Civil Cases 7–35

I. THE FORBIDDEN REASONING

7–01 According to a fundamental common law rule of evidence, subject to few exceptions, evidence may not be tendered in-chief against the accused that directly or indirectly reveals his criminal record or bad character. The rule reflects the fear, shared by other exclusionary rules of evidence, that the particular evidence might "have a prejudicial influence on the minds of the jury which would be out of proportion to its true evidential value".[1] Bad character evidence is notoriously prejudicial. Once introduced into court, it "irreversibly changes the chemistry of the trial" so that "it becomes almost impossible for the accused to be tried dispassionately on the facts of the case."[2] By its nature, this type of evidence encourages the jury to engage in a "forbidden reasoning", potentially to infer present guilt from past misdeed. Proof of the accused's criminal past may prompt the view that it is unlikely the accused reformed himself and more likely he repeat-offended. Even if not fully convinced of the accused's guilt beyond a reasonable doubt, the jury may consider that the accused should be punished for his past behaviour. In such a trial, the presumption of innocence can have little real effect. The tendency of jurors to label the accused has been highlighted by Ellsworth, who found that jurors "do not seem to spend a great deal of time trying to define the legal categories, evaluating the admissibility of evidence they are using, or testing their final conclusion against a standard of proof. In fact, many jurors simply

---

[1] *R. v Christie* [1914] A.C. 545 at 559, *per* Lord Moulton (HL).
[2] Murphy, "Character Evidence: the Search for Logic and Policy Continues" [1998] 2 E. & P. 71 at 73.

appear to select a sketchy stereotyped theme to summarise what happened (eg. 'cold-hearted killer plots revenge', 'nice guy panics and overreacts') and then choose a verdict on the basis of the severity of the crime as they perceive it".[3]

7–02 The risks of prejudice in criminal proceedings are rightly considered far too serious to justify a broad discretionary determination of the admissibility of bad character evidence. It is a matter for resolution by the trial judge, having regard to the rules and principles developed by the common law courts, and subject in Ireland to the invariable obligation to ensure that the accused receives a fair trial for the purpose of Art.38(1) of the Constitution. The decision is necessarily made in the jury's absence in the *voire dire*;[4] where erroneously admitted, any resulting conviction is likely to be quashed owing to the necessarily prejudicial nature of this type of evidence. In criminal cases where spontaneous inadmissible references are made to the accused's criminal record or bad character, the trial judge must exercise his discretion to direct the jury to disregard the statement or, where the evidence is extremely prejudicial, to discharge the jury.[5] Evidence of the accused's criminal past deemed by the trial judge to be admissible in-chief, or cross-admissible as between multiple complainants in a joined trial, is commonly referred to as "similar fact evidence," a designation that has endured largely for reasons of convenience. Once admitted, the evidence is probative of the facts at issue, and may supply corroboration of other evidence in the case.[6] The extent to which an accused who chooses to testify may be cross-examined upon his bad character and criminal record is discussed in Chapter 8.

II. THE *MAKIN* AND *BOARDMAN* PRINCIPLES

7–03 The common law's current body of similar fact evidence rules has its origins in a much quoted decision by Lord Herschell in *Makin v Attorney-General for New South Wales*.[7] The centre-piece findings of *Makin* are, first, confirmation of the general prohibition against admitting evidence of the accused's criminal record for the purpose of inferring his present guilt (the forbidden reasoning), and, second, a qualification to this rule:

"It is undoubtedly not competent for the prosecution to adduce evidence

---

[3] Ellsworth, "Some Steps between Attitudes and Verdicts" in Hastie (ed.), *Inside the Juror: The Psychology of Juror Decision Making* (Cambridge, 1993) at pp.47–8.
[4] *cf.* para.**1–24** *et seq.*
[5] In *People (DPP) v Marley* [1985] I.L.R.M. 17, the Court of Criminal Appeal considered that inadmissible reference to acquittal of the accused in a previous trial for murder should have led to the discharge of the jury in his later trial for forgery. By contrast, in *People (DPP) v Kavanagh* (CCA, July 7, 1997), a warning to disregard an inadmissible reference by a witness to an assault by the accused on his wife was considered appropriate to mitigate any resulting prejudice to the accused in a trial for murder.
[6] *cf.* para.**5–10**.
[7] [1894] A.C. 57 (PC): *cf.* appendix at 1.

tending to shew that the accused has been guilty of criminal acts other than those covered by the indictment, for the purpose of leading to the conclusion that the accused is a person likely from his criminal conduct or character to have committed the offence for which he is being tried. On the other hand, the mere fact that the evidence adduced tends to shew the commission of other crimes does not render it inadmissible if it be relevant to an issue before the jury, and it may be so relevant if it bears upon the question whether the acts alleged to constitute the crime charged in the indictment were designed or accidental, or to rebut a defence which would otherwise be open to the accused."[8]

7–04 *Makin* failed to identify principles or guides by which future courts might limit the admissibility of bad character evidence notwithstanding its relevance, and it continues to divide the critics.[9] The *Makin* decision has been repeatedly endorsed by the Irish courts, though on the understanding that the qualification it identifies is limited to exceptional cases.[10] Of obvious concern is the apparent breadth of the qualification identified by Lord Herschell, whose premise is that proof of the accused's criminal record is admissible if tendered not to infer his present guilt but to bear upon some specifically relevant issue in the trial.[11] The practice of the courts, however, has been to apply the qualification sparingly in the light of the strict principle that bad character evidence is prima facie inadmissible against the accused. Lord Sumner explained in *Thompson v R*.[12] that the "mere theory that a plea of not guilty puts everything material in issue is not enough for this purpose. The prosecution cannot credit the accused with fanciful defences in order to rebut them at the outset with some damning piece of prejudice". In *People (Attorney-General) v Kirwan*,[13] evidence that the accused had recently served a four-year prison sentence was admitted to rebut his claim that the £200 found in his possession after his brother's murder was his own. The evidence was also capable of proving the identity of the murderer in the "special signature" sense envisaged by the English cases:[14] the deceased's body had been dismembered by a person skilled in butchery, skills the accused had learned whilst in prison.

---

[8] *ibid.* at 65, *per* Lord Herschell C.J.
[9] Mirfield, "Similar facts – Makin out?" [1987] C.L.J. 83 writes that *Makin* "continues to exert a baneful influence both upon the cases and upon much of the academic commentary on them". By contrast, Allan, "Similar Fact Evidence and Disposition: Law, Discretion, and Admissibility" (1985) 48 M.L.R. 253 at 263 asserts that Lord Herschell's double-barrel distinction is still the most coherent statement of the law, and that "the standard of cogency to be satisfied in the particular case [should] depend on the function that the similar fact evidence is tendered to perform". He advocates that propensity evidence be subject to a test that balances the probative value of the evidence in light of its likely prejudicial effect, and that non-propensity similar fact evidence be subject to a relevance based test.
[10] *People (Attorney-General) v Kirwan* [1943] I.R. 279 at 297, *per* Murnaghan J. (CCA).
[11] *R. v Dossett* 2 C. & K. 306, approved in *Makin*.
[12] [1918] A.C. 221 at 232 (HL).
[13] [1943] I.R. 279 (CCA).
[14] *cf.* para.7–13.

7–05 *Makin* was for some time assumed to encourage a categorical approach to bad character evidence, as evidence relevant to show a system or *modus operandi*, or to establish the accused's identity by proof of special signature, or to rebut specific defences such as the defence of innocent association[15] between the accused and the complainant.[16] Although Lord Herschell did not employ the words "striking similarities", it is subtextually clear from his review of the case law and his findings of fact that bad character evidence was potentially relevant to establish a system or pattern of the accused based upon an appeal to peculiar similarities between the current offence and the accused's past deeds. *Makin* was one of the clearest instances of a case with striking similarities. The accused couple had been charged with the murder of an adopted infant whose body had been discovered buried in their back garden. The trial judge permitted the prosecution to admit evidence showing that the bodies of 13 other babies received by the accused on similar terms had been found buried in the gardens of houses previously occupied by them. The admissibility of the evidence was upheld on appeal since it had a crucial bearing on the question of whether the death had been designed or accidental and was relevant to rebut a defence of death by natural causes (a defence not actually raised in the case).

7–06 Most of the reported cases after *Makin* featured "striking similarities". In *R. v Smith*,[17] "the brides in the bath case", similar fact evidence was admitted to rebut the defence of accidental death. The evidence established that on two subsequent occasions the accused married women who drowned in similar circumstances in his bath; further, that on each occasion the accused claimed the drowning had been induced by epileptic fit; and further, that he stood to benefit from each death, having ensured that his wives arranged life insurance policies. Unusual similarities also existed in *R. v Armstrong*,[18] where the evidence was admitted to rebut a defence of innocent purpose, here with respect to the purchase of arsenic. The evidence revealed that eight months after his wife's death by poisoning, the accused had secretly administered the same poison to another person. In *R. v Straffen*,[19] the accused had been committed to Broadmoor, after he was deemed unfit to plead by reason of insanity during his trial for the murder of two girls. He escaped for four hours, in which time another woman was murdered in the area. When recaptured—the murder as yet unknown to the police—he said, "I didn't kill her". Although there remained the slim possibility that another passer-by committed the murder, evidence of his past murders was admitted due to their striking similarities: each woman had been killed by manual strangulation without any attempt to commit a sexual

---

[15] *People (Attorney-General) v Dempsey* [1961] I.R. 288 (CCA); *R. v Armstrong* [1922] 2 K.B. 555.
[16] As enumerated in Cross, *Evidence* (4th ed., Butterworths, London, 1974) at pp.319–38. These remain valid bases for the admissibility of similar fact evidence: *People (DPP) v BK* [2000] 2 I.R. 199 at 210–11 (CCA).
[17] [1915] W.N. 309.
[18] [1922] 2 K.B. 555 (CA).
[19] [1952] 2 Q.B. 911 (CA).

assault; the murders appeared motiveless; and on no occasion had an attempt been made to conceal the body.

7–07 Gradually, the courts began to insist upon a high degree of similarity to justify admitting evidence of prior misdeed,[20] thereby forging the now well-entrenched (if sometimes misleading) term, similar fact evidence. The importance of establishing striking similarities was affirmed by the House of Lords in its landmark decision of *Boardman v DPP*.[21] Praised by some as "an intellectual breakthrough" in English law,[22] the decision is perhaps best interpreted as authority for a test based less upon category than upon a requirement that the evidence possess a probative force sufficiently strong to justify being heard in the trial notwithstanding its clear prejudicial effect. Lord Wilberforce found:

> "The basic principle must be that the admission of similar fact evidence … is exceptional and requires a strong degree of probative force. This probative force is derived, if at all, from the circumstance that the facts testified to by the several witnesses bear to each other such a striking similarity that they must, when judged by experience and common sense, either all be true, or have arisen from a cause common to the witnesses or from pure coincidence".[23]

7–08 In *R. v Mansfield*,[24] the similar fact evidence derived from circumstantial details so strikingly similar as to make coincidence unlikely. The Court of Appeal affirmed the trial judge's directions on the cross-admissibility of evidence relating to three counts of arson, on grounds (*inter alia*) of the following striking similarities. The first fire occurred in a hotel where the accused was living, the second and third in a hotel where he worked. All three fires were started by sprinkling flammable liquid onto the carpet and igniting it. The accused was discovered in the vicinity of all three fires, and he had ample time on each occasion to avoid appearing suspicious to the police. He was one of the few occupants who managed to escape fully clothed from the hotel during the first fire. A waste paper bin belonging to his room was discovered close to the third fire. Two of the fires started in areas of the hotels to which staff alone had had access.

---

[20] *R. v Robinson* (1953) 37 Cr. App. R. 95 (CA); *R. v Carter* [1956] Crim. L.R. 772 (CA).
[21] [1974] 3 All E.R. 887 (HL): *cf.* appendix 23. In *Boardman*, evidence given by each of two boys on counts of buggery was deemed cross-admissible and mutually corroborative against the accused headmaster on grounds of striking similarities in the manner in which the acts were allegedly committed. In retrospect, the evidence lacked the high level of peculiarity which the principles expressed in the case appear to require. Rather vaguely, the House felt that the form of words used by the headmaster to enlist the boys' co-operation was sufficiently striking, as was his request that each boy assume an active (or penetrative) role in the buggery.
[22] Hoffman, "Similar Facts after *Boardman*" (1975) 91 L.Q.R. 193.
[23] [1974] 3 All E.R. 887 at 897 (HL): *cf.* appendix 23. See also Lord Morris of Both-Y-Gest at 895, Lord Cross at 911, and Lord Salmon at 913.
[24] [1978] 1 All E.R. 134 (CA).

7–09 The Irish and English courts have recently interpreted "striking similarities" to be a guide and not a fixed test,[25] although it is not difficult to appreciate its attractiveness as a benchmark for admissibility of evidence fraught with concerns of prejudice. Strikingly similar features naturally reduce the likelihood of coincidental association between the various events, as well as limiting the reception of bad character evidence to exceptional cases. In this sense, the courts' preference for striking similarities is protective of the accused. For instance, in *R. v Beggs*,[26] the accused had been charged with one count of murder and five counts of unlawful wounding. The trial judge refused to sever the indictments and ruled that the evidence was cross-admissible between counts. The accused's appeal against the trial judge's decision succeeded upon the basis that this case in fact contained striking dissimilarities as between the offences. The wounding charges were with respect to non-vulnerable parts of the victims' bodies, who had been four fellow students and a 50-year-old man. By contrast, the murder offence had involved cutting the victim's throat, and the victim had been a practising homosexual who met the accused at a nightclub. The court emphasised that in a case of this type, where the prejudicial effect of the similar fact evidence was likely to be enormous, it was correspondingly necessary to establish that the similarities were striking.

7–10 On the other hand, judicial reference to similarities and patterns linking evidence of prior crimes committed by the accused with the present charges creates a wall of prejudice often impossible or highly difficult to surmount. The capacity of judicial directions at the close of the trial to mitigate this prejudice may seriously be questioned. On this point, Allan observes that when evidence of a criminal history is admitted because it is strikingly similar, "the danger of resort by the jury to the forbidden reasoning will be considerable" to the extent that the jury may treat the evidence "as proving that the accused has a highly specific disposition to commit exactly the type of crime charged".[27] In a similar vein, Mee asserts that strikingly similar and unusual details have been allowed to justify the reception of evidence revealing the accused to be of a type or disposition likely to repeat-offend, and thus to encourage recourse to the forbidden reasoning.[28] Reference to striking similarity is perhaps best regarded as an expression of the exceptional nature of similar fact evidence, an uncertain but distant line beyond which the prosecution must pass before it may request the court to infer the accused's present guilt by analogical reference to the accused's similar bad conduct on prior occasions. Lord Wilberforce famously recognised in *Boardman*,

> "[M]uch depends ... on the experience and common sense of the judge. ... [E]xperience plays as large a part as logic. And in matters of experience it is for the judge to keep close to current mores. What is striking in one

---

[25] *DPP v P* [1991] 2 A.C. 447 (HL); *B v DPP* [1997] 3 I.R. 140 (HC); *cf.* para.7–12 *et seq.*
[26] (1990) 90 Cr. App. R. 430 (CA).
[27] Allan, "Similar Fact Evidence and Disposition: Law, Discretion, and Admissibility" (1985) 48 M.L.R. 253 at 259.
[28] Mee, "Similar Fact Evidence: Accusation = Guilt?" [1991] Ir. Crim. L.J. 122 at 125.

age is normal in another; the perversions of yesterday may be the routine or the fashion of tomorrow".[29]

7–11 Judges will not always agree upon what constitutes "striking" or "peculiar", and the potential for inconsistency is great, as was illustrated by the starkly divergent responses of the Court of Appeal in the *R. v Novac*[30] and *R. v Johannsen*.[31] In *Novac*, Bridge L.J. considered that evidence by three boys that the accused had on different occasions offered to provide them with shelter for the night in his house before committing buggery were "commonplace features" of such crimes, neither unique nor striking. His Lordship further concluded that the fact that the accused had picked the boys up at amusement arcades was merely evidence of surrounding circumstances, and it was insufficiently proximate to the crimes to justify cross-admissibility as similar fact evidence. In *Johannsen*, the accused was charged with buggery and indecent assault in similar circumstances to the accused in *Novac*. Lawton L.J. "without hesitation" found that evidence that the accused had picked each boy up at an amusement arcade, and had enticed each boy to his house by treats and the offer of accommodation, before committing the crimes, bore the stamp of striking similarity sufficient to justify cross-admissibility between counts.

7–12 Once willing to overturn conviction where the trial judge failed to apply the "striking similarity" test,[32] the English courts have gradually departed from making central reference to it. Not long after *Boardman*, in *R. v Scarrott*,[33] Scarman L.J. took pains to emphasise the following:

> "Hallowed though by now the phrase 'strikingly similar' is ... it is no more than a label and is not to be confused with the substance of the law which it labels. ... We therefore have to reach a judgment on the evidence of this particular case, and to determine whether the evidence adduced, that is the similar fact evidence adduced, possesses such features that it is a proper exercise of judgment to say that the evidence is logically probative, that it has positive probative value in assisting to determine the truth".

7–13 In *DPP v P*,[34] the House of Lords reinterpreted *Boardman* principally to require a high degree of probative force sufficient to justify the likely prejudice, and it rejected the view that striking similarity was necessarily a pre-requisite test for admissibility of the evidence in-chief or cross-admissibility of the evidence between counts. Although the House approved *Boardman*, it focused instead on its references to the need to balance the evidence's probative

---

[29] [1974] 3 All E.R. 887 at 898 (HL).
[30] (1976) 65 Cr. App. R. 107 (CA).
[31] (1977) 65 Cr. App. R. 101 (CA).
[32] *e.g. R. v Clarke* (1977) 67 Cr. App. R. 398 (CA).
[33] [1978] 1 All E.R. 672 at 676 (CA).
[34] [1991] 2 A.C. 447 (HL).

worth against its likely prejudicial effect. The House favoured retaining the requirement of striking similarity where the identity of the accused is at issue, in which case the evidence may show "a signature or other special feature" to enable the court to identify the accused as the actor common to the past events and the circumstances surrounding the present offence.[35] More recently, this last vestige of the striking similarity test was abandoned in *John W.*,[36] where the Court of Appeal concluded that striking similarity is not a pre-requisite for admissibility of bad character evidence bearing upon the identification of the wrongdoer.

7–14 *DPP v P* was endorsed by the High Court in *B v DPP*,[37] also a case where the accused, charged with various acts of sexual abuse of his daughters, sought to have the indictment severed and separate trials conducted to avoid excessive prejudice by the cross-admissibility of evidence between counts. Budd J. agreed that striking similarity is just "one of the ways in which evidence may exhibit the exceptional degree of probative force required for admissibility, so that to insist upon it in all cases would be incorrect".[38] Having regard to the facts in this case, Budd J. considered the daughters' evidence to be strikingly similar—that the abuse had occurred when their mother was absent, that all had involved acts of sexual self-gratification on the part of the father, that the abuse had involved threats of violence, and that the accused had paid for abortions undergone by the daughters. It is of note that Budd J. regarded the fact alone of multiple accusation against the accused to be a striking feature justifying admissibility upon an appeal to the unlikelihood of coincidence.[39] This view has since been endorsed to justify cross-admissibility of evidence between counts against the accused in a joined trial with multiple complainants.[40] It is of note, however, that Budd J. acknowledged, for cases of multiple accusation involving a number of complainants in the same trial, that the trial judge must ensure the jury considers and eliminates the prospect of collusion between the complainants, and he must carefully tailor any corroboration warnings to the jury in light of any particular challenges made by the accused to the evidence.[41]

7–15 *DPP v P* was applied further in *People (DPP) v BK*,[42] although the court in this case was to a much greater extent steered by the absence of striking

---

[35] *ibid.* at 460: was approved by Barron J. in *People (DPP) v BK* [2000] 2 I.R. 199 at 209 (CCA). This view implicitly favours the proposition by Lord Hailsham in *Boardman* [1974] 3 All E.R. 887 at 906: "If [the perpetrator] left a particular symbol behind or always performed the offence wearing a Red Indian head-dress, the scale would probably be tipped" in favour of admitting the similar fact evidence.
[36] [1998] 2 Cr. App. R. 289 (CA). The court had reached a contrary view, however, in *R. v West* (1996) 2 Cr. App. R. 374 (CA).
[37] [1997] 3 I.R. 140 (HC, SC): *cf.* appendix 48.
[38] *ibid.* at 154.
[39] *ibid.* at 157.
[40] *People (DPP) v LG* [2003] 2 I.R. 517 *per* Keane C.J. (CCA).
[41] *ibid. cf.* para.**5–51** *et seq.*
[42] [2000] 2 I.R. 199 (CCA).

similarities in the case. The accused was charged with buggery of one boy, and the attempted buggery of two other boys, at a residential centre where he worked. The offences were alleged to have occurred with respect to two boys in a caravan, and with respect to one boy in a dormitory at night. In considering whether the trials should have been separated, Barron J. applied the probative versus prejudicial test to assess whether the evidence was cross-admissible between counts, in which event a joined trial was proper. The test was not fulfilled in this case, since there were material differences in the stories and events recounted by one boy, and since the abuse alleged by the other two boys was strikingly different from the allegations of the first boy.

III. Ambit of Similar Fact Evidence Rules

7–16 Similar fact evidence is not limited to evidence of previous similar offences for which the accused was actually convicted[43] or to evidence showing a demonstrably bad character.[44] The similar fact evidence must, however, be sufficiently cogent to warrant admissibility. It must do more than merely deepen suspicion.[45]

7–17 Similar fact evidence rules apply equally to the defence as to the prosecution. In *R. v Redgrave*,[46] the accused attempted to tender evidence of numerous romantic liaisons with women immortalised in a bundle of love letters, to show that he was heterosexual by nature and therefore unlikely to have importuned male police officers for an immoral purpose in a public urinal. The Court of Appeal found that the accused had been bound by the principles in *Makin* precluding the admission of evidence showing disposition or

---

[43] *R. v Downey* [1995] 1 Cr. App. R. 547 (CA); *R. v Barnes* [1995] 2 Cr. App. R. 491 (CA).
[44] So held in *R. v Barrington* [1981] 1 All E.R. 1132 (CA), where the accused was charged with indecent assault of three girls who had allegedly been induced to his house on false pretences, shown pornographic photos, asked to pose nude for similar photos, and then sexually assaulted. Evidence was accepted from three other girls who testified that the accused had invited them to his home and behaved similarly before each had escaped. The Court of Appeal affirmed the evidence's admissibility on grounds that it rebutted a defence of innocent association (babysitting) and because it was highly probative.
[45] This was not the case in *Harris v DPP* [1952] A.C. 694 (HL). The accused employee was charged with eight counts of larceny, and was convicted on one count. Evidence showed that on each occasion someone had entered the office by the same method, stealing only some of the available money. The only evidence connecting the accused with seven of the thefts was that none of them had occurred when he was on leave. The evidence connecting him with the eight theft was that he had been found on duty near the office after the burglary alarm went off, close to where the money had been hidden in a bin. The House of Lords quashed conviction upon the basis that the trial judge had failed to warn the jury that evidence of the first seven counts could not confirm the eight. See also *R. v Tricoglus* (1977) 65 Cr. App. R. 16 (CA), where evidence by two witnesses—establishing an unaccepted offer of a lift by a bearded man in a mini close to where the two complainants had been raped—had been wrongly admitted: the evidence was irrelevant and at most established that the accused was a kerb-crawler.
[46] (1982) 74 Cr. App. R. 10 at 14 (CA).

proclivity,[47] and further by the principle in *R. v Rowton*[48] that, when seeking to establish his good character, the accused is limited to proof of his *general reputation*.[49]

7-18 The English courts currently prefer to emphasise that relevance and probative force is the linchpin of similar fact evidence rules.[50] By itself, however, probative relevance is too minimal a test to advance any understanding of the use and effect of similar fact evidence, and is less a legal test than a more rigorous version of the prerequisite of relevance that any item of evidence must first satisfy before the issue of admissibility arises. Although the inherent relevance of past comparable action to the present trying of an offence has often been questioned, it is fair to assume that many observers would readily accept to varying degrees that this type of evidence is relevant. The history of similar fact evidence rules amounts in the end to an attempt to limit the admissibility of such evidence, less because it is unhelpful and irrelevant, and more because it imports risks of insurmountable prejudice that ultimately may drain the trial of fundamental fairness. As Lord Cross explained in *Boardman*, "the reason for this general rule is not that the law regards such evidence as inherently irrelevant, but because it is believed that if it were generally admitted jurors would in many cases think that it was more relevant that it was—so that, as it is put, its prejudicial effect would outweigh its probative value".[51] Following an effort to test the impact of evidence of previous convictions upon jury deliberations, a recent Law Commission consultation paper in England asserted a great need to tighten current rules on similar fact evidence, despite a sense by the courts that there was a need to relax them.[52] The report confirms the prevailing assumption that proof of recent similar convictions increases the probability of further conviction (although oddly, its test cases suggested that recent dissimilar convictions reduced the probability of conviction, and that jurors may be swayed more by evidence of pattern or system).

7-19 Irish law has made no significant contribution to this body of law in terms of developing the applicable principles. This owes much to the fact that the bulk of Irish appeals upon evidence matters are concerned with a breach of the accused's constitutional rights, and the rule against admissibility of bad character evidence has not been asserted as a negative constitutional right, although clearly it is fundamental to the constitutional right to a fair trial. The

---

[47] *cf.* para.**7–20**.
[48] (1865) Le. & Ca. 520.
[49] *cf.* para.**8–27**.
[50] *e.g. R. v Burns* [1996] Crim. L. R. 323 (CA): in admitting tapes that the accused had previously utilised to blackmail his victims, the Court of Appeal spoke of a strong probative force created by the strong similarities between the tapes and the method of blackmail.
[51] [1974] 3 All E.R. 887 at 908 (HL), adapting *dicta* by Lord Simon in *DPP v Kilbourne* [1973] A.C. 729 at 756 (HL).
[52] Law Commission Consultation Paper No.141, *Evidence in Criminal Proceedings: Previous Misconduct of a Defendant* (H.M.S.O., 1996).

probative versus prejudicial test is undoubtedly appropriate to Irish law, being consistent with a constitutionalised criminal justice model and also with recent legislative references to the trial judge's residual discretion to disapply various rules and provisions where not in the "interests of justice". This approach was evident in *DPP v Keogh*,[53] where the court considered bad character evidence in the context of s.8(1) of the Criminal Law (Sexual Offences) Act 1993. Section 8(1) provides that a garda may direct a person to leave a street or public place where he has reasonable cause to suspect the person to be loitering with intent to solicit or importune another for the purposes of prostitution. In rejecting garda evidence that the accused had frequented a place well-known as a "red light" area for two and a half years, Kelly J. decided that s.8(1), which was silent on the point, must be construed in conformity with the common law and constitutional concept of justice according to which "evidence of character or of previous convictions shall not be given at a criminal trial except at the instigation of the accused".[54] The evidence was on the one hand probatively "vague and imprecise", and on the other hand prejudicial in the extreme since "exceedingly difficult to rebut".[55]

IV. The Accused's Criminal Propensity

7–20 The *Makin* decision prohibits bad character evidence tendered in-chief to show that the accused is by type or by nature more likely to have committed the offence with which he is charged. On the other hand, it recognises the admissibility of this evidence where specifically relevant in the trial. Decisions subsequent to *Makin* cultivated principles and criteria in a bid to circumscribe the bases upon which the evidence may be deemed sufficiently probative to justify the inevitable prejudice to the defence. It remains the case, however, that bad character or similar fact evidence, irrespective of the logic that deems it admissible, intrinsically enables, if not encourages, the jury to engage in the forbidden reasoning. Once admitted, the prejudice is difficult to overcome, however strongly the trial judge phrases his closing directions. Although in principle the prosecution may not tender similar fact evidence "for the purpose" of showing on grounds of type or disposition the greater likelihood that the accused committed the offence, the prosecution may offer the evidence to establish other relevant facts, independent of an appeal to the accused's propensity or disposition. The distinction is generally defended upon the basis that the relevance of the bad character evidence is supplied by the specific detail of the acts, and not by inferences arising from his generally bad character. Much then depends upon the extent to which the prosecution is able to justify the evidence for specific reasons that do not seem primarily rooted in the accused's propensity or disposition—a dichotomy often wholly unrealistic in the context of jury trials, and reliant upon a doublethink evocative of the

---

[53] [1998] 1 I.L.R.M. 71 (HC).
[54] *ibid*. at 78, citing *King v Attorney-General* [1981] I.R. 233 at 241–42 (SC).
[55] *ibid*. at 79.

distinction often drawn between hearsay and original evidence when justifying the acceptance of prejudicial pre-trial statements.[56]

7–21 The use of propensity evidence to establish identity was first sanctioned by the House of Lords in *Thompson v R.*,[57] a decision now greatly impaired by the controversy and criticism it subsequently courted. Articles found in the accused's possession after arrest (powder puffs and photos of naked boys) were admitted as circumstantial evidence of the peculiarity of his disposition. According to Lord Atkinson, the incriminating articles were admissible "to show, when taken together in connection with the facts proved, that the prisoner harboured on that day an intent to commit an act of indecency with these boys should occasion offer".[58] According to Lord Sumner, the photos were admissible as "an incident in the habitual gratification of a particular propensity which not only takes [him] out of the class of ordinary men gone wrong but stamps [him] with the hall-mark of a specialised and extraordinary class as much as if [he] carried on [him] some physical peculiarity. ... It was accordingly admissible evidence of his identity".[59]

7–22 *Thompson*—with its proselytising language, its preoccupation with sexual peccadillo,[60] and the strong stench of entrapment in the case—had fallen decidedly out of favour in England by the 1970s, although it was perceived to retain some relevance in the broader context of establishing identity by reference to "unusual" dispositional traits.[61] Although the case against Thompson appeared strong, and the explanations given in defence uncompelling, the decision indulged in a dangerous logic, founded more upon pre-judgment than proof. Articles or traits suggesting that the accused was prey to deviant urges of a peculiar kind do not prove that the accused on the material occasion yielded to those urges. In any case of sexual offence where the possession of suggestive articles (*e.g.* pornography) or background detail

---

[56] *cf.* para.**9–20**.
[57] [1918] A.C. 221 (HL).
[58] *ibid.* at 230, *per* Lord Atkinson.
[59] *ibid.* at 234–35.
[60] *Thompson* had subsequently been invoked to enable reception of evidence of homosexual tendencies in all cases involving offences of a homosexual nature. In *R. v King* [1967] 2 Q.B. 338, for instance, the Court of Appeal decided that it was right to ask the accused in a sexual offence case whether he was homosexual, no less than it was right to ask him about indecent photographs found in his possession. In *R. v Horwood* [1970] 1 Q.B. 133 (CA), however, the court insisted that sexual orientation must first be shown to be relevant to the charges, and, somewhat paradoxically, that evidence of homosexuality should not be taken to infer the greater probability that the accused committed a criminal offence. In *Boardman* [1974] 3 All E.R. 887 at 897 (HL), Lord Wilberforce stoutly rejected the idea that the "particular form" a sexual proclivity has been shown to take may be enough to justify the admission of such evidence: "all sexual activity has some form or other and the varieties are not unlimited: how particular must it be for a special rule to apply?".
[61] *e.g.* Pattenden (1996) at pp.468–9, for whom cases like *Pfenning v The Queen* (1995) 182 C.L.R. 461 and *Thompson v R.* [1918] A.C. 221 (HL) show that "similar facts which are not 'strikingly similar' in combination with other evidence may be so probative on an issue of identity that if the evidence is accepted there is no reasonable explanation other than that the accused is guilty of the offence charged".

(*e.g.* conversations with prostitutes) is submitted by the prosecution as evidence, the possibility of false association and forbidden reasoning should be the court's dominant concern when assessing its admissibility, and where these have been discounted, they should nonetheless require careful directions to the jury at the close of the trial.

7-23 The admissibility of sexually suggestive material has become contentious in recent years, owing to the more rigorous prosecution of sexual offence and abuse cases. A decision to approve the reception of paedophiliac magazines and articles in *R. v Lewis*[62] was roundly criticised at the time for failing to apply the *Makin* and *Boardman* prescriptions. There was some support for routine reception of similar fact evidence in this way, however. Spencer, for one, argues that the character evidence rule "is distinctly generous to accuseds because in the nature of things evidence of paedophilia on a paedophilie charge tells us something important and more directly relevant than, say, evidence of previous dishonesty in a trial for theft or previous violence in a trial for wounding or assault".[63] A proposal along these lines was sensibly rejected by a majority of the Criminal Law Revision Committee due to "the danger of injustice".[64]

7-24 In *R. v Wright*,[65] the appellant headmaster had been convicted on numerous counts of buggery and indecent assault of his pupils. One ground of appeal was that the trial judge had wrongly admitted two incriminating articles found in the accused's office bureau and at his residence. The first was a travel guide for gay men, which was admitted in-chief on the basis that it suggested its owner was homosexual; and the second was a pornographic gay video, which was proven during cross-examination to rebut the appellant's assertion of good character. The accused denied possession of the items, and suggested, not uncommonly, that they were planted. Giving judgment for the Court of Appeal, Mustill L.J. accepted that such evidence is inadmissible to show the accused is homosexual and therefore more likely to commit the offence, whether the offence is sexual or otherwise, and that evidence of sexual orientation is not *per se* relevant to guilt. Accordingly, the book ought not to have been admitted. The learned judge's response to the video was less certain, although he accepted that evidence of bad character (broader in kind than similar fact evidence) may be admitted to rebut an accused's assertion under cross-examination of his good character, but that such evidence is relevant to credit and not issue under s.1(f) of the Criminal Evidence Act 1898 (in Ireland, s.1(f) of the Criminal Justice (Evidence) Act 1924).[66] One senses, however, that Mustill L.J. considered the video too prejudicial and not probative enough to justify admissibility.

---

[62] (1983) 76 Cr. App. R. 33 (CA).
[63] "Reforming the Law on Children's Evidence in England: the Pigot Committee and After" in Dent and Flin (eds.), *Children as Witnesses* (Chichester, 1992) at p.119.
[64] Criminal Law Revision Committee, *Eleventh Report: Evidence*, 1972, Cmnd. 4991, at para.89.
[65] (1990) 90 Cr. App. R. 325 (CA).
[66] *cf.* para.**9–01**.

7–25 *Wright* was faithfully followed in *R. v Burrage*[67] where conviction for indecent assault was again overturned. The prosecution had been permitted to question the accused about gay pornography found in his possession, in order to rebut the accused's assertion (in response to questioning) that he was sexually interested only in adult women. The Court of Appeal considered that *Wright* "ought to be more widely known", and that evidence seeking to establish sexual orientation as a fact tending to prove guilt (whether directly or indirectly) is pure dispositional evidence and as such is inadmissible.

7–26 It follows from this approach that evidence of sexual orientation—whether it be the accused's pre-trial response to questions, or proof that the accused possessed pornography suggesting a particular form of sexuality, or indeed proof that he had had sexual relations with a type of person—is not particularly relevant to the specific charges, and tends to prove no more than sexual disposition. Moreover, the evidence is extremely damaging to the defence, as demonstrated by the convictions initially secured in *Wright* and *Burrage*. Although the relevance or probative force of sexual disposition may in exceptional cases be proved, the degree of probative force must be particularly high, given the devastating prejudice likely to be caused to the defence, the effect of which is unlikely to be cured by closing directions, howsoever worded by the trial judge. A recent test of jury deliberations by the Law Commission in England found that where it was made known to the jury that the accused had been previously convicted for child sexual abuse, the jury was instantly negative towards him, and significantly more willing to disbelieve and convict him of any crime: by contrast, disclosure of other convictions, even of dishonesty, had negligible effect unless conviction was for a recent similar offence.[68]

V. SIMILAR FACT EVIDENCE IN JOINED TRIALS

7–27 Similar fact evidence issues commonly arise in joined trials, where the accused is tried on a number of counts with respect to similar offences against a number of complainants. The court's decision not to sever the counts, in the event of a challenge, tends to be based upon its view of whether the evidence for each count may be cross-admissible with respect to the other counts.[69] This derives from a concern to avoid undue prejudice to the defence and unfairness in the trial, and does not reflect a rule that joined trials may not take place where evidence of complainants is not cross-admissible.[70] In a joined trial, the same jury will hear all the evidence for each offence, in many cases

---

[67] [1997] Crim. L.R. 440 (CA).
[68] Law Commission Consultation Paper No. 141, *Evidence in Criminal Proceedings: Previous Misconduct of a Defendant* (H.M.S.O., 1996).
[69] Archbold, *Criminal Pleading and Practice* (Sweet & Maxwell, London, 1997) at p.1253.
[70] *R. v Sims* [1946] 1 K.B. 534 (CA) is authority for the view that there is no inflexible rule against joined trials in which the evidence for one count is not admissible in respect of other counts: approved in *People (DPP) v LG* [2003] 2 I.R. 517 (CCA).

by numerous different complainants, during the course of a single trying of the accused.[71] The process is fraught with possibilities of prejudice and contamination, particularly where serious doubts exist with respect to individual complainants, doubts which are far less apparent when evidence is heard from multiple complainants supplementing and strengthening each other's evidence. The defence is entitled to continue throughout the trial to seek severance of the counts on grounds of prejudice, and the trial judge may at any point accede to the request or become obliged to do so if there has been a material change in circumstances since the original decision to uphold joinder of the indictments.[72] Although it is preferable that the trial judge make a decision on cross-admissibility when determining if a joined trial may continue or be split,[73] a decision on this matter may be affected by the course of the trial and the evidence that emerges spontaneously from witness testimony. The trial judge's decision will naturally be reflected in the directions and warnings given to the jury at the close of the trial, although the capacity of warnings to overcome prejudice may seriously be questioned.[74]

7–28 Where in joined trials with multiple complainants, evidence on one count is judged cross-admissible for the purpose of another count, the prosecution commonly attempts to resolve any gaps in the account given by a single complainant's account (*e.g.* details of an assailant's identity) by reference to the other complainant's account, and to assert that the testimony of the complainants, if accepted, are mutually corroborative or mutually supporting,[75] whether cumulatively[76] or sequentially.[77] In such cases, the trial judge must caution the jury to evaluate each complainant's evidence separately for the purpose of deciding whether the prosecution has proved the accused's guilt as charged, before proceeding to ascertain whether the complainants have corroborated each other. In *People (DPP) v LG*,[78] convictions were quashed in a joined trial despite the cross-admissibility of the complainants' evidence

---

[71] *e.g. People v Wallace* (CCA, November 22, 1982). The three accused were convicted for larceny of leather jackets and suits on one date and for an attempt to steal clothing at the same store on another date. Upon appeal, the court upheld the cross-admissibility of evidence on each count, finding that they shared distinct and unusual characteristics: on both occasions, the thieves had brought with them an empty cardboard box covered by sellotape into which they intended to conceal the garments.

[72] *R. v John Wright* (1990) 90 Cr. App. R. 325 (CA).

[73] *People (DPP) v LG* [2003] 2 I.R. 517 *per* Keane C.J. (CCA).

[74] Black J. once remarked that the "naïve assumption that all prejudicial effects can be overcome by instructions to the jury ... all practising lawyers know to be unmitigated fiction": *Krulevitch v US* (1949) 336 U.S. 440 at 443. A similar sentiment may have been implicit in an observation by the Court of Criminal Appeal in *People (DPP) v Kavanagh* (July 7, 1997) to wit, that warning the jury to disregard the evidence may sometimes serve to underscore rather than diminish the effect of the inadmissible evidence (in this case, a witness' assertion in a murder trial that the accused had previously assaulted his own wife).

[75] *B v DPP* [1997] 3 I.R. 140 at 154 (HC); *cf.* para.**6–13** *et seq.* and *cf.* appendix 48.

[76] As in *Attorney-General v McCabe* [1927] I.R. 129 (CCA) and *R. v Downey* [1995] 1 Cr. App. R. 547 (CA); *cf.* para.**5–46**.

[77] As in *R. v Black* [1995] Crim. L. R. 640 (CA).

[78] [2003] 2 I.R. 517 at 525, *per* Keane C.J. (CCA).

between counts, since the trial judge had failed "to direct the jury in clear terms that they should consider the evidence in respect of the counts relating to the first complainant on the one hand and the second complainant on the other hand, separately," before proceeding to examine the evidence cumulatively. The omission to do so may have led the jury wrongly to presume that they were entitled to evaluate the evidence as one piece.

7–29 The very similarities which at first appeared to justify a joinder of trials may later, when considering the question of mutual corroboration, require the court to rule out the possibility that the evidence is misleadingly plausible or that it arises from collusive accusation against the accused. These issues were considered by the House of Lords in *R. v H.*, where the defence appealed against conviction for sexual offences committed at different times on his stepdaughter and adopted daughter.[79] The House was asked to decide how a trial judge should treat similar fact evidence from multiple complainants in the same trial where the defence has established a risk that the evidence is contaminated by collusion and other factors. Whilst recognising that combined allegations may be tainted innocently (as where the complainants discussed the matters together) or tainted deliberately (as where the complainants decided to pool or to exaggerate their allegations against the accused), the House unanimously rejected the contention that the risk alone affects the evidence's cross-admissibility or that it requires a specific *voire dire* investigation. The House reasoned, it is submitted sensibly, that matters such as the possibility of collusion are often not capable of proper estimation until all the evidence is heard at the trial, and that to require the prosecution to rule out the possibility of collusion in advance of the full trying of the issues before the jury would be to "load the scales unfairly" against "the interests of those who cannot protect themselves".[80] It would also, according to Lord Griffiths, "strike root and branch at the very reason we have jury trial".[81] Neither Lord Mustill nor Lord Griffith could envisage a situation where the prosecution would be willing to bring charges on foot of evidence so patently contaminated that its admissibility would be dubious enough to require the trial judge to conduct an initial *voire dire*.

7–30 *R. v H* instead favours the use of tailored warnings to the jury at the close of the trial. If the trial judge is satisfied that no reasonable jury could accept the evidence to be free from collusion, the jury must be directed that they can no longer consider that evidence when deciding the accused's guilt. Otherwise, if the defence has raised the risk of collusion and contamination, the judge should direct the jury to it, indicating how it might have occurred in the case, and explaining that if the jury is not satisfied that the evidence is free from contamination, they must no longer have regard to it. This approach appears consistent with Irish law. The necessity to rule out the possibility of

---

[79] [1995] 2 W.L.R. 737.
[80] *ibid*. at 753, *per* Mustill L.J.
[81] *ibid*. at 750.

collusion in the trial judge's closing directions to the jury was confirmed by Budd J. in *B v DPP*.[82]

7–31 In numerous other decisions, the courts have emphasised that where cross-admissible evidence has been challenged on grounds of collusion, and there is a "real" risk that the evidence is contaminated or that it is not "truly independent", the trial judge must not direct the jury that the evidence is capable of being mutually corroborative as between the complainants.[83] The Court of Criminal Appeal expressed a similar view in *People (DPP) v Morrissey*,[84] holding that, in cases where the accused claims the complainant has falsely accused him in collusion with another witness (in this case, the complainant's mother), the trial judge may not direct the jury that the evidence of the witnesses is capable of being mutually corroborative. In such cases, if corroboration is to be found, it must be supplied by a source of evidence independent from the witnesses alleged to have acted collusively.

VI. Evidence to Explain the Background of an Act

7–32 A distinction is sometimes drawn between evidence relevant and admissible to explain the background of an act and evidence inadmissible to show prior misconduct. The distinction was explained in the following terms by Kennedy J. in *R. v Bond*:[85]

> "The general rule [against admitting similar fact evidence] cannot be applied where the facts which constitute distinct offences are at the same time part of the transaction which is the subject of the indictment. Evidence is necessarily admissible as to acts which are so closely and inextricably mixed up with the history of the guilty act itself as to form part of one chain of relevant circumstances, and so could not be excluded in the presentment of the case before the jury without the evidence being thereby rendered unintelligible".

7–33 In *Attorney-General v Joyce and Walsh*,[86] evidence of a previous attempt by the first accused to poison the second accused's husband, and the second accused's knowledge of the plan, was deemed cross-admissible as against both accused since the prior attempt formed part of the background to the relationships of each party. The fact that a prior act occurred some time in the past is, according to Sullivan P., a matter properly affecting the weight but not admissibility of the evidence. In *Attorney-General v Fleming*, "background

---

[82] [1997] 3 I.R. 140 (HC); *cf.* para.**5–51** *et seq.* and *cf.* appendix 48.
[83] In *R. v Ananthanarayanan* [1994] 2 All E.R. 847 (CA), conviction was overturned upon this basis. The multiple complaints against the accused shared a common source, a local social services department which had solicited complaints against the accused.
[84] CCA, July 10, 1998.
[85] [1906] 2 K.B. 389 at 400.
[86] [1929] I.R. 526 (CCA) .

evidence" was similarly admitted to show the accused's previous attempt to poison his wife.[87] In *R. v Ball*,[88] evidence of previous incest between a brother and sister was admitted not to establish *mens rea* but "to establish guilty relations between the parties and the existence of a sexual passion between them as elements in proving that they had illicit connection in fact on or between the dates charged". The distinction has emerged more recently in the specific context of establishing the background history of the accused's relationship with a single complainant. In *R. v B*,[89] the Court of Appeal accepted that evidence of prior sexual assault or rape by the accused against the complainant is admissible to show the background to their relationship. The approach was affirmed in *R. v Underwood*[90] in the context of evidence showing the accused's history of violence towards his partner. In *R. v Dolan*,[91] however, the court ordered a retrial because evidence should not have been admitted in a trial for infanticide showing the accused to have a violent temper and a propensity to strike inanimate objects. The evidence was insufficiently probative and unduly prejudicial. The court wisely expressed the view that evidence of the accused's temperament should only be admitted as "background evidence" for reasons of necessity and high probative force of the evidence.

7–34 The distinction between "background facts" and "similar fact evidence" makes sense only if "background" facts are restricted to aspects of the accused's relationship with the complainant or victim of directly relevence to the offence being tried. Complications may, however, emerge in joined trials with multiple complainants, aspects of whose evidence may or may not be cross-admissible.[92] Greater clarity would be achieved by recognising the potential admissibility of this type of evidence under existing similar fact evidence rules, to show the nature and history of the accused's relationship with the complainant or deceased (to rebut the frequent assertion in defence that the association was innocent, a basis recognised by similar fact evidence rules to be relevant and admissible if sufficiently probative).

VII. CIVIL CASES

7–35 In principle, similar fact evidence rules apply in civil proceedings, although the practice is undoubtedly affected by the fact that the bulk of civil cases are now heard by judge alone.[93] For this and other reasons specific to

---

[87] [1934] I.R. 15 (CCA). The court accepted the admissibility of evidence that the accused had previously tried to poison his wife before 15 months later murdering her by blows to the head. Although there was dissimilarity in the method and performance of each act, the circumstantial fact that the accused had made a promise to marry his mistress disclosed a motive and design common to each.
[88] [1911] A.C. 47 at 71, *per* Lord Loreburn L.C. (HL).
[89] [1997] Crim. L.R. 220 (CA).
[90] [1999] Crim. L.R. 227 (CA).
[91] [2003] Crim. L.R. 41 (CA).
[92] *cf.* para.7–27 *et seq.*
[93] In *Browne v Eastern and Midland Railway Co.* (1880) 22 Q.B.D. 391 at 393, Stephen J.

the nature of criminal prosecution, the admissibility of similar fact evidence is less contentious in the civil context, and depends upon a more discretionary balancing of the probative or logical value of the evidence against the risks of fairness to the defence.[94] Thus, in *Mood Music Publishing Company Ltd. v De Wolfe Ltd.*,[95] a case where the plaintiffs sought to rebut the defence of innocent copying by advancing evidence that the defendant had infringed copyright in the past, Lord Denning M.R. considered that evidence of past similar facts may be admitted if it is "logically probative ... provided that it is not oppressive or unfair to the other side: and also that the other side has notice of it and is able to deal with it".

7–36 The civil courts often entertain dispositional evidence where called upon to consider the welfare of children and the dangers to which they may be exposed. In *Re P.*,[96] Stephen Brown L.J. ordered the removal of an infant ward of court from her family having heard evidence that her siblings had each been sexually abused. His Lordship explained that "in these cases, which are difficult and anxious, the court is not trying an allegation of a criminal offence, it is assessing the needs of the court's ward".[97]

---

found that "evidence of events similar to the one under inquiry, on account of their general similarity, is not admissible. You must not prove, *e.g.* that a particular engine driver is a careless man in order to prove that a particular accident was caused by his negligence on a particular occasion". These *dicta* were endorsed by the Court of Criminal Appeal in *People (DPP) v Shortt (No.1)* [2002] 2 I.R. 686 at 694.

[94] Examples of earlier civil cases admitting evidence of similar fact or prior misconduct include *Brown v Eastern and Midlands Railway Co* (1889) 22 Q.B.D. 391, a case of public nuisance in which evidence of prior acts of public nuisance was admitted; and *Moore v Ransome's Dock* (1898) 14 T.L.R. 539, a case where evidence of prior accidents on the dock was admitted as evidence relevant to show knowledge by the proprietors that the dock was dangerous. See also *West Midlands Passenger Executive v Singh* [1988] 2 All E.R. 873 (CA), where the court admitted evidence of an employer's history of discriminatory work practices.

[95] [1976] Ch. 119 at 127 (CA).

[96] [1987] 2 F.L.R. 467 (CA). See also *Re G. (A Minor) (Child Abuse: Standard of Proof)* [1987] 1 W.L.R. 1461. In its decision in *Smyth and Genport v Twomey* (April 8, 1997), the Supreme Court chose not to consider the wider issues of similar fact evidence in civil cases.

[97] [1987] 2 F.L.R. 467 at 471 (CA).

Further Reading

Allan, "Similar Fact Evidence and Disposition: Law, Discretion, and Admissibility" (1985) 48 M.L.R. 253.

Baker, "Once a Rapist? Motivational Evidence and Relevance in Rape Law" (1997) 110 Harv. L.J. 563.

Carter, "Forbidden Reasoning Permissible: Similar Fact Evidence a Decade after *Boardman*" (1985) 48 M.L.R. 29.

Cross, "Fourth Time Lucky—Similar Fact Evidence in the House of Lords" [1975] Crim. L.R. 62.

Elliott, "The Young Person's Guide to Similar Fact Evidence" [1983] Crim. L.R. 284, 352.

Hoffman, "Similar Facts after *Boardman*" (1975) 91 L.Q.R. 193.

Mahoney, "Similar Fact Evidence and the Standard of Proof" [1993] Crim. L.R. 185.

McEwan, "Previous Misconduct at the Crossroads: Which Way Ahead?" [2002] Crim. L.R. 180.

Mee, "Similar Fact Evidence: Accusation = Guilt?" [1991] Ir. Crim. L.J. 122.

Mee, "Similar Fact Evidence: Still Hazy after All these Years" (1994) 16 D.U.L.J. 83.

Mirfield, "Similar Facts—Makin Out?" [1987] C.L.J. 83.

Mirfield, "Proof and Prejudice in the House of Lords" (1996) 112 L.Q.R. 1.

Munday, "Comparative Law and English Law's Character Evidence Rules" (1993) 13 Oxford J.L. Studies 589.

Munday, "Similar Fact Evidence: Identity Cases and Striking Similarity" [1999] C.L.J. 45.

Murphy, "Character Evidence: the Search for Logic and Policy Continues" [1998] 2 E. & P. 71.

Nair, "Similar Fact Evidence—Prejudice and Irrelevance Revisited" [1993] Crim. L.R. 432.

Pattenden, "Similar Fact Evidence and Proof of Identity" (1996) 112 L.Q.R. 446.

Yates, "How Many Counts to an Indictment?" [1976] Crim. L.R. 428.

Zuckerman, "Similar Fact Evidence—the Unobservable Rule" (1987) 104 L.Q.R. 187.

CHAPTER 8

CROSS-EXAMINATION OF THE ACCUSED UPON BAD CHARACTER

I. Introduction 8–01
II. Parameters of Section 1(f) 8–04
III. Section 1(f)(i): Admissible Similar Fact Evidence 8–22
IV. Section 1(f)(ii): Character Put in Issue by the Defence 8–26
    The Accused's Good Character 8–26
    Imputations against the Character of the Prosecutor 8–36
V. Section 1(f)(iii): Evidence by the Accused Against a
    Co-Accused 8–61

I. INTRODUCTION

8–01 An accused who chooses to testify in his defence may not be cross-examined upon matters likely to expose his bad character or criminal record, save in the circumstances identified by s.1(f) of the Criminal Justice (Evidence) Act 1924. Prior to s.1, the accused had not been competent to testify as a witness in his own trial. The 1924 Act embraced the reforms undertaken earlier in England under the Criminal Evidence Act 1898,[1] by which the accused was for the first time permitted but not obliged to testify in his defence, and his failure to so testify could not be made the subject of comment by the prosecutor.[2] The simple reform accomplished by these provisions transformed the criminal trial into the now familiar testimonial contest between prosecution witnesses and the accused. The prohibition against cross-examination upon bad character or criminal record appears in s.1(f) of the 1924 Act as a qualification to a general rule under s.1(e) that the prosecution is entitled to cross-examine an accused who has chosen to give evidence in-chief notwithstanding that it would tend to incriminate him in the offences for which he is being tried.

---

[1] 7 Dáil Eireann, *Parliamentary Debates*, 1924, at p.2650.
[2] Criminal Justice (Evidence) Act 1924, s.1(a)–(b).

Section 1(e)

"A person charged and being a witness in pursuance of this Act may be asked any question in cross-examination notwithstanding that it would tend to criminate him as to the offence charged."

Section 1(f)

"A person charged and called as a witness in pursuance of this Act shall not be asked, and if asked shall not be required to answer, any question tending to show that he has committed or been convicted of or been charged with any offence other than that wherewith he is then charged, or is of bad character, unless—

(i) the proof that he has committed or been convicted of such other offence is admissible evidence to show that he is guilty of the offence wherewith he is then charged; or

(ii) he has personally or by his advocate asked questions of the witnesses for the prosecution with a view to establish his own good character, or has given evidence of his good character, or the nature or conduct of the defence is such as to involve imputations on the character of the prosecutor or the witnesses for the prosecution; or

(iii) he has given evidence against any other person charged with the same offence."

8–02 Section 1(f) clearly asserts that the accused shall not be asked or required to answer any question tending to show that he is of bad character or that he has committed or been convicted of or been charged with any offence other than that for which he is being tried, unless one of three situations arise during the trial, namely: (1) the information has already been admitted in-chief upon the basis that it constitutes similar fact evidence;[3] or (2) the accused has put character in issue (expressly or by implication) by asserting his own good character or by impugning the character of a prosecution witness; or (3) the accused has given evidence against a co-accused in the case.

8–03 Section 1(f) has survived as a worthy, if sometimes problematic, compromise between competing policy concerns. On the one hand, it reflects the view that the accused should not be treated as an ordinary witness when giving testimony in his own trial. In this respect, s.1(f) implicitly exempts the accused from s.6 of the Criminal Procedure Act 1865, by which witnesses may be cross-examined upon their previous convictions.[4] If the accused were

---

[3] *cf.* para.7–02.
[4] Section 6 of the 1865 Act is itself an exception to the rule governing the finality of a witness' answers to *collateral* questions (or questions relevant to credit): *cf.* para.3–13 *et seq.*

treated as an ordinary witness, he would be vulnerable to cross-examination upon all his past convictions to diminish his credibility as a witness in his own cause.[5] Bad character and similar fact evidence is notoriously prejudicial, and may be the last ounce that turns the scale against the accused.[6] The prejudicial content of the information might predictably be mishandled by the jury when deciding his guilt, leading in turn to irrational decision-making. An accused, howsoever innocent, may be deterred from telling his story under oath, due to the fear that he might do his case more damage than good if exposed to a trawl through his past offences. On the other hand, if the accused were given a complete immunity from cross-examination upon character, flowing from his privilege against self-incrimination,[7] he would be in a disproportionately better position than other witnesses.[8] Admissible similar fact evidence could not be put to him. He would have a licence to smear his accusers and any co-accused without risk of compromise under cross-examination and without sanction aside from perjury (which may be feared less than conviction for a present offence).

II. PARAMETERS OF SECTION 1(F)

8–04 Over the years following the enactment of s.1(f), the English courts resolved numerous interpretative questions, many of them addressed in the House of Lords' decision in *Jones v DPP*.[9] The House interpreted s.1(e) to permit questions directly implicating the accused in the present offence, and s.1(f) to restrict questions indirectly incriminating him by means of bad character evidence. A preferable view holds that s.1(e) permits questions directly or indirectly incriminating the accused, but that s.1(f) restricts questions whose effect is to reveal the accused's bad character or criminal record.[10]

8–05 "Tending to show" was interpreted to mean tending to reveal to the jury for the first time. According to Lord Reid: "If the obvious purpose of this proviso is to protect the accused from possible prejudice, as I think it is, then "show" must mean "reveal" because it is only a revelation of something new which could cause such prejudice".[11] The accused had been charged with the murder of a young girl. His defence of alibi—that he had been with a prostitute at the time, and had arrived home late to be reprimanded by his wife—was identical word-for-word to an explanation he gave at an earlier trial in which he had been found guilty of the rape of a young girl. The prosecution, wishing to spare his earlier victim the ordeal of testifying again, did not seek to introduce similar fact evidence of the previous rape. Under cross-examination, the accused

---

[5] *cf. R. v Flynn* [1963] 1 Q.B. 729 (CA) and para.**3–06**.
[6] *Maxwell v DPP* [1935] A.C. 309 at 323, *per* Sankey V.-C. (HL).
[7] *cf.* para.**13–80**.
[8] Heydon, *Evidence: Cases & Materials* (Butterworths, London, 1991) at p.285.
[9] [1962] A.C. 635 at 664 (HL).
[10] *R. v Miller* [1952] 2 All E.R. 667 (CA).
[11] [1962] A.C. 635 at 664 (HL).

let it slip that he had "been in trouble with the police" before. Up to this point in the cross-examination, the jury had the vague knowledge that the accused had either been charged with or convicted of an offence on an earlier occasion important enough to have been reported in the Sunday papers. Upon this basis and to show how implausible his present defence was, the trial judge permitted the prosecution to cross-examine him upon the similarity of the two alibis. His appeal against the trial judge's decision to permit s.1(f) cross-examination failed: his own evidence had revealed his criminal record to the jury, and thus he had voluntarily abandoned his shield of protection under s.1(f).

8–06 The central proposition of *Jones* is that where the jury has already been made aware of the accused's bad character, the accused may be cross-examined upon it. It rests upon a particular interpretation of "reveal" as "show", and appears consistent with s.1(f)(i), which permits the accused to be cross-examined upon similar fact evidence where earlier admitted in-chief at the trial in accordance with the relevant rules.[12] The House's application of the principle to the facts in the *Jones* decision was questionable, however. A vague admission by the accused under cross-examination was permitted to justify an unfettered cross-examination upon his criminal record for similar offences, ostensibly because his bad character had already been "revealed" to the jury. Lord Denning's dissent is arguably more consistent with the spirit and policy of s.1: "I do not think that it is open to the prosecution to throw out prejudicial hints and insinuations—from which a jury might infer that the man had been charged before—and then escape censure under the cloak of ambiguity ... It is one thing to confess to having been in trouble before. It is quite another to have it emphasised against you with devastating detail".[13] In this regard, it is to be noted that Irish law appears, from the few reported judgments addressing the parameters of s.1(f), to adopt a markedly more protective stance against exploration in the trial of the accused's bad character.[14]

8–07 A narrow approach to "tending to reveal" may be necessary to counteract any risks that an accused's criminal record has already been conveyed implicitly to the jury. Special protection may have been arranged for members of the jury, thereby creating an impression of the accused's potential dangerousness.[15] A police officer may unforeseeably have caused it to be known that photographs of the accused were retained in police files,[16] or that the accused has a criminal record,[17] or that he was in trouble with the police before.[18] Attempts ought to be made by the trial judge to reduce the prejudice thereby caused, notwithstanding that it is not necessarily the result of prosecutorial strategy. Depending upon the degree of likely prejudice, this may require a

---

[12] *cf.* para.**7–01** *et seq.*
[13] [1962] A.C. 635 at 667 (HL).
[14] *People (DPP) v McGrail* [1990] 2 I.R. 38 (CCA): *cf.* appendix 34 and para.**8–48** *et seq.*
[15] *R. v Dodd* (1981) 74 Cr. App. R. 50 (CA); *R. v Ling* [1987] Crim. L.R. 495 (CA).
[16] *R. v Wattam* (1941) 28 Cr. App. R. 80 (CA).
[17] *R. v Sutton* (1969) 53 Cr. App. R. 504 (CA).
[18] *R. v Weaver* [1968] 1 Q.B. 353 (CA).

retrial with a new jury,[19] or instead careful directions by the trial judge to the existing jury against engaging in the "forbidden reasoning" (inferring the present guilt of the accused from evidence of his past crimes).[20]

8–08 Section 1(f) prohibits, subject to exception, any questions bearing upon "any past offences the accused has committed or been convicted of or been charged with", or upon his bad character. Cross-examination pursuant to s.1(f)(i) is stated to be with respect to offences the accused has "committed" or been "convicted" of, where evidence of those offences has been admitted in the trial under "similar fact evidence" rules.[21] Whilst s.1(f)(i) permits cross-examination upon a more limited form of "similar fact evidence", it enables evidence elicited testimonially from the accused to become evidence probative of the issue in showing "that he is guilty of the offence wherewith he [is] charged". By contrast, cross-examination under s.1(f)(ii)-(iii) is not limited to criminal record, and extends to the accused's general moral reputation and disposition to lie,[22] although evidence elicited from the accused becomes evidence relevant to his lack of credit and is not probative of the issues at trial.

8–09 "Any offence" clearly includes offences committed before the accused was charged with the offence for which he is being tried. According to at least one English decision, cross-examination may extend to crimes and acts committed *after* the offence for which the accused is tried, at least to the extent that it is necessary to avoid misinterpretation of the accused's claim to an unblemished record: "If the accused endeavours to show that he is of good character when he is in fact of bad character, he presents a false view of the case, and the prosecution are not only entitled but bound to do what they can to prove to the jury that he ought not to be placed upon the high pedestal which he desires to occupy".[23] On the other hand, evidence tending to reveal the commission of offences, whether before or after the accused was charged, is evidence tending to reveal the accused's bad character, and accordingly attracts the s.1(f) shield.[24]

8–10 In *Stirland v DPP*,[25] the House of Lords interpreted the word "charged" to be limited to occasions when the accused had been "brought before a court" in respect of a criminal offence. The accused, charged with forgery, had asserted his good character by calling a witness to testify that he had never before been charged with a criminal offence. Upon this basis, the trial judge decided to allow the cross-examiner to question him about an incident when a former

---

[19] As in *R. v Tyrer, The Times*, October 13, 1988. The Court of Appeal added that the prejudice must be serious, and defence counsel should have made immediate objection to the wrongful admission of the bad character evidence.
[20] As in *R. v Ling* [1987] Crim. L.R. 495 (CA).
[21] *cf.* para.**7–01** *et seq*.
[22] So found in *Stirland v DPP* [1944] 2 All ER 13 (HL), approved in *People (Attorney-General) v Coleman* [1945] I.R. 237 at 246 (CCA).
[23] *R. v Wood* [1920] 2 K.B. 179 at 182, *per* Earl of Reading C.J. (CA).
[24] *People (Attorney-General) v Coleman* [1945] I.R. 237 (CCA).
[25] [1944] 2 All E.R. 13 (HL).

employer had accused him of forgery. Overturning conviction, the House of Lords reasoned that the incident lacked the requisite degree of relevance whilst wreaking untold prejudice for the accused. More generally, the House observed that even the most virtuous may occasionally be suspected of wrongdoing and that such evidence is not generally relevant to show bad character.

8–11 In *Maxwell v DPP*,[26] the House of Lords considered whether the words "charged" and "committed" include offences for which an accused was charged but acquitted. The accused had been tried for manslaughter in the course of procuring an abortion. After giving evidence of his good character, he was cross-examined about a previous similar charge of which he had been acquitted. Viscount Sankey concluded that the mere fact of a charge is not generally evidence of bad character but rather evidence of misfortune. Such evidence is not only irrelevant but dangerous in that it may "lead the minds of the jury astray into false issues".[27] This did not, however, mean that the word "charged" was redundant in s.1(f), or that the operability of s.1(f) was dependent upon proof that the accused committed a past crime. There would sometimes be exceptional cases where the accused said something in a previous trial that cast real doubt over something he said in a current trial, in which case the fact of the previous charge would fall to be established under cross-examination as a preliminary step.

8–12 The decisions in *Jones v DPP* and *People (Attorney-General) v Kirwan*,[28] although they each relate to previous convictions, are illustrative of the extent to which some element of the previous trial or sentence may subsequently be relevant in a later trial. In *Jones*, the accused's alibi was identical to a conversation he had detailed at an earlier trial for the rape of a schoolgirl. The similarities were judged "remarkable" and "highly relevant"[29] to show that the accused's alibi lacked credit (although cross-examination was rightly restricted to the terms of each alibi, and reference to the details of the prior conviction were tactfully avoided). In *Kirwan*, the Supreme Court upheld the admissibility of evidence showing the fact of the accused's previous criminal conviction and recent release from prison, upon the basis that it was necessary to establish the following relevant facts, in line with the principles in *Makin*:[30] (1) that the accused was found in possession of a large sum of money, which he could not have earned in the short time between his release and the murder, and which had earlier been in the deceased's possession; (2) that the deceased's body had been dismembered by a person specially skilled to do so, such as the accused, since he had learned butchery skills in prison; and (3) that on the evening of the murder, the deceased's servant boy had been put to sleep by the administration of a drug the accused had been prescribed in prison.

---

[26] [1935] A.C. 309 (HL). See also *R. v Cokar* [1960] 2 Q.B. 207 (CA).
[27] [1935] A.C. 309 at 323, *per* Viscount Sankey L.C. (HL).
[28] [1943] I.R. 279 (SC).
[29] *Jones v DPP* [1962] A.C. 635 at 664 (HL), *per* Lord Reid at 661, *per* Lord Morris at 674–80.
[30] *cf.* para.**7–04**.

8–13 The purpose of allowing cross-examination of the accused under s.1(f)(ii) and (iii) is to affect the accused's *credibility* as a witness by permitting in exceptional situations questions calculated to show that the accused is of bad *character* and thus a discredited witness in his own cause. By contrast, when the accused is cross-examined under s.1(f)(i) in relation to similar fact evidence already ruled admissible and tendered in-chief, questions may be asked that are calculated to show not only that the accused is of bad character but that his past crimes *ipso facto* suggest that he has committed the offence for which he is at present tried. The trial judge is required to explain this distinction to the jury if it arises. Failure to do so is likely to necessitate a retrial.[31]

8–14 It is sometimes proposed that the distinction between credit-relevance and issue-relevance is both meaningless and anomalous: meaningless, insofar as evidence that discredits an accused tends inevitably to affect a person's concept of the accused's guilt as charged; anomalous, given that evidence of the accused's *good* character may be accepted as evidence relevant to credit and issue.[32] Although often of enormous practical importance, the distinction has been accused of forcing juries to attempt "intellectual acrobatics" when unscrambling *post-hoc* judicial directions.[33] For this reason, where the prejudicial effect of the character evidence is likely greatly to outweigh its probative force, a trial judge should exercise his discretion to reject the evidence, rather than later seek to mitigate its prejudice by means of difficult directions when summing-up. Judicial warnings are often inadequate to undo the prejudice caused once bad character evidence has been admitted.[34] Indeed, it has been observed that "the judge's cautionary instruction may do more harm than good. It may emphasise the jury's awareness of the censured remark—as in the story, by Mark Twain, of the boy told to stand in the corner and not think of a white elephant".[35] On the other hand, in the absence of judicial direction, the jury is in danger of assuming themselves free to use the evidence as they see fit, not merely to show that the accused may be an unreliable witness, but further that his past crimes make it more probable that he is guilty of the crimes as charged.[36]

---

[31] e.g. *People (Attorney-General) v Bond* [1966] I.R. 214 (CA); *Murdoch v Taylor* [1965] 1 All E.R. 406 (HL).
[32] cf. para.**8–28**; Pattendon, "The Purpose of Cross-Examination under s.1(f) of the Criminal Evidence Act 1898" (1982); Munday, "Stepping Beyond the Bounds of Credibility" (1986).
[33] *R. v Watts* [1983] 3 All E.R. 101 at 104, *per* Lane L.C.J. (CA). According to Mustill L.J. in *R. v Wright* (1990) 90 Cr. App. R. 325 at 333 (CA), "the distinction between matters going directly to the primary issues and those going to credit of those who give evidence on the issue is hard to operate in practice, and possibly unsound in theory".
[34] On which, see: Doob and Kirshenbaum, "Some Empirical Evidence on the Effect of Section 12 of the Canada Evidence Act upon an Accused" (1972) 15 Crim. L.Q. 88; and Wissler and Saks, "On the Inefficacy of Limiting Instructions: When Jurors Use Prior Conviction Evidence to Decide on Guilt" (1985) 9 *Law and Human Behavior* 37.
[35] *US v Antonelli Fireworks Co.* (1946) 155 F. 2d 631 at 656, *per* Jerome Frank J.
[36] *People (Attorney-General) v Bond* [1966] I.R. 214 (CCA).

8–15 In *R. v Watts*,[37] the Court of Appeal attempted to limit cross-examination to previous convictions for dishonesty, upon the basis that s.1(f) evidence is relevant to establish the accused's discreditable nature, by contrast with similar fact evidence admitted in-chief as evidence probative of his present guilt. The decision in *Watts* acknowledges that evidence of past criminal offences identical to the offence under trial is often devastatingly prejudicial. In *Watts*, the accused was a man of subnormal intelligence accused of indecent assault in a case where identity was at issue; the evidence sought to be introduced was of previous convictions for sexual offences. Lord Lane C.J. reasoned as follows:

> "The jury in the present case was charged with deciding the guilt or innocence of a man against whom an allegation of indecent assault on a woman was made. They were told that he had previous convictions for indecent assaults of a more serious kind on young girls. They were warned that such evidence was not to be taken as making it more likely that he was guilty of the offence charged, which it seems it plainly did, but only as affecting his credibility, which it almost certainly did not. ... The direction was, of itself, sound in law but in the circumstances of this case it would have been extremely difficult, if not practically impossible, for the jury to have done what the judge was suggesting. The prejudice which the appellant must have suffered in the eyes of the jury when it was disclosed that he had previous convictions for offences against young children could hardly have been greater. The probative value of the convictions, on the sole issue on which they were admissible was, at best, slight".

8–16 *Watts* has since been qualified by the principle of indivisibility of character, affirmed by the Court of Appeal in *R v Powell*.[38] According to this principle, all convictions are relevant to credit, although the trial judge should exercise discretion to exclude the evidence where it would be "fraught with results which immeasurably outweigh the result of questions put by the defence and which make a fair trial of the accused almost impossible".[39] Under *Powell*, if one is being tried for theft, one may be cross-examined in relation to previous convictions for trespass or rape, or indeed in relation generally to bad reputation. The fact that the previous offences are identical or highly similar to the current offence is a factor that may, but not must, cause the trial judge to disallow the cross-examination. This may be hard to reconcile with the rationale

---

[37] [1983] 3 All E.R. 101 (CCA). This distinction was upheld in *R. v Lawrence* [1995] Crim. L.R. 815 (CA) where conviction was quashed upon the basis that the jury might have been led to believe that the accused's previous convictions established a propensity to commit crime, whereas under s.1(f) cross-examination upon previous convictions is relevant to the accused's credit as a witness.

[38] (1985) 82 Cr. App. R. 167 (CA). Previously recognised in *R. v Samuel* (1956) 40 Cr. App. R. 8 at 11, *per* Goddard L.C.J. (CA): "[I]f a prisoner puts his character in issue, he puts his whole character in issue, not such parts as may be convenient to him, leaving out the inconvenient parts".

[39] Approved in *R. v McLeod* [1994] 3 All E.R. 257 (CA).

underpinning similar fact evidence rules. The very evidence that the courts must be vigilant to exclude may suddenly assume centre-stage when the accused is deemed to have lost his protected status. The only formal difference is that its admission *via* cross-examination under s.1(f)(ii) and (iii) bears only upon his credibility as a witness, although the trial judge's warning to that end may have nominal effect only.

8–17 The Court of Appeal stressed in *Powell* that where the previous offences are of a highly similar nature, and therefore carry greater prejudicial effect for the accused, the trial judge must take extra care to warn the jury that cross-examination upon the past offences is relevant to the credibility of the accused as a witness and not to proof of the facts at issue. In *R. v Davinson-Jenkins*,[40] the inability of judicial directions to mitigate the enormous prejudice caused by reference to identical past convictions resulted in a retrial. The accused, a well-educated career woman, had been charged with shoplifting at a chemist. She was cross-examined upon a string of previous convictions for shoplifting. The Court of Appeal concluded it was unrealistic to imagine that the jury, after judicial direction, could put the fact of those convictions to the back of their mind when considering the accused's guilt. The highly similar nature of the previous convictions made it extremely unlikely that the jury would not interpret that evidence to establish propensity, and this was a prejudice that no amount of judicial direction could unravel.

8–18 Where the offence is clearly of a minor nature, the trial judge ought to balance the likely prejudice against the probative worth of the evidence, and ought to exercise discretion to disallow cross-examination unless the prosecution shows good cause why it is specifically appropriate in the context of the case. Counsel ought to obtain the leave of the trial judge in all but the clearest scenarios, given the danger that a conviction will be quashed subsequently due to improper cross-examination.

8–19 Cross-examination ought to be upon *relevant* issues only. Character may be a fact at issue,[41] in which case character evidence is highly relevant to the determination of the trial or hearing. In most cases, however, character is not directly relevant, and the purpose of introducing the evidence is to discredit the accused's testimony (by showing him to be of bad character) or in exceptional cases indirectly to infer his present guilt (by reference to prior guilt). As explained by Viscount Sankey L.C. in *Maxwell v DPP*: "When it is sought to justify a question it must not only be brought within the terms of the permission, but also must be capable of justification according to the general rules of evidence and in particular must satisfy the test of relevance".[42] In this light, evidence that the accused was previously charged but acquitted for a

---

[40] [1997] Crim. L.R. 816 (CA).
[41] In *Hill v Examiner* [2001] 4 I.R. 219 (SC), evidence of the plaintiff's bad character was considered relevant to establish the extent of his loss to reputation in defamation proceedings.
[42] [1935] A.C. 309 at 319 (HL).

similar offence is irrelevant *per se* upon the basis that factually it does not tend to prove that the accused lacks credibility. Cross-examination under s.1(f) is often in response to the accused's decision to put character in issue, whether his own or that of a prosecution witness or co-accused. The questioning may, however, seek validly to establish relevant facts whose *indirect* effect is to suggest the accused's bad character (as in *Jones* and *Kirwan*),[43] although in this situation, a higher degree of relevance is normally required to justify the potential prejudice to the accused.

8–20 The test of relevance would seem to apply equally where cross-examination *directly* concerns the accused's character within the parameters of s.1(f). This is evident in decisions emphasising the need to establish that such cross-examination is necessary to rebut a particular claim made by the accused in-chief, for instance that he is of particularly good character. The relevance requirement, intended to be protective of the accused, is further evident in decisions asserting that where s.1(f) sanctions cross-examination upon the fact of prior conviction, it is not normally permissible to admit, or to interrogate the accused upon, the *details* or particulars of those crimes, unless to establish relevant facts whose importance outweighs the likely prejudice to the accused.[44] In *R. v France*,[45] conviction was overturned upon the basis that the trial judge had wrongly permitted character cross-examination to stray beyond legitimate bounds in revealing the *detail* as opposed to the fact of the accused's previous convictions. The court's decision was founded on the distinction between cross-examination upon credibility (for which the fact but not the details of conviction are relevant) and cross-examination upon a fact at issue (for which the details of the conviction may, depending on the case, be relevant).

8–21 The accused may lose his shield of protection from cross-examination upon bad character, if any of the following three events occur: (1) the evidence has already been tendered in-chief as admissible similar fact evidence; (2) the accused has put his own good character in issue, or has impugned the character of the prosecution or one of its witnesses; or (3) the accused has given evidence against a co-accused in the case.

III. Section 1(f)(i): Admissible Similar Fact Evidence

8–22 Cross-examination of the accused pursuant to s.1(f)(i) is not dependent upon a loss of the shield arising from the conduct of the defence. If the accused elects to testify, he is exposed to cross-examination upon evidence admitted in-chief by the prosecution in compliance with "similar fact evidence" rules,[46] where such evidence proves that the accused "committed" or was "convicted"

---

[43] *cf.* para.**8–12**.
[44] *R. v Khan* [1991] Crim. L.R. 51 (CA).
[45] [1979] Crim L.R. 48 (CA).
[46] *cf.* para.**7–01** *et seq.*

of other criminal offences. Section 1(f)(i) ensures the continued admissibility of "similar fact evidence", where it establishes the *fact* of prior criminal offence, throughout the trial. The accused may not be cross-examined, under the s.1(f)(i) exception, with respect to offences for which he was charged but not convicted, nor upon his bad character, disposition, or propensity.

8–23 A further point of distinction is that evidence established under cross-examination pursuant to s.1(f)(i) is evidence that may be probative of the issue. It becomes evidence the jury are entitled to consider when determining proof of the accused's guilt. By contrast, evidence admitted under ss.1(f)(ii)–(iii) is admissible as evidence relevant to credit, tending to establish the accused's character and, more broadly, whether or not he is worthy of belief.

8–24 Section 1(f)(i) might be taken implicitly to envisage cross-examination upon evidence already presented to the court as part of the prosecution's evidence in-chief—where deemed admissible by the trial judge after specific consideration in a *voire dire*, and where limited to proof of his criminal record. Although this is the typical sequence, s.1(f)(i) is by no means confined to it. Under *Makin*, similar fact evidence may be admitted where relevant to rebut a defence. Where the true nature of the defence has become apparent during the accused's evidence in-chief but not before, the prosecution may seek to tender similar fact evidence in rebuttal. The first time the jury hears this evidence, then, may be during the accused's cross-examination.

8–25 This scenario occurred in *R. v Anderson*.[47] The appellant and her co-accused had been identified as members of the IRA and charged with planning to plant a number of bombs in and around London. Her defence, expressed from the witness box and unanticipated by the prosecution, was that she had instead been attempting to smuggle prison escapees from Ireland to Denmark. To rebut this live explanation, the prosecution sought and was granted leave to show that she had been "wanted" by the police in connection with other offences, and that it was therefore unlikely that she would have been chosen to assist other "wanted" persons eluding the authorities. Her appeal against conviction failed before the Court of Appeal. Lord Lane C.J. put it as follows:

> "[Subject to the *Makin* principles,] if the prosecution know that a particular defence is going to be advanced, they may (subject to the judge's discretion) call evidence to rebut it as part of their own substantive case even if that tends to show the commission of other crimes. The accused can plainly then be cross-examined about the matter. If the prosecution do not know of the defence in advance, then they may call evidence to rebut it and the accused can then be recalled, if that is desired, to deal with the rebutting evidence. The judge in the present case—wisely, the evidence not being in dispute—allowed the somewhat laborious process to be short-circuited. The result however was just as much in accordance

---

[47] [1988] Q.B. 678 at 685–89 (CA).

with authority [and the Act of 1924] as if the procedure had been carried out *in extenso*".

IV. SECTION 1(F)(II): CHARACTER PUT IN ISSUE BY THE DEFENCE

The Accused's Good Character

8–26 The defence may choose specifically to assert the accused's good character—by written pleading, by calling "character witnesses", or by oral submissions to the effect. When it does so, character becomes an issue in the trial which the prosecution is entitled to rebut by evidence revealing the accused's bad character. Although technically it is evidence going to credit only, good character evidence has the implicit effect of inviting the jury to infer innocence. It is thus right that the court has the opportunity to hear the other side of the story. This is the "tit for tat" element implicit in s.1(f)(ii).

8–27 The founding case of *R. v Rowton*[48] adopted the view that character evidence (whether good or bad) was limited to the accused's general reputation, as was evidence tendered in rebuttal. The principle was upheld in a modern setting in *R. v Redgrave*.[49] According to Cockburn C.J., the facility to tender good character evidence arose not from a sense of the relevance of such evidence (since it is irrelevant to show innocence, just as bad character evidence is generally irrelevant to show guilt), but rather, "from the fairness of our laws ... [as] an anomalous exception to the general rule". In answer to the charge that he had "persistently importuned for an immoral purpose"—specifically that he had masturbated before undercover policemen in a public urinal—the accused sought to admit evidence tending to show that his sexual proclivity was heterosexual. The puported evidence was five bundles of love letters addressed to girlfriends, and various photographs of him in a romantic posture with women. In an attempt to restrict the extent to which an accused could tender such evidence in future cases, Lawton L.J. made the following observations. The practice at common law of permitting an accused to testify that he had enjoyed a stable monogamous life with his wife or partner arose not from an accused's right but from judicial indulgence. In the instant case, the offence did not discriminate on grounds of sexuality, so strictly speaking the evidence was irrelevant. More generally, the learned judge commented that it "may well be that in many cases, perhaps in most cases, those who have homosexual dispositions and commit homosexual acts, do not have much inclinations towards heterosexual activity, but this is not always so. It is a matter of both history and judicial experience that many who commit homosexual acts also indulge in heterosexual activity".[50] According to the rule in *Rowton*, "the accused could do no more than say, or call witnesses to prove, that he was not by general reputation the kind of young man who would

---

[48] (1865) Le. & Ca. 520.
[49] (1982) 74 Cr. App. R. 10 (CA).
[50] *ibid.* at 13.

have behaved in the kind of way that the [prosecution] alleged".[51] The virtues of the rule were, in his opinion, demonstrated in the case—it was against the public interest to permit an accused to testify to his sexual intimacy with various women, or to encourage a climate where former partners could be compelled to testify to confirm whether or not they had had sexual intercourse with the accused.

8–28 In cases where the accused's assertion of good character has gone unchallenged by the prosecution, the accused is entitled to have the issue put to the jury and adequately dealt with in the trial judge's summing-up. The English courts have recently begun to require a specific judicial direction at the close of the trial, indicating the relevance of good character evidence. In *R. v Berrada*,[52] the Court of Appeal directed that trial judges should direct the jury that a person of good character might be less likely to lie in court or to have committed a criminal offence as alleged. Waterhouse J. considered it preferable that the trial judge explain the use to which good character evidence may properly be put, namely that it may be relevant both to questions of credit and questions of issue, but that it is "primarily relevant to the question of [the accused's] *credibility*" as a witness.[53] The judge seemed to regard reference to credit-relevance as obligatory and reference to issue-relevance (that a good character makes it less likely the accused committed the crime) as preferable.[54]

8–29 The view that good character evidence is potentially relevant both to credit and issue logically entails that the accused who asserts his good character may in turn lose his s.1(f) shield and expose himself to cross-examination upon evidence of bad character with a view not only to discredit the accused as a witness, but further to infer his present guilt by reference to past crimes and offences. Lord Goddard C.J. seemed to accept this as inevitable: "It is very difficult to see how if it is permissible to cross-examine a prisoner with regard to convictions, for instance, if he is a thief and he is cross-examined upon previous convictions of larceny, the jury is not, in effect, being asked to say: 'The prisoner is just the sort of man who will commit these crimes and therefore it is highly probable he did'".[55]

8–30 By *R. v Vye*,[56] the good character direction had become mandatory in applicable cases. The Court of Appeal extended it to cases in which the accused

---

[51] *ibid.* at 15.
[52] (1990) 91 Cr. App. R. 131 (CA): conviction was quashed due to non-direction upon good character. See also *R. v Bryant and Oxley* (1978) 67 Cr. App. R. 157, [1978] 2 All E.R. 689 (CA), which proposes that the trial judge should explain how good character evidence is relevant not only to bolster the accused's credibility as a witness, but also to show that because the accused exhibited a good character up to the present, it is less likely he committed the crime as alleged: applied in *R. v Cohen* (1990) 91 Cr. App. R. 124 at 129 (CA).
[53] (1990) 91 Cr. App. R. 131 at 133 (CA) (emphasis added).
[54] So interpreted in *R. v Cohen* (1990) 91 Cr. App. R. 125 at 130 (CA).
[55] *R. v Samuel* (1956) 40 Cr. App. R. 8 at 12 (CA).
[56] [1993] 3 All E.R. 241 (CA).

chooses not to testify but instead relies upon pre-trial exculpatory statements, and further to joined trials, even if a good character direction for one accused inevitably suggests that the other accused is of bad character. In *R. v Aziz*,[57] the House of Lords unanimously sanctioned the Court of Appeal's preference in *Vye* for a mandatory "good character direction", and it agreed that this direction should be relevant both to show credibility of the accused and to establish his propensity not to commit the offence with which he is charged. Lord Steyn explained this development as follows:

> "[I]n modern practice a judge almost invariably reminds the jury of the principal points of the prosecution case. At the same time he must put the defence case before the jury in a fair and balanced way. Fairness requires that the judge should direct the jury about good character because it is evidence of probative significance. Leaving it entirely to the discretion of judges to decide whether to give directions on good character led to inconsistency and to repeated appeals".[58]

8–31 The House made it clear that the accused was entitled to a full good character direction whenever it was the case that he had a "clean record"—notwithstanding a decision on his part not to testify or the fact that he mounted a "cut throat defence" implicating a co-accused, both occurrences in *Aziz*. Where the accused has made exculpatory statements, they become evidence in the case, and therefore the credibility of the maker of the statement, as well as the likelihood of his committing the offence, are matters of evidential significance to be considered by the jury.

8–32 By way of exception to the mandatory rule, the House was prepared to recognise that the rule might not apply where an accused without previous criminal convictions is shown beyond doubt to have been guilty of serious criminal behaviour similar to the offence with which he is charged: "A sensible criminal justice system should not compel a judge to go through the charade of giving directions in accordance with *R. v Vye* in a case where the accused's claim to good character is spurious".[59]

8–33 This transformation of previous judicial indulgence to fixed mandatory direction, although founded intuitively upon fair play, is not necessarily a wise direction to pursue, particularly in England where excessive categorisation of evidentiary directions and warnings has already been known to generate needless appeals. Munday criticises the development for equating "the absence of tangible evidence discrediting an accused with evidence positively enhancing his standing in the eyes of a tribunal of fact".[60] A more workable template was approved by the New Zealand Court of Appeal in *Falealilt*.[61] On the one

---

[57] [1995] 3 All E.R. 149 (HL).
[58] *ibid.* at 156.
[59] *ibid.* at 158.
[60] Munday, "What Constitutes Good Character?" [1997] Crim. L.R. 247 at 249.
[61] [1996] 3 N.Z.L.R. 664 (CA).

hand, the court accepted the need for a mandatory good character direction in cases that attracted it. On the other hand, it rejected the view that the direction was necessary in all cases where the accused is shown not to have a criminal record. Positive evidence is required to show that the accused is of good character and therefore deserving of a good character direction. The court also favoured a non-formulaic direction: "because of the variety in the circumstances in which the need will arise, the direction will no doubt be tailored to meet those circumstances".[62]

8–34 In the decisions, testimonial assertions by the accused that he is a religious man[63] or that he has a clean record has proved sufficient assertion of good character for the purpose of exposure to bad character cross-examination under s.1(f)(ii).[64] Mere repudiation of the charges does not by itself amount to an assertion of good character under s.1(f)(ii), nor is reference by the accused during his evidence to the fact that he has taken the oath.[65] The s.1(f) shield is not lost when a different witness for the defence asserts the good character of the accused without being asked to do so by defence counsel,[66] nor where the good character evidence is given in-chief by a prosecution witness or under cross-examination by the defence.[67] This approach protects the accused from exposure to a highly prejudicial line of questioning merely because unplanned remarks were inadvertently made about his good character. If, however, the accused calls witnesses for the purposes of testifying to his good character, questions relevant to his character may be put to him.

---

[62] *ibid.* at 667.
[63] In *R. v Ferguson* (1909) 2 Cr. App. R. 250, an assertion that the accused was a "regular attender at mass" was interpreted to put his good character in issue.
[64] In *R. v Coulman* (1927) 20 Cr. App. R. 106, defence counsel had asserted the accused was a "family man in regular work". By contrast, in *R. v Stronach* [1988] Crim. L.R. 48 (CA), where the accused was charged with knowingly dealing with goods for which excise duty had not been paid, an incidental reference to the fact that the accused was a married man and in the employ of London Transport was deemed insufficient to expose his character to interrogation. His conviction, since it was secured after disclosure of his previous convictions for evasion of import taxes, was quashed. The distinction would seem to be based on the difference between *asserting* good character and simply giving an account of the events including their background. This was evident in *Malindi v The Queen* [1967] 1 A.C. 439 (PC). Charged with a conspiracy to commit acts of violence, the accused gave evidence of various clandestine meetings where he had spoken out against the use of violence in the group's campaign. Lord Morris of Borth-y-Gest (at 453) reasoned as follows: "He gave his version of events and of conversations. He did no more. He did not, independently of giving his account of what had actually happened and of what has actually been said, assert that he was a man of good character".
[65] *R. v Robinson* [2001] Crim. L.R. 478 (CA), where the court also considered that the accused had not asserted his good character to the requisite degree by brandishing a bible in his hands whilst giving testimony (which the trial judge had wrongly considered to be a cynical ploy sufficient to expose him to cross-examination upon bad character).
[66] See *R. v Redd* [1923] 1 K.B. 104 (CA). The accused did not attempt to give evidence of his good character. A witness, who had been called to produce letters, volunteered information of the good character of the accused from the witness box. Upon appeal, it was decided that the trial judge had erred in permitting s.1(f) cross-examination in these circumstances.
[67] *Malindi v R.* [1967] 1 A.C. 439 (PC).

8–35 In *People (DPP) v Ferris*,[68] the Court of Criminal Appeal was called upon to interpret the following words in s.1(f)(ii): "where he has personally or by his advocate asked questions of the witnesses for the prosecution with a view to establishing his own good character, or has given evidence of his good character". According to Fennelly J., the accused's shield was not necessarily lost where the defence had called witnesses who at some point in their testimony referred to his good character. In the case, two aunts of the complainant had been called as witnesses for the defence, and they testified that they had left their own boys in the company of the accused on occasion and that it had given rise to no difficulties or complaints. In these circumstances, the prosecution was not entitled to recall the accused for the purpose of cross-examination upon bad character and criminal record. The prosecution was entitled instead to call other witnesses to rebut the defence's claim of good character (subject to the similar fact evidence rules).

Imputations against the Character of the Prosecutor

8–36 The second limb of s.1(f)(ii) is similarly founded upon the "tit for tat" rationale, exposing the accused to character cross-examination where "the nature or conduct of the defence is such as to involve imputations upon the character of the prosecutor or the witnesses for the prosecution". Lord Pearce put it that: "If the accused is seeking to persuade the jury that the prosecutor behaved like a knave, then the jury should know the character of the man who makes these accusations, so that it may judge fairly between them instead of being in the dark as to one of them".[69]

8–37 At its simplest, the provision exposes the accused to an interrogation of his own character whenever he has besmirched the character of a witness for the prosecution in an attempt to devalue the evidence levelled against him. In determining whether or not the accused's testimony has the effect of casting aspersions upon another witness' character, the court will engage predominantly in an objective assessment of its actual effect.[70] The findings of fact on this point may be expected to fluctuate according to the sensibilities of the day. In *People (Attorney-General) v Coleman*,[71] where the accused ultimately was convicted of criminal abortion and sentenced to 15 years of penal servitude, he was deemed to have made sufficient imputation after claiming that the prosecution witness in respect of whom the charges were brought had used contraceptives contrary to Catholic teaching, and that she had conspired with her husband to make false accusations against the accused in an attempt to deflect attention from their own guilt.

---

[68] CCA, June 10, 2002.
[69] *Selvey v DPP* [1970] A.C. 304 at 353 (HL).
[70] In *R. v Owen* (1986) 83 Crim. App. R. 100, the Court of Appeal considered it was immaterial that defence counsel had done his best to avoid making the imputations, since the effect of the line of questioning had to be judged objectively as a question of fact.
[71] [1945] I.R. 237 (CA).

8–38 The most divisive application of s.1(f)(ii) is to imputations made against police officers involved in the investigation and prosecution of the offence. It is rightly acknowledged that the mere entering of a non-guilty plea—although it may *imply* that those against him lie—ought not to be treated as an imputation sufficient to put his own character in issue. The extent to which an accused may further challenge the bona fides of the prosecution's allegations without necessarily exposing himself to a prejudicial interrogation of character, is naturally a matter of grave practical concern to the criminal trial. The Irish courts have consciously diverged from the English authorities on this issue.[72] Although English case law has been for the most part piece-meal and unprincipled, usefully for our purposes, there has been an abundance and variety of reported cases.

8–39 Prior to the House of Lords' consolidating decision in *Selvey v DPP*,[73] the following shifts could be discerned. In *R. v Rouse*,[74] it was decided that merely to call one's accuser "a liar" is insufficient "imputation", since this allegation is in real terms a denial (albeit forcibly) of the charges: "Merely to deny a fact alleged by the prosecution is not necessarily to make an attack upon the character of the prosecution or his witnesses. Such a denial is necessary and inevitable in every case where a prisoner goes into the witness-box, and is nothing more than a traverse of the truth of an allegation made against him; to add in cross-examination that the prosecutor is a liar is merely an emphatic mode of denial, and does not affect its essential quality".[75] On the other hand, in *R. v Rappolt*,[76] the accused's assertion that the witness was such a "horrible liar" that his own brother would not speak to him was construed—perhaps by dint of its additional detail—as an attack upon the "general character" of the witness sufficient to put the accused's character in issue.

8–40 In *R. v Preston*,[77] the accused claimed, incidentally to his defence, that the identification parade had been improperly tampered with by a police inspector testifying for the prosecution. The Court of Appeal reasoned that it is implicit in s.1(f)(ii) "that if the defence is so conducted, or the nature of the defence is such as to involve the proposition that the jury ought not to believe the prosecutor or one of the witnesses for the prosecution on the ground that his conduct—not his evidence in the case, but his conduct outside the evidence given by him—makes him an unreliable witness ... it then becomes admissible to cross-examine the prisoner as to his antecedents and character".[78] In the case, the allegation of improper conduct was "very near the line", but not enough to expose the accused to cross-examination upon bad character. In light of the fact that the identification parade had failed to produce a positive

---

[72] *People (DPP) v McGrail* [1990] 2 I.R. 38 (CCA): *cf.* appendix 34 and para.**8–48** *et seq.*
[73] [1970] A.C. 304 (HL).
[74] [1904] 1 K.B. 184 (C.C.R.).
[75] *ibid.* at 187, *per* Darling J.
[76] (1911) 6 Cr. App. R. 156 (CA).
[77] [1909] 1 K.B. 568 (CA).
[78] *ibid.* at 575, *per* Channell J.

result, and that the accused's imputation had not formed part of the "nature and conduct of the defence" but was more in the nature of an ad hoc, ill-considered remark from the witness box, s.1(f)(ii) did not operate to penalise him by exposure to cross-examination upon character.

8–41 The Court of Appeal temporarily distanced itself from these refinements when it reconsidered the issue in *R. v Hudson*.[79] Lord Alverstone C.J. asserted that it was encumbent upon the court to adopt a strict literal interpretation of the section, and that the words "unless the nature or conduct of the defence is such as to involve imputations" must be given an ordinary interpretation. It was "not legitimate to qualify the words by adding or inserting 'unnecessarily,' or 'unjustifiably,' or 'for purposes other than that of developing the defence,' or other similar words".[80] *Hudson* was subsequently qualified in the context of rape cases by the Court of Appeal's decision in *R. v Turner*,[81] holding that the accused was free to claim that the complainant consented to the act without placing himself in peril of cross-examination upon character, even where to do so implied that the witness was a liar or was sexually active or promiscuous.[82] Humphrey J. rightly recognised that times have changed, and that whereas calling another person a liar was once insulting enough to prompt a duel, it had become a commonplace assertion in courts of law as a matter of adversarial tactic, effectively "upping the ante" of proof required by the prosecution. Given that in rape cases there are three vital facts at issue—that of sexual intercourse, lack of consent, and identity of the rapist—it is important to safeguard the accused's right broadly to deny the charges. Humphreys J. envisaged that the accused could make further imputations so long as the questions and the evidence are directed to the facts at issue, here the complainant's consent. The questions asked under cross-examination had related to her conduct throughout the sexual act, and had not attempted to express or imply that the complainant was promiscuous, a situation the judge implied would activate s.1(f)(ii).

8–42 Some further inroads were achieved in *R. v Flynn*,[83] where the court reverted to the principle of discretion: that at the end of the day, the trial judge exercises discretion to allow or disallow cross-examination upon the basis that an imputation has been made against the prosecution. In the case, the

---

[79] [1912] 2 K.B. 464 (CA).
[80] *ibid.* at 471.
[81] [1944] K.B. 463 (CA).
[82] *R. v Turner* was approved in *R. v Selvey* [1970] A.C. 305 at 337 (HL) by Dilhorne V.C. upon the basis that even though the allegation of consent necessarily makes imputations against the character of the prosecution witness, it is essentially a traverse or denial of an issue raised by the prosecution. *Turner* was applied in *R. v Krausz* (1973) 57 Cr. App. Rep. 466 (CA) to permit evidence tending to show that the complainant was of loose morals, upon the basis that the evidence was relevant to establish consent. The decision was based upon the view that an accused can attack the complainant's character without thereby subjecting his own character to attack, and that this includes the freedom to scrutinise the complainant's sexual history. Given the changes to this area of the law (*cf.* para.**3–24** *et seq.*), the decision is of doubtful authority now.
[83] [1963] 1 Q.B. 729 (CA).

accused was charged with robbing another person of a sum of money in a public lavatory, which the accused claimed was "hush money" the other had given him after his indecent overtures were rebuffed. Under cross-examination, counsel for the accused suggested that the other party had made the homosexual advances, and in consequence the accused was cross-examined upon his character and previous convictions. Upon appeal, the Court of Criminal Appeal concluded that the imputations were sufficient to entitle the trial judge to consider allowing the cross-examination, but that the trial judge should have exercised his discretion to disallow it, and trial judges should do so in all cases where "the very nature of the defence *necessarily* involves an imputation against a prosecution witness or witnesses".[84]

8–43 Despite the qualifications to *Hudson*, the English courts had embarked upon a view of s.1(f)(ii) that seriously restricted the grounds of defence open to accused persons anxious to exclude evidence of their previous offences from the trial. In each of the following illustrative cases, the accused was exposed to cross-examination upon character and record: in *R. v Cook*[85] because he claimed that the police had induced him to confess by threatening to charge his wife; in *R. v Clark*[86] because he claimed that the police had dictated the confession and forced him to sign (which the court interpreted as an allegation that the statement had been concocted, and therefore constituted an attack upon the general character and conduct of the police inspector); and in *R. v Billings*[87] because he claimed that the police had actively suppressed evidence in the case.

8–44 Presented with the opportunity in *Selvey v DPP*,[88] the House of Lords embarked upon a full review of the law in a decision that became the leading authority in England. The accused's defence to the charge of buggery was as follows. The complainant had approached him, telling him that he had already committed buggery that day with another man for £1, and that he could do the same with the accused; after the accused declined the offer, the complainant planted indecent photos on him. The House upheld the trial judge's decision to allow cross-examination upon the accused's previous convictions for homosexual offences then on the statute books, and reasoned as follows:

8–45 The House unanimously rejected the submission that s.1(f)(ii) ought to be interpreted in a "benevolent" or protective light with respect to the accused. Affirming *Hudson*, the court reasoned that the section must be given its "ordinary natural meaning".[89] According to this approach, only the "traversing" or "mere denial" (including emphatic denials) of the prosecution's charges

---

[84] *ibid.* at 737, *per* Slade J. (emphasis added).
[85] [1959] 2 Q.B. 340 (CA).
[86] [1955] 2 Q.B. 469 at 477, *per* Goddard L.C.J. (CA), citing *R. v Preston* [1909] 1 K.B. 568 at 575 (CA).
[87] [1961] V.R. 127 (CA).
[88] [1970] A.C. 304 (HL).
[89] *ibid.* at 355, per Pearce L.J.

preserves the accused's protection from cross-examination upon character and record.[90] This was otherwise in the instant case where the accused made imputations that were "additional to a denial" of the charges and a blackening of the character of a prosecution witness.[91] Dilhorne V.C. took the view that cross-examination under s.1(f)(ii) was admissible even where imputations were necessary to enable the accused to establish his defence, and especially where the imputation referred to the reliability of the prosecution witness independently of the evidence he had given.

8–46 Each of the judges in *Selvey* counterbalanced his finding on this first issue by acknowledging that the trial judge retains a discretion to disallow cross-examination upon character or criminal record even though the accused has been deemed to lose his shield.[92] To Lord Guest, this discretion "springs from the inherent power of the judge to control the trial before him and to see that justice is done in fairness to the accused".[93] According to Lord Hodson, it is in the exercise of this discretion—rather than in the interpretation of s.1(f)(ii)—that the court ought to show benevolence towards the accused, and that the trial judge might for instance decide to refuse cross-examination where the imputations are "of little weight or of relatively minor significance in proportion to the character of the accused as revealed by his record".[94] This perspective has not proved popular. Jurists have tended to view *Selvey* less as an advocate of the discretion-based model than of freer cross-examination of the accused upon criminal record and bad character. Mirfield,[95] for instance, draws a line between *Selvey* and the *dicta* of Lord Devlin earlier in *Jones v DPP*,[96] to wit: "If a witness cannot be cross-examined to test the veracity and accuracy of his evidence in-chief, he cannot be cross-examined at all". This, according to Mirfield, compromises the "no stymie principle" which has antecedents in the English common law and according to which neither prosecution and defence should be hampered when attempting to cross-examine a witness with a view to establishing that he has lied under oath.

8–47 The Irish decisions have consciously adopted an interpretation of s.1(f)(ii) that is benevolent and protective of the accused. This was first suggested in *Attorney-General v O'Shea*,[97] where Kennedy C.J. decided that

---

[90] The English Court of Appeal has since accepted that where a prosecution witness given two conflicting versions of events, a challenge to that witness' truthfulness does not necessarily go beyond emphatic denial of the charges: *R. v Desmond* [1999] Crim. L.R. 313 (CA).
[91] *ibid.* at 352, *per* Guest L.J.
[92] This follows the dominant view that the trial judge is not obliged to permit cross-examination upon character or record where s.1(f)(ii) permits it: *R. v Christie* [1914] A.C. 545 (HL); *Stirland v DPP* [1944] A.C. 315 (HL); *Jones v DPP* [1962] A.C. 631 (HL). A contrary view had been favoured in *R. v Fletcher* (1913) 9 Cr. App. R. 53 at 56 (CA).
[93] [1970] A.C. 304 at 352 (HL).
[94] *ibid.* at 348.
[95] Mirfield, "The Argument from Consistency for Overruling *Selvey*" [1991] C.L.J. 490.
[96] [1962] A.C. 631 at 708 (HL).
[97] [1931] I.R. 713 at 723 (CCA).

"legitimate cross-examination, however severe, is not ... such a conduct of the defence as to involve imputations upon the character of the witnesses for the prosecution". Sufficient imputations were, however, made in *People (Attorney-General) v Coleman*,[98] where the accused claimed that a detective sergeant was in a conspiracy with business rivals of his, and that the conspirators had concocted evidence in an attempt to keep him out of business. In deciding that the accused had impugned the witness' character sufficiently to put his own character in issue, Sullivan C.J. was influenced by the fact that "the proper conduct of the defence did not necessitate the making of any of the imputations in question".[99]

8–48 The leading Irish authority on the matter is the decision of Hederman J. in *People (DPP) v McGrail*.[100] The accused was charged with various offences under the Firearms Act 1964. The prosecution's case was that the accused had been arrested whilst trying to escape from a house the gardaí had entered on foot of a search warrant, and that he had made a number of incriminating statements upon arrest and directed the gardaí to where the firearms were hidden. The accused had subsequently refused to sign statements produced by the gardaí, and throughout the trial he denied ever having made them—the very scenario that had justified character cross-examination in cases like *R. v Clarke*[101] upon the basis that a denial of having made the statement implied it had been concocted by the policeman. In *McGrail*'s case, under cross-examination, it was specifically put to the garda witnesses that the accused had made none of those statements. Upon the basis that this constituted an imputation against the character of a prosecution witness, counsel sought leave to cross-examine the accused upon his criminal record.

8–49 It was argued for the accused that, given the prosecution's case, the only defence open to him was a challenge to the authenticity of the statements, and that such a challenge, if accepted, would unavoidably lead to an inference that the prosecution witnesses had invented the statements: this was the central issue in the case, and as such the accused was entitled to give evidence relevant to it without exposing himself to cross-examination upon bad character. The trial judge permitted s.1(f)(ii) cross-examination upon the basis that it was now common practice to put the character of the accused in issue wherever he alleged improper practice on the part of prosecution witnesses and gardaí, for which propositions he referred to *Attorney-General v Campbell*[102] and *R. v Britzman & Hall*.[103] In *McGrail*'s case, the accused's record was revealed to include seven past convictions for unlawful taking of motor cars and one conviction (set aside upon appeal) for possession of housebreaking implements. He was convicted of the firearms offences.

---

[98] [1945] I.R. 237 at 247 (CCA).
[99] *ibid*.
[100] [1990] 2 I.R. 38 (CCA): *cf.* appendix 34.
[101] *cf.* para.**8–43**.
[102] [1945] I.R. 237 (SC).
[103] [1983] 1 W.L.R. 350 (CA).

8–50 McGrail's appeal to the Court of Criminal Appeal succeeded. In a judgment impressive for its clarity of exposition, Hederman J. authoritatively stated the view that for the purposes of s.1(f)(ii), the accused may make imputations against the character of a prosecution witness without exposing himself to bad character cross-examination where the imputations were "reasonably necessary" to enable him to establish his defence. This is otherwise only where his imputations are "unconnected with the proofs of the instant case" or "independent of the facts of the case":

> "A distinction must be drawn between questions and suggestions which are reasonably necessary to establish either the prosecution case or the defence case, even if they do involve suggesting a falsehood on the part of the witness of one or the other side, on one hand and, on the other hand, an imputation of bad character introduced by either side relating to matters unconnected with the proofs of the instant case. ... This court is of the view that the principles of fair procedures must apply. A procedure which inhibits the accused from challenging the veracity of the evidence against him at the risk of having his own previous character put in evidence is not a fair procedure".[104]

8–51 In *McGrail*, Hederman J. logically proceeded upon the basis that s.1(f)(ii) required a particular interpretation, in direct contrast with the view adopted by the House of Lords in *Selvey* that the words were to be interpreted in light of their "ordinary and natural" meaning and required no gloss.[105] In this, the learned judge was correct; the words "imputation upon the character" of a prosecution witness are not self-evident in their scope. The criminal trial is awash with imputation, from the fact of prosecution to the denial of guilt, and it therefore falls upon the court to calibrate by principle the type of imputations that are capable of divesting the accused of his shield under s.1(f)(ii).

8–52 Hederman J. further reasoned that the accused is free to deny having made or signed the statements upon which the prosecution relies, even where this implies or asserts that the statements have been concocted by the gardaí appearing for the prosecution. He is not likewise free to claim with impunity that a garda witness is wont to engage in improper practices or that he is *generally* of bad character and upon this basis ought not to be believed.[106]

---

[104] [1990] 2 I.R. 38 at 50 (CCA).
[105] *cf.* para.**8–45**.
[106] Hederman J. clearly had in mind *R. v Britzman* [1983] 1 W.L.R. 350 (CA). The accused claimed that the police officers had been "mistaken" in believing him to have made admissions during interviews with the police and in a shouting match with his co-accused across adjoining cells. His appeal against cross-examination under s.1(f)(ii) was unsuccessful. According to the Court of Appeal, an inference had been cast unavoidably suggesting that the police had invented false evidence to secure a conviction. According to Lawton L.J. (at 353): "Any denial that the conversations had taken place at all necessarily meant by implication that the police officers had given false evidence which they had made up in order to get the appellants convicted".

Thus it appears that the accused has a right to impugn the conduct of a prosecution witness where the impugned conduct is relevant to the witness' participation in, or investigation of, the proceedings wherein the accused is charged, without losing his shield, but no further:

> "Such a course of conduct is inevitable if an accused person is not to be seriously hampered in the conduct of his defence. Any ruling otherwise would have the effect of inhibiting the conduct of the defence in that an accused person, who may have a criminal record, may be intimidated into abandoning an effort to put in issue the truth of the evidence of a prosecution witness lest his own character outside the facts of the trial be put in issue".[107]

8–53 By contrast with *Selvey*, the decision in *McGrail* implicitly favours a rule-based approach to s.1(f)(ii). The trial judge has no discretion to permit cross-examination upon bad character where the imputations cast by the accused are proof-related and reasonably necessary to establish his defence. The judge's discretion arises only where s.1(f)(ii) *enables* cross-examination upon character. The prevailing sentiment in *McGrail* is that cross-examination upon character or record should be confined to exceptional circumstances, and that the accused should not be restricted unduly in choosing how to challenge the veracity of the prosecution's evidence. A similar view of s.1(f)(ii) had been expressed well by Slade J. in *R. v Flynn*:

> "If it were otherwise, it comes to this, that the Act of 1898, the very Act which gave the charter, so to speak, to an accused person to give evidence on oath in the witness box, would be a mere trap because he would be unable to put forward any defence, no matter how true, which involved an imputation on the character of the prosecution or any of his witnesses, without running the risk, if he had the misfortune to have a record, of his previous convictions being brought up in court while being tried on a wholly different matter".[108]

8–54 *McGrail* ultimately asserts that constitutional justice and public policy require that the accused be free to choose a defence with impunity, and it goes so far as to say that this includes his freedom to divert the blame to a prosecution witness without thereby exposing himself to the privations of s.1(f)(ii). In a sense, this was less an interpretation of s.1(f)(ii) than the development of a free-standing principle of Irish law. Hederman J. rooted his findings quite subtly in the need to permit an accused person to put "the truth" into evidence without fear of penalty. One can alternatively, and it is submitted more usefully, view *McGrail* as an attempt to ensure that the accused is free to consider how best to put the prosecution to proof of the offences. This ensures that the presumption of innocence operates in a very real and concrete manner. The

---

[107] [1990] 2 I.R. 38 at 49 (CCA).
[108] [1963] 1 Q.B. 729 at 737, *per* Slade J. (CA).

prosecution is required to convince the court that the accused is the guilty party, and the accused is protected from the prospect of being judged by his past life and character by a principle precluding indirectly relevant but highly prejudicial evidence whose introduction in the trial would serve significantly to lighten the prosecution's burden to prove and persuade. The *McGrail* judgment can also be viewed as part of a wider concern, deeply embedded in Irish law but not in English law, to subject confession evidence to rigorous scrutiny. Whilst genuine confession evidence is rightly regarded, particularly by members of the public, as good and strong evidence, Irish evidence law treats it with an appreciable degree of suspicion once it has been contested by the accused.[109] *McGrail* clearly reflects this culture in its concern to give the accused an unfettered right to challenge the veracity of inculpatory statements elicited from the accused by investigators under conditions greatly dissimilar to the courtroom trial.

8–55 This view that cross-examination of the accused upon character and record should be restricted to exceptional cases commands support in other common law jurisdictions.[110] The decision whether or not to expose the jury to information relating to the accused's past—information inevitably absorbed by the jury as indicative of the type of man the accused really is—is so crucial to the outcome of criminal trials that it is difficult to see merit in an approach that encourages recourse to discretion in favour of stable rules and principles. The principled approach adopted in *McGrail* is for this reason greatly to be preferred to the House of Lords' decision in *Selvey*. Under the Irish model, the trial judge must follow the rules and principles enunciated in *McGrail*, and may exercise a discretion to permit or refuse cross-examination upon character or record only where s.1(f)(ii) clearly enables such cross-examination. Under the current English model, the accused is exposed to possible cross-examination upon character or record in significantly more cases, and this depends upon how the trial judges exercise their discretion. The Irish experience indicates that the rule-based approach is also more likely to reduce appeals, whilst the English experience suggests that the House of Lords was wrong when it supposed in *Selvey* that a discretion-based test would achieve this end.[111]

---

[109] *cf.* para.**10–15** *et seq.*

[110] In Australia, imputations against prosecution witness are restricted to imputations that are extraneous to the witness' conduct in the investigation and prosecution: the Evidence Act 1995. In New South Wales, a distinction is made between imputations cast upon the prosecutor as distinct from prosecution witnesses: Crimes Act 1900–74, ss.413A–B.

[111] Law Commission, Consultation Paper No 141, *Criminal Law—Evidence in Criminal Proceedings: Previous Misconduct of an Accused*, 1996, at p.266. The Law Commission proposed that loss of the s.1(f)(ii) shield should be restricted to imputations that are extraneous to the witness' conduct in the investigation and prosecution, a concept drawn from the Evidence Act 1995 in Australia. The proposal is considered by some to be too narrow—failing to cover, for example, an allegation that a police officer fabricated confessions in other cases: Roberts, "The Law Commission Consultation Paper on Previous Misconduct: (1) All the Usual Suspects" [1997] Crim. L.R. 75 at 88.

8–56 Numerous decisions since *Selvey* have given rise to useful observations, however. In considering how to exercise the discretion to permit or refuse s.1(f)(ii) cross-examination in response to spontaneously cast imputations by the accused, the trial judge should first consider the possibility of "mistake, misunderstanding or confusion", given the "strain of being in the witness-box and the exaggerated use of language which sometimes results from such strain or lack of education or mental instability".[112] The accused may have been needled into making the imputations by shrewd cross-examining tactics. *McGrail* makes it clear that the extent to which the imputations have been central to the "nature and conduct" of the accused's defence is a factor material to the trial judge's discretion. The trial judge might also be guided by whether or not the case against the accused is strong enough not to depend upon the character issue. Where the case appears to depend considerably upon the balance of credibility, there is a greater need to banish bad character evidence from the courtroom.

8–57 Discretion should be exercised to disallow character cross-examination where on the one hand the impugning remarks made by the accused are slight and on the other hand the evidence of past record is likely to be very prejudicial.[113] If the accused's imputation against a prosecution witness relates only to one of numerous counts, the trial judge may and probably should exercise discretion against cross-examination where evidence of the accused's criminal record would unduly prejudice him.[114] Making imputations ought not be permitted to open the floodgates to an unfettered character assassination of the accused, particularly where he has a record of past crimes similar or identical to the crime being tried. Accordingly, the trial judge ought to explain, when summing-up, that evidence of the accused's bad character or record, if accepted by the jury, may affect their view of the accused's credibility or truthfulness as a witness but must not be taken to be inferential of his guilt as charged. The English courts have overturned conviction specifically upon this basis, even in cases where the trial judge explained that the evidence was not probative of guilt.[115]

8–58 The trial judge should warn the accused that his shield is likely to be lost if he pursues a certain direction,[116] although by itself the failure to so warn will not necessarily result in the quashing of conviction. For this reason, the trial judge should be informed in advance of the trial that the accused has a criminal record that should not be disclosed to the jury.[117]

8–59 It has been reasoned by the English Court of Appeal that s.1(f) cross-examination should be allowed in circumstances where the accused claims

---

[112] *R. v Britzman* [1983] 1 W.L.R. 350 at 355, *per* Lawton L.J. (CA).
[113] *R. v Watts* [1983] 3 All E.R. 101 (CA).
[114] *R. v Curbishley* [1963] Crim. L.R. 778 (CA).
[115] As in *R. v Prince* [1990] Crim. L.R. 49 (CA).
[116] *R. v Cook* [1959] 2 Q.B. 340 (CA).
[117] *R. v Ewing* [1983] 2 All E.R. 645 (HL).

that a prosecution witness is an accomplice for the purpose of subjecting that witness' testimony to the rules governing corroboration.[118] It is very doubtful that an Irish court would reach this same view, given that Irish law enforces a stricter corroboration rule for accomplice evidence,[119] and given recent experiences in Ireland with respect to unreliable accomplice witnesses.[120]

8–60 The Court of Appeal decided in *R. v Miller*[121] that s.1(f)(ii) cross-examination is permissible where the accused makes imputations against a person who has not given *viva voce* evidence, out of fear, but whose statement was read in court. In a decision that was not expected in England, the court decided that s.1(f) applies to all persons with material evidence to give, whether by deposition or statement or orally, whether dead, beyond the seas, unfit, fearful or unwilling to attend court. The findings have clear relevance to the provisions recently introduced in Ireland for the taking of testimony by vulnerable witnesses in advance of the trial.[122]

V. SECTION 1(F)(III): EVIDENCE BY THE ACCUSED AGAINST A CO-ACCUSED

8–61 Section 1(f)(iii) permits cross-examination upon bad character or record where the accused "has given evidence against any other person charged with the same offence". As for s.1(f)(ii), cross-examination under s.1(f)(iii) is only for the purpose of establishing the accused's lack of credit.[123] There is curiously little reported Irish authority upon the scope of s.1(f)(iii).

8–62 In *Murdoch v Taylor*,[124] Lord Morris emphasised that "giving evidence against" is a far more robust and decisive criterion than "tending to incriminate". Given the serious repercussions for the co-accused following cross-examination upon his criminal record, it requires strict proof. Lord Morris proposed the following test: "If, while ignoring anything trivial or casual, the positive evidence given by the witness would rationally have to be included in any survey or summary of the evidence in the case which, if accepted, would warrant the conviction of 'the other person charged with the same offence', then the witness would have given evidence against such other person."[125] Accordingly, the incriminating evidence must be evidence probative of a fact at issue, tending to prove the other co-accused's guilt as charged. Inconvenience or inconsistency with the other's defence is not of itself sufficient to activate s.1(f)(iii).[126]

---

[118] *R. v Manley* (1962) 126 J.P. 316 (CA).
[119] *cf.* para.**5–21** *et seq.*
[120] *cf.* para.**5–24** *et seq.*
[121] [1997] Crim. L.R. 217 (CA).
[122] *cf.* para.**1–56** *et seq.*
[123] *Murdoch v Taylor* [1965] A.C. 574 (HL).
[124] *ibid.* applied in *R. v Fitzpatrick* [1998] Crim. L.R. 63 (CA).
[125] [1965] A.C. 574 at 584 (HL).
[126] *R. v Varley* [1982] 2 All E.R. 519 (CA).

8–63 According to well-settled authority, the court determines whether or not a co-accused has given evidence against a fellow co-accused by looking objectively at the effect of his evidence for the running of the other's defence. In *R. v Bruce*,[127] the Court of Appeal found that evidence that appears to *undermine* a co-accused's defence does not necessarily amount to "evidence against" him; what is required is evidence that, if believed by the court, makes his acquittal less likely. In this case, eight men had been charged with robbery. A first co-accused admitted there had been a plan to commit robbery, but denied he had been a party to its execution. A second co-accused contradicted him by testifying that there had been no plan. In response to this development, counsel for the first co-accused was permitted to cross-examine the second upon his previous convictions. Upholding the appeal by the second co-accused, the Court of Appeal reasoned that he had actually provided the first co-accused with a better defence, and if anything had served to undermine the prosecution's case.

8–64 Under this test, the co-accused's motives or intentions are irrelevant.[128] Whereas in *Bruce* one co-accused's contradiction of the other's account unwittingly weakened the prosecution's case against the other, in *R. v Hatton*[129] it had the unintended effect of weakening the other's defence and it thereby exposed the first co-accused to cross-examination upon his bad character and criminal record. The appellant and two co-accused were charged with stealing scrap metal. The appellant testified that he and the first accused had been party to plans to take the scrap metal, but denied that they had acted dishonestly since they had believed they were entitled to take it. This was held by the Court of Appeal to be "evidence against", since it confirmed a material part of the prosecution's case that there had been a plan to rob the metal. *Bruce* was distinguished upon the basis that the accused in that case "had merely denied a part of the prosecution's case which [the co-accused] had admitted", but had not supported the prosecution's case in any material respect.[130]

8–65 Once a co-accused gives evidence against a fellow co-accused, thereby losing his shield, the trial judge has no discretion to disallow cross-examination upon bad character or record; nor, according to the House of Lords in *Murdoch*, should the cross-examination be "fettered in any way".[131] In this one crucial respect, s.1(f)(iii) differs from the two preceding subsections, which tend to be governed by a proportionality test balancing the probative force of the evidence against its likely prejudicial effect. The distinction is generally justified by the severity of the situation in which a co-accused finds himself when a fellow co-accused has tendered evidence against him; facing possible criminal conviction and loss to liberty, fairness requires that he be free to mount a cut-

---

[127] [1975] 1 W.L.R. 1252 (CA). See also *R. v Kirkpatrick* [1998] Crim. L.R. 63 (CA).
[128] *R. v Varley* [1982] 2 All E.R. 519 (CA).
[129] (1977) 64 Cr. App. R. 88 (CA).
[130] *ibid.* at 91.
[131] [1965] A.C. 574 at 416, *per* Donovan L. (HL).

throat attack upon his co-accused's character.[132] This view of s.1(f)(iii) cross-examination as a matter of right rather than discretion is not without its detractors. Elliot denounces the logic as "pious justification" concealing the fact that in reality this dynamic relieves the prosecution of much of its burden of proof and that the "system relies heavily on this mutual bloodletting for the conviction of people who would otherwise escape their just desserts".[133]

8–66 Section 1(f)(iii) often works an injustice. Where a first co-accused testifies that a second co-accused was responsible for the crime, the second—who may be innocent of all charges though possessing a criminal record—is forced to testify to refute the allegations, and in so doing may incur exposure of his criminal record. This situation would not have occurred had the persons accused not been jointly tried. Further, s.1(f)(iii) will naturally work to the advantage of the co-accused with no criminal record who has little to lose and everything to gain by prejudicing his co-accused's case.

8–67 Section 1(f)(iii) applies only where the co-accused has been "charged with the same offence". The provision originally envisaged two or more co-accused persons in a relationship akin to a criminal joint venture, where one of them, "endeavouring to save himself", gives evidence against the other.[134] As it stands, however, it fails to address the situation where a co-accused charged in the same proceedings but not jointly for the same offence, gives evidence against his co-accused. This evidence is likely to be severely prejudicial given that co-accused persons tend to have shared a relationship equal or akin to that of accomplices. Yet the co-accused in this position appears not to have a *statutory* right to cross-examine the other upon his character and reliability.

8–68 The few reported English cases to consider this limitation demonstrate its anomalousness. In *R. v Roberts*,[135] one accused was charged with fraudulent conversion and the other with false pretences. After one of them gave evidence against the other, the trial judge permitted s.1(f)(ii) cross-examination. Conviction was quashed upon the basis that the accused had been charged with different offences, and accordingly s.1(f)(iii) did not apply to facilitate cross-examination upon bad character. In *R. v Lauchlan*,[136] two men each charged in the same trial with assaulting the other were deemed not to be charged with the same offence, as different facts had to be established to justify each person's convictions. In *R. v Rockman*,[137] s.1(f)(iii) was again deemed not to apply, given that the first co-accused was charged with assaulting the second co-accused, and in the same trial the second co-accused was charged with wounding the first.

---

[132] First authoritatively decided in *R. v Ellis* [1961] 1 W.L.R. 1064, [1961] 2 All E.R. 928 (CA).
[133] Elliot (1991) at p.5.
[134] 60 *Dáil Debates* Col. 720.
[135] [1936] 1 All E.R. 23 (CA).
[136] CCA, June 15, 1976.
[137] CCA, November 22, 1977.

8–69 Reviewing the law in *R. v Hills*,[138] Viscount Dilhorne concluded that s.1(f)(iii) arose only where the co-accused are charged jointly with the "same offence" and not with different offences in the one indictment. The "same offence" was found to mean "the same in all material circumstances including the time at which the offence is alleged to have been committed".[139] Upon this basis, "a distinct and separate offence similar in all material respects to an offence committed later, no matter how short the interval between the two, cannot properly be regarded as 'the same offence'."[140] There must accordingly be a convergence not merely in the nature of the offence, but also in its material particulars including the time the offence was alleged to have been committed. By way of mitigation, the learned judge asserted that s.1(f)(iii) may yet apply where the court forms the view that the co-accused *could have been charged jointly* with the same offence. For the purposes of s.1(f)(iii), the court may look behind the counts—which these days are tersely drafted with minimal detail disclosed—and may, for instance, examine the depositions to see "what further particulars of the offence charged would have been given if applied for".[141]

8–70 When this unnecessary limitation—and it would seem, oversight— was highlighted by the House of Lords in *R. v Hills*, it provoked a swift response from Parliament,[142] which amended s.1(f)(iii) of the Criminal Evidence Act 1898 by replacing the words "charged with the same offence" with "charged in the same proceedings".[143] It is hoped that the Irish legislature similarly amends s.1(f)(iii). As Viscount Dilhorne acknowledged, it is unjust that "when one of two co-accused gives evidence against the other, the right of the co-accused against whom the evidence is given should depend on what charges the prosecution has thought it right to bring".[144]

---

[138] [1980] A.C. 27 (CA).
[139] *ibid.* at 34.
[140] *ibid.*
[141] *ibid.* at 33.
[142] [1980] A.C. 27 (HL), decided in July 1978.
[143] Criminal Evidence Act 1979, s.1.
[144] [1980] A.C. 27 at 35 (HL).

Further Reading

Cohen, "Challenging Police Evidence of Interviews and the Second Limb of Section 1(f)(ii)—Another View" [1981] Crim. L.R. 523.

Dennis, "Evidence Against a Co-Accused" [1983] *Current Legal Problems* 177.

Elliot, "Cut Throat Tactics: the freedom of an accused to prejudice a co-accused" [1991] Crim. L.R. 5.

Mirfield, "The Argument from Consistency for Overruling *Selvey*" [1991] C.L.J. 490.

Munday, "Irregular Disclosure of Evidence of Bad Character" [1990] Crim. L.R. 92.

Munday, "Stepping Beyond the Bounds of Credibility" [1986] Crim. L.R. 511.

Munday, "The Paradox of Cross-Examination to Credit—Simply too Close for Comfort" [1994] C.L.J. 303.

Munday, "What Constitutes Good Character?" [1997] Crim. L.R. 247.

Pattenden, "The Purpose of Cross-Examination under s.1(f) of the Criminal Evidence Act 1898" [1982] Crim. L.R. 707.

Seabrooke, "Closing the Credibility Gap: A New Approach to Section 1(f)(ii) of the Criminal Evidence Act 1898" [1987] Crim. L.R. 231.

Chapter 9

THE RULE AGAINST HEARSAY

I. Principles and Definitions	9–01
Rationale of the Hearsay Rule	9–09
Strictness of the Rule	9–12
Right to Cross-Examine	9–16
II. Distinguishing Hearsay from Original Evidence	9–20
III. Implied Assertions	9–31
IV. Documentary Evidence	9–36
V. Hearsay in Civil Cases	9–40
Child Witnesses and Family Law	9–43
VI. Hearsay at Pre-Trial and Interlocutory Stages	9–48
VII. Hearsay and Tribunals	9–53
VIII. Miscellaneous	9–55
Expert Evidence	9–55
Identification Evidence	9–56
IX. Exceptions to the Hearsay Rule	9–59
Statutory Exceptions	9–59
Common Law Exceptions	9–62

I. Principles and Definitions

9–01 The rule against hearsay, traditionally one of the strictest of the common law rules of evidence, operates to exclude statements as evidence probative of any assertion therein save where made directly by a witness while giving testimony in the case[1] and unless falling within a recognised common law or statutory exception. Although there are a number of different contexts in which statements may be admitted in a limited evidentiary capacity—*e.g.* as relevant to credibility in the event of a challenge,[2] or as original evidence[3]—the courts often preventatively reject statements to which a hearsay objection has been made, in light of the risk of prejudice and irregularity for the trial or hearing if

---

[1] This definition of the scope of the hearsay rule derives from an authoritative formulation expressed by Cross, *Cross on Evidence* (5th ed., Butterworths, London, 1979) at p.6, to wit, that "a statement other than one made by a person while giving oral evidence in the proceedings is inadmissible as evidence of any fact stated".
[2] *cf.* para.**3–07** *et seq.*
[3] *cf.* para.**9–20** *et seq.*

the statement creates undue prejudice or is erroneously construed to be probative of the issues.

9–02 An obvious example of hearsay, true to its dictionary meaning, is an utterance made by an untraceable bystander who was heard to identify the accused fleeing the scene of the crime. The third-party bystander's direct assertion, heard by another who wishes to testify to that effect, constitutes pure hearsay. In such a case, the sincerity, memory, or perceptual ability of the declarant cannot be tested in court, nor his demeanour observed as the information is conveyed. The prohibited words may constitute double or multiple hearsay, depending upon how many people passed on the original assertion. Although this third-party/absent declarant dimension to the rule is naturally its most exigent, and most strictly applied, the rule applies equally to preclude the reception of pre-trial statements made by a party present and willing to testify as a witness.[4]

9–03 A pre-trial statement made by a witness, consistent with the testimony he is about to give or has given, is inadmissible as proof of its contents, save where it benefits from a common law or statutory exception; as a general rule, the witness must testify to the relevant facts *de novo*. This strand, also called the principle against self-corroboration,[5] is less contentious where the witness is present and cross-examinable, and there are now so many statutory exceptions to it that its survival has been slim and is constantly under threat.[6] Where not exempted by statute, however, the rule strictly applies, and it may form a strong basis for appeal where the statement created prejudice which was unmitigated by oral evidence in the case and material to the verdict. Conviction for the offence of threatening to kill was quashed in *People (DPP) v McDonagh*[7] in circumstances where the trial court had permitted a garda to recount an interview with the accused in which the garda had repeated the complainant's allegation that the accused phoned her to tell her that when he got out of court that morning he was going to come after her and kill her. Although the parties were present in court and available for cross-examination, the statement constituted inadmissible hearsay, and the prosecutor had been under a duty to exclude the contents of the question put to the accused in interview prior to the trial, which "were undoubtedly highly prejudicial, particularly as the actual

---

[4] This was not always the case, however. *Halsbury's Laws of England* (Vol.13) and Phipson's *Law of Evidence* (9th ed.) phrased the rule as follows: "statements made by persons not called as witnesses are inadmissible to prove the truth of the facts stated". Although Cross (*op. cit.*, n.1) expressed the rule to include all statements "other than one made by a person while giving oral evidence", he had earlier criticised the eventual extension of the rule to parties amenable to cross-examination. He wrote (1956) at p.101 that "although it is undoubtedly the law that a witness cannot normally narrate a previous statement of his own as evidence of its truth, the basic reason for the exclusion of such evidence is that it would be superfluous, and it certainly seems to be etymologically incorrect to speak of it as hearsay".
[5] *cf.* para.**2–50**.
[6] *cf.* para.**9–59** *et seq.*
[7] CCA, May 29, 2003.

wording was considerably more explicit than the evidence of [the complainant] herself".[8]

9–04 With respect to witnesses, the rule applies only to out-of-court statements sought to be repeated testimonially as proof of some assertions expressed or implied in the statements. Lord Wilberforce authoritatively stated the principle in *Ratten v R.* as follows:[9]

> "The mere fact that evidence of a witness includes evidence as to words spoken by another person who is not called, is no objection to its admissibility. Words spoken are facts just as much as any other action by a human being. If the speaking of the words is a relevant fact, a witness may give evidence that they were spoken. A question of hearsay only arises when the words spoken are relied on 'testimonially,' i.e., as establishing some fact narrated by the words."

9–05 A statement is commonly relevant and admissible upon a limited basis to challenge the credibility of a witness, where the statement diverges from his account given from the witness box, although the jury must be instructed by the close of the trial that the statement is relevant only to the question of the witness' credit and is not evidence tending to prove any of the assertions expressed or implied in the statement.[10] Whereas the hearsay rule excludes out-of-court statements as evidence of the factual truth of their assertions, the rule against narrative prohibits the reception of consistent statements as evidence of the credibility of the witness. Both rules share a common rationale in the avoidance of self-manufactured and unreliable evidence. By way of exception to the rule against narrative, a complaint of sexual offence, if made sufficiently early, may be admitted as evidence tending to show the complainant's consistency or credit, although not as evidence probative of an issue; the trial judge's failure to direct the jury sufficiently on this distinction has led to the quashing of conviction in a number of cases.[11]

9–06 Statements are often received by the court without infringing the hearsay rule if they are admissible as evidence to establish or to rebut some specific relevant issue or claim in the case, where this does not require the court to determine the truth or accuracy of any assertion made in the statement. In this capacity, statements have been categorised as *original evidence*. The admission of statements as original evidence has flourished in the reported appeals in England in recent decades, and there has been a correlative decline in recourse to the common law exceptions, many of them now under-developed as a result. The common law exceptions have been further outstripped by statute, which increasingly addresses the hearsay question in a contextual light.[12]

---

[8] *ibid.*, *per* Geoghegan J.
[9] [1972] A.C. 378 at 387 (PC).
[10] *cf.* para.**3–08** *et seq.*
[11] *cf.* para.**3–51** *et seq.*
[12] *e.g.* Proceeds of Crime Act 1996, ss.8(1)(b) and 8(5); Copyright and Related Rights Act 2000, s.127. *cf.* para.**9–59** *et seq.*

The Rule against Hearsay

9–07 Where a statement has been deemed generally or partially admissible under a common law or statutory exception to the hearsay rule, or where the statement is admitted in a limited evidentiary capacity such as to show discredit or to prove a particular relevant fact, the trial judge must take especial care to explain the evidential use to which the statement may properly be put by the jury in the trial. If the statement is admissible for the purposes of one count, such as perverting the course of justice in *R. v Watson*,[13] but not for other counts, such as possession of drugs with intent to supply, the failure of the trial judge to highlight this distinction may result in the quashing of conviction.

9–08 The rule against hearsay evidence typically applies to written or oral statements made before the trial, and with respect to express or implied assertions contained within the statements. For some time, however, the rule has been considered to apply beyond statements to include non-verbal implied assertions derived from conduct or behaviour (*e.g.* the distressed and hysterical state of the complainant fleeing the accused, being an implied assertion that he has been attacked by him). The application of the rule to implied assertions has precipitated much debate and confusion on the distinction between evidence of assertion and other forms of evidence such as real evidence. At root, the hearsay rule attaches to evidence that makes an assertion by or on behalf of a person. If the *assertions* within the evidence are not made or generated with human input—such as passive assertions arising from an image mechanically photographed and unadapted—it is not hearsay. This distinction is troublesome where human participation in the information is partial, as in the case of photofits[14] or ticket stubs retained after a trip or event.[15] Ultimately, the court must assess whether the evidence is actually assertive, whether it derives from personal input, and whether the truth of the assertion is relevant to the proceedings.

Rationale of the Hearsay Rule

9–09 Wigmore described the hearsay rule, with characteristic enthusiasm, as "a rule which may be esteemed, next to jury trial, as the greatest contribution of that eminently practical legal system to the world's methods of procedure".[16] The rule against hearsay had taken root by the close of the seventeenth century, two centuries after the emergence of the modern trial of proof by witness testimony.[17] Whilst historians have agreed roughly on the rule's dating, they differ significantly on the underlying causes and motives. Wigmore attributed the development to a gathering mistrust of the jury's ability to evaluate hearsay evidence.[18] Morgan attributed it to the perceived need to test assertions by

---

[13] [1997] Crim. L.R. 680 (CA).
[14] *cf.* para.**6–32**.
[15] *cf.* para.**9–26**.
[16] *Evidence in Trials at Common Law* (3rd ed., Little Brown & Co., Boston, 1974) at p.28.
[17] Choo, *Hearsay and Confrontation in Criminal Trials* (Clarendon Press, Oxford 1996) at pp.3–7.
[18] Wigmore, *op. cit.* n.16 at p.29.

effective cross-examination.[19] Holdsworth considered that the strict prohibition emerged due to the absence of a general corroboration requirement for allegations of crime (as existed in continental jurisdictions).[20] Cross prudently assumed the rule to be prompted by each of these concerns, and concluded that there might not be a single coherent explanation for its development.[21] The hearsay rule has weathered an unparalleled level of scrutiny and challenge in recent decades, chiefly arising from the inconvenience or injustice wrought by its technical application in specific contexts where the concerns associated with the rule are absent or present to an insignificant degree. Although many of the objectionable side-effects to the rule have been removed on a piecemeal basis by the legislatures in Ireland and England, the rule endures and applies generally, if with less dominance.

9–10 The hearsay rule presupposes that pre-trial statements are inherently likely to suffer from ambiguity, insincerity, misperception, or error.[22] It reflects the concern, particularly in cases of multiple hearsay, that a statement loses its accuracy when it is retold by a number of people, and that a mistruth gains momentum by the sheer force of repetition. Trankell reported the results of various tests on story-telling within chains of six people, and found "the interesting thing is not that the account has thinned out, but rather that on its way to the final station it has also gathered details which were not originally present."[23] In this respect, the hearsay rule reflects elements of the "best evidence" principle,[24] and similarly may be seen to encourage law enforcers to search for better evidence against the accused.[25]

9–11 The rule was popularly justified by Lord Normand in *R. v Teper*[26] upon the basis that hearsay evidence is a weak form of evidence since it is second-hand, it is not delivered on oath, and it cannot be tested under cross-examination. Against this, it has been argued that hearsay is often the best evidence in a case, especially where the speaker is dead and the statements were written down, and further that the oath is no longer a guarantee of the truth.[27] Statements made soon after an event may be more valuable and reliable than those testified to years later in the heated context of the courtroom trial.[28] The rule may tend to confuse witnesses by preventing them from telling their story in a natural way. It is frequently asserted that underpinning its strict

---

[19] *Some Problems of Proof under the Anglo-American System of Litigation* (1956) at p.117.
[20] *A History of English Law* (Vol. 9, Methuen & Co., London 1926) at pp.217–8.
[21] Cross and Tapper, *Evidence* (8th ed., Butterworths, London, 1995) at p.566.
[22] So recognised by the Law Commission, *Evidence in Criminal Proceedings: Hearsay and Related Topics*, Consultation Paper, No.136, 1995, at para.640.
[23] Trankell, *Reliability of Evidence* (Rotobeckman A.B., Stockholm, 1972) at pp.56–64.
[24] *cf.* para.**1–14**.
[25] Allan, "Implications of Modern Psychological Knowledge" (1991) at p.228.
[26] [1952] A.C. 480 at 486 (PC).
[27] Guest, "The Scope of the Hearsay Rule" (1985) at p.401.
[28] Heydon, *Evidence: Cases and Materials* (3rd ed., Butterworths, London, 1991) at p.322.

application is a strong mistrust of the jury.[29] Lord Mansfield C.J. once observed that "no man can tell what effect it may have upon [the] minds" of the jury.[30] The rule, like many other rules of evidence in criminal trials, protects the accused from the prospect that jurors may attach too much weight to hearsay assertions inadequately tested in court, or may otherwise become unduly prejudiced against the accused. It further protects him from the prospect that the jury will fail adequately to take account of the possibilities of concoction or mistake.[31] In this sense, the rule operates in a bifurcated court to enable the trial judge to screen and filter forms of admissible from inadmissible evidence.[32] This is illustrated by the comparative scarcity of hearsay rules in civil law jurisdictions operating unitary courts.

Strictness of the Rule

9–12 One of the most recurring criticisms of the hearsay rule is that it is applied too strictly. The objection is particularly forceful in English law, in light of the House of Lords' declarations that judicial innovation of the rule has ceased and that any further exceptions must be accomplished by the legislature—an absolutism the Irish courts have wisely avoided.[33] This view was first expressed in *Myers v DPP*[34]—a case much cited as an example of the clear divorce of the hearsay rule from its rationale. The accused was prosecuted for stealing motorcars and reselling them with the logbooks of older cars. The prosecution was forced to rely upon cylinder lock numbers indelibly stamped on the engines, and it therefore sought to call into evidence the records retained by the motor manufacturers. The officer in charge of the records was asked to produce microfilms prepared from cards recording the cylinder numbers of manufactured cars inputted by unidentifiable assembly line workers. The Court of Appeal upheld the evidence because of "the inherent probability that it [would] be correct rather than incorrect".[35] The House of Lords disagreed, although with evident reluctance. The records constituted inadmissible hearsay evidence, since they were out of court assertions by unidentifiable workmen. Lord Reid reluctantly defended the need to preserve the rule even if "absurdly technical" in individual cases, and considered that the case for creating new

---

[29] Morgan, *op. cit.*, n.19 at p.117. For an English view, see Cross, *op. cit.*, n.1 at pp.6-9, 478-80.
[30] *Berkeley Peerage Case* (1811) 4 Camp. 401 at 415. See also *R. v Kearly* [1992] 2 W.L.R. 656 at 679, *per* Ackner L.J. (HL).
[31] Some published research findings appear to contradict this view. A study by Miene, Park, and Borgida in "Juror Decision Making and the Evaluation of Hearsay Evidence" (1992) 76 Minn. L. Rev. 683 prompted the researchers to consider that the jurors may ultimately have accorded the hearsay statements too little weight. Bull, Kovera, Penrod, and Park in "Jury's Perceptions of Hearsay Evidence" (1992) 76 Minn. L. Rev. 703 found little variation in conviction rates between courts that had admitted hearsay statements and courts that had not.
[32] Damaska, *Evidence Law Adrift* (Yale University Press, New Haven, 1997) at p.41.
[33] *cf.* para.**9–62**.
[34] [1965] A.C. 1001 (HL): repeated in *R. v Kearly* [1992] 2 W.L.R. 656 at 679, *per* Lord Oliver (H.L).
[35] *ibid.* at 1023.

exceptions was a matter properly for parliament. (The application of the hearsay rule to industrial records was reversed by the legislature in England in 1965[36] and in Ireland in 1992.[37])

9–13 Dissenting, Lord Pearce remarked that the anonymity and reliability of modern industrial records of mass production was a new social fact that the common law ought to embrace. The industrial records constituted the only evidence in *Myers*. No suggestion was made that the workmen had had any incentive to concoct false numbers. The only possibility was that mistakes may have been made, although the chances of this were highly slim given the number of cars concerned in the case. It is clear, as Guest has observed, that the *Myers* decision revealed a genuine fear that "to open up the hearsay rule to an examination in each judicial instance of the reliability of the evidence would effectively destroy the convenience of the practice whereby potentially unreliable evidence is eliminated without further discussion".[38]

9–14 In light of heated debate in England over the viability of many aspects of its application, the rule against hearsay has recently undergone major reconstruction in England, culminating in the abolition of the rule in its strict form in civil proceedings,[39] and in a much debated proposal by the Law Commission for a softer version of the rule in criminal proceedings.[40] The model legislation proposed by the Commission would establish a general inclusionary discretion to admit hearsay evidence where the court is satisfied that its probative value is such that the interests of justice require it to be admitted. It would further exclude unintended assertions from the ambit of the rule (to avoid the effect of the unpopular decision in *Kearly*);[41] and it would extend the range of exceptions to the rule to include first-hand oral and documentary statements of identifiable persons who are unavailable to testify because dead, ill, or uncontactable. All statements where admitted, whether consistent or inconsistent with the witness' testimony, would be admissible generally, and potentially as probative evidence, thereby avoiding the need to give elaborate directions to the jury on the limited extent to which they may consider a statement to be relevant to credibility but not issue.[42] The proposal addresses a long-running debate on the characterisation of contemporanous notes a witness may be permitted to consult when giving his testimony.[43]

---

[36] Criminal Evidence Act 1965, replaced ultimately by the Criminal Justice Act 1988, as amended by the Criminal Evidence Act 1995. In the civil context, documentary hearsay exceptions were created under the Civil Evidence Acts 1968 and 1972, since replaced by the Civil Evidence Act 1995.
[37] *cf.* para.**9–36** *et seq.*
[38] Guest, "The Scope of the Hearsay Rule" (1985) at p.388.
[39] Section 1(1) of the Civil Evidence Act 1995 provides: "In civil proceedings, evidence shall not be excluded on the ground that it is hearsay".
[40] Law Commission, *Evidence in Criminal Proceedings: Hearsay and Related Topics*, No.245 (1997).
[41] *cf.* para.**9–28** *et seq.*
[42] *cf.* para.**3–08** *et seq.*
[43] *cf.* para.**2–45**.

The Rule against Hearsay

Hearsay concerns have thus far been avoided by viewing the notes as *aides memoires* or props to memory, rather than as independent sources of information or evidence in the case. The Commission recommends admissibility of the notes or statements so long as made by the witness at a time when the events were fresh in his mind, although it proposes a number of safeguards, such as a requirement of advance notice to the defence, the admissibility in-chief of evidence challenging the credibility of the absent declarant, and an acknowledgment that the court has a duty to acquit or direct an acquittal if the case against the accused depends wholly or substantially upon unconvincing hearsay evidence.

9–15 Finally, to temper such a general dilution of the hearsay rule, and to pre-empt a challenge under Art.6(3) of the European Convention on Human Rights, the Commission recommended provision to the effect that "unsupported hearsay should not be sufficient proof of any offence".[44] This latter recommendation proved unpopular with the judges consulted, who considered it unwise to encourage the evolution of a new corroboration rule at a time when corroboration rules were being dismantled in England (although the Commission had wisely eschewed reference to "corroboration" since that had become associated with the restrictive *Baskerville* test, and it favoured reference instead to the broader category of evidence loosely called "supporting evidence").[45] The proposals as a whole have attracted a mixture of modest support and severe criticism, the latter chiefly upon the basis that the proposed rules lack any discernible principles within which they may be framed.

Right to Cross-Examine

9–16 The justification for the strictness of the hearsay rule in more recent years is the opponent's lack of opportunity to cross-examine the declarant upon the accuracy or reliability of the information narrated or implied in the statement. Wigmore famously described cross-examination as "beyond any doubt the greatest legal engine ever invented for the discovery of truth. However difficult it may be for the layman, the scientist, or the foreign jurist to appreciate this its wonderful power, there has probably never been a moment's doubt upon this point in the mind of a lawyer of experience".[46] Lord Ackner expressed the view in *R. v Kearly*,[47] that the hearsay rule "is a recognition of the great

---

[44] Law Commission, Consultation Paper No.138, at para.9.5.
[45] *cf. paras* **6–06** *et seq.*, **5–48**.
[46] Wigmore, *Evidence in Trials at Common Law* (Chadbourn rev., Little Brown & Co., Boston, 1981) at para.1367, p.29. A divergent view was reached by the Australian Law Reform Commission which regarded cross-examination as "arguably the poorest of the techniques employed at present in the common law courts" (Research Paper No.8, *Manner of Giving Evidence*, 1982, chap.10, para.5). In England, the Law Commission (1995, *op. cit.*, n.22 at para.662) acknowledged research indicating that witnesses give less accurate evidence in response to direct or leading questions, and commented that "the absence of cross-examination is the most valid justification for the hearsay rule, but even this justification is not valid for all hearsay, and it does not justify the current form of the hearsay rule".
[47] [1992] 2 W.L.R. 656 at 679 (HL).

difficulty, even more acute for a juror than for a trained judicial mind, of assessing what, if any, weight can be properly given to a statement by a person whom the jury has not seen or heard and which has not been subject to any test of reliability by cross-examination".

9–17 Central to the concept of natural justice developed by the Irish courts is the necessity to be presented with direct oral evidence in circumstances where a person has a right to an oral hearing, not only in criminal proceedings but potentially in any proceedings where adverse findings may be drawn against the person and serious consequences may ensue in consequence. This principle has been applied regularly by the Irish courts to tribunals exercising *quasi*-judicial functions, in response to the argument that the rules of evidence are more flexible in this context. In *Kiely v Minister for Social Welfare*,[48] the appeals enquiry had wrongly permitted a written statement by a doctor, engaged by the Department of Social Welfare, to prevail over evidence given testimonially by two doctors called as witnesses for the applicant. Henchy J. observed:

> "Tribunals exercising *quasi*-judicial functions are frequently allowed to act informally—to receive unsworn evidence, to act on hearsay, to depart from the rules of evidence, to ignore courtroom procedures, and the like—but they may not act in such a way as to imperil a fair hearing or a fair result. ... Of one thing I feel certain, that natural justice is not observed if the scales of justice are tilted against one side all through the proceedings. *Audi alteram partem* means that both sides must be fairly heard. That is not done if one party is allowed to send in his evidence in writing, free from the truth-eliciting processes of a confrontation which are inherent in an oral hearing, while his opponent is compelled to run the gauntlet of oral examination and cross-examination".[49]

9–18 Where a committee or body has been established by statute, there is a strict presumptive requirement of constitutional justice and fair procedures.[50] In *Borges v Medical Council*,[51] the Fitness to Practise Committee of the Medical Council, exercising its powers under the Medical Practitioners Act 1978, instituted a professional misconduct enquiry of the applicant, but decided to confine itself to documents, which included transcripts from witnesses who had testified against the applicant at similar professional misconduct proceedings in England, the findings of the General Medical Council, and the judgment of the Privy Council. The High Court ruled that the Committee could not proceed with its enquiry into allegations of misconduct against the applicant unless it called complainants to give oral evidence of the allegations. Ó Caoimh J. reasoned that justice required that the doctor be afforded the opportunity to

---

[48] [1977] I.R. 267 (SC).
[49] *ibid.* at 281, *per* Henchy J.
[50] *East Donegal Co-Operative v Attorney-General* [1970] I.R. 317 at 341, *per* Walsh J. (SC).
[51] HC, March 5, 2003.

The Rule against Hearsay

confront his accusers and to test their evidence against him. The Supreme Court affirmed his findings.[52]

9–19 Neither the rule against hearsay nor the right to cross-examine have been classified as stand-alone constitutional rights, the breach of which would have strict technical effect, but instead as fundamental elements of the *genus* constitutional right to fair procedures or a fair trial, the nature of which differs from case to case.[53] This characterisation of the right not to be prejudiced by hearsay evidence may ultimately be a matter of form, given the court's consistent assertion of the requirement of oral evidence in trials, hearings, and enquiries, and it is consistent with the Irish courts' characterisation of other evidential and procedural rights, such as the right to confront one's accuser[54] and the right to be identified in criminal cases by means of a formal identification parade.[55] The approach of the European Court of Human Rights has been formally similar. Whilst the accused has a right under Art.6(3)(d) of the European Convention on Human Rights in criminal proceedings to "examine or have examined witnesses against him", the court has interpreted this to require that the accused be given adequate opportunity to challenge witnesses either when they are making their statement or at some subsequent stage in the proceedings.[56] It is not viewed as a stand-alone right, but as a component of the more general right to fair procedures before and during the trial.

II. Distinguishing Hearsay from Original Evidence

9–20 An important distinction has been drawn between admitting a statement as hearsay and admitting it in an alternative capacity as "original evidence" probative of some relevant fact whose proof does not require the court to consider the truth of any assertions expressed or implied in the statement. Statements may be relevant irrespective of their accuracy or truth. The making of a statement may be a fact at issue,[57] as in defamation and passing off actions; or the effect of the words may be relevant, as where the defences of duress and provocation are raised. In principle, however, statements admitted upon this basis are admissible as evidence probative only of the relevant fact that justified admissibility, and not more generally as evidence probative of the facts at issue. A hearsay statement should not be admitted as original evidence where the court is invited to consider the truth or accuracy of the assertions made in the statement; where the validity of the assertions are relevant to the facts at issue, and acceptance of the evidence is likely to prejudice the defence, the

---

[52] SC, January 30, 2004.
[53] *Murphy v GM PB PC Ltd. and GH* (HC, June 4, 1999) *per* O'Higgins J.
[54] *cf.* para.**1–60** *et seq.*
[55] *cf.* para.**6–18**.
[56] *Kostovski v The Netherlands* (1990) 12 E.H.R.R. 434.
[57] In *People (DPP) v Nevin* (March 14, 2003), the Court of Criminal Appeal approved reference in the trial to conversations the deceased had had on political matters, which was admissible to rebut an allegation by the accused during her evidence that the deceased had been a member of the I.R.A.

statement should not be admitted save where otherwise admissible as an exception to the hearsay rule.

9–21 A clear illustration of the distinction between hearsay and original evidence arose in *Subramaniam v Public Prosecutor*.[58] In response to the charge of unlawful possession of ammunition, the accused claimed he had acted under duress after he was kidnapped and threatened into cooperation by terrorists. The trial judge refused to permit reference to what the terrorists had said to him upon his capture. His appeal to the Privy Council succeeded upon the basis that the only purpose of introducing the evidence was to show that threats had been made whose effect was to cause the accused to fear for his life and to comply with the terrorists' demands under duress. Since reference to the statements was not concerned to establish the truth of the assertions therein—namely that the terrorists actually intended to kill him (the terrorists not being tried)—the evidence was not hearsay in kind, and the hearsay rule did not arise. A definitive statement of the rule was propounded by Lord de Silva M.R:

> "It is hearsay and inadmissible when the object of the evidence is to establish the truth of what is contained in the statement. It is not hearsay and is admissible when it is proposed to establish by the evidence, not the truth of the statement, but the fact that it was made".[59]

9–22 In *DPP v O'Kelly*,[60] the High Court reiterated *dicta* by Kingsmill Moore J. in *Cullen v Clarke*,[61] inspired by Lord de Silva M.R in *Subramaniam*, to wit:

> "[T]he utterance of the words may itself be a relevant fact, quite apart from the truth or falsity of anything asserted by the words spoken. To prove, by the evidence of a witness who heard the words, that they were spoken, is direct evidence, and in no way encroaches on the general rule against hearsay".

9–23 In *O'Kelly*, McCracken J. answered the appeal question by ruling that original evidence may be given by a second garda of the fact that the member in charge of the station informed the accused of his rights and gave him the requisite notice in compliance with Art.8 of the Treatment of Persons in Custody Regulations of 1987.[62] Article 8 did not impose upon the member in charge a duty to ensure that communication of his rights was actually understood by the accused, and therefore the court was not required to examine the substance of the communication and the accused's response: the "only evidence that was

---

[58] [1956] 1 W.L.R. 965 (PC) (*cf.* appendix 7); approved in *Cullen v Clarke* [1963] I.R. 368 at 378 (SC) (*cf.* appendix 8); *Re Haughey* [1971] I.R. 217 at 264 (SC).
[59] [1956] 1 W.L.R. 965 at 970 (PC).
[60] HC, February 10, 1998.
[61] [1963] I.R. 368 at 378 (SC).
[62] *cf.* para.**10–26** *et seq.*

required to be given was that the words were spoken and the notice handed over. Garda Lynn (the prosecuting garda) heard the words spoken in the presence of the accused and saw the notice being handed over. He was entitled to give evidence of these facts, and he did so".

9–24 In *Ratten v R.*,[63] the Privy Council revisited these issues and admitted a critical statement in a murder trial in the capacity of original evidence rather than as hearsay properly admissible under the more appropriate *res gestae* exception.[64] The defence to the charge that the accused had shot and murdered his wife was that the gun had fired accidentally whilst he was cleaning it. The evidence established that a shot had been fired between 1.12 a.m. and 1.20 a.m. A telephonist from the local exchange gave evidence that at 1.15 a.m. she received a telephone call from Ratten's house by a woman who asked for the police in an hysterical voice. Lord Wilberforce upheld the trial court's decision to admit the statement as original evidence upon the basis that it was relevant to rebut the accused's testimonial account that no telephone call had been made from the house around that time (and that there was no one else in the house besides himself, his wife, and their small children), and additionally to rebut his claim that the gun had fired accidentally (since the caller had phoned in a distressed state).

9–25 To the extent that the statement rebutted the denial of a phonecall in *Ratten*, admissibility did not require the court to consider the truth of any assertions implicitly generated by the words. To the extent that it rebutted the accused's account by showing the distress of the caller, admissibility depended upon accepting as truthful the implied assertion that the caller was in distress and fear. Whether or not in principle this evidence required the court to consider its truth, its undeniable probative thrust was that the caller was in fear for her life at the material time. Whereas in the *Subramaniam* case, it did not matter that the terrorists' threats were genuinely intended or not (since the terrorists were not on trial), in *Ratten* it mattered critically to know whether or not the wife had been in fear, and the manner in which her words were spoken inevitably engendered an evidential inference that her fears were genuine. The statement was more appropriately admissible in *Ratten* as a *res gestae* exception to the hearsay rule, upon which Lord Wilberforce expounded in *obiter dicta* later approved by the House of Lords in *Andrews*.[65] The equality of opportunity in admitting the statement either as original evidence or as *res gestae* did not exist to the extent assumed by Lord Wilberforce. Under the *res gestae* exception, the statement was admissible without qualification, a preferable result; admissible as original evidence, it was in principle probative only of the relevant issue and, as such, was amenable generally to exclusion if the prejudicial effect of the evidence outweighed the probative basis upon which it was formally admitted.

---

[63] [1972] A.C. 378 (PC): *cf.* appendix 17.
[64] *cf.* para.**9–68**.
[65] *cf.* para.**9–69**.

9–26 It is clear from the English case law that the hearsay/original evidence distinction has given judges considerable scope to side-step application of the hearsay rule by recasting the evidential use and basis of the statement in question. In *R. v Rice*,[66] the contentious evidence was a used airline ticket bearing the accused's name, found with other used tickets retained by the airline (now admissible, by way of legislative exception, as documentary information compiled in the ordinary course of business).[67] The person who collected the ticket—who, it was argued, had implicitly made a statement that the ticket had been received from Mr Rice—was unidentified. The Court of Appeal preferred not to characterise the ticket stub as implied assertion hearsay but instead as an item of real evidence on a par with a passport that "is more likely on the whole to be in the possession of the person to whom it was issued".[68] The ticket had been produced "from proper custody" and from a "place where tickets used by passengers would in the ordinary course be found".[69] The ticket was alternatively admissible as original evidence establishing a relevant circumstantial fact bearing upon the question whether a man named Mr Rice had taken the flight in question (though not probative of whether or not the flight had been booked by a Mr Rice).[70]

9–27 A much less convincing re-characterisation of relevant issue and evidential basis arose in *Woodhouse v Hall*,[71] where the accused was prosecuted for running a brothel masquerading as a massage parlor. The trial court's refusal to admit evidence that the undercover guards had received unsolicited offers of "hand jobs" from the masseuses was criticised upon appeal. Applying *dicta* in *Ratten* and *Subramaniam*, Donaldson L.J. reasoned, opaquely, that this was not a case for application of the hearsay rule: "[The] justices ... may have thought that they had to be satisfied as to the truth of what the ladies said ... that the words were not a joke but were meant seriously. ... But this is not a matter of truth or falsity. It is a matter of what was really said—the quality of the words, the message being transmitted. The relevant issue is did these ladies make these offers?"[72] Yet the central relevant issue in *Woodhouse* was whether or not the place was being run as a brothel. Offers made by masseuses were only relevant in the context of the particular criminal charge; if not accepted to have been intended, the offers were not independently relevant. In criticism of the strange ruling in *Woodhouse*, it has also been remarked that an offer is never true or false, but may be made sincerely or flippantly, and it offends the

---

[66] [1963] 1 Q.B. 857 (CCA).
[67] *cf.* para.**9–36** *et seq.*
[68] *ibid.* at 871–2, *per* Winn J.
[69] *ibid.*
[70] *ibid.* at 872, *per* Winn J. Allen in *Practical Guide to Evidence* (Clarendon, London, 1998) at pp.132–3 justifies the admission of the ticket upon an alternative basis—that the combination of words and context in the case amounted to the performance of an action (or "performative utterance"), which thus had no independent assertive truth-value capable of attracting the hearsay rule.
[71] (1981) 72 Cr. App. R. 39 (CA).
[72] *ibid.* at 42.

The Rule against Hearsay

rationale of the hearsay rule to introduce second-hand evidence of an offer by someone who is not present at the trial to testify to its sincerity.[73]

9–28 In *R. v Kearly*,[74] the House of Lords was presented with a number of difficult hearsay questions over five days of submissions that ultimately divided the bench. The accused was charged with possessing drugs with intent to supply, after the police had raided his flat and discovered drugs and related paraphernalia. Whilst in the flat, the police officers received 10 telephone calls and answered the door to seven people, each asking to speak to the accused and looking for drugs. The prosecution did not summon the callers, but sought to rely upon evidence by the police of receipt of the calls. Lord Oliver considered the evidence to constitute a new variant—what was sought to be established by the prosecution was not necessarily the accuracy of the words uttered by the callers, but, rather, inferences as to the actions and intentions of the accused drawn from the combination of words used by the speakers and the circumstances in which they were uttered. The prosecution, in other words, sought to exploit the distinction between original and hearsay evidence by admitting the evidence ostensibly not to prove its accuracy but to establish relevant facts (the callers' beliefs) that cumulatively might engender an inference of the accused's guilt.

9–29 A majority of the House decided that the calls implied the callers believed the accused to be a dealer in drugs. Even if the callers had testified, their *belief* as to the accused's intentions would be irrelevant and unreceivable. If this was so for inferences arising from express assertions, it was also so with respect to implied assertions. Evidence of the calls could be relevant only through that which made them inadmissible under the hearsay rule: that is, as evidence of the accused's intention to supply drugs.

9–30 Lords Browne-Wilkinson and Griffiths dissented, and their alternative reasoning is worth noting given that the *Kearly* decision—though resting upon clear logic and principle—has been roundly condemned in England for dragging the law of hearsay into disrepute.[75] The minority took the view that there is no violation of the hearsay rule where evidence of what the callers said is not relied upon testimonially to prove the truth of the words, but instead as original evidence to explain the callers' purpose in making the calls, and to establish that there was a market ready and willing to purchase drugs from the accused. This did not require the court to accept the truth of the individual beliefs of the absent parties, but instead to establish relevant circumstantial facts. The dissenting approach is consistent with a line of American authority. In the

---

[73] Ashworth and Pattenden, "Reliability, Hearsay Evidence and the English Criminal Trial" (1986) 102 L.Q.R. 293 at 313.
[74] [1992] 2 W.L.R. 656 (HL).
[75] Lord Griffiths (*ibid*. at 659) suggested that the layman would consider the law an ass not to admit evidence of 17 calls by customers to the accused's apartment as *relevant* to charges of drug dealing. Tapper, "Hearsay and Implied Assertions" (1992) 109 L.Q.R 524 at 528, writes that *Kearly* "seems unlikely to be followed or approved, and may condemn the law of hearsay in England to wallow in a parochial mass of technicality".

context of prosecutions for illegal gambling, numerous courts decided to interpret such calls as original circumstantial evidence showing that illegal gambling was taking place at the address where the call was made, and that this evidence is not dependent upon accepting that the callers wished to place a bet or truly believed that bets were being accepted at the address phoned.[76]

III. IMPLIED ASSERTIONS

9–31 Several cases have applied the hearsay rule to assertions of fact implicit in a statement. The first reported decision in *Wright v Doe d. Tatham*[77] concerned a dispute over a will made by an apparently incompetent testator who from youth had been branded a simpleton and till death treated as a dependent by relatives and servants. The will was contested by the heir-at-law, and supported by the principal beneficiary. The latter sought to rely upon letters written by friends to the deceased, containing phrases such as "you are blessed with health" which, it was argued, implied that the testator had been competent. Parke B. adopted the view that to the extent that the letters implied qualities the deceased was alleged to have possessed, "those letters may be considered in this respect to be on the same footing as if they had contained a direct and positive statement that he was competent. For this purpose they are mere hearsay evidence, statements of the writer, not on oath, of the truth of the matter in question".[78]

9–32 *R. v Teper*[79] was another case of implied assertion hearsay. The accused was convicted for the arson of a shop belonging to his wife. His defence was based upon alibi. The prosecution sought to rely upon evidence by a policeman that some 26 minutes after the fire began, he heard a woman bystander remark as the accused took flight, "your place burning and you going away from the fire!" The accused's conviction was quashed upon the basis that the hearsay rule precluded the court from admitting a hearsay statement alleged to have been made by an absent declarant; the statement in this case implicitly asserted the identity of the accused and its only function had been to establish his presence near the shop and the peculiarity of his conduct.

9–33 The further application of the hearsay rule to cases of non-verbal implied assertion, or non-narrative hearsay, was first recognised in *Wright v Doe d. Tatham*.[80] By 1956, with respect at least to *intended* implied assertions, Cross could write that "[n]o one has ever doubted that the rule against hearsay applies to conduct which was intended to be assertive".[81] The House of Lords in *R. v*

---

[76] *People v Radley* (1945) 157 P. (2d) 426; *US v Zenni* (1980) 492 F. Supp. 464; *McGregor v Stokes* [1952] V.L.R. 347.
[77] (1838) 7 Ad. & E. 313.
[78] *ibid*. at 385.
[79] [1952] A.C. 480 (PC).
[80] (1838) 7 Ad. & E. 313.
[81] (1956) at 94, 95: asking, "is there any reason why a witness' report of a doctor's statement

Kearly[82] confirmed the equal application of the rule against hearsay to implied assertion. Although not much commented upon by the Irish judges to date, the converse seems implicit in Kingsmill Moore J.'s observation in *Cullen v Clarke* that "[s]peaking is as much an act as doing".[83]

9–34 Whilst it is accepted that the hearsay rule does not apply to non-assertive behaviour, such as the leaving of fingerprints, there is considerable uncertainty over the application of the hearsay rule to statements or conduct not intended to be assertive but resting upon some fact *assumed* by the maker of the statement or the doer of the act from which the court may draw inference.[84] In *Wright v Doe d. Tatham*,[85] Parke B. (*obiter*) identified numerous examples of non-verbal hearsay. Not all of them appear appropriate to the rule, such as: the observed conduct of a deceased sea captain who, after examining every part of his vessel, embarks upon it with his family (as an implied assertion that the boat was seaworthy); or a description by another person of a doctor's conduct in permitting a patient to make a will (as an implied assertion on the doctor's part that he believed the patient to be competent to do so). To justify the strict application of the hearsay rule to implied assertions, however, it should be clear that the contended justification demonstrably gives rise to the assertion in question, where admitted. The above examples of non-verbal conduct provided by Parke B. are ones where no public conventions or rules of meaning are adopted by the actors (such as silence in response to questions, or the raising of one's palm as a signal to another to stop).[86] The action or performance in each instance is ambiguous: the sea captain may yet have been reckless as to the safety of the vessel; the doctor may implicitly have believed it was not his duty to query the patient's competence to make the dying bequest. These examples are alternatively classed as *unintended implied assertions*. According to one view, unintended implied assertions are equally prone to error and inaccuracy, since the speaker will not have been as conscious of the need to be careful with respect to his unintended or presumptive assertions.[87] They are less likely to engender concerns that the assertion was affected or concocted, however, or to merit the application of the hearsay rule upon the basis that they are in fact assertive.

9–35 The hearsay rule should not strictly apply to implied assertions that are not clear or unambiguous in the circumstances. The admissibility of statements of this kind is more properly a question of the evidence's relevance to the case having regard to its likely prejudicial effect, and its value a matter for the

---

that the person he had examined was dead should be distinguished from the witness' account of the placing of the body on a mortuary van by the doctor after the examination?".

[82] [1992] 2 W.L.R. 656 (HL); *cf.* para.**9–28** *et seq.*
[83] [1963] I.R. 368 at 381 (SC): *cf.* appendix 8.
[84] Heydon, *op. cit.*, n.28 at p.326.
[85] (1838) 7 Ad. & E. 313 at 388.
[86] Guest, "The Scope of the Hearsay Rule" (1985) at p.398.
[87] Pattenden, "Conceptual versus Pragmatic Approaches to Hearsay" (1993) at p.142. For a contrary view, see Allan, "Implied Assertions as Hearsay" (1992) at p.1194 and Heydon, *op. cit.*, n.28 at p.327.

weight of the evidence having regard to its reliability. The Law Commission in England has recommended that if application of the hearsay rule to implied assertions is to be retained, it should be limited to cases where the person can be said to have intended another to believe or to act upon the assertion implied in the statement or conduct. The hearsay rule should not proscribe all assumptions and implied facts to be drawn from what a person said, as occurred in *R. v Kearly*[88] which precluded evidence of intercepted phone calls upon the basis that they implied the callers' belief that the recipient was a drug dealer.[89] This approach was adopted in the US, motivated by similar concerns to prosecute drug dealers.[90] The removal of unintended implied assertions from the scope of the rule in other jurisdictions has derived from a sense that incidental or unintended assertions (such as "Hello Daddy", as an implied assertion that the other person was the speaker's father)[91] are less likely to have been mistaken or affected.[92] It has also been recognised that if the distinction between intended and unintended assertions is not drawn, potentially every statement or act would attract the hearsay rule to a proliferating degree, dragging the law and its well-meaning logic into disrepute.[93]

IV. DOCUMENTARY EVIDENCE

9–36 Part II of the Criminal Evidence Act 1992 created a broad statutory exception permitting the admissibility in criminal proceedings of documentary information produced in the ordinary course of business. The provisions implicitly acknowledge the reliability of statements and information recorded in documents where compiled in the ordinary course of business and supplied by unidentified persons who had personal knowledge of the matters. "Document" is defined with appropriate breadth to *include* maps, plans, graphs, drawings, photographs, and any information in non-legible form reproduced in permanent legible form.[94] Part II admits information in documentary form where either compiled in the ordinary course of business, or supplied by a first person (whether or not he compiled it or is identifiable) to a second person

---

[88] *cf.* para.**9–28** *et seq.*
[89] Law Commission (1995), *op. cit.*, n.22.
[90] US Rule 801 of the Federal Rules of Evidence, applied in *US v Long* (1990) 905 F. 2d 1572 at 1579. A similar approach has been taken in Australia under the Uniform Evidence Acts 1995, s.59(1), which provides that the hearsay rule applies to implied assertions only to the extent that they are intended.
[91] This statement divided the Australian High Court, prior to s.59(1) of the Uniform Evidence Acts 1995, in *Walton v R.* (1989) 166 C.L.R. 283 (HC, Aust.).
[92] Australian Law Reform Commission *Report on Evidence*, Interim Report No. 26 and Final Report No. 38.
[93] *ibid.*
[94] Section 2. After prior definitions proved unduly restrictive, the English legislature similarly opted for an open-ended and technologically non-specific definition in s.13 of the Civil Evidence Act 1995, amending the Criminal Justice Act 1988, which provides that "document" means "anything in which information of any description is recorded, and 'copy', in relation to a document, means anything onto which information recorded in a document has been copied, by whatever means, and whether directly or indirectly".

who may reasonably be supposed to have had personal knowledge of the matters in question.[95] The information may have been supplied directly or indirectly, although where indirectly, only if the person to whom it was supplied received it in the ordinary course of business.[96]

9–37 Part II contains a number of safeguards against abuse of documentary hearsay. Under s.8, the court has a discretion to exclude the document "in the interests of justice", having regard in particular to circumstances suggesting it is unreliable or inauthentic or would result in unfairness to the accused. Evidence is admissible to challenge the credibility of the documentary information, as if the information had been tendered personally in-chief.[97] A copy of the document must be served upon the accused not later than 21 days prior to the trial, pursuant to s.6(1) of the Criminal Procedure Act 1967.[98] Under s.6, a certificate affirming that the information was compiled in the ordinary course of a business (and other details) "shall be evidence of any matter stated or specified therein". Although the certificate, and the advance notice of intention to tender documentary evidence under Pt II, appear to have been intended to function as prerequisites to admissibility—s.5 provides for admissibility "subject to this Part"—the Court of Criminal Appeal in *People (DPP) v Byrne*[99] appears to have interpreted Pt II to enable admissibility without these restrictions.

9–38 *Byrne* was a similar case to *DPP v Myers*,[100] and concerned the admissibility of statements and records by various persons who had received a doctored car in the course of business and recorded entries at the relevant stages. Although Keane C.J. did not explain the basis upon which he believed the statements to be admissible, the implicit view appears to have been that they were admissible under Pt II of the 1992 Act and that this was not necessarily dependent upon advance certification and notice. The witnesses in the case who testified to affirm the information they personally recorded would have been entitled to refer to contemporaneous records as notes to refresh their memory,[101] and alternatively their declarations may have been admissible as *res gestae* statements accompanying and explaining contemporaneous acts.[102] This was not the case for the officer from the Revenue Commissioners and the officer from the Motor Taxation Office, however, since they had not personally compiled the information they attested, and the admissibility of their recorded statements was a matter to be proven by reference to the exceptions to the hearsay rule.

---

[95] Section 5(1).
[96] Section 5(2).
[97] Section 9.
[98] Sections 7, 10.
[99] [2001] 2 I.L.R.M. 134 (CCA).
[100] [1965] A.C. 1001 (HL); *cf.* para.**9–12** *et seq.*
[101] *cf.* para.**2–41** *et seq.*
[102] *cf.* para.**9–74** *et seq.*

9–39 The statutory exception for admissibility of documentary evidence has not yet been extended to civil proceedings. In *Hughes v Staunton*,[103] Lynch J. observed the technicality of the hearsay rule in civil cases. If all the nurses and doctors who provided entries in the medical records discovered from the English hospitals were requested to testify, and each was questioned about their entries, each would invariably testify that he had now no present recollection of the circumstances surrounding the entry but was confident that it was accurate and reliable. In other words, in cases of this type, where documents have been produced in the course of a customary working duty, there is no essential need to require the authors to testify, since if they testified they would usually be compelled to consult the document entries as contemporaneous notes to refresh their memory,[104] and the hearsay rule would thus be circumnavigated in the accustomed manner.

V. HEARSAY IN CIVIL CASES

9–40 The hearsay rule applies in principle with like effect to civil hearings, although in the civil context parties are free to waive their objection to evidence that technically constitutes hearsay, such as expert reports and documentary information, as a matter of procedural convenience or mutual benefit.[105] In *Hughes v Staunton*,[106] for instance, the parties mutually consented to the admission of various medical records discovered from an English hospital, thereby avoiding the need to require the travel and attendance at court of numerous medical personnel. Lynch J. decided to treat the records as "giving a reasonably accurate account of the events which they purport to record". The records would be rejected only where contradicted by sworn evidence and unsupported by oral evidence that the judge preferred.

9–41 The court may not accept documentary hearsay evidence where contradicted by oral evidence in the case. In *Moloney v Jury's Hotel plc.*,[107] the Supreme Court directed a rehearing in negligence proceedings, after finding that the High Court erred when it accepted hospital notes as evidence capable of diminishing the weight of the plaintiff's testimony. The author of the notes was not made available for cross-examination, and the possibility that the notes were inaccurate had not adequately been explored by the court.

9–42 Given the administrative inconveniences occasioned by a strict technical application of the hearsay rule to documentary information in civil cases, it

---

[103] HC, February 16, 1990.
[104] *cf.* para.**2–41** *et seq.*
[105] *e.g. Shelley-Morris v Bus Atha Cliath* [2003] 1 I.R. 232 at 238 (SC), with respect to an agreement of the parties in personal injury proceedings to substitute expert medical reports for *viva voce* evidence.
[106] HC, February 16, 1990.
[107] SC, November 12, 1999.

The Rule against Hearsay

has been argued for some time that the rule should be suspended or rewritten for civil proceedings. In 1988, the Law Reform Commission recommended that the exclusionary rule be replaced in civil cases by an inclusionary rule subject to judicial discretion to exclude statements of insufficient probative value and to a requirement of advance notice.[108] In England, the Law Commission similarly proposed abolition in civil cases,[109] and this was accomplished by the Civil Evidence Act 1995.[110]

Child Witnesses and Family Law

9–43 In recent years, the legislature has made special provision for child witnesses, who prior to the reform had been exposed to the full rigours of common law rules governing their competence to testify and eligibility to take the oath, the rule against hearsay, and strict corroboration rules.[111] The past inability of the prosecution in criminal proceedings to refer to a young child's pre-trial statement—even where the trial occurred years after the recorded contemporaneous account—and the ongoing ability of the defence to refer selectively to that statement where it diverged from particulars given in the witness' live testimony,[112] created a situation where the child witness was shown repeatedly to be an unreliable witness *per se*, and the prosecution of child abuse cases was correspondingly more difficult. For criminal proceedings, the Criminal Evidence Act 1992 removed each of these fundamental obstacles, in particular the requirement of live *viva voce* testimony in open court and physical confrontation with and re-identification of the accused,[113] the necessity to show eligibility to take the oath in order to avoid the strict effect of corroboration rules,[114] and the rule against hearsay (to the extent it applied to interview statements made by a complainant under 14 years to a garda).[115] Until the Children Act of 1997, the law did not permit the reception of unsworn testimony of children in civil cases;[116] nor was there a power to accept pre-trial statements as an exception to the hearsay rule; nor was there a right to give testimony by television link with an intermediary as existed in criminal proceedings for sexual or violent offences since the Criminal Evidence Act 1992.[117] If the complainant was too young or traumatised to give evidence directly in court, other parties, such as childcare workers, were restricted in making reference to what the child had told them.

9–44 In the meantime, the courts circumvented the strict effects of the hearsay

---

[108] Law Reform Commission (1988) at pp.6–7.
[109] Law Commission, *The Hearsay Rule in Civil Cases*, Report No.216, 1993.
[110] Section 1(1) of the Civil Evidence Act 1995 provides: "In civil proceedings, evidence shall not be excluded on the ground that it is hearsay".
[111] *cf.* para.**2–08** *et seq.*
[112] *cf.* para.**3–07** *et seq.*
[113] *cf.* para.**1–60** *et seq.*
[114] *cf.* para.**2–07** *et seq.*
[115] *cf.* para.**1–65**.
[116] *Mapp v Gilhooley* SC, April 23, 1991; *cf.* para.**2–15**.
[117] *cf.* para.**1–53** *et seq.*

rule in family law proceedings by various routes. One of these was, and is, to consider reports provided to the court by child psychiatrists and psychologists in which assertions made to the expert by the child and his parents are narrated and assessed.[118] In *Matter of M, S, & W Infants*,[119] a wardship application, the High Court justified receiving hearsay evidence from a speech therapist and a social worker (including a video-taped interview), upon the basis that the hearsay rule had never been strictly applied in Ireland to wardship proceedings, which are not *lis inter partes* or adversarial in nature but instead akin to an investigation into the welfare of the child under the court's *parens patria* jurisdiction. Costello P. reasoned that although the court has discretion in wardship cases to admit hearsay evidence, and to accord more or less weight to the statement depending upon how reliable it appears, the court must first be satisfied of the necessity to admit the statement. Notwithstanding, and perhaps because of, the admissibility of hearsay in wardship cases, the procedures otherwise followed must be "scrupulously fair".[120] In deciding whether to act on the statement, the court must consider whether there were any motives or influences that precipitated the allegation or suggestion of wrongdoing. If the child's statement was made in the context of an embittered matrimonial dispute, the court must investigate the possibility that the allegations were the product of undue influence on the part of one of the child's parents, and upon this basis refuse to act on it.[121]

9–45 In *Southern Health Board v CH*,[122] the appeal was fought over the use of videotaped interviews with the six-year-old complainant detailing the sexual abuse she suffered from her father, in the context of fit persons proceedings to appoint a named guardian for the child. Costello P. likened the application to wardship proceedings, since in each event the court is obliged to act in the best interests of the child and the proceedings are therefore more inquisitorial. As for wardship cases, the judge should exercise his discretion to admit the evidence only where satisfied that it is necessary to do so—either because the child is too young to give evidence or because he is unable to do so. Additionally, where videotapes are admitted, a copy of the tape must be furnished to the party against whom the allegations are made so that that party has an opportunity to rebut any inferences that may be drawn from the tapes. Upon appeal, the Supreme Court adopted a different justification for the reception of this type of evidence, and it reasoned that the court was entitled to permit an expert witness, such as a counsellor, to furnish the court with the material upon which he based his expert opinion, and that the court should hear "the basic evidence from which [the expert's] conclusion was reached".[123] The reasoning of the Supreme Court appears tenable only upon the basis that

---

[118] Pursuant to s.47 of the Family Law Act 1995 and s.20 of the Child Care Act 1991.
[119] [1996] 1 I.L.R.M. 370 (HC).
[120] *ibid*. at 381.
[121] *ibid*.
[122] [1996] 1 I.R 219 (SC): *cf.* appendix 50.
[123] *ibid*. at 238, *per* O'Flaherty J., following *State (D and D) v Groarke* [1990] 1 I.R. 305 (SC).

it is limited to family proceedings affecting the welfare of a child. Whilst an expert witness may properly base his expert judgment upon research and findings published by other experts in his field, the common law generally requires him to prove the primary facts upon which his conclusion rests, and only insofar as those primary facts are admissible.[124] The principle that a judge in family law proceedings may hear and act upon pre-hearing assertions conveyed by one person to a counsellor later appearing as expert witness does not elsewhere sit easily, and certainly not in criminal proceedings where the assertions are material to guilt.

9–46 Section 23 of the Children Act 1997 has effectively suspended the application of the hearsay rule as it applies to statements made by a child who has been considered too young or traumatised to give testimony in the proceedings. Challenges to such statements now affect the weight but not admissibility of the evidence, and s.24 itemises various factors that may weigh with the court, such as whether: "(a) the original statement was made contemporaneously with the occurrence or existence of the matters stated; (b) the evidence involves multiple hearsay; (c) any person involved has any motive to conceal or misrepresent matters; (d) the original statement was an edited account or was made in collaboration with another for a particular purpose; and (e) the circumstances in which the evidence is adduced as hearsay are such as to suggest an attempt to prevent proper evaluation of its weight". Section 25 provides that where evidence of the child is given in this documentary form, the defence is entitled to admit evidence in-chief, where it is otherwise admissible, to challenge the child's credibility as if the child had testified.

9–47 Section 23 does not formally affect the broader discretion, identified by the Supreme Court in *CH*, to permit an expert witness to refer to assertions made to him by the child and other parties to the proceedings. The common law discretion to admit hearsay evidence in wardship and fit persons proceedings, as recognised by Costello P. in *M, S, & W* and *CH*, is broader than s.23, and potentially could include forms of multiple hearsay and implied assertion. This general (now residual) discretion may logically extend beyond the wardship and fit persons proceedings to include guardianship and custody disputes under the Guardianship of Infants Act 1964. Although such disputes may begin as private proceedings, and are not as procedurally inquisitorial as the wardship or fit persons proceedings, the potential involvement of the health board in the proceedings,[125] and the constitutional duty of the court to safeguard the interests of the child[126] enshrined in s.3 of the 1964 Act, make these

---

[124] *R. v Abadom* [1983] 1 W.L.R. 126 (CA). *cf.* paras **9–55, 12–24**.
[125] By virtue of s.20 of the Child Care Act 1991.
[126] According to McCracken J. in *Eastern Health Board v District Judge J.P. McDonnell* [1999] 1 I.R. 174 at 183 (HC): "it is the function of the Courts, and not of local authorities or Health Boards, to ensure that the constitutional guarantees given to an individual are upheld. Therefore, where the welfare of a citizen, and in particular of a child who is in need, is concerned there would have to be very clear delegation of powers if the obligation is to be imposed upon somebody other than the courts".

proceedings inherently more public and inquisitorial. Where hearsay is submitted upon this basis, however, the courts are likely to be guided by the considerations identified by s.24 as being of particular relevance to the weight of the evidence.

VI. HEARSAY AT PRE-TRIAL AND INTERLOCUTORY STAGES

9–48 The courts have recognised that the rules of evidence apply more flexibly at the pre-trial and pre-hearing stages. In the criminal context, it was confirmed in *DPP v Sweeney*[127] that when deciding whether to issue a search warrant, a chief superintendent (or other relevant authority) must conclude that there are "reasonable grounds" for the warrant, but he is not required to seek direct oral evidence of a type that would be admissible at the trial. Hearsay evidence, based upon information from an unidentified source, to the extent it was believed to be reliable, constituted reasonable grounds for the purposes of the application for a warrant in the case.

9–49 In *People (DPP) v McGinley*,[128] the Supreme Court distinguished the bail application from civil interlocutory applications, and observed that whilst evidence rules are not as strictly applied for either, there is a greater need in applications for bail to ensure integrity in the criminal process and to protect the accused person's constitutional right to liberty. The court approved *People (Attorney-General) v O'Callaghan*[129] for the principle that an applicant for bail is generally entitled to have the evidence against him given *viva voce* under oath and amenable to cross-examination. By way of exception to this, however, the court may dispense with the need to hear oral evidence where it believes "there are sufficient grounds for not requiring the witness to give *viva voce* evidence".[130] In allowing the appeal in the case, the Supreme Court concluded that the judge had insufficiently considered the alternative option of adjourning the application so that oral evidence could be arranged, and had erred in admitting hearsay statements of persons objecting to the bail application upon the grounds that the applicant had threatened and intimidated them. Likewise, in *DPP v McNamara*,[131] the Supreme Court confirmed that hearsay evidence may be heard in bail applications, but remitted the decision on bail for rehearing as the garda's evidence had been substantially hearsay.

9–50 Order 40, r.4 of the Rules of the Superior Courts permits hearsay evidence and statements of belief in affidavits for the purpose of interlocutory hearings.[132] In this type of application, time tends to be of the essence, and in

---

[127] HC, March 26, 1996.
[128] [1998] 2 I.L.R.M. 233 (SC).
[128] [1966] I.R. 501 (SC).
[130] [1998] 2 I.L.R.M. 233 at 238, *per* Keane J. (SC).
[131] SC, June 21, 2002, *per* Hardiman J.
[132] The High Court rejected submissions in *Walsh v Harrison* [2003] 2 I.L.R.M. 161 that an affidavit filed by the defendant in defamation proceedings was inadmissible by reason of its scandalous allegations and third-party hearsay.

The Rule against Hearsay

principle, though not always in practice, the court does not make final determinations on the facts at issue in the proceedings. It was argued in *Murphy v GM*[133] that if the effect of Ord.40, r.4 was that hearsay assertions were admissible in affidavits for the purposes of s.3 of the Proceeds of Crime Act 1996, pursuant to which the court could freeze the respondent's assets without requiring an undertaking as to damages (usually essential in cases of pre-hearing injunctive relief), s.3 was unconstitutional in effect. The court approved *M v D*,[134] where Moriarty J. had accepted that the procedures under the 1996 Act are similar to those for Mareva injunctions, whereby an "appreciable measure of hearsay evidence is considered acceptable in Affidavits filed on behalf of parties". Although the rule against hearsay may be assumed indirectly to confer upon an accused a right not to have hearsay evidence tendered against him in criminal proceedings, O'Higgins J. reasoned that such a right is not distinct but may be taken to derive from the *genus* constitutional right to a fair trial and to fair procedures. In this case, it was material that the respondent had been given the opportunity to cross-examine the deponent, and had not availed of it. The affidavit in question was admissible, its probative value thereafter a matter of weight at the discretion of the court.

9–51 Despite the flexibility in interlocutory applications, the court should not, save with good reason, accept hearsay evidence at the expense of rebutting oral evidence. In *Moloney v Jury's Hotel Plc.*,[135] the Supreme Court overturned a decision of the trial judge to dismiss the plaintiff's claim for injunctive relief after accepting entries in two medical notes and rejecting oral evidence given by the plaintiff and her medical witnesses. As Barrington J. recognised, the notes were not evidence in the case, and, as the persons who made the entries had not been called for the purposes of oral evidence and cross-examination, the court could not be sure that the entries were not mistaken or inaccurate.

9–52 The courts have expressed the view that hearsay evidence is often inappropriate and dangerous in the context of interlocutory applications for injunctive relief. In *Smithkline Beecham Plc. v Antigen Pharmaceuticals Ltd*,[136] a passing-off case requiring evidence of whether pharmacists and consumers were confused by the similarity in the names of the parties' painkillers, the dangers of being influenced by hearsay when determining the balance of convenience were clear to the court. The plaintiffs and the defendant had filed affidavits based upon hearsay accounts apparently given by pharmacists and consumers to the deponent and reaching opposite conclusions upon whether pharmacists were confused. McCracken J. observed generally that "survey evidence is of little or no value in interlocutory applications, where that evidence is not tested by cross-examination, and indeed all the background facts relating to that evidence, such as the actual questionnaires and answers, are not put in evidence".[137]

---

[133] HC, June 4, 1999.
[134] [1998] 3 I.R. 175 at 178 (HC).
[135] SC, November 12, 1999.
[136] [1999] 2 I.L.R.M. 190 (HC).
[137] *ibid.* at 197.

VII. HEARSAY AND TRIBUNALS

9–53 With respect to tribunals exercising *quasi*-judicial functions, it has been assumed that the rules of evidence do not necessarily apply as strictly, although the Supreme Court has articulated on occasion that all the rules of evidence that exist for the protection of a person accused in criminal proceedings and that are considered critical to fair procedures, in particular the rule against hearsay, must be adhered to by tribunals. In considering hearsay evidence to be anathema to a fair hearing, the courts have placed emphasis upon the inability of the applicant to cross-examine under oath the author of the adverse statements. In *Kiely v Minister for Social Welfare*,[138] the appeals enquiry had wrongly permitted a written statement by a doctor, engaged by the Department of Social Welfare, to prevail over evidence given testimonially by two doctors called as witnesses for the applicant. Henchy J. observed: "Tribunals exercising *quasi*-judicial functions are frequently allowed to act informally—to receive unsworn evidence, to act on hearsay, to depart from the rules of evidence, to ignore courtroom procedures, and the like—but they may not act in such a way as to imperil a fair hearing or a fair result".[139] Specifically in the *Kiely* case, the Supreme Court was called upon to interpret the effect of Art.11(5) of the Social Welfare Regulations of 1952, enabling an appeals officer to admit any duly authenticated written statement "as *prima facie* evidence of any fact". It was open to the court to reason that the effect of that provision was to enable the officer to accept such a written statement as evidence of any fact unless and until rebutted by other evidence in the case. The court went further, however, and ruled that not only is such prima facie proof under Art.11(5) capable of being displaced by rebutting oral evidence, but that where oral evidence has been tendered in an enquiry and it tends to rebut or contradict the inference to be drawn by the statute from the certified statement, the statement is no longer admissible under that provision.

9–54 *Kiely* was applied by the Supreme Court in *Gallagher v Revenue Commissioners*,[140] where it upheld the High Court's orders quashing the respondents' decision to dismiss the applicant from his post in Customs and Excise following an allegation that he had deliberately undervalued imported vehicles and had cost the State significant losses in revenue. In relying to a significant extent upon hearsay evidence—documentary information from British customs authorities detailing previous sales with relevant vehicles—without oral testimony or the opportunity to cross-examine the source of the information, the applicant had been deprived of his constitutional right to fair procedures and natural justice.

---

[138] [1977] I.R. 267 (SC).
[139] *ibid*. at 281, *per* Henchy J.
[140] [1995] 1 I.L.R.M. 241 (SC).

VIII. MISCELLANEOUS

Expert Evidence

9–55 When expert witnesses give testimony in court, their views will typically be informed by the research and findings of other experts and peers in their field, and will tend to represent an accumulation of information and assertion from a variety of sources. The courts permit a measure of leeway in this regard without attracting the hearsay rule. This is partly for reasons of convenience, but also because experts testify on foot of their professional standing or expertise, which it is often appropriate that the courts accept. To limit the testimony of experts to statements based upon evidence proved in court would greatly frustrate the trial and expose it to a range of proliferating issues.[141] In *R. v Abadom*,[142] the Court of Appeal held that an expert forensic scientist was required to prove the basic facts upon which his opinion rested—here the refractive index of glass, in the context of assessing whether the glass found embedded in the accused's shoes was part of the glass smashed during a robbery. The expert was entitled to rely upon general statistical research undertaken by the Home Office, so long as he identified his sources to the court and so long as their credibility was amenable to examination.

Identification Evidence

9–56 The law governing identification evidence has come under the scrutiny of relatively recent rules and principles, chief amongst them the requirement of a special warning in every case where the prosecution tenders disputed evidence of identification.[143] The rules reflect the critical influence that identification evidence has upon the jury and the special need to exercise caution against accepting positive identification at face-value. In light of the ability of the identification warning to address any specific infirmities in the evidence, the English courts, in a number of cases addressing the point, have been content to avoid a mechanical application of the hearsay rule to evidence establishing who the witness selected at an identification parade where the evidence establishes that a positive identification was made at the parade. In *R. v Osbourne and Virtue*,[144] the witness could not recall having selected anyone at the parade, and a policeman wished to testify that she had positively identified the accused. Lawton L.J. asked "why, when a witness has forgotten what she did, evidence should not be given by another witness with a better memory to establish what, in fact, she did when the events were fresh in her mind".[145] The court considered it unnecessary to apply the hearsay rule, as the witness was available in court for cross-examination, and it was appropriate that her

---

[141] *cf.* the collateral issue rule at para.**3–01** *et seq.*
[142] [1983] 1 W.L.R. 126 (CA).
[143] *cf.* para.**6–01** *et seq.*
[144] [1973] 1 Q.B. 678 (CA): followed in *R. v Smith* [1976] Crim. L.R. 511 (CA), admitting a sketch of a suspect made by a police officer at the direction of a witness who was not called to testify in the trial.
[145] [1973] 1 Q.B. 678 at 690 (CA).

uncertainty should instead affect her credibility as a witness and the weight to be given to her evidence.

9–57 In *R. v McCay*,[146] a witness had made a positive identification of the accused at a parade by telling the police "it is number 8", which had been recorded. The witness did not consult the witness statement before the trial, and when questioned he identified the accused again in court; in his testimony, however, he could not recollect the number he had called at the parade. The trial judge permitted the police inspector to give this number in his evidence. Upholding his decision, Russell L.J. reasoned that "it is number 8" was a contemporaneous statement accompanying a relevant act (the identification), and as such admissible as a *res gestae* exception to the rule against hearsay.[147] The statement was not relevant to identify the assailant, but to establish whether a past identification had been made by the witness.

9–58 The courts have also considered hearsay concerns arising from cases where information was given informally by bystander witnesses to the police. Unlike the context in which witness statements are given, confirmed, and signed in the presence of police officers under controlled conditions, the informal giving and recording of information that a garda or other witness wishes to convey and that the original witness no longer remembers with precision engenders obvious hearsay concerns of unreliability. In numerous cases, the bystander observed and noted the registration number of a vehicle, reported it to a policeman at the scene of the crime, but later at the trial no longer possessed a record or memory of the number and was forced to rely upon the details recorded by the policeman. Although earlier cases ruled that this was defeated by the hearsay rule, eventually the English courts recognised a means of circumventing its application by encouraging the police to take a contemporaneous note of the witness' observation or recollection, approved by the witness at the time and later functional as an *aide memoire* to activate the witness' memory of the details.[148] As the note is viewed as *aide* to memory rather than source of information, and as it is not characterised as evidence in the case, the hearsay issue is thereby circumvented, however disingenuously.[149] In *R. v Kelsey*,[150] the Court of Appeal decided that the hearsay rule did not arise where the witness' recollection is taken down in writing 'under the supervision' of the officer and where the witness had an opportunity at the time to verify his account by either rereading the record taken by the policeman

---

[146] [1990] 1 W.L.R. 645 (CA).
[147] *cf.* para.**9–74** *et seq.*
[148] *cf.* para.**2–41** *et seq.*
[149] Described by the Law Reform Commission in 1980 as "of a type which get the law of evidence a bad name" (1980) at p.60.
[150] (1982) 74 Cr. App. R. 213 (CA). These requirements the court considered important in light of the fact that at common law a contemporaneous note could only function as a witness' *aide memoire* where the note had been written by the witness personally or, if written by some other person, where written contemporaneously, and "seen, read and adopted as accurate" by the witness: *R. v Mills and Rose* (1962) 1 W.L.R. 1152 at 1156, *per* Winn J.

or having it read back to him (although, where the witness did not physically read the police officer's note but heard the words and approved them, this fact must be established in evidence by the police officer). These conditions[151] are deemed prudent in light of the danger that "this mode of proof might, if permitted, open the doors to allowing a witness' whole account of an incident, which he had dictated to an officer at the time and since forgotten, to be given at the trial by the officer".[152]

IX. EXCEPTIONS TO THE HEARSAY RULE

Statutory Exceptions

9–59 The hearsay rule's general aversion to pre-trial statements is evocative historically of the common law's insistence in a non-technological era upon proof by oral live testimony. With the means now available for alternatives to the traditional form of *viva voce* confrontation, and a sense that vulnerable witnesses ought to be protected from the pressures of fully open testimony, recent statutory modifications have enabled the giving and the recording of testimony (by videotape or deposition) in advance of a criminal trial,[153] the admission of videotaped garda interviews with a complainant under 14 years in criminal proceedings for sexual offence,[154] and the admission of statements by a child in civil proceedings under the Children Act 1997.[155]

9–60 The legislature has tended to suspend the hearsay rule in specific contexts in a piecemeal manner, often where there has ceased to be any rationale for its continued application, as with Pt II of the Criminal Evidence Act 1992 which created an exception for documentary information produced or compiled in the ordinary course of a business.[156] Numerous other exceptions have been created for reasons of procedural convenience—to discontinue the wasteful necessity of requiring all persons with direct knowledge of relevant facts to testify, and to dispense with the need for formal proof where unnecessary. Section 21 of the Criminal Justice Act 1984 provided for the admissibility of statements as proof of fact in criminal proceedings, save where objection is made in writing within 21 days of receipt of notice of intention to tender the statement.[157] Section 6(1) of the Criminal Justice (Miscellaneous Provisions) Act 1997 permits, upon the first appearance of the accused before the District

---

[151] They were not fulfilled in *R. v McLean* (1968) 52 Cr. App. R. 80 (CA), where conviction was quashed following admission in the trial court of the record of a car number that had apparently been dictated by the witness, recorded by a police officer, but not read out to the witness to clarify his confirmation.
[152] (1982) 74 Cr. App. R. 213 at 217, *per* Taylor J. (CA).
[153] Criminal Procedure Act 1967, s.4F-G, inserted by Criminal Justice Act 1999, s.9; Children Act 2001, s.253; *cf.* para.**1–56** *et seq.*
[154] Criminal Evidence Act 1992, s.16(1)(b); *cf.* para.**1–65**.
[155] *cf.* para.**9–43** *et seq.*
[156] *cf.* para.**9–36** *et seq.*
[157] Following the Law Reform Commission's proposals (1980) at p.203.

Court, the admission of a certificate signed by the arresting or charging garda, where not below the rank of sergeant, to establish the fact of the arrest and charge. Under s.6(2), a certificate may be given in evidence to establish that the garda who signed it commenced or remained on duty at the scene of the crime, that no person entered the place without his permission, and no evidence was disturbed, whilst he was on duty. The above provisions are qualified by the right of the accused to seek, and the power of the court in any event to direct in the interests of justice, that evidence of the matters stated in the certificate ought instead to be given orally at an adjourned date.[158] Section 11(2) provides that a certificate may be given in evidence to establish that the garda who signed it copied the image of the fingerprints or palm-prints taken from the accused, and that the copy corresponds to the prints of the accused.

9–61 Where the statutory suspension of the hearsay rule is likely to have draconian effect for a party in the proceedings, the courts tend to interpret the provision restrictively. The Supreme Court recently considered the effect of s.8(5) and s.8(7) of the Criminal Assets Bureau Act 1996, which provide that a bureau officer may act upon "any information received by him/her from another bureau officer" and that it "shall be admitted in evidence in any subsequent proceedings". In *Criminal Assets Bureau v Hunt*,[159] Keane C.J. observed that the precise scope of this abridgment of the rule against hearsay was uncertain, and he favoured the view that s.8 did not intend to waive the rule so as to render information conveyed by one bureau officer to another officer admissible, which would have the absurd result of enabling one officer to convey inadmissible information to achieve admissibility. The court considered that s.8 instead operated to suspend the hearsay rule only so far as to admit in evidence "as truthful an unsworn statement made out of court by a bureau officer to the bureau officer who gives evidence that he acted on foot of the information in question" (a statement that would have been potentially admissible, in any event, as original evidence). Thus, the only means by which the court could accept bank statements on which the officer acted was where these had been proved under the provisions of the Bankers Books Evidence Acts, 1879-1959; as this had not been effected in the case, the proceedings against the respondents should have been dismissed.

Common Law Exceptions

9–62 The exception created for confessions—as statements made against the interests of the declarant—remains the most significant common law exception to the hearsay rule, and is considered separately in the next chapter. Numerous other common law exceptions endure, largely in the form they had assumed by the close of the nineteenth century. Aside from the popular *res gestae* exception, however, they have fallen out of use due to the emergence of particular statutory exceptions to the rule and the option of admitting

---

[158] Section 6(4).
[159] SC, March 19, 2003.

statements as original evidence.[160] Despite the implausible specificity of many of the exceptions, the English judiciary, most notably in *DPP v Myers*,[161] have resisted cultivating a more residual judicial discretion to exempt statements from the hearsay rule. This has not been the preference in other jurisdictions, however. The Irish courts have not ruled out extension or contraction of the rule against hearsay by judicial development, and this proposition in *Myers* has not been formally approved.[162] In *Matter of M, S, & W Infants*,[163] a wardship case, Denham J. refused to accept that the hearsay rule or its exceptions were "set in stone". In *Ares v Venner*,[164] the Canadian Supreme Court rejected the majority view in *Myers*, approving instead the minority sentiments expressed by Lords Donovan and Pearce:

> "The common law is moulded by the judges and it is still their province to adapt it from time to time so as to make it serve the interests of those it binds. Particularly is this so in the field of procedural law. Here the question posed is—'Shall the courts admit as evidence of a particular fact authentic and reliable records by which alone the fact may be satisfactorily proved?' I think the courts themselves are able to give an affirmative answer to the question".

9–63 Despite the House of Lord's adherence to the view that further development of the hearsay rule is a matter for the legislature and not the courts,[165] numerous changes have been undertaken which, it has been argued,[166] constitute new exceptions to the rule. One of those was to decide in *R. v Duncan*[167] that "mixed confession" statements tendered in evidence by the defence are admissible generally in the trial and for the benefit of the accused, where they contain sufficient inculpatory content to constitute a "confession" at law, and despite the fact that they contain exculpatory elements favourable to the defence. Another of those was to decide in *Myers v DPP*[168]

---

[160] *cf.* para.**9–20** *et seq.*
[161] *cf.* para.**9–12** *et seq.*
[162] The Court of Criminal Appeal reserved the question in *People (DPP) v Marley* [1985] I.L.R.M. 17 and *People (DPP) v Prunty* [1986] I.L.R.M. 716.
[163] SC, January 29, 1999.
[164] (1970) 14 D.L.R. (3d) 4 at 16 (SC), *per* Hall J. A similar view was expressed in New Zealand in *Smith v Police* [1969] N.Z.L.R. 856 at 860.
[165] *People (DPP) v Myers* [1965] A.C. 1001 at 1021 *per* Lord Reid (HL); repeated in *R. v Kearly* [1992] 2 W.L.R. 656, *per* Lord Bridge at 673, *per* Lord Oliver at 687 (HL). By contrast, Lord Griffiths, dissenting, (at 659) considered that "the judges of today should accept the responsibility of reviewing and adapting the rules of evidence to serve present society".
[166] Ashworth and Pattenden, "Reliability, Hearsay Evidence and the English Criminal Trial" (1986) at p.301; Hartshorne and Choo, "Hearsay-fiddles in the House of Lords" (1999) at p.293.
[167] (1981) 73 Cr. App. Rep. 359 (CA); approved by the House of Lords in *R. v Sharp* [1988] 1 W.L.R. 7 (HL); *cf.* para.**10–67** *et seq.*
[168] [1997] 3 W.L.R. 552 (HL)—overruling previous decisions such as *Lui Mei Lin v The Queen* [1989] A.C. 288 (PC), where it was acknowledged that a co-accused could cross-examine another co-accused upon a prior inconsistent confession, but that the trial judge was obliged to caution the jury when summing-up that the inconsistent statement

that a first co-accused could tender evidence, in a probative capacity, of a confession statement made by a second co-accused but not tendered in evidence by any other party—a development seriously at odds with the rationale that has informed the hearsay rule to date, and one unlikely to find favour in this jurisdiction, despite the liberal approach to "mixed statements" favoured by the Court of Criminal Appeal in *People (DPP) v Clarke*.[169]

9–64 When admitted under a common law exception to the rule, the hearsay evidence is often permitted to function as evidence fully probative of the facts asserted therein. In this respect, there is a significant difference between admitting the statement as original evidence to establish a particular relevant fact and admitting it as hearsay; however, it is not always clear in decisions such as *Ratten* that this is so.[170] Although the courts are prone to inconsistency, statements are sometimes generally admissible, and sometimes admissible upon a limited basis to establish a particular assertion, depending upon the particular exception.

(1) The *Res Gestae* Exception

9–65 The *res gestae* exception is the most recurrent basis upon which spontaneous statements are admitted, and it is not limited to first-hand hearsay.[171] There are four specific types of spontaneous statement to which the genus *res gestae* exception applies. They each require that the maker of the statement be dead or otherwise unavailable for the trial, and they share a common requirement of contemporaneity with the event, as a safeguard against concoction or mistake. The *res gestae* exception is substantially defined by the requirement of contemporaneity, such that it is typically reasoned that where a statement is so bound up in time with an act or event, it may be taken to form part of the act or event itself and is admissible alongside evidence of that act or event. The requirement of contemporaneity is also a safeguard against the possibility that the speaker had time to disengage from the event, to reflect critically upon it, and to affect a statement or allegation in response. In this vein, Wigmore explained that the admissibility of spontaneous *res gestae* exclamations is based upon the experience that, under certain external circumstances of physical shock, a stress of nervous excitement may be produced that stills the reflective faculties and removes their control, so that the resulting utterance is a spontaneous and sincere response to what he has perceived.[172]

---

was only relevant to the credibility of the co-accused and was not evidence probative of any facts asserted therein; *cf.* para.**10–63** *et seq.*
[169] [1994] 3 I.R. 289 (CCA); *cf.* appendix 46 and para.**10–68** *et seq.*
[170] *cf.* para.**9–24** *et seq.*
[171] Ormerod, "Redundant Res Gestae" (1998) at p.310.
[172] Wigmore, *op. cit.* n.46 at para.1747.

The Rule against Hearsay

(i) Spontaneous statements made by a participant in the act or observer of the act

9–66 The requirement of spontaneity or contemporaneity was at one stage applied with notorious strictness by the courts, of which the classic example is *R. v Bedingfield*.[173] The accused was charged with murdering the deceased by cutting her throat. His defence was that she had committed suicide. The evidence disclosed that the deceased had walked about 20 yards out of the room in which the accused was then found, and had said, pointing to her throat, "See what Harry has done!" She died 10 minutes later. Her statement was deemed inadmissible and not to benefit from the *res gestae* exception since, when the words were spoken, the "transaction" had been at an end, the mortal wound was already inflicted, and all alleged action upon the accused's part over.

9–67 As the opportunities arose, the courts gradually departed from the strict view of time and tense to one which focused on whether the statement was a spontaneous exclamation or, instead, a detached observation. In *Teper v R.*,[174] the statement by a bystander identifying the accused fleeing his burning shop was made 26 minutes after the fire began and at some distance from the shop. Setting aside conviction in a case depending substantially upon proof of the source of the fire, Lord Normand indicated it is essential that the words sought to be proven should, if not absolutely contemporaneous with the event, be at least so closely associated with it in time, place, and circumstances, that the words form part of the thing done akin to an item of real evidence and not merely a reported statement. Lord Normand's formulation was approved by the Court of Criminal Appeal in *People (Attorney-General) v Crosbie*,[175] where the court deemed admissible a statement by the deceased identifying his assailant moments after infliction of a stab wound.

9–68 This more rationale-based approach to *res gestae* is favoured today, and was signalled by Lord Wilberforce in *Ratten v R.*[176] Although the deceased's telephone request for the police was admitted as original evidence,[177] the learned judge made it clear that if it had been hearsay, it would have been admissible under the *res gestae* exception. In *obiter dicta* since celebrated and approved, Lord Wilberforce proposed that the test for *res gestae* should not be the uncertain one of whether it forms part of the transaction in *time*, but rather whether the:

> "statement was so clearly made in circumstances of spontaneity or involvement in the event that the possibility of concoction can be disregarded ... [I]f the drama, leading up to the climax, has commenced

---

[173] (1879) 14 Cox C.C. 341.
[174] [1952] A.C. 480 at 487 (PC).
[175] [1966] I.R. 490 (CCA): *cf.* appendix 15.
[176] [1972] A.C. 378 (PC): *cf.* appendix 17.
[177] *cf.* para.**9–24** *et seq.*

and assumed such intensity and pressure that the utterance can safely be regarded as a true reflection of what was unrolling or actually happening, it ought to be received".[178]

9–69 Conversely, if the trial judge considers that the statement was made as narrative of a detached past event and that the speaker was sufficiently disengaged from the event as to be able to construct or adapt it, the statement should be excluded. These *dicta* were affirmed by the House of Lords in *R. v Andrews*.[179] The deceased had heard a knock on the door, opened it, and was stabbed by two people who then robbed his flat. Minutes later, the police arrived. In response to questions, the victim told them the names of the two men. The man died from the wounds two months later. The House of Lords decided that the deceased's oral statement was admissible since made in circumstances of spontaneity and contemporaneity when the person's mind was still dominated by the event and where the risk of concoction was low. Any question of malice or mistake on the part of the maker of the statement affected the weight of the evidence and not its admissibility—specifically in this case with respect to the allegation that the deceased had borne the two men grudges since he had blamed them for an earlier break-in, and also with respect to an allegation that the deceased had consumed some alcohol.

9–70 The *Andrews* test was applied in *Mills v R*.[180] to a statement uttered by the victim of a fatal machete wound shortly before he died. Although the statement was admissible as a dying declaration in a case of murder or manslaughter as evidence tending to prove the cause of his death,[181] it was alternatively admissible as *res gestae* to the extent that the words had been uttered "in conditions of approximate contemporaneity ... [when] the victim's grave wounds, would have dominated his thoughts ... [such] that the possibility of concoction or distortion could be disregarded".[182]

9–71 The next specific instances of *res gestae* are equally subject to the principles outlined in *Ratten* and *Andrews*, and to the requirement that the statement be a "spontaneous exclamation" by a party unavailable to testify. This was confirmed recently in *R. v Callender*,[183] where the Court of Appeal rejected the contended application of the exception to statements explaining the purpose of an accompanying act (possession of incendiary devices), since concern that the hearsay statement was inaccurate and unreliable persisted in a case where the maker of the statement (the accused) had declined to give testimony at his trial.

---

[178] [1972] A.C. 378 at 389–90 (PC).
[179] [1987] A.C. 281 (HL).
[180] [1995] 3 All E.R. 865 (PC).
[181] *cf.* para.**9–83** *et seq*.
[182] [1995] 3 All E.R. 865 at 876, *per* Lord Steyn (PC).
[183] [1998] Crim. L.R. 337 (CA).

(ii) Spontaneous statements showing state of mind

9–72 Res gestae statements may be admitted to establish, where relevant, the contemporaneous state of mind or emotions of the speaker, as evidence, for instance, of the state of knowledge or beliefs of the person at a particular time. It is clear, however, that an exception like this coincides with the notion of original evidence, akin to its use in *Subramaniam*, where hearsay utterances were admitted to show that threats, whether or not genuine, had been made by terrorists and had caused the accused to act under duress.[184]

9–73 Market research surveys, which had been admitted for some time in civil cases as a matter of practice beyond the scrutiny of the hearsay rule, have been characterised as admissible under this *res gestae* exception to show the opinions and beliefs of the persons surveyed.[185] Consumer surveys are particularly relevant in civil proceedings for passing-off and infringement of intellectual property, although their accuracy or credibility is frequently challenged as a matter of their weight or, if serious enough, their admissibility. In *R. Griggs Group v Dunnes Stores*,[186] where the plaintiff claimed the defendants had passed-off their Doc Marten boots as their own, the High Court criticised a survey asking passer-bys at night in poor conditions of light to judge the similarity of the two pairs of boots. McCracken J. observed generally that such survey evidence may be worthless if incapable of being tested by cross-examination. In *Smithkline Beecham Plc. v Antigen Pharmaceuticals Ltd.*,[187] where hearsay evidence was tendered by both the plaintiffs and defendant to show contradictory views upon whether pharmacists were likely to be confused by the similarity in the names of their respective painkillers, McCracken J. observed that "survey evidence is of little or no value in interlocutory applications, where that evidence is not tested by cross-examination, and indeed all the background facts relating to that evidence, such as the actual questionnaires and answers, are not put in evidence".

(iii) Spontaneous statements explaining an accompanying act

9–74 Spontaneous utterances or declarations that accompanied a particular act may be admitted where the particular act is independently relevant[188] as evidence of the intention with which the act was performed or of the reason why it was done. Significantly, however, the exception does not permit the statement to be probative of the factual basis of the reason advanced by the speaker. In *Skinner v Shew*,[187] where the plaintiff claimed the defendant had unlawfully induced a third party to breach its contract with the plaintiff, a letter from the third party to the plaintiff was admitted to show the reasons given by the third party, upon the basis that the letter had been contemporaneous with his decision to repudiate the contract and had purported to explain its

---

[184] *cf.* para.**9–21**.
[185] *Hanafin v Minister for the Environment* [1996] 2 I.R. 321 at 331–4 (HC), approving *Customglass Boats Ltd. v Salthouse Bros. Ltd.* [1976] R.P.C. 589 (SC, N.Z.).
[186] HC, October 4, 1996.
[187] [1999] 2 I.L.R.M. 190 at 197 (HC).

act. The letter was admissible under this exception to show the actor's intentions and purpose at the time of the act, but was not admissible to establish that threats had actually been made by the defendant against the third party. Upon this basis, the decision in *R. v Edwards*[190] has been criticised. A statement by the deceased was admitted in light of the fact that it accompanied the act of leaving an axe and a knife at her neighbour's house and that it explained she did so because her husband kept attacking her. Cross questioned the admission of the reference to prior attacks by her husband, which could have no probative value unless accepted to be true; he accepted, however, that the statement was admissible for this purpose under the alternative exception created for spontaneous statements establishing the state of mind of the declarant.[191]

9–75 In *Cullen v Clarke*,[192] the plaintiff sought to establish, in an application under the Workmen's Compensation Act 1934, that though he had recovered from his work-related injury, he had not been able to secure employment, and accordingly should be deemed "totally" rather than "partially" incapacitated. The Circuit Court refused to permit the plaintiff to quote statements made by employers refusing him work, upon the basis that reference to those statements would have been for the purpose of proving the employers' reasons in their absence, and would thereby have offended the hearsay rule. The Supreme Court, it is submitted rightly, resisted the argument that these letters constituted original evidence, and preferred to assess them under the *res gestae* principle. After a review of the common law exceptions to the hearsay rule, Kingsmill Moore J. decided that the statements were admissible as *res gestae* since they accompanied and explained a relevant act and therefore constituted part of the act and were not "secondary or hearsay".[193] Although the learned judge accepted that when admitted in this way, a statement becomes evidence tending to establish the intent of the actor (but not the factual basis of that intent), Kingsmill Moore J. cautioned that the court should bear in mind in cases of absent declarants that the statement may be false. In the case at hand, "the reason why an employer refused to employ him is not necessarily the same thing as the reason given by an employer for refusing to employ him".[194]

(iv) Spontaneous statements of physical sensation

9–76 Spontaneous statements of contemporaneous physical sensation felt by the maker of the statement have traditionally been admissible at common law to prove, for instance, that the speaker said he was suffering pain from a

---

[188] *Gresham Hotel v Manning* (1867) I.R. 1.
[189] [1894] 2 Ch.D. 581.
[190] (1872) 12 Cox C.C. 230.
[191] Cross, "The Scope of the Rule against Hearsay" (1956) at p.109.
[192] [1963] I.R. 368 (SC): *cf.* appendix 8.
[193] Approving *Lloyd v Powell Duffryn Steam Coal Co. Ltd.* [1914] A.C. 733 at 757, *per* Lord Moulton (HL).
[194] [1963] I.R. 368 at 381 (SC).

The Rule against Hearsay

stab wound, where contemporaneous with the painful sensation. The statement was not, however, admissible to explain the causes of the wound. In *Manchester Brewery v Combs*,[195] evidence that the defendant's customers had left the beer after tasting it (implied assertion hearsay) was admitted as evidence probative of the issue whether the plaintiff had supplied the defendant with good beer. Prejudicial statements made in the absence of the person against whom their admission is sought are treated with more caution.[196] In *R. v Black*,[197] the appeal was fought on the admissibility of comments made by the deceased wife of the accused complaining of painful symptoms after taking medication procured by the accused: "If it had appeared that these were statements made behind the back of the appellant, it would have required grave consideration whether they could have been admitted, but the court is satisfied that they were made in his presence in such circumstances as to require some answer or comment from him, and that the absence of any such comment was evidence from which the jury might draw inferences".

(2) Confessions

9–77 A confession statement admitting guilt of a criminal offence is admissible as an exception to the rule against hearsay, chiefly upon the basis that because the statement is against the interests of its maker, it is more likely to be true.[198] Despite anchorage in this rationale, the courts have permitted the accused to rely upon a "mixed statement" to establish a defence, despite contextually not against his interests, and have resisted imposing a duty upon the trial judge to direct the jury that the exculpatory aspects of the statement are less likely to be true since not made against interest.[199] Admissions or statements against the interest of their maker are generally admissible, where relevant, in civil proceedings upon a broader basis, given the absence of concerns over the statement's intrinsic reliability in the context of interrogative pressures. As a general rule, such admissions are only admissible as against their maker but not against other parties to legal proceedings.[200]

(3) Declarations and Statements by a Deceased Person

9–78 These old common law exceptions render declarations by deceased persons fully admissible as probative of their assertions, where the evidence would have been admissible if the declarant was alive to testify to it.[201] These were recognised and applied by the common law judges in a very technical manner, although their potential application endures beyond the principles

---

[195] (1900) 82 L.T. 347.
[196] Cross, (1956) at p.113.
[197] (1922) 16 Cr. App. R. 118 at 120, *per* Avory J. (CA).
[198] *cf.* para.**10–01**.
[199] *cf.* para.**10–68** *et seq.*
[200] *Willey v Synan* (1937) 57 C.L.R. 200; *cf.* para.**10–65** *et seq.*
[201] *R. v Pike* (1829) 3 C. & P. 598, where the deceased had been four-years-old at the time and, according to the rules operative at the time, incompetent to testify; *Sturla v Freccia* (1880) 5 App. Cas. 623, where the declaration itself was founded upon hearsay.

and rationales that informed them in an earlier age. In light of a judicial unwillingness in recent decades not to expand by common law principle the hearsay rule or exceptions thereto, the courts have instead preferred, where possible, to assess the statement as *res gestae*[202] or as original evidence.[203] The specific instances of declaration, listed below, have for some time been regarded as archaic and arbitrary in their operation—for instance that dying declarations showing cause of death are admissible in trials only for murder and manslaughter, but not in trials for death by dangerous driving or other serious offences. Whilst the judges have recognised this limitation on a number of occasions, they have not undertaken any significant revision of the exceptions, save to recognise that the landmark decisions in *Ratten* and *Andrews* have clearly signalled a principled shift from rule to probative value of the statement in light of the concerns of the hearsay rule.[204]

(i) Declarations by a deceased person against a pecuniary or proprietary interest

9–79 This exception is now of most relevance to civil proceedings involving disputes over land or contracts. It has not been extended to declarations against *penal* interest—thus, admissions by the deceased of criminal guilt are not later admissible in proceedings against another for the same crime.[205] The exception presupposes that a statement that the deceased owed an amount of money to another, or an admission that he did not actually own certain lands or that they were subject to public and general rights, is likely to be true.[206] Admissibility depends upon establishing that the deceased had personal knowledge of the facts as stated, and that he knew that the declaration was against his interests. This was not the case in *Tucker v Oldbury Urban Council*.[207] The deceased workman's answer to a query by a colleague with respect to a work injury he had just sustained was held inadmissible because at the time the workman had no knowledge that he or his dependents could or would sue for compensation for the injury. Over and above this, the deceased's response was a natural description of the injury and was not intended as a declaration against interest.

(ii) Written declarations by a deceased person in the course of a duty

9–80 The exception applies only to facts and not opinions, and rests upon an assumption that it is significantly less likely, where information is made or recorded for the purposes of work, that the declarant lied or erred. The statement must have been made in the course of a duty to record or report the information

---

[202] e.g. *Mills v R* [1995] 3 All E.R. 865 at 876, *per* Lord Steyn (PC).
[203] e.g. *R. v Ratten* [1972] A.C. 378 (PC): *cf.* appendix 17.
[204] *Mills v R* [1995] 3 All E.R. 865 at 876, *per* Lord Steyn (PC).
[205] *R. v Blastland* [1986] A.C. 41 (HL); *cf.* para.**10–04**.
[206] e.g. *Flood v Russell* (1891) 29 L.R. I.R. 91, with respect to a statement that her husband had only given her a life interest in his estate.
[207] [1912] 2 K.B. 317 (CA).

The Rule against Hearsay

in question, and the statements must have been contemporaneous with the acts recorded.[208]

(iii) Declarations by a deceased person relating to pedigree

9–81 The exception rested upon an assumption that members of a family talk amongst themselves in a truthful manner where no interest is to be gained by mistruth. It required the declarant to be a blood relative or spouse of a blood relative of the person whose pedigree is at issue,[209] and that the declaration was made before the dispute occurred.

(iv) Declarations by a deceased person explaining the contents of his will

9–82 Declarations by a deceased testator are admissible to explain, if necessary, the contents of his will. The exception has been explained to arise from necessity in cases where the deceased's declarations are the only means of proving due execution, and in a context associated with trustworthiness and solemnity.[210] It was held in *Goods of Ball*[211] that declarations made by a testator before or after executing a will are, in the event of its loss, admissible as secondary evidence of its content.

(v) Dying declarations tending to establish the cause of the declarant's death

9–83 Dying declarations are admissible in murder or manslaughter trials potentially to establish the cause of the speaker's death and the identity of his killer.[212] The declaration must have been made under a settled and hopeless expectation of death, and the speaker must have been competent. The exception derives from a religious perspective, to wit, that a dying man "who is immediately going into the presence of his Maker, will not do so with a lie upon his lips"[213]—thus the rigid requirement of settled and hopeless expectation of death. This was expressed by Eyre C.B. in *R. v Woodcock*,[214] to wit, that such declarations are admissible "when the party is at the point of death, and when every hope of this world is gone; when every motive to falsehood is silenced, and the mind is induced by the most powerful considerations to speak the truth".

9–84 The exception focusses less on the form of the declaration—which

---

[208] Applied in *Harris v Lambert* H.C. [1932] I.R. 504 (HC) to entries made by a deceased solicitor in his work diaries. See also *Dillon v Tobin* (1879) 12 I.L.T.R. 32 (Prob); *Danville v Calwell* [1907] 2 I.R. 617 (KBD); *Power v United Dublin Tramways Co.* [1926] I.R. 302 (SC).
[209] *In re Holmes: Beamish v Smeltzer* [1934] I.R. 693.
[210] Cross, "The Scope of the Rule against Hearsay" (1956) at pp.101–2.
[211] (1890) 25 L.R. Ir. 556.
[212] *R. v Moseley* (1825) 1 Mood C.C. 97.
[213] *R. v Osman* (1881) 15 Cox C.C. 1 at 3, *per* Lord Coleridge C.J. (CCR).
[214] (1789) 1 Leach 500 at 502.

may be written or oral, and which may be in response to questions so long as the deceased was not prompted[215]—and chiefly on the requirement that the words were spoken at a time when the deceased laboured under a settled and hopeless expectation of death (although the exception does not require that the declarant actually died soon after).[216] The court considered the declarant not to have resigned himself to death to the requisite degree in *R. v Jenkins*.[217] The declaration commenced with the words "with no present hope of my recovery ...", which suggested the declarant had held out some future hope for recovery.

(4) Statements contained in public documents

9–85 The *locus classicus* for the exception is *Sturla v Freccia*[218] where it was described to apply to "a document that is made by a public officer for the purposes of the public making use of it and being able to refer to it. It is meant to be where there is a judicial or *quasi*-judicial duty to enquire". As a general rule, the public document must be made under a strict duty to enquire into all the relevant information recorded; it must be concerned with a public matter; and it must be intended to be retained for public inspection, as in the case of records of births, deaths, and marriages, and public surveys and reports. In such circumstances, the documents (in original or certified form) are presumed reliable, and they function as prima facie evidence of the facts contained therein. If the facts established by the documents are contradicted by oral evidence, the court is entitled to decide that the prima facie inference has been rebutted.[219]

9–86 The exception at this stage amounts to a residual discretion at common law, given that it has been superceded in many cases by statutory provision exempting specific certificates[220] and documentary hearsay compiled in the ordinary course of work.[221] The common law exception does not apply to documents or certificates produced by public authorities but not made available to the public, as in *R. v Boam*[222] with respect to a confiscation order under drugs trafficking legislation recording the court's determination of the value of the proceeds of crime (comparable to the admissibility of an officer's belief of the valuation of property and the proceeds of crime in Ireland under s.8(1)(b) of the Proceeds of Crime Act 1996).[223]

---

[215] *R. v Fitzpatrick* (1912) 46 I.L.T.R. 173.
[216] *R. v Bernadotti* (1869) 11 Cox C.C. 316.
[217] (1869) 11 Cox C.C. 250 (CA).
[218] (1880) 5 App. Cas. 623 at 643, *per* Lord Blackburn (HL).
[219] *Kiely v Minister for Social Welfare* [1977] I.R. 267 (SC).
[220] e.g. Registration of Births and Deaths (Ireland) Act 1883, Marriages (Ireland) Act 1844, and the Bankers Books Evidence Act 1879 and 1959.
[221] *cf.* para.**9–36** *et seq.*
[222] [1998] Crim. L.R. 206 (CA).
[223] In *McK (F) v F (A)* (January 30, 2002) the Supreme Court accepted that the provision was draconian in admitting affidavit evidence founded upon hearsay in applications for orders at interlocutory level.

Further Reading

Allan, "Implications of Modern Psychological Knowledge" (1991) 44 *Current Legal Problems* 217.
Allan, "Implied Assertions as Hearsay" (1992) 142 New L.J. 1194.
Ashworth and Pattenden, "Reliability, Hearsay Evidence and the English Criminal Trial" (1986) 102 L.Q.R. 293.
Baker, *The Hearsay Rule* (Sir Isaac Pitman & Sons, London, 1950).
Carter, "Hearsay: Whether and Whither?" (1993) 109 L.Q.R. 573.
Cross, "The Scope of the Rule against Hearsay" (1956) 72 L.Q.R. 91.
Doherty, "Recent Cases on Hearsay Evidence in Civil Child Sexual Abuse Proceedings" (1996) I.L.T. 284.
Finman, "Implied Assertion as Hearsay" (1962) 14 Stanford L. Rev. 682.
Guest, "The Scope of the Hearsay Rule" (1985) 101 L.Q.R. 385.
Jackson, "Hearsay: the Sacred Cow that won't be Slaughtered?" Int. J. Ev. & P.166.
Jackson and Doran, "Judge and Jury: Towards a New Division of Labour in Criminal Trials" (1997) 60 M.L.R. 759.
Hartshorne and Choo, "Hearsay-fiddles in the House of Lords" (1999) 62 M.L.R. 290.
Law Commission, *Evidence in Criminal Proceedings: Hearsay and Related Topics*, Consultation Paper, No.136, London: L.C., 1995.
Law Reform Commission Working Paper No. 9, *The Rule Against Hearsay* 9–1980.
Law Reform Commission Report, *The Rule Against Hearsay in Civil Cases* 25–1988.
Murphy, "Previous Consistent and Inconsistent Statements: A Proposal to Make Life Easier for Juries" [1985] Crim. L.R. 270.
O'Higgins, "Hearsay Evidence in Bail Applications" (1998) 4 Bar Rev. 129.
Ormerod, "Redundant Res Gestae" [1998] Crim. L.R. 301.
Pattenden, "Conceptual versus Pragmatic Approaches to Hearsay" (1993) 56 M.L.R. 138.
Rein, "The Scope of Hearsay" (1994) 110 L.Q.R. 431.
Spencer, "Orality and the Evidence of Absent Witnesses" [1994] Crim. L.R. 628.
Tapper in "Hearsay and Implied Assertions" (1992) 109 L.Q.R. 524.
Tapper, "Hearsay in Criminal Cases" [1997] Crim. L.R. 771.
Zuckerman, "Law Commission Consultation Paper No. 138 on Hearsay: the Futility of Hearsay" [1996] Crim. L.R. 4.

CHAPTER 10

CONFESSION EVIDENCE

    I. General Principles **10–01**
            Confessions **10–01**
            Form of Confession **10–05**
            Persons in Authority **10–08**
            Proof of Admissibility and the *Voire Dire* **10–10**
            Tests of Admissibility **10–15**
    II. The Judges' Rules **10–17**
   III. Treatment of Persons in Custody Regulations **10–26**
   IV. Requirement of Voluntariness **10–30**
            Threats and Inducements **10–32**
            Oppressive Questioning **10–35**
            Threats, Inducements, and Oppression from Third Parties **10–37**
            Causation **10–40**
            The Subjective Test **10–41**
    V. Requirements of Fairness and Reliability **10–43**
   VI. Compliance with the Constitutional Rights of the Accused **10–48**
            Rights of Access to Legal Advice **10–50**
  VII. Fruit of the Poisoned Tree **10–58**
 VIII. Confession as Evidence Against a Co-Accused **10–63**
   IX. "Mixed Statements" **10–67**
    X. The Corroboration Warning **10–72**

I. GENERAL PRINCIPLES

Confessions

10–01 Confession statements and admissions voluntarily made by the accused are generally admissible in criminal trials as probative evidence tending to establish the accused's guilt. They are technically admissible against the confessor as an exception to the rule against hearsay, upon the basis that, since they are *inculpatory* and against his interests, they are more likely to be true and less likely to engender the suspicions of unreliability with which the hearsay rule is intrinsically concerned.[1]

---

[1] *People (DPP) v Pringle* (1981) 2 Frewen 57 at 78, *per* O'Higgins C.J. (CCA); *R. v Smith* (1966) 51 Cr. App. R. 22 at 27 (CA); *R. v Hardy* (1794) 24 St. Tr. 199 at 1093. Wigmore expressed the rationale as follows: "Now, assuming the making of a confession

Confession Evidence

10–02 Proof of admissibility of the confession statement is borne by the prosecution, and must be discharged, in the event of challenge, by proof beyond reasonable doubt. To constitute a "confession" for the purposes of the exception to the rule against hearsay, the admission must have been made voluntarily to a "person in authority" such as a member of the Garda Síochána. An inculpatory statement made to a person unconnected with "a person in authority" has the status of an "admission" and is similarly admissible against the interests of the declarant.[2] This is justified upon the basis that a man does not usually make a statement against his interests unless it is true, although it has usefully been queried whether it should not instead be premised upon the assumption that a person does not normally make an adverse statement unless *he believes it to be true*.[3] Instances of bare admissions are scarce, given that the type of admission upon which prosecutions are brought tends to be confession statements obtained from the accused by persons in authority under more formal conditions amenable to proof.[4] A confession or admission is only admissible if the speaker had personal knowledge of the matter addressed.[5] In *R. v Chatwood*,[6] statements by the accused that the substance found in his possession was heroin were admissible in light of the fact that the declarant was a habitual drug user and had personally sampled the drugs. By contrast, in *Surujpaul v R.*,[7] the accused, charged as accessory before the fact to a murder, lacked direct personal knowledge of the relevant circumstances when he made the admission that the murder had been committed. As the accused had not been present during the murder, his admission therefore constituted multiple hearsay, and it was not proper to receive it in evidence.

10–03 Confession statements in criminal proceedings are otherwise categorised as *informal admissions*, to be contrasted with *formal admissions inter partes* (or concessions made in the course of pleadings or submissions for the purpose of dispensing with the need for formal proof).[8] A plea of

---

to be a completely proved fact—its authenticity beyond question and conceded—then it is certainly true that we have before us the highest sort of evidence. The confession of crime is usually as much against a man's permanent interests as anything well can be ... [I]t carries a persuasion which nothing else does, because a fundamental instinct of human nature teaches each of us its significance" (*Treatise on the American System of Evidence at Common Law,* 3rd ed.). This rationale was acknowledged again recently in *R. v Myers* [1997] 3 W.L.R. 552 at 569, *per* Hope L (HL).

[2] Admissions are similarly admissible in civil hearings: e.g. *Bord na gCon v Murphy* [1970] I.R. 301 (SC).
[3] Ashworth and Pattendon, "Reliability, Hearsay Evidence and the Criminal Trial (1986) 102 L.Q.R. 292 at 304.
[4] e.g. *Rumping v DPP* [1964] A.C. 814 (CA), with respect to a letter written by the accused to his wife confessing to murder, which had been entrusted to another shipmate to pass on to the wife but had instead been handed up to the police after his arrest.
[5] *Comptroller of Customs v Western Lectric Co.* [1966] A.C. 367 at 371 (PC).
[6] (1980) 70 Cr. App. R. 39 (CA).
[7] [1958] 1 W.L.R. 1050 (PC). See also *Comptroller of Customs v Western Lectern Co Ltd* [1966] A.C. 367 (PC), where the admissions were worthless because the declarant had no personal knowledge of the origins of the goods.
[8] e.g. Criminal Justice Act 1984, s.22: *cf.* para.**1–14**. By way of exception, the common law courts precluded formal admissions in cases seeking a declaration of interest in property: *Williams v Powell* [1894] W.N. 141.

guilty is a formal admission by the accused of commission of the offence as charged,[9] although is not taken to be an acceptance of the truth of the assertions made in the statements upon which the prosecution relied.[10] The practical difference between formal and informal admissions is that where the informal admission is ruled to be admissible, the accused remains free to challenge the status and weight of the confession, and the court is entitled ultimately to accept or reject all or part of the confession statement having regard to the surrounding circumstances and other evidence in the case.

10–04 The exception to the hearsay rule in criminal proceedings is operative only with respect to the accused's confession. Extra-judicial statements made by a third party confessing to the crime for which the accused is later tried remain strictly inadmissible, subject to the ordinary exceptions to the hearsay rule permitting dying declarations and *res gestae* statements, etc.[11] This was confirmed by the House of Lords in *R. v Blastland*[12] with respect to a confession made to the police by a third party, and it was applied more recently in *R. v Callan*[13] with respect to a spontaneous statement by a woman, with whom the accused was discovered upon arrest, that the gun in question belonged to her. The US Supreme Court, by contrast, has determined that a reliable confession by a third party should be admitted as a declaration against interest, and that it is unfair and unjust to exclude it from another person's trial.[14]

Form of Confession

10–05 Although police practice—reflected in rule 9 of the Judges' Rules[15]— requires statements made by the accused to be taken down in writing and signed by him, in principle, a confession may be given orally[16] or in writing and in some cases by means of conduct.[17] If written, the statement may be signed or unsigned—although it is a prerequisite for admissibility that the person who transcribed the statement testifies to establish that the document was read out to the accused and acknowledged by him at the time to be a correct record of what he had said.[18] The form into which the content has been reduced (whether typed, written, signed or unsigned, recorded on audio or videotape) raises questions of fact to be resolved upon the evidence, and may affect the weight to be attached to the original statement or, in cases where the prosecution relies solely upon the confession, the adequacy of the

---

[9] Walsh, *Criminal Procedure* (Thomson Round Hall, Dublin, 2002) at p.799.
[10] *R. v Riley* 18 Cox C.C. 285 at 295, *per* Hawkins J. (CCR).
[11] *cf.* para.**9–62** *et seq.*
[12] [1986] A.C. 41 (HL).
[13] (1993) 98 Cr. App. R. 467 (CA).
[14] *Chambers v Mississippi* 410 U.S. 295 (1973) (SC).
[15] *cf.* para.**10–17**.
[16] *McMahon v Judges of the Special Criminal Court*, High Court, July 30, 1998.
[17] As in *Li-Shu-Ling v R.* [1989] A.C. 270 (PC), where the police had videotaped the accused physically recreating the crime.
[18] *People v Keane* (1976) 110 I.L.T.R. 1 (CCA).

prosecution's case against the accused.[19] Where statutory powers exist to detain the suspect for questioning in a garda station, and where facilities have been put into place to enable audio or visual recording of interviews, recourse by the gardai to general common law powers to question the suspect *en route* to the station is likely to generate weak or inadmissible evidence of self-incrimination.[20]

10–06 The video-recording of interviews in which inculpatory statements are made and later relied upon by the prosecution supplies probative and useful evidence in the event of a challenge to the voluntariness of the statement. Section 27 of the Criminal Justice Act 1984 enables the electronic or video recording of garda interviews with respect to crimes carrying a sentence of five years imprisonment or more.[21] Regulations for the electronic recording of confessions were not introduced until 1997, however.[22] A video recording scheme, pursuant to s.27 of the 1984 Act, was commenced in 1999.[23] According to the then Minister for Justice, the videotape of the interview would be relied upon in any case where the statement was challenged. The correlation between the videotape of the interview and the note written down by the attending garda has not so far been addressed by the law. In the absence of specific new rules governing the videotape, and amending rule 9 of the Judges' Rules (which requires the garda to give the accused an opportunity to confirm the content of the statement before signing it), the videotape is likely to function in the short-term as secondary evidence relevant in the event of a challenge to the admissibility of the confession allegedly confirmed and signed by the accused in the interview.

10–07 Although described as mandatory, the Regulations fall short of effecting this, insofar as they become mandatory only where the proper equipment has been provided and installed in the station,[24] and in any case may not be utilised if it is "not practicable" to do so.[25] The courts have observed that it would be a serious matter for the admissibility of untaped confessions if the gardai detained the accused in a station lacking the facilities when they could reasonably have detained him in a station properly equipped.[26] In *People*

---

[19] In *People (DPP) v Geoghan and Bourke* (Central Criminal Court, November 18, 2003), McKecknie J. directed an acquittal in a murder case upon the basis that the confession made by the accused was inadmissible (due to the making of an inducement) and the only other evidence against him was an oral conversation with a garda of which no record had been taken; *cf.* para.**10–34**.
[20] See *People (DPP) v Connolly* [2003] 2 I.R. 1 (CCA): *cf.* para.**10–07**.
[21] As had been recommended by the O'Briain Committee Report of 1978.
[22] Criminal Justice Act 1984 (Electronic Recording of Interviews) Regulation 1997 (S.I. No.74 of 1997).
[23] As had been recommended by the Report of the Committee to Enquire into Certain Aspects of Criminal Procedure (1990) (Martin Committee Report).
[24] Article 3(1). The Fennelly Report (Report of the Working Group on the Jurisdiction of the Courts, July 15, 2003) has observed "optimal deployment", noting that some 225 rooms in 128 stations have been equipped with the necessary devices.
[25] Article 4(3)(b).
[26] *People (DPP) v Holland* (CCA, June 15, 1998).

(DPP) v Connolly,[27] Hardiman J. emphasised the need to ensure that proper audio-visual facilities are installed and utilised, not only to establish an important procedural safeguard for detainees, but to provide secondary evidence capable of corroborating confessions later repudiated by the accused at his trial—concerns clearly underpinning the mandatory corroboration warning introduced by s.10 of the Criminal Procedure Act 1993 for uncorroborated confessions.[28] The learned judge asserted:

> "Its failure to become routine ... nearly twenty years after statutory provision for it was first made, has ceased to be a mere oddity and is closely approaching the status of an anomaly. ... The courts have been very patient, perhaps excessively patient, with delays in this regard. The time cannot be remote when we will hear a submission that, absent extraordinary circumstances (by which we do not mean that a particular garda station has no audio visual machinery or that the audio visual room was being painted), it is unacceptable to tender in evidence a statement which has not been so recorded."[29]

Persons in Authority

10–08 To constitute a "confession" for the purpose of the exception to the hearsay rule, the statement must have been made to a "person in authority". A "person in authority" traditionally refers to "someone engaged in the arrest, detention, examination or prosecution of the accused or someone acting on behalf of the prosecution".[30] Although in all but the fewest cases the "person in authority" is an official law enforcer, in principle it is sufficient that when the accused made the statement, he acted in the belief, rightly or wrongly, that the person to whom he confessed was close to the police and would have some role to play in his arrest, detention, or prosecution. In *People v Murphy*,[31] a citizen, enlisted by a garda for help and who urged the accused to cooperate with the garda "for his own good", constituted a "person in authority" for the purposes of the suspect's subsequent admissions.[32] A school headmistress has constituted a "person in authority" with respect to a schoolgirl.[33] More commonly, a doctor, called by the gardaí to examine the accused, is likely to constitute a "person in authority".[34]

10–09 Conversely, not every prosecution witness to whom statements were

---

[27] [2003] 2 I.R. 1 at 5 (CCA).
[28] *cf.* para.**10–75**.
[29] [2003] 2 I.R. 1 at 18 (CCA).
[30] *People (DPP) v McCann* [1998] 4 I.R. 397, *per* O'Flaherty J (CCA), citing *R. v William Boughton* (1910) 6 Cr. App. R. 8 (CA) and *Deokinanan v R.* [1969] 1 A.C. 20 (PC).
[31] [1947] I.R. 236 (CCA).
[32] Byrne J. was influenced by the facts that the citizen had acted in concert with the garda, and that the inducement had been made in the presence of the garda from whom no demur was made.
[33] *R. v McLintock* [1962] Crim. L.R. 549 (CA).
[34] *Sullivan v Robinson* [1954] I.R. 161 (SC).

uttered or given constitutes a person in authority. The test depends primarily upon whether subjectively the accused believed he was confessing to a person in authority. In *Deokinanan v R.*,[35] a trusted friend of the accused was held not to constitute a person in authority, despite his collusion with the persons in authority, since the collusion had not been known to the accused when he made his statements. The Privy Council rightly recognised, however, that for the purposes of testing the voluntariness of the admissions, it matters not whether the threat, inducement, or oppression emanated from a person in authority or other person, since a confession made to a trusted friend may similarly suffer the effects of an inducement, if given, for instance, in response to a bribe.[36] This was clarified in England by s.76(2) of the Police and Criminal Evidence Act 1984, which abolished the requirement of communication to a "person in authority". Thus, although statements against interest to persons not in authority are equally admissible as an exception to the hearsay rule, they are equally subject to the strict tests of admissibility.

Proof of Admissibility and the *Voire Dire*

10–10 The burden of proof of admissibility of a confession is upon the prosecution,[37] and where the confession is challenged by the defence, this must be proved by the criminal standard.[38] The accused does not bear an evidential burden when making such a challenge, and in principle is not required to admit evidence to justify putting the prosecution to proof on the admissibility of the confession, although the challenge needs to be clearly made,[39] and should be indicated to the prosecution prior to the trial to avoid prejudicial reference to the confession. The Court of Criminal Appeal has directed that where the defence intends to challenge the admissibility of confession statements, this issue should be dealt with fully at the beginning of the trial to avoid the practical difficulties deriving from the jury's absence, sometimes for weeks, in cases where evidence has already been heard.[40]

10–11 A majority of the Supreme Court in *People (DPP) v Conroy*[41] ruled that a decision on the admissibility of confessions is made by the trial judge in the *voire dire* in the absence of the jury, and that the former practice of considering the admissibility of statements in the presence of the jury should

---

[35] [1969] 1 A.C. 20 (PC).
[36] Departing from *R. v Row* (1809) Russ. & Ry. 153 and *R. v Moore* (1852) 2 Den. 522.
[37] *People (Attorney-General) v Murphy* [1946] I.R. 236 (CCA).
[38] *R. v Sartori* [1961] Crim. L.R. 397 (CA); *R. v McLintock* [1962] Crim. L.R. 549 (CA).
[39] This has been incorporated into s.78 of the Police and Criminal Evidence Act 1984 (UK). "Represented" has been interpreted to require the defence to indicate the nature of its challenge without bearing a burden as such upon this issue. A mere suggestion in the course of cross-examination is not sufficient, however: *R. v Liverpool Juvenile Court Ex p. R* [1988] Q.B. 1.
[40] *People (DPP) v Quinn* (CCA, March 23, 1998), per O'Flaherty J. (*ex tempore*). The same point was made by Kennedy C.J. in *Attorney-General v McCabe* [1927] I.R. 129 at 134 (CCA).
[41] [1986] I.R. 460 (SC): *cf.* appendix 29.

cease as it infringed the constitutional right of the accused to a "trial with a jury from whose knowledge there is excluded any evidence of guilt which is inadmissible at law".[42] The purpose of the *voire dire* is to assess whether the evidence is admissible, and not whether the account provided in the confession is true. If a decision has been made to admit the statement in evidence, the trial judge, at the close of the trial, directs the jury that it is for them to decide the probative value or weight properly to be attached to the statements, having regard to other evidence in the trial.[43] In *People (DPP) v Quillegan and O'Reilly (No.3)*,[44] it was unsuccessfully argued that the trial judge was required additionally to submit the voluntariness issue to the jury for their determination—in other words, not to restrict the jury from considering the issues of fact upon which the trial judge's assessment of the admissibility of the confession had earlier been based. In their trial, both of the accused gave *voire dire* evidence in the jury's absence asserting that their confessions had been bullied and threatened out of them; and they continued to refute the confessions when giving trial testimony in the jury's presence. Upon appeal, they submitted that the trial judge had erred when he directed the jury at the close of the trial to consider whether the confession statements were true and genuine, and when he did not further direct the jury to consider whether the statements had been made voluntarily. A majority of the Supreme Court rejected the argument upon an application of the division of labour between judge and jury on questions of law and fact identified by the Supreme Court earlier in *Conroy*. McCarthy J., dissenting, could not "reconcile the constitutional guarantee of trial by jury with an exclusive right in the trial judge to determine the issue as to whether or not a confession was voluntarily made".[45]

10–12 The accused is entitled to give evidence in the *voire dire* without abandoning his "right to silence" by exposure to examination in the main trial.[46] The evidence the accused gives in the *voire dire*—in *Wong Kam Ming v R.*[47] an admission that he had been involved in the attack in question—is not subsequently admissible in the trial, and if the accused elects to give evidence he may not be cross-examined upon remarks or admissions made in the absence of the jury in the *voire dire* unless the confession was ruled admissible.[48]

10–13 The trial judge should not reveal to the jury, when they are recalled after the *voire dire*, that the confession has been deemed voluntary—since this may cause undue prejudice to the accused by suggesting that the trial judge had reached a concluded view upon the credibility of prosecution witnesses

---

[42] *ibid.* at 472, *per* Finlay C.J. (SC); *cf.* para.1–25.
[43] *ibid.* at 488, *per* Henchy J. (SC).
[44] [1993] 2 I.R. 305 (SC).
[45] [1986] I.R. 460 at 488 (SC).
[46] *People (DPP) v Conroy* [1986] I.R. 460 at 494, *per* Griffin J. (SC); *R. v Brophy* [1982] A.C. 476 at 481, *per* Lord Fraser of Tullybelton (HL).
[47] [1980] A.C. 427 (PC).
[48] Applied in *R. v Brophy* [1982] A.C. 476 (CA), quashing conviction upon the basis that the trial judge had improperly permitted the prosecution to refer to admissions of membership of the IRA made by the accused in the *voire dire*.

and the accused.[49] The defence has a right to continue to contest the confession throughout the trial despite a ruling of admissibility in the *voire dire*.[50] This was made clear in *People (Attorney-General) v Ainscough*,[51] where the Court of Criminal Appeal quashed conviction because the trial judge had failed to ensure that the accused was aware of this right, and because the jury may have assumed that his objections to the confession had been unsustainable. If the trial judge decides upon the *voire dire* that the confession is admissible, but having heard evidence throughout the trial arrives at a contrary decision, he may decide to exclude the statement from the trial, or (if it is the only material evidence against the accused) to direct the jury to acquit the accused, or in more extreme cases to order a re-trial.[52]

10–14 Where the accused denies having made the statement upon which the prosecution relies, and thereby implies that the statement was fabricated, he does not lose his shield of protection from cross-examination upon bad character for the purposes of s.1(f)(ii) of the Criminal Justice (Evidence) Act 1924,[53] since Irish law holds that the accused may make imputations upon the character of a prosecution witness with impunity where those imputations are "reasonably necessary" to enable him to establish his defence.[54]

Tests of Admissibility

10–15 The laws of evidence have developed rigorous tests to assess the validity and authenticity of confessions disputed by the accused. In a sense, these reflect the "exceptional" nature of confession evidence within a system of justice characterised by its preference for independent proof of the accused's guilt by the State prosecutor—a dynamic suggested by the right to silence[55] and the requirement that trial judges give corroboration warnings in any case where the prosecution tenders disputed confession statements.[56] Irish law supports the accused's right to put the prosecution to full proof by repudiating a confession statement without necessarily exposing himself to cross-examination upon criminal record or bad character arising from the imputations against the character of garda witnesses.[57] The caution with which common law judges treat confession statements tendered by the prosecution but

---

[49] *Mitchell v Queen* [1998] 2 W.L.R. 839 (PC). The court decided not to overturn conviction, however, upon the basis that the evidence against the accused was compelling, although the court may also have been influenced by the fact that defence counsel had challenged the admissibility of the confession in the presence of the jury before a *voire dire* had been arranged.
[50] *People (DPP) v Conroy* [1986] I.R. 460 at 487, *per* Henchy J. (SC): *cf.* appendix 29.
[51] [1960] I.R. 136 (CCA).
[52] *R. v Watson* [1980] 2 All E.R. 293 (CA); *R. v Sat-Bhambra* (1988) 88 Cr. App. R. 55 (CA).
[53] *cf.* para.**8–48** *et seq.*
[54] *(People) DPP v McGrail* [1990] 2 I.R. 38 at 50, *per* Hederman J. (CCA): *cf.* appendix 34.
[55] *cf.* para.**13–84** *et seq.*
[56] *cf.* para.**10–72** *et seq.*
[57] *cf.* para.**8–48** *et seq.*

repudiated by the accused is therefore begotten of principle as much as of practice.

10–16 There are four fundamental sources of rules that must be complied with before a confession statement is properly admissible in Ireland in criminal trials, although the extent to which each source affects admissibility of the confession differs: (1) the Judges' Rules under the common law; (2) the Regulations of 1987 on the Treatment of Persons in Custody; (3) the common law rules testing the voluntariness of the confession; and (4) the accused's constitutional rights having regard to statutory provisions defining and circumscribing gardaí powers. Of these, non-compliance with the voluntariness requirement alone *necessarily* requires a finding of inadmissibility, and remains the touchstone test of a confession's admissibility. Although infringement of any constitutional right of the accused is a very serious matter for the admissibility of evidence subsequently obtained by the gardaí (whether confessions or real evidence), the evidence may yet be admissible if it was not causatively obtained as a direct result of the breach or in any case if there were "extraordinary excusing circumstances" justifying the violation of constitutional right.[58]

II. THE JUDGES' RULES

10–17 The Judges' Rules were first formulated by the judges of the King's Bench Division in 1912, as guides for the police when dealing with suspects, following a request by the Home Secretary. The first four rules appeared in the report for *R .v Voisin*,[59] where it was recognised that the rules "have not the force of law; they are administrative directions the observance of which the police authorities should enforce upon their subordinates as tending to the fair administration of justice".[60] Although they were intended as guiding principles with no force of law, it was gradually recognised that breach of the rules could entitle a court in its discretion to exclude the confession.[61] The Supreme Court approved their status on this footing in *McCarrick v Leavy*[62] and *People v Cummins*,[63] the latter acknowledging that all nine of the rules form part of Irish law. The rules implicitly address non-custodial questioning by gardai, although they have been construed to apply equally to persons detained for questioning under statutory powers governed by the 1987 Custody Regulations.[64] The rules, as narrated in *Cummins*,[65] are as follows.

"(1) When a police officer is endeavouring to discover the author of a

---

[58] *cf.* para.**11–21** *et seq.*
[59] [1918] 1 K.B. 531.
[60] *ibid.* at 539, *per* Lawrence J.
[61] *R. v May* (1952) 36 Cr. App. R. 91 at 93, *per* Lord Goddard C.J. (CA).
[62] [1964] I.R. 225 (SC).
[63] [1972] I.R 312 (SC): *cf.* appendix 18.
[64] *People (DPP) v Darcy* (CCA, July 29, 1997).
[65] [1972] I.R 312 at 317–8 (SC).

crime there is no objection to his putting questions in respect thereof to any person or persons, whether suspected or not, from whom he thinks that useful information may be obtained.

(2) Whenever a police officer has made up his mind to charge a person with a crime, he should first caution such person before asking any questions or any further questions as the case may be.

(3) Persons in custody should not be questioned without the usual caution being first administered.

(4) If the prisoner wishes to volunteer any statement, the usual caution should be administered. It is desirable that the last two words of such caution should be omitted, and that the caution should end with the words 'be given in evidence.'

(5) The caution to be administered to a prisoner when he is formally charged should therefore be in the following words: "Do you wish to say anything in answer to the charge? You are not obliged to say anything unless you wish to do so, but whatever you say will be taken down in writing and may be given in evidence." Care should be taken to avoid the suggestion that his answers can only be used in evidence *against* him, as this may prevent an innocent person making a statement which might assist to clear him of the charge.

(6) A statement made by a prisoner before there is time to caution him is not rendered inadmissible in evidence merely because no caution has been given, but in such a case he should be cautioned as soon as possible.

(7) A prisoner making a voluntary statement must not be cross-examined, and no questions should be put to him about it except for the purpose of removing ambiguity in what he has actually said. For instance, if he has mentioned an hour without saying whether it was morning or evening, or has given a day of the week and day of the month which do not agree, or has not made it clear to what individual or what place he intended to refer in some part of his statement, he may be questioned sufficiently to clear up the point.

(8) When two or more persons are charged with the same offence and their statements are taken separately, the police should not read these statements to the other persons charged, but each of such persons should be given by the police a copy of such statements and nothing should be said or done by the police to invite a reply. If the person charged desires to make a statement in reply the usual caution should be administered.

(9) Any statement made in accordance with the above rules should, whenever possible, be taken down in writing and signed by the person making it after it has been read to him and he has been invited to make any corrections he may wish."

10–18 Breach of any of the Judges' Rules will not *necessarily* render a confession inadmissible, although it has been observed that they are "departed from at peril".[66] In principle, the question of inadmissibility arises only where it is shown that the evidence in question was precipitated by the breach of a rule.[67] In cases where a causative association is established, the trial judge has a discretion to admit the statement notwithstanding,[68] and will chiefly be guided by the extent to which the breach had a material bearing upon the voluntariness of the statement[69] and fairness in the proceedings against the accused.[70] This was emphasised in *R. v Voisin*.[71] The accused was convicted of the murder of a woman, whose body parts had been discovered in a parcel upon which a piece of paper was affixed bearing the words "Bladie Belgiam". During questioning, the police officer had asked the accused to write down the words "Bloody Belgian", following which he had written "Bladie Belgiam". The admissibility of the evidence was upheld upon appeal despite the fact that the accused had not been cautioned before asked to write the words down.

10–19 Breach of the Judges' Rules, as a matter of principle and fact, therefore, is distinct from the requirement of voluntariness. This was further evident in *People (Attorney-General) v Cummins*,[72] considering the effect of a breach of rule 3. The accused had been taken into custody for questioning on a number of different charges. When a garda asked him "What about Premier Tailors? I believe you did it", he replied "We did and we got £255". The garda then cautioned the accused and invited him to make a statement, to which the accused declined with the luckless words "Do you want me to hang myself?" In answer to the question referred by the Circuit Court, Walsh J. decided that the trial judge erred when he considered that a breach of the Judges' Rules was a matter necessarily affecting the voluntariness or admissibility of the statement.

10–20 This distinction between breach of the Judges' Rules and involuntariness was further demonstrated in *People (DPP) v Buckley*,[73] a case which indicates that breaches may subsequently be cured by compliance with the rules prior to obtaining another or successive confession from the accused. In his first interview, the accused was given the caution as required by rule 3. Following this, however, a statement made by a co-accused was read out to him, and he was invited to reply. (The statement he gave in response, following the breach of rule 8, was later ruled inadmissible by the Special Criminal Court in its discretion.) Shortly after the first interview, the co-accused was brought into the room and a conversation took place between them. (The admissions made in this conversation were also ruled inadmissible upon the ba-

---

[66] *People (DPP) v Farrell* [1978] I.R. 13 at 21, *per* O'Higgins C.J. (CCA).
[67] *People (DPP) v Murphy* (SC, July 12, 2001).
[68] See, *e.g. People (DPP) v O'Connell* [1995] 1 I.R. 244 (CCA); *People (DPP) v Darcy* (CCA, July 29,1997); *People (DPP) v Smith* (CCA, November 22, 1999).
[69] *People (DPP) v Darcy* (CCA, July 29, 1997).
[70] *R. v Miller* [1998] Crim. L.R. 209 (CA).
[71] [1918] 1 K.B. 531: *cf.* appendix 3.
[72] [1972] I.R. 312 (SC): *cf.* appendix 18.
[73] [1990] 1 I.R. 14 (CCA): *cf.* appendix 32.

sis that the entry of the co-accused constituted a *novus actus interveniens*, necessitating a fresh caution.) A third interview was conducted with the accused, and after the caution was given, he made a third incriminating statement. The issue upon appeal was whether the Special Criminal Court had been right to conclude that statements from the third interview were admissible. The Court of Criminal Appeal acknowledged that where by reason of a threat, promise, or inducement, a statement is deemed involuntary and inadmissible, subsequent statements not made immediately after the taint may be inadmissible if the court considers that the effect had remained when the accused made the statement.[74] On the other hand, where there has been a breach of the Judges' Rules only, and it was rectified by a fresh caution, subsequent statements in accordance with the rules are not tainted by the circumstances of the earlier breach.

10–21 Rules 1 and 2 do not require a garda to administer the caution immediately upon discovery of the accused in suspicious circumstances, if at the time the garda had not decided to charge the accused with respect to an offence. As was decided in *DPP v Byrne*,[75] a case where the gardaí had come upon the accused's car when it was stationary with the ignition on and surrounded by a small crowd, the garda is entitled to ask preliminary questions to ascertain if, and by whom, any offence has been committed. Latitude at the preliminary stage of investigation was similarly affirmed in *Moore v Martin*,[76] where the failure of the garda to caution a person alleged by another driver to have caused his own car to crash was interpreted not to constitute a breach of the rules.

10–22 The necessity for a fresh caution before the accused is interviewed in garda custody, expressed in rule 3, has been asserted upon the basis that "in the anxiety of being arrested and questioned by those in authority it is possible to forget the rights of which a person has been earlier informed".[77] A fresh caution is not necessarily required each time a person is questioned in custody, so long as the full caution was given at the commencement of his questioning in the garda station and so long as its effect is understood to continue.[78] Because of the discretionary effect for the resultant evidence of a breach of the Rules, the courts have from time to time overlooked divergence where otherwise voluntariness and fairness prevailed, such as in *People (DPP) v Morgan*[79] where the garda told the accused prior to questioning that the "caution still applies".

10–23 Rule 8 has featured highly in the case law, given that police questioning and interrogation has tended to harness the pressure exerted upon suspects

---

[74] *cf.* para.**10–58** *et seq.*
[75] [1999] 1 I.L.R.M. 500 (SC).
[76] HC, May 29, 2000.
[77] *R. v Miller* [1998] Crim. L.R. 209 (CA).
[78] *People (DPP) v Morgan* (CCA, *ex tempore*, July 28, 1997).
[79] CCA, July 28, 1997.

when the content of statements made by other persons with knowledge of the case is revealed to them. The objective of the rule has been expressed to prevent a police officer from revealing in evidence before the jury the nature or contents of any statements made by other parties charged with respect to the same offence where that person, by virtue of being jointly charged, may not be called as a witness.[80]

10–24 The courts have sometimes adopted a literal interpretation of the rule. In *R. v Williamson*,[81] the Court of Criminal Appeal interpreted it not to have been breached when the person on whose statement the accused was questioned, had not yet been "charged". In *People (DPP) v Burke and O'Leary*,[82] the court, again upon the basis that the other party had not been charged with respect to the crime, decided the rule had not been breached in circumstances where the gardaí told the accused that another person had made a statement implicating him in the crime, and had not instead permitted the accused to read or hear the full statement as provided. More recently, however, the courts have suggested a purposive approach to the Rules. In *People (DPP) v Palmer*,[83] neither of the witness statements read out to the applicant were tendered in evidence, although the statement by the applicant's brother had been read out to the jury following an admissibility challenge to the statement allegedly provided by the accused. The Court of Criminal Appeal recognised that the "spirit" of the rule had been breached when a statement by the applicant's brother had been read out to him when in garda custody in the presence of his brother. The "spirit" of the rule had also been offended by reading another witness statement to the applicant. Neither was of consequence for the appeal, however. The "essential admissions" had been made by the applicant later in the evening, and the trial judge had been entitled in his discretion to admit the statements.

10–25 Rule 9 has been interpreted not to require that every statement by the accused be taken down in writing. In *People (DPP) v McKeever*,[84] the gardaí were found not to have breached the rule by failing to record general conversations with the accused once everything of consequence had been recorded and signed by the accused. Frequently in their discretion, however, the courts exclude notes of admissions made by the accused in interview with the gardaí where these were not recorded and signed contemporaneously.[85]

---

[80] *R. v Mills and Lemon* [1947] 1 K.B. 297 (CA).
[81] [1964] Crim. L.R. 126 (CA).
[82] (1986) 3 Frewen 92 (CCA).
[83] CCA, March 22, 2002.
[84] [1994] 2 I.L.R.M. 186 (CCA).
[85] *People (DPP) v Reddan* [1995] 3 I.R. 560 at 566 (CA): in the case, the gardai had contemporaneously recorded a subsequent interview, which was then signed by the accused in compliance with rule nine of the Judges' Rules.

III. TREATMENT OF PERSONS IN CUSTODY REGULATIONS

10–26 The Criminal Justice Act (Treatment of Persons in Custody in Garda Síochána Stations) Regulations of 1987 supplement the Judges' Rules by setting down more detailed preconditions for the conduct of interviews and the treatment of persons in custody. Similar to breaches of the Judges' Rules, non-compliance does not require a finding of admissibility, and their effect upon the reliability of confession statements is more indirect by contrast with the requirement of voluntariness. Section 7 of the Criminal Justice Act 1984, under which the Regulations were adopted, provides that the failure of a garda "to observe any provision of the regulations shall not of itself ... affect the lawfulness of the custody of the detained person or the admissibility in evidence of any statement made by him". The extent to which this is the case, as a matter of practice, largely depends upon whether the breach affected the voluntariness of the confession (*e.g.* where made in an intoxicated or sleep-deprived state), or whether instead the breach was technical by nature (*e.g.* unrelated defects in the record of custody and arrest required by regs 6 and 7).[86] In *People (DPP) v McFadden*,[87] Keane C.J. of the Court of Criminal Appeal considered that discretion should be exercised in favour of inadmissibility where the breach was not of a "trivial or inconsequential nature".

10–27 The prosecution must adduce proof that there has been compliance with the Criminal Justice Act 1984 and the 1987 Regulations, and the defence does not have to put the prosecution to proof on these issues.[88] The Regulations of most concern to the admissibility or weight of confession statements are as follows.

10–28 Arrested persons under the age of 17 years may not be questioned in relation to an offence or asked to make a written statement in the absence of their parent or guardian[89] (unless it is impossible to contact one, or one has not attended within a reasonable time, or it is not practicable for one to attend within a reasonable time), except where the member in charge authorises the questioning because there are reasonable grounds to believe a delay would involve "a risk of injury to persons or serious loss of or damage to property, destruction of or interference with evidence or escape of accomplices". Where the member in charge has reasonable grounds for believing that the person is not below the age of 17 years, the Regulations are deemed to apply to the person as if he had already attained that age.[90] These rules have been enacted

---

[86] See *People (DPP) v Smith* (CCA, November 22, 1999) and *People (DPP) v O'Driscoll* (CCA, *ex tempore*, July 19, 1999).
[87] [2003] 2 I.L.R.M. 201 at 208 (CCA). The breach was fundamental where it related to the garda's failure to explain the basis for the intended search of the accused as soon as the cooperation of the accused had been withdrawn; *cf.* para.**11–59** *et seq.*
[88] *DPP v Spratt* [1995] 2 I.L.R.M. 117 (HC).
[89] Article 13(1). The High Court had proposed in *Travers v Ryan* [1985] I.R. 586 (HC), *per* Finlay P., that suspects under 14 years should not be questioned in the absence of their parent or guardian.
[90] Article 2(4).

in supplementary form by ss.56–63 of the Children Act 2001,[91] which apply to all persons under the age of 18 years, and which specifically set out requirements of notification of material information to the child's parent or guardian and to the solicitor arranged for the child. Section 57 specifically requires that when the child is arrested and brought to a garda station, the member in charge must, without delay, inform the child or cause him to be informed of the offence for which is arrested, his right of access to a solicitor and "how this entitlement can be availed of", and that a parent or guardian is being informed of his custody. The information must be given "in a manner and in language that is appropriate to the age and level of understanding of the child". As for the Custody Regulations, breach of any of the provisions under ss.56–63 and 65 "shall not of itself ... affect the lawfulness of the custody of the detained child or the admissibility in evidence of any statement made by the child".[92]

10–29 Article 12 governs the conduct of interrogation (or "the interview"). Questioning must be conducted "in a fair and humane manner". Not more than two gardaí may question the arrested person at any one time, and not more than four gardaí may be present at any one time throughout. The person may not be interviewed for more than four successive hours, at which point the interview must be terminated or adjourned for a reasonable time (even if the accused requests continuation of the interview).[93] An arrested person may not be questioned between midnight and 8 a.m. except with the authority of the member in charge of the station, which may be given only on the grounds that: (1) he has been taken to the station during that period; or (2) there are reasonable grounds to believe a delay would involve "a risk of injury to persons or serious loss of or damage to property, destruction of or interference with evidence or escape of accomplices"; or (3) in cases where the person is detained for questioning (prior to being charged) under s.4 of the Criminal Justice Act 1984 and the detainee has refused in writing to agree to a suspension of his questioning. Where the person requests the presence of a solicitor, "he shall not be asked to make a written statement in relation to an offence until a reasonable time for the attendance of the solicitor has elapsed". A person who is under the influence of alcohol or drugs "to the extent that he is unable to appreciate the significance of questions put to him or his answers" may not be questioned so long as he remains in that condition, except with the authority of the member in charge upon the basis that there are reasonable grounds to believe a delay would involve "a risk of injury to persons or serious loss of or damage to property, destruction of or interference with evidence or escape of accomplices".

---

[91] Section 66(4) provides that the duties imposed upon the gardai under the Act for treatment of children in custody are "without prejudice to any other duties imposed on them in that respect by or under any other enactment".
[92] Section 66.
[93] *People (DPP) v Reddan* [1995] 3 I.R. 560 at 570 (CCA), *per* Blayney J: "If a waiver were permitted, a difficulty could then arise as to how long the interview should be allowed to continue thereafter".

IV. REQUIREMENT OF VOLUNTARINESS

10–30 The voluntariness of a confession statement is a strict prerequisite to its admissibility, and if the trial judge, upon an application of the relevant common law principles, finds that the statement was not voluntarily given, he has no discretion to admit it[94]—a principle that applies equally to statements received by parties other than the gardaí or persons in authority.[95]

10–31 Voluntariness must be considered in the light of the legally sanctioned practice of interrogation. This is why, according to the law, a statement may be voluntary "though not necessarily volunteered".[96] The extent to which interrogation becomes oppressive, and the confession involuntary, depends in part upon the particular attributes and circumstances of the arrested person. Although the principles underpinning the legal concept of voluntariness have been agreed for some time, application of the tests has proven varied. This is inevitable given the individual nature of the person's will, but also because the test "is essentially situational rather than self-operating" and depends on all the circumstances of the case.[97]

Threats and Inducements

10–32 The traditional test at common law focused on the presence of a threat (fear of prejudice) or inducement (hope of an advantage). It was expressed in authoritative form by Lord Sumner in *Ibrahim v R.*,[98] and was first endorsed in Ireland by the Court of Criminal Appeal in *State v Treanor*[99] and by the Supreme Court in *People (Attorney-General) v McCabe*.[100] In more recent years, the courts have favoured a test based upon the extent to which the questioning leading to the confession was "oppressive", and this development was first adopted in Ireland in *People (DPP) v McNally and Breathnach*[101] and affirmed by the Supreme Court in *People (DPP) v Lynch*.[102]

10–33 In *Attorney-General v Cleary*,[103] the threat that drained the confession of its voluntariness was a statement by the garda that he would take the accused to a doctor to see if she recently had a baby. In *People (DPP) v Ward*,[104] threats by the interviewing gardaí to summon the detainee's girlfriend and elderly parents to the station, amongst other things, rendered his subsequent confession inadmissible. Many of the remarks construed by the courts to constitute an

---

[94] *People (Attorney-General) v Cummins* [1972] I.R. 312 at 323 (SC): *cf.* appendix 18.
[95] *cf.* para.**10–37** *et seq.*
[96] *People (Attorney-General) v McCabe* [1927] I.R. 129 at 134, *per* Kennedy C.J. (CCA).
[97] *People (DPP) v Hoey* [1987] I.R. 637 at 652, *per* Henchy J. (SC).
[98] [1914] A.C. 599 (PC).
[99] [1924] 2 I.R. 193 (CCA).
[100] [1927] I.R. 129 (SC).
[101] (1981) 2 Frewen 43 (CCA).
[102] [1982] I.R. 64 (SC): *cf.* appendix 27.
[103] (1938) 72 I.L.T.R. 84 (CCA).
[104] Special Criminal Court, November 27, 1998.

inducement have appeared innocent on their face, although the basis for exclusion was their possible effect upon the accused in terms of suggesting an incentive to confess.[105] The courts have on occasion assumed the making of an inducement in circumstances where the accused's *volte face* is otherwise inexplicable, as in *People (Attorney-General) v Flynn*.[106] The accused, after two hours of being "completely uncooperative", was visited by a second garda during his lunch break, the result of which was in a short time the making of a confession. In light of his allegations that the confession had been bullied out of him by inducements and threats (which had been rejected by the trial judge under *voire dire*), and the fact that he was not released from custody until he made the statements, the Court of Criminal Appeal could not be sure the statements had been voluntarily made and his conviction was quashed. Similarly, in *People (DPP) v Ward*,[107] the Special Criminal Court accepted the accused's claim that he had confessed following threats and inducements. Given that the confession was made suddenly after the accused had maintained silence throughout five intensive interrogation sessions (14 and a half hours), it was "a remarkable *volte face* which gives rise to unease".[108]

10–34 A confession may be ruled inadmissible where it was given in consequence of some inducement or hope of advantage intimated to the detainee by the garda. In *People (DPP) v Geoghan and Bourke*,[109] McKecknie J. directed an acquittal upon the basis that the prosecution's case against the accused for murder depended solely upon a confession statement given by the accused after a garda told him it would be in his interest to make an admission of guilt and that the matter would then proceed as a prosecution for assault in which bail would be granted. An inducement may be given by a garda wittingly or not, and can arise in the form of a response to a question by the accused. In *R. v Northam*,[110] the accused asked the policeman if a confession to the crime under investigation would be considered in his pending trial for other offences, to which the policeman replied that he had no objection to that occurring. In the circumstances, the court deemed the policeman's response to constitute an implicit inducement to confess. The court considered authority for the view that where the threat or inducement derives from a person *not* in authority, the test is whether in fact the confession was induced,[111] whereas if the threat or inducement was made by a person in authority, the proper test is "was any offer or promise made which was capable of constituting an inducement, as distinct from one which in fact induced? It is what the average, normal, probably quite unreasonable person in the position of the appellant at the time might

---

[105] e.g. in *R. v Richards* [1967] 1 All E.R. 829 (CA): "I think it would be better if you made a statement and told me exactly what happened".
[106] [1963] I.R. 255 (CCA).
[107] Special Criminal Court, November 27, 1998.
[108] *ibid.*, per Barr J. The courts have also expressed unease with *voltes faces* of this nature in the context of "oppressive questioning", as in *People (DPP) v McNally and Breathnach* (1981) Frewen 43 at 49, 53 (CCA): *cf.* appendix 26.
[109] CCC, November 18, 2003.
[110] (1967) 52 Cr. App. R. 97 (CA).
[111] *R. v Richards* [1967] 1 W.L.R. 653 at 655 (CA).

have thought was likely to result to his advantage from the suggestion agreed to by the police officer".[112]

Oppressive Questioning

10–35 A test of voluntariness based upon the absence of threats and inducements had the effect of focusing attention on the conduct of the investigating police, rather than on the subjective effect of all the circumstances on the accused, and as such it was unduly narrow. In more recent years, the courts have endorsed and developed a more amenable filter in the form of "oppressive questioning". This test was applied by the Court of Criminal Appeal in *People (DPP) v Breathnach*,[113] where the accused eventually made inculpatory statements after 40 hours in custody and repeated requests for a solicitor. In these circumstances, the court could not be satisfied beyond reasonable doubt that the confession was a voluntary one. The court approved the tests of "oppressive questioning" authoritatively stated in *R. v Priestly* and in *R. v Prager*, as follows.

> "[Oppressive questioning is] something which tends to sap, and has sapped, that free will which must exist before a confession is voluntary. ... First, was there in fact something which could properly be styled or might well be oppression? Secondly, did whatever happened in the way of oppression or likely oppression induce the statement in question?"[114]

> "[Oppressive questioning is] questioning which by its nature, duration or other attendant circumstances (including the fact of custody) excites hopes (such as the hope of release) or fears, or so affects the mind of the subject that his will crumbles and he speaks when otherwise he would have stayed silent."[115]

10–36 In *People (DPP) v Shaw*,[116] Griffin J. illustrated various types of conduct on the part of the gardaí certain to render a confession involuntary (most of them forbidden under the Treatment of Persons in Custody Regulations of 1987).[117] The learned judge asserted that a statement is involuntary "if it was wrung from its maker by physical or psychological pressures, by threats or promises made by persons in authority, by the use of drugs, hypnosis, intoxicating drink, by prolonged interrogation or excessive questioning, or by any one of a diversity of methods which have in common the result or the risk

---

[112] *R. v Northam* (1967) 52 Cr. App. R. 97 at 103–4, *per* Winn L.J. (CA).
[113] (1981) 2 Frewen 43 (CCA). The test of "oppressive questioning" was again approved by the Court of Criminal Appeal later that year in *People (DPP) v Pringle* (1981) 2 Frewen 57; *cf.* para.**10–41**.
[114] (1966) 51 Cr. App. R. 1 at 1, *per* Sachs J. (CA).
[115] (1972) 56 Cr. App. R. 151 at 161, *per* Edmund Davies L.J. (CA), applying a formulation given in an address by Lord McDermott to the Bentham Club in 1968.
[116] [1982] I.R. 1 at 60–61 (SC).
[117] *cf.* para.**10–26** *et seq.*

that what is tendered as a voluntary statement is not the natural emanation of a rational intellect and a free will".

Threats, Inducements, and Oppression from Third Parties

10–37 Only threats, inducements or oppressive questioning on the part of the "person in authority" are capable of draining the confession of its voluntariness, according to *People (DPP) v McCann*.[118] In this light, pressure exerted upon the accused by family members urging him to cooperate with the gardaí did not affect the "voluntariness" of the statement. In *People (DPP) v Egan*,[119] two visits by family members had predated the accused's confession, and the last had precipitated it. The Court of Criminal Appeal appeared to assume that the fact the relatives had been present at the request of the accused foreclosed any question of voluntariness. This is likely to be otherwise, however, where the threat or inducement was made by a person *not* in authority, such as a bystander or witness or friend, but in the presence of a person in authority who said nothing to remove the threat or inducement. In such cases, the resulting confession may be deemed involuntary as if the threat or inducement had been made by the person in authority.[120]

10–38 If the accused is influenced by the intervention or presence of relatives—in *McCann* by persuasion on the part of his siblings to confess to the crime—it cannot be said that the confession was secured by threats or inducements made by the persons in authority. This is otherwise if the police intimate to the accused that any of his friends or family will be adversely affected by his continued silence, as in *People (DPP) v Ward*.[121] The English courts have likewise ruled that self-generated fears that family or friends might also be implicated do not affect the admissibility of the confession.[122]

10–39 The voluntariness requirement applies equally to inspectors or officers armed with statutory powers (typically the power to require information upon pain of penal liability, as a qualification of the right to silence).[123] In *Matter of National Irish Bank*,[124] Barrington J. construed "the right not to have involuntary confessions accepted in evidence at a criminal trial" to derive from the right to be tried in accordance with the law for the purposes of Art.38(1) and Art.40(3) of the Constitution.

---

[118] [1998] 4 I.R. 397 (CCA).
[119] [1989] I.R. 681 (CCA).
[120] *R. v Cleary* (1963) 48 Cr. App. R. 116 (CA).
[121] *cf.* para.**10–33**.
[122] *R. v Rennie* [1982] 1 W.L.R. 64 (HL), in the context of the reliability ground (PACE 1984, s.72).
[123] *cf.* para.**13–92** *et seq. In the Matter of National Irish Bank* [1999] 1 I.L.R.M. 321 at 353 (SC), *per* Barrington J., considering the powers of inspectors appointed by the Minister for Enterprise and Employment under s.8 of the Companies Act 1990.
[124] *ibid.* at 359.

Causation

10–40 As a general rule, the accused must establish that the threat, inducement, or oppression caused the accused to make an inculpatory statement he would not otherwise have made.[125] In *People (DPP) v Pringle*,[126] a threat by the garda that unless the accused accounted for his movements on the day in question, his girlfriend would be charged as an accessory did not invalidate the confession, as the effect upon the accused had been removed shortly afterwards when his solicitor assured him that his girlfriend could not be so charged.

The Subjective Test

10–41 The Irish courts favour an application of a test that is subjective to the accused.[127] This may favour the accused, as in *People (Attorney-General) v Flynn*,[128] or act against him as in *People (DPP) v Pringle*.[129] In *Pringle*, the accused appealed against his conviction for the offence of capital murder of a garda who had been fatally shot in the midst of a bank raid. Prior to giving the confession tendered against him in his trial, he had been interviewed during lengthy periods over a weekend under s.30 of the Offences Against the State Act 1939. He had regular access to legal advice over this period, and spoke with his solicitor for two hours after his arrest and a subsequent four times throughout his detention. At one point, he remarked to a garda, "I know that you know I was involved, but upon the advice of my solicitor I am saying nothing and you will have to prove it all the way". The remark was accepted by the Special Criminal Court to constitute an admission of guilt. Upon the basis that the statement critically influenced the court in finding him guilty, the applicant appealed to the Court of Criminal Appeal, where admissibility of the statement was upheld. O'Higgins C.J. adopted the view that oppression is relative to context, and he endorsed *dicta* in *Priestly*,[130] to wit: "What may be oppressive as regards a child, an invalid or an old man or somebody inexperienced in the ways of this world may turn out not to be oppressive when one finds that the accused person is of a tough character and an experienced man of the world". The learned judge rejected the view that "the mere length of ... questioning" entails a finding of unfairness or oppressiveness.[131] In deciding that the accused's unintended slip constituted an admissible confession, the court was clearly influenced by the regularity of the legal advice the accused received throughout his detention (by contrast with the detainee in *Breathnach*).[132] It could thus be inferred in *Pringle's* case

---

[125] *cf.* para.**11–13** *et seq*. This was recognised in *DPP v Ping Lin* [1976] A.C. 574, *per* Lord Salmon (HL) as "the vital question".
[126] (1981) 2 Frewen 57 (CCA).
[127] The English courts have likewise acknowledged that the fundamental test of voluntariness is the state of the accused's mind when he made the confession and not the intention of the investigators: *DPP v Ping Lin* [1976] A.C. 574 (HL).
[128] [1963] I.R. 235 (CCA); *cf.* para.**10–41**.
[129] (1981) 2 Frewen 57 (CCA).
[130] (1965) 51 Cr. App. R. 1 at 1, *per* Sachs J. (CA).
[131] (1981) 2 Frewen 57 at 97 (CCA).
[132] (1981) 2 Frewen 43 (CCA); *cf.* para.**10–34** and appendix 26.

that any oppression that arose due to the rigour and intensity of the interrogation had dissipated by the time he made the critical remark.

10–42 In *People (DPP) v Hoey*,[133] the accused had been arrested under s.30 of the Offences against the State Act 1939 and questioned for extensive periods, throughout which he refused to say anything incriminating upon the advice of his solicitor. At one point, the detective inspector said to him: "Will I have to get some member to go up to your family and find out from them if anybody ... is going to take responsibility for the property in the house?" The accused then made incriminating statements. The Court of Criminal Appeal considered that, although the words had the effect of inducing the accused to confess, they merely indicated that further investigation would be necessary and that this might inconvenience other persons. In doing so, the gardaí had not acted improperly. The Supreme Court disagreed, and found the confession to be involuntary due to an improper inducement causing the accused to believe his family would be left alone if he admitted responsibility. A majority of the court favoured the view that the question of voluntariness is to be decided by reference to the effect of the inducement or threat upon the person to whom it is put and not the subjective test of what was intended or hoped for by the person in authority. Male fides was not necessary on the part of the person in authority. The crucial factor was the effect upon the accused's will and whether it had been overborne by the words used.

V. REQUIREMENTS OF FAIRNESS AND RELIABILITY

10–43 In *People (DPP) v Shaw*,[134] Griffin J. identified a two-tiered test for the admissibility of confessions: first, whether voluntary; and second, even if voluntary, whether obtained in circumstances of fairness. One of the learned judge's findings was rejected subsequently by the Supreme Court—namely, his view that the *O'Brien* rule excluding unconstitutionally obtained evidence was not intended to apply equally to confessions. Of more weight was the learned judge's assertion that confessions must also be tested against basic standards of fairness, a view reached in the light of how "our constitutional postulates the observance of basic or fundamental fairness of procedures".[135] The courts have made reference to fairness alongside voluntariness consistently since.[136] In *People (DPP) v Ward*,[137] the Special Criminal Court considered that the accused had a "basic constitutional right to fair procedures and treatment while in custody". Characterisation of the requirement of fairness in this way logically attracts the application of the *O'Brien* exclusionary rule against

---

[133] [1987] I.R. 637 (SC).
[134] [1982] I.R. 1 (SC): *cf.* appendix 25.
[135] *ibid.* at 61.
[136] *People (DPP) v Breathnach* (1981) 2 Frewen 43 (CCA); *People (DPP) v Lynch* [1982] I.R. 64 (SC); *People (DPP) v Conroy* [1986] I.R. 460 (SC); *People (DPP) v Healy* [1990] 2 I.R. 73 (SC).
[137] Special Criminal Court, November 27, 1998.

Confession Evidence 299

unconstitutionally obtained evidence,[138] although the courts on the whole prefer to subject confession statements to the test of voluntariness developed at common law, given that a substantial body of precedent has developed on this, and given that it applies with strict effect to render involuntary statements inadmissible in the trial. Although the juridical basis for a ruling of inadmissibility due to unfairness exists at common law in terms of the trial judge's inherent discretion in criminal proceedings to exclude relevant evidence upon the basis that its likely prejudicial effect outweighs its probative effect,[139] it is now more appropriate to locate its basis in the constitutional imperative of the trial court to ensure that the accused is tried "in accordance with the law" for the purpose of Art.38(1) of the Constitution, specifically by ensuring that only evidence obtained fairly is tendered against him.

10–44 English law now recognises that a confession, although otherwise valid, may be excluded on grounds that it is unreliable evidence. Section 78(2) of the Police and Criminal Evidence Act 1984 in effect provides a second test which the confession statement must pass, namely that it was not "in consequence of anything said or done ... unreliable". The statutory unreliability basis is considered to be broader than the voluntariness test,[140] and may have encouraged a more exclusionary approach in England to confession evidence, although it is not without its limitations (chief amongst which is the rule that corroboration evidence obtained subsequent to the confession, such as the discovery of physical or real evidence referred to in the confession, is not relevant to the reliability of the confession).[141]

10–45 The Irish courts have on occasion recognised unreliability as a more general basis for rejecting confession statements, notwithstanding compliance with the Judges' Rules, Custody Regulations, the requirement of voluntariness, and the constitutional rights of the accused. To what extent the unreliability of a confession may constitute a separate ground requiring a strict finding of inadmissibility is a matter of some consequence, although as yet it is unresolved. As a basis unto itself, a finding of inadmissibility could be made notwithstanding the inability of the defence to establish improper conduct (threats, inducements, or oppression) on the part of the gardaí or a causative association between the statement and the conduct. The Irish courts have not yet considered the parameters of this ground, and there has been a tendency to date to refer to unfairness casually in the context of the total effect of the various other factors (breach of Rules or Regulations, threats or inducements, etc.).[142]

10–46 A general unreliability ground might enable confessions to be excluded because of some characteristic of the accused generally or at the time he made

---

[138] *cf.* para.**11–27**.
[139] *People (DPP) v Meleady (No.3)* [2001] 4 I.R. 16 at 31, *per* Geoghegan J. (CCA).
[140] *e.g. R. v Walker* [1998] Crim. L.R. 211 (CA), finding that this was not limited to conduct on the part of the police, and is a basis broader than the common law rules.
[141] *Andrews and Hirst on Criminal Evidence* (Jordans, Bristol, 2001) at p.579.
[142] *People (DPP) v Ward* (Special Criminal Court, November 27, 1998).

the confession, despite an absence of misconduct or irregularity on the part of the investigating gardaí. Drunkenness has been regarded on a number of occasions as not sufficient to warrant a ruling that the statement is inadmissible (although the weight of the statement may accordingly suffer).[143] The possibility that the accused was on drugs or "strung out" is also unlikely by itself to constitute a ground for exclusion if the court accepts the garda's evidence that when making the statement the accused appeared rational and sober.[144] The English courts have likewise ruled that the accused's drugs dependency, and his alleged willingness to say anything in order to be released to obtain drugs, is not relevant to the consideration of "unreliability"[145]—a stance clearly at odds with the otherwise operative principle that the true test of a confession's voluntariness and reliability is the state of mind of the accused when questioned.[146] Other decisions, however, have been prepared to accept that a statement may be unreliable where the accused was suffering acute symptoms of withdrawal from drugs,[147] or where he took drugs prior to his confession.[148] It was emphasised in *R. v Crampton*[149] that if the police are in any doubt as to the detainee's fitness for interrogation, they must summon a doctor to clarify this fact. *Crampton* was approved in *People v Ward* in the context of the legality of the accused's detention.[150]

10–47 By contrast with the drugs-based argument, the courts more readily accept that the mental age and aptitude of the accused are highly relevant to a confession's reliability. In *R. v Everett*,[151] the Court of Appeal quashed a 42-year-old man's confession to indecent assault upon the basis that his mental age had been about eight years and his statement ought not to have been

---

[143] In *People (Attorney-General) v Sherlock* (1975) 1 Frewen 383 (CCA), the defence challenged a confession made by the accused two hours after he had arrived at the station under the influence of intoxicants and shortly before he vomited. The court regarded the condition of the accused to be relevant to the weight of the statement but not by itself to entail inadmissibility: "The fact that his debilitated condition may have either prompted him or not restrained him from making his statement which incriminated himself ... does not make the statements involuntary." This perspective was repeated more recently by O'Flaherty J. in *People (DPP) v Cormack* [1999] 1 I.L.R.M. 398 at 400 (SC), where challenge was made to a roadside confession by a drunken accused after his car had ended up in a ditch: "Any admission said by a person, drunk or sober, is *prima facie* admissible in evidence". The effect of the declarant's drunkenness is a matter, therefore, that principally affects the weight to be accorded subsequently by the fact finders to the statement.
[144] *People (DPP) v Murphy* (SC, July 12, 2001).
[145] *R. v Goldenberg* (1988) 88 Cr. App. R. 285 (CA).
[146] *Murphy on Evidence* (Blackstone, London, 1997) at p.243.
[147] *R. v Effick* (1992) 95 Cr. App. R. 427 (CA).
[148] *R. v Walker* [1998] Crim. L.R. 211 (CA).
[149] (1991) 92 C.A.R. 369 (CA).
[150] Special Criminal Court, October 23, 1998. On the facts, the court rejected the applicant's submission that he had been suffering symptoms of withdrawal from heroin, noting that throughout his custody he had not been observed to show any physical signs of withdrawal, he had appeared to have "his wits about him", and he had only requested physeptone (a heroin substitute) once.
[151] [1988] Crim. L.R. 826 (CA).

admitted. In *People (DPP) v Quinn*,[152] the co-accused, then aged 13, had been charged with two other persons of rape and sexual assault, and his two confession statements constituted the only evidence implicating him. Upon appeal, O'Flaherty J. accepted that there was no evidence of a breach of the Custody Regulations, nor of "undue oppression". There were, however, numerous inconsistencies and ambiguities within the statements, and as against the complainant's account, which on the whole suggested that when making his confession the co-accused had had "an imperfect knowledge of what is involved in sexual intercourse". Evidence had been given in the trial that the co-accused's mental capacity lay between seven and eight years. O'Flaherty J. criticised the gardaí's decision to opt for formal compliance with the Regulations—by arranging for the child's parents to attend rather than a member of staff from St Lawrence's home where the co-accused had lived each week and had developed good relationships. The arrival of his mother, "who would not be able to be of much assistance to him", made the resulting confession uncertain. The elements, when viewed together, rendered the confession statement "totally unreliable"—and although the decision to overturn conviction was formally made on the weight of the evidence, rendering any observations on admissibility of the statements technically *obiter*, O'Flaherty J. expressed the view that the case should have been withdrawn from the jury.

VI. Compliance with the Constitutional Rights of the Accused

10–48 If evidence has been obtained against the accused in breach of his constitutional rights, the evidence is strictly inadmissible in his trial, save where "extraordinary excusing circumstances" are shown to have existed.[153] The leading Irish authority upon the matter is *People (Attorney-General) v O'Brien*,[154] where Walsh J. ruled that "[e]vidence obtained in deliberate and conscious violation of constitutional rights of an accused should, save in extraordinary excusing circumstances, be absolutely inadmissible". In *People (DPP) v Lynch*,[155] O'Higgins C.J. asserted that the *O'Brien* test applies equally to confession statements as it does to real evidence, thereby ensuring the early demise of a contrary ruling by Griffin J. in *People (DPP) v Shaw*.[156] In the context of a confession obtained after extensive periods of questioning and sleep-deprivation, described in the case as "oppressive circumstances", O'Higgins C.J. declared in *People (DPP) v Lynch*:

"Once the Constitution has been violated for the purpose of securing a

---

[152] CCA, March 23, 1998, O'Flaherty J. (*ex tempore*).
[153] *cf.* para.**11–01** *et seq.*
[154] [1965] I.R. 142 at 170 (SC): *cf.* appendix 12. First applied to confession evidence in *People (DPP) v Madden* [1977] I.R. 336 (CCA).
[155] [1982] I.R. 64 (SC): *cf.* appendix 27.
[156] [1982] I.R. 1 at 37–41 (SC): *cf.* appendix 25. Griffin J. had proposed that where a confession was voluntary under the common law rules, it was admissible in the trial save, at the discretion of the court, where the statement had been obtained in circumstances of unfairness.

confession, the fruits of that violation must be excluded from evidence on that ground alone. Nor can it be said that the matter can safely be left to a decision on fairness or the voluntary nature of the statement." [157]

10–49 Where a law has been breached by the gardaí, or improper strategies employed to obtain the evidence, without the infringement of a recognised constitutional right of the accused, determination of admissibility is discretionary. Where the gardaí lack lawful authority, or in exercising their powers fail to comply with a suspect's fundamental rights, an illegality becomes an unconstitutionality.[158] In terms of relevance to unconstitutionally obtained confession statements, the most recurring examples are unlawful arrest, unlawful detention, unlawful questioning, and denial of access to legal advice.[159] If the arrest or detention is unlawful, the accused's constitutional right to be detained only in accordance with the law, and his right to liberty, have been infringed contrary to Arts. 40.4.1 and 40.5 of the Constitution. Although the constitutional right of the accused of reasonable access to legal advice has been narrowly sketched,[160] the effect of violation is strict. The Court of Criminal Appeal reasoned in *People (DPP) v Madden*[161] that its effect was to render the detention unlawful; by contrast, the court in *People (DPP) v Breathnach*[162] considered that prolonged interrogation of an accused who had not consulted a solicitor, despite frequent requests, affected the voluntariness of his statement. The association between denial of access to legal advice and the unlawfulness of the detention may serve substantially to dilute, or to obviate, the requirement of proof of causation,[163] as was evident in *People (DPP) v Finnegan*,[164] where prima facie the accused would not have made the statement had he not remained in detention. In *Finnegan*, Barrington J. of the Court of Criminal Appeal found that the right of reasonable access necessitates a private consultation with the solicitor, in person or by telephone, and where this right has been infringed, detention of the accused is unlawful and subsequent statements inadmissible, save where extraordinary excusing circumstances are proven to have existed.

Rights of Access to Legal Advice

10–50 The right of reasonable access to a solicitor during detention, and its potential effect on the admissibility of evidence, was first acknowledged in *People (DPP) v Madden*.[165] The right was incorporated into the Criminal Justice Act (Treatment of Persons in Custody in Garda Síochána Stations) Regulations 1987. The relevant provisions are scattered throughout the

---

[157] [1982] I.R. 64 at 79 (SC): *cf.* appendix 27.
[158] *cf.* para.**11–07** *et seq.*
[159] *cf.* para.**11–28**: *et seq.*
[160] *cf.* para.**10–50** *et seq.*
[161] [1977] I.R. 336 (CCA): *cf.* appendix 26.
[162] (1981) 2 Frewen 43 (CCA).
[163] *cf.* para.**11–14**.
[164] CCA, July 15, 1997.
[165] [1977] I.R. 336 (CCA).

Regulations, lacking a principled base and often very vague. Moreover, they exist in a body of requirements the breach of which "shall not of itself ... affect the lawfulness of the custody of the detained person or the admissibility in evidence of any statement made by him".[166] Article 11(1) provides that an "arrested person shall have reasonable access to a solicitor of his choice and be enabled to communicate with him privately". Article 8(1)(b) requires the "member in charge" of the garda station[167] to inform the person in custody that "he is entitled to consult a solicitor".[168] Where the person requests a solicitor, the member in charge is required to ensure that the solicitor is contacted, and if he cannot be contacted within a reasonable time or is unwilling or unable to attend, the person must be given an opportunity to request another solicitor.[169] Where the person requests the presence of a solicitor, "he shall not be asked to make a written statement in relation to an offence until a reasonable time for the attendance of the solicitor has elapsed".[170] Where the arrested person has not had access to legal advice, and a solicitor "whose presence [had] not been requested by the arrested person presents himself at the station and informs the member in charge that he wishes to visit that person, the person shall be asked if he wishes to consult the solicitor and, if he does so wish" he is entitled to reasonable access and private communication with that solicitor. The arrested person is entitled to consult the solicitor out of hearing, although in sight of, a garda.[171]

10–51 The right of reasonable access was first recognised as a constitutional right, the breach of which would attract the strict *O'Brien* exclusionary rule, in the Supreme Court's decision in *DPP v Healy*.[172] Prior to this, the judges had been guarded lest the right attract the strict effect of the *O'Brien* rule. In *People v Farrell*,[173] O'Higgins C.J. found: "none of the judgments goes so far as to declare that every person under suspicion of, or faced with, a charge of a criminal offence has a constitutional right to have the services of a solicitor and doctor before being questioned by an investigating Garda". *Farrell* was

---

[166] Criminal Justice Act 1984, s.7(3).
[167] According to art.4(3) "[a]s far as practicable, the member in charge shall not be a member who was involved in the arrest of a person for the offence in respect of which he is in custody in the station or in the investigation of that offence".
[168] The right of detainees to be informed of their entitlement of reasonable access to legal advice would appear germane to the utility of the constitutional right of reasonable access upon an application of the reasoning employed by the Supreme Court in *People (DPP) v Healy* [1990] 2 I.R. 73 (SC): *cf.* para.**10–52** and appendix 33. In this light, the High Court's finding in *DPP v Spratt* [1995] 1 I.R. 585 (HC) that it must not be a constitutional right since it is listed in the custody regulations as a statutory right, appears logically unconvincing. In *People (DPP) v Reddan* [1995] 3 I.R. 560 at 566 (CCA), two minutes of discussion was deemed adequate for the purposes of communicating the right of access to a solicitor.
[169] Article 9(2).
[170] Article 12(6).
[171] Article 11(3).
[172] [1990] 2 I.R. 73 (SC): *cf.* appendix 33. The principle applies also to persons entitled to criminal legal aid, following the principles in *State (Healy) v Donoghue* [1976] I.R. 325 (SC).
[173] [1978] I.R. 13 at 20 (CCA).

disapproved by Walsh J. in *People (DPP) v Conroy*[174] to the extent that it might have suggested that the accused had no constitutional right to a solicitor if he requested one.

10–52 In *Healy*,[175] the Supreme Court reasoned that the right of reasonable access entails a correlative right to be informed of the arrival of a solicitor whether personally requested by the accused or arranged for him by others. In the case, the solicitor had been arranged for the accused by his family. Upon arrival at the station, the solicitor requested access to the detainee, but was told he would have to wait until questioning was over. According to Finlay C.J., the accused had had "an immediate [constitutional] right … to be told of the arrival" of the solicitor.[176] The right of access to a solicitor was so fundamental that to classify it as an illegality rather than a violation of constitutional rights would be to undermine its importance. The Supreme Court was unimpressed by the argument that telling the accused that his solicitor had arrived would have hindered the interrogation and diminished the prospect of a confession. Finlay C.J. considered the right of reasonable access to legal advice to be necessary to enable the accused to decide freely whether or not to make an incriminating statement.

10–53 Recent cases suggest that the courts are back-tracking from the propulsion to the constitutional plane of the right of access to legal advice following arrest, presumably because the effects of a breach of constitutional rights (as opposed to an otherwise unlawful act or illegality) have a much stricter effect on the admissibility of the evidence at the trial. The courts have, however, recognised that the accused has a right to communicate with his solicitor in private, and that the constitutional right of access identified in *Healy* would be meaningless without it. In *People (DPP) v Finnegan*,[177] the court found that this right existed with respect to personal and telephonic communication between the solicitor and the accused. The European Court of Human Rights has similarly reasoned that the right of an accused to consult with his solicitor in private and in confidence is one of the basic requirements of a fair trial for the purposes of Art.6(3)(c).[178] Without it, the right of access to legal advice would be useless. It would appear to be the case, currently, that the detainee's solicitor is not entitled to insist on behalf of his client that the questioning adopt a particular form, such as that it be videotaped on the basis that it would provide material evidence to rebut inferences potentially to be drawn from the accused's silence under the Offences Against the State (Amendment) Act 1998.[179] It appears also to be the case in Ireland, in stark

---

[174] [1986] I.R. 460 (SC): *cf.* appendix 29.
[175] [1990] I.L.R.M. 313 (SC): *cf.* appendix 33.
[176] *ibid.* at 320 (SC).
[177] CCA, July 15, 1997.
[178] *S v Switzerland* (1991) E.H.R.R. 670.
[179] *Lavery v Member-in-Charge, Carrickmacross Garda Station* [1992] 2 I.R. 390, *per* O'Flaherty J. (SC): *cf.* para.**13**–**107**.

Confession Evidence   305

contrast to the Miranda law in the US,[180] that a detainee does not have a right, constitutional or otherwise, to insist that questioning take place in the solicitor's presence.[181]

10–54 In a number of other decisions, however, the courts rightly regard the accused's deprivation of legal advice to raise a matter of considerable seriousness. In *People (DPP) v O'Connell*,[182] the confession was deemed inadmissible as a result of the garda's incorrect remark to the accused prior to his confession that a solicitor had been arranged for him. In *McSorley v Governor Mountjoy Prison*,[183] the failure of the trial judge to tell an unrepresented accused at his trial that he had a constitutional right to legal aid was serious enough to overturn conviction.

10–55 The Treatment of Persons in Custody Regulations fall short of requiring the gardaí to *obtain* a solicitor.[184] The right of access to a solicitor logically requires that the investigating gardaí make *attempts* to locate a solicitor, however. If a solicitor is specifically named by the detainee but cannot be procured, the gardaí must make reasonable attempts to contact another solicitor.[185] The courts have limited this correlative duty to making all reasonable attempts to secure a solicitor. It appears to be the case that where all reasonable attempts have been made, the fact that they were unsuccessful and the accused made a confession prior to the eventual arrival of the solicitor does not infringe any constitutional right of the accused.[186] In *People (DPP) v Buck*,[187] it was argued before the Supreme Court that when deciding whether to detain a person for questioning prior to charging him, the gardaí must first have regard to the difficulties in providing the person with access to a solicitor, and further that the spirit of reg.12(6) of the Custody Regulations requires the gardaí to refrain from questioning the arrested person until a reasonable time has elapsed for the arrival of the solicitor. In the case, the confession was given after the arrival of the solicitor, although it was argued that since inadequate effort had been made to arrange legal advice, his detention had been unlawful *ab initio* and the confession upon this basis was inadmissible.

10–56 In *Buck*, the Supreme Court found that the failure to suspend

---

[180] *Miranda v Arizona* 384 U.S. 436 (1966). The decision essentially required police officers when questioning a suspect, prior to access to legal advice, to obtain a waiver of his constitutional right to remain silent and his right to speak first to a lawyer: see generally, Symposium (1998) 50 Stanford L.R. 1057–1180.
[181] *People (DPP) v Pringle* (1981) 2 Frewen 57 (CCA); *Barry v Waldron* (HC, May 23, 1996, *ex tempore*); *Lavery v Member in Charge* [1999] 2 I.R. 390 at 396 (SC).
[182] [1995] 1 I.R. 244 (CCA).
[183] [1996] 2 I.L.R.M. 331 (HC).
[184] *People (DPP) v Reddan* [1995] 3 I.R. 560 at 573 (CCA).
[185] *People (DPP) v Holland* (CCA, June 15, 1998).
[186] *People (DPP) v Darcy* (CCA, July 29, 1997): after unsuccessful attempts had been made to contact three solicitors and before the arrival of the fourth, the accused had made his confession.
[187] [2002] 2 I.R. 268 (SC): *cf.* appendix 64.

questioning until the arrival of the solicitor was not *per se* a denial of the person's constitutional right of access to a solicitor, once arrangements had been made for a solicitor to attend. (Although there was a conflict of evidence over when the detainee first requested a solicitor, the evidence established that a solicitor was not secured until over five hours of detention had passed. The gardai gave evidence that solicitors were thin on the ground in Clonmel the Sunday of the arrest and detention as it was a summer day and a large golfing event was taking place.) Surprisingly, the court appeared to attach little or no consequence to the fact that questioning of the accused had commenced before any attempt had been made to organise the attendance of a solictor. The court considered that where a request for a solicitor is made by the person, and bona fide attempts are made by the gardaí to secure one, the question of the admissibility of any confession statements made by the accused prior to the arrival of the solicitor should be determined by the trial judge as a matter of common law discretion having regard to principles of fairness and public policy already identified by the courts. The court accepted, however, that in any case where the person's right of access to a solicitor has been infringed, the detention is unlawful.

10–57 It appears that the tentativeness with which the courts recognise an accused person's right of access to legal advice stems from a concern not to subject the admissibility of confessions received after the person had legal advice to the strict *O'Brien* exclusionary rule. The difficulty is a practical one—for some time, access to unnominated solicitors has been at the mercy of availability and *pro bono* services.[188] There is no statutory provision for a "stopping of the clock" with respect to time spent in detention to facilitate the obtaining of a solicitor.[189] It may seriously be doubted that current Irish law on the right of access to legal advice adequately protects a detainee under the Criminal Justice (Drug Trafficking) Act 1996 or the Offences Against the State (Amendment) Act 1998, where silence is response to questions may later engender inferences capable of amounting to corroboration of the prosecution's case against him. Whilst *Buck* was not decided in the context of an adverse inference generating detention—the accused had been detained under the Criminal Justice Act 1984—the findings of the Supreme Court appear generally stated. The facility to draw adverse inferences from the silence of detainees suspected of serious offences was of concern to the European Court of Human Rights in *Murray v UK*[190] and is considered further in Chapter 13[191]:

> "[A]t the beginning of a police interrogation, an accused is confronted with a fundamental dilemma relating to his defence. If he chooses to remain silent, adverse inferences may be drawn against him in accordance

---

[188] Keane, "Detention Without Charge and the Criminal Justice (Drug Trafficking Act) 1996" [1997] Ir. Crim. L.J. 3.
[189] McFadden, "The Right to a Solicitor: Recent Developments" (2002) 7 *Bar Review* 390 at 391.
[190] (1996) 22 E.H.R.R. 29 at 67.
[191] *cf.* para.**13–100** *et seq.*

with the provisions of the Order. On the other hand, if the accused opts to break his silence during the course of the interrogation, he runs the risk of prejudicing his defence without necessarily removing the possibility of inferences being drawn against him. Under such conditions the concept of fairness enshrined in Article 6 requires that the accused has the benefit of the assistance of a lawyer already at the initial stages of police interrogation."

VII. Fruit of the Poisoned Tree

10–58 The fruit of the poisoned tree principle addresses the effect of an inadmissible confession on evidence subsequently obtained by the police (whether real evidence gathered on foot of information disclosed in the inadmissible confession, or whether a second confession). The principle was developed as a strict exclusionary rule by the courts in North America with respect to all evidence and facts obtained as a result of inadmissible confessions, and is considered in more detail in Chapter 11.[192]

10–59 With respect to confessions, successive statements may be inadmissible, even though not following immediately after the first, where the effect of the original taint (be it inducement, threat, oppressive questioning, or the absence of statutory authority) has remained.[193] Thus, where an inadmissible confession has been given, the investigators must seek to remove the taint by expressly informing the detainee that his earlier admission may not be effective and that he need not speak solely in the belief that "the cat is now out of the bag" or that his situation has become hopeless because of his earlier admissions. Harlan J. put it thus in *Darwin v Connecticut*:[194] "It would be neither conducive to good police work, nor fair to a suspect, to allow the erroneous impression that he has nothing to lose to play the major role in a defendant's decision to speak a second or third time". It has been said that there should be a genuinely "meaningful intervening event" that cures the taint, such as consultations with lawyers, friends, or family.[195] The so-called "cat out of the bag" principle has found favour in a number of English decisions. In *R. v McGovern*,[196] Farquharson C.J. observed: "One cannot refrain from emphasising that when an accused person has made a series of admissions as to his or her complicity in a crime at a first interview, the very fact that those admissions have been made [is] likely to have an effect upon her during the course of the second interview".

---

[192] *McNabb v US* (1942) 318 U.S. 332; *Mallory v US* (1957) 354 U.S. 449; *Wong Sun v US* (1963) 371 U.S. 471; *cf.* para.**11–01** *et seq*.
[193] *People (DPP) v Buckley* [1990] 1 I.R. 14 (CCA): *cf.* appendix 32.
[194] (1968) 391 U.S. 346.
[195] Thus expressed in a dissenting judgment by Brennan J. in *Oregon v Elstad* (1985) 470 U.S. 298 at 341, and favoured by Mirfield (1996).
[196] (1990) 92 Cr. App. R. 229 (CA).

10–60 The extent to which an original taint has not been "cured" will depend not only upon the circumstances of the accused but also the nature of the "taint" (whether on the one hand a threat, or on the other hand a technical failure to observe the letter of a statute). In *People (DPP) v Cleary*,[197] a technically faulty exercise of the garda's power to detain a suspect for questioning under s.4 of the Criminal Justice Act 1984 did not invalidate his confession later in the station, as the confession had been determined, persistent, and "was a free, unconditioned and detached decision to continue in the same vein".[198]

10–61 If in a second interview the garda refers to earlier admissions made by the suspect that were not received in compliance with his rights, his subsequent reiteration of the admissions may also be deemed inadmissible upon the basis that they were "improperly" obtained and suffer the taint of the preceding irregularity.[199]

10–62 The English courts have not generally adopted the fruits of the poisoned tree doctrine, and the common law rule was that physical or real evidence obtained on foot of an inadmissible confession was not also inadmissible in evidence if the discovered evidence could be "fully and satisfactorily proved" without any reference to the inadmissible confession.[200] This was otherwise where the discovered evidence was so closely and intimately connected with the confession as to have been produced by the accused as part of his confession. This approach has been strengthened in recent years in England by statute.[201]

VIII. CONFESSION AS EVIDENCE AGAINST A CO-ACCUSED

10–63 A confession statement is admissible only as against the interests of the confessor, and therefore is not admissible as evidence for the purpose of the prosecution's case against a co-accused.[202] Given the significant risks of prejudice to a co-accused's defence, it is encumbent upon the trial judge to warn the jury in specific terms not to treat the unsworn statement of one co-accused as evidence against another co-accused.[203] In *People (Attorney-*

---

[197] HC, December 7, 2001.
[198] *ibid.*, per Herbert J.
[199] As occurred in *People (DPP) v Cleary* HC, December 7, 2001.
[200] *R. v Warickshall* [1783] 1 Leach 263, approved in *Lam Chi-Ming v R.* [1991] 2 A.C. 212 (PC).
[201] The admissibility of evidence obtained in consequence of an inadmissible confession is governed in England by s.76 of the Police and Criminal Evidence Act 1984. See further: *Kuruma v R.* [1955] A.C. 197 (PC); *Fox v Gwent Chief Constable* [1985] 1 W.L.R. 1126 (HL); *R. v Sang* [1980] A.C. 402 (HL); *R. v Christie* [1980] A.C. 402 (HL); *R. v Khan* [1996] 2 Cr. App. R. 440 (CA).
[202] *People v Keane* (1976) 110 I.L.T.R. 1 (CCA); *R. v Lake* (1976) 64 Cr. App. R. 172 (CA).
[203] *People (DPP) v Ferris* (CCA, March 11, 1997, *ex tempore*).

General) v Sherlock,[204] the appeal upon this issue failed as the trial judge had adequately directed the jury on admissibility of the statements, and each co-accused had made a statement incriminating himself in the murder. In *People (DPP) v Palmer*,[205] the appeal on this ground also failed after the court found that the statement by the co-accused did not sufficiently implicate the applicant to justify the direction. In fact, the applicant had made a statement implicating the co-accused in question, and that correctly had attracted the specific direction against cross-admissibility.

10–64 If the accused chooses to testify during his trial, a co-accused is entitled to cross-examine him subject to the ordinary rules of evidence and procedure, and subject in particular to the prohibition against questions tending to expose the other's criminal record or bad character. A co-accused's right to cross-examine another is dependent only upon the other electing to give testimony in his own defence. This right is not dependent upon the other having implicated the co-accused, although if this occurred the witness loses his "shield of protection" from questions upon record and character by virtue of s.1(f) of the Criminal Justice (Evidence) Act 1924.[206]

10–65 The right of one co-accused to cross-examine another co-accused, where both have elected to testify, in principle enables a co-accused to seek the limited admission, upon a credit-relevant basis, of a prior inconsistent confession statement made by the other but not admitted in the trial. Such a statement, although not relied upon by the prosecution during the trial, must be disclosed to the defence.[207] In *Lui Mei Lin v Queen*[208]—where a "mixed confession" statement incriminating a co-accused had earlier been deemed inadmissible upon the basis that it had been induced and was not voluntary—the Privy Council reasoned that the general right to cross-examine a witness upon any previous inconsistent statements made by him in writing ought to be unfettered where the witness is a co-accused who seeks to defend himself by arguing that the other co-accused is unworthy of belief. The trial judge, however, was obliged to caution the jury when summing-up that the inconsistent statement was relevant to the credibility of the co-accused but was not evidence probative of the facts asserted therein. This development was strengthened in *R. v Myers*,[209] where the two accused were charged with fatally stabbing a taxi driver. One of them admitted to the police officers, in the absence of the usual caution, that she had killed the driver but that they had only intended to rob him. At the trial, the prosecution decided not to rely upon this statement. The co-accused sought to cross-examine the other co-accused upon it. The right to do so was endorsed by the House of Lords upon the basis that "the trial judge does not have a discretionary power, *as between co-defendants*, to

---

[204] (1975) 1 Frewen 383 (CCA).
[205] CCA, March 22, 2002.
[206] *cf.* para.**8–61** *et seq.*
[207] *cf.* paras **1–42** *et seq.*, **3–38**.
[208] [1989] 1 A.C. 288 (PC).
[209] [1997] 3 W.L.R. 552 (HL).

exclude relevant evidence on the ground that he is choosing the lesser course which involves the lesser injustice as between the defendants".[210] Lord Slynn went further, however, and expressed the view that a co-accused should also be entitled to refer to the prior statement as probative evidence.[211] This places the co-accused who made an inadmissible confession in a very precarious position, since if the trials had been conducted singly, the rule in *R. v Blastland*[212] would have prevented reference to the other party's confession upon the basis that it was third party hearsay.

10–66 A qualification to the rule that a confession by one co-accused is not cross-admissible against another co-accused exists for a declaration made separately by one party that tends to establish that both parties were involved in a conspiracy or common enterprise. Admissibility requires the prosecution to prove that the statement was made at a time when the alleged conspiracy existed, and it is limited to cases where both parties are prosecuted jointly and the prosecution alleges a common enterprise or conspiracy. The declaration is not treated as a "confession" for the purposes of the Rules, but as something which was part of the planning and implementation of the joint purpose. The prosecution may rely upon the declaration as evidence tending to prove the common design between them.[213] For the purposes of the rule, however, it is essential to establish that the offences were jointly planned and executed. This was not the case in *R. v Gray*[214]—although the parties had colluded over the telephone and disseminated information for the purposes of insider trading, each had committed the offence separately (in other words, there was evidence of a common agreement but this did not relate to a jointly committed offence).[215]

IX. "MIXED STATEMENTS"

10–67 According to recent English and Irish case law, where a statement is partly inculpatory and also partly exculpatory (in terms of laying the basis for a defence, or in terms of casting the blame upon another), the statement may yet be admitted in the trial as a "statement against the interests" of the declarant probative of the facts asserted therein. In light of the fact that the accused may be required to adduce evidence tending to show a reasonable possibility of the existence of the facts upon which a fresh issue defence is based,[216] the statement assumes a particular importance in cases where the accused elects not to testify.

10–68 The view that a "mixed statement" ought to be admitted generally as a confession was affirmed by the Court of Criminal Appeal in *People (DPP) v*

---

[210] *ibid.* at 571, *per* Lord Hope of Craighead (HL).
[211] *ibid.* at 563–4.
[212] [1986] A.C. 41 (HL).
[213] *R. v Duffield* (1851) 5 Cox C.C. 404.
[214] [1995] 2 Cr. App. R. 100 (CA).
[215] See also, *People (DPP) v Rose* CCA, February 21, 2002.
[216] *cf.* para.**4–23** *et seq.*

Clarke.[217] The accused made a statement to the gardaí, implicating himself in a murder and providing details relevant to his subsequent plea of self-defence. The accused later exercised his right to silence, and chose not to testify at his trial. The trial judge deemed the pre-trial statement admissible as a confession. In his directions to the jury, however, he pointed out that pre-trial statements are not equivalent to giving sworn testimony in open court when cross-examination may take place and the jury may assess the accused's demeanour and credibility. Ordering a retrial, O'Flaherty J. disagreed with the trial judge's directions, and ruled that "once a statement is put in evidence ... it then and thereby becomes evidence in the real sense of the word, not only against the person who made it but for him as to facts contained in it favourable to his defence or case".[218] He added that the trial judge had an *obligation* to remind the jury that the accused had squarely raised the issue of self-defence in his statement and that it was an issue they ought to consider.

10–69 In *Clarke*, the court approved, and broadly followed, the approach favoured by the English Court of Appeal in *R. v Duncan*.[219] In *Duncan*, as in *Clarke*, the accused had declined to testify, and elements of his statement confessing to murder had lain the basis for a defence of provocation and constituted the only evidence in the trial tendered in support of it. The trial judge refused to admit the statement on the ground that it was "self-serving", and withdrew the issue of provocation from the jury upon the basis that no evidence had been heard in support of it. Upon appeal, Lord Lane C.J. expressed the view that in cases such as this, it would be simpler and therefore more just if the entire statement was admitted in evidence as probative of the issue. The learned judge proposed, in keeping with the rationale of the hearsay rule, that there was no reason why a trial judge should not remark to the jury that inculpatory aspects of the statement are more likely to be true (since made *against* the interests of the accused), and to make contrary "comment in relation to the exculpatory remarks upon the election of the accused not to give evidence".[220] This latter proposition in *Duncan* was not explored in *Clarke*, which instead approved *Duncan* to the extent that it recognised a discretion, as opposed to strict obligation, upon the trial judge to advise the jury as to the weight of the exculpatory statements.

10–70 The rationale for the general admissibility of "mixed statements" relied upon by the accused derives from a sense that "that which is (evidentially) sauce for the goose is held to be sauce for the gander too".[221] Although the

---

[217] *People (DPP) v Clarke* [1994] 3 I.R. 289 (CCA): *cf.* appendix 46. *Clarke* was approved in *People (DPP) v Kenny* (CCA, November 19, 2002), a decision based on the extent to which the court must decide the weight of the evidence in the context of an application to withdraw issues from the jury: *cf.* para.**1–50**.
[218] [1994] 3 I.R. 289 at 303 (CCA).
[219] (1981) 73 Cr. App. R. 359 (CA): approved by the House of Lords in *R. v Sharp* [1988] 1 W.L.R. 7 (HL).
[220] (1981) 73 Cr. App. R. 359 at 365, *per* Lord Lane C.J. (CA).
[221] Birch, "The Sharp End of the Wedge: Use of Mixed Statements by the Defence" [1997] Crim. L.R. 416.

view that the statement should be admissible in its entirety has the support of old authority,[222] it presents certain difficulties for a co-accused. A confession statement is admissible as an exception to the rule against hearsay upon the basis that it is a statement made *against* interest and therefore is less likely to be inaccurate, unreliable, manufactured, or untrue.[223] An admission of guilt that also lays the foundation for a specific defence may be in the accused's *best* interests, given that it may constitute sufficient evidence to justify putting the issue to the jury,[224] whether or not the accused has made himself available for cross-examination (which, under current rules of evidence, may not occur unless he elects to give evidence in his defence).[225] Therefore, to admit the confession in its entirety may be to expose the court to assertions not amenable to adequate testing. Although mixed confession statements are in principle admissible against the interests of the confessor where tendered by the prosecution,[226] and therefore are not admissible as evidence against a co-accused,[227] a statement implicating a co-accused may unfairly prejudice his defence without giving him a correlative right to require the implicating accused to submit to cross-examination. These concerns were reflected in an earlier ruling by the English Court of Appeal in *R. v Donaldson*,[228] where James L.J. drew a distinction between mixed statements tendered by the prosecution as evidence against the accused, which ought to be admitted in their entirety, and mixed statements tendered by the accused and being "entirely of a self-serving nature", which ought to remain inadmissible as proof of the issues.[229] On the other hand, it has been recognised that since the accused retains the right to challenge an admissible confession throughout the trial,[230] it is right that he be able to point to exculpatory passages in the mixed statement to indicate that the statement is not essentially a "confession" of his guilt.

10–71 The options facing the trial judge in this regard are either to admit the statement unedited (as favoured by *Clarke*) and to warn the jury that the statement is admissible against its maker but not cross-admissible against the co-accused, or, where the risk of prejudice to a co-accused is likely not to be cured by a warning, to accede to a request to order separate trials of the co-accused.

---

[222] *R. v Paine* (1696) 5 Mod. 163 at 167; *R. v Jones* (1827) Car. & P. 629.
[223] *cf.* para.**9–77**.
[224] *cf.* para.**4–23** *et seq.*
[225] *cf.* para.**2–17**.
[226] According to the House of Lords in *R. v Aziz* [1995] 3 All E.R. 149 at 155, this precludes the accused from tendering a statement (even though mixed) that is not being relied upon by the prosecution.
[227] *cf.* para.**10–63**.
[228] (1976) 64 Cr. App. R. 59 (CA).
[229] *ibid.* at 65.
[230] *cf.* para.**10–03**.

Confession Evidence 313

X. THE CORROBORATION WARNING

10–72 Overriding the position of the common law with respect to uncorroborated confession statements,[231] s.10 of the Criminal Procedure Act 1993 provides that where confession evidence has been tendered in the trial of an indictable offence, and is not corroborated, the trial judge must caution the jury to have "due regard to the absence of corroboration". Although this is stated to require no fixed set of words, it is irreducibly necessary that the direction explain how the evidence may be corroborated in the trial, and why the law prefers that such evidence be corroborated. In numerous cases, warnings were deemed defective upon appeal for misidentifying evidence capable of constituting corroboration in the trial.[232]

10–73 The legislature enacted s.10 in response to anxieties precipitated by a series of high-profile cases of miscarriage of justice, including those of the "Guilford Four" and "Birmingham Six" in England and Nicky Kelly in Ireland.[233] It was additionally influenced by the findings of the Martin Committee, which had expressed the need to establish strong procedural safeguards to ensure that confessions are properly obtained, chief amongst which should be the recording of all statements made by suspects and detainees to the gardai. In this latter respect, the Committee was impressed by the experience in Canada, where a requirement that interviews be taped had virtually eliminated *voire dire* enquiries upon the voluntariness of confession statements and had been enthusiastically endorsed there by criminal defence lawyers.[234]

10–74 The importance of corroboration in prosecutions that rely upon repudiated confessions was acknowledged by Hardiman J. in *Braddish v DPP*[235] in the context of the duty on the prosecution to retain and disclose material evidence. In response to the prosecution's explanation that the surveillance videotape had been destroyed after a decision was made to rely solely upon a confession statement made by the accused, Hardiman J. asserted that the prosecution had been under a duty to give the defence an opportunity to inspect and consider the videotape prior to any decision to destroy it, and that this may have provided vital evidence for the accused to challenge the legality of his detention (in terms of rebutting a claim that the gardaí had "reasonable suspicion" that he committed the offence).[236] The videotape may also have provided evidence relevant to establishing whether corroboration existed in the case or not. In the absence of the videotape, the identification (which purported to be by means of stills taken from the videotape) was

---

[231] *People (DPP) v Quillegan and O'Reilly (No.3)* [1993] 2 I.R. 305 (SC).
[232] *cf.* para.**5–40** *et seq.*
[233] Byrne and Binchy, *Annual Review of Irish Law 1993* (Round Hall Sweet & Maxwell, Dublin, 1996) at p.228.
[234] Committee to Inquire into Certain Aspects of Criminal Procedure, 1990, at p.36.
[235] [2001] 3 I.R. 127 (SC): *cf.* appendix 63 and para.**1–42** *et seq.*
[236] *cf.* para.**11–43** *et seq.*

inadmissible, and accordingly the disputed confession statement was uncorroborated. Hardiman J. observed that the law had recognised corroboration to be an essential safeguard against unreliable confessions, adding that "relatively recent history both here and in the neighbouring jurisdiction has unfortunate examples of the risks of excessive reliance on confession evidence".[237]

10–75 In *People (DPP) v Connolly*,[238] a successful challenge was brought against the trial judge's directions on the uncorroborated state of the confession statement tendered by the prosecution as the sole evidence against the accused in the case. The confession, which had been written down and signed by the accused, had allegedly been conveyed to a garda on duty. A second garda had joined them while the statement was being concluded and was present to hear the statement read over to the accused and to witness him signing it. The accused repudiated the statement during the trial, claiming that its content had been concocted and drafted by the first garda, and that he had been induced to sign it. The trial judge dealt with the issue by instructing the jury that they "should bear in mind" that the statement was "unsupported by exterior evidence" and that there was no "corroboration, tending to support it". Upon appeal, the applicant submitted that this did not constitute "due regard to the absence of corroboration" and that the warning required more detailed reference to the reasons why the law prefers that such evidence be corroborated and to the significance of its absence, in a manner similar to the terms of the warning tailored by the Supreme Court for identification evidence in *People (AG) v Casey (No. 2)*.[239] Overturning conviction, Hardiman J. found that, whilst the content of the trial judge's warning will vary from case to case and need not be given in any particular form of words, it must be "sufficiently explanatory"[240] and a trial judge's direction that the absence of corroboration in any case is "something [the jury] should bear in mind" was not forceful enough. Reference ought to be made, in appropriate cases, to the concerns underpinning the requirement in s.10, which may be achieved neutrally, without implying misfeasance on the part of garda witnesses, by referring to the findings of the Martin Committee, that "there have been a number of instances in the past where admissions have subsequently been proved to be unreliable".[241] The trial judge ought also to explain the meaning of 'corroboration' having regard to the factual nature of the prosecution's case; to this end, the "facts of the individual case will suggest appropriate illustrations."[242] Hardiman J. helpfully outlined a warning that would satisfy the s.10 requirement in similar cases:[243]

"This case stands or falls on the confessions which the prosecution allege

---

[237] [2001] 3 I.R. 127 at 133 (SC).
[238] [2003] 2 I.R. 1 at 5 (CCA).
[239] [1963] I.R. 33 (SC): *cf.* para.**6–01** *et seq.*
[240] [2003] 2 I.R. 1 at 17.
[241] *ibid.* at 16.
[242] *ibid.*
[243] *ibid.* at 16–17.

the accused made. Either you are satisfied beyond reasonable doubt that that confession is true and reliable, in which case you will convict, or you are not so satisfied, in which case you will acquit. The law requires me to point out to you that there is no corroboration of the evidence of the confession. Corroboration means independent confirmation. In a case like this, it would mean some evidence independent of that of the gardai who say they heard the accused confess, which you could fairly and reasonably regard as confirming the truth of the confession. There might have been forensic evidence placing the accused in the injured party's house, which would certainly confirm the truth of the alleged confession. He might have been found in possession of the stolen property or he might have been identified by some person as the robber. On the other hand, there are cases which, of their nature, make it hard to find corroboration. You must consider what sort of case this is from the point of view of corroboration. When you are considering whether you can feel sure that the statement is true and reliable beyond reasonable doubt, you must ask yourselves whether the absence of any corroboration or independent confirmation of the statement should reduce your trust in it to the point where you are not confident of its truth beyond reasonable doubt. Since the earliest times, people faced with important decisions have sought to make their task easier by looking for independent confirmation of one view or another. It is very natural and prudent to do so, and very comforting if you find it. But if it is absent, the decision still has to be made. If it is absent where you would expect to find it, that fact in itself may affect the decision.

I am obliged to give you this warning because of a law passed by the Oireachtas in 1993, which says that I must advise you to give due regard to the absence of corroboration. It is essential that you do so. You must also bear in mind that, despite the absence of corroboration, you are perfectly entitled to convict if you are indeed satisfied of the truth of the accused's confession beyond reasonable doubt. The law does not say that you cannot convict without corroboration, merely that you should specifically consider the absence of corroboration and what weight, if any, you should give to this factor. Once you do this, your decision is a matter for your own good sense and conscience."

Further Reading

Birch, "The Sharp End of the Wedge: Use of Mixed Statements by the Defence" [1997] Crim. L.R. 416.

Costelloe, "Detention for Questioning and Oppressive Interrogation" (2001) 11(1) I.C.L.J. 12.

Dein, "Non Tape Recorded Cell Confession Evidence—On Trial" [2002] Crim. L.R. 630.

McFadden, "The Right to a Solicitor: Recent Developments" (2002) 7 *Bar Review* 390.

McGuckian, "Recent Developments in the Law governing the Admissibility of Confessions in Ireland" (1999) 9(1) I.C.L.J. 8.

Mirfield, Silence, *Confessions and Improperly Obtained Evidence* (2nd ed., Sweet & Maxwell, London, 1997).

Mirfield, "Successive Confessions and the Poisonous Tree" [1996] Crim.L.R. 554.

Smith, "Exculpatory Statements and Confessions" [1995] Crim. L.R. 280.

Thornton, "The Prejudiced Defendant: Unfairness by a Defendant in a Joined Trial" [2003] Crim. L.R. 433.

White, "The Confessional State—Police Interrogation in the Irish Republic" (2000) 10(1) I.C.L.J. 17 and 10(2) I.C.L.J. 2.

Wolchover and Heaton-Armstrong, *Confession Evidence* (Sweet & Maxwell, London, 1996).

Wolchover and Heaton-Armstrong, "Tape Recording Witness Statements" (1997) New L.J. 855.

Chapter 11

EVIDENCE OBTAINED UNCONSTITUTIONALLY AND ILLEGALLY

I. Evidence Obtained in Breach of the Accused's Constitutional Rights 11–01
    The Exclusionary Rule 11–01
    Constitutional Rights and the Obtaining of Evidence 11–07
    Proof of a Causative Link 11–13
    "Deliberate and Conscious Violation" 11–16
    "Extraordinary Excusing Circumstances" 11–21
II. Evidence Obtained Illegally or Improperly 11–23
III. Gardaí Powers of Arrest, Detention, Search, and Seizure 11–28
    Arrest and Detention 11–28
    Powers of Search and Seizure 11–52
IV. Application of the Exclusionary Rule in Civil Cases 11–69

I. EVIDENCE OBTAINED IN BREACH OF THE ACCUSED'S CONSTITUTIONAL RIGHTS

The Exclusionary Rule

11–01 The judgment of Walsh J. in *People (Attorney-General) v O'Brien*,[1] the Supreme Court's first authoritative analysis on the matter, has become the *locus classicus* for determining the admissibility of evidence obtained in violation of a constitutional right of the accused:

> "The courts in exercising the judicial powers of government of the State must recognise the paramount position of constitutional rights and must uphold the objection of an accused person to the admissibility at his trial of evidence obtained or procured by the State or its servants or agents *as a result of a deliberate and conscious violation of the constitutional rights of the accused person where no extraordinary excusing circumstances*

---

[1] [1965] I.R. 142 (SC): *cf.* appendix 12.

exist, such as the imminent destruction of vital evidence or the need to rescue a victim in peril."[2]

11–02 The *O'Brien* exclusionary rule was originally sketched in terms of respect for the accused's constitutional rights: "The vindication and the protection of constitutional rights of the citizen is a duty superior to that of trying such citizen for a criminal offence."[3] In more recent years, it has additionally been justified by the public interest in deterring unlawful police conduct. In *Spano v New York*,[4] considered by Finlay C.J. in *People (DPP) v Kenny*,[5] the deterrence principle was justified as follows: "The abhorrence of society to the use of involuntary confessions does not turn alone on their inherent untrustworthiness. It also turns on the deep-rooted feeling that the police must obey the law; that in the end life and liberty can be as much endangered from illegal methods used to convict those thought to be criminals as from the actual criminals themselves". There are, however, significant differences between an exclusionary rule founded on vindication of rights and a rule founded on deterrence concerns. In his majority judgment in *Kenny*,[6] now of much influence, Finlay C.J. endorsed a principle of exclusion accommodating the goals of both the vindication and deterrent models, upon the basis that it is "likely to protect constitutional rights in more instances". Finlay C.J. accepted that the "absolute protection" rule often had the effect of depriving the fact finders of highly probative evidence and that, in furtherance of other goals, "it constitutes a potential limitation on the capacity of the courts to arrive at the truth and so most effectively to administer justice".[7] In this sense, it aims to protect the basic rights of an accused, fairness and due process, and not the detection or punishment of crime.[8] The learned judge expressed the "absolute protection" model of due process as follows:

> "To exclude only evidence obtained by a person who knows or ought reasonably to know that he is invading a constitutional right is to impose a negative deterrent. ... To apply, on the other hand, the absolute protection rule of exclusion whilst providing also that negative deterrent, incorporates as well a positive encouragement to those in authority over the crime prevention and detection services of the State to consider in detail the personal rights of the citizens as set out in the Constitution, and the effect of their powers of arrest, detention, search and questioning in relation to such rights."[9]

11–03 In *People (DPP) v Shaw*,[10] there was significant disagreement in the

---

[2] *ibid.* at 170 (emphasis added).
[3] *ibid., per* Walsh J.
[4] (1959) 360 U.S. 315 at 320 *per* Warren C.J. (CA, NY).
[5] [1990] I.L.R.M. 569 at 579 (SC): *cf.* appendix 36.
[6] *ibid.* at 578.
[7] *ibid.*
[8] *ibid.* at 579.
[9] *ibid* at 578.
[10] [1982] I.R. 1 (SC): *cf.* appendix 25.

Supreme Court on the logic and methodology by which the *O'Brien* exclusionary rule ought to be applied, although the judges agreed that it did not operate in the case to render the crucial evidence inadmissible. The case gave rise to issues regarding the legality of the accused's detention and his subsequent confession, since upon arrest he had not been brought to a District Court at the first reasonable opportunity and not until two days later after the gardaí had concluded a successful investigation into the disappearance and murder of two women. Whilst the court was agreed that the inculpatory statements had been voluntarily given and were admissible, a majority (Griffin, Henchy, Kenny and Parke JJ.) favoured the view that following the accused's arrest, the gardaí were entitled and responsible to weigh his constitutional right to liberty and due process against the constitutional rights of the woman who had recently disappeared and whose life was believed to be in danger. As the rights and interests had been properly balanced, his detention was lawful and his confession ordinarily admissible.

11–04 The approach of the majority judges in *Shaw* presents numerous problems, not least because it encourages the gardaí to resolve conflicts between fundamental constitutional rights at a localised level upon an "ends justify the means" basis. It is contingent on acceptance of the view that where "extraordinary excusing circumstances" exist, a violation of the constitutional right of the accused does not occur, a view that appears textually and logically at variance with the exclusionary rule formulated by Walsh J. in *O'Brien*. The words "extraordinary *excusing* circumstances" necessarily refer to some anterior infringement of a constitutional right.[11] The statement is concerned with the effects of *illegalities* and *breaches* of constitutional rights for the admissibility of evidence, and it presupposes that resolution of the delicate balance between the violation of a constitutional right and justifying circumstances is undertaken latterly by the courts when determining, by *voire dire*, whether or not the resultant evidence is admissible. As such, Walsh J.'s interpretation in *Shaw* of his own ruling in *O'Brien* is the only tenable one to adopt so long as these *dicta* remain the definitive expression of the exclusionary rule in Ireland. In *Shaw*, Walsh J. reasoned that when the gardaí failed to bring the accused to a District Court at the first reasonable opportunity, they had infringed a constitutional right of the accused, which rendered his detention unlawful, but that the evidence thereby obtained was admissible as the infringement had been justified by the presence of "extraordinary excusing circumstances" (specifically, the perceived need to rescue a victim in peril). The learned judge correctly reasoned that "nothing in the admissibility rule renders lawful what was and is unlawful. By definition, the question of admissibility arises only because there was an illegality".[12]

11–05 This preferable view of the *O'Brien* rule had the support of the High

---

[11] A view shared by Casey, *Constitutional Law in Ireland* (3rd ed., Round Hall Sweet & Maxwell, Dublin, 2000) at p.533 and O'Connor, "The Admissibility of Unconstitutionally Obtained Evidence in Irish Law" (1982) 17 Ir. Jur. 257 at 269.
[12] [1982] I.R. 1 at 33 (SC).

Court in *DPP v Delaney*,[13] where Morris J. stated that the *O'Brien* rule is not authority for "the general proposition that a member of the Garda Síochána may violate a constitutional right providing that there are 'extraordinary excusing circumstances' ".[14] Rather, it means "that where such a violation occurs and evidence is harvested as a result, it is for the court of trial to decide all issues as to the admissibility of this evidence including a consideration of any extraordinary excusing circumstances alleged, upon the criteria stated in [*O'Brien* and *Shaw*]".[15] These findings were approved in *Freeman v DPP*[16] by Carney J., who considered that in a case where the gardaí had entered the suspect's dwelling without warrant or consent, the arrest had been unlawful, but that since the gardaí had discovered the suspect *in flagrante delicto* (moving goods believed to be stolen from a van into a house), the arrest had been effected in "extraordinary excusing circumstances" and therefore admissibility of the evidence was justified. Carney J. proposed that to "attribute too wide a scope to the exception in the case of the imminent destruction of evidence may undermine the rationale of a rule which by its nature is invoked in circumstances where well meaning haste on the part of the gardaí may lead to unconstitutional acts".[17]

11–06 The Supreme Court, however, opted for Griffin J.'s interpretation of the *O'Brien* rule, when it considered *DPP v Delaney*.[18] In the case, the gardaí had decided forcibly to enter the accused persons' dwelling without warrant and then to arrest and charge them, which they sought to justify upon the basis that a hostile crowd had gathered outside the flat and had threatened to burn it down, where the gardaí believed that young children were inside the premises. By way of consultative case stated, the Supreme Court was asked if there was justification at law for the apparent infringement of the right of the occupier to the inviolability of his dwelling under Art.40.5 of the Constitution. In a decision that does not rigorously address operation of the exclusionary rule, O'Flaherty J. applied Griffin J.'s views on the necessity of the gardaí to balance constitutional rights, and Finlay C.J.'s more recent pronouncement in *Kenny*, to wit, that evidence obtained in breach of a constitutional right of the accused must be excluded save where there are "extraordinary excusing circumstances which justify the admission of the evidence".[19] O'Flaherty J. considered that the principle expressed in *Kenny* had "nothing to say to the concept of a hierarchy of rights".[20] The gardaí had acted in an "extremely fraught situation" and when they chose to act in defence of the life and limb of others, and to subordinate the right of another to inviolability of the dwelling, they were fulfilling the requirements of the Constitution.

---

[13] [1996] 3 I.R. 556 (HC).
[14] *ibid.* at 561.
[15] *ibid.*
[16] [1996] 3 I.R. 565 at 575 (HC).
[17] *ibid.* at 576.
[18] [1997] 3 I.R. 453 (SC).
[19] [1990] 2 I.R. 110 at 134 (SC).
[20] [1997] 3 I.R. 453 at 459 (SC).

Constitutional Rights and the Obtaining of Evidence

11–07 In order to justify a strict application of the *O'Brien* test, it must be established that an actual constitutional right of the accused[21] was violated as a result of which the evidence was obtained. The courts have thus far reasoned that incriminating evidence obtained as a result of unauthorised entry onto premises not belonging to, or occupied by, the accused does not necessarily constitute evidence obtained in breach of constitutional rights for the purposes of attracting the *O'Brien* rule.[22] In other words, the *O'Brien* rule is concerned only to exclude evidence obtained in breach of the constitutional rights of the accused. The only constitutional right seemingly affected by entry onto premises for the purposes of investigation and search is Art.40.5, which guarantees that the "dwelling of every citizen shall be inviolable and shall not be forcibly entered save in due course of law". The Irish courts have not so far been swayed to identify unenumerated rights to inviolability or privacy with respect to business premises or offices.[23] In *Kennedy v Law Society of Ireland*,[24] it was established that the respondent had acted in excess of its statutory powers by the manner in which it conducted an investigation into the accounts and practice of the appellant solicitor. The appellant had not identified the constitutional right supposedly infringed, and the court could identify none equivalent to the constitutional rights to liberty and inviolability of the person and dwelling recurrent in the criminal cases. Accordingly, the evidence obtained by the inspectors had been obtained illegally but not unconstitutionally, and its admissibility was dependent to a more appreciable extent upon judicial discretion (which, in the event, was exercised in favour of the appellant).[25]

11–08 It is clear from decisions justifying unauthorised obtaining of evidence in "extraordinary excusing circumstances" that the accused does not possess an unqualified right to have excluded from his trial all evidence obtained in violation of his constitutional rights.[26] One's attitude to characterisation or scope of this right depends partly upon whether one adopts the view that evidence obtained in "extraordinary excusing circumstances", where the constitutional rights of others prevail over the constitutional rights of the accused, is not obtained in violation of the accused's constitutional rights.[27] O'Connor has expressed the view that the accused benefits from such a right in consequence of the duty of the courts, recognised by the Supreme Court in *O'Brien* and *Kenny*, to defend and vindicate the constitutional rights of the

---

[21] *People (DPP) v Lawless* (CCA, November 28, 1985) illustrates that evidence incriminating the accused (such as a stash of heroin flushed down a toilet) is unaffected by the *O'Brien* rule where someone else's constitutional right had been violated (such as, here, the actual owner or tenant of the house which the gardai entered on foot of a defective warrant).
[22] *People (DPP) v Lawless* (CCA, November 28, 1985).
[23] e.g. *DPP v McMahon, McMeel and Wright* [1986] I.R. 393 (SC), with respect to entry onto licensed premises not constituting a "dwelling".
[24] [2002] I.R. 458 (SC).
[25] *cf.* para.11–23 *et seq.*
[26] *cf.* para.11–21.
[27] *cf.* para.11–22.

accused.[28] On the other hand, US Supreme Court authority, considered by the Supreme Court in *O'Brien* and *Kenny*, has not recognised this associated constitutional right,[29] but favours instead the view that such exclusionary rules constitute a "judicially created remedy designed to safeguard Fourth Amendment rights generally through its deterrent effect, rather than a personal constitutional right of the party aggrieved".[30]

11–09 Where evidence has causatively been obtained by an infringement of the accused's constitutional rights, the evidence is strictly inadmissible under the *O'Brien* rule save where there existed "extraordinary excusing circumstances". The infringement of rights most likely to precipitate and later to invalidate confession statements in practice flow from unlawful arrest, detention, questioning, and denial of access to legal advice. In *People (DPP) v Madden*,[31] an incriminating statement, made voluntarily and after due caution, was deemed inadmissible since it had been made a few hours after the expiration of the accused's lawful period of detention under s.30 of the Offences Against the State Act 1939, and therefore had been obtained in violation of the detainee's constitutional right to liberty under Art.40.4.1°. In *People (DPP) v Cleary*,[32] the accused had made a confession while he was questioned in his sister's house, purportedly pursuant to s.4 of the Criminal Justice Act 1984, which empowers gardaí to detain a suspect for questioning without charge for up to 12 hours. Despite the fact that the admissions were voluntary and in compliance with the Judges' Rules, and despite the fact that neither the accused nor his father objected to the questioning, the statements were deemed inadmissible since elicited in circumstances where the accused's constitutional right to liberty had been violated. The infringement of rights most likely to render non-confession or real evidence strictly inadmissible flow from unlawful arrest, unlawful search of the person or dwelling house, and unlawful seizure of evidence.[33]

11–10 Irish law affords greater and more principled protection of the right to privacy than does English law. Whereas it has been recognised in England that the common law does not enforce a generic right to privacy, and accordingly that evidence of incriminating telephone calls are obtained unfairly but not illegally,[34] the Irish courts have recognised a distinct constitutional right to privacy, which specifically entails a right to freedom from covert telephone

---

[28] The question was posed by O'Connor (1982) at p.290, and answered in the affirmative.
[29] *Brewer v Williams* (1977) 430 U.S. 387 at 421 (SC); *US v Callandra* (1974) 414 U.S. 338 (SC).
[30] *US v Leon* (1983) 468 U.S. 897 at 906, *per* White J (SC).
[31] [1977] I.R. 336 (CCA). See also *People (DPP) v Farrell* [1978] I.R. 13 (CCA).
[32] HC, December 7, 2001.
[33] *cf.* para.**11–54** *et seq.*
[34] *Malone v Metropolitan Police Commissioners* [1979] 2 All E.R. 620. The European Court of Human Rights found, however, in the same case, that the British Government had infringed the applicant's right to privacy under Art.8 of the Convention since the surveillance had been undertaken without any lawful authority: *Malone v UK* (1984) 7 E.H.R.R. 14 at 39–41.

surveillance. The right is not absolute and "its exercise may be restricted by the constitutional rights of others, by the requirements of the common good and ... [by] the requirements of public order and morality".[35] In *Kennedy and Arnold v Ireland and Attorney-General*,[36] the plaintiffs' phones had been tapped by agents of the State without formal justification or recourse to the system safeguards previously declared by Ministers for Justice. Awarding damages (including aggravated damages) against the defendants for violation of their constitutional right to privacy (an unenumerated personal right protected by Art.40.1), Hamilton P. found that the "dignity and freedom of an individual in a democratic society cannot be ensured if his communications of a private nature, be they written or telephonic, are deliberately, consciously and unjustifiably intruded upon and interfered with".[37]

11–11 In consequence of the High Court's declaration of a general constitutional right to privacy, Irish law on investigative State bugging and interception of phone calls and mail made the transition from administrative control to statutory regulation subject to identifiable safeguards. Section 2(1) of the Interception of Postal Packets and Telecommunications Messages (Regulation) Act 1993 enables the Minister for Justice to authorise interception, by means of a warrant (or in exceptional cases orally, followed by a warrant), solely for the purposes of criminal investigation or the interests of State security. An individual application must be made in writing to the Minister. The Minister, before issuing the warrant, must form the opinion that the interception is necessary for an ongoing investigation, that the investigation would fail without the interception, and that there is a reasonable prospect that the interception will provide material results. The Act is stated to apply to the investigation of a "serious offence or a suspected serious offence" and activities endangering the security of the State. The warrant may remain in force for up to three months, although it may be renewed by the Minister for further periods of three months.[38] When considering whether to authorise or extend an interception, the Minister *may* consult with a judge of the High Court who has been designated to review the operation of the Act and to report to the Taoiseach on compliance at intervals of not more than 12 months.[39] It has been questioned, despite these safeguards, whether the provisions sufficiently comply with the jurisprudence of the European Court of Human Rights.[40] The court has asserted that when balancing the individual's right to privacy against the public interest in prosecuting crime, each State must have primary regard to process and justification, including: provision for the definition of categories of persons whose telephones are liable to be tapped; the nature of offences for which phone tapping is legitimate; the setting of time-limits for the duration of cov-

---

[35] *Kennedy and Arnold v Ireland and Attorney General* [1988] I.L.R.M. 472 at 476, *per* Hamilton J. (HC).
[36] [1988] I.L.R.M. 472 (HC).
[37] *ibid.* at 477.
[38] Section 2(5).
[39] Sections 2(7) and 8.
[40] Ní Raifeartaigh, "The European Convention on Human Rights and the Irish Criminal Justice System" (2001) *Bar Review* 111 at 114.

ert surveillance; precautions to be taken for the communication of such recordings to the court and to the defence;[41] and the systematic review of legislation and rules governing covert surveillance.[42]

11–12 In the absence of statutory authority under the 1993 Act, s.98 of the Postal and Telecommunications Services Act 1983 prohibits the interception and recording of telephonic messages by any person without the agreement of the caller (or the person on whose behalf the message is transmitted) *and* the person who is intended by him to receive the message. This amounts to a broad prohibition, requiring consent additionally by the intended caller, and it therefore prohibits unauthorised interception and recording of calls made to a seized phone. In *People (DPP) v Dillon*,[43] the Court of Criminal Appeal allowed an appeal against the trial judge's decision to admit evidence of a phone conversation on the accused's mobile phone between the arresting garda (who spontaneously assumed an alias) and a caller. Without the consent of the person who called *and* the person intended to receive the call (as opposed to the actual recipient), s.98 was infringed, and accordingly the call had been intercepted in violation of the constitutional right to telephonic privacy of the caller and the intended addressee. Hardiman J. also concluded that the criminal import of the call is not an *ex turpi non causa sua* bar to the application of the *O'Brien* rule, and that if it were, unlawful bugging and interception would regularly recur with impunity.

Proof of a Causative Link

11–13 The absence of a causative association between violation of a constitutional right and the disputed evidence is frequently conclusive against inadmissibility in cases of non-confession evidence where the accused was obliged under law to provide the evidence or to permit the search upon pain of separate criminal liability for his failure so to do. In *Walsh v District Judge O'Buachalla & DPP*,[44] the appellant had been convicted of drunken driving. Upon appeal, he claimed he had requested and been refused access to a solicitor. According to the evidence, he had not requested a solicitor throughout the 40 minutes it took for a doctor to arrive on the scene to arrange a specimen of urine. The garda had refused in the belief that the request was a delaying tactic. In Blayney J.'s opinion, even if the garda's refusal had breached the suspect's constitutional rights (which seemed unlikely, in light of case law to date),[45] the certificate was admissible since the specimen obtained had not been causatively linked to the breach. No amount of legal advice would have altered the fact that the person was legally obliged to comply with the taking of the specimen, upon pain of summary prosecution for non-compliance.

---

[41] *Huvig v France* (1990) 12 E.H.R.R. 528.
[42] *Klass v Germany* (1978) 2 E.H.R.R. 214.
[43] [2003] 4 I.R. 501 (CCA).
[44] [1991] 1 I.R. 56 (HC).
[45] *cf.* para.**10–50** *et seq.*

Evidence obtained Unconstitutionally and Illegally 325

Similar reasoning was adopted in *People (DPP) v Cullen*,[46] where Finlay C.J. refused to identify a causative link between the accused's lack of legal advice at the time of his search and evidence obtained as a result of the search. Failure to submit to a personal search under s.7(1) of the Criminal Law Act 1976 constituted a statutory offence, and no person has a constitutional right to consider whether or not to commit a criminal offence.

11–14 Decisions to date suggest that in cases where the accused's constitutional right of access to legal advice has been infringed, and a confession is obtained thereafter, the relevant causative association for the purpose of the *O'Brien* rule is as between the fact that the accused was in unlawful detention and the fact that his confession was given whilst he was in unlawful detention. In *People (DPP) v Finnegan*,[47] Barrington J. of the Court of Criminal Court found that the right of reasonable access necessitates a private consultation with the solicitor, in person or by telephone. Following *People (DPP) v Madden*,[48] the learned judge reasoned that where this right has been infringed, the suspect's detention is unlawful and his subsequent statements are inadmissible. In *People (DPP) v Buck*,[49] it was argued that since inadequate thought had been given to the availability of legal advice prior to questioning the accused, his detention was unlawful *ab initio* and his confession in this context was inadmissible. The Supreme Court rejected the view that the right of reasonable access is necessarily breached when questioning begins after the accused has requested a solicitor and before his solicitor arrives. The Supreme Court disposed of the appeal upon the basis that the confession had been given after the accused had consulted his solicitor, and so it was causatively unrelated to an earlier period of questioning throughout which the accused had made no incriminating statements.

11–15 The rationale for the causation requirement has too infrequently been addressed by the courts, and sits uneasily with the Supreme Court's espousal of the "negative deterrent" element of the "absolute protection" rule described by Finlay C.J. in *Kenny*. A causation requirement implicitly derives from a view that the *O'Brien* exclusionary rule aims to protect the constitutional rights of the *accused* and not more generally. This was evident in earlier *dicta* by Finlay C.J. in *State (Trimbole) v Governor of Mountjoy Prison*,[50] to wit that where the constitutional rights of an accused have been infringed, the court seeks to "restore as far as possible the person damaged to the position in which he would be if his rights had not been so invaded".[51] The learned judge coupled this with an objective curiously akin to the concept of unjust enrichment familiar to equity, to wit, that the court must "ensure as far as possible that persons

---

[46] CCA, March 30, 1993.
[47] CCA, July 15, 1997.
[48] [1977] I.R. 336 (CCA).
[49] [2002] 2 I.R. 268 (SC): *cf.* appendix 64 and para.**10–55** *et seq.*
[50] [1985] I.R. 550 (SC).
[51] *ibid.* at 573; approved in *Quinlivan v Governor of Portlaoise Prison* [1998] 1 I.R. 456 at 462 (SC).

acting on behalf of the Executive who consciously and deliberately violate the constitutional rights of citizens do not themselves or their superiors obtain the planned results of that invasion".[52] These negative deterrent and unjust enrichment strands are obscurely incompatible with the compensatory focus of the causation requirement as currently applied, however.

"Deliberate and Conscious Violation"

11–16 Interpretation of the phrase "deliberate and conscious" in the *O'Brien* exclusionary rule has proved noticeably contentious in the Irish courts, within which rival views of criminal justice and evidence have been fought out. The phrase, originally coined by Walsh J. in *O'Brien*, was applied in that case to validate evidence obtained on foot of a search warrant of whose technical defect the gardaí had been unaware. A majority of Irish decisions since *O'Brien*, however, have chosen to interpret "deliberate and conscious" not by reference to an intention on the part of the gardaí to infringe a constitutional right of the accused, but instead to their intention to act or behave in such a way that a constitutional right of the accused would be breached whether innocently or not. This particular view of the *O'Brien* rule was asserted by the Court of Criminal Appeal in *People (DPP) v Madden*,[53] to wit, that evidence obtained in breach of constitutional rights is inadmissible, save for extraordinary excusing circumstances, where *the acts or conduct giving rise to* the breach (but not necessarily the breach) were effected "deliberately and consciously" by the gardaí and not inadvertently or by accident. In the context of a case where the gardaí continued to take and record the accused's confession a few hours after the expiry of his lawful period of detention (48 hours, under s.30 of the Offences Against the State Act 1939), O'Higgins C.J. rejected a submission that evidence may be excluded only upon proof of some male fides or intentional violation on the part of the investigators. Even if effected "for the best of motives and in the interests of the due investigation of crime", it had been "done or permitted without regard to the right of liberty guaranteed to this defendant by Article 40 of the Constitution and to the State's obligation under that Article to defend and vindicate that right".[54] This view was repeated in *People (DPP) v Walsh*,[55] which interpreted the *O'Brien* rule to apply strictly to cases where "a man is consciously and deliberately kept in custody ... without a charge ... and without being brought before a court as soon as reasonably possible". It was irrelevant for the purposes of the rule that the garda was not conscious of the illegality or breach of constitutional right once he was "conscious of the actual circumstances which existed".[56]

11–17 In *People (DPP) v Shaw*,[57] however, Griffin J. of the Supreme Court

---

[52] *ibid.*
[53] [1977] I.R. 336 (CCA); applied in *People (DPP) v Farrell* [1978] I.R. 13 (CCA).
[54] *ibid.* at 347.
[55] [1980] I.R. 294 (SC); approved in *People (DPP) v Kenny* [1990] I.L.R.M. 569 at 576 (SC).
[56] *ibid.* at 317, *per* Walsh J.
[57] [1982] 1 I.R. 1 at 56 (SC): *cf.* appendix 25.

(with whom Henchy, Kenny and Parke JJ. concurred) reasoned that evidence was not unconstitutionally obtained in a case where the garda did not know that what he was doing was illegal or unconstitutional, and therefore that "it is the violation of the person's constitutional rights, and not the particular act complained of, that has to be deliberate and conscious for the purpose of ruling out a statement". According to this perspective, the *mens rea* prerequisite for inadmissibility relates to the violation of the right: as the gardaí in *Shaw* had followed standard practice at the time and had not acted prior to receiving a search warrant, no intention had been manifest to violate the dwelling of the accused. This remains a minority interrpetation of *O'Brien*. In his dissenting judgment in *Shaw*, worthier than the putative majority judgment, Walsh J. asserted that the *O'Brien* rule does not make inadmissibility contingent upon the violator's knowledge of the Constitution or the law, and that to import any such interpretation would be to put a premium on ignorance of the law.[58]

11–18 A majority of the judgments since *Shaw* supports the view articulated by Walsh J. that application of the *O'Brien* rule does not require proof that the investigator intended to breach a constitutional right of the accused, although the second view is a discernible slipstream running through Irish criminal jurisprudence on the exclusionary rule. It re-emerged noticeably in a minority decision led again by Griffin J. in *People (DPP) v Kenny*,[59] and supported by a second dissenting judgment of Lynch J. who asserted, in opposition to the absolute protection model espoused by the majority: "The inviolability of the citizen's dwelling must be upheld but this does not mean that evidence obtained in breach of it must always be rejected however relevant it may be to the case at hearing. It must be rejected if there is any element of blame or culpability or unfairness ... in relation to the breach of the right on the part of those who obtained the evidence unless there are adequate excusing circumstances".[60]

11–19 In *O'Brien*, the Supreme Court considered that the strict exclusionary rule did not apply to inadvertent breaches—in this case to a typographical error on a search warrant (118 Cashel Road instead of 118 Captain's Road). The view that inadvertent errors do not strictly attract the *O'Brien* rule was echoed by Finlay C.J. in *Kenny*, where the learned judge nonetheless advocated an absolute protection model of exclusion. In his view, evidence obtained in breach of constitutional rights may yet be admitted at the discretion of the court where satisfied that "the act constituting the breach of constitutional rights was committed unintentionally or accidentally, or ... that there are extraordinary excusing circumstances which justify the admission".[61] The alternative to qualification of the *O'Brien* rule in this way is the re-characterising of "extraordinary excusing circumstances" to form a broader basis of justification. This option was mooted by Lynch J., who favoured the phrase "adequate excusing circumstances" in his dissenting judgment in *Kenny*.[62]

---

[58] *ibid*. at 33–34.
[59] [1990] I.L.R.M. 569 (SC).
[60] [1990] I.L.R.M. 569 at 587 (SC): *cf.* appendix 36.
[61] *ibid*. at 579.
[62] *ibid*. at 578.

11–20 In *People (DPP) v Balfe*,[63] Murphy J. drew a distinction between a search warrant issued without authority, which "has no value in law", and a search warrant issued within jurisdiction but containing a mistake in the recording of the order, which does not necessarily attract the application of the *O'Brien* rule. The defect arising in *O'Brien* and *Balfe* was of the second kind insofar as the warrants misidentified the accused's dwelling. In *Balfe*, Murphy J. considered that since the error was patent and a matter evident to the person to whom the warrant was produced, the addressee had been entitled to object to the warrant upon that basis and to refuse to cooperate with the search; where he had not done so, the *O'Brien* rule did not subsequently arise. Despite the court's recognition of inadvertence or accidental mistake as a ground for the non-application of the *O'Brien* rule, some decisions indicate that where the infringed constitutional right is of fundamental importance contextually to the evidence obtained, justification along the lines of inadvertence will be rejected by the court. In *DPP v O'Connell*,[64] the garda in charge failed to organise a solicitor for the accused after he was mistakenly told the accused had already had a consultation with a solicitor: despite apparent inadvertence, the garda's failure was deemed "deliberate and conscious" for the purpose of the rule.

"Extraordinary Excusing Circumstances"

11–21 The burden is upon the prosecution to establish that there were "extraordinary excusing circumstances" justifying the breach of constitutional right and consequential obtaining of evidence. The question is determined by the trial judge under *voire dire* in the absence of the jury.[65] In *O'Brien*, Walsh J. illustrated as instances of "extraordinary excusing circumstances" the imminent destruction of vital evidence and the need to rescue victims in peril. In *People (DPP) v McCann*,[66] the preservation of vital evidence—forensic evidence gathered from the burnt-out remains of the accused's family home—was a concern capable of constituting "extraordinary excusing circumstances". An unwillingness to disrupt questioning already underway when a solicitor arrives on behalf of the accused is not capable of justifying the violation of the accused's constitutional right of access to his solicitor.[67] The investigation of crime in itself is insufficient justification, and a person may not be detained unlawfully to accomplish that end save where extraordinary excusing circumstances otherwise exist.[68] Response to the presence of a number of people positioned outside a building and threatening to the people inside the building justified entry without a warrant in *People (DPP) v Delaney*.[69] Where

---

[63] [1998] 4 I.R. 50 at 60 (CCA).
[64] [1995] 1 I.R. 244 (CCA).
[65] *cf.* para.**1–24** *et seq.*
[66] [1998] 4 I.R. 397 (CCA). See also *People (DPP) v Lawless* (1985) 3 Frewen 30 (CCA), where the imminent destruction of drugs was considered sufficient justification for a precipitous entry on foot of an invalid warrant.
[67] *DPP v Healy* [1990] 2 I.R. 73 (SC): *cf.* appendix 33.
[68] *People v O'Loughlin* [1979] I.R. 85 (CCA).
[69] [1997] 3 I.R. 453 (SC).

a person is discovered *in flagrante delicto*, the gardaí may enter a private dwelling for the purposes of an arrest, although, in the absence of a valid warrant or express statutory authority, only upon the basis that this constitutes an "extraordinary excusing circumstance".[70]

11–22 In *Shaw*, the accused had been unlawfully detained for three days, which was explained upon the basis that the gardaí suspected him of the abduction and possible murder of two young women, one of whom was hoped to be alive. The accused subsequently made a statement confessing to the rape and murder of one of the girls, and brought the gardaí to the site of the body in Connemara. Appealing against conviction for rape and murder, the accused submitted that since his detention had been unlawful, the confession and physical evidence obtained thereafter had been inadmissible. Amongst the different methodologies employed by the Supreme Court,[71] Walsh J. reasoned that the detention had been unlawful and in breach of the accused's constitutional rights, but that the evidence could be deemed admissible by reason of "extraordinary excusing circumstances" arising from the need to protect the life of one of the girls. Griffin J.—with whom Henchy, Parke and Kenny JJ. concurred—adopted a different approach, reasoning that the accused's constitutional right to liberty had to yield to the obligation of the State to vindicate another person's constitutional right to life (constituting "extraordinary excusing circumstances"), and therefore that the detention was lawful. This approach is not consistent with the wording of the *O'Brien* rule, however, namely that the circumstances *excuse* the anterior breach of constitutional rights and unlawfulness.

II. EVIDENCE OBTAINED ILLEGALLY OR IMPROPERLY

11–23 Evidence has been obtained *illegally* if the investigator acted without or beyond his lawful authority under statute or the common law, or if it was obtained by the commission of a crime, tort, or breach of contract. Evidence has been obtained *improperly* where the investigator exercised trickery, deception, bribery, or other ruse to obtain the evidence. In *O'Brien*, Kingsmill Moore J. opted for a less rigid rule with respect to evidence obtained illegally but not in breach of the constitutional rights of the accused. This approach vests a broader admissibility discretion in the trial judge to balance the public interests of the State in admitting probative evidence of criminal activity against the interest of the citizen to be protected from illegal or irregular invasions of civil liberties.[72] The answer to the question, in the learned judge's view, would depend upon all the circumstances of the case and "the nature and extent of the illegality"—in particular whether the illegality was intentional, whether it was "the result of an *ad hoc* decision or ... a settled or deliberate policy", whether the evidence was obtained in "circumstances of urgency or emer-

---

[70] *Freeman v DPP* [1996] 3 I.R. 565 (HC).
[71] *cf.* para.**11–03** *et seq.*
[72] Drawing from *Lawrie v Muir* (1950) S.C. 19 at 26.

gency", and whether it was of a "trivial and technical nature or ... a serious invasion of important rights the recurrence of which would involve a real danger to necessary freedoms".[73] Whilst Walsh J.'s judgment in *O'Brien* subsequently became sanctified *dicta* for the admissibility of evidence obtained in breach of constitutional rights, his view of illegally obtained evidence has not formed part of Irish law on the issue,[74] and it resembles the approach favoured in England to the extent it reasons that the trial judge has no discretion to exclude probative evidence merely upon the basis that it was illegally obtained.[75]

11–24 Section 7(3) of the Criminal Justice Act 1984 provides that a breach of any regulation adopted pursuant to the 1984 Act—including the Treatment of Persons in Custody in Garda Síochána Stations Regulations of 1987—"shall not ... of itself affect the lawfulness of the custody of the detained person or the admissibility in evidence of any statement made by him". Whilst this provision does not expressly address non-confession evidence, its reference to the lack of automatic effect for the "lawfulness of the custody" achieves this effect.

11–25 The effect of improper conduct of the investigator was considered in *People (Attorney-General) v Cummins*.[76] Walsh J. affirmed the discretionary rule, though he observed that a statement may be excluded at the discretion of the trial judge where "the initial effect of a false pretence, such as stating falsely to an accused person that his alleged accomplices have already made a full confession and have incriminated the accused, in certain circumstances could conceivably lead an innocent person to make a confession of guilt or of partial guilt as an act of despair in the hope that in some way it might mitigate the punishment which would otherwise fall upon him if he were to be convicted on the false testimony of alleged accomplices".[77] On the other hand, if "an accused person who is in fact guilty believes, because of his own assessment of the situation, that in the long run it might be advantageous to him to admit his guilt rather than to conceal it, any confession which he makes as a result of

---

[73] [1965] I.R. 142 at 160 (SC): *cf.* appendix 12.
[74] *ibid.* at 168.
[75] Debate in the English courts has centred on whether or not the trial judge is *entitled* to exclude evidence unfairly or improperly obtained. In *Jeffrey v Black* [1978] Q.B. 490 (CA), Widgery C.J. expressed the view that judges have discretion to exclude relevant evidence where obtained by trickery, by deception, oppression, or unfairness on the part of the investigator. A significant limitation was imposed on this principle in *R. v Sang* [1980] A.C. 402, where the House of Lords ruled that judges have no discretion to exclude evidence that the accused committed the crimes with which he is charged, even though the evidence was obtained by entrapment, although with respect to other evidence obtained by entrapment the judge may decide to exclude it in his discretion. See also *R. v Smurthwaite* [1994] 1 All E.R. 898 (CA). It has, however, been acknowledged that statements made to undercover police officers, who adopted a disguise to circumvent the Judges' Rules and Code, ought not be admitted: *R. v Bryce* (1992) 95 Cr. App. R. 320 (CA); *R. v Lin, Hung and Tsui* [1995] Crim. L.R. 817 (CA).
[76] [1972] I.R. 312 (SC): *cf.* appendix 18 and para.**10–19**.
[77] *ibid.* at 325.

such calculation is not to be impugned even though the accused's assessment of the situation may have been incorrect—once it is shown that the confession was in fact voluntary".[78]

11–26 Thus, where an unlawful or improper act was committed when obtaining the evidence, but no constitutional right of the accused deliberately and consciously breached, the evidence "shall be admissible unless the court in its discretion excludes it" according to the Supreme Court's unanimous decision in *DPP v McMahon*.[79] The court also acknowledged that when exercising its discretion, the court may balance the fundamental interests identified in *O'Brien*, namely: the public interest in the detection and punishment of crime, measured against the public interest in the repression of illegal or improper investigative methods by the police. In *DPP v McMahon*,[80] the Supreme Court upheld the admissibility of evidence obtained by the gardaí after entering premises to investigate breaches of the gaming legislation, in circumstances where the gardaí had behaved as trespassers without a search warrant or statutory authority to enter. McCarthy J. observed, however, that should such a practice of entering without lawful authority emerge later as a pattern, a different stance might be adopted by the courts to deter it.

11–27 The trial judge is under an ongoing duty at common law to exclude evidence unfairly obtained in order to prevent abuse of the court's own processes.[81] There also exists a constitutional duty "more ample and dominant" in breadth.[82] The development in recent years of the accused's *genus* constitutional right to fair procedures may have served substantially to convert this discretion into an obligation to exclude illegally or unfairly obtained evidence, having regard to the court's duty to ensure the accused is tried in "due course of law" for the purposes of Arts 40.4.1 and 38.1. Where the illegality or impropriety compromises a constitutional right of the accused, any evidence thereby obtained is in violation of his constitutional rights and as such attracts the rigours of the exclusionary rule in *O'Brien*.

III. GARDAÍ POWERS OF ARREST, DETENTION, SEARCH, AND SEIZURE

Arrest and Detention

11–28 If a confession statement is elicited, or non-confession evidence obtained, following an unlawful arrest or subsequent to the expiry of the lawful period of detention, and the suspect has not clearly given his consent to

---

[78] *ibid.* at 327.
[79] [1987] I.L.R.M. 87 at 92, *per* Finlay C.J. (SC). See also *McKenna v Deerey* [1998] 1 I.R. 62 (SC).
[80] *ibid.* at 92, *per* Finlay C.J. (SC): following *People (DPP) v Madden* [1977] I.R. 336 (SC).
[81] *State (Trimbole) v Governor of Mountjoy Prison* [1985] I.R. 550 at 573, *per* Finlay C.J.
[82] *ibid.*

remaining in garda custody,[83] the suspect's constitutional right to liberty has been infringed and the evidence is prima facie inadmissible under the *O'Brien* exclusionary rule.[84]

11–29 An arrest has been described in traditional terms as "the seizure or touching of a person's body accompanied by a form of words which indicate to that person that he is under restraint".[85] Words alone suffice to effect an arrest, however, where "they are calculated to bring, and do bring, to the person's notice that he is under restraint and he submitted to the compulsion".[86] The communication of arrest does not have to be made in any particular formula of words,[87] although it is vital that the person is informed of the factual basis and the legal authority.[88] A number of decisions have recognised flexibility with respect to citation of specific provisions, so long as the gist of the provision was conveyed and the accused suffered no actual prejudice. In *DPP v Connell*,[89] the garda when arresting the accused for drunken driving had incorrectly cited the legal basis as s.49(8) of the Road Traffic Act 1994, instead of s.49(8) of the Road Traffic Act 1961 (as had been inserted by s.10 of the Road Traffic Act 1994). In upholding the arrest, Geoghegan J. of the High Court adopted the view that an arrest is valid if the legal authority is adequately identified and if the person is adequately informed of the general reason for the arrest. The learned judge approved *Christie v Leachinsky*,[90] for the proposition that the necessity to inform the arrested person of the reasons for his arrest does not exist in circumstances where the person must already know the general nature of the alleged offence for which he is detained. Applying the principles to the case, Geoghegan J. concluded that it had been obvious which statutory offence the accused had been arrested for (even though incorrectly cited), and that the garda had sufficiently communicated in layman's terms that the reason for the arrest was suspected drunken driving.

11–30 The circumstances of a case may make strict compliance with the duty to communicate authority reasonably impracticable, as in *People v Walsh*.[91] In upholding the arrest, the court was influenced by evidence showing that the accused had not immediately been informed of the reasons for his arrest because it had taken place in a crowded bar, and further that he had not actively requested the information and was at any rate given the reasons upon his arrival at the station. O'Higgins C.J. invoked the House of Lords' decision in *Christie v Leachinsky*[92] for the view that what "must be avoided [is] the

---

[83] *Dunne v Clinton* [1930] I.R. 366 at 372 (HC): *cf.* appendix 4.
[84] *People (DPP) v Byrne* [1989] I.L.R.M. 613 (SC).
[85] *DPP v McCreesh* [1992] 2 I.R. 239 at 250, *per* Hederman J. (SC).
[86] *ibid.*, approving *Alderson v Booth* [1969] 2 Q.B. 216.
[87] *People v Walsh* [1980] I.R. 294 at 305, *per* O'Higgins C.J. (SC), applied in *People (DPP) v Cleary* (HC, December 7, 2001).
[88] *Re O'Laighleis* [1960] I.R. 93 (SC).
[89] [1998] 3 I.R. 62 (HC).
[90] [1947] A.C. 573 at 587, *per* Simon L.J. (HL).
[91] [1980] I.R. 294 (SC).
[92] [1947] A.C. 573 (HL).

deliberate concealment of the cause of arrest either by refusing to give the information when asked or by giving a false response".[93]

11–31 The requirement to identify the correct legal authority may be less strict for provisions taking effect *after arrest*, such as s.13 of the Road Traffic Act 1994, which states that persons arrested under s.49(8) of the Road Traffic Act 1961 may be requested and required to provide a blood or urine sample and that the failure to provide a sample constitutes a criminal offence. In *DPP v McGarrigle*,[94] the Supreme Court asserted the necessity for clear communication of the request for a blood or urine sample in the context of an arrest for suspected drink driving. Finlay C.J. recognised that the arrested driver has a right to be informed of any legal obligation that is subject to penal sanction; he did not accept, however, that a suspect had a right to be volunteered such information as "the seriousness of the consequences of refusal so as to permit him to decide whether or not to commit a criminal offence." According to the Supreme Court in *Brennan v DPP*,[95] upon arrest it is necessary to "invoke the operative section", since arrest encroaches on a person's constitutional right to liberty. Following arrest, however, "no policy or purpose is served by requiring members of the gardaí to invoke the actual section on which the requirement is based".[96] Where the nature and effect of the provision was conveyed to the arrested person without citing the precise Act and section, the arrest remains lawful and evidence thereupon obtained is admissible. In *Madigan v Devally and DPP*,[97] the garda who detained the driver for drunken driving, and who requested a blood or urine sample, incorrectly cited the repealed statutory provisions (under the Road Traffic Act 1978), instead of s.49(8) of the Road Traffic Act 1961 (newly inserted by s.10 of the Road Traffic Act 1994) and s.13(1)(b) of the Road Traffic Act 1994, respectively, which had been in force 27 days by the time of the arrest. Given that the wording of the repealed and newly inserted provision for the refusal offence was identical, and given that the garda had correctly identified the powers being invoked, "no question of disadvantage or injustice to the applicant [arose] by reason of any mix up on the part of the garda between the 1978 and the 1994 Act".[98]

11–32 The gardai have various powers of arrest on foot of a warrant or summarily without warrant. Sources of the non-summary power of arrest are scattered throughout the statute books.[99] The powers of summary arrest are now governed by the Criminal Law Act 1997. Previously under the common law, the garda had the power to arrest summarily any person he reasonably

---

[93] [1980] I.R. 294 at 307, *per* O'Higgins C.J. (SC).
[94] SC, June 22, 1987: applied in *People (DPP) v Hand* [1994] 1 I.R. 577 (SC).
[95] [1996] 1 I.L.R.M. 267 (SC).
[96] *ibid*. at 271.
[97] [1999] 2 I.L.R.M. 141 (SC).
[98] *ibid*. at 152, *per* Lynch J.
[99] See Walsh, *Criminal Procedure* (Thomson Round Hall, Dublin, 2002), at pp.156–76.

suspected of *having committed* a felony or the crime of treason.[100] The power did not extend to arrest for misdemeanours, except for breaches of the peace. The Criminal Law Act 1997 abolished the distinction between misdemeanours and felonies, and applies to "arrestable offences" (being offences attracting a penalty of imprisonment of 5 years or more, including attempts to commit such offences)[101] save where statute elsewhere creates specific powers of arrest for particular offences. The common law power of the garda and citizen to effect a summary arrest for breaches of the peace is formally unaffected by the 1997 Act;[102] however, that offence has been superceded by s.8 of the Criminal Justice (Public Order) Act 1994, which created the offence of failing to comply with a garda's request to desist from engaging in disorderly conduct. Under s.4(1)–(2) of the Criminal Law Act 1997, the garda may arrest without warrant any person he observes or reasonably suspects to be in the act of committing an arrestable offence; or, where an arrestable offence has been committed, any person he reasonably suspects of having committed it. A citizen may lawfully effect such an arrest only where (1) he has reasonable cause to believe that the offender "would otherwise attempt to avoid, or is avoiding, arrest by a member of the Garda Siochana" and (2) the citizen transfers the suspect into the custody of the gardai as soon as practicable.[103] The garda, but not a citizen, may arrest without warrant any person he suspects with reasonable cause to have committed an arrestable offence where the garda has reasonable cause to believe (but does not know) that an arrestable offence was committed.[104] Specific other powers of summary arrest have been created by statute, such as: the Misuse of Drugs Act 1977, s.25; Offences Against the State Act 1939, s.30(1); the Criminal Assets Bureau Act 1996, s.16; the Control of Horses Act 1996, s.4; the Domestic Violence Act 1996, s.18; the Litter Pollution Act 1997, s.23(6); and the Children Act 2001, s.254.

11–33 A garda may, with a valid warrant, enter onto and search any premises, including a dwelling, where the person is or where the garda, with reasonable cause, suspects that person to be, pursuant to s.6(1) of the Criminal Law Act 1997. A garda may, without a warrant, enter onto and search any premises, including a dwelling, where the person is or where the garda, with reasonable cause, suspects that person to be, pursuant to s.6(2); although where the premises constitutes a "dwelling" and the garda has not obtained the consent of the occupier, he may only enter where: he observed the suspect entering the dwelling, or he "with reasonable cause, suspects that before a warrant of arrest

---

[100] *People v Walsh* [1980] I.R. 294 at 306, *per* O'Higgins C.J. (SC); *People (DPP) v Shaw* [1982] I.R. 1 at 28, *per* Walsh J. (SC). See also *Madigan v Devally* [1999] 2 I.L.R.M. 141 (SC), where Lynch J. rejected a submission that the gardai had a common law right and duty, parallel to statute, to arrest a person suspected of drunken driving (save possibly in the event of suspected manslaughter following a fatality on the road).
[101] If the offence carries a lesser penalty, a warrant must be obtained: *DPP v Bradley* (HC, December 9, 1999).
[102] Walsh, *op cit.* n.99 at p.157.
[103] Section 4(1)–(2), (4)–(5).
[104] Section 4(3).

could be obtained the person will either abscond for the purpose of avoiding justice or will obstruct the course of justice", or he "with reasonable cause, suspects that before a warrant of arrest could be obtained the person would commit an arrestable offence", or the suspect ordinarily resides at that dwelling in question.

11–34 Under s.39(1) of the Road Traffic Act 1994, a garda may for the purpose of arresting a driver believed to have caused injury under s.106(3A) of the Road Traffic Act 1961, "enter without warrant (if needs be by use of reasonable force) any place (including a dwelling) where the person is or where the member, with reasonable cause, suspects him to be and, in case the place is a dwelling, the member shall not so enter unless he or another such member has observed the person enter the dwelling concerned." Under s.39(2) of the 1994 Act, a garda may, for the purpose of arresting a person for drink driving offences under ss.49(8) or 50(10) of the 1961 Act, "enter without warrant (if need be by use of reasonable force) any place (including the curtilage of a dwelling but not including a dwelling) where the person is or where the member, with reasonable cause, suspects him to be".

11–35 These provisions responded to the natural reluctance of the courts to recognise at common law—in the absence of specific legislation—gardaí powers, without warrant, to enter onto the curtilage of private property and into dwellings for the purposes of effecting arrests. Although the courts had invalidated arrests effected without warrant on the private property of suspects resisting arrest,[105] in *DPP v Forbes*[106] the Supreme Court was prepared to uphold the lawfulness of arrests effected on the forecourt of the private property of *other persons*, in the absence of evidence establishing that the consent of the occupier had actually been withheld. Whilst the findings were couched in the context of an arrest on the forecourt but not within the dwelling-house of another person—therefore where no constitutional right was being waived or breached—the court expressed a general principle of implied consent that is likely to support the new provisions enabling arrests on private property under

---

[105] With respect to arrests for drunken driving and for the purpose of requiring a blood or urine sample, the House of Lords' decision in *Morris v Beardmore* [1980] A.C. 446 (HL) was followed by the Supreme Court in *DPP v Gaffney* [1987] I.R. 173 and *DPP v McCreesh* [1992] 2 I.R. 239. In *McCreesh*, Hederman J. (at 254) found that "the right of arrest given [under the Road Traffic Acts] should not be construed as extending to the infringement of any fundamental right other than the right of freedom from arrest without warrant by a member of the Garda Síochána". See also *Freeman v DPP* [1996] 3 I.R. 565, where Carney J. of the High Court considered that, although s.41(1) of the Larceny Act 1916 was wide enough to assume the power to arrest on private property, the courts should not construe such a power in the absence of express statutory words, and that this literal approach to powers of arrest was necessary in light of the fact that Art.40.5 of the Constitution had expressly elevated the right of inviolability of the dwelling to the constitutional plane. The learned judge was, however, prepared to recognise that an arrest of persons apprehended *in flagrante delicto* (here moving goods, believed to be stolen, from their van to a house) was one effected in "extraordinary excusing circumstances" for the purposes of the *O'Brien* exclusionary rule.

[106] [1994] 2 I.R. 542 (SC).

the Criminal Law Act 1997 and Road Traffic Act 1994. According to O'Flaherty J:

> "It must be regarded as axiomatic that any householder gives an implied authority to a member of the garda to come onto the forecourt of his premises to see to the enforcement of the law or prevent a breach thereof ... Could it be said what danger the driver of such a car might have posed for the occupants of that dwellinghouse? In the circumstances of this case, the gardaí were clearly acting in the execution of their duties. This must be the acid test. ... For them to have ignored the defendant's conduct on this occasion would have bordered on a dereliction of duty on their part. To suggest that they would be perfectly entitled to arrest the defendant if he was on the public road but not if he was on a third party's property would constitute, as was suggested in the course of the debate before us, a massive absurdity".[107]

11–36 Where statutory provision does not expressly authorise arrest for the particular offence on the curtilage of a person's private property, the gardaí are entitled to assume they have an "implied authority" to effect the arrest,[108] although this applies only so far as the authority or consent has not been withdrawn by the owner or occupier of the premises. In *DPP v Molloy*,[109] McCracken J. found that the arrest of a drunken driver for the offence of refusal to provide a blood or urine sample (under s.13 of the Road Traffic Act 1994), if effected on the curtilage of the driver's private premises, was unlawful in circumstances where he had clearly withdrawn the "implied authority" identified in *Forbes* and where he had resisted arrest. In *DPP v Delaney*,[110] O'Caoimh J. similarly reasoned that where an arrest had been attempted on the curtilage of a third party's private premises, in circumstances where it could not be said that the owners impliedly gave the gardaí consent, the arrest was unlawful, the gardaí were trespassers, and any evidence thereby obtained was inadmissible. The striking feature of the decision was its assumption that the gardaí had no implied authority to effect the arrest where the owner of the premises transpired to be the brother of the suspect, and as such *Delaney* amounts to a significant qualification to the general principle advanced in *Forbes*.

11–37 An arrest may be lawful and the subsequent detention unlawful, although the converse does not occur. If an arrest is for some reason feared to be invalid or unlawful, the arrestee must be released from custody, but he may subsequently be re-arrested and detained.[111] In *Quinlivan v Governor of Portlaoise Prison*,[112] the Supreme Court reasoned that where an administrative

---

[107] *ibid.* at 548 (SC).
[108] *DPP v O'Rourke* (HC, February 17, 2003), finding that the s.34 of the Road Traffic Act 1994 does not modify the garda powers identified in *Forbes*.
[109] SC, February 28, 2003.
[110] [2003] 1 I.R. 363 (HC).
[111] *People (DPP) v O'Shea* (1981) 2 Frewen 57 (CCA).
[112] [1998] 1 I.R. 456 at 463, *per* Barron J. (SC).

error has the effect of invalidating an aspect of the accused's detention (here the fact that the Special Criminal Court had not been properly constituted when it made its decision to remand the accused into custody), there is a "positive" obligation on the authorities from the time the error is discovered to ensure that the suspect is returned to garda custody so that he may be brought before an appropriate court. According to Barron J: "This positive duty was performed by the prompt release of the applicant by the respondent followed by his immediate arrest by the gardaí".[113] In response to the submission that he had never properly been released prior to his re-arrest (since it had taken place outside the prison gates and on prison property), Barron J. observed: "The law would surely be an ass if it denied the right of the gardaí to arrest a person on private property where the person arrested had no chance of escaping arrest in favour of permitting the arrest on the public street, where he would have had the same lack of chance of escaping".[114]

11–38 Upon arrest, the person must be conveyed to a garda station with reasonable dispatch.[115] The absence of statutory authority and proven justification for the 20 minutes roadside detention of suspected drink drivers prior to testing their breath for signs of alcohol necessarily entailed the view, according to the Supreme Court in *DPP v Finn*,[116] that their detention was unlawful and any samples thereby obtained prima facie inadmissible. The court acknowledged, however, that a temporary delay or detention after an arrest is permissible where for the purposes of performing a particular procedure that the gardaí are entitled to perform and where necessary to give effect to the purpose for which the power of arrest was created.[117] Where the delay is for a "reasonable" period of time, it does not have to be objectively justified by the prosecution. Murray J. did not consider a 20 minutes delay necessarily to be "unreasonable"; however, since this delay was "a prescribed and conscious prolongation of an arrested person's period of detention" by the gardaí,[118] following internal garda guidelines, its reasonableness was required to be proven testimonially by the prosecution beyond reasonable doubt for the purpose of establishing the legality of the detention.[119]

---

[113] *ibid.* at 463.
[114] *ibid.* at 462–3. Similar decisions were made in *Duncan v Governor of Portlaoise Prison* [1998] 1 I.R. 433 (HC) and *Cully v Governor of Portlaoise Prison* [1998] 1 I.R. 443 (HC).
[115] *People (DPP) v Walsh* [1980] I.R. 294 (SC): affirmed again recently in *People (DPP) v Cleary* (HC, December 7, 2001).
[116] [2003] 1 I.R. 372 (SC).
[117] *ibid.* at 385, *per* Hederman J.
[118] *ibid.* at 379, *per* Murray J.
[119] In *DPP v McNeice* [2003] 2 I.R. 614, the Supreme Court decided that temporary detention for the purpose of securing the reliability of the results of the intoxilyser test was lawful where evidence was given by a qualified operator of the test establishing the necessity of the delay to ensure that the results were not affected by the presence of alcohol in the mouth of the driver. The court further ruled that a second twenty minute delay upon arrival at the station was lawful where it was considered appropriate to ensure the reliability of the test results under more controlled circumstances.

11–39 With respect to the forming of suspicion and the decision to charge, "everything depends on the circumstances of the case", according to Walsh J. in *Hannigan v District Judge Clifford*.[120] Once an arrested person has been charged, he must be brought before a court at the first reasonable opportunity[121] for the purposes of determining whether he is to remain in custody or to be released upon bail.[122] According to Hanna J. in *Dunne v Clinton*: "No hard and fast rule can be laid down to cover every case. It must depend on many circumstances, such as the time and place of the arrest, the number of the accused, whether a [judge] is easily available, and such other matters as may be relevant".[123]

11–40 The traditional view of the common law right to liberty and the power to effect an arrest was stated by Hanna J. in *Dunne v Clinton*,[124] to wit, that "there can be no half-way house between the liberty of a suspect, unfettered by restraint, and an arrest", and the practice of detaining suspects prior to making a formal arrest or laying charges, is, in the absence of specific lawful authority, an illegal one. This perspective may be considered implicit in Art.40.4.1 of the Constitution: "No citizen shall be deprived of his personal liberty, save in accordance with law". The assertions in *Dunne* hold true today only to the extent that they underscore the necessity for strict proof of lawful authority for the arrest and detention. Their broader perspective of the function of arrest—for the purpose of bringing charges and not for the purpose of investigative detention of the suspect—has been weakened considerably over recent years in Ireland by the enactment of general and specific gardaí powers to detain suspects, following an arrest, for the purposes of criminal investigation prior to making a decision whether to charge the suspect. These amount to a significant re-characterisation of the function of arrest prior to formal charging. The common law view of arrest, expressed by Walsh J. in *Shaw*, was that it was "simply a process of ensuring the attendance at court of the person so arrested" and it was unlawful (and tantamount to false imprisonment) to arrest a person (with or without a warrant) for the purpose of interrogation or the eliciting of useful evidence.[125] The learned judge was prepared to accept that questioning was legitimate only so long as the desire to interrogate was not the justification or basis for the arrest.

11–41 The gardaí may detain without charge for the purposes of searches under the Misuse of Drugs Acts 1977 and 1984, and for the taking of blood and urine samples under the Road Traffic Acts. An accused may be detained in a garda station for questioning for up to 12 hours under s.4 of the Criminal Justice Act 1984 (where arrested for offences carrying a sentence of five years imprisonment or more, and where considered necessary for investigation of

---

[120] [1990] I.L.R.M. 65 at 68 (SC).
[121] *People (DPP) v Walsh* [1980] I.R. 294 (SC); *People (DPP) v Shaw* [1982] I.R. 1 (SC).
[122] *Dunne v Clinton* [1930] I.R. 366 at 374, *per* Hanna J. (HC): *cf.* appendix 4.
[123] *ibid.*
[124] *ibid.* at 372.
[125] [1982] I.R. 1 at 29–30 (SC).

an offence). Under s.30 of the Offences Against the State Act 1939,[126] the gardaí have the power to detain persons suspected of having committed a scheduled offence, for up to 48 hours—and under s.10 of the Offences Against the State (Amendment) Act 1998, for a further 24 hours by order of a District Court judge,[127] a provision that was enacted on a short-term basis but has since been renewed annually in the context of ongoing investigation and trial of persons guilty of directing terrorist organisations. More recently—in response to the policy drive to prosecute drug traffickers—s.2 of the Criminal Justice (Drug Trafficking) Act 1996 gave gardaí inspectors the power to detain persons suspected of trafficking in controlled drugs for up to six hours of questioning; which may be increased by 18 hours and then a further 24 hours if sanctioned by a chief superintendent (where considered necessary to properly investigate the suspected offence); and which may be increased by a further 72 hours and a further 48 hours if sanctioned by a Circuit or District Court judge (culminating potentially in seven days of detention without charge). The reasonableness of the belief in the necessity of the detention must subsequently be proved at the trial or the detention will be deemed unlawful and any consequential confession inadmissible. The European Court of Human Rights acknowledged in *Murray v UK*[128] that the suspicion necessary to ground an arrest for detention may be based upon information from a confidential source, so long as reliable, and that the level of factual justification required at the investigative stage may be affected by the special exigencies in the investigation of serious crimes such as drug trafficking and terrorism.

11–42 Of more general application, s.4 of the Criminal Justice Act 1984 enables the gardaí to apprehend a person "whom he, with reasonable cause, suspects of having committed an offence to which this section applies" (indictable offences attracting imprisonment of at least five years), and, upon the authority of the member in charge of the station, to detain the suspect in a garda station without charge initially for up to six hours where "there are reasonable grounds for believing that his detention is necessary for the proper investigation of the offence", and for a further six hours with the authority of a superintendent or garda of higher rank. If the suspect is arrested at night, and given the requisite rest period between midnight and 8 a.m., the person may be detained in total for up to 20 hours.[129]

---

[126] In *People (DPP) v Quillegan and O'Reilly (No.3)* [1993] 2 I.R. 305 (SC); *cf.* appendix 42, the Supreme Court upheld the constitutionality of s.30, and it rejected submissions that s.30 arbitrarily discriminated between detainees, reasoning that a s.30 detainee implicitly benefits from the full range of rights and protection afforded to persons detained for non-scheduled offences.

[127] The requirement of judicial authority for further hours of detention was prompted by the decision of the European Court of Human Rights in *Brogan v UK* (1989) 11 E.H.R.R. 117.

[128] (1996) 22 E.H.R.R. 29: *cf.* appendix 49.

[129] Keane, "Detention Without Charge and the Criminal Justice (Drug Trafficking Act) 1996" [1997] 7 I.C.L.J. 3 at 6.

11–43 The parameters of "reasonable belief" have been canvassed in a number of cases, and in *Walshe and Bedford*[130] culminated in an award of €275,000 to two plaintiffs who had been arrested and detained unlawfully for three days under s.30 of the Offences Against the State Act 1939, in circumstances where the gardaí lacked a reasonable belief in the necessity of the detention. In *People (DPP) v Cleary*[131] it was argued upon appeal that because the garda had already formed the *belief* that the accused murdered the deceased, before he detained the accused under s.4, the provision had been improperly invoked since there were no longer any "reasonable grounds" for requiring detention to "investigate" the offence. Herbert J. reasoned as follows:

> "The whole object and purpose, in my view, of Section 4 of the Criminal Justice Act 1984 is to give to the member of An Garda Síochána effecting an arrest adequate time, but no more, through proper investigation to progress, if necessary through belief, from a suspicion based upon a reasonable cause for that suspicion to a position where that member of An Garda Síochána has enough evidence to prefer a charge against the arrested person for the offence".[132]

11–44 Herbert J. rejected the notion that s.4 applies only to arresting gardaí with lesser degrees of apprehension of the guilt of the suspect. An admission by the suspect does not necessarily constitute enough evidence to prefer a charge, and the garda is entitled to consider that the admission might be "mischievous or baseless, or might at any stage during the subsequent proceedings become inadmissible in evidence".[133]

11–45 By s.2 of the Criminal Justice (Miscellaneous Provisions) Act 1997, however, where the garda at any point ceases to believe that the suspect's detention is necessary for the purposes of investigating the offence, he must be released. Section 2 also provides that if, during detention for the investigation of one offence the garda has reasonable cause to suspect the person of having committed another or a different offence, the garda may consider the detention for the first offence to be detention for the purposes of investigation of the second offence.

11–46 Given that the power of detention for questioning is regarded by the common law to constitute a serious abridgment of a person's right to liberty, its legal basis is subject to strict and literal interpretation by the courts.[134] In bringing the person into garda custody, "reasonable expedition" must be observed, according to common law principle.[135] In *People (DPP) v Cleary*,[136]

---

[130] HC, May 2003.
[131] HC, December 7, 2001.
[132] *ibid.*
[133] *ibid.*
[134] *Clarke v Member in Charge* [2001] 4 I.R. 173 at 178, *per* Keane C.J. (SC).
[135] *People v Walsh* [1980] I.R. 294 *per* O'Higgins C.J. (SC).
[136] HC, December 7, 2001.

a delay of 10 minutes before the suspect was driven to the station did not constitute unreasonable delay. By contrast, a delay of two hours—during which time the suspect was searched for drugs in a shed—was unreasonable and invalidated the arrest in *DPP v Boylan*.[137] The place of detention authorised by the provisions is "a Garda Síochána station, a prison or some other convenient place". If a garda purports to exercise s.4 in an alternative manner—as in *People (DPP) v Cleary*[138] by questioning the suspect in his sister's house prior to taking the detainee to the station—the lawful authority for the interview is lost and any resulting admissions are generally inadmissible. "Some other convenient place" has been interpreted, in accordance with the *ejusdem generis* principle, to refer to a convenient building such as a station or prison but not to a vehicle.[139] The words "Garda Síochána station, a prison or some other convenient place" implicitly import the plural—and upon this basis, detention in three different stations did not exceed the bounds of the statutory power in *People (DPP) v Kelly (No.2)*.[140] According to O'Higgins C.J.: "The place of such detention is a secondary consideration and is indicated in general terms as a "Garda Síochána station, a prison or some other convenient place". As long as the duration of the detention is within the permitted period and the detention is effected for the purpose of removing the detainee to, or keeping him in, a place which complies with the description given, in my view the detention is permitted by the subsection".[141]

11–47 The detention must be continuous, although the courts have recognised that there may be temporary disruptions to the detention, if necessary in the circumstances of the case—as in *People (DPP) v Farrell*[142] for the purpose of a two-hour car drive to enable the accused to indicate relevant places; and as in *Clarke v Member in Charge*[143] for the purpose of the accused's attendance at the District Court. In such cases, this is not a removal of the accused for the purpose of detention in another place, but a continuation of the same detention, and it "should not be excluded in reckoning the period of detention permitted by the section".[144] In *Farrell*[145] and other cases,[146] the temporary removal of a detainee to a garda car for the purpose of a drive in the hope of discovering evidence was not viewed to be incompatible with the continuity of the detention. In each case, the courts were influenced by the fact that the detainee had accompanied the gardaí voluntarily. In *People v Kelly (No.2)*,[147] the Supreme

---

[137] [1991] 1 I.R. 477 (CCA).
[138] HC, December 7, 2001.
[139] *People (DPP) v Farrell* [1978] I.R. 13 (CCA).
[140] [1983] I.R. 1 (SC), with respect to detention under s.30 of the Offences Against the State Act 1939.
[141] *ibid.* at 20–21.
[142] [1978] I.R. 13 (CCA).
[143] [2001] 4 I.R. 171 (SC).
[144] *Clarke v Member in Charge ibid.* at 179, *per* Keane C.J.
[145] [1978] I.R. 13 (CCA).
[146] *State (Walsh) v Maguire* [1979] I.R. 372 (SC); *People (DPP) v McGrath* (CCA, December 2, 2002).
[147] [1983] I.R. 1 (CCA).

Court pointed out that where the removal of the detainee from one station to another is effected with mala fides, or to harass the accused, or to deprive him of access to legal advice, the detention becomes unlawful.

11–48 Where a person is detained with respect to one offence and also questioned with respect to other offences, his detention is lawful only if there is a reasonable and genuine connection between the detention and the offence the detainee is suspected of having committed. The practice of "holding charges"—arresting persons for less serious charges in order to interrogate them on other crimes—has been challenged on a number of occasions in the context of recourse by the gardaí to powers of arrest for offences attracting lengthy periods of detention. In *People (DPP) v Quillegan and O'Reilly*,[148] the accused had been detained under s.30 of the Offences Against the State Act 1939 with respect to the scheduled offence of malicious damage to a house in which the deceased had been discovered. The Supreme Court unanimously approved the detention for the purpose of questioning on that offence and also the non-scheduled offence of murder. The court accepted that the mode of arrest gave the gardaí "the advantage of having persons whom they wished to question in a position where such persons could not walk away from them".[149] Each of the judges emphasised the need to establish, however, that the arresting garda had a genuine suspicion that the accused had been involved in the scheduled offence, and that the arrest and detention was bona fide for the purpose of that alleged offence, even if it involved questioning on a related offence of a more serious nature.

11–49 In *People (DPP) v Howley*,[150] Finlay C.J. approved *Quillegan*, and rejected the contended application of a predominant purpose test of arrest and detention. The s.30 power of detention was validly utilised for the purpose of questioning on a non-scheduled offence (in the case, murder) where there remained a genuine suspicion that the accused committed the scheduled offence for which he was arrested (in the case, cattle maiming) and so long as the interrogation was genuinely directed towards investigation of that offence. This link between the offence for which the accused was ostensibly detained, and the offences in respect of which he was actually questioned during that detention, did not exist in *Criminal Assets Bureau v Craft*.[151] The High Court asserted that a person may not be detained under the Criminal Justice (Drug Trafficking) Act 1996 for the purposes of an investigation into suspected revenue offences.

11–50 A person may be questioned voluntarily in a police station, although as soon as it is intended to charge the person, he is formally "in custody" and there must be a legal basis for the continued detention, the absence of which

---

[148] [1987] I.L.R.M. 606 (SC).
[149] *ibid., per* Walsh J.
[150] [1989] I.L.R.M. 629 (SC): *cf.* appendix 31.
[151] [2001] 1 I.R. 121 (HC).

exposes the detainer to civil liability for unlawful imprisonment.[152] In *People (DPP) v O'Loughlin*,[153] the accused voluntarily accompanied the gardaí to the station to help them with their enquiries into the theft of agricultural machinery, and he made a first statement in the morning. By 2 p.m., the gardaí had ascertained that the information in his statement was false. After questioning, he made a second statement at 10 p.m implicating himself in the theft. The second statement was ruled inadmissible upon the basis that from 2 p.m. on, it had become reasonable and therefore necessary to charge the accused; he had not been free to leave the station (although he did not know this himself), and no lawful authority had been invoked by the gardaí to justify his detention prior to the time he made a confession.

11–51 Where the suspect has been charged with an offence, he may no longer be questioned with respect to it, although he may be questioned on his involvement in other offences so long as he is lawfully detained for that purpose.[154] There are qualified provisions for re-arrest subsequent to expiry of the lawful period of detention and prior to a decision to charge the detainee, under s.10 of the Criminal Justice Act 1984, s.4 of the Criminal Justice (Drug Trafficking) Act 1996, and s.30A of the Offences Against the State Act 1939.[155] Under these provisions, the person generally may not be detained in connection with the offence for which he was earlier detained, or for another offence of which he ought reasonably to have been suspected upon his earlier arrest, save with the authority of a judge of the District Court (in the case of the 1984 and 1939 Acts) or a judge of the District or Circuit Court (in the case of the 1996 Act), and only where it is established upon sworn information that "further information has come to the knowledge" of the gardaí since his release with respect to the person's suspected involvement in the offence. Each of the Acts facilitates re-arrest, as a qualification to this rule, where for the purposes of "charging him or her with that offence forthwith".[156]

Powers of Search and Seizure

11–52 The question of the admissibility of real evidence is alternatively, although indirectly, an enquiry into the existence and scope of a valid legal basis for the garda's search of the accused's person or house prior to seizure of the evidence. Search and seizure in the absence of due legal authority constitutes a violation of the person's constitutional rights, chiefly with respect to the inviolability of his dwelling house and his right to bodily integrity. The gardaí are entitled to search and seize on foot either of: (1) a specific statutory basis; (2) the person's consent; (3) a lawful arrest; or (4) a valid search warrant.

---

[152] *Dunne v Clinton* [1930] I.R. 366 (HC) *cf.* appendix 4 and para.**11–40**.
[153] [1979] I.R. 85 (CCA).
[154] *R. v Buchan* [1964] 1 All E.R. 502, 1 W.L.R. 365 (CA).
[155] Inserted by the Offences Against the State (Amendment) Act 1998, s.11.
[156] Considered in the context of s.4 of the Criminal Justice (Drug Trafficking) Act 1996 in *DPP v Early* [1998] 3 I.R. 158 (HC).

11–53 Regulation 17(1) of the Custody Regulations of 1987 provides: "A member conducting a search of a person in custody shall ensure, so far as practicable, that the person understands the reason for the search and that it is conducted with due respect for the person being searched". Whilst breach of this or any other provision of the regulations—*per* s.7(3) of the Criminal Justice Act 1984—does not necessarily render the detention unlawful or the consequential evidence inadmissible, the courts may nonetheless draw that conclusion in its discretion, as for breaches of the Judges' Rules.[157] In *People (DPP) v McFadden*,[158] Keane C.J. of the Court of Criminal Appeal considered that discretion should be exercised in favour of inadmissibility where the garda failed to explain the basis for the intended search of the accused as soon as the accused had withdrawn his cooperation (in the case, with respect to inspection of a wallet the garda found in the accused's pocket in the context of a search to which the accused initially consented).

(1) Statutory Authority

11–54 Numerous statutes confer powers upon the gardaí to detain persons without warrant for the purpose of a search, upon reasonable suspicion of having committed a statutory offence.[159] The courts have repeatedly stated that, as a prerequisite to their valid exercise, the citizen must be informed of the statutory authority being invoked before the search commences. The most significant statutory bases are as follows.

11–55 Section 23(1) of the Misuse of Drugs Act 1977 empowers a garda to search without warrant any person whom he has reasonable cause to suspect to be in possession of a controlled substance in the terms of the Act, and to detain him for such time as is reasonably necessary for the purpose of being so searched. Section 23(1)(b) empowers a garda to stop and search any vehicle, vessel, or aircraft that he suspects to carry drugs, and requires the person in control of the vehicle, vessel, or aircraft to stop it or keep it stationary. Section 30(1) of the Offences against the State Act 1939 empowers a garda without warrant to stop, search, interrogate, or arrest any person whom he suspects to have committed or to be involved in the commission of a scheduled offence. Section 30(2) provides that the garda may stop and search any vehicle or vessel that he suspects to contain such a person. Section 29 of the Dublin Police Act 1842 empowers a garda generally to "stop, search, and detain any vessel, boat, cart or carriage in or upon which there shall be reason to suspect that any thing stolen or unlawfully obtained may be found". Section 8 of the Criminal Law

---

[157] *cf.* para.**10–18** *et seq.*
[158] [2003] 2 I.R. 105, [2003] 2 I.L.R.M. 201 (CCA) *cf.* para.**11–59**.
[159] *e.g.* Intoxicating Liquor Act 1960, s.22(3), empowering a garda to require a driver to halt a vehicle for the purpose of a search where there are reasonable grounds for suspecting that the vehicle is being used in connection with the commission of the offences of moving stills and spirits; and Wildlife Act 1976, s.72(2), empowering a garda or authorised person to stop a person and require him to give his name and address where reasonably suspected of having committed an offence under Pt II or under ss.45, 47, 51 or 53 of the Act.

Act 1976 empowers a garda to stop drivers, upon reasonable suspicion, to ascertain whether the occupants of the vehicle have committed or are about to commit a scheduled offence and whether evidence may be obtained in relation to the commission or intended commission of a scheduled offence, and to search the vehicle or any person in or accompanying the vehicle or vessel.[160]

11–56 Section 109 of the Road Traffic Act 1961 is worded differently to the above provisions in that, rather than empowering a garda to stop a vehicle, it requires the driver of a vehicle "to stop on being so required" by a garda. In *DPP (Stratford) v Fagan*,[161] the appellant argued that this did not give the gardaí power to conduct random tests on drivers or to stop a vehicle without any prior reasonable suspicion of the commission of an offence under the Road Traffic Act. The Supreme Court accepted that s.109 does not vest a power in the gardaí to require a driver to stop his vehicle, and that instead it imposes a duty upon the driver to stop when requested to do so by a garda.[162] The court rejected the appeal, however, upon the basis that the common law imposes a duty on the gardaí, and gives them authority, to take all necessary steps to keep the peace and to prevent crime.[163] In her dissent, Denham J. noted that the legislature had carefully limited the garda power requiring drivers to stop and therefore that it arose only in specific scenarios and subject to strict terms. The learned judge rejected the application of a "broad sweep" of principle suggested in some of the English decisions, and asserted "that such an important and fundamental matter [as the curtailment of the right to freedom of movement] cannot be implied into such a section".[164]

11–57 The gardaí are not required to effect an arrest prior to the search; a reasonable period of detention is permitted for the purposes of a search prior to the decision to arrest.[165] If incriminating objects are found upon the person, the garda is *obliged* to arrest, charge, and to take the person into custody. In *O'Callaghan v Ireland*,[166] where it was argued that s.23 of the Misuse of Drugs Act 1977 operated unconstitutionally to permit detention without charge, thereby creating an unprecedented state of uncertainty for the suspect, Finlay C.J. reasoned that the power was an "extension of the ordinary power of arrest on suspicion of the commission of an offence". The learned judge upheld the provision, observing that it would in most cases "be in ease of a suspect".[167] He found further that a detainee has "appropriate rights concerning access to legal advice, freedom from harassment, interrogation or assault, and all the other rights that are appropriate to an arrested person."[168]

---

[160] Being murder, manslaughter, scheduled offences under the Offences Against the State Act, and other statutory offences.
[161] [1994] 2 I.L.R.M. 349 (SC).
[162] *ibid.* at 355, *per* Blayney J., approving *Steel v Goacher* [1983] R.T.R. 98 at 103.
[163] *ibid.* at 355, *per* Blayney J., approving *Glasbrook Brothers Ltd. v Glamorgan CC* [1925] A.C. 270 at 277 and *Rice v Connolly* [1966] 2 Q.B. 414 at 419.
[164] [1994] 2 I.L.R.M. 349 at 363 (SC).
[165] *DPP v Rooney* [1993] I.L.R.M. 61 at 63, *per* O'Hanlon J. (HC).
[166] [1994] 1 I.R. 555 at 562 (SC).
[167] *ibid.* at 563.
[168] *ibid.* at 563.

11–58 It has been reasoned[169] that although temporary detention for the purpose of a search is not as drastic in effect as an arrest, where a garda purports to exercise such a power, the legal authority and reason for the search must adequately be communicated to the suspect, in line with the principles established in *Christie v Leachinsky*[170] and recent Irish case law.[171] If the suspect clearly cooperates with the garda and consents to the search, it is not strictly necessary that the garda invoke and communicate the appropriate powers of compulsion under common law or statute, although clearly there is more certainty and less scope for contention later if the appropriate powers are duly invoked and explained.

(2) Consent

11–59 The necessity for invocation and communication of the lawful basis for compulsory search arises where the suspect has not volunteered to cooperate and submit to the search. In *People (DPP) v O'Donnell*,[172] the accused, detained upon suspicion of membership of the I.R.A. contrary to s.21 of the Offences Against the State Act 1939, had initially cooperated with the garda and submitted the right-hand pocket of his jacket for a search. When he withdrew his consent prior to a search of the left-hand pocket, the garda cautioned him that he was arresting him under s.30 of the 1939 Act upon suspicion of membership of an unlawful organisation, and that he would use force if necessary to search the other pocket. A search of the other pocket revealed explosive substances. The conviction for an offence contrary to s.4 of the Explosive Substances Act 1883 was affirmed by the Court of Criminal Appeal upon the basis that it had not been necessary for the garda to invoke or explain his powers of compulsory search whilst the suspect had consented to the search, and that this necessity arose only when the suspect's consent and cooperation was withdrawn. By contrast, the garda's failure to explain the basis for his search had a material effect on the evidence discovered in *People (DPP) v McFadden*,[173] since the unexplained search proceeded withdrawal by the accused of his cooperation to the search. The accused had initially consented to a search of his person, but when the garda discovered a wallet in his pocket he had told the garda "not to go near the wallet". In these circumstances when cooperation was withdrawn, it had been encumbent upon the garda to explain the basis and authority for the search, and the failure to do so compromised the rights of the accused sufficiently to entail inadmissibility of the evidence consequentially obtained.

11–60 Consent to a search of the person may be, and often is, given tacitly—for instance, where the suspect holds out his arm in response to a request. With the suspect's continued acquiescence, the holding out of an arm may

---

[169] *DPP v Rooney* [1993] I.L.R.M. 61 at 63, *per* O'Hanlon J. (HC).
[170] [1946] 1 K.B. 124 (CA): *cf.* appendix 6.
[171] *cf.* para.**11–29** *et seq.*
[172] [1995] 3 I.R. 551 (CCA).
[173] [2003] 2 I.L.R.M. 201 (CCA) *cf.* para.**11–53**.

11–61 Consent to a search of the house in which evidence is found may dispense with the need to invoke statutory authority or to obtain a warrant for the search.[175] A person may impliedly consent to entry by the gardaí onto his private premises, and it would appear that unless the consent is expressly withdrawn the courts may interpret the subsequent search and gathering of evidence to have been effected by consent.[176] This was evident recently in *People (DPP) v McCann*,[177] where the appellant's submission that he had consented only to the entry of the gardaí to the public bar and not to the annexed private quarters was defeated by evidence that the appellant had not withdrawn his consent to the gardaí moving into the remains of the private home.

11–62 Whether the burnt-out remains of a house may constitute a dwelling-house for the purposes of the constitutional right to "inviolability of the dwelling house" was doubted by O'Flaherty J. in *McCann*. The case was not decided upon the point, however, as the evidence supported a finding that the accused had impliedly given his consent to the entry.

(3) Arrest

11–63 Upon arrest, a person's immediate environment may be searched. The gardaí have power, when effecting a lawful arrest, to seize (without a search warrant) goods in the possession or custody of the arrested person if they believe it is necessary to do so in order to prevent the destruction of the goods and where the goods are: (a) evidence in support of the criminal charge on foot of which the arrest was made; or (b) evidence in support of any other criminal charge against the person arrested then being contemplated; or (c) reasonably believed to be stolen property or to be property unlawfully in the possession of the person arrested.[178] There are many statutory and common law bases for arrest.[179] It was stressed in *Jeffrey v Black*,[180] however, that it is not lawful to institute a search of an arrested person's house or premises for the purpose of obtaining evidence unrelated to the offence for which the person was arrested. In *Jeffrey*, the accused had been arrested for the theft of a sandwich in a public house, and then brought to his home where the police seized quantities of cannabis resin. His conviction for possession of the drug was quashed due to the unlawfulness of the search in the absence either of his consent, a search warrant, or an adequate correlation with the arrest.

---

[174] HC, December 7, 2001.
[175] *People (DPP) v Cleary, ibid.*
[176] *cf.* para.**11–35**.
[177] [1998] 4 I.R. 397 (CCA).
[178] So held by O'Keefe J. in *Jennings v Quinn* [1968] I.R. 305 at 309 (SC), approving *Elias v Pasmore* [1934] 2 K.B. 164 (K.B.D.): *cf.* appendix 14.
[179] *cf.* para.**11–32**.
[180] [1978] 1 All E.R. 555 (QBD).

(4) Search Warrants

11–64 In the absence of statutory authority to search without warrant, or sufficient grounds for an arrest, or the consent of a suspect, the gardaí must obtain a valid search warrant prior to a search and seizure. On foot of a valid search warrant, the gardaí may, in general seize: (1) goods specifically mentioned in the warrant; (2) goods reasonably implied by the warrant; (3) goods whose identity the warrant states (*e.g.* goods in a certain box); and (4) evidence in support of the offence to which the warrant relates. The common law frowns upon the concept of a "general ransack". Thus, search warrants are implicitly spent after the first search, and must be acted upon as soon as is reasonably practicable. Section 10 of the Criminal Justice (Miscellaneous Provisions) Act 1997 provides that search warrants obtained for "serious crimes" expire after one week from issue of the warrant. Section 7 of the Child Trafficking and Pornography Act 1998 provides that the gardaí may enter premises within seven days from the date of the warrant. Section 26(2) of the Misuse of Drugs Act 1977 provides for the execution of a warrant at any time or times within one month from the date of issue of the warrant. By contrast, where a search warrant has been issued by a senior member of the gardaí, based upon suspicion of drug trafficking offences pursuant to s.8 of the Criminal Justice (Drug Trafficking) Act 1996, the warrant expires after 24 hours from the time of issue.

11–65 In seeking a declaration of invalidity of the warrant, the applicant bears the burden of proof, since a warrant benefits from a presumption of legality.[181] In the event of challenge, however, the validity must strictly be proved. This principle is an old one. In 1765, Camden C.J. asserted: "Our law holds the property of every man so sacred, that no man can set his foot upon his neighbour's close without his leave: if he does he is a trespasser, though he does no damage at all: if he will tread upon a neighbour's ground he must justify it by law".[182] Further, in light of the unqualified protection afforded to the dwelling house by Art.40.5 of the Constitution, search warrants must formally "be in clear, complete, accurate and unambiguous terms".[183] The necessity for "close scrutiny and express justification" exists equally in cases where the warrant compromises other constitutional rights, enumerated or unenumerated. This was indicated by Kinlen J. in *Hanahoe v Hussey*,[184] in the context of a warrant issued under s.64 of the Criminal Justice Act 1994 against solicitors who retained files sought by the gardaí to establish that the lawyers' clients had profited from drug trafficking: "This court accepts without question that any such intrusion on the personal rights of a citizen, building, privacy, property and the inviolability of a dwelling-house must therefore be closely

---

[181] *Hanahoe v Hussey* [1998] 3 I.R. 69 at 99, *per* Kinlen J. (HC).
[182] *Entick v Carrington* [1876] 2 Wils 275.
[183] *DPP v Dunne* [1994] 2 I.R. 337 at 540, *per* Carney J. (HC), declaring a search warrant invalid due to the inadvertent crossing-out of "on the premises" without which words the terms made no sense.
[184] [1998] 3 I.R. 69 at 92 (HC).

scrutinised and expressly justified. ... The court must be ever conscious of the fact that this is a new and serious invasion of constitutional rights including the invasion of privacy and possibly the invasion of confidential relationships".[185]

11–66 Search warrants are for the most part issued by a District Court judge or peace commissioner after receiving adequate information under oath from a member of the gardaí that there is "reasonable cause for suspecting" that incriminating evidence will be obtained.[186] Where a warrant was issued by the peace commissioner or District judge within his jurisdiction, "the courts will not interfere with the [decision] unless it can be shown that no reasonable District Judge would have come to the conclusion, which she did, based on the evidence before her".[187] The grant of a search warrant is contingent upon receiving adequate justifying information under oath and upon making adequate enquiries.[188] The basis for the "reasonable suspicion" must subsequently be proven in court by the attendance of the person who issued the warrant.[189] Conviction was quashed in *DPP v Yamanoha*[190] due to the invalidity of a search warrant issued under s.26(1) of the Misuse of Drugs Act 1977 upon unsworn information. In *Byrne v Grey*,[191] the High Court concluded that a peace commissioner had acted beyond the bounds of his authority by failing to ascertain the basis for the garda's suspicion that quantities of cannabis were to be found at the accused's dwelling, in circumstances where the gardaí instead discovered quantities of heroin there. According to Hamilton P: "these powers encroach on the liberty of the citizen and the inviolability of his dwelling as guaranteed by the Constitution and the courts should construe a statute which authorises such encroachment so that it encroaches on such rights no more than the statute allows, expressly or by necessary implication".[192]

11–67 A similar failure arose in *People (DPP) v Kenny*,[193] with respect to the failure of a peace commissioner to ascertain by adequate enquiry whether sworn information in writing stating a general suspicion of drug trafficking in Rathmines constituted reasonable grounds for issuing a warrant. A majority of the Supreme Court endorsed an absolute protection model of due process

---

[185] *ibid.* at 94.
[186] In *DPP v Edgeworth* (SC, March 29, 2001), the court rejected a technical challenge to the validity of a search warrant that was headed by the words "the District Court" but had been issued by a peace commissioner. The court found that the Misuse of Drugs Act 1977 had not specified a particular form for the heading of the warrant issued by a peace commissioner.
[187] *Hanahoe v Hussey* [1998] 3 I.R. 69 at 95, *per* Kinlen J. (HC).
[188] See *Hanahoe v Hussey* [1998] 3 I.R. 69 (HC), where the District Court judge was found to have made adequate enquiry into the reasonableness of the suspicion.
[189] *People (DPP) v Byrne* [1987] I.R. 363 (SC); *People (DPP) v Owens* [1999] 2 I.R. 17 (SC).
[190] [1994] 1 I.R. 565 (CCA): the detective sergeant in the case swore his oath *after* he had given the information orally to the peace commissioner.
[191] [1988] I.R. 31 (HC): *cf.* appendix 30.
[192] *ibid.* at 38.
[193] [1990] I.L.R.M. 569 (SC).

and quashed conviction due to the inadmissibility of evidence of drugs obtained on foot of an invalid search warrant. The court rejected the submission that the breach had been unintentional and accidental—a stance consistent with the view of a majority of the judges that "deliberate and conscious" in *O'Brien* refers to proof that the act in question (submitting a standard form warrant) was deliberate, and not that it was done deliberately in violation of the suspect's constitutional rights.

11–68 Numerous statutes now provide, upon an exceptional basis, that warrants may be issued internally by senior garda officers in circumstances of urgency. Under s.14 of the Criminal Assets Bureau Act 1996, a garda bureau officer may issue a warrant (with a 24-hour duration) in circumstances of urgency where it would be impracticable to seek a warrant from a District judge. Under s.8(2) of the Criminal Justice (Drug Trafficking) Act 1996, a garda officer not below the rank of superintendent may issue a search warrant where satisfied that: a warrant is necessary for the proper investigation of a drug trafficking offence; that there are circumstances of urgency giving rise to the need for immediate issue of a warrant; and that it would be impracticable to apply to a judge for the warrant. The Court of Criminal Appeal recently signalled grave doubts over the legality of the gardaí's internal authorisation of lengthy extensions of detention, however.[194] Hardiman J. expressed the view that attempts must first be made to obtain a warrant upon sworn information, from a District judge or peace commissioner, in cases particularly where the search follows a lengthy surveillance operation.

IV. APPLICATION OF THE EXCLUSIONARY RULE IN CIVIL CASES

11–69 The *O'Brien* exclusionary rule, since premised not only upon deterrence against unlawful investigative practice but also protection of a party's constitutional rights, applies with similar effect in civil cases.[195] In *O'C v TC*,[196] McMahon J. excluded evidence in family law proceedings obtained after an unlawful search by one spouse of the other spouse's dwelling in violation of Article 40.5. In *P McG v AF*,[197] Budd J. ruled that a court-appointed medical inspector was not entitled to base his findings upon a personal diary seized by one of the parties in violation of the respondent's constitutional right to privacy. The application of the *O'Brien* rule to administrative and disciplinary hearings has not yet been addressed in Ireland, and it has been

---

[194] *People (DPP) v Byrne* (CCA, October 30, 2003).
[195] So found by Fennelly J. in *Kennedy v Law Society of Ireland (No.3)* [2002] 2 I.R. 458 at 489 (SC). See also *Universal City Studios Inc v Mulligan (No.2)* [1999] 3 I.R. 392 (HC), where Laffoy J. endorsed *People (DPP) v Kenny* [1990] 2 I.R. 110 (SC; cf. para.**11–02** and appendix 36), a case where the Supreme Court espoused the optimal protection model for evidence obtained in violation of the constitutional rights.
[196] HC, December 8, 1981.
[197] HC, January 28, 2000.

proposed that it may apply in appropriate cases but that its application "must necessarily be extremely limited".[198]

11–70 A discretionary rule similarly applies to evidence obtained *illegally* or *improperly*. In *Universal City Studios Inc v Mulligan (No.2)*,[199] the plaintiff was unable to prove the existence of the warrant authorising him to search the defendant's car for evidence of copyright infringement. As this had not violated a distinct constitutional right of the accused (such as inviolability of his dwelling), the evidence obtained on foot of the unauthorised search and seizure had been *illegally* obtained. In the circumstances of the case, Laffoy J. considered the evidence to be admissible against the defendant. On the other hand, in *Kennedy v. Law Society of Ireland*,[200] the Supreme Court adopted the view that a report produced by accountants following an *ultra vires* investigation of the applicant by the respondent had been an "integral" part of the tainted investigation, and upon this basis the court quashed a decision against the applicant by the respondent's Compensation Fund Committee.

---

[198] *Kennedy v Law Society of Ireland* [2002] I.R. 458 at 490 *per* Fennelly J. (SC).
[199] [1999] 3 I.R. 392 (HC).
[200] [2002] I.R. 458 (SC).

Further Reading

Dawson, "The Exclusion of Unlawfully Obtained Evidence: A Comparative Study" (1982) 31 I.C.L.Q. 513.

Keane, "Detention Without Charge and the Criminal Justice (Drug Trafficking Act) 1996" [1997] 7 I.C.L.J. 3.

Ní Raifeartaigh, "The European Convention on Human Rights and the Irish Criminal Justice System" (2001) *Bar Review* 111.

O'Connor, "The Admissibility of Unconstitutionally Obtained Evidence in Irish Law" (1982) 17 Ir. Jur. 257.

Robertson, "Entrapment Evidence: Manna from Heaven, or Fruit of the Poisoned Tree?" [1994] Crim. L.R. 805.

Ryan, "The Criminal Justice (Drug Trafficking) Act 1996: Decline and Fall of the Right to Silence?" [1997] 7 I.C.L.J. 22.

"The Rationale for the Exclusionary Rule of Evidence" [1992] 2 I.C.L.J. 1.

Uglow, "Covert Surveillance and the European Convention on Human Rights" [1999] Crim. L.R. 287.

CHAPTER 12

OPINION AND EXPERT EVIDENCE

I. General Principles **12–01**
II. The Expert Witness **12–05**
    Experts in the Criminal Trial **12–05**
    Forensic Evidence and DNA **12–12**
    Expertise and its Limits... **12–16**
    Expert Witnesses in Civil Proceedings **12–18**
III. Expert Evidence and Hearsay.. **12–24**
VI. Non-Expert Opinion Evidence **12–27**

I. GENERAL PRINCIPLES

12–01 As a general rule, witnesses are permitted to testify to their knowledge of facts as they perceived them, but they are not permitted to express opinions or inferences arising from those facts. In principle, the trial judge, or the jury where sitting, is solely responsible to draw inferences from the relevant facts established by the evidence, and a witness who expresses his view upon, for instance, the causes or intent of a party's behaviour, is said to usurp the function of the court. The common law recognised a significant exception to this general rule, enabling the court to receive evidence of "the opinion of scientific men upon proven facts [to] be given by men of science within their own science".[1] In principle, the function of the expert witness—authoritatively stated in *Davie v Edinburgh Magistrates*[2]—"is to furnish the judge or jury with the necessary scientific criteria for testing the accuracy of their own conclusions, so as to enable the judge or jury to form their independent judgment by the application of these criteria to the facts proved in evidence". The exception has broadened considerably over the years to facilitate evidence of relevant specialist analysis and judgment by persons duly qualified and expert in their field. Routine examples in criminal proceedings include forensic scientists, pathologists, psychiatrists, DNA analysts, and fingerprint experts; and in civil proceedings, medical experts, actuaries, financial consultants, and surveyors.

12–02 The rule against opinion evidence is often not applied severely to ad

---

[1] So established by Lord Mansfield in *Folkes v Chaad* (1782) 3 Doug. K.B. 157.
[2] [1953] S.C. 34, *per* Cooper L.J: approved in: *People (DPP) v Pringle* (1981) 2 Frewen 57 at 87, *per* O'Higgins C.J. (CCA); *L(P) v DPP* (HC, April 16, 2002) *per* Herbert J.

hoc opinion expressed spontaneously by a witness under examination, as in *People (DPP) v Malocco*,[3] where a garda witness commented "in my mind [I] tried to think was there anything in the file which would indicate his innocence in this matter". The court regarded the risk the jury would draw prejudicial inferences from this comment to be remote, and in the circumstances of the case that it had neither required a direction by the trial judge nor the jury's discharge from the proceedings. The rule, to the extent that it remains generally stated and subject to little elaboration by the courts, depends for its effectiveness upon the pragmatism and discretion of the trial judge. In deciding whether to require the witness not to express further opinion, or whether to direct the jury to disregard the opinion stated by the witness, or whether to discharge the jury and direct a retrial in cases where the resulting prejudice is incurable, the trial judge will be steered by the relative contentiousness and importance of the opinion, comment, or train of thought expressed by the witness, having regard to the facts at issue upon which the court is asked ultimately to decide.

12–03 A narrower version of the rule against opinion evidence is that it restrains a witness only from expressing an opinion upon an "ultimate issue" before the court. This would apply, for instance, in a criminal prosecution for assault under s.2 of the Non-Fatal Offences Against the Person Act 1997 with the effect that a witness would be permitted to testify that he saw the accused hit the other person but would be precluded from expressing the view that the accused assaulted the other person without justification. The witness would otherwise be free to express opinions upon other relevant, circumstantial facts, such as whether the accused was observed in possession of a weapon. A witness, such as a garda (who is not normally treated as an expert witness), may convey information and impressions based upon his experience of the streets and relevant to the scale and nature of the drugs found in the possession of the accused;[4] although the garda may not express the opinion that the accused is guilty as charged.[5] The so-called "ultimate issue" rule operated in *R. v Davies*[6] with the effect that a witness in proceedings for drink driving was permitted to testify that he observed the accused consume alcohol, but was not permitted to testify that the accused was unfit to drive due to his drunkenness. Where the witness was an expert, he was permitted to specify the extent to which the accused was drunk, but not that the accused was so drunk that he was unfit to drive his car as charged. (Although these findings are illustrative of the "ultimate issue rule", a contrary conclusion on the issue of perceived drunkenness was reached by a majority of the Supreme Court in *Attorney-General (Ruddy) v*

---

[3] CCA, May 23, 1996.
[4] *R. v Bryan* (CA, November 8, 1984), followed in *R. v Hodges and Walker* [2003] Crim. L.R. 472 (CA). A police officer with experience of the use of drugs in his locality is not, however, competent to give evidence of the tolerance of drug users to particular drugs such as ecstasy, which must be established only by a person duly qualified in toxicology or pharmacology: *R. v Edwards* (2001) 9 *Archbold News* 1 (CA).
[5] For which conviction was overturned in *R. v Jeffries* [1997] Crim. L.R. 819 (CA).
[6] [1962] 3 All E.R. 97 (CMAC).

Opinion and Expert Evidence 355

Kenny,[7] considered within.) The courts have not always displayed consistency in applying the ultimate issue rule, however. In *DPP v A & BC Chewing Gum Ltd*,[8] the evidence of a child psychiatrist was accepted to show that images on the picture cards sold by the accused were likely to corrupt and deprave children (in a case where the accused was charged with obscenity). By contrast, in *R. v Anderson and Neville*,[9] Widgery J. excluded evidence purporting to establish that an article was "obscene", finding that this was a matter "exclusively for the jury" to decide.

12–04 Although each party to a hearing or trial is entitled to tender relevant expert evidence to establish or rebut a particular proposition, the courts have always been concerned to ensure that the critical facts at issue are not obscured by excessive expert esotericism and supposition. The courts are often apt to determine the admissibility of expert evidence in terms of whether the expertise seeks to testify to matters upon which the jury may be assumed to be sufficiently knowledgeable, a principle expressed in *R. v Turner*[10] and acknowledged in *People (DPP) v Kehoe*.[11] Whilst opinions on an ultimate issue are naturally more likely to engender subsequent appeals, the rule against opinion evidence operates more broadly to preclude a witness from attempting a leap from perceived fact to inference, since this not only trespasses upon a critical function of the jury, it additionally deprives the fact-finders of an opportunity to discern the methodology and premises upon which the witness' recollection and perception have been constructed.

II. THE EXPERT WITNESS

Experts in the Criminal Trial

12–05 Common law jurisprudence on the purpose and scope of expert testimony has for the most part concerned the expert in criminal trials, in which context the courts are considerably more vigilant to ensure that expert testimony does not purport to establish the critical facts at issue, such as the accused's state of mind, which the court is obliged to establish independently to its own satisfaction. For this reason, the evidence of psychiatrists is received with much more restraint in criminal than in civil proceedings. Whilst the evidence of

---

[7] (1960) 94 I.L.T.R. 185 (SC); *cf.* para.**12–08** *et seq.*
[8] [1968] 1 Q.B. 159. In *R. v Land* [1998] Crim. L.R. 70 (CA), the court considered expert evidence inadmissible upon the question whether the person in an indecent photo was a "child". This particular issue was addressed in Ireland by s.2(3) of the Child Trafficking and Pornography Act 1998, which provides that in proceedings for an offence under ss.3, 4, 5 or 6 of the Act: "a person shall be deemed, unless the contrary is proved, to be or have been a child, or to be or have been depicted or represented as a child, at any time if the person appears to the court to be or have been a child, or to be or have been so depicted or represented, at that time".
[9] [1971] 3 All E.R. 1152 (CA).
[10] [1975] 1 Q.B. 834 (CA).
[11] [1992] I.L.R.M. 481 (CCA): *cf.* appendix 40.

psychiatrists is often useful and sometimes necessary in criminal proceedings to explain the nature, pathology, and consequences of diseases or defects of the mind, the expert psychiatrist in principle may not express an opinion in court upon matters relating to the *mens rea*, such as whether or not the accused had been provoked. This was made clear by the Court of Appeal in *R. v Turner*,[12] where Lawton L.J. drew an important distinction between the obvious *relevance* of a psychiatrist's views of the accused and the *admissibility* of such views under common law rules:

> "If on the proven facts a judge or jury can form their own conclusions without help, then the opinion of an expert is unnecessary. In such a case if it is given dressed up in scientific jargon it may make judgment more difficult. The fact that an expert witness has impressive scientific qualifications does not by that fact alone make his opinion on matters of human nature and behaviour within the limits of normality any more helpful than that of the jurors themselves; but there is a danger that they may think it does."

12–06 The *Turner* principles were approved in *People (DPP) v Kehoe*,[13] where O'Flaherty J. decided that a psychiatrist had been permitted to stray beyond his proper role as witness in the trial by expressing an opinion on whether the accused had been provoked to such an extent that he did not intend to kill the deceased: "These are clearly matters four square within the jury's function and a witness no more than the trial judge or anyone else is not entitled to trespass on what is the jury's function".

12–07 In *People (DPP) v Pringle*,[14] the accused appealed against the trial court's limited acceptance of forensic evidence relating to fibres taken from a pullover the accused was wearing at the time of the bank raid and fibres taken from the getaway cars. Although the Special Criminal Court had accepted that the prosecution failed to establish that any of the fibres from the cars came from the accused's pullover, it had considered the forensic evidence to be consistent with the finding of guilt the court was prepared to make upon the accused's admission.[15] Expert evidence in the case established that one point of comparison existed between the fibres, that they each shared the same colour. Before the Court of Criminal Appeal, it was argued that the expert evidence had been inadmissible in the trial as the witness had not been in a better position than the court to determine the points and extent of the comparison, and that rather than deferring to the expert witness on this matter, the judges ought to have examined the fibres themselves. The court rejected the submission, upon the basis that the witness was an expert in forensic science and had been entitled to give his conclusions. Any questions or doubts arising from the expert's findings raised matters that appropriately affected the weight of the evidence.

---

[12] [1975] 1 Q.B. 834 at 841, *per* Lawton L.J. (CA).
[13] [1992] I.L.R.M. 481 at 485 (CCA): *cf.* appendix 40.
[14] (1981) 2 Frewen 57 (CCA).
[15] *cf.* para.**10–41**.

The court considered the argument that the judges should personally have conducted "laboratory experiments ... for visual comparisons" to be "novel and wholly inappropriate".[16]

12–08 Expert evidence by psychiatrists is regularly admissible in sexual offence cases to rationalise the complainant's delay in bringing a complaint against the accused, in the context of attempts by judicial review to restrain prosecution of alleged sexual offences committed in the distant past.[17] Such evidence is critical in murder trials to establish whether the accused suffered a disease of the mind capable of divesting him of criminal responsibility for the purpose of the *M'Naghten rules*.[18] An expert psychiatrist may give an opinion on the accused's *capacity* to commit the crime in question, although he may not tender a view on whether the accused committed the crime *intentionally* or not. In *R. v Toner*,[19] it was permissible for a doctor to testify in a trial for attempted murder that the accused was suffering from a condition causing low blood sugar levels and that the condition was likely to prevent him forming a murderous intent at the material time. In *Lowery v R.*,[20] controversially, the evidence of a psychiatrist was admitted to show that one of two accused was more likely than the other to have killed the deceased, although the decision was subsequently limited to its "special facts".[21] It was permissible in *R. v Lupien*[22] for a psychiatrist to testify to the view that the accused was likely to react violently to homosexual advances. On the other hand, in *R. v Chard*,[23] it was impermissible for a medical witness to testify to his view of the accused's intention to kill or cause serious harm, which, in the absence of any issue as to sanity, was inadmissible and a matter more properly to be determined by the jury. The distinction upon which decisions such as *Lupien* and *Chard* hinge is clearly delicate and difficult to enforce. Although the court in *Chard* doubted the admissibility of expert psychiatric evidence in murder trials where insanity had not been entered as a defence, subsequent decisions in England have affirmed the relevance and admissibility of such evidence in cases where defences such as provocation and duress rest upon a mental or personality abnormality of the accused.[24]

---

[16] (1981) 2 Frewen 57 at 88, *per* O'Higgins C.J. (CCA).
[17] This assesses whether prosecutorial or complainant delay is so excessive as to hamper the accused in preparing a defence and to engender the prospect of unfairness in the trial. The reliability and quality of psychological evidence was described by Kearns J. to be "of paramount importance" in *W. (A.) v DPP* (HC, November 23, 2001). In *JL v DPP* [2000] 3 I.R. 122 at 149, Hardiman J. expressed "the need for caution and for very full and impartial presentation of psychiatric or psychological evidence". See also *PC v DPP* [1999] 2 I.R. 25 (HC); *PO'C v DPP* [2000] 3 I.R. 87 (SC); *D(V) v DPP* (HC, November 23, 2001); and *BJ v DPP* (HC, February 12, 2002).
[18] *R. v M'Naghten* (1843) 4 St. Tr. 847.
[19] (1991) 93 Cr. App. R. 382 (CA).
[20] [1974] A.C. 85 (PC).
[21] *R. v Toohey* [1965] A.C. 595 (HL).
[22] [1982] W.A.R. 171 (SC, Can.).
[23] (1971) 56 Cr. App. R. 268 (CA).
[24] *R. v Morhall* [1996] 1 A.C. 90 (HL); *R. v Smith (Morgan)* [2000] 4 All E.R. 289 (HL); *R. v Emery* (1993) 14 Cr. App. R. 394 (CA).

12–09 For some time under the common law, a psychiatrist or other expert was strictly precluded from commenting upon whether the accused was to be believed, or whether his testimony was reliable in the light of his mental condition. This, the rule in *R. v Gunewardene*,[25] was overruled by the House of Lords in *R. v Toohey*.[26] It is of note that *Toohey* was decided as matter of fairness to the defence, from which perspective the exclusionary rules of evidence operate more strictly given that the risks of prejudice are heightened in the punitive context. The evidence in the case was an opinion by a psychiatrist that the complainant was more prone to hysteria than the average person, and that drink may have heightened his condition and culminated in accusations of assault against the three men accused. Lord Pearce was of the view that "when a witness through physical (in which I include mental) disease or abnormality is not capable of giving a true or reliable account to the jury, it must surely be allowable for medical science to reveal this vital hidden fact from them".[27] The Court of Appeal in *R. v O'Brien*[28] subsequently permitted a psychiatrist to express his views on the reliability of a confession statement signed but later repudiated by the accused, where it was alleged the accused suffered an abnormality or "significant deviation from the norm" sufficient to raise doubts as to the reliability of his confession. *O'Brien* follows a series of decisions[29] that incrementally departed from the rule in *R. v Weightman*[30] limiting the evidence to cases based upon mental abnormality.

12–10 Whilst the courts have adopted a more indulgent attitude to evidence of psychiatrists sought to be admitted by the defence to challenge a witness' credibility, they continue to preclude expert psychiatric or psychological opinion on a witness's reliability or truthfulness under oath.[31] In deciding whether a particular form of specialist evidence is admissible, the trial judge will also be guided by the rule limiting credibility challenges on collateral issues.[32] In *R. v JP*,[33] the Court of Appeal resisted an attempt to permit the defence in a sexual offence case to admit evidence by an expert in cults and fringe religious movements on whether the complaints were reliable or whether instead they had been affected by false memory syndrome. The decision was based upon a rejection of the assertion that the complainant had in fact participated in a form of deliverance ministry, although the court observed that even if this claim had been sustained, the expert on cults was not competent to express "expert" views upon the complainant's reliability. The robust line adopted by

---

[25] [1951] 2 K.B. 600 (CA).
[26] [1965] A.C. 595 (HL).
[27] [1965] A.C. 595 at 608 (HL).
[28] CA, January 25, 2000.
[29] *R. v Raghip* [1991] T.L.R. 562 (CA); *R. v Ward* (1993) 96 Cr. App. R. 1 (CA).
[30] (1991) 92 Cr. App. R. 291 (CA), refusing to admit evidence on behalf of the defence relevant as to whether the accused suffered an attention-seeking disorder.
[31] *R. v Turner* [1975] 1 Q.B. 834 at 842 (CA), *per* Lawton L.J., limiting a contrary decision in *Lowery v R.* [1974] A.C. 85 (PC) to its special facts; *cf. R. v Mackenney* (1981) 76 Cr. App. R. 271 (CA).
[32] *cf.* para.**3–01** *et seq.*
[33] [1999] Crim. L.R. 401 (CA).

the court, in a case of horrifying sexual abuse by the accused of his two daughters, has been praised as "a good example of evidence which ought never to be admitted unless its evidential significance is clearly established, for it has almost unparalleled potential to distract, prejudice and confuse a jury".[34]

12–11 If hypnosis or other forms of therapy have been performed on a complainant to recover suppressed memory of sexual or other offences, the therapist ought to be present at the trial for questioning under oath as to the procedures involved. The absence of this safeguard, along with evidential uncertainties about the date and circumstances of the complainant's recovered memory, prompted the Supreme Court to prohibit further prosecution of the accused in *NC v DPP*.[35] In the absence of an "effective test or control of the mechanism of alleged recovered memory", the situation for the accused was "fraught with risk of unfairness".[36] The courts have not, however, considered recovered memory inadmissible, although concerns arising from the circumstances surrounding the recovery greatly affect their weight. The Home Office Guidelines issued in 1987 for use in pre-trial interviews with witnesses require that the hypnotherapist make a resumé of the witness' recollections prior to hypnosis, that the session be videotaped and the tape transcribed, that the hypnotherapist himself make a witness statement, and that any additional information emerging from the session be written down in a witness statement within 24 hours. Details of any hypnosis session must be disclosed to the defence, even if unsuccessful. The failure of the prosecution to adhere to the guidelines constituted a material irregularity in the trial of *R. v Browning*.[37]

Forensic Evidence and DNA

12–12 The *Turner* judgment invoked another, more contemporary concern—namely, that the views expressed by an expert witness, introduced to the court as a person of distinction and intelligence, are liable to be accorded disproportionate weight by the jury, or worse, to be treated as self-validating authority upon the issue.

12–13 Whilst science progressively facilitates increasingly sophisticated and accurate means of proof, by fingerprints or other tissue samples and now by DNA profile, one of the peculiar dangers for proof and truth posed by scientific evidence is the possibility that it is allowed to assume the status of fixed irrefutable inference in the case, in circumstances where its actual unreliability may not yet be discerned. In 1997, the fingerprint bureau of Scotland Yard made its first admission of mistake since its formation in 1901. Independent checks revealed that a fingerprint match in a burglary investigation had been faulty and had led to charges against the wrong person who had served two

---

[34] Commentary [1998] Crim. L.R. 403.
[35] SC, July 5, 2001.
[36] *ibid. per* Hardiman J. See also *JL v DPP* [2000] 3 I.R. 122 (SC).
[37] [1995] Crim. L.R. 227 (CA).

months in prison by the time the error was uncovered.[38] One of the most high-profile examples of false positive association in recent years was the case of the "Birmingham Six".[39] The so-called *Griess* test had produced a positive result in their trial, which Home Office scientists interpreted to render it 99 per cent certain that the accused had been in the vicinity of high explosives prior to their arrest. The *Griess* test was later shown to react positively with a number of chemicals other than nitroglycerine and could have resulted from exposure to a number of household detergents and soaps. Yet the trial judge referred to the *Griess* test result at the time as "the clearest and most overwhelming evidence I have ever heard".

12–14 Similarly, DNA evidence, which is an increasingly effective means of eliminating possibilities, is at risk of assuming conclusiveness at the risk of proof of guilty intent, following proof of a physical connection between the accused and the scene of the crime. DNA fingerprinting or profiling—now used to construct genetic "bar codes" from tissue samples—was discovered in 1985 by Sir Alec Jeffreys of the University of Leicester. A debate has emerged in Ireland upon the merits of establishing a national DNA database, and whether this should be restricted to the DNA of persons already convicted of criminal offences (which has been the preference in other jurisdictions) or whether, in an attempt to avoid the negative effects this may have upon partiality in future criminal investigations, this should include the DNA of every citizen of the State.[40] In the first publicised case of its use in England, DNA evidence sensationally led to the withdrawal of charges of rape and murder against a 17-year-old man, and the preferral of charges against the accused, leading to conviction, in *R. v Pitchfork*.[41] The case, however, revealed a hidden danger. The accused had initially evaded capture by providing a sample of a friend's DNA instead of his own. In the absence of cast-iron safeguards against distortion or error, the evidence is capable of mechanically precipitating injustice. In *People (DPP) v Horgan*,[42] where the accused was convicted following DNA evidence establishing contact with the deceased, a defence DNA expert from Scotland strongly criticised the procedures in place in Ireland, upon the basis that they fail to address numerous risks of contamination. Although samples had been corked in the case, they had not been sealed, and documentary evidence failed to establish adequate continuity between the time the sample had been obtained and the time of the results. This possibility prompted the court in *People (DPP) v Howe*[43] to direct an acquittal in a murder trial where the prosecution had relied upon evidence of a match between DNA samples of a bloodstain found on the broken window through which the gun

---

[38] *Sunday Times*, April 6, 1997.
[39] *R. v McIlkenny* (1991) 93 Cr. App. R. 287 (CA).
[40] McConnell, *Irish Times*, August 20, 2003; O'Connell, *Irish Times*, August 27, 2003.
[41] January 23, 1988; *cf.* Fennell, *Law of Evidence in Ireland* (2nd ed., Butterworths, Dublin, 2003) at p.186; Hibbs, "Application of DNA fingerprinting—truth will out" (1989) 139 N.L.J. 619.
[42] Central Criminal Court, 2003.
[43] Central Criminal Court, October 14, 2003.

Opinion and Expert Evidence 361

was fired and samples later taken from the accused's hair. The decision was based upon the fact that the evidence was uncorroborated, and the prosecution had tendered insufficient expert evidence on the statistical probabilities of a false match (the closest thought to be where the identical blood belonged to a brother, a chance of about one in 10,000).

12–15 In trials where DNA evidence is relied upon, the trial judge may be obliged to administer a full corroboration warning to mitigate the prejudicial effect of the appearance of scientific conclusiveness in the proceedings.[44] In *Z v DPP*,[45] the Supreme Court addressed a submission, by way of judicial review, that the accused would not obtain a fair trial in circumstances where the prosecution had indicated in its Book of Evidence an intention to tender the results of DNA tests, and where the media had already publicised the apparent existence of conclusive results. Dismissing the appeal, the court accepted that difficult matters of prejudice may emerge from publicity or advance reference to DNA results, but it reasoned that "it is well within the capacity of the trial judge to avoid any potential unfairness" by means of careful directions to the jury in terms of the evidence it must consider and the matters it must ignore when determining guilt.[46] Where the DNA evidence is not ultimately received by the court—whether following a *voire dire* finding of inadmissibility, or a decision by the prosecution not to admit it—and there is a prospect in the case that members of the jury were aware of the possible existence of DNA evidence, the trial judge should, in keeping with the presumption of innocence, make an "unambiguous and clear charge" to the jury that they must "try the case on a presumption that whatever DNA testing took place did not in any way implicate the accused in the offences with which he was charged."[47]

Expertise and its Limits

12–16 The party calling the expert witness bears the burden of proving the witness' credentials as an expert in the relevant field, which is typically achieved by way of preliminary questions in-chief after the witness takes the oath. It has been argued that to qualify properly as expert testimony, the evidence must relate to a discipline that is consistent (although not necessarily uniform), methodical, cumulative, and predictive—of which medicine is usually proffered as the paradigm.[48] In America, the courts have often addressed the effects for

---

[44] *cf.* para.**5–19** *et seq.*
[45] [1994] 2 I.L.R.M. 481 (SC).
[46] *ibid.* at 501, *per* Finlay C.J.
[47] *ibid.* at 502, *per* Finlay C.J.
[48] Kenny (1983). In *R. v Gilfoyle* (CA, December 20, 2000), the novelty of an expert psychologist's methodology for determining whether the deceased had committed suicide, in a case where her husband was charged with her murder, was one reason why the Court of Appeal affirmed the trial court's decision to dismiss the appellant's application to tender the evidence. Although the psychologist was distinguished in his field, he had never before performed a "psychological autopsy", and there were no criteria available to the court for the purpose of independently testing his conclusions. The court further

evidence of the burgeoning of specialist knowledge in past decades, and the extent to which this ought to be reflected in the varieties of expert evidence admissible before the courts. Liberal admissibility rules run the risk of obfuscating the issues in each case, estranging the court from the central issues or usurping its inference-drawing function, whilst encouraging the exploitation of "junk science" in court. In light of these concerns, the US Supreme Court in *Daubert v Merrell Dow Pharmaceuticals Inc.*, sought to impose new limits by requiring that to qualify as "scientific knowledge", the "expertise" must have validated its theory or technique by proper scientific methodology.[49]

12–17 The actual and potential limitations of expert science have been highlighted in recent years by the inexactitude of psychiatric evidence. Although psychiatrists are medically qualified and therefore persons of science, there is a greater than usual difficulty in reaching consensus upon key issues. Further, within psychiatry and, to a much greater extent, psychology, "it is uniquely difficult to draw a line between matters of fact and matters of value"; the latter "may involve the tacit conveyance of a decision on principle and policy which it is not the province of the expert to make".[50] The courts are often invited to accept expert evidence by psychiatrists in criminal cases as evidence tending to establish the accused's capacity to commit the crime, and in civil cases to assess whether or not it could reasonably have been foreseen that a particular person would have harmed himself or others. Many theories have been constructed to explain aggressive or sociopathic behaviour: psychological experiences as a child such as exposure to adult violence; the biochemistry of the brain; and the link between chromosomal abnormality and deviance.[51] Many, such as the chromosomal theory, have been invalidated.[52] According to Diamond, the chief stumbling block in the path of predicting dangerousness is the lack of any clear-cut association between mental illness and dangerous behaviour.[53] Upon this basis, he proposes that psychiatrists should assert in

---

considered that the psychologist had purported to deal with matters that were within the competence of the court to determine.
[49] (1993) 113 S.C. 2786.
[50] Kenny, "The Expert in Court" (1983) 99 L.Q.R. 197 at 208.
[51] See generally: Diamond, "The Psychiatric Prediction of Dangerousness" (1974) 123 *University of Pennsylvania Law Review* 439; Megargee, "The Prediction of Dangerous Behaviour" (1976) 3 *Criminal Justice & Behavior* 3; Monahon, "The Prevention of Violence" in Monahon (ed.), *Community Mental Health and the Criminal Justice System* (New York, Pergamon Press, 1976); and Shah, "Dangerousness: A paradigm for exploring some issues in law and psychology" (1978) 33 *American Psychologist* 224.
[52] Center for Studies of Crime and Delinquency, National Institute of Mental Health, *Report of the XYY Chromosomal Abnormality* 33–34, Public Health Service Pub. No.2103, 1970.
[53] Studies have revealed that mental illnesses that most often lead to dangerousness, such as schizophrenia and other psychoses, are not more prevalent in the criminal class than in general society. Non-mental conditions such as sociopathy, alcoholism, and drug dependency have frequently been associated with criminality, however. See: Guze, Goodwin, and Crane, "Criminality and Psychiatric Disorders" (1969) 20 *Archives of General Psychiatry* 583; Guze, Tuason, Gatfield, Stewart, and Ricker, "Psychiatric Illness and Crime with Particular Reference to Alcoholism: A Study of 223 Criminals" (1962) 134 *Journal of Nervous & Mental Disorders* 512; and Cloninger and Guze, "Psychiatric

evidence that they cannot with any certainty calculate the dangerousness of a person.[54] In exonerating a psychiatric decision to maintain a schizophrenic patient as an out-patient in circumstances where the patient subsequently committed suicide, Griffin J. for the Ontario High Court commented: "Psychology and psychiatry are inexact sciences and the practice thereof should not be fettered with rules so strict as to exact an infallibility on the part of the practitioners which they could not humanly possess".[55] If this principle applies in civil proceedings taken against a psychiatrist for failing to anticipate a patient's dangerousness, it is also applies, and more exigently, in criminal proceedings to views regarding the accused's criminal or violent temperament.

Expert Witnesses in Civil Proceedings

12–18 Although the foregoing principles apply to civil cases, expert witnesses occupy a more confident position in the civil context wherein the admissibility of evidence is not constrained by concern to avoid punitive prejudice to an accused. Expert witnesses are frequently critical to the verdict, as in cases of professional negligence and proceedings seeking nullity of marriage. The expert is often permitted to draw and articulate conclusions on whether or not the defendant's conduct is causatively related to the plaintiff's or whether a party to the proceedings suffered a psychiatric or psychological illness, although the courts reserve the right to accept or reject any expert evidence tendered.[56]

12–19 The practical implication of the professional standard model of liability for medical negligence,[57] established in Ireland by *Dunne v National Maternity Hospital*[58] and in England by *Bolam v Friern Hospital*,[59] is often that the plaintiff fails to prove his case where the defendant produces credible expert opinion to support the course he took in the given circumstances: in the light of traditional medical negligence principles, the courts are disinclined to find negligence where there appears to be an honest difference of opinion between doctors,[60] so long as each view appears to represent an approved or respectable strand of medical thought.[61] It is thus usually the case that the *defendant's* expert medical testimony is pivotal to the action.

12–20 The dominance of expert medical witnesses in medical negligence

---

Illness and Female Criminality: The Role of Sociopathy and Hysteria in the Antisocial Woman" (1970) 127 *American Journal of Psychiatry* 303.
[54] Diamond, *op. cit.*, n.51 at p.452.
[55] *Haines v Bellissimo* (1977) 82 D.L.R. (3d) 215.
[56] A point emphasised by Laffoy J. in the context of nullity proceedings in which psychiatrists gave contradicting views on the petitioner's emotional ability to enter into and sustain a normal marital relationship: *PC v CH* (HC, January 11, 1996).
[57] See further, Healy, *Medical Negligence: Common Law Perspectives* (Sweet & Maxwell, London, 1999), chap.3.
[58] [1989] I.R. 91 (SC).
[59] [1957] 2 All E.R. 118.
[60] *Daniels v Heskin* [1954] I.R. 73 (SC).
[61] *Bolitho v City and Hackney H.A.* [1998] A.C. 232 (HL).

hearings for many years retarded the development of the common law duty on doctors to disclose material medical information to patients at the pre-treatment stage, otherwise known as the informed consent action. The tendency of the *Dunne* or *Bolam* model of liability to precipitate mechanically anomalous results was illustrated vividly in cases like *Gold v Haringey H.A.*[62] The plaintiff challenged the defendants' non-disclosure of two risks—a 0.2–0.6 per cent risk that her sterilisation could fail and lead to conception, and the comparatively safer 0.05 per cent risk of failure inherent in a male vasectomy. She argued that if these risks had been disclosed, she would have foregone the procedure in favour of her husband obtaining a vasectomy. Fortunately for this plaintiff, and rather unusually, all the defence's experts conceded that they personally would have advised the plaintiff of those failure rates and alternatives. In theory, however, it was not general practice to do so, and one expert estimated that some 50 per cent would not have made the contended disclosure. Upon appeal, Lloyd L.J. rejected the trial judge's description of the *Bolam* test as "exceptional", and asserted that that test is "of general application whenever a defendant professes any special skill".[63] The strange result for the plaintiff was that, although each expert witness personally endorsed disclosure of the relevant risks and alternatives, the defence succeeded because a rough estimate of general practice amongst the relevant sector of the medical community suggested that most doctors would not have disclosed the information in question.

12–21 In more recent years, the Irish courts have disentangled the medical non-disclosure claim from the professional standard test of reasonable care.[64] In doing so, they have expressed general support for the reasonable patient test or "informed consent" model first advanced in 1972 in the celebrated case of *Canterbury v Spence*,[65] where Robinson J. explained: "Respect for the patient's right to self-determination on particular therapy demands a standard set by law for physicians rather than one which physicians may or may not impose upon themselves. ... [T]he patient's right of self-decision shapes the boundaries of the duty to reveal". Under this model, expert medical evidence establishing what the defendant was required to disclose as a matter of general or approved clinical practice is no longer pivotal to determination of the facts at issue, although it remains relevant.[66]

12–22 The tendency of experts to be partisan, whether or not consciously, is stoked by the gladiatorial or adversarial nature of the common law trial. Describing her experiences as an expert medical witness, Dr Yolande Lucire observes that when "perceived to be useful, the medical practitioner is wooed

---

[62] [1988] 1 Q.B. 481 (CA).
[63] *ibid.* at 489.
[64] *Geoghegan v Harris* [2000] 3 I.R. 536, *per* Kearns J. (HC): applied in *Callaghan v Gleeson and Lavelle* (HC, July 19, 2002) *per* Johnson J.
[65] (1972) 464 F 2d 772 at 784–86, *per* Robinson J.
[66] See further, Craven, "Consent to Treatment—Disclosure Revisited" (2000) 6 *Bar Review* 111; Healy, "A Little Knowledge ... Medical Negligence: A Timely Breakthrough in the Duty to Disclose" (1999) 94(8) *Law Society Gazette* 16.

in the most flattering of tones, but when advice is inimical to the issue at hand the medical practitioner is subjected to insults in an attempt to rile and to discredit by causing the doctor to lose her cool".[67] This, Lucire accepts, derives from the nature of the adversary system, "a variant of hand to hand combat of selected gladiators, within the most rigidly formal and structured conditions".[68] On occasion, the judges have acknowledged this problem. In *Abbey National Mortgages Plc. v Key Surveyors Ltd.*, Hicks J. observed that "expert witnesses instructed upon behalf of parties to litigation often tend, if called as witnesses at all, to espouse the cause of those instructing them to a greater or lesser extent, on occasion becoming more partisan than the parties".[69] In a similar vein, Taylor has written that although medical experts are unlikely ever to "wilfully misrepresent what they think, ... their judgments become so warped by their regarding the subject in one point of view, that even when conscientiously disposed they are incapable of forming independent opinion".[70] The director of the Action for Victims of Medical Accidents in England—which holds a database of about 2,000 potential experts for plaintiffs—has stated that it "the best paid Saturday job on the market".[71] The extent to which experts can unwittingly become hired guns for one side of a dispute, and the damaging implications this may have for the integrity of the profession they represent, was highlighted by a study of 500 psychiatrists for the Institute of Psychiatry in England.[72] 25 per cent of those surveyed conceded that they had been asked to alter or edit their reports. 50 per cent of these agreed to make crucial changes even to their conclusions. In many instances, selective editing had been performed by lawyers: indeed 90 per cent of the requests to amend had been made by solicitors. In a test of claims against the Workers' Compensation Board of New York, it was found that while 99.5 per cent of doctors consulted by claimants concluded that their claimants were suffering a disability, only 24 per cent of doctors for the insurers reached the same conclusion.[73]

12–23 The critical importance of medical expert evidence in negligence proceedings presents numerous difficulties for plaintiffs seeking to establish medical negligence, not least the difficulty of obtaining national medical experts willing to censure the conduct of the defendant—a situation addressed in England by the establishment of panels of expert witnesses appointed to give evidence on behalf of the court rather than the parties. This difficulty—expressed in the context of the State of California—was observed eloquently by Justice Carter of the Supreme Court, as follows: "[P]hysicians who are

---

[67] Lucire, "The Expert Witness Self-Examined" in Winfield (ed.), *The Expert Medical Witness* (Federation Press, Sydney, 1989) at p.89.
[68] *ibid.*
[69] [1996] 1 W.L.R. 1534 at 1542 (CA).
[70] Taylor, *Treatise on the Law of Evidence* (12th ed., Maxwell, London, 1931) at p.59.
[71] Cited in Bawdon, "A crowded thoroughfare" (1996) *New Law Journal Supplement* 1742-3.
[72] Reported in *Sunday Times*, May 12, 1996.
[73] Haddad, "Analysis of 2932 Workers' Compensation back injury cases" (1987) 12 *Spine* 765.

members of medical societies flock to the defense of their fellow member charged with malpractice and the plaintiff is relegated, for his expert testimony, to the occasional lone wolf or heroic soul, who for the sake of truth and justice has the courage to run the risk of ostracism by his fellow practitioners and the cancellation of his public liability insurance policy".[74] That is to say that members of professions tend to be institutionally and socially collegial.[75] One research survey of medical professionals revealed that in the hypothetical (and grossly negligent) scenario of a doctor who mistakenly removed a patient's good kidney instead of his diseased kidney, merely 31 per cent of specialists and 27 per cent of general practitioners expressed a willingness to testify on behalf of the plaintiff patient.[76] The problem is compounded further by an undeveloped assumption that the plaintiff is required in every medical negligence action to advance some expert medical evidence in support of his case;[77] in this endeavour, "rightly or wrongly there tends to be safety in numbers",[78] as was evident in the case of *Dunne v National Maternity Hospital*.[79] By contrast, it is the case that defendants, better placed to corral support within the medical profession, tend often to dominate the trial with a display of numerical supremacy. This tendency to flood the court with "big battalions of expert witnesses" has occasionally been criticised by judges.[80] Nonetheless, it persists. Indeed, one judge recently decided, albeit with some reluctance, that the court lacks the power to deny expert evidence or to limit the number of experts even where it feels that the evidence is not strictly necessary.[81]

III. EXPERT EVIDENCE AND HEARSAY

12–24 An expert witness is subject to the same rules of evidence as a non-expert witness, and this includes the rule against hearsay. Accordingly, the expert must testify personally—although throughout his testimony, he may refer to notes he made contemporaneously with the events in question.[82] The

---

[74] *Huffman v Lindquist* (1951) 234 P. 2d 34 at 46.
[75] Belli, "An Ancient therapy Still Applied: The Silent Medical Treatment" (1956) 1 *Villanova Law Review* 255.
[76] Referred to in *Morris v Metriyakool* (1981) 309 N.W. 2d 910.
[77] This is suggested by the wording of the *Bolam* test [1957] 2 All E.R. 118 at 121, which emphasises that the "true test ... is whether [the defendant] *has been proved* to be guilty of such failure as no doctor of ordinary skill would be guilty of if acting with ordinary care". The court was presented with an untypical scenario in *Thake v Maurice* [1984] 2 All E.R. 513 at 521–2. On the one hand, the plaintiff had failed to produce expert testimony; on the other, the defendant admitted that he erred in failing to give a warning. In these circumstances, the court felt that to raise the *Bolam* argument against the plaintiff would be to turn an "utterly artificial argument" to mere "tactical advantage". This was endorsed by the Court of Appeal in *Thake v Maurice* [1986] 1 All E.R. 497 at 506.
[78] McMahon and Binchy, *Irish Law of Torts* (2nd ed., Butterworths, Dublin, 1990) at p.264.
[79] [1989] I.R. 91 (SC).
[80] *Midland Bank Trust v Hett, Stubbs & Kemp* [1978] 3 All E.R. 571 at 582, *per* Oliver J.
[81] *Rawlinson v Westbrook*, reported in *The Times*, January 25, 1995.
[82] *cf.* para.**2–41** *et seq.*

Opinion and Expert Evidence 367

courts have recognised some flexibility with respect to the application of the hearsay rule to experts. Expert witnesses are generally free to draw upon research and premises established by others in their specialised field, although they must identify their sources and methodology to the court so that they may be tested in the event of challenge.[83] The expert is required to identify all the "primary facts" upon which his professional opinion is based, such as in *R. v Abadom* [84] the refractive index of glass used to assess the particles of glass found embedded in shoes worn by the accused.

12–25 The Irish courts appear to have recognised a potentially broad qualification to the rule against hearsay, at least in civil proceedings affecting the welfare of a child, permitting the admissibility of videotaped interviews between the expert and the child where necessary to enable the court to appraise the merits of the expert's opinion on the sexual abuse as alleged.[85] This view was repeated by the Supreme Court in *Southern Health Board v CH*,[86] where the court approved the admissability of videotaped interviews with the child complainant upon which the social worker, as expert witness, had formed an opinion of sexual abuse. The direction seems fated to undermine the certainty of the hearsay rule, and it is useful to consider the extent to which it will be developed in light of the fact that the legislature, by enacting the Children Act 1997 shortly after *CH*, addressed the hearsay rule in child welfare cases, suspending the rule as it applies to pre-hearing statements by the child in proceedings affecting the welfare of a child.[87]

12–26 The delicate issues arising from the reception of videotaped interviews between children and social workers or child counsellors was carefully considered by the Court of Appeal in *Re N*,[88] and these are likely to be of considerable guidance in Ireland, given recent provision here for the admissibility of videotaped interviews in civil proceedings pursuant to the Children Act 1997, and to a more limited extent in criminal proceedings pursuant to s.16 of the Criminal Evidence Act 1992.[89] The court found that expert evidence is admissible to shed light upon statements made in such interviews, the emotions and body language of the complainant, and any signs of fantasy or unreliability. (The court did not, however, consider that social workers possessed the requisite specialist training, and that competence to give expert evidence on these matters necessitates qualifications and experience specifically in the area of child psychology or psychiatry.) The expert is restricted, however, to observing consistencies or inconsistencies in the complainant's accounts, and may not properly comment upon whether the complainant is to be believed (since this would be to trespass upon the inference-

---

[83] *cf.* para.**9–55**.
[84] [1983] 1 W.L.R. 126 (CA).
[85] *State (D and D) v Groarke* [1990] 1 I.R. 305 (SC).
[86] [1996] 1 I.R. 219 (SC): *cf.* appendix 50.
[87] *cf.* para.**9–46** *et seq.*
[88] CA, March 14, 1996.
[89] *cf.* para.**1–65** *et seq.*

drawing and fact-finding responsibility of the court). Although this line is naturally difficult to enforce when an expert is invited to comment upon the consistency of an account, the trial judge is in a position to supervise examination of the expert and to mitigate any inadmissible opinions by means of judicial direction. In *Re N.*, the matter was returned for rehearing, on the basis that the trial judge had too readily accepted the inadmissible opinion of the complainant's guardian *ad litem* that the complainant was being truthful—further, the interview had been given under pressurised conditions driven by the child protection team, and this along with other factors such as lapse of time, engendered acute risks that the interview was contaminated.

IV. NON-EXPERT OPINION EVIDENCE

12–27 In many cases, statements of perceived fact by witnesses belie their underlying assumptions and opinions; the task of disentangling the interpretative elements of the witness' perception and recollection falls chiefly to the cross-examiner. Ordinary witnesses are sometimes permitted to express opinions arising from the facts narrated in their testimony. In general, the witness may be permitted to convey ordinary observations in their description of people or events, such as that a person appeared young or agitated, where intrinsic to the relevant facts perceived by him[90] and where not an excessive intrusion upon the function of the court to determine the ultimate issues before it. The witness may express opinions on his own condition. Witnesses who are acquainted with the handwriting of a person relevant to the proceedings may give evidence for the purpose of recognition of the handwriting. The argument that only a handwriting expert was competent to do so was rejected in *People (DPP) v Malocco*.[91] Further, s.8 of the Criminal Procedure Act 1865 (Denman's Act) provides that witnesses may, for the purposes of establishing the genuineness of a piece of "disputed writing", compare it "with any writing provided to the satisfaction of the judge to be genuine."

12–28 A witness may be permitted by statute to express an admissible opinion.[92] Section 3(2) of the Offences Against the State (Amendment) Act 1972 provides, for the purpose of the charge of membership of an unlawful organisation contrary to s.21 of the Offences Against the State Act 1939, that when a garda officer, not below the rank of chief superintendent, states in

---

[90] May, *Criminal Evidence* (4th ed., Sweet & Maxwell, London, 1999) at p.164.
[91] CCA, May 23, 1996.
[92] For instance, under s.3(4)(b) of the Domestic Violence Act, 1996, to obtain a barring order against a co-habitant to whom he is not married, the applicant must possess an interest in the dwelling at least equal to the respondent's, and for the purpose of the application the applicant is permitted to state his belief that he has a legal or beneficial interest in the dwelling not less than that of the respondent. Section 4 of the Competition (Amendment) Act 1996 reflects the general common rule permitting expert evidence by a person with due qualifications and experience: in proceedings relating to an offence under s.2 of the Act, the opinion of any witness possessing the appropriate qualities or expertise relevant to his evidence shall be admissible.

evidence that "he believes that the accused was at a material time a member of an unlawful organisation, the statement shall be evidence that he was then such a member". In *Attorney-General v O'Leary*,[93] Costello J. rightly interpreted this provision to function as an exception to the rule against opinion evidence, rendering "admissible in evidence in certain trials statements of belief which would otherwise be inadmissible", but that it did not render the garda's opinion conclusive of the fact of membership. The court is free to accept or reject the garda's belief, testimonially asserted, that the accused was a member of an unlawful organisation at the material time. The draconian nature of s.3(2) was evident in *People (DPP) v Gannon*,[94] where the Court of Criminal Appeal ruled that if a decision is taken not to cross-examine the garda or to tender evidence to rebut his belief, the court may accept the garda's evidence and convict the accused upon it "without in any way infringing the principles of natural justice or the constitutional rights of the accused". McCracken J. further ruled that the cogency and weight of the witness' asserted belief that the accused was a member of an unlawful organisation is enhanced by the accused's failure to testify. A challenge to the witness' opinion must be made directly, and a plea of guilty does not of itself detract from the opinion, which, if unchallenged, may be weighty notwithstanding that the witness was not asked to explain the factual basis for his testimonial belief.

12–29 Evidence given by the gardaí with respect to road traffic offences is treated as non-expert opinion evidence in Ireland for the purposes of the rule. The admissibility of the garda's evidence as to the apparent drunkenness of the accused is not, in principle, contingent upon proof that forensic assessment of his condition was duly conducted,[95] although in trials of offences for which speed of the car is a fact at issue, the prosecution must corroborate the garda's evidence of the car's apparent speed by evidence from another source or witness.[96] A garda is permitted as an ordinary witness in the case to give evidence of his view that the accused was drunk or intoxicated at the material time, and he may also express a view as to how drunk the accused was, even where the inference goes to the issue, as in prosecutions for drink driving. This view was adopted by the High Court and the Supreme Court in *Attorney-General (Ruddy) v Kenny*,[97] where a garda testified that the accused driver had appeared "bleary" and "smelling of drink". Davitt P. found: "Drunkenness, unfortunately, is a condition which is not so exceptional or so much outside the experience of the ordinary individual, that it should require an expert to diagnose it. In my opinion a Garda witness, or an ordinary witness, may give

---

[93] [1991] I.L.R.M. 454 (HC): *cf.* appendix 39. See also *People (Attorney-General) v Ferguson* (CCA, October 27, 1975).
[94] CCA, April 2, 2003, *per* McCracken J. See also *Attorney-General v Ferguson* (CCA, October 17, 1975).
[95] In *People (DPP) v Quirke* (HC, March 3, 2003), admissibility of the garda's testimonial assertion that the accused was drunk at the material time was unaffected by the alleged unreliability of the alcolyser test administered (20 minutes not having been allowed to elapse after the time of arrest); *cf.* para.**11–38**.
[96] Road Traffic Act 1961, s.105; *cf.* para.**5–18**.
[97] (1960) 94 I.L.T.R. 185 (HC/SC).

evidence of his opinion on whether a person is drunk".[98] Davitt P. was further of the view that where an ordinary witness is permitted to express an opinion as to whether the accused was drunk or not, "it should be admissible for him to express an opinion as to *how* drunk he was".[99]

12–30 In so finding, Davitt P. approved the view expressed in *R. v German*[100] that an ordinary witness may testify to matters of identity, the apparent age of a person, and the speed of movement. The learned judge was also influenced by the prospect that an ordinary witness to the scene of a crime or an arrest may be in the best position to give accurate, sensible evidence of the state of mind, appearance, or behaviour of the accused, as it might have taken some time for a doctor or other qualified expert to arrive. The court emphasised that its decision was based upon the admissibility of the evidence and that any challenges to the accuracy or reliability of the opinion would affect the weight properly to be attached to it by the trial court. A majority of the Supreme Court was "completely in accord" with the principles established by Davitt P; Lavery J. observed: "When it is a matter of thick speech, uncertainty of gait, inability to walk a straight line (in any event a most unreliable guide), smell from breath, drowsiness, truculence, argumentativeness, and other observable symptoms, I think any reasonable person can express a view based upon the sum total of his observations".[101]

12–31 Whilst the courts' findings upon the range of questions an ordinary witness is permitted to answer appears sensible and appropriate, the correctness of the courts' approach in the specific context of drink driving is questionable having regard to the general rule that a witness is not competent to form and express inferences upon the ultimate issues before the court. In this regard, Kingsmill-Moore J.'s dissent is cogent, resting upon the traditional confinement of witnesses to the narration of facts observed directly by one or more of their senses. Kingsmill-Moore J. proposed instead that the witness be permitted "to describe the appearance, movements, demeanour, actions and words of a person whose condition is in question and leaving it to the District Justice to draw his own conclusions".[102]

---

[98] *ibid.* at 187.
[99] *ibid.*
[100] *English and Empire Digest*, vol. 2 at p.124.
[101] (1960) 94 I.L.T.R. 185 at 189 (HC/SC).
[102] *ibid.* at 192.

Further Reading

Alldridge, "Scientific Expertise and Comparative Criminal Procedure" (1999) 3 Int. J. E. & P. 141.
Balding and Donnelly "The Prosecutor's Fallacy and DNA Evidence" [1994] Crim. L.R. 711.
Howard, "The Neutral Expert: A Plausible Threat to Justice" [1991] Crim. L.R. 98.
Jackson, "The Ultimate Issue Rule: One Rule Too Many" [1984] Crim. L.R. 75.
Kenny, "The Expert in Court" (1983) 99 L.Q.R. 197.
Mackay and Colman, "Equivocal Rulings on Expert Psychological and Psychiatric Evidence" [1996] Crim. L.R. 88.
Ormerod, "Scientific Evidence in Court" [1968] Crim. L.R. 240.
Ormerod, "The Evidential Implications of Psychological Profiling" [1996] Crim. L.R. 863.
Pattenden, "Expert Evidence Based on Hearsay" [1982] Crim. L.R. 85.
Roberts, "Science in the Criminal Process" (1994) 14 Oxford J. L.S.
Sheldon and MacLeod, "From Normative to Positive Date: Expert Psychological Evidence Re-Examined" [1991] Crim. L.R. 811.
Sheldrick, "Expert Evidence, Sexual Assault, and the Testimony of Children: *R. v D.D.*" (2001) 5 Int. J. E. & P. 199.
Spencer, "The Neutral Expert: An Implausible Bogey" [1991] Crim. L.R. 106.
Ward, "Law, Common Sense and the Authority of Science: Expert Witnesses and Criminal Insanity in England, CA. 1840–1940" (1997) 6 *Social and Legal Studies* 343.
Ward, "Psychiatric Evidence and Judicial Fact-Finding" (2000) Int. J. E. & P. 180.
Young, "DNA Evidence: Beyond Reasonable Doubt" [1991] Crim. L.R. 264.

CHAPTER 13

PRIVILEGE

I. Private Privilege: General Principles	13–01
Secondary Evidence	13–08
Waiver	13–10
Communications in Furtherance of Crime or Iniquity	13–13
Family Law Proceedings Affecting the Welfare of Children	13–17
Proceedings under the Succession Act 1965	13–19
II. Legal Professional Privilege	13–20
Scope of Protected "Communications"	13–25
Disclosure of Expert Witness Reports	13–28
Distinction between Legal Advice and Legal Assistance	13–33
Communications in Furtherance of Settlement	13–36
Documents in Existence Prior to Legal Advice	13–39
Communications to Third Parties	13–41
Documents Created for Mixed Purposes	13–42
Advice to Remain Silent and Adverse Inferences	13–45
III. Confidential Relationships	13–47
Sacerdotal Privilege	13–49
Counsellors' Privilege	13–52
IV. Privileges Against Revealing Informants	13–53
Common Law Privileges	13–54
The Constitution: Executive and Parliamentary	13–62
V. Marital Privacy	13–66
VI. Public Interest Privilege	13–69
VII. Privilege Against Self-Incrimination	13–80
The Right to Silence	13–84
Compulsorily Acquired Self-Incriminating Evidence	13–92
Adverse Inferences from Silence	13–100

I. PRIVATE PRIVILEGE: GENERAL PRINCIPLES

13–01 A private privilege operates so that the person to whom it attaches, whether or not party to legal proceedings, may decline to answer certain questions or to produce certain documents, howsoever relevant and admissible in the proceedings, and he may compel others from doing so. Privilege raises a bar against revealing particular *information*, and as such it is distinct from competence and compellability to testify:[1] a competent witness compelled to testify may invoke a privilege to resist answering certain questions during his testimony, or may waive his privilege against doing so, as the case may be. The issue of privilege is also distinct from the issue of admissibility. Hearsay evidence does not change its character when a witness waives his privilege against saying it. In addition to the public interest privilege, there are now a number of different private privileges—chief amongst them the privilege against self-incrimination and the related right to silence; the legal professional privilege; informer privilege; sacerdotal and counselling privilege; and marital privilege. The bulk of reported case law on privilege has arisen in the context of disputes over discovery of documentation in civil proceedings, and over the privilege against self-incrimination and the right to silence in criminal proceedings.

13–02 Traditionally under the common law, once a private privilege applied, it did so absolutely by rule and not discretion. The question of disclosure was decided in terms of whether the privilege applied, and it did not entitle the court to determine the matter by weighing competing interests. In Ireland, as in other common law jurisdictions, private privilege has become a public matter, and it is now necessarily decided by reference to rights and public interests developed under the Constitution. The Irish courts routinely decide the question of disclosure or discovery after weighing the public interest served by the private privilege against the public interest (and right of the other party) in placing all the material evidence before the court.[2] Whilst this has altered the nature and methodology of privilege law in Ireland, it has not led to any significant expansion of the basis or type of privilege now recognised. The courts repeatedly express the public interest in restricting privileges and promoting the admission of material evidence before the court.[3] Private privilege has similarly been constitutionalised and renovated in other jurisdictions such as Canada and Australia. In *Solosky v R*,[4] the Supreme Court of Canada, following an extensive review of case law, acknowledged that privilege had outstripped its status "merely as a rule of evidence which acts as a shield to prevent privileged materials from being tendered in evidence", and that the courts had effectively elevated privilege to a new plane, extended beyond its traditional bounds.

13–03 English law has differed, adhering to the strict application of private privileges. Cross was notably sceptical about subjecting private privilege to judicial discretion, arguing that it would engender uncertainty with respect to the range of matters over which privilege could be claimed.[5] The issue came

---

[1] *cf.* para.**2–03** *et seq.*
[2] *Smurfit Paribas Bank v A.A.B. Export Finance* [1990] 1 I.R. 469, *per* Finlay C.J. (SC): *cf.* appendix 35.
[3] Expressed in *Calcraft v Guest* [1898] 1 Q.B. 759 and more recently by the Supreme Court in *Smurfit Paribas Bank, ibid.*
[4] (1979) D.L.R. (3d) 745 at 757 (SC, Can.).
[5] *Cross on Evidence* at p.422.

to the fore eventually in England in *R. v Derby Magistrates Ex p.B*,[6] which proceeded a Court of Appeal decision encouraging judges to engage in a discretionary weighing with respect to discovery of privileged documents likely to exonerate an accused in criminal proceedings (which, by tradition, the common law had sanctioned only in the context of the informer privilege).[7] In *Derby Magistrates*, the witness claimed privilege over documents created in the context of earlier trials, when he had at first confessed to the murder of the girl in question, but then made a statement, leading to his acquittal, in which he asserted that he had been present during the murder and that it had been committed by his stepfather. Under cross-examination at the stepfather's trial, the witness refused to answer questions with respect to advice he received from his solicitor prior to his decision to confess to the murder. The trial judge, applying favourable authority in *R. v Ataou*,[8] considered that the interest served by the privilege fell to be balanced against the competing interest served by disclosure, and that in this case the stepfather's right to a fair trial (with all the material evidence placed before it) outweighed the witness' interest in preserving the confidentiality of past legal advice. The House of Lords, after a lengthy review of the history of the privilege, disagreed upon the basis that once a private privilege applies, it does so absolutely. Whilst the court went to considerable pains to emphasise the fundamental public interest served by the legal professional privilege, it refused to develop the privilege in tandem with the approach adopted generally for public privilege.[9]

13–04 As a result of the strict effect of privilege in England, its courts are more likely to balance any competing interests and to exercise judicial discretion when deciding the *scope* of the privilege and the communications to which the privilege applies.[10] Given the freer hand that Irish judges have to balance any competing interests on a case-by-case basis, there is less need in Ireland to adopt an unduly strict or technical approach to the scope of privilege or range of communications attracting privilege, despite decisions such as *Smurfit Paribas Bank v A.A.B. Export Finance*.[11]

13–05 The Supreme Court decided in *Bula Ltd. (in receivership) v Crowley*[12] that where privilege is claimed in response to a request for discovery, the deponent must individually list the documents and identify the privilege respectively claimed, so "as would convey to the reader of the affidavit the general nature of the document concerned in each individual case together with the broad heading of privilege being claimed for it."[13] The judges may inspect a document to ascertain if the claim of privilege is well-founded.

---

[6] [1996] A.C. 487 (HL).
[7] *R. v Ataou* [1988] Q.B. 709 (CA); *cf.* para.**13–58** *et seq.*
[8] *ibid.*
[9] Commentary [1996] Crim. L.R. 191.
[10] *e.g. Waugh v British Railways Board* [1980] A.C. 521 (HL); *cf.* para.**13–40**.
[11] [1990] 1 I.R. 469 (SC): *cf.* para.**13–31** *et seq.*
[12] [1990] I.L.R.M. 756 (SC): *cf.* appendix 38.
[13] *ibid.* at 758, *per* Finlay C.J.

13–06 The high level of pre-hearing discovery and disclosure generally provided in civil proceedings has not been mirrored in criminal proceedings, due chiefly to the more rigid approach to admissibility rules in the criminal context and the traditionally narrow scope of statutory pre-trial disclosure required from the prosecution under the Criminal Procedure Act 1967, as amended.[14] The pre-trial duty on the prosecutor to seek out, preserve, and disclose relevant evidence for the benefit of the defence has been developed by the present Supreme Court in recent years, however, in a series of cases applying principles of constitutional and criminal justice.[15] As this duty develops, so too may the scope and quality of documentary disclosure to be made by the prosecutor.[16] The rules of court governing discovery in civil proceedings have been construed not to apply to criminal proceedings.[17] The matter was considered by the Supreme Court in *Sweeney v Director of Rape Crisis Centre*,[18] in the context of an appeal against an order of non-party discovery made in favour of the accused and against the Rape Crisis Centre. Following consideration of the ancestry of discovery in Equity and the open-ended nature of the Rules of the Supreme Court (Ireland) 1905 (referring to discovery in the context of 'any cause or matter'), Geoghegan J. observed that discovery orders had never been made in criminal proceedings and that it "would have been clear that the rules relating to discovery would not have been intended to include criminal proceedings." The learned judge distinguished the prosecutor's duty to furnish adequate pre-trial disclosure of relevant evidence from discovery procedures. The former springs from the constitutional requirement of fair procedures; it requires that the prosecution reveal its hand to the defence prior to the trial, but it does not apply mutually to require the accused to do likewise (save in exceptional cases, where for instance the defence of alibi is raised). Finding in favour of the appellant, Geoghegan J. approved a decision in *People (DPP) v Flynn and Keely*,[19] where Moriarty J. refused the application (*inter alia*) because:

---

[14] *cf.* para.**1–66**.
[15] *cf.* para.**1–42** *et seq.*
[16] It is clear that recent development of this duty has influenced the framing of grounds of appeal. In *People (DPP) v Nevin* (CCA, March 14, 2003), one of the grounds of appeal was that the prosecution's refusal to disclose documentation relevant to an investigation of Jack White's pub for paramilitary association had unfairly hampered the accused's defence. The court rejected the claim having regard to the fact that an association with paramilitary activity had been ruled out by the gardai and the probative value of the documentation was minimal.
[17] It was recently argued before the Supreme Court in *McKevitt v DPP* (March 18, 2003), however, that the failure of the prosecution to organise disclosure of documents in a comparable manner to civil discovery affected the fairness of the trial process. Keane C.J. declined to express a view upon the failure to catalogue, index, or collate the relevant material. For the purpose of the judicial review application, he decided that the Special Criminal Court had acted within jurisdiction when deciding the extent of disclosure required in the applicant's trial for membership of an illegal organisation and the new crime of directing terrorism, contrary to the Offences Against the State (Amendment) Act 1998.
[18] [2001] 4 I.R. 101 (SC).
[19] [1996] 1 I.L.R.M. 317 at 319 (Cir. C).

"The principle that each party should be entitled to know from the other in advance any information that would enhance his own case or destroy his adversary's case was less applicable in criminal proceedings where the entire burden of proof rested on the prosecution. Discovery was intended to be mutual between the parties and it could not be mutual in a criminal case because it would not be ordered against the accused. It followed that a non-party should not be subjected to a greater obligation than could be imposed on the accused."

13–07 A person or witness must himself assert his privilege, and in judicial proceedings a trial judge is under no duty to claim it on behalf of the party or to advise him accordingly, unless the party is an accused in criminal proceedings protected by the right to silence.[20] The privileges are highly personal in effect, so that no other party can complain about the privileged party's decision to waive privilege over the matters in question; nor may adverse inferences be drawn from a person's recourse to the privilege.[21]

Secondary Evidence

13–08 Generally, if evidence is deemed inadmissible, secondary evidence of it, such as a copy, is also inadmissible. With respect to privilege, by contrast, the *information* and matters contained in privileged material may be proved by other means—such as by testimony from a different witness, or skilful cross-examination of the privileged party. Although a privilege may attach to a document for the benefit of a particular person, secondary evidence of the information that derives from sight of the original document may sometimes be accepted from another source. In the controversial and somewhat unpopular decision in *Calcraft v Guest*,[22] witnesses who had copied original privileged documents, accidentally left in their possession, were permitted to prove their contents. The Court of Appeal reasoned that this would be permissible even if the documents had fallen into another's hands by unlawful or improper means— an approach that instantly appears incompatible with the preference in Ireland for balancing constitutional rights and considerations of public interest. *Calcraft* was followed in *R. v Tompkins*,[23] with respect to handwritten notes discovered on the floor of the court by opposing counsel and in which the accused revealed incriminating information. This ill considered perspective has been abandoned in more recent years. In *I.T.C. Film Distributors Ltd. v Video Exchange Ltd.*,[24] Warner J. asserted that obtaining another party's documents when in the courts, whether by trick (as in this case) or by stealth, and then putting them in evidence in affidavits for motions, amounted to a contempt of court, and the court certainly should not admit the documents or any copies made of them at the request of the filcher. In *English and American Insurance Co. Ltd. v Herbert*

---

[20] *cf.* para.**2–18** *et seq.*
[21] *Wentworth v Lloyd* (1864) 10 HL Cas. 589.
[22] [1898] 1 Q.B. 759 (CA).
[23] (1977) 67 Cr. App. R. 181 (CA).
[24] [1982] 1 Ch. 431.

Smith & Co.,[25] the privileged documents were mistakenly rerouted with a batch of papers by a law clerk to the opponent's solicitors. Although the court did not formally overrule *Calcraft*, Brown-Wilkinson V.-C. noted other cases of similar circumstances where the privilege had been enforced,[26] and he found for the plaintiffs, observing that it would be "most undesirable if the security which is the basis of that freedom [of speech between lawyer and client were] to be prejudiced by mischances which are of everyday occurrence leading to documents which have escaped being used by the other side".

13–09 The common law recognises that privilege may be waived by the party who is entitled to claim or assert the privilege. It further recognises by way of a general exception that privilege does not attach to communications in furtherance of a crime or fraud. Beyond these two formal cut-off points, where the proceedings are less adversarial, private privilege may be applied more in the nature of an interest to be weighed against other competing interests: as in cases affecting the welfare of children; or of inherent jurisdiction such as wardship proceedings; or of proceedings governed by statute such as the Succession Act 1965.

Waiver

13–10 A private privilege may be waived by the party entitled to claim the privilege. In this sense, an arrested person may impliedly waive his right to silence, following due caution of his rights.[27] Where he testifies at his trial, he waives another aspect of this right to the extent that he may be asked questions tending directly to implicate him in the offence with which he is charged,[28] although he retains the privilege against self-incrimination with respect to his involvement in other offences, and he benefits from a prohibition against cross-examination upon his character or criminal record.[29]

13–11 As a general rule, only the maker of a statement may waive privilege over it.[30] The party entitled to claim or waive the legal professional privilege is the client, not the lawyer,[31] although case law recognises, applying agency principles, that privilege may be lost following revelation by the lawyer of the information contained in the document,[32] and where the lawyer is not acting outside the bounds of his instructions. This flows from the principle that

---

[25] [1988] F.S.R. 232.
[26] *Ashburton v Pape* [1913] 2 Ch. 469 (CA); *Goddard v Nationwide Building Society* [1987] Q.B. 670 (CA).
[27] *cf.* paras **10–17** *et seq.*, **10–26**.
[28] Criminal Justice (Evidence) Act 1924, s.1(e).
[29] *cf.* para.**8–01** *et seq.*
[30] So held in *Hehir v Commissioners of Police of the Metropolis* [1982] 1 W.L.R. 715 (CA), finding that the defendant could not waive privilege over a statement made by the plaintiff for the purpose of an internal investigation by the defendant into the alleged misconduct of two police officers.
[31] *McMullen v Carty* (SC, January 27, 1998); *cf.* para.**13–23**.
[32] *Burnwell v British Transport Commission* [1956] 1 Q.B.D. 187.

privilege may implicitly and constructively be waived. The Supreme Court acknowledged in *McMullen v Carty*[33] that where a client sues his solicitor for alleged negligence in the conduct of earlier proceedings, he implicitly waives his privilege with respect not only to communications between the solicitor and himself but also as between the solicitor and counsel retained for the case. He has done so by putting the communications in issue. In *Great Atlantic Insurance v Home Insurance Co.*,[34] the Court of Appeal decided that where some part of the privileged document is adduced as evidence in judicial proceedings, the court has a right to insist upon seeing the entire document unless the remainder may be severed distinctly from the other part. This view stems from the principle that parties cannot edit their evidence.[35]

13–12 The English courts have recently considered the effect of reference in the trial to information contained in privileged documents, and whether incidental or intentional reference has a knock-on effect in shedding the document and other related documents of its privileged status through implied waiver. Phipson has long been of the view that English law unnecessarily protects against the loss of privilege in this way, and that where a party reveals part of his hand, privilege should be lost extensively.[36] This sentiment was endorsed by Auld L.J. in the Divisional Court in *R. v Secretary of State Transport and Factortame Ltd.*[37] Whilst it was accepted that reference to information in one document may cause privilege to be lost in respect of a broad set of documents privileged upon the same basis, this will not occur if the partially disclosed material does not bear upon the matters at issue with respect to the privilege claimed. As the reference had been made to a distinct period, the documents were thereby impliedly waived, but were clearly severable from documents relating to different periods of time.

Communications in Furtherance of Crime or Iniquity

13–13 According to this common law exception, communications in furtherance of a crime, fraud, or iniquity are not privileged. Upon the basis that the document was being used to suborn witnesses in *People (Attorney-General) v Coleman*,[38] all claims to marital or legal professional privilege were lost when it was discovered that the note, intercepted by a prison warder during an interview between the accused and his wife, listed other women for whom the accused had performed unlawful abortions.

13–14 The scope of the exception as developed by the courts is indirectly a question of the true scope of the privilege. In *R. v Cox*,[39] where the exception

---

[33] SC, January 27, 1998.
[34] [1981] 1 W.L.R. 529 (CA).
[35] Recognised also by Mustill J. in *Nea Kateria Maritime Co. Ltd. v Atlantic Corp. and Great Lakes Steamship* (1981) COMM L.R. 138.
[36] *Phipson on Evidence* (14th ed., Sweet & Maxwell, London, 1990) at p.527.
[37] Divisional Court, May 6, 1997.
[38] [1945] I.R. 237 (CCA).
[39] (1884) 14 Q.B.D. 153.

was authoritatively discussed in the context of lawyer-client correspondence, Stephen J. rationalised it upon the basis that a "communication in furtherance of a criminal purpose does not come within the ordinary scope of professional employment".[40] In principle, the court explained, the result is the same where the lawyer had no actual knowledge of the criminal purpose that prompted the client's request for legal advice or assistance. Privilege is not necessarily lost, however, if the lawyer warns the client that unless he acts in a certain way he will be liable to prosecution—as held in *Butler v Board of Trade*[41]—since the common law recognises that a legitimate function of legal advice is to warn clients of the possible consequences of their actions. In *Butler*, the court rejected a broader test that would withdraw privilege in any case where the communication was *relevant to* the commission of a crime or fraud. Instead, it favoured the view that the communication must have been "*in furtherance of* a crime or fraud". The exception did not, however, apply to a letter in which a solicitor urged her client to take care not to incur serious consequences for his conduct, since this lacked "any element of vice which the umbrella or confidence may not in general cover".[42]

13–15 For privilege to be lost on this ground, the party seeking disclosure must usually establish the other party's involvement in an offence or conduct proscribed as moral turpitude, fraud, criminal dishonesty, or "conduct constituting a direct interference with the administration of justice".[43] Initially identified with respect to criminal purposes, the exception was subsequently applied to cases of corporate fraud[44] and civil conspiracy to injure another trade or business.[45] In *Crawford v Treacy*,[46] the argument was made, but rejected as a matter of fact, that communications between a solicitor and client were not privileged because they were in furtherance of an attempt to enable the deceased to defeat the legal entitlement of his wife under the Succession Act 1965. The allegation of statutory offence or tort, such as unlawful inducement to breach a contract[47] or trespass,[48] does not *of itself* justify loss of the privilege where unaccompanied by reprehensible behaviour. By contrast, improper conduct that has the effect of abusing the process of the courts, such as the bringing of a malicious prosecution,[49] divests the communication of privilege.

---

[40] *ibid.* at 166.
[41] [1971] 1 Ch. 680.
[42] *ibid.* at 689, *per* Goff J.
[43] *Bula Ltd. v Crowley (No.2)* [1994] 2 I.R. 54 at 58, *per* Finlay C.J. (SC).
[44] *Williams v Quebrada Railway, Land and Copper Ltd.* [1895] 2 Ch. 751, with respect to the claim that charges had unlawfully been created at a time the company was insolvent in an attempt to defeat the claims of floating charge holders.
[45] *Gamlen Chemical Co. (U.K.) Ltd. v Rochem Ltd.* [1983] R.P.C. 1.
[46] HC, November 4, 1998.
[47] *Crescent Farm (Sidcup) Sports Ltd. v Sterling Offices Ltd.* [1972] Ch. 553.
[48] *Dubai Aluminum Co. Ltd. v Al Alawi* [1999] 1 All E.R. 703.
[49] As occurred in *Murphy v Kirwan* [1993] 3 I.R. 501 (SC).

13–16 In *Murphy v Kirwan*,[50] the Supreme Court was divided on the level of proof required to substantiate an allegation of malicious prosecution raised by the counter-claiming defendants in an attempt to defeat the plaintiff's claim to legal professional privilege over communications with his lawyers. Proof was particularly at issue in the case given that the privilege was claimed in the context of discovery prior to a hearing of the substantive issues. Finlay C.J., in his majority judgment, favoured the view that the party seeking disclosure should establish that his allegation is "plausible or viable", whilst Egan J., dissenting, considered that "[t]here must be some prima facie evidence that the allegation has a foundation in fact".[51] Although the wording of the respective tests do not appear substantially different, prima facie proof may require some element of persuasive evidence sufficient to justify a reasonable inference in favour of the proposition. The difference was evident in the judges' respective findings of fact. Finlay C.J. concluded that the counter-claiming defendants had made a plausible case for the allegation in a series of affidavits filed to date in the proceedings, whilst Egan J. concluded that an insufficient case had been established upon proof merely that the earlier proceedings had been dismissed and that a charge of malicious prosecution had been made and repeated in various affidavits of the defendant. The test of "viable and plausible proof" was applied in *Corbett v DPP*[52] against an accused who alleged abuse of the court processes—including a misdirected communication and an "infelicitous phrasing" of a letter by a garda—described by O'Sullivan J. to be "close to the innocuous end of the scale".[53]

Family Law Proceedings Affecting the Welfare of Children

13–17 In recent years, the courts have acknowledged that the legal professional privilege does not operate strictly in the context of wardship proceedings, upon the basis that procedurally these are not adversarial and that the court is entrusted to ensure that all the relevant evidence is placed before it in order to ascertain the welfare or best interests of the ward.[54] For a time, the view prevailed that this approach did not similarly apply in private custody disputes under the Children Act 1989,[55] equivalent to proceedings in Ireland under the Guardianship of Infants Act 1964. Rulings to that effect were overruled by the English Court of Appeal in *Oxfordshire CCC v M*.[56] In so deciding, the court was influenced by statutory provision, equivalent to s.3 of the 1964 Act in Ireland, stating that in such proceedings the welfare of the child is the court's "first and paramount consideration". This view was enthusiastically endorsed in *L(T) v L(V)*[57] by McGuinness J., who recognised

---

[50] *ibid.*
[51] Approving *O'Rourke v Darbshire* [1920] A.C. 581 (HL).
[52] [1999] 2 I.R. 179 (HC).
[53] *ibid.* at 191.
[54] *Re A. (Minors: Disclosure of Material)* [1991] 2 F.L.R. 473.
[55] *Barking and Dagenham LBC v O* [1993] 4 All E.R. 59.
[56] [1994] 2 All E.R. 269 (CA).
[57] [1996] F.L.R. 126 (Cir.C.): *cf.* appendix 47.

the public interest in disclosure of relevant evidence in child welfare cases, noting that the Supreme Court had recognised a comparable public interest in the context of the crime/fraud exception in *Murphy v Kirwan*.[58]

13–18 McGuinness J. found, accordingly, that in any proceedings affecting the welfare of children, "the desirability of disclosure must on the facts of the case be weighed against the desirability of maintaining the privilege and a decision taken in the light of the interests of the child concerned".[59] It is worth noting that McGuinness J. expressed the view that the power to override the legal professional privilege should be exercised rarely, and she did not apply it in this case to order discovery of diary notes the respondent had made of matters relevant to the custody and care of his children following a request to do so by his solicitor. With respect to such notes, McGuinness J. accepted that family lawyers frequently advise their clients to draft a diary or log of relevant events intended to be of assistance later to the solicitor or counsel, and she accepted that these were privileged. The learned judge did not accept that the public interest lay in the disclosure of what in essence were instructions to lawyers. McGuinness J. noted that the contentious English cases had concerned reports prepared by experts, in which context the argument for disclosure is strong, but that the "same considerations do not necessarily apply to other matters normally covered by legal professional privilege".[60]

Proceedings under the Succession Act 1965

13–19 Applications under the Succession Act 1965—whether seeking directions or disputing due execution or testamentary capacity—are, it is said, not proceedings *inter partes*, and it is more important in this context that any one party to the dispute is not seized, by virtue of private privilege, of more information than the court upon the vital questions at issue. The inquisitorial nature of these proceedings is illustrated by the old principle that a witness who attested the relevant will or codicil may be cross-examined by counsel for the party who called him, since in this context the witness does not belong to any party, but is present to assist the court in getting to the truth of the matters under scrutiny.[61] The effect of the inquisitorial nature of the proceedings upon privilege was considered in *Estate of Fuld Deceased*,[62] with respect to a claim that statements by witnesses who attested the will and which were brought into existence for the purposes of anticipated litigation, were privileged, and the witnesses could not be asked about their content in court. Scarman J. subjected the legal professional privilege to a balancing of competing interests, acknowledging the direct conflict between the court's right in probate cases to know all that a witness knows about the execution of a contested will and the right of a party to privilege over communications passing between a solicitor

---

[58] *cf.* para.**13–16**.
[59] [1996] F.L.R. 126 at 137 (HC).
[60] *ibid.*
[61] *Jones v Jones* (1908) 24 T.L.R. 839.
[62] [1965] 2 All E.R. 657.

and a witness in advance of contemplated litigation. Probate proceedings were observed to be more inquisitorial, and upon this basis the right of the court to know all that a witness knows about the execution of the disputed will prevailed. In *Crawford v Treacy*,[63] an application in which the wife claimed a legal right share in her husband's estate, the principles in *Fuld's* case were approved, although O'Sullivan J. did not consider that the public interest was served by disclosure of various letters of legal advice, much of which was already known to the court from recitals in the pleadings to date

II. LEGAL PROFESSIONAL PRIVILEGE

13–20 Legal professional privilege is specific to communications emanating from legal advice and litigation. It is not part of a wider professional privilege,[64] nor does it apply beyond communications between a lawyer, client, and third parties to protect against disclosing identities, sources, or facts of which any party has knowledge, subject to other rules and privileges applying.[65] The public interest is said to lie in preserving the integrity of the litigation process by protecting the confidentiality of the relationship between lawyer and client, which, it is reasoned, would not function effectively if strained by the prospect of compulsory disclosure.[66] The rationale for this limitation on discovery of documentation was expressed well by Knight-Bruce L.J., as follows: "Truth, like all other good things, may be loved unwisely—may be pursued too keenly—may cost too much. And surely the meanness and mischief of prying into one's confidential relations with his legal adviser, the general evil of infusing reserve and dissimulation, uneasiness and suspicion, and fear into those communications which must take place, and which, unless in a condition of perfect security, must take place uselessly or worse, are too great a price to pay for truth itself".[67]

13–21 Legal professional privilege is now identified throughout the common law as a substantive right rather than merely a rule of evidence.[68] As such, the necessity to preserve the "professional secrecy" between lawyer and client has been characterised as fundamental to a fair trial under Art.6 of the European Convention on Human Rights.[69] This development was recognised by Lord Taylor C.J. in *R. v Derby Magistrates Ex p.B*,[70] to wit that "[l]egal professional

---

[63] HC, November 4, 1998.
[64] *Greenough v Gaskell* (1833) 1 My. & K. 98 at 103, *per* Lord Brougham L.C.
[65] *Bursill v Tanner* (1883) 16 Q.B.D. 1.
[66] *Holmes v Baddeley* (1844) 1 Ph. 476 at 480–1, *per* Lord Lyndhurst L.C.
[67] *Pearse v Pearse* (1846) 1 De G. & Sm. 12 at 28–29.
[68] One of the first courts to recognise this was the Supreme Court of Canada in *Descoteaux v Mierzwinksi* (1982) 141 D.L.R. (3d) 590.
[69] So ruled by the European Court of Human Rights in *Niemitz v Germany* (1992) 16 E.H.R.R. 97, where a search warrant of a solicitor's offices was deemed unnecessary and disproportionate since founded upon authority that lacked special provision protecting the lawyer's need to preserve professional confidentiality.
[70] [1996] A.C. 487 (HL).

privilege is ... much more than a mere rule of evidence ... It is a fundamental condition on which the administration of justice as a whole rests".[71] In *Miley v Flood*,[72] Kelly J. approved this view of the legal professional privilege. The implications of characterising the privilege as a constitutional right are that, in this form, it does not absolutely defeat disclosure, but must be weighed against any competing constitutional right or public interest—in contrast to the old common law view that a private privilege applied absolutely.[73] The necessity to balance the competing interests prior to making the order has been a central feature of the public interest privilege for years.[74] It is of recent origins in private privilege law, however, featuring previously only as an exception to the privilege against revealing informants.[75]

13–22 Legal professional privilege arises in the context of communications for the purposes of litigation and/or the obtaining of legal advice. The litigation privilege covers communications between a lawyer and a client (such as instructions),[76] client and third party, or lawyer and third party (typically, a barrister or expert witness) in preparation of contemplated litigation. The advice privilege likewise applies to communications between lawyer and client for the purposes of obtaining or giving legal advice, including communications to and from a third party.[77] Third parties with a common interest in the relevant matters—such as co-complainant or co-tenant—may, in appropriate cases and where party to the advice, claim the same privilege as against outsiders to the confidential exchanges over the period of time the common interest existed.[78] The status of the DPP was considered in *Breathnach v Ireland (No.3)*,[79] where he was described to be potentially both lawyer and client, "since he formulates the legal opinion on which the institution or non-institution of a prosecution is based and he then becomes one of the parties to the subsequent litigation". Communications to and from the DPP[80] or Attorney General[81] naturally attract the legal professional privilege, though the courts instead favour application of the broader privilege based upon public interest.[82]

---

[71] *ibid.* at 507.
[72] [2001] 1 I.L.R.M. 489 at 504–7 (HC); *cf.* paras **13–27, 13–31** and appendix 62.
[73] *cf.* para.**13–02** *et seq.*
[74] *cf.* para.**13–69** *et seq.*
[75] *cf.* para.**13–58** *et seq.*
[76] In *L (T) v L (V)* [1996] F.L.R. 126 (HC), privilege was found to attach to diary entries compiled by the respondent client after a request by his solicitor to keep a running account of matters relevant to the custody and care of the parties' children in the context of judicial separation proceedings. Privilege was found not to attach, however, to diary entries written by the respondent prior to the instituting of proceedings and which recorded financial information relevant to his private medical practice.
[77] e.g. *Bula Ltd. v Crowley* [1990] I.L.R.M. 756 (SC): *cf.* appendix 38; *Re Getty (Sarah C.) Trust* [1985] Q.B. 956.
[78] *Wheeler v Le Marchant* (1881) 17 Ch. D. 675.
[79] [1993] 2 I.R. 458 at 471, *per* Keane J (HC).
[80] *Breathnach v Ireland* [1993] 2 I.R. 458 (HC).
[81] *Horgan v Murray* [1999] 1 I.L.R.M. 257 (HC).
[82] *cf.* para.**13–79**.

13–23 By common law principle, the privilege enures for the benefit of the client only, and the client must consent to any waiver of the privilege.[83] According to *Calcraft v Guest*,[84] once privileged, always privileged. Thus, privilege remains over documents relating to earlier concluded litigation for the benefit of the former litigant and may be asserted by his successors in title as though they were inherited in the manner of property rights.[85] The need to preserve confidentiality may be much less when the client is dead, however, and there appears no objection in principle to subjecting such claims to a discretionary balancing of the relevant interests. This was opted for by the US Supreme Court in *Swindler and Berlin v US*,[86] when the court chose to lift the lid on the privilege as it applies in criminal proceedings to communications over which a deceased client had privilege. The court preferred to subject such disputes to a balancing of interests between fairness and accuracy on the one hand and the interest served by the privilege on the other.[87]

13–24 Where legal professional privilege attaches to communications between Departments of State and lawyers for the purposes of contemplated litigation, the legal professional privilege tends to be claimed instead of the public interest privilege. In *Silver Hill Duckling Ltd. and Steele v Minister for Agriculture, Ireland, and the Attorney General*[88]—a dispute over compensation due to the plaintiffs following the slaughter of their ducks—the court accepted that litigation must have been contemplated at an early state in the plaintiffs' communications with the Department of Agriculture and certainly as soon as it was clear that the parties were in serious disagreement over the value of the claim. O'Hanlon J. upheld the claim to both forms of the legal professional privilege over communications between the Minister and his advisers following the date when litigation was apprehended (assessed at seven weeks after the slaughter) and to earlier communications made for the purposes of processing the applicants' claim. O'Hanlon J. considered that a claim to public interest privilege did not arise in the case, save for reference in the documents to the minutes of an EEC committee meeting which were ordinarily discoverable. In *Corbett v DPP*,[89] however, it was rightly recognised that in many cases the claim by a body or agent of the State to public interest privilege is coterminous with a claim to legal professional privilege, where the communications were for the purposes of legal advice or contemplated litigation. O'Sullivan J. decided that two documents sent by the DPP to the Chief State Solicitor, each state solicitor, and the Garda Commissioner did not attract legal professional privilege; it was equally open to the respondent, however, to claim privilege

---

[83] *Schneider v Leigh* [1955] 2 Q.B. 195 (CA), with the effect that the doctor who wrote the report of the plaintiff's injuries on behalf of the defendant to civil proceedings could not later claim privilege over that report when the former plaintiff sued him for defamation: *cf.* para.**13–11**.
[84] [1898] 1 Q.B. 759 at 761, *per* Lord Lindley M.R (CA).
[85] *Russell v Jackson* (1851) 9 Hare 387.
[86] (1998) 118 S.Ct. 2081 (US, SC).
[87] Ho, "Legal Professional Privilege after Death of Client" (1999) 115 L.Q.R. 27.
[88] [1987] I.R. 289 (HC).
[89] [1999] 2 I.R. 179 (HC).

Privilege

based upon "the public interest in the prevention and prosecution of crime". Having scrutinised the documents, the court refused to order disclosure of material containing legal advice, which for reasons of public interest were privileged, but ordered discovery of paragraphs in the documents not containing legal advice.

Scope of Protected "Communications"

13–25 The privilege protects "communications" in the broadest sense of the word, so long as confidential and for the purposes of either legal advice or contemplated litigation. Affirmative evidence may be necessary, in the event of a dispute, to establish that the document was actually confidential. Confidentiality did not exist in *Bord na gCon v Murphy*,[90] a case where the disputed statement was conveyed by the defendant to his solicitor in the expectation that his solicitor would convey it to the Board in response to written complaints against the defendant that he had infringed provisions of the Greyhound Industry Act 1958. Legal professional privilege has been deemed not to attach to a legal document such as a lease or a will created following legal advice, since this is not a "communication for the purposes of litigation or legal advice".[91]

13–26 In considering the range of communications protected because they make reference to confidential legal advice, the courts have often turned to the rationale of the privilege rather than to rule or precedent. In *Bula Ltd. v Crowley*,[92] Murphy J. of the High Court considered the view that in general a second document is privileged where it repeats confidential legal advice but that a second document that discusses the legal advice is not so privileged.[93] The learned judge rejected the contended distinction, favouring instead a non-categorical approach to the question. He observed that the form (whether a full opinion by counsel, or a letter resolving to make a lodgment into court) matters less than the question whether discovery of the documents "would of necessity disclose to a material extent confidential legal advice given to one or other of the two defendants in pursuit of their common interest".[94]

13–27 According to *R. v Central Criminal Court Ex p. Francis*,[95] the common law has not confined "communications" to statements or documents, and they potentially include physical items such as a blood sample.[96] The legal professional privilege does not in general attach to information regarding

---

[90] [1970] I.R. 301 (SC).
[91] *Balabel v Air India* [1988] 2 All E.R. 246 (CA).
[92] HC, December 19, 1989, Murphy J. (*ex tempore*).
[93] Favoured in *Style and Hollander on Documentary Evidence* (2nd ed., Longman, London, 1987) at p.103.
[94] HC, December 19, 1989, Murphy J. (*ex tempore*).
[95] [1989] A.C. 346 (HL).
[96] As in *R. v R.* [1995] 1 Cr. App. R. 183 (CA), in the context of s.10(1) of the Police and Criminal Evidence Act 1984.

the client's identity or residence,[97] save in exceptional circumstances.[98] The prevailing common law view is that such information is "collateral" to legal advice,[99] and not by nature confidential;[100] the legal professional privilege protects "communications" between the parties but it does not attach to facts the solicitor has observed or learned during the process.[101] In other words, the facts of a client's identity or his residence are not within the scope of privileged communications between lawyer and client. A different approach, though achieving the same result, was adopted by Kelly J. in *Miley v Flood*[102] upon an application of the uncertain distinction between legal advice and legal assistance introduced in *Smurfit Paribas*.[103] Kelly J. concluded that disclosure may not, by way of exception, be ordered "where (a) the naming of the client would incriminate or (b) where the identity of the client is so bound up with the nature of the advice sought, that to reveal the client's identity would be in fact to reveal that advice".[104]

Disclosure of Expert Witness Reports

13–28 A significant exception to the legal professional privilege was created with respect to expert reports in personal injury cases. The new rules were added to the Rules of the Superior Courts (1986) by S.I. 391 of 1998.[105] In High Court personal injury proceedings, the parties must, following service of the Notice of Trial and exchange of a Schedule of Reports, exchange (*inter alia*) all reports and statements prepared by experts whom they intend to call as witnesses and "containing the substance of the evidence to be adduced" by them. An "expert" is defined illustratively, followed by the words "and/or any

---

[97] *Re Cathcart Ex p.* (1870) 5 Ch. App. 703 (CA).
[98] Such a derogation was expressly acknowledged in *International Credit and Investment Co. (Overseas) Ltd. v Adham (Disclosure)* (*The Times*, February 10, 1997), and is implicit in the principles favoured in *Federal Commissioners of Taxation v Coombes* (1999) 164 A.L.R. 131, discussed by Kelly J. in *Miley v Flood* [2001] 1 I.L.R.M. 489 at 514–7 (HC); *cf.* appendix 62.
[99] *Re Cathcart Ex p.* (1870) 5 Ch. App. 703 at 705, *per* James L.J. (CA).
[100] *United States of America v Mammoth Oil Company* [1925] 2 D.L.R. 966 at 970, *per* Hodgkins J.A.
[101] *Federal Commissioners of Taxation v Coombes* (1999) 164 A.L.R. 131.
[102] [2001] 1 I.L.R.M. 489 (HC): *cf.* appendix 62.
[103] *cf.* para.**13-33** *et seq.*
[104] [2001] 1 I.L.R.M. 489 (HC).
[105] Rules of the Superior Courts (No. 6) (Disclosure of Reports and Statements) (S.I. No. 391 of 1998), pursuant to s.45 of the Courts and Court Officers Act 1995, and inserting rr.45–51 into Ord.39 of the Rules of the Superior Courts 1986. The new rules apply to all personal injury actions instituted on or after September 1, 1997. See generally: Delaney and McGrath, *Civil Procedure in the Superior Courts* (Round Hall Sweet & Maxwell, Dublin, 2001) at Chap.17; Barr, "Expert Evidence – A Few Personal Observations and the Implications of Recent Statutory Developments" (1999) 4 Bar Rev. 185; Brady, "The Disclosure and Exchange of Experts' Reports in Personal Injuries Litigation" (1999) Bar Rev. 181; Carolan, "New Superior Court Rules on Disclosure of Expert Reports in Personal Injury Actions – A Sea Change in Irish Law" (1999) 3 I.I.L.R. 3; O'Neill, "Disclosure in Personal Injuries Actions" (1997) 4 Bar Rev. 77; Pierse, "Disclosure of Reports and Information in Personal Injuries Litigation: the 1998 Rules" (1999) Bar Rev. 42.

expert whatsoever", and thus appears referable both to the party's intended use of the witness and the court's own sense of what constitutes expertise having regard to appropriate principles.[106] This is evident in s.45(3) of the Courts and Courts Officers Act 1995, which defines expert as a person who is "qualified to give expert evidence." A party is precluded from calling an expert in evidence whose report was not disclosed to the opposing party in compliance with these rules.[107]

13–29 The rules only apply to reports by experts intended to be called in evidence.[108] In *Kincaid v Aer Lingus Teoranta*,[109] the Supreme Court found that where an expert report originally listed in the schedule of reports served upon the opponent is withdrawn before the hearing because the party no longer intends to call the witness to testify, legal professional privilege re-attaches to the report and the opponent may not require its disclosure.

13–30 The rules demarcate the scope of "statement" by requiring disclosure of "the substance of the evidence to be adduced".[110] If a statement – expressed, for instance, in a follow-up letter by an expert—is peripheral to the report, or discursive of matters raised in the report, disclosure may not strictly be required, although this distinction has not yet been explored by the Irish courts. The practice in England after the introduction of earlier rules (enabling the court to order an exchange of expert reports)[111] was to request the expert to draft one report for the purpose of compliance with the disclosure requirement, wherein conclusions on responsibility were avoided, and to draft a second confidential report candidly addressing the merits of the cause of action. This practice was swiftly exposed and condemned in *Ollett v Bristol Aerojet Ltd.*[112] Ackner J. emphasised that the expert witness' role in legal proceedings is to furnish an expert *opinion* for the purposes of the proceedings and that this opinion must clearly and fully be stated in the disclosed report.

13–31 The answer to the question "how far must disclosure go for the purpose of disclosing the substance of the expert's report" may only be determined by reference to the purpose of the new rules, since the rules do not themselves specify the extent of disclosure. This purpose may either be (1) to prevent one party ambushing the other at the hearing by introducing issues not anticipated by the other, or (2) to promote disclosure in general of all material expert evidence prior to the hearing.[113] The second option would entail a more general erosion of the legal professional privilege as it applies to expert reports in personal injury litigation. The fact that the words "the substance of the

---

[106] *cf.* para.**12–05** *et seq.*
[107] Order 39, r.46(1) and r.48.
[108] *Galvin v Murray* [2001] 2 I.L.R.M. 234 at 239, *per* Murphy J. (SC).
[109] [2003] 2 I.R. 314 (SC).
[110] Order 39, r.45(1)(e).
[111] Rules of the Superior Courts, Ord.38, r.38, since replaced.
[112] [1979] 1 W.L.R. 1197.
[113] Delaney and McGrath, *op. cit.* n.105 at p. 473.

evidence" were added to the new rules at a late stage following representations by the Bar Council, may be taken to indicate that the intention ultimately was to avoid a general erosion of the privilege. The limited case-law on the rules to date suggest that the Irish courts may endorse this perspective by identifying the dominant purpose of the rules to be the avoidance of surprise at the hearing rather than the general advancement of disclosure of relevant documentation. In *Galvin v Murray*,[114] Murphy J. found as follows: "Clearly the disclosure rules are designed to forewarn other parties of expert evidence with which they may be confronted. The rules have no role to play in investigating the strengths or weaknesses of an opponent's case." This view was reiterated by Geoghegan J. in *Kincaid v Aer Lingus Teoranta*:[115] "the purpose of the rules is not to disclose the strength and weaknesses of each other's case but rather to prevent surprise evidence being thrown up at a trial which the other party at that stage is unable to deal with."

13–32 A similar approach to the English provisions[116] was adopted in *Ollett v Bristol Aerojet Ltd.*,[117] where Ackner J. remarked: "The whole purpose of [the rules] is, in relation to expert evidence, to save expense by dispensing with the calling of experts when there is in reality no dispute and, where there is a dispute, by avoiding parties being taken by surprise as to the true nature of the dispute and thereby being obliged to seek adjournments." In *Kenning v Eve Construction*,[118] the English High Court considered whether a party is obliged to disclose documentary information received from an expert which the party does not intend to elicit from the expert witness under examination in-chief but which, if disclosed, would cast a different light upon the question of liability. The court was thus asked to consider whether disclosure is reserved to information the party intends to advance in *support* of his claim, or whether instead a party must disclose all the findings and queries expressed by the expert in documentary form even where actually or potentially injurious to the interests of the calling party. In opposing such an extension, it was persuasively argued that a general requirement of disclosure of all of the expert's opinion would stultify the recording of experts' reports and introduce defensive practice to the process. The submission was rejected by the High Court, which reasoned that a party is required to weigh up the pros and cons of calling the witness (in

---

[114] [2001] 2 I.L.R.M. 234 at 239–40 (SC).
[115] [2003] 2 I.R. 314 (SC).
[116] English law also requires disclosure of "the substance of [the expert witness'] evidence to the other parties in the form of a written report": Rules of the Superior Courts, Ord.25, r.8(1)(b).
[117] [1979] 1 W.L.R. 1197.
[118] [1989] 1 W.L.R. 1189. Accidental disclosure was made of a cover letter written by a defence expert and attached to his full report. The plaintiff sought to amend his statement of claim, which the defendant opposed upon the basis that it was influenced by the privileged, non-disclosable letter. Since the High Court held that the plaintiff had an ordinary right to make the amendments, and that these probably would have been made even if the letter had not been disclosed, the court's findings on the extent of due disclosure constitute *obiter dicta*. The court clearly regarded the letter to be subject to the disclosure requirement.

light partly of the obligation to disclose). If a decision is taken to call the witness in evidence, his full opinion upon potential liability – including parts favourable and unfavourable to the client – are required to be disclosed to the opponent; the failure to make *adequate* disclosure of the expert's communicated views entitles the court to decide that the expert may not be called by the client.

Distinction between Legal Advice and Legal Assistance

13–33 In the past, the legal professional privilege was applied to routine communications between lawyers and clients.[119] A judgment by Finlay C.J. in *Smurfit Paribas Bank v A.A.B. Export Finance*[120] purports to make inroads into this aspect of the privilege. Notwithstanding the broad nature of the principles sketched by the old authorities, and notwithstanding the fact that the judges used the terms legal assistance interchangeably with legal advice, Finlay C.J. regarded a claim of privilege over a communication for the purpose of obtaining "legal assistance" as one that would necessitate an "expansion" of the scope of the legal professional privilege. The learned judge did not specify or illustrate the types of duties a lawyer may perform by way of legal assistance exclusive of legal advice, although he considered that letters between the client and solicitor in this case constituted legal assistance upon the basis that they pertained to the creation of a floating charge, and comprised instructions and clarifications of instructions to the solicitor. Such a distinction is very difficult to discern, however. Virtually all cases of legal assistance, including straightforward leases and wills, engender some degree of pre-emptive consideration of the possibility of future dispute and litigation. The effect of introducing an unclear distinction within the legal professional privilege may be to undermine the public interest served by the privilege, namely the preservation of lawyer-client candour unstrained by the threat of publicity, and to invite more frequent challenge to documentation claimed to be privileged as legal advice.

13–34 The common law traditionally sketched private privilege broadly where it applied to lawyer-client communications. In *Wheeler v Le Marchant*,[121] Lord Jessell M.R. phrased the privilege as applying to "all things reasonably necessary in the shape of communication to the legal advisers ... in order that legal advice may be obtained safely and sufficiently". The English courts have wisely disapproved of a "nit-picking approach to documents".[122] Judgments after *Smurfit Paribas Bank* have continued to refer to legal professional privilege broadly. In a subsequent judgment in *Bula Ltd. v Crowley (No.2)*,[123]

---

[119] *Belabel v Air India* [1988] Ch. 317 (CA).
[120] [1990] 1 I.R. 469 (SC): *cf.* appendix 35.
[121] (1881) 17 Ch. 675 at 681, approved by the Supreme Court in *Gallagher v Stanley & National Maternity Hospital* [1998] 2 I.R. 267.
[122] *Belabel v Air India* [1988] Ch. 317 (CA); *R. v Manchester Crown Court Ex p.* [1999] 1 W.L.R. 832 at 839.
[123] [1994] 2 I.R. 54 at 58 (SC), approving *Minter v Priest* [1929] 1 K.B. 655.

Finlay C.J. referred to legal professional privilege attaching to "such communications with a lawyer as pass as professional communications in a professional capacity". In *Gallagher v Stanley & National Maternity Hospital*,[124] the Supreme Court referred to legal professional privilege attaching to "confidential communications passing between lawyer and client for the purpose of obtaining legal *advice or assistance*" or in contemplation of litigation. The distinction established in *Smurfit Paribas Bank* between advice and assistance was, however, applied by the High Court in *Miley v Flood*[125] in refusing a challenge by a solicitor against a demand by the Tribunal of Inquiry into Certain Planning Matters and Payments that he reveal the identity of a client who was the beneficial owner of various companies.

13–35 Whilst it makes little sense to subject each communication between lawyer and client to the scrutiny of uncertain tests, or to disarm lawyer-client candour by the ongoing risk of publicity, a distinction ought to be recognised in appropriate cases between documents that reflect or record legal advice sought or obtained and documents of merely administrative content. Upon this basis in *R. v Manchester Crown Court Ex p. Rogers*,[126] Lord Bingham considered a solicitor bound to disclose records of whether on a particular date the accused had arranged or attended a consultation with his solicitor. For such cases, it is submitted, it makes little sense to construct fine lines and tests of distinction, and better to ask whether disclosure of the type of document in dispute would strike at the rationale for the privilege, namely to foster the free exchange of legal advice and communication between lawyer and client unhampered by the threat of publicity.

Communications in Furtherance of Settlement

13–36 It was decided in *Horgan v Murray*[127] that a communication made for the purpose of attempting a compromise of a dispute is in principle privileged due to the public interest in encouraging settlements and despite constituting a communication for the purpose of *avoiding* litigation. O'Sullivan J. observed that "the purposes of litigation include attempts to compromise it",[128] and further rejected the contention that the privilege is lost over documents that one party intended to give to the other before changing his mind, as frequently occurs in the context of "to and fro negotiations".

13–37 "Without prejudice" letters are routinely protected by privilege—it would appear, upon a separate basis beyond the privilege that protects lawyer-client relations—although the party must establish to the satisfaction of the court that the purpose of the document was genuinely to attempt a settlement, and that it was intended to be confidential in the event the settlement failed.

---

[124] [1998] 2 I.R. 267 at 271, *per* O'Flaherty J. (SC).
[125] [2001] 1 I.L.R.M. 489 (HC): *cf.* para.13–33 *et seq.* and appendix 62.
[126] [1999] 1 W.L.R. 832.
[127] [1999] 1 I.L.R.M. 257 (HC).
[128] *ibid.* at 260.

The words "without prejudice" cannot be used as a cloak.[129] Upon this basis, several "without prejudice" letters were found not to be privileged in *Ryan v Connolly*.[130] The Supreme Court asserted in *Ryan* that the court may be obliged to balance the interest in disclosure against the public interest in encouraging settlements in cases where the disclosure is sought not for the purpose of holding an opponent to admissions made in the "without prejudice" offer "but simply to demonstrate why a particular course had been taken".[131] The court is not precluded from considering and acting upon such communications in the context of submissions that the defendant induced the claimant to believe that a settlement would be reached and that there was no necessity to institute proceedings within the relevant limitation period.

13–38 A "without prejudice" letter may be admissible without the consent of the author or the recipient for the purpose of enforcing a binding agreement to settle, where proceedings were compromised in reliance upon, or arising out of, the communication.[132] It would appear that this is limited to cases where either party to the settlement, but not a third party such as insurer, wishes to tender the document in evidence.[133] Oral assertions, admissions, and statements advanced to the other side in a "without prejudice" settlement meeting are also privileged upon this basis. The English Court of Appeal so found in *Unilever plc. v Proctor & Gamble Co.*,[134] approving the following *dicta* by Oliver L.J. in *Cutts v Head*:[135]

> "That the rule rests, at least in part, on public policy is clear from many authorities, and the convenient starting point of the inquiry is the nature of the underlying policy. It is that the parties should be encouraged so far as possible to settle their disputes without resort to litigation and should not be discouraged by the knowledge that anything that is said in the course of such negotiations (and that includes, of course, as much the failure to reply to an offer as an actual reply) may be used to their prejudice in the course of the proceedings. They should, as it was expressed by Clauson J. in *Scott Paper Co. v Drayton Paper Works Ltd.*,[136] be encouraged freely and frankly to put their cards on the table. ... The rule applies to exclude all negotiations genuinely aimed at settlement whether oral or in writing from being given in evidence".

Documents in Existence Prior to Legal Advice

13–39 Privilege does not attach retroactively to documents in existence before

---

[129] *Cutts v Head* [1984] Ch. 290.
[130] [2001] 2 I.L.R.M. 174 (SC).
[131] *ibid.* at 181.
[132] As in *Tomlin v Standard Telephones and Cables Ltd.* [1969] 3 All E.R. 201 (CA), where a dispute subsequently arose over the terms of the settlement agreed by the parties.
[133] *Rush & Tomkins Ltd. v Greater London Council* [1989] A.C. 1280 (HL).
[134] [2001] 1 All E.R. 783 (CA).
[135] [1984] 1 All E.R. 597 at 605–6 (CA).
[136] (1927) 44 R.P.C. 151 at 156.

the client decided to obtain the relevant legal advice. The issue arose in a number of cases with respect to forged documents. In *R. v Peterborough Justices*,[137] the client had sent a forged document onto a solicitor for the purpose of gaining legal advice. After a warrant issued to search the premises of the solicitor, the document was seized. In finding that the document was not privileged, the court reasoned that the document had been liable to seizure when it was in the client's hands; since a solicitor holds a document in the right of his client, he cannot assert in respect of its seizure any greater authority than the client himself possessed. In *R. v King*,[138] another case of forged documents, the Court of Appeal reasoned that privilege may be lost where the solicitor to whom the documents were entrusted sends them onto a third party, however expert. Dunn L.J. commented: "It would be strange if a forger could hide behind a claim of legal professional privilege by the simple device of sending all the incriminating documents in his possession to his solicitor to be examined by an expert".[139]

13–40 Despite decisions such as *Calcraft*,[140] it has been said that if an original document is privileged, so too is any copy of the document made by the solicitor;[141] there is no reason to doubt this principle where the originals and the copies remain confidential. It was conversely stated by Lord Denning M.R. in *Buttes Gas & Oil Co. v Hammer (No.3)*[142] that where an original document is not privileged, neither is any copy of it, even if acquired by the solicitor for the purposes of legal advice or litigation. This was at issue in *Tromso Sparebank v Beirne*.[143] Costello J. followed the principle in *Buttes*, noting that the public interest lay in encouraging rather than reducing the range of relevant evidence before the court. A copy of a document to which privilege never attached was equally unprivileged, and the defendant in the proceedings would have been entitled to obtain the documents by means of third party discovery or, if necessary, by *subpoena ad duces tecum*.

Communications to Third Parties

13–41 Communications between a solicitor or a client and a third party (most commonly, an insurer or expert) are privileged where for the purposes of contemplated litigation. The privilege attaches to communication to and from the expert, but not to the documents or chattels upon which the expert formed his opinion.[144] It is sufficient that the possibility of litigation was apprehended

---

[137] [1978] 1 All E.R. 225.
[138] [1983] 1 All E.R. 929 (CA).
[139] *ibid.* at 931.
[140] *cf.* para.**13–08**.
[141] *Chadwick v Bowman* (1886) 16 Q.B. 223: approved in *Estate of Fuld* [1965] 2 All E.R. 657 at 658–9, per Scarman J; and *Buttes Gas & Oil Co. v Hammer (No. 3)* [1981] Q.B. 223, per Denning M.R. (HL). The view was also expressed in *Dubai Bank Ltd. v Galadari* [1990] Ch. 98 at 104 (CA).
[142] [1981] Q.B. 223 (HL).
[143] [1989] I.L.R.M. 257 (HC).
[144] *Harmony Shipping Co. v Davis* [1979] 3 All E.R. 177 at 181 (CA).

and not necessarily the cause of action.[145] The focus chiefly is on whether the material was designed to enable a lawyer to give legal advice on the matter. This would include communications between lawyers and witnesses but not necessarily a mere request by letter for information without reference to litigation (even if the litigation was in fact contemplated or ongoing).[146]

Documents Created for Mixed Purposes

13–42 Although communications to and from the offices of lawyers benefit from a congruence of the legal advice and litigation basis for legal professional privilege, and a presumptive public interest in maintaining their confidentiality, this is not the case for documents and material produced elsewhere and for mixed purposes. The purpose issue commonly arises in the context of post-accident reports prepared initially for internal administration but used later for legal purposes. For privilege to attach to the resulting document, its dominant purpose must have been preparation for litigation, according to the leading authorities in Ireland and England—although some other jurisdictions apply a sole purpose test.[147] In *Waugh v British Railway Board*,[148] the House of Lords asserted that "unless the purpose of submission to the legal adviser in view of litigation is at least the dominant purpose to which the relevant document was prepared, the reasons which require privilege to be extended to it cannot apply".[149] The document in dispute was a joint internal report incorporating witness statements, of a type compiled by the Railway Board in the event of occupational injuries, and for the purpose of submission to the inspectorate and then to the Minister for the Environment. The report in this case disclosed on its heading that it was also to be sent to a firm of solicitors. The court found, despite its heading, that the report had been prepared for dual purposes of equal rank—to prepare for litigation, and to inform the Board of the circumstances of the accident so that steps could be taken to avoid recurrence—and, as such, it was not privileged.

13–43 When assessing the purpose of the document, the courts tend to favour disclosure where possible. This is increasingly so for civil actions. The public interest is currently perceived to lie in encouraging an early exchange of reports between the parties as a spur to settlement and a reduction of delay. This attitude was evident in *Gallagher v Stanley & National Maternity Hospital*,[150] a medical negligence case. It concerned the disclosure of witness statements made by three nurses in the immediate aftermath of the plaintiff's complicated delivery. The statements had been organised by the matron, who claimed at a later stage in the proceedings that she had been solely motivated by the possibility of litigation. O'Flaherty J. rejected the submission. Although litigation may have

---

[145] *Alfred Compton Amusement Machines Ltd. v Customs and Excise Commissioners (No.2)* [1972] 2 Q.B. 102 (CA).
[146] *Anderson v Bank of British Columbia* (1876) 2 Ch. D. 644 (CA).
[147] *e.g. Grant v Downs* (1976) 135 C.L.R. 674 (HC, Aust.).
[148] [1980] A.C. 521 (HL).
[149] *ibid*. at 533, *per* Lord Wilberforce.

been in her mind, she was likely to have been primarily motivated by her management duties. O'Flaherty J. expressed support for the dominant purpose test. In deciding that the legal professional privilege did not in this case attach to the statements, he was influenced by the rationale for the privilege and the fact that a witness statement was distinct from legal advice and instruction. The purpose of the privilege "is to aid the administration of justice, not to impede it. In general, justice will be best served where there is the greatest candour and where all relevant documentary evidence is available".[151]

13–44 Privilege attaches, however, to communications between a lawyer and third party, such as the client's insurer, for the purposes of contemplated litigation, such as letters addressing the merits and scope of a claim, whether actual or potential.[152] Privilege now routinely and strictly attaches to reports and communications sent by clients to their insurers for the purposes of alerting them to possible legal claims. In *Andrews v Northern Ireland Railways Co. Ltd.*,[153] Carswell J characterised this type of communication as one not for mixed purposes but for a "first and immediate purpose" of alerting the insurers, and in turn their lawyers, to the possibility of a claim. *Andrews* turned upon discovery of two reports forwarded by the conductor and the driver of the train to the defendant's insurers five days after the plaintiff's accident. In response to the plaintiff's assertion that legal professional privilege over the documents could not then have ripened since the defendant did not know the plaintiff would issue proceedings, Carswell J. located "ample authority for the proposition that if litigation is in *reasonable prospect* documents brought into existence for the purpose of obtaining legal advice *or in connection with* the conduct of such litigation are privileged."[154] The learned judge adopted the view that legal professional privilege does not depend upon proof that the immediate purpose of the communication was the obtaining of legal advice to defend a claim, nor that the document was sent directly to lawyers. It was sufficient if the purpose of the communication was "to report the accident to insurers, where it is *probable* that litigation will ensue, in order to allow them to assess the strength of the case of the insured and to advance their investigations".[155] The reports in this case were discoverable. They had been brought into existence at the request of the insurer "in order to allow them to assess the case and advance their investigation, with the ultimate purpose of preparing the defence of any claim against the insured which *might* ensue".[156]

---

[150] [1998] 2 I.R. 267 (SC).
[151] *ibid.* at 271.
[152] *Power City Ltd. v Monahan* (HC, October 14, 1996). See also *Coss v National Maternity Hospital* (1949) 83 I.L.T. 103 (HC), finding that a Notice of Accident Form sent by a person to his insurers is not privileged.
[153] [1992] N.I. 1.
[154] *ibid.* at 6 (emphasis added).
[155] *ibid.* (emphasis added).
[156] *ibid.* at 8 (emphasis added).

Advice to Remain Silent and Adverse Inferences

13–45 The recent provisions enabling inferences to be drawn in exceptional cases from an accused's silence may exert undue strain on the legal professional privilege.[157] This has already occurred in England, where a general power to draw inferences from silence exists in criminal proceedings.[158] In *R. v Roble*,[159] for instance, the accused had made "no comment" upon the advice of his solicitor when questioned by the police in custody. At his trial, he stated in evidence that he had acted in self-defence and had not provided this account to the police when questioned because he had been advised to do so by his solicitor. Upon appeal from the trial judge's directions to the jury, the Court of Appeal reasoned that a defence submission of this nature did not constitute a waiver of legal professional privilege. The court expressed the view, however, that in the absence of a waiver of the privilege explaining the basis for the solicitor's advice to remain silent, and in the absence of direct evidence by the solicitor, an explanation of this nature is unlikely to inhibit the jury from drawing adverse inferences, and the trial judge was right to permit the jury to draw those inferences.[160]

13–46 Evidence of the pressure this exerts upon the legal professional privilege was striking in *R. v Bowden*.[161] During the trial, the prosecution invited the court to draw inferences from the accused's silence in custody, and made no reference to a statement provided by the solicitor to the police indicating the reasons for his advice that the accused remain silent. To avoid adverse inferences, defence counsel referred to the solicitor's statement. The trial judge construed this to constitute implied waiver of his legal professional privilege. The Court of Appeal affirmed. Whilst it accepted that an explanation by the accused at his trial that he remained silent upon the advice of his solicitor does not in itself lead to loss of the privilege, the court took the view that where a statement is made by a solicitor with the authority of the client explaining the basis for his legal advice, or where evidence is tendered in the trial of the grounds on which the advice was given, the client may be taken implicitly to have waived his claim to legal professional privilege and may accordingly be cross-examined upon the nature of that advice and the factual premises underlying it, including information given confidentially by the client to the solicitor.

---

[157] *cf.* para.**13–100** *et seq.*
[158] *cf.* para.**13–103** *et seq.*
[159] [1997] Crim. L.R. 448 (CA). See also *R. v Argent* [1997] 2 Cr. App. R. 27 (CA); *R. v Condron* [1997] 1 W.L.R. 827 (CA).
[160] *R. v Howell* [2003] Crim. L.R. 405 (CA) similarly ruled that silence is not objectively justifiable merely upon the basis that it was in response to legal advice received in detention, and that to rule otherwise would be to thwart the policy of the legislature to prompt disclosure by the accused.
[161] [1999] 1 W.L.R. 823 (CA).

III. CONFIDENTIAL RELATIONSHIPS

13–47 The confidential nature of a communication or relationship—whether in the public interest or not—is entirely distinct from the status of privilege. Privilege does not attach to a communication merely because it was intended or required to be confidential. The courts are entitled to uphold the confidential nature of the communication, however, after balancing the public interest in its maintenance against the public interest in disclosure of material evidence.[162] In developing a new basis for the sacerdotal privilege in *Cook v Carroll*[163] Gavan Duffy J. approved four criteria favoured by Wigmore for the general purpose of conferring privilege upon communications by virtue of the confidential nature of the relationship between the communicants.[164] According to these criteria, privilege may be established where the court is satisfied that: (1) the communication was confidential; (2) confidentiality is essential to the satisfactory maintenance of the relationship; (3) the relationship is one the community deems necessary to foster; and (4) the likely harm caused by mandatory disclosure outweighs the benefit to be gained in the instant case by it.

13–48 Wigmore's criteria have been endorsed on numerous occasions now by the Irish courts as appropriate to cases raising untested claims to private privilege. The criteria draw implicitly from public interests, of a type already underpinning the existing private privileges. Where the communication, however privately confidential, involves an organ of the State or a public body, the matter is more appropriately assessed as a claim of public interest privilege, however. The High Court concluded thus in *Goodman International v Hamilton (No.3)*,[165] with respect to information conveyed to members of the Oireachtas. The counselling privilege identified in *ER* and *Johnston*, considered next, and the privilege over communications between a member of the Oireachtas and an informant identified in *Goodman International (No.3)*, are examples of new types of privilege—alternatively as new relationships to which existing forms of privileges have been extended. Although the superior courts have an inherent discretion to confer a right akin to privilege in a specific case where the public interest lies in supporting the confidence, it is as frequently recognised by the courts that public policy is opposed to the restriction of evidence by the recognition of new categories of privilege.

Sacerdotal Privilege

13–49 In *Cook*, Gavan Duffy J. recognised an absolute privilege over

---

[162] So found in *Cooper Flynn v Radio Telefís Éireann* [2000] 3 I.R. 344 at 351, *per* Kelly J. (HC), with respect to the identity of clients claimed to have participated in tax evasion schemes.
[163] [1945] I.R. 515 (HC).
[164] Wigmore, *Anglo-American System of Evidence* (3rd ed., vol. viii Boston, 1940) at paras 2380–91.
[165] [1993] 3 I.R. 320 (HC); *cf.* para.**13–63**.

Privilege

confidential communications made by a parishioner to a priest, and applied it in the case to uphold a priest's refusal in evidence to answer questions relating to a conversation he had had with the defendant. The learned judge rejected the submission that the question of privilege should be decided by reference to the English common law—which had largely brushed the sacerdotal privilege aside[166]—since its precedents had been established subsequent to a Reformation rejected as heresy by the Catholic majority in Ireland. It was appropriate, then, that the common law principles governing this question of privilege be developed in Ireland "in harmony with the national spirit" and the "special position" afforded by the Constitution to the Roman Catholic Church.[167]

13–50 According to *Cook*, the sacerdotal privilege cannot be waived by the confider, and any waiver must be made by the priest in question (which the court accepted as unlikely given the inviolable secrecy of the sacrament of penance). It was clearly Gavan Duffy J.'s view that priests automatically satisfy the test advanced by Wigmore,[168] and that the confidence between a parish priest and his people "wears a sacred character of immense potential benefit to the community, both to resolve the most delicate problems of life and to shield the flock from public scandal in things of shame".[169] Gavan Duffy J. assumed in *Cook* that the sacerdotal privilege vesting in the parish priest operated in an absolute sense—in other words, that it did not entitle the court to consider the question of disclosure by weighing competing interests in the balance. In light of the significant expansion of the courts' constitutional jurisprudence since *Cook*, the judicial recognition of constitutional imperatives, and the yielding of the private privileges to constitutional considerations, this aspect of the sacerdotal privilege remains appropriately amenable to reconsideration.

13–51 Privilege may not exist where confidentiality of relationship and exchange is absent. In *Forristal v Forristal*,[170] Deale J. noted that Gavan Duffy J. had confined his ruling in *Cook* to private exchanges between a priest and his parishioner. In the context of defamation proceedings, a priest unsuccessfully invoked the privilege over a letter sent to him by the defendant in which he claimed that his brother, the plaintiff, had failed to honour his obligations to take care of their mother under a family trust. In distinguishing *Cook*, Deale J. was influenced by the fact that the writer of the letter was not the priest's parishioner and that a relationship of confidentiality had not preceded the sending of the letter through the mail.

Counsellors' Privilege

13–52 Privilege was found to attach to communications with a marriage

---
[166] *e.g. Wheeler v Le Marchant* (1881) 17 C. D. 675 at 681.
[167] [1945] I.R. 515 at 519 (HC).
[168] *cf.* para.**13–47**.
[169] [1945] I.R. 515 at 519 (HC).
[170] (1966) 100 I.L.T.R. 182 (Cir.C.).

guidance counsellor (who was also a religious officer) in *ER v JR*.[171] Without directly addressing whether the privilege was available upon equal terms to marriage counsellors who were not also priests, Carroll J. applied the four criteria identified by Wigmore and approved in *Cook*,[172] and found that the relationship possessed the requisite confidentiality.[173] The privilege identified by Carroll J. was clearly different in effect to the sacerdotal privilege vesting in the priest. In *ER*, privilege was found to vest only in the clients (the married couple) and not in the counsellor.[174] Therefore, only the clients were capable of waiving the privilege. This aspect of the privilege was directly at issue in *Johnston v Church of Scientology*,[175] with respect to notes made in the course of "auditing" the plaintiff's personality in counselling sessions at the defendant's centre. Geoghegan J. drew a clear distinction between the confidentiality issues raised by secular counselling and the operation of sacerdotal privilege. The sacerdotal privilege has its origins in pre-Reformation common law antiquity, and it applies strictly to confessional communications between priest and layman. As an "absolute unwaivable privilege [it] is *sui generis* and is not capable of development". Privilege may attach to other relationships of confidence, such as counselling, but by contrast it may only be claimed or waived by the client.

IV. PRIVILEGES AGAINST REVEALING INFORMANTS

13–53 Numerous variants of privilege now potentially exist with respect to non-disclosure of the sources of allegations, deriving from the common law and provisions of the Constitution, and at present in varying degrees of development.

Common Law Privileges

13–54 The common law recognised a specific privilege that a public prosecutor could claim against a request to reveal the identity of a source. Established in *Attorney-General v Briant*,[176] it has since been developed as a public privilege requiring the court to consider the question of disclosure after weighing the public interest in preserving the anonymity of police informers against the public interest in hearing the evidence. The privilege was accepted in this form in *Director of Consumer Affairs v Sugar Distributors Ltd*.[177] Costello J. approved Lord Diplock's speech in *D v N.S.P.C.C.*, where the rationale underpinning the privilege was expressed as follows: "If [the] identity

---

[171] [1981] 1 I.L.R.M. 125 (HC).
[172] *cf.* para.**13–47**.
[173] *cf.* para.**13–49**.
[174] Following *Pais v Pais* [1970] W.L.R. 830.
[175] [2001] 1 I.R. 682 (HC, SC). The defendant's appeal to the Supreme Court succeeded on a different ground, namely that the documents in question were not in the defendant's custody or power of procurement.
[176] (1846) 15 M. & W. 169.
[177] [1991] 1 I.R. 225 (HC).

[of police informers] were liable to be disclosed in a court of law, these sources of information would dry up and the police would be hindered in their duty preventing and detecting crime".[178] The common law privilege against disclosure of sources did not initially apply beyond public prosecutors, although in recent years it has been extended to watchdog and enforcement bodies established by statute[179] such as the N.S.P.C.C.[180] and the DPP.[181] In non-public spheres, however, the privilege does not arise (save potentially with respect to journalists, considered below). Thus a solicitor does not benefit from a privilege against disclosure of the identity of his client or the source of his instructions, and nor, according to case law, may either party claim legal professional privilege with respect to such information where deemed "collateral" to the legal advice.[182]

13–55 Further extension of the privilege has been achieved in public spheres. In *Goodman International (No.3) v Hamilton*,[183] the High Court decided that members of the Oireachtas generally benefit from the privilege at common law, and may not be compelled to divulge their sources, since it is in the public interest that matters of importance be brought to the attention of political representatives without fear that confidences may be dishonoured. Geoghegan J. preferred to treat the matter as public interest privilege, since it concerned communications involving an organ of the State, rather than a new private privilege sustainable upon an application of the criteria identified by Wigmore.[184] Despite the deference to classification of privilege as either public or private, the practical effect is usually the same (save where the privilege has been classed as absolute, such as the sacerdotal privilege),[185] since each privilege requires the court to balance the competing interests before deciding whether on balance disclosure. A privilege comparable to that recognised in *Goodman International (No.3) v Hamilton*[186] was asserted by politicians against the Morris tribunal with respect to information given in confidence to them as members of the Oireachtas (in circumstances where no utterance was made in the Oireachtas capable of attracting parliamentary privilege under Art 15.12). In *Howlin v Morris Tribunal*,[187] the claim was made by reference to common law privilege but also parliamentary privilege upon the basis that Art.15 provides that each House has the power "to protect its official documents and the private papers of its members". The High Court found that an absolute privilege attached to the telephone records in question as "private papers" for the purpose of Art.15,[188] and it was unnecessary to consider the potential

---

[178] [1978] A.C. 171 at 218 (HL).
[179] *R. v Lewes Justices Ex p. R* [1973] A.C. 388 (HL).
[180] *D v N.S.P.C.C.* [1978] A.C. 171 (HL).
[181] *Director of Consumer Affairs v Sugar Distributors Ltd.* [1991] 1 I.R. 225 (HC).
[182] *Miley v Flood* [2001] 1 I.L.R.M. 489 (HC); *cf.* para.**13–33** *et seq.*
[183] [1993] 3 I.R. 320 (HC).
[184] *cf.* para.**13–47**.
[185] *cf.* para.**13–50**.
[186] [1993] 3 I.R. 320 (HC): *cf.* appendix 45.
[187] HC, October 13, 2003.
[188] *cf.* para.**13–64**.

application of common law principle. Kearns J. reasoned that legal and public policy was against subjecting private parliamentary papers to judicial scrutiny for discovery purposes, which "would leave the judicial branch in potential collision with either House".

13–56 The specific question of disclosure by gardaí—and, it would appear, all servants or agents of the State[189]—of statements or information relevant to the identity of an informant is now more properly a matter to be decided by reference to the rules governing public interest privilege,[190] which derived from the old common law executive privilege. The practical effect is the same since the "private" informer privilege is not absolute but is treated as raising a public interest that the court may weigh in each case against competing interests such as disclosure of the evidence.

13–57 The privilege has traditionally applied only to exempt bodies with the power to prosecute from revealing the identity of informants of *criminal* activity. Upon this basis, it was deemed in *Buckley v Incorporated Law Society*[191] not to attach to letters sent to the Law Society reporting alleged instances of professional misconduct on the part of a solicitor. In so ruling upon the scope of the privilege, Costello J. followed the Supreme Court's expressed preference in *Smurfit Paribas Bank*[192] for judicial weighing of the competing interests served respectively by privilege or disclosure. The cut-off point identified in *Buckley* is regrettably arbitrary and at variance with the otherwise fluid approach advocated by the Irish courts to questions of privilege and disclosure. A more principled approach—one more conducive to expansion or retrenchment of the privilege, according to the nature of the confidentiality requesting protection—had been adopted mere months before in *Goodman International (No. 3) v Hamilton*.[193] Geoghegan J. approved the exclusionary discretion identified by Lord Edmund-Davies in *D v N.S.P.C.C.*,[194] to wit: "where (i) a confidential relationship exists (other than that of lawyer and client) and (ii) disclosure would be in breach of some ethical or social value involving the public interest, the court has a discretion to uphold a refusal to disclose relevant evidence provided it considers that, on balance, the public interest would be better served by excluding such evidence". The "sole touchstone" for the question of non-disclosure was "the public interest"—and it was not necessary to establish the presence or absence of central government in the matter, nor that the informant acted under a duty, and nor (according to Geoghegan J.) that the communication was confidential, although each of these

---

[189] Upon the basis that the informer privilege claimed by a prison governor was treated as raising a private and not a public privilege, the decision in *State (Comerford) v Governor of Mounjoy Prison* [1981] I.L.R.M. 86 (HC) has been criticised by Fennell, *The Law of Evidence in Ireland* (Butterworths, Dublin, 1992) at p.190.
[190] *DPP (Hanley) v Holly* [1984] I.L.R.M. 149 (HC); *cf.* para.**13–78**.
[191] [1994] 2 I.R. 44 (HC).
[192] [1990] 1 I.R. 469 (SC): *cf.* appendix 35 and para.**13–33** *et seq.*
[193] [1993] 3 I.R. 320 (HC): *cf.* appendix 45.
[194] [1978] A.C. 171 at 245 (HL).

factors may be relevant to the cogency of the arguments in favour of or against disclosure.

13–58 The common law privilege is not absolute. A person may be required to reveal his sources where disclosure would exonerate an accused in criminal proceedings. In *Marks v Beyfus*,[195] Lord Esher M.R. ruled that this exception does not confer a discretion upon the court, but that where it arises in a case the court must require disclosure:

> "[I]f upon a trial of a prisoner the judge should be of opinion that the disclosure of the name of the informant is necessary or right in order to shew the prisoner's innocence, then one public policy is in conflict with another public policy, and that which says that an innocent man is not to be condemned when his innocence can be proved is the policy that must prevail".

13–59 The exception was applied in *Ward v Special Criminal Court*,[196] where the accused sought disclosure of up to 40 statements made by 20 persons to the gardaí throughout the investigation of the murder of Veronica Guerin; not being called as witnesses, the persons were classifiable as informants, whose lives, it was claimed, required protection from feared reprisal. The Special Criminal Court had opted for a compromise whereby defence lawyers could inspect the statements but were forbidden from revealing their content to the accused. Carney J. of the High Court disagreed with this direction, which was fraught with difficulty not least in "fundamentally altering the established relationship between defence lawyers and their client".[197] The trial judge reasoned that in a case of this nature, the court should scrutinise the documents and ascertain what documents, if any, might be useful in tending to prove innocence of the accused. Carney J.'s ruling was upheld upon appeal by the Supreme Court.

13–60 In Ireland, journalists are not *per se* entitled to refuse to disclose their sources, according to *Re Kevin O'Kelly*.[198] It has since been recognised, however, in *Burke v Central Independent Television Plc*.[199] that journalists may benefit from privilege in extreme circumstances, such as where necessary to protect the lives of their informants. In the context of libel proceedings against a journalist's publishers arising from allegations that the plaintiffs were involved in the nerve centre of the IRA, the Supreme Court assessed the question of disclosure upon a weighing of the competing interests. In this case, the interests were both constitutional in status—namely the protection of citizens from the risk of death or bodily injury against the protection and vindication of the good name of citizens, in which balance the former interest clearly

---

[195] (1890) 25 Q.B.D. 494 at 498 (CA).
[196] [1998] 2 I.R. 493 (SC).
[197] HC, November 13, 1998.
[198] (1974) 109 I.L.T.R. 97 (CCA).
[199] [1994] 2 I.R. 61 (SC).

prevailed. The court was prepared to assume the truth of the defendant's submission of risk to life at that stage in the proceedings.

13–61 In more recent years, the English legislature has created a privilege enabling journalists to withhold identity of source save where outweighed by a countervailing interest in disclosure.[200] This option was rejected by the Law Reform Commission which considered it preferable that the issues be weighed by the court upon a case-by-case basis, having regard to the confidentiality of the information and the criteria identified by Wigmore and endorsed in *Cook v Carroll*.[201] The choice of maintaining the inclusionary rule (subject to non-disclosure in exceptional cases) or of enacting a new exclusionary rule (by creating specific provision subject to exceptions) may ultimately be one of form in Ireland, given that private privilege has been constitutionalised by the Irish courts with the result that privilege is less categorical and subject to a greater extent to the specific interests raised in each case.

The Constitution: Executive and Parliamentary

13–62 The Constitution has had the effect of conferring absolute privilege upon executive and parliamentary communications, in some cases expressly and in others implicitly. Article 15.12 created a privilege—since interpreted to be absolute, and often referred to as an "immunity"—over "[a]ll official reports and publications of the Oireachtas or of either House thereof and utterances made in either House wherever published". The privilege is limited to publications and utterances first made within the Dáil and Seanad, and Art.15.12 has not been interpreted to apply more loosely to communications first made in the context of tribunals or committees established by the Oireachtas.[202] Article 15.13 bolstered the privilege by means of the principle of non-amenability for parliamentarians: "The members of each House of the Oireachtas ... shall not, in respect of any utterance in either House, be amenable to any court or any authority other than the House itself".[203]

13–63 In *Attorney-General v Hamilton (No.2)*,[204] the Supreme Court considered whether parliamentary privilege is lost when the allegation or information is repeated by the member outside the Dáil or Seanad, such as where he repeats the allegation before a tribunal of enquiry. The High Court had decided that since parliamentary privilege is absolute it should be narrowly construed, and upon this basis the privilege did not implicitly extend to

---

[200] Contempt of Court Act 1981, s.10. The Irish Government waived its privilege in *Reynolds v Times Newspapers Ltd.* [1999] 1 All E.R. 609 (HL).
[201] *cf.* para.**13–47**.
[202] *Attorney-General v Hamilton (No.2)* [1993] 3 I.R. 227 at 270, *per* Finlay C.J. (SC).
[203] The principle of non-amenability was considered by Geoghegan J. in the High Court in *Attorney-General v Hamilton (No.2) ibid.* at 246, and was found to apply only to cases where the member was exposed to penalty or sanction for refusal to disclose (such as would arise from contempt of court).
[204] [1993] 3 I.R. 227 (SC).

"statements" repeated by the member outside the Oireachtas or tendered as evidence before a tribunal of enquiry. The Supreme Court disagreed, and found that the true construction of Arts 15.12 and 15.13 was that any utterance first made in either House of the Oireachtas, wheresoever published, remains privileged in the context of any legal proceedings. Thus the privilege was not lost upon "factually similar" repetition of the information by the member outside the Oireachtas, and the source of the information remained confidential. The court's findings were influenced chiefly by the wording of Art.15.13, which operated in the case as an ouster of jurisdiction rather than as a privilege in bar against disclosure of publications and utterances originating in the Oireachtas. The ouster could be waived, although the court considered that the repetition and elaboration of original allegations for the purpose of assisting a tribunal of enquiry did not amount to a specific waiver, and that compelling a member of the Oireachtas to reveal the sources of allegations first uttered in the Oireachtas, upon pain of penalty for contempt of court, was precisely what Art.15.13 had prohibited.[205]

13–64 In *Howlin v Morris Tribunal*,[206] Kearns J. explored the application of parliamentary privilege to records of telephone conversations. The learned judge found as a matter of fact that records of conversations between members of the public and their political representatives constitute "private papers" for the purpose of attracting privilege under Art.15. Although the words "private papers" are not used in Art.15.12 or 15.13, they appear in Art.15.10 in the context of a provision declaring the ability of each House to "make its own rules and standing orders, with power ... to ensure freedom of debate, and to protect its official documents and the private papers of its members". In *Howlin's* case, it was claimed by the respondent that since the Committee on Procedure and Privileges—upon whom the Oireachtas had conferred its powers under Art.15.10—had failed to pass a motion specifically conferring immunity or privilege upon the applicant's papers, privilege did not arise. This view of the operation of parliamentary privilege was doubted by Kearns J., who found in any event that it was sufficiently clear from the outset that the Committee was in attendance at the Morris Tribunal to assert the applicant's right to assert privilege over those papers. On a more general level, the learned judge emphasised that the components of Art.15 must be read schematically, and a clear underlying principle is the "freedom of debate" identified in Art.15.10. Kearns J. expressed the following view of the nature of parliamentary privilege arising under Art.15:

> "The power, it seems to me, can only be seen as creating a complete protection in the nature of a privilege, being one of a unique character which is created by the Constitution and which is either self-executing or which requires only the expression of the will of the House to give it full constitutional effect. Any interpretation that the power is somehow

---

[205] *ibid.* at 273, *per* Finlay C.J.
[206] HC, October 13, 2003.

qualified would leave the judicial branch on a potential collision course with either House whenever exercising its power under Article 15.10, precisely the opposite of what the Article is intended to achieve".

13–65 In *Attorney-General v Hamilton (No.1)*,[207] the Supreme Court interpreted the Art.28 requirement that the Government meet and act with "collective authority" and "collective responsibility" implicitly to require the absolute confidentiality of all discussions between members of the Government prior to making decisions. The demarcation is jurisdictional, given the separation of powers between the executive and the judiciary envisaged by Art.6.1 of the Constitution; accordingly, the court may not lift the veil and examine the substance of the claim by weighing the relevant competing interests, nor may the privilege be waived by an individual member of Government.

V. MARITAL PRIVACY

13–66 Marital privilege was not common law in origin, and was first enacted by s.3 of the Evidence Amendment Act 1853 protecting against mandatory disclosure by either spouse of communications between them. Since neither the accused nor his spouse were competent witnesses in criminal proceedings—not until the Criminal Evidence Act 1898 in England and the Criminal Justice (Evidence) Act 1924 in Ireland—it was at this time of relevance to civil proceedings. The common law privilege was implicitly acknowledged by s.1 of the Criminal Justice (Evidence) Act 1924. Although s.1 rendered the spouse of the accused *competent* to testify at the behest of the accused, and provides that the prosecution cannot invite adverse inferences from the failure of the spouse to testify, the spouse remained non-compellable at the behest of the accused for policy reasons, chiefly to promote marital harmony, and to minimise the prospect of intimidation between spouses.[208] Marital privilege received additional strength in Ireland by reason of the weighty protection afforded the married family under the Constitution, in particular by Art.41, although when the Supreme Court considered the matter of marital *privacy* in *McGhee v Attorney-General*,[209] a majority reasoned that the right derived from Art.40(3) as an unenumerated personal right, whilst only Walsh J. considered that marital privacy was protected by Art.41 as an incident of the status afforded to the married family. Although Art.41 is clearly the principal source in the Constitution for the protected status of the married family, and although it does not confer absolute rights of self-governance upon the family, its present wording renders it an unwieldy bulwark against compromise; to the extent that Art.40 confers personal rights more amenable to being balanced against

---

[207] [1993] 2 I.R. 250 (SC).
[208] For a thoughtful analysis of the vagaries of these rules under the common law and the Irish constitution, see the judgment of Walsh J. in *People (DPP) v T* (1988) 3 Frewen 141.
[209] [1974] I.R. 284 (SC).

Privilege 405

competing interests, and to the extent that it applies without formal discrimination between the marital family and other domestic units,[210] it provides a more appropriate basis for balancing the interests served by privilege or disclosure.

13–67 The current rationale for marital privilege is based upon upholding the institution of marriage, although this has come under considerable attack in recent years,[211] and the privilege was abolished in England by s.80(9) of the Police and Criminal Evidence Act 1984. In its application to criminal proceedings, marital privilege was substantially eroded by Pt IV of the Criminal Evidence Act 1992.[212] In cases of violence against the spouse or a child, or sexual offences against a child, the spouse of the accused, where not jointly charged, is compellable to testify at the behest of the prosecution or the co-accused. In explaining this direction—which ran counter to the Law Reform Commission's proposal that in no circumstances should the spouse of the accused be compellable for the prosecution[213]—the Minister for Justice explained to the Dáil that the Court of Criminal Appeal indicated in *People (DPP) v T*[214] that common law or statutory rules limiting compellability of the spouse may prove unconstitutional, in cases of suspected child abuse at least.[215] Part IV further provides that the spouse, unless jointly charged, is in all cases competent to testify either for the prosecution, or the defence, or a co-accused. Overturning the common law position, s.23 provides that the spouse, unless jointly charged, is also, in general, compellable at the behest of the accused in any criminal proceedings. To the extent that a spouse or former spouse is not compellable under Pt IV, marital privilege remains enforceable, as acknowledged by s.26.[216]

13–68 As with the other privileges, marital privacy implicitly distinguishes between form and content, so that information imparted in an oral communication made by one spouse to the other may, if overheard, be proven by the third party in evidence.[217] Although in principle, a privilege is distinct from a person's competence and compellability to testify as a witness[218]—for

---

[210] In *People (DPP) v T* (1988) 3 Frewen 141 Walsh J., followed *Re Nicolaoue* [1966] I.R. 567 (SC) and proposed that "if the family happens to be one which, in ordinary parlance is such, even though not based in marriage and therefore not within the provision of Art.41, it is within the provisions of Art.40".
[211] Criticised by: Jackson, "Part IV of the Criminal Evidence Act 1992" (1993) 15 D.U.L.J. 202; O'Connor, "Competence and Compellability of Spouses as Witnesses for the Prosecution" (1985) I.L.T. 204, and Creighton, "Spouse Competence and Compellability" [1990] Crim. L.R. 34.
[212] *cf.* para.**2–22** *et seq.*
[213] Law Reform Commission, *Report on Competence and Compellability of Spouses as Witnesses*, 13–1985 at p.49.
[214] *People (DPP) v T* (1988) 3 Frewen 141, *per* Walsh J.
[215] 416 *Dáil Debates* Cols 1287–1288, March 3, 1992. For further discussion of this, see Jackson, "Part IV of the Criminal Evidence Act 1992" (1993) 15 D.U.L.J. 202.
[216] *cf.* para.**2–25** *et seq.*
[217] *R. v Smithies* 5 C. & P. 321; *R. v Simons* 6 C. & P. 540.
[218] *cf.* para.**2–04**.

instance, a witness may agree to testify, or be compelled to testify, and then invoke the privilege against self-incrimination to resist answering certain questions—this rule does not appear to hold for marital privilege. Peter Pain J. emphasised upon appeal in *R. v Pitt*[219] that if such a witness—here the wife of the accused—refuses to answer questions properly put to her, she may be deemed a hostile witness; given this possibility, trial judges should caution a non-compellable spouse of the implications of his decision prior to taking the oath or affirmation. Upon this basis, where a spouse, despite being non-compellable as a witness against his spouse, elects to give testimony, he thereby waives his claim to marital privilege, and may be asked and required to answer questions as an ordinary witness, subject to, and with the benefit of, the other rules of evidence and other applicable privileges. The witness retains the right not to answer questions that would expose him to charge or penalty (the privilege against self-incrimination), although this right does not enable the witness to refuse to answer questions that would expose the witness' spouse or other person to charge or penalty.[220]

VI. PUBLIC INTEREST PRIVILEGE

13–69 This is variously called executive or State privilege, although the more popular reference to public interest privilege is aptly reflective of its broader scope in recent years. The privilege remains principally concerned with the confidential communications and inner workings of organs, bodies, and agents of the State. It was affirmed by the High Court in Ireland in *Leen v President of the Executive Council (No.1)*[221] upon the basis that it was rooted in public policy and not in immunities previously enjoyed by the Crown, which, it was supposed, had not survived the creation of the Free State.[222] The privilege reflects the view that evidence, howsoever relevant, should be privileged where its discovery would damage national interests, such as the effective operation of the public service and enforcement agencies. There are no clear rules governing the privilege, although the courts have shown themselves not unwilling to order total or partial discovery of such documents, and have repeatedly expressed the need to scrutinise the documents before deciding whether the claim of privilege outweighs the public interest in the proper administration of justice by production of all the material evidence.

13–70 At one time, the courts refused to examine claims of public privilege—then more stoutly called *immunity*—where duly certified by the relevant minister. The House of Lords broke from this tradition in *Conway v Rimmer*[223] when it affirmed judicial discretion to examine the documents over which public privilege was claimed before deciding whether the document should be

---

[219] [1982] 3 All E.R. 63.
[220] *R. v Minihane* (1921) 16 Cr. App. R. 38 (CA).
[221] [1926] I.R. 456 (HC).
[222] Casey, *Constitutional Law in Ireland* (Sweet & Maxwell, London, 1987) at p.54.
[223] [1968] A.C. 910 (HL).

discovered or concealed. The issues arose in the context of a suit by a former constable against his former Superintendent for malicious prosecution upon the charge of stealing a torch. The Home Secretary objected to the production of five internal reports for senior officers upon the basis that production would be injurious to the public interest. Four of the reports related to the plaintiff's conduct as probationary officer, and the fifth to an alleged theft. The House of Lords considered that the Home Secretary's certification of privilege was not final, and that the court had the power to scrutinise the documents privately before reaching its own view. In addressing the question of discovery, the court should balance the State's interest in non-disclosure against the public interest in the proper administration of justice.

13–71 This development in the public interest privilege was approved by the Supreme Court in a constitutional setting in *Murphy v Dublin Corporation and Minister for Local Government*.[224] In a case seeking disclosure of an inspector's report made prior to a compulsory purchase order against the applicant by Dublin Corporation, the court stressed that the nature of the documents over which a private privilege or a public immunity is sought must be particularised and the grounds for the privilege or immunity individually set out. Public privilege could not be claimed generally over broad classes of document. It behoves the court to scrutinise the claim of immunity, given that the court is constitutionally encharged to secure the proper administration of justice. *Murphy* was affirmed by the Supreme Court in *Ambiorix v Minister for the Environment*,[225] where it was reiterated that judges must resolve the competing interests when public interest privilege is claimed over a document. Finlay C.J. observed that the judge is not required to inspect every document over which privilege is sought, but may decide that privilege applies or not after a survey of the particulars and reasons advanced in support of the claim. It is open to the judge to decide that inspection is necessary, however.

13–72 *Murphy* was applied in *Folens Co. v Minister for Education*,[226] where Costello J. observed that while the courts should protect confidential communications between members of an executive organ, the court should study the communication first to ascertain that its contents are in fact confidential. In *Walker v Ireland*,[227] the High Court ordered disclosure of a document sent to the Irish Government by the Attorney General for the UK and Northern Ireland, and in doing so was influenced by the fact that the British Attorney-General had not objected to discovery. The court confirmed that there is no absolute privilege attaching to communications between sovereign states, and that the question of disclosure falls to be assessed in line with the principle articulated in *Murphy*.

---

[224] [1972] I.R. 215 (SC); *cf.* appendix 16; applied in *Geraghty v Minister for Local Government* [1975] I.R. 300 (HC).
[225] [1992] 1 I.R. 277 (SC).
[226] [1981] I.L.R.M. 21 (HC).
[227] [1997] 1 I.L.R.M. 363 (HC).

13–73 It was acknowledged in *Incorporated Law Society of Ireland v Minister for Justice*[228] that the public interest lies in preserving confidential and uninhibited communication within the public service, but that ultimately when weighing the competing interests, the court should assess the extent to which, as a matter of likelihood, non-disclosure would adversely affect the opponent, and, on the other hand, the extent to which disclosure would injure the public interest in preserving confidential communications within the public service. In *Breathnach v Ireland (No.3)*,[229] Keane J. considered it important also to consider the extent to which disclosure would weaken the claimant's case—a factor not formally appropriate to the issues engendered by public privilege, though coterminous with analysis of its effect upon the opponent's case.

13–74 The development in *Murphy* has been described by Morgan as "an example of the Irish judiciary's characteristic preference for individual rights over and against the smooth running of government administration which may benefit large numbers of people".[230] English law differs from the view adopted in *Murphy* and later cases that privilege cannot be claimed over classes or categories of documents, and it recognises the appropriateness of a class claim over communications by police officers in the course of their duty. This option was rejected by Keane J. in *DPP (Hanley) v Holly*,[231] where Keane J. emphasised that the party claiming public privilege over a document must set out the specific type of possible damage that may result to the public interest, so the court can privately consider the merits of the claim. In *Breathnach v Ireland (No.3)*,[232] a suit for malicious prosecution, Keane J. repeated this view and ordered disclosure of notes taken during the course of interrogation of the plaintiff. More recently, in *Hughes v Garda Commissioner*,[233] where the plaintiff garda instituted civil proceedings after a demotion for refusing to name an informant to his superiors, Laffoy J. ordered discovery of various documents containing confidential information received by gardaí in the course of investigating subversive crime, upon the basis that they were "so centrally germane" to the facts at issue.

13–75 The strong public interest in confidentiality of communications by or to the gardaí has, however, been accepted by the courts. In *Corbett v DPP*,[234] an individual claim for privilege over a communication between the DPP and a garda prior to applying for an adjournment of a prosecution for assault was successful upon the basis that there is a high public interest in preserving the confidentiality of such communications. In *Skeffington v Rooney*,[235] the

---

[228] [1987] I.L.R.M. 42 at 44 (HC).
[229] [1993] 2 I.R. 458 at 472 (HC).
[230] Morgan, *The Separation of Powers in the Irish Constitution* (Round Hall Sweet & Maxwell, Dublin, 1997) at p.157.
[231] [1984] I.L.R.M. 149 (HC).
[232] [1993] 2 I.R. 458 at 472 (HC).
[233] HC, January 20, 1998.
[234] [1999] 2 I.R. 179 (HC).
[235] [1997] 2 I.L.R.M. 56 (SC).

Supreme Court acknowledged that although the court can investigate each claim of public privilege, it may accept that certain types of documents are generally privileged in a case. It is open to the legislature to create new types of specific privilege, which would have the effect of overriding the common law rules,[236] although clear and express words are required to create a privilege, and the creation of a duty to keep certain information confidential does not necessarily give rise to such a claim.[237] Given the separation of powers logic upon which *Murphy* and other decisions were based, however, a provision purporting to immunise a class of executive communication not clearly authorised by the Constitution would engender certain suspicions of unconstitutionality.

13–76 There is a formal distinction between the public interest privilege and a private privilege, although increasingly this seems rooted in tradition and not in principle, particularly in Ireland where private privileges have been developed in line with constitutional imperatives. The formal distinction at common law had the following effects. A privilege was a private right to suppress certain evidence, upheld for the benefit of clearly identified parties; if waived, no one could object to the waiver;[238] secondary evidence of the privileged document or information could be admitted;[239] where the privilege was absolute, no question of balancing competing interests and rights arose. A public privilege, then called immunity, differs in the following respects: the non-disclosure of documents or information is viewed for reasons of public policy as a duty as well as a right; secondary evidence is inadmissible; and inbuilt in the determination of discovery is the balancing of competing interests (since the administration of justice on the one hand, and the public interest in preserving the confidentiality of State communications on the other, are both interests of the State). As has been discussed earlier,[240] the Irish courts have developed private privileges in the context of rights and interests protected by the Constitution, and in this light the formal distinction between the two is unsustainable save by reference to the Constitution and the balancing of interests thereby facilitated.

13–77 Due to the formal and lineal distinction between public and private privilege, it has been reasoned by the English courts that the public interest privilege cannot be waived, and upon this basis it was referred to as an "immunity" by the House of Lords in *Air Canada v Secretary of State for Trade (No.2)*.[241] The view that a public interest privilege may not be waived entails the view that it must be claimed and then fought by the relevant public official or authority. Yet this view has come under increasing attack in England,

---

[236] *PB v AL* [1996] 1 I.L.R.M. 154 at 158, *per* Costello P. (HC).
[237] As in *Skeffington v Rooney* [1997] 2 I.L.R.M. 56 at 71 (SC) with respect to s.12 of the Garda Síochána (Complaints) Board Act 1986.
[238] *cf.* para.**13–10** *et seq.*
[239] *cf.* para.**13–08**.
[240] *cf.* para.**13–02**.
[241] [1983] 2 A.C. 394, *per* Lord Fraser (HL).

not least because it suggests an eagerness on the part of the State in some cases to suppress vital evidence of public corruption (and in this regard, President Nixon's claim of executive privilege in the Watergate enquiry lingers in the collective memory). It is also not borne out in practice, as public privilege is frequently not claimed in cases.[242] The House of Lords ruled in *R. v Chief Constable West Midlands Police Ex p. Wiley*[243] that a minister is not obliged to sign public interest certificates over documents sought to be discovered. Upon the question of waiver—which is distinct from, although related to, the question of claiming the privilege—the House considered that a person responsible for the communication could decline to claim the privilege, though not waive it, and that this would be a factor to be considered by the court when deciding whether the public interest lay in suppressing the evidence.[244] The Irish courts have not yet analysed this issue in depth, although the Supreme Court indicated recently in *McDonald v RTÉ.*,[245] with little fuss, that public interest privilege may be waived, though not implicitly by mere reference to the documents in the context of a consultation meeting, nor individually by servants or agents of the State such as garda officers.

13–78 The specific question of disclosure by gardaí—and, it would appear, all servants or agents of the State—of statements or information relevant to the identity of an informant is decided by reference to the rules governing public interest privilege.[246] The public interest in withholding identity is likely to be lost where the informant has no wish to remain anonymous (although the privilege is not technically private by nature and so is not capable of being claimed or waived by parties without a requisite degree of authority). This was the conclusion of the Court of Appeal in the unusual circumstances of *Savage v Chief Constable of Hampshire*,[247] where the informant had taken civil proceedings against the police for allegedly reneging on an agreement to pay him in return for valuable information.

13–79 By the same logic, documents sent by gardaí to the DPP do not engender legal professional privilege but instead attract, automatically, a public interest privilege against disclosure. In so ruling, Keane J. observed in *Breathnach v Ireland (No.3)*[248] that the extent to which freedom of communication between the gardaí and the DPP might be inhibited by the prospect of subsequent disclosure in court proceedings raises an issue of essential public interest.

---

[242] Ganz, "Matrix Churchill and Public Interest Immunity" (1993) 56 M.L.R. 564 at 565.
[243] [1994] 2 W.L.R. 433.
[244] Following *Hehir v Commissioner of Police of the Metropolis* [1982] 1 W.L.R. 715 at 723, *per* Brightman L.J. (CA).
[245] [2001] 2 I.L.R.M. 1 (SC), *per* Fennelly J.
[246] *cf.* para.**13–78**.
[247] [1997] W.L.R. 1061 (CA).
[248] [1993] 2 I.R. 458 at 472 (HC).

VII. PRIVILEGE AGAINST SELF-INCRIMINATION

13–80 The privilege against self-incrimination operates to exempt a person from answering questions, or producing documents, that have the effect of exposing him to criminal charge, penalty, or forfeiture.[249] The privilege is of general application to any person at any stage prior to and during criminal or civil proceedings whenever incriminating information is sought from him. To the extent that the privilege affects the accused in criminal proceedings, it becomes the right to silence,[250] and it is manifest in the rules rendering the accused incompetent as a witness for the prosecution and non-compellable in general.[251] Both the privilege against self-incrimination[252] and the right to silence[253] have been accorded constitutional status by the courts. The classic formulation of the privilege against self-incrimination was given by Goddard L.J. in *Blunt v Park Lane Hotel Ltd*:[254] "no one is bound to answer any question if the answer thereto would, in the opinion of the judge, have a tendency to expose the deponent to any criminal charge, penalty or forfeiture which the judge regards as reasonably likely to be preferred or sued for".

13–81 The trial judge may choose to hear *in camera* the witness' response to the question asked during the proceedings, to decide if the privilege applies. If a trial judge wrongly denies the accused his privilege, what he was subsequently compelled to say may be excluded from subsequent trials upon the basis that it was involuntary.[255] The case law has consistently emphasised that there must be a real and appreciable fear that the witness' answer will expose him to charge or penalty.[256] Upon this basis in the past, the courts have found the privilege not to apply to a witness' anticipated exposure to ecclesiastical censure.[257] Although the privilege was originally limited to feared exposure to *criminal* charges, penalties, or forfeiture,[258] it has expanded sufficiently to include monetary penalties recoverable in civil proceedings and to apply to directors as a bar against questions tending to incriminate their company.[259] The privilege has also been extended to apply to answers

---

[249] The inclusion of forfeiture derived from an old equity principle against discovery for the purposes of forfeiture of property: *Mexborough (Earl of) v Whitwood U.D.C.* [1897] 2 Q.B. 111 at 115 (CA), following *Pye v Butterfield* 5 B. & S. 829. In England, the effect of the privilege upon questions relating to the forfeiture of property was abolished by s.16(1)(a) of the Civil Evidence Act 1968.
[250] *cf.* para.**13–80**.
[251] *cf.* para.**2–17**.
[252] *Re Haughey* [1971] I.R. 217 (SC).
[253] *Attorney-General v O'Leary* [1991] I.L.R.M. 454 at 460, *per* Costello J. (HC); *Heaney and McGuinness v Ireland* [1994] 3 I.R. 593 at 605, *per* Costello J. (HC).
[254] [1942] 2 K.B. 253 at 257 (CA).
[255] *R. v Garbett* (1847) 1 Den. 236.
[256] *R. v Boyes* (1871–3) All E.R. 172.
[257] *Blunt v Park Lane Hotel* [1942] 2 K.B. 253 (CA), Lord Goddard C.J. ruling that the prospect of ecclesiastical censure for adultery was now obsolete and a "fanciful" risk.
[258] *e.g. S v E* [1967] 1 Q.B. 371, where the privilege did not apply to questions ascertaining the results of a blood test establishing paternity of the parties' child (given that the witness was not liable to *penalty*).
[259] In *Rio Tinto Zinc Corp. v Westinghouse Electric* [1978] A.C. 547, privilege was held by

incriminating the witness under foreign law, so long as there is a reasonable possibility that criminal proceedings may be taken abroad and that the individual may be extradited to the other jurisdiction.[260]

13–82 The privilege only relates to the answers that a person may not be compelled to make, and it does not preclude questions being put to him.[261] Notwithstanding the privilege, however, a person may, under a number of statutes, face conviction for the separate offence of failing to provide the requested information,[262] and an accused may, under exceptional provisions introduced in Ireland for drug trafficking and offences against the State, incur adverse inferences in his trial arising from his failure to mention matters when questioned in custody later relied upon in his defence.[263]

13–83 Unless specifically abrogated by statute, any person may assert the privilege against self-incrimination so long as it properly applies to the information being withheld. The courts have accepted that statutes that confer powers upon bodies to elicit information from persons, and that legally compel persons to provide the information, do not necessarily abrogate the privilege, so long as the information obtained by the body is not used in future criminal proceedings against that person. In *M v D*,[264] the High Court considered the submission that an order for discovery under s.9 of the Proceeds of Crime Act 1996 infringed the respondent's privilege against self-incrimination by requiring him to furnish particulars of his property, income, and sources over the past 10 years. Moriarty J. rejected the view that compulsory disclosure of assets did not amount to self-incrimination;[265] but he granted the discovery order in exchange for an undertaking from the DPP that the information thereby obtained would not prejudice the respondent in any future criminal proceedings. This approach, favoured previously by the House of Lords,[266] was followed again in the context of s.9 in *Gilligan v Criminal Assets Bureau*.[267] The High Court

---

the House of Lords to attach to documents upon the basis that they would expose the parties to substantial fines by the European Commission for infringement of competition laws. This constituted "exposure to penalties", and it did not matter that they were enforceable in civil proceedings.

[260] So held by O'Dalaigh C.J. in *State (McGee) v O'Rourke* [1971] I.R. 205 (SC), departing from the traditional view favoured in *Wigmore on Evidence* (vol.81, at para.2258, p.342) that "incrimination" was limited to penalties under domestic law, and favouring instead the view expressed in *Cross on Evidence* (2nd ed., Sweet & Maxwell, London, 1963) at p.232.

[261] *Allhusen v Labouchere* (1878) 3 Q.B.D. 654 at 660 (CA), where privilege was upheld in response to interrogatories.

[262] *cf.* para.**13–88**.

[263] *cf.* para.**13–100** *et seq.*

[264] [1998] 3 I.R. 175 at 178 (HC).

[265] Rejecting the English Court of Appeal's decision in *Re Thomas (Disclosure Order)* [1992] 4 All E.R. 814.

[266] *Istel Ltd. v Tully* [1993] A.C. 45 (HL).

[267] [1998] 3 I.R. 185 (HC): upheld by the Supreme Court at [2001] 4 I.R. 113. *M v D* and *Gilligan* were applied in *Carroll v Law Society of Ireland (No.2)* [2003] 1 I.R. 284 (HC). The court found that any evidence compulsorily acquired against the applicant in the context of professional misconduct proceedings before the Education Committee of

rejected the view that the true effect of s.9 was not actually to *compel* a person to comply with the request for particulars of his property, income, and sources. Section 9 empowered the courts to require such discovery upon pain of imprisonment for contempt of court. In this light, McGuinness J. considered an undertaking from the DPP not to profit from the compelled disclosure in future criminal proceedings to be "essential in virtually every case where an order under s.9 is granted".[268]

The Right to Silence

13–84 A suspect may remain silent, and an accused may choose not to testify,[269] flowing from the common law (and constitutional) right to silence and presumption of innocence.[270] Within the adversarial system of law, this is assumed necessary to ensure that the State prosecutor discharges its burden of proof after the adduction of independent evidence meeting proof to the requisite standard.[271] If the accused elects to testify, he waives his right to silence and his privilege against self-incrimination in so far as they apply to questions tending directly to incriminate him in the offences for which he is being tried.[272] If the accused exercises his right to silence and elects not to testify, adverse inferences may not be drawn from this fact during the trial. The prosecution may not comment upon the failure of the accused to testify[273]—nor may the trial judge invite the jury to draw inferences from the accused's decision not to give evidence in defence.[274] The trial judge is under an obligation, when summing-up, to advise the jury that the accused has a right to silence, and that no adverse inferences may be drawn from his decision not to testify.[275]

13–85 The privilege against self-incrimination and the right to silence have been invested with lofty symbolic status in judicial *dicta* over the years, although chiefly in bygone eras when legislation had not yet subjected the privilege to the numerous restrictions that exist today in the public interest. Described as "most sacred" by one judge,[276] and by another as a "general rule established

---

the Law Society was inadmissible for the purposes of subsequent proceedings against him. Despite the very close nexus between the Education Committee and the respondent, the court refused to grant orders restraining the enquiry, and was influenced by the expressed acceptance by the respondent that the applicant's right to silence would be respected in the proceedings.

[268] [1998] 3 I.R. 185 at 233 (HC).
[269] *cf.* para.**2–17**.
[270] *Attorney-General v O'Leary* [1991] I.L.R.M. 454 at 460, *per* Costello J. (HC) (*cf.* appendix 39); *Heaney and McGuinness v Ireland* [1994] 3 I.R. 593 (SC) (*cf.* appendix 51).
[271] *cf.* para.**4–07**.
[272] Criminal Justice (Evidence) Act 1924, s.1(e); *cf.* para.**8–03** *et seq.*
[273] Criminal Justice (Evidence) Act 1924, s.1(b); *cf.* para.**2–18**.
[274] Conviction was quashed upon this basis in *Attorney-General v Quinn* (CCA, March 23, 1998).
[275] *People (DPP) v Finnerty* [1999] 4 I.R. 364 at 376, *per* Keane J. (SC) (*cf.* appendix 59).
[276] *R. v Worrall Ex p.* (1820) 1 Buck 531 at 540, *per* Eldon L.C. (CA).

with great justice and tenderness",[277] the right to silence was famously sanctified in American constitutional jurisprudence by the Fifth Amendment. The European Court of Human Rights, somewhat controversially (given the privilege's origins in the English common law), found against the respondent in *Saunders v UK*,[278] and declared that the privilege and the right now constituted fundamental international standards central to the rule of law.

13–86 Views differ upon the causes and dating of the privilege against self-incrimination and the maxim *nemo tenetur seipsum prodere*, to wit, that no person is bound to betray himself. Wigmore was notably sceptical of its status as a self-existing right, and formed the view that it had been employed as a lever in a jurisdictional conflict between the common law courts and rival courts adopting inquisitorial methods.[279] He observed that interrogation of suspects had survived in the common law courts by the early eighteenth century, long after the abolition of the Star Chamber tribunals and High Commission of the ecclesiastical courts in the 1640s, and that it did not apply as a general rule to all witnesses and in all criminal and civil proceedings until the Restoration period.[280] Whilst other writers posit the privilege in a continuous common law tradition,[281] the view that the privilege fully emerged no earlier than the nineteenth century has been approved by the Criminal Law Revision Committee[282] and by the Royal Commission on Criminal Procedure,[283] which concluded, similarly to Wigmore, that the privilege against self-incrimination and the right to silence emerged without any clear justification, and that they functioned chiefly to mitigate the disadvantages to the accused flowing from the prohibition against appearing as a witness in his own defence[284] and the poor quality of juries and legal representation then existing.

13–87 Although the right was described recently in *Matter of National Irish Bank*[285] as a common law principle borne of "the revulsion of the judges for forced confessions as being both unjust and unreliable in practice", the extent to which the right to silence and the privilege against self-incrimination amount to fundamental rights unto themselves, rather than illustrative instances of the presumption of innocence, has not always been clear in Ireland. Recent judicial pronouncements upon the right to silence have tended to posit it in a practical

---

[277] *Harrison v Southcote and Moreland* (1751) 2 Ves. Se. 389 at 394, *per* Lord Hardwicke L.C. (CA).
[278] (1996) 23 E.H.R.R. 313 at 337; *cf.* para.**13–93** and appendix 52.
[279] Wigmore (1902) at p.610.
[280] Wigmore, *A Treatise on Evidence* (vol.VI, Little Brown & Co., Boston) at pp.289–91.
[281] Maguire, "The Attack of the Common Lawyers on the Oath *Ex Officio*" in Witthe (ed.), *Essays in History and Political Theory in Honour of C.H. McIlwain* (Harvard University Press, 1956); Levy, *Origins of the Fifth Amendment* (Oxford University Press, New York, 1968).
[282] *Eleventh Report—Evidence (General)*, 1972, Cmnd. 4991, at para 21.
[283] Cmnd. 8092, 1981, at paras 1:13–121.
[284] *cf.* paras **2–16, 8–01**.
[285] [1999] 1 I.L.R.M. 321 at 350, *per* Barrington J. (SC): *cf.* appendix 57. See also *R. v Director of Serious Fraud Ex p. Smith* [1993] A.C. 1 (HL).

context as the first refuge of the guilty. In *Heaney and McGuinness v Ireland*,[286] O'Flaherty J. observed: "Where a person is totally innocent of any wrongdoing as regards his movements, it would require a strong attachment to one's apparent constitutional rights not to give such an account when asked pursuant to statutory requirement. So, the court holds, that the matter in debate here, can more properly be approached as an encroachment against the right not to have to say anything that might afford evidence that is self-incriminating".[287] In *People (DPP) v Foley*,[288] the Court of Criminal Appeal considered the effect, for the right to silence and the burdens of proof, of a statutory reverse-onus clause, in a case where the co-accused, who explained that he had called around to the house where the firearms were found to join a friend for tea, was acquitted, whilst the other co-accused who offered no explanation was convicted. In response to the appellant's submission that the provision effectively penalised the accused who invoked his constitutional right to silence, Budd J. reasoned:

> "What the 'right to silence' amounts to is that an accused is entitled in the first instance to call on the prosecution to prove its case. *Prima facie*, his situation is that he does not have to give an explanation or give evidence. But if proof of guilt is forthcoming—if circumstances are laid before the court of trial that point to the guilt of the accused—then an accused must attempt to rebut the prosecution case by evidence or else suffer the consequences."[289]

13–88 In a number of statutes, the legislature has created powers to compel the disclosure of information by creating separate criminal offences for refusal to answer particular questions. Under s.52 of the Offences Against the State Act 1939, the refusal of a detainee under s.30 of the Act to account for his movements at a particular time or the involvement of other persons in a scheduled offence constitutes a separate offence punishable by up to six months imprisonment. The section does not address the use to which the information may subsequently be put as evidence in criminal proceedings—in other words, whether the provision requires him to self-incriminate for the purposes of a future prosecution against him. In *Heaney and McGuinness v Ireland*,[290] the European Court of Human Rights ruled that this infringed the accused's right to a fair trial in his prosecution for the s.52(2) offence of refusing to provide information. By contrast, ss.15–16 of the Criminal Justice Act 1984 make it an offence not to account for firearms or ammunition found in one's possession, but they provide that information demanded from the person may not be used against the informer in any proceedings. Under s.7 of the Criminal Law Act

---

[286] [1996] I.R. 580, [1997] 1 I.L.R.M. 117 (SC); *cf.* appendix 51.
[287] [1997] 1 I.L.R.M. 117 at 124 (SC).
[288] [1995] 1 I.R. 267 (CCA). The court was asked to consider s.27A of the Firearms Act 1964, and its effect for the burdens of proof by providing that a person is guilty of an offence if a firearm is found in his possession or under his control such as to "give rise to a reasonable inference that he has not got it in his possession or under his control for a lawful purpose"; *cf.* para.**4–41**.
[289] *ibid.* at 292.
[290] (2001) 33 E.H.R.R. 264; *cf.* para.**13–97** and appendix 61.

1976, it is an offence not to furnish the gardaí with various information such as name and address. Under s.107 of the Road Traffic Act 1961 the gardaí may demand various types of information from drivers, such as their name and address (which, if undisclosed, authorises the garda to make an arrest without warrant), and information relating to the use of the vehicle. Under ss.13 and 15 of the Road Traffic Act 1994, a driver commits a criminal offence where he refuses to submit to a blood or urine sample following a request by a garda who suspects him of drink driving. Other examples include the Customs Consolidation Act 1876, the Companies Acts 1963–1990, the Income Tax Acts and Finance Acts, and the Social Welfare (Consolidation) Act 1993.[291] Although the statutes clearly abrogate the privilege against self-incrimination in specified cases, the courts are apt often to construe them as an acknowledgment of a person's duty to cooperate with the authorities and to provide appropriate information. In *DPP v Elliot*,[292] the High Court rejected a submission that since s.15 of the Road Traffic Act 1994 did not formally provide for an arrest prior to the request for a blood or urine sample, the garda was required to advise the driver that, although he could be convicted for refusal to give the sample, he had the benefit of the privilege of self-incrimination and was at liberty to leave the scene if he wished. O'Flaherty J. commented: "If the Oireachtas imposes an obligation on a person to perform some act which may be self-incriminating, I do not think either the Constitution or the common law can dilute that obligation by requiring the person to be given an opportunity to avoid complying with the obligation".[293]

13–89 More controversially, a number of recent statutes have made inroads into the pre-trial right to silence, and the principle that no adverse inferences ought to be drawn from the accused's refusal to speak. These have been considered earlier in the context of corroboration, since they each provide that corroborative inferences may be drawn from the accused's silence or non-cooperation.[294] They include: ss.18–19 of the Criminal Justice Act 1984; s.3 of the Criminal Justice (Forensic Evidence) Act 1990; s.7 of the Criminal Justice (Drug) Trafficking Act 1996; and s.5 of the Offences Against the State (Amendment) Act 1998. These enable the court to draw "such inferences ... as appear proper" from the specified silence or omission—in the case of the 1984 Act, this is the accused's failure to explain his presence in a particular place, or his possession of a particular thing; in the case of the 1990 Act, this is his refusal to consent to the taking of various tissue samples from his person; and in the case of the 1996 and 1998 Acts, this is his refusal to mention information when questioned in custody that he later relies upon in his defence.

13–90 Thus far, legislative curtailment of the privilege against self-

---

[291] For a review of the ad hoc manner in which the legislature has impinged upon the right to silence, see *Heaney and McGuinness v Ireland* [1997] 1 I.L.R.M. 117 at 124–6 (SC): *cf.* appendix 51.
[292] [1997] 2 I.L.R.M. 156 (HC).
[293] *ibid.* at 160.
[294] *cf.* para.**5–11** *et seq.*

incrimination and the right to silence in Ireland has been reserved to specified contexts. The provisions have survived constitutional challenge before the Irish courts, where they have consistently been justified upon the basis that the right to silence is not an absolute right, and that so long as the encroachment is necessary and proportionate and no broader than the interest requires, it is constitutional. It is of note that the Supreme Court in *Heaney and McGuinness v Ireland*[295] was also influenced by the exceptional nature of prosecutions for offences against the State. Costello J. adopted the view in the High Court that the common law right to silence was protected as an element of the right to a fair trial under Art.38.1.[296] In the Supreme Court,[297] O'Flaherty J. instead considered that the right was protected as a correlative element of the constitutional right to freedom of expression under Art.40.6. Whilst the latter approach has the benefit of unifying the constitutional reference point for both the privilege against self-incrimination and the right to silence, the right to freedom of expression appears inappropriate to support these specific claims.[298] In both cases, the right to silence was viewed to be a right qualified by considerations of public order or morality, so that legislative encroachment upon the right was constitutional so long as proportionate to the public interest and no wider than that interest required.

13–91 In *Rock v Ireland & Attorney-General*,[299] the Supreme Court appeared to regard the right to silence to affect principally the accused's constitutional right to a fair trial under Art.38.1, in a decision upholding the constitutionality of ss.18–19 of the Criminal Justice Act 1984. Whilst this is consistent with the approach of the European Court of Human Rights—which *perforce* considers inferences from silence in a trial to raise a question of the fairness of the trial for the purposes of Art.6 of the Convention—the distinction may yet serve to declassify the right, or to establish it as a right that is not self-existing and from whose breach strict consequences may not always flow, so long as the accused is fairly tried on balance. A similar approach has been adopted by the Irish courts to the rights to cross-examine,[300] to formal identification,[301] and to confrontation.[302] It is not necessarily appropriate, however, to subordinate the right to silence in this way, given that the adversarial system constructed over the centuries by the common law is tilted procedurally and symbolically in favour of the presumption of innocence and the rule that the prosecution must prove the accused's guilt as charged.

---

[295] [1997] 1 I.L.R.M. 117 at 127, *per* O'Flaherty J. (SC): *cf.* appendix 51.
[296] [1994] 3 I.R. 593 at 601 (HC).
[297] [1997] 1 I.L.R.M. 117 (SC).
[298] The courts had previously restricted the right of freedom of expression to the expression of opinion and not facts: *cf.* McGrath, *Annual Review of Irish Law 1996* (Dublin, Round Hall Sweet & Maxwell, 1997), at pp. 330-1; *Attorney-General v Paperlink* [1984] I.L.R.M. 373 (HC); *Kearney v Minister for Justice* [1986] I.R. 116 (HC).
[299] [1997] I.R. 484, [1998] 2 I.L.R.M. 35 (SC); *cf.* para.**5–13** and appendix 55.
[300] *cf.* para.**9–19**.
[301] *cf.* para.**6–18**.
[302] *cf.* para.**1–60** *et seq.*

Compulsorily Acquired Self-Incriminating Evidence

13–92 It is logically clear that where evidence is given following the unlawful or improper exercise by another of a statutory power to compel the information, the evidence has been obtained illegally, unconstitutionally, and (possibly) involuntarily.[303] In the *Heaney* case, the Supreme Court had declined to consider the question whether information lawfully obtained under s.52 of the Offences Against the State Act 1939 was admissible later in criminal proceedings against the person compelled to give the information, and whether evidence initially provided in response to another person's exercise of powers to compel the information is exempt from the requirement of voluntariness. The status of compelled evidence lawfully elicited and later tendered against the compelled person in criminal proceedings was unclear until this and other related issues were addressed by the Supreme Court in *Matter of National Irish Bank*.[304] Shortly before, the European Court of Human Rights in *Saunders v UK*[305] had ruled that similar legislation in England—s.434 of the Companies Act 1985—was a prima facie violation of the accused's right to silence and privilege against self-incrimination, since it compelled a person, upon pain of separate conviction, to furnish information to inspectors that could be admitted as evidence against him in a future prosecution for participation in illegal share support schemes.

13–93 A majority of the court in *Saunders* found that "the public interest cannot be invoked to justify the use of answers compulsorily obtained in a non-judicial investigation to incriminate the accused during the trial proceedings".[306] As observed by Martens and Kuris JJ. in their dissent, the majority decision of the court effectively elevates the privilege against self-incrimination by conflating it with the right to silence as a fundamental principle. The future difficulties these findings suggest for confiscation orders under the Proceeds of Drugs Act 1996 and the other numerous statutes compelling disclosure of incriminating information are self-evident, and they are likely to have a chilling effect upon recourse to the provisions in Ireland and a correlative preference for recourse to ordinary warrants issued upon sworn information given to a District judge or peace commissioner.[307] It is of note, however, that the court in *Saunders* did not address, or appear to foresee any controversy arising from the admissibility of evidence obtained consequentially upon information given in statements under compulsion, although the emergence of a fruits of the poisoned tree principle[308] in criminal proceedings against a person compelled to self-incriminate, cannot be ruled out.

---

[303] A conclusion of involuntariness was reached in *R. v Garbett* (1847) 1 Den. 236 upon the basis that the trial judge failed to ensure that the accused enjoyed his right to silence during his trial.
[304] [1999] 1 I.L.R.M. 321 at 350, *per* Barrington J. (SC): *cf.* appendix 57.
[305] (1996) 23 E.H.R.R. 313 at 340; *cf.* appendix 52.
[306] *ibid.*
[307] Dillon-Malone, "The Privilege against Self-Incrimination in Light of *Saunders v United Kingdom*" (1997) 3 *Bar Review* 132 at 134: *cf.* para.**11–66** *et seq.*
[308] *cf.* para.**10–58** *et seq.*

13–94 The *National Irish Bank* case[309] concerned s.10 of the Companies Act 1990, which compels officers and agents of a company to cooperate with inspectors appointed to investigate the affairs of a company suspected of having acted unlawfully, and to furnish documents and to answer questions as and when requested by the inspectors. Both the High Court and the Supreme Court accepted that despite the absence of express words to the effect, s.10 entirely abrogated the privilege against self-incrimination as it applied to the officers or agents questioned, but that the encroachment was proportionate to, and no greater than, the public interest served by the measure. Barrington J. adopted a different view to the High Court with respect to the *use* to which compelled answers could later be put in criminal proceedings—an issue affecting the right to silence, to the extent that the accused in criminal proceedings was the party earlier compelled to provide the self-incriminating evidence. Considering s.18 of the 1990 Act (that answers given by an officer or agent of a company "may be used in evidence against him"), Barrington J. reasoned that this did not mean that compelled answers were automatically admissible against him in later proceedings. The court must still ascertain that the statement in question had been provided voluntarily: if not, admission of the statement would be in breach of the accused's right to a fair trial under Art.38.1.

13–95 As regards whether information elicited pursuant to a compulsory power is necessarily involuntary, the court considered the decision in *Saunders*, where the European Court of Human Rights had ruled that the "public interest cannot be invoked to justify the use of answers compulsorily obtained in a non-judicial investigation to incriminate the accused during the trial proceedings",[310] irrespective of whether the evidence was obtained before a charge had been preferred against the accused. Barrington J. adopted a more tentative approach, however. On the one hand, the learned judge acknowledged: "The fact that inspectors are armed with statutory powers or may even have invoked them does not necessarily mean that a statement made in reply to their questions is not voluntary".[311] On the other hand, he ruled that where the statement is subsequently tendered by the prosecution as evidence against the accused in criminal proceedings, it must be established that the alleged confession was a voluntary confession, and "it is immaterial whether the compulsion or inducement used to extract the confession came from the executive or from the legislature."[312] Barrington J. reasoned that evidence compelled by inspectors under s.10 of the Companies Act 1990 is not tainted evidence; and he drew an analogy with evidence obtained under a search warrant lawfully issued pursuant to statutory powers. The court appeared to consider that this reasoning applies equally to compelled evidence subsequently used as evidence against the same person; in other words, where the powers of compulsion are lawfully and properly exercised, and the information is

---

[309] [1991] 1 I.L.R.M. 321 (SC); *cf.* appendix 57.
[310] (1996) 23 E.H.R.R. 313 at 340.
[311] [1999] 1 I.L.R.M. 321 at 353 (SC).
[312] *ibid.* at 359.

otherwise given "voluntarily", the information and any evidence obtained consequentially may be admitted against him.

13–96 Yet the elements that traditionally have rendered confessions unreliable and strictly inadmissible under the common law—a preceding threat, inducement, or oppressive questioning—are intrinsic to the exercise of compulsory powers to elicit information upon pain of criminal charge, penalty, or adverse inference. This formed part of the reasoning of the court in *Saunders*: "The right not to incriminate oneself, in particular, presupposes that the prosecution in a criminal case seek to prove their case against the accused without resort to evidence obtained through methods of coercion or oppression in defiance of the will of the accused".[313] The Supreme Court's disinclination in *National Irish Bank* to equate information given by statutory compulsion with involuntariness will certainly beget a case-by-case approach to this issue in the short-term, though guided by a clear principle laid down by Barrington J. at the close of his judgment, to wit that "what is objectionable under Article 38 of the Constitution is compelling a person to confess and then convicting him upon the basis of his compelled confession",[314] a principle at the heart of the judgment in *Saunders*.[315]

13–97 Section 52(2) of the Offences Against the State Act 1939 is not alone as a provision that creates powers to compel disclosure but omits to specify the use to which the evidence may subsequently be put. This is not unusual in Ireland or England, where the rules of evidence are traditionally anchored in common law tradition and precedent. In admonishing the failure of s.52 to specify the uses of the compelled information in *Heaney and McGuinness v Ireland*,[316] the European Court of Human Rights was solely concerned with the resulting fairness for the accused in a prosecution for failure to provide the information under s.52(2). The decision is likely more broadly to prompt greater specificity and detail in future statutory provisions on information, privilege, and admissibility of evidence, which ought to be welcomed to the extent it would advance transparency and certainty in the law. In the meantime, it is clear from *National Irish Bank* that where a statute fails to address the evidential consequences of its evidence-eliciting provisions, the relevant Irish common law and constitutional principles and rules of evidence apply.

13–98 The approach of the Irish courts to these issues may diverge in future cases from the jurisprudence of the European Court of Human Rights. The Irish courts are for now rightly wedded to the common law and constitutional principles and rules that have informed their criminal jurisprudence, to the extent these have not been abrogated by statute, and they observe strict distinctions based upon the admissibility and function of statements as evidence. As demonstrated in *Saunders*, the concern of the European Court of Human

---

[313] (1996) 23 E.H.R.R. 313 at 337.
[314] [1999] 1 I.L.R.M. 321 at 360 (SC).
[315] *cf.* para.**13–93**.
[316] (2001) 33 E.H.R.R. 264; *cf.* appendix 61.

Privilege

Rights is with fairness in a specific case as a net issue, and upon this basis the court tends to identify standards, rather than distinctions, of evidence, having regard to the overarching requirement of fairness in matters of trial and proof. Both the Commission and a majority of the court were concerned not with the admissibility or evidential function *per se* of the compelled statements, but instead with the accumulated unfairness in the trial by reason of the fact that the compelled statements had formed "a not insignificant part of the evidence against him at his trial".[317] In considering the extent to which the privilege against self-incrimination operated to preclude statements compelled from the accused in a non-judicial capacity, the court ruled that the privilege applies equally as against the use of the statements to undermine the credibility of the accused in subsequent proceedings as it does to their use as probative evidence against him in criminal proceedings. The court further reasoned that compelled statements that appear on their face to be exculpatory and not self-incriminating may similarly be inadmissible where the person's knowledge of the information is itself incriminating.

13–99 Also of concern to Irish law is the European Court of Human Right's reluctance to date to recognise generally that the privilege against self-incrimination may be overridden in appropriate cases in the public interest. The court has observed a distinction between statutory powers to obtain evidence that has an existence independent of the will of the person from whom it is elicited (such as tissue samples, articles, and clothing), which does not affect the right to silence, and evidence obtained in defiance of the will of the person (such as incriminating information), which affects the right to silence. Applying the distinction in *Funke v France*,[318] the court found that the applicant's right to silence had been infringed in a case where he had been convicted for failing to produce bank statements when under investigation for non-payment of customs duties. Upon this basis recently in *JB v Switzerland*,[319] the court found that the accused's right to a fair trial had been infringed where he was prosecuted for failing to provide a prosecutor in tax evasion proceedings with documents relating to all the companies in which he had invested money. Although the contrary argument appears equally sustainable, the court considered in both cases that this documentary information was protected as evidence that did not exist independently of the person's will, and accordingly that the applicant's privilege against self-incrimination had been breached.

Adverse Inferences from Silence

13–100 The accused retains all the rights incidental to his right to silence and presumption of innocence, save where not expressly, clearly, and constitutionally withdrawn by a particular statute.[320] The accused's right not to tes-

---

[317] (1996) 23 E.H.R.R. 313 at 331, *per* Commission.
[318] (1993) 16 E.H.R.R. 257.
[319] European Court of Human Rights, May 3, 2001.
[320] *People (DPP) v Finnerty* [1999] 4 I.R. 364 (SC); *R. v Taylor* [1998] Crim. L.R. 77 (CA).

tify is unaffected by the inferences-from-silence provisions under ss.18–19 of the Criminal Justice Act 1984, s.7 of the Criminal Justice (Drug) Trafficking Act 1996, and s.5 of the Offences Against the State (Amendment) Act 1998, none of which create powers to draw inferences from the failure of the accused to testify at his trial. Thus the prosecution may not comment upon his decision not to testify,[321] nor may the trial judge invite the jury to draw inferences from it.[322] The trial judge is under an affirmative duty to advise the jury when summing-up that the accused has a right to silence, and that no adverse inferences may be drawn from his decision not to give evidence.[323]

13–101 Where a court, pursuant to a statute, accepts an instance of silence as inferential evidence in the case, or permits the jury to do so, the inference capable of being drawn is limited to the specific instance of silence or non-cooperation enabled by the statute. The court is not entitled to go further and permit inferences to be drawn from the accused's general uncooperativeness or recourse to silence, or other omissions on his part. In *People (DPP) v Finnerty*,[324] it was argued upon appeal that the trial judge had erred by permitting the prosecution to cross-examine the accused upon his conduct in detention—specifically his failure to mention information later relied on in his defence—and by failing to remind the jury when summing-up that the accused benefited from a right to silence. The accused had been arrested and detained under s.4 of the Criminal Justice Act 1984, which makes no provision for inferences from an accused's silence in detention or his failure to mention information later relied on in his defence, by contrast with the exceptional provisions introduced by the Criminal Justice (Drug Trafficking) Act 1996 and the Offences Against the State (Amendment) Act 1998. The fact that the 1984 Act created two specific instances when adverse inferences could be drawn—arising from the failure of the accused to account for his possession of certain objects or his presence in a particular place, pursuant to ss.18–19— necessitated the view that the Oireachtas did not intend a more general abridgment of the right to silence in the manner chosen in England.[325] The Supreme Court reversed conviction, and ruled that under no circumstances should the accused have been questioned about his failure to answer any question in detention. The court favoured the defence's submission that the prosecution ought instead have informed the jury that the applicant had been detained under the 1984 Act but that nothing of probative value had emerged from that detention. In the present case, the jury may well have been left under the impression that they were entitled to draw adverse inferences from the failure of the accused to give his version of events when questioned in the garda station, which may have affected the jury's assessment of his credibility in proceedings for rape.

---

[321] Criminal Justice (Evidence) Act 1924, s.1(b); *cf.* para.**2–18**.
[322] Conviction was quashed upon this basis in *Attorney-General v Quinn* (CCA, March 23, 1998).
[323] *People (DPP) v Finnerty* [1999] 4 I.R. 364 at 376, *per* Keane J. (SC): *cf.* appendix 59.
[324] *ibid.*
[325] *ibid.* at 380–1; *cf.* para.**13–103**.

13–102 The inferences-from-silence provisions under the Criminal Justice (Drug Trafficking) Act 1996 and the Offences Against the State (Amendment) Act 1998 have rightly been challenged and criticised on a number of fronts.[326] In an adversarial context, their justification must rest for the most part upon a fear that the failure of the accused to disclose his defence until the trial "may prevent any checking of its validity by the prosecution, so that it appears to be an ambush or concoction".[327] Their true effect is inquisitorial, however, to the extent that they pressurise a suspect into defending himself at an early stage in the proceedings. This systemic shift was in the mind of the sponsors of the legislation at the time.[328] The type of pressure exerted may, depending upon the suspect and the surrounding circumstances, be unfairly oppressive. To avoid adverse inferences after being informed of the possibility by the interviewing garda, a suspect must endeavour to anticipate the charge that will ultimately be preferred and to mention every fact that he could reasonably be expected to rely upon in defence to the likely charge.[329] It cannot strongly be argued, however, that the Irish provisions are designed to exert pressure upon a suspect to attempt proof of his innocence upon pain of incurring circumstantial inferences of guilt, which is the undeniable thrust of the general measure in place in England under s.34 of the Criminal Justice (Public Order) Act 1994.[330] Mirfield has described that measure as tantamount to recruiting the suspect in an active capacity for the purposes of investigating his own crime.[331] Since it applies generally, it is likely to work unjustly against persons who genuinely cooperated with the police but who for one reason or another neglected to mention a crucial fact later relied upon in the trial.

13–103 The English courts have faced many difficulties with respect to the admissibility and evidential function of inferences from silence enabled by statute.[332] According to one view, they "continue to provide an extraordinarily

---

[326] See Keane, "Detention Without Charge and the Criminal Justice (Drug Trafficking) Act 1996" (1997) 7 I.C.L.J. 1, Ryan, "The Criminal Justice (Drug Trafficking) Act 1996: Decline and Fall of the Right to Silence?" (1997) 7 I.C.L.J. 22, and Opinion, "Offences Against the State (Amendment) Act 1998—Two Views" (1998) *Bar Review* 5.

[327] Branston, "The Drawing of an Adverse Committal from Silence" [1998] Crim. L.R. 189 at 191.

[328] During the Dáil Debates for the Drug Trafficking Bill 1996 (*Dáil Debates*), Liz O'Donnell asserted: "The time has come to carry out an examination as to whether the legal system should be made more inquisitorial in nature. There is a public perception that the guilty use the adversarial nature of the criminal justice system to escape justice".

[329] Keane, "Detention Without Charge and the Criminal Justice (Drug Trafficking) Act 1996" (1997) 7 I.C.L.J. 1 at 8.

[330] This followed the introduction of the Criminal Evidence (Northern Ireland) Order in 1988, which permitted the court to draw inferences from the accused's silence and failure to testify: see generally Greer and Morgan (eds.), *The Right of Silence Debate* (1990).

[331] "Two Side Effects of Sections 34 to 37 of the Criminal Justice and Public Order Act 1994" (1995) C.L.R. 534 at 540.

[332] In *R. v Cowan* [1995] 4 All E.R. 939 at 944–45 (HL), Lord Taylor C.J. approved a specimen direction drafted by the Judicial Studies Board, which recommended that inferences may be drawn from an accused's silence "if the evidence [he] relies on presents

rich source of problems, out of all proportion to the value of the evidence generated for the prosecution".[333] The importance of the English experience as a salutary warning to the Irish legislators cannot be overestimated. The English courts have been criticised for conceding only minimal exceptions to ss.34–35, such that it is said that in England "the absence of evidence—inferences from silence—may be admitted more readily than will positive evidence in the shape of a confession which is contested on the basis of unreliability".[334] This was evident in the unpopular decisions in *R. v Friend*[335] to permit and uphold inferences from the silence of an accused aged 14 years and five months who had an estimated mental age of nine and a notably low I.Q. described by one expert witness as "within the handicapped bracket". The Court of Appeal decided that under the 1994 Act, reference to 14 years of age as the benchmark age for receiving the evidence of a child witness must be understood in a chronological sense, and the trial judge was not wrong to invite the jury to draw inferences from this accused's silence since no exception had been identified under the legislation for persons with a low mental age.

13–104 It is now acknowledged in England that, since the drawing of inferences from pre-trial silence operates to imply that the accused has fabricated his post-interview defence, communication between a solicitor and the accused prior to the police interview may thus be probative in rebutting any such inferences.[336] The advice to remain silent may have taken root in strategic concerns that ought not to be taken to infer guilt, for instance to exert pressure upon the prosecution to disclose more evidence, or as a temporary device to buy time in order to consider all the available options. In any event, it has been decided that where the accused seeks to explain the basis for his silence, the trial judge should caution him that he runs the risk of losing his legal professional privilege by constructive waiver.[337] In most cases, it is necessary that reference to a "no comment" interview with the accused should be restricted to the fact of his silence, although the Court of Appeal has acknowledged that the trial judge may properly ask to hear evidence of the interview and the surrounding circumstances before he decides whether or not it is "proper" to invite the jury to draw inferences from the accused's refusal to answer questions put to him.[338] The regularity with which the legal advice argument has been made recently in England suggests that it is only a matter of time before an accused begin to argue that the legal advice he received was dogmatically given so as to render it impossible in the circumstances to make

---

no adequate explanation for his absence from the witness box", or if "the only sensible explanation for his decision not to give evidence is that he has no answer to the case against him, or none that could have stood up to cross-examination".

[333] Birch, Commentary on *R. v Taylor* [1999] Crim. L.R. 77 at 78.
[334] Sharpe, "Vulnerable Defendants and Inferences from Silence" (1997) New L.J. 842 at 842.
[335] [1997] Crim L.R. 817 (CA).
[336] *R. v Daniel* [1998] 2 Cr. App. R. 373 (CA).
[337] *R. v Condron and Condron* [1997] 1 Cr. App. R. 185 (CA).
[338] *R. v Griffin* [1998] Crim. L.R. 418 (CA).

an informed choice between whether to disclose or instead to make "no comment".

13–105 The European Court of Human Rights has upheld, subject to safeguards, the drawing of adverse inferences from an accused's silence where a prima facie case has already been established against him and it is appropriate in the circumstances to require some explanation from him. In *Murray v UK*,[339] the court approved, as one such safeguard, provision that the accused may not be convicted "solely or *mainly* [from his] silence"; the Irish measures are qualified by provision that "a person shall not be convicted of an offence *solely* upon an inference drawn from such failure or refusal".[340] Of equal concern to the court is the fairness of the trial judge's advice and directions to the jury upon the inferences that may be drawn from the silence. In *Condron v UK*,[341] for instance, the court condemned a direction by a trial judge to the jury that led them to believe they were entitled to draw adverse inference against the accused arising from his silence in detention even where satisfied that his explanation for maintaining silence was plausible (in the case, that he stayed silent upon the advice of his solicitor who considered him unfit to answer questions because he was withdrawing from drugs).

13–106 Of particular concern to Irish jurisprudence is a principle, currently gaining strength, that where the accused is detained under legislation permitting the drawing of adverse inferences from his silence, the accused must first have access to legal advice. Whilst in *Murray*, the court found that the drawing of inferences against the accused was not unreasonable in the circumstances of the case, it found that his right of access to a solicitor had been breached in so far as he had been in custody and remained silent for 48 hours before a solicitor arrived. In *Averill v UK*,[342] the court similarly reasoned that an accused's right of access to legal advice had been breached where he had remained silent for 24 hours in custody prior to the arrival of a solicitor: "access to a lawyer should have been guaranteed to the applicant before his interrogation began."[343] In both cases, it was the lack of legal advice and representation during the time in which the detainee remained silent, rather than the drawing of inferences from his silence, that constituted the breach of the accused's right to a fair trial under Art.6 of the Convention. In *Magee v UK*,[344] the court explained that an accused must, as a matter of procedural fairness, have "access to a solicitor at the initial stages of interrogation as a counterweight to the

---

[339] (1996) 22 E.H.R.R. 29 at 60 (emphasis added): *cf.* appendix 49. The *Murray* decision explored the effect of adverse inferences from silence under the Criminal Evidence (Northern Ireland) Order in 1988.
[340] *cf.* para.**5–14**.
[341] [2001] E.H.R.R. 1.
[342] (2001) 31 E.H.R.R. 839. In the case, the applicant's right to a fair trial had not been infringed, however, as he had not been convicted solely upon the basis of inferences but primarily in light of forensic and testimonial evidence.
[343] *ibid.*
[344] (2001) 31 E.H.R.R. 822 at 835.

intimidating atmosphere specifically devised to sap his will and make him confide in his interrogators".

13–107 This evolving principle—that an accused detained under inference-generating legislation is entitled to heightened access to legal advice—is capable of applying with strict effect to render adverse inferences inadmissible where the period of silence predated the arrival of a solicitor. It is alternately capable of applying more extensively to render detention of a suspect unlawful, although this type of broad *ab initio* reasoning was rejected recently by the Supreme Court in *People (DPP) v Buck*.[345] The principle had been favoured by McGuinness J. of the High Court in *Lavery v Member-in-Charge, Carrickmacross Garda Station*,[346] before it was rejected by the Supreme Court upon appeal. The accused had been arrested under s.30 of the Offences Against the State Act 1939, upon suspicion of membership of an unlawful organisation. The appeal focused on the effect of the failure of the gardaí to cooperate with requests by the accused's solicitor to inspect notes taken of interviews with the accused predating the solicitor's arrival at the station. The requests had been made to enable the solicitor to appraise whether or not it was recorded that any question considered material to the investigation had already been put to the accused, and whether he had replied in a false or misleading way—in other words, matters that would have enabled the solicitor to formulate advice as to whether and to what extent his client was already liable to incur adverse inferences during his trial. Overturning McGuinness J.'s decision to release the accused upon the basis that his detention had been unlawful from the moment when the solicitor's request was refused, O'Flaherty J. of the Supreme Court (with whom Hamilton C.J., Barrington, Keane, Murphy JJ. concurred), disposed of the matter tersely by reiterating the view that a solicitor is not entitled to be present during interrogation of his client, nor is it open to the client or the solicitor to prescribe the manner by which interviews in detention may be conducted.

13–108 Irish law has thus far, and it is submitted rightly, guarded the right to silence from the type of general dilution experienced in England and elsewhere in the common law. Reform along the lines undertaken in England would be wholly inappropriate without first effecting fundamental adjustments to the law and practice relating to access of detainees to legal advice prior to and throughout interrogation by the gardaí—a safeguard considered essential by the European Court of Human Rights in any case where a detainee's silence in detention exposes him to adverse inferences later in his trial.[347]

13–109 Curtailment of the right to silence significantly affects the burden of proof which in the adversarial system rests as a fundamental principle upon the prosecution. The adversarial system is specifically constructed on this premise and does not contain the checks and balances that would be necessary

---

[345] [2002] 2 I.R. 268 (SC); *cf.* para.**10–55** *et seq.* and appendix 64.
[346] HC, October 2, 1998; [1992] 2 I.R. 390 (SC): *cf.* appendix 58.
[347] *cf.* para.**13–106**.

if the burden were placed upon the accused.[348] The procedural safeguards variously adopted by civil law jurisdictions are illustrated by the involvement of judges at the investigative stage of criminal cases and throughout subsequent examination and hearing stages. It is of note in this regard that when, on the few occasions the judicial role was removed from inquisitorial proceedings abroad, the growth of a detailed body of exclusionary rules of evidence ensued.[349] Without the drafting of a principled framework operative for crimes in general, within which to posit existing rights and new rules, piecemeal adjustments operate visibly to compromise fundamental principles of law and to precipitate a miscellany of rules. Whilst it is appropriate that account be taken of the special nature of serious crimes, and that legislative curtailment of the right to silence be made upon an exceptional basis in the public interest, care must be taken to preserve the application of the measures to appropriate cases, and that the exception does not eventually devour the rule entire. It has often been acknowledged by individual members of the European Court of Human Rights—which consistently has approved withdrawal of the right to silence in appropriate cases[350]—that attempts to combat terrorism can be as dangerous for democracy and the rule of law as the affliction itself, and that the courts "should therefore be given an even more careful protection in view of the intensity of national interests in taking repressive measures against crime".[351]

---

[348] See generally Foster, *German legal System and Laws* (2nd ed., Blackstone, London, 1996); Heyde, *Justice and the Law in the Federal Republic of Germany* (Muller, Heidelberg, 1994); Kahn-Freund et al, *A Sourcebook on French Law* (3rd ed., Oxford University Press, Oxford, 1991); Merryman, *The Civil Law Tradition* (Stanford University Press, California, 1969); von Mehren and Gordley, *Civil Law System* (2nd ed., Little, Brown, Boston, 1977); and Wegerich and Freckmann, *The German Legal System* (Sweet & Maxwell, London, 1997).

[349] As occurred in Germany after the abolition of the investigating judge in 1975: see Wegerich and Freckmann, *The German Legal System* (Sweet & Maxwell, London, 1997).

[350] *cf.* para.**13–105**.

[351] *Murray v UK* (1995) 19 E.H.R.R. 193 at 243, *per* Jambrek J., dissenting.

Further Reading

Allen, "Public Interest Immunity and Statutory Privilege" (1983) 42 C.L.J. 118.
Cahill, *Discovery in Ireland* (Roundhall Sweet & Maxwell, Dublin, 1996).
Collins, "Community Law and its Impact on the Law of Privilege" (1997) I.C.L.R. 2–9.
Conlon, "Once Privileged Always Privileged: *Quinlivan v Tuohy*" (1995) I.L.T. 56.
Delaney and McGrath, *Civil Procedure in the Superior Courts* (Round Hall Sweet & Maxwell, Dublin, 2001).
Dennis, "Instrumental Protection, Human Right or Functional Necessity? Reassessing the Privilege against Self-Incrimination" (1995) C.L.J. 342.
Dillon-Malone, "The Privilege against Self-Incrimination in Light of *Saunders v United Kingdom*" (1997) 3 *Bar Review* 132.
Fennelly, "Legal Professional Privilege in Community Law" (1997) I.C.L.R. 2–1.
Fitzpatrick, "The Changing Face of Discovery" (2003) (April) G.L.S.I. 14.
Ganz, "Volte Face on Public Interest Immunity" (1997) 60 M.L.R. 552.
Greer, "The Right to Silence" (1990) 53 M.L.R. 710.
Ho, "Legal Professional Privilege after Death of Client" (1999) 115 L.Q.R. 27.
Hogan, "The Right to Silence after *National Banks* and *Finnerty*" (1999) 21 D.U.L.J. 176.
Hunt, "Whither Professional Privilege in Ireland" (2002) 15 Ir. Tax Rev. 278.
Keane, "Detention Without Charge and the Criminal Justice (Drug Trafficking) Act 1996" (1997) 7 I.C.L.J. 1.
Kharam, "Crown Privilege in Criminal Cases" (1971) Crim. L. Rev. 675.
Lourie, "Exposing Truth While Keeping Secrets: Publicity, Privacy and Privilege" (2000) 35 Ir. Jur. 17.
McDermott, "Silence as a Criminal Offence" (2001) 11(1) C.L.J. 9.
McGrath, "Public Interest Privilege" (2000) 22 D.U.L.J. 75.
McGrath, "Legal Professional Privilege" (2001) 36 Ir. Jur. 126.
McNair, "The Early Development of the Privilege Against Self-Incrimination" (1990) Oxford J.L.S. 66.
McSherry, "Confidential Communication between Clients and Mental Health Care Professionals: the Public Interest Exceptions" 37 (2002) I.J. 269.
Munday, "Inferences from Silence and European Human Rights Law" [1996] Crim. L. Rev. 370.
Ní Raifeartaigh, "The Criminal Justice System and Drug Related Offending: Some Thoughts on Procedural Reform" (1998) *Bar Review* 15.
Ní Raifeartaigh, "The European Convention on Human Rights and the Irish Criminal Justice System" (2001) *Bar Review* 111.
Noctor, "Legal Professional Privilege and the Public Safety Exception" (1999) I.L.T. 230.
Nokes, "Professional Privilege" (1950) 66 L.Q.R. 88.
O'Connell, "The European Court of Human Rights in the Context of the Right to Silence" (1996) I.L.T. 185.

O'Connor and Cooney, "Criminal Due Process, the Pre-Trial Stage and Self Incrimination" (1980) 15 Ir. Jur. 219.

Opinion, "Offences Against the State (Amendment) Act 1998—Two Views" (1998) *Bar Review* 5.

Redmond, "The Privilege against Self-Incrimination in the Context of the 1990 Companies Act" (1993) 3 I.C.L.J. 118.

Ring, "The Right to Silence: *Rock v Ireland and Others*" (1997) 3(5) *Bar Review* 132.

Russell, "A Privilege of the State" (1967) II Ir. Jur. 88.

Ryan, "The Criminal Justice (Drug Trafficking) Act 1996: Decline and Fall of the Right to Silence?" (1997) 7 I.C.L.J. 22.

Wigmore, "The History of the Privilege Against Self-Incrimination" (1902) 15 Harv. L.R. 610.

APPENDICES

1. Makin v A.G. for New South Wales

Privy Council, December 21, 1893
[1894] A.C. 57 at 65–68

Herschell L.C.J:

... In their Lordships' opinion the principles which must govern the decision of the case are clear, though the application of them is by no means free from difficulty. It is undoubtedly not competent for the prosecution to adduce evidence tending to shew that the accused has been guilty of criminal acts other than those covered by the indictment, for the purpose of leading to the conclusion that the accused is a person likely from his criminal conduct or character to have committed the offence for which he is being tried. On the other hand, the mere fact that the evidence adduced tends to shew the commission of other crimes does not render it inadmissible if it be relevant to an issue before the jury, and it may be so relevant if it bears upon the question whether the acts alleged to constitute the crime charged in the indictment were designed or accidental, or to rebut a defence which would otherwise be open to the accused. The statement of these general principles is easy, but it is obvious that it may often be very difficult to draw the line and to decide whether a particular piece of evidence is on the one side or the other.

The principles which their Lordships have indicated appear to be on the whole consistent with the current of authority bearing on the point, though it cannot be denied that the decisions have not always been completely in accord.

The leading authority relied on by the Crown was the case of *Reg. v Geering* 18 L. J. (N.S.) (M.C.) 215, where on the trial of a prisoner for the murder of her husband by administering arsenic evidence was tendered, with the view of shewing that two sons of the prisoner who had formed part of the same family, and for whom as well as for her husband the prisoner had cooked their food, had died of poison, the symptoms in all these cases being the same. The evidence was admitted by Pollock C.B., who tried the case; he held that it was admissible, inasmuch as its tendency was to prove that the death of the husband was occasioned by arsenic, and was relevant to the question whether such taking was accidental or not. The Chief Baron refused to reserve the point for the consideration of the judges, intimating that Alderson B., and Talfourd J., concurred with him in his opinion.

This authority has been followed in several subsequent cases. And in the case of *Reg. v Dossett* 2 C. & K. 306, which was tried a few years previously, the same view was acted upon by Maule J., on a trial for arson, where it appeared that a rick of wheat-straw was set on fire by the prisoner having fired a gun near to it. Evidence was admitted to shew that the rick had been on fire the previous day, and that the prisoner was then close to it with gun in his hand. Maule J., said: "Although the evidence offered may be proof of another felony, that circumstance does not render it inadmissible, if the evidence be otherwise receivable. In many cases it is an important question whether a thing was done accidentally or wilfully."

The only subsequent case to which their Lordships think it necessary to refer to specifically is that of *Reg. v Gray* 4 F. & F. 1102, where on a trial for arson with intent to defraud an insurance company, Willes J., admitted evidence that the prisoner had made claims on two other insurance companies, in respect of fires which had occurred in two other houses which he had occupied previously and in succession, for the purpose of shewing that the fire which formed the subject of the trial was the result of design and not of accident. The learned judge after consulting Martin B., refused to reserve the point for the consideration of the Court for Crown Cases Reserved. The fact that the learned judge took this course after consulting Martin B., is important, because a decision of that learned judge was mainly relied on in opposition to the authorities to which attention has been drawn. ...

Their Lordships do not think it necessary to enter upon a detailed examination of the evidence in the present case. The prisoners had alleged that they had received only one child to nurse; that they had received 10s. a week whilst it was under their care, and that after a few weeks it was given back to the parents. When the infant with whose murder the appellants were charged was received from the mother she stated that she had a child for them to adopt. Mrs. Makin said that she would take the child, and Makin said that they would bring it up as their own and educate it, and that he would take it because Mrs. Makin had lost a child of her own two years old. Makin said that he did not want any clothing; they had plenty of their own. The mother said that she did not mind his getting £3 premium so long as he took care of the child. The representation was that the prisoners were willing to take the child on payment of the small sum of £3, inasmuch as they desired to adopt it as their own.

Under these circumstances their Lordships cannot see that it was irrelevant to the issue to be tried by the jury that several other infants had been received from their mothers on like representations, and upon payment of a sum inadequate for the support of the child for more than a very limited period, or that the bodies of infants had been found buried in a similar manner in the gardens of several houses occupied by the prisoners. ...

2. R v Baskerville
Court of Appeal, July 31, 1916
[1916] 2 K.B. 658 at 664–667

Reading L.C.J:

... As the rule of practice at common law was founded originally upon the exercise of the discretion of the judge at the trial, and, moreover, as it is anomalous in its nature, inasmuch as it requires confirmation of the testimony of a competent witness, it is not surprising that this rule should have led to differences of opinion as to the nature and extent of the corroboration required, although there are propositions of law applicable to corroboration which are beyond controversy. For example, "confirmation does not mean that there should be independent evidence of that which the accomplice relates, or his testimony would be unnecessary": *Reg. v Mullins* 3 Cox, C.C. 526, 531, *per* Maule J. Indeed, if it were required that the accomplice should be confirmed in every detail of the crime, his evidence would not be essential to the case, it would be merely confirmatory of other and independent testimony. Again, the corroboration must be by some evidence other than that of an accomplice, and therefore one accomplice's evidence is not corroboration of the testimony of another accomplice: *Rex v Noakes* (1832) 5 C. & P. 326. The difference of opinion has arisen in the main in reference to the question whether the corroborative evidence must connect the accused with the crime. The rule of practice as to corroborative evidence has arisen in consequence of the danger of convicting a person upon the unconfirmed testimony of one who is admittedly a criminal. What is required is some additional evidence rendering it probable that the story of the accomplice is true and that it is reasonably safe to act upon it. If the only independent evidence relates to an incident in the commission of the crime which does not connect the accused with it, or if the only independent evidence relates to the identity of the accused without connecting him with the crime, is it corroborative evidence? There are some expressions to be found in the books which imply that it may be, and in *Rex v Birkett* (1813) R. & R. 251 the judges were of opinion that an accomplice did not require confirmation as to the person he charged, if he was confirmed as to the particulars of his story. The case is very imperfectly reported, and the evidence is not stated. It was not argued by counsel, but was stated verbally to a meeting of the judges by the judge who tried the case. There are other cases where it has been held that a conviction on such evidence could not be quashed by the Court, but the *ratio decidendi* is that as an accomplice is a competent witness and the jury thought him worthy of credit, the verdict was in accordance with law: *Rex v Atwood* 1 Leach, 464; *Rex v Jones* (1809) 2 Camp. 131. There are other cases where it has been held that on such evidence the case cannot be withdrawn from the jury: *Rex v Hastings* (1835) 7 C. & P. 152; *Reg. v Andrews* 1 Cox, C.C. 183, *per* Coleridge J., *Reg. v Avery* 1 Cox, C.C. 206. After examining these and other authorities to the present date, we have come to the conclusion that the better opinion of the law upon this point is that stated in *Reg. v Stubbs* Dears. 555 by Parke B., namely, that the evidence of an accomplice must be confirmed not only as to the circumstances of the crime, but also as to the identity of the prisoner. The learned Baron does not mean that there must be confirmation of all the circumstances of the crime; as we have already stated, that is unnecessary. It is sufficient if there is confirmation as to a material circumstance of the crime and of the identity of the accused in relation to the crime. Parke B. gave this opinion as a result of twenty-five years' practice; it was accepted by the other judges, and has been much relied upon in later cases. ...

We hold that evidence in corroboration must be independent testimony which affects the accused by connecting or tending to connect him with the crime. In other words, it must be evidence which implicates him, that is, which confirms in some material particular not only the evidence that the crime has been committed, but also that the prisoner committed it. The test applicable to determine the nature and extent of the corroboration is thus the same whether the case falls within the rule of practice at common law or within that class of offences for which corroboration is required by statute. ...The nature of the corroboration will necessarily vary according to the particular circumstances of the offence charged. It would be in high degree dangerous to attempt to formulate the kind of evidence which would be regarded as corroboration, except to say that corroborative evidence is evidence which shows or tends to show that the story of the accomplice that the accused committed the crime is true, not merely that the crime has been committed, but that it was committed by the accused.

The corroboration need not be direct evidence that the accused committed the crime; it is sufficient if it is merely circumstantial evidence of his connection with the crime. A good instance of this indirect evidence is to be found in *Reg. v Birkett* 8 C. & P. 732. Were the law otherwise many crimes which are usually committed between accomplices in secret, such as incest, offences with females, or the present case, could never be brought to justice. ...

3. R v Voisin
King's Bench Division, February 11, 1918
[1918] 1 K.B. 531 at 537–539

Lawrence J:

... The alleged misreception of evidence relates to a paper writing containing the words "Bladie Belgiam." This was written by the prisoner at the request of the police at a time while he was being detained at Bow Street. The trunk of the body of the murdered woman had been found contained in a parcel in Regent Square with a label containing these words upon it. The police were making investigations. They had requested the prisoner to go to Bow Street and to account for his movements at the supposed time of the murder. He had just made a statement which had been taken down in writing, and after he had done so he was asked whether he would have any objection to write down the two words "Bloody Belgian." He said "Not at all" and then wrote them down as above. It was argued that that writing was inadmissible in evidence on the ground that it was obtained by the police without having first cautioned the prisoner and while he was in custody. A number of cases were called to our attention in which different views had been entertained by judges as to when statements by prisoners should and when they should not be excluded from consideration by the jury. It is clear, and has been frequently held, that the duty of the judge to exclude statements is one that must depend upon the particular circumstances of each case. The general principle is admirably stated by Lord Sumner in his judgment in the Privy Council in *Ibrahim v Rex* [1914] A.C. 699 at 609, 610 as follows: "It has long been established as a positive rule of English criminal law, that no statement by an accused is admissible in evidence against him unless it is shewn by the prosecution to have been a voluntary statement, in the sense that it has not been obtained from him either by fear of prejudice or hope of advantage exercised or held out by a person in authority." The point of that passage is that the statement must be a voluntary statement; any statement which has been extorted by fear of prejudice or induced by hope of advantage held out by a person in authority is not admissible. As Lord Sumner points out, logically these considerations go to the value of the statement rather than to its admissibility. The question as to whether a person has been duly cautioned before the statement was made is one of the circumstances that must be taken into consideration, but this is a circumstance upon which the judge should exercise his discretion. It cannot be said as a matter of law that the absence of a caution makes the statement inadmissible; it may tend to show that the person was not upon his guard as to the importance of what he was saying or as to its bearing upon some charge of which he has not been informed. In this case the prisoner wrote these words quite voluntarily. The mere fact that the words were written at the request of police officers, or that he was being detained at Bow Street, does not make the writing inadmissible in evidence. Those facts do not tend to change the character of handwriting, nor do they explain the resemblance between his handwriting and that upon the label, or account for the same misspellings occurring in both. There was nothing in the nature of a "trap" or of the "manufacture of evidence"; the identity of the deceased woman had not at this moment been established, and the police, though they were detaining the prisoner in custody for inquiries, had not then decided to charge him with this crime; indeed, if the writing had turned out other than it did and other circumstances had not subsequently transpired, it is certain that he, like others who were similarly detained, would have been discharged. It is desirable in the interests of the community that investigations into crime should not be cramped. The Court is of opinion that they would be most unduly cramped if it were to be held that a writing voluntarily made under the circumstances here proved was inadmissible in evidence. ...

[T]he mere fact that a statement is made in answer to a question put by a police constable is not in itself sufficient to make the statement inadmissible in law. It may be, and often is, a ground, for the judge in his discretion excluding the evidence; but he should do so only if he thinks the statement was not a voluntary one in the sense above mentioned, or was an unguarded answer made under circumstances that rendered it unreliable, or unfair for some reason to be allowed in evidence against the prisoner. ...

4. Dunne v Clinton
High Court, May 28, 1930
[1930] I.R. 366 at 372–375

Hannah J:

… The first question that arises is whether this detention is something different from arrest or imprisonment. In law there can be no half-way house between the liberty of the subject, unfettered by restraint, and an arrest. If a person under suspicion voluntarily agrees to go to a police station to be questioned, his liberty is not interfered with, as he can change his mind at any time. If, having been examined, he is asked and voluntarily agrees, to remain in the barracks until some investigation is made, he is still a free subject, and can leave at any time. But a practice has grown up of "detention" as distinct from arrest. It is, in effect, keeping a suspect in custody, perhaps under as comfortable circumstances as the barracks will permit, without making any definite charge against him, and with the intimation in some form of words or gesture that he is under restraint, and will not be allowed to leave. As, in my opinion, there could be no such thing as notional liberty, this so-called detention amounts to arrest, and the suspect has in law been arrested and in custody during the period of his detention. The expression "detention" has no justification in law in this connection, and the use of it has in a sense helped to nurture the idea that it is something different from arrest and that it relieves the guards from the obligation to have the question of the liberty of the suspected person determined by a peace commissioner or the Court. If the word "detention" were deleted from the police vocabulary and the word "arrest" substituted there would be a clearer understanding as to the obligations upon the guards. If it is necessary or advisable for the investigation of crime that there should be some intermediate period conforming to the present practice, it must be authorised by the Legislature. It is a deprivation of the liberty of the subject, and it is fundamental that that cannot occur in cases such as this, save by the order of a peace commissioner or a court.

There is no reported case on this point in Ireland, but it was considered in the Court of Criminal Appeal on 9th April, 1929, in the case of *Attorney-General v Cox*, unreported, before the Chief Justice, the President of the High Court, and myself. I have referred to my own note of the case and the decision. The accused had been convicted of murder, and at his trial certain statements made by him to the guards had been admitted in evidence. The admissibility of these statements depended on whether they were made at a time when the accused was in custody and under arrest. This question formed one of the grounds of appeal. The facts were very similar to the present case, and in pursuance of the same practice of the guards. A number of men, including the accused, had gone to the barracks at the request of the guards, voluntarily, and had been examined as to their movements and other matters relevant to the crime. The men, other than the accused, went away after they had made their statements, but the accused was detained, but not charged or formally arrested. There was a conflict as to whether the statement was made before or after he was detained. The Chief Justice, in giving the judgment of the Court, said: "The police contend that this man was only in detention, and not under arrest ... There is no doubt that at some time on the night of the 22nd-23rd of December he was not a free man, and was detained, as the police say." His Lordship then considered the evidence, and stated the view of the Court, that the statement was made before there was any detention, but added: "The Court cannot accept this distinction between detainer where a person is not a free agent, and arrest or imprisonment as it is commonly understood in law, and I am trying to avoid it. ..."

It is, in my opinion, clearly the law that, once a person is detained by the guards, or, in other words, in custody of the guards, on suspicion of having committed a felony, it is the duty of the police-officer arresting him to take him with reasonable expedition before a peace commissioner. He can be retained in custody only during such a time as is reasonable for that purpose. Any question of the time necessary to investigate the offence, or to obtain evidence upon which to found a charge, is quite irrelevant. It is for the peace commissioner and not the guard to determine whether the suspected person is to remain in custody or to be released on bail.

Many of the old cases have been cited to us, but it is not necessary to go further afield than the judgment of Mr. Justice Gibson in *R. (Rea.) v Davison* [1913] 2 I.R. 342 at p.360. The question in that case was as to the delay in the execution of a warrant, the suggestion being made that it was due to a desire to bring the accused before a particular magistrate. At p.359 Gibson J. says: "No time was fixed for the execution of the warrant: 'The law has fixed a time, for by law the officer is bound to carry immediately before the magistrate. If he delay any time, it is against the duty of office': Parker C.J., in *Reg. v Derby Fortescue* at p.143. Powis J. in the same case said that where a warrant was to bring before a particular Justice, the officer might carry before another, if nearer. Unreasonable detention on the part of a constable or magistrate was actionable: *Wright v Court* 4 B. & C. 596 *Davis v Capper* 10 B. & C. 28. ... He [the officer] was not a prosecutor, but merely a ministerial functionary. The power of election is founded mainly on convenience, in order to enable the arrested person to be dealt with as expeditiously as possible, in his interest, and not to enable the constable to exercise a quasi right of challenge. What would Coke, whose report of *Foster's Case* 5 Co. 59 is the primary authority on this point, have said to such pretension on the constable's part, in the days of Shakespeare? What would have been the opinion of Powis J. in such a case is certain from what he said: see *Reg. v Derby*. The law is stated in Nun and Walsh, edition 1841, p.185, as follows: "The choice is not to be capriciously made, or such as to put the prisoner to any unnecessary inconvenience. The officer therefore will not be justified in carrying the prisoner to a distance when there is a magistrate near at hand; it is his duty, unless there be some very sufficient reason for not doing so, to proceed to the next Justice. *Wright v Court*, a case of arrest without warrant, is explicit as to the principle. The judgment is as follows: 'But, it is the duty of a person arresting anyone on suspicion of felony to take him before a Justice as soon as he reasonably can, and the law gives no authority even to a Justice to detain a person suspected, but for a reasonable time till he may be examined.' Where there was no warrant it was the duty of the arresting officer to take the prisoner with all convenient speed before some neighbouring Justice."

The principle enunciated by Mr. Justice Gibson applies equally in the case of arrest, under the common law of arrest on reasonable suspicion of having committed a felony, and clearly indicates immediate and convenient speed. Now, what is a reasonable time after arrest? No hard and fast rule can be laid down to cover every case. It must depend on many circumstances such as the time and place of the arrest, the number of the accused, whether a peace commissioner is easily available, and such other matters as may be relevant.

... It is obvious that the guards thought that they had the right to detain the plaintiffs in pursuance of their practice, which, in my opinion, is unlawful, and would have further detained them but for the challenge of the plaintiffs' solicitor. ...

5. Woolmington v D.P.P.

House of Lords, May 23, 1935
[1935] A.C. 462 at 469–475, 480–483

Viscount Sankey L.C.:

My Lords, the appellant, Reginald Woolmington, after a trial at the Somerset Assizes at Taunton on January 23 ... was convicted at the Bristol Assizes on February 14 of the wilful murder of his wife on December 10, 1934, and was sentenced to death. He appealed to the Court of Criminal Appeal, substantially upon the ground that the learned judge had misdirected the jury by telling them that in the circumstances of the case he was presumed in law to be guilty of the murder unless he could satisfy the jury that his wife's death was due to an accident. ...

The facts are as follows. Reginald Woolmington is 21½ years old. His wife, who was killed, was 17½ years old last December. They had known each other for some time and upon August 25 they were married. Upon October 14 she gave birth to a child. Shortly after that there appears to have been some quarrelling between them and she left him upon November 22 and went to live with her mother. Woolmington apparently was anxious to get her to come back, but she did not come. The prosecution proved that at about 9.15 in the morning of the 10th Mrs. Daisy Brine was hanging out her washing at the back of her house at 25 Newtown, Milborne Port. While she was engaged in that occupation, she heard voices from the next door house, No. 24. She knew that in that house her niece, Reginald Woolmington's wife, was living. She heard and could recognize the voice of Reginald Woolmington saying something to the effect "are you going to come back home?" She could not hear the answer. Then the back door in No. 24 was slammed. She heard a voice in the kitchen but could not tell what it said. Then she heard the sound of a gun. Upon that she looked out of the front window and she saw Reginald Woolmington, whose voice she had heard just before speaking in the kitchen, go out and get upon his bicycle, which had been left or was standing against the wall of her house, No. 25. She called out to him but he gave no reply. He looked at her hard and then he rode away.

According to Reginald Woolmington's own story, having brooded over and deliberated upon the position all through the night of December 9, he went on the morning of the 10th in the usual way to the milking at his employer's farm, and while milking conceived this idea that he would take the old gun which was in the barn and he would take it up that morning to his wife's mother's house where she was living, and that he would show her that gun and tell her that he was going to commit suicide if she did not come back. He would take the gun up for the purpose of frightening her into coming back to him by causing her to think that he was going to commit suicide. He finished his milking, went back to his father's house, had breakfast and then left, taking with him a hack saw. He returned to the farm, went into the barn, got the gun, which had been used for rook shooting, sawed off the barrels of it, then took the only two cartridges which were there and put them into the gun. He took the two pieces of the barrel which he had sawn off and the hack saw, crossed a field about 60 yards wide and dropped them into the brook. Having done that, he returned on his bicycle, with the gun in his overcoat pocket, to his father's house and changed his clothes. Then he got a piece of wire flex which he attached to the gun so that he could suspend it from his shoulder underneath his coat, and so went off to the house where his wife was living. He knocked at the door, went into the kitchen and asked her: "Are you coming back?" She made no answer. She came into the parlour, and on his asking her whether she would come back she replied she was going into service. He then, so he says, threatened he would shoot himself, and went on to show her the gun and brought it across his waist, when it somehow went off and his wife fell down and he went out of the house. He told the jury that it was an accident, that it was a pure accident; that whilst he was getting the gun from under his shoulder and was drawing it across his breast it accidentally went off and he was doing nothing unlawful, nothing wrong, and this was a pure accident. There was considerable controversy as to whether a letter in which he set out his grievances was written before or after the above events. But when he was arrested at 7.30 on the evening of the 10th and charged with having committed murder he said: "I want to say nothing, except I done it, and they can do what they like with me. It was jealousy I suppose. Her mother enticed her away from me. I done all I could to get her back. That's all."

The learned judge in summing-up the case to the jury said: "If you accept his evidence, you will have little doubt that she died in consequence of a gunshot wound which was inflicted by a gun which he had taken to this house, and which was in his hands, or in his possession, at the time that it exploded. If you come to the conclusion that she died in consequence of injuries from the gun which he was carrying, you are put by the law of this country into this position: The killing of a human being is homicide, however he may be killed, and all homicide is presumed to be malicious and murder, unless the contrary appears from circumstances of alleviation, excuse, or justification. 'In every charge of murder, the fact of killing being first proved, all the circumstances of accident, necessity, or infirmity are to be satisfactorily proved by the prisoner, unless they arise out of the evidence produced against him: for the law will presume the fact to have been founded in malice until the contrary appeareth.' That has been the law of this country for all time since we had law. Once it is shown to a jury that somebody has died through the act of another, that is presumed to be murder, unless the person who has been guilty of the act which causes the death can satisfy a jury that what happened was something less, something which might be alleviated, something which might be reduced to a charge of manslaughter, or was something which was accidental, or was something which could be justified."

At the end of his summing-up he added: "The Crown has got to satisfy you that this woman, Violet Woolmington, died at the prisoner's hands. If they must satisfy you of that beyond any reasonable doubt. If they satisfy you of that, then he has to show that there are circumstances to be found in the evidence which has been given from the witness-box in this case which alleviate the crime so that it is only manslaughter or which excuse the homicide altogether by showing that it was a pure accident." ...

It is true as stated by the Court of Appeal that there is apparent authority for the law as laid down by the learned judge. But your Lordships' House has had the advantage of a prolonged and exhaustive inquiry dealing with the matter in debate from the earliest times, an advantage which was not shared by either of the Courts below. Indeed your Lordships were referred to legal propositions dating as far back as the reign of King Canute (994-1035). But I do not think it is necessary for the purpose of this opinion to go as far back as that. Rather would I invite your Lordships to begin by considering the proposition of law which is contained in Foster's Crown Law, written in 1762, and which appears to be the foundation for the law as laid down by the learned judge in this case. It must be remembered that Sir Michael Foster, although a distinguished judge, is for this purpose to be regarded as a text-book writer, for he did not lay down the doctrine in any case before him, but in an article which is described as the "Introduction to the Discourse of Homicide." In the folio edition, published at Oxford at the Clarendon Press in 1762, at p.255, he states:

> "In every charge of murder, the fact of killing being first proved, all the circumstances of accident, necessity, or infirmity are to be satisfactorily proved by the prisoner, unless they arise out of the evidence produced against him; for the law presumeth the fact to have been founded in malice, until the contrary appeareth. And very right it is, that the law should so presume. The defendant in this instance standeth upon just the same foot that every other defendant doth: the matters tending to justify, excuse, or alleviate, must appear in evidence before he can avail himself of them."

Now the first part of this passage appears in nearly every text-book or abridgment which has been since written. ...

The question arises, Is that statement correct law? ... *M'Naughton's case* (1843) 4 St. Tr. (N. S.) 847 stands by itself. It is the famous pronouncement on the law bearing on the question of insanity in cases of murder. It is quite exceptional and has nothing to do with the present circumstances. In *M'Naughton's case* the onus is definitely and exceptionally placed upon the accused to establish such a defence. ...

If at any period of a trial it was permissible for the judge to rule that the prosecution had established its case and that the onus was shifted on the prisoner to prove that he was not guilty and that unless he discharged that onus the prosecution was entitled to succeed, it would be enabling the judge in such a case to say that the jury must in law find the prisoner guilty and so make the judge decide the case and not the jury, which is not the common law. It would be an entirely different case from those exceptional instances of special verdicts where a judge asks the jury to find certain facts and directs them that on such facts the prosecution is entitled to succeed. Indeed, a consideration of such special verdicts shows that it is not till the end of the evidence that a verdict can properly be found and that at the end of the evidence it is not for the prisoner to establish his innocence, but for the prosecution to establish his guilt. Just as there is evidence on behalf of the prosecution so there may be evidence on behalf of the prisoner which may cause a doubt as to his guilt. In either case, he is entitled to the benefit of the doubt. But while the prosecution must prove the guilt of the prisoner, there is no such burden laid on the prisoner to prove his innocence and it is sufficient for him to raise a doubt as to his guilt; he is not bound to satisfy the jury of his innocence.

This is the real result of the perplexing case of *Rex v Abramovitch* (1914) 11 Cr. App. R. 45, which lays down the same proposition, although perhaps in somewhat involved language. Juries are always told that, if conviction there is to be, the prosecution must prove the case beyond reasonable doubt. This statement cannot mean that in order to be acquitted the prisoner must "satisfy" the jury. This is the law as laid down in the Court of Criminal Appeal in *Rex v Davies* 29 Times L. R. 350; 8 Cr. App. R. 211, the headnote of which correctly states that where intent is an ingredient of a crime there is no onus on the defendant to prove that the act alleged was accidental. Throughout the web of the English Criminal Law one golden thread is always to be seen, that it is the duty of the prosecution to prove the prisoner's guilt subject to what I have already said as to the defence of insanity and subject also to any statutory exception. If, at the end of and on the whole of the case, there is a reasonable doubt, created by the evidence given by either the prosecution or the prisoner, as to whether the prisoner killed the deceased with a malicious intention, the prosecution has not made out the case and the prisoner is entitled to an acquittal. No matter what the charge or where the trial, the principle that the prosecution must prove the guilt of the prisoner is part of the common law of England and no attempt to whittle it down can be entertained. When dealing with a murder case the Crown must prove (a) death as the result of a voluntary act of the accused and (b) malice of the accused. It may prove malice either expressly or by implication. For malice may be implied where death occurs as the result of a voluntary act of the accused which is (i) intentional and (ii) unprovoked. When evidence of death and malice has been given (this is a question for the jury) the accused is entitled to show, by evidence or by examination of the circumstances adduced by the Crown that the act on his part which caused death was either unintentional or provoked. If the jury are either satisfied with his explanation or, upon a review of all the evidence, are left in reasonable doubt whether, even if his explanation be not accepted, the act was unintentional or provoked, the prisoner is entitled to be acquitted. ... We cannot say that if the jury had been properly directed they would have inevitably come to the same conclusion.

In the result ... we order that the appeal should be allowed and the conviction quashed. ...

6. Leachinsky v Christie

Court of Appeal, July 17, 1945
[1946] 1 K.B. 124 at 133–136

Scott L.J:

... The preceding references to and reflections on our old procedural law, justify, I think, the following conclusions as to a constable's power of arrest. (1) Arrest on a criminal charge always was and still is a mere step on the procedural road towards committal, trial, verdict, judgment, and punishment or acquittal, as may result. (2) The power of arrest conferred by the law is limited to the purpose of the particular proceeding scil, the specific charge formulated. (3) The arrest must be made on that charge only; and the person arrested must be told by the constable at the time of arrest what the charge is. The constable cannot lawfully keep an open mind, and remain still undecided at the moment of arrest: he must make up his mind and formulate the charge on which he decides, and then arrest on that charge. (4) If, having told the accused, before arresting, what the charge is, he then either changes his mind or becomes undecided, he has no longer any power to arrest on that charge; and if he does so arrest, he acts illegally and is guilty of the tort of false imprisonment. (5) If he arrests on a specific charge, but before he has brought the prisoner before the appropriate judicial authority he changes his mind and decides to keep him on another charge, his power to detain automatically ceases and it becomes his immediate legal duty then to release the prisoner and make a new arrest on the new charge. To prevent misunderstanding, it is well to add, that in discussing the procedural character of arrest without warrant (whether by a constable or a private person) and pointing out how limited is the scope of the power conferred by the law, I am, of course, not suggesting that the initial absence, or the subsequent cessation, of the legal right to arrest or detain will of itself affect the jurisdiction of the court to deal with the accused person when he has once been brought before it. Quite different considerations apply to that question. Neither the committing magistrate nor the trial court will lose jurisdiction merely because it appears by evidence or admission that the prisoner has been arrested in circumstances which, for any of the reasons I have stated, made the arrest unlawful, although that fact may well influence discretion as to bail; but the person so wronged will have his cause of action against the person who arrested him unlawfully; and in an action for false imprisonment every harm to the plaintiff causally resulting from the original wrong will be matter for the jury to consider in assessing the quantum of general damages, and of course it is open to the jury to give exemplary damages. Again, to prevent misunderstanding, it may be well to point out that once a prisoner has been lawfully arrested on a definite charge, and brought before a magistrate's court for committal, there is nothing in the law of arrest to prevent a more serious charge being added to or substituted for the existing charge. That question appertains not to the law of arrest but to the procedural law of the court.

The aspect of the law of arrest which is most directly relevant to the present appeal is that of the purpose for which the arrest is made. The ultimate object which the law has in view in authorising arrest is, of course, the protection of society, but arrest is not an end in itself. What the law grants is not a right, but only a power, although it may also be imposing a duty, especially on a constable. When effected, the arrest is in essence just a step in the administration of criminal justice, and not the less so because it is the first step, or at any rate the first step *inter partes*—for process may begin by information and warrant, or summons, at a stage before the accused is involuntarily made party to the *lis* between the prosecutor and him. It is by bringing him in person before the court, whether committing magistrate or judge and jury, that he is made a party, and the whole purpose of arrest, just as much as of the initial steps of information, warrant or summons, is to give the court jurisdiction over the alleged offender, in order that justice may be done, and that he, if found guilty, may be punished. The corporal presence of the offender is just as essential to trial, verdict and judgment, as to punishment, and, if he be innocent it is equally essential to him, as well as to the prosecution. English justice could not be what it is without that fundamental feature. In short, in our administration of justice the presence of the offender is basically the original starting point of any criminal proceeding: and none the less so because on the one hand bail may be substituted for the body of the accused by judicial order, or on some occasions at the early stage before he comes before the magistrate, by permission of the executive, namely, the police: and on the other hand the presence of the accused in court is not essential in some summary cases. Consideration of the last mentioned requisite of criminal procedure—the presence of the accused in court, which apart from minor exceptions is essential—leads logically to another essential rule of this branch of law, which also is pertinent to the present appeal. An arrest must not only be on a definite charge and for the purpose of prosecuting that charge, but it must be expressly stated at the time to be on that charge. The law does not allow an arrest *in vacuo*, or without reason assigned, and the reason assigned must be that the arrest is for the purpose of a prosecution on the self-same charge, as is the justification for the arrest. It follows, and it is a principle lying at the very roots of English freedom, that if a man is arrested on one charge he is entitled to his release the moment the prosecution of that charge is abandoned. The prosecution cannot arrest on one charge, abandon their intention to proceed on that charge and then keep him in cold storage, still nominally on that charge, while they inquire into the possibility of putting forward a different charge. To do that they must first release him: then, when they propose to put forward some other charge, they can make that new charge the occasion of a new arrest. That is still the law to-day, when the vast majority of prosecutions are public, just as truly as it was in earlier times when they were mostly private; and by public and private I mean conducted by a public authority and by a private individual respectively.

It follows from what I have said that the practice, if there be one, which the learned judge obviously had in mind, of arresting a supposed murderer, for instance, on a minor charge, as a means of preventing his escape from justice at a time when the police suspect, but have not sufficient clues to constitute reasonable and probable cause for arresting the suspect for the suspected crime, is in my opinion illegal, and gives the person arrested a cause of action for false imprisonment. In practice the police would, as a rule, incur no liability for substantial damages, except where their anticipatory suspicions prove ill-founded, but it is important, for the sake of the great principle of the liberty of the subject, that the illegality of the practice should be widely known to judges, to the legal profession, to the police and to the public. It is better that an occasional criminal should escape punishment, than that the judges should let in the thin edge of the wedge for discretionary arrest at the instance of the executive. The rule of law today is that unless the limiting conditions at common law, or by statute, are strictly observed by the constable, the arrest he makes is illegal and constitutes an actionable wrong for which the arrested person may sue him in trespass, the damages being at large. It is this right of action in the King's courts for any unauthorised arrest or detainment by the executive which, above all other legal rights, is, under our constitution, the foundation upon which the freedom of the individual rests. ...

7. Subramaniam v Public Prosecutor

Privy Council, July 9, 1956
[1956] 1 W.L.R. 965 at 967–968, 970, 973

de Silva M.R.:

... It was common ground that on April 29, 1955, at a place in the Rengam District in the State of Johore, the appellant was found in a wounded condition by certain members of the security forces; that when he was searched there was found around his waist a leather belt with three pouches containing 20 live rounds of ammunition; no weapon of any description was found upon him or in the immediate vicinity.

The defence put forward on behalf of the appellant was that he had been captured by terrorists, that at all material times he was acting under duress, and that at the time of his capture by the security forces he had formed the intention to surrender, with which intention he had come to the place where he was found. ...

In ruling out peremptorily the evidence of conversation between the terrorists and the appellant the trial judge was in error. Evidence of a statement made to a witness by a person who is not himself called as a witness may or may not be hearsay. It is hearsay and inadmissible when the object of the evidence is to establish the truth of what is contained in the statement. It is not hearsay and is admissible when it is proposed to establish by the evidence, not the truth of the statement, but the fact that it was made. The fact that the statement was made, quite apart from its truth, is frequently relevant in considering the mental state and conduct thereafter of the witness or of some other person in whose presence the statement was made. In the case before their Lordships statements could have been made to the appellant by the terrorists, which, whether true or not, if they had been believed by the appellant, might reasonably have induced in him an apprehension of instant death if he failed to conform to their wishes. ...

Their Lordships feel unable to hold with any confidence that had the excluded evidence, which goes to the very root of the defence of duress, been admitted the result of the trial would probably have been the same. ...

8. Cullen v Clarke
Supreme Court, February 27, 1959
[1963] I.R. 368 at 378–382

Kingsmill Moore J:

... I think the learned Judge was in error, if he held, as he appears to have held, that he could only come to a conclusion under para. (b) if there was positive evidence given by prospective employers as to their reasons for not employing the workman. Such reasons may be deduced from a variety of circumstances. Admittedly the most satisfactory evidence of this would be the testimony of the employers, given in open court and subject to cross-examination. There may, however, be practical difficulties in producing a number of such employers as witnesses. If so, the workman must fall back on other evidence. Can he, as part of such evidence, testify to what the employers said in refusing him work? This is the question on which the learned Judge invited the assistance of the Court.

I do not think such a question can be answered satisfactorily in the abstract. To do so would involve a disquisition on the nature of hearsay evidence and the so-called exceptions to the rule. The actual question put and the object for which it was put in each case has to be considered. In view of some of the arguments addressed to the Court, it is necessary to emphasise that there is no general rule of evidence to the effect that a witness may not testify as to the words spoken by a person who is not produced as a witness. There is a general rule, subject to many exceptions, that evidence of the speaking of such words is inadmissible to prove the truth of the facts which they assert; the reasons being that the truth of the words cannot be tested by cross-examination and has not the sanctity of an oath. This is the rule known as the rule against hearsay. In answer to the invitation of the trial Judge, I may perhaps call attention to some of the cases in which evidence may properly be given of words uttered by persons who are not called as witnesses.

First: the utterance of the words may itself be a relevant fact, quite apart from the truth or falsity of anything asserted by the words spoken. To prove, by the evidence of a witness who heard the words, that they were spoken, is direct evidence, and in no way encroaches on the general rule against hearsay. In the present case the refusal of an employer to engage the workman is a relevant fact. A workman could give evidence that, on asking the employer for a job the employer said, " No."

Second: where a fact or transaction is in issue declarations which accompany or explain the fact or transaction are generally admitted under the somewhat vague principle that they form part of the *res gestae*. If the employer had said, "No, but ask me again in a week's time," the statement would be admissible as being really an intrinsic part of the act, showing that the refusal was not absolute and unqualified but might yield to altered circumstances. Again, in so far as the evidence of the words spoken is offered merely to explain or qualify the nature of the act, there is no breach of the hearsay rule.

Third: the statements accompanying the act may be offered as showing the mind of the actor at the time of the doing of the act. Here there is a breach of the hearsay rule, in so far as reliance is placed on the truth of the words uttered, a truth which is not sanctified by an oath or capable of being tested by cross-examination. But here resort can be had to another well-established practice, sometimes regarded as falling within the *res gestae* extension, sometimes as an exception to the hearsay rule. "When the motive or reason of a person for doing an act, or the intention with which he does it, is relevant to the issue, his statement made at the time of the doing of the act is evidence of his motive, reason or intention": *Law of Hearsay Evidence*, Tregarthen, at p.55. Whenever the bodily or mental feelings of a person are material to be proved, the usual expression of such feelings made at or about the time in question may be given in evidence. If they were the natural language of the affection, whether of body or mind, they furnish original and satisfactory evidence of its existence, and the question whether they were real or feigned is for the jury to determine": *Phipson's Law of Evidence*, 8th ed., 1942, at p. 71. ...

Fourth, as to the admissibility of declarations as to state of mind, where such declarations are made prior to or subsequent to an act and unconnected therewith, the authorities are not uniform, but the modern tendency is to admit such declarations. "... [W]herever it is material to prove the state of a person's mind, or what was passing in it, and what were his intentions, there you may prove what he said, because that is the only means by which you can find out what his intentions were": *Sugden v St. Leonards* L.R. 1 P.D. 154, *per* Mellish L.J. at p.251. "It is well established in English jurisprudence, in accordance with the dictates of common sense, that the words and acts of a person are admissible as evidence of his state of mind. Indeed, they are the only possible evidence on such an issue. It was urged at the Bar that although the acts of the deceased might be put in evidence, his words might not. I fail to understand the distinction. Speaking is as much an act as doing.

"It must be borne in mind that there is nothing in the admission of such evidence which clashes with the rooted objection in our jurisprudence to the admission of hearsay evidence. The testimony of the witnesses is to the act, i.e., to the deceased speaking these words, and it is the speaking of the words which is the matter put in evidence and which possesses evidential value. The evidence is, therefore, not in any respect open to the objection that it is secondary or hearsay evidence": *Lloyd v Powell Duffryn Steam Coal Co., Ltd.* [1914] A.C. 7.13, *per* Lord Moulton, at p.757. The remarks of the Lord Justice, in so far as they hold that the admission of evidence of words spoken by a person

Appendices

who is not a witness in order to prove the state of his mind is not a transgression of the general hearsay rule must, I think, be confined to cases where such words are the spontaneous and unrehearsed expression of contemporary feelings, words which reveal rather than declare the condition of the mind. A man's statement as to what are his motives, intention, or other his state of mind may be rehearsed, and may be false, and to admit such a statement as evidence of the true condition of his mind is contrary to the general hearsay rule and can only be allowed as an exception to that rule. Nevertheless, such statements, if contemporary with a relevant act, have regularly been admitted. Thus in *Fellowes v Williamson* (1829) Moo. & Mal. 3011 the question was whether the plaintiffs had sold to A certain goods because of a representation made by the defendant that A was solvent. Evidence was admitted that, when the plaintiffs were approached by A for the goods, they stated that they had received a favourable account of A and would accordingly send the goods. The case was decided in 1829 when the parties to a case were not competent witnesses, and so the evidence in regard to the declaration by the plaintiffs of their motives must have been given by some third person, or must have been contained in a letter. Again, in *Skinner & Co. v Shew & Co.* [1894] 2 Ch. 581, the question was whether the plaintiff had lost the benefit of a contract which he was on the point of concluding, by reason of the defendants' threats of legal proceedings made to the other party to the intended contract. The other party had broken off negotiation by a letter from their legal adviser which, after referring to a letter from the defendants, went on to say: "Under these circumstances it is absolutely impossible for our clients to continue any negotiations for an agreement. However useful your invention may be, they cannot submit themselves to the risk of a law suit." The letter was admitted as evidence not merely of repudiation, but also of the reason and motive for such repudiation. Mr. Justice North was careful to point out that though admissible, the evidence was by no means conclusive, as the truth of the statement of motive could be questioned.

Finally: in a case under the analogous English section, *Cowell v Taylor, Walker & Co., Ltd.* 33 B. W. C. C. 275, MacKinnon L.J., at p. 279 says :—"He [the workman] was asked the question: 'Why did all those people, or why did some of them, refuse to employ you?' The question was objected to on the ground that if he was allowed to give that evidence it would be giving hearsay evidence of what was said by somebody else, and it is said the learned County Court Judge upheld the objection and, therefore, he was not allowed to state the reason given by the employers to whom he had applied as to why they would not give him work. For my part I am inclined to think that the question was admissible. It was not really hearsay; it was a fact which it was necessary for the man to prove and I think the question ought to have been admitted." The view expressed was *obiter*, for the learned Judge went on to decide in the workman's favour' on other evidence. The other judges of the Appeal Court did not express any general view, but du Parcq L.J. as well as MacKinnon L.J. relied on a conversation between the workman and the secretary of his original employers, in which the secretary had stated that they would not give him work as they were afraid he would hurt his foot again. I find difficulty in seeing how the proposed evidence would not be hearsay. Undoubtedly the reason why the employers refused to give the workman a job was a fact to be proved in any legal way. But the reason why an employer refused to employ him is not necessarily the same thing as the reason given by an employer for refusing to employ him. It may or may not be the same. If reliance is placed on the truth of what is stated by a person not called as a witness it is hearsay evidence, admissible only if it falls within one of the exceptions to the rule excluding hearsay. Here, and in *Cowell's Case* 33 B.W C.C. 275 the reasons and motives of a prospective employer were clearly relevant facts: and statements as to those reasons, certainly if made contemporaneously with the refusal to employ him, would, although hearsay, be admissible as coming within the exception already stated. But such statements, though admissible, must be acted on with caution; for the statements may be false. An employer, for instance, might refuse to employ a man because of gross disfigurement or because he was a foreigner, but he would not be likely to assign those reasons. He would be more likely to say that he had no job available. ...

9. McGowan v Carville

Supreme Court, April 30, 1959
[1960] I.R. 330 at 354–356, 350–352

Lavery J:

... [I]t is clear that the Legislature understands very well how to prescribe the manner of proof of the offence of not holding a licence required by law and how to make the non-production of a particular licence an offence in itself. Davitt P. has shown this by quoting s. 56, sub-s. 4, of the Road Traffic Act, 1933, dealing with compulsory insurance. ...

The Oireachtas seems to me clearly to have seen the distinction in dealing with the respective offences and the manner of proof. Any person found driving a motor vehicle on a public road must produce his licence to a guard demanding it either then or within five days (s. 39, sub-s. 1). If he fails to produce it he is required to give his name and address (s. 39, sub-s. 2) and if he refuses or fails to give his name and address he may be arrested (s. 39, sub-s. 3). A licensing authority is required to keep a register of driving licences (Clause 11, Road Traffic (Driving Licence) Regulations 1934 (S.R. & 0., 1934, No. 151)). The garda authorities can, therefore, quite simply by enquiring ascertain whether a licence has been issued, and I should think that proof that no such licence had been issued to the person concerned by the licensing authority for the area indicated by the address given would be ample proof to shift the burden of proof that he had a licence obtained lawfully in some other area on to the person involved.

Davitt P. has made it clear that it is for the District Justice to determine whether the burden of proof has been shifted.

Mr. McCarthy referred the Court to *Best on the Principles of the Law of Evidence* (12th ed., 1922) at p.252, para. 275. The passage is very much in point. I quote:

> "This rule [that the burden of proof lies on the person who wishes to support his case by a particular fact which lies more peculiarly within his own knowledge, or of which he is supposed to be cognisant: para. 274] is of very general application: it holds good whether the proof of the issue involves the proof of an affirmative or of a negative, and has even been allowed to prevail against presumption of law. But the authorities are by no means agreed as to the *extent* to which it ought to be carried. In *R. v Turner* 5 M. & S. 206 at 211, Bayley J. says, 'I have always understood it to be a general rule, that if a negative averment be made by one party, which is peculiarly within the knowledge of the other, the party within whose knowledge it lies, and who asserts the affirmative, is to prove it, and not he who avers the negative.' But in *Elkin v Janson* 13 M. & W. 655 at 662, Alderson B., on this dictum being quoted, said. 'I doubt, as a general rule, whether those expressions are not too strong. They are right as to the *weight* of the evidence, but there should be some evidence to start it, in order to cast the onus on the other side.' And in *R. v Burdett* 4 B. & A. 95 at 140, Holroyd J. states in the most explicit terms that the rule in question 'is not allowed to supply the want of necessary proof, whether direct or presumptive, against a defendant of the crime with which he is charged; but when such proof has been given, it is a rule to be applied in considering the weight of the evidence against him, whether direct or presumptive, when it is unopposed, unrebutted, or not weakened, by contrary evidence which it would be in the defendant's power to produce, if the fact directly or presumptively proved were not true.'"

I should mention that the case of *Minister for Industry and Commerce v Steele* [1952] 1 I.R. 304 appears to me clearly to support the proposition that the onus of proof of every ingredient of an offence lies in the first instance on the prosecutor: see *per* Murnaghan J., at p.315.

In that case the Court held that the evidence was sufficient to shift the onus to the person charged.

It is therefore, to be borne in mind that it is not for the prosecutor to prove that the person charged is not the holder of a licence but it is for him to give such evidence as will, if not displaced by further evidence offered by the defendant, justify a finding that he had not a licence. ...

Maguire C.J. (dissenting):

... In a criminal case the burden of proof as a matter of law and pleading lies upon the prosecutor. ... [U]nless it is otherwise directed by statute the presumption of innocence casts on the prosecutor the burden of proving every ingredient of the offence even though negative averments be involved therein.

To this rule there are commonly said to be two exceptions, that is, cases in which the burden of proof does not rest upon the party substantially asserting the affirmative or which if they occur during the trial will cause such burden to shift to his opponent. The first is where a disputable presumption of law exists or a *prima facie* case has been proved. The second, under which it is said this case falls, is where the subject-matter of a party's allegation (whether affirmative or negative) is peculiarly within the knowledge of his opponent. In such a case it lies upon the latter to rebut such allegation.

The principle of this exception has been recognised chiefly in older cases and by the Legislature. Instances given are offences against the game laws or proceedings against an apothecary for practising without a certificate. According to Phipson, "The better opinion now appears to be that some *prima facie* evidence must be given by the complainant in order to cast a burden upon his adversary." In Stephen's *Digest of the Laws of Evidence* (9th ed., art. 96), the rule is stated as follows: "In considering the amount of evidence necessary to shift the burden of proof the Court has regard to the opportunities of knowledge with respect to the fact to be proved which may be possessed by the parties respectively." This statement of the law was approved of in *Rex v Kakelo* [1923] 2 K.B. 793, at 795. This case has been approved of by this Court in *Steele's Case* [1952] I.R. 304. Both Mr. Justice Murnaghan, at p.315, and Mr. Justice O'Byrne, at p.317, cite with approval the above statement of the rule and apply it.

In my opinion the onus of proving that he has a licence is cast upon a person driving a vehicle for which a licence is required, by the Act itself, or if not by the Act by the application of the rule just quoted. Section 3, sub-s. 4. of the Motor Car Act, 1903, provided that a licence must be produced by any person driving a motor car when demanded by a police constable. The Act of 1933 does not alter this save to the extent that a driver is not obliged to have his licence with him. If he has it with him he is required to produce it: if he has not got it with him, as already pointed out, he is required to produce it within five days at a Garda Station (s. 39). ...

In face of [the statutory provisions] it seems to me bordering on the absurd to suggest that if a person is charged with the offence of driving a mechanically propelled vehicle the onus is upon the prosecution to give any evidence beyond that given in this case. Even if the terms of the Act did not speak so clearly, I am of opinion that once it is shown that a person was in control of a vehicle for the driving of which a licence is required, the onus of proving that he has a licence is cast upon him because the knowledge that he has an effective licence, *viz.*, a licence duly granted and signed by him is peculiarly within his knowledge. ...

10. Bratty v A-G. for Northern Ireland

House of Lords, October 3, 1961
[1963] A.C. 386 at 405–406

Viscount Kilmuir L.C.:

... [T]he decision in *Woolmington's* case [1935] A.C. 462 did not mean that the judge must deal in his summing-up with the issues of accident and provocation merely because these defences were raised. There must be some evidence of accident or provocation on which a reasonable jury could act. ...

It is necessary that a proper foundation be laid before a judge can leave "automatism" to the jury. That foundation, in my view, is not forthcoming merely from unaccepted evidence of a defect of reason from disease of the mind. There would need to be other evidence on which a jury could find non-insane automatism. What the Court of Criminal Appeal say about the onus of proof must be read in the context of evidence directed simultaneously to defences of insanity and automatism. ...

[F]or a defence of automatism to be "genuinely raised in a genuine fashion", there must be evidence on which a jury could find that a state of automatism exists. By this I mean that the defence must be able to point to some evidence, whether it emanates from their own or the Crown's witnesses, from which the jury could reasonably infer that the accused acted in a state of automatism. Whether or not there is such evidence is a matter of law for the judge to decide. In the case before your Lordships, in my opinion, McVeigh J. was right in ruling that there was no evidence on this point fit to be left to the jury. I have already dealt with the unsuccessful attempt to prove psychomotor epilepsy and the concession before us that there was nothing in the evidence to show or suggest that there was any other pathological cause. If one subtracts the medical evidence directed to the establishment of psychomotor epilepsy, I am of opinion that there was not any evidence on which a jury could properly have considered the existence of automatism. Counsel for the appellant directed our attention to the appellant's statement, to his evidence and to his previous conduct. In my view they do not provide evidence fit to be left to a jury on this question. They could not form the basis of reasonable doubt. ...

11. People (A.G.) v Casey (No. 2)
Supreme Court, December 21, 1962
[1963] I.R. 33 at 37–40

Kingsmill Moore J:

... It is the function of a judge in his charge to give to the jury such direction and warnings as may in his opinion be necessary to avoid the danger of an innocent man being convicted, and the nature of such directions and warnings must depend on the facts of the particular case. But, apart from the directions and warnings suggested by the facts of an individual case, judicial experience has shown that certain general directions and warnings are necessary in every case and that particular types of warnings are necessary in particular types of case.

Such accumulated judicial experience eventually tends to crystallise into established rules of judicial practice, accepted rules of law and statutory provisions. Thus the general directions which must be given in every case as to the onus of proof and the necessity of establishing guilt beyond reasonable doubt have arisen from experience of the fallibility of human testimony in general, whether due to mendacity, imperfect observation, auto-suggestion or other causes. The suggestibility and lack of responsibility of children of tender age find recognition in the statutory provision that their unsworn evidence shall not be sufficient to convict of an offence, unless corroborated by other material evidence implicating the accused, and even when such evidence is received under oath it is customary for judges to tell juries that they should not convict unless they have weighed the evidence with the most extreme care. Similarly the opportunities for giving false evidence afforded to an accomplice and to a person who alleges that a sexual offence has been committed against him or her, coupled with the extreme temptation to give false evidence frequently present in such cases, have given rise to the rule that a judge must warn the jury that it is always dangerous to convict on the evidence of such persons unless it is corroborated in some material particular implicating the accused.

The category of circumstances and special types of case which call for special directions and warnings from the trial judge cannot be considered as closed. Increased judicial experience, and indeed further psychological research, may extend it. It is submitted by Mr. Sorahan, counsel for the prisoner that the time has come for such an extension, that accumulated experience has demonstrated the necessity for warning a jury as to the mistakes which can be made, and which have been made, in the identification by witnesses of persons accused and, in particular, that a jury should be told that an identification parade, though the best available method of confirming identification, is very far from infallible.

Mr. Sorahan referred to cases such as the *Beck Case* and the *Slater Case*, which have passed into legal history as classical examples of erroneous identification and to two recent cases in our jurisdiction where persons had been convicted on what appeared to be entirely satisfactory identification but where subsequent investigation proved the identification to have been wrong. Judicial experience, including that of some members of this Court, could provide further instances where positive and honest identification was shown to be mistaken. There is unfortunately no record of the number of cases where a witness purported to identify as the offender a person who was present at an identification parade merely to make up the requisite number of the parade, nor can we know in how many cases a person may have been convicted on an erroneous identification which there was no method of proving to be erroneous. Recent judicial utterances reveal an increasing awareness of the potentialities of error in visual identification, however honest, however convinced, and convictions have been set aside on the production of fresh evidence casting doubt on the identification: *R. v Ashinan* [1954] Crim. L.R. 382; *R. v Harrigan* [1957] Crim. L.R. 52; *R. v Williams* [1956] Crim. L.R. 833; *R. v Parks* [1961] Crim. L.R. 825.

The necessity of giving a special direction where identification rests on the evidence of only one witness has already been judicially recognised. Thus in *The People (Attorney General) v Francis Hughes* 92 I.L.T.R. 179, Maguire C.J., giving the judgment of the Court of Criminal Appeal, said: "Nevertheless having regard to the circumstances that the case depended upon the identification of the applicant by one witness and that the accused was not professionally represented at the trial, this Court is of opinion that the greatest care was required in charging the jury, as to the way in which they should approach the case and particularly of the dangers inherent in evidence of visual identification."

In *The People v Keffard* (unreported) Mr. Justice Kenny, giving the judgment of the Court of Criminal Appeal, said in reference to the possibility that the jury had convicted on the evidence of one identification witness: "If they were entitled to do so this Court is satisfied that they could have done so only when they had been warned in the most specific terms of the dangers involved in visual identification ... There have been so many instances of mistakes in visual identification, and the possibilities of error in this type of evidence are so numerous, that the jury should be directed on the necessity of exercising care in all cases where the visual identification is that of one witness only." The Court set aside the conviction because the evidence of identification was presented to the jury as a ground upon which they were entitled to convict the accused, without any reference to the caution with which they should regard such evidence. ...

We are of opinion that juries as a whole may not be fully aware of the dangers involved in visual identification nor of the considerable number of cases in which such identification has been proved to be erroneous; and also that they may be inclined to attribute too much probative effect to the test of an identification parade. In our opinion it is desirable that in all cases, where the verdict depends substantially on the correctness of an identification, their attention should be called in general terms to the fact that in a number of instances such identification has proved erroneous, to the possibilities of mistake in the case before them and to the necessity of caution. Nor do we think that such warning should be confined to cases where the identification is that of only one witness. Experience has shown that mistakes can occur where two or more witnesses have made positive identifications. We consider juries in cases where the correctness of an identification is challenged should be directed on the following lines, namely, that if their verdict as to the guilt of the prisoner is to depend wholly or substantially on the correctness of such identification, they should bear in mind that there have been a number of instances where responsible witnesses, whose honesty was not in question and whose opportunities for observation had been adequate, made positive identifications on a parade or otherwise, which identifications were subsequently proved to be erroneous; and accordingly that they should be specially cautious before accepting such evidence of identification as correct; but that if after careful examination of such evidence in the light of all the circumstances, and with due regard to all the other evidence in the case, they feel satisfied beyond reasonable doubt of the correctness of the identification they are at liberty to act upon it.

This direction is not meant to be a stereotyped formula. It may be too condensed to be fully appreciated by a jury without some further explanation and the facts of an individual case may require it to be couched in stronger or more ample terms, as when the witness or witnesses had no previous acquaintance with the appearance of the accused or had only an indifferent opportunity for observation. It does, however, contain a minimum warning which should be given, in any case which depends on visual identification. No specific reference is made to "corroboration in a material particular implicating the accused." An item of evidence falling within this formula may, according to its nature, have very little or very great probative value. This consideration is meant to be covered by the words, "in the light of all the circumstances, and with due regard to all the other evidence in the case," and it is for the judge to deal with the lesser or greater probative value of any item of corroborative evidence.

In the case which has been referred to us a finding of the guilt of the accused depends substantially if not entirely on the acceptance of the identification by two witnesses, neither of whom had any previous acquaintance with the prisoner. One was a boy aged eleven at the date of the occurrence. The other had only a momentary view in the light of the headlamps of his motor-car. The trial Judge put fairly to the jury the particular considerations against accepting the identifications, but did not give them the general warning which we think necessary. The particular considerations would undoubtedly gain added emphasis and importance when seen against the background of the general warning. As no such warning was given the Court is of opinion that there should be a new trial.

12. People (D.P.P.) v O'Brien
Supreme Court, December 14, 1964
[1965] I.R. 142 at 150–152, 159–162, 168–170

Kingsmill Moore J:

… Is evidence procured by the guards in the course of, and as a result of, a domiciliary search, unauthorised by a search warrant, admissible in subsequent criminal proceedings? The argument covered a wider field and embraced the whole question as to how far evidence was admissible which had been obtained by irregular or illegal means, whether by State functionaries or private persons. …

There would appear to be no Irish decision on the question binding on this Court, though there are decisions of lower courts to which we were referred. We were also referred to English, Scottish and United States decisions, which exhibit a great diversity of views between the Courts of these countries. As the question has been referred to us as a matter of exceptional public importance, and is of first instance in this Court, consideration may properly be given to the opinions expressed in courts of other jurisdictions administering a similar common law, though ultimately our decision must rest on our own view of the principles involved.

English law, at all events until recently, was uncompromising and admitted all relevant evidence not excluded by any of the recognised rules of evidence, even if the facts sought to be proved had been ascertained illegally. Thus, though confessions which were extorted by fear or induced by promises by a person in authority could not be proved, yet evidence procured as a result of what was said in such a confession was admissible: *R. v Warickshall* (1783) 1 Leach 263; *R. v Barker* [1941] 2 K. B. 381 at p.384. In *Jones v Owens* 34 J.P.

759 an illegal search of the person of the accused revealed in his pockets a number of salmon smolts and this evidence was admitted on a charge of illegal fishing, Mellor J. stating broadly that "it would be a dangerous obstacle to the administration of justice if we were to hold, because evidence was obtained by illegal means, it could not be used against a party charged with an offence." In *R. v Leatham* 8 Cox C.C. 498 Crompton J., admitting secondary evidence of a document the production of the original of which was withheld on grounds of privilege, said: "It matters not how you get it; if you steal it even, it would be admissible. Other English cases exemplify the same rule. I forbear to cite them as the matter has recently received full consideration in the Privy Council in the case of *Kuruma v The Queen* [1955] A.C. 197. *Kuruma* had been searched illegally and two cartridges were found on him. He was convicted of being in unlawful possession of ammunition, an offence which, at the time and place of the search, involved the penalty of death, and he was sentenced to death. He appealed to the Privy Council on the ground that evidence obtained by an illegal search was inadmissible. The Privy Council held it to be admissible. Lord Goddard, giving the judgment of the Privy Council, said, at p.203: "In their Lordships' opinion the test to be applied in considering whether evidence is admissible is whether it is relevant to the matters at issue. If it is, it is admissible and the court is not concerned with how the evidence was obtained. While this proposition may not have been stated in so many words in any English case there are decisions which support it, and in their Lordships' opinion it is plainly right in principle." (Lord Goddard's words, though cast in a general form, must of course, be read *secundum materiam subjectam* and as meaning that if the evidence is relevant it is not made inadmissible solely on the ground that it was obtained by illegal means. Evidence is relevant if it is logically probative: it is admissible if it is legally receivable. The rules of evidence exclude from admission many facts which are logically relevant to the issues, and I do not interpret Lord Goddard's words as in any way intended to cut down such established rules). Lord Goddard continues, at p.204: "No doubt in a criminal case the judge always has a discretion to disallow evidence if the strict ruins of admissibility would operate unfairly against the accused. This was emphasised in the case before this Board of *Noor Mohamed v The King* [1949] A.C. 182 at pp. 191–2 and in the recent case in the House of Lords, *Harris v Director of Public Prosecutions* [1952] A.C. 694 at 707. If, for instance, some admission of some piece of evidence, e.g., a document, had been obtained from a defendant by a trick, no doubt the judge might properly rule it out." He then refers to a number of Scottish cases in which the judges considered the question whether the illegal action of the police could be excused, and concludes: "In their Lordships' opinion, when it is a question of the admission of evidence strictly it is not whether the method by which it was obtained is tortious but excusable but whether what has been obtained is relevant to the issue being tried. ..."

None of the cases to which I have referred are binding on this Court and the problem must be approached on a basis of principle rather than authority. Three answers are possible. First, that if evidence is relevant it cannot be excluded on the ground that it was obtained as a result of illegal action: second, that if it was obtained as a result of illegal action it is never admissible: third, that where it was obtained by illegal action it is a matter for the trial judge to decide, in his discretion, whether to admit it or not, subject, in cases where the evidence has been admitted, to review by an appellate court.

It seems to me that neither the first nor the second answer is sustainable. The first answer represents the earlier portion of Lord Goddard's judgment in *Kuruma's Case* but even Lord Goddard found it necessary to allow exceptions to the rule, namely, where the strict rules of admissibility would operate unfairly against the accused, instancing the obtaining of a document by a trick. Courts both in England and Ireland have frequently refused to admit evidence which was undoubtedly relevant where the probative value of the evidence would be slight and its prejudicial effect would be great: *Noor Mohamed v The King* [1949] A.C. 182 at p.192. I can testify to the existence of a similar practice in Ireland from my own experience of the criminal courts both as advocate and judge. This Court in *McCarrick v Leavy* [1964] I.R. 225 has recently affirmed that a judge has discretion to exclude evidence of a confession which, though relevant and strictly admissible, had been taken in a manner which contravened the principles laid down in the "Judge's Rules. ..."

The second answer would open up equal difficulties. The exclusionary rule laid down in *Weeks v United States* 232 U.S. 383 was not accepted in many of the State courts. An absolute exclusionary rule prevents the admission of relevant and vital facts where unintentional or trivial illegalities have been committed in the course of ascertaining them. Fairness does not require such a rule and common sense rejects it.

Some intermediate solution must be found. As pointed out by the Lord Justice-General in *Lawrie v Muir* (1950) S.C. (J.) 19 and by Holmes J. in *Olmstead's Case* 277 U.S. 438 a choice has to be made between desirable ends which may be incompatible. It is desirable in the public interest that crime should be detected and punished. It is desirable that individuals should not be subjected to illegal or inquisitorial methods of investigation and that the State should not attempt to advance its ends by utilising the fruits of such methods. It appears to me that in every case a determination has to be made by the trial judge as to whether the public interest is best served by the admission or by the exclusion of evidence of facts ascertained as a result of, and by means of, illegal actions, and that the answer to the question depends on a consideration of all the circumstances. On the one hand, the nature and extent of the illegality have to be taken into account. Was the illegal action intentional or unintentional, and, if intentional, was it the result of an *ad hoc* decision or does it represent a settled or deliberate policy? Was the illegality one of a trivial and technical nature or was it a serious invasion of important rights the recurrence of which would involve a real danger to necessary freedoms? Were there circumstances of urgency or emergency which provide some excuse for the action? Lord Goddard in *Kuruma's Case* mentions as a ground for excluding relevant evidence that it had been obtained by a "trick" and the Lord Justice-General in *Lawrie's Case* refers to an "unfair trick." These seem to me to be more dubious grounds for exclusion. The police in the investigation of crime are not bound to show their hand too openly, provided they act legally. I am disposed to lay emphasis not so much on alleged fairness to the accused as on the public interest that the law should be observed even in the investigation of crime. The nature of the crime which is being investigated may also have to be taken into account. ...

It would not be in accordance with our system of jurisprudence for this Court to attempt to lay down rules to govern future hypothetical cases. We can do no more than decide the case now before us, and to lay down that, in future cases, the presiding judge has a discretion to exclude evidence of facts ascertained by illegal means where it appears to him that public policy, based on a balancing of public interests, requires such exclusion. If he decides to admit the evidence an appeal against his decision should lie to a superior Court which will decide the question according to its own views and will not be bound to affirm the decision of the trial judge if it disagrees with the manner in which the discretion has been exercised, even if it does not appear that such discretion was exercised on wrong principles. The result of such decisions, based on the facts of individual cases, may in time give rise to more precise rules.

I turn to the facts of the case now before us. It appears that the circumstances were such that on the information sworn by Sergeant Healy a warrant to search 118 Captain's Road would have been signed almost as a matter of course. The issue of a warrant to search for goods suspected to have been stolen was authorised even by the common law. No reason has been suggested why a warrant should not have as readily been issued for a search of 118 Captain's Road as for 118 Cashel Road. The mistake was a pure oversight and it has not been shown that the oversight was noticed by anyone before the premises were searched. I can find no evidence of deliberate treachery, imposition, deceit or illegality; no policy to disregard the provisions of the Constitution or to conduct searches without a warrant; nothing except the existence of an unintentional and accidental illegality to set against the public interest of having crime detected and punished. Assuming that the Judge had a discretion to exclude or receive evidence of what was discovered in the course of the search because the search was illegal, I am of opinion that such discretion was rightly exercised in receiving the evidence. ...

Mr. Justice Walsh, in the judgment, which he is about to deliver, is of opinion that where evidence has been obtained by the State or its agents as a result of a deliberate and conscious violation of the constitutional (as opposed to the common law) rights of an accused person it should be excluded save where there are "extraordinary excusing circumstances," and mentions as such circumstances the need to prevent an imminent destruction of vital evidence or rescue of a person in peril, and the seizure of evidence obtained in the course of and incidental to a lawful arrest even though the premises on which the arrest is made have been entered without a search warrant. I agree that where there has been such a deliberate and conscious violation of constitutional rights by the State or its agents evidence obtained by such violation should in general be excluded, and I agree that there may be certain "extraordinary excusing circumstances" which may warrant its admission. I would prefer, however, not to attempt to enumerate such circumstances by anticipation. The facts of individual cases vary so widely that any hard and fast rules of a general nature seem to me dangerous and I would again leave the exclusion or non-exclusion to the discretion of the trial judge. The views expressed in this judgment may seem to be a departure from what has hitherto been considered the law or the initiating of a principle in a field where up to now our law has been undefined. The further development of that principle should await clarification in the light of actual cases. I have already given my reasons for considering that in this particular case the evidence should not be excluded. This case is not one of deliberate and conscious violation, but of a purely accidental and unintentional infringement of the Constitution. In such cases, as Mr. Justice Walsh indicates, the evidence normally should not be excluded.

Walsh J:

... It is of interest to note that in his judgment in *Lawrie v Muir* (1950) S.C. (J.) 19 which has been referred to by Mr. Justice Kingsmill Moore, Lord Cooper, the Lord Justice-General, says, at p.27: "In particular, the case may bring into play the discretionary principle of fairness to the accused which has been developed so fully in our law in relation to the admission in evidence of confessions or admissions by a person suspected or charged with a crime." Accepting as I do that this is the principle upon which, in Scotland, involuntary or improperly induced statements or confessions are inadmissible, then the Scottish decisions upon evidence obtained as the result of illegal searches and seizures can be understood as being an extension of this principle of "fairness" because the deliberate adoption of an illegal procedure by the police would, to use the words of the Lord Justice-General in the same case, be "with a view to securing the admission of evidence obtained by an unfair trick." In the United States of America the exclusionary rule, as it is called, does not appear to have been based on a principle of "fairness" to the prisoner but for the express purpose of enforcing compliance on the part of the police with the constitutional rights of the accused person. This is clear from the many decisions of the Supreme Court of the United States and the latest expression of it is in the judgment of that Court in *Stone v State of California* (delivered the 23rd March, 1964). It would also appear that at least in cases of illegal search and seizure upon premises, the rule seems to be confined to cases where the violation has been that of the constitutional rights of the defendant. "It must be the defendant's own privacy which is invaded by the officers. Evidence obtained in violation of the rights of only third persons is not excludable by the defendant" (*Wigmore on Evidence*, (revised), 1961, vol. 8, at s. 2184a (viii) and the cases noted thereunder).

In my judgment the law in this country has been that the evidence in this particular case is not rendered inadmissible and that there is no discretion to rule it out by reason only of the fact that it was obtained by means of an illegal as distinct from an unconstitutional seizure. Members of the police make illegal searches and seizures at their peril and render themselves liable to the law of tort and in many instances also to the criminal law. In my view it would properly be within the province of a court which learns in the course of a trial that evidence preferred has been obtained as a result of an illegal search and seizure, whether on the property of the accused or any other person, knowingly and deliberately carried out by the police, to publicly draw attention to that fact and in that, though perhaps remote, way effectually to control the actions of the police. But to render the evidence inadmissible on that account only and for the purpose of controlling the police would be to prefer the latter purpose to the competing but primary one of conducting a fair trial. If a stage should be reached where this Court was compelled to come to the conclusion that the ordinary law and police disciplinary measures have failed to secure compliance by the police with the law, then it would be preferable that a rule of absolute exclusion should be formulated rather than that every trial judge, when the occasion arises, should also be asked to adjudicate upon the question of whether the public good requires the accused should go free without full trial rather than that the police should be permitted the fruits of the success of their lawless ventures. Apart from the anomalies which might be produced by the many varying ways in which that discretion could be exercised by individual judges, the lamentable state of affairs which would call for such a change in the existing law of evidence would certainly justify absolute exclusion rather than a rule which might appear to lend itself to expediency rather than to principle.

I come now to deal with the ground which was based upon the Constitutional issue. Article 40, para. 5, of the Constitution provides as follows: "The dwelling of every citizen is inviolable and shall not be forcibly entered save in accordance with law." That does not mean that the guarantee is against forcible entry only. In my view, the reference to forcible entry is an intimation that forcible entry may be permitted by law but that in any event the dwelling of every citizen is inviolable save where entry is permitted by law and that, if necessary, such law may permit forcible entry. In a case where members of a family live together in the family house, the house as a whole is for the purpose of the Constitution the dwelling of each member of the family. If a member of a family occupies a clearly defined portion of the house apart from the other members of the family, then it may well be that the part not so occupied is no longer his dwelling and that the part he separately occupies is his dwelling as would be the case where a person not a member of the family occupied or was in possession of a clearly defined portion of the house. In this case the appellants are members of a family living in the family dwelling-house and also appear to have their own respective separate bedrooms. Each of the appellants would therefore have a constitutional right to the inviolability of No. 118 Captain's Road. I have already referred, in the earlier part of this judgment, to what are sometimes, regrettably, the competing interests of the trial and conviction of criminals and the frustration of police illegalities. When the illegality amounts to infringement of a constitutional right the matter assumes a far greater importance than is the case where the illegality does not amount to such infringement. The vindication and the protection of constitutional rights is a fundamental matter for all courts established under the Constitution. That duty cannot yield place to any other competing interest. In Article 40 of the Constitution, the State has undertaken to defend and vindicate the inviolability of the dwelling of every citizen. The defence and vindication of the constitutional rights of the citizen is a duty superior to that, of trying such citizen for a criminal offence. The courts in exercising the judicial powers of government of the State must recognise the paramount position of constitutional rights and must uphold the objection of an accused person to the admissibility at his trial of evidence obtained or procured by the State or its servants or agents as a result of a deliberate and conscious violation of the constitutional rights of the accused person where no extraordinary excusing circumstances exist, such as the imminent destruction of vital evidence or the need to rescue a victim in peril. A suspect has no constitutional right to destroy or dispose of evidence or to imperil the victim. I would also place in the excusable category evidence obtained by a search incidental to and contemporaneous with a lawful arrest, although made without a valid search warrant.

In my view evidence obtained in deliberate conscious breach of the constitutional rights of an accused person should, save in the excusable circumstances outlined above, be absolutely inadmissible. It follows therefore that evidence obtained without a deliberate and conscious violation of the accused's constitutional rights is not excludable by reason only of the violation of his constitutional right.

In the present case it is abundantly clear from the evidence that it was through an error that the wrong address appeared on the search warrant and that the searching officers were unaware of the error. There was no deliberate or conscious violation of the right of the appellants against arbitrary intrusion by the Garda officers. The evidence obtained by reason of this search is not inadmissible upon the constitutional ground.

For the reasons I have given as to both grounds, the appeal should be dismissed.

13. A.G. v Quinn
Supreme Court, December 18, 1964
[1965] I.R. 366 at 375–376, 379–384

Walsh J:
The appellant was convicted of the offence of manslaughter on the 18th January, 1963, by a jury at Limerick and on the 22nd January was sentenced to a term of twelve months' imprisonment with hard labour by the presiding judge, the President of the Circuit Court.

The charge arose from an incident on the 19th May, 1962, between the deceased and the appellant who up to then had been close friends. On that evening the deceased and the appellant had had a number of drinks together in a public house and then left the public house, apparently to walk home. They were observed to be on friendly terms while they were in the public house. On the way home some disagreement or altercation arose between them on the roadway in the course of which the appellant struck the deceased a blow with his fist on his face which caused the deceased to fall striking his head upon the ground. His skull was fractured by the fall and this caused his death on the following day. A witness present had heard the deceased say to the appellant: "If you don't bring back that fork I will send up the sergeant to you," to which the accused had replied: "Michael Burke told me to take. ..." That was all the witness heard and he next heard the thud of a man's body falling on the ground. He came back to the scene and found the deceased lying on the road. The appellant's account is that on the way home the deceased accused him, in effect, of stealing a fork belonging to one, Michael Burke, and that the appellant had told him that he had Burke's permission to take it and that he then sought to leave the deceased but that the deceased held his arm to detain him, aimed a blow at him with his fist which he, the appellant, avoided by ducking and the appellant then replied with a blow of his fist to the deceased's face which he maintained was delivered in self-defence. That was the blow which caused the deceased to fall and which led to his death. Before he learned of the death of the deceased the appellant had made a statement to the civic guards in which he told the same story, save that there was no mention of the deceased holding his arm to detain him. This statement was in evidence during the prosecution case. In the course of cross-examination by counsel for the appellant the mother of the deceased said that she had been informed by the deceased after his injury that he had had "a bit of a scuffle." In giving evidence on his own behalf the appellant maintained that he had only struck one blow and that was in self-defence. ...

In the course of his charge to the jury the learned trial Judge in dealing with the question of self-defence quoted to the jury from Archbold a passage from Lindley J. in *Rex v Knock* 14 Cox C.C. 1: "I mention that because on this question of self-defence the judge has to direct the jury as to what it means. It is quite sufficient if you have a reasonable doubt whether this was a case of self-defence or not. If so, you are entitled to acquit the accused, but the State makes the case contrary, that there is no such evidence in this case; that viewing the evidence as a whole this is the case of a man going home with another man and because of a few words over a fork the man who was killed grabbed the accused and made a blow at him which apparently was not delivered; that he then received a heavy blow which struck him to the ground and resulted in his death. The case for the prosecution is that there is no question of self-defence. They must satisfy you it was manslaughter. The defence need not satisfy you if it was self-defence, if you have a real doubt about it. The State says that you should have no doubt." The first difficulty which arises with regard to this passage is that the learned trial Judge was in fact putting the defence case as the prosecution case. Notwithstanding the correct statement from *Rex v Knock* the effect of this passage might well have left the jury in a position where they sought in vain for the defence case and might well have left them with the impression that upon that evidence there could not be any question of self-defence.

What is not at all clear from the transcript is what was the case the prosecution was making when they invited the jury to decide this issue against the appellant. It does not appear that the jury was being asked to reject the story which the accused told, save in one respect possibly, namely, the accused's reference to the deceased catching him by the arm before attempting to strike him. Nor is it clear that the prosecution was suggesting that no self-defence was necessary or that the method of self-defence employed went beyond the necessities of the occasion.

Furthermore, that last line of the passage above quoted from the Judge's charge touched upon the question of the onus of proof. A few lines further on the trial Judge said to the jury. ... "The legality of the blow cannot be justified at all on any ground except self-defence and that is put forward for the defence. The defence does not have to prove that as a matter of certainty and I have only to tell you again that there is only one count." That was the concluding line of the charge to the jury. ... In the opinion of this Court the Judge's charge to the jury on the question of the onus of proof might reasonably have left them under the impression that while there was no onus upon the defence to establish self-defence beyond reasonable doubt or as a matter of certainty yet there was some obligation to make a sufficient impression in the jury's mind to create at least a doubt about the State case. The learned Judge's reply to Mr. Kinlen's requisition rather suggests that this was in fact his view. This appears also to have been the interpretation put upon his observation by the judgment of the Court of Criminal Appeal when they held that he had charged the jury properly and adequately on this point. ...

In the opinion of this Court the directions of the learned trial Judge introduced such an element of doubt on the question of the onus of proof that the conviction cannot be allowed to stand. As the matter assumes an added importance because of the terms in which the Court of Criminal Appeal approved the Judge's directions to the jury this Court considers it necessary to state the correct position clearly. ...

When the evidence in a case, whether it be the evidence offered by the prosecution or by the defence, discloses a possible defence of self-defence the onus remains throughout upon the prosecution to establish that the accused is guilty of the offence charged. The onus is never upon the accused to raise a doubt in the minds of the jury. In such case the burden rests on the prosecution to negative the possible defence of self-defence which has arisen and if, having considered the whole of the evidence, the jury is either convinced of the innocence of the prisoner or left in doubt whether or not he was acting in necessary self-defence they must acquit. Before the possible defence can be left to the jury as an issue there must be some evidence from which the jury would be entitled to find that issue in favour of the appellant. If the evidence for the prosecution does not disclose this possible defence then the necessary evidence will fall to be given by the defence. In such a case, however, where it falls to the defence to give the necessary evidence it must be made clear to the jury that there is a distinction, fine though it may appear, between adducing the evidence and the burden of proof and that there is no onus whatever upon the accused to establish any degree of doubt in their minds. In directing the jury on the question of the onus of proof it can only be misleading to a jury to refer to "establishing" the defence "in such a way as to raise a doubt." No defence has to be "established" in any case apart from insanity. In a case where there is evidence, whether it be disclosed in the prosecution case or in the defence case, which is sufficient to leave the issue of self-defence to the jury the only question the jury has to consider is whether they are satisfied beyond reasonable doubt that the accused killed the deceased (if it be a case of homicide) and whether the jury is satisfied beyond reasonable doubt that the prosecution has negatived the issue of self-defence. If the jury is not satisfied beyond reasonable doubt on both of these matters the accused must be acquitted.
...

In the result, the conviction will be quashed. A new trial should be directed

Appendices 463

as in my opinion there is an issue on self-defence which can be decided only by a jury.

14. Jennings v Quinn and Dooris
Supreme Court, July 28, 1966
[1968] I.R. 305 at 308–310

O'Keefe J:

... Before considering the question whether property taken at the time of the arrest of an accused person can properly be sent out of the State, it is desirable to consider what right, if any, the persons making the arrest have to seize the property at all. In the case of *Dillon v O'Brien and Davis* 20 L.R. Ir. 300 it was held by the Exchequer Division (Palles C.B., Dowse B. and Andrews J.) that, when a person is lawfully arrested to be brought before a court on a criminal charge, property seized at the time of the arrest and which is to be used as evidence on that charge may lawfully be retained for that purpose by the police. The Chief Baron, who delivered a judgment with which the other members of the court concurred, rested his decision on the principle that the State has an interest in having a person, who is guilty of a crime, brought to justice; and in ensuring that a prosecution, once commenced, is determined in accordance with law. In the course of his judgment, at p.317 of the report, he said: "But the interest of the State in the person charged being brought to trial in due course necessarily extends as well to the preservation of material evidence of his guilt or innocence as to his custody for the purpose of trial. His custody is of no value if the law is powerless to prevent the abstraction or destruction of this evidence, without which a trial would be no more than an empty form. But if there be a right to production or preservation of this evidence, I cannot see how it can be enforced otherwise than by capture." In *Elias v Pasmore* [1934] 2 K. B. 164 the King's Bench Division in England based, on the same considerations of public interest, a decision that at the time of arrest the police are entitled to seize and retain, for the purpose of a criminal charge not merely property which is evidence relating to that charge on which the arrest is made but property which is evidence relating to any other criminal charge. Horridge J., who tried the case, referred to the Scottish decision of *Pringle v Bremner and Stirling* 5 Macph. (H.L.) 55 to the same effect; but he was not content to rest his decision on this precedent without considering the question of principle afresh in order to determine whether it could be applied to a seizure of documents in England.

In my opinion the public interest requires that the police when effecting a lawful arrest, may seize, without a search warrant, property in the possession or custody of the person arrested when they believe it necessary to do so to avoid the abstraction or destruction of that property and when that property is:

(a) evidence in support of the criminal charge upon which the arrest is made, or

(b) evidence in support of any other criminal charge against that person then in contemplation, or

(c) reasonably believed to be stolen property or to be property unlawfully in the possession of that person; and that they may retain such property for use at the trial of the person arrested, or of any other person or persons on any criminal charge in which the property is to be used as evidence in support of the charge or charges; and that thereafter they should return the property to the person from whom it was seized, unless the disposal of the property otherwise has been directed by a court of competent jurisdiction.
...

It appears to me that the public interest also requires that property, which the police might lawfully retain for use as material evidence in a charge against a person arrested if that charge were brought against him within the jurisdiction, may also be retained lawfully by them for the purpose of sending it, and that they may send it, into another jurisdiction where a charge on which that property is material evidence has been laid against the person arrested, at least in cases where the lawful arrest of the person within the jurisdiction was made in aid of the jurisdiction of the country in which the charge is laid. For this reason I would be prepared to hold that the defendants might lawfully retain in their possession any of the property which has come into their possession at the time of, or shortly after, the arrest of the plaintiff and which is required as material evidence on a charge laid against the plaintiff in the United Kingdom.
...

15. People (Attorney General) v Crosbie and Meehan

Court of Criminal Appeal, September 7, 1966
[1966] I.R. 490 at 491–492, 496–498

Kenny J:

... Christopher Noel Murphy was killed on the 21st of May, 1965, during a fight in what is called "the read room" in the docks in Dublin. The dockers seeking work meet in this room and those who are to be employed for the shifts during the day hear their names being read out by the representatives of the stevedores. Murphy was killed at 8.30 a.m. when there were about 500 persons in this room. His death was caused by a stab-wound inflicted on him by Crosbie who made a statement to the Guards in which he admitted that he had a knife with him at the time of the fight. There was abundant evidence on which the jury would have been entitled to find that the stab-wound which caused Murphy's death was inflicted by Crosbie. ...

Crosbie entered the read room by the lower door on the east side when Meier was standing near the stevedores' door. The two Meehans, Bolger and Crosbie passed where Noel Murphy was standing and went towards Meier who was struck with a bar by James Meehan. Meier then ran towards the lower door on the eastern side of the room and escaped. Crosbie and the two Meehans were then attacked by three brothers, Liam Callaghan, Tony Callaghan and Joseph Callaghan, and Crosbie and James Meehan were driven into the porch. When Meier fled, Noel Murphy went down towards the porch and there was evidence that Noel Murphy was trying to separate Crosbie and one of the Callaghans in the porch while another of the witnesses said that Noel Murphy had got to the entrance of the porch when he was stabbed. Noel Murphy then staggered from the door of the porch into the read room, Crosbie came to the door of the porch leading into this room and Noel Murphy then said when Crosbie was standing near him: "He has a knife, he stabbed me." There was no evidence that either of the Meehans or Bolger was near Crosbie or Noel Murphy when this remark was made. Crosbie, who had a knife in his hand, was then attacked by Michael Murphy who succeeded in getting it from him. Noel Murphy died on the 21st May as the result of a stab-wound on the right hand side of his chest. …

The Court is of opinion that evidence of the statement made by Noel Murphy immediately after he had been stabbed by Crosbie was admissible in evidence against all the accused, although it was hearsay, because it formed part of the criminal act for which the accused were being tried or for those who prefer to use Latin phrases, because it formed part of the *res gestae*. In *Director of Public Prosecutions v Christie* [1914] A. C. 545 the accused was charged with indecently assaulting a boy who was five years of age. The boy's mother stated that he left her at about 10 o'clock in the morning, that she saw him again at about 10.30 a.m. and that she took him across a field: the accused was then fetched after the mother had spoken to somebody else. The mother's evidence was that the boy said "That is the man, Mum", as they were going towards the accused. A policeman, who was standing near the accused asked what man and the boy then went up to the accused and gave a description of the acts which had been done: the accused then said: "I am innocent." The policeman's evidence was that the boy in answer to the question, "Which is the man," went up to the accused, touched him on the sleeve and said: "That is the man," and that the boy then gave an account of the acts done by the accused. The main matter debated in the case was whether the account given by the boy of what the accused had done to him was admissible in evidence and no objection seems to have been taken to the admissibility of the statement, "That is the man." The Attorney General argued that the entire statement of the boy was admissible and relied on four separate grounds in support of this. One of these was that what the boy said was admissible as part of the *res gestae*. In the course of his speech Lord Reading C.J. said, at p.566: "The statement under review formed no part of the incidents constituting the offence. It was not made whilst the offence was being committed or *immediately thereafter*" (italics mine). "It took place after Christie had left the boy, and the mother had found him and taken him across the fields and had spoken to another man. In my view it was not so immediately connected with the act of assault as to form part of the *res gestae*." In *Lejzor Teper v The Queen* [1952] A.C. 480 Lord Normand when giving the advice of the Privy Council said, at p. 486:

"The rule against the admission of hearsay evidence is fundamental. It is not the best evidence and it is not delivered on oath. The truthfulness and accuracy of the person whose words are spoken to by another witness cannot be tested by cross-examination, and the light which his demeanour would throw on his testimony is lost. Nevertheless, the rule admits of certain carefully safeguarded and limited exceptions, one of which is that words may be proved when they form part of the *res gestae*. The rules controlling this exception are common to the jurisprudence of British Guiana, England and Scotland. It appears to rest ultimately on two propositions, that human utterance is both a fact and a means of communication, and that human action may be so interwoven with words that the significance of the action cannot be understood without the correlative words, and the dissociation of the words from the action would impede the discovery of truth. But the judicial applications of these two propositions, which do not always combine harmoniously, have never been precisely formulated in a general principle. Their Lordships will not attempt to arrive at a general formula, nor is it necessary to review all of the considerable number of cases cited in the argument. This, at least, may be said, that it is essential that the words sought to be proved by hearsay should be, if not absolutely contemporaneous with the action or event, at least so clearly associated with it, in time, place and circumstances, that they are part of the thing being done, and so an item or part of real evidence and not merely a reported statement. ..."

The words spoken by Noel Murphy were spoken within one minute of the stabbing. They related directly to the incident which was being investigated (the stabbing), and they were spoken immediately after it. If the words of Lord Normand are adopted, the words were so clearly associated with the stabbing in time, place and circumstances that they were part of the thing being done and so an item or part of real evidence and not merely a reported statement.

This Court is accordingly of opinion that the words spoken by Noel Murphy were admissible in evidence against all the accused. ...

16. Murphy v Dublin Corporation and Minister for Local Government

Supreme Court, July 14, 1971
[1972] I.R. 215 at 232–239

Walsh J:

... As will be seen from the documents already cited, the claim to privilege was made on two grounds: first, that production of the inspector's report would be contrary to public policy and detrimental to the public interest and service and, secondly, that in any event it was within a class of documents which on grounds of public interest ought to be withheld from production and disclosure.

The action in which the present question arises is a civil suit *inter partes*, one of the parties being the Minister for Local Government. Therefore, the court has not to review the considerations which might arise if in the course of a criminal prosecution an effort was made to obtain the disclosure of communications passing between members of the police force or from informants to the police and, on the other side of the coin, it is not necessary to examine the considerations which might arise in a criminal prosecution where the refusal to disclose certain evidence relevant to the trial could result in the condemnation of an innocent accused.

The present claim of privilege is that in a civil action the executive organ of government may by its own judgment withhold relevant evidence from the organ of government charged with the administration of justice and engaged in the determination of the rights of the litigants, and that this may be done when the claim of privilege is made on either or both of the grounds already mentioned.

Under the Constitution the administration of justice is committed solely to the judiciary in the exercise of their powers in the courts set up under the Constitution. Power to compel the attendance of witnesses and the production of evidence is an inherent part of the judicial power of government of the State and is the ultimate safeguard of justice in the State. The proper exercise of the function of the three powers of government set up under the Constitution, namely, the legislative, the executive and the judicial, is in the public interest. There may be occasions when the different aspects of the public interest "pull in contrary directions"—to use the words of Lord Morris of Borth-y-Gest in *Conway v Rimmer* [1968] A.C. 910, 965. If the conflict arises during the exercise of the judicial power then, in my view, it is the judicial power which will decide which public interest shall prevail. This does not mean that the court will always decide that the interest of the litigant shall prevail. It is for the court to decide which is the superior interest in the circumstances of the particular case and to determine the matter accordingly. As the legislative, executive, and judicial powers of government are all exercised under and on behalf of the State, the interest of the State, as such, is always involved. The division of powers does not give paramountcy in all circumstances to any one of the organs exercising the powers of government over the other. It is clear that when the vital interests of the State (such as the security of the State) may be adversely affected by disclosure or production of a document, greater harm may be caused by ordering rather than by refusing disclosure or production of the document. In such a case the courts would refuse the order but would do so on their own decision. The evidence that the courts might choose to act upon to arrive at that decision would be determined by the courts, having regard to the circumstances of the case. Again, taking the example of the safety of the State, it might well be that the court would be satisfied to accept the opinion of the appropriate member of the executive or of the head of the Government as sufficient evidence of the fact upon a claim being made for non-disclosure or non-production, as the case may be, on that ground. I have referred to non-disclosure and non- production as distinct matters because in certain circumstances the very disclosure of the existence of a document, apart altogether from the question of its production, could in itself be a danger to the security of the State. As this is not such a case it is unnecessary to deal further with this aspect of public interest.

It is, however, impossible for the judicial power in the proper exercise of its functions to permit any other body or power to decide for it whether or not a document will be disclosed or produced. In the last resort the decision lies with the courts so long as they have seisin of the case.

A case such as the present one is far removed from the considerations which would apply in matters concerning the safety or security of the State. That is not to say that in the ordinary day-to-day administration of the executive branch of government matters may not arise whose disclosure would be contrary to the public interest. Where documents come into existence in the course of the carrying out of the executive powers of the State, their production may be adverse to the public interest in one sphere of government in particular circumstances. On the other hand, their non-production may be adverse to the public interest in the administration of justice. As such documents may be anywhere in the range from the trivial to the vitally important, somebody or some authority must decide which course is calculated to do the least injury to the public interest, namely, the production of the document or the possibility of the denial of right in the administration of justice. It is self evident that this is a matter which falls into the sphere of the judicial power for determination. In a particular case the court may be able to determine this matter having regard to the evidence available on the subject and without examining the document in question, but in other cases it may be necessary, as the court may think, to produce the document to the court itself for the purpose of inspecting it and making the decision having regard to the conflicting claims made with reference to the document. As has been pointed out, this is a type of exercise which the courts frequently engage in when they examine statements or confessions and decide what parts of them, if any, may be permitted to go into evidence or to be disclosed to any person other than the person into whose custody the document came.

Having regard to the nature of the powers of the courts in these matters, it seems clear to me that there can be no documents which may be withheld from production simply because they belong to a particular class of documents. Each document must be decided upon having regard to the considerations which apply to that particular document and its contents. To grant or withhold the production of a document simply by reason of the class to which it belongs would be to regard all documents as being of equal importance notwithstanding that they may not be. In my view, once the court is satisfied that the document is relevant, the burden of satisfying the court that a particular document ought not to be produced lies upon the party, or the person, who makes such a claim. It follows therefore that, before any claim can be made in support of the non-production of a document by the executive, a claim must be made in relation to the particular document or documents and the ground of the claim must be stated.

I do not accept the view expressed by Lord Reid in *Conway v Rimmer* at p.943 and adopted by Mr. Justice Kenny in the present case that "cases would be very rare in which it could be proper to question the view of the responsible Minister that it would be contrary to the public interest to make public the contents of a particular document." It may well be that it would be rare or infrequent for a court, after its own examination, to arrive at a different conclusion from that expressed by the Minister, but that is a far remove from accepting without question the judgement of the Minister. Mr. Justice Kenny expressed the view that the court should accept such a judgement on the part of the Minister unless (a) it is shown not to have been formed in good faith, or (b) it is one which no responsible Minister could form, or (c) it is based on a misunderstanding of the issues in the case in which production of the document is sought. I have already indicated that in my view the onus would in any event be upon the Minister to make the case for non-production. ...

In my view, in the present case Mr. Justice Kenny was not correct in accepting without examination the Minister's judgement on this matter, namely, that the production of the report would be contrary to public policy and detrimental to the public interest and service. ... Whatever the Minister's grounds may be, he has not disclosed them and his certificate or order simply states a conclusion. In my view, a case has not been made for the non-production of the document concerned and in that event the learned trial judge ought to have directed production of the document, at least for his own inspection, when he could then decide the matter. ...

This case does not end at that point. Up to this I have been dealing with the case on the basis that the claim made was a claim of executive privilege not to produce a document. Such a claim is, of course, one made with reference to a document brought into being in the course of the carrying out of the executive functions of the State. It does not appear to me that this is such a document.

The Housing Act, 1966 (at article 5 of the third schedule) constitutes the Minister for Local Government as the adjudicating authority upon the dispute which arises between the owner of the land which is made the subject of a compulsory purchase order and the local authority making such order. The executive powers of government of the State are vested in the Government: see s. 2 of Article 28 of the Constitution. Different Departments of State are set up to deal with the business of executive government which are assigned to these Departments: see s. 12 of Article 28. The Government is collectively responsible for the Departments of State administered by the members of the Government assigned as Ministers over particular Departments (s. 4, sub-s. 2, of Article 28), and the powers, duties and functions of the Department are assigned to and administered by the Minister named.

The function which is given to the Minister by Article 5 of the third schedule of the Act of 1966 is not an executive power of the State assigned to his Department or a power which vested in the Government as an executive power from the State. He is *persona designata* in that the holder of the office of the Minister for Local Government is the person designated for that function. If the Oireachtas had so enacted, the Act could just as easily have assigned the function to the chairman of Coras Iompair Éireann, or to the chairman of the Electricity Supply Board, or to the head of any other State-controlled or semi-State corporation; if it had done so, there could be no question of such person seeking or being granted the executive privilege of non-production of the document in question. The fact that the Minister for Local Government was the person chosen by the Oireachtas to carry out this function does not *per se* confer upon the function the character of the exercise of the executive power of the State. ...

In my view, in the exercise of the function which he was performing in this case, it was not open to the Minister to refuse to produce the inspector's report on the ground that it is a document for which the executive privilege of non-production is available if granted by the Court; I refer to "executive privilege" for want of a better term. It follows that it was not open to the High Court to refuse to order production of the document in question on the grounds given by Mr. Justice Kenny. I would allow the appeal.

17. Ratten v The Queen

Privy Council, October 11, 1971
[1972] A.C. 378 at 387–392

Wilberforce L.J:

... The mere fact that evidence of a witness includes evidence as to words spoken by another person who is not called, is no objection to its admissibility. Words spoken are facts just as much as any other action by a human being. If the speaking of the words is a relevant fact, a witness may give evidence that they were spoken. A question of hearsay only arises when the words spoken are relied on "testimonially," i.e., as establishing some fact narrated by the words. Authority is hardly needed for this proposition, but their Lordships will restate what was said in the judgment of the Board in *Subramaniam v Public Prosecutor* [1956] 1 W.L.R. 965, 970. ...[1]

The evidence relating to the act of telephoning by the deceased was, in their Lordship's view, factual and relevant. It can be analysed into the following elements.

(1) At about 1.15 p.m. the number Echuca 1494 rang. I plugged into that number.

(2) I opened the speak key and said "Number please."

(3) A female voice answered.

(4) The voice was hysterical and sobbed.

(5) The voice said "Get me the police please."

The factual items numbered (1)–(3) were relevant in order to show that, contrary to the evidence of the appellant, a call was made, only some 3–5 minutes before the fatal shooting, by a woman. It not being suggested that there was anybody in the house other than the appellant, his wife and small children, this woman, the caller, could only have been the deceased. Items (4) and (5) were relevant as possibly showing (if the jury thought fit to draw the inference) that the deceased woman was at this time in a state of emotion or fear (cf. *Averson v Lord Kinnaird* (1805) 6 East 188, 193, *per* Lord Ellenborough C.J.). They were relevant and necessary, evidence in order to explain and complete the fact of the call being made. A telephone call is a composite act, made up of manual operations together with the utterance of

---

[1] *cf.* appendix 7.

words (cf. *McGregor v Stokes* [1952] V.L.R. 347 and remarks of Salmond J. therein quoted). To confine the evidence to the first would be to deprive the act of most of its significance. The act had content when it was known that the call was made in a state of emotion. The knowledge that the caller desired the police to be called helped to indicate the nature of the emotion—anxiety or fear at an existing or impending emergency. It was a matter for the jury to decide what light (if any) this evidence, in the absence of any explanation from the appellant, who was in the house, threw upon what situation was occurring, or developing at the time.

If then, this evidence had been presented in this way, as evidence purely of relevant facts, its admissibility could hardly have been plausibly challenged. But the appellant submits that in fact this was not so. It is said that the evidence was tendered and admitted as evidence of an assertion by the deceased that she was being attacked by the accused, and that it was, so far, hearsay evidence, being put forward as evidence of the truth of facts asserted by his statement. It is claimed that the Chief Justice so presented the evidence to the jury and that, therefore, its admissibility, as hearsay, may be challenged.

Their Lordships, as already stated, do not consider that there is any hearsay element in the evidence, nor in their opinion was it so presented by the trial judge, but they think it right to deal with the appellant's submission on the assumption that there is: i.e., that the words said to have been used involve an assertion of the truth of some facts stated in them and that they may have been so understood by the jury. The Crown defended the admissibility of the words as part of the "res gestae" a contention which led to the citation of numerous authorities.

The expression "res gestae", like many Latin phrases, is often used to cover situations insufficiently analysed in clear English terms. In the context of the law of evidence it may be used in at least three different ways:

1. When a situation of fact (e.g. a killing) is being considered, the question may arise when does the situation begin and when does it end. It may be arbitrary and artificial to confine the evidence to the firing of the gun or the insertion of the knife, without knowing in a broader sense, what was happening. Thus in *O'Leary v The King* (1946) 73 C.L.R. 566 evidence was admitted of assaults, prior to a killing, committed by the accused during what was said to be a continuous orgy. As Dixon J. said at p. 577:

    "Without evidence of what, during that time, was done by those men who took any significant part in the matter and especially evidence of the behavior of the prisoner, the transaction of which the alleged murder formed an integral part could not be truly understood and, isolated from it, could only be presented as an unreal and not very intelligible event."

2. The evidence may be concerned with spoken words as such (apart from the truth of what they convey). The words are then themselves the res gestae or part of the res gestae, i.e., are the relevant facts or part of them.

3. A hearsay statement is made either by the victim of an attack or by a bystander—indicating directly or indirectly the identity of the attacker.

The admissibility of the statement is then said to depend on whether it was made as part of the res gestae. A classical instance of this is the much debated case of *Reg. v Bedingfield* (1879) 14 Cox C.C. 341, and there are other instances of its application in reported cases. These tend to apply different standards, and some of them carry less than conviction. The reason, why this is so, is that concentration tends to be focused upon the opaque or at least imprecise Latin phrase rather than upon the basic reason for excluding the type of evidence which this group of cases is concerned with. There is no doubt what this reason is: it is twofold. The first is that there may be uncertainty as to the exact words used because of their transmission through the evidence of another person than the speaker. The second is because of the risk of concoction of false evidence by persons who have been victims of assault or accident. The first matter goes to weight. The person testifying to the words used is liable to cross-examination: the accused person (as he could not at the time when earlier reported cases were decided) can give his own account if different. There is no such difference in kind or substance between evidence of what was said and evidence of what was done (for example between evidence of what the victim said as to an attack and evidence that he (or she) was seen in a terrified state or was heard to shriek) as to require a total rejection of one and admission of the other.

The possibility of concoction, or fabrication, where it exists, is on the other hand an entirely valid reason for exclusion, and is probably the real test which judges in fact apply. In their Lordships' opinion this should he recognised and applied directly as the relevant test: the test should be not the uncertain one whether the making of the statement was in some sense part of the event or transaction. This may often be difficult to establish: such external matters as the time which elapses between the events and the speaking of the words (or vice versa), and differences in location being relevant factors but not, taken by themselves, decisive criteria. As regards statements made after the event it must be for the judge, by preliminary ruling, to satisfy himself that the statement was so clearly made in circumstances of spontaneity or involvement in the event that the possibility of concoction can be disregarded. Conversely, if he considers that the statement was made by way of narrative of a detached prior event so that the speaker was so disengaged from it as to be able to construct or adapt his account, he should exclude it. And the same must in principle be true of statements made before the event. The test should be not the uncertain one, whether the making of the statement should be regarded as part of the event or transaction. This may often be difficult to show. But if the drama, leading up to the climax, has commenced and assumed such intensity and pressure that the utterance can safely be regarded as a true reflection of what was unrolling or actually happening, it ought to be received. The expression "res gestae" may conveniently sum up these criteria, but the reality of them must always be kept in mind: it is this that lies behind the best reasoned of the judges' rulings.

A few illustrations may be given. One of the earliest and as often happens also the clearest, is that of Holt C.J. at nisi prius in *Thompson v Trevanion*

(1693) Skin. 402. He allowed that "what the wife said immediate upon the hurt received, and before that she had time to devise or contrive anything for her own advantage" might be given in evidence, a statement often quoted and approved. *Reg. v Bedingfield*, 14 Cox C.C. 341 is more useful as a focus for discussion, than for the decision on the facts. Their Lordships understand later indications of approval (*Rex v Christie* [1914] A.C. 545; *Teper v The Queen* [1952] A.C. 480) to relate to the principle established, for, though in a historical sense the emergence of the victim could be described as a different "res" from the cutting of her throat, there could hardly be a case where the words uttered carried more clearly the mark of spontaneity and intense involvement.

In a lower key the evidence of the words of the careless pedestrian in *O'Hara v Central S.M.T. Co. Ltd.*, 1941 S.C. 363 was admitted on the principle of spontaneity. The Lord President (Normand) said that there must be close association: the words should be at least de recenti and not after an interval which would allow time for reflection and concocting a story: see p.381. Lord Fleming said, at p.386: "Obviously statements made after there has been time for deliberation are not likely to be entirely spontaneous, and may, indeed, be made for the express purpose of concealing the truth" and Lord Moncrieff refers to the "share in the event" which is taken by the person reported to have made the statement. He contrasts an exclamation "forced out of a witness by the emotion generated by an event" with a subsequent narrative (pp.389-90). The Lord President reaffirmed the principle stated in this case in an appeal to this board in *Teper v The Queen* [1952] A.C. 480, stressing the necessity for close association in time, place and circumstances between the statement and the crucial events. ...

[T]here is ample support for the principle that hearsay evidence may be admitted if the statement providing it is made in such conditions (always being those of approximate but not exact contemporaneity) of involvement or pressure as to exclude the possibility of concoction or distortion to the advantage of the maker or the disadvantage of the accused.

Before applying it to the facts of the present case, there is one other matter to be considered, namely the nature of the proof required to establish the involvement of the speaker in the pressure of the drama, or the concatenation of events leading up to the crisis. On principle it would not appear right that the necessary association should be shown only by the statement itself, otherwise the statement would be lifting itself into the area of admissibility. There is little authority on this point. In *Reg. v Taylor* [1961] 3 S.A.L.R. 616 where witnesses said they had heard scuffles and thuds during which the deceased cried out "John, please don't hit me any more, you will kill me," Fannin J. said that it would be unrealistic to require the examination of the question (sc. of close relationship) without reference to the terms of the statement sought to be proved. "Often the only evidence as to how near in time the making of the statement was to the act it relates to, and the actual relationship between the two, will be contained in the statement itself" (p.619). Facts differ so greatly that it is impossible to lay down any precise general rule: it is difficult to imagine a case where there is no evidence at all of connection between statement and principal event other than the statement itself, but whether this is sufficiently shown must be a matter for the trial judge. Their Lordships would be disposed to agree that, amongst other things, he may take the statement itself into account.

In the present case, in their Lordships' judgment, there was ample evidence of the close and intimate connection between the statement ascribed to the deceased and the shooting which occurred very shortly afterwards. They were closely associated in place and in time. The way in which the statement came to be made (in a call for the police) and the tone of voice used, showed intrinsically that the statement was being forced from the deceased by an overwhelming pressure of contemporary event. It carried its own stamp of spontaneity and this was endorsed by the proved time sequence and the proved proximity of the deceased to the accused with his gun. Even on the assumption that there was an element of hearsay in the words used, they were safely admitted. The jury was, additionally, directed with great care as to the use to which they might be put. On all counts, therefore, their Lordships can find no error in law in the admission of the evidence. They should add that they see no reason why the judge should have excluded it as prejudicial in the exercise of discretion. ...

18. People (Attorney General) v Cummins
Supreme Court, July 26, 1972
[1972] I.R. 312 at 322–327

Walsh J:

... It should be said at once that a trial judge has no discretion to admit an inculpatory or an exculpatory confession, or statement, made by an accused person which is inadmissible in law because it was not voluntary. It is a matter for the trial judge to decide, when he has heard the evidence on the point, whether or not he will admit a statement, but if he is satisfied that it was not voluntary then his decision can be only to exclude it. In so far as admissions, alleged to have been made by an accused person, are tendered in evidence and were made or obtained in circumstances which are in contravention of what are known as "the Judges' Rules", then the learned trial judge has a judicial discretion to admit or not to admit the admissions in question provided that he is satisfied that they were voluntary. If they were not voluntary they must be excluded: see the decision of this Court in *McCarrick v Leavy* [1964] I.R. 226.

The Judges' Rules which are in force in this country are the ones mentioned in *McCarrick v Leavy*; they are sometimes called the Judges' Rules of 1922 though they first appeared in 1912 when the judges in England, at the request of the Home Secretary, drew up four rules as a guide for police officers in respect of communications with prisoners or persons suspected of crime. The Rules were signed by Lord Chief Justice Alverstone and were then four in number; they were printed at the end of the report of *R. v Voisin* [1918] 1 K.B. 631. In the judgment of the Court of Criminal Appeal given in that case, the following statement appears at p.539 of the report: "These Rules have not the force of law; they are administrative directions the observance of which the police authorities should enforce upon their subordinates as tending to the fair administration of justice. It is important that they should do so, for statements obtained from prisoners, contrary to the spirit of these rules, may be rejected as evidence by the judge presiding at the trial." The origin of the Rules is again mentioned in *R. v Cook* (1918) 34 T.L.R. 616. By 1922 the rules mentioned in those cases had increased to a total of nine. These nine rules are the ones which have been followed in this State since that date. The first four of them are the ones which were originally formulated in 1912 and they are mentioned in the cases decided in 1918. The fact that the Judges' Rules which are now in force in Great Britain are different from the ones in force here has been noted, and the distinction was made in the argument in this Court.

I now turn to the facts of the present case. The first matter to be noted is that, according to the evidence in the transcript, the reference to the accused being in custody on the 9th January, 1968, in Store Street Garda Station makes it quite clear that he was in custody not on the charges which related to Premier Tailors but on other charges; that is to say, he was already in custody on some other charge when approached in the Station by Detective Inspector Lalor. Rule 3 of the Judges' Rules refers to the necessity to give a caution to a person in custody before he is questioned, and that rule has been held to apply to a person in custody although the custody is not related to the matter in respect of which he is being questioned. Under the Judges' Rules, therefore, Inspector Lalor should have cautioned the accused before asking him about Premier Tailors and before making the statement "I believe you did it" to which the accused made what amounted to an admission of guilt. Subject to the question of whether this statement on the part of the accused was voluntary or not, it was open to the trial judge to exercise his discretion to exclude this piece of evidence on the grounds that it was obtained in violation of the Judges' Rules. The judge did not do so, however, and therefore the question of whether he exercised his judicial discretion or not in this respect does not arise because the judge's ruling on this first question related only to the question of whether the statements were voluntary or not; the judge does not seem to have directed his mind, or had it directed, to the question of exercising his discretion in regard to a violation of the Judges' Rules. …

It appears to me that the learned trial judge had in his mind to some extent rule 2 of the Judges' Rules, but he seems to have fallen into the same error as the District Justice in *McCarrick v Leavy* in apparently having the belief that therefore the statement was to be regarded as necessarily not voluntary, and inadmissible. Furthermore, the learned trial judge appears to have assumed that the expression of the Inspector's belief, whether it be a true or false expression of his belief, was evidence that the Inspector had already made up his mind to charge the accused. Even if the Inspector had been in a position to charge the accused, which apparently he was not, that was not quite the same thing as having made up his mind to do so; and in so far as that itself was an issue of fact it was one which the Judge would have to decide. He does not appear to have decided as a fact that the Inspector had made up his mind to charge the accused.

So far as the Judge's ruling concerned the admissibility or otherwise of

Inspector Lalor saying "What about Premier Tailors? I believe you did it" and the accused replying "We did it and we got 255 in an envelope in the safe and a brooch, a bracelet and ear-rings," I am of opinion that the learned trial judge did not exercise his discretion at all in this matter. ...

In my view, the trial judge was wrong in rejecting the evidence on the ground that it was not voluntary, first, because he appears to have assumed that evidence obtained in breach of the Judges' Rules is to be treated in the same way as a confession obtained in circumstances which render it not voluntary and, secondly, because he does not appear to have directed his mind at all towards the question of whether it was calculated to produce from the accused a confession which was not voluntary. He did express the view that it was calculated to give the accused the impression that there was only one answer to it because the guards already had in their possession evidence which would convict him of the offence, but I interpret that as meaning that it was calculated to give the accused the impression that it would be fruitless for him to endeavour to conceal his guilt rather than calculated to give him the impression that it would be beneficial for him to admit guilt instead of maintaining silence or, indeed, of protesting his innocence. If an accused person who is in fact guilty believes, because of his own assessment of the situation, that in the long run it might be advantageous to him to admit his guilt rather than to conceal it, any confession which he makes as a result of such calculation is not to be impugned even though the accused's assessment of the situation may have been incorrect once it is shown that the confession was in fact voluntary. ...

19. R. v Hester

House of Lords, November 22, 1972
[1973] A.C. 296 at 324–325, 328

Diplock L.J:

... This makes it necessary to examine the concept of corroboration at common law apart from statute. The rule adopted in legal systems based on the civil law that an accused could not be convicted on the testimony of a single witness never took root in the common law. The only exception was in the case of perjury—a crime which was originally punished in the Court of Star Chamber, whose procedure prior to its abolition was influenced by the civil law. Apart from statute and with this one exception inherited from the practice of the Star Chamber, ever since trial by jury assumed its modern form it has always been open to juries to convict an accused of any offence on the unsupported testimony of a single witness. But common sense, the mother of the common law, suggests that there are certain categories of witnesses whose testimony as to particular matters may well be unreliable either because they may have some interest of their own to serve by telling a false story, or through defect of intellect or understanding or, as in the case of those alleging sexual acts committed on them by others, because experience shows the danger that fantasy may supplant or supplement genuine recollection. For brevity I will hereafter refer to evidence of this kind as 'suspect' evidence and the witnesses who give it 'suspect' witnesses.

At common law the risk of unreliability was dealt with in different ways according to its cause. The more draconian way was to classify the witness as incompetent to give evidence in the proceedings at all. Until the Evidence Act 1843, persons who had a proprietary or pecuniary interest in the outcome of civil or criminal proceedings were incompetent witnesses in those proceedings. So in civil proceedings were the parties and their spouses until the Evidence Act 1851; and the incompetence of the accused to give evidence in criminal proceedings against him continued until it was at last removed by the Criminal Evidence Act 1898. Persons incapable of understanding the nature of an oath, whether because of infancy or defect of intelligence, were also incompetent at common law to testify in civil and criminal proceedings alike. The only statutory inroad on this disability is that which is now contained in s. 38 (1) of the Children and Young Persons Act 1933.

But a witness whose evidence on a particular matter might be expected to be of doubtful reliability for reasons which did not bring him within the category of an incompetent witness was always admissible at common law. It was for the jury to determine what credence they attached to it. In law they were entitled to base their verdict on it, and on it alone, if they were satisfied of its truth. But in criminal cases, for the protection of the accused it became the practice of judges in the second quarter of the 19th century to warn the jury of the danger of convicting on such testimony unless it was corroborated by evidence from some other source. ...

The danger sought to be obviated by the common law rule in each of these three categories of witnesses is that the story told by the witness to the jury may be inaccurate for reasons not applicable to other competent witnesses; whether the risk be of deliberate inaccuracy, as in the case of accomplices, or unintentional inaccuracy, as in the case of children and some complainants in cases of sexual offences. What is looked for under the common law rule is confirmation from some other source that the suspect witness is telling the truth in some part of his story which goes to show that the accused committed the offence with which he is charged. ...

Only too often the sort of direction given to the jury is to tell them at the outset that they must not convict unless they are satisfied beyond reasonable doubt by the evidence put before them that the accused is guilty of the offence with which he is charged. Then, as respects the unsworn evidence of a young child tendered by the prosecution, they are instructed that they are prohibited by statute from paying any regard to that evidence unless it is corroborated by some other evidence, and one of the *Baskerville* [1916] 2 K.B. 658, [1916-17] All E.R. Rep. 38 formulae—for there are several in that judgment—is used to explain what 'corroboration' means. Next they are told that it is for the judge to say whether there is other evidence capable of amounting to corroboration of the child's evidence and their attention drawn to the evidence which falls within this category, but they are then told that it is for the jury not the judge to decide whether that evidence does amount to corroboration and that only if they do so decide are they entitled to pay any regard to the unsworn child's evidence in deciding to convict. ...

My Lords, if a summing-up is to perform its proper function in a criminal trial by jury it should not contain a general disquisition on the law of corroboration couched in lawyer's language but should be tailored to the particular circumstances of the case.

It would be highly dangerous to suppose that there is any such thing as a model summing-up appropriate to all cases of this kind. No doubt if there is unsupported evidence on oath of a child complainant fit to be left to the jury, the judge should tell them that it is open to them to convict on her evidence alone, although he should remind them forcibly of the danger of doing so. But there is no need for him to tell them of what kind of evidence could amount to corroboration of her story, if in fact there is none at all. ...

20. D.P.P. v Kilbourne

House of Lords, January 31, 1973
[1973] A.C. 729 at 747–749

Hailsham of St. Marylebone L.C.:

... The other ground upon which the general proposition may be defended is the bald proposition that one accomplice cannot corroborate another. In support of this proposition were cited *R. v Noakes* (1832) S.C. & P. 326 *per* Littledale J., *R. v Gay* (1909) 2 Cr. App. Rep. 327, *R. v Prater* [1960] 1 All E.R. at 299, [1960] 2 Q.B. at 465 *per* Edmund Davies J., *R. v Baskerville* [1916] 2 K.B. at 664, [1916-17] All E.R. Rep. at 41 citing *R. v Noakes* and *R. v Cratchley* (1913) 9 Cr. App. R. 232.

I believe these citations have been misunderstood. They all refer to fellow accomplices: see *per* Lord Diplock in *Director of Public Prosecutions v Hester* [1972] 3 All E.R. at 1073, 1074, [1972] 3 W.L.R. at 929, 930. Obviously where two or more fellow accomplices give evidence against an accused their evidence is equally tainted. The reason why accomplice evidence requires corroboration is the danger of a concocted story designed to throw the blame on the accused. The danger is not less, but may be greater, in the case of fellow accomplices. Their joint evidence is not 'independent' in the sense required by *R. v Baskerville* [1916] 2 K.B. at 667, [1916-17] All E.R. Rep. at 43, and a jury must be warned not to treat it as a corroboration. But this illustrates the danger of mistaking the shadow for the substance. I feel quite sure that, for instance, where an unpopular officer in the army or the unpopular headmaster of a school could have been the victim of a conspiracy to give false evidence of this kind as the suggestion was in *R. v Bailey* [1924] 2 K.B. 300, [1924] All E.R. Rep. 466 a similar warning should be given. As Lord Hewart C.J. said in that case [1924] 2 K.B. at 305, [1924] All E.R. Rep at 467 (which turned, however, on a wholly different point):

> "The risk, the danger, the logical fallacy is indeed quite manifest to those who are in the habit of thinking about such matters. It is so easy to derive from a series of unsatisfactory accusations, if there are enough of them,

an accusation which at least appears satisfactory. It is so easy to collect from a mass of ingredients, not one of which is sufficient, a totality which will appear to contain what is missing."

On the other hand, where the so-called accomplices are of the third class listed by Lord Simonds L.C. in *Davies v Director of Public Prosecutions* [1954] A.C. at 400 the danger is or may be nugatory. The real need is to warn the jury of the danger of a conspiracy to commit perjury in these cases, and, where there is the possibility of this, it is right to direct them not to treat as corroborative of one witness the evidence of another witness who may be part of the same conspiracy, but who cannot be an accomplice because if the evidence is untrue there has been no crime committed. This prompts me to point out that although the warning must be given in every appropriate case, the dangers to be guarded against may be quite different. Thus the evidence of accomplices is dangerous because it may be perjured. The evidence of Lady Wishfort complaining of rape may be dangerous because she may be indulging in undiluted sexual fantasy. A Mrs. Frail making the same allegation may need corroboration because of the danger that she does not wish to admit the consensual intercourse of which she is ashamed. In another case the danger may be one of honestly mistaken identity as when the conviction of the accused depends on an identification by a single uncorroborated witness to whom he was previously unknown. These matters should, in suitable cases, be explored when the nature and degree of danger is being discussed, as suggested in *R. v Price* [1969] 1 Q.B. at 546. I do not, therefore, believe that there is a general rule that no persons who come within the definition of accomplice may be mutually corroborative. It applies to those in the first and second of Lord Simonds L.C.'s categories and to many other cases where witnesses are not or may not be accomplices. It does not necessarily apply to all witnesses in the same case who may deserve to be categorised as 'accomplice'. In particular it does not necessarily apply to accomplices of Lord Simonds L.C.'s third class, where they give independent evidence of separate incidents, and where the circumstances are such as to exclude the danger of a jointly fabricated story.

Whatever else it is, the rule about fellow accomplices is not authority for the proposition that no witness who may himself require corroboration may afford corroboration for another to whom the same consideration applies, and this alone is what would help the respondent. When a small boy relates a sexual incident implicating a given man he may be indulging in fantasy. If another small boy relates such an incident it may be a coincidence if the detail is insufficient. If a large number of small boys relate similar incidents in enough detail about the same person, if it is not conspiracy it may well be that the stories are true. Once there is a sufficient nexus it must be for the jury to say what weight is given to the combined testimony of a number of witnesses. ...

21. People (A.G.) v Taylor
Court of Criminal Appeal, July 30, 1973
[1974] I.R. 97 at 98–100

Walsh J:

... [The accused] was found guilty of murder at a trial in the Central Criminal Court presided over by Mr. Justice Pringle. At the trial the question of provocation was raised by the defence, and a great deal turned upon whether the death was the result of a carefully premeditated act for which the weapon had been obtained in advance or whether the circumstances leading up to the death were, to a large extent, unforeseen and whether the weapon which was used for killing the deceased was a weapon which was just found to be at hand and used there and then in the heat of the moment in circumstances which the defence contend amounted to provocation.

During the examination-in-chief of one of the prosecution witnesses, the widow of the deceased, an application was made by counsel for the prosecution to have her treated as a hostile witness and that application was granted by the learned judge. The basis of the application, which was made in the absence of the jury, was that the witness had previously made a statement to the guards which differed on a material matter (the type of weapon used) from the evidence she was now giving in the witness-box. In the statement she had said that the stabbing had been done with a knife, and in her evidence in court she said that it was done with a pair of scissors. This application was made in the absence of the jury but on the strength of the difference between the statement to the guards and the evidence in the witness-box of the witness as to whether it was a knife or a pair of scissors. The judge permitted the witness to be treated as hostile.

When the jury were recalled to court, the cross-examination of the witness immediately commenced by counsel for the prosecution referring to the fact that the witness had made a statement to the civic guards that the weapon used was a knife. The object of this cross-examination, and the introduction of the statement made by her, was to discredit her testimony because her testimony in relation to the circumstances leading up to the stabbing referred to matters which, if accepted, the defence would ask the jury to accept as the basis of the claim of provocation. In point of fact in the cross-examination the witness was never asked which of her statements was the true one—the one in the witness-box referring to a pair of scissors or the statement to the civic guards referring to a knife. That simply underlines the view that the nature of the weapon (whether it was a pair of scissors or a knife) was not regarded as of importance in the case: but what was of extreme importance was the question of the credibility of the witness in her account of the circumstances on which the plea of provocation was based which might be accepted by the jury. The fact that she had made the statement obviously impressed itself on the jury's mind because the transcript discloses that the jury, during the course of considering their verdict, actually came back and asked to be given a copy of the statement. It appears to the Court that the procedure was, to say the least of it, telescoped by the prosecution.

The proper procedure, if it is desired to have a witness treated as hostile, is to make the application to the judge and put before him the material upon which it is sought to have the witness declared to be a hostile witness. This, of course, should be done in the absence of the jury and, if the judge rules that the witness may be treated as hostile, then the witness may be cross-examined. That is something quite different and distinct from the rules and procedure which govern the admissibility of written statements in cross-examination. This particular witness had been allowed to be treated as hostile and, when the jury were recalled to court, the proper procedure for the prosecution was to have put to the witness that she had on another occasion made a statement which differed materially from or contradicted the one she was making in the witness-box. If she were to deny that, then the proper procedure would have been to have her stand down from the box, and to prove in fact that she did in fact make a statement by putting into the box the person who took the statement, proving it in the ordinary way without revealing the contents of the statement at that stage. The earlier witness should then have been put back in the box and the statement put to her for identification, and then her attention should have been directed to the passage in which the alleged contradiction or material variation appears. If she had agreed that there was such a contradiction or material variation, that should have been the end of the matter in so far as the question of impugning her credibility was concerned because there would then have been before the jury an admission from the witness—to the effect that she had made contrary statements on the same matter. The statement might then be put in evidence, though that would not be strictly necessary at that stage when the admission had been made. If she had persisted in denying the contradiction, then the statement, having already been proved, would have gone in as evidence of the fact that the witness had made a contrary statement.

It must at all times be made clear to the jury that what the witness said in the written statement is not evidence of the fact referred to but is only evidence on the question of whether or not she has said something else—it is evidence going only to her credibility.

What was vital in the present case was whether or not the stabbing occurred in the circumstances alleged by the wife which were that there had been a situation created in which the jury could hold that there had been provocation, or whether the killing had been previously planned and had been premeditated. The introduction of the statement in the present case touched directly on that point in a manner highly prejudicial to the accused. In the view of the Court, the prosecution did not establish the necessary basis for introducing the written statement made to the Guards and, that being so, the statement should not have been received in evidence.

Having regard to the fact that the jury by their verdict obviously rejected the claim of provocation, this Court cannot say that they would have done so if the statement had not been admitted. In the circumstances, therefore, the conviction should be quashed and a new trial ordered.

22. People (A.G.) v Byrne

Court of Criminal Appeal, November 20, 1973
[1974] I.R. 1 at 2–4, 6–9

Kenny J:

... The case raises the question as to the form of charge which should be given by a judge to the jury in relation to the onus of proof in criminal cases and so is of considerable importance. ...

The judge ... told the jury that they had to be satisfied of the guilt of the accused, and he equated "satisfied" with "beyond a reasonable doubt." He did not tell the jury that the accused were entitled to the benefit of the doubt. The only case cited to us was *R. v Hepworth* [1955] 2 Q.B. 600 in which the Court of Criminal Appeal in England held that it was not sufficient for a judge to tell the jury that they had to be satisfied of the guilt of the accused, and in which a judge used these words and the conviction was set aside.

Until 1949 judges in criminal cases in Ireland invariably told the jury that the prosecution had to prove the guilt of the accused beyond reasonable doubt. In that year Lord Goddard cast doubt on this way of stating the matter, and since then there have been many judgments given in England on this subject which are difficult to reconcile or to explain. It has been held that it is sufficient for a judge to tell the jury that they must be sure of the prisoner's guilt; while a direction that they must be satisfied has been held to be inadequate. This Court thinks that the departure from the time-honoured formula is unfortunate because it is still the best way of indicating the degree of proof which is required in a criminal case.

For at least 150 years it has been usual for judges to tell the jury that the State must prove the guilt of the accused beyond reasonable doubt. Evidence that this had become established law in 1865 is given by the report of *R. v White* (1865) 4 F. & F. 383 in which Baron Martin, in summing up a criminal case to the jury, is reported to have said to them that in order to enable them to return a verdict against the prisoner they must be satisfied, beyond any reasonable doubt, of his guilt "and this as a conviction created in their minds, not merely as a matter of probability; and if it was only an impression of probability, their duty was to acquit." ...

In *R. v Hepworth* [1955] 2 Q.B. 600 [Lord Goddard] held that a charge in which a judge used the word "satisfied" when explaining the burden of proof was insufficient and a conviction in which such a charge was given was set aside. It is obvious that Lord Goddard had become uneasy about the effect of his remarks in *Kritz's Case* [1950] 1 K.B. 82 and in *Summers' Case* [1952] 1 All E.R. 1059):

> "Another thing that is said in the present case is that the recorder only used the word 'satisfied'. It may be, especially considering the number of cases recently in which this question has arisen, that I misled courts because I said in *Reg. v Summers* [1952] 1 All E.R. 1059) 'You must feel sure of the prisoner's guilt' ... Comment has been made on the use by the recorder of the word 'satisfied' only, and we have come to the

conclusion that the summing-up was not satisfactory; but again I emphasize that this is a case of receiving and in such a case it is always important that the onus of proof should be emphasized and explained."

The latest case on the matter is *R. v Allan* [1969] 1 W.L.R. 33, 36 in which Lord Justice Fenton Atkinson said:

"It has been said a good many times in cases—which it is not necessary to cite—that merely to say that the jury must be 'satisfied' without any clear indication of the degree of satisfaction required is an inadequate direction. But equally it has been said a good many times that it is not a matter of some precise formula or particular form of words being used. The important question is whether the direction as a whole was such as to bring to the minds of the jury that they must be sure of the guilt of the accused."

A different view has been taken by the High Court of Australia. ... In the later case of *Dawson v The Queen* [1961] 106 C.L.R. 1 Chief Justice Dixon, when speaking of the charge of the trial judge, said at p.18 of the report:

"But the incident makes it proper to say that in my view it is a mistake to depart from the time-honoured formula. It is, I think, used by ordinary people and is understood well enough by the average man in the community. The attempts to substitute other expressions, of which there have been many examples not only here but in England, have never prospered. It is wise as well as proper to avoid such expressions ..."

This Court agrees with the views expressed in the House of Lords, the Privy Council and the High Court of Australia. The correct charge to a jury is that they must be satisfied beyond reasonable doubt of the guilt of the accused, and it is helpful if that degree of proof is contrasted with that in a civil case. It is also essential, however, that the jury should be told that the accused is entitled to the benefit of the doubt and that when two views on any part of the case are possible on the evidence, they should adopt that which is favourable to the accused unless the State has established the other beyond reasonable doubt.

In this case the trial judge used the words "satisfied" and "to your satisfaction" on many occasions when explaining the onus of proof. He then said that "being satisfied" means the same thing as "beyond a reasonable doubt." This is not correct because one may be satisfied of something and still have a reasonable doubt. The judge made no attempt to explain to the jury what degree of satisfaction is required and it is in this respect that the time-honoured words "beyond reasonable doubt" are of such assistance; nor did the judge tell the jury that the accused were entitled to the benefit of the doubt. The Court thinks that jurymen understand the meaning of the expression "beyond reasonable doubt", particularly when it is associated with a comparison of the standard of proof in a civil case.

For these reasons the Court is of opinion that the judge's charge to the jury was not correct and, as the error related to a vital matter, it has decided that the conviction should be set aside and a new trial ordered. ...

23. Boardman v D.P.P.

House of Lords, November 13, 1974
[1974] 3 All E.R. 887 at 896–898, 903–906, 910–912

Wilberforce L.J:

... Questions of this kind arise in a number of different contexts and have, correspondingly, to be resolved in different ways. I think that it is desirable to confine ourselves to the present set of facts, and to situations of a similar character. In my understanding we are not here concerned with cases of 'system', 'underlying unity' (compare *Moorov v H.M. Advocate* 1930 J.C. 68), words whose vagueness is liable to result in their misapplication, nor with a case involving proof of identity, nor an alibi, nor, even, is this a case where evidence is adduced to rebut a particular defence. It is sometimes said that evidence of 'similar facts' may be called to rebut a defence of innocent association—a proposition which I regard with suspicion since it seems a specious manner of outflanking the exclusionary rule. But we need not consider the validity or scope of this proposition. The Court of Appeal dealt with the case on the basis, submitted by the appellant's counsel, that no defence of innocent association was set up; in my opinion we should take the same course.

This is simply a case where evidence of facts similar in character to those forming the subject of the charge is sought to be given in support of the evidence on that charge. Though the case was one in which separate charges relating to different complainants were tried jointly, the principle must be the same as would arise if there were only one charge relating to one complainant. If the appellant were being tried on a charge relating to Said, could the prosecution call Hamidi as a witness to give evidence about facts relating to Hamidi? The judge should apply just as strict a rule in the one case as in the other. If, as I believe, the general rule is that such evidence cannot be allowed, it requires exceptional circumstances to justify the admission. This House should not, in my opinion, encourage erosion of the general rule.

We can dispose at once of the suggestion that there is a special rule or principle applicable to sexual, or to homosexual, offences. This suggestion had support at one time—eminent support from Lord Sumner in *Thompson v R.* [1918] A.C. 221 at 235—but is now certainly obsolete (see *per* Lord Reid and other learned Lords in *Kilbourne* [1973] 1 All E.R. 440 at 456, [1973] A.C. 729 at 751). Evidence that an offence of a sexual character was committed by A against B cannot be supported by evidence that an offence of a sexual character was committed by A against C, or against C, D and E.

The question certified suggests that the contrary may be true if the offences take a 'particular form'. I do not know what this means; all sexual activity has some form or other and the varieties are not unlimited: how particular must it be for a special rule to apply? The general salutary rule of exclusion must not be eroded through so vague an epithet. The danger of it being so is indeed well shown in the present case, for the judge excluded the (similar fact) evidence of one boy because it showed 'normal' homosexual acts while admitting the (similar fact) evidence of another boy because the homosexual acts assumed a different, and, in his view, 'abnormal' pattern. Distinctions such as this, rightly called fine distinctions by the judge, lend an unattractive unreality to the law.

If the evidence was to be received, then, it must be on some general principle not confined to sexual offences. There are obvious difficulties in the way of formulating any such rule in such a manner as, on the one hand, to enable clear guidance to be given to juries, and, on the other hand, to avoid undue rigidity

The prevailing formulation is to be found in the judgment of the Court of Criminal Appeal in *R. v Sims* [1946] 1 All E.R. 697 at 700 where is was said:

> "The evidence of each man was that the accused invited him into the house and there committed the acts charged. The acts they describe bear a striking similarity. That is a special feature sufficient in itself to justify the admissibility of the evidence. ... The probative force of all the acts together is much greater than one alone; for, whereas the jury might think that one man might be telling an untruth, three or four are hardly likely to tell the same untruth unless they were conspiring together. If there is nothing to suggest a conspiracy, their evidence would seem to be overwhelming."

R. v Sims has not received universal approbation or uniform commentary, but I think it must be taken that this passage has received at least the general approval of this House in *Director of Public Prosecutions v Kilbourne* [1973] 1 All E.R. 440, [1973] A.C. 729. For my part, since the statement is evidently related to the facts of that particular case, I should deprecate its literal use in other cases. It is certainly neither clear nor comprehensive. A suitable adaptation, and, if necessary, expansion should be allowed to judges in order to suit the facts involved. The basic principle must be that the admission of similar fact evidence (of the kind now in question) is exceptional and requires a strong degree of probative force. This probative force is derived, if at all, from the circumstance that the facts testified to by the several witnesses bear to each other such a striking similarity that they must, when judged by experience and common sense, either all be true, or have arisen from a cause common to the witnesses or from pure coincidence. The jury may, therefore, properly be asked to judge whether the right conclusion is that all are true, so that each story is supported by the (others).

I use the words 'a cause common to the witnesses' to include not only (as in *R. v Sims*) the possibility that the witnesses may have invented a story in concert but also that a similar story may have arisen by a process of infection from media of publicity or simply from fashion. In the sexual field, and in others, this may be a real possibility; something much more than mere similarity and absence of proved conspiracy is needed if this evidence is to be allowed. This is well illustrated by *Kilbourne's* case where the judge excluded 'intra group' evidence because of the possibility as it appeared to him, of collaboration between boys who knew each other well. This is, in my respectful opinion, the right course rather than to admit the evidence unless a case of collaboration or concoction is made out.

If this test is to be applied fairly, much depends in the first place on the experience and common sense of the judge. As was said by Lord Simon of

Glaisdale in *Kilbourne's* case, in judging whether one fact is probative of another, experience plays as large a place as logic. And in matters of experience it is for the judge to keep close to current mores. What is striking in one age is normal in another; the perversions of yesterday may be the routine or the fashion of tomorrow. The ultimate test has to be applied by the jury using similar qualities of experience and common sense after a fair presentation of the dangers either way of admission or of rejection. Finally, whether the judge has properly used and stated the ingredients of experience and common sense may be reviewed by the Court of Appeal.

The present case is, to my mind, right on the borderline. There were only two relevant witnesses, Said and Hamidi. The striking similarity as presented to the jury was and was only the active character of the sexual performance to which the accused was said to have invited the complainants. In relation to the incident which was the subject of the second charge, the language used by the boy was not specific; the 'similarity' was derived from an earlier incident in connection with which the boy used a verb connoting an active role. I agree with, I think, all your Lordships in thinking that all of this, relating not very specifically to the one striking element, common to two boys only, is, if sufficient, only just sufficient. Perhaps other similarities could have been found in the accused's approaches to the boys (I do not myself find them particularly striking), but the judge did not rest on them or direct the jury as to their 'similarity'. I do not think that these ought now to be relied on. The dilution of the 'striking' fact by more prosaic details might have weakened the impact on the jury rather than strengthening it. The judge dealt properly and fairly with the possibility of a conspiracy between the boys. ...

Hailsham of St. Marylebone L.J:

... This statement [in *Makin*] may be divided into its component parts. The first sentence lays down a general rule of exclusion. 'Similar fact' evidence, or evidence of bad character, is not admissible for the purpose of leading to the conclusion that a person, from his criminal conduct or character, is likely to have committed the offence for which he is being held.

Two theories have been advanced as to the basis of this, and both have respectable judicial support. One is that such evidence is simply irrelevant. No number of similar offences can connect a particular person with a particular crime, however much they may lead the police, or anyone else investigating the offence, to concentrate their enquiries on him as their prime suspect. According to this theory, similar fact evidence excluded under Lord Herschell L.C.'s first sentence has no probative value and is to be rejected on that ground. The second theory is that the prejudice created by the admission of such evidence outweighs any probative value it may have. An example of this view is to be found in the speech of Lord Simon of Glaisdale in *Kilbourne* [1973] 1 All E.R. at 461, [1973] A.C. at 757 where he said:

> "The reason why the type of evidence referred to by Lord Herschell L.C. in the first sentence of the passage is inadmissible is, not because it is irrelevant, but because its logically probative significance is considered

to be grossly outweighed by prejudice to the accused, so that a fair trial is endangered if it is admitted..."

With respect, both theories are correct. When there is nothing to connect the accused with a particular crime except bad character or similar crimes committed in the past, the probative value of the evidence is nil and the evidence is rejected on that ground. When there is some evidence connecting the accused with the crime, in the eyes of most people, guilt of similar offences in the past might well be considered to have probative value (*cf* the statutory exceptions to this effect in the old law of receiving and under the Theft Act 1968). Nonetheless, in the absence of a statutory provision to the contrary, the evidence is to be excluded under the first rule in *Makin* [1894] A.C. 57, [1891-94] All E.R. Rep. 24 because its prejudicial effect may be more powerful than its probative effect, and thus endanger a fair trial because it tends to undermine the integrity of the presumption of innocence and the burden of proof. In other words, it is a rule of English law which has its root in policy, and by which, in Lord du Parcq's phrase [1949] 1 All E.R. at 371, [1949] A.C. at 194, logicians would not be bound.

But there is a third case, to which the second rule in *Makin* applies. The mere fact that the evidence adduced tends to show the commission of other crimes does not by itself render it inadmissible if it is relevant to an issue before the jury and it may be so relevant if it bears on the question whether the acts alleged to constitute the crime charged in the indictment were designed or accidental, or to rebut a defence which would otherwise be open to the accused.

Contrary to what was suggested in argument for the appellant, this rule is not an exception grafted on to the first. It is an independent proposition introduced by the words: 'On the other hand', and the two propositions together cover the entire field. If one applies, the other does not. ...

It is perhaps helpful to remind oneself that what is *not* to be admitted is a chain of reasoning and not necessarily a state of facts. If the inadmissible chain of reasoning be the only purpose for which the evidence is adduced as a matter of law, the evidence itself is not admissible. If there is some other relevant, probative, purpose than the forbidden type of reasoning, the evidence is admitted, but should be made subject to a warning from the judge that the jury must eschew the forbidden reasoning. The judge also has a discretion, not as a matter of law, but of good practice, to exclude evidence whose prejudicial effect, though the evidence be technically admissible on the decided cases, may be so great in the particular circumstances as to outweigh its probative value to the extent that a verdict of guilty might be considered unsafe or unsatisfactory if ensuing (*cf per* Lord Simon in *Harris* [1952] 1 All E.R. at 1048, [1952] A.C. at 707). In all these cases it is for the judge to ensure as a matter of law in the first place, and as a matter of discretion where the matter is free, that a properly instructed jury, applying their minds to the facts, can come to the conclusion that they are satisfied so that they are sure that to treat the matter as pure coincidence by reason of the 'nexus', 'pattern', 'system', 'striking resemblances' or whatever phrase is used, is 'an affront to common sense'. In this the ordinary rules of logic and common sense prevail, whether the case is one of burglary and the burglar has left some 'signature' as the mark of his presence, or false pretences, and the pretences alleged have too many common characteristics to have happened coincidentally, or whether the dispute is one of identity and the accused in a series of offences has some notable physical features or behavioural or psychological characteristics, or, as in some cases, is in possession of incriminating articles, like a jemmy, a set of skeleton keys, or, in abortion cases, the apparatus of the abortionist. Attempts to codify the rules of common sense are to be resisted. The first rule in *Makin* is designed to exclude a particular kind of inference being drawn which might upset the presumption of innocence, by introducing more heat than light. When that is the only purpose for which the evidence is being tendered, it should be excluded altogether, as in *R. v Horwood* 1938 J.C. 152. Where the purpose is an inference of another kind, subject to the judge's overriding discretion to exclude, the evidence is admissible, if in fact the evidence be logically probative. Even then it is for they jury to assess its weight, which may be greater or less according as to how far it accords with other evidence, and according as to how far that other evidence may be conclusive.

There are two further points of a general character that I would add. The 'striking resemblances' or 'unusual features', or whatever phrase is considered appropriate, to ignore which would affront common sense, may be either in the objective facts, as for instance in 'Brides in the Bath' [*R. v Smith* [1914-15] All E.R. Rep. 262] or *Straffen* [1952] 2 Q.B. 911, or they may constitute a striking similarity in the accounts by witness of disputed transactions. For instance, whilst it would certainly not be enough to identify the culprit in a series of burglaries that he climbed in through a ground floor window, the fact that he left the same humorous limerick on the walls of the sitting room, or an esoteric symbol written in lipstick on the mirror, might well be enough. In a sex case, to adopt an example given in argument in the Court of Appeal, whilst a repeated homosexual act by itself might be quite insufficient to admit the evidence as confirmatory of identity or design, the fact that it was alleged to have been performed wearing the ceremonial head-dress of an Indian chief or other eccentric garb might well in appropriate circumstances suffice. ...

Cross of Chelsea L.J:

... Before I come to the particular facts of this case there is one other matter to which I wish to refer. When in a case of this sort the proposition wishes to adduce 'similar fact' evidence which the defence says is inadmissible, the question whether it is admissible ought, if possible, to be decided in the absence of the jury at the outset of the trial and if it is decided that the evidence is inadmissible and the accused is being charged in the same indictment with offences against the other men the charges relating to the different persons ought to be tried separately. If they are tried together the judge will, of course, have to tell the jury that in considering whether the accused is guilty of the offence alleged against him by A, they must put out of mind the fact—which they know—that B and C are making similar allegations against him. But, as the Court of Criminal Appeal said in *R. v Sims* [1946] K.B. 531, it is asking too much of any jury to tell them to perform mental gymnastics of this sort. If the charges are tried together it is inevitable that the jurors will be influenced, consciously or unconsciously, by the fact that the accused is being charged not with a single offence against one person but with three separate offences against three persons. It is said, I know, that to order separate trials in all these cases would be highly inconvenient. If and so far as this is true it is a reason for doubting the wisdom of the general rule excluding similar fact evidence. But so long as there is that general rule the courts ought to strive to give effect to it loyally and not, while paying lip service to it, in effect let in the inadmissible evidence by trying all the charges together. ...

It is by no means unheard of for a boy to accuse a schoolmaster falsely of having made homosexual advances to him. If two boys make accusations of that sort at about the same time independently of one another then no doubt the ordinary man would tend to think that there was 'probably something in it'. But it is just this instinctive reaction of the ordinary man which the general rule is intended to counter and I think that one needs to find very striking peculiarities common to the two stories to justify the admission of one to support the other. The feature in the two stories on which attention was concentrated in the courts below is that both youths said that the appellant suggested not that he should bugger them but that they should bugger him. This was said to be an 'unusual' suggestion. If I thought that the outcome of this appeal depended on whether such a suggestion was in fact 'unusual' I would be in favour of allowing it. It is no doubt unusual for a middle-aged man to yield to the urge to commit buggery or to try to commit buggery with youths or young men but whether it is unusual for such a middle-aged man to wish to play the passive rather than the active role I have no idea whatever and I am not prepared, in the absence of any evidence on the point, to make any assumption one way or the other. As I see it, however, the point is not whether what the appellant is said to have suggested would be, as coming from a middle-aged active homosexual, in itself particularly unusual, but whether it would be unlikely that two youths who were saying untruly that the appellant had made homosexual advances to them would have put such a suggestion into his mouth. In one passage in his summing-up the judge touched on this aspect of the matter and said that the jury might think it more likely that if their stories were untrue Said and Hamidi would have said that the appellant wished to bugger or did bugger them than that he wished them to bugger or induced them to bugger him. There is, I think, force in that observation; but I do not think that this similarity standing alone would be sufficient to warrant the admission of the evidence. My noble and learned friends, Lord Morris, Lord Hailsham and Lord Salmon point, however, to other features common to the two stories which, it may be said, two liars concocting false stories independently of one another would have been unlikely to hit on and, although I must say that I regard this as very much a borderline case, I am not prepared to dissent from their view that the 'similar fact' evidence was admissible here and that the appeal should be dismissed.

24. R v Turnbull
Court of Appeal, July 9, 1976
[1977] 1 Q.B. 224 at 228–231

Widgery L.C.J:

... Each of these appeals raises problems relating to evidence of visual identification in criminal cases. Such evidence can bring about miscarriages of justice and has done so in a few cases in recent years. The number of such cases, although small compared with the number in which evidence of visual identification is known to be satisfactory, necessitates steps being taken by the courts, including this court, to reduce that number as far as is possible. In our judgment the danger of miscarriages of justice occurring can be much reduced if trial judges sum up to juries in the way indicated in this judgment.

First, whenever the case against an accused depends wholly or substantially on the correctness of one or more identifications of the accused which the defence alleges to be mistaken, the judge should warn the jury of the special need for caution before convicting the accused in reliance on the correctness of the identification or identifications. In addition he should instruct them as to the reason for the need for such a warning and should make some reference to the possibility that a mistaken witness can be a convincing one and that a number of such witnesses can all be mistaken. Provided this is done in clear terms the judge need not use any particular form of words.

Secondly, the judge should direct the jury to examine closely the circumstances in which the identification by each witness came to be made. How long did the witness have the accused under observation? At what distance? In what light? Was the observation impeded in any way, as for example by passing traffic or a press of people? Had the witness ever seen the accused before? How often? If only occasionally, had he any special reason for remembering the accused? How long elapsed between the original observation and the subsequent identification to the police? Was there any material discrepancy between the description of the accused given to the police by the witness when first seen by them and his actual appearance? If in any case, whether it is being dealt with summarily or on indictment, the prosecution have reason to believe that there is such a material discrepancy they should supply the accused or his legal advisers with particulars of the description the police were first given. In all cases if the accused asks to be given particulars of such descriptions, the prosecution should supply them. Finally, he should remind the jury of any specific weaknesses which had appeared in the identification evidence.

Recognition may be more reliable than identification of a stranger; but, even when the witness is purporting to recognise someone whom he knows, the jury should be reminded that mistakes in recognition of close relatives and friends are sometimes made.

All these matters go to the quality of the identification evidence. If the quality is good and remains good at the close of the accused's case, the danger of a mistaken identification is lessened; but the poorer the quality, the greater the danger.

In our judgment, when the quality is good, as for example when the identification is made after a long period of observation, or in satisfactory conditions by a relative, a neighbour, a close friend, a workmate and the like, the jury can safely be left to assess the value of the identifying evidence even though there is no other evidence to support it; provided always, however, that an adequate warning has been given about the special need for caution. Were the courts to adjudge otherwise, affronts to justice would frequently occur. A few examples, taken over the whole spectrum of criminal activity, will illustrate what the effects on the maintenance of law and order would be if any law were enacted that no person could be convicted on evidence of visual identification alone.

Here are the examples. A had been kidnapped and held to ransom over many days. His captor stayed with him all the time. At last he was released but he did not know the identity of his kidnapper nor where he had been kept. Months later the police arrested X for robbery and as a result of what they had been told by an informer they suspected him of the kidnapping. They had no other evidence. They arranged for A to attend an identify parade. He picked out X without hesitation. At X's trial, is the trial judge to rule at the end of the prosecution's case that X must be acquitted?

This is another example. Over a period of a week two police officers, B and C, kept observations in turn on a house which was suspected of being a distribution centre for drugs. A suspected supplier, Y, visited it from time to time. On the last day of the observation B saw Y enter the house. He at once signalled to other waiting police officers, who had a search warrant to enter. They did so; but by the time they got in, Y had escaped by a back window. Six months later C saw Y in the street and arrested him. Y at once alleged that C had mistaken him for someone else. At an identity parade he was picked out by B. Would it really be right and in the interests of justice for a judge to direct Y's acquittal at the end of the prosecution's case?

A rule such as the one under consideration would gravely impede the police in their work and would make the conviction of street offenders such as pickpockets, car thieves and the disorderly very difficult. But it would not only be the police who might be aggrieved by such a rule. Take the case of a factory worker, D, who during the course of his work went to the locker room to get something from his jacket which he had forgotten. As he went in he saw a workmate, Z, whom he had known for years and who worked near him in the same shop, standing by D's open locker with his hand inside. He hailed the thief by name. Z turned round and faced D; he dropped D's wallet on the floor and ran out of the locker room by another door. D reported what he had seen to his chargehand. When the chargehand went to find Z, he saw him walking towards his machine. Z alleged that D had been mistaken. A directed acquittal might well be greatly resented not only by D but by many others in the same shop.

When, in the judgment of the trial judge, the quality of the identifying evidence is poor, as for example when it depends solely on a fleeting glance or on a longer observation made in difficult conditions, the situation is very different. The judge should then withdraw the case from the jury and direct an acquittal unless there is other evidence which goes to support the correctness of the identification. This may be corroboration in the sense lawyers use that word; but it need not be so if its effect is to make the jury sure that there has been no mistaken identification. For example, X sees the accused snatch a woman's handbag; he gets only a fleeting glance of the thief's face as he runs off but he does see him entering a nearby house. Later he picks out the accused on an identity parade. If there was no more evidence than this, the poor quality of the identification would require the judge to withdraw the case from the jury; but this would not be so if there was evidence that the house into which the accused was alleged by X to have run was his father's. Another example of supporting evidence not amounting to corroboration in a technical sense is to be found in *R. v Long* (1973) 57 Cr. App. R. 871. The accused, who was charged with robbery, had been identified by three witnesses in different places on different occasions, but each had only a momentary opportunity for observation. Immediately after the robbery the accused had left his home and could not be found by the police. When later he was seen by them he claimed to know who had done the robbery and offered to help to find the robbers. At his trial he put forward an alibi which the jury rejected. It was an odd coincidence that the witnesses should have identified a man who had behaved in this way. In our judgment odd coincidences can, if unexplained, be supporting evidence.

The trial judge should identify to the jury the evidence which he adjudges is capable of supporting the evidence of identification. If there is any evidence or circumstance which the jury might think was supporting when it did not have this quality, the judge should say so. A jury, for example, might think that support for identification evidence could be found in the fact that the accused had not given evidence before them. An accused's absence from the witness box cannot provide evidence of anything and the judge should tell the jury so. But he would be entitled to tell them that when assessing the quality of the identification evidence they could take into consideration the fact that it was uncontradicted by any evidence coming from the accused himself.

Care should be taken by the judge when directing the jury about the support for an identification which may be derived from the fact that they have rejected an alibi. False alibis may be put forward for many reasons: an accused, for example, who has only his own truthful evidence to rely on may stupidly fabricate an alibi and get lying witnesses to support it out of fear that his own evidence will not be enough. Further, alibi witnesses can make genuine mistakes about dates and occasions like any other witnesses can. It is only when the jury are satisfied that the sole reason for the fabrication was to deceive them and there is no other explanation for its being put forward, that fabrication can provide any support for identification evidence. The jury should be reminded that proving the accused has told lies about where he was at the material time does not by itself prove that he was where the identifying witness says he was.

In setting out these guidelines for trial judges, which involve only changes of practice, not law, we have tried to follow the recommendations set out in the report which Lord Devlin's committee made to the Secretary of State for the Home Department in April 1976. We have not followed that report in using the phrase 'exceptional circumstances' to describe situations in which the risk of mistaken identification is reduced. In our judgment, the use of such a phrase is likely to result in the build-up of case law as to what circumstances can properly be described as exceptional and what cannot. Case law of this kind is likely to be a fetter on the administration of justice when so much depends on the quality of the evidence in each case. Quality is what matters in the end. In many cases the exceptional circumstances to which the report refers will provide evidence of good quality, but they may not; the converse is also true.

A failure to follow these guidelines is likely to result in a conviction being quashed and will do so if in the judgment of this court on all the evidence the verdict is either unsatisfactory or unsafe. ...

25. People (D.P.P.) v Shaw

Supreme Court, December 17, 1980
[1982] I.R. 1 at 32–34, 36–38, 40–42, 54–56, 60–63

Walsh J:

... I feel that I should elaborate a little upon my reference to *The People (Attorney General) v O'Brien* [1965] I.R. 142 as, from time to time, there appears to be some confusion as to what the case decided. As I had the advantage of being a member of the Court which gave that decision, I feel that I am in a position to deal with it. The case and the decision dealt primarily with two matters concerning the admissibility of evidence. The first was the question of the admissibility of evidence which was obtained illegally but where the illegality did not amount to an infringement of a constitutional right of the accused person. The second point was the question of the admissibility of evidence obtained by illegal methods which constituted infringements of the accused's constitutional rights. With regard to the first point, the majority of the Court decided that evidence obtained illegally could be admissible at the discretion of the judge, whereas the minority members of the Court took the view that such evidence was always admissible provided that it was relevant and probative. With regard to the second point, the basic proposition was that an objection to the admissibility at a criminal trial of evidence obtained or procured by the State, its servants or agents, as a result of a deliberate and conscious violation of the constitutional rights of the accused person must be upheld, subject to certain exceptions. This general proposition was contained in my own judgment and was agreed to by all the members of the Court. I expressed the view that an exception to this general rule would be where "extraordinary excusing circumstances" existed and I gave three examples, namely, the imminent destruction of vital evidence, the need to rescue a victim in peril, and also evidence obtained by a search which was incidental to and contemporaneous with a lawful arrest, though made without a valid search warrant. I said that, in addition to these "extraordinary excusing circumstances", evidence obtained without a deliberate and conscious violation of an accused's constitutional rights was not inadmissible by reason only of the existence of a violation of his constitutional right. In other words, accidental and unintentional infringements of the Constitution would not be sufficient to exclude such evidence.

It is important to emphasise that "extraordinary excusing circumstances" and "accidental and unintentional infringement of the Constitution" are quite separate matters. Kingsmill Moore J. in his judgment accepted the general proposition and also agreed that there might be certain "extraordinary excusing circumstances" which would warrant the admissibility of such evidence, but he preferred not to attempt to enumerate such extraordinary excusing circumstances by anticipation. He also expressly agreed that an accidental and unintentional infringement of the Constitution would not normally exclude evidence so obtained. His disinclination to attempt to enumerate all the cases which might amount to excusing circumstances was shared by all the members of the Court. He was thus leaving open the question of what could amount to extraordinary excusing circumstances and he was not prepared to enumerate them by anticipation. He took the view that circumstances of cases vary so widely that it would be a matter for the discretion of the trial judge to decide whether or not the circumstances which were pleaded in excuse of the violation of the constitutional right in question were such as to amount to "extraordinary excusing circumstances." The examples of these given in my own judgment were simply illustrative and did not claim to be exhaustive.

O'Brien's Case was examined recently by this Court in *The People v Walsh* [1980] I.R. 294 and the views I now express were the views of the Court in that case. It is also necessary to emphasise that nothing in the admissibility rule renders lawful what was and is unlawful. By definition the question of admissibility arises only because there was an illegality.

I might add that there is nothing whatever in *O'Brien's Case* to suggest that the admissibility of the evidence depends upon the state or degree of the violator's knowledge of constitutional law or, indeed, of the ordinary law. To attempt to import any such interpretation of the decision would be to put a premium on ignorance of the law. The maxim *ignorantia legis neminem excusat* does not permit an intentional and deliberate act or omission to be shorn of its legal consequences. It is appropriate to point out that the opinion of this Court on a similar subject was expressed as follows at p.134 of the report of *The State (Quinn) v Ryan* [1965] I.R. 70:

> "A belief, or hope, on the part of the officers concerned that their acts would not bring them into conflict with the Courts is no answer, nor is an inadequate appreciation of the reality of the right of personal liberty guaranteed by the Constitution."

To hold otherwise would be to hold what to many people would be an absurd position, namely, that the less a police officer knew about the Constitution and, indeed, of the law itself, the more likely he would be to have the evidence which he obtained in breach of the law (and/or the Constitution) admitted in court. If such indeed were the position, it could well lead to a demand that the interests of equality of treatment should permit an accused person to be allowed to be heard to the effect that he did not know that the activity of which he was charged, and which has been proved against him, amounted to a breach of the criminal law. ...

The appellant was first arrested at about 11.30p.m. on Sunday, the 26th September, 1976, at Salthill in the county of Galway. At that time the appellant was a passenger in a car driven by Geoffrey Evans. Evans was told that he was being arrested on suspicion of being in possession of a stolen car. Whether the garda had in mind the offence of receiving property known to have been stolen or the offence of unlawful possession which is made an arrestable offence by virtue of s. 13 of the Criminal Justice Act, 1951, does not really matter as, in either event, the garda officer had lawful authority to effect the arrest of Evans. The appellant was also arrested but was told that he was being taken to the garda station for questioning. ...

During the course of the Monday both Evans and the appellant were interrogated by the garda authorities in the Galway station about the disappearance of Elizabeth. During the period of this interrogation the arrest of both Evans and the appellant had ceased to be lawful and they were at that time unlawfully imprisoned. That was deliberately and consciously done in the hope of obtaining information concerning both Elizabeth and Mary, and also in the hope and expectation that there might still be a possibility of discovering Mary alive. The garda officers did not believe, and had no reason to believe, that Elizabeth was still alive. Their concern was the possibility of Mary being alive. Throughout the Monday the appellant was questioned at length. Towards the end of the day he became so distressed that the interrogating officers felt that there was no further purpose in continuing the questioning and he was allowed to go to bed. In the meanwhile it appears that sometime on the same evening Evans, who had been questioned separately in another part of the station, had signed what, in effect, was a full confession admitting the murder of Elizabeth by himself and the appellant. According to the evidence, the gardaí who had been interrogating the appellant were unaware of that situation. However, it is quite clear that by the evening of Monday, the 27th September, the garda authorities in that station had sufficient evidence upon which to found a reasonable belief that both Evans and the appellant had committed a murder. If the gardaí had chosen to do so, that would have been sufficient to charge both men with that offence and the custody could thus have again become lawful. However, at no stage on the Monday was the appellant informed of the fact that a statement incriminating him had been made by Evans, nor was any suggestion made to the appellant that he was being held in respect of the death of Elizabeth.

Being in a distressed condition, the appellant was permitted to go to bed at 11.15 p.m. At 4 a.m. on the following (Tuesday) morning, he was brought upstairs again for further questioning. He was described as being then completely different in his condition from that of the previous night, and as being relaxed and calm. He was then told by one of the detective officers present that he should tell the truth, and the detective officer said: "I know everything, I have just been with Geoffrey"—which was a reference to Evans. The appellant then made a statement to the gardaí and concluded it at about 6.50 a.m. The statement amounted to a confession that the appellant was guilty of all the offences of which he was subsequently convicted. The officer who interviewed the appellant after his interrogation had recommenced at 4 a.m.

on the Tuesday morning was already aware that Evans had made a statement admitting to the murder of Elizabeth, and incriminating the appellant. Evans had not made any reference to the fate of Mary. The officer interrogating the appellant on the Tuesday morning was aware of these facts and, when he told the appellant that he had been speaking to Evans and that he "knew the whole story", he did not tell the appellant that Evans had been speaking only of Elizabeth. That interrogating officer knew that Evans had stated that Elizabeth had been kept alive for a considerable time before she was killed and, to use his own words, the officer felt "that there was a possibility that, if they had been involved in the disappearance of Mary, there was a hope that she was still alive some place and I was very concerned to establish the truth."

The procedure adopted in this interrogation was directly authorised by Detective Superintendent Reynolds in the hope that both Elizabeth and Mary might be still alive; he took the considered decision that to continue to detain the appellant and Evans in the garda station and to interrogate them was more important than bringing them before a court on charges. There has never been any claim, even if it were relevant, that Detective Superintendent Reynolds was at any time unaware of the law dealing with the disposal of arrested persons, or of their constitutional rights. He regarded the charge on which both men had been held (i.e., the possession of a car believed to have been stolen) to be simply a minor offence by comparison with the safety of the girls which was his concern. As Detective Superintendent Reynolds had actually been engaged in the taking of the statement from Evans at 10 p.m. on the Monday night, he was aware from that statement that Elizabeth was already dead. He felt that there was such a similarity between the disappearance of Elizabeth and that of Mary that he should continue pressing his inquiries in the hope that Mary might still be alive. With regard to the position or the possible whereabouts of Mary, he considered that the fact that Elizabeth had been kept alive for almost 24 hours before she met her death (according to Evans) suggested that there was a hope that Mary might still be found while alive. ...

When the appellant had confessed to the murder of Mary, Detective Superintendent Reynolds contacted the Director of Public Prosecutions by telephone and informed him of the statements which Evans and the appellant had made. Following his discussion with the Director of Public Prosecutions, he made arrangements to take the two men out to Lough Inagh where, it was alleged, the body of Mary had been disposed of, and to take them to other places where she had been detained and where certain items of her clothing etc. had been burned and where other items had been concealed. Evans and the appellant had volunteered to go with the gardaí to these places for the purpose of pointing out such places. After this journey, which was referred to generally in the evidence as "the Connemara episode," the gardaí and the two men arrived back in Galway. At no stage was either of them charged in Galway or brought before any court or peace commissioner. As stated already, the appellant and Evans were then brought to the garda station in Wicklow; they appeared before a court for the first time in Wicklow on Wednesday, the 29th September. ...

The net question is whether an arrest or imprisonment which is not in accordance with law can be rendered lawful by a belief that such arrest or imprisonment may vindicate one or more of those rights of another citizen which the Constitution in Article 40, s. 3, guarantees to defend, protect and vindicate. In the instant case there arises the question of a belief that another person's life, already imperilled, may be saved by effecting or maintaining an unlawful arrest or detention. In my opinion the answer must be that the unlawful character of the act remains unchanged however well intentioned it may be.

The Constitution expressly provides that no person may be deprived of his personal liberty save in accordance with law: Article 40, s. 4, sub-s. 1. There is nothing in the Constitution which authorises the commission of an unlawful act. If an act is unlawful and the law or the laws which render it unlawful is or are not inconsistent with, or invalid having regard to the provisions of the Constitution, it is quite clear that the Constitution cannot and does not purport to render lawful an act which is unlawful and that no court is competent or permitted to do so. To suggest that an effort in vindicating the life of another person, e.g., to enable that person to gain the benefit of the constitutional provision for the protection or vindication of his life, is sufficient in itself to render lawful any act however unlawful, provided it is motivated by an honest desire to save or vindicate a life, is simply to state that the end may justify the means, unlawful though they may be. The specific question raised in the certificate of the Court of Criminal Appeal, namely, whether the arrest and imprisonment of the appellant after 10.30 a.m. on Monday, the 27th September, 1976, was lawful by reason of the obligation of the gardaí to attempt to vindicate the right to life appears to me to beg the question. The Constitution, by reason of its express provision that no person shall be deprived of his personal liberty save in accordance with law, means what it says. It entrenches the law and raises it to the level of a constitutionally guaranteed right. To take the example which was considered by the trial judge, if an application for the release of the appellant at the time in question had been made to the High Court under Article 40 of the Constitution and the only justification which could be offered by the custodians, namely, the Garda Síochána, was their belief, albeit a reasonable one, that holding the appellant under continued arrest might lead to the saving of the life of Mary, the High Court would have had no alternative but to order the release of the appellant forthwith on the grounds that he was not being detained in accordance with the law. The custodians would not have been able to point to any law which justified the appellant's continued detention. If it were sought simply to justify it by showing a good motive, such as an effort or a hope to save a life in so doing, the court would have had to hold, in accordance with Article 40, s. 4, sub-s. 2, of the Constitution, that such detention, however well intentioned, was not in accordance with the law—whether it be the law stated in the Constitution or the law in force by virtue of statute or common law. To do otherwise would be to disobey the mandatory express injunction of Article 40. Therefore, I am of opinion that the statements would not have been admissible because such arrest and imprisonment were contrary to law and, therefore, amounted to a breach of the constitutional rights of the appellant. For the reasons I have already given, the answer to that question does not govern this case.

So far as paragraph 1 of the grounds of appeal is concerned, the answer must be that the provisions of the Constitution did not permit the Garda

Síochána to deprive the appellant of his personal liberty for the period in question in the belief that such deprivation might vindicate the constitutional right or rights of another citizen. For the reasons already given, that arrest and imprisonment were unlawful. But, for the reasons already given, in the circumstances of this case such unlawful arrest did not render inadmissible the incriminating evidence furnished by the appellant during the period of the unlawful arrest. The circumstances prevailing at the time the appellant made his Galway confession were capable of amounting in law to extraordinary excusatory circumstances. For the reasons I have given I would dismiss this appeal. ...

Griffin J. (with whom Henchy, Kenny, Parke JJ. agreed):

... The real question which arises in this case is whether there were circumstances in which the right to personal liberty conferred by Article 40, s. 4, sub-s. 1, may be said to have been limited or qualified. Unless there was justification for limiting or qualifying the right of the appellant to personal liberty, on the facts proved there was a reasonable prospect on the 27th and 28th September, 1976, that Mary's competing right to life and to the protection of her person would be seriously and irretrievably endangered. In my opinion, where such a conflict arises, a choice must be made. It is the duty of the State to protect the more important right, even at the expense of another important, but less important, right. Therefore, the State must weigh each right for the purpose of evaluating the merits of each and strike a balance between them and, having done so, take such steps as are necessary to protect the more important right. Although the right to personal liberty is one of the fundamental rights, if a balance is to be struck between one person's right to personal liberty for some hours or even days and another person's right to protection against danger to his life, then in any civilised society, in my view, the latter right must prevail in circumstances such as those which confronted Superintendent Reynolds.

Applying these principles to this case, Superintendent Reynolds had to make a choice between vindicating the right of the appellant to personal liberty and endeavouring to save the life of Mary, which latter course would have the necessary consequence of continuing the detention of the appellant. He made that choice and, viewing the matter objectively from the point of view of foresight and not hindsight, in my opinion he made the correct choice and, indeed, the only choice which he could reasonably have made in the circumstances. Accordingly, in continuing the detention of the appellant, the superintendent was not acting unlawfully but was doing what was necessary to protect the constitutional rights of Mary under Article 40, s. 3, sub-s. 2, of the Constitution.

With regard to the statements made and the evidence given in relation to what was pointed out by the appellant and what was found as a result of the places visited on the Connemara journey, it is in my view irrelevant whether the appellant was in lawful or unlawful custody at the time this journey was made. This was a journey undertaken at his own express request. He it was who volunteered to go and to point out the different places to which he and the accompanying gardaí subsequently went. In this respect the appellant was a free agent, as the trial judge found, and all the evidence which was obtained on that journey and which connected him with the offences was discovered directly as a consequence of his own voluntary acts. In my view, therefore, there was no ground upon which that evidence could have been excluded at the trial.

However, I should like to add that in my view the appellant's detention was not unlawful at that time. The explanation of Superintendent Reynolds for permitting that journey was that, although the appellant had confessed to the killing of Mary, he (the superintendent) could not take the risk of accepting the accuracy of the statements of the appellant and Evans. The superintendent believed that, notwithstanding the admission of the appellant, there was still a chance that Mary might be alive and that her life might be saved. The trial judge fully accepted that explanation. I agree with the Court of Criminal Appeal that it was the duty of the superintendent to pursue even a remote chance that she might have been alive, and that the chance that she was still alive, though remote, was sufficient to render the continued detention of the appellant lawful. Indeed, if the superintendent had not permitted the journey when the appellant volunteered to undertake it, and if the body of Mary had been found subsequently not in Lough Inagh but tied up in a wood or in a remote building, it would surely be said with hindsight that the superintendent had neglected his duty to the State and to Mary.

Accordingly, my answer to the question of law set out in the certificate of the Court of Criminal Appeal would be that the continued detention of the appellant after 10.30 a.m. on Monday, the 27th September, 1976, was lawful, and that the statements made by him on the 27th and 28th September, 1976, were admissible.

I have had an opportunity of reading the judgment which Mr. Justice Walsh has just delivered. ... I do not think it is correct to state without qualification that no person may be arrested with or without a warrant for the purpose of interrogation or the securing of evidence from that person. Nor do I find myself able to support the opinion that a person's statement is to be ruled out as evidence obtained in deliberate and conscious violation of his constitutional rights, even though the taker of the statement may not have known that what he was doing was either illegal or unconstitutional. I consider the authorities to be to the contrary effect. For example, in *The People (Attorney General) v O'Brien* [1965] I.R. 142 Kingsmill Moore J. (who gave the majority judgment), having held that evidence obtained in deliberate and conscious violation of constitutional rights should be excluded except in "extraordinary excusing circumstances" (which he preferred to leave unspecified), excused as "a purely accidental and unintentional infringement of the Constitution" the violation complained of in that case—see p.162 of the report. See also *The People v Madden* [1977] I.R. 336 at p.346 where a "factor such as inadvertence" was recognised as capable of being one of the extraordinary excusing circumstances" envisaged in *O'Brien's Case*. In my opinion, it is the violation of the person's constitutional rights: and not the particular act complained of, that has to be deliberate and conscious for the purpose of ruling out a statement. In the present case, I would rank the superintendent's well-founded anxiety for the life of Mary as an example of an extraordinary excusing circumstance for keeping the appellant in custody for what otherwise would have been an impermissibly long period. ...

The circumstances which will make a statement inadmissible for lack of voluntariness are so varied that it would be impossible to enumerate or categorise them fully. It is sufficient to say that the decided cases show that a statement will be excluded as being involuntary if it was wrung from its maker by physical or psychological pressures, by threats or promises made by persons in authority, by the use of drugs, hypnosis intoxicating drink, by prolonged interrogation or excessive questioning or by any one of a diversity of methods which have in common the result or the risk that what is tendered as a voluntary statement is not the natural emanation of a rational intellect and a free will. As to the present case, there is no question but that the questioned statements were made voluntarily.

Secondly, even if a statement is held to have been voluntarily obtained in the sense indicated, it may nevertheless be inadmissible for another reason. Because our system of law is accusatorial and not inquisitorial, and because (as has been stated in a number of decisions of this Court) our Constitution postulates the observance of basic or fundamental fairness of procedures, the judge presiding at a criminal trial should be astute to see that, although a statement may be technically voluntary, it should nevertheless be excluded if by reason of the manner or of the circumstances in which it was obtained, it falls below the required standards of fairness. The reason for exclusion here is not so much the risk of an erroneous conviction as the recognition that the minimum of essential standards must be observed in the administration of justice. Whether the objection to the statement be on constitutional or other grounds, the crucial test is whether it was obtained in compliance with basic or fundamental fairness, and the trial judge will have a discretion to exclude it "where it appears to him that public policy, based on a balancing of public interests, requires such exclusion"—*per* Kingsmill Moore J. at p.161 of the report of *O'Brien's Case*. This is a fairer and more workable test than a consideration of whether the questioned statement complies with specific constitutional provisions, because most of the criminal trials in this State are held in courts (the District Court, the Circuit Court and the Special Criminal Court) which, in terms of their judicial personnel, judicial experience and vested jurisdiction, are not designed for constitutional interpretation or for the balancing of constitutional rights, or for the preferment of one invoked constitutional provision over another.

The test of basic fairness, based on a due consideration of the rights of the accused coupled with the requirements, in the interests of the common good, of the prosecution, superimposed on the need for voluntariness, has the merit of ensuring, if the judicial discretion is correctly exercised, that an accused will not be wrongly or unfairly convicted out of his own mouth.

Applying those two tests to the facts of the present case, the elucidation I have given earlier in this judgment of the circumstances in which, and the purpose for which, the questioned statements were taken shows that both those tests were satisfied. Therefore, I would dismiss this appeal.

Appendices 501

Kenny J:

I have had the advantage of reading the judgment of Mr. Justice Griffiths and am in complete agreement with it. ...

When the people enacted the Constitution of 1937, they provided (Article 40, s. 3) that the State guaranteed in its laws to respect, and, as far as practicable, by its laws to defend and vindicate the personal rights of the citizen and that the State should, in particular, by its laws protect as best it might from unjust attack and, in the case of injustice done, vindicate the life, person, good name and property rights of every citizen. I draw attention to the use of the words "the State." The obligation to implement this guarantee is imposed not on the Oireachtas only but on each branch of the State which exercises the powers of legislating, executing and giving judgment on those laws: Article 6. The word "laws" in Article 40, s. 3, is not confined to laws which have been enacted by the Oireachtas but comprehends the laws made by judges and by ministers of State when they make statutory instruments or regulations. ...

When a conflict of constitutional rights arises, it must be resolved by having regard to (a) the terms of the Constitution, (b) the ethical values which all Christians living in the State acknowledge and accept and (c) the main tenets of our system of constitutional parliamentary democracy.

When passing judgment on the actions of the Garda Síochána, we must remember that they have to make many immediate decisions and cannot possibly get a court decision to guide them. Our function is to decide whether the choice they made in the priority of constitutional or legal rights was correct. I have no doubt that the decision made by Detective Superintendent Reynolds to regard Mary's right to life as ranking higher than the appellant's right to personal liberty for three days was the correct one. The detention of the appellant by the gardaí until Wednesday the 29th September, 1976, when he was brought before the District Court, was lawful in my opinion.

It follows that the statements and admissions made by him during the period from 10.30 a.m. on the 27th September until Wednesday the 29th September, 1976, were admissible in evidence. It was not a question of the end justifying the means—a doctrine which most ethical teachers since Aristotle have repudiated. It was a question of vindicating a higher ranking constitutional right.

26. People (D.P.P.) v McNally and Breathnach

Court of Criminal Appeal, February 16, 1981
(1981) 2 Frewen 43 at 44, 48–51, 53–56

Finlay P:

... The facts established without contradiction before the trial Court indicated that on the early morning of 31st March, 1976, a number of armed persons stopped a train carrying mail at Palmerstown, Co. Dublin; boarded it and under threat of shooting the staff and employees on the train, stole from it a number of mailbags. In general, the evidence indicated an extremely carefully prepared crime in which a number of persons were involved and which was carried out as a result of careful planning. ...

The grounds on which this Court decided that the conviction of the applicant Bernard McNally should be set aside, and that he should be released (as indicated in the ruling), were connected with the admission by the Court of trial of the alleged verbal admissions of the applicant. ...

At the time of the first of these alleged verbal admissions the applicant had been in custody for a continuous period of approximately 44 hours, and during the entire of the questioning and interviewing which he had undergone up to that time, had consistently denied involvement in the commission of the crime or any knowledge of it, and had consistently given an account of his movements which was exculpatory.

It is clear from the transcript of evidence that the applicant gave a very different account of the alleged making of these statements from that which is briefly summarised in this Judgment, and in particular made lengthy and detailed allegations of ill-treatment, physical cruelty and threatening behaviour. ...

This Court ... accepts and adopts the decision of the Court of Criminal Appeal in the *People v Farrell* [1978] I.R. 13 with regard to the effect and consequence of the Judges' Rules and of a breach of them. At page 21 in the judgment of the Court read by the Chief Justice it is stated as follows:

> "The Judges' Rules are not rules of law. They are rules for the guidance of persons taking statements. However, they have stood up to the test of time and will be departed from at peril. In very rare cases such as *R. v Mills and Lemon* [1947] K.B. 297 a statement taken in breach may be admitted in evidence but in very exceptional circumstances. Where, however, there is a breach of the Judges' Rules, such as a failure to make a written record of the alleged confession or a failure to invite the accused to accept or reject the statements, each of such breaches calls for an adequate explanation. The breaches and the explanations (if any) together with the entire circumstances of the case are matters to be taken into consideration by the trial Judge before exercising his judicial discretion as to whether or not he will admit such statement in evidence." ...

... [T]his Court is not satisfied that the Court of trial was correct in law in admitting these verbal statements into evidence. No explanation other than a previous course of conduct was tendered to the trial Court for the failure of the two Garda witnesses directly concerned to make a note of the alleged verbal admissions made by the applicant and to afford to him an opportunity for correcting, amending or rejecting them. Bearing in mind that each of these alleged verbal admissions occurred in what are usually described as the small hours of the morning after very lengthy periods of questioning and interview extending over 44 hours interrupted by one night's sleep only, this Court is not satisfied that there were any circumstances proved before the Court of trial which would justify the exercise of its discretion in favour of admitting in evidence these verbal statements notwithstanding the undoubted breach of the Judges' Rules. Since at the trial there was no other evidence connecting this applicant with the commission of the crime which had occurred this Court was satisfied that the conviction should be set aside and the applicant released.

The grounds on which the Court has decided and ruled that the conviction of the applicant Breathnach should be set aside are those contained at Grounds Nos. 8, 9, 10, 11 and 12 of the Grounds of Appeal of this applicant as originally furnished. ...

This Court accepts with approval the description of oppressive questioning given by Lord McDermott in an address to the Bentham Club and adopted by the Criminal Division of the Court of Appeal in England in *R. v Prager* [1972] 56 Cr. App. R. 151. In that address Lord McDermott described it as "questioning which by its nature, duration or other attendant circumstances (including the fact of custody) excites hopes (such as the hope of release) or fears, or so affects the mind of the subject that his will crumbles and he speaks when otherwise he would have stayed silent".

This Court would further adopt with approval the definition of oppression in the context of questioning contained in the judgment of Sachs J. in *R. v Priestley* [1967] 51 Cr. App. R. 1 where he defined it as follows:

> "[T]o my mind, this word in the context of the principles under consideration imports something which tends to sap, and has sapped, that free will which must exist before a confession is voluntary. ..."

Applying these standards and principles to the evidence in the case of this applicant the following factors or circumstances become relevant:

(a) the unexplained change of attitude of this applicant to questioning concerning the crime after a period of forty hours in custody;

(b) the fact that the questioning which immediately preceded the making of the statement took place not in a regular or normal room appropriate to the interview of a suspected person by a policeman but rather in what must be considered as the possibly menacing environment of an underground passage-way in a Garda Station;

(c) the fact that the making of the alleged voluntary statement occurred at the early hours of the morning when the applicant had been disturbed from a night's sleep; and

(d) the fact that, notwithstanding the expressed desire on the occasion of this detention of the applicant to have the advice and assistance of a solicitor and his consistent refusal on a previous occasion to be questioned without that assistance and advice, no solicitor had been obtained for him before the questioning and the making of the alleged voluntary statements occurred. ...

Working on the basis that all the primary findings of fact made by the Court of trial are correct or beyond the reach of correction in this Court, we are not satisfied beyond reasonable doubt, nor do we think that the Court of trial was entitled to be satisfied beyond reasonable doubt, under either head of the test laid down by the Supreme Court in *Shaw's Case*, that the statements made by this applicant were voluntarily made or that the manner in which they were made satisfied the basic requirements of fairness. ...

The combination of these and other factors is such that, in the opinion of this Court, it would not be open to the Court of trial to conclude, beyond a reasonable doubt, that the statements were voluntary in the legally accepted meaning of that word, or even if they were, that the circumstantial context in which they were made passes the test of basic fairness. The statements, therefore, should not have been admitted in evidence. Without them, there was not enough evidence to connect this applicant with the crime. This Court, for this reason, treated the application for leave to appeal as the hearing of the appeal, allowed the appeal against both conviction and sentence and ordered the release of this applicant. ...

27. People (D.P.P.) v Lynch
Supreme Court, February 19, 1981
[1982] I.R. 64 at 74–79

O'Higgins C.J:

... I have come to the conclusion that the learned trial judge was incorrect in the decision he came to and in the manner in which he exercised his discretion. It is not open to this Court to question his findings of fact on the allegations made by the appellant as to not being allowed to go home, or as to being ill-treated. The judge was entitled to prefer the evidence from the various garda officers to the effect that all these allegations were untrue. Nevertheless, so obtrusive and dominating a feature of this interrogation was its length, that such should not have been ignored or overlooked. The fact that for almost 22 hours the appellant was subjected to sustained questioning, that he never had the opportunity of communicating with his family or friends, and that he never was permitted to rest or sleep until he made an admission of guilt, all amount to such circumstances of harassment and oppression as to make it unjust and unfair to admit in evidence anything he said. The trial judge exercised his discretion to admit these statements on the basis that the allegations made by the appellant were untrue. In so doing, he ignored the features of oppression, harassment and fatigue which I have mentioned and which should have caused the statements, even if *prima facie* voluntary, to be excluded. For this reason I think his discretion was exercised on a wrong basis and, accordingly, I concluded that the statements should not have been admitted, that the appeal should be allowed and that the conviction of the appellant should be quashed. ...

In view ... of the wide range of argument advanced, it seems to me that something should be said of a general nature with regard to the admissibility of evidence which is alleged to have been obtained irregularly in the course of a garda investigation, such as took place in this case. In the first place it should be accepted that such an investigation is conducted on behalf of the State and that there is a direct public interest in its success. Equally important, however, is the fact that every such investigation takes place in a democratic State which is subject to the Constitution and to the laws which operate thereunder. There is always a public concern that criminals should be brought to justice and a public interest that the rights of the individual citizen, which the Constitution guarantees, will be protected.

Most garda investigations, certainly of major crimes, involve a painstaking search for clues, the following up of leads, the questioning of many people who may be able to add to the information available and so help in bringing those responsible to justice. Often in such investigations the Gardaí, for one reason or another, do not get the co-operation and assistance which they seek and require. Moreover, they are frequently confronted with an organised conspiracy to shield the culprit, to hamper the investigation and generally to defeat the ends of justice. In so far as they are faced with such problems and have to overcome such difficulties, they are entitled to the sympathy and understanding of both the general body of the public and of judges who preside at subsequent trials. Sympathy for, and understanding of, difficulties is one thing: to excuse irregular means which have been adopted because of those difficulties, in order to secure evidence at a trial, is quite another. I use the word "irregular" deliberately in order to comprehend both methods or means which under our legal system are illegal in the sense that they offend the ordinary common or statute law and also such methods or means which offend and violate the Constitution.

In countries which do not possess a written constitution the word "illegal" is sufficiently wide to cover both technical and minor breaches of the common law and serious and deliberate interferences with the accepted civil rights of citizens. In such countries it is possible to lay down a general policy which can be applied to all situations in which illegality of any kind is used in the securing of evidence. ...

Where, however, there exists a written constitution which guarantees rights to citizens and prohibits specified acts and conduct in violation of such rights, quite different considerations must apply. In countries governed by a written constitution one may expect the judges, by their oath and office, to be bound to uphold the constitution and its provisions and to do so on all occasions in the courts in which they preside. In the United States the Federal Supreme Court has established in a series of decisions a rule strictly excluding evidence obtained in breach of constitutional provisions: *Weeks v United States* (1914) 232 U.S. 383; *Mapp v Ohio* (1961) 367 U.S. 643 and *Terry v Ohio* (1968) 392 U.S. 1. In the last-mentioned case Warren C.J. explained the reason at page 13 of the report in the following words:

"Courts which sit under our Constitution cannot and will not be made party to lawless invasions of the constitutional rights of citizens by permitting unhindered governmental use of the fruits of such invasions. Thus in our system evidentiary rulings provide the context in which the judicial process of inclusion and exclusion approves some conduct as comporting with constitutional guarantees and disapproves other actions by state agents. A ruling admitting evidence in a criminal trial, we recognize, has the necessary effect of legitimizing the conduct which produced the evidence, while an application of the exclusionary rule withholds the constitutional imprimatur."

It was exactly this question which was considered by this Court under certificate from the Court of Criminal Appeal in *The People (Attorney General) v O'Brien* [1965] I.R. 142. In that case the judgment of Kingsmill Moore J. (which had the approval, in one of two respects, of a majority of the Court, and, in the other, of the entire Court) has always been regarded as laying down two clear principles to be applied in considering the admission of evidence irregularly obtained. The first of these principles is that evidence obtained as result a deliberate and conscious violation of the Constitution should be excluded unless there is some extraordinary excusing circumstance which warrants its admission. The second principle is that, in relation to evidence obtained by illegal means which fall short of a violation of constitutional rights the presiding judge has a discretion to exclude such evidence where it appears to him that public policy, based on a balancing of public interest, requires such exclusion. Since 1965 these principles have been applied in a large number of cases, of which I will only mention the most recent: *The People v Madden* [1977] I.R. 336, *The People v O'Loughlin* [1979] I.R. 85 and *The People v Walsh* [1980] I.R. 294.

Recently, however, in the course of his judgment in *The People v Shaw* [1982] I.R. 1, Mr. Justice Griffin questioned the application of the *ratio decidendi* of *O'Brien's Case* to statements of an inculpatory nature made by an accused. He pointed out, as was the fact, that the disputed evidence in *O'Brien's Case* consisted of property found in premises which had been entered without a lawful warrant. He contrasted such "real evidence" with the evidence of a statement which is, in his words, "evidence emitted by, or extracted from, the accused and, as such, requires to be tested for admissibility primarily by the manner in which the accused was led, or came, to produce a confessional or inculpatory statement which the prosecution wishes to adduce in evidence against him." He then suggested that the proper and appropriate test as to the admissibility of such statements, whether the objection be on constitutional or other grounds, should be whether they were obtained in compliance with basic or fundamental fairness and that, in this respect, the trial judge should have a discretion to exclude where the public interest requires such exclusion. I fear that I cannot agree with these views, either in relation to the ambit of the decision in *O'Brien's Case* or in relation to the generality of the test which he suggests for the admission or exclusion of statements. I do not think that any such test could ever be applied in circumstances which involve a deliberate and conscious breach of constitutional rights. ...

It is true that the admission of incriminating statements as such was not considered, except as coming within the general category of evidence obtained by irregular means. The reason for this is easy to see in that such statements generally fall to be excluded on the grounds that they are not voluntary. The Court was divided as to the admissibility of evidence obtained by illegal, as opposed to unconstitutional, means; but it was unanimous "that where evidence has been obtained by the State or its agents as a result of a deliberate and conscious violation of the constitutional (as opposed to the common law) rights of an accused person it should be excluded save where there are 'extraordinary excusing circumstances' ..." *per* Kingsmill Moore J. at p.162 of the report. In relation to the admissibility of the particular evidence in that case, which was obtained both illegally and in breach of the Constitution, Kingsmill Moore J. added: "This case is not one of deliberate and conscious violation, but of a purely accidental and unintentional infringement of the Constitution. ..."

Once the Constitution has been violated for the purpose of securing a confession, the fruits of that violation must be excluded from evidence on that ground alone. Nor can it be said that the matter can safely be left to a decision on fairness or the voluntary nature of the statement. In *The People v Madden* the statement was held to be voluntary at the trial, although it was secured by a violation of constitutional rights. It could be that the deprivation of liberty, contrary to the express provisions of the Constitution, would in itself lead to a voluntary confession of guilt by an accused. If such a confession were ever admitted in evidence because it was voluntary or because it was fairly taken, or for any other reason then, in the words of Warren C.J., the courts would "be made party to lawless invasions of the constitutional rights of citizens by permitting unhindered governmental use of the fruits of such invasions." I cannot accept that such a result could ever be permissible under the Constitution.

One further matter deserves comment. In this case, apart from the defence that the incriminating statements were involuntary or obtained unfairly, it was also part of the defence that these had been secured in breach of the appellant's constitutional rights. This latter issue seemed to depend on whether, as the gardaí swore, the appellant had remained in the garda station of his own free will and had never asked to go home or to be put in touch with his wife, or whether (as he swore) he was detained against his will and, although requesting to be allowed to leave, was not permitted to go. The trial judge disbelieved the appellant and, therefore, did not consider further any question of illegal detention or breach of constitutional rights. In my view, this fact alone rendered this trial unsatisfactory. This conflict of evidence and the true facts, ought to have been decided by the jury. On the jury's finding as to where the truth lay, the trial judge could decide whether or not there had been an illegal detention. In my view, the jury, either by a specific question or by an appropriate direction ought to have been asked to decide, as a question of fact material to the defence, whether the appellant's evidence that he had been held against his wishes was or was not true.

28. R. v. Galbraith

Court of Appeal, May 19, 1981
[1981] 2 All E.R. 1060 at 1061–1062

Lord Lane C.J:

.... At the close of the Crown's evidence, a submission was made by counsel for the applicant that there was no case for the applicant to answer. The judge rejected that submission. The principal ground of appeal to this court is that he was wrong in so doing. ...

There are two schools of thought: (1) that the judge should stop the case if, in his view, it would be unsafe (alternatively unsafe or unsatisfactory) for the jury to convict; (2) that he should do so only if there is no evidence on which a jury properly directly could properly convict. Although in many cases the question is one of semantics, and though in many cases each test would produce the same result, this is not necessarily so. A balance has to be struck between on the one hand a usurpation by the judge of the jury's functions and on the other the danger of an unjust conviction. ...

There is ... a ... solid reason for doubting the wisdom of [the first] test. If a judge is obliged to consider whether a conviction would be 'unsafe' or 'unsatisfactory', he can scarcely be blamed if he applies his views as to the weight to be given to the Crown's evidence and as to the truthfulness of their witnesses and so on. That is what Lord Widgery C.J. said in *R. v Barker* (1977) 65 Cr. App. R. 287 at 288 was clearly not permissible:

> "... even if the judge had taken the view that the evidence could not support a conviction because of the inconsistencies, he should nevertheless have left the matter to the jury. It cannot be too clearly stated that the judge's obligation to stop the case is an obligation which is concerned primarily with those cases where the necessary minimum evidence to establish the facts of the crime has not been called. It is not the judge's job to weigh the evidence, decide who is telling the truth, and to stop the case merely because he thinks the witness is lying. To do that is to usurp the function of the jury ..." (Our emphasis) ...

How then should the judge approach a submission of 'no case'? (1) If there is no evidence that the crime alleged has been committed by the defendant, there is no difficulty. The judge will of course stop the case. (2) The difficulty arises where there is some evidence but it is of a tenuous character, for example because of inherent weakness or vagueness or because it is inconsistent with other evidence. (a) Where the judge comes to the conclusion that the Crown's evidence, taken at its highest, is such that a jury properly directed could not properly convict on it, it is his duty, on a submission being made, to stop the case. (b) Where however the Crown's evidence is such that its strength or weakness depends on the view to be taken of a witness's reliability, or other matters which are generally speaking within the province of the jury and where on one possible view of the facts there is evidence on which a jury could properly come to the conclusion that the defendant is guilty, then the judge should allow the matter to be tried by the jury. It follows that we think the second of the two schools of thought is to be preferred.

There will of course, as always in this branch of the law, be borderline cases. They can safely be left to the discretion of the judge. ...

29. People (D.P.P.) v Conroy

Supreme Court, July 31, 1986
[1986] I.R. 460 at 486–488, 490–491, 493, 472, 480–481

Henchy J:

... The suggestion ... that the contested issues of fact governing the admission or exclusion of an inculpatory statement or other incriminating evidence should be decided by the jury rather than by the judge sitting without the jury, is novel and, so far as can be ascertained, is not supported by either statutory or judicial authority. Indeed, it would seem to be in conflict with all judicial authority in this jurisdiction since *The State v Treanor* [1924] 2 I.R. 193. It is therefore necessary to examine its implications from the point of view of principle and practice. The principle which appears to underlie the change proposed in *The People v Lynch* [1982] I.R. 64 is that all issues of fact must be decided by the jury rather than by the judge. That, of course, is the general principle, but the well-established exceptions to it make the invocation of the principle inappropriate for present purposes. I find the law on the matter stated clearly and correctly in Salmond, *Jurisprudence*, 11th ed. (ed. Glanville Williams), p. 68:

> "The general rule is that questions of law ... are for the judge, but that questions of fact (that is to say, all other questions) are for the jury. This rule, however, is subject to numerous and important exceptions. ... The interpretation of a document, for example, may be, and very often is, a pure question of fact and nevertheless falls within the province of a judge. So the question of reasonable probable cause for a prosecution—which arises in actions for malicious prosecution—is one of fact and yet one for the judge himself. So it is the duty of the judge to decide whether there is any sufficient evidence to justify a verdict for the plaintiff; and if he decides that there is not, the case is withdrawn from the jury altogether; yet this is a mere matter of fact, undetermined by any authoritative rule of law. By an illogical though convenient usage of speech, any question which is thus within the province of the judge instead of the jury is called a question of law, even though it may be in the proper sense a pure question of fact. It is called a question of law because it is committed to and answered by the authority which normally answers questions of law only."

To the list of exceptions there set out must be added all questions of admissibility of evidence, which are reserved exclusively for the judge even though such questions may involve, or rest entirely on findings of fact. The commonest example is an incriminating statement which the defence contends should be held inadmissible for lack of voluntariness. The standard procedure for dealing with that situation is for the judge to send out the jury and to hold a trial-within-the-trial, known as the *voir dire*. Both prosecution and defence may call evidence and the matter may be pursued with a thoroughness and an openness which might not be proper—indeed might prejudice the defence or otherwise invalidate the trial—if the jury were present. If the judge is not satisfied beyond a reasonable doubt that the questioned statement was voluntary, he will exclude it. If he is satisfied beyond a reasonable doubt that it was voluntary, he will rule it to be admissible. The jury will then be recalled to the court and the prosecution will give evidence of the making of the statement. However, the defence will then be free, so far as is thought prudent, to re-agitate before the jury, by way of cross-examination, the matters on which it had relied on earlier in the absence of the jury as rendering the statement inadmissible. Indeed it has been held that where an unrepresented accused unsuccessfully used the *voir dire* to cross-examine the police officer who took a confessional statement from him, with a view to having it ruled out as not being voluntary, and where the judge did not inform the accused that he could again cross-examine the police officer in the presence of the jury, the conviction was set aside as unsatisfactory and a new trial ordered: The *People v Ainscough* [1960] I.R. 136. A similar statement of the law by the Privy Council is to be found in *R. v Chan Wei Keung* [1967] 2 A.C. 160, where it was pointedly added that it is not for the trial judge who admits a statement as voluntary to tell the jury that they too must be satisfied beyond a reasonable doubt that it was voluntary. The function of the jury in such circumstances would appear to be to decide whether in all the circumstances the statement is worthy of being relied on by them. It is, in my opinion, a well-entrenched principle of trial by jury that in circumstances such as arose in this case it is for the judge, and for the judge alone, to rule on the admissibility of the statements.

Principle apart, the change in the respective functions of judge and jury suggested in *The People v Lynch* would be capable of producing grave practical problems. If it were mandatory that issues such as whether a statement was voluntary, whether a detention was lawful, or whether there was a conscious and deliberate violation of constitutional rights, be tried by the jury, there might be grave prejudicial consequences for the accused. When admissibility on such grounds is decided by the judge in the absence of the jury the defence is able to question or give evidence to rebut the prosecution case on the matter, with freedom from the risk of prejudicing the jury. Cross-examination of prosecution witnesses may be pursued in the course of the *voir dire* along lines which would frequently be incompatible with the prudent conduct of the defence in the presence of the jury. For example, questions may be put to prosecution witnesses which, if put in the presence of the jury, would disclose previous convictions or allow the accused's character to be put in evidence by the prosecution. To conduct the trial-within-the-trial in the presence of the jury would frequently be so restrictive of the defence and so capable of undue prejudice as to be incompatible with a fair trial. It does not come as a surprise, therefore, to learn that the United States Supreme Court has held that such a mode of trial is incompatible with due process: *Jackson v Denno* (1964) 378 U.S. 368. The Court there ruled that the determination of admissibility (in that case voluntariness) must be "in a proceeding separate and apart from the body trying guilt or innocence."

Another practical defect in a trial-within-the-trial in the presence of the jury is that it would frequently make the jury trying the particular issue governing admissibility unfit to try the general issue of guilt or innocence.

This would be particularly so where the jury's special verdict ruled out the questioned statement and there was other evidence which might justify a conviction. A jury thus informed of the circumstances and contents of the rejected statement would lack the characteristics of an impartial jury for the trial of the issue of guilt or innocence. A verdict of guilty thus resulting could not be allowed on appeal to stand. The alternative to such a mistrial would be, after the trial-within-the-trial was over, to try the issue of guilt or innocence before another jury. This, however, would be inconsistent with the unitary and unbroken trial with a jury which is necessarily postulated by the constitutional right to trial with a jury: see *The People v McGlynn* [1967] I.R. 232. What Article 38, s. 5 of the Constitution guarantees is a single trial with a jury, not a succession of trials.

All things considered, I am of the opinion that the trial-within-the-trial of an issue of or involving admissibility of evidence cannot be had before the jury. It is for the judge, and the judge alone, to hear and determine the question of the admissibility of a questioned statement of an incriminating nature, including the factual background of its making. But it is also for the judge, when at the end of the case he addresses the jury, to direct their attention to the circumstances of the questioned statement and to tell them that it is for them to decide, having regard to all the evidence, what probative value, if any, they should give to the statement. ...

Griffin J:

... Prior to the decision in *The People v Lynch* [1982] I.R. 64, the universal procedure in this jurisdiction had been that the judge alone decided whether the prosecution had proved beyond reasonable doubt whether the inculpatory statement alleged to have been made by the accused was voluntary or had not been obtained in deliberate and conscious breach of the constitutional rights of the accused. For this purpose, a trial-within-the-trial (the *voir dire*) took place in the absence of the jury. If the statement survived that test, it was admissible in evidence and was put before the jury as part of the evidence for the prosecution, the truth of the statement being a crucial question for the jury. It was then the right of counsel for the defence to cross-examine again, in the presence of the jury, the witnesses who had given evidence in their absence, in the hope of persuading the jury that the statement had been improperly obtained and was therefore unreliable. It was the function of the jury (after proper direction in that behalf by the trial judge) to give to the statement such weight and value as in all the circumstances of the particular case they thought it deserved.

This procedure of a trial-within-the-trial was stated by the Court of Criminal Appeal to be the one which should thereafter be adapted in confession cases in *The State v Treanor* [1924] 2 I.R. 193—the first reported decision of the Court of Criminal Appeal within a matter of months of the establishment of our courts under the Courts of Justice Act. 1924. In the course of delivering the judgment of the Court in that case, FitzGibbon J. said at p.208:

"A confession made to any person under the influence of a promise or threat held out by a person in authority, calculated to induce the confession, is inadmissible, unless it be clearly proved to the satisfaction of the judge, whose duty it is to decide the question, that the promise or threat did not operate upon the mind of the accused, and that the confession was voluntary notwithstanding, and that the accused was not influenced to make it by the previous promise or threat.

The Court is further of opinion that if evidence is tendered to prove the inadmissibility of evidence *prima facie* admissible, it is the duty of the judge to receive it, and to decide the question of admissibility, before the evidence is given in the hearing of the jury. ...

This procedure may be inconvenient ... but it is better that some inconvenience should be endured rather than that evidence should be given in the hearing of the jury which might, and probably would, affect their decision, no matter how emphatically they may be exhorted to expunge it from their recollections. ..."

Since 1924, there have been a great number of cases in which the procedure laid down in the *Treanor Case* was followed, and also a great number of cases in which that procedure was accepted by the Court of Criminal Appeal and by this Court as being the correct procedure, and in which it was never questioned until the *Lynch Case*. ...

If and when it is proposed to change a procedure which has been universally approved and adopted in our courts for upwards of almost sixty years, and which is in line with one almost universally approved and adopted in most democratic countries of the western world, in my opinion there should be compelling reasons for making the proposed change. The change in procedure proposed in *The People v Lynch* was a fundamental change in the procedure to be adopted on the trial of criminal cases on indictment. In my opinion, there are no such compelling reasons for change in the case of the procedures in question in this case. On the contrary, there are, as the Chief Justice and Mr. Justice Henchy have emphasised in their judgments, compelling reasons in the interests of the accused and of justice generally, why the procedures should not be changed. ...

Finlay C.J. (Hederman J. concurring):

... I am ... satisfied that the constitutional right to a trial in due course of law as interpreted by this Court would involve as a fundamental matter the right to trial with a jury from whose knowledge there is excluded any evidence of guilt which is inadmissible at law. For this reason I have the greatest possible difficulty in conceiving circumstances under which, with justice, it would be possible to leave to a jury at the conclusion of the case evidence the admissibility of which is being challenged, simply giving to them a direction on the issue of fact which is involved and a warning that if they should resolve that issue in favour of the accused they should ignore the incriminating evidence which they had heard. Experience as a judge indicates that even as a trained lawyer there is a very significant difficulty in excluding from one's mind incriminating evidence on the trial of a criminal case which is inadmissible. In my view, it would be an unreal task to seek to impose on a jury of lay persons, and the risk of real injustice flowing from it would be great. ...

Walsh J. (dissenting):

... The constitutional function of the jury is to decide questions of fact. In the type of criminal case in which the success of the whole prosecution depends upon the admissibility of a statement by an accused person (cases of which seem to have become more frequent in recent years) it would seem incongruous if the most vital facts of the case, namely those which will govern the admissibility of the evidence without which the prosecution must fail, should be taken away from the jury. Admittedly until the *Lynch Case* [1982] I.R. 64 it was always the practice for the trial judge alone to decide these matters but the whole question of evidence obtained by unconstitutional methods only surfaced with *The People v O'Brien* [1965] I.R. 142. The law as expounded in the *Lynch Case* was to adapt to the new situation, as indeed the law did when the Judges' Rules were formulated and various other rules of evidence dealing with corroboration etc. The whole purpose of judge made rules is to adapt the law to changing conditions. The purpose of the rule enunciated in the *Lynch Case* was to ensure that the essential facts in a case are to be decided by the tribunal whose exclusive function it is to decide facts, namely, the jury. In the case of a court of a single judge or several judges which act without a jury, both functions, namely, the finding of fact and the legal ruling based upon the resolution of the issue of facts, must be made by the same tribunal, which thus makes for a much more difficult situation than when the task is divided between the judge and the jury. ...

If the procedure suggested in the *Lynch Case*, namely to have a special issue tried by the jury, is adopted then that is the end of that particular matter and it does not have to be repeated. If the judge chooses himself to decide the matter in the first instance and in the result to admit the contested statement, he must then be extremely careful in his final directions to the jury who will then have before them the incriminating statement. In a matter such as the present one he would have to explain it to them very carefully and put a special question or questions to enable the jury to find as a question of fact whether at the time when that statement was made the accused person was being detained in circumstances which the judge would have already explained to them would be illegal. If they so find they must therefore ignore the statement and try to put out of their minds any prejudicial effect it may have had upon them. It would seem to me to be a much easier course in most cases to get the jury to decide this during the case without the statement being put before them, and after which the judge could then make his ruling in law as to admissibility. It has also been urged that in some cases it would be difficult if not impossible to have the circumstances of the taking of statements investigated without reference to the contents of it, and to do that in the presence of a jury might be highly prejudicial to the accused. That could well be, but in my view not so prejudicial as letting the jury retire finally with the same prejudice without a chance of any further instructions. Furthermore it leaves out of account the fact that the accused person can always waive the procedure of having the matter decided in the first instance by a jury if he is of opinion that the effect might be prejudicial. There may indeed be very many cases where the accused would prefer it to be done in the presence of a jury. If in such circumstances, the judge rules evidence inadmissible upon the jury's findings, then he is in a much better position to emphasise to the jury that from that moment and for the rest of the trial they are to have no regard whatever to the statement. ...

30. Byrne v Grey

High Court, October 9, 1987
[1988] I.R. 31 at 38-41

Hamilton P.:

... It is quite clear from a consideration of the terms of s. 26 of the Misuse of Drugs Act, 1984, that a search warrant issued in accordance with the provisions of s. 26, sub-s. 1 of the Misuse of Drugs Act, 1977, confers considerable powers on members of the Garda Síochána.

It authorises them within one month of the date of issue of the warrant, to enter (if need be by force) the premises or other lands named in the warrant; to search such premises or other land and any persons found therein; to examine any substance, article or other thing found thereon or therein; to inspect any book, record or other document found thereon; and if there is reasonable ground for suspecting that an offence is being or has been committed under this Act in relation to a substance, article or other thing found on such premises or other land or that documents so found are documents mentioned in sub-s. (1)(b) of s. 26 or is a record or other document which the member has reasonable cause to believe to be a document which may be required as evidence in proceedings for an offence under the Act, to seize and detain the substance, article, document or other thing as the case may be and further gives them authority to arrest without warrant any person or persons found on such premises or other land for the purpose of searching him or them and so arrest any such person and keep him or them as may be appropriate under arrest until such time as such of the powers of search for examination as he wishes to exercise pursuant to the warrant have been exercised by him.

These powers encroach on the liberty of the citizen and the inviolability of his dwelling as guaranteed by the Constitution and the courts should construe a statute which authorises such encroachment so that it encroaches on such rights no more than the statute allows, expressly or by necessary implication.

The statute authorising such encroachment provides at s. 26 thereof that a justice of the District Court or a peace commissioner must be satisfied by information on oath of a member of the Garda Síochána that there is reasonable ground for the suspicion before he is entitled to issue the search warrant I mentioned in the Act as amended.

In construing this section, a court ought, in the words of Lord Diplock in the course of his judgment in *Reg. v I.R.C., Ex p. Rossminister Ltd.* [1980] A.C. 952, at p.1008:

"... to remind itself, if reminder should be necessary, that entering a man's house or office, searching it and seizing his goods against his will are tortious acts against which he is entitled to the protection of the court unless the acts can be justified either at common law or under some statutory authority. So if the statutory words relied on as authorising the acts are ambiguous or obscure a construction should be placed upon them that is least restrictive of individual rights which would otherwise enjoy the protection of the common law. But judges in performing their constitutional function of expounding what words used by Parliament in legislation mean, must not be over-zealous to search for ambiguities or obscurities in words which on the face of them are plain, simply because the members of the court are out of sympathy with the policy to which the Act appears to give effect."

In this country, the individual rights referred to as enjoying the protection of the common law also enjoy the protection of the Constitution.

It is quite clear that the warrant impugned in this application was issued by the first respondent, and is so stated to have been issued, pursuant to s. 26 of the Misuse of Drugs Acts, 1977 and 1984.

The warrant states that the Peace Commissioner was satisfied by the information on oath of Detective Garda Michael Doyle that there was reasonable ground for suspecting that a plant of the genus cannabis was being cultivated contrary to s. 17 of the Misuse of Drugs Acts, 1977 and 1984, on the premises at 50, White Brook Park, Tallaght in the City of Dublin.

Section 26 makes it a condition precedent to the issue of the warrant that the District Justice or peace commissioner should himself be satisfied by information on oath that facts exist which constitute reasonable ground for suspecting that an offence has been or is being committed.

The information sworn in this case by Det. Garda Michael Doyle merely stated as follows:

"I am a member of the Garda Síochána and I have reasonable grounds for suspecting that a plant of the genus cannabis is being cultivated contrary to s.17 of the Misuse of Drugs Act, 1977 and 1984, on or in the premises or other land at 50, White Brook Park, Tallaght, Dublin 24."

In the course of his judgment in *Reg. v I.R.C., Ex p. Rossminister* [1980] A.C. 957 Lord Salmon states at p.1019 of the report that:

"Section 20 C makes a wide inroad into the citizen's basic human rights, the right to privacy in his own home and business premises and the right to keep what belongs to him. It allows the Inland Revenue the power to force its way into a man's home or offices and deprive him of his private papers and books. In my view, it provides only one real safeguard against an abuse of power. That safeguard is not that the Inland Revenue is satisfied that there is reasonable ground for suspecting that an offence involving fraud in relation to tax has been committed, but that the judge who issues the search warrant is so satisfied after he has been told on oath by the Inland Revenue full details of the facts which it has discovered. That is why I am inclined to the view that it is implicit in section 20 C that a search warrant signed by the judge should state that he is so satisfied, i.e., that the warrant should always give the reason for its issue. In any event, I hope that in the future the practice will always be that such warrants state plainly that the judge who signed them is so satisfied.

I am however, convinced that search warrants like the present are invalid because they recite as the reason for their issue only that an officer of the Inland Revenue has stated on oath that there is reasonable ground for suspecting that an offence involving fraud in relation to tax has been committed. If the judge gives that as his reason for issuing the warrant, it seems to me to follow that his reason for issuing it cannot be that he is so satisfied by the information given to him on oath by an officer of the Inland Revenue of the detailed facts which the officer has ascertained; but that the judge's reason for issuing the warrant was because the officer had stated on oath that there is reasonable ground to suspect, etc."

In my view, these words apply with equal force to the issue of search warrants pursuant to the provisions of s. 26 of the Misuse of Drugs Act, 1977.

It is quite clear that the District Justice or peace commissioner issuing the warrant must himself be satisfied that there is reasonable ground for suspicion. He is not entitled to rely on a mere averment by a member of the Garda Síochána that he, the member of the Garda Síochána, has reasonable grounds for suspicion. A member of the Garda Síochána seeking the issue of a warrant pursuant to the provisions of s. 26 of the Misuse of Drugs Acts, 1977 and 1984 must be in a position to so satisfy either the District Justice or the peace commissioner of the relevant facts so that the District Justice or the peace commissioner can satisfy himself in accordance with the requirements of the section. He is not entitled to rely on the suspicion of the member of the Garda Síochána applying for the warrant. ...

It is quite clear that in deciding whether or not to issue the warrant the first respondent was obliged to act judicially. As stated by Lord Justice Atkin in *Rex v Electricity Commissioners, London Electricity Joint Committee Co. (1920) Ex parte* [1924] 1 K.B. 171 at p.205:

"Wherever any body of persons having legal authority to determine questions affecting the rights of subjects, and having the duty to act judicially, act in excess of their legal authority they are subject to the controlling jurisdiction of the King's Bench Division exercised in these writs. ..."

31. People (D.P.P.) v Howley

Supreme Court, July 29, 1988
[1989] I.L.R.M. 629 at 632–635

Walsh J:

... In effect two points were made in the submissions to this Court; firstly, that the arrest under the provisions of s. 30 of the Offences Against the State Act, in respect of cattle maiming was but a colourable device to deprive the appellant of his liberty so as to provide an opportunity for the members of the Garda Síochána to question him in respect of what, it was submitted, was really uppermost in their minds, namely, a murder investigation. It was also submitted to this Court that even if the arrest was not a colourable device that after the expiration of the 24 hours the further extension granted by the Chief Superintendent had been granted by him at the request of the investigating gardaí without it being disclosed to him that they were also pursuing a murder enquiry and wished to question him in respect of that. It was submitted that the lawfulness of the detention endured during the extension period can only be established if it is shown that the predominant interest of the Garda Síochána in detaining the applicant was the investigation of the cattle maiming offence.

With regard to the first submission it appears that the arrest as such complied with all the necessary formalities as laid down by the judgment of this Court in *The People v Quillegan* [1987] I.L.R.M. 606. With regard to the offence of cattle maiming the maiming in question had occurred in February 1984 and at that time a complaint was made to the Garda Síochána in respect of that offence. The complaint was extensively investigated by the members of the gardaí and that was clearly established in evidence before the trial judge in the present case in the 'trial within the trial'. At that time suspicion rested upon the applicant and on his brother as being the persons responsible for the cattle maiming. A garda file on the matter was opened and, as shown in the evidence in the 'trial within the trial', not only did suspicion settle upon the appellant and his brother but in fact consideration was given to arresting them under s. 30 of the Offences Against the State Act in respect of that offence. This had all occurred a considerable time before the death of Lily Ormsby. There was also evidence to the effect that the investigations were re-activated and continued from time to time and that the Garda Síochána had never ceased to take an active interest in the investigation of that particular crime. When, after the death of Lily Ormsby, the appellant was arrested by the members of the Garda Síochána under s. 30 in respect of this cattle maiming offence he was, during the first 24 hours, when interrogated mostly asked about the cattle maiming episode. When the investigating gardaí asked the Chief Superintendent to grant an extension of time, they did so on the basis that they were continuing their investigation into cattle maiming and that they would require an extension of the time to continue that investigation. They did not expressly tell the Chief Superintendent that they were also asking questions about the alleged murder, and the Chief Superintendent in his evidence, while saying that he had not been so told, nevertheless agreed that he would have been surprised if they had not been asking questions about that matter during the period of detention. However he was adamant that he granted the extension of time for the pursuit of the cattle maiming offence. Therefore if the evidence of the Garda Síochána were to be accepted by the judge for the purpose of coming to a decision on the 'trial within the trial' the Chief Superintendent's action had complied with the requirements laid down by this Court in *The People v Byrne* [1987] I.R. 363.

In the event the learned trial judge came to the conclusion that the Garda Síochána while they were also investigating to a greater or lesser extent a murder suspicion they were also genuinely seeking to detect the culprit in the cattle maiming offences. In my view, there is ample evidence on which he could have come to such a conclusion and that in fact is the conclusion he came to. Therefore I am satisfied that on the evidence the judge was justified in holding that the arrest in respect of the cattle maiming charge was not in any sense a colourable device and that it was a serious, genuine investigation of what itself was quite a serious offence. In my view, the first submission in this case must fail in so far as it seeks to establish that the detention for the first 24 hours was unlawful.

With regard to the period of the extension of detention I do not see any grounds for holding that that detention was unlawful. Undoubtedly if a Chief Superintendent is deceived into making an extension of a detention order by being misled by the investigating Garda so as, in effect, to be caused to entertain a suspicion as a result of what was said to him which the gardaí making the representations did not themselves entertain then the extension would not be lawful as it would have been obtained fraudulently. However that is not the present case. It is submitted on behalf of the appellant, partly by relying upon the decision of this Court in *The People v Quillegan* [1987] I.L.R.M. 606 and the decision of *The People v Patrick Walsh* [1986] I.R. 722 and partly on some English decisions dealing with administrative law that if the predominant element in the investigation during the period of extension was concerned with the murder and not with cattle maiming the extension was unlawful.

Insofar as *The People v Quillegan* and *The People v Walsh* are concerned reliance appears to be placed on the fact that in those cases the scheduled offences in respect of which the accused in each case were arrested were comparatively minor cases and the arrest was rendered lawful only by the fact that in each case that these comparatively minor matters were inextricably mixed with the murder offence in each case.

It is true that the offences in each of those cases, which were the scheduled offences, were by comparison with the murder case comparatively trivial and if they had had no connection at all with the murder case it would certainly have lent substance to an allegation that the arrests and detention effected by virtue of s. 30 of the Offences Against the State Act 1939 at a time when the Garda Síochána were really only investigating murder offences were simply colourable devices for securing the detention of the suspected persons for the purposes of questioning about the murder.

However, the submission made is to misunderstand the decisions. What these decisions were concerned with was whether the Garda Síochána were genuinely pursuing the scheduled offences, even though they were comparatively trivial. The courts concerned were satisfied that the Garda Síochána were genuinely pursuing these offences, and that the genuineness of the pursuit was evidenced by the fact that these offences were inextricably mixed with the murder offences because it was clear in each case that whoever had been guilty of the lesser offences was quite obviously involved in the murder offences. Therefore what the cases established is that when an arrest for a scheduled offence effected under s. 30 of the Offences Against the State Act 1939, not only must the arresting garda have the necessary reasonable suspicion concerning the particular offence in question, but that in fact there must be a genuine desire and intent to pursue the investigation of that offence or suspected offence and that the arrest must not simply be a colourable device to enable a person to be detained in pursuit of some other alleged offence. The decisions do not provide any basis for asserting that where a person has been genuinely arrested for the purpose of investigating a scheduled offence, and when the arrest itself is not otherwise flawed, it must be established that there is a link between the two offences to maintain the lawfulness of the detention if in the course of the detention the detained person is questioned in respect of the other suspected offence whether it be a scheduled offence or not. It is already well established by the decision of this Court in *The People v Kelly* [1983] I.L.R.M. 271 that it is quite permissible for members of the Garda Síochána to put questions to a person in custody under s. 30 of the Act of 1939 in respect of offences other than that for which he was arrested but that of course there is no obligation whatever upon such person to answer any such questions or indeed any questions relating to the suspected offence on which he was arrested save the statutory questions permitted by s. 30 of the Act in question. It is also established that any statements or admissions made in reply to such question or during the custody are not rendered inadmissible only by reason of the fact that they were made in those circumstances. There is nothing in the decisions of any Irish courts to suggest that the lawfulness of the detention, or as in this case the extension of the detention, is dependent upon the offence or the suspected offence which is the occasion of the detention being the dominant concern of the members of the Garda Síochána when, as the occasion arises, they may wish to question such detained person in respect of an offence or offences other than that in respect of which the detention order was made.

...

Either his detention is lawful or it is not. There is no intermediate position. There can be no question of competing or predominant issues which can determine that question. If the arrest is not lawful it is not rendered so by the seriousness or importance of the offence being investigated and if it be lawful it is not rendered in anyway unlawful by the fact that the offence in respect in which the arrest is made is far less serious than some other offence also under investigation. What cannot be lawfully done is to arrest a person by virtue of the powers given in s. 30 of the Offences Against the State Act simply to make him available for the investigation of some other alleged offence. See the decision of this Court in *Trimbole v Governor of Mountjoy Prison* [1985] I.L.R.M. 465. It is not legally possible to justify an illegal detention even though where extraordinary excusing circumstances can be proved to exist it may be excused so far as the admissibility of evidence is concerned. Where a person is suffering illegal detention the High Court and this Court is bound by the Constitution to order his release and there can be no question of any consideration being given to permitting the detention to continue because of some dominant motive. But as was also pointed out by this Court in *Trimbole's* case the necessary release from illegal detention does not carry with it any immunity from the proper enforcement of the due process of the law to make such person amenable to answer criminal offences in the courts. ...

32. People (D.P.P.) v Buckley
Court of Criminal Appeal, July 31, 1989
[1990] 1 I.R. 14 at 15–17

Finlay C.J:

... The applicant was arrested pursuant to s. 30 of the Offences Against the State Act, 1939, on suspicion of having committed a scheduled offence under the Firearms Act, 1964, being the use of firearms in connection with the robbery. He was then brought to Tralee garda station and was interviewed by a number of members of the Garda Síochána.

Relevant to the issues arising in this case are three interviews. The first of those was an interview with Gardaí Hanley and Walsh, at which there was supplied to the applicant a statement alleged to have been made by one of his co-accused, Mr. Galvin. Upon being given that statement the applicant, on the evidence, asked the gardaí to read it to him and they did so. After the conclusion of the reading the applicant asked the gardaí certain questions concerning the statement and after that he was asked by the members of the gardaí present to tell the truth. Having been so asked, he made the remark: "Haven't ye got the story there?"

This verbal admission was ruled inadmissible by the Special Criminal Court on the grounds that the request by the gardaí to the applicant after the reading of the statement by his fellow accused constituted an invitation to make a reply to that statement and that accordingly it was in breach of Rule VIII of the Judges' Rules, and the court exercised its discretion to exclude it as evidence.

Shortly after that had occurred, two other members of the Garda Síochána entered the room in which the applicant was with the co-accused, Mr. Galvin. A conversation then took place between Mr. Galvin and the applicant, and this conversation was tendered in evidence. The Special Criminal Court held that the entry of Mr. Galvin into the room was a *novus actus interveniens* and that a new caution should have been given to the applicant, though he had been previously cautioned, and that in those circumstances certain statements made by the applicant which were incriminatory in nature should be ruled out of evidence as inadmissible. This interview had concluded at approximately 5.00 to 5.15 p.m.

A further interview then commenced at approximately 6.45 p.m. between the applicant and Detective Sergeant Dillon and Detective Garda Mahony. On the evidence as accepted by the trial court, the applicant was then cautioned and was asked to tell the truth about the Sunday night. In reply to that the following conversation took place. The applicant said: "Ye know all about that", and, on being asked what he meant: "Sure Galvin told you who loaded the lorry. I'll give ye no names anyhow." He was then asked to tell his own part in the affair and his reply was: "You know I was on the job and I told the other two lads. It was hard luck that I was stopped so near that farm place." He was then asked about the robbery and he stated: "I was there. Ye know that. I am saying nothing more about that."

It is in respect of these last verbal statements at the interview commencing at approximately 6.45 p.m. which were admitted in evidence by the trial court that the whole issue on this appeal arises.

It was submitted on behalf of the applicant that by reason of the fact that the applicant had already, on two separate occasions, made incriminatory statements to other members of the Garda Síochána, in circumstances which have been ruled inadmissible by the trial court, this must be taken to have coloured the making of the subsequent statements, notwithstanding the intervening caution, and in particular, that he must no longer be considered to have had a free will in relation to whether or not he would admit guilt at the time of the making of these statements.

Reliance was placed on *The People (Director of Public Prosecutions) v Lynch* [1982] I.R. 64; *R. v Meynell* (1834) 2 Lew C.C. 122; *R. v Rue* (1876) 13 Cox C.C. 209; and on *R. v Smith* [1959] 2 Q.B. 35. Reference was also made on behalf of the respondent to the decision in *The People (Attorney General) v Galvin* [1964] I.R. 325. This court is satisfied that the cases to which reference has been made would appear to establish a principle that where an accused person makes a statement which is incriminatory in nature and has previously been induced to make a statement either by promise, threat or oppression, also incriminatory in nature, which is by that fact rendered inadmissible, the court must, in respect of the later statement, even though no immediate circumstances of oppression, threat or inducement surround it, have regard to the possibility that the threat or inducement remains so as to affect the free will of the party concerned and, therefore, the voluntary nature of the statement.

The court is, however, satisfied that very different considerations apply and arise in a case where a previous admission of guilt has been made which is rendered inadmissible, not by virtue of any oppressive circumstances, nor by the holding out of any inducement or threat, but rather by the exercise by the court of a discretion concerning a breach of the Judges' Rules.

In this case the court is satisfied that having regard to the lapse of time and having regard to the uncontested evidence that, at the interview which commenced at 6.45 p.m. on the evening of the 2nd September the applicant was duly and properly cautioned, and that a very short time after that he made these incriminating statements, the Special Criminal Court was correct in reaching a conclusion that since they were not tainted by the continuance of any oppression, inducement or threat, and since the earlier statements had been ruled out on a different ground from that of inducement or threat, they were properly admissible in evidence. The court is satisfied that once that ruling was correct, there was sufficient evidence to support a conviction in this case and, accordingly, the application for leave to appeal must be refused.

33. People (D.P.P.) v. Healy

Supreme Court, December 5, 1989
[1990] 2 I.R. 73 at 75, 78–82, 88–90

Finlay C.J:

... The only evidence tendered by the prosecution against the defendant which would associate him with participation in the crimes which had been committed was a statement in writing made by him to members of the Garda Síochána whilst in their custody following upon his arrest pursuant to s. 30 of the Offences Against the State Act, 1939.

The admissibility of this statement was challenged by the defence on the ground that prior to the completion of it a solicitor retained by the defendant's family had arrived at the garda station and requested an interview with the defendant. He was not permitted to see him nor was the defendant informed of his presence until after the completion and signing of the statement. ...

The right in issue in this case is the right of a detained person to have access during his detention to a solicitor whose attendance he has requested or whose attendance has been requested by other persons *bona fide* acting on his behalf. No question arises as to any right that a detained person might have to be informed of his right of access to a solicitor by the gardaí who are detaining him, or of any possible right of a detained person to have a solicitor present while he is being interrogated. I express no view on either of these two rights which may arise for determination in other cases.

Clearly the right which is in question could be defeated in the case of a detainee who himself requests the presence of his solicitor, either by failure to convey such request to the solicitor or by failure upon the arrival of such solicitor to grant the actual access.

In the case of a solicitor who has arrived at a garda station on a request made on behalf of a detained person, which is the present case, the right could be defeated either by failing to inform the detainee of the solicitor's arrival or, on the detainee having become aware of such arrival and having requested access to the solicitor, by refusing to grant it.

Counsel for the Director did not seek to distinguish between the right of access arising from the detainee's own request for a solicitor and that arising from the presence of a solicitor sought on his behalf.

Having regard to the view I reached as a judge of the High Court in *The State (Harrington) v Commissioner of An Garda Síochána* (Unreported, High Court, Finlay P., 14th December 1976) and to the approval of that view contained in the judgment of the Court of Criminal Appeal in *The People (Director of Public Prosecutions) v Pringle* (1981) 2 Frewen 57, I am satisfied that no such distinction exists.

The existence of a right of access to a solicitor by a person in detention has been identified and dealt with by judgments of this Court in the following cases: *In re Emergency Powers Bill, 1976* [1977] I.R. 159, *The People v Shaw* [1982] I.R. 1, and *The People (D.P.P.) v Conroy* [1986] I.R. 460. It has been dealt with by the Court of Criminal Appeal in the following cases: *The People v Madden* [1977] I.R. 336, *The People v Farrell* [1978] I.R. 13, and *The People*

(Director of Public Prosecutions) v Pringle (1981) 2 Frewen 57. ...

In *The People v Shaw* [1982] I.R. 1 Walsh J. in the course of his judgment firmly identified the right of access to a solicitor in the following passage, at p.35:

"While he was in custody on the Sunday night, the appellant asked the garda officer in charge if he 'could get him a solicitor'. He was informed that the officer had no function in 'getting him a solicitor'. In evidence the officer stated that he understood the request to be that he, the officer, should choose a solicitor for him. This was accepted by the trial judge ... As was pointed out in *The People v Madden* [1977] I.R. 336 at pp. 355-356 of the report, while there may be no legal obligation on the Garda Síochána to proffer, without request, the assistance of a legal adviser to a person under arrest, a refusal of a request of reasonable access to a legal adviser would render the detention illegal." ...

The matter was again dealt with by Walsh J. in *The People (D.P.P.) v Conroy* [1986] I.R. 460 where he stated at p.478:

"It may or may not be the case, and I do not have to decide this at the moment, that there is a constitutional obligation upon the police to ask a person if he wishes to have a solicitor and that was the point which was before the Court in the *Farrell Case*, but I am satisfied that if he does ask for a solicitor he is entitled to have one. In so far as the *Farrell Case* might appear to decide the contrary, in my view, it ought not to be followed. The constitutional right of the appellant in the present case to have a solicitor, if he asked for one, is based upon the constitutional obligation imposed upon the Garda Síochána to abide by the provisions of Article 40, s. 3 of the Constitution, which postulates the observance of basic or fundamental fairness of procedures during interrogations by members of the Garda Síochána. If such basic fairness of procedure is not so observed by members of the Garda Síochána then it is the duty of the Courts to implement constitutional guarantees by excluding the evidence so obtained: see the decision of this Court in *The People v Shaw* [1982] I.R. 1.

In my view it could not reasonably be held that a failure to comply with the request of a person in custody, who was being interrogated throughout the night in respect of a possible charge of murder, could not be regarded as an unfair procedure of the type which Article 40, s. 3 of the Constitution requires to be avoided. Even if a solicitor is sent for in such circumstances but the members of the Garda Síochána decide to press ahead with the interrogation before the arrival of the solicitor, I would regard it as a constitutionally forbidden procedure."

The judgment of Walsh J. in *Conroy's* case was, as to the main issue arising in that case (the question as to whether or not the findings of fact necessary to rule on the admissibility of an alleged statement should be made by the judge or by the jury), a dissenting judgment. The issue of the request alleged to have been made by the defendant for the services of a solicitor was not dealt with in any of the other three judgments delivered by the majority of the Court.

The provisions of s. 5 of the Criminal Justice Act, 1984, which imposes an obligation on the Garda Síochána, where persons are detained pursuant to s. 4 of that Act, to inform them of their entitlement to consult a solicitor and to notify the solicitor if one is named, had not come into operation at the date of the detention of the defendant in this case and have no bearing, in my view, on the issues that arise in this case. The legislative provision contained in that section cannot be taken by the Court as any guide to the status of the right of access to a solicitor, that is, whether it is constitutional or merely legal in origin. ...

The undoubted right of reasonable access to a solicitor enjoyed by a person who is in detention must be interpreted as being directed towards the vital function of ensuring that such person is aware of his rights and has the independent advice which would be appropriate in order to permit him to reach a truly free decision as to his attitude to interrogation or to the making of any statement, be it exculpatory or inculpatory. The availability of advice from a lawyer must, in my view, be seen as a contribution, at least, towards some measure of equality in the position of the detained person and his interrogators.

Viewed in that light, I am driven to the conclusion that such an important and fundamental standard of fairness in the administration of justice as the right of access to a lawyer must be deemed to be constitutional in its origin, and that to classify it as merely legal would be to undermine its importance and the completeness of the protection of it which the courts are obliged to give.

The vital issue which arises, therefore, if a breach of the right of access to a solicitor has occurred as a result of a conscious and deliberate act of a member of the Garda Síochána, is whether there is a causative link between that breach and the obtaining of an admission.

A right of reasonable access to a solicitor by a detained person, I am satisfied, means, in the event of the arrival of a solicitor at the garda station in which a person is detained, an immediate right of that person to be told of the arrival and, if he requests it, immediate access. The only thing that could justify the postponement of informing the detained person of the arrival of the solicitor or of immediately complying with a request made by the detained person when so informed, for access to him, would be reasons which objectively viewed from the point of view of the interest or welfare of the detained person, would be viewed by a court as being valid. I reject completely the submission made on behalf of the Director of Public Prosecutions that the test to be applied to the question of reasonable access is a subjective test in the mind of the jailer of the detained person. The test is whether the superintendent's refusal of access was a conscious and deliberate act, as it clearly was. The fact that he may not have appreciated that his refusal was a breach of the defendant's constitutional right is immaterial. Furthermore, I would also reject the submission made on behalf of the Director that the fact that a detained person was in the course of making a statement, whether it was exculpatory of incriminatory, at the time of the arrival of the solicitor could possibly be an objectively valid reason for postponing informing him of that arrival, and asking him whether he wished to suspend the making of the statement in order to have access to the solicitor.

Having regard to these conclusions, it is clear on the evidence in this case that the defendant should have been informed at 4.00 p.m. of the arrival of the solicitor, and if he had asked to see him at that time, should have been permitted to see him. The failure to follow that course and the postponement both of the access to the solicitor and of the informing of the defendant of the presence of the solicitor until after the completion of the statement was, in my view, both a deliberate and conscious violation of the defendant's constitutional right and also a complete failure to observe reasonable standards of fairness in the procedure of his interrogation. ...

McCarthy J:

... In my view, if "conscious and deliberate" is a term of art appropriate to be used in the context of constitutional rights and their violation, the only test is whether or not the act or omission that constituted such violation was itself a conscious and deliberate act; the fact that the violator did not realise he was in breach of a constitutional right is irrelevant. If it were otherwise, then if one jailor could distance himself from the others, as the superintendent did in the instant case, there need never be such a violation. It is not the state of mind of the violator that matters; it is the objective assessment of the conscious acts or omissions. A violation of constitutional rights is not to be excused by the ignorance of the violator no more than ignorance of the law can enure to the benefit of a person who, at common law, and by statute law (Criminal Justice Act, 1964, s. 4, sub-s. 2) is presumed to have intended the natural and probable consequences of his conduct. If it were otherwise, there would be a premium on ignorance. ...

[McCarthy J. considers *dicta* by Griffin J., with which Henchy, Kenny and Parke JJ. concurred, in *The People v Shaw* [1982] I.R. 1 at p.55.][2] The Supreme Court was there dealing with the admissibility of a confession obtained during an otherwise impermissibly long period of detention, which detention was in the hope of producing a result that would save Mary's life. It was a far remove from the circumstances of the instant appeal, in particular since the superintendent was well aware that the continued detention was *prima facie* unlawful but, in what the Court of Criminal Appeal described as "these unique circumstances" (p.21) the continued detention was, because of an extraordinary excusing circumstance, not unlawful. In *Shaw*, therefore, the Court decided the appeal on the assumption that the test of admissibility was:

> "[F]irst, whether each was a statement taken in deliberate and conscious violation of the appellant's constitutional rights and, secondly, if so, whether it should nevertheless be held admissible because of extraordinary excusing circumstances." ([1982] I.R. 1 at p.57).

It would appear to follow that the examination of *The People (Attorney*

---

[2] *Cf.* appendix 25.

General) v O'Brien [1965] I.R. 142 and its reasoning was not necessary for the decision in *Shaw*.

34. People (D.P.P.) v McGrail

Court of Criminal Appeal, December 18, 1989
[1990] 2 I.R. 38 at 45–46, 48–51

Hederman J:

... At the end of the State case on the second day of the trial, counsel for the applicant applied for a direction. The learned trial judge refused his application. Having dealt with the application Mr. Vaughan Buckley, counsel for the accused, said to the learned trial judge: "One other matter My Lord, Mr. O'Connell has indicated that if the accused was to give evidence in this case, there would be an application made to permit him to cross-examine the accused as to his character. He is alleging apparently, that by my cross-examination of the Gardaí, relating to the alleged verbal statements put to the accused, in particular I think he will be alleging that, by putting it to one of the gardaí that he invented the verbal statements, I put the accused's character in issue. I would submit that that issue, as to the question of whether the accused made verbal statements or not in this case, is the central issue in the trial and that to put it to a garda, who was giving evidence concerning those alleged verbal admissions that he invented them, which could be the only proper inference if the accused's instructions are correct, that I would submit is a central issue in this case and I would submit that by doing that I certainly did not put my client's character in issue." Mr. O'Connell for the prosecution submitted to the trial judge: "... that the nature and conduct of the defence in this case involved imputations on the character and credibility of the *gardaí* witnesses. Mr. Vaughan Buckley specifically put it to Detective Garda Mitchell bluntly that he was inventing verbal statements against his client. There is a lot of recent authority on it, I do not think on this particular aspect there is any Irish case." At this stage the learned trial judge intervened and said to counsel for the prosecution: "I think the practice up to now has been to allow the accused's character in issue following what I might call general accusations of either malpractice or indeed improper practice." Mr. O'Connell for the prosecution: "I think the proper legal position is that, even if your Lordship were to hold that the conduct of the defence involved imputations against the character of prosecution witnesses, your Lordship still has a discretion in the matter whether or not to permit cross-examination of the accused in relation to previous convictions, in the interest of overall fairness of the trial, but certainly there are a number of recent authorities from the English courts arising out of very similar circumstances to what occurred in this particular case." Counsel for the prosecution then went on to cite from *R. v Britzman*; *R. v Hall* [1983] 1 W.L.R. 350. He also referred to the most recent edition of Archbold, at para. 4 of page 360. Mr. Vaughan Buckley then submitted to the learned trial judge that the applicant's previous convictions were motoring offences, and he said: "Just to let your Lordship know in relation to that, but, in relation to the situation generally, I could not have defended Mr. McGrail in this case without making the accusations I made. We are alleging he was 'verballed' by the *gardaí*; how could he be defended except he had to put this to the *gardaí*." Counsel for the defence further submitted to the learned judge that he had never heard of a court in this land to go so far as to grant leave to the prosecution under those circumstances.

The learned trial judge stated: "What I am primarily concerned with is the guilt or innocence of the accused man on the charges before this court, and this is of course what I will tell the jury; nevertheless it does appear to me that on the authority of *Attomey General v Campbell* (1928) 62 I.L.T.R. 30 that, as a grave imputation has been made against the character of the prosecuting witnesses, the character of the accused man has been put in issue and I am supported also by *R. v Tanner* (1977) 66 Cr. App. Rep. 56 and *R. v Britzman; R. v Hall* [1983] 1 W.L.R. 350. ...

In the view of the court the trial judge erred in principle in ruling that the case made by the defence put the character of the prosecution witnesses in question.

Every criminal trial involves an imputation as to the character of somebody. The mere fact that an accused is accused of a criminal offence and that evidence is offered to support that view is in effect an imputation against the character of the accused. If the accused, either by giving evidence or through his counsel's cross-examination of the witnesses for the prosecution, suggests to them that they are not to be believed, that is also an imputation as to their character in as much as it is suggested that they are telling an untruth, if that is the way the matter is put to them. The defence may even require, in its efforts to rebut the prosecution case, to suggest to the witness and to the court that in fact the real author of the crime, if it has been proved to have been committed, is not the accused but one or other, perhaps, of the witnesses for the prosecution. Such a course of conduct is inevitable if an accused person is not to be seriously hampered in the conduct of his defence. Any ruling otherwise would have the effect of inhibiting the conduct of the defence in that an accused person, who may have a criminal record, may be intimidated into abandoning an effort to put in issue the truth of the evidence of a prosecution witness lest his own character outside the facts of the trial be put in issue. For example, in a prosecution for rape, if the accused's case is that the alleged sexual intercourse was by consent, to put that case to the complainant is in effect to say that she was guilty of immoral, although not unlawful, conduct. Such suggestion or inference is not based on any matter independent of the evidence given by the complainant. It would be a totally different matter if it was put to the complainant that she behaved in a similar immoral fashion on occasions or in situations quite independent of the facts of the case in issue. Such an attack on the character of the complainant is now restricted by s. 3 of the Criminal Law (Rape) Act, 1981. Thus to suggest to her that she was a common prostitute or had had sexual relations by consent with other persons independently of the accused would be to put her character in issue for the purpose of discrediting her testimony.

Similarly, when the case against an accused person is based on confessions alleged to have been made by him and he denies that he made any such statements to the police, the inescapable inference is of course that the police are not telling the truth. But that again is a matter which is not independent of the facts of the case. It would be different if it had been suggested to the policemen that this was their usual practice in respect of any persons they prosecuted, for the purpose of discrediting their testimony in the case at hearing. It would be quite an intolerable situation if an accused person, in the conduct of the defence in cross-examining prosecution witnesses the veracity of whose evidence he was challenging, should be required to confine himself to suggesting a mistake or other innocent explanation to avoid the risk of having his own character put in issue.

The provisions of the Criminal Justice (Evidence) Act, 1924, prohibit putting in evidence the bad character of the accused unless "the nature or conduct of the defence is such as to involve imputations on the character of the prosecutor or the witnesses for the prosecution." The question is what construction is to be put on the words "imputations on the character of the prosecutor or the witnesses for the prosecution". In the view of the court this must be construed as applying only to imputations made on the character of the prosecutor or his witnesses independent of the facts of the particular case, as, for example, when it is suggested that the witnesses are of such general ill-repute that they are persons who are not to be believed. To put to a prosecution witness that he fabricated the evidence he is giving, or that he and other witnesses for the prosecution combined together to fabricate evidence for the particular trial in question, may be necessary to enable the accused to establish his defence, if in fact his defence is that he made no such statement to one or more of the prosecution witnesses. It seems immaterial whether the allegation of untruthfulness is made directly to the witness or witnesses or is a necessary inference on the questions put. If the accused gives evidence and if, for example, he denies the facts of the offence alleged against him and it is put to him that he is not telling the truth, is that to be taken as an attack by the prosecution on his character? The court thinks not. A distinction must be drawn between questions and suggestions which are reasonably necessary to establish either the prosecution case or the defence case, even if they do involve suggesting a falsehood on the part of the witness of one or the other side, on one hand and, on the other hand, an imputation of bad character introduced by either side relating to matters unconnected with the proofs of the instant case.

Even in such an event as the latter one, the danger of unfairness to an accused person who has had previous convictions cannot be overlooked and, in such an event, the trial judge has a discretion, when he thinks proper, to refuse leave to cross-examine an accused person about his previous convictions or his alleged bad character. In the view of the court he has no discretion to permit cross-examination of the accused when the matters complained of relate directly to the evidence given in the case at hearing, either by way of suggesting the untruthfulness of witnesses or an agreement between the prosecution witnesses to concoct a case against the accused. There can be many instances where it could be shown that witnesses for the prosecution have a financial interest in the conviction of an accused person. If they were asked if their evidence was coloured by the fact, it could scarcely be objected to.

In the present case the learned trial judge relied upon the decision of the former Court of Criminal Appeal in *Attorney General v Campbell* (1928) 62 I.L.T.R. 30. In that case the allegation made was that a detective sergeant had coerced the witness into giving false evidence, that the detective sergeant in question had conspired with business competitors of the accused person to keep him out of business, and that, for this extraneous purpose, they were ready to concoct evidence. This was held to amount to a direct imputation on the character of the persons who gave evidence, namely, the merchants in question and the detective sergeant. It involved a general conspiracy to ruin anybody who might come into commercial competition with the dealers in question.

This decision, which was the very first given under the terms of the 1924 statute in relation to this matter, appears to the court to have been an over-literal interpretation of the statute, in so far as the case dealt with the suggestions made to the detective sergeant that his evidence was untrue. In so far as the defence case imputed the existence of a general conspiracy to ruin anybody in competition with the other dealers concerned, it probably did fall within the terms of the statute. The court is of opinion that this decision should not be followed in so far as it dealt with imputations or suggestions of untruthfulness in the evidence of the detective sergeant but, in so far as it was suggested that he was a party to a general conspiracy to ruin competitors, that was a different matter. In our view the decisions in *R. v Tanner* (1977) 66 Cr. App. Rep. 56 and *R. v Britzman; R. v Hall* [1983] 1 W.L.R. 350 should not be followed in so far as they hold that a challenge to the veracity of the evidence of the prosecution is sufficient to open the way to a cross-examination of the accused as to his character, or to render admissible evidence of his previous character. This court is of the view that the principles of fair procedures must apply. A procedure which inhibits the accused from challenging the veracity of the evidence against him at the risk of having his own previous character put in evidence is not a fair procedure. The gratuitous introduction of material by way of cross-examination or otherwise to show that the witness for the prosecution has a general bad character, divorced from the facts of the case at hearing, is a different matter.

In the opinion of the court the learned trial judge misdirected himself in indicating that he would permit the accused's character to be put in issue, and the course taken subsequent to the case was brought about by that decision. In view of the court this application for leave to appeal should be allowed, the application should be treated as the hearing of the appeal and the conviction should be quashed and a new trial ordered.

35. Smurfit Paribas Bank v A.A.B. Export Finance

Supreme Court, February 15, 1990
[1990] 1 I.L.R.M. 588 at 590–595

Finlay C.J:

This is an appeal brought by the defendant against an order made in the High Court on 13th March 1989 by Costello J. directing the further discovery of all correspondence or other instructions passing between the defendant and the solicitor then acting for the defendant in relation to the defendant's floating charge which is in issue in these proceedings. The defendant had, upon the making of an original discovery in the case, claimed privilege for this correspondence and these other instructions.

The learned trial judge reserved judgment on the motion brought by the plaintiff for further discovery and then inspected the documents in respect of which the disputed claim for privilege had been made. Having done so, he came to the conclusion:

(a) That they did not request and did not contain any legal advice about the proposed transaction.

(b) That they contained references to the instructions which the defendant's solicitors received from the defendant and further instructions and clarifications of instructions given by the defendant to the solicitors.

(c) That these instructions were given to enable the defendant's solicitors to draft the documentation necessary to complete the transaction which their client was entering into or to advise later on draft documents which other parties to the transaction might prepare for their consideration.

Having reached these conclusions as to the nature of the documents concerned with which, having inspected the documents on the hearing of this appeal, I agree the learned trial judge then came to the conclusion that they were not privileged from disclosure and inspection on the following grounds:

(1) That they do not request and do not contain any legal advice.

(2) That they contain no information nor remarks that can he regarded as in any way being confidential.

(3) That they are statements of fact as to the transaction which the defendants indicate they wish to have completed by the drafting of the necessary legal documents. In reaching that conclusion he placed reliance upon the decision of *Smith-Bird v Blower* [1939] 2 All E.R. 406, in which a letter written to the solicitors by a defendant, not for the purpose of obtaining legal advice, but in answer to an inquiry as to whether he had agreed to sell the property in question, was not privileged. ...

For the purpose of determining which of these conflicting submissions is correct in law it is, in my view, necessary to try and ascertain what the underlying principles of the doctrine of privilege of communications between a client and his lawyers are.

The existence of some such privilege would appear to have been clearly identified at common law from the early nineteenth century.

However, the question as to whether or not a party to litigation will be privileged to refuse to produce particular evidence is a matter within the sole competence of the courts: 'Power to compel the attendance of witnesses and the production of evidence is an inherent part of the judicial power of government of the State and is the ultimate safeguard of justice in the State'

(*Murphy v The Corporation of Dublin* [1972] I.R. 215 at 233).

In the same case at p.234 the court also held that it is for the courts to decide which is the superior interest in the circumstances of the particular case and to determine the matter of privilege from disclosure accordingly.

For a considerable period conflicting decisions appear to have been reached at common law as to whether a privilege for communications between a client and his lawyer applied only where litigation was in existence or in contemplation or whether it also applied in relation to communications seeking legal advice where no litigation existed or was in contemplation. Before that conflict of decision appears to have been firmly resolved Jessel M.R. in *Anderson v The Bank of British Columbia* (1876) 2 Ch. D. 644 stated what he believed to be the underlying principle in the following words:

> "The object and meaning of the rule is this: that as, by reason of the complexity and difficulty of our law, litigation can only be properly conducted by professional men, it is absolutely necessary that a man in order to prosecute his rights or to defend himself from an improper claim, should have recourse to the assistance of professional lawyers, and it being so absolutely necessary, it is equally necessary, to use a vulgar phrase, that he should be able to make a clean breast of it to the gentleman whom he consults with a view to the prosecution of his claim, or the substantiating of his defence against the claim of others; that he should be able to place unrestricted and unbounded confidence in the professional agent and that the communications he so makes to him should be kept secret unless with his consent (for it is his privilege and not the privilege of the confidential agent) that he should be enabled properly to conduct his litigation. That is the meaning of the rule."

I would adopt this statement as far as it goes as identifying the requirement of the superior interest of the common good in the proper conduct of litigation which justified the immunity of communications from discovery in so far as they were made for the purpose of litigation as being the desirability in that good of the correct and efficient trial of actions by the courts. In the case of *Greenough v Gaskill* (1833) 1 M.Y.& K. 98 which is usually accepted as the first identification of this particular type of privilege and which Jessel M.R. in the passage which I have just quoted is purporting to summarise. Lord Brougham L.C. said, at p.102 of the report:

> "... the protection would be insufficient if it only included communications more or less connected with judicial proceedings; for a person oftentimes requires the aid of professional advice upon the subject of his rights and his liabilities, with no reference to any particular litigation and without any other reference to litigation generally than all human affairs have, in so far as every transaction may, by possibility, become the subject of judicial inquiry."

It is clear that this view of the extent of privilege as being outside actual or contemplated litigation eventually became accepted as a common and unanimous view. In the course of his judgment in the Court of Appeal in *Minter v Priest* [1929] 1 K.B. 655 Lawrence L.J. slated as follows:

> "It has long since been established that it is not necessary for the purpose of obtaining protection from disclosure that the communications should be made either during or relating to an actual or expected litigation and that it is sufficient that they pass as professional communications in a professional capacity."

The same view was expressed in that court by Greer L.J. where he stated:

> "After some difference of opinion it has been established that the privilege is not confined to the conduct of litigation or to advice obtained for the purposes of existing or contemplated litigation. It applies to communications between client and solicitor in respect of all matters that come within the ordinary scope of professional employment."

Although this decision of the Court of Appeal was reversed by the House of Lords, that reversal would appear to have been based not on any difference as to the scope of the privilege applicable to communications between a client and solicitor but rather as to the question as to whether the occasion of the particular communication arising in *Minter v Priest* was a communication between a client and a solicitor acting as such. Lord Buckmaster L.J. with whom Tankerton L.J. agreed, in the course of his judgment in that case, reported at [1930] A.C. 558, spoke of the existence of the privilege in wide terms as being necessary for the protection of society. Lord Atkin in his speech in the same case would appear to have related a necessary confidential element in the communication between a solicitor and client which attracts privilege to the fact that it was a communication passing for the purpose of getting legal advice. His speech does not, however, seem to direct itself to the question as to whether there is a distinction to be made between legal advice and legal assistance. Some of the many decisions which have arisen with regard to questions of a claim of privilege for professional communications between solicitors and clients in the years between 1820 and the present, speak of the necessity for it to be the obtaining of legal advice and assistance and some speak of the necessity of obtaining legal advice. Some would appear to support a contention that it is sufficient if legal assistance other than advice only were sought.

The existence of a privilege or exemption from disclosure for communications made between a person and his lawyer clearly constitutes a potential restriction and diminution of the full disclosure both prior to and during the course of legal proceedings which in the interests of the common good is desirable for the purpose of ascertaining the truth and rendering justice. Such privilege should, therefore, in my view, only be granted by the courts in instances which have been identified as securing an objective which in the public interest in the proper conduct of the administration of justice can be said to outweigh the disadvantage arising from the restriction of disclosure of all the facts.

It is necessary to bear these general considerations in mind in attempting to ascertain the underlying principle which appears to have led to the expansion of the privilege for communications with a lawyer from cases of actual or contemplated litigation to cases of communications seeking legal advice and/or legal assistance other than advice.

The decided cases do not appear to me to provide any satisfactory explanation of this expansion.

For the expansion to be justified, having regard to the considerations which I have just set out in this judgment, it would appear necessary that it should be closely and proximately linked to the conduct of litigation and the function of administering justice in the courts.

Where a person seeks or obtains legal advice there are good reasons to believe that he necessarily enters the area of potential litigation. The necessity to obtain legal advice would in broad terms appear to envisage the possibility of a legal challenge or query as to the correctness or effectiveness of some step which a person is contemplating. Whether such query or challenge develops or not, it is clear that a person is then entering the area of possible litigation.

Having regard to those considerations I accept that where it is established that a communication was made between a person and his lawyer acting for him as a lawyer for the purpose of obtaining from such lawyer legal advice, whether at the initiation of the client or the lawyer, that communication made on such an occasion should in general be privileged or exempt from disclosure, except with the consent of the client.

Similar considerations do not, however, it seems to me, apply to communications made to a lawyer for the purpose of obtaining his legal assistance other than advice. There are many tasks carried out by a lawyer for his client, and properly within the legal sphere, other than the giving of advice, which could not be said to contain any real relationship with the area of potential litigation. For such communications there does not appear to me to be any sufficient public interest or feature of the common good to be secured or protected which could justify an exemption from disclosure.

Accepting as I do, therefore, the inferences drawn by the learned trial judge from his perusal of the documents which he was entitled to and indeed bound to carry out, I also find myself in agreement with the principles of law applied by him to the inferences thus raised and accordingly would affirm his decision and dismiss this appeal. ...

36. People (D.P.P.) v Kenny

Supreme Court, March 20, 1990
[1990] I.L.R.M. 569 at 571–573, 575–579, 582–584, 586–587

Finlay C.J:

... On 2 October 1984 two members of An Garda Siochana were in hiding casing out a surveillance of a premises at 1, Belgrave Place, Rathmines, in the City of Dublin, in which the accused was then residing.

They observed activity outside the house and in and around Flat No. 1 ...

on the ground floor, which included activity by the accused and which appeared to them as constituting some form of trafficking in drugs.

By wireless telephone, one of the gardaí requested a colleague to bring to him a search warrant which had been obtained from a peace commissioner, pursuant to s.26(1) of the Act of 1977, in respect of the premises Flat No. 1 on the ground floor of 1 Belgrave Place. The search warrant was brought to the garda concerned and he, having sought entry by demand, made forcible entry through a window, found the accused on the premises, and found a quantity of controlled drugs on the premises for which, on his evidence, the accused took responsibility. That was the only evidence associating the accused with the controlled drugs. No issue arose in this case by reason of the fact that the search warrant was issued by a peace commissioner. ...

The Court of Criminal Appeal in its judgment of 15 June 1989, delivered by McCarthy J., found that the warrant issued in this case was invalid by reason of the fact that there was no evidence that the peace commissioner was himself satisfied that there were reasonable grounds for suspecting the existence of controlled drugs on the premises, but rather that the only evidence was to the effect that he relied in its entirety on the information in writing submitted to him by the Garda Siochana, in other words, that he relied on the fact, that the garda had grounds for so suspecting.

Counsel for the respondent accepts that this portion of the judgment of the Court of Criminal Appeal was correct. Quite independently of that concession, I am satisfied that it was. ...

The Court of Criminal Appeal in its judgment of 30 November 1989 delivered by O'Hanlon J. having concluded that the warrant was invalid, held that reliance upon it was not in deliberate or conscious violation of the constitutional rights of the accused. ...

In reaching that conclusion the Court of Criminal Appeal relied upon the decision of the Supreme Court of the United States in *United States v Leon* (1983) 468 U.S. 897, and expressed the view that it was an echo of the views expressed by Kingsmill Moore J. in *People (Attorney General) v O'Brien* [1965] I.R. 142.

The decision in *United States v Leon* is clearly and expressly based upon the principle of deterrence rather than the principle of absolute protection of the constitutional right concerned, in applying the exclusion of evidence rule to the obtaining of evidence by unconstitutional means.

In the course of the judgment of White J. delivering the opinion of the court, it is stated as follows at p. 906:

> "The rule thus operates as a 'judicially created remedy' designed to safeguard Fourth Amendment rights generally through its deterrent effect, rather than a personal constitutional right of the party aggrieved."

I do not find this to constitute an echo of the judgment of Kingsmill Moore J. in *People (Attorney General) v O'Brien* [1965] I.R. 142.

The greater part of that judgment deals with evidence obtained by illegal as distinct from unconstitutional, means and constitutes a review of the English and Scottish authorities in which, of course, no question of any differentiation between illegality and unconstitutionality arises. ...

This expression of opinion which formed the majority view of the court in *O'Brien's* case, clearly leaves unresolved in relation to the admissibility of unconstitutionally obtained evidence the choice raised by the arguments in this case between the deterrent and absolute protection principles.

In *People v Walsh* [1980] I.R. 294, Walsh J. in the course of his judgment, at p.317, stated as follows:

> "If a man is consciously and deliberately kept in custody in a garda station or anywhere else without a charge being preferred against him and without being brought before a court as soon as reasonably possible, he is in unlawful custody and there has been a deliberate and conscious violation of his constitutional right to be at liberty. That this was the position in the present case is abundantly clear from the evidence given by the police officer at the trial. The fact that the officer or officers concerned may not have been conscious that what they were doing was illegal or that even if they did know it was illegal, they did not think it was a breach of the Constitution does not affect the matter. They were conscious of the actual circumstances which existed." [emphasis added]

This judgment of Walsh J. in that case was a dissenting judgment, but not by reason of the principles of law enunciated in it, but rather by reason of the view taken as to whether on the facts of the case the detention of the applicant was or was not unlawful.

Delivering the majority judgment of the court in *Walsh's* case, with which Kenny J. agreed, O'Higgins C.J., at p.299, having recited the submission made on behalf of the appellant that evidence of fingerprints taken whilst the accused was in unlawful custody was inadmissible, stated as follows:

> "I wish to say at once that this submission should succeed if the imprisonment or detention in Store Street cannot be justified in law. I have had the benefit of reading the judgment of Walsh J. in which he reviews the authorities on this important aspect of constitutional law. I am in complete agreement with the manner in which he states the law. However, in my view this is not the crucial question. In my view the crucial question—indeed, the only question—is whether the arrest of the appellant and his detention immediately thereafter on the night of 23 January was or was not lawful. ..."

Griffin J. delivered the majority judgment of the court in [*People v Shaw* [1982] I.R. 1], with which Henchy, Kenny and Parke JJ. agreed. It contained a very clear disagreement with the views expressed by Walsh J. ...

In *D.P.P. v Healy* [1990] I.L.R.M. 313, I in my judgment and McCarthy J. in his adopted what I have described as the absolute protection test for evidence obtained by reason of a breach of a detained person's constitutional right of access to a lawyer.

The constitutional rights with which all these cases are concerned are personal rights, being either the right to liberty (*Walsh's* case; *Madden's* case;

Shaw's case), or the inviolability of the dwelling (*O'Brien's* case and the instant case).

The duty of the court pursuant to Article 40.3.1° of the Constitution is as far as practicable to defend and vindicate such rights.

As between two alternative rules or principles governing the exclusion of evidence obtained as a result of the invasion of the personal rights of a citizen, the court has, it seems to me, an obligation to choose the principle which is likely to provide a stronger and more effective defence and vindication of the right concerned.

To exclude only evidence obtained by a person who knows or ought reasonably to know that he is invading a constitutional right is to impose a negative deterrent. It is clearly effective to dissuade a policeman from acting in a manner which he knows is unconstitutional or from acting in a manner reckless as to whether his conduct is or is not unconstitutional.

To apply, on the other hand, the absolute protection rule of exclusion whilst providing also that negative deterrent, incorporates as well a positive encouragement to those in authority over the crime prevention and detection services of the State to consider in detail the personal rights of the citizens as set out in the Constitution, and the effect of their powers of arrest, detention, search and questioning in relation to such rights.

It seems to me to be an inescapable conclusion that a principle of exclusion which contains both negative and positive force is likely to protect constitutional rights in more instances than is a principle with negative consequences only.

The exclusion of evidence on the basis that it results from unconstitutional conduct, like every other exclusionary rule, suffers from the marked disadvantage that it constitutes a potential limitation of the capacity of the courts to arrive at the truth and so most effectively to administer justice.

I appreciate the anomalies which may occur by reason of the application of the absolute protection rule to criminal cases.

The detection of crime and the conviction of guilty persons, no matter how important they may be in relation to the ordering of society, cannot, however, in my view, outweigh the unambiguously expressed constitutional obligation 'as far as practicable to defend and vindicate the personal rights of the citizen'.

After very careful consideration I conclude that I must differ from the view of the majority of this Court expressed in the judgment of Griffin J. in *Shaw's* case. I am satisfied that the correct principle is that evidence obtained by invasion of the constitutional personal rights of a citizen must be excluded unless a court is satisfied that either the act constituting the breach of constitutional rights was committed unintentionally or accidentally, or is satisfied that there are extraordinary excusing circumstances which justify the admission of the evidence in its (the court's) discretion.

In the instant case there cannot be any question but that the acts of the gardaí which obtained the warrant by the submission to the peace commissioner of the sworn written information in the form in which I have recited it, and which then forcibly entered the dwellinghouse were neither unintentional nor accidental, and counsel for the respondent agrees that there are no extraordinary excusing circumstances in this case. Even though, then, I would accept that neither of the two gardaí concerned had any knowledge that they were invading the constitutional rights of the accused and would also accept that they were carrying out the process of obtaining and executing a search warrant in a manner which has been customary over a long period with the gardaí, I am satisfied that the evidence obtained as a result of the forcible entry into the house should not have been admitted at the trial of the accused, and that accordingly, the conviction of the accused should not have occurred.

I would, therefore, allow this appeal and I would quash the conviction entered against the accused.

Griffin J. (dissenting):

... My judgment in *Shaw's* case had the support of Henchy, Kenny and Parke JJ. Having carefully considered all the arguments advanced in this case I can see no reason why I should resile from what I said in that case. ...

I agree with the submission of counsel for the Director of Public Prosecutions that, in the cases on which the applicant's counsel relied, other than *O'Brien's* case and *Shaw's* case, there was in each of those cases a deliberate and conscious decision to detain the persons in custody in breach of their rights. In *Madden's* case, the superintendent knew full well that he had no power to detain a suspect for longer than 48 hours, and that s.30 of the Offences Against the State Act 1939, required that, unless the person detained was charged before the District Court or a Special Criminal Court within the period of 48 hours, he must be released at the expiration of that time. He was neither charged nor released within that time and any statement thereafter made or completed by him was therefore inadmissible.

In *O'Loughlin's* case, the Court of Criminal Appeal held that the detention of the accused was not due to either inadvertence or oversight. "It was done by experienced garda officers who must have had a special knowledge of citizens' rights in such circumstances. It could only have been the result of a deliberate decision of these officers who were aware of the applicant's rights. These rights were disregarded and swept aside ..." *per* O'Higgins C.J. at p.91.

In *D.P.P. v Healy*, the superintendent in charge of the investigation deliberately delayed, in circumstances which amounted to denying, the detained person's right of access to his solicitor, because the former was in the process of being interviewed and it 'would be bad manners' to interrupt it.

In the instant case, Garda Conway, for the purpose of obtaining a search warrant, adopted a procedure which had been in almost universal use throughout the country for very many years, and from my own experience I would suspect at least thirty to forty years, i.e. by means of a standard form, suitably adapted for the particular case. This practice was not confined to cases in which the misuse of drugs was involved, but is in use in respect of obtaining search warrants for many other purposes, such as, for example, s.42 of the Larceny Act 1916. Even if only one such warrant was issued each day in the greater Dublin area (a highly unlikely circumstance) that would amount to a total in excess of 10,000 warrants in 30 years. It is likely that there must have been upwards of 100,000 or more such warrants issued in the same way in that period. In recent years, a large number of similar warrants must have been obtained pursuant to s.26 of the Misuse of Drugs Act 1977, having regard to the enormous increase in the use of drugs, by reason of the huge profits to be made by dealers in drugs, and to the numbers of those who are now what is known as 'hooked' on drugs. The Oireachtas, in enacting s.26 of the Act of 1977, has provided that warrants should be issued only after the detached intervention of a neutral district justice or peace commissioner, who for that purpose is interposed between the gardaí and the person in respect of whose dwelling the search warrant is sought. In my view the error which invalidated this search warrant was that of the peace commissioner.

Garda Conway, having obtained what was an ostensibly valid warrant, went to the applicant's flat. He knocked on the door, and shouted 'Gardai, open up'. There was a lot of movement inside the flat but the door was not opened. Although he did not say so in evidence, as an experienced member of the drugs squad, he must have been aware that by reason of their nature, the drugs he was hoping to find could be destroyed in a matter of seconds by flushing down the toilet, or by throwing them in the fire, or by consuming them. He went to the window of the room in which he had heard the movement, stood on the window-sill and again shouted 'Gardai, open up'. There were two people in that room and he put his ID card against the window, and, as no effort was made to open the door, he broke the window and gained entrance to the flat. The drugs the subject of the charge in this case were subsequently found in the course of a search of the premises.

In my opinion, the act of Garda Conway in breaking into the flat in the circumstances in which he did so, did not constitute a deliberate and conscious violation of the constitutional rights of the applicant. Like my colleague Lynch J., a copy of whose judgment I have had the advantage of reading in advance, I can see no distinction between this case and *O'Brien's* case. The evidence of the finding of the drugs in the applicant's flat was, in my opinion, correctly admitted at his trial. The decision of the Court of Criminal Appeal in dismissing the applicant's application for leave to appeal was in my view correct, and I would accordingly dismiss this appeal. ...

Lynch J. (dissenting):

... The courts must be zealous to vindicate and uphold the citizens' constitutional rights. Any hint of a deliberate disregard by the gardaí for such constitutional rights must result in evidence obtained thereby being rejected unless there are adequate excusing circumstances. I prefer the term 'adequate' to 'extraordinary' in view of decisions which suggest that inadvertence may be a sufficient excuse.

In the present case the forcible entry of the applicant's dwelling was of course deliberate but the violation of the applicant's constitutional rights in relation to his dwelling under Article 40.5 was neither conscious nor deliberate. On the contrary the gardaí showed respect for the constitutional inviolability of the applicant's dwelling by applying for the issue of the warrant to the appropriate civil (as distinct from garda) authority on an information believed for many years to be the correct form of information to lead to the issue of such warrants under the Misuse of Drugs Act 1977. The gardaí further showed respect for the applicant's constitutional rights in relation to his dwelling by bringing the warrant with them and showing it to the applicant and I can see nothing in the conduct of the gardaí to support an inference of a conscious and deliberate intention to violate the applicant's constitutional rights in relation to his dwelling.

Insofar as there was any fault leading to the invalidity of the warrant that fault must rest rather with the peace commissioner who is interposed between the garda authorities and the citizen to see that the citizen's dwelling is not entered without due cause and on whom s.26 of the 1977 Act imposes the duty of satisfying himself by proper evidence that there is due cause for such entry on the citizen's dwelling. The peace commissioner is independent of the gardaí and if not satisfied by proper evidence he must refuse the warrant unless and until he becomes so satisfied by additional evidence. ...

The inviolability of the citizen's dwelling must be upheld but this does not mean that evidence obtained in breach of it must always be rejected however relevant it may be to the case at hearing. It must be rejected if there is any element of blame or culpability or unfairness (including any such clement to be inferred by the reasonable application of the doctrine *ignorantia juris haud excusat*) in relation to the breach of the right on the part of those who obtained the evidence unless there are adequate excusing circumstances. ...

37. People (D.P.P.) v O'Reilly

Court of Criminal Appeal, April 26, 1990
[1990] 2 I.R. 415 at 417–424

O'Flaherty J:

... Mrs. Farrell, a widow aged 81 years, was alone in her house on the 30th November, 1988. She was in her front garden plucking some chrysanthemums when two men appeared on the scene; one offered to do a painting job for her which she refused and he then asked for a drink of water. He had come out of a red car which had pulled up at Mrs. Farrell's gateway. While she was providing this man with a drink of water another man came into her house and he had a big bedspread around his head and, as Mrs. Farrell described him he had "a most notorious face, an awful face" and Mrs. Farrell thought that he was insane or an idiot or something. She said that she got "a most dangerous fright" and that he burst through and "banged" this old quilt about for about ten minutes or so when she said to him "I can't stay here all day, I have some little jobs to do" and the first man (who had offered to do the painting) was looking in and keeping an eye and he said at one stage "I think I hear a car".

The man with the blanket offered to sell it to her for £50 and Mrs. Farrell described him in evidence as "a stout butt of a fair haired man". She could not describe his exact height but thought that he was small. Neither could she describe his age as she said she was very bad for describing ages. This all happened at about 3.30 p.m. and, in evidence, Mrs. Farrell recounted that a short time later, about 4.00 p.m. she discovered the money, £850 or thereabouts, was missing. In the statement that she made to a garda later that evening she seemed to think that the time she noticed her money was missing was at about

6.30 p.m. It had been kept in a tea canister which, in turn, was kept in a biscuit tin. This was in a room off the main living-room.

The *gardaí* ascertained that the applicant had bought a red Ford Sierra Saloon car from a garage in Newbridge, County Kildare, some time previously and, it will be recalled, that Mrs. Farrell had noticed a red car outside her house on the day in question. Suspicion centred on the applicant and he was detained under s.4 of the Criminal Justice Act, 1984. ….

[O]n the 26th January, 1989, at about 10.30 a.m. Mrs. Farrell was brought to Edgeworthstown in a garda car. She was seated in the front passenger seat with Garda Coen in the driver's seat and Garda Garvey in the back seat. At about 11.00 a.m., after Mrs. Farrell had had an opportunity of seeing about twenty or thirty people passing by, there approached a group, three in front (two women and a man) and two men behind and she said to Garda Coen "I think that's him there" and when asked by Garda Coen if she was sure, she said "I didn't get a good look at him". Garda Coen and Mrs. Farrell remained in the car with Garda Garvey outside and evidence was given that at about 12.05 p.m. about four people emerged from a building (in fact it was the courthouse) and Mrs. Farrell said to Garda Coen "that's him, that's him", "the fellow with the ugly face". She pointed out the applicant as being the person with the blanket who had been in her house on 30th November, 1988.

Counsel for the accused cross-examined Garda Coen as to why no identification parade had been held. He said that he was twenty three years in the guards and that he was eight or nine years in the plain clothes division. He said that he had never held an identification parade because he never had occasion to do so. It will be recalled that at the first "partial identification" the leading group consisted of two women and a man but Garda Coen in his evidence said that this group consisted of two men and a woman; on cross-examination he changed back to what had been contained in his original statement. He was not able to give any details as regards the other two men who were in the group (aside from Mr. O'Reilly) in relation to the first "partial identification". The upshot of this evidence was that the *gardaí* were not in a position to give any description of what the other people passing up and down on the street on that day looked like. It was put to Garda Coen that if there had been a formal identification parade that certain details would have been noted such as the number of people present, their ages, descriptions, their height and so forth. None of these matters were noted in respect of the informal identification that was attempted in the circumstances of this case.

When it was put to Garda Coen that he should have held an official formal parade he said:

> "Well to me, my lord, it is far more beneficial to the defendant. If a person holds an official I.D. parade you bring a person into a room with a number of people in the room, they are expecting to see that person there. If you bring a person on to a street, I didn't know when I went to Edgeworthstown how many people would be passing that street, there could be ten, twenty, forty or a hundred, and it is much more difficult to pick out a person walking the street than it is and it is a much more fairer way, to me, than having an official I.D. parade."

Mrs. Farrell, in the course of her evidence, also recounted the events in Edgeworthstown and also identified the accused man in court. Under cross-examination certain discrepancies between what she had said in her original statement to the *gardaí* on the 30th November, 1988, and what she said in court were explored but since no point has been made on these possible discrepancies at the hearing of the appeal the Court would propose to say no more about them. Mrs. Farrell agreed that she had only a few minutes in which to observe the man who had been in her house. She agreed and, indeed, it was corroborated by the garda who went to her house on the evening of the incident that she was very upset but she was very definite in her identification in court that the accused was the man and that she was not mistaken in her identification of the accused.

It can be stated that the single issue at the trial was whether the identification of the applicant was adequate. While mention was made of a red motor car it was not established in evidence that the car seen outside Mrs. Farrell's house by Mrs. Farrell and another witness belonged to the accused.

This case bears many similarities to *The People (Attorney General) v Fagan* (1974) 1 Frewen 375. In that case, too, the only issue at the trial was whether the identification of the applicant was adequate. There the accused had never seen the man before the particular robbery and the identification took place outside the Circuit Court. The judgment of the Court of Criminal Appeal recounts that no identification parade was held. The reason given was that the applicant did not live at home and "was not always that readily available". The Court categorised this explanation for not holding a formal identification parade as "less than satisfactory". At p.377 of Frewen the judgment goes on:

> "In *The People (Attorney General) v Martin* [1956] I.R. 22 the Supreme Court held that there is no rule of law or practice that requires visual identification of a person to be proved by means of an identification parade; each case must be considered on its own facts. It is readily understandable that other types of identification may in certain circumstances be fairer and more dependable than a formal identification parade which, because of its surroundings, atmosphere, range of choice and limited opportunity for observation, may be a less than satisfactory means of achieving a reliable identification. But the acceptability of an alternative method must always depend on the circumstances of the case."

Here the explanation for not holding a formal identification parade must also be accounted less that satisfactory. The reason given was that it might be "more beneficial" to the defendant not to hold one. While it is right that those in charge of prosecutions should be scrupulous in looking to the rights of the accused, nonetheless, the decision as to what is most beneficial for an accused, in the preparation and conduct of his defence, must be primarily a matter for the decision of the accused and his legal adviser (if he has a legal adviser at the time). It should be said that the Court is in no doubt that Garda Coen acted out of a dutiful though mistaken conception as to what was right and proper in the circumstances of this case.

Mr. Murphy, counsel for the applicant on the appeal but who did not represent him at the trial, referred the Court to Chief Justice O'Higgins' well known dictum in *The State (Healy) v Donoghue* [1976] I.R. 325 at page 348:

> "In the first place the concept of justice, which is specifically referred to in the preamble [to the Constitution] in relation to the freedom and dignity of the individual, appears again in the provisions of Article 34 which deal with the Courts. It is justice which is to be administered in the Courts and this concept of justice must import not only fairness, and fair procedures, but also regard to the dignity of the individual."

He submitted that this was a case where there should have been a formal identification parade. Here was an old lady who suffered from arthritis, who, it was common case, had sustained a severe fright and was in a state of shock; where her chances of observing the features of whoever were in her house were limited; who had not known the accused before—all these would point to the inescapable need for the holding of a formal identification parade. Counsel said that the way in which such parades were held was not in doubt. It involves that there are assembled eight or nine people of similar age, height, appearance, dress and walk in life to the suspect; that the parade will be supervised by an independent garda (that is, one not concerned with the actual investigation); that full details will be kept of the description of the various people making up the parade and that the witness should not have any opportunity of seeing the suspect in advance of the holding of the parade. This is not intended to be an exhaustive list for such parades and, on occasion, the way in which an identification parade has been held has, itself, been subject to criticism (see, for example, *The People (Attorney General) v O'Driscoll* (1972) 1 Frewen 351).

There will be circumstances where it is not possible or practicable to hold an identification parade. If, for example, the suspect is of singular appearance it may not be possible to get together sufficient people to make up a fair parade. The holding of an identification parade would probably be a redundant exercise if the witness knew the suspect previously—though a warning would still have to be given in accordance with the principles laid down in *The People (Attorney General) v Casey (No. 2)* [1963] I.R. 33.

Neither is one concerned with a situation where a suspect will not agree to go on an identification parade or attempts to frustrate it once it is assembled. If that is the course a suspect, afterwards an accused, takes then that is the particular option that he has exercised and he may have to live with the consequences. However, the situation in this case is that the accused man was given no such option at all.

The Court is clearly of the opinion that this is a case that required the holding of an identification parade and the Court will deprecate any suggestion that the holding of formal identification parades have outlived their usefulness; they are important in that they provide a filter for both prosecution and defence. If a suspect is not picked out at an identification parade, then very often the prosecution may go no further. Conversely, if a suspect is identified he may well think that the time has arrived to reach an accommodation with the prosecution by pleading guilty to the alleged offence.

The Court is also mindful that an important difference between a formal identification parade and an informal identification, such as in the instant case, is that in the former the accused (and his legal adviser if one is present) has full knowledge about the composition of the parade and may object if it is perceived to be unfair. Furthermore, the court of trial will have the benefit of a detailed account of the parade and a description of those who participated in it. By contrast, an accused has no input where there is an informal identification and is unlikely even to have knowledge of its happening. Therefore, he may be seriously inhibited in challenging its fairness at the trial. The Court, however, would emphasise as was emphasised by the Supreme Court in its decision in *The People (Attorney General) v Casey (No.2)* [1963] I.R. 33 that the result of an identification is not conclusive and the warnings required in relation to the dangers of visual identification apply also when someone has been identified in a formal identification parade.

The Court will add one further point. It was stated in the course of the hearing of the appeal that, in fact, photographs were shown to Mrs. Farrell (including a photograph of the accused) prior to her visit to Edgeworthstown. The dilemma facing the defence counsel at the trial was that if he referred to the photographs it would have the connotation that the accused was possibly a person of bad character; so the defence was left with Hobson's choice and decided that no mention should be made of the photographs. Mr. Murphy, in the course of the hearing of the appeal, made no particular point about the photographs except to draw the Court's attention to this fact but it adds weight to the Court's concern that this was an identification which was obtained in unusual and doubtful circumstances which renders the conviction unsafe. The trial judge's ruling should certainly have been sought on the admissibility of the identification evidence obtained in such frail circumstances.

A complaint is also made that the learned trial judge failed adequately to warn the jury along the lines required by the Supreme Court in *The People (Attorney General) v Casey (No.2)* [1963] I.R. 33.

It is nearly thirty years since that landmark decision was handed down and since there is a danger that one of the matters that the Court adverted to may happen, *viz.* that the direction to be given will be treated as a "stereotyped formula", the Court thinks it would be a help to reiterate again what was decided by the Court in *The People (Attorney General) v Casey (No. 2)* [1963] I.R. 33. ...[3]

In this case there is no doubt that the learned trial judge complied in full with the first part of the direction and, indeed, he went on to deal with the particular circumstances in which the injured party observed the accused man. He told the jury:

> "You have to weigh up very carefully the opportunity that she had to observe him, the time during which she observed him, the circumstances in which she observed him. All those things are important. How far she was standing from him, what time of day it was, what sort of person you think she is, as to whether she would get an identification wrong or otherwise. You have to weigh up all those factors in your mind and

---
[3] *Cf.* appendix 11.

approach it with caution bearing in mind always that even in identification parades or even other circumstances where the opportunity to observe the person was very good that nevertheless mistakes have been made in the past. But I have to say to you, ladies and gentlemen, that having weighed up those factors and having considered all those matters, if you are nevertheless confident at the end of the case that Mrs. Farrell has properly identified Mr. O'Reilly, in those circumstances if you are satisfied beyond all reasonable doubt that that evidence is correct and trustworthy then you are entitled to act on it and to proceed to convict the accused. If you are not so satisfied you are obliged to acquit the accused."

Mr. Murphy complains that this remains too general and that the charge required that the judge should have given firmer guidance to the jury as regards the particular infirmities that of necessity afflicted this case, *viz.* the fact that the lady was elderly; that she was in a state of shock; that she suffered a good deal of pain from an arthritic condition; and had only a short period in which to observe the men in her house. Furthermore, the deficiencies in the actual identification that was made at Edgeworthstown should have been highlighted to assist the jury. In other words, while the first part of *The People (Attorney General) v Casey (No. 2)* [1963] I.R. 33 formula was observed, the second part was not.

The Court is of opinion that in the circumstances of this case the judge's directions to the jury should have been much more specific as regards the danger of acting on the evidence of Mrs. Farrell. While he pointed to the fact that mistakes can be made even where there is a formal identification parade he did not put the converse, which was this case, where there was no formal identification parade at all and the infirmities that surrounded the actual identification that was made in Edgeworthstown should have been emphasised in greater detail to the jury.

In fairness to the learned trial judge it must be said that he was not asked to re-direct the jury on this aspect of his charge.

The only distinction that the Court can draw between this and *The People (Attorney General) v Fagan* (1974) 1 Frewen 375 is that the witness in the *Fagan* case was shaken severely in cross-examination on his identification and, indeed, admitted to the strong possibility that he had made a mistake.

Mrs. Farrell, it would appear, was made of sterner stuff and age has not dimmed any of the obvious exuberance of her character. However, it is central to the need to give warnings in cases of visual identification that people, young and old, tend to be certain. If they are not certain their evidence will fall to the ground anyway. No matter how certain a witness appears to be, the requirement laid down in *Casey's* case is that the warning of the danger of convicting on visual identification only remains.

The Court cannot think that what was defective in the original trial can now be put right and there would be no point in ordering a re-trial in these circumstances. ...

38. Bula Ltd. (in Receivership) v Crowley

Supreme Court, June 29, 1990
[1990] I.L.R.M. 756 at 757–758

Finlay C.J:

... In an *ex tempore* judgment delivered as the agreed judgment [in *Bula Ltd. v Tara Mines Ltd.*] by Walsh J. (5th February 1990), a transcribed copy of which has been approved by him, he dealt shortly but extremely comprehensively with the format required in respect of documents in which such a claim of privilege is being made in an affidavit of discovery. He stated as follows:

> "The format suggested by the plaintiff in his claim here appears to me to be at least in effect what the rules of court require, because unless documents are identified and properly indicated no particular claim of privilege should be made about anything. One must know what the claim is. The court directs that the rules of court should be followed in the format envisaged by the rules and so far as I am concerned the format indicated or sought in the motion today by the plaintiffs is in effect what the rules require. Therefore the schedule of documents should follow that format."

A consideration of the motion in that case and the appeal from the order of the High Court clearly indicate that what was required by this judgment and what the plaintiff was seeking in that case was an individual listing of the documents with the general classification of privilege claimed in respect of each document indicated in such fashion by enumeration as would convey to a reader of the affidavit the general nature of the document concerned in each individual case together with the broad heading of privilege being claimed for it. Such a requirement, irrespective of what may have been a habitual form of affidavit of discovery in the past, seems necessary to comply with .the principles laid down by this Court in the recent case of *Smurfit Paribas Bank Ltd v AAB Export Finance Ltd.* [1990] I.L.R.M. 588. ...

With regard to the second ground of appeal in the motion against the defendant Laurence Crowley, dealing with the communications between him and the defendant McKay and Schnellmann Ltd. subsequent to 2nd July 1986, the position in my view is as follows. In the course of an *ex tempore* judgment delivered on 19th December 1989 Murphy J., on the hearing of this motion in the High Court, stated as follows:

> "Discovery is a procedure which is left to the integrity of the parties themselves. The party who fails to make an adequate discovery is precluded from relying upon that document. The deponent who swears the affidavit has the final word on what is relevant and it is difficult, if not impossible, for the court to go behind that."

I am not satisfied that such an absolute protection of the decision by a deponent with regard to the question of discovery is warranted on principle. I accept that a court should be satisfied, as a matter of probability, that an error has occurred in an omission from an affidavit of discovery of documents on the basis of irrelevancy before making any order for further discovery and that it should not, in particular, permit the opposing party to indulge in an exploratory or fishing operation. ...

39. O'Leary v Attorney General
High Court, October 26, 1990
[1993] 1 I.R. 102 at 104–113

Costello J:

On the 19th November, 1987, the plaintiff was convicted by the Special Criminal Court of (1) membership of an unlawful organisation contrary to s.21 of the Offences Against the State Act, 1939 (as amended) and (2) possession of incriminating documents contrary to s.12 of the same Act, both offences having been committed on the 18th April, 1987. On the 29th July, 1988, his application for leave to appeal against his convictions was refused by the Court of Criminal Appeal but his sentence of five years imprisonment for membership of an unlawful organisation was reduced to four. The year following, on the 27th July, 1989, these proceedings were instituted. In them he claims declarations (i) that s.24 of the Act of 1939 and (ii) that s.3, sub-s.2 of the Offences Against the State (Amendment) Act, 1972, are unconstitutional. To explain the issues which have been raised I must briefly refer to the proceedings at the plaintiff's trial.

The plaintiff was indicted on two counts, a count which charged that on the 18th April, 1987, he was a member of an unlawful organisation, to wit, an organisation styling itself the Irish Republican Army, otherwise Oglaigh na hÉireann, otherwise the IRA contrary to s.21 of the Offences Against the State Act, 1939, as amended by s.2 of the Criminal Law Act, 1976; and a count which charged that on the same day he had in his possession incriminating documents, namely 37 posters containing the words "IRA calls the shots", contrary to s.12 of the Act of 1939. Neither of the sections referred to in the indictment is challenged in this action. In the course of the trial (in which the plaintiff entered a not guilty plea) the prosecution adduced evidence as follows. Chief Superintendent McKeon swore that it was his belief that on the 18th April, 1987, the accused was a member of an unlawful organisation known as the IRA. This evidence was challenged in cross-examination but he maintained it and in addition expressed his belief that at the time of the trial the accused was still a member of a subversive organisation. In adducing this evidence the prosecution relied on s.3, sub-s 2 of the Act of 1972 which provides:

> "Where an officer of the Garda Síochána, not below the rank of Chief Superintendent, in giving evidence in proceedings relating to an offence under the said section 21, states that he believes that the accused was at a material time a member of an unlawful organisation, the statement shall be evidence that he was then such a member."

In addition to the evidence of the Chief Superintendent the prosecution produced evidence of finding in the plaintiff's possession 37 copies of a poster showing the picture of a man in a paramilitary uniform brandishing a rifle and with the words "IRA calls the shots" prominently displayed on it. The prosecution submitted (and this submission has not been challenged at any time by the plaintiff) that these posters were "incriminating documents" within the meaning of s.2 of the Act of 1939, which defines an incriminating document as one *inter alia* issued by or emanating from an unlawful organisation. The prosecution relied on the fact of possession by the plaintiff of these incriminating documents and the legal effect of these facts brought about by s.24 of the Act of 1939 which provides that:

> "On the trial of a person charged with the offence of being a member of an unlawful organisation, proof to the satisfaction of the court that an incriminating document relating to the said organisation was found on such person or in his possession or on lands or in premises owned or occupied by him or under his control shall, without more, be evidence until the contrary is proved that such person was a member of the said organisation at the time alleged in the said charge."

At the close of the prosecution case the plaintiff gave evidence. He denied that he was a member of an unlawful organisation. He accepted that the posters were in his possession but he said that he had them as a member of Sinn Fein. The Special Criminal Court rejected his evidence. It accepted that the belief of the Chief Superintendent was correct and that it was corroborated by the evidence of the finding of the posters in the possession of the plaintiff.

The claims that the impugned sections are unconstitutional are based on the following arguments. The plaintiff, it is submitted, like every other person accused of a criminal charge, had a right to the presumption of innocence at his trial before the Special Criminal Court. This right is a constitutionally protected one and so a statute which infringes it must be invalid. The invalidity attached to s.24 of the Act of 1939 results because:

(a) the presumption of innocence which every accused enjoys casts a burden on the prosecution to prove the guilt of every accused, and

(b) this burden is removed from the prosecution in a case when the prosecution relies on s.24, for that section has the effect of placing a burden on an accused of establishing that he is not a member of an unlawful organisation once possession of an incriminating document is established. It is submitted that this shifting of the burden of proof on to an accused unconstitutionally deprives him of the protection of the presumption of innocence.

A similar argument is advanced in the attack on s.3, sub-s 2 of the Act of 1972. By providing that the statement of the belief of a Chief Superintendent is to be evidence that an accused person is a member of an unlawful organisation the section, it is said, shifts the burden of proof on to an accused person and requires him to establish, once the evidence is adduced, that he is not a member of an unlawful organisation thus depriving him of the presumption of innocence to which he is entitled.

I have little difficulty in accepting the basic contention on which these arguments are posited and in construing the Constitution as conferring on every accused in every criminal trial a constitutionally protected right to the presumption of innocence. This right is now widespread and indeed enjoys universal recognition. Article 11 of the United Nations Universal Declaration of Human Rights, 1948, provides that "Everyone charged with a penal offence has the right to be presumed innocent until proved guilty according to law . . ." Article 6(2) of the European Convention on Human Rights and Fundamental Freedoms, 1950, provides that "Everyone charged with a criminal offence shall be presumed innocent until proved guilty according to law . . ." Article 8(2) of the American Convention on Human Rights, 1969, prepared within the Organisation of American States provides that "Every person accused of a criminal offence has the right to be presumed innocent so long as his guilt has not been proven according to law.": Article 7 of the African Charter on Human and Peoples' Rights provides that every individual has the right to have his cause heard and declares that this, *inter alia*, comprises "the right to be presumed innocent until proven guilty by a competent Court or tribunal."

By construing the Constitution in the light of contemporary concepts of fundamental rights (as I am entitled to do; see *The State (Healy) v Donoghue* [1976] I.R. 325) the plaintiff's claim obtains powerful support. But in addition, although the Constitution was enacted before these international instruments were adopted in 1937, the presumption of innocence had long been an integral part of the common law tradition which constituted an important part of the legal order which this State then adopted (as pointed out by McCarthy J. in *Ryan v Director of Public Prosecutions* [1989] I.R. 399). The Constitution of course contains no express reference to the presumption but it does provide in Article 38 that "no person shall be tried on any criminal charge save in due course of law." It seems to me that it has been for so long a fundamental postulate of every criminal trial in this country that the accused was presumed to be innocent of the offence with which he was charged that a criminal trial held otherwise than in accordance with this presumption would, prima facie, be one which was not held in due course of law. It would follow that *prima facie* any statute which permitted such a trial so to be held would be unconstitutional. The contentious issue in the case, therefore, is not whether the plaintiff had a constitutionally protected right to the presumption of innocence but whether the impugned provisions of the Acts of 1939 and 1972 infringed that right.

Before considering the sections which are now challenged there are four observations of a general nature which should be made.

Firstly, there are a considerable number of statutes (for example, the Libel Act, 1843, the Explosives Substances Act, 1883, the Merchandise Marks Act, 1884, the Forgery Act, 1913, the Prevention of Corrupt Practices Act, 1916, the Larceny Act, 1916, and in more recent times the Criminal Law (Jurisdiction) Act, 1976, the Misuse of Drugs Act, 1977, and the Misuse of Drugs Act, 1984) which contain provisions which have the effect of shifting the onus of proof in certain circumstances from the prosecution to the accused. There is no standard form by which this is brought about. For example, s.28 of the

Larceny Act, 1916, provides that any person found at night having in his possession without lawful excuse, "the proof whereof shall lie on such person", a housebreaking implement is guilty of an offence, whilst s.22 of the Misuse of Drugs Act, 1977, provides that in any proceedings for an offence under the Act where the defendant claims that he has a controlled drug lawfully in his possession by virtue of s.4 of the Act "the onus of proving such lawful possession . . . shall be on the defendant." The two sections challenged in these proceedings are different from these sections and different from each other. Section 3, sub-s 2 of the Act of 1972 provides that the statement of the belief of a Chief Superintendent that an accused was a member of an unlawful organisation "shall be evidence that he was then such a member", whilst s.24 of the Act of 1939 provides that the fact of possession of an incriminating document "shall, without more, be evidence until the contrary is proved" that a person in possession of the document is a member of an unlawful organisation. It is obvious that the difference in the manner in which the statute shifts the onus of proof may produce different legal consequences and so any statute which does so must be carefully considered to appreciate exactly the effect it may have on an accused's constitutional rights. But there is one feature in common which a number of these statutes possess. By providing that once a fact is established (the possession of the housebreaking implement under the Larceny Act, 1916, the possession of a controlled drug under the Misuse of Drugs Act, 1977, the possession of a document which is an incriminating document under the Act of 1939), the court is then required to draw an inference which is specified in the section. It is the nature and effect of the inference or conclusion that requires careful analysis.

Secondly, it is important to bear in mind that the phrase "the burden of proof" is used in two entirely different senses and that when it is said that a statute "shifts" the burden of proof onto the accused this may mean two entirely different things. The phrase is used firstly to describe as a matter of substantive law the burden which is imposed on the prosecution in a criminal trial to establish the case against the accused beyond a reasonable doubt. This burden is fixed by law and remains on the prosecution from the beginning to the end of the trial. It is this burden which arises from the presumption of the accused's innocence and it is the removal of this burden by statute that may involve a breach of the accused's constitutional rights. It is now usual to refer to this burden as the legal or persuasive burden of proof. But the phrase is also used to describe the burden which is cast on the prosecution in a criminal trial of adducing evidence to establish a case against an accused, a burden which is now usually referred to as the evidential burden of proof. In criminal cases the prosecution discharges this evidential burden by adducing sufficient evidence to raise a "*prima facie*" case against an accused. It can then be said that an evidential burden has been cast on to the accused. But the shifting of the evidential burden does not discharge the legal burden of proof which at all times rests on the prosecution. The accused may elect not to call any evidence and will be entitled to an acquittal if the evidence adduced does not establish his or her guilt beyond a reasonable doubt. Therefore if a statute is to be construed as merely shifting the evidential burden no constitutional infringement occurs. (For a discussion on the two meanings see: Glanville

Williams, *Criminal Law*, 1961 ed., paras 287 and 288 and *Phipson on Evidence*, 1982 ed., chapter 4.)

Whilst it may not be desirable or indeed possible to lay down any hard and fast rule for the construction of statutes involving the shifting of a burden of proof, it is clear that if the effect of the statute is that the court must convict an accused should he or she fail to adduce exculpatory evidence then its effect is to shift the legal burden of proof (thus involving a possible breach of the accused's constitutional rights) whereas if its effect is that notwithstanding its terms the accused may be acquitted even though he calls no evidence because the statute has not discharged the prosecution from establishing the accused's guilt beyond a reasonable doubt then no constitutional invalidity could arise.

Thirdly, it does not necessarily follow that a statute is unconstitutional merely because its effect is that the failure of an accused to adduce exculpatory evidence must result in a conviction. The statute may merely give legal effect to an inference which it is reasonable to draw from facts which the prosecution establish. The presumption of the accused's innocence is therefore rebutted not by the statute but by the inference. An example is to be found in s.27A of the Firearms Act, 1964 (inserted by s.8 of the Criminal Law (Jurisdiction) Act, 1976) which provides that where a person has a firearm in his possession in such circumstances as give rise to a reasonable inference that he has not or does not possess it for a lawful purpose he shall be guilty of an offence "unless he has it in his possession . . . for a lawful purpose". As the inference exists apart from the statute I do not think that the statute can thereby be invalidated by the Constitution.

Fourthly, the Constitution should not be construed as absolutely prohibiting the Oireachtas from restricting the exercise of the right to the presumption of innocence. The right is to be implied from Article 38, which provides that trials are to be held "in accordance with law", and it seems to me that the Oireachtas is permitted in certain circumstances to restrict the exercise of the right because it is not to be regarded as an absolute right whose enjoyment can never be abridged. This is how the European Convention has been construed. The European Commission on Human Rights was required to consider a provision of a statute of the United Kingdom in which a man living with or habitually in the company of a prostitute is presumed to be knowingly living on the earnings of prostitution unless he proves otherwise (*X v United Kingdom* 5124/71 referred to in Jacobs, *The European Convention on Human Rights*, pages 113-114). In the course of its opinion the Commission stated that the provision:

> "creates a rebuttable presumption of fact which the defence may, in turn, disprove. The provision in question is not, therefore, as such a presumption of guilt. The Commission recognises however that this form of provision could, if widely or unreasonably worded, have the same effect as a presumption of guilt. It is not therefore sufficient to examine only the form in which the presumption is drafted. It is necessary to examine the substance and effect."

Because the presumption was restrictively worded and because it was neither irrebuttable nor unreasonable the statute did not infringe Article 6 of the Convention. The right to the presumption in the United Nations Universal Declaration is subject to article 29 which provides that in the exercise of his rights and freedoms "everyone shall be subject only to such limitations as are determined by law solely for the purpose of securing due recognition and respect for the rights and freedoms of others and of meeting the just requirements of morality, public order and the general welfare in a democratic society." The Canadian Charter of Rights and Freedoms provides that any person charged with an offence has the right to be presumed innocent until proven guilty according to law (s.11(d)) but this right, like the other rights and freedoms which the Charter guarantees is "subject only to such reasonable limits prescribed by law as can be demonstrably justified in a free and democratic society" (s. 1).

The Supreme Court of the United States has recognised that the presumption of innocence in a criminal trial is constitutionally protected and it has held that the due process clause of the Fifth Amendment may be breached by a statute which created a statutory presumption which failed to pass a "rational connection test", so that "a statutory presumption cannot be sustained if there is no rational connection between the fact proved and the ultimate fact presumed, if the inference of the one from the other is arbitrary because of lack of connection between the two in common experience": *Tot v United States* (1943) 319 U.S. 463 and *Leary v United States* (1969) 395 U.S. 6. But if the statute does pass the "rational connection" test then it is constitutionally valid even though it may adversely bear on an accused's right to be presumed innocent of the offence with which he is charged: *County Court of Ulster County, New York v Allen* (1979) 442 U.S. 140.

If I conclude, therefore, that either of the statutory provisions I am now considering *prima facie* infringes the plaintiff's right to the presumption of innocence it would then be necessary to consider the principles which would justify the Oireachtas in restricting the enjoyment of the presumption, for if the statute complied with those principles then no constitutional invalidity would arise. But firstly I must consider whether the statutes operate so as to infringe the right asserted. To that task I will now turn. ...

I fail to see how [s.3, sub-s 2 of the Act of 1972] affects in any way the plaintiff's right to enjoy the presumption of innocence. What this section does is to make admissible in evidence in certain trials statements of belief which would otherwise be inadmissible. The statement of belief if proffered at the trial becomes "evidence" by virtue of this section in the prosecution case against the accused. Like other evidence it has to be weighed and considered and the section cannot be construed as meaning that the court of trial must convict the accused in the absence of exculpatory evidence. The accused need not give evidence, and he may ask the court to hold that the evidence does not establish beyond a reasonable doubt that he is a member of an unlawful organisation. Should the court agree he must be acquitted.

Although s.24 of the Act of 1939 is differently worded to s.3, sub-s 2 of the Act of 1972 and although its object is different (the latter making admissible in evidence a statement of belief; the former enabling an inference to be drawn if certain facts are established) I think that this section does not infringe the plaintiff's constitutionally protected rights. It is important to appreciate how the section is drafted. It provides that proof of possession by an accused of an incriminating document (that is one emanating from an unlawful organisation) "shall, without more, be evidence until the contrary is proved" that the accused in whose possession the document was found was a member of the unlawful organisation. But this does not impose an obligation on an accused to give evidence so as to avoid a conviction. The section, it seems to me, only shifts an evidential burden on to an accused to whom it is applied. An "incriminating document" is defined in the Act in very wide terms so that it would embrace for example a letter from the leader of an unlawful organisation to the accused as well as a propaganda leaflet or poster extolling the aims of an unlawful organisation. "Possession" in the Act is a wide concept and an accused could have in his "possession" an incriminating document in different circumstances; it could be when hidden under the floorboards of the house in which he was living or, at the other end of the scale, when distributing it at a public meeting. So, the nature of the incriminating document and the circumstances in which it is possessed may in some cases give rise to a very strong inference of the accused's association with an unlawful organisation whilst in others any such inference might be very slight. If it was intended that the court could not evaluate the evidence and that it "must" convict in the absence of exculpatory evidence I think the section would have been differently worded. As actually drafted it seems to me that the court may evaluate and assess the significance of the evidence of possession and if it has a reasonable doubt as to the accused's guilt of membership of an unlawful organisation it must dismiss the charge, even in the absence of exculpatory evidence. If this is so then the section does not infringe an accused's right to the presumption of innocence. I must therefore decline to make the declarations which the plaintiff has sought. ...

40. People (D.P.P.) v Kehoe

Court of Criminal Appeal, November 6, 1991
[1992] I.L.R.M. 481 at 482–486, 488–489

O'Flaherty J:

... The facts, shortly stated, are that the accused had been friendly with Miss Sheila Murphy and she had had a child by him, and then, much to the accused's distress, it appears that Pat Harvey who had up to then been his best friend appears to have started a relationship with Miss Murphy and there is no doubt that this caused the accused acute jealousy and a form of suppressed rage which led, some short time before the actual events with which we are concerned, to the accused assaulting Pat Harvey by striking him some blows. Also, in a letter to Miss Murphy, the accused wrote that he had in his heart a wish to kill him (Harvey). So that was the background to his state of mind when, on the day of the occurrence, that is, on 1st March 1990, he met Miss Murphy and there appears to have been a certain amount of social intercourse between them, a considerable number of drinks were consumed and she, invited him back to her apartment at Willow House, Mounttown Flats, Dun Laoghaire.

There is no doubt that at that stage there was a good relationship between the two parties, and when he arrived at Miss Murphy's apartment he went into the sittingroom, and then at a certain stage he went to the toilet, and he thought of going into one of the bedrooms with the idea of seeing his son, that is, the son to which he was the father and to which Miss Murphy was the mother. He went in and instead he saw Pat Harvey in the bedroom, and (at Vol. D of the transcript, at p. 23a) counsel asked him what effect this had on his feelings, when he discovered that it was not his baby that was there but that it was Pat Harvey (who was probably asleep), he said:

> "I couldn't believe it. I was shocked. I was upset. I couldn't understand why I was brought up there if he could have been there, you know? I shouldn't have been brought up there."

Further when he was asked:

> "Now, you were shocked, you were upset. You were in the process of describing your reaction. ... Anything else you felt when you discovered the young man was in the bed and not the baby?"

He said: 'I just felt annoyed'.

The accused left the bedroom, went to the kitchen where he got a knife and ran back and stabbed Harvey. The accused's actions afterwards are not of any great importance, except to say that on the next day he went and saw the gardaí and made a full statement which was in line with his evidence at the trial.

Now, it is clear from that that the only course the case could take was to come down to whether the accused was guilty of murder or manslaughter; the only defence the accused had was a defence of provocation. It is not necessary to review what is involved in that defence because it is accepted in this case that proper directions were given in accordance with the case of *People (D.P.P.) v MacEoin* [1978] I.R. 27. The obligation on the prosecution, once such a defence is brought forward, is that the prosecution must establish beyond reasonable doubt that the accused was not provoked to such an extent that having regard to his temperament, character, and circumstances he lost control of himself at the time of the wrongful act. Then the jury should be told that they must consider whether the acts or words, or both, of provocation if found by them to have occurred, when related to the accused, bear a reasonable relation to the amount of force used.

If the prosecution prove beyond reasonable doubt that the force used was unreasonable and excessive, having regard to the provocation, the defence of provocation fails.

Provocation was the defence, and the only defence, as has been said, that the accused had in this case, and it was sought to buttress that defence by introducing the evidence of Dr. Behan.

It is important to point out that Dr. Behan was not called to establish a defence of insanity, or any form of mental illness or any form of derangement that might have occurred by the accused's use of drugs and alcohol in regard to which it appears he had become dependent. While the evidence of a psychiatrist is, undoubtedly, relevant and admissible in such circumstances, as it will be if the defence of diminished responsibility or such is given recognition in our law it is clear to the court that Dr. Behan could not in this case give any relevant, admissible evidence in relation to the state of mind, the temperament and these other matters that are referred to in *McEoin's* case, that the accused could not do himself. But he attempted to do so, and this approach, if it might be summarised, was to say that he had a great deal of experience of people who had been through emotional upset, people who had become involved with drink and drugs, and so forth, and that, therefore, he was in a strong position to give a clinical pronouncement on the reality of the defence that the accused man was putting forward. ...

There is no doubt that Dr. Behan was attempting to articulate in a fuller way what the accused had stated, rather briefly, *viz* his annoyance and upset but on which he based his defence of provocation.

The Court is of the opinion that the accused's defence was properly to be considered by the jury without such elaboration and that, further, in the course of his evidence it is clear that Dr. Behan overstepped the mark in saying that he believed the accused did not have an intention to kill and that the accused was telling the truth. These are clearly matters four-square within the jury's function and a witness no more than the trial judge or anyone else is not entitled to trespass on what is the jury's function. This has been stressed over and over again in many cases, most recently in a decision of the Supreme Court in *People (D.P.P.) v Egan* [1990] I.L.R.M. 780. So it appears to the court that the correct approach, where there is any doubt in the matter, is for the defence to canvass the view of the trial judge in the first instance as to whether psychiatric evidence is properly admissible, because the view of the Court is that this was not a case for the admission of psychiatric evidence, and it would appear to be, as far as criminal cases are concerned, properly confined to the matters already mentioned, such as the defence of insanity or the like.

The Court of Appeal (Criminal Division) in England was confronted with a similar problem in a case of *R. v Turner* [1975] Q.B. 834. The court was comprised of Lawton L.J., Neild and Cantley JJ. The facts were not dissimilar from this case, except that the provocation alleged was offered by a girlfriend of the accused and she, thinking that she was pregnant by him taunted him— at least he said that she taunted him—with the fact that she had relations with other men, and there was an attack made on her leading to her death. ... Lawton L.J., giving the judgment of the court, went on to say:

> "We all know that both men and women who are deeply in love can, and sometimes do, have outbursts of blind rage when discovering unexpected wantonness on the part of their loved ones; the wife taken in adultery is the classical example of the application of the defence of 'provocation'; and when death or serious injury results, profound grief usually follows. Jurors do not need psychiatrists to tell them how ordinary folk who are not suffering from any mental illness are likely to react to the stresses and strains of life. It follows that the proposed evidence was not admissible to establish that the defendant was likely to have been provoked. The

same reasoning applies to its suggested admissibility on the issue of credibility. The jury had to decide what reliance they could put on the defendant's evidence. He had to be judged as someone who was not mentally disordered. This is what juries are empanelled to do. The law assumes they can perform their duties properly. The jury in this case did not need, and should not have been offered, the evidence of a psychiatrist to help them decide whether the defendant's evidence was truthful."

It seems to the court that the law in Ireland is the same. ...

The court would wish to say, firstly, that at the very outset of his charge, without any doubt, the learned trial judge made clear that the findings of fact and their assessment of the evidence was a matter exclusively for the jury and not for him. Secondly, and with regard to the other passages which have been quoted, it seems to the court that the judge was indicating to the jury the effect of Dr. Behan's evidence which is in accord with this Court's assessment of his evidence. In other words, it is not so much that he was adversely commenting on Dr. Behan's evidence *qua* Dr. Behan as a witness, but the judge was saying that his testimony could not prove or could not assist in proving anything that was not in the case already and put there by the accused. The judge was pointing out that the evidence of the psychiatrist had the infirmities that the *Turner* case predicted such evidence would have. So, in a sense, the learned trial judge was not adversely commenting on a witness as much as stating the correct law on the matter.

If one were to take the passage to the effect that the jury should not have any regard to Dr. Behan's opinion as simply a comment on a witness who had given relevant admissible evidence, the court is in no doubt that the judge would have done well to reiterate the warning that the matter was, in the last analysis, for the jury. Increasingly, it is the experience in this jurisdiction as it is in other jurisdictions that a trial judge abstains from offering any view of the evidence, good, bad or indifferent. That is not to say that trial judges are not entitled to offer a view, but more and more trial judges consider that juries are best left to see evidence through a glass clearly rather than to have it either magnified or diminished by the judge's intervention.

So, in summary, the court has reached the conclusion that this ground of misdirection, or mistrial, has not been made out. The court has carefully considered the other grounds of appeal, which are that there is a suggestion that the learned trial judge did not adequately direct the jury that all questions on disputed fact were for them but it is clear that he did make clear that the resolution of these matters was exclusively for the jury and the Court is of the opinion that this ground has not been made out either. ...

41. People (D.P.P.) v Brophy

Court of Criminal Appeal, January 30, 1992

[1992] I.L.R.M. 709 at 711–712, 714–716, 721

O'Flaherty J:

... The complainant, with a schoolgirl companion, called to the accused's shop on Thursday, 21st December 1989, where there were heard conversations between the accused and the two girls. According to the accused, corroborated by the complainant's companion, it was at that stage that the accused offered to make two of these pendulums for the girls. ...

It was agreed that they set out in the accused's car to his house which was a comparatively short distance away about a ten or fifteen minute drive. Again, it is more or less agreed that they spent about one hour in the house. The complainant alleged that several acts of molestation took place while they were in his sitting room. This involved touching the complainant's breasts outside her shirt and underneath her shirt on a number of occasions. The accused's version of events was that he was engaged in fulfilling the order; that the complainant engaged in cordial conversation with him; was interested in examining his large collection of videotapes as well as other curios, including his large collection of the stones, to which reference has already been made. Further, that there was no question of any interference at all with the complainant and that at about 1.15 pm he got a phone call on his mobile phone from Mr. O'Connor, the bank official, with whom he had arranged a meeting at 1 o'clock and Mr. O'Connor was understandably angry that he was not keeping that appointment because Mr. O'Connor, who had journeyed from College. Street, Dublin, was anxious to make the 2 o'clock first race at Leopardstown racecourse. ...

Sometime between 1.15 and 1.30 p.m. it seems clear that the accused drove the complainant back to the shopping centre, gave her some money (it may have been £4 or £5) and this, it was said, was to pay her bus fare to and from Lucan and, in the presence of a security man at the shopping centre, she alighted from the car and did not show any sign of distress; in fact, according to the security man she said to the accused; 'I'll see you tomorrow'. Thereafter, the complainant made the journey to her mother's house in Templeogue, where she stayed for some time and to whom she did not complain of any assault. Neither did she complain to others to whom she might have complained before meeting her mother. She then met up with some three girl companions before meeting with her father who had come in from Lucan with the intention of meeting her at about 3.00 pm and with the intention that she would stay with him for some time. The complainant was in a distressed condition when she met her three companions as when she met her father. Further reference will be made to the significance of this later in the judgment. ...

It will be recalled that the complainant had an opportunity to complain to several persons and, certainly, she had an opportunity of complaining to her mother and it appears that she was in her mother's house for some appreciable length of time and did not complain. She did, however, complain to three of her companions and she also complained, separately, to her father. However the prosecution took the view that since the complaint had not been made at the first opportunity after the offence which reasonably offered itself they should not give the terms of the complaints but felt free to give evidence of the fact of the making of complaints. ... [W]hat we have to decide is whether evidence of the fact of the making of a complaint was admissible in circumstances where, it is conceded, the complaint was not made at the first opportunity which reasonably presented itself.

The history of the admissibility of complaints in sexual cases is recounted in *Cross on Evidence* (seventh edition) at p. 282:

> "In the Middle Ages it was essential that the victim should have raised the hue and cry if an appeal of rape were to succeed. By the beginning of the eighteenth century, when the modern law of evidence was beginning to take shape, the absence of complaint was no longer an absolute bar to success, but Hawkins still referred to the strong presumption against a prosecutrix in a case of rape if she made no complaint within a reasonable time of the alleged offence. If the absence of such complaint could tell against a prosecutrix it seemed to follow that the fact of having made a complaint ought to tell in her favour, and if failure to complain could be proved by the defence then the fact of making a complaint should be capable of proof by the prosecution. Such proof does however raise problems since it grates against the rule excluding previous consistent statements, the hearsay rule and the rule against self-corroboration."

In the old law it was only the fact of complaint that was admissible and it was not until *R. v Lillyman* [1896] 2 Q.B. 167 that the Court for Crown Cases Reserved extended admissibility of a complaint to its terms. It seems to the court, therefore, that either evidence of a complaint having been made is admissible, or it is not. If it is admissible, then, subject to the discretion of the trial judge to prevent unnecessary prejudicial repetition, the terms of the complaint are also admissible. It is for the trial judge to rule on the matter in the first instance. In this case, the trial judge's ruling was not sought in advance. The evidence given by the complainant was as follows. Having recounted the visit to her mother and her meeting with three girlfriends, she was asked in examination-in-chief what she did when she met them. She replied:

> "I burst out crying and told them the story.
>
> Do you remember seeing your father?
>
> Yes. My friends told me that I should tell somebody. So, my father came down with the car and I got in the car and said goodbye to my mother, and on the way home I told my father in the car and burst out crying. He brought me back to my mother's house and asked my mother to ring the police."

Mr. Hardiman S.C. on behalf of the accused made an application, in short, to have the jury discharged on the basis that this evidence was inadmissible.

Mr. Marrinan, for the prosecution, said that there had been agreement that the fact of the complaint could be tendered in evidence but not its terms. As we have held already there seems no room for half measures in regard to this; either the fact of a complaint is admissible or it is not. Indeed, in the case of *Lillyman* which established the entitlement of the prosecution to introduce details of the complaint as well as the fact of the complaint it was made clear that the admissibility of evidence of the fact that the complaint was made was subject to the condition that it was made 'as speedily after the acts complained of as could reasonably be expected' (at p. 171 of the report). The prosecution conceded that the complaint was not made as speedily as possible. Since the prosecution were clearly of the view that the terms of the complaint were not admissible, then the fact of the complaint should not have been admitted either.

The judge ruled that he would not discharge the jury and, in the ordinary way, the discharging of a jury in any trial must be a very extreme remedy but we are of the opinion that in this case, where the prosecution depended on the uncorroborated evidence of the complainant, the requirement that a balance had to be kept to preserve fairness in the trial since the evidence was so minimal required that the jury should have been discharged when this evidence got in.

Everyone, thereafter, was very careful not to advert to this evidence of complaint at all and, indeed, the three girl companions were not even called as witnesses though the father did give evidence of the fact of a complaint and of the distressed condition in which the complainant was at the time that he met her. But the point of this evidence was not explained to the jury.

In the circumstances, it might be useful if we recapitulated the law on this topic of admissibility of complaints. It is as follows:

(a) Complaints may only be proved in criminal prosecutions for a sexual offence.

(b) The complaint must have been made as speedily as could reasonably be expected and in a voluntary fashion, not as a result of any inducements or exhortations. Once evidence of the making of a complaint is admissible then particulars of the complaint may also be proved.

(c) It should always be made clear to the jury that such evidence is not evidence of the facts on which the complaint is based but to show that the victim's conduct in so complaining was consistent with her testimony.

(d) While there is mention in one of the older cases, *R. v Osborne* [1905] 1 K.B. 551 of a complaint being 'corroborative of the complainant's credibility' this does not mean that such a complaint amounts to corroboration of her testimony in the legal sense of that term but as pointing to the consistency of her testimony. Corroboration in the strict sense involves independent evidence, that is evidence other than the complainant's evidence.

(e) The law on complaints should not be confused with what takes place once the police institute their inquiries.

That is a separate matter. A complaint made to the police may, as such, be admissible or not under the guidelines set out above but just because a complaint is not made at the first opportunity to the police does not, of course, inhibit their inquiries. ...

However, on the basis of our findings in respect of the other grounds of appeal we hold that the conviction in this case is unsafe and unsatisfactory and for this reason we order that the conviction should be quashed. ...

We think this is not a case to exercise our discretion to order a retrial because, aside altogether from the infirmities in the evidence which we have delineated, no court would be justified in imposing any further sentence of imprisonment on Mr. Brophy should he be convicted on a retrial. ...

42. People (D.P.P.) v Quillegan and O'Reilly (No. 3)

Supreme Court, July 14, 1992
[1993] 2 I.R. 305 at 321–322, 332–433, 351–352

Finlay C.J:

... Where a person has been arrested pursuant to s.30 of the [Offences Against the State] Act of 1939 he has got, in the view of this Court, the following protections.

1. If the arresting garda does not have a *bona fide* suspicion based on reason of one or other of the matters provided for in the section the arrest is unlawful and he may be released by an order pursuant to Article 40 of the Constitution – *The State (Trimbole) v The Governor of Mountjoy Prison* [1985] I.R. 550.

2. At the time of the arrest the suspect must be informed, if he does not already know, of the offence pursuant to the Act of 1939 or scheduled for its purposes, of which he is suspected, otherwise his arrest will be unlawful – *The People (Director of Public Prosecutions) v Walsh* [1980] I.R. 294.

3. The person detained has, during his detention, a right to legal assistance, and the refusal to grant it to him when reasonably requested can make his detention unlawful – *In re The Emergency Powers Bill, 1976* [1977] I.R. 159, and *Director of Public Prosecutions v Healy* [1990] I.L.R.M. 313.

4. The right to medical assistance – *In re The Emergency Powers Bill, 1976* [1977] LR. 159.

5. The right to access to the courts – *In re The Emergency Powers Bill, 1976* [1977] LR. 159.

6. The right to remain silent and the associated, right to be told of that right – *The People (Director of Public Prosecutions) v Quilligan* [1986] I.R. 495.

7. The Judges' Rules with their provisions in regard to the giving of cautions and the abstention from cross-examination of a prisoner apply to a person

in detention under s.30 – *The People (Director of Public Prosecutions) v Quilligan* [1986] I.R. 495.

8. A person detained under s.30 must not, in the words of Walsh J. in *The People (Director of Public Prosecutions) v Quilligan* [1986] I.R. 495, "be subject to any form of questioning which the courts would regard as unfair or oppressive, either by reason of its nature, the manner in which it is conducted, its duration or the time of day or of its persistence into the point of harassment, where it is not shown that the arrested person has indicated clearly that he is willing to continue to be further questioned".

9. If the detention of a person arrested under s.30 is extended by a Chief Superintendent for a further period after the first period of twenty-four hours, he must entertain also the necessary *bona fide* suspicion of the suspect that justified his original arrest and must be satisfied that his further detention is necessary for the purposes provided for in the section – *The People (Director of Public Prosecutions) v Eccles, McPhillips and McShane* (1986) 3 Frewen 36.

The Court having considered all these protections, any of which can be made effective either by, where appropriate, the release of the person detained from his detention, pursuant to an order made under Article 40 of the Constitution or can be given effect to by the exclusion of evidence obtained in violation of any of these rules applicable to detention under s.30, is satisfied that having regard to the purposes of the section as outlined in the judgment of Walsh J. in *The People (Director of Public Prosecutions) v Quilligan* [1986] I.R. 495, to which reference has already been made, that s.30 has not been established as constituting a failure by the State as far as practicable by its laws to defend and vindicate the personal right of immediate liberty of the citizen. ...

At the trial each of the accused gave evidence concerning the circumstances surrounding the taking of statements from him at the trial within a trial as a result of which the learned trial judge ruled that the statements taken were admissible in evidence before the jury. Broadly speaking, the allegations made by each of the accused at that hearing were to the effect that they were harassed, threatened and, to an extent, assaulted and that they were induced to make statements by an inducement involving in each case the situation of their respective wives who were in custody. In each case, also, it was stated by the accused that the statements were not of their own creation but that words were written down or dictated by members of the Garda Síochána, and they were induced or cajoled or bullied into signing the document so written out.

At the trial, in the presence of the jury, these allegations were repeated and the two accused, each of whom gave evidence before the jury on his own trial, in addition to denying participation in the crime and giving an account of his movements on the evening when the crime was committed, gave again the evidence in substantially identical terms to what had been sworn to by them in the trial within a trial, in the absence of the jury.

In those circumstances, it was specifically contended on behalf of each of the accused, prior to the commencement of the judge's charge that the learned trial judge should direct the jury that apart from reaching a conclusion with regard to whether the confessions which had been admitted in evidence were true and genuine, that they should firstly reach a conclusion as to whether they were voluntarily made and accordingly should have been admitted into evidence, and in effect, that if they concluded that they were not voluntarily made that they should not make any further inquiry as to whether they were or were not true.

This application was rejected by the learned trial judge, and I am satisfied that he was correct in so doing.

Having regard to the decision of this Court in *The People (Director of Public Prosecutions) v Conroy* [1986] I.R. 460, it is clear that the function of ruling on the admissibility of confessions or incriminating statements alleged to have been made by an accused is a mixed question of fact and law which falls within the function, in a trial had with a jury, of the trial judge. I am satisfied that it follows from that fact that there cannot be, as it were, any question of an appeal from or review by the jury of the decision of the trial judge to admit statements into evidence. If a judge should err, either in the principles which he applied or by acting on insufficient or non-existent evidence in reaching a conclusion that statements were admissible, then, he must be corrected on appeal by an appellate court.

Where, as has occurred in this case, the issue with regard to the admissibility of statements turns largely on allegations of threats, assault, inducement or harassment, or of what is described as the "planting" of statements, then, the function of the jury is, I am satisfied, as follows.

It must be clearly directed by the trial judge to have regard to all the evidence which is before it, including all the evidence suggesting that the statement has been obtained by any of the unlawful methods which I have mentioned above for the purpose of ascertaining whether they are satisfied beyond a reasonable doubt that the confession or incriminating statement made by the accused is true and is a sufficient proof of his guilt.

A jury is not bound by a finding of fact made by a trial judge in the course of his ruling on the admissibility of a statement such as, for example, a rejection by him of an allegation that a member of the Garda Síochána assaulted the accused whilst in his custody and thus obtained the statement from him. It must be made clear, whether by specific warning or by a positive direction to a jury that their function in having to be satisfied beyond a reasonable doubt as to the truth of a voluntary statement admitted into evidence before them necessarily involves an examination by them of allegations of any description which are relevant to the question as to whether the statement was truly voluntarily given or not. It should be made clear to them that if they have a reasonable doubt as to whether a statement was truly voluntarily given that that would form a very solid ground for also entertaining a reasonable doubt as to whether it was true.

I have very carefully considered the entire charge of the learned trial judge in this case. In considerable detail, notwithstanding the length of the case, and with complete accuracy, he put before the jury the allegations of every description made by each of the accused, going to the question as to whether these statements were voluntarily given. The terms of his charge clearly made that question relevant, and highly relevant, to the question as to whether the statements could be satisfactorily accepted by the jury beyond a reasonable doubt as being true. Having regard to that conclusion concerning the nature of the charge, I am satisfied that this ground of appeal must also fail. ...

McCarthy J:

... Trial includes the resolution of all issues of fact. ... I am unable to reconcile the constitutional guarantee of trial by jury with an exclusive right in the trial judge to determine the issue as to whether or not a confession was voluntarily made. In *The People (Director of Public Prosecutions) v Lynch* [1982] I.R. 64, as referred to in *The People (Director of Public Prosecutions) v Conroy* [1986] I.R. 460, Walsh J. said at p. 86 of the report:

> "A similar situation arises with regard to the voluntary character of a statement. It is for the trial judge, in the first instance, to decide upon the admissibility; but he cannot decide upon the truth of the statement. A judge in such a case must direct the jury that they must be satisfied that the statement is true, or true in material respects, before they can accept it as evidence to be acted upon. In many cases consideration of this matter may involve the jury in considering and arriving at a conclusion on the circumstances under which the statement was made or obtained."

Clearly, a statement may be involuntary, being obtained by threats, but true (historically, it was only statements obtained under torture that were accepted as true); statements made voluntarily may be untrue; involuntary statements may be untrue and voluntary statements may be true. There is no norm. In my view, to exclude the jury from a consideration of whether or not a statement was voluntarily made is to deny the accused the constitutional right to trial by jury. That right is not ensured by limiting the jury's function to a determination of whether or not the statement is true even while directing the jury that the determination of truth or otherwise may depend upon their view as to the various allegations of impropriety against, as in this case, the gardaí. Apart from the reference at citation (c) in the charge of Costello J., there is no indication given to the jury that they are concerned with whether or not the confession was given voluntarily; in context, I believe the expression "given voluntarily" there was in no sense an invitation to the jury to enter into that inquiry. From my experience at the Bar, I am aware of a number of instances in which, the judge having ruled in favour of admission of the statement as having been voluntarily made, the issue was further left to the jury for their consideration at the end of the case.

43. Lindsay v Mid-Western Health Board
Supreme Court, December 18, 1992
[1993] 2 I.R. 147 at 178–185

O'Flaherty J:

This is an appeal from the judgment and order of the High Court (Morris J.) of the 30th May, 1991, holding in favour of the plaintiff in an action for damages for personal injuries brought on her behalf for the alleged negligence of the defendant, its servants or agents in regard to matters surrounding a surgical procedure carried out at Limerick Regional Hospital on or about the 16th March, 1982. ...

The plaintiff, Beatrice Lindsay, then aged eight years, was admitted to Limerick Regional Hospital on the 15th March, 1982, with stomach pains. She was diagnosed as having an acute appendicitis or, as an alternative, mesenteric adonitis. This latter condition is an inflammation of the lymph glands in the mesentery. The symptoms of this condition mimic the symptoms of an inflamed appendix and, indeed, that is what happened in this case because after the appendix was removed and was subsequently subjected to pathological examination it was found not to have been the cause of the plaintiff's original troubles. No point is made on this as it is accepted that it was reasonable to operate to remove the appendix in the circumstances of this case. ...

The evidence of the anaesthetists was to the effect that the relevant anaesthetic procedures were put in place and that nothing untoward happened in the course of the operation. The plaintiff was removed to the recovery room when she was described by Dr. McDermott as being absolutely normal. Although she appeared to be commencing to regain consciousness she did not do so and then she developed seizures which proved extremely difficult to control. She eventually became comatose and unresponsive. This was at about 2 a.m. on the morning of the 16th March, the anaesthetic having been administered at about 12.35 a.m. Later, on neurological examination, a C.T. scan showed generalised brain oedema. E.E.G. showed bilateral diffuse symmetrical slow activity, in keeping with a diffuse form of neuronal dysfunction. The plaintiff has irreversible brain damage, is in a coma and will not come out of it. At the date of the trial she had a life expectancy of about 15 years. ...

In my judgment, the submission that *res ipsa loquitur* does not apply in the circumstances of this case should be rejected. It is true that a precise circumstance of negligence cannot be pointed to – such as in the classical cases of bags of sugar falling on a passing pedestrian (*Scott v London and St. Katherine Docks Co.* (1865) 3 H. & C. 596) or a motor car driven onto a footpath (*Murray v Gilmore*, Unreported, Supreme Court, 20th December, 1973) – but it seems to me that if a person goes in for a routine medical procedure, is subject to an anaesthetic without any special features, and there is a failure to return the patient to consciousness, to say that that does not call for an explanation from defendants would be in defiance of reason and justice. Equally, however, it seems to me that in this case the most that the defendants should be required to do is to show that they exercised all reasonable care and that they were not negligent, and that they should not be required to take the further step of proving, on a balance of probabilities, what did cause the plaintiff's brain damage. The distinction between a negligent act and causation requires to be emphasised. ...

The learned trial judge, having held that the effect of the application of the maxim *res ipsa loquitur* was to throw the burden of proof onto the defendant to prove, on the balance of probabilities, what caused the plaintiff's brain damage, and it having failed to do so – having propounded possibilities only of what caused her condition – that that would amount to the court adopting a theory based on pure speculation; that was not sufficient for the defendant to meet the case and, therefore, he held that negligence was to be inferred. On that basis, he found for the plaintiff.

As I have set out, the trial judge rejected hypoxia as a cause of the plaintiff's condition. Mr. Sutton S.C. for the plaintiff has submitted, however, that the trial judge did so only in regard to the assertion made on behalf of the plaintiff that hypoxia was the cause of the plaintiff's brain damage; that, however, it remains as something that could still be in the case and something that the defendant has not disproved as it is required to do once the maxim *res ipsa loquitur* comes into play. I would reject this submission as being at variance with the judge's findings. He had before him the clear evidence of all the defence witnesses, especially the two anaesthetists, that no hypoxic occurrence took place in the course of the anaesthetic procedures and he also accepted the evidence of the expert defence witnesses in this regard. The only conclusion that can be drawn is that hypoxia is out of the case. While the plaintiff's advisers did not have to assert any particular cause for the plaintiff's condition, it is the case, I believe, that hypoxia as a possible cause would have had to be disproved in any event. So nothing turns on the fact that the plaintiff's advisers propounded it as a cause in the first instance.

With hypoxia out of the case, it follows inexorably that the anaesthetists must be acquitted of any blame because the only thing that could have resulted if anything had been remiss with the way the anaesthetic was administered was hypoxia: nothing else.

I believe that the trial judge was, however, correct in regarding this as a *res ipsa loquitur* case. Disparity between the situation of the respective parties is crucial in this regard. As O Dalaigh C.J. said in *Dowd v Kerry County Council* [1970] IR 27 at p. 41 of the report:

> "It should also be said that in an action with regard to a surgical operation the patient rarely knows anything; what has happened is known only to the defendants."

In the decision of the British Columbia Supreme Court (Andrews J.) *Girard v Royal Columbian Hospital et al.* (1976) 66 D.L.R. (3d) 676 which was cited to the learned High Court Judge as well as to us, Andrews J. agreed with the description of *res ipsa loquitur* contained in Fleming, *The Law of Torts* (See now 7th edition at p. 291):

> "In some circumstances, the mere fact that an accident has occurred raises

an inference of negligence against the defendant. A plaintiff is never obliged to prove his case by direct evidence. Circumstantial evidence is just as probative, if from proof of certain facts other facts may reasonably be inferred. *Res ipsa loquitur* is no more than a convenient label to describe situations where, notwithstanding the plaintiff's inability to establish the exact cause of the accident, the fact of the accident by itself is sufficient in the absence of an explanation to justify the conclusion that most probably the defendant was negligent and that his negligence caused the injury. The maxim contains nothing new; it is based on common sense, since it is a matter of ordinary observation and experience in life that sometimes a thing tells its own story. Unfortunately, the use of a Latin phrase to describe this simple notion has become a source of confusion by giving the impression that it represents a special rule of substantive law instead of being only an aid in the evaluation of evidence, an application merely of the general method of inferring one or more facts in issue from circumstances proved in evidence'. (*Davis v Bunn* (1936) 56 C.L.R. 246 at 268)."

I, too, would adopt this as an apt description of the scope of the maxim. Andrews J. went on to say (at p. 691):

"The human body is not a container filled with a material whose performance can be predictably charted and analysed. It cannot be equated with a box of chewing tobacco or a soft drink (*Pillars v R.J. Reynolds Tobacco Co.* (1918) Miss. 490, 78 So. 365 (S.C.); and *Donoghue v Stevenson* [1932] A.C. 562). Thus, while permissible inferences may be drawn as to the normal behaviour of these types of commodities the same kind of reasoning does not necessarily apply to a human being. Because of this medical science has not yet reached the stage where the law ought to presume that a patient must come out of an operation as well or better than he went into it. From my interpretation of the medical evidence the kind of injury suffered by the plaintiff could have occurred without negligence on anyone's part. Since I cannot infer there was negligence on the part of the defendant doctors the maxim of *res ipsa loquitur* does not apply."

I would adopt this reasoning to the circumstances of the present case.

I believe at the end of all the evidence in this case the situation was that the plaintiff had clearly established a *prima facie* case on two different bases. One was the evidence of Professor Keane that postulated the probability that there had been an hypoxic occurrence. This, as I have said, was rejected by the trial judge. Further, for the reasons I have suggested as regards how unique and unusual this occurrence was, and because of the respective positions of the litigants, clearly an answer was required from the defendant. That answer could be provided in two ways. It could have proved, on the balance of probabilities, that the plaintiff met her injuries in a particular manner that caused her condition but which was not connected with the administration of the anaesthetic. This it failed to do. The furthest the defendant got was to suggest as possibilities other means by which the plaintiff sustained her injuries. I believe this evidence is not, however, to be regarded as totally inadmissible. It was legitimate, I believe, for the defendant to adduce evidence of possibilities, remote though they might be, as an explanation; in contradistinction to saying that it could not offer *any* explanation of any description whatsoever. It went to provide some corroboration, as well, that there was no negligence on its part in the administration of the anaesthetic. The other course was for the defendant to establish that from beginning to end of this anaesthetic procedure there was no negligence on its part. This it did decisively and, in those circumstances, it appears to me that it rebutted the burden of proof that rested on it to displace the maxim *res ipsa loquitur* and so the case returned to the plaintiff's bailiwick to prove negligence.

I believe that it is necessary to ensure that the rule embodied in the maxim does not put a burden on defendants which is so onerous as to produce an unjust result. Each case must, of course, be dealt with in accordance with its own particular facts but, as I have said, I believe that in the circumstances here the defendant has met the *prima facie* case made against it as fully as could be expected. It would be an unjustifiable extension of the law to say that in the absence of an explanation that could be proved, on the balance of probabilities, negligence on the part of the defendant must be inferred. It has often been said that medical science is not an exact one and it is safe to prophesy that medical science and its technology will advance past frontiers which are not within anyone's contemplation at this time and so matters at present not amenable to explanation will be capable of resolution.

Accordingly, I would reverse the order of the High Court.

44. Hardy v Ireland and Ors. (No.2)

Supreme Court, March 18, 1993
[1994] 2 I.R. 550 at 563–569

Hederman J. (with whom O'Flaherty J. and Blayney J. agreed):

... The sole ground argued in this Court on behalf of the appellant was an assertion that s.4, sub-s.1 of the Explosive Substances Act, 1883, was inconsistent with the Constitution and had not been carried over in accordance with Article 50 thereof.

I take the following summary of the facts of the actual case from *The People (Director of Public Prosecutions) v Hardy* (Court of Criminal Appeal, 22nd June, 1992, *ex tempore*):

> "... the [applicant] was coming through the customs clearance at Rosslare, was asked to open the bag he was carrying by customs officials there, and they became suspicious of what he was carrying and of his conduct. He sought to run away from them, was apprehended and brought back, and they then found in his bag a quantity of what eventually transpired to be sodium chlorate, and also ten mercury tilt switches. Evidence was given by a Dr. McDermott, which was not challenged by any contradictory

evidence, that sodium chlorate was a substance which was capable of being used, and was used, for the purpose of making an explosion, together with other substances. And evidence was given by a Garda McArdle who is an expert in these matters, and again was not challenged. He was cross-examined but no contradictory evidence was given; his evidence was that mercury tilt switches could be one of the components, and were used as one of the component parts in what are described as car bomb explosions."

Section 4, sub-s.1 of the Explosive Substances Act, 1883, provides:

"Any person who makes or knowingly has in his possession or under his control any explosive substance, under such circumstances as to give rise to a reasonable suspicion that he is not making it or does not have it in his possession or under his control for a lawful object, shall, unless he can show that he made it or had it in his possession or under his control for a lawful object, be guilty of felony, and, on conviction, shall be liable to penal servitude for a term not exceeding fourteen years, or to imprisonment for a term not exceeding two years with or without hard labour, and the explosive substance shall be forfeited. ...."

In my judgment, in a trial alleging an offence under the section the prosecution has to prove beyond reasonable doubt (I take the basic ingredients contained in the section and I leave aside alternate wording):

(1) That the accused knowingly had in his possession a substance which it proves is an explosive substance;

(2) that he had it under such circumstances as to give rise to a reasonable suspicion that he did not have it in his possession for a lawful object and that, in turn, means that there is an onus on the prosecution to prove that the accused could not show that he had it in his possession for a lawful object.

Once those ingredients are in place, it is still open to the accused to demonstrate in any one of a number of ways, such as by cross-examination, submissions or by giving evidence, that a *prima facie* situation pointing to his guilt should not be allowed to prevail.

I believe that this analysis complies with our well-established criminal law jurisprudence in regard to having trials in due course of law. That constitutional requirement applies whether the offence is made an offence under a pre- or post-constitutional enactment. It protects the presumption of innocence; it requires that the prosecution should prove its case beyond all reasonable doubt; but it does not prohibit that, in the course of the case, once certain facts are established, inferences may not be drawn from those facts and I include in that the entitlement to do this by way even of documentary evidence. What is kept in place, however, is the essential requirement that at the end of the trial and before a verdict can be entered the prosecution must show that it has proved its case beyond all reasonable doubt.

I would dismiss the appeal.

Egan J:

The only issue permitted to be argued by the Court was whether or not s.4, sub-s.1 of the Explosive Substances Act, 1883, was carried forward having regard to the provisions of Article 50 of Bunreacht na hÉireann.

The principal argument by the applicant was that the effect of the section was to change the burden of proof so that an accused person might be found guilty without his guilt having been proved beyond reasonable doubt and that this was inconsistent with the presumption of innocence which was a necessary ingredient for a trial in due course of law.

The argument on behalf of the State was that insofar as any burden of proof was cast on an accused under the section it was an evidential one and did not infringe an accused's constitutional rights. It was argued that in relation to all aspects of the offence the principles of (a) the benefit of the doubt, (b) the benefit of accepting an explanation which could be true and (c) the benefit of accepting the innocent explanation in a case where two or more explanations were equally open, must be applied in favour of the accused person.

A careful look at the subsection makes it clear that the State must prove:

(1) possession or control of an explosive substance;

(2) that the accused "knowingly" had such possession or control; and

(3) that the possession or control was in such circumstances as to give rise to a reasonable suspicion that he did not have it in his possession or control for a lawful object.

The onus lies fairly and squarely on the State to prove these matters and they must be proved beyond reasonable doubt. It may seem perhaps contradictory that a "reasonable suspicion" must be proved beyond reasonable doubt but this is not so. If the court or jury is not satisfied beyond reasonable doubt that a suspicion has been raised and that it is a reasonable suspicion, an essential ingredient of the offence will be missing and the prosecution will fail.

If, however, all the above ingredients are proved beyond reasonable doubt the accused must be convicted unless "he can show that he made it or had it in his possession or under his control for a lawful object". *Prima facie* these words place an onus on the accused but they are in a saving or excusatory context and this is of relevance. Insanity, for instance, is something which must be established by an accused person in a criminal prosecution if he wishes to rely on it.

It is true that when the evidence in a case, whether offered by the prosecution or the defence, discloses a possible defence of self-defence, the onus remains on the prosecution to negative the possible defence of self defence. See the judgments of Walsh J. in *The People v Quinn* [1965] I.R. 366 and *The People v Dwyer* [1984] I.R. 416.

The onus in regard to self-defence springs from the common law. In the present case, however, we are dealing with a statute and the words used are very clear. If the saving clause is to be relied upon, I am satisfied that the onus shifts to the accused. The words are "unless he can show ... [etc.]". These words cannot be construed as meaning that the raising of a doubt would be a sufficient discharge. The onus, not being an onus resting on the prosecution, does not require proof beyond reasonable doubt. It is sufficient if there is proof on the balance of probabilities.

The conclusion which I have reached to the effect that the onus of proof can shift does not determine the matter. There is nothing in the Constitution to prohibit absolutely the shifting of an onus in a criminal prosecution or to suggest that such would inevitably offend the requirement of due process. For these reasons I am satisfied that the subsection is not repugnant to the Constitution and that the appeal should be dismissed.

Murphy J:

The only issue argued before the Court on this appeal was whether s.4 of the Explosive Substances Act, 1883, was inconsistent with the provisions of Bunreacht na hÉireann. That section was considered and, in my view, properly interpreted by Lord McDermott L.C.J. delivering the judgment of the Court of Criminal Appeal in Northern Ireland in *Regina v Fegan* [1972] N.I.L.R. 80 at p. 82 in the following terms:

> "This provision illustrates a means of meeting a legislative problem recently considered by the House of Lords in *Reg. v Warner* [1969] 2 A.C. 256; in relation to a charge of possessing drugs – the problem of how to curb a grave evil which postulates a guilty mind or mental element on the part of offenders, when proof of that guilty mind or mental element is likely to be a matter of inherent difficulty. Section 4(1) of the Act of 1883 may be said to proceed by way of compromise. It does not make it an offence to possess explosive substances for an unlawful purpose, nor does it create an absolute offence by prohibiting the mere possession of explosive substances. Instead, its two limbs provide for a dual inquiry (1) Was the person charged knowingly in possession under such circumstances as to give rise to a reasonable suspicion that his possession was not for a lawful object? and (2) If the answer to (1) is in the affirmative, has the person charged shown that his possession was for a lawful object? If the answer to (1) is in the affirmative and the answer to (2) is the negative a conviction follows; otherwise there must be an acquittal. The first limb allows for a conviction on a reasonable *suspicion*. The second allows what may be very much a subjective defence, with the accused and his or her spouse permitted by section 4(2) (as an exception to the then existing law) to give evidence on oath as ordinary witnesses."

Having reviewed the facts of the particular case Lord McDermott L.C.J. held that the summing up by the trial judge was defective in that:

> "... it makes the guilt of the accused depend altogether on the establishment of a reasonable suspicion, whereas under section 4 it remains open to an accused person, despite the clearest proof of circumstances giving rise to a reasonable suspicion, to show that his object in having possession was in fact lawful, and to do so on a balance of probabilities."

The view which the Court of Criminal Appeal in Northern Ireland expressed to the effect that the burden which an accused undertakes where he chooses to rely on the second limb of s.4, sub-s.1 of the Explosive Substances Act, 1883, is proof "on the balance of probabilities" is supported by the speech of Lord Roskill delivering the unanimous decision of the House of Lords in *Reg. v Berry* [1985] 1 A.C. 246 in which he commented on the effect of the section (at p. 254) as follows:

> "The respondent was therefore liable to conviction unless he could thereupon discharge the burden which the subsection at that stage casts on him, a burden which only has to be discharged on a balance of probabilities."

It seems to me that what Lord McDermott describes as the first limb of s.4, sub-s.1 of the Act of 1883 casts upon the prosecution the burden of proving first the possession of the explosive substance, secondly, that the accused "knowingly" had the explosive substance in his possession and thirdly, the existence of such circumstances as to give rise to a reasonable suspicion that the accused did not have the explosive substance in his possession for a lawful object. The burden of proof that falls on the State in respect of each and every one of those three ingredients is "... proof beyond reasonable doubt". Accordingly, if any reasonable doubt exists in relation to the proof of any of those ingredients or if the facts of the case admit of an innocent explanation as an alternative to a guilty one, then the accused must be acquitted. These principles flow from the presumption of innocence of an accused to any charge made against him. However, the second limb of the section deals not with the charge but with a statutory exoneration or exculpation from a charge already made and sustained beyond reasonable doubt. I am convinced that the burden which the accused must discharge if he is to avail of that procedure is a duty to satisfy the jury of the statutory condition, that is to say, the existence of a lawful object on the balance of probabilities.

However, I do not see that there is any inconsistency between a trial in due course of law as provided for by Article 38, s.1 of the Constitution and a statutory provision such as is contained in s.4 of the Explosive Substances Act, 1883, which affords to an accused a particular defence of which he can avail if, but only if, he proves the material facts on the balance of probabilities.

Accordingly, I too would dismiss the appeal.

45. Goodman International v Hamilton (No. 3)

High Court, May 27, 1993
[1993] 3 I.R. 320 at 325–330

Geoghegan J:

... In a case where it is thought appropriate to apply the Wigmore test, I am satisfied that each of the four conditions must in general apply to the particular relationship and that in considering, for instance, the application of the fourth condition, the facts of the particular case before the court or tribunal are not relevant. That was the approach of Gavan Duffy J. in *Cook v Carroll* [1945] I.R. 515 and of Carroll J. in the later case of *E.R. v J.R.* [1981] I.L.R.M. 125 where she held that the relationship of priest/marriage counsellor to spouses did comply with the conditions. Carroll J. however observed that the court should be slow to admit new categories of privilege. I respectfully agree with this view, having regard to the other line of Irish authorities to which I will briefly refer concerning public policy privilege in connection with discovery of documents. The Irish courts have disapproved of class privilege in relation to documents. By the same token any unnecessary extension of privilege by reference to fixed categories of relationships would seem to me to offend the jurisprudence of the Irish courts.

An attractive argument can undoubtedly be put forward that the relationship between a member of the public and a member of the Oireachtas in the context of information of public interest being conveyed on an understanding that the informant's identity would not be disclosed does comply with the Wigmore conditions. But there would be real problems of definition of the relationship and indeed limitation, for, as counsel for the applicants have pointed out, the same privilege might be argued for in the case of the relationship between informant and county councillor and other analogous relationships.

In my view the Wigmore rules, which are nothing more than a summing up by a distinguished textbook writer are, are an inappropriate test to apply to the privilege claimed here which has a direct public interest dimension far beyond the mere private interest in confidentiality The Wigmore rules are appropriate *prima facie* rules where the privilege is sought in respect of a private relationship analogous to that of lawyer and client, but not where a direct public interest is a major factor in favour of upholding the privilege claimed. I have used the word "direct" because in a sense, as has been pointed out in some of the more modern cases, all privilege is grounded on public policy. But the public element is much more directly present where the claimed privilege relates to communications involving organs of State or public bodies. I find myself able to decide this case without reference to the Wigmore conditions as such and on a narrow basis relating to the actual facts before me. In these circumstances I find it unnecessary to consider whether there should be an additional recognised category of relationships to which privilege would attach.

I have made reference in passing to a second line of Irish authorities relating to public policy privilege. I am referring to *Murphy v Corporation of Dublin* [1972] I.R. 215; *Geraghty v Minister for Local Government* [1975] LR.300; *Ambiorix Ltd. v The Minister for the Environment* [1992] 1 I.R. 277, and some

High Court decisions which have applied the principles ennunciated in those cases. The common factor in these cases was a rejection of any kind of class or category privilege. Underlining them is the public interest in the administration of justice. The exclusion of admissible and relevant evidence is in general contrary to that public interest. It is for the courts to decide on the merits of a plea of privilege in any particular case. But in no Irish case has it ever been held that there are no circumstances where the general public interest in the non-exclusion of admissible and relevant evidence cannot be overridden by a conflicting public interest in a particular case in favour of non-disclosure. This view is confirmed by Walsh J. in *In re Kevin O'Kelly* (1974) 108 I.L.T.R. 97 when he observed at p. 101 of the report:

> "The fact that a communication was made under terms of expressed confidence or implied confidence does not create a privilege against disclosure. So far as the administration of justice is concerned the public has a right to every man's evidence except for those persons protected by a constitutional or other established and recognised privilege."

For the purpose of this case I must assume that the informants were acting *bona fide*, though of course that may not in fact be the case. I must further assume that they fully expected that, having been promised by the members of the Oireachtas in question that their identity would not be disclosed, that promise would be honoured. I think that most Irish people would regard it as important that matters of actual or potential public concern may be brought to the attention of elected national public representatives without fear of the confidence being broken. But I do not believe that most people would expect an absolute rule of non-disclosure that could brook no exceptions. If disclosure of the source was relevant to the guilt or innocence of an accused in a trial for a serious criminal offence then justice and the public interest might require disclosure.

In arriving at my decision in the instant case, the case which I have found most helpful is *D. v N.S.P.C.C.* [1978] A.C. 171. This is not because the House of Lords laid down any definitive rules. On the contrary, although there was unanimity on a narrow issue which actually determined the case, the discussion in the four carefully thought out speeches revealed numerous differences of opinion among the Law Lords as to the wider issues of privilege. But the case is of considerable assistance in identifying the different kinds of privilege and the different sets of circumstances in which they may arise. The uncertainty of the law is highlighted by the fact that the House of Lords overturned the decision of the Court of Appeal which in turn was divided in that Lord Denning M.R. dissented to the views of Scarman L.J., as he then was, and Sir John Pennycuick. But the House of Lords, although reversing the Court of Appeal, rejected Lord Denning's views on confidentiality and privilege. The Court of Appeal had overturned a judgment of Croom-Johnson J. which was highly praised by the House of Lords. The High Court judgment itself overturned a decision of a Senior Master who was apparently a distinguished expert on the law of evidence.

I mention all this so as to highlight the state of flux in which this branch of the law was in England at least in 1977. None of the more recent English cases have finally clarified it.

One clear principle that does emerge from the speeches in the House of Lords in *D. v N.S.P.C.C.* [1978] A.C. 171 is that confidentiality alone is never a ground for non-disclosure but it may be a relevant factor in determining whether there is a public interest in non-disclosure or as Lord Hailsham of St. Marylebone, at p. 230 of the report, put it:

> "Confidentiality is not a separate head of immunity. There are however cases when confidentiality is itself a public interest..."

Any Irish court would agree also with the following sentiments of Lord Hailsham as contained in his reported speech, at p. 223:

> "I start with the assumption that every court of law must begin with a determination not as a general rule to permit either party deliberately to withhold relevant and admissible evidence about the matters in dispute. Every exception to this rule must run the risk that because of the withholding of relevant facts justice between the parties may not be achieved. Any attempt to withhold relevant evidence therefore must be justified and requires to be jealously scrutinised."

But Lord Hailsham went on to sound the following caution:

> "The facts disclosure of which is required must be required for the purpose of deciding the dispute. A collateral purpose is not justified and must be disregarded."

In the context of the Beef Tribunal, therefore, any understandable and legitimate desire of the applicants to have sources identified so that defamation or other proceedings can be instituted must be completely discounted in any consideration as to whether non-disclosure of sources be permitted.

Subject to slight modifications necessitated by *Cook v Carroll* [1945] I.R. 515 and *E.R. v J.R.* [1981] I.L.R.M. 125, I accept and adopt the summary of the legal rules relating to permitted non-disclosure of information contained in the speech of Lord Edmund-Davies in *D. v N.S.P.C.C.* [1978] A.C. 171 which, at p. 245 of the report, reads as follows:

> I. In civil proceedings a judge has no discretion, simply because what is contemplated is the disclosure of information which has passed between persons in a confidential relationship (other than that of lawyer and client), to direct a party to that relationship that he need not disclose that information even though its disclosure is (a) relevant to and (b) necessary for the attainment of justice in the particular case. If (a) and (b) are established, the doctor or the priest must be directed to answer if, despite the strong dissuasion of the judge, the advocate persists in seeking disclosure. This is also true of all other confidential relationships in the absence of a special statutory provision. ...

II. But where (i) a confidential relationship exists (other than that of lawyer and client) and (ii) disclosure would be in breach of some ethical or social value involving the public interest, the court has a discretion to uphold a refusal to disclose relevant evidence provided it considers that, on balance, the public interest would be better served by excluding such evidence.

III. In conducting the necessary balancing operation between competing aspects of public interest, the presence (or absence) of involvement of the central government in the matter of disclosure is not conclusive either way, though in practice it may affect the cogency of the argument against disclosure. ...

IV. The sole touchstone is the public interest, and not whether the party from whom disclosure is sought was acting under a 'duty' as opposed to merely exercising 'powers'. A party who acted under some duty may find it easier to establish that public interest was involved than one merely exercising powers, but that is another matter.

V. The mere fact that relevant information was communicated in confidence does not necessarily mean that it need not be disclosed. But where the subject matter is clearly of public interest, the additional fact (if such it be) that to break the seal of confidentiality would endanger that interest will in most (if not all) cases probably lead to the conclusion that disclosure should be withheld. And it is difficult to perceive of any judicial discretion to exclude relevant and necessary evidence save in respect of confidential information communicated in a confidential relationship.

VI. The disclosure of all evidence relevant to the trial of an issue being at all times a matter of considerable public interest, the question to be determined is whether it is clearly demonstrated that in the particular case the public interest would nevertheless be better served by excluding evidence despite its relevance. If, on balance, the matter is left in doubt, disclosure should be ordered."

Even though some of these rules may not be relevant to the case, I thought it best to set out the suggested rules in full so as to place those which are relevant in context. I should also add that I can see no relevant difference in principle between information given on a confidential basis to the intent that it would not be disclosed and information given with a view to its being publicly aired but on the understanding that the identity of the informant would not be disclosed. The principles on which the confidence in each should be maintained by a court or tribunal are the same.

In my view the combination of the second and sixth principles as enunciated by Lord Edmund-Davies gave the respondent a discretion as to whether he would insist on disclosure. Having regard to all the surrounding circumstances and in particular the fact that the unknown informants could not reasonably have expected that, through an accidental and erroneous understanding of constitutional privilege, the members of the Oireachtas laid themselves open to being forced to disclose and the fact that the respondent has at all times made clear that no hearsay evidence will be admitted to undermine the good names of the applicants, the discretion in my view would have to be exercised in favour of non-disclosure. I have therefore arrived at the same decision as the respondent by a different route. ...

46. People (D.P.P.) v Clarke
Court of Criminal Appeal, July 6, 1994
[1994] 3 I.R. 289 at 302–304

O'Flaherty J:

... The learned trial judge dealt with this matter as follows:

> "... A statement made to the guards is not in the same category as evidence in the case. Evidence in a case is somebody getting into the witness box, taking the oath, giving his evidence orally and allowing the jury to assess his evidence as he gives it, listen to a cross-examination if there is one and see whether a person is shaken in any way in his evidence. ... [A] statement made to the guards is not at all in the same category as a statement made on oath subject to cross-examination subject to the jury assessing what they think of the witness and whether they are convinced by his evidence or not. I say that because at some stages in his closing address to the jury Mr. McDowell spoke to you about the statement as though it were evidence. It is only evidence of what the accused man said to the guards the day after."

The judge then went on to point out that an accused had no obligation to give evidence and he then went on to point to the corrections that the accused had made to his original statement in particular as regards who had accompanied him on the last fatal mission and so forth. The sole point for resolution in dealing with this ground of appeal is the direction that should be given to a jury in relation to a statement made by an accused which contains incriminatory as well as exculpatory matter. ...

The law on this topic was reviewed extensively in the decision of the Court of Criminal Appeal in *The People (Attorney General) v Crosby* (1961) 1 Frew. 231. The Court comprised Maguire C.J., McLoughlin and Teevan JJ. The judgment in the case was given by Teevan J.

The true position in law, as established by that case, and which we take this opportunity of reiterating, is that once a statement is put in evidence, as in this case by the prosecution, it then and thereby becomes evidence in the real sense of the word, not only against the person who made it but for him as to facts contained in it favourable to his defence, or case. A jury is not bound to accept such favourable facts as true, even if unrefuted by contrary evidence, but they should be told to receive, weigh and consider them as evidence.

It appears that the learned trial judge's approach was to draw a distinction between the incriminating parts and the exculpatory parts of the original statement. For some time this approach held sway in England but it appears now that it no longer prevails: see the judgment of the Court of Appeal, Criminal Division in *R. v Duncan* (1981) 78 Cr. App. R. 359. The Court, in the course of its judgment, at p. 365, said as follows:

> "Where a mixed statement [meaning thereby one that contains incriminatory as well as exculpatory matter] is under consideration by the jury in a case where the defendant has not given evidence, it seems to us that the simplest, and, therefore, the method most likely to produce a just result, is for the jury to be told that the whole statement, both the incriminating parts and the excuses or explanations, must be considered by them in deciding where the truth lies. It is, to say the least, not helpful to try to explain to the jury that the exculpatory parts of the statement are something less than evidence of the facts they state. Equally, where appropriate, as it usually will be, the judge may, and should, point out that the incriminating parts are likely to be true (otherwise why say them?), whereas the excuses do not have the same weight. Nor is there any reason why, again where appropriate, the judge should not comment in relation to the exculpatory remarks upon the election of the accused not to give evidence."

This has been affirmed as a correct statement of the law in England by the House of Lords in *R. v Sharp* [1988] 1 W.L.R. 7.

With reference to the present case, while the judge was entitled to comment unfavourably on certain changes that had been made in regard to the accused's original statement there was an obligation on him when dealing with the statement to remind the jury that the accused had raised the defence of self-defence fairly and squarely in the course of his first statement and that they thus had to consider that defence. It would have been appropriate, too, to point out that that statement was made at a very early stage before the accused had got any legal advice and was made spontaneously to the gardaí. It was necessary to remind the jury that the accused had never departed from the essential stance that he had taken as regards why he shot the deceased. The jury might have believed that explanation or disbelieved it and, either way, might still have held against the accused. But his explanation should have been laid before the jury as part of the evidence in the trial. Then they could accept it as true or reject it as false and resolve the issue of guilt or innocence having regard to the onus of proof that rested on the prosecution.

The Court is of the opinion that this ground, too, has been made out. ...

47. L.(T.) v L.(V.)

Circuit Court, November 10, 1994
[1996] F.L.R. 126 at 128–132, 134, 137

McGuinness J:

In these proceedings, the applicant seeks a decree of judicial separation from the respondent husband, together with a number of ancillary orders regarding *inter alia* the custody of the children, periodic and lump sum maintenance and a division of the family property. ...

This Motion was issued on 5th October 1994 and by the time it was listed for hearing, the respondent had in fact filed his affidavit of discovery. However, counsel for the applicant submitted that there were a number of items missing from the respondent's Discovery including in particular a 'blue book' or diary which, it was alleged, contained financial information concerning the respondent's private medical practice. On 7th November, counsel informed the court that most of the outstanding items had been dealt with but no discovery of the 'blue book' had been made. Counsel for the respondent submitted that no diary of the type alleged existed. She produced in court pocket diaries for 1993 and 1994. She argued that most of the material in these diaries consisted of notes made at the suggestion of the respondent's solicitor with a view to instructing the said solicitor and as such were covered by legal professional privilege. Counsel for the applicant, Mr. Durcan, submitted that such notes in the diary were not specifically documents of instructions to solicitor and counsel and were thus not covered by legal professional privilege. In the alternative, he argued that where documents contained matters relevant to the welfare of children, legal professional privilege should not be applied to them and they should be disclosed. In making this argument, Mr. Durcan relied on a number of English cases referred to in detail below.

As a method of procedure, counsel agreed that I should read the diaries in question with a view to deciding (a) whether the matters contained therein were relevant to the proceedings, and (b) whether any relevant matters were to be covered by legal professional privilege. ...

On my reading of the respondent's pocket diaries for 1993 and 1994, it appears to me that a considerable amount of the matters noted therein is relevant to the present proceedings and therefore I must consider whether these matters should be discovered or whether they are covered by legal professional privilege. The relevant notes in the diaries fall into two categories. The first category consists of some sparse notes made from time to time of what appear to be fees received from private patients. It is clear that this material is proper for discovery and I am accordingly providing counsel for both parties with a list of the pages in the 1993 diary on which this type of note appears and these pages are to be discovered by the provision of photocopies of the relevant pages to the applicant's solicitor. None of this type of material appears in the 1994 diary.

The second category of material—contained in the 1994 diary—consists of day to day notes concerning the parties and their children. It should be noted that these entries do not occur until after the issue of the applicant's proceedings on 11 February 1994.

Most solicitors and counsel who regularly practise in the field of family law will be familiar with the advice which is frequently given to matrimonial litigants to keep careful notes of current developments and happenings, both as they affect the parties and more importantly, as they affect the children. These notes are made for the specific purpose of instructing solicitor and counsel and as preparation for the trial of the action.

On reading the respondent's 1994 diary, I felt strongly that the material therein was of this nature and I would accept the submission of Ms. Clissmann on behalf of the respondent that the diary was prepared for the purpose of litigation and thus would, in the normal way, fall to be covered by legal professional privilege.

I must therefore go on to consider the submission made by Mr. Durcan on behalf of the applicant that where documents contain matters relevant to the welfare of children, legal professional privilege should not be applied to them and they should be disclosed.

The specific issue of possible conflict between legal professional privilege and the paramount welfare of children has not, so far as I am aware, been argued or decided to date in this jurisdiction and learned counsel were also unable to discover any Irish decision on the matter. There is, however, some indication of the balancing of statutory privilege and the welfare of children to be found in the judgement of the learned Mr. Justice Finlay then President of the High Court, in the case of *M.(S.) and M.(M.) v M.(G.) and Others* [1985] ILRM 186. The proceedings in that case involved *inter alia* a claim by the plaintiffs, who were prospective adoptive parents for an order dispensing with the consent of the mother, who was one of the defendants, and an order for interim custody and the claim by the mother for custody. The Adoption Board and the Adoption Society were amongst the other defendants. In affidavits of discovery filed on behalf of the Board and the Society, privilege was claimed in relation to certain documents based on section 8 of the Adoption Act, 1976. This section prohibits an order for the discovery, inspection, production or copying of any book, document or record of the Board unless the court is satisfied that it is in the best interests of any child concerned to do so. In regard to the issue of discovery, the learned judge stated at p. 187 of the report:

> "I have no doubt that the best interests of the child in regard to the determination of these proceedings when considered in the context of discovery depends upon discovery of such documents being made as would enable all the parties to those proceedings to present their case to the full.
>
> "In detail this means that the plaintiffs, as prospective adoptive parents, should be in a position to adduce the maximum amount of evidence establishing their suitability as custodians of the child and to defend themselves against any challenges or criticisms of that suitability and that the mother should have a like advantage and opportunity.
>
> "The provisions of section 8 of the 1976 Act clearly indicate an intention on the part of the legislature that the necessary confidentiality of documents and other papers, the property of the Adoption Board,

should be maintained unless the best interests of the child concerned in a particular case is established to my satisfaction as a matter of probability to require their discovery or production. Once, however, that has been established there cannot arise in my view any question of balancing the interests of an individual child concerned in a particular case against the general proceedings and efficiency of the activities of the Adoption Board."

Thus where the interests of a child were at stake, those interests overrode the statutory privilege claimed by the Board.

In regard to the issue of legal professional privilege, it appears to be settled law in the English jurisdiction that in wardship proceedings, the court may, in the interests of the welfare of a child, override legal professional privilege, at least in the case of experts' reports. Hershman and McFarlane in their comprehensive work *Children: Law and Practice* (stating the law as at 1st September 1994) describe the position as follows:

"In ordinary litigation the court has no power to override the privilege attaching to material produced for a party by expert witnesses. However the court sitting in wardship proceedings does have the power in appropriate cases to override the legal professional privilege attached to an expert's report and order its disclosure. The power, which stems from the parental non-adversarial character of wardship proceedings, should only be exercised rarely giving due consideration to the need for parties not to feel inhibited from obtaining such reports and not to be left with a feeling of injustice and only if the interests of the child require disclosure." [Section D, para. 1392 A]

It appears that this position was based on the fact that wardship proceedings were of their nature inquisitorial rather than adversarial.

Some doubt arose as to whether this position in regard to privilege was carried over into proceedings under the Children Act 1989 which is a comprehensive and reforming statute now covering proceedings in regard to children in the English jurisdiction. ...

The issue was then considered by the English Court of Appeal in the case of *Oxfordshire County Council v M. and Anor.* [1994] 2 All E.R. 269. Here the Court of Appeal overruled the *Barking and Dagenham v O and Another* case [1993] 4 All E.R. 59 and approved the judgement of Thorpe J. in *Re R (a minor)* [1993] 4 All E.R. 702. In this case, the question was one of disclosure of a psychiatrist's report on children where child sexual abuse was alleged. As is stated in the headnote, the Court of Appeal held that proceedings under the Children Act, 1989 are not adversarial and the court's duty is to investigate and to seek to achieve a result which is in the interests of the welfare of the child or children the subject of the proceedings. Such proceedings are not similar to ordinary civil litigation in cases between party and party in which the doctrine of professional privilege applies but fall into a special category where the court is bound to undertake all necessary steps to arrive at an appropriate result in the paramount interests of the welfare of the child.

Accordingly the court has power to override legal professional privilege and order disclosure where a party wishes not to disclose an unfavourable expert's report obtained with the leave of the court ....

I would note in passing that the principle that in certain circumstances legal professional privilege may be overruled has recently been reaffirmed in the Supreme Court in the case of *Murphy v Kirwan* [1994] 1 I.L.R.M. 293, where it was held that professional privilege must not be applied so as to be injurious to the interests of justice and to those in the administration of justice where persons have been guilty of conduct of moral turpitude or of dishonest conduct, even though it may not be fraud. This of course was not a case concerning the welfare of children but it nevertheless accepts and affirms the principle that legal professional privilege may be overruled in the interests of a higher priority such as justice.

However, I would also emphasise the limitations placed on disclosure in children's cases by the English decisions. Firstly the cases refer solely to medical and expert reports and clearly such reports are the type of material which would normally require to be disclosed in this context. The same considerations do not necessarily apply to other matters normally covered by legal professional privilege. In each case the desirability of disclosure must on the facts of the case be weighed against the desirability of maintaining the privilege and a decision taken in the light of the interests of the child concerned.

Secondly, I accept that the power to override the normal privilege in such cases should, as was said by Johnston J. in *Re A. (Minors: Disclosure of Material)* [1991] 2 F.L.R. 473, be exercised only rarely and only when the court is satisfied that it is necessary.

In the light of these principles, I have carefully considered the material contained in the respondent's 1994 pocket diary. In no sense does it contain or refer to any medical or other expert's report. While reference is made to day to day happenings in regard to the children, I do not feel that the material in regard to the children is of such a nature that the interests of the children require that it be disclosed by way of discovery in these proceedings. As I have said the notes in the diary are in the nature of instructions to solicitor and counsel. I will therefore refuse discovery of the respondent's pocket diary of 1994. ...

48. B. v D.P.P.

High Court, October 9, 1995
[1997] 3 I.R. 140 at 152, 154, 157–158

Budd J:

... The applicant contends that the large number of counts in the indictment is unfair. The allegations of the three complainants in this case are strikingly consistent and similar. Each alleges that she was abused from a very young age in the absence of her mother and each says that she was subjected to acts of sexual self-gratification on the part of the father accompanied by threats of violence in the event of resistance or disclosure. Each complains of coercion through force, fear and shame. As a general rule it is not open to the prosecution to adduce evidence of the bad character of the accused in any form. The exclusionary rule also precludes proof of the commission of discreditable acts which are not themselves criminal and of any discreditable propensity which may make the accused appear as more likely to have committed the act charged. The reason for the rule is that such evidence is simply irrelevant, because no number of similar offences in themselves can connect a person with a particular crime. The second reason is that prejudice created by such evidence outweighs any probative value it might have. Evidence is inadmissible if it does no more than to suggest that the accused is the sort of person who might commit the offence charged, but it may be admissible if it goes further and becomes part of the proof that he did commit it. [The learned judge next quoted *dicta* from *Makin v Attorney General for New South Wales* [1894] A.C. 57 at 65 and *R. v Boardman* [1975] A.C. 421 at 441, 462, 444]. ...[4]

More recently stress has been laid on the positive probative value of the evidence rather than the use of "striking similarity" as the test for admissibility in cases. This is because striking similarity is just one of the ways in which evidence may exhibit the exceptional degree of probative force required for admissibility, so that to insist upon it to an equal degree in all cases would be incorrect. I have set out the above principles because the principles to be applied in cases of multiple charges and accusations do not differ materially from those applicable where similar fact evidence is used to rebut an explanation otherwise open to an accused. Indeed, the function of evidence of multiple accusers is often to rebut such an explanation. Where an accused faces more than one allegation of a similar nature, the evidence of one accuser may be admissible to support the evidence of another. Such evidence may be corroborative. In a recent English case *Director of Public Prosecutions v P.* [1991] 2 A.C. 447, the House of Lords held that striking similarity is not a prerequisite of admissibility. P. was convicted of rape and incest, the victims being his two daughters. Before the start of the trial the judge refused the defendant's application that the counts relating to each girl should be tried separately. The Court of Appeal, with reluctance, quashed the convictions on the ground that, in the absence of any striking similarity between their stories, the allegation of one girl should not have been admitted to support those of the other. Mackay L.J. on the appeal to the House of Lords allowed the prosecutor's appeal and reviewed the development of the authorities in this area of the law. Having explained that since *Reg. v Boardman* [1975] A.C. 421, the law has required some feature of similarity beyond what has been described as the paederast's or the incestuous father's stock-in-trade before one victim's evidence can be properly admitted upon the trial involving another victim. Having outlined the views expressed in *Makin* and *Boardman*, Mackay L.J. at p. 460 said:

> "From all that was said by the House in *Reg. v Boardman* I would deduce the essential feature of evidence which is to be admitted is that its

---

[4] *cf.* appendices 1 and 23.

probative force in support of the allegation that an accused person committed a crime is sufficiently great to make it just to admit the evidence, notwithstanding that it is prejudicial to the accused in tending to show that he was guilty of another crime. Such probative force may be derived from striking similarities in the evidence about the manner in which the crime was committed and the authorities provide illustrations of that of which *Reg. v Straffen* [1952] 2 Q.B. 911 and *Rex v Smith* (1915) 11 Cr. App. R. 229 provide notable examples. But restricting the circumstances in which there is sufficient probative force to overcome prejudice of evidence relating to another crime to cases in which there is some striking similarity between them is to restrict the operation of the principle in a way which gives too much effect to a particular manner of stating it, and is not justified in principle. *Hume on Crimes*, 3rd ed. (1844), vol. II, p. 384, said long ago:

> 'the aptitude and coherence of the several circumstances often as fully confirm the truth of the story, as if all the witnesses were deponing to the same facts.'

"Once the principle is recognised, that what has to be assessed is the probative force of the evidence in question, the infinite variety of circumstances in which the question arises, demonstrates that there is no single manner in which this can be achieved. Whether the evidence has sufficient probative value to outweigh its prejudicial effect must in each case be a question of degree. ...

In the present case the evidence of both girls describes a prolonged course of conduct in relation to each of them. In relation to each of them force was used. There was a general domination of the girls with threats against them unless they observed silence and a domination of the wife which inhibited her intervention. The defendant seemed to have an obsession for keeping the girls to himself, for himself. The younger took on the role of the elder daughter when the elder daughter left home. There was also evidence that the defendant was involved in regard to payment for the abortions in respect of both girls. In my view these circumstances taken together gave strong probative force to the evidence of each of the girls in relation to the incidents involving the other, and was certainly sufficient to make it just to admit that evidence, notwithstanding its prejudicial effect. This was clearly the view taken by the Court of A ppeal and they would have given effect to it were it not for the line of authority in the Court of Appeal to which I have referred. ..."

In *Director of Public Prosecutions v P.*, the evidence was admissible because each girl independently described a prolonged course of conduct involving the general domination of the family by the accused, who seemed obsessed with keeping the girls to himself. I should add that the mere existence of multiple accusations of similar offences does not mean that the evidence will be admissible as it is still essential that there should be a sufficient degree of probative force to overcome the prejudicial effect of such evidence. Whether the accounts of each of several complainants are corroborative and also the risk of collusion, either by conspiracy or where one witness has been unconsciously influenced by another, may well be relevant factors at the trial. It seems that the underlying principle is that the probative value of multiple accusations may depend in part on their similarity, but also on the unlikelihood that the same person would find himself falsely accused on various occasions by different and independent individuals. The making of multiple accusations is a coincidence in itself, which has to be taken into account in deciding admissibility. Applying these criteria to the applicant's case, it seems to me that the evidence of all three complainants may well be admissible on the basis of the principles enunciated in *Director of Public Prosecutions v P*. If the complaints of all three daughters are dealt with in the one trial, then this may well involve a considerable number of counts. Of course, it is the duty of the trial judge to ensure that the applicant is only arraigned on such number of counts as permit a fair trial. In short, it is for the trial judge to ensure that the defence is not unfairly embarrassed by a plethora of counts. I have no doubt that the trial judge will follow the usual practice of ensuring that a limited number of counts are selected and accordingly the presence of a large number of counts in the indictment at this stage is not a ground for prohibition. ...

49. Murray v United Kingdom

European Court of Human Rights, February 8, 1996
(1996) 22 E.H.R.R. 29 at 60–67

45. ... Although not specifically mentioned in Article 6 (art. 6) of the Convention, there can be no doubt that the right to remain silent under police questioning and the privilege against self-incrimination are generally recognised international standards which lie at the heart of the notion of a fair procedure under Article 6 (art. 6) (See the *Funke* judgment (1993) 16 E.H.R.R. 257). By providing the accused with protection against improper compulsion by the authorities these immunities contribute to avoiding miscarriages of justice and to securing the aims of Article 6 (art. 6).

46. The Court does not consider that it is called upon to give an abstract analysis of the scope of these immunities and, in particular, of what constitutes in this context "improper compulsion". What is at stake in the present case is whether these immunities are absolute in the sense that the exercise by an accused of the right to silence cannot under any circumstances be used against him at trial or, alternatively, whether informing him in advance that, under certain conditions, his silence may be so used, is always to be regarded as "improper compulsion".

47. On the one hand, it is self-evident that it is incompatible with the immunities under consideration to base a conviction solely or mainly on the accused's silence or on a refusal to answer questions or to give evidence himself. On the other hand, the Court deems it equally obvious that these immunities cannot

and should not prevent that the accused's silence, in situations which clearly call for an explanation from him, be taken into account in assessing the persuasiveness of the evidence adduced by the prosecution.

Wherever the line between these two extremes is to be drawn, it follows from this understanding of "the right to silence" that the question whether the right is absolute must be answered in the negative.

It cannot be said therefore that an accused's decision to remain silent throughout criminal proceedings should necessarily have no implications when the trial court seeks to evaluate the evidence against him. In particular, as the Government have pointed out, established international standards in this area, while providing for the right to silence and the privilege against self-incrimination, are silent on this point. Whether the drawing of adverse inferences from an accused's silence infringes Article 6 (art. 6) is a matter to be determined in the light of all the circumstances of the case, having particular regard to the situations where inferences may be drawn, the weight attached to them by the national courts in their assessment of the evidence and the degree of compulsion inherent in the situation.

48. As regards the degree of compulsion involved in the present case, it is recalled that the applicant was in fact able to remain silent. Notwithstanding the repeated warnings as to the possibility that inferences might be drawn from his silence, he did not make any statements to the police and did not give evidence during his trial. Moreover under Article 4 (5) of the Order he remained a non-compellable witness. Thus his insistence in maintaining silence throughout the proceedings did not amount to a criminal offence or contempt of court. Furthermore, as has been stressed in national court decisions, silence, in itself, cannot be regarded as an indication of guilt.

49. The facts of the present case accordingly fall to be distinguished from those in *Funke* where criminal proceedings were brought against the applicant by the customs authorities in an attempt to compel him to provide evidence of offences he had allegedly committed. Such a degree of compulsion in that case was found by the Court to be incompatible with Article 6 (art. 6) since, in effect, it destroyed the very essence of the privilege against self-incrimination.

50. Admittedly a system which warns the accused – who is possibly without legal assistance (as in the applicant's case) – that adverse inferences may be drawn from a refusal to provide an explanation to the police for his presence at the scene of a crime or to testify during his trial, when taken in conjunction with the weight of the case against him, involves a certain level of indirect compulsion. However, since the applicant could not be compelled to speak or to testify, as indicated above, this factor on its own cannot be decisive. The Court must rather concentrate its attention on the role played by the inferences in the proceedings against the applicant and especially in his conviction.

51. In this context, it is recalled that these were proceedings without a jury, the trier of fact being an experienced judge. Furthermore, the drawing of inferences under the Order is subject to an important series of safeguards designed to

respect the rights of the defence and to limit the extent to which reliance can be placed on inferences. In the first place, before inferences can be drawn under Article 4 and 6 of the Order appropriate warnings must have been given to the accused as to the legal effects of maintaining silence. Moreover, as indicated by the judgment of the House of Lords in *R. v Kevin Sean Murray* the prosecutor must first establish a *prima facie* case against the accused, i.e. a case consisting of direct evidence which, if believed and combined with legitimate inferences based upon it, could lead a properly directed jury to be satisfied beyond reasonable doubt that each of the essential elements of the offence is proved.

The question in each particular case is whether the evidence adduced by the prosecution is sufficiently strong to require an answer. The national court cannot conclude that the accused is guilty merely because he chooses to remain silent. It is only if the evidence against the accused "calls" for an explanation which the accused ought to be in a position to give that a failure to give any explanation "may as a matter of common sense allow the drawing of an inference that there is no explanation and that the accused is guilty". Conversely if the case presented by the prosecution had so little evidential value that it called for no answer, a failure to provide one could not justify an inference of guilt (*ibid*.). In sum, it is only common-sense inferences which the judge considers proper, in the light of the evidence against the accused, that can be drawn under the Order.

In addition, the trial judge has a discretion whether, on the facts of the particular case, an inference should be drawn. As indicated by the Court of Appeal in the present case, if a judge accepted that an accused did not understand the warning given or if he had doubts about it, "we are confident that he would not activate Article 6 against him" (see paragraph 31 above). Furthermore in Northern Ireland, where trial judges sit without a jury, the judge must explain the reasons for the decision to draw inferences and the weight attached to them. The exercise of discretion in this regard is subject to review by the appellate courts.

52. In the present case, the evidence presented against the applicant by the prosecution was considered by the Court of Appeal to constitute a "formidable" case against him (see paragraph 26 above). It is recalled that when the police entered the house some appreciable time after they knocked on the door, they found the applicant coming down the flight of stairs in the house where Mr L. had been held captive by the IRA. Evidence had been given by Mr L. – evidence which in the opinion of the trial judge had been corroborated – that he had been forced to make a taped confession and that after the arrival of the police at the house and the removal of his blindfold he saw the applicant at the top of the stairs. He had been told by him to go downstairs and watch television. The applicant was pulling a tape out of a cassette. The tangled tape and cassette recorder were later found on the premises. Evidence by the applicant's co-accused that he had recently arrived at the house was discounted as not being credible.

53. The trial judge drew strong inferences against the applicant under Article

6 of the Order by reason of his failure to give an account of his presence in the house when arrested and interrogated by the police. He also drew strong inferences under Article 4 of the Order by reason of the applicant's refusal to give evidence in his own defence when asked by the court to do so.

54. In the Court's view, having regard to the weight of the evidence against the applicant, as outlined above, the drawing of inferences from his refusal, at arrest, during police questioning and at trial, to provide an explanation for his presence in the house was a matter of common sense and cannot be regarded as unfair or unreasonable in the circumstances. ...

Nor can it be said, against this background, that the drawing of reasonable inferences from the applicant's behaviour had the effect of shifting the burden of proof from the prosecution to the defence so as to infringe the principle of the presumption of innocence.

55. The applicant submitted that it was unfair to draw inferences under Article 6 of the Order from his silence at a time when he had not had the benefit of legal advice. In his view the question of access to a solicitor was inextricably entwined with that of the drawing of adverse inferences from pre-trial silence under police questioning. In this context he emphasised that under the Order once an accused has remained silent a trap is set from which he cannot escape: if an accused chooses to give evidence or to call witnesses he is, by reason of his prior silence, exposed to the risk of an Article 3 inference sufficient to bring about a conviction; on the other hand, if he maintains his silence inferences may be drawn against him under other provisions of the Order.

56. The Court recalls that it must confine its attention to the facts of the present case. The reality of this case is that the applicant maintained silence right from the first questioning by the police to the end of his trial. It is not for the Court therefore to speculate on the question whether inferences would have been drawn under the Order had the applicant, at any moment after his first interrogation, chosen to speak to the police or to give evidence at his trial or call witnesses. Nor should it speculate on the question whether it was the possibility of such inferences being drawn that explains why the applicant was advised by his solicitor to remain silent.

Immediately after arrest the applicant was warned in accordance with the provisions of the Order but chose to remain silent. The Court, like the Commission, observes that there is no indication that the applicant failed to understand the significance of the warning given to him by the police prior to seeing his solicitor. Under these circumstances the fact that during the first 48 hours of his detention the applicant had been refused access to a lawyer does not detract from the above conclusion that the drawing of inferences was not unfair or unreasonable.

Nevertheless, the issue of denial of access to a solicitor, has implications for the rights of the defence which call for a separate examination (see paragraphs 59-69 below).

57. Against the above background, and taking into account the role played by

inferences under the Order during the trial and their impact on the rights of the defence, the Court does not consider that the criminal proceedings were unfair or that there had been an infringement of the presumption of innocence.

58. Accordingly, there has been no violation of Article 6 paras. 1 and 2 (art. 6-1, art. 6-2) of the Convention.

B. Access to lawyer

59. The applicant submitted that he was denied access to a lawyer at a critical stage of the criminal proceedings against him. He pointed out that in Northern Ireland the initial phase of detention is of crucial importance in the context of the criminal proceedings as a whole because of the possibility of inferences being drawn under Articles 3, 4 and 6 of the Order. He was in fact denied access to any legal advice for 48 hours. During that time Article 3 and Article 6 cautions had been administered without his having had the benefit of prior legal advice. He was interviewed on twelve occasions without a solicitor being present to represent his interests. When he was finally granted access to his solicitor he was advised to remain silent partly because he had maintained silence already during the interview and partly because the solicitor would not be permitted to remain during questioning. The silence which had already occurred prior to seeing his solicitor would have triggered the operation of both Articles 3 and 6 at any subsequent trial, even had he chosen to give an account to the police. Having regard to the very strong inferences which the trial judge drew under Articles 4 and 6 of the Order, the decision to deny him access to a solicitor unfairly prejudiced the rights of the defence and rendered the proceedings against him unfair contrary to Article 6 paras. 1 and 3 (c) (art. 6-1, art. 6-3-c) of the Convention. ...

62. The Court observes that it has not been disputed by the Government that Article 6 (art. 6) applies even at the stage of the preliminary investigation into an offence by the police. In this respect it recalls its finding in the *Imbrioscia v Switzerland* judgment[5] that Article 6 (art. 6) – especially paragraph 3 (art. 6-3) – may be relevant before a case is sent for trial if and so far as the fairness of the trial is likely to be seriously prejudiced by an initial failure to comply with its provisions (art. 6-3) (Series A no. 275, p. 13, para. 36). As it pointed out in that judgment, the manner in which Article 6 para. 3 (c) (art. 6-3-c) is to be applied during the preliminary investigation depends on the special features of the proceedings involved and on the circumstances of the case.[6]

63. National laws may attach consequences to the attitude of an accused at the initial stages of police interrogation which are decisive for the prospects of the defence in any subsequent criminal proceedings. In such circumstances Article 6 (art. 6) will normally require that the accused be allowed to benefit from the

---

[5] (1994) 17 E.H.R.R.
[6] *Loc. cit.*, at p.14, para.38.

assistance of a lawyer already at the initial stages of police interrogation. However, this right, which is not explicitly set out in the Convention, may be subject to restrictions for good cause. The question, in each case, is whether the restriction, in the light of the entirety of the proceedings, has deprived the accused of a fair hearing.

64. In the present case, the applicant's right of access to a lawyer during the first 48 hours of police detention was restricted under section 15 of the Northern Ireland (Emergency Provisions) Act 1987 on the basis that the police had reasonable grounds to believe that the exercise of the right of access would, *inter alia*, interfere with the gathering of information about the commission of acts of terrorism or make it more difficult to prevent such an act.

65. It is observed that the applicant did not seek to challenge the exercise of this power by instituting proceedings for judicial review although, before the Court, he now contests its lawfulness. The Court, however, has no reason to doubt that it amounted to a lawful exercise of the power to restrict access. Nevertheless, although it is an important element to be taken into account, even a lawfully exercised power of restriction is capable of depriving an accused, in certain circumstances, of a fair procedure.

66. The Court is of the opinion that the scheme contained in the Order is such that it is of paramount importance for the rights of the defence that an accused has access to a lawyer at the initial stages of police interrogation. It observes in this context that, under the Order, at the beginning of police interrogation, an accused is confronted with a fundamental dilemma relating to his defence. If he chooses to remain silent, adverse inferences may be drawn against him in accordance with the provisions of the Order. On the other hand, if the accused opts to break his silence during the course of interrogation, he runs the risk of prejudicing his defence without necessarily removing the possibility of inferences being drawn against him.

Under such conditions the concept of fairness enshrined in Article 6 (art. 6) requires that the accused has the benefit of the assistance of a lawyer already at the initial stages of police interrogation. To deny access to a lawyer for the first 48 hours of police questioning, in a situation where the rights of the defence may well be irretrievably prejudiced, is – whatever the justification for such denial – incompatible with the rights of the accused under Article 6 (art. 6). ...

There has therefore been a breach of Article 6 para. 1 in conjunction with paragraph 3 (c) (art. 6-1 and art. 6-3-c) of the Convention as regards the applicant's denial of access to a lawyer during the first 48 hours of his police detention.

50. Southern Health Board v C.H.

Supreme Court, March 11, 1996
[1996] 1 I.R. 219 at 237–240

O'Flaherty J:

... The Court thinks it important in the first instance to assign a description to the proceedings in issue. They are in essence an inquiry as to what is best to be done for the child in the particular circumstances pertaining. The Court holds that the nature of these proceedings is similar to proceedings where a court is exercising its wardship jurisdiction. Section 3 of the Guardianship of Infants Act, 1964, provides that where in any proceedings before any court the custody, guardianship or upbringing of an infant is in question, the court in deciding that question shall regard the welfare of the infant as the first and paramount consideration. The Act defines welfare as comprising of the "religious and moral, intellectual, physical and social welfare of the infant." The Act of 1964, itself a statutory statement of what is inherent in the Constitution, reinforces the common law position that the court is entrusted with the responsibility of the child's welfare. This is of the utmost importance. At the outset it must be emphasised that the proceedings are not of a criminal nature, nor are they a *lis inter-partes*. Here, the Court must undertake an investigation of what is in the best interests of the child: whether to be placed with the father or the Board.

We adopt what Lord Devlin said in the course of his speech in *In re K. (Infants)* [1965] A.C. 201 at p. 240, when he marked the dichotomy between the role of a judge as arbitrator and the role of a judge as a protector of persons when he said:

> "Where the judge sits as an arbiter between two parties, he need consider only what they put before him. If one or other omits something material and suffers from the omission, he must blame himself and not the judge. Where the judge sits purely as an arbiter and relies on the parties for his information, the parties have a correlative right that he should act only on information which they have had the opportunity of testing. Where the judge is not sitting purely, or even primarily, as an arbiter but is charged with the paramount duty of protecting the interests of one outside the conflict, a rule that is designed for just arbitrament cannot in all circumstances prevail."

So, the first point to note about this case is that the judge is in essence required to inquire as to what is in the best interests of the child. It is true, of course, that the rights of the father must be safeguarded, as far as practicable, consistent with discharging that primary obligation. But when the consequences of any encroachment on the respective rights is considered, it is easy to comprehend that the child's welfare must always be of far graver concern to the Court. We must, as judges, always harken to the constitutional command which mandates, as prime consideration, the interests of the child in any legal proceedings. Rules that have been laid down by the judges over the years, or by the legislature (*cf* s.27 of the Criminal Evidence Act, 1992) may not suffice in the particular circumstances calling for resolution.

In this case, allegations of sexual misconduct on the part of the father were raised by the Board, and, it is suggested, were supported by video recordings based on an interview or interviews between the social worker, Mr. O'Leary, and the child. As such, these allegations raise a serious matter in regard to the child's welfare and the District Judge, in protecting the interests of the child, must inquire into such allegations.

The kernel of the submission made on behalf of the respondent is that the evidence of the social worker, in regard to the videos, constituted hearsay evidence, and therefore, was inadmissible. However, the Court is of the opinion that the correct approach is to regard the evidence of Mr. O'Leary as expert testimony. In *State (D. and D.) v Groarke* [1990] 1 I.R. 305, and in which one of the issues was the admissibility of video recordings to support claims by a medical doctor of sexual abuse in relation to the child at the centre of the case, Finlay C.J. held that in order to determine whether the conclusion reached by the doctor who had interviewed the infant was sound, the court should have had the basic evidence from which such conclusion was reached, which was the video tapes, before evidence of such conclusion had been given. In that case, the admissibility of hearsay evidence was not raised, instead the court looked to the expert evidence of the medical doctor.

The District Judge in this case has obviously commenced the necessary inquiry; he has taken proper bearings and set a course which should lead to a just result, but nonetheless, in the course of the advice that we give in this judgment, we point out that the key evidence as far as this part of the case is concerned will be that offered by the social worker, Mr. Jim O'Leary. In a sense, the tapes are simply material that will back up his testimony. Essentially, however, the important evidence will be his expert testimony. It will be for the District Judge to accept or reject that evidence, having given the father every opportunity to engage his own expert testimony in that regard.

It would seem to be necessary, too, that since the child is now six and a half years old that the District Judge should establish anew that she is, indeed, incompetent to give evidence. He will hear such expert evidence as he thinks right and if he receives confirmation that the child is incompetent to give evidence, or, as a distinct condition, if he finds that the trauma that she would suffer would make it undesirable that she come to give evidence, then he will be justified in allowing in the evidence of the video recordings. In this regard, it is well to point out that a courtroom is, in general, an unsuitable environment for a child of such tender years as this child.

As already indicated, counsel for the Board recommended for our consideration the approach of the Supreme Court of Canada in *R. v Khan* [1990] 2 S.C.R. 531. The question for resolution in that case was whether a court could admit the evidence of a child's mother as to statements made by the child to her in a prosecution against a medical doctor for sexual assault. The child was three and a half years of age and had been held by the trial judge not to be a competent witness.

McLachlin J. (speaking for the Court) concluded (at p. 548):

"... hearsay evidence of a child's statement on crimes committed against the child should be received, provided that the guarantees of necessity and reliability are met, subject to such safeguards as the judge may consider necessary and subject always to considerations affecting the weight that should be accorded to such evidence. This does not make out-of-court statements by children generally admissible; in particular the requirement of necessity will probably mean that in most cases the children will still be called to give *viva voce* evidence."

Earlier (at pp. 546–547) the learned judge had described situations where the reception of the hearsay evidence is "necessary", when she said:

"Necessity for these purposes must be interpreted as 'reasonably necessary'. The inadmissibility of the child's evidence might be one basis for a finding of necessity. But sound evidence based on psychological assessments that testimony in court might be traumatic for the child or harm the child might also serve. There may be other examples of circumstances which could establish the requirement of necessity.

The next question should be whether the evidence is reliable. Many considerations such as timing, demeanour, the personality of the child, the intelligence and understanding of the child, and the absence of any reason to expect fabrication in the statement may be relevant on the issue of reliability. I would not wish to draw up a strict list of considerations for reliability, nor to suggest that certain categories of evidence (for example the evidence of young children on sexual encounters) should be always regarded as reliable. The matters relevant to reliability will vary with the child and with the circumstances, and are best left to the trial judge."

Two points of distinction from the Canadian case should be noted: first, it was concerned with a re-telling of oral communications (without the benefit of video recordings) and it was concerned with a criminal trial not involving the welfare of the infant but rather the question of the guilt or innocence of an accused.

We are concerned, of course, not with a criminal trial but with a particular inquiry, as already related, to do with the welfare of the child.

In the circumstances, we recommend a different emphasis as regards how this evidence of the tape interviews should be adopted. In this case, it is necessary to point out that the father is not arraigned. The focus of the District Judge's inquiry will be exclusively on the welfare and best interests of the child. The tapes are not to be admitted as the independent evidence of the child but rather as a portion of the material on which the expert evidence of Mr. O'Leary will be based. The District Judge will approach the evidence of Mr. O'Leary as he would the evidence of any other expert witness. Mr. O'Leary will be subject to cross-examination. The respondent has already seen the tapes and will have the right to adduce such expert or other evidence, in rebuttal or otherwise, as it thinks best.

We think this approach meets the paramount rights of the child but protects, as far as practicable, the rights of the father. ...

51. Heaney and McGuinness v Ireland and Attorney General

Supreme Court, July 23, 1996
[1997] 1 I.L.R.M. 117 at 121–128

O'Flaherty J:

This is an appeal from the judgment and order of the High Court (Costello J., as he then was) of the 29th June, 1994, (see [1994] 3 I.R. 593), dismissing the plaintiffs' claim for a declaration that s.52 of the Offences Against the State Act, 1939, is invalid having regard to the provisions of the Constitution.

The impugned section

Section 52 of the Offences Against the State Act, 1939, provides:

(1) Whenever a person is detained in custody under the provisions in that behalf contained in Part IV of this Act, any member of the Garda Síochána may demand of such person, at any time while he is so detained, a full account of such person's movements and actions during any specified period and all information in his possession in relation to the commission or intended commission by another person of any offence under any section or sub-section of this Act or any scheduled offence.

(2) If any person, of whom any such account or information as is mentioned in the foregoing sub-section of this section is demanded under that sub-section by a member of the Garda Síochána, fails or refuses to give to such member such account or any such information or gives to such member any account or information which is false or misleading, he shall be guilty of an offence under this section and shall be liable on summary conviction thereof to imprisonment for a term not exceeding six months.

Background facts

On the 25th October 1990, each of the plaintiffs was required, pursuant to this provision, to provide an account of their respective movements during stated periods in the preceding days. They both refused to do so. On the 26th June 1991, they were each convicted of an offence under the section. They were sentenced to imprisonment for six months, which sentences have been served. Nonetheless, appeals against conviction are pending in the Court of Criminal Appeal and they await the disposal of these proceedings. ...

The court concludes that the learned trial judge was right in his conclusion that the section did not infringe the Constitution. While the learned trial judge held that Article 38 was applicable to a case such as this, the court does not reach any conclusion on whether Article 38 is applicable or not. It is clear on the facts of the cases grounding the instant appeal that, on each plaintiff not answering in accordance with the requirement of the section, an offence contrary to the section was made out. While, therefore, nothing touching the due course of a trial arose as a result of the plaintiffs' failure so to answer, the court accepts that on occasion what happens prior to trial may have an adverse impact on the trial. Pre-trial activities concerning the obtaining of confession statements, or the failure to allow an accused to prepare for his trial by withholding essential information, are but two examples of what might be held to vitiate a trial so that it could not properly be said to be a trial held in due course of law.

Freedom of expression clause

The court prefers instead, to rest its judgment of the proposition that the right to silence is but a corollary to the freedom of expression that is conferred by Article 40 of the Constitution. This approach is in harmony with the decision of the Court in *Educational Company of Ireland Ltd. v Fitzpatrick (No 2)* [1961] I.R. 345 to the effect that just as a person has a constitutional right to join an association, equally a person is entitled to disassociate.

Then, the question is: can this right be abrogated or qualified.

Qualification of right

Just as the freedom of expression clause in the Constitution is itself qualified, so must the entitlement to remain silent be qualified. Before coming to relevant statute law, it is, of course, well established that so far as the administration of justice is concerned the exercise of the judicial power carries with it the entitlement of a judge to compel the attendance of witnesses and, *a fortiori*, the answering of questions by witnesses. "This is the ultimate safeguard of justice in the State, whether it be in pursuit of the guilty or the vindication of the innocent": *per* Walsh J., delivering the judgment of the Court of Criminal Appeal in the case of *In re O'Kelly* (1974) 108 I.L.T.R. 97 at p. 101 (*cf. Murphy v Dublin Corporation* [1972] I.R. 215). Of course, at common law no witness is punishable for refusing to answer a question which he claims may incriminate him. As Dr. Glanville Williams has pointed out "the rule has not been doubted for four centuries" (Glanville Williams, *The Proof of Guilt: A Study of the English Criminal Trial*, 3rd ed. (1963), p. 52).

However, the immunity is expressly abrogated in the case of an accused who gives evidence (section 1 (e) of the Criminal Justice (Evidence) Act, 1924).

Misprision of felony

Going outside the confines of the courtroom, the offence of misprision of a felony is committed if a person conceals or procures the concealment of a felony known to have been committed. It is the duty of all citizens to disclose to the proper authorities all material facts as to the commission of a felony of which the citizen has definite knowledge.

Self-incrimination

There is a dichotomy to be noticed: it is between the absolute entitlement to silence as against the entitlement to remain silent when to answer would give rise to self-incrimination. Where a person is totally innocent of any wrongdoing as regards his movements, it would require a strong attachment to one's apparent constitutional rights not to give such an account when asked pursuant to statutory requirement. So the Court holds that the matter in debate here can more properly be approached as an encroachment against the right not to have to say anything that might afford evidence that is self-incriminating.

Statutory interference

To move then to some examples of statutory interference with the right against self-incrimination, as Lord Mustill pointed out in the course of his speech in *R. v Director of Serious Fraud Office, ex p. Smith* [1993] A.C. 1, at p. 40, "statutory interference with the right is almost as old as the right itself." He went on to say:

> "Since the 16th century, legislation has established an inquisitorial form of investigation into the dealings and assets of bankrupts which is calculated to yield potentially incriminating material, and in more recent times there have been many other examples, in widely separated fields, which are probably more numerous than is generally appreciated.
>
> These statutes differ widely as to their aims and methods. In the first place, the ways in which the overriding of the immunity is conveyed are not the same. Sometimes it is made explicit. More commonly, it is left to be inferred from general language which contains no qualification in favour of the immunity. Secondly, there are variations in the effect on the admissibility of information obtained as a result of the investigation. The statute occasionally provides in so many terms that the information may be used in evidence; sometimes that it may not be used for certain purposes, inferentially permitting its use for others; or it may be expressly prescribed that the evidence is not to be admitted; or again, the statute may be silent. Finally, the legislation differs as to the mode of enforcing compliance with the questioner's demands. In some instances failure to comply becomes a separate offence with prescribed penalties; in others, the court is given a discretion to treat silence as if it were a contempt of court."

The Irish legislative experience is somewhat akin to what has been enacted in Britain but with an important qualification, touching the primacy of the Constitution, which will be considered hereafter.

A selection, but not an exhaustive list, of statutes in diverse areas which require disclosure include: the Customs Consolidation Act 1876; the Road Traffic Act 1961; the Companies Acts 1963 to 1990; the Income Tax Acts and Finance Acts; the Offences Against the State (Amendment) Act 1972; the Criminal Law Act 1976; the Criminal Justice Act 1984; the Bankruptcy Act 1988; the Criminal Justice (Forensic Evidence) Act, 1990; the Pensions Act 1990 and the Social Welfare (Consolidation) Act 1993.

These statutes differ considerably in their substance and objectives. The language may vary with regard to the means and type of disclosure. In some the duty to disclose is express, while in others it is implied. Section 10 of the

Companies Act 1990 employs mandatory language in terms of a "duty" to disclose information, whereas in s.24 of the Bankruptcy Act 1988, such a duty is to be inferred from the provisions penalising a failure to answer. The Companies Act 1963 (s.293, sub-s.1 (a)) speaks in terms of full disclosure. The Criminal Justice Act 1984 (s.15) requires persons to give information. The circumstances in which disclosure is to be made differ: pursuant to the Road Traffic Act 1961, disclosure is to a member of the Garda Síochána; under the Companies Acts 1963 to 1990, it is to a liquidator or examiner; under the Bankruptcy Act 1988, it is to the court; and under the Social Welfare (Consolidation) Act 1993, it is the Minister who may require information.

The purpose to which such information may ultimately be put varies: under the Criminal Justice Act 1984, (s.15, sub-s.4) information is expressly stated to be inadmissible in evidence "in any proceedings civil or criminal", whereas s.52 of the Offences Against the State Act 1939 is silent on this matter and while the case of *The People (Director of Public Prosecutions) v McGowan* [1979] I.R. 45, a decision of the Court of Criminal Appeal, suggests that information which is lawfully obtained pursuant to this statutory provision may be used in evidence, the court expressly reserves its position on whether this is correct or not.

Finally, there are differences in penalties imposed for non-compliance with a disclosure order. In some instances failure to comply is treated as a separate offence with prescribed penalties; for example s.18, sub-s.5 of the Pensions Act 1990, imposes a fine and/or imprisonment on summary conviction. But, in other instances, punishment is at the discretion of the court, e.g. under s.10, sub-s.5 of the Companies Act 1990, an inspector can certify a refusal which is then treated similarly to contempt of court.

This short analysis indicates the *ad hoc* and varied manner in which the legislation impinges on the right to silence. These statutes are as diverse as they are many. In light of the inconsistencies between each, it would be idle to engage in summarising or parsing the various statutes any further; however, they each serve to illustrate that in certain circumstances a person may be required to disclose information under threat of penal sanction. They evoke a legislative intent to abrogate, to various extents, the right to silence, in a myriad of contrasting circumstances.

Support for and opposition to immunity

Counsel for the plaintiffs have cited many venerable approbations for the right to silence, i.e. it is "a maxim of our law as settled, as important and as wise as almost any other in it", *R. v Scott* (1856) Dears & B. 47, 61 (Coleridge J.); a "most important right", *Orms v Crockford* (1824) 13 Price 376, 388 (Alexander L.C.B.); and "most sacred", *Ex parte Cessens* (1820) 1 Back 531, 540 (Lord Eldon); as well as Blackstone (IV Commentaries 296) and Gilbert, *The Law of Evidence* (Dublin, 1794) which states in the following terms:

> "our law ... differs from the Civil Law, that it will not force any man to accuse himself and in this we certainly follow the law of nature, which commands every man to endeavour his own preservation and therefore

pain and force may compel men to confess what is not the truth. ...."

Other jurists, however, were less enamoured of the immunity. Bentham, for one, regarded it as a misguided concession to the guilty (see Ian Dennis, "Instrumental Protection, Human Right or Functional Necessity Reassessing the Privilege Against Self-Incrimination" [1995] C.L.J. 342). And Sir James Fitzjames Stephen, writing in 1860, referred to "the old and now exploded maxim, that a man cannot be a witness in his own cause" – "The Criminal Law and the Detection of Crime" *Cornhill Magazine* 2, 697 (July–December 1860). See Hostettler, *Politics and Law in the Life of Sir James Fitzjames Stephen* (Barry Rose Law Publisher, 1995).

Two observations have to be made about the old expressions of support for the immunity. They relate to a time when, as far as criminal trials were concerned, an accused was not competent to give evidence in his or her own defence and, in any event, a statutory provision must always prevail over the common law. A statutory provision is subject only to the Constitution.

Conclusion

In the light of these cross-currents of judicial and juristic opinion, as well as the various statutes already cited, the court is of the opinion that the matter calling for resolution on this appeal is whether the power given to the Garda Síochána in the circumstances by the section is proportionate to the objects to be achieved by the legislation. As previously pointed out, the case falls to be resolved under a Constitution which guarantees liberty for the exercise of certain rights including the right of citizens to express freely their convictions and opinions. The right to freedom of expression necessarily implies the right to remain silent. The provisions of statutes of the British parliament are not necessarily a safe guide to what is constitutionally permissible for the Irish legislature. However, it is clear that the right to freedom of expression is not absolute. It is expressly stated in the Constitution to be subject to public order and morality. The same must hold true of its correlative right – the right to silence.

The Offences against the State Act 1939 is described in its long title to be *inter alia*:

> "An Act to make provision in relation to actions and conduct calculated to undermine public order and the authority of the State . . ."

Section 52, the section complained of, appears in Part V of the Act. Part V is in the nature of an exceptional provision. It comes into operation only when the Government is satisfied that the ordinary courts are inadequate to secure the effective administration of justice and the preservation of public peace and order and makes and publishes a proclamation to that effect pursuant to the provisions of s.35 of the Act. The Government made such a proclamation on the 26th May 1972, and it is still in force. Dáil Éireann has power at any time, under the provisions of s.35, to pass a resolution annulling the Government proclamation, but it has not done so.

It is in this context that the problem which arises in the present case falls to be resolved. On the one hand, constitutional rights must be construed in such a way as to give life and reality to what is being guaranteed. On the other hand, the interest of the State in maintaining public order must be respected and protected. We must, therefore, ask ourselves whether the restriction which s.52 places on the right to silence is any greater than is necessary having regard to the disorder against which the State is attempting to protect the public.

As was said in *Cox v Ireland* [1992] 2 I.R. 503 at p. 522:

> "The court is satisfied that the State is entitled, for the protection of public peace and order, and for the maintenance and stability of its own authority, by its laws to provide onerous and far-reaching penalties and forfeitures imposed as a major deterrent to the commission of crimes threatening such peace and order and State authority, and is also entitled to ensure as far as practicable that amongst those involved in the carrying out of the functions of the State, there is not included persons who commit such crimes."

That case was concerned with penalties and forfeitures arising on conviction in the Special Criminal Court for an offence amenable to the legislation; we can adapt the language, however, to the situation here: the State is entitled to encroach on the right of the citizen to remain silent in pursuit of its entitlement to maintain public peace and order. Of course, in this pursuit the constitutional rights of the citizen must be affected as little as possible. As already stated, the innocent person has nothing to fear from giving an account of his or her movements, even though on grounds of principle, or in the assertion of constitutional rights, such a person may wish to take a stand. However, the court holds that the *prima facie* entitlement of citizens to take such a stand must yield to the right of the State to protect itself. *A fortiori*, the entitlement of those with something relevant to disclose concerning the commission of a crime to remain mute must be regarded as of a lesser order.

The court concludes that there is a proper proportionality in the provision between any infringement of the citizen's rights with the entitlement of the State to protect itself.

Accordingly, the decision of the court is to disallow the appeal and decline to hold that it has been established that the provision in question is invalid having regard to the provisions of the Constitution.

52. Saunders v United Kingdom

European Court of Human Rights, December 17, 1996
(1996) 23 E.H.R.R. 313 at 337–340

67. ... The Court first observes that the applicant's complaint is confined to the use of the statements obtained by the DTI inspectors during the criminal proceedings against him. While an administrative investigation is capable of involving the determination of a "criminal charge" in the light of the Court's

case-law concerning the autonomous meaning of this concept, it has not been suggested in the pleadings before the Court that Article 6 para. 1 (art. 6-1) was applicable to the proceedings conducted by the inspectors or that these proceedings themselves involved the determination of a criminal charge within the meaning of that provision (art. 6-1).[7] In this respect the Court recalls its judgment in *Fayed v the United Kingdom* where it held that the functions performed by the inspectors under section 432 (2) of the Companies Act 1985 were essentially investigative in nature and that they did not adjudicate either in form or in substance. Their purpose was to ascertain and record facts which might subsequently be used as the basis for action by other competent authorities – prosecuting, regulatory, disciplinary or even legislative.[8] As stated in that case, a requirement that such a preparatory investigation should be subject to the guarantees of a judicial procedure as set forth in Article 6 para. 1 (art. 6-1) would in practice unduly hamper the effective regulation in the public interest of complex financial and commercial activities (*ibid.*, p. 48, para. 62).

Accordingly the Court's sole concern in the present case is with the use made of the relevant statements at the applicant's criminal trial.

68. The Court recalls that, although not specifically mentioned in Article 6 of the Convention (art. 6), the right to silence and the right not to incriminate oneself are generally recognised international standards which lie at the heart of the notion of a fair procedure under Article 6 (art. 6). Their rationale lies, *inter alia*, in the protection of the accused against improper compulsion by the authorities thereby contributing to the avoidance of miscarriages of justice and to the fulfilment of the aims of Article 6 (art. 6).[9] The right not to incriminate oneself, in particular, presupposes that the prosecution in a criminal case seek to prove their case against the accused without resort to evidence obtained through methods of coercion or oppression in defiance of the will of the accused. In this sense the right is closely linked to the presumption of innocence contained in Article 6 para. 2 of the Convention (art. 6-2).

69. The right not to incriminate oneself is primarily concerned, however, with respecting the will of an accused person to remain silent. As commonly understood in the legal systems of the Contracting Parties to the Convention and elsewhere, it does not extend to the use in criminal proceedings of material which may be obtained from the accused through the use of compulsory powers but which has an existence independent of the will of the suspect such as, *inter alia*, documents acquired pursuant to a warrant, breath, blood and urine samples and bodily tissue for the purpose of DNA testing.

In the present case the Court is only called upon to decide whether the use made by the prosecution of the statements obtained from the applicant by the inspectors amounted to an unjustifiable infringement of the right. This question

---

[7] See, *inter alia*, the *Deweer v Belgium* judgment of February 27, 1980, Series A no. 35, pp.21–24, paras.42–47.
[8] (1994) 18 E.H.R.R. 393 at para.61
[9] See *Murray v U.K.* (1996) 22 E.H.R.R. 29 at 49, para. 45 and the above-mentioned *Funke* (1993) 16 E.H.R.R. 257 at para. 44.

must be examined by the Court in the light of all the circumstances of the case. In particular, it must be determined whether the applicant has been subject to compulsion to give evidence and whether the use made of the resulting testimony at his trial offended the basic principles of a fair procedure inherent in Article 6 para. 1 (art. 6-1) of which the right not to incriminate oneself is a constituent element.

70. It has not been disputed by the Government that the applicant was subject to legal compulsion to give evidence to the inspectors. He was obliged under sections 434 and 436 of the Companies Act 1985 to answer the questions put to him by the inspectors in the course of nine lengthy interviews of which seven were admissible as evidence at his trial. A refusal by the applicant to answer the questions put to him could have led to a finding of contempt of court and the imposition of a fine or committal to prison for up to two years and it was no defence to such refusal that the questions were of an incriminating nature.

71. ... [B]earing in mind the concept of fairness in Article 6 (art. 6), the right not to incriminate oneself cannot reasonably be confined to statements of admission of wrongdoing or to remarks which are directly incriminating. Testimony obtained under compulsion which appears on its face to be of a non-incriminating nature – such as exculpatory remarks or mere information on questions of fact – may later be deployed in criminal proceedings in support of the prosecution case, for example to contradict or cast doubt upon other statements of the accused or evidence given by him during the trial or to otherwise undermine his credibility. Where the credibility of an accused must be assessed by a jury the use of such testimony may be especially harmful.

It follows that what is of the essence in this context is the use to which evidence obtained under compulsion is put in the course of the criminal trial.

72. In this regard, the Court observes that part of the transcript of answers given by the applicant was read to the jury by counsel for the prosecution over a three-day period despite objections by the applicant. The fact that such extensive use was made of the interviews strongly suggests that the prosecution must have believed that the reading of the transcripts assisted their case in establishing the applicant's dishonesty. This interpretation of the intended impact of the material is supported by the remarks made by the trial judge in the course of the *voir dire* concerning the eighth and ninth interviews to the effect that each of the applicant's statements was capable of being a "confession" for the purposes of section 82(1) of the Police and Criminal Evidence Act 1984. Similarly, the Court of Appeal considered that the interviews formed "a significant part" of the prosecution's case against the applicant. Moreover, there were clearly instances where the statements were used by the prosecution to incriminating effect in order to establish the applicant's knowledge of payments to persons involved in the share-support operation and to call into question his honesty. They were also used by counsel for the applicant's co-accused to cast doubt on the applicant's version of events.

...

74. [The court] does not accept the Government's argument that the complexity of corporate fraud and the vital public interest in the investigation of such fraud and the punishment of those responsible could justify such a marked departure as that which occurred in the present case from one of the basic principles of a fair procedure. Like the Commission, it considers that the general requirements of fairness contained in Article 6 (art. 6), including the right not to incriminate oneself, apply to criminal proceedings in respect of all types of criminal offences without distinction from the most simple to the most complex. The public interest cannot be invoked to justify the use of answers compulsorily obtained in a non-judicial investigation to incriminate the accused during the trial proceedings. It is noteworthy in this respect that under the relevant legislation statements obtained under compulsory powers by the Serious Fraud Office cannot, as a general rule, be adduced in evidence at the subsequent trial of the person concerned. Moreover the fact that statements were made by the applicant prior to his being charged does not prevent their later use in criminal proceedings from constituting an infringement of the right.

75. It follows from the above analysis and from the fact that section 434 (5) of the Companies Act 1985 authorises, as noted by both the trial judge and the Court of Appeal, the subsequent use in criminal proceedings of statements obtained by the inspectors that the various procedural safeguards to which reference has been made by the respondent Government cannot provide a defence in the present case since they did not operate to prevent the use of the statements in the subsequent criminal proceedings.

76. Accordingly, there has been an infringement in the present case of the right not to incriminate oneself.

53. Gilligan v Criminal Assets Bureau and Ors.

High Court, June 26, 1997
[1998] 3 I.R. 185 at 229–230, 233

McGuinness J:

... The plaintiff next challenged the [Proceeds of Drugs Act 1996] on the basis that it infringed the privilege against self-incrimination or the right to silence. The plaintiff argues that the structure of the Act forces him to give evidence in regard to the property affected by orders under s.2 and s.3 and that this evidence could be self-incriminating. ...

Section 9 provides:

> "At any time during proceedings under s.2 or 3 or while an interim order or an interlocutory order is in force, the Court or, as appropriate, in the case of an appeal in such proceedings, the Supreme Court may by order direct the respondent to file an affidavit in the Central Office of the High Courts specifying—

> (a) the property of which the respondent is in possession or control, or
> (b) the income, and the sources of the income, of the respondent during such period (not exceeding ten years) ending on the date of the application for the order as the court concerned may specify, or both."

In dealing with the general argument made by the plaintiff in regard to the privilege against self-incrimination the defendants submit that a respondent to proceedings under the Act is not in any way forced to give evidence which could be self-incriminating. He has an option. He can give evidence freely and seek to realise his assets, or he can decline to say anything that might incriminate him, or he can give evidence omitting any particulars that might incriminate him. Furthermore, even though an obligation is imposed upon a respondent to displace the evidence which has been adduced by the applicant in proceedings under the Act there is no obligation *per se* on the respondent himself to give any evidence. He can seek to displace the evidence that has been tendered by the applicant by means of cross-examination, or by means of third party evidence, or by means of independent "real" evidence. The defendants argue that there is no obligation necessarily imposed by the Act for the respondent to say anything or to give evidence himself.

The defendants' argument here seems me to tend towards a sophisticated version of the "the innocent have nothing to fear", which I would not accept as being sufficient in itself to offset a threat to the privilege against self-incrimination. There have been sufficient miscarriages of justice in the history of crime in this and in other jurisdictions to indicate that a belief that "the innocent have nothing to fear" is not necessarily the whole answer. The defendants' argument also rather blithely passes by the fact that a failure to give evidence by the respondent will in all probability result in the disposal of the respondent's assets.

The provisions of section 9 do not offer the respondent the same type of choice. Here the court may direct the swearing of an affidavit, and presumably a refusal or failure to do so would amount to contempt. ...

It is clear from *Heaney's* case that the privilege against self-incrimination, or the right to silence, is by no means absolute. This decision is, of course, binding on me. It is certainly arguable that any encroachment on that privilege contained in ss.2, 3 and 9 of the Proceeds of Crime Act 1996 is in pursuit of the State's entitlement "to maintain public peace and order". However, this is qualified by the caveat that "the constitutional rights of the citizen must be affected as little as possible". In order to minimise any encroachment on the citizen's rights and in order to operate the procedures under the Act in a way which in accordance with constitutional justice, it seems to me that the court would need to take particular care in deciding whether to make an order under s.9 requiring disclosure. This is especially so when one bears in mind the wide scope of the discovery which may be ordered. I note that even in the *M v D* case, where the primary evidence presented by the applicant was full and convincing, the learned judge required an undertaking to be given by the D.P.P. not to profit from any disclosure which might take place in those proceedings in a future prosecution of the respondent. Moriarty J. referred to "the degree of nexus between the applicant and the office of the D.P.P." The evidence given in the instant case shows an even clearer nexus than Moriarty J. might have envisaged between the personnel of the Criminal Assets Bureau and the criminal investigation section of the Garda Siochana. It appears to me that the type of undertaking sought by Moriarty J. in the *M v D* case would be essential in virtually every case where an order under s.9 is granted. Even then there may well be difficulty in operating such an undertaking in a secure and watertight manner. ...

54. R. v McQuiston

Court of Appeal, July 9, 1997
[1998] 1 Cr. App. R. 139 at 141–142

Otton L.J:

... In *R. v Rawlings and Broadbent* [1995] 1 W.L.R. 178, this Court held that it is a matter for the trial judge's discretion as to whether or not to grant a request from the jury to have the video replayed. The Court emphasised, however, that it was necessary to guard against unnecessary unfairness resulting from the replay only of the evidence in-chief and of no other evidence. If the jury wished to be reminded of what the witness said it is sufficient and most expeditious to remind them from the judge's own note. If, however, the jury are concerned with how the words were spoken, the judge may exercise his discretion to allow the whole or the relevant part of the video to be replayed. If the judge allows the video to be replayed, he should comply with three requirements:

1. The replay should be in court with judge, counsel and defendant present.

2. The judge should warn the jury not to give the complainant's evidence in-chief disproportionate weight simply because it is repeated well after all the other evidence, and to bear in mind the other evidence in the case.

3. After the replay of the video, the judge should remind the jury of the complainant's cross-examination and re-examination from his notes.

By parity of reasoning, we take the view that where a judge exercises his discretion that the video should not be replayed and where he reads *verbatim* and substantially from the transcript he should still warn the jury not to give the complainant's evidence in that form disproportionate weight simply because it is repeated well after all the other evidence and to bear in mind the other evidence in the case. In particular, it is still incumbent upon the judge to remind the jury of the complainant's cross-examination and re-examination from his notes and, where appropriate, any relevant part of the defendant's own evidence.

Accordingly, we concluded that there was a material irregularity in the latter part of the trial. We are clearly of the view that the learned judge at this stage disturbed the balance he had so carefully struck in his summing-up. He went too far by giving such a long recapitulation *verbatim*. By failing to give an appropriate warning and to remind the jury of the other relevant evidence, he produced an unbalanced state of affairs when the jury finally retired. Consequently we harbour a real suspicion that the convictions are unsafe and should be quashed. ...

55. Rock v Ireland
Supreme Court, November 19, 1997
[1997] 3 I.R. 484 at 497–498, 501

Hamilton C.J:

... It is clear from ... the provisions of s.18 of [the Criminal Justice Act 1984] that, while a court may draw such inferences from an accused's failure or refusal to account for the presence of an object, substance or mark in the circumstances provided for in the section, it is not obliged to draw any inference from such failure or refusal. It is, however, entitled to draw such inferences as appear proper.

It is purely a matter for the court, or subject to the judge's directions, the jury, to decide whether any inferences should be drawn or what inferences may be properly drawn from the failure or refusal of the accused person to account for the presence of such substances.

In deciding what inferences may properly be drawn from the accused person's failure or refusal, the court is obliged to act in accordance with the principles of constitutional justice and having regard to an accused person's entitlement to a fair trial must be regarded as being under a constitutional obligation to ensure that no improper or unfair inferences are drawn or permitted to be drawn from such failure or refusal.

As stated by O'Flaherty J. in delivering the judgment of this Court in *O'Leary v The Attorney General* [1995] 1 I.R. 254 at p. 266:

> "Courts, whether comprising a judge sitting with a jury or a judge or judges only, will not act as automatons in the assessment of evidence. With a statutory provision setting out what is to be regarded as evidence – and whether it is called a presumption or not is of no moment – the court must always approach its task in a responsible manner and have regard to the paramount place that the presumption of innocence occupies in any criminal trial."

It is clear from the provisions of the said section that it does not interfere in any way with the accused person's right to the presumption of innocence or the obligation on the prosecution to establish guilt beyond all reasonable doubt. The burden of proof which rests on the prosecution in a criminal charge is not in any way affected by the provisions of the impugned sections, which merely provide a factor which may be adduced as evidence in the course of the trial.

If inferences are properly drawn, such inferences amount to evidence only;

they are not to be taken as proof. A person may not be convicted of an offence solely on the basis of inferences that may properly be drawn from his failure to account; such inferences may only be used as corroboration of any other evidence in relation to which the failure or refusal is material. The inferences drawn may be shaken in many ways, by cross-examination, by submission, by evidence or by the circumstances of the case.

The Court is satisfied that the provisions of ss.18 and 19 of the Act of 1984 do not constitute an attack on, or interference with, an accused person's constitutional right to the "presumption of innocence" and is satisfied that it has not been established by the applicant that the provisions of the said sections are repugnant to the provisions of the Constitution. ...

While it is true that ss.18 and 19 could lead to an accused being convicted of a serious offence in circumstances where he or she might otherwise have been acquitted, there are two important, limiting factors at work. Firstly, an inference cannot form the basis for a conviction in the absence of other evidence. As the learned trial judge pointed out:

"... there is no doubt a strengthening of the State's case but in no sense is it final and in neither event is the accused required to exculpate himself."

Secondly, only such inferences "as appear proper" can be drawn: that is to say, an inference adverse to the accused can only be drawn where the court deems it proper to do so. If it does not, then neither judge nor jury will be permitted to draw such inference. Thus, for example, a court could refuse to allow an inference in circumstances where its prejudicial effect would wholly outweigh its probative value as evidence.

The Court is not satisfied that the provisions of the impugned sections are so contrary to reason and fairness as to constitute an unjust attack on the applicant's constitutional rights and the appeal herein must be dismissed.

56. Donnelly v Ireland
Supreme Court, January 22, 1998
[1998] 1 I.R. 321 at 338, 342–343, 345–346, 348, 356–358

Hamilton C.J:

This is an appeal brought by the above-named Anthony Donnelly (hereinafter called the plaintiff), against the judgment of the then President of the High Court (Costello P.) delivered on the 9th December 1996 and the order made in pursuance thereof on that date whereby the plaintiff's claims for:

(1) a declaration that ss.12, 13 (1) and (2) and 18 of Part III of the Criminal Evidence Act 1992, are invalid insofar and to the extent that they are repugnant to the provisions of Bunreacht na hÉireann and in particular Articles 38.1, 38.5 and 40.3 thereof;

Appendices

(2) a declaration that s.13 (3) of the Criminal Evidence Act 1992, is invalid insofar as the said provision is repugnant to the provisions of Bunreacht na hÉireann and in particular Articles 6, 34, 38.1 and 40.3 thereof;

(3) an order of certiorari in respect of the plaintiff's conviction by the Dublin Circuit Criminal Court on the 18th March 1994 ....

The plaintiff was charged with an offence of sexual assault contrary to s.2 of the Criminal Law (Rape Amendment) Act 1990, and after a seven day trial was found guilty of the offence by a jury on the 17th February 1994. ...

The complainant, who was under seventeen years of age gave her evidence through a live television link. She was in fact fourteen years of age at the date of trial.

As appears from the judgment of the learned trial judge it was not considered necessary in the course of the hearing before him to give evidence as to the manner in which evidence under s.13 was given at the trial. The learned trial judge ... assumed, without objection, that the live television link was operated in the manner set forth in detail by Kinlen J. in the course of his judgment in *White v Ireland* [1995] 2 I.R. 268.

The learned trial judge, however, noted that:

(i) the witness was seen at all times by judge, jury and counsel on monitors;

(ii) the witness had a monitor and when being questioned could see the questioner;

(iii) the system was under the control of the trial judge;

(iv) the witness did not see the accused; and

(v) the witness could be and was cross-examined.

The plaintiff did not have the opportunity of confronting physically his accuser in open court. ...

It is clear from a consideration of the learned trial judge's judgment that he recognised the primacy of an accused person's right to fair procedures as guaranteed by the provisions of Article 38.1 of the Constitution as interpreted by the courts, in particular in *The State (Healy) v Donoghue* [1976] I.R. 325.

Having quoted certain passages from the judgment of O'Higgins CJ. in that case [Costello P.] went on to say at p. 334:

> "If, therefore, the constitutional guarantee of fair procedures is breached then the court will declare a statute which does so to be unconstitutional. What the Court must do in this case is to see whether or not s.13(1)(a) breaches that guarantee. If it does so then there can be no question of balancing conflicting rights – if the procedures are unfair this section must be condemned."

[Costello P.] then went on to consider the issue as to whether the procedures permitted by s.13 of the Act of 1992 were unfair to the plaintiff and stated:

> "The plaintiff in this case had, in his trial in the Dublin Circuit Court the

benefit of all the procedures which the Supreme Court identified as being necessary to constitute a fair trial. He had notice of the evidence which was to be given against him. He was represented by counsel. The witnesses were examined and cross-examined and were seen at all times by the jury (as well as the trial judge and counsel) by means of the television link. What has to be determined, therefore, is whether the trial was unfair because the children who accused him of the crime with which he was charged did not give evidence in his presence. The unfairness involved, it is submitted, was this; (a) it is well recognised that it is more difficult for a false accuser to lie successfully in the presence of the person wrongfully accused than in his or her absence and (b) if the safeguard which the physical presence of an accuser and the accused is withdrawn (as is done by the impugned section) the trial becomes unfair.

It is, of course, an undeniable fact that children may be manipulated by malevolent adults or, in some cases, by over-zealous social workers into making false accusations of sexual abuse and it is obvious that fair procedures require that there are proper means to assess the credibility of all the testimony in the prosecution case, including that of child witnesses. The question, therefore, is whether the existing procedures without a physical confrontation, are fair to the accused. I think they are. It may well have been considered necessary at the end of the 18th century when criminal procedures were very different to what they are today to require a face-to-face confrontation between the accused and his or her accuser. I do not think that in modern Ireland a criminal trial becomes unfair if there is not such confrontation. The jury in a trial in which the s.13 procedures are adopted will see the witness at all times. It will be able to evaluate the manner in which the child gives his or her testimony, and his or her reaction to any suggestion that he or she is lying or that he or she has been manipulated. It seems to me that the absence of a physical confrontation between the witness and the accused will have no significant effect on the ability of a false accuser to mislead a jury and I do not think that the jury's assessment of the credibility of a witness will be compromised by the fact that the witness does not see the accused when giving evidence. It follows, therefore, that the procedures allowed by the section are not unfair."

Having held that the section did not infringe the plaintiff's constitutional right to fair procedures he went on to say that:

"As a corollary to this it follows that the right to a physical confrontation by an accused of his or her accusers is not a constitutionally protected right. ..."

It is well established in our constitutional jurisprudence that an accused person's right to a fair trial is one of the most fundamental constitutional rights accorded to persons and that in so far as it is possible or desirable to construct a hierarchy of constitutional rights it is a superior right. ...

The impugned provisions of the Act of 1992 do not restrict in any way the rights of an accused person as established by the constitutional jurisprudence of this Court and in particular by *In re Haughey* [1971] I.R. 217 and *The State (Healy) v Donoghue* [1976] I.R. 325.

What they do permit in the case of proceedings for the offences set forth in s.12 of the Act of 1992 is the giving of evidence by persons under 17 years (unless the court sees good reason to the contrary) and by any other person, with the leave of the court, through a live television link.

It is accepted that the reason for the procedure permitted by s.13 of the Act of 1992 was that it is generally accepted that young persons under the age of 17 are likely to be traumatised by the experience of giving evidence in court and that its purpose is to minimise such trauma. ...

The Court recognises, as did the learned trial judge, that it is an undeniable fact that children may be manipulated by malevolent adults, or in some cases, by over-zealous social workers into making false accusations of sexual abuse and that fair procedures require that there are proper means to assess the credibility of all the testimony in the prosecution case, including the testimony of child witnesses.

The Court is satisfied, however, that the assessment of such credibility does not require that the witness should be required to give evidence in the physical presence of the accused person and that the requirements of fair procedures are adequately fulfilled by requiring that the witness give evidence on oath and be subjected to cross-examination and that the judge and jury have ample opportunity to observe the demeanour of the witness while giving evidence and being subjected to cross-examination. In this way, an accused person's right to a fair trial is adequately protected and vindicated. Such right does not include the right in all circumstances to require that the evidence be given in his physical presence and consequently there is no such constitutional right.

The accused person's right to a fair trial is further protected by the fact that it is open to the court not to permit the giving of evidence by a young person through a live television link if the accused person establishes that 'there is good reason to the contrary' and that the leave of the court is required before any other person may give evidence in this manner. A judge considering either of these issues will be obliged to have regard to the accused person's right to a fair trial.

It was submitted on behalf of the plaintiff that, even if an accused person had no constitutionally protected right to a physical confrontation with his or her accuser the procedures permitted by s.13 of the Act of 1992 and adopted during the course of his trial were unfair (and therefore unconstitutional) because (i) they did not require a case by case determination of the need to apply such procedures and (ii) they place an unfair onus on an accused to require him to establish the witnesses' competence to undertake a face-to-face confrontation with the accused.

Once it is established that an accused person has no constitutional right to have a witness give evidence in his presence and in effect "confront" him, then the circumstances in which evidence is given other than in his presence is a matter for the Oireachtas.

The impugned sections of the Act of 1992, the procedures outlined therein and the circumstances in which they may be employed, enjoy the presumption of constitutionality and the onus is on the plaintiff to establish that they are repugnant to the Constitution and are not fair procedures. Such repugnancy must be clearly established.

Fair procedures do not require a case by case determination as to whether a person under the age of 17 years would be traumatised by giving evidence in court in the presence of the accused person and the Oireachtas was entitled to enact legislation permitting the giving of evidence by such persons through a live television link unless the court sees good reason to the contrary.

The Court is satisfied that the plaintiff has failed to discharge that onus and that the procedures complained of are not unfair and do not amount to an interference with an accused person's right to a fair trial and that his appeal should be dismissed and the order of the High Court affirmed.

57. In the Matter of National Irish Bank

Supreme Court, January 21, 1999
[1999] 1 I.L.R.M. 321 at 350–354, 359–361

Barrington J:

... The right to silence had its origins in the common law but was elevated into a constitutional principle by the 5th Amendment to the American Constitution. It grew out of the revulsion of the judges for forced confessions as being both unjust in their origin and unreliable in practice. Some judges also seemed to have felt that it was unfair to place a man in a position where he was condemned no matter what he did. As Lord Mustill put the matter in *R. v The Director of Serious Fraud Office* [1993] A.C. 1 at 32:

> "Next there is the instinct that it is contrary to fair play to put the accused in a position where he is exposed to punishment whatever he does. If he answers, he may condemn himself out of his own mouth; if he refuses he may be punished for his refusal. ..."

An American Judge had the same idea in mind when he referred to "the cruel trilemma of self accusation, perjury or contempt" (see *Murphy v Waterfront Commissioners* 378 U.S. 52 at 55 (1964).

The right to silence or privilege against self incrimination was a judge made law and could be abridged or abolished at any time by a sovereign parliament. The most the judges could do was to insist that, if parliament wished to abolish such a cherished doctrine of the common law it should state its intention clearly. ...

If however one regards the right to silence as not merely a common law privilege but as a constitutional right, one must ask oneself 'What is the extent of it and what limitations can be placed upon it? Is a confession to be rejected because it was obtained by the application of executive power but to be accepted if obtained solely by the application of legislative power? Or is it the element of compulsion which makes the confession unacceptable?"

The provisions of our Constitution invoked by the appellant as assisting his submission are Article 40.6.1, Article 40.3 and Article 38.1.

The relevant parts of these three constitutional provisions read as follows:

Article 40.6.1

The State guarantees liberty for the exercise of the following rights, subject to public order and morality;

(i) the right of the citizens to express freely their convictions and opinions.

Article 40.3

1. The State guarantees in its laws to respect, and, as far as practicable, by its laws to defend and vindicate the personal rights of the citizen.

2. The State shall, in particular, by its laws protect as best it may from unjust attack and, in the case of injustice done, vindicate the life, person, good name, and property rights of every citizen.

Article 38

1. No person shall be tried on any criminal charge save in due course of law.

In the context of the present case the effect of Article 40.3 is merely to reinforce the other two constitutional guarantees the first of which, as interpreted by this court, applies to the right to silence generally and the second of which applies to the conduct of a criminal trial.

Article 40.6

This Court in *Heaney v Ireland* [1996] 1 I.R. 580 derived the general right to silence from the right to freedom of expression guaranteed to citizens by Article 40.6. The court held that the constitutional right of freedom of expression carried with it, by necessary implication, the correlative right to remain silent. In this respect the court followed the reasoning of an earlier Supreme Court in the *Educational Company v Fitzpatrick (No. 2)* [1961] I.R. 345 which derived from the constitutional right of freedom of association the correlative right to refuse to associate. In this respect the present Supreme Court differed from the then President of the High Court Mr. Justice Costello who had derived the right to silence from Article 38.1 of the Constitution. But the court held that the right to silence was not absolute but might in certain circumstances have to give way to the exigencies of the common good provided the means used to curtail the right of silence were proportionate to the public object to be achieved.

In the *Heaney* case the court was dealing with a provision of the Offences against the State Act, 1939 which was an Act dealing with threats to the security of the State and the court held that the curtailment to the right of silence contained in s.52 of the Act was no more than was necessary in the circumstances.

The present case deals with the investigation of commercial fraud. No doubt this may often be a much less serious matter than the matter under investigation by the court in the *Heaney* case but nevertheless potentially it is a matter of great importance in modern society. ...

It appears to me that the powers given to the inspectors under s.10 of the Companies Act, 1990, as set out earlier in this judgment, are no greater than the public interest requires. Their meaning is clear and they pass the proportionality test. Accordingly it appears to me that interviewees are not entitled to refuse to answer questions properly posed to them by the inspectors pursuant to the inspectors' powers under the Act.

Article 38.1

Article 38.1 deals with a different matter. That Article, as reinforced by Article 40.3, deals with the conduct of a criminal trial and provides that no person is to be tried on any criminal charge "save in due course of law." The phrases "due course of law" and "due process of law" like the phrase "equality before the law" embody dynamic constitutional concepts into which lawyers have obtained deeper insights as society has evolved. But it is doubtful if the principle of proportionality—so important in other branches of constitutional law—can have any useful application here. A criminal trial is conducted "in due course of law" or "with due process of law" or it is not. The question then arises would a trial, at which a confession obtained from the accused under penal sanction imposed by statute, was admitted in evidence against the accused, be a trial in due course of law?

Should the court attempt to give guidance at this stage

A preliminary difficulty arises in attempting to answer this question. The difficulty is that the conduct of a criminal trial in due course of law is primarily a matter for the trial judge. The question of whether a statement is or is not a voluntary statement depends upon the circumstances in which it was made. The fact that inspectors are armed with statutory powers or may even have invoked them does not necessarily mean that a statement made in reply to their questions is not voluntary. ...

The Saunders case

Earlier in this judgment I have referred to the fact that the majority judges in the European Court in the *Saunders* case (17th December 1996) found powers such as those vested in the inspectors in the present case to be necessary to enable the public authorities to investigate fraud. At the same time the court found that some of the answers given by Saunders in reply to inspectors in that case were self incriminating and that the use made by the prosecution, at the subsequent criminal trial, of Saunder's replies to the inspectors was such as to deny him a "fair trial" within the meaning of Article 6 paragraph 1 of the European Convention on Human Rights. At paragraph 74 of its judgment the court stated:

"The public interest cannot be invoked to justify the use of answers compulsorily obtained in a non-judicial investigation to incriminate the accused during the trial proceedings ... Moreover the fact that statements were made by the applicant prior to his being charged does not prevent their later use in criminal proceedings from constituting an infringement of the right." ...

[A] trial in due course of law requires that any confession admitted against an accused person in a criminal trial should be a voluntary confession and that any trial at which an alleged confession other than a voluntary confession were admitted in evidence against the accused person would not be a trial in due course of law within the meaning of Article 38 of the Constitution and that it is immaterial whether the compulsion or inducement used to extract the confession came from the executive or from the legislature.

Section 18

The relevant provisions of s.18 of the Companies Act, 1990 may be abbreviated to read as follows:

"An answer by a person to a question put to him in exercise of powers conferred by (a) s.10 may be used in evidence against him".

There is no doubt that the quoted provision covers civil cases but it is necessary to address the problem of whether the quoted provision is broad enough to cover the admission of involuntary confessions in criminal cases. One could argue that if it was intended to remove the common law privilege against self-incrimination the statute should have said so. On the other hand it can be argued that the statute expressly preserves legal professional privilege (see s.23) but does not mention the common law privilege against self-incrimination. It is therefore possible to argue that had it been intended to preserve the common law privilege against self-incrimination the statute would have said so.

However this line of reasoning becomes irrelevant once one is satisfied that Article 38 of the Constitution confers on accused persons a right not to have involuntary confessions accepted in evidence at a criminal trial and that this right is reinforced by the general provisions of Article 40.3 of the Constitution. The Companies Act, 1990 is a post constitutional statute and must therefore be presumed to be constitutional. ...

Accordingly the better interpretation of s.18 in the light of the Constitution is that it does not authorise the admission of forced or involuntary confessions against an accused person in a criminal trial, and it can be stated, as a general principle, that a confession, to be admissible at a criminal trial must be voluntary. Whether however a confession is voluntary or not must in every case in which the matter is disputed be a question to be decided, in the first instance, by the trial judge.

The Fruits

The judgment in this case follows the decision in *Heaney v Ireland* [1996] 1 I.R. 580 insofar as that case decided that there may be circumstances in which the right of the citizen to remain silent may have to yield to the right of the State authorities to obtain information. It is not inconsistent with the decision in *Rock v Ireland* [1998] 2 I.L.R.M. 37 that there may be circumstances in which a court is entitled to draw fair inferences from the accused having remained silent when he could have spoken. It follows *The People v Cummins* [1972] I.R. 312 insofar as that case decided that for a confession to be admissible in a criminal trial it must be voluntary.

In the course of the submissions the question arose of what would be the position of evidence discovered by the inspectors as a result of information uncovered by them following the exercise by them of their powers under s.10. It is proper therefore to make clear that what is objectionable under Article 38 of the Constitution is compelling a person to confess and then convicting him on the basis of his compelled confession. The courts have always accepted that evidence obtained on foot of a legal search warrant is admissible. So also is objective evidence obtained by legal compulsion under, for example, the drink driving laws. The inspectors have the power to demand answers under s.10. These answers are in no way tainted and further information which the inspectors may discover as a result of these answers is not tainted either. The case of *The People v O'Brien* [1965] I.R. 142, which deals with evidence obtained in breach of the accused's constitutional rights has no bearing on the present case. In the final analysis however, it will be for the trial judge to decide whether, in all the circumstances of the case, it would be just or fair to admit any particular piece of evidence, including any evidence obtained as a result or in consequence of the compelled confession.

In these circumstances I would uphold the decision of the learned High Court judge but would add the statement that a confession of a bank official obtained by the inspectors as a result of the exercise by them of their powers under s.10 of the Companies Act, 1990 would not, in general, be admissible at a subsequent criminal trial of such official unless, in any particular case, the trial Judge was satisfied that the confession was voluntary.

58. Lavery v Member in Charge, Carrickmacross Garda Station

Supreme Court, February 23, 1999
[1999] 2 I.R. 390 at 394–396

O'Flaherty J:

… The point at issue in these proceedings is a net one. It is not in doubt that s.30 [of the Offences Against the State Act 1939] permits the arrest and detention of suspected persons, where a member of the Garda Síochána suspects that a person has committed or is about to commit, or is or has been concerned in the commission of an offence under any section or sub-section of the Act of 1939 (including amending Acts) or an offence which, for the time being, is a scheduled offence for the purposes of Part V of the 1939 Act, or whom he suspects of carrying a document in relation to the commission or the intended commission of any such offence, or whom he suspects of being in possession of information in relation to the commission or intended commission of any such offence as aforesaid. Section 52 of the Act of 1939 permits a person who has been lawfully arrested under s.30 to be questioned in respect of the matters specified in that section and makes it an offence to refuse to give the information sought, or to give information which is false or misleading. It is beyond debate that a person thus detained has a constitutional right to access to a legal advisor: see the court's judgments in *Re Emergency Powers Bill* 1976 [1977] I.R. 159; *The People v Shaw* [1982] I.R. 1 and *The People (D.P.P.) v Pringle* 2 Frewen 57. However, the right of access is one of reasonable access. As stated in the judgment of the Court of Criminal Appeal in the *Pringle* case, at p. 96:

> "This court is satisfied that the Garda Síochána have a right to interrogate a person in lawful custody provided that such interrogation is carried out in a fair and reasonable manner. The court is also satisfied, as has been clearly established, that a person in lawful custody is entitled to *reasonable* (emphasis added) access to his lawyer or solicitor. These two rights must, to some extent, be balanced and there are no grounds for holding that either right can or should be exercised to the unreasonable exclusion of the other."

While there is no suggestion that Mr. MacGuill was not given reasonable access in the understood sense of that term, the complaint before the High Court, brought pursuant to Article 40, s.4 of the Constitution, was that the new legislation required that the solicitor should be given access to the documents that he required and, once he was refused, the respondent's detention became unlawful and he should be set free.

When the matter came for hearing before the High Court (McGuinness J.) on the evening of 2nd October, 1998, she held with the submissions advanced on behalf of Mr. Lavery and ordered his release. It should be noted, in passing, that while a complaint had been made at the garda station that no notes had been taken of the earlier interviews, this suggestion was not put to Superintendent White in the course of his evidence before the learned High Court judge.

The State appeals to this court. The question for resolution is this: Does such deprivation, as the solicitor for the detained man suffered in this case mean that the detention of the respondent was rendered unlawful? Without any doubt, if a person in custody is denied blanket access to legal advice, or if he is subjected to ill treatment by way of assaults, for example, then that would render his detention unlawful.

However, the gardaí must be allowed to exercise their powers of interrogation as they think right, provided they act reasonably. Counsel for the State submitted to the High Court Judge that in effect what Mr. MacGuill was seeking was that the gardaí should give him regular updates and running accounts of the progress of their investigations and that this was going too far. I agree. The solicitor is not entitled to be present at the interviews. Neither was it open to the respondent, or his solicitor, to prescribe the manner by which the interviews might be conducted, or where. The point of whether there were adequate notes taken of any interview might, or might not, be of significance if there was a subsequent trial.

I think all the members of the court were struck by the apparent inconsistency in the State's attitude: that although the detained man could see the notes of the interviews, his solicitor could not. While this may have been a somewhat incongruous course of conduct, it does not render the detention unlawful. It should be noted, too, that of course if a charge had followed on the detention both the accused and his legal advisors would have been entitled to all relevant documentation. This matter was explored comprehensively in the recent decision of this court in *Ward v Special Criminal Court* [1998] 2 I.L.R.M. 493.

I hold that the respondent's detention was in accordance with law and that he should not have been released under Article 40 of the Constitution. I would, accordingly, reverse the order made by the learned High Court Judge. ...

59. People (D.P.P.) v Finnerty

Supreme Court, June 17, 1999
[1999] 4 I.R. 364 at 376–377, 379–382

Keane J:

... This case is solely concerned with the claimed right of a person detained under s.4 of the [Criminal Justice] Act of 1984, to refuse to answer questions put to him by the gardaí during the course of his detention and the corollary of that right i.e. the need to ensure that no inferences adverse to him are drawn at any subsequent trial from the exercise of that right.

The history of the law prior to the enactment of the Act of 1984, is relevant. Our criminal law, deriving ultimately from the Anglo-American system, historically reflected a tension between two competing principles. The first was the right and duty of the police to investigate crime of every sort in the interests of the community as a whole and the corresponding obligation on citizens to assist them in that task. The second was the right of a suspect at a defined stage in the investigation to refuse to answer any questions and the obligation on the police to inform him of that right in the almost universally known formula of the traditional police caution. ...

The Act of 1984, accordingly, did not modify in any way the right of a person whom the gardaí suspect of having committed a crime to refuse to answer questions put to him by the gardaí and his entitlement under the Judges' Rules to be reminded of that right before any questioning begins. That right would, of course, be significantly eroded if at the subsequent trial of the person concerned, the jury could be invited to draw inferences adverse to him from his failure to reply to those questions and, specifically, to his failure to give the questioning gardaí an account similar to that subsequently given by him in evidence. It would also render virtually meaningless, the caution required to be given to him under the Judges' Rules.

It must also be borne in mind that it is a usual practice for solicitors to advise their clients while they are in custody, not to answer any questions put to them by the gardaí, if they consider that it would not be in their interests to do so. However, if the jury could be invited to draw inferences from the failure to reply to such questions, the result would be that persons in custody would have to be advised by solicitors that, notwithstanding the terms of the caution, it might be inimical to their client's interests not to make a full statement to the gardaí, thereby eroding further the right of silence recognised at common law.

Had the Oireachtas intended to abridge the right of silence in this manner, it would have expressly so legislated. Sections 18 and 19 of the Act of 1984 enable the court of trial to draw inferences from the failure or refusal of a person arrested by the gardaí, to account for the presence of certain objects in his possession, or his having been found at a particular place. Such inferences may afford corroboration of any evidence, but the person may not be convicted of an offence solely on the basis of such inferences. This leads to the inevitable conclusion that no such general abridgement of the right of silence was intended to be effected where a person declined to answer questions put to him by the gardaí during the course of such a detention.

It is also noteworthy that such an alteration in the law was effected, in England, in circumstances of acute controversy, by s.34 of the Criminal Justice (Public Order) Act, 1994, which provides *inter alia* that, where a person, on being questioned under caution by an investigating police officer, fails to mention any fact relied on in his defence in the proceedings, the court or jury:

"... may draw such inferences from the failure as appears proper."

That in turn led to an amendment in that Act of the traditional form of caution which, as set out in Code C, para. 10.4, is now as follows:

"You do not have to say anything but it may harm your defence if you do not mention when questioned something which you later rely on in court. Anything you do say may be given in evidence."

The absence of any such provisions in the Act of 1984 speaks for itself.

In the case of the Offences Against the State Act, 1939, the right of silence was modified in so far as s.52 of that Act made a failure to account for one's movements, when requested to do so under that Act, a punishable offence. In *Heaney v Ireland* [1994] 3 I.R. 593, Costello J., as he then was, concluded that the right of silence modified by this provision was a constitutional right deriving from Article 38.1 of the Constitution guaranteeing that no person would be tried on any criminal charge "save in due course of law". He held, however, that the abridgement of the right of silence effected by s.52 was proportionate to the objectives intended to be achieved by the legislation. He, accordingly, rejected the challenge to the constitutionality of the provision and his decision was upheld by this Court, although in the judgment of O'Flaherty J., the constitutional right to remain silent is traced to a different source, i.e. as being a corollary to the freedom of expression also recognised by the Constitution. The same principles were applied by this Court in *Rock v Ireland* [1997] 3 I.R.

484, where the constitutionality of ss.18 and 19 of the Act of 1984 were upheld. (See also the decision of Barrington J., speaking for the court, in *Re National Irish Bank Ltd.* ([1999] 3 I.R. 145.)

It follows that the right of suspects in custody to remain silent, recognised by the common law, is also a constitutional right and the provisions of the Act of 1984, must be construed accordingly. Absent any express statutory provisions entitling a court or jury to draw inferences from such silence, the conclusion follows inevitably that the right is left unaffected by the Act of 1984, save in cases coming within ss.18 and 19, and must be upheld by the courts.

Counsel for the applicant, who argued this case on behalf of the applicant with conspicuous ability, accepted that he would have had no complaint if the prosecution had simply informed the court that the applicant had been detained under the Act of 1984, but that nothing of probative value had emerged from the detention. He urged, however, that that was not what had happened in this case: on the contrary, evidence was adduced by the prosecution to the jury as to what transpired during the detention, after the complainant had been cross-examined, with the avowed intention of cross-examining the applicant as to his failure to give such an account during the course of his detention, when he came to give evidence, a course of action strenuously objected to on behalf of the defence, but permitted by the learned trial judge.

Again, while counsel for the applicant accepted that he had not objected to the cross-examination when it eventually took place, he also pointed out that at that stage, the trial judge had already made his ruling on the matter and that, in any event, the damage was done so far as the defence was concerned once the cross-examination on this topic was under way. While also accepting that it was open to him at that stage to apply to the trial judge to discharge the jury, he submitted that this was a dubious course for the defence to adopt in a case where the jury had been presented with two diametrically opposed versions of what had happened on that evening between the complainant and the applicant and the defence might justifiably have hoped that the jury would be left with a reasonable doubt as to whether the complainant's version was true.

The court is satisfied that counsel for the applicant's submissions are well founded. The defence should not have been put at any disadvantage on the hearing of the appeal by the decision, reasonable in all the circumstances, not to object to the cross-examination or apply for the discharge of the jury.

The principles applicable in a case such as the present where a defendant while detained under the provisions of the Act of 1984 has refused to answer questions put to him, can be stated as follows:

1. Where nothing of probative value has emerged as a result of such a detention, but it is thought desirable that the court should be aware that the defendant was so detained, the court should be simply informed that he was so detained, but that nothing of probative value emerged.

2. Under no circumstances should any cross-examination by the prosecution as to the refusal of the defendant, during the course of his detention, to answer any questions, be permitted.

3. In the case of a trial before a jury, the trial judge in his charge should, in general, make no reference to the fact that the defendant refused to answer

questions during the course of his detention.

The application of the first and second of these principles to the present case must result in the appeal being allowed. Unfortunately, the difficulties were compounded by the passage in the trial judge's charge, which was by implication, critical of the applicant for having made statements as to what transpired during the course of his detention, which had not been put to the gardaí and which, the trial judge invited the jury to infer, had not been transmitted to his legal advisers.

It must be said, in fairness to the trial judge that, once the misapprehension he was under when making those observations was made clear to him, he might have been prepared to rectify the matter when the jury was recalled. The defence, however, adopted the position, as they were entitled to do, that the matter was beyond rectification and sought the discharge of the jury, a course opposed by the prosecution which the trial judge did not adopt. The jury accordingly, in deliberating on the guilt or innocence of the accused, might well have been under the impression that they were not only entitled to draw adverse inferences from the failure of the defendant to give his version of events in detail in the garda station, but that they were also entitled to draw such inferences from the supposed failure of the applicant to instruct his legal advisers as to what had transpired during the course of that questioning.

Any inferences which the jury might have drawn to that effect would have been in direct violation of the applicant's constitutionally guaranteed right to remain silent, and might well have been a factor in the jury's assessment of the credibility of the applicant's account, of what happened between him and the complainant on that night. The verdict of the jury cannot, accordingly, in those circumstances be regarded as safe or satisfactory. ...

60. People (D.P.P.) v J.E.M.
Supreme Court, February 1, 2000
[2001] 4 I.R. 385 at 400–403

Denham J:

... [Section] 7 of the Criminal Law (Rape)(Amendment) Act 1990 ... is quite clear in stating that it is for the judge to decide in his discretion, having regard to the evidence, whether the jury should be given a warning about the danger of convicting the person on the uncorroborated evidence of the other person.

The trial judge had heard counsel debate the issue of corroboration. The law does not make the warning mandatory in all cases; whether or not it should be given is a matter for the discretion of the trial judge. This represented a change in the law. ...

Reference to the current law is to be found in a number of cases. Thus, in *The People (Director of Public Prosecutions) v J.C.* (Unreported, Court of Criminal Appeal, 7th November, 1994) the court at p. 8 of the transcript stated:

"It has to be emphasised that the matter of whether the corroboration warning should or should not be given is a matter for the trial judge. ...."

In *R. v Makanjuola* [1995] 1 W.L.R. 1348 at 1350-2, the court was invited to give guidance as to the circumstances which, as a matter of discretion, a judge ought, in summing up to a jury, urge caution in regard to a particular witness and the terms in which it should be given. Lord Taylor of Gosforth C.J. summarized, at pp. 1351 and 1352, as follows:

"(1) Section 32(1) abrogated the requirement to give a corroboration direction in respect of an alleged accomplice or a complainant of a sexual offence simply because a witness falls into one of those categories.

(2) It is a matter for the judge's discretion what, if any, warning he considers appropriate in respect of such a witness, as indeed in respect of any other witness in whatever type of case. Whether he chooses to give a warning and in what terms will depend on the circumstances of the case, the issues raised and the content and quality of the witness's evidence.

(3) In some cases, it may be appropriate for the judge to warn the jury to exercise caution before acting upon the unsupported evidence of a witness. This will not be so simply because the witness is a complainant of a sexual offence nor will it necessarily be so because a witness is alleged to be an accomplice. There will need to be an evidential basis for suggesting that the evidence of the witness may be unreliable. An evidential basis does not include mere suggestions by cross-examining counsel.

(4) If any question arises as to whether the judge should give a special warning in respect of a witness, it is desirable that the question be resolved by discussion with counsel in the absence of the jury before final speeches.

(5) Where the judge does decide to give some warning in respect of a witness, it will be appropriate to do so as part of the judge's review of the evidence and his comments as to how the jury should evaluate it rather than as a set-piece legal direction.

(6) Where some warning is required, it will be for the judge to decide the strength and terms of the warning. It does not have to be invested with the whole florid regime of the old corroboration rules.

(7) It follows that we emphatically disagree with the tentative submission made by the editors of *Archbold* in the passage at para. 16-36 quoted above. Attempts to re-impose the straitjacket of the old corroboration rules are strongly to be deprecated.

(8) Finally, this court will be disinclined to interfere with a trial judge's exercise of his discretion save in a case where that exercise is unreasonable in the *Wednesbury* sense (see *Associated Provincial*

Picture Houses Ltd. v Wednesbury Corp. [1947] 2 All E.R. 680, [1948] 1 K.B. 223)."

Whereas the wording of the legislation of England and Wales is not exactly the same as the wording of the legislation in this State, the underlying approach to abrogate the pre-existing requirement as to warnings in relation to uncorroborated evidence in sexual offence cases is comparable. The legal principle underpinning both statutes is similar. This court endorses the approach indicated by Lord Taylor in relation to the approach in a sexual offence trial, with the exception of para. 8. This court approves the analysis by Taylor L.C.J. at p. 1351 where he stated:

"Given that the requirement of a corroboration direction is abrogated in the terms of s.32(1), we have been invited to give guidance as to the circumstances in which, as a matter of discretion, a judge ought in summing up to a jury to urge caution in regard to a particular witness and the terms in which that should be done. The circumstances and evidence in criminal cases are infinitely variable and it is impossible to categorise how a judge should deal with them. But it is clear that to carry on giving 'discretionary' warnings generally and in the same terms as were previously obligatory would be contrary to the policy and purpose of the 1994 Act. Whether, as a matter of discretion, a judge should give any warning and if so its strength and terms must depend upon the content and manner of the witness's evidence, the circumstances of the case and the issues raised. The judge will often consider that no special warning is required at all. Where, however, the witness has been shown to be unreliable, he or she may consider it necessary to urge caution. In a more extreme case, if the witness is shown to have lied, to have made previous false complaints, or to bear the defendant some grudge, a stronger warning may be thought appropriate and the judge may suggest it would be wise to look for some supporting material before acting on the impugned witness's evidence. We stress that these observations are merely illustrative of some, not all, of the factors which judges may take into account in measuring where a witness stands in the scale of reliability and what response they should make at that level in their directions to the jury. We also stress that judges are not required to conform to any formula and this court would be slow to interfere with the exercise of discretion by a trial judge who has the advantage of assessing the manner of a witness's evidence as well as its content."

This general analysis is useful as the policy and purpose of s.7 of the Irish statute and s.32 of the English statute are similar. Both address a similar underlying principle. This analysis is relevant and helpful when considering the Irish legislation.

The Irish legislation is clear. The Criminal Law (Rape) (Amendment) Act 1990, states that in a trial, such as this, where evidence is given by the person in relation to whom the offence is alleged to have been committed, it is for the judge to decide in his discretion, having regard to all the evidence given, whether the jury should be given a warning. This is a clear statement of principle and law.

The trial judge in this case exercised his discretion. This was a long trial where the issue of corroboration was debated by counsel before the judge. In light of the issues raised, the circumstances and the evidence given, the trial judge exercised his discretion not to give a warning. No reason has been given upon which this court could interfere with the trial judge's exercise of discretion. Consequently, this ground of appeal fails. ...

61. Heaney and McGuinness v Ireland

The European Court of Human Rights, December 21, 2000
(2001) 33 E.H.R.R. 264 at paras 40–48, 53–55, 58–59

40. ... The Court recalls its established case-law to the effect that, although not specifically mentioned in Article 6 of the Convention, the rights relied on by the applicants, the right to silence and the right not to incriminate oneself, are generally recognised international standards which lie at the heart of the notion of a fair procedure under Article 6. Their rationale lies, *inter alia*, in the protection of the accused against improper compulsion by the authorities, thereby contributing to the avoidance of miscarriages of justice and to the fulfilment of the aims of Article 6. The right not to incriminate oneself, in particular, presupposes that the prosecution in a criminal case seek to prove their case against the accused without resort to evidence obtained through methods of coercion or oppression in defiance of the will of the accused. In this sense the right in question is closely linked to the presumption of innocence contained in Article 6 § 2 of the Convention.[10] The right not to incriminate oneself is primarily concerned, however, with respecting the will of an accused person to remain silent. The Court would note, in this context, that the present case does not concern a request, through the use of compulsory powers, of material which had an existence independent of the will of the applicants, such as documents or blood samples.[11]

41. The Court observes that the applicants complained under Article 6 of the Convention about having been punished, through the application of section 52 of the 1939 Act, for relying on their rights to silence, against self-incrimination and to be presumed innocent during police questioning in the course of a serious criminal investigation. It recalls that the autonomous meaning of the expression "charge" in Article 6 § 1 of the Convention means that a person can be considered to have been "charged" for the purposes of that Article when that individual's situation has been "substantially affected".[12]

---

[10] See *Saunders v United Kingdom* December 17, 1996, Reports of Judgments and Decisions 1996-VI, at p.2064, §68.
[11] *ibid.* at pp. 2064–2065, §69.
[12] See *Serves v France* October 20, 1997, Reports of Judgments and Decisions 1996-VI, at p.2172, §42.

42. While the present applicants had not yet been formally charged on 24 October 1990 when the section 52 requests were made, the Court considers that they were, at that stage, "substantially affected" and therefore "charged", in the above-noted sense, with membership of the IRA and with some involvement in the bombing in October 1990.

The High Court noted that it was suspected that the bombing had been carried out by the IRA and that the applicants had been arrested on suspicion of membership of the IRA and of involvement in that bombing. The Government confirmed this in their observations. They were arrested within approximately twenty-four hours of the bombing in a house close to the site of the explosion while that house was being searched by the police on the basis of a warrant. They were expressly arrested and detained under section 30 of the 1939 Act. Having been cautioned, they were questioned, *inter alia*, about the bombing. The subsequent section 52 requests related to the applicants' movements around the time of that bombing.

43. However, it is true that, while the applicants may have been so charged within the meaning of Article 6 when the section 52 requests were made, they were acquitted in the substantive proceedings relating to the charge of membership of the IRA. The Court recalls that an accused's acquittal, in general, precludes that person from claiming to be a victim of a violation of the procedural guarantees of Article 6.[13]

44. Nevertheless, the Court notes that this latter principle has been refined in certain circumstances. ...

45. In the *Allenet de Ribemont* case, the Court explained this refinement, pointing out that the Convention, including Article 6 § 2, must be interpreted in such a way as to guarantee rights which are practical and effective as opposed to theoretical and illusory.[14] Applying this approach to the present case, the Court observes that, if the applicants were unable to rely on Article 6, their acquittal in the substantive proceedings would exclude any consideration under Article 6 of their complaints that they had been, nevertheless, already punished prior to that acquittal for having defended what they considered to be their rights guaranteed by Article 6 of the Convention.

46. In such circumstances, the Court finds that the applicants can rely on Article 6 §§ 1 and 2 in respect of their conviction and imprisonment under section 52 of the 1939 Act.

2. Compliance with Article 6 §§ 1 and 2 of the Convention
47. The Court accepts that the right to silence and the right not to incriminate oneself guaranteed by Article 6 § 1 are not absolute rights.[15]

---

[13] See, *e.g. Byrn v Denmark*, Application No. 13156/87, Commission Decision of July 1, 1992, Decisions and Reports 73, at p.5.
[14] See *Allenet de Ribemont v France* February 10, 1995, Series A no. 308, at p.16, §35.
[15] See *Murray v United Kingdom* February 8, 1996, Reports 1996–I, at pp.49–50, §47.

48. However, it is also recalled that Mr. Funke's criminal conviction for refusing to provide information requested by the customs authorities was considered to amount to a violation of Article 6 § 1. In that case, the Court noted that the customs authorities had secured Mr. Funke's conviction in order to obtain certain documents which they believed existed, although they were not certain of the fact. The Court found that the customs authorities, being unable or unwilling to procure them by some other means, attempted to compel Mr. Funke himself to provide the evidence of offences he had allegedly committed. The special features of customs law were found insufficient by the Court to justify such an infringement of the right of anyone charged with a criminal offence, within the autonomous meaning of that expression in Article 6, to remain silent and not to contribute to incriminating himself.

In the *John Murray* judgment, the Court described the *Funke* case, pointing out that the "degree of compulsion" which had been applied through the initiation of criminal proceedings against Mr. Funke was found to have been incompatible with Article 6 because "in effect, it destroyed the very essence of the privilege against self-incrimination".[16] ...

53. The Court considers that the legal position as regards the admission into evidence of section 52 statements was particularly uncertain in October 1990 when the applicants were questioned.

It notes that the text of section 52 of the 1939 Act is silent on this point. The Government did not refer to any domestic case-law prior to October 1990 which would have authoritatively excluded the later admission into evidence against the applicants of any statements made by them pursuant to those requests. Nor did the Government exclude the possibility that, prior to October 1990, statements made pursuant to section 52 had in fact been admitted in evidence against accused persons. The Government's position was rather that, in any event, the situation had been clarified for the future by the January 1999 judgment in the *National Irish Bank Ltd* case.[17] This uncertainty about the domestic legal position in October 1990 is underlined by the comments of the Supreme Court in the present applicants' constitutional proceedings on the judgment of the Court of Criminal Appeal in the earlier *McGowan* case.[18]

In any event, the applicants were provided with conflicting information in this respect by the questioning police officers on 24 October 1990. At the beginning of their interviews they were informed that they had the right to remain silent. Nevertheless, when the section 52 requests were made during those interviews, they were then effectively informed that, if they did not account for their movements at particular times, they risked six months' imprisonment. The only reference during the interviews to the possible use of statements made by the applicants in any later proceedings was to inform them that anything they did say would be written down and might be used against them.

---

[16] See *Murray v United Kingdom*, ibid. at p.50, §49.
[17] *In the Matter of National Irish Bank Ltd. and the Companies Act 1990* [1999] 1 I.L.R.M. 343.
[18] *People (D.P.P.) v McGowan* [1979] I.R. 45.

54. Given this uncertainty, the position in October 1990 as regards the later admission into evidence of section 52 statements could not have, in the Court's view, contributed to restoring the essence of the present applicant's rights to silence and against self-incrimination guaranteed by Article 6 of the Convention.

The Court is not, therefore, called upon in the present case to consider the impact on the rights to silence or against self-incrimination of the direct or indirect use made in later proceedings against an accused of statements made pursuant to section 52 of the 1939 Act.

55. Accordingly, the Court finds that the "degree of compulsion" imposed on the applicants by the application of section 52 of the 1939 Act with a view to compelling them to provide information relating to charges against them under that Act in effect destroyed the very essence of their privilege against self-incrimination and their right to remain silent. ...

[The] Court recalls that in the *Saunders* case[19] it found that the argument of the United Kingdom government that the complexity of corporate fraud and the vital public interest in the investigation of such fraud and the punishment of those responsible could not justify such a marked departure in that case from one of the basic principles of a fair procedure. It considered that the general requirements of fairness contained in Article 6, including the right not to incriminate oneself, "apply to criminal proceedings in respect of all types of criminal offences without distinction from the most simple to the most complex". It concluded that the public interest could not be relied on to justify the use of answers compulsorily obtained in a non-judicial investigation to incriminate the accused during the trial proceedings. ...

58. The Court, accordingly, finds that the security and public order concerns relied on by the Government cannot justify a provision which extinguishes the very essence of the applicants' rights to silence and against self-incrimination guaranteed by Article 6 § 1 of the Convention.

59. It concludes, therefore, that there has been a violation of the applicants' right to silence and their right not to incriminate themselves guaranteed by Article 6 § 1 of the Convention.

Moreover, given the close link, in this context, between those rights guaranteed by Article 6 § 1 of the Convention and the presumption of innocence guaranteed by Article 6 § 2 (see paragraph 40 above), the Court also concludes that there has been a violation of the latter provision.

---

[19] *Saunders v United Kingdom* December 17, 1996, Reports of Judgments and Decisions 1996-VI at pp. 2066–67, §74.

62. Miley v Flood

High Court, January 24, 2001
[2001] 1 I.L.R.M. 489 at 504–506, 517–518

Kelly J:

... Legal professional privilege is more than a mere rule of evidence. It is a fundamental condition on which the administration of justice as a whole rests. That is the conclusion which I reached in *Duncan v Governor of Portlaoise Prison* [1997] 1 I.R. 558. In that case I quoted with approval a passage from the speech of Lord Taylor of Gosforth in *R. v Derby Magistrates Court; Ex parte B.* [1996] 1 A.C. 487 where, having set forth the history of legal professional privilege in English law he concluded at p. 507 as follows:

> "The principle which runs through all these cases, and the many other cases which were cited, is that a man must be able to consult his lawyer in confidence, since otherwise he might hold back half the truth. The client must be sure that what he tells his lawyer in confidence will never be revealed without his consent. Legal professional privilege is thus much more that an ordinary rule of evidence, limited in its application to the facts of a particular case. It is the fundamental condition on which the administration of justice as a whole rests."

My decision in *Duncan v Governor of Mountjoy Prison* [1997] 1 I.R. 558 was upheld by the Supreme Court in an *ex tempore* decision (Unreported, Supreme Court, 5th March, 1997).

Similar conclusions as to the fundamental nature of legal professional privilege have been reached by courts of other jurisdictions. For example in *Descoteaux v Mierzwinksi* (1982) 141 D.L.R. (3d) 590 the Supreme Court of Canada took the view that the right to legal confidentiality had developed from a rule of evidence into a substantive right. Lamar J., in delivering of the judgment of the court, said ... at p. 601:

> "there is no denying that a person has a right to communicate with a legal adviser in all confidence, a right that is 'founded upon the unique relationship of solicitor and client' (*Solosky, supra*). It is a personal and extra patrimonial-right which follows a citizen throughout his dealings with others. Like other personal, extra patrimonial rights, it gives rise to preventive or curative remedies provided for by law, depending on the nature of the aggression threatening it or of which it was the object. Thus a lawyer who communicates a confidential communication to others without his client's authorisation could be sued by his client for damages; or a third party who had accidentally seen the contents of a lawyers file could be prohibited by injunction from disclosing them."

At p. 603 he said:

> "The following statement by Wigmore ... of the rule of evidence is a

good summary, in my view, of the substantive conditions precedent to the existence of the right of the lawyers client, to confidentiality: 'Where legal advice of any kind is sought from a professional legal adviser in his capacity as such, the communications relating to that purpose, made in confidence by the client, are at his instance permanently protected from disclosure by himself or by the legal adviser, except the protection be waived'.

Seeking advice from a legal advisor includes consulting those who assist him professionally (for example, his secretary or articling student) and who have as such had access to the communications made by the client for the purpose of obtaining legal advice.

There are exceptions. It is not sufficient to speak to a lawyer or one of his associates for everything to become confidential from that point on. The communication must be made to the lawyer or his assistants in their professional capacity; the relationship must be a professional one at the exact moment of the communication. Communications made in order to facilitate the commission of a crime or fraud will not be confidential either, regardless of whether or not the lawyer is acting in good faith."

In *Esso Australia Resources Ltd. v Sir Daryl Dawson* [1999] F.C.A. 363, the Federal Court of Australia had this to say on the topic at para. 26:

"Legal professional privilege has long been the subject of controversy. It operates to exclude evidence not because of its unreliability but to advance other objectives. Jeremy Bentham regarded the exclusion of probative evidence as 'one of the most pernicious and most irrational notions that ever found its way into the human mind': *Rationale of Judicial Evidence* (J. S. Mill ed.) (1827) at 193–194. But the judgment of the common law has been that while the central objective of the legal system is the search for truth, it is more important that some communications be kept secret. In the case of legal professional privilege, secrecy is defended on the basis is that it would promote the administration of justice. 'The systemic benefits of the privilege are commonly understood to outweigh the harm caused by excluding critical evidence': *Swidler v United States* (1998) 141 L ed. 2d 379 at 389 *per* O'Connor J. (in dissent)."

Notwithstanding that controversial history however, the Federal Australian Court nonetheless said at para. 14:

"Historically, legal professional privilege was justified as a vindication of the oath and honour of the lawyer. But it came to be recognised that the privilege has a more solid foundation. In the absence of the privilege a client would not freely consult with his lawyer. He would not make a full and frank disclosure of the material facts upon which the lawyer's advice is sought. Thus is said that one effect of the denial of the privilege could, some say that it would, greatly inhibit the professional advice and assistance given by a lawyer. This inhibition would significantly undermine the proper functioning of the adversarial system of justice. These considerations, among others, have lead courts to accept that the privilege is not merely a rule of evidence but a basic principle of the common law: a principle that transcends the normally predominant principle that all rational means for ascertaining the truth should be employed in the curial process.

Legal professional privilege is also protected by the European Convention on Human Rights. In *Niemitez v Germany* (1992) 16 E.H.R.R. 97 the European Court of Human Rights took the view that a warrant which permitted the search of a lawyers office was 'not necessary in a democratic society'. The power, which took no account of any special protection which might be desirable in relation to the lawyer's premises was disproportionate to its purposes. The court took the view (at p. 141) that where a lawyer is involved '... an encroachment on professional secrecy may have repercussions on the proper administration of justice and hence on the rights guaranteed by Article 6 of the Convention'."

This short survey of the international scene demonstrates that in all of the leading common law countries, legal professional privilege exists and is regarded as being very much more than a rule of evidence. Rather, just as in this jurisdiction, it constitutes an essential condition upon which the administration of justice rests. In the context of European human rights it is protected by art. 6 of the European Convention on Human Rights. ...

Having considered all of [the] authorities, I have come to the conclusion that the applicant is not entitled as a matter of Irish law to maintain a claim of privilege over the identity of persons who provided him with his instructions on behalf of the company. Any such claim of privilege would be inconsistent with the views of the Supreme Court in *Smurfit Paribas Bank Ltd. v A.A.B. Export Finance Ltd. (No. 1)* [1990] 1 I.R. 469 which are binding upon me.

Even in England where a wider form of legal privilege exists the position would, on the basis of the English authorities, be no different.

In the foreign jurisdictions where the law of privilege is not the same as in this jurisdiction, there is nonetheless a strong body of legal authority reaffirming the general principle that a solicitor is not entitled to maintain a claim to privilege in respect of the identity of his client.

A dilution of this general principle arises where (a) the naming of the client would incriminate or (b) where the identity of the client is so bound up with the nature of the advice sought, that to reveal the client's identity would be in fact to reveal that advice. There is no evidence whatsoever to suggest that the naming of these persons by the applicant would incriminate them, nor is there any evidence that the identity of these persons is so bound up with the nature of the advice sought that to reveal the identity would be in fact to reveal the advice. Consequently even if this exception to the general principle were to apply it would have no bearing upon the instant case.

In these circumstances the applicant is not entitled to the declaration which he seeks and it is refused. The respondent was in my view entitled to require of him the disclosure of the identity of the persons who furnished him with instructions on behalf of the company and he must now furnish that information to the respondent.

This application is dismissed.

63. Braddish v D.P.P.

Supreme Court, May 18, 2001
[2001] 3 I.R. 127 at 129–135

Hardiman J:

On the 2nd July 1997 a robbery took place in a shop in Limerick. The premises were protected by video surveillance and it appears from the statements exhibited in the affidavits herein that a Detective Garda O'Neill viewed the videotape. He believed that the videotape showed the robbery in progress and that the applicant was the person shown committing it. On this basis he arrested the applicant on the 14th October 1997. The applicant was detained pursuant to s.4 of the Criminal Justice Act 1984. During his detention, which was extended pursuant to the Act, the applicant is alleged to have made and signed a statement admitting to the robbery.

The applicant was released from custody on the 14th October 1997. He was not charged with the robbery until the 2nd July 1998, a period of approximately nine months. It is alleged by the applicant, and doubted but not expressly denied by the first-named respondent, that on the first appearance in the District Court the applicant's then solicitor requested any signed statements, any video footage and any stills of such video footage.

This request was subsequently repeated in correspondence in December 1998. Finally, in January 1999, the applicant's then solicitor was told in correspondence:

> "In relation to the videos these are no longer available as they were returned to the owners after the accused admitted the crime". ...

A retrial took place on the 20th April 1999 before His Honour Judge Haugh and a jury. On this trial, objection was taken to the introduction in evidence of stills which had been made from the video tape while it was in the possession of the gardaí. The learned trial judge excluded the stills from evidence on the basis that it was unfair to produce them when the video film from which they had been taken was not available. ...

Judicial Review Proceedings

On the 14th June 1999 the applicant was granted leave to seek judicial review. He sought to restrain the further prosecution of the indictment preferred against him on the grounds that:

> "(1) The applicant cannot have a fair trial in due course of law and according to law as is required by the provisions of Article 38.1 and

Article 40.4.1 of the Constitution of Ireland because the first-named respondent herein has failed refused and/or neglected to furnish to the applicant's legal advisers copies of and/or an opportunity to inspect the originals of (a) original still photographs, (b) video."

Shortly before the hearing in the High Court Detective Garda O'Neill filed a further affidavit in which he stated that the video was returned to the owner of the shop where the robbery took place "mistakenly on an unknown date between ... the 3rd July 1998 and the 23rd December 1998 when Mr. Murray raised queries with the gardaí regarding the video and other matters enquired into by the Defence".

Issues

It will be seen that the issue raised by the applicant is a net one. Does the fact that the video tape is unavailable because the guards parted with possession of it require in the circumstances that the further prosecution of the applicant be restrained? In addressing this issue it is important to recall that the video allegedly shows the crime in progress and allows the identification of the perpetrator. No other identification evidence was apparently available and no person was asked to see if he or she could identify the applicant even though it appears from the papers that there was at least one eye witness to the robbery.

The High Court Order

In a very detailed judgment delivered the 21st December 2000 O'Caoimh J. refused the relief sought. He did so on the basis that the prosecution case was not one relying on visual identification itself, but one which rested on the statement alleged to have been made by the applicant when arrested by the gardaí. He observed however that if the prosecution were to rely on the photographic stills, a real problem would exist because the applicant would be deprived of his opportunity of testing the evidence as the video tape was missing. He stated that he was influenced by the fact that the written request for the videos was not made until about eighteen months after the applicant had been arrested. The learned judge held that he could not conclude that if a timely application had been made, the applicant would have been deprived of an opportunity of viewing the video evidence. The learned judge also held that the applicant had not moved promptly for relief by way of judicial review.

Entitlement to items of evidence

It is well established that evidence relevant to guilt or innocence must, so far as necessary and practicable, be kept until the conclusion of a trial. This principle also applies to the preservation of articles which may give rise to the reasonable possibility of securing relevant evidence.

These propositions were established in the judgment of Lynch J. in *Robert Murphy v D.P.P.* [1989] I.L.R.M. 71. In his judgment the learned judge surveys authorities going back well over a century. These include the judgment of

Palles C.B. in *Dillon v O'Brien and Davies* [1887] 20 L.R. I.R. 300. There, the learned Chief Baron said:

> "The interest of the State in the person charged to being brought to trial in due course necessarily extends as well to the preservation of material evidence of his guilt or innocence as to his custody for the purpose of the trial."

In *Murphy v D.P.P.*, the applicant had been charged with stealing a car and driving offences. The car was in the possession of the guards and the applicant's solicitor had made clear his wish to inspect and test the car, notably for finger print evidence, at an early stage. Nevertheless, the guards parted with the car without either examining it forensically themselves or notifying the applicant's solicitor that they intended to part with it. Lynch J. held that their action "in the circumstances amounted to a breach of the rule of fair procedures". This was so even though it had not and could not be established that the applicant would in fact have found anything of evidential use on an examination of the car. The learned judge held that "The applicant has been deprived of the reasonable possibility of rebutting the evidence proffered against him. It is also clear that there is no way in which this loss to the applicant of possibly corroborative evidence can now be remedied by any further inspection of the car".

The learned judge concluded:

> "The authorities established that evidence relevant to guilt or innocence must so far as is necessary and practicable be kept until the conclusion of the trial. These authorities also apply to the preservation of articles which may give rise to the reasonable possibility of securing relevant evidence."

I would respectfully concur with the judgment of Lynch J. and with the authorities which he cites. …

In the criminal trial for this robbery, the applicant is pleading not guilty despite the alleged existence of an inculpatory statement signed by him. This statement was allegedly made while he was in garda custody after an arrest allegedly based wholly on the videotape evidence. If the applicant wished to object to the statement on the basis of the illegality of his detention it is difficult to see how he could do so unless he could show that the ground put forward for his arrest did not in fact support it and could not reasonably be supposed to do so. This seems impossible to do without the videotape. The stills, certainly in the form of which they were presented to this Court, are quite useless for identification purposes.

More fundamentally, this is a videotape which purports actually to show the robbery in progress. It is not acceptable, in my view, to excuse the absence of so vital and direct a piece of evidence simply by saying that the prosecution are not relying on it, but prefer to rely on an alleged confession. Firstly, the confession is hotly disputed. Secondly, a confession should if possible be corroborated and relatively recent history both here and in the neighbouring jurisdiction has unfortunate examples of the risks of excessive reliance on confession evidence. Thirdly the videotape has a clear potential to exculpate as well as to inculpate.

This videotape was real evidence and the gardaí were not entitled to dispose of it before the trial. It is now admitted that they should not have done so. Lest however the sentence already quoted from the State Solicitor's letter (and which can only have been based on his instructions from the gardaí) can be read to suggest that because the prosecution was based wholly on an alleged confession, other items of evidence can be destroyed or rendered unavailable, I wish to state emphatically that this is not so. It is the duty of the gardaí, arising from their unique investigative role, to seek out and preserve all evidence having a bearing or potential bearing on the issue of guilt or innocence. This is so whether the prosecution proposes to rely on the evidence or not, and regardless of whether it assists the case the prosecution is advancing or not. ...

There are other possible explanations for the prosecution's unwillingness to deploy in evidence material which was used in the investigation. But the fact that such material is not used can never justify its destruction or unavailability, or the destruction of notes or records about it. This is because a particular fact or piece of real evidence which it would be irrelevant or counter productive for the prosecution to deploy may (perhaps for that very reason) be very useful to the defence. It must therefore be preserved and disclosed. The prosecution are not entitled to take the view that once they have better evidence, or evidence more convenient to them to deploy, they are entitled to destroy the evidence which came first to hand. They are not entitled to say, for instance, "This is a confession case; we will stand or fall on the confession and are therefore entitled to ignore the video tape".

It is important to bear in mind that the evidential items to which the foregoing applies are not only those with a direct and established evidential significance but include those which, in the words of Lynch J., "may give rise to the reasonable possibility of securing relevant evidence". In assessing whether this criterion is met it is useful to bear in mind what was said in the leading Irish authority on discovery as to the scope of the material which must be discovered to the other side. In *Sterling-Winthrop Group Ltd. v Fabenfabriken Bayer A.G.* [1967] I.R. 97, dealing exclusively with the question of documents, the Court held that the documents to be produced on discovery were not confined to those which would be evidence either to prove or disprove any matter in question in the action, but extended to:

> "Every document relating to the matters in question in the action, which not only would be evidence upon any issue, but which, is it is reasonable to suppose, contains information which *may* – not which *must* – enable the party requiring the affidavit to advance his own case or to damage the case of his adversary. ... " (emphasis in original).

The same principles apply to evidential materials other than documents. ...

It would be difficult to think of evidence more directly relevant than a purported videotape showing the commission of the crime. But in cases where the evidence is not of such direct and manifest relevance, the duty to preserve and disclose has to be interpreted in a fair and reasonable manner. It must be recalled that, in the words of Lynch J., the duty to preserve evidence is to do so "so far as is necessary and practicable". A duty so qualified cannot be precisely or exhaustively defined in words of general application. Certainly, it cannot be interpreted as requiring the gardaí to engage in disproportionate commitment of manpower or resources in an exhaustive search for every conceivable kind of evidence. The duty must be interpreted realistically on the facts of each case. ...

Conclusion

I would reverse the order of the learned High Court judge and grant the applicant the order he seeks against the first-named respondent restraining him for further prosecuting the applicant on Bill No. 37/1998, County of Limerick, on the basis of the non-availability of the video tape due to the action of the gardaí.

64. People (D.P.P.) v Buck
Supreme Court, April 17, 2002
[2002] I.R. 268 at 277–281, 283

Keane C.J:

... The law as to the admissibility in evidence of confessions of guilt has for long been the subject of anxious consideration by courts in this and other jurisdictions. Three propositions are firmly established in our law:

(1) a confession, whether made to a police officer or any other person will not be admitted in evidence unless it is proved beyond reasonable doubt to have been voluntarily made;
(2) even where voluntarily made, a trial judge retains a residual discretion to exclude such a statement where it is made to a police officer otherwise than in accordance with certain procedures, accepted in Ireland as being embodied in the English Judges' Rules;
(3) such a statement will also be excluded where it has been obtained as the result of a conscious and deliberate violation of the accused's constitutional rights.

There has been much judicial discussion as to the underlying policy reasons for the second and third of these principles. While considerations of fairness to the accused person are naturally prominent, they are not the sole reason for the existence of the principles, as Kingsmill Moore J. observed in *The People (Attorney General) v O'Brien* [1965] I.R. 142 at p. 160:

> "I am disposed to lay emphasis not so much on alleged fairness to the accused as on the public interest that the law should be observed even in the investigation of crime."

As the recent Australian cases of *R. v Swaffield, Pavic v The Queen* [1998] H.C.A. 1 demonstrate, considerations of fairness to the accused on the one hand and public policy on the other will frequently overlap. However, in the context of the present case, it is not necessary to consider the application of the first and second of these principles, since it is conceded that the trial judge was entitled to conclude in the *voir dire* that the inculpatory statement had been voluntarily made and that there had been no breach of the Judges' Rules necessitating consideration by him of his residual discretion to exclude the statement.

In the present case, however, the inculpatory statements were made at a time when the defendant was being detained in custody under the provisions of the [Criminal Justice Act 1984]. Where a person is so detained, whether under that Act or some other statutory provision, he or she is entitled to the benefit of specific constitutional protections, in addition to the common law safeguards to which I have already referred. Giving the judgment of this court in *Re Emergency Powers Bill, 1976* [1977] I.R. 159, O'Higgins C.J., said at p. 173:

> "While it is not necessary to embark upon an exploration of all the incidents or characteristics which may not accompany the arrest and custody of a person under [the impugned section], it is nevertheless desirable, in view of the submissions made to the court, to state that the section is not to be read as an abnegation of the arrested person's rights (constitutional or otherwise) in respect of matters such as the right of communication, *the right to have legal and medical assistance*, and the right of access to the courts. ...." [emphasis added]

In *People (Director of Public Prosecutions) v Healy* [1990] 2 I.R. 73, it was held by a majority of this court that the right of a person in garda custody to reasonable access to his solicitor was derived from, and protected by, the Constitution, and was not merely legal in origin. It was further held that, where a breach of that constitutional right of access to a solicitor occurred as a result of the deliberate and conscious acts of a member of An Garda Síochána, any admission subsequently obtained from a person detained in custody was inadmissible in evidence.

The right of a person in garda custody to reasonable access to a solicitor is also now enshrined in the Act of 1984 and the Regulations of 1987, the relevant provisions of which are referred to in more detail below.

In this case, it is submitted on behalf of the defendant that the questioning of him by the gardaí after he had requested that a solicitor be obtained and before the solicitor arrived was a conscious and deliberate breach of his constitutional right of access to his solicitor which rendered his detention unlawful and any evidence obtained while he was in such unlawful detention inadmissible.

In *People (Director of Public Prosecutions) v Conroy* [1986] I.R. 460, Walsh J. said at p. 479:

> "Even if a solicitor is sent for in such circumstances [in response to a

request to that effect by a person in custody] but the members of the Garda Síochána decide to press ahead with the interrogation before the arrival of the solicitor, I would regard it as a constitutionally forbidden procedure."

That was said by the judge in the course of a dissenting judgment in that case and the matter was not dealt with in any of the other three judgments delivered by the majority of the court. Accordingly, the question as to whether inculpatory statements made by a person in custody who is subjected to questioning by a garda after he has requested the presence of a solicitor (but before the solicitor arrives) are admissible, cannot be regarded as having been authoritatively resolved.

In such a case, it cannot be said that the constitutional right of access to a solicitor has necessarily been denied. In this context, the facts in *People (Director of Public Prosecutions) v Healy* [1990] 2 I.R. 73 should be borne in mind. In that case, the defendant was arrested and detained by members of An Garda Síochána pursuant to s.30 of The Offences Against the State Act, 1939, on suspicion of being in unlawful possession of firearms. After he had been interviewed for several hours by gardaí in relation to an attempted armed robbery of which he was suspected he began to make a statement. Shortly thereafter, a solicitor who had been retained by a member of the defendant's family arrived at the garda station and sought an interview with him. He was informed that the defendant was being interviewed and, despite his protests, was told that he would have to wait. He was eventually permitted to see the defendant, but at that stage the taking of the statement had been completed. The trial judge ruled that the statement was inadmissible, because the defendant had been, without any excuse, denied a right of instant access to his solicitor and he the trial judge, could not be satisfied that the incriminating admissions contained in the statement were made prior to the denial of that right of access.

Upholding the trial judge's ruling, the Supreme Court *per* Finlay C.J. said that the failure by the gardaí to permit the solicitor to see the defendant as soon as he arrived at the station constituted a deliberate and conscious violation of his constitutional right of access to a solicitor and was also a complete failure to observe "reasonable standards of fairness" in the conduct of the interrogation. ...

It would seem to be implicit in that finding of the Chief Justice that if the trial judge in that case had been satisfied that the incriminating statement had been made prior to the arrival of the solicitor, it would have been admissible in evidence, since, at that point, there would have been no deliberate and conscious violation of the applicant's constitutional right of access to a solicitor or so total a failure to observe reasonable standards of fairness as to require the exclusion of the statement.

It is also to be noted that there is no express statement in the judgment of the Chief Justice in that case or in the separate judgments delivered by Griffin and McCarthy JJ. that the detention of the defendant must be regarded as having been unlawful as from the time when the solicitor was refused access to him. The crucial issue, in the view of Finlay C.J., not dissented from by Griffin and McCarthy JJ., was whether there was a causative link between the breach of the right of access to a solicitor by the gardaí and the obtaining of an admission.

A slightly different approach is apparent in other authorities to which we were referred. In *People (Director of Public Prosecutions) v Madden* [1977] I.R. 336, O'Higgins C.J., delivering the judgment of the Court of Criminal Appeal, said at p. 355:

> "This court is satisfied that a person held in detention by the Garda Síochána, whether under the provisions of the [Offences Against the State Act 1939] or otherwise, has got a right of reasonable access to his legal advisers and that a refusal of a request to give such reasonable access would render his detention illegal."

Those remarks were *obiter*, since there had been no such request in that case. However, the question also arose in *The People (Director of Public Prosecutions) v Finnegan* (Unreported, Court of Criminal Appeal, 15th July, 1997), where the defendant, while in detention, was allowed to speak to his solicitor on the telephone but the member in charge of the garda station remained in earshot while the defendant was speaking to his solicitor. Barrington J., delivering the judgment of the Court of Criminal Appeal, having cited the passages to which I have referred from the judgments of O'Higgins C.J. in *People (Director of Public Prosecutions) v Madden* [1977] I.R. 336 and Finlay C.J. in *People (Director of Public Prosecutions) v Healy* [1990] 2 I.R. 73, said of the latter at p. 41:

> "The implication of this is that any statement made after 4.00 p.m. [when the solicitor arrived and was denied access] would have been inadmissible presumably because the prisoner was from that hour in unlawful detention because of the denial of his constitutional right of access to his solicitor and any statement obtained from him was therefore inadmissible. ... In the present case there was a breach of Mr. Finnegan's constitutional rights when he was denied private access by telephone to his solicitor. From that point on he was in unlawful detention. No evidence was adduced to show that this unlawful detention came to an end at any particular time nor indeed was the point addressed at the trial."

Whether or not it was a necessary implication of the passage in question in *People (Director of Public Prosecutions) v Healy* [1990] 2 I.R. 73 that the defendant was regarded as being in unlawful detention from the time that he was denied access to his solicitor, it would seem in any event to be a logical corollary of the statement of the law by this court in *The Emergency Powers Bill 1976* [1977] I.R. 159, i.e., that the detention of a person against his or her will pursuant to a statutory power is permissible only where his constitutional right of reasonable access to a solicitor is observed. It would seem to follow inexorably that his or her detention becomes unlawful as soon as that right is denied.

Assuming that, in the present case, the trial judge was entitled to conclude that the arrest and detention of the defendant was lawful and did not constitute a *mala fide* attempt to ensure that he was without legal advice while he was being interrogated and that the gardaí made *bona fide* attempts to secure the presence of a solicitor when the defendant requested them to do so, it would follow that there was in this case no deliberate and conscious breach of his constitutional right of reasonable access to a solicitor and, on that assumption, his detention remained lawful. It would also seem to me that, where a person being detained under a statutory provision asks for a solicitor to be present and the gardaí make *bona fide* attempts to comply with that request, the admissibility of any incriminating statement made by the person concerned before the arrival of the solicitor should be decided by the trial judge as a matter of discretion in the light of the common law principles to which I have referred, based on considerations of fairness to the accused and public policy. Such an approach would seem preferable to a rigid exclusionary rule that would treat such statements as inadmissible without any regard to the circumstances prevailing in the particular case. ...

Since the trial judge was, on the evidence, entitled to conclude that there had been no conscious and deliberate violation of the defendant's right of access to a solicitor, it follows that he was at no time in unlawful custody and that, accordingly, the inculpatory statements made by him were properly not treated as inadmissible on the ground that he was in unlawful custody when they were made. Even if the continuation of the questioning by the gardaí between the time that he asked for a solicitor and the arrival of the solicitor who visited the defendant at 8.33 p.m. could be regarded as a conscious and deliberate violation of his constitutional rights, there was no causative link between the breach in question and the making of the incriminating statements. The defendant had not made any incriminating statements prior to the arrival of the solicitor and, on the trial judge's findings, had been advised by him as to his right not to make any statement. The trial judge also accepted the solicitor's evidence that, at that point, the defendant was relaxed and not showing any signs of stress. It follows inevitably that there was, on the evidence, no causative link between any breach of the defendant's constitutional rights arising from the questioning before the solicitor arrived and the making of the incriminating statements. ...

65. Dunne v D.P.P.

Supreme Court, April 25, 2002
[2002] 2 I.R. 305 at 307–309, 313, 315–317, 319, 322, 325, 328, 342–344

McGuinness J:

I have had the advantage of reading in draft form the judgments about to be delivered by Mr. Justice Hardiman and Mr. Justice Fennelly. Both judgments extensively review the facts of this case and the applicable law. I do not consider that I have anything relevant to add either in regard to the facts or in regard to the law. I shall therefore confine myself to a few brief remarks regarding the conclusions to be drawn in this case.

In his judgment Hardiman J. refers to and relies on what he rightly describes as *"the main point of principle"* in his earlier judgment (with which Denham J. and Geoghegan J. agreed) in *Braddish v D.P.P.* [2001] 3 I.R. 127. In that judgment he stated:

> "It is the duty of the Gardai, arising from their unique investigative role, to seek out and preserve all evidence having a bearing or potential bearing on the issue of guilt or innocence."

In the instant case, the Applicant, Mr. Dunne, is charged with the robbery of a sum of money from the Parkway Filling Station in Palmerstown on the 18th January 1998. The evidence of Mr. Torley, the owner of the filling station, is that the various areas of the filling station were all covered by video camera surveillance. On previous occasions relevant videotapes from the filling station had been acquired by the Gardai in the course of other investigations. Mr. Torley, however, cannot recall whether the Gardai either requested or obtained the videotapes covering the period of the robbery on the 18th January 1998. He is, however, certain that the video cameras were operative on that date.

The evidence of Detective Garda Denis Kenny, who is the officer in charge of the investigation but who was not present at the filling station on the night of the robbery is that no videotape of the events that occurred at the Parkway Filling Station was given to or obtained by any member of the Garda Síochána. This evidence is uncontradicted. No affidavit was sworn by the garda or *gardaí* who actually attended at the scene of the robbery.

Since there is no evidence that the videotapes in question were ever in the possession of the Garda Síochána, there can be no question of a failure to preserve that evidence, as there was in the *Braddish* case or, for example, in *Murphy v D.P.P.* [1989] I.L.R.M. 71. The decision of this Court turns, therefore, on whether the further prosecution of the applicant should be prohibited on the ground that the Garda Síochána failed in their duty to "seek out" evidence which had "a bearing or potential bearing on the issue of guilt or innocence".

In his judgment Fennelly J. expresses the view that to impose on the Gardai such a duty to seek out evidence represents a "very significant new step in the law". He envisages a danger that "there will develop a tendency to shift the focus of criminal prosecution on to the adequacy of the police investigation rather than the guilt or innocence of the accused" and that trials will be prohibited wherever a Court can be persuaded that the Gardai have failed to seek out any identifiable evidence which might even possibly tend to exonerate the accused. It seems to me that Fennelly J.'s anxieties in this regard are reasonable and that such dangers do exist. It is essential that a duty on the part of the Gardai to seek out relevant evidence should not be too widely interpreted. As was stated by Hardiman J. in *Braddish v D.P.P.*, such a duty "cannot be interpreted as requiring the Gardai to engage in a disproportionate commitment of manpower or resources in an exhaustive search for every conceivable kind of evidence. The duty must be interpreted realistically on the facts of each case."

Where a court would be asked to prohibit a trial on the grounds that there was an alleged failure to seek out evidence, it would have to be shown that any such evidence would be clearly relevant, that there was at least a strong probability that the evidence was available, and that it would in reality have a bearing on the guilt or innocence of the accused person. It would also be necessary to demonstrate that its absence created a real risk of an unfair trial.

On the facts of the present case, and bearing in mind in particular that the only other evidence against the Applicant is a brief inculpatory statement, I agree with the reasoning and conclusions of Hardiman J. I would allow the appeal and grant an order prohibiting the Respondent from proceeding further with the prosecution of the Applicant on the charge relating to the Parkway Filling Station. ...

Hardiman J:

... If science or technology can provide certainty in matters of great importance which would otherwise be determined on human testimony which may be fallible or worse, who but a guilty man would not willingly invoke its aid? On this theory both individuals on whom suspicion has fallen (mandatorily) and whole populations (voluntarily) have been submitted to scientific and technological tests. The balance has long been struck in favour of the use of technology in the search for the perpetrators of crime, even when the processes involved are minimally invasive or transiently painful or undignified for innocent people. The greater good prevails. This development is due in large measure to the development of techniques of previously unimagined sophistication, from the telephoto lens and the video camera to the extraordinary precision of DNA analysis. Additionally, and at much the same time, our faith in some older techniques has been undermined. From visual identification to alleged confessions, the last three decades have provided excellent reason for avoiding over reliance on them.

This case does not challenge any of these developments. It seeks to take them further. It raises the question, is it open to the authorities on whom such wide powers and resources have been conferred by law or by technology, to decide in a particular case, that they will not use them? Alternatively, if for no stated reason the authorities simply do not avail of some technical assistance in the detection of crime, which might have inculpated or exculpated the suspect, is this relevant to their ability to prosecute him using evidence of a more traditional sort? ...

In my judgment in *Braddish v D.P.P.* [2001] 3 I.R. 127... having recited the facts of the case and referred to the cases I said:

> "It is the duty of the gardaí, arising from their unique investigative role, to seek out and preserve all evidence having a bearing or potential bearing on the issue of guilt or innocence. This is so whether the prosecution proposes to rely on the evidence or not, and regardless of whether it assists the case the prosecution is advancing or not. ..."

In general, I agree with the statement of the facts of this case in the judgment about to be delivered by Mr. Justice Fennelly. It seems particularly important that there was a video system in operation on the premises allegedly robbed, consisting of a number of cameras covering the forecourt, the inside of the shop and the till area including the security hatch. The owner also said that there was a standard procedure in the event of a robbery: the gardaí would be notified and they would arrive and view the video. The tape would then be given to the gardaí. The owner was certain that the video system was in operation at the time of the robbery and was "likely to have captured the events immediately prior to and subsequent to same, including the culprits moving to and from the said hatch area". ...

It is perfectly true, as Mr. Justice Fennelly points out, that the facts of this case are distinguishable from those of *Braddish*. There, the video tape had undoubtedly been in the possession of the gardaí and used by them. They had voluntarily parted with possession of the tape, leading directly to its non-availability. Here, there is no positive proof that the gardaí ever had the tape. It may not be necessary to follow the learned trial judge in holding that they probably did obtain it: in any event it is clear that they could have done so. ...

If the duty of the gardaí were limited to preserving evidence which actually comes into their hands the respondent would be entitled to win on this argument. But since their duty extends also to taking reasonable steps to seek out material evidence, I do not believe that these averments go far enough. Indeed, if these averments were sufficient it would constitute a positive incentive to investigators not to seize or request permission to take evidence which might contradict their suspicions or undermine the reliability of other evidence. ...

I believe there is only one test to be applied on such an application. It is that deriving from the judgment of Denham J. in *B. v D.P.P.* [1997] 3 I.R. 140, at 196:

> "The communities right to have offences prosecuted is not absolute but is to be exercised constitutionally, with due process. If there is a real risk that the applicant would not receive a fair trial then, on the balance of these constitutional rights the applicant's right would prevail ..." ....

The "real risk of an unfair trial", on the other hand, does not necessarily involve blaming any person. The main focus in these applications should be on the fairness of the intended trial without the missing evidence, and not on whose fault it is that the evidence is missing, and what the degree of that fault may be. The latter factors, however, are not always irrelevant.

I would also add that, in my view, parting with possession of a video tape, or failing to take possession of it in the first place, can never be justified solely on the basis that a garda has formed the view that the tape is not helpful or is unlikely to be helpful.

Furthermore, if, on the balance of probabilities, video evidence is likely to have been available I believe that there is an onus on the gardaí or the Director to give some explanation as to why it was not sought or obtained. ...

I would, however, repeat that view in the present case, where of course it is central to the resolution of the issue, and not *obiter*. It must of course be read in the context of the limiting statement also to be found in my judgment in *Braddish*:

"It would be difficult to think of evidence more directly relevant, than a purported video tape showing the commission of the crime. But in cases where the evidence is not of such direct and manifest relevance, the duty to preserve and disclose it has to be interpreted in a fair and reasonable manner. It must be recalled that, in the words of Lynch J., the duty to preserve evidence is to do so 'so far as is necessary and practicable'. A duty so qualified cannot be precisely or exhaustively defined in words of general application. Certainly, it cannot be interpreted as requiring the gardaí to engage in disproportionate commitment of manpower or resources in an exhaustive search for every conceivable kind of evidence. The duty must be interpreted realistically on the facts of each case".

In the absence of a limitation such as this, there might indeed be ground for apprehension that, as Fennelly J. expresses it "… where an accused person is in a position to show that the gardaí have failed to seek evidence which would have had a potential bearing on the innocence of the accused, that will suffice to meet the test of a real and serious risk to a fair trial".

I do not think that this is so. The emphasis, which is quite explicit both in *Braddish* and in this judgment, on the need for the obligation to seek out, and indeed to preserve, evidence to be *reasonably* interpreted requires, I hope, that no remote, theoretical or fanciful possibility will lead to the prohibition of a trial. But we are not dealing with anything of that sort here. On the evidence in the present case it is overwhelmingly likely that a video camera recorded the actual conduct of this robbery by its unmasked perpetrators. In those circumstances it appears to be not a possibility or even a mere probability, but a near certainty, that the video tape would indeed constitute evidence bearing vitally on the question of guilt or innocence.

I do not believe that to insist that such evidence be produced, or at least that some explanation be given for its non-production, is to take a novel conceptual step. On the contrary, as I have indicated above, I believe that the substantive conceptual step required was taken before the end of the Victorian era. … I do not believe that the long recognised right and duty to make all reasonably obtainable evidence available in a criminal case is properly open to criticism on the basis that it will open the floodgates to arguments based on potential relevance of a purely theoretical nature.

The near ubiquity of video cameras in urban settings is such that it demands the specific attention of the courts if their judgments are to be realistic in a contemporary setting. The innovation required is one of adaptation to new technology rather than one of principle. For many years, in the cognate area of eyewitness visual identification, it has been usual to seek the views of as many eye witnesses able to identify or describe a person as possible. This done, the prosecution must either call all such witnesses, whether they identify or describe the accused or not, or (at least on request) make the defence aware of the names and addresses, and give the statements, of the unused witnesses. This is so even, and indeed especially, if their testimony contradicts the description of the suspect given by those on whom the prosecution wish to rely.

There would be grave concern if a garda failed to note the names and addresses of such witnesses to a robbery, failed to ascertain what they have to say, or failed to preserve statements unhelpful to the prosecution for the possible use of the defence. In the age of video cameras, not to enquire whether a tape of the crime is available, not to take possession of it and not to preserve it is the precise equivalent. An indistinct video may still be of use to a defendant, just an eyewitness who does not identify the defendant may be.

To require that the same steps be taken by way of inquiry after, and preservation of, video tapes as witness testimony is not to require anything new in principle or unreasonably onerous in terms of work or expense. And it must be recalled that while a witness whose name or statement is not taken may, after all, be found by the defence, a video tape not taken for preservation will almost certainly be wiped or recorded over in a very short time. It is thus impracticable in most cases for responsibility for the seeking and finding of video tape evidence to rest anywhere but on the police. ...

In those circumstances it would seem to me to be harsh to disqualify the applicant from relief to which he was otherwise entitled on the grounds of delay. He is, I think, entitled to have it assumed in his favour that he knew nothing of a robbery at the Parkway Filling Station until he was charged with it on the 11th August 1998. There is nothing to show that he should have been alerted to the possible presence of a video at any particular time thereafter. ...

Fennelly J. (dissenting):

.... The underlying principle must be to ensure that the applicant has a fair trial. This must, I think, be determined objectively. Evidence, which has existed, may have ceased to exist before trial for a multitude of reasons. A material witness may have died or have become unavailable; evidence may have been destroyed in a fire or simply been lost. None of the cases suggest, nor could they, that an accused person should be allowed to evade trial because such random events have possibly prevented him from finding exculpatory evidence. However, effect on the fairness of a trial of the absence of evidence is the same whether or not it has been in the hands of the police. In my view, the determining element in the cases is that the missing evidence has been in the hands of the prosecution. This was so in all four of the cases cited. The rationale of the decision of Lynch J. in *Murphy v D.P.P.* [1989] I.L.R.M. 71 is that the gardaí had evidence in their possession which could possibly be of assistance to the accused. They could not be allowed to pass judgment on whether it would, in fact, have assisted him. For that reason, it is correct to apply a standard based on possibility combined with real and serious risk of unfairness. All this takes place in the context of a possible trial and it is of the greatest importance that the courts ensure that the police force behaves with impeccable fairness in its handling of evidence. If it had been established, in this case, that the contested video had, in fact, been given to the gardaí, I believe that the same result should have been applied as in *Braddish*.

In this case, however, the relevant garda officer, Detective Garda Kenny, has denied repeatedly and emphatically and in the clearest terms, that it ever came into Garda possession.

I have already explained why I do not think it suffices for the applicant to place the inferential evidence of Mr. Torley in contradiction of such clear denials. It must be recalled that the burden on the applicant is to show a real or serious risk that he will not have a fair trial. His case, on the evidence, would have to be paraphrased as stating that there was a possibility that videotapes which may or may not have come into Garda possession contained evidence tending to exculpate him. Quite obviously, the evidence does not meet that standard.

The difference of opinion between myself and Hardiman J. is not entirely limited to our different approaches to the assessment of the facts. In truth, the difference in that respect is not very great.

The more important issue is that Hardiman J. says that the principle enunciated in *Braddish* is that:

> "It is the duty of the Gardai, arising from their unique investigative role, to *seek out* and preserve all evidence having a bearing or potential bearing on the issue of guilty or innocence" (emphasis added).

On the facts of *Braddish,* the video evidence had actually been in the possession of the gardaí. For that reason, the decision of the Court was consistent with the line of authorities commencing with the judgment of Lynch J. in *Murphy v D.P.P.*. Where the passage, just cited, goes further so as to encompass evidence which the gardaí should have sought out, I believe it is *obiter*. More importantly, it represents a very significant new step in the law. The passage states that the gardaí are under a duty to "seek out and preserve all evidence having a bearing or potential bearing on the issue of guilt or innocence." That is no doubt a reasonable statement of the duties of policemen in the performance of their work. It does not, however, necessarily follow that, where an accused person is in a position to show that the gardaí have failed to seek evidence which would have had a potential bearing on the innocence of the accused, that will suffice to meet the test of a real and serious risk to a fair trial. On such an assumption, a trial will be prohibited, wherever a court can be persuaded that the gardaí have failed to seek out any identifiable evidence which might even possibly tend to exonerate the accused. I cannot agree that our criminal law should go so far. It is difficult to say where the line will be drawn. Giving the increasing prevalence of CCTV in our towns, it is to be anticipated that there will be a rash of applications for prohibition wherever video evidence is not produced. Even where it does not cover the crime scene, why should it not be arguable that video recordings of activity in surrounding areas should be obtained. The danger is that there will develop a tendency to shift the focus of criminal prosecution onto the adequacy of the police investigation rather than the guilt or innocence of the accused. ...

INDEX

Accomplice witness
definition, 5–26
mandatory corroboration warning
co-accused, 5–29
convicted accomplice, 5–28
effect, 5–21
English law, 5–34
fellow accomplices, 5–33
necessity for, 5–23—5–25
prosecution witness, 5–22
spouse of accomplice, 5–28
status, determination by jury, 5–30—5–32
types of accomplice, 5–27
Witness Protection Programme, 5–23

Accused
bad character,
cross-examination upon, *see* **Cross-examination**
evidence generally, *see* **Bad character evidence**
competence and compellability,
co-accused, 2–17, 2–20
evidence in own defence, 2–19
historical background, 1–02, 2–16
principles generally, 2–17
right to silence, 2–18
confession by, *see* **Confession**
lies by,
false alibi, etc, 3–21
peripheral or collateral issue, 3–18—3–20
pre-trial disclosure by, 1–47
right to silence, *see* **Silence**
spouse, competence and compellability,
Australian law, 2–26
former spouse, 2–24
historical background, 2–21, 2–22

Accused—*contd*.
spouse, competence and compellability—*contd*.
marital privacy, 2–21, 13–66—13–68
principles generally, 2–23, 2–25

Adjectival law, 1–05

Admissibility
confession evidence, *see* **Confession**
hearsay evidence, *see* **Hearsay evidence**
illegally or improperly obtained evidence, 11–23—11–27
principles generally, 1–17
question of law, 1–22
unconstitutionally obtained evidence, *see* **O'Brien exclusionary rule**
voire dire enquiry, *see* **Voire dire**
weight of evidence, and, 1–20—1–23

Arrest, *see also* **Detention**
definition, 11–29
charging and bringing before court, 11–39
citizen, by, 11–32
conveyance to garda station, 11–38
entry powers of gardaí, 11–33—11–35
implied authority, 11–36
information requirements, 11–29—11–31
legal authority for, 11–29—11–31
search and seizure following, 11–61
statutory powers of gardaí, 11–32—11–36
summary arrest without warrant, 11–32

Arrest—*contd.*
unlawful,
exclusion of evidence obtained, 11–28
release and re-arrest, 11–37

Bad character evidence
admissibility, 7–02
criminal propensity of accused,
identity, establishing, 7–21, 7–22
principles generally, 7–20
sexually suggestive material and sexual orientation, 7–22—7–26
cross-examination of accused, *see* **Cross-examination**
forbidden reasoning, 7–01
similar fact evidence, *see* **Similar fact evidence**
voire dire, 7–02
Best evidence principle, 1–14
Biased witness, 3–10—3–12
***Boardman* principle**, 7–07
Book of evidence, 1–66n, 3–38
Burden of proof
Defences, *see* **Defence**
evidential burden
legal burden distinguished, 4–15—4–18
nature of, 4–10
prima facie case, 4–10, 4–11
tactical or provisional burden, 4–12
legal burden,
definition, 4–05
accused, on, 4–09
evidential burden distinguished, 4–15—4–18
extent, 4–06
presumption of innocence, and, 4–07, 4–08
prosecution, on, 4–07, 4–08
risk of non-persuasion, 4–05
presumptions of law, 4–13, 4–14
principles generally, 4–01—4–04
reversal of
common law principle,
civil cases, *res ipsa loquitur*,
definition, 4–59
access to information, and, 4–67—4–69

Burden of proof—*contd.*
reversal of—*contd.*
common law principle—*contd.*
civil cases, *res ipsa loquitur*—*contd.*
causation distinguished, 4–64
effect of inference, 4–62
extraordinary event,
evidence of, 4–50
maxim generally, 4–14, 4–59, 4–66
medical negligence, 4–70—4–71
rebuttal of inference, 4–63, 4–65
rejection of inference, 4–61
criminal cases,
Edwards/Hunt approach, 4–55—4–58
peculiar knowledge principle, 4–50—4–54
statutory reversal,
desertion, 4–44
English law, 4–38, 4–39
evidential burden generally, 4–32
legal burden generally, 4–32, 4–33
offences against the state, 4–34—4–37, 4–40
possession of explosive, 4–42, 4–43
possession of firearm, 4–41
proceeds of crime, 4–49
reverse-onus clauses generally, 4–31
right to silence, 4–41, 4–48
road traffic legislation, 4–31, 4–45
summary proceedings, 4–46, 4–47

Child witness
competence and compellability
civil proceedings, 2–15
common law rules, 2–10
historical background, 2–08
intelligibility criterion, 2–11, 2–12
modern view, 2–09

Index 645

Child witness—*contd.*
competence and compellability—*contd.*
statutory provisions, 2–12—2–15
voire dire, 2–14
discretionary corroboration warning, 5–49, 5–50
hearsay evidence in family law proceedings, 9–43—9–47
oath, comprehension of, 2–07, 2–10
television link, testimony via, *see* **Television link measures**
unsworn testimony
civil proceedings, 2–15
statutory provisions, 2–12
value of, 2–07, 2–10
videotaped interview, *see* **Videotaped interview of child complainant**
Circumstantial evidence
definition, 1–34
conviction upon, 1–36, 1–37
direct evidence distinguished, 1–35
relevant fact, proving, 1–16, 1–34
types of, 1–34
weight of, 1–36, 1–37
Civil proceedings
course of trial, *see* **Course of trial**
documentary hearsay evidence, 9–39—9–42
expert witnesses, *see* **Expert evidence**
facts at issue, 1–15
illegally or improperly obtained evidence, 11–69
O'Brien exclusionary rule, 11–69
rules of evidence generally, 1–04
similar fact evidence, 7–35, 7–36
standards of proof, 4–79—4–80
Collateral facts, 1–19
Collateral issue rule
collateral issue, test for, 3–03—3–05
exceptions, 3–06
purpose of, 3–02
statement of rule, 3–01
Common law trial
accusatorial and adversarial nature, 1–10
inquisitorial system distinguished, 1–12

Common law trial—*contd.*
jury, effect on rules of evidence, 1–09
modern developments, 1–11
rules of evidence generally, 1–10
Confession
admissibility,
burden of proof, 10–02, 10–10
exception to hearsay rule, 9–77, 10–01, 10–02, 10–04
tests generally, 10–15, 10–16
voire dire, 10–11—10–13
co-accused, evidence against,
conspiracy or common enterprise, 10–66
cross-examination by co-accused, 10–64, 10–65
direction against cross-admissibility, 10–63
previous inconsistent statements, 10–65
constitutional rights of accused,
access to legal advice,
attempt to locate solicitor, 10–55
deprivation of legal advice, effect of, 10–54
incorporation of right in regulations, 10–50
notice of arrival of solicitor, 10–52
private consultation right, 10–53
questioning in presence of solicitor, 10–53
questioning pending arrival of solicitor, 10–56
recognition as constitutional right, 10–51
silence, and adverse inferences, 10–57
breach of, *O'Brien* exclusionary rule, 10–48
rights generally, 10–48,
corroboration warning, 10–07, 10–72, 10–74
denial of, and cross-examination upon bad character, 10–14, 10–15
electronic recording, 10–06
fairness test, 10–43
form of, 10–05, 10–06

Confession—*contd*.
  formal and informal admissions
      distinguished, 1–14n, 10–03
  fruit of poisoned tree
      English law, 10–62
      nature of taint, 10–60
      successive statements, 10–59,
          10–61
      US law, 10–58
  Judges' Rules
      breach of
          effect, 10–18
          involuntariness distinguished,
              10–19, 10–20
      historical background, 10–17
      rule 1, 10–21
      rule 2, 10–21
      rule 3, 10–22
      rule 8, 10–23, 10–24
      rule 9, 10–25
      statement of rules, 10–17
  mixed statements, general
      admissibility, 10–67—10–71
  person in authority, 10–08, 10–09
  principles generally, 10–01—10–04
  reliability
      alcohol and drugs, 10–46
      English law, 10–44
      Irish law, 10–45
      mental age and aptitude, 10–47
  Treatment of Persons in Custody
      Regulations
      arrested person under 17 years,
          10–28
      conduct of interrogation, 10–29
      non-compliance, effect of,
          10–26
      proof of compliance, 10–27
  video recording, 10–06
  voluntariness
      causation, 10–40
      involuntary statement,
          inadmissibility, 10–30
      oppressive questioning, 10–35,
          10–36
      requirement generally, 10–30,
          10–31
      subjective test, 10–41, 10–42
      third party threat or inducement,
          10–37—10–39
      threat or inducement, 10–32—
          10–34

Constitutional rights
  confession statements, *see*
      Confession
  evidence obtained unconstitutionally,
      see **O'Brien exclusionary
      rule**
  rights generally, 1–06
Corroboration
  definition, 5–04, 5–47
  car speed, 5–18, 12–29
  discretionary warning,
      child witness, 5–49, 5–50
      mutual corroboration, 5–51,
          5–52
      principles generally, 5–35
      sexual offences, *see* **Sexual
          offence case**
  English law, 5–01
  identification evidence, and, 6–06—
      6–09
  independent proof requirement
      accomplices, 5–06
      admission, etc. by accused,
          5–10
      complainants, etc. conspiring
          against accused, 5–06
      lies by accused, 5–07—5–09
      refusal of accused to co-operate,
          5–11
      self–corroboration, 5–05
      sexual offence cases, 5–42—
          5–46
      silence of accused, 5–12—
          5–16
  mandatory warning
      accomplice witnesses, *see*
          Accomplice witness
      confession evidence, 10–72,
          10–74
      duty of trial judge, 5–19
      form of, 5–20
  mutual corroboration, 5–51, 5–52
  perjury, 5–18
  principles generally, 5–01—5–03
  requirement of, 5–17, 5–18
  Scots law, 5–01n
  silence, adverse inferences, 5–12—
      5–16
  treason, 5–18
Counsellors' privilege, 13–48, 13–52
Course of trial
  application to dismiss, 1–48n

Index

Course of trial—*contd.*
  close of case, evidence after,
    1–49n
  cross-examination, 1–52
  evidence *en bloc*, exceptions,
    1–49
  examination-in-chief, 1–51
  judge's power to call or question
    witness, 1–53
  no case to answer, 1–50
  order of proceedings, 1–48
  preliminary examination in District
    Court, 1–48n
  summing-up, 1–54
Criminal proceedings
  course of trial, *see* **Course of trial**
  expert witnesses, *see* **Expert evidence**
  facts at issue, 1–15
  rules of evidence generally, 1–03
  standards of proof, 4–71—4–73
Cross-examination
  accused generally, 1–52, 2–19
  bad character of accused,
    accused's good character, defence
      asserting
      credit-relevance and issue-
        relevance, 8–29
      examples of assertions,
        8–34
      general reputation, 8–27
      good character direction,
        8–28, 8–30—8–32
      principles generally, 8–26
      whether defence asserting,
        8–35
    admissible similar fact evidence,
      8–22—8–25
    co-accused, evidence by accused
      against,
      effect, 8–65
      objective test, 8–62—8–64
      potential injustice, 8–66
      principles generally, 8–61
      same offence requirement,
        8–67—8–70
    historical background, 8–01
    indivisibility of character,
      8–16
    loss of shield of protection,
      situations generally, 8–02,
        8–21

Cross-examination—*contd.*
  bad character of accused—*contd.*
    parameters of statutory provisions
      credit-relevance and issue-
        relevance, 8–13—
        8–20
      minor offences, 8–18
      offences committed, convicted
        of or charged with,
        8–08—8–12
      principles generally, 8–04
      tending to show, 8–05—
        8–07
    prosecution witness, imputations
      against
      Australian law, 8–55n
      English discretion-based
        approach, 8–39—8–46,
        8–55—8–60
      Irish rule-based approach,
        8–47—8–55
      principles generally, 8–36—
        8–38
    witness statement read in
      court, 8–60
    statutory provisions generally,
      8–01—8–03
  hearsay evidence, and, 9–16—9–19
  hostile witness, 2–31, 2–34, 2–36
  principles generally, 1–52
  witness credibility, *see* **Witness**
  witness notes, 2–47

Death, presumption of, 4–14
Defence
  evidence, and burdens of proof,
    4–19—4–28
  insanity
  civil standard of proof, 4–30
  legal burden on accused, 4, 09,
    4–29
Detention
  expiry of lawful period, re-arrest
    following, 11–51
  holding charges, 11–48
  information requirements, 11–29
  legal basis for, 11–40
  unlawful
    exclusion of evidence obtained,
      11–28
    release and re-arrest, 11–37
  voluntary questioning, 11–50

Detention—*contd.*
without charge, for questioning
continuity of detention, 11–47
non-scheduled offences, 11–48,
11–49
reasonable belief requirement,
11–43, 11–44
statutory powers, 11–40—11–45
strict interpretation by courts,
11–46—11–51
Direct evidence
definition, 1–29
circumstantial evidence
distinguished, 1–35
hearsay evidence distinguished,
1–29
Directed verdict, 1–23
DNA evidence
expert evidence, 12–12—12–15
identification by, 6–25
Documentary evidence
definition, 1–33, 9–36
hearsay evidence
civil proceedings, 9–39—9–42
statutory exception for
admissibility, 9–36—9–38
primary and secondary, 1–33
Drugs
confession, effect on, 10–46
dealing
hearsay and original evidence,
9–28—9–30
implied assertions, 9–35
detention without charge, 11–41,
11–51, 11–57
opinion evidence by garda, 12–03
search and seizure powers, 11–55,
11–64, 11–66
statutory evidential inferences,
4–31n, 4–36n
trafficking, and right to silence,
4–48, 5–14, 10–57
Treatment of Persons in Custody
Regulations, 10–29
Drunkenness
arrest for drunken driving, 11–29,
11–31, 11–34, 11–36
confession, effect on, 10–46
expert evidence, 12–03
garda opinion evidence, 12–29
Treatment of Persons in Custody
Regulations, 10–29

Dying declaration
cause of death, establishing, 9–83,
9–84
hearsay rule, exception to, 9–78
pecuniary or proprietary interest,
against, 9–79
pedigree, as to, 9–81
principles generally, 9–78
will, explaining, 9–82
written declaration in course of duty,
9–80

**European Convention on Human
Rights**, 1–06, 13–21
European Court of Human Rights,
1–06, 1–07
Evidence
definition, 1–13
laws and theory,
adjectival law, as, 1–05
codification in foreign
jurisdictions, 1–05
constitutionalisation, 1–06
evolution, 1–08
exclusionary rules, as, 1–01
principles generally, 1–01—1–06
sources, 1–01, 1–06, 1–08
Examination-in-chief, 1–51
Expert evidence
civil proceedings,
medical negligence, 12–19—
12–23
principles generally, 12–18
criminal proceedings,
forensic evidence and DNA,
12–12—12–15
judges' role, 12–07
limitations, 12–16, 12–17
psychiatric evidence, 12–05,
12–06, 12–08—12–11
Griess test, 12–13
hearsay rule, and, 9–55, 12–24—
12–26
legal professional privilege, and
disclosure of reports, 13–28—
13–32
principles generally, 12–01—12–04
ultimate issue rule, 12–03

Facts
collateral facts, 1–19
facta probantia, 1–15

Index

Facts—*contd.*
  facts at issue, 1–15
  relevant facts, 1–16
  witness credibility, 1–18
Family law proceedings
  child witness, hearsay evidence,
    common law discretion, 9–44,
      9–45, 9–47
    historical background,
      9–43
    statutory provisions, 9–36,
      9–47
  inquisitorial nature, 1–53n
  legal professional privilege, 13–17,
    13–18
  television link facility, 1–55
Fingerprints
  expert evidence, 12–13
  identification by, 6–25
Forensic evidence, 12–12—12–15

Hearsay evidence
  bail applications, 9–49
  civil proceedings,
    child witness in family law
      proceedings, 9–43—
      9–47
    documentary hearsay evidence,
      9–39—9–42
  direct evidence distinguished,
    1–29
  documentary evidence
    civil proceedings, 9–39—9–42
    statutory exception for
      admissibility, 9–36—
      9–38
  expert evidence, 9–55, 12–24—
    12–26
  identification evidence, 9–56—
    9–58
  implied assertions
    non-verbal, 9–33, 9–34
    rule against hearsay, application
      of, 9–08, 9–31, 9–32
    unintended, 9–34, 9–35
  interlocutory applications, 9–50—
    9–52
  original evidence distinguished
    case illustrations, 9–21—9–30
    principles generally, 1–30—1–32,
      9–20
  pre-trial, 9–48

Hearsay evidence—*contd.*
  rule against hearsay,
    definition, 9–01
    common law exceptions,
      confessions, 9–77, 10–01,
        10–02, 10–04
      dying declarations, *see* **Dying**
        declaration
      principles generally, 9–62—
        9–64
      res gestae, *see* **Res gestae**
        exception
      statements in public
        documents, 9–85, 9–86
    cross-examination, and, 9–16—
      9–19
    English Law Commission
      recommendations, 9–14,
      9–15
    principles generally, 9–02—9–08
    rationale for, 9–09—9–11
    statutory exceptions, 9–59—
      9–61
    strict application, 9–12—9–15
  rule against narrative distinguished,
    2–50
  tribunal proceedings, 9–53, 9–54
  videotaped interview of child
    complainant, 1–65
Hostile witness
  definition, 2–30
  cross-examination, 2–30, 2–34,
    2–36
  impeachment of adverse witness,
    and, 2–35
  pre-trial statements, 2–30, 2–37—
    2–40
  principles generally, 2–30
  unfavourable witness distinguished,
    2–34
  voire dire, 2–32, 2–33

Identification evidence
  Devlin Committee findings, 6–02
  hearsay rule, and, 9–56—9–58
  means of identification,
    deferred identification, 6–16
    dock identification, 6–15
    identification parade,
      advantage of, 6–18
      constitutional rights, and,
        6–18

Identification evidence—*contd.*
  means of identification—*contd.*
    identification parade—*contd.*
      defective procedure, *Casey* warning, 6–23
      exceptions to requirement, 6–20
      procedure, 6–19, 6–21
      refusal of accused to participate, 6–22
      witness's failure to identify accused, 6–24
    photofits and identikits, 6–32
    photographs, fingerprints, DNA, etc.
      attitude of courts, 6–25
      photographs, 6–26, 6–27
      video footage and stills, 6–28—6–31
    pre-trial identification generally, 6–15, 6–16
    second identification in open court, 6–17
    voice identification, 6–33, 6–34
  pre-trial disclosure, 6–03, 6–35—6–38
  principles generally, 6–01—6–03
  warning
    Casey direction, 6–04
    English law, 6–11
    mutual and cumulative identifications, 6–13, 6–14
    recognition cases, 6–10, 6–11
    sexual offence cases, 6–12
    supporting evidence, reference to, 6–06—6–09
    weak and unsupported evidence, 6–05

Identikits, use in identification, 6–32

Illegally or improperly obtained evidence
  definition, 11–23
  admissibility, discretionary rule, 11–23, 11–25—11–27
  civil proceedings, 11–69
  lawfulness of custody, and, 11–24

Informer privilege
  common law privilege, 13–54
  disclosure by gardaí, 13–56, 13–78
  disclosure exonerating accused, 13–58, 13–59
  journalists, 13–60, 13–61

Informer privilege—*contd.*
  members of Oireachtas, 13–55
  public prosecutors, 13–54
  rationale for, 13–51
  scope of, 13–57

Innocence, presumption of
  principles generally, 4–07, 4–08, 4–14
  reversal of burden of proof, and *see* **Reversal of burden of proof**

Insanity defence, 4–09, 4–29, 4–30

Judge
  common law trial, 1–10, 1–11
  division of function between jury, and, 1–22
  inquisitorial system, 1–12
  judicial notice, 1–39, 1–41
  power to call or question witness, 1–53
  summing–up, 1–54
  witness, as, 2–01n

Judicial evidence, 1–13

Judicial notice
  principles generally, 1–39
  substantive law, of, 1–41

Jury
  common law trial generally, 1–09, 1–11
  division of function between judge, and, 1–22
  voire dire enquiry, presence during, 1–25, 1–26

Leading questions
  cross-examination, 1–52
  examination-in-chief, 1–51
  hostile witnesses, 2–30, 2–34
  videotaped interview of child complainant, 1–75

Legal professional privilege
  advice privilege, 13–22
  communications in furtherance of settlement, 13–38—13–40
  deceased client, 13–23
  documents existing prior to advice, 13–39, 13–40
  DPP communications, 13–22
  duration, 13–23
  expert witness reports, disclosure of, 13–28—13–32
  fundamental right, 13–21

Legal professional privilege—*contd.*
  legal advice and assistance
    distinguished, 13–35—13–37
  litigation privilege, 13–22
  mixed purpose documents, 13–42—13–44
  principles generally, 13–20—13–24
  rationale for, 13–20
  scope of protected communications, 13–25—13–27
  silence of accused, adverse inferences, 13–43, 13–46
  state department communications, 13–24
  third party communications, 13–41
  waiver, 13–23
Lies
  accused, by
    corroboration, and, 5–07—5–09
    false alibi, etc, 3–21
    peripheral or collateral issue, 3–18—3–20
    lie detector test, 3–15n
    Lucas rules, 3–18—3–21
    witness's reputation for lying, 3–15—3–17

M'Naghten rules, 4–29
Makin principle, 7–03
Marital privacy, 2–21—2–26, 13–66—13–68
Medical negligence
  expert evidence,
    adversarial nature, 12–22
    plaintiff's difficulty in obtaining, 12–23
  professional standard model of liability, 12–19, 12–20
  reasonable patient test, 12–21
  res ipsa loquitur, 4–70—4–71
Mental disability, person suffering
  competence and compellability
    child's competence, and, 2–28
    historical background, 2–27
    legislation, application of, 2–29
    test of specific competence, 2–27
    voire dire, 2–28
  television link, testimony via, *see* **Television link measures**
  witness credibility, 3–22

Narrative, rule against *see* **Rule against narrative**
***O'Brien* exclusionary rule**
  causative link between violation and evidence, 11–13—11–15
  civil proceedings, 11–67
  constitutional rights and obtaining of evidence
    confession evidence, 11–09
    entry onto premises, 11–07
    real evidence, 11–09
    right to privacy, 11–10—11–12
    scope of accused's rights, 11–08
    unlawful arrest or detention, 11–28
  deliberate and conscious violation, 11–16—11–20
  deterrence and vindication principles, 11–02
  extraordinary excusing circumstances, 11–21, 11–22
  operation of rule generally, 11–03—11–06
  statement of rule, 11–01
Oath or affirmation, 2–01, 2–05—2–07
Offences against the State
  detention for questioning, 11–41, 11–48, 11–51
  garda opinion evidence, 4–34n, 12–28
  identification of defence witnesses, 1–47n
  incriminating documents, reverse-onus clause, 4–34
  right to silence, and, 4–48, 5–14, 10–57
  search and seizure powers, 11–55, 11–59
  statutory power of arrest, 11–32
  voluntariness of confession, subjective test, 10–41, 10–42
Opinion evidence
  expert evidence, *see* **Expert evidence**
  non-expert evidence, 12–27—12–31
  rule against, 12–01—12–03

Parliamentary privilege
  constitutional basis, 13–62
  members of government, 13–65
  records of telephone conversations, 13–64
  tribunal of enquiry, 13–63
Percipient evidence, 1–29
Phone calls and mail, interception of, 11–10—11–12
Photofit identifications, 6–32
Photographic evidence, use in identification, 6–26, 6–27
Physical disability, witness suffering from, 3–22
Pre-trial disclosure, etc.
  constitutional requirement, 1–42
  criminal record of witness, 3–14, 3–38
  identification evidence, 6–03, 6–35—6–38
  prosecutor's duty to seek out, preserve and disclose material evidence, 1–42
  right to fair trial, and, 1–44, 1–45
  scope of duty, 1–43
  summary proceedings, 1–46
  test for prospective unfairness, 1–44
  the accused, 1–47
  videotaped interview of child complainant, 1–66
  witness credibility, 3–38
  witness notes, 2–49
Presumptions of law, 4–13, 4–14
Previous convictions
  accused, cross-examination on, *see* **Cross-examination**
  witness, 3–13, 3–14
Previous inconsistent statements, 2–37—2–40, 3–07—3–09
Privacy
  constitutional right, 11–10
  interception of phone calls and mail, 11–10—11–12
Private privilege
  communications in furtherance of crime, etc, 13–09, 13–13—13–16
  constitutionalisation, 13–02
  discovery and disclosure, and, 13–05, 13–06
  effect, 13–07

Private privilege—*contd.*
  English law, 13–03
  family law proceedings, 13–17, 13–18
  forms of, 13–01
  person asserting, 13–07
  principles generally, 13–01—13–07
  public interest privilege distinguished, 13–76
  secondary evidence, 13–08, 13–09
  testamentary proceedings, 13–19
  waiver, 13–10—13–12
Privilege
  competence and compellability distinguished, 2–03, 13–01
  confidential relationships
    counsellors' privilege, 13–48, 13–52
    sacerdotal privilege, 13–49—13–51
  informer privilege, *see* **Informer privilege**
  legal professional privilege, *see* **Legal professional privilege**
  marital privacy, 2–21—2–26, 13–66—13–68
  parliamentary privilege, *see* **Parliamentary privilege**
  private privilege, *see* **Private privilege**
  public interest privilege, *see* **Public interest privilege**
  self-incrimination, against, *see* **Self-incrimination, privilege against**
Proof
  best evidence principle, 1–14
  burden, *see* **Burden of proof**
  possibility and probability, 1–13
  standard, *see* **Standard of proof**
Psychiatric evidence
  criminal capacity, 12–08
  hypnotherapy, etc, 12–11
  limitations, 12–17
  principles generally, 12–05, 12–06
  sexual offence cases, 12–08
  witness reliability, 12–09, 12–10
Public document, exception to hearsay rule, 9–85, 9–86

Index 653

Public interest privilege
  communications between gardaí and DPP, 13–79
  disclosure of informant by gardaí, 13–56, 13–78
  investigation of claim by court, 13–70—13–75
  principles generally, 13–69
  private privilege distinguished, 13–76
  waiver, 13–77
Rationalism, 1–08
Real evidence, 1–38
Recognition evidence, 6–10, 6–11
Relevant facts, 1–16
Res gestae **exception**
  contemporaneity requirement, 9–65
  principles generally, 9–65
  spontaneous statements
    explaining accompanying act, 9–74, 9–75
    participant or observer, by, 9–66—9–71
    physical sensation, 9–76
    showing state of mind, 9–72, 9–73
  res ipsa loquitur, *see* **Reversal of burden of proof**
Rule against narrative
  exceptions, 2–51
  rule against hearsay distinguished, 2–50
  sex offence cases, early complaint rule
    broadening of rule, 2–60
    complaint rebutting claim by accused, 2–59
    corroboration, and, 2–56, 5–05
    extension to offences not involving consent, 2–53
    first reasonable opportunity, 2–57
    lack of spontaneity due to prompting, 2–58
    male complainants, application to, 2–53
    purpose of, 2–54
    special exception, 2–52
    strict application, 2–53
    third party evidence, 2–55
  statement of rule, 2–50

Sacerdotal privilege, 13–49—13–51
Search and seizure
  arrest, following, 11–61
  consent to, 11–59—11–60
  powers of gardaí generally, 11–52, 11–53
  search warrant,
    issue of, 11–64—11–68
    powers under, 11–64
    time for executing, 11–64
    validity, 11–67
  statutory powers, 11–54—11–58
  Treatment of Persons in Custody Regulations, 11–53
Self-incrimination, privilege against
  compulsorily acquired self-incriminating evidence, 13–92—13–99
  compulsory disclosure of assets, 13–83
  principles generally, 13–80—13–82
Sexual history evidence
  common law rule, 3–23, 3–24
  current statutory provisions
    analysis, 3–28
    application procedure, 3–25
    prosecution raising expressly or impliedly, 3–29
    sexual experience, 3–27
    strict admissibility test, 3–26
    unfairness to accused, 3–26
  English law, 3–34—3–37
  reasons for limiting, 3–30—3–33
Sexual offence cases
  difficulties of proof, 5–38
  discretionary corroboration warning
    Canadian law, 5–47
    circumstances requiring, 5–39, 5–40
    cumulative effect of evidence, 5–46, 5–47
    English law, 5–47
    evidence of distress, 5–43, 5–44
    form of, 5–39, 5–41
    independent proof requirement, 5–42
    mutual corroboration, 5–51, 5–52
    rationale for, 5–37, 5–38
    sexually transmitted disease, 5–45
    statutory provisions, 5–36
    supporting evidence, use of terminology, 5–48

Sexual offence cases—*contd.*
  identification evidence warning,
    6–12
  psychiatric evidence, 12–08
  rule against narrative, special
    exception, *see* **Rule against
    narrative**
  sexual history evidence, *see* **Sexual
    history evidence**
Silence
  adverse inferences from,
    access to legal advice, and,
      13–106—13–108
    corroborative inferences, 5–12—
      5–16
    English law, 13–102—13–104
    European Court of Human
      Rights, 13–105
    legal professional privilege, and,
      13–43, 13–46
    statutory provisions, 13–89,
      13–100—13–102
  curtailment of right generally,
    13–109
  freedom of expression, and,
    13–90
  origin of right, 13–86
  privilege against self–incrimination,
    and, 13–81
  reverse-onus clauses, and, 4–41,
    4–48, 13–87
  right generally, 13–84—13–87
  right to fair trial, and, 13–91
  statutory curtailment of right,
    13–88—13–90
Similar fact evidence
  definition, 7–02
  ambit of rules,
    defence, application to,
      7–17
    principles generally, 7–16
    probative versus prejudicial test,
      7–18, 7–19
    background facts, and, 7–23—
      7–34
  Boardman principle,
    statement of principle, 7–07
    striking similarity test, 7–06—
      7–15
  civil cases, 7–35, 7–36
  cross-examination of accused upon,
    8–22—8–25

Similar fact evidence—*contd.*
  joined trials,
    collusion, 7–28—7–31
    cross-admissibility generally,
      7–27
  Makin principle,
    statement of principle, 7–03
    system, *modus operandi* or
      special signature, 7–04,
      7–05
Sources of law, 1–01, 1–06, 1–08
Spontaneous statements, *res gestae*
  exception, *see* **Res gestae
  exception**
Standard of proof
  definition, 4–02
  civil proceedings,
    artificial life support, request to
      discontinue, 4–80
    "balance of probabilities",
      4–80
    nullity proceedings, 4–80
    referendum application, 4–80
    serious and weighty matters
      generally, 4–80
    testamentary proceedings, 4–80
  criminal proceedings, "beyond all
    reasonable doubt", 4–72—
    4–73
  principles generally, 4–01, 4–02
subpoena *duces tecum*, 2–01
subpoena *ad testificandum*, 2–01
Succession Act, proceedings under
  declaration by deceased explaining,
    9–82
  private privilege, 13–19
  standard of proof, 4–80
Survey evidence, *res gestae* **exception**,
  9–73

Television link measures
  application of, 1–55
  constitutionality, 1–59—1–63
  English law, 1–59
  intermediary, questioning by, 1–58
  introduction of, 1–55
  pre-trial interview, *see* **Videotaped
    interview of child
    complainant**
  principles generally, 1–57
  re-identification of accused in court,
    1–57

Index

Television link measures—*contd.*
right of direct physical
confrontation, and, 1–60—
1–63
US law, 1–61
videotaping requirement, 1–57
wig or gown, wearing prohibited,
1–57
Testimony
live television link, via, *see*
Television link measures
pre-trial,
child complainant, *see*
**Videotaped interview of
child complainant**
principles generally, 1–56
viva voce, 1–28, 1–55
witnesses generally, *see* **Witness**
Trial-within-trial, *see* **Voire dire**
Tribunal, hearsay evidence, 9–53,
9–54

**Video surveillance footage, use in
identification**, 6–28—6–31
**Videotaped interview of child
complainant**
admissibility, 1–65
closing directions as to, 1–71
cross-examination on, 1–65, 1–69
discretion of trial judge, 1–67, 1–73
edited version, 1–65
evidence-in-chief, in lieu of, 1–64
guidelines as to use in court, 1–70,
1–76
hearsay, and, 1–65
leading questions, 1–75
pre-trial disclosure, 1–66
statement subsequently retracted or
revised, 1–74
transcript, retention by jury, 1–68,
1–72
***Viva voce* evidence**
definition, 1–28
common law requirement, 1–28,
1–55
testimony via live television link,
and, *see* **Television link
measures**
Voice identification, 6–33, 6–34
Voire dire
definition, 1–24
bad character evidence, 7–02

Voire dire—*contd.*
confession evidence, 10–11—10–13
constitutional rights, and, 1–25
English law, 1–26
Fennelly Report, 1–27
hostile witness, 2–32, 2–33
witness competence,
child witness, 2–14
enquiry generally, 2–02
person suffering mental disability,
2–28

Weight of evidence
definition, 1–21
admissibility, and, 1–20
circumstantial evidence, 1–36,
1–37
jury instructions, 1–23
question of fact, 1–22
Will
declaration by deceased explaining,
9–82
proceedings as to
private privilege, 13–19
standard of proof, 4–80
Witness
accomplice, *see* **Accomplice witness**
child witness, *see* **Child witness**
competence and compellability,
accused, *see* **Accused**
banker, 2–01n
child, *see* **Child witness**
diplomat, 2–01n
judge, 2–01n
onus of proof, 2–02
person suffering mental disability,
2–27—2–29
principles generally, 2–01
privilege distinguished, 2–03,
13–01
spouse of accused, *see* **Accused**
waiver of non-compellability,
2–04
credibility,
bias, 3–10—3–12
collateral issue rule, *see*
Collateral issue rule
lack of veracity, 3–15—3–17
physical or mental disability,
3–22
pre-trial disclosure by
prosecution, 3–38

Witness—*contd.*
  credibility—*contd.*
    previous convictions, 3–13, 3–14
    previous inconsistent statements,
      3–07—3–09
    relevant facts, 1–18
    sexual history, *see* **Sexual history
      evidence**
  cross-examination, 1–52
  examination-in-chief, 1–51
  expert witness, *see* **Expert evidence**
  hostile witness, *see* **Hostile witness**
  hypnosis, 2–42n
  judge's power to call or question,
    1–53
  memory, notes refreshing,
    corroboration, and, 2–46, 5–05
    cross-examination on, 2–47
    inspection by judge and jury,
      2–45
    non-contemporaneous notes,
      2–44

Witness—*contd.*
  memory, notes refreshing—*contd.*
    permission of trial judge as to
      use, 2–42
    policeman's record, 2–48
    pre-trial disclosure, 2–49
    rationale for rule, 2–41
    rereading of statements, etc. pre-
      trial, 2–43, 2–44
    sufficiently contemporaneous
      notes, 2–42
    use of terminology, 2–45
  oath or affirmation, 2–01, 2–05—
    2–07
  opinion evidence, *see* **Opinion
    evidence**
  rule against narrative, *see* **Rule
    against narrative**
  veracity and the
    Richardson rules, 3–15—3–17
***Woolmington* principle**, 4–07, 4–09,
  4–34, 4–49, 4–50